Webster's
New Explorer
LARGE PRINT
Dictionary
THIRD EDITION

Webster's
New Explorer
LARGE PRINT
Dictionary
THIRD EDITION

Created in Cooperation with the Editors of
Merriam-Webster

FEDERAL
STREET
PRESS

A Division of Merriam-Webster, Incorporated
Springfield, Massachusetts

This edition published Federal Street Press,
a division of Merriam-Webster, Incorporated
PO Box 281
Springfield, MA 01102

Federal Street Press books are available for bulk purchase
for sales promotion and premium use.
For details write the manager of special sales,
Federal Street Press, P.O. Box 281, Springfield, MA 01102

ISBN   978-1-59695-146-4

Printed in Canada
9th Printing   Marquis, Toronto, ON   9/2019 Jouve

"New Words and the Dictionary" was originally published under a different title in
New Routes / Disal and is used with permission.

**This Large Print Book carries the
Seal of Approval of NAVH**

Contents

Preface

We are happy to be able to offer this new edition of *Webster's New Explorer Large Print Dictionary* for readers who appreciate a large print book. The format will be familiar to users of the previous edition, but there are a number of new features here, including a supplement of new words and an essay on how words get entered into the dictionary.

This dictionary is a reference of the very core of the English vocabulary, and while the type size is generous, the scope of the book is necessarily quite limited. It is intended to serve as a handy, one-volume quick reference for those in need of help with such matters as spelling, pronunciation, end-of-line hyphenation, and idiomatic usage of the most common words in everyday use.

This dictionary has been produced in cooperation with the editors of Merriam-Webster Inc., and as such it draws on the vast resources of that company. Aside from the new words supplement in the front, the dictionary is made up of two distinct parts: the main A-Z vocabulary section followed by a section on common abbreviations.

The need for concise presentation requires a treatment that is unique to this book in many respects, and we urge a thorough reading of the section Using this Dictionary, in the following pages. A key to the symbols used in the pronunciation system follows that.

New Words and the Dictionary

Most people don't think too often about their dictionary. They probably assume that it has all the words they will ever need, and trust it to serve as a kind of policeman of language, pointing to correct spelling and settling arguments about meaning. A dictionary, according to this idea, should keep the citizens of a language (that is, the words themselves) in order and protect them from sabotage and outsiders (that is, make sure that words don't shift in spelling or meaning and keep out unwanted new or foreign words).

But there's a big problem with this model. While we know that languages follow rules, they don't follow orders. Language changes constantly, sometimes in ways that delight us and sometimes in ways that dismay us. Especially today, with ever-faster means of communication changing the way we learn and work, language change is a fact of life. English absolutely needs a word like *blog*, for example; and if that word seems trendy, consider this: the word *hello* only entered the language around 1877.

So how does a dictionary keep up with change? By being in a near-constant state of change itself.

The question most frequently asked of a lexicographer—a person who writes dictionaries—is this one: How does a word get into the dictionary? The answer begins with the simple act of reading. We read to find evidence of words as they are really used, and this becomes the data and the raw material of our research. We read to find words that are new to English (like *ciabatta* and *crowdsourcing*) as well as new meanings of words that are already part of the language (like *spam* or *slider*). Dictionary editors read a little bit at the office every day from publications such as newspapers and from magazines about parenting, sailing, or wine. We read novels, textbooks, law reviews, and math journals. We even read restaurant menus and soup-can labels. Online sources are naturally examined as well. We look for a clear example of a word used in a particular way, along with all necessary context—anything from the surrounding words to several sentences to whole paragraphs of text—and all this is added to our ever-growing language database. Each individual word that we make note of, along with its context and its source, is called a citation. Citations may then be printed out on index cards, so that they can later be studied either electronically or on paper.

There are other ways of finding new words, of course. Sometimes an ordinary dictionary user will write to alert us to a new word. More often, analysis of vocabulary using electronic means can turn up words that are new to the language, perhaps by searching the various online databases now available for language research. You might think of this process as taking a census of the English language.

Once a citation for a given word is created, that word has taken its first step toward becoming an entry in the dictionary. It is by no means certain that it will become an entry, however. We need to see many citations from many publications showing the same word used the same way over a few years in order to indicate that the word is a permanent addition to English. We don't want to add a trendy word that will quickly drop from use, and we aren't interested in a pet word used by just one writer or found repeatedly in only one publication. Not that there's anything wrong with odd new words or this year's college slang—they just don't belong in the dictionary until they achieve a more enduring and general acceptance. The next step, therefore, is the collection of more citations, in order to measure the word's currency (evidence that it is used in current published writing) as well as its frequency (how often it is used).

When it's time to look at the newly collected citations for a revision of one of our dictionaries, the accumulated evidence of each word is assembled and an editor goes about the task of deciding whether the word has shown up often enough to deserve a new entry or, if the word is already in the dictionary, whether it has acquired a new meaning.

The definer begins work with a basic question: Is this word used by many people in many places? If the answer is "yes," then a second question presents itself: How is the word used?

This second question leads to a string of others: What part of speech does the word represent? Does the word have one meaning or several? Does it have alternative spellings? How is it pronounced? Where is it used? When did it enter the English language? What are its origins? Is it technical jargon? Is it slang? If it's a noun, does it form its plural in a conventional way? If it's a verb, is it transitive, intransitive, or both? Does it often appear in a phrase with a particular meaning that must be defined? Does it have a clear synonym or antonym? Is there controversy about how to use it?

Lexicographers, clearly, must make distinctions that most people never have to make, and all of them must be derived from the citations. Thus, the editor has begun as a spy by observing language, but must continue as a detective by getting answers from clues left behind as evidence. Seeking those answers makes today's editors high-tech investigators of language. There are now online collections of 18th-century American newspapers, Renaissance literature, and Civil War-era correspondence, for example, all of which are valuable sources of information about language. Tracing the history of words and expressions can now be done quickly and precisely. Lightning-fast searches make it possible to confirm suspicions about how a word is used and what other words it's used with (for example, to discover that *kind of* is much more common than *sort of*). It's even easier than ever to distinguish American English from British English; for example, we can now easily confirm that *different to* is extremely rare in American English by comparison with *different from* (by a ratio of 1:34), but not nearly so rare in British English (the British ratio is about 1:7).

If a word is always used in italics or between quotation marks when found in publications, it is probably so new or foreign that it is not yet a "naturalized citizen" of English—not yet ready to be included except in the largest dictionaries. A word that is a trademark needs to have developed a general meaning (like *Kleenex* or the verb *google*) in order to be added. Names of notable persons, places, or events like *Eiffel Tower* or *George Washington* may be omitted from a dictionary, but those that are often used with general meanings, such as *Romeo* ("a male lover"), *Hollywood* ("the American motion-picture industry"), and *Waterloo* ("a decisive or final defeat"), will usually be found in a college or desk dictionary. Two-, three-, and four-word entries are allowed in a good-sized dictionary, but only if they are impossible to understand without explanation. (Think of the difference between *cattle ranch*, which would not be entered because its meaning is obvious, and *dude ranch*, which isn't quite so obvious.)

Once the research is complete, the editor must write a definition that follows the dictionary's strict style guidelines. One of the most important rules is that a definition must normally be worded so that it could be substituted in a sentence for the word itself. Another traditional rule is that the definition must be as brief as possible, so that the dictionary can hold the maximum number of definitions. An unabridged dictionary, for example, may have nearly half a million defined words—far more than a college dictionary, which may have one third that number, or smaller paperback and student dictionaries, which may have fewer still.

But change—there's that word again—has now come to the dictionary format itself. The limitations of the printed page are rapidly being dissolved by the possibilities of the Internet, where space limitations have become irrelevant. The future will likely bring dictionaries with longer definitions, greater usage guidance, and more examples of each word in context—as well as audio pronunciations and even video lessons. The dictionary is gaining more flexibility as a reference at the same time as it has become accessible from anywhere. For the dictionary, joining the electronic revolution has been just the latest phase in a constant history of change.

Peter Sokolowski
Editor at Large for Merriam-Webster

A Selection of New Words

Modern Culture

abaya \ə-ˈbī-ə\ *n* : a loose-fitting full-length robe worn by some Muslim women

BFF *abbr* best friends forever

boomerang child *n* : a young adult who returns to live at his or her family home esp. for financial reasons

bromance \ˈbrō-ˌman(t)s\ *n* : a close nonsexual friendship between men — **bromantic** \brō-ˈman-tik\ *adj*

haram \hä-ˈräm\ *adj* : forbidden by Islamic law

hijab \hē-ˈjäb, -ˈjab\ *n* : the traditional covering for the hair and neck that is worn by Muslim women

honor killing *n* : the traditional practice in some countries of killing a family member who is believed to have brought shame on the family

LGBT *abbr* lesbian, gay, bisexual, and transgender

man cave *n* : a room or space (as in a basement) designed according to the taste of the man of the house to be used as his personal area for hobbies and leisure activities

speed dating *n* : an event at which each participant converses individually with all the prospective partners for a few minutes in order to select those with whom dates are desired

Eating and Drinking

acai *also* **açai** \ˌä-ˌsä-ˈē, -sī-ˈē\ *n* : a small dark purple fleshy berrylike fruit of a tall slender palm of tropical Central and South America that is often used in beverages

agnolotti \ˌän-yə-ˈlä-tē, -ˈlȯ-\ *n, pl* **agnolotti** : pasta in the form of semicircular cases containing a filling (as of meat, cheese, or vegetables)

ciabatta \chə-ˈbä-tə\ *n* : a flat oblong bread having a moist interior and a crispy crust

edamame \ˌe-də-ˈmä-mä\ *n* : immature green soybeans usu. in the pod

flexitarian \ˌflek-sə-ˈter-ē-ən\ *n* : one whose normally meatless diet occasionally includes meat or fish — **flexitarian** *adj*

goji \\'gō-'jē\ *n* : the dark red mildly tart berry of a thorny chiefly Asian shrub that is typically dried and used in beverages

kettle chip *n* : a type of potato chip made so as to be thicker and crunchier than the typical potato chip

locavore \\'lō-kə-ˌvȯr\ *n* : one who eats foods grown locally whenever possible

mojito \mō-'hē-tō\ *n, pl* **-tos** : a cocktail made of rum, sugar, mint, lime juice, and soda water

panino \pə-'nē-nō\ *n, pl* **panini** \pə-'nē-nē\ : a usu. grilled sandwich made with Italian bread

pescatarian *or* **pescetarian** \ˌpe-skə-'ter-ē-ən\ *n* : one whose diet includes fish but no other meat

rugelach *also* **rugalach** \\'rü-gə-lək\ *n, pl* **-lach** : a pastry made with cream-cheese dough that is rolled around a filling (as nuts, jam, or chocolate) and baked

slid·er \\'slī-dər\ *n* : a very small meat sandwich (as a hamburger) typically served on a bun

stevia \\'stē-vē-ə, -vyə\ *n* : a white powder derived from the leaves of a tropical stevia plant and used as noncaloric sweetener

udon \\'ü-ˌdän\ *or* **udon noodle** *n* : a thick Japanese noodle made from wheat flour and usu. served in a soup

white tea *n* : tea that is light in color and made from buds and immature leaves that undergo little to no oxidation before drying

za *or* **'za** \\'zä\ *n, slang* : pizza

Ecology

biowaste \\'bī-ō-ˌwāst\ *n* : waste (as manure, sawdust, or food scraps) that is composed chiefly of organic matter

carbon footprint *n* : the amount of greenhouse gases and specif. carbon dioxide emitted by something (as a personʃs activities or a productʃs manufacture and transport) during a given period

eco–friendly \ˌē-kō-'fren(d)-lē, ˌe-kō-\ *adj* : not environmentally harmful

green–collar \'grēn-'kä-lər\ *adj* : of, relating to, or involving actions for protecting the natural environment

HEPA \'he-pə\ *adj* : being, using, or containing a filter usu. designed to remove 99.97% of airborne particles measuring 0.0003 millimeters or greater in diameter passing through it

Electronics and Electronic Communications

blog \'blȯg, 'bläg\ *n* : a Web site that contains an online personal journal with reflections, comments, and often links to other sites provided by the writer — **blog** *vb* — **blog·ger** *n*

blogosphere \'blä-gə-ˌsfir\ *n* : all of the blogs on the Internet as a collective whole

cloud computing *n* : the practice of storing regularly used computer data on multiple computers in a network that can be accessed through the Internet

cyberbullying \'sī-bər-ˌbu̇-lē-iŋ, -'bə-\ *n* : the electronic posting of mean-spirited messages about a person (as a student) often done anonymously — **cyberbully** \-ˌbu̇-lē, -ˌbə-\ *n or vb*

DVR *abbr* digital video recorder

e–reader \'ē-ˌrē-dər\ *n* : a handheld electronic device designed to be used for reading e-books and similar material

FAQ \'fak, ˌef-ˌā-'kyü\ *n* : a document (as on a Web site) that provides answers to a list of typical questions that users might ask regarding a particular subject; *also* : a question included in such a document

goo·gle \'gü-gəl\ *vt* **goo·gled; goo·gling** \-g(ə-)liŋ\ *often cap* : to use the Google search software to obtain information about (something or someone) on the World Wide Web

HDMI \ˌāch-ˌdē-ˌem-'ī\ *trademark* — used for a digital video interface capable of transmitting information in high definition

IM \'ī-'em\ *vb* **IM'd; IM'ing** : to send an instant message to : to communicate by instant message

instant messaging *n* : a means or system for transmitting electronic messages instantly — **instant message** *n or vb*

LOL *or* **lol** *abbr* laugh out loud; laughing out loud

netbook \'net-ˌbu̇k\ *n* : a small portable computer designed primarily for wireless Internet access

OMG *or* **omg** *abbr* oh my God

photoshop \'fō-(ˌ)tō-ˌshäp\ *vt, often cap* : to alter (a digital image) with Photoshop software or other image-editing software esp. in a way that distorts reality (as for deliberately deceptive purposes)

RSS \ˌär-ˌes-'es\ *n* : a computer document format that enables updates to Web sites to be easily distributed

sexting \'sek-stiŋ\ *n* : the sending of sexually explicit messages or images by cell phone

SIM card \'sim\ *n* : a card that is inserted into a device (as a cell phone) and that is used to store data (as phone numbers or contact information)

smartphone \'smärt-ˌfōn\ *n* : a cell phone that includes additional software functions (as e-mail or an Internet browser)

social media *n pl but sing or pl in constr* : forms of electronic communication (as Web sites for social networking) through which users create online communities to share information, ideas, personal messages, and other content (as videos)

TiVo \'tē-(ˌ)vō\ *vt* : to record (as a television program) with a DVR

tweet *vi* : to post a message to the Twitter online message service

wiki \'wi-kē, 'wē-\ *n* : a Web site that allows visitors to make changes, contributions, or corrections

Entertainment

after–party \'af-tər-ˌpär-tē\ *n* : a party for invited guests that follows a main party or event

beer pong \-'päŋ, -'pȯŋ\ *n* : a game in which a set of beer-containing cups is placed at two ends of a table and in which a player scores by bouncing or tossing a Ping-Pong ball into an opponentʃs cup from which the opponent then has to drink the beer

Bollywood \'bä-lē-ˌwůd\ *n* : the motion-picture industry in India

crunk \'krəŋk\ *n* : a style of Southern rap music featuring repetitive chants and rapid dance rhythms

dude ranch *n* : a vacation resort offering activities (as horseback riding) typical of western ranches

flash mob *n* : a group of people summoned (as by e-mail or text message) to a designated location at a specified time to perform an indicated action before dispersing

gentleman's club *n* : a nightclub for men that features scantily clad women dancers

mixtape \'miks-ˌtāp\ *n* : a compilation of songs recorded (as onto a cassette tape or a CD) from various sources

pole dancing *n* : usu. solo dancing performed while using a fixed vertical pole as a prop — **pole dance** *n or vi* — **pole dancer** *n*

racino \rə-'sē-(ˌ)nō\ *n, pl* -nos : a racetrack at which slot machines are available for gamblers

sudoku \sü-'dō-kü\ *n* : a puzzle in which several numbers are to be filled into a 9x9 grid of squares so that every row, every column, and every 3x3 box contains the numbers 1 through 9

Texas Hold'em \-'hōl-dəm\ *n* : poker in which each player is dealt two cards facedown and all players share five cards dealt faceup

Ultimate Frisbee *n, often not cap* : a game played on a rectangular field between two seven-player teams in which a plastic disc is advanced by being thrown from player to player and in which a team scores by catching a throw in the opponentʃs end zone — called also *Ultimate*

zip line *n* : a cable suspended above an incline to which a pulley and harness are attached for a rider — **zip–line** *vi*

Health and Medicine

African swine fever *n* : an acute highly contagious usu. fatal disease of swine that is indigenous to Africa

andropause \\'an-drə-ˌpȯz\ *n* : a gradual and highly variable decline in the production of androgenic hormones and esp. testosterone in the human male that is held to occur during and after middle age — called also *male menopause*

blood–borne \\'bləd-ˌbȯrn\ *adj* : carried or transmitted by the blood

cardio *n* : exercise intended to strengthen the heart and blood vessels

feeding tube *n* : a flexible tube passed into the stomach for introducing fluids and liquid food into the stomach

first responder *n* : a person (as a police officer or an emergency medical technician) who is among those responsible for going immediately to the scene of an accident or emergency to provide assistance

germophobe \\'jər-mə-ˌfōb\ *n* : a person who has an abnormal fear of germs — **germophobic** \\ˌjər-mə-'fō-bik\ *adj*

medial collateral ligament *n* : a ligament of the inner knee that helps to stabilize the knee joint

Norwalk virus \\'nȯr-ˌwȯk-\ *n* : a highly infectious virus that causes acute inflammation of the stomach and the intestines in humans

physician assistant *n* : a person certified to provide basic medical services usu. under the supervision of a licensed physician — called also *PA, physician's assistant*

swine flu *n* : influenza in humans that is marked esp. by fever, sore throat, cough, chills, body aches, fatigue, and sometimes diarrhea and vomiting

West Nile *n* : a virus that causes an serious illness and that is spread esp. from birds to humans by mosquitoes

Science

dark energy *n* : a hypothetical form of energy that produces a force that opposes gravity and is thought to be the cause of the accelerating expansion of the universe

Kuiper Belt \\'kī-pər-\ *n* : a band of small celestial bodies beyond the orbit of Neptune from which many comets are believed to originate

dwarf planet *n* : a celestial body that orbits the sun and has a spherical shape but is not large enough to disturb other objects from its orbit

multiverse \\'məl-tē-ˌvərs\\ *n* : a theoretical reality that includes a possibly infinite number of parallel universes

Weapons and the Military

biosecurity \\ˌbī-(ˌ)ō-si-'kyùr-ə-tē\\ *n* : measures taken to ensure security from exposure to harmful biological agents

dirty bomb *n* : a bomb designed to release radioactive material

IED *abbr* improvised explosive device

RPG *abbr* rocket-propelled grenade

sleeper cell *n* : a terrorist cell whose members work under cover in an area until sent into action

waterboarding \\'wȯ-tər-ˌbȯr-diŋ, 'wä-\\ *n* : an interrogation technique in which water is forced into a detainee's mouth and nose so as to induce the sensation of drowning

yellowcake \\'ye-lō-ˌkāk, 'ye-lə-\\ *n* : partially refined uranium ore that is often used as an intermediate step in the production of nuclear weapons

Generic

air quotes *n pl* : a gesture made by raising and flexing the index and middle fingers of both hands that is used to call attention to a spoken word or expression

Amber Alert *n* : a widely publicized bulletin that alerts the public to a recently abducted or missing child

black box *n* : a device intended to be able to survive a crash that is in aircraft for recording cockpit conversations and flight data

bucket list *n* : a list of things that one has not done before but wants to do before dying

buzzkill \\'bəz-ˌkil\\ *n* : one that has a depressing or negative effect

crowdsourcing \\'kraùd-ˌsȯr-siŋ\\ *n* : the practice of obtaining needed services, ideas, or content by soliciting contributions from a large group of people

cube farm *n, slang* **:** an office in which employees work in cubicles

dry–erase board *n* **:** a hard smooth white surface used for writing or drawing on with erasable markers

elliptical trainer *n* **:** a stationary exercise device on which the user stands on two small rimmed platforms and moves them forward and back in an approximately elliptical path

fair trade *n* **:** a movement whose goal is to help producers in developing countries to get a fair price for their products so as to reduce poverty, provide for the ethical treatment of workers and farmers, and promote environmentally sustainable practices

fist bump *n* **:** a gesture in which two people bump their fists together (as in greeting or celebration) — **fist–bump** *vb*

frenemy \ˈfre-nə-mē\ *n, pl* **-mies** **:** one who pretends to be a friend but is actually an enemy

game changer *n* **:** a newly introduced element or factor that changes an existing situation or activity in a significant way

ginormous \jī-ˈnȯr-məs\ *adj* **:** extremely large

helicopter parent *n* **:** a parent who is overly involved in the life of his or her child

kitten heel *n* **:** a short stiletto-like heel on womenſs shoes

labradoodle \ˈla-brə-ˌdü-dᵊl\ *n, often cap* **:** a dog that is a cross between a Labrador retriever and a poodle

memory foam *n* **:** a dense foam that becomes more pliable when in contact with heat

mental health day *n* **:** a day that an employee takes off from work in order to relieve stress or renew vitality

mission creep *n* **:** the gradual broadening of the original objectives of a mission or organization

muscle shirt *n* **:** a close-fitting usu. sleeveless T-shirt

panic attack *n* **:** an episode of intense fear or apprehension that comes on suddenly

perfect storm *n* : a critical or disastrous situation created by a powerful concurrence of factors

person of interest : a person who is believed to be possibly involved in a crime but has not been charged or arrested

plan B *n* : an alternative plan of action for use if the original plan should fail

shero \'shir-(ˌ)ō\ *n, pl* **sheroes** : a woman regarded as a hero

shovel–ready \'shə-vəl-ˌre-dē\ *adj* : ready for the start of work (as of a construction project or site)

snitty \'sni-tē\ *adj* **snittier; -est** : disagreeably ill-tempered

staycation \'stā-'kā-shən\ *n* : a vacation spent at home or nearby — **staycationer** \'stā-'kā-sh(ə-)nər\ *n*

subprime \'səb-ˌprīm\ *adj* : having or being an interest rate that is higher than a prime rate and is extended esp. to low-income borrowers

ta–da *also* **ta–dah** \tä-'dä\ *interj* — used as mock fanfare to call attention to something remarkable

tase \'tāz\ *vt* **tased; tasing** *often cap* : to shoot with a Taser gun

tighty–whities *also* **tighty–whiteys** \'tī-tē-'wī-tēz\ *n pl, slang* : snug white underpants for men

T–note \'tē-ˌnōt\ *n* : a U.S. government bond usu. with a maturity of not less than one year or more than seven years

woo–hoo *or* **whoo–hoo** \'wü-'hü, ˌwü-\ *interj* — used to express exuberant delight or approval

Using this Book

Vocabulary Entries

Main entries follow one another in alphabetical order. Centered dots within the entries show points at which a hyphen may be put at the end of a line:

ag·gre·gate

Homographs of closely related origin are run into a single main entry, with second and succeeding homograph spellings represented by a swung dash:

as . . . *adv* **1 :** to the same degree **2 :** for example ∼ *conj* **1 :** in the same way or degree as **2 :** while **3 :** because **4 :** though ∼ *pron*—used after *same* or *such* ∼ *prep* : in the capacity of

Homographs of distinctly different origin are given separate entries with preceding raised numerals:

¹**clove** . . . *n* **:** section of a bulb
²**clove** *past of* CLEAVE
³**clove** *n* **:** dried flower bud of an East Indian tree used as a spice

Variant spellings that are quite common appear at the main entry following a comma:

dem·a·gogue, dem·a·gog

Inflected forms, such as the plurals of nouns, the principal parts of verbs, and the comparative and superlative forms of adjectives and certain adverbs, are shown when they are irregular, when adding the inflectional suffix makes a change in the base form of the word, such as the dropping of a final *e,* or when there might be doubt about their spelling. They are given either in full or cut back to a convenient point of end-of-line hyphenation:

> **emerge** . . . *vb* **emerged; emerg·ing**
> **have** . . . *vb* **had** . . . **hav·ing** . . . **has**
> **mouse** . . . *n, pl* **mice**
> **mys·ti·fy** . . . *vb* **-fied; -fy·ing**
> **pet·ty** . . . *adj* **-ti·er; -est**
> **ra·bies** . . . *n, pl* **rabies**

Common variants of inflected forms are also shown even if they are regular:

> **equi·lib·ri·um** . . . *n, pl* **-ri·ums** *or* **-ri**a . . . **:** state of
> balance

When the inflected forms of a verb involve no irregularity except the doubling of a final consonant, the doubled consonant is shown instead of full or cutback inflected forms:

> **ex·tol** . . . *vb* **-ll- :** praise highly

This means the inflected forms of *extol* are *extolled; extolling.*

Several other kinds of entries are also found in this dictionary. A variant or inflected form whose alphabetical place is distant from the main entry is entered at its own place as a **cross-reference entry** with the referenced main entry shown in small capital letters:

> **²fell** *past of* FALL

A **run-in entry** is a term that is related to the main entry and that is defined or identified within a definition. The run-in entry appears within a definition in boldface type set off by parentheses:

> **ha·zel** . . . *n* **1 :** . . . small tree bearing edible nuts
> **(hazel·nuts)**

An **undefined run-on entry** may appear after all definitions of a main entry, set off by a dash:

heal . . . *vb* **:** make or become sound or whole—**healer** *n*

The meaning of an undefined run-on entry word can be inferred easily from the meaning of the main entry where it appears and that of another main entry, often a suffix, elsewhere in the dictionary.

A **run-on phrase** is a group of two or more words involving the main entry as its major element and having a special meaning of its own. The run-on phrase always has a definition and it comes at the end of an entry, following an undefined run-on entry if there is one:

take . . . *vb* . . . —**tak·er** *n*—**take advantage of :** profit by . . .

Self-Explanatory Words

Lists of undefined words whose meanings can be inferred from the meaning of a prefix and that of a word entered at its own place in the dictionary will be found at the following prefix entries: *anti-, bi-, co-, counter-, extra-, hyper-, in-, inter-, mini-, multi-, non-, over-, post-, pre-, re-, self-, sub-, super-, un-,* and *vice-.*

Pronunciation

Information about the **pronunciation** is placed within slant lines:

ac·com·pa·ny \ə'kəmpənē\ . . .

Where the pronunciation or a portion of a pronunciation is implied by a preceding pronunciation or by another entry, the specific pronunciation information may be omitted or indicated in a cutback form which shows the information for that portion in question:

¹**bull** \\'bu̇l\ *n* **:** large adult male animal . . .
²**bull** *n* **1 :** papal letter . . .
bull·dog *n* **:** compact short-haired dog
bull·doze \-ˌdōz\ *vb* **1 :** move or level with a . . .

A full list of the symbols used to indicate pronunciation is shown on page xii of this dictionary.

Functional Labels

Every main entry has an italic label indicating its grammatical function. The traditional parts of speech are indicated by abbreviations:

awake *adj* (adjective)
aloud *adv* (adverb)
al·though *conj* (conjunction)
amen *interj* (interjection)
²**capital** *n* (noun)
semi- *prefix* (prefix)
ev·ery·body *pron* (pronoun)
mis·quote *vb* (verb)

Other italic functional labels either are spelled out or are combinations of one or more part-of-speech elements:

an *indefinite article*
the *definite article*
ought *verbal auxiliary*
-able, -ible *adj suffix*
eigh·teen *adj or pron*
eye·glass·es *n pl*
-like *adj comb form*
un·der·hand·ed *adj or adv*
-ize *vb suffix*
-ness *n suffix*

Guide Words

At the top of every two-page spread are printed the first and last boldface words to be found on those pages. The guide word on the left-hand page is the alphabetically first bold word, and the guide word on the right-hand page is the alphabetically last bold word.

The guide words indicate the range of boldface entries to be found on the pages, and this includes all boldface words: main entry words, variant spellings, inflected forms, run-in entries, undefined run-on entries, and defined run-on phrases. At the top of page 2, for example, is the guide word **abeyance**, which is the first main entry on that page; the guide word for page 3 is **abstract,** which is the last main entry on that page.

But the guide words indicating the alphabetically first and last words need not be just main entries. On page 20 is the guide word **alternately,** an undefined run-on at the entry **alternate** (which starts on page 19). It is used as a guide word because it is earlier alphabetically than the first main entry on page 20, **alternating current**. The guide word at the top of page 21 is **amicably,** a run-on at the main entry **amicable**. This tells you that all of the words alphabetically between *alternately* and *amicably* will be found on this two-page spread.

The only exception to this rule of using the alphabetically first and last words for guide words occurs when following the rule would make the guide words on successive pages out of alphabetical order. On page 71, the guide is **boned,** even though the alphabetically last boldface words is **boning**. This happens because the first guide word on page 72 is **boneless,** and **boned** is chosen for page 71 to keep the guide words in alphabetical sequence.

Abbreviations

All abbreviations used in the dictionary are listed, along with a number of other common abbreviations, in a special section immediately following the dictionary proper.

Pronunciation Symbols

ə banana, collide, abut; raised \ə\ in \ᵊl, ᵊn\ as in battle, cotton; in \lᵊ, mᵊ, rᵊ\ as in French table, prisme, titre

ˈə, ˌə humbug, abut

ər operation, further

a map, patch

ā day, fate

ä bother, cot, father

à father as pronounced by those who do not rhyme it with *bother*

au̇ now, out

b baby, rib

ch chin, catch

d did, adder

e set, red

ē beat, nosebleed, easy

f fifty, cuff

g go, big

h hat, ahead

hw whale

i tip, banish

ī site, buy

j job, edge

k kin, cook

k̲ German ich, Buch

l lily, cool

m murmur, dim

n nine, own; raised \ⁿ\ indicates that a preceding vowel or diphthong is pronounced through both nose and mouth, as in French *bon* \bōⁿ\

ŋ sing, singer, finger, ink

ō bone, hollow

ȯ saw, cork

œ French boeuf, German Hᶺlle

œ̄ French feu, German Hohle

ȯi toy, sawing

p pepper, lip

r rarity

s source, less

sh shy, mission

t tie, attack

th thin, ether

t̲h̲ then, either

ü boot, few \ˈfyü\

u̇ put, pure \ˈpyu̇r\

ᴜe German füllen

ᴜ̄e French rue, German fühlen

v vivid, give

w we, away

y yard, cue \ˈkyü\; raised \ʸ\ indicates that a preceding \l\, \n\, or \w\ is modified by the placing of the tongue tip against the lower front teeth, as in French *digne* \dēnʸ\

z zone, raise

zh vision, pleasure

\ slant line used in pairs to mark the beginning and end of a transcription

ˈ mark at the beginning of a syllable that has primary (strongest) stress: \ˈpen-mən͵ship\

ˌ mark at the beginning of a syllable that has secondary (next-strongest) stress: \ˈpenmən͵ship\

Webster's
New Explorer
LARGE PRINT
Dictionary
THIRD EDITION

A

¹a \ˈā\ *n, pl* **a's** *or* **as** \ˈāz\ : 1st letter of the alphabet

²a \ə, ˈā\ *indefinite article* : one or some — used to indicate an unspecified or unidentified individual

aard·vark \ˈärd₁värk\ *n* : ant‑eating African mammal

aback \ə'bak\ *adv* : by surprise

aba·cus \ˈabəkəs\ *n, pl* **aba·ci** \ˈabə₁sī, -₁kē\ *or* **aba·cus·es** : calculating instrument using rows of beads

abaft \ə'baft\ *adv* : toward or at the stern

ab·a·lo·ne \₁abə'lōnē\ *n* : large edible shellfish

¹aban·don \ə'bandən\ *vb* : give up without intent to re‑claim — **aban·don·ment** *n*

²abandon *n* : thorough yielding to impulses

aban·doned \ə'bandənd\ *adj* : morally unrestrained

abase \ə'bās\ *vb* **abased; abas·ing** : lower in dignity — **abase·ment** *n*

abash \ə'bash\ *vb* : embarrass — **abashment** *n*

abate \ə'bāt\ *vb* **abat·ed; abat·ing** : decrease or lessen

abate·ment \ə'bātmənt\ *n* : tax reduction

ab·at·toir \ˈabə₁twär\ *n* : slaughterhouse

ab·bess \ˈabəs\ *n* : head of a convent

ab·bey \ˈabē\ *n, pl* **-beys** : monastery or convent

ab·bot \ˈabət\ *n* : head of a monastery

ab·bre·vi·ate \ə'brēvē₁āt\ *vb* **-at·ed; -at·ing** : shorten — **ab·bre·vi·a·tion** \ə₁brēvē'āshən\ *n*

ab·di·cate \ˈabdi₁kāt\ *vb* **-cat·ed; -cat·ing** : renounce — **ab·di·ca·tion** \₁abdi'kāshən\ *n*

ab·do·men \ˈabdəmən, ab'dōmən\ *n* **1** : body area between chest and pelvis **2** : hindmost part of an insect — **ab·dom·i·nal** \ab'dämənᵊl\ *adj* — **ab·dom·i·nal·ly** *adv*

ab·duct \ab'dəkt\ *vb* : kidnap — **ab·duc·tion** \-'dəkshən\ *n* — **ab·duc·tor** \-tər\ *n*

abed \ə'bed\ *adv or adj* : in bed

ab·er·ra·tion \₁abə'rāshən\ *n* : deviation or distortion — **ab·er·rant** \a'berənt\ *adj*

abet \ə'bet\ *vb* **-tt-** : incite or encourage — **abet·tor, abet·ter** \-ər\ *n*

abey·ance \ə'bāəns\ *n* : state of inactivity

ab·hor \əb'hȯr, ab-\ *vb* **-rr-** : hate — **ab·hor·rence** \-əns\ *n* — **ab·hor·rent** \-ənt\ *adj*

abide \ə'bīd\ *vb* **abode** \-'bōd\ *or* **abid·ed; abid·ing** **1** : endure **2** : remain, last, or reside

ab·ject \'ab,jekt, ab'-\ *adj* : low in spirit or hope — **ab·jec·tion** \ab'jekshən\ *n* — **ab·ject·ly** *adv* — **ab·ject·ness** *n*

ab·jure \ab'ju̇r\ *vb* **1** : renounce **2** : abstain from — **ab·ju·ra·tion** \,abjə'rāshən\ *n*

ablaze \ə'blāz\ *adj or adv* : on fire

able \'ābəl\ *adj* **abler** \-blər\; **ablest** \-bləst\ **1** : having sufficient power, skill, or resources **2** : skilled or efficient — **abil·i·ty** \ə'bilətē\ *n* — **ably** \'āblē\ *adv*

-able, -ible \əbəl\ *adj suffix* **1** : capable of, fit for, or worthy of **2** : tending, given, or liable to

ab·lu·tion \ə'blüshən, a'blü-\ *n* : washing of one's body

ab·ne·gate \'abni,gāt\ *vb* **-gat·ed; -gat·ing** **1** : relinquish **2** : renounce — **ab·ne·ga·tion** \,abni'gāshən\ *n*

ab·nor·mal \ab'nȯrməl\ *adj* : deviating from the normal or average — **ab·nor·mal·i·ty** \,abnər'malətē, -nȯr-\ *n* — **ab·nor·mal·ly** *adv*

aboard \ə'bōrd\ *adv* : on, onto, or within a car, ship, or aircraft ～ *prep* : on or within

abode \ə'bōd\ *n* : residence

abol·ish \ə'bälish\ *vb* : do away with — **ab·o·li·tion** \,abə'lishən\ *n*

abom·i·na·ble \ə'bämənəbəl\ *adj* : thoroughly unpleasant or revolting

abom·i·nate \ə'bämə,nāt\ *vb* **-nat·ed; -nat·ing** : hate — **abom·i·na·tion** \ə,bämə'nāshən\ *n*

ab·orig·i·nal \,abə'rijənəl\ *adj* **1** : original **2** : primitive

ab·orig·i·ne \-'rijənē\ *n* : original inhabitant

abort \ə'bȯrt\ *vb* : terminate prematurely — **abor·tive** \-'bȯrtiv\ *adj*

abor·tion \ə'bȯrshən\ *n* : spontaneous or induced termination of pregnancy

abound \ə'bau̇nd\ *vb* : be plentiful

about \ə'bau̇t\ *adv* : around ～ *prep* **1** : on every side of **2** : on the verge of **3** : having as a subject

above \ə'bəv\ *adv* : in or to a higher place ～ *prep* **1** : in or to a higher place than **2** : more than

above·board *adv or adj* : without deception

abrade \ə'brād\ *vb* **abrad·ed; abrad·ing** : wear away by rubbing — **abra·sion** \-'brā-zhən\ *n*

abra·sive \ə'brāsiv\ *n* : substance for grinding, smoothing, or polishing ∼ *adj* **1** : tending to abrade **2** : causing irritation — **abra·sive·ly** *adv* — **abra·sive·ness** *n*

abreast \ə'brest\ *adv or adj* **1** : side by side **2** : up to a standard or level

abridge \ə'brij\ *vb* **abridged; abridg·ing** : shorten or condense — **abridg·ment, abridge·ment** *n*

abroad \ə'brȯd\ *adv or adj* **1** : over a wide area **2** : outside one's country

ab·ro·gate \'abrəgāt\ *vb* **-gat·ed; -gat·ing** : annul or revoke — **ab·ro·ga·tion** \ˌabrə'gā-shən\ *n*

abrupt \ə'brəpt\ *adj* **1** : sudden **2** : so quick as to seem rude — **abrupt·ly** *adv*

ab·scess \'abˌses\ *n* : collection of pus surrounded by inflamed tissue — **ab·scessed** \-ˌsest\ *adj*

ab·scond \ab'skänd\ *vb* : run away and hide

ab·sent \'absənt\ *adj* : not present ∼ **ab·sent** \ab'sent\ *vb* : keep oneself away — **ab-sence** \'absəns\ *n* — **absen-tee** \ˌabsən'tē\ *n*

ab·sent·mind·ed \ˌabsənt-'mīndəd\ *adj* : unaware of one's surroundings or action — **ab·sent·mind·ed·ly** *adv* — **ab·sent·mind·ed·ness** *n*

ab·so·lute \'absəˌlüt, ˌabsə'-\ *adj* **1** : pure **2** : free from restriction **3** : definite — **ab·so·lute·ly** *adv*

ab·so·lu·tion \ˌabsə'lüshən\ *n* : remission of sins

ab·solve \əb'zälv, -'sälv\ *vb* **-solved; -solv·ing** : set free of the consequences of guilt

ab·sorb \əb'sȯrb, -'zȯrb\ *vb* **1** : suck up or take in as a sponge does **2** : engage (one's attention) — **ab·sor·ben·cy** \-'sȯrbənsē, -'zȯr-\ *n* — **ab·sor·bent** \-bənt\ *adj or n* — **ab·sorb·ing** *adj*

ab·sorp·tion \əb'sȯrpshən, -'zȯrp-\ *n* : process of absorbing — **ab·sorp·tive** \-tiv\ *adj*

ab·stain \əb'stān\ *vb* : refrain from doing something — **ab·stain·er** *n* — **ab·sten·tion** \-'stenchən\ *n* — **ab·sti·nence** \'abstənəns\ *n*

ab·ste·mi·ous \ab'stēmēəs\ *adj* : sparing in use of food or drink — **ab·ste·mi·ous·ly** *adv* — **ab·ste·mi·ous·ness** *n*

ab·stract \ab'strakt, 'abˌ-\ *adj* **1** : expressing a quality apart from an object **2** : not representing something specific ~ \\'ab̩-\\ *n* : summary ~ \\ab'-, 'ab̩-\\ *vb* **1** : remove or separate **2** : make an abstract of — **ab·stract·ly** *adv* — **ab·stract·ness** *n*

ab·strac·tion \\ab'strakshən\\ *n* **1** : act of abstracting **2** : abstract idea or work of art

ab·struse \\əb'strüs, ab-\\ *adj* : hard to understand — **ab·struse·ly** *adv* — **ab·struse·ness** *n*

ab·surd \\əb'sərd, -'zərd\\ *adj* : ridiculous or unreasonable — **ab·sur·di·ty** \\-ətē\\ *n* — **ab·surd·ly** *adv*

abun·dant \\ə'bəndənt\\ *adj* : more than enough — **abun·dance** \\-dəns\\ *n* — **abun·dant·ly** *adv*

abuse \\ə'byüz\\ *vb* **abused; abus·ing** **1** : misuse **2** : mistreat **3** : attack with words ~ \\-'byüs\\ *n* **1** : corrupt practice **2** : improper use **3** : mistreatment **4** : coarse and insulting speech — **abus·er** *n* — **abu·sive** \\-'byüsiv\\ *adj* — **abu·sive·ly** *adv* — **abu·sive·ness** *n*

abut \\ə'bət\\ *vb* **-tt-** : touch along a border — **abut·ter** *n*

abut·ment \\ə'bətmənt\\ *n* : part of a bridge that supports weight

abys·mal \\ə'bizməl\\ *adj* **1** : immeasurably deep **2** : wretched — **abys·mal·ly** *adv*

abyss \\ə'bis\\ *n* : immeasurably deep gulf

-ac \\̩ak\\ *n suffix* : one affected with

aca·cia \\ə'kāshə\\ *n* : leguminous tree or shrub

ac·a·dem·ic \\̩akə'demik\\ *adj* **1** : relating to schools or colleges **2** : theoretical — **academic** *n* — **ac·a·dem·i·cal·ly** \\-iklē\\ *adv*

acad·e·my \\ə'kadəmē\\ *n, pl* **-mies** **1** : private high school **2** : society of scholars or artists

acan·thus \\ə'kanthəs\\ *n, pl* **acan·thus** **1** : prickly Mediterranean herb **2** : ornament representing acanthus leaves

ac·cede \\ak'sēd\\ *vb* **-ced·ed; -ced·ing** **1** : become a party to an agreement **2** : express approval **3** : enter upon an office

ac·cel·er·ate \\ik'selə̩rāt, ak-\\ *vb* **-at·ed; -at·ing** **1** : bring about earlier **2** : speed up — **ac·cel·er·a·tion** \\-̩selə'rāshən\\ *n*

ac·cel·er·a·tor \\ik'selə̩rātər, ak-\\ *n* : pedal for controlling the speed of a motor vehicle

ac·cent \\'ak̩sent\\ *n* **1** : distinctive manner of pronunciation **2** : prominence given to one syllable of a word **3**

: mark (as ´, `, ^) over a vowel in writing or printing to indicate pronunciation ∼ \'ak͵-, ak'-\ *vb* : emphasize — **ac·cen·tu·al** \ak'senchəwəl\ *adj*

ac·cen·tu·ate \ak'senchə͵wāt\ *vb* **-at·ed; -at·ing** : stress or show off by a contrast — **ac·cen·tu·a·tion** \-͵senchə'wā-shən\ *n*

ac·cept \ik'sept, ak-\ *vb* **1** : receive willingly **2** : agree to — **ac·cept·abil·i·ty** \ik͵septə'bilətē, ak-\ *n* — **ac·cept·able** \-'septəbəl\ *adj* — **ac·cep·tance** \-'septəns\ *n*

ac·cess \'ak͵ses\ *n* : capability or way of approaching — **ac·ces·si·bil·i·ty** \ik͵sesə'bilətē, ak-\ *n* — **ac·ces·si·ble** \-'sesəbəl\ *adj*

ac·ces·sion \ik'seshən, ak-\ *n* **1** : something added **2** : act of taking office

ac·ces·so·ry \ik'sesərē, ak-\ *n, pl* **-ries 1** : nonessential addition **2** : one guilty of aiding a criminal — **accessory** *adj*

ac·ci·dent \'aksədənt\ *n* **1** : event occurring by chance or unintentionally **2** : chance — **ac·ci·den·tal** \͵aksə'dentᵊl\ *adj* — **ac·ci·den·tal·ly** *adv*

ac·claim \ə'klām\ *vb or n* : praise

ac·cla·ma·tion \͵aklə'māshən\ *n* **1** : eager applause **2** : unanimous vote

ac·cli·mate \'aklə͵māt, ə'klīmət\ *vb* **-mat·ed; -mat·ing** : acclimatize — **ac·cli·ma·tion** \͵aklə'māshən, -͵klī-\ *n*

ac·cli·ma·tize \ə'klīmə͵tīz\ *vb* **-tized; -tiz·ing** : accustom to a new climate or situation — **ac·cli·ma·ti·za·tion** \-͵klīmətə'zāshən\ *n*

ac·co·lade \'akə͵lād\ *n* : expression of praise

ac·com·mo·date \ə'kämə͵dāt\ *vb* **-dat·ed; -dat·ing 1** : adapt **2** : provide with something needed **3** : hold without crowding

ac·com·mo·da·tion \ə͵kämə-'dāshən\ *n* **1** : quarters — usu. pl. **2** : act of accommodating

ac·com·pa·ny \ə'kəmpənē\ *vb* **-nied; -ny·ing 1** : go or occur with **2** : play supporting music — **ac·com·pa·ni·ment** \-nəmənt\ *n* — **ac·com·pa·nist** \-nist\ *n*

ac·com·plice \ə'kämpləs, -'kəm-\ *n* : associate in crime

ac·com·plish \ə'kämplish, -'kəm-\ *vb* : do, fulfill, or bring about — **ac·com·plished** *adj* — **ac·com·plish·er** *n* — **ac·com·plish·ment** *n*

ac·cord \ə'kȯrd\ *vb* **1** : grant **2** : agree ∼ *n* **1** : agreement **2** : willingness to act — **ac·cor·dance** \-'kȯrdᵊns\ *n* — **ac·cor·dant** \-ᵊnt\ *adj*

ac·cord·ing·ly \ə'kȯrdiŋlē\ *adv* : consequently

according to *prep* **1** : in conformity with **2** : as stated by

ac·cor·di·on \ə'kȯrdēən\ *n* : keyboard instrument with a bellows and reeds ∼ *adj* : folding like an accordion bellows — **ac·cor·di·on·ist** \-nist\ *n*

ac·cost \ə'kȯst\ *vb* : approach and speak to esp. aggressively

ac·count \ə'kau̇nt\ *n* **1** : statement of business transactions **2** : credit arrangement with a vendor **3** : report **4** : worth **5** : sum deposited in a bank ∼ *vb* : give an explanation

ac·count·able \ə'kau̇ntəbəl\ *adj* : responsible — **ac·count·abil·i·ty** \-ˌkau̇ntə'bilətē\ *n*

ac·coun·tant \ə'kau̇ntᵊnt\ *n* : one skilled in accounting — **ac·coun·tan·cy** \-ᵊnsē\ *n*

ac·count·ing \ə'kau̇ntiŋ\ *n* : financial record keeping

ac·cou·tre, ac·cou·ter \ə'kütər\ *vb* **-tred** *or* **-tered; -tring** *or* **-ter·ing** \-'kütəriŋ, -'kütriŋ\ : equip

ac·cou·tre·ment, ac·cou·ter·ment \ə'kütrəmənt, -'kütər-\ *n* **1** : accessory item — usu. pl. **2** : identifying characteristic

ac·cred·it \ə'kredət\ *vb* **1** : approve officially **2** : attribute

— ac·cred·i·ta·tion \-ˌkredə-'tāshən\ *n*

ac·crue \ə'krü\ *vb* **-crued; -cru·ing** : be added by periodic growth — **ac·cru·al** \-əl\ *n*

ac·cu·mu·late \ə'kyümyəˌlāt\ *vb* **-lat·ed; -lat·ing** : collect or pile up — **ac·cu·mu·la·tion** \-ˌkyümyə'lāshən\ *n*

ac·cu·rate \'akyərət\ *adj* : free from error — **ac·cu·ra·cy** \-rəsē\ *n* — **ac·cu·rate·ly** *adv* — **ac·cu·rate·ness** *n*

ac·cursed \ə'kərst, -'kərsəd\ **ac·curst** \ə'kərst\ *adj* **1** : being under a curse **2** : damnable

ac·cuse \ə'kyüz\ *vb* **-cused; -cus·ing** : charge with an offense — **ac·cu·sa·tion** \ˌakyə'zāshən\ *n* — **ac·cus·er** *n*

ac·cused \ə'kyüzd\ *n, pl* **-cused** : defendant in a criminal case

ac·cus·tom \ə'kəstəm\ *vb* : make familiar through use or experience

ace \'ās\ *n* : one that excels

acer·bic \ə'sərbik, a-\ *adj* : sour or biting in temper, mood, or tone

acet·amin·o·phen \ə,sētə-'minəfən\ *n* : pain reliever

ac·e·tate \'asəˌtāt\ *n* : fabric or plastic derived from acetic acid ace·tic acid \ə'sētik-\ *n* : acid found in vinegar

acet·y·lene \ə'set°lən, -°l₁ēn\ *n* : colorless gas used as a fuel in welding

ache \'āk\ *vb* ached; ach·ing 1 : suffer a dull persistent pain 2 : yearn — ache *n*

achieve \ə'chēv\ *vb* achieved; achiev·ing : gain by work or effort — achieve·ment *n* — achiev·er *n*

ac·id \'asəd\ *adj* 1 : sour or biting to the taste 2 : sharp in manner 3 : of or relating to an acid ~ *n* : sour water-soluble chemical compound that reacts with a base to form a salt — acid·ic \ə'sidik\ *adj* — acid·i·fy \ə'sidə₁fī\ *vb* — acid·i·ty \-ətē\ *n* — acid·ly *adv*

ac·knowl·edge \ik'nälij, ak-\ *vb* -edged; -edg·ing 1 : admit as true 2 : admit the authority of 3 : express thanks for — ac·knowl·edg·ment *n*

ac·me \'akmē\ *n* : highest point

ac·ne \'aknē\ *n* : skin disorder marked esp. by pimples

ac·o·lyte \'akə₁līt\ *n* : assistant to a member of clergy in a religious service

acorn \'ā₁korn, -kərn\ *n* : nut of the oak

acous·tic \ə'küstik\ *adj* : relating to hearing or sound —

acous·ti·cal \-stikəl\ *adj* — acous·ti·cal·ly \-klē\ *adv*

acous·tics \ə'küstiks\ *n sing or pl* 1 : science of sound 2 : qualities in a room that affect how sound is heard

ac·quaint \ə'kwānt\ *vb* 1 : inform 2 : make familiar

ac·quain·tance \ə'kwānt°ns\ *n* 1 : personal knowledge 2 : person with whom one is acquainted — ac·quain·tance·ship *n*

ac·qui·esce \₁akwē'es\ *vb* -esced; -esc·ing : consent or submit — ac·qui·es·cence \-'es°ns\ *n* — ac·qui·es·cent \-°nt\ *adj* — ac·qui·es·cent·ly *adv*

ac·quire \ə'kwīr\ *vb* -quired; -quir·ing : gain

ac·qui·si·tion \₁akwə'zishən\ *n* : a gaining or something gained — ac·qui·si·tive \ə'kwizətiv\ *adj*

ac·quit \ə'kwit\ *vb* -tt- 1 : pronounce not guilty 2 : conduct (oneself) usu. well — ac·quit·tal \-°l\ *n*

acre \'ākər\ *n* 1 *pl* : lands 2 : 4840 square yards

acre·age \'ākərij\ *n* : area in acres

ac·rid \'akrəd\ *adj* : sharp and biting — acrid·i·ty \a'kridətē, ə-\ *n* — ac·rid·ly *adv* — ac·rid·ness *n*

ac·ri·mo·ny \'akrə,mōnē\ *n,
pl* **-nies** : harshness of language or feeling — **ac·ri·mo·ni·ous** \,akrə'mōnēəs\ *adj*
— **ac·ri·mo·ni·ous·ly** *adv*

ac·ro·bat \'akrə,bat\ *n* : performer of tumbling feats —
ac·ro·bat·ic \,akrə'batik\ *adj*

across \ə'krȯs\ *adv* : to or on
the opposite side ∼ *prep* **1**
: to or on the opposite side of
2 : on so as to cross

acryl·ic \ə'krilik\ *n* **1** : plastic
used for molded parts or in
paints **2** : synthetic textile fiber

act \'akt\ *n* **1** : thing done **2**
: law **3** : main division of a
play ∼ *vb* **1** : perform in a
play **2** : conduct oneself **3**
: operate **4** : produce an effect

ac·tion \'akshən\ *n* **1** : legal
proceeding **2** : manner or
method of performing **3** : activity **4** : thing done over a period of time or in stages **5**
: combat **6** : events of a literary plot **7** : operating mechanism

ac·ti·vate \'aktə,vāt\ *vb* **-vat·ed; -vat·ing** : make active or
reactive — **ac·ti·va·tion** \,aktə-'vāshən\ *n*

ac·tive \'aktiv\ *adj* **1** : causing action or change **2**
: lively, vigorous, or energetic
3 : erupting or likely to erupt
4 : now in operation — **active**
n — **ac·tive·ly** *adv*

ac·tiv·i·ty \ak'tivətē\ *n, pl*
-ties 1 : quality or state of being active **2** : what one is actively doing

ac·tor \'aktər\ *n* : one that
acts

ac·tress \'aktrəs\ *n* : woman
who acts in plays

ac·tu·al \'akchəwəl\ *adj* : really existing — **ac·tu·al·i·ty**
\,akchə'walətē\ *n* — **ac·tu·al·iza·tion** \,akchəwələ-'zāshən\ *n* — **ac·tu·al·ize**
\'akchəwə,līz\ *vb* — **ac·tu·al·ly** *adv*

ac·tu·ary \'akchə,werē\ *n, pl*
-ar·ies : one who calculates
insurance risks and premiums
— **ac·tu·ar·i·al** \,akchə-'werēəl\ *adj*

ac·tu·ate \'akchə,wāt\ *vb* **-at·ed; -at·ing** : put into action —
ac·tu·a·tor \-,wātər\ *n*

acu·men \ə'kyümən\ *n* : mental keenness

acu·punc·ture \'akyù,pəŋk-chər\ *n* : treatment by puncturing the body with needles
— **acu·punc·tur·ist** \,akyù-'pəŋkchərist\ *n*

acute \ə'kyüt\ *adj* **acut·er;
acut·est 1** : sharp **2** : containing less than 90 degrees **3**
: mentally alert **4** : severe —
acute·ly *adv* — **acute·ness** *n*

ad \'ad\ *n* : advertisement

ad·age \'adij\ *n* : old familiar
saying

ad·a·mant \\'adəmənt, -ˌmant\ *adj* : insistent — **ad·a·mant·ly** *adv*

adapt \ə'dapt\ *vb* : adjust to be suitable for a new use or condition — **adapt·abil·i·ty** \əˌdaptə'bilətē\ *n* — **adapt·able** *adj* — **ad·ap·ta·tion** \ˌadˌap'tāshən, -əp-\ *n* — **adap·ter** *n* — **adap·tive** \ə'daptiv\ *adj*

add \'ad\ *vb* **1** : join to something else so as to increase in amount **2** : say further **3** : find a sum — **ad·di·tion** \ə'dishən\ *n*

ad·der \'adər\ *n* **1** : poisonous European snake **2** : No. American snake

ad·dict \'adikt\ *n* : one who is psychologically or physiologically dependent (as on a drug) ~ \ə'dikt\ *vb* : cause to become an addict — **ad·dic·tion** \ə'dikshən\ *n* — **ad·dic·tive** \-'diktiv\ *adj*

ad·di·tion·al \ə'dishənəl\ *adj* : existing as a result of adding — **ad·di·tion·al·ly** *adv*

ad·di·tive \'adətiv\ *n* : substance added to another

ad·dle \'ad°l\ *vb* **-dled; -dling** : confuse

ad·dress \ə'dres\ *vb* **1** : direct one's remarks to **2** : mark an address on ~ \ə'dres, 'adˌres\ *n* **1** : formal speech **2** : place where a person may be reached or mail may be delivered

ad·duce \ə'düs, -'dyüs\ *vb* **-duced; -duc·ing** : offer as proof

ad·e·noid \'adˌnȯid, -°nȯid\ *n* : enlarged tissue near the opening of the nose into the throat — usu. pl. — **adenoid, ad·e·noi·dal** \-əl\ *adj*

adept \ə'dept\ *adj* : highly skilled — **adept·ly** *adv* — **adept·ness** *n*

ad·e·quate \'adikwət\ *adj* : good or plentiful enough — **ad·e·qua·cy** \-kwəsē\ *n* — **ad·e·quate·ly** *adv*

ad·here \ad'hir, əd-\ *vb* **-hered; -her·ing** **1** : remain loyal **2** : stick fast — **ad·her·ence** \-'hirəns\ *n* — **ad·her·ent** \-ənt\ *adj or n*

ad·he·sion \ad'hēzhən, əd-\ *n* : act or state of adhering

ad·he·sive \-'hēsiv, -ziv\ *adj* : tending to adhere ~ *n* : adhesive substance

adieu \ə'dü, -dyü\ *n, pl* **adieus** *or* **adieux** \-'düz,-'dyüz\ : farewell

ad·ja·cent \ə'jās°nt\ *adj* : situated near or next

ad·jec·tive \'ajiktiv\ *n* : word that serves as a modifier of a noun — **ad·jec·ti·val** \ˌajik-'tīvəl\ *adj* — **ad·jec·ti·val·ly** *adv*

ad·join \ə'join\ *vb* : be next to

ad·journ \ə'jərn\ *vb* : end a meeting — **ad·journ·ment** *n*

ad·judge \ə'jəj\ *vb* **-judged; -judg·ing 1** : think or pronounce to be **2** : award by judicial decision

ad·ju·di·cate \ə'jüdi‚kāt\ *vb* **-cat·ed; -cat·ing** : settle judicially — **ad·ju·di·ca·tion** \ə‚jüdi'kāshən\ *n*

ad·junct \'aj‚eŋkt\ *n* : something joined or added but not essential

ad·just \ə'jəst\ *vb* : fix, adapt, or set right — **ad·just·able** *adj* — **ad·just·er, ad·jus·tor** \ə'jəstər\ *n* — **ad·just·ment** \-mənt\ *n*

ad·ju·tant \'ajətənt\ *n* : aide esp. to a commanding officer

ad–lib \'ad'lib\ *vb* **-bb-** : speak without preparation — **ad–lib** *n or adj*

ad·min·is·ter \əd'minəstər\ *vb* **1** : manage **2** : give out esp. in doses — **ad·min·is·tra·ble** \-strəbəl\ *adj*

ad·min·is·tra·tion \əd‚minə-'strāshən, ad-\ *n* **1** : process of managing **2** : persons responsible for managing — **ad·min·is·tra·tive** \əd'minə‚strātiv\ *adj* — **ad·min·is·tra·tive·ly** *adv*

ad·min·is·tra·tor \əd'minə‚strātər\ *n* : one that manages

ad·mi·ra·ble \'admərəbəl\ *adj* : worthy of admiration — **ad·mi·ra·bly** \-blē\ *adv*

ad·mi·ral \'admərəl\ *n* : commissioned officer in the navy ranking next below a fleet admiral

ad·mire \əd'mīr\ *vb* **-mired; -mir·ing** : have high regard for — **ad·mi·ra·tion** \‚admə-'rāshən\ *n* — **ad·mir·er** *n* — **ad·mir·ing·ly** *adv*

ad·mis·si·ble \əd'misəbəl\ *adj* : that can be permitted — **ad·mis·si·bil·i·ty** \-‚misə-'bilətē\ *n*

ad·mis·sion \əd'mishən\ *n* **1** : act of admitting **2** : admittance or a fee paid for this **3** : acknowledgment of a fact

ad·mit \əd'mit\ *vb* **-tt- 1** : allow to enter **2** : permit **3** : recognize as genuine — **ad·mit·ted·ly** *adv*

ad·mit·tance \əd'mit°ns\ *n* : permission to enter

ad·mix·ture \ad'mikschər\ *n* **1** : thing added in mixing **2** : mixture

ad·mon·ish \ad'mänish\ *vb* : rebuke — **ad·mon·ish·ment** \-mənt\ *n* — **ad·mo·ni·tion** \‚admə'nishən\ *n* — **ad·mon·i·to·ry** \ad'mänə‚tōrē\ *adj*

ado \ə'dü\ *n* **1** : fuss **2** : trouble

ado·be \ə'dōbē\ *n* : sun-dried building brick

ad·o·les·cence \ˌad³l'es³ns\ *n* : period of growth between childhood and maturity — **ad·o·les·cent** \-³nt\ *adj or n*

adopt \ə'däpt\ *vb* **1** : take (a child of other parents) as one's own child **2** : take up and practice as one's own — **adop·tion** \-'däpshən\ *n*

adore \ə'dōr\ *vb* **adored; ador·ing** **1** : worship **2** : be extremely fond of — **adorable** *adj* — **ador·ably** *adv* — **ad·o·ra·tion** \ˌadə'rāshən\ *n*

adorn \ə'dȯrn\ *vb* : decorate with ornaments — **adornment** *n*

adrift \ə'drift\ *adv or adj* **1** : afloat without motive power or moorings **2** : without guidance or purpose

adroit \ə'drȯit\ *adj* : dexterous or shrewd — **adroit·ly** *adv* — **adroit·ness** *n*

adult \ə'dəlt, 'ad,əlt\ *adj* : fully developed and mature ~ *n* : grown-up person — **adult·hood** *n*

adul·ter·ate \ə'dəltə,rāt\ *vb* **-at·ed; -at·ing** : make impure by mixture — **adul·ter·a·tion** \-,dəltə'rāshən\ *n*

adul·tery \ə'dəltərē\ *n, pl* **-ter·ies** : sexual unfaithfulness of a married person — **adul·ter·er** \-tərər\ *n* — **adul·ter·ess** \-tərəs\ *n* — **adul·ter·ous** \-tərəs\ *adj*

ad·vance \əd'vans\ *vb* **-vanced; -vancing** **1** : bring or move forward **2** : promote **3** : lend ~ *n* **1** : forward movement **2** : improvement **3** : offer ~ *adj* : being ahead of time — **advance·ment** *n*

ad·van·tage \əd'vantij\ *n* **1** : superiority of position **2** : benefit or gain — **ad·van·ta·geous** \ˌad,van'tājəs, -vən-\ *adj* — **ad·van·ta·geous·ly** *adv*

ad·vent \'ad,vent\ *n* **1** *cap* : period before Christmas **2** : a coming into being or use

ad·ven·ti·tious \ˌadvən'tishəs\ *adj* : accidental — **ad·ven·ti·tious·ly** *adv*

ad·ven·ture \əd'venchər\ *n* **1** : risky undertaking **2** : exciting experience — **ad·ven·tur·er** \-chərər\ *n* — **ad·ven·ture·some** \-chərsəm\ *adj* — **ad·ven·tur·ous** \-chərəs\ *adj*

ad·verb \'ad,vərb\ *n* : word that modifies a verb, an adjective, or another adverb — **ad·ver·bi·al** \ad'vərbeəl\ *adj* — **ad·ver·bi·al·ly** *adv*

ad·ver·sary \'advər,serē\ *n, pl* **-sar·ies** : enemy or rival — **adversary** *adj*

ad·verse \ad'vərs, 'ad-,\ *adj* : opposing or unfavorable — **ad·verse·ly** *adv*

ad·ver·si·ty \ad'vərsətē\ *n, pl* **-ties** : hard times

ad·vert \ad'vərt\ *vb* : refer

ad·ver·tise \'advər₁tīz\ *vb* -**tised**; -**tis·ing** : call public attention to — **ad·ver·tise·ment** \₁advər'tīzmənt, əd'vərtəz-mənt\ *n* — **ad·ver·tis·er** *n*

ad·ver·tis·ing \'advər₁tīziŋ\ *n* : business of preparing advertisements

ad·vice \əd'vīs\ *n* : recommendation with regard to a course of action

ad·vis·able \əd'vīzəbəl\ *adj* : wise or prudent — **ad·vis·abil·i·ty** \-₁vīzə-'bilətē\ *n*

ad·vise \əd'vīz\ *vb* -**vised**; -**vis·ing** : give advice to — **ad·vis·er, ad·vis·or** \-'vīzər\ *n*

ad·vise·ment \əd'vīzmənt\ *n* : careful consideration

ad·vi·so·ry \əd'vīzərē\ *adj* : having power to advise

ad·vo·cate \'advəkət, -₁kāt\ *n* : one who argues or pleads for a cause or proposal ∼ \-₁kāt\ *vb* -**cat·ed**; -**cat·ing** : recommend — **ad·vo·ca·cy** \-vəkəsē\ *n*

adze \'adz\ *n* : tool for shaping wood

ae·gis \'ējəs\ *n* : protection or sponsorship

ae·on \'ēən, 'ē₁än\ *var of* EON

aer·ate \'ar₁āt\ *vb* -**at·ed**; -**at·ing** : supply or impregnate with air — **aer·a·tion** \₁ar'ā-shən\ *n* — **aer·a·tor** \'ar-₁ātər\ *n*

ae·ri·al \'arēəl\ *adj* : inhabiting, occurring in, or done in the air ∼ *n* : antenna

ae·rie \'arē, 'irē\ *n* : eagle's nest

aer·o·bic \₁ar'ōbik\ *adj* : using or needing oxygen

aer·o·bics \-biks\ *n sing or pl* : exercises that produce a marked increase in respiration and heart rate

aero·dy·nam·ics \₁arōdī'nam-iks\ *n* : science of bodies in motion in a gas — **aero·dy·nam·ic** \-ik\ *adj* — **aero·dy·nam·i·cal·ly** \-iklē\ *adv*

aero·nau·tics \₁arə'nȯtiks\ *n* : science dealing with aircraft — **aero·nau·ti·cal** \-ikəl\ *adj*

aero·sol \'arə₁säl, -₁sȯl\ *n* **1** : liquid or solid particles suspended in a gas **2** : substance sprayed as an aerosol

aero·space \'arō₁spās\ *n* : earth's atmosphere and the space beyond — **aerospace** *adj*

aes·thet·ic \es'thetik\ *adj* : relating to beauty — **aes·thet·i·cal·ly** \-iklē\ *adv*

aes·thet·ics \-'thetiks\ *n* : branch of philosophy dealing with beauty

afar \ə'fär\ *adv* : from, at, or to a great distance — **afar** *n*

af·fa·ble \'afəbəl\ *adj* : easy to talk to — **af·fa·bil·i·ty**

\ˌafəˈbilətē\ *n* — **af·fa·bly** \ˈafəblē\ *adv*

af·fair \əˈfar\ *n* : something that relates to or involves one

¹**af·fect** \əˈfekt, a-\ *vb* : assume for effect — **af·fec·ta·tion** \ˌafˌekˈtāshən\ *n*

²**affect** *vb* : produce an effect on

af·fect·ed \əˈfektəd, a-\ *adj* **1** : pretending to some trait **2** : artificially assumed to impress — **af·fect·ed·ly** *adv*

af·fect·ing \əˈfektiŋ, a-\ *adj* : arousing pity or sorrow — **af·fect·ing·ly** *adv*

af·fec·tion \əˈfekshən\ *n* : kind or loving feeling — **af·fec·tion·ate** \-shənət\ *adj* — **af·fec·tion·ate·ly** *adv*

af·fi·da·vit \ˌafəˈdāvət\ *n* : sworn statement

af·fil·i·ate \əˈfilēˌāt\ *vb* **-at·ed; -at·ing** : become a member or branch — **af·fil·i·ate** \-ēət\ *n* — **af·fil·i·a·tion** \-ˌfilēˈāshən\ *n*

af·fin·i·ty \əˈfinətē\ *n, pl* **-ties** : close attraction or relationship

af·firm \əˈfərm\ *vb* : assert positively — **af·fir·ma·tion** \ˌafərˈmāshən\ *n*

af·fir·ma·tive \əˈfərmətiv\ *adj* : asserting the truth or existence of something ∼ *n* : statement of affirmation or agreement

af·fix \əˈfiks\ *vb* : attach

af·flict \əˈflikt\ *vb* : cause pain and distress to — **af·flic·tion** \-ˈflikshən\ *n*

af·flu·ence \ˈafˌlüəns; aˈflü-, ə-\ *n* : wealth — **af·flu·ent** \-ənt\ *adj*

af·ford \əˈfōrd\ *vb* **1** : manage to bear the cost of **2** : provide

af·fray \əˈfrā\ *n* : fight

af·front \əˈfrənt\ *vb or n* : insult

af·ghan \ˈafˌgan, -gən\ *n* : crocheted or knitted blanket

afire \əˈfīr\ *adj or adv* : being on fire

aflame \əˈflām\ *adj or adv* : flaming

afloat \əˈflōt\ *adj or adv* : floating

afoot \əˈfüt\ *adv or adj* **1** : on foot **2** : in progress

afore·said \əˈfōrˌsed\ *adj* : said or named before

afraid \əˈfrād, *South also* əˈfred\ *adj* : filled with fear

afresh \əˈfresh\ *adv* : anew

aft \ˈaft\ *adv* : to or toward the stern or tail

af·ter \ˈaftər\ *adv* : at a later time ∼ *prep* **1** : behind in place or time **2** : in pursuit of ∼ *conj* : following the time when ∼ *adj* **1** : later **2** : located toward the back

af·ter·life \ˈaftərˌlīf\ *n* : existence after death

af·ter·math \-ˌmath\ *n* : results

af·ter·noon \ˌaftər'nün\ *n* : time between noon and evening

af·ter·thought *n* : later thought

af·ter·ward \'aftərwərd\, **af·ter·wards** \-wərdz\ *adv* : at a later time

again \ə'gen, -'gin\ *adv* **1** : once more **2** : on the other hand **3** : in addition

against \ə'genst\ *prep* **1** : directly opposite to **2** : in opposition to **3** : so as to touch or strike

agape \ə'gāp, -'gap\ *adj or adv* : having the mouth open in astonishment

ag·ate \'agət\ *n* : quartz with bands or masses of various colors

age \'āj\ *n* **1** : length of time of life or existence **2** : particular time in life (as majority or the latter part) **3** : quality of being old **4** : long time **5** : period in history ∼ *vb* : become old or mature

-age \ij\ *n suffix* **1** : aggregate **2** : action or process **3** : result of **4** : rate of **5** : place of **6** : state or rank **7** : fee

aged *adj* **1** \'ājəd\ : old **2** \'ājd\ : allowed to mature

age·less \'ājləs\ *adj* : eternal

agen·cy \'ājənsē\ *n, pl* **-cies** **1** : one through which something is accomplished **2** : office or function of an agent **3** : government administrative division

agen·da \ə'jendə\ *n* : list of things to be done

agent \'ājənt\ *n* **1** : means **2** : person acting or doing business for another

ag·gran·dize \ə'granˌdīz, 'agrən-\ *vb* **-dized; -diz·ing** : make great or greater — **ag·gran·dize·ment** \ə'grandəzmənt, -ˌdīz-; ˌagrən'dīz-\ *n*

ag·gra·vate \'agrəˌvāt\ *vb* **-vat·ed; -vat·ing** **1** : make more severe **2** : irritate — **ag·gra·va·tion** \ˌagrə'vāshən\ *n*

ag·gre·gate \'agrigət\ *adj* : formed into a mass ∼ \-ˌgāt\ *vb* **-gat·ed; -gat·ing** : collect into a mass ∼ \-gət\ *n* **1** : mass **2** : whole amount

ag·gres·sion \ə'greshən\ *n* **1** : unprovoked attack **2** : hostile behavior — **ag·gres·sor** \-'gresər\ *n*

ag·gres·sive \ə'gresiv\ *adj* **1** : easily provoked to fight **2** : hard working and enterprising — **ag·gres·sive·ly** *adv* — **ag·gres·sive·ness** *n*

ag·grieve \ə'grēv\ *vb* **-grieved; -griev·ing** **1** : cause grief to **2** : inflict injury on

aghast \ə'gast\ *adj* : struck with amazement or horror

ag·ile \ajəl\ *adj* : able to move quickly and easily — **agil·i·ty** \ə'jilətē\ *n*

ag·i·tate \'ajə₁tāt\ *vb* **-tat·ed;** **-tat·ing** **1** : shake or stir back and forth **2** : excite or trouble the mind of **3** : try to arouse public feeling — **ag·i·ta·tion** \₁ajə'tāshən\ *n* — **ag·i·ta·tor** \'ajə₁tātər\ *n*

ag·nos·tic \ag'nästik, əg-\ *n* : one who doubts the existence of God

ago \ə'gō\ *adj or adv* : earlier than the present

agog \ə'gäg\ *adj* : full of excitement

ag·o·nize \'agə₁nīz\ *vb* **-nized;** **-niz·ing** : suffer mental agony — **ag·o·niz·ing·ly** *adv*

ag·o·ny \'agənē\ *n, pl* **-nies** : extreme pain or mental distress

agrar·i·an \ə'grerēən\ *adj* : relating to land ownership or farming interests — **agrarian** *n* — **agrar·i·an·ism** *n*

agree \ə'grē\ *vb* **agreed; agree·ing** **1** : be of the same opinion **2** : express willingness **3** : get along together **4** : be similar **5** : be appropriate, suitable, or healthful

agree·able \-əbəl\ *adj* **1** : pleasing **2** : willing to give approval — **agree·able·ness** *n* — **agree·ably** *adv*

agree·ment \-mənt\ *n* **1** : harmony of opinion or purpose **2** : mutual understanding or arrangement

ag·ri·cul·ture \'agri₁kəlchər\ *n* : farming — **ag·ri·cul·tur·al** \₁agri'kəlchərəl\ *adj* — **ag·ri·cul·tur·ist** \-rist\, **ag·ri·cul·tur·al·ist** \-rəlist\ *n*

aground \ə'graúnd\ *adv or adj* : on or onto the bottom or shore

ague \'āgyü\ *n* **1** : fever with recurrent chills and sweating **2** : malaria

ahead \ə'hed\ *adv or adj* **1** : in or toward the front **2** : into or for the future **3** : in a more advantageous position

ahead of *prep* **1** : in front or advance of **2** : in excess of

ahoy \ə'hói\ *interj* — used in hailing

aid \'ād\ *vb* : provide help or support ∼ *n* : help

aide \'ād\ *n* : helper

AIDS \'ādz\ *n* : serious disease of the human immune system

ail \'āl\ *vb* **1** : trouble **2** : be ill

ai·le·ron \'ālə₁rän\ *n* : movable part of an airplane wing

ail·ment \'ālmənt\ *n* : bodily disorder

aim \'ām\ *vb* **1** : point or direct (as a weapon) **2** : direct one's efforts ∼ *n* **1** : an aiming or the direction of aiming **2** : object or purpose — **aim·less** *adj* — **aim·less·ly** *adv* — **aim·less·ness** *n*

air \\'ar\\ *n* **1** : mixture of gases surrounding the earth **2** : melody **3** : outward appearance **4** : artificial manner **5** : compressed air **6** : travel by or use of aircraft **7** : medium of transmission of radio waves ~ *vb* **1** : expose to the air **2** : broadcast — **air·borne** \\-ˌbōrn\\ *adj*

air–condition *vb* : equip with an apparatus (**air conditioner**) for filtering and cooling the air

air·craft *n, pl* **aircraft** : craft that flies

Aire·dale terrier \\'ar,dāl-\\ *n* : large terrier with a hard wiry coat

air·field *n* : airport or its landing field

air force *n* : military organization for conducting warfare by air

air·lift *n* : a transporting of esp. emergency supplies by aircraft — **airlift** *vb*

air·line *n* : air transportation system — **air·lin·er** *n*

air·mail *n* : system of transporting mail by airplane — **airmail** *vb*

air·man \\-mən\\ *n* **1** : aviator **2** : enlisted man in the air force in one of the 3 ranks below sergeant

airman basic *n* : enlisted man of the lowest rank in the air force

airman first class *n* : enlisted man in the air force ranking just below sergeant

air·plane *n* : fixed-wing aircraft heavier than air

air·port *n* : place for landing aircraft and usu. for receiving passengers

air·ship *n* : powered lighter=than-air aircraft

air·strip *n* : airfield runway

air·tight *adj* : tightly sealed to prevent flow of air

air·waves \\'ar,wāvz\\ *n pl* : medium of transmission of radio waves

airy \\'arē\\ *adj* **air·i·er; -est** **1** : delicate **2** : breezy

aisle \\'īl\\ *n* : passage between sections or rows

ajar \\ə'jär\\ *adj or adv* : partly open

akim·bo \\ə'kimbō\\ *adj or adv* : having the hand on the hip and the elbow turned outward

akin \\ə'kin\\ *adj* **1** : related by blood **2** : similar in kind

-al \\əl\\ *adj suffix* : of, relating to, or characterized by

al·a·bas·ter \\'alə,bastər\\ *n* : white or translucent mineral

alac·ri·ty \\ə'lakrətē\\ *n* : cheerful readiness

alarm \\ə'lärm\\ *n* **1** : warning signal or device **2** : fear at sudden danger ~ *vb* **1** : warn **2** : frighten

alas \ə'las\ *interj* — used to express unhappiness, pity, or concern

al·ba·tross \'albə,tros, -,träs\ *n, pl* **-tross** *or* **-tross·es** : large seabird

al·be·it \ȯl'bēət, al-\ *conj* : even though

al·bi·no \al'bīnō\ *n, pl* **-nos** : person or animal with abnormally white skin — **al·bi·nism** \'albə,nizəm\ *n*

al·bum \'albəm\ *n* **1** : book for displaying a collection (as of photographs) **2** : collection of recordings

al·bu·men \al'byümən\ *n* **1** : white of an egg **2** : albumin

al·bu·min \-mən\ *n* : protein found in blood, milk, egg white, and tissues

al·che·my \'alkəmē\ *n* : medieval chemistry — **al·che·mist** \'alkəmist\ *n*

al·co·hol \'alkə,hȯl\ *n* **1** : intoxicating agent in liquor **2** : liquor — **al·co·hol·ic** *adj*

al·co·hol·ic \,alkə'hȯlik, -'häl-\ *n* : person affected with alcoholism

al·co·hol·ism \'alkə,hȯl,izəm\ *n* : addiction to alcoholic beverages

al·cove \'al,kōv\ *n* : recess in a room or wall

al·der·man \'ȯldərmən\ *n* : city official

ale \'āl\ *n* : beerlike beverage — **ale·house** *n*

alert \ə'lərt\ *adj* **1** : watchful **2** : quick to perceive and act ~ *n* : alarm ~ *vb* : warn — **alert·ly** *adv* — **alert·ness** *n*

ale·wife *n* : fish of the herring family

al·fal·fa \al'falfə\ *n* : cloverlike forage plant

al·ga \'algə\ *n, pl* **-gae** \'al,jē\ : any of a group of lower plants that includes seaweed — **al·gal** \-gəl\ *adj*

al·ge·bra \'aljəbrə\ *n* : branch of mathematics — **al·ge·bra·ic** \,aljə'brāik\ *adj* — **al·ge·bra·i·cal·ly** \-'brāəklē\ *adv*

alias \'ālēəs, 'ālyəs\ *adv* : otherwise called ~ *n* : assumed name

al·i·bi \'alə,bī\ *n* **1** : defense of having been elsewhere when a crime was committed **2** : justification ~ *vb* **-bied; -bi·ing** : offer an excuse

alien \'ālēən, 'ālyən\ *adj* : foreign ~ *n* **1** : foreign-born resident **2** : extraterrestrial

alien·ate \'ālēə,nāt, 'ālyə-\ *vb* **-at·ed; -at·ing** : cause to be no longer friendly — **alien·ation** \,ālēə'nāshən, ,ālyə-\ *n*

alight \ə'līt\ *vb* : dismount

align \ə'līn\ *vb* : bring into line — **align·er** *n* — **align·ment** *n*

alike \ə'līk\ *adj* : identical or very similar ~ *adv* : equally

al·i·men·ta·ry \ˌalə'mentərē\ *adj* : relating to or functioning in nutrition

al·i·mo·ny \'alə,mōnē\ *n, pl* **-nies** : money paid to a separated or divorced spouse

alive \ə'līv\ *adj* **1** : having life **2** : lively or animated

al·ka·li \'alkə,lī\ *n, pl* **-lies** *or* **-lis** : strong chemical base — **al·ka·line** \-kələn, -,līn\ *adj* — **al·ka·lin·i·ty** \ˌalkə'linətē\ *n*

all \'ȯl\ *adj* **1** : the whole of **2** : greatest possible **3** : every one of ~ *adv* **1** : wholly **2** : so much **3** : for each side ~ *pron* **1** : whole number or amount **2** : everything or everyone

Al·lah \'älə, 'al-\ *n* : God of Islam

all–around *adj* : versatile

al·lay \ə'lā\ *vb* **1** : alleviate **2** : calm

al·lege \ə'lej\ *vb* **-leged; -leg·ing** : assert without proof — **al·le·ga·tion** \ˌali'gāshən\ *n* — **al·leg·ed·ly** \ə'lejədlē\ *adv*

al·le·giance \ə'lējəns\ *n* : loyalty

al·le·go·ry \'alə,gōrē\ *n, pl* **-ries** : story in which figures and actions are symbols of general truths — **al·le·gor·i·cal** \ˌalə'gȯrikəl\ *adj*

al·le·lu·ia \ˌalə'lüyə\ *interj* : hallelujah

al·ler·gen \'alərjən\ *n* : something that causes allergy — **al·ler·gen·ic** \ˌalər-'jenik\ *adj*

al·ler·gy \'alərjē\ *n, pl* **-gies** : abnormal reaction to a substance — **al·ler·gic** \ə'lərjik\ *adj* — **al·ler·gist** \'alərjist\ *n*

al·le·vi·ate \ə'lēvē,āt\ *vb* **-at·ed; -at·ing** : relieve or lessen — **al·le·vi·a·tion** \ə,lēvē'ā-shən\ *n*

al·ley \'alē\ *n, pl* **-leys** **1** : place for bowling **2** : narrow passage between buildings

al·li·ance \ə'līəns\ *n* : association

al·li·ga·tor \'alə,gātər\ *n* : large aquatic reptile related to the crocodiles

al·lit·er·a·tion \ə,litə'rāshən\ *n* : repetition of initial sounds of words — **al·lit·er·a·tive** \-'litə,rātiv\ *adj*

al·lo·cate \'alə,kāt\ *vb* **-cat·ed; -cat·ing** : assign — **al·lo·ca·tion** \ˌalə'kāshən\ *n*

al·lot \ə'lät\ *vb* **-tt-** : distribute as a share — **al·lot·ment** *n*

al·low \ə'lau̇\ *vb* **1** : admit or concede **2** : permit — **al·low·able** *adj*

al·low·ance \-əns\ *n* **1** : allotted share **2** : money given regularly for expenses

al·loy \'al,ȯi\ *n* : metals melted together — **al·loy** \ə'lȯi\ *vb*

all right *adv or adj* **1** : satisfactorily **2** : yes **3** : certainly

all·spice \'ȯlspīs\ *n* : berry of a West Indian tree made into a spice

al·lude \ə'lüd\ *vb* **-lud·ed; -lud·ing** : refer indirectly — **al·lu·sion** \-'lüzhən\ *n* — **al·lu·sive** \-'lüsiv\ *adj*

al·lure \ə'lu̇r\ *vb* **-lured; -lur·ing** : entice ~ *n* : attractive power

al·ly \ə'lī, 'al͵ī\ *vb* **-lied; -ly·ing** : enter into an alliance — **al·ly** \'al͵ī, ə'lī\ *n*

-al·ly \əlē\ *adv suffix* : -ly

al·ma·nac \'ȯlmə͵nak, 'al-\ *n* : annual information book

al·mighty \ȯl'mītē\ *adj* : having absolute power

al·mond \'ämənd, 'am-, 'ȯlm-, 'älm-\ *n* : tree with nutlike fruit kernels

al·most \'ȯl͵mōst, ȯl'-\ *adv* : very nearly

alms \'ämz, 'älmz, 'almz\ *n, pl* **alms** : charitable gift

aloft \ə'lȯft\ *adv* : high in the air

alo·ha \ä'lōhä\ *interj* — used to greet or bid farewell

alone \ə'lōn\ *adj* **1** : separated from others **2** : not including anyone or anything else — **alone** *adv*

along \ə'lȯŋ\ *prep* **1** : in line with the direction of **2** : at a point on or during ~ *adv* **1** : forward **2** : as a companion

along·side *adv or prep* : along or by the side

alongside of *prep* : alongside

aloof \ə'lüf\ *adj* : indifferent and reserved — **aloof·ness** *n*

aloud \ə'lau̇d\ *adv* : so as to be heard

al·paca \al'pakə\ *n* **1** : So. American mammal related to the llama **2** : alpaca wool or cloth made of this

al·pha·bet \'alfə͵bet, -bət\ *n* : ordered set of letters of a language — **al·pha·bet·i·cal** \͵alfə'betikəl\, **al·pha·bet·ic** \-'betik\ *adj* — **al·pha·bet·i·cal·ly** \-klē\ *adv*

al·pha·bet·ize \'alfəbə͵tīz\ *vb* **-ized; -iz·ing** : arrange in alphabetical order — **al·pha·bet·iz·er** *n*

al·ready \ȯl'redē\ *adv* : by a given time

al·so \'ȯlsō\ *adv* : in addition

al·tar \'ȯltər\ *n* : structure for rituals

al·ter \'ȯltər\ *vb* : make different — **al·ter·a·tion** \͵ȯltə'rāshən\ *n*

al·ter·ca·tion \͵ȯltər'kāshən\ *n* : dispute

al·ter·nate \'ȯltərnət, 'al-\ *adj* **1** : arranged or succeeding by turns **2** : every other ~ \-͵nāt\ *vb* **-nat·ed; -nat·ing** : occur or cause to occur

by turns ~ \-nət\ *n* : substitute — **al·ter·nate·ly** *adv* —
al·ter·na·tion \ˌȯltər'nāshən,
ˌal-\ *n*

alternating current *n* : electric current that regularly re-
verses direction

al·ter·na·tive \ȯl'tərnətiv,
al-\ *adj* : offering a choice —
alternative *n*

al·ter·na·tor \'ȯltərˌnātər, 'al-\
n : alternating-current generator

al·though \ȯl'thō\ *conj* : even
though

al·tim·e·ter \al'timətər, 'altə-
ˌmētər\ *n* : instrument for
measuring altitude

al·ti·tude \'altəˌtüd, -ˌtyüd\ *n*
1 : distance up from the
ground **2** : angular distance
above the horizon

al·to \'altō\ *n, pl* **-tos** : lower
female choral voice

al·to·geth·er \ˌȯltə'gethər\
adv **1** : wholly **2** : on the
whole

al·tru·ism \'altrùˌizəm\ *n*
: concern for others — **al·tru·
ist** \-ist\ *n* — **al·tru·is·tic**
\ˌaltrù'istik\ *adj* — **al·tru·is·
ti·cal·ly** \-tiklē\ *adv*

al·um \'aləm\ *n* : crystalline
compound containing alu-
minum

alu·mi·num \ə'lümənəm\ *n*
: silver-white malleable ductile light metallic element

alum·na \ə'ləmnə\ *n, pl* **-nae**
\-ˌnē\ : woman graduate

alum·nus \ə'ləmnəs\ *n, pl* **-ni**
\-ˌnī\ : graduate

al·ways \'ȯlwēz, -wāz\ *adv* **1**
: at all times **2** : forever

am *pres 1st sing of* BE

amal·gam \ə'malgəm\ *n* **1**
: mercury alloy **2** : mixture

amal·gam·ate \ə'malgəˌmāt\
vb **-at·ed; -at·ing** : unite —
amal·ga·ma·tion \-ˌmalgə-
'māshən\ *n*

am·a·ryl·lis \ˌamə'riləs\ *n*
: bulbous herb with clusters of
large colored flowers like lilies

amass \ə'mas\ *vb* : gather

am·a·teur \'aməˌtər, -ˌtùr,
-ˌtyùr, -ˌchùr, -chər\ *n* **1**
: person who does something
for pleasure rather than for
pay **2** : person who is not expert — **am·a·teur·ish** \ˌamə-
'tərish, -'tùr-, -'tyùr-\ *adj*
— **ama·teur·ism** \'aməˌtər-
ˌizəm, -ˌtùr-, -ˌtyùr-, -ˌchùr-,
-chər-\ *n*

am·a·to·ry \'aməˌtōrē\ *adj*
: of or expressing sexual love

amaze \ə'māz\ *vb* **amazed;
amaz·ing** : fill with wonder
— **amaze·ment** *n* — **amaz·
ing·ly** *adv*

am·a·zon \'aməˌzän, -zən\ *n*
: tall strong woman — **am·a·
zo·ni·an** \ˌamə'zōnēən\ *adj*

am·bas·sa·dor \am'basədər\
n : representative esp. of a

government — **am·bas·sa·do·ri·al** \-ˌbasə'dō-rēəl\ *adj* — **am·bas·sa·dor·ship** *n*

am·ber \'ambər\ *n* : yellowish fossil resin or its color

am·ber·gris \'ambərˌgris, -ˌgrēs\ *n* : waxy substance from certain whales used in making perfumes

am·bi·dex·trous \ˌambi'dek-strəs\ *adj* : equally skilled with both hands — **am·bi·dex·trous·ly** *adv*

am·bi·ence, am·bi·ance \'am-bēəns, 'ämbēˌäns\ *n* : pervading atmosphere

am·big·u·ous \am'bigyəwəs\ *adj* : having more than one interpretation — **am·bi·gu·i·ty** \ˌambə'gyüətē\ *n*

am·bi·tion \am'bishən\ *n* : eager desire for success or power — **am·bi·tious** \shəs\ *adj* — **am·bi·tious·ly** *adv*

am·biv·a·lence \am'bivələns\ *n* : simultaneous attraction and repulsion — **am·biv·a·lent** \-lənt\ *adj*

am·ble \'ambəl\ *vb* **-bled; -bling** : go at a leisurely gait — **amble** *n*

am·bu·lance \'ambyələns\ *n* : vehicle for carrying injured or sick persons

am·bu·la·to·ry \'ambyələˌtōrē\ *adj* **1** : relating to or adapted to walking **2** : able to walk about

am·bush \'amˌbush\ *n* : trap by which a surprise attack is made from a place of hiding — **ambush** *vb*

ame·lio·rate \ə'mēlyəˌrāt\ *vb* **-rat·ed; -rat·ing** : make or grow better — **ame·lio·ra·tion** \-ˌmēlyə'rāshən\ *n*

amen \'ā'men, 'ä-\ *interj* — used for affirmation esp. at the end of prayers

ame·na·ble \ə'mēnəbəl, -'men-\ *adj* : ready to yield or be influenced

amend \ə'mend\ *vb* **1** : improve **2** : alter in writing

amend·ment \-mənt\ *n* : change made in a formal document (as a law)

amends \ə'mendz\ *n sing or pl* : compensation for injury or loss

ame·ni·ty \ə'menətē, -'mē-\ *n, pl* **-ties 1** : agreeableness **2** *pl* : social conventions **3** : something serving to comfort or accommodate

am·e·thyst \'aməthəst\ *n* : purple gemstone

ami·a·ble \'āmēəbəl\ *adj* : easy to get along with — **ami·a·bil·i·ty** \ˌāmēə'bilətē\ *n* — **ami·a·bly** \'āmēəblē\ *adv*

am·i·ca·ble \'amikəbəl\ *adj* : friendly — **am·i·ca·bly** \-blē\ *adv*

amid \ə'mid\, **amidst** \-'midst\ *prep* : in or into the middle of

amino acid \ə'mēnō-\ *n* : nitrogen-containing acid

amiss \ə'mis\ *adv* : in the wrong way ～ *adj* : wrong

am·me·ter \'am,ētər\ *n* : instrument for measuring electric current

am·mo·nia \ə'mōnyə\ *n* **1** : colorless gaseous compound of nitrogen and hydrogen **2** : solution of ammonia in water

am·mu·ni·tion \,amyə'nishən\ *n* **1** : projectiles fired from guns **2** : explosive items used in war

am·ne·sia \am'nēzhə\ *n* : sudden loss of memory — **am·ne·si·ac** \-zē,ak, -zhē-\, **am·ne·sic** \-zik, -sik\ *adj or n*

am·nes·ty \'amnəstē\ *n, pl* **-ties** : a pardon for a group — **amnesty** *vb*

amoe·ba \ə'mēbə\ *n, pl* **-bas** *or* **-bae** \-,bē\ : tiny one-celled animal that occurs esp. in water — **amoe·bic** \-bik\ *adj*

amok \ə'mək, -'mäk\ *adv* : in a violent or uncontrolled way

among \ə'məŋ\ *prep* **1** : in or through **2** : in the number or class of **3** : in shares to each of

am·o·rous \'amərəs\ *adj* **1** : inclined to love **2** : being in love **3** : indicative of love —

am·o·rous·ly *adv* — **am·o·rous·ness** *n*

amor·phous \ə'mȯrfəs\ *adj* : shapeless

am·or·tize \'amər,tīz, ə'mȯr-\ *vb* **-tized; -tiz·ing** : get rid of (as a debt) gradually with periodic payments — **amor·ti·za·tion** \,amərtə'zāshən, ə,mȯrt-\ *n*

amount \ə'maunt\ *vb* **1** : be equivalent **2** : reach a total ～ *n* : total number or quantity

amour \ə'mur, ä-, a-\ *n* **1** : love affair **2** : lover

am·pere \'am,pir\ *n* : unit of electric current

am·per·sand \'ampər,sand\ *n* : character & used for the word *and*

am·phib·i·ous \am'fibēəs\ *adj* **1** : able to live both on land and in water **2** : adapted for both land and water — **am·phib·i·an** \-ən\ *n*

am·phi·the·ater \'amfə,thē-ətər\ *n* : oval or circular structure with rising tiers of seats around an arena

am·ple \'ampəl\ *adj* **-pler** \-plər\; **-plest** \-pləst\ **1** : large **2** : sufficient — **am·ply** \-plē\ *adv*

am·pli·fy \'amplə,fī\ *vb* **-fied; -fy·ing** : make louder, stronger, or more thorough — **am·pli·fi·ca·tion** \,ampləfə-

'kāshən\ *n* — **am·pli·fi·er** \'amplə,fīər\ *n*

am·pli·tude \-,tüd, -,tyüd\ *n* **1** : fullness **2** : extent of a vibratory movement

am·pu·tate \'ampyə,tāt\ *vb* **-tat·ed; -tat·ing** : cut off (a body part) — **am·pu·ta·tion** \,ampyə'tāshən\ *n* — **am·pu·tee** \,ampyə'tē\ *n*

amuck \ə'mək\ *var of* AMOK

am·u·let \'amyələt\ *n* : ornament worn as a charm against evil

amuse \ə'myüz\ *vb* **amused; amus·ing** **1** : engage the attention of in an interesting and pleasant way **2** : make laugh — **amuse·ment** *n*

an \ən, 'an\ *indefinite article* : a — used before words beginning with a vowel sound

-an \ən\, **-ian** \ēən\, **-ean** \ēən\ *n suffix* **1** : one that belongs to **2** : one skilled in ~ *adj suffix* **1** : of or belonging to **2** : characteristic of or resembling

anach·ro·nism \ə'nakrə,nizəm\ *n* : one that is chronologically out of place — **anach·ro·nis·tic** \ə,nakrə'nistik\ *adj*

an·a·con·da \,anə'kändə\ *n* : large So. American snake

ana·gram \'anə,gram\ *n* : word or phrase made by transposing the letters of another word or phrase

anal \'ānᵊl\ *adj* : relating to the anus

an·al·ge·sic \,anᵊl'jēzik, -sik\ *n* : pain reliever

anal·o·gy \ə'naləjē\ *n, pl* **-gies** **1** : similarity between unlike things **2** : example of something similar — **an·a·log·i·cal** \,anᵊl'äjikəl\ *adj* — **an·a·log·i·cal·ly** \-iklē\ *adv* — **anal·o·gous** \ə'naləgəs\ *adj*

anal·y·sis \ə'naləsəs\ *n, pl* **-y·ses** \-,sēz\ **1** : examination of a thing to determine its parts **2** : psychoanalysis — **an·a·lyst** \'anᵊlist\ *n* — **an·a·lyt·ic** \,anᵊl'itik\, **an·a·lyt·i·cal** \-ikəl\ *adj* — **an·a·lyt·i·cal·ly** \-iklē\ *adv*

an·a·lyze \'anᵊl,īz\ *vb* **-lyzed; -lyz·ing** : make an analysis of

an·ar·chism \'anər,kizəm, -,när-\ *n* : theory that all government is undesirable — **an·ar·chist** \-kist\ *n or adj* — **an·ar·chis·tic** \,anər'kistik\ *adj*

an·ar·chy \'anərkē, -,när-\ *n* : lack of government or order — **an·ar·chic** \a'närkik\ *adj* — **an·ar·chi·cal·ly** \-iklē\ *adv*

anath·e·ma \ə'nathəmə\ *n* **1** : solemn curse **2** : person or thing accursed or intensely disliked

anat·o·my \ə'natəmē\ *n, pl* **-mies** : science dealing with the structure of organisms — **an·a·tom·ic** \ˌanə'tämik\, **an·a·tom·i·cal** \-ikəl\ *adj* — **an·a·tom·i·cal·ly** *adv* — **anat·o·mist** \ə'natəmist\ *n*

-ance \əns\ *n suffix* **1** : action or process **2** : quality or state **3** : amount or degree

an·ces·tor \'anˌsestər\ *n* : one from whom an individual is descended

an·ces·tress \-trəs\ *n* : female ancestor

an·ces·try \-trē\ *n* **1** : line of descent **2** : ancestors — **an·ces·tral** \an'sestrəl\ *adj*

an·chor \'aŋkər\ *n* **1** : heavy device that catches in the sea bottom to hold a ship in place **2** : anchorperson ∼ *vb* : hold or become held in place by or as if by an anchor — **an·chor·age** \-kərij\ *n*

an·chor·per·son \'aŋkərˌpərsən\ *n* : news broadcast coordinator

an·cho·vy \'anˌchōvē, an'chō-\ *n, pl* **-vies** *or* **-vy** : small herringlike fish

an·cient \'ānshənt\ *adj* **1** : having existed for many years **2** : belonging to times long past — **ancient** *n*

-ancy \ənsē\ *n suffix* : quality or state

and \ənd, 'and\ *conj* — used to indicate connection or addition

and·iron \'anˌdīərn\ *n* : one of 2 metal supports for wood in a fireplace

an·drog·y·nous \an'dräjənəs\ *adj* **1** : having characteristics of both male and female **2** : suitable for either sex

an·ec·dote \'anikˌdōt\ *n* : brief story — **an·ec·dot·al** \ˌanik'dōtᵊl\ *adj*

ane·mia \ə'nēmēə\ *n* : blood deficiency — **ane·mic** \ə'nēmik\ *adj*

anem·o·ne \ə'nemənē\ *n* : small herb with showy usu. white flowers

an·es·the·sia \ˌanəs'thēzhə\ *n* : loss of bodily sensation

an·es·thet·ic \ˌanəs'thetik\ *n* : agent that produces anesthesia — **anes·thetic** *adj* — **anes·the·tist** \ə'nesthətist\ *n* — **anes·the·tize** \-thəˌtīz\ *vb*

an·eu·rysm, an·eu·rism \'anyəˌrizəm\ : blood-filled bulge of a blood vessel

anew \ə'nü, -'nyü\ *adv* : over again

an·gel \'ānjəl\ *n* : spiritual being superior to humans — **an·gel·ic** \an'jelik\, **an·gel·i·cal** \-ikəl\ *adj* — **an·gel·i·cal·ly** *adv*

an·ger \'aŋgər\ *n* : strong feeling of displeasure ∼ *vb* : make angry

an·gi·na \an'jīnə\ *n* : painful disorder of heart muscles — **an·gi·nal** \an'jīnᵊl\ *adj*

¹**an·gle** \'aŋgəl\ *n* **1** : figure formed by the meeting of 2 lines in a point **2** : sharp corner **3** : point of view ~ *vb* **-gled; -gling** : turn or direct at an angle

²**angle** *vb* **an·gled; an·gling** : fish with a hook and line — **an·gler** \-glər\ *n* — **an·gle·worm** *n* — **an·gling** *n*

an·go·ra \aŋ'gōrə, an-\ *n* : yarn or cloth made from the hair of an Angora goat or rabbit

an·gry \'aŋgrē\ *adj* **-gri·er; -est** : feeling or showing anger — **an·gri·ly** \-grəlē\ *adv*

an·guish \'aŋgwish\ *n* : extreme pain or distress of mind — **an·guished** \-gwisht\ *adj*

an·gu·lar \'aŋgyələr\ *adj* **1** : having many or sharp angles **2** : thin and bony — **an·gu·lar·i·ty** \,aŋgyə'larətē\ *n*

an·i·mal \'anəməl\ *n* **1** : living being capable of feeling and voluntary motion **2** : lower animal as distinguished from humans

an·i·mate \'anəmət\ *adj* : having life ~ \-,māt\ *vb* **-mat·ed; -mat·ing** **1** : give life or vigor to **2** : make appear to move — **an·i·mat·ed** *adj*

an·i·ma·tion \,anə'māshən\ *n* **1** : liveliness **2** : animated cartoon

an·i·ma·tron·ic \,anəmə'tränik\ : relating to an elec-trically animated mechanical figure

an·i·mos·i·ty \,anə'mäsətē\ *n, pl* **-ties** : resentment

an·i·mus \'anəməs\ *n* : deep-seated hostility

an·ise \'anəs\ *n* : herb related to the carrot with aromatic seeds (**ani·seed** \-,sēd\) used in flavoring

an·kle \'aŋkəl\ *n* : joint or region between the foot and the leg — **an·kle·bone** *n*

an·nals \'anᵊlz\ *n pl* : chronological record of history — **an·nal·ist** \-ᵊlist\ *n*

an·neal \ə'nēl\ *vb* **1** : make less brittle by heating and then cooling **2** : strengthen or toughen

an·nex \ə'neks, 'an,eks\ *vb* : assume political control over (a territory) ~ \'an,eks, -iks\ *n* : added building — **an·nex·a·tion** \,an,ek'sāshən\ *n*

an·ni·hi·late \ə'nīə,lāt\ *vb* **-lat·ed; -lat·ing** : destroy — **an·ni·hi·la·tion** \-,nīə'lāshən\ *n*

an·ni·ver·sa·ry \,anə'vərsərē\ *n, pl* **-ries** : annual return of the date of a notable event or its celebration

an·no·tate \'anə,tāt\ *vb* **-tat·ed; -tat·ing** : furnish with notes — **an·no·ta·tion** \,anə-'tāshən\ *n* — **an·no·ta·tor** \'anə,tātər\ *n*

an·nounce \ə'naúns\ *vb*
-nounced; -nounc·ing : make
known publicly — **an·nounce-
ment** *n* — **an·nounc·er** *n*

an·noy \ə'nói\ *vb* : disturb or
irritate — **an·noy·ance** \-əns\
n — **an·noy·ing·ly** \-'nóiiŋlē\
adv

an·nu·al \'anyəwəl\ *adj* **1**
: occurring once a year **2**
: living only one year — **annual** *n* — **an·nu·al·ly** *adv*

an·nu·i·ty \ə'nüətē, -'nyü-\
n, pl **-ties** : amount payable
annually or the right to such a
payment

an·nul \ə'nəl\ *vb* **-ll-** : make
legally void — **an·nul·ment** *n*

an·ode \'an‚ōd\ *n* **1** : positive
electrode **2** : negative battery terminal — **an·od·ic**
\a'nädik\ *adj*

anoint \ə'nóint\ *vb* : apply oil
to as a rite — **anoint·ment** *n*

anom·a·ly \ə'näməlē\ *n, pl*
-lies : something abnormal or
unusual — **anom·a·lous**
\ə'nämələs\ *adj*

anon·y·mous \ə'nänəməs\ *adj*
: of unknown origin — **an·o-
nym·i·ty** \‚anə'nimətē\ *n* —
anon·y·mous·ly *adv*

an·oth·er \ə'nəthər\ *adj* **1**
: any or some other **2** : one
more ~ *pron* **1** : one more **2**
: one different

an·swer \'ansər\ *n* **1** : something spoken or written in reply to a question **2** : solution
to a problem ~ *vb* **1** : reply
to **2** : be responsible **3** : be
adequate — **an·swer·er** *n*

an·swer·able \-rəbəl\ *adj* : responsible

ant \'ant\ *n* : small social insect — **ant·hill** *n*

-ant \ənt\ *n suffix* **1** : one that
performs or causes an action
2 : thing that is acted upon ~
adj suffix **1** : performing an
action or being in a condition
2 : causing an action or
process

ant·ac·id \ant'asəd\ : agent
that counteracts acidity

an·tag·o·nism \an'tagə‚nizəm\
n : active opposition or hostility — **an·tag·o·nist** \-ənist\ *n*
— **an·tag·o·nis·tic** \-‚tagə-
'nistik\ *adj*

an·tag·o·nize \an'tagə‚nīz\ *vb*
-nized; -niz·ing : cause to be
hostile

ant·arc·tic \ant'ärktik, -'ärtik\
adj : relating to the region
near the south pole

antarctic circle *n* : circle parallel to the equator approximately
23°27' from the south pole

an·te·bel·lum \‚anti'beləm\
adj : existing before the U.S.
Civil War

an·te·ced·ent \‚antə'sēdᵊnt\ *n*
: one that comes before — **an-
tecedent** *adj*

an·te·lope \'antᵊl‚ōp\ *n, pl*
-lope *or* **-lopes** : deerlike
mammal related to the ox

an·ten·na \an'tenə\ *n, pl* **-nae** \-ˌnē\ *or* **-nas** **1** : one of the long slender paired sensory organs on the head of an arthropod **2** *pl* **-nas** : metallic device for sending or receiving radio waves

an·te·ri·or \an'tirēər\ *adj* : located before in place or time

an·them \'anthəm\ *n* : song or hymn of praise or gladness

an·ther \'anthər\ *n* : part of a seed plant that contains pollen

an·thol·o·gy \an'thäləjē\ *n, pl* **-gies** : literary collection

an·thra·cite \'anthrəˌsīt\ *n* : hard coal

an·thro·poid \'anthrəˌpȯid\ *n* : large ape — **anthropoid** *adj*

an·thro·pol·o·gy \ˌanthrə-'päləjē\ *n* : science dealing with humans — **an·thro·po·log·i·cal** \-pə'läjikəl\ *adj* — **an·thro·pol·o·gist** \-'päləjist\ *n*

anti- \ˌantē, -ˌtī\ **ant-, anth-** *prefix* **1** : opposite in kind, position, or action **2** : opposing or hostile toward **3** : defending against **4** : curing or treating

an·ti·bi·ot·ic \ˌantēbī'ätik, -bē-\ *n* : substance that inhibits harmful microorganisms — **antibiotic** *adj*

List of self-explanatory words with the prefix *anti-*

antiabortion	antiburglar	anticonservation
antiacademic	antiburglary	anticonservationist
antiadministration	antibusiness	anticonsumer
antiaggression	anticancer	anticonventional
antiaircraft	anticapitalism	anticorrosion
antialien	anticapitalist	anticorrosive
antiapartheid	anti–Catholic	anticorruption
antiaristocratic	anticensorship	anticrime
antiart	anti–Christian	anticruelty
antiauthoritarian	anti–Christianity	anticult
antiauthority	antichurch	anticultural
antibacterial	anticigarette	antidandruff
antibias	anticlerical	antidemocratic
antiblack	anticollision	antidiscrimination
antibourgeois	anticolonial	antidrug
antiboycott	anticommunism	antidumping
antibureaucratic	anticommunist	antiestablishment

an·ti·body \'anti₁bädē\ *n* : bodily substance that counteracts the effects of a foreign substance or organism

an·tic \'antik\ *n* : playful act ~ *adj* : playful

an·tic·i·pate \an'tisə₁pāt\ *vb* **-pat·ed; -pat·ing 1** : be prepared for **2** : look forward to — **an·tic·i·pa·tion** \-₁tisə'pā-shən\ *n* — **an·tic·i·pa·to·ry** \-'tisəpə₁tōrē\ *adj*

an·ti·cli·max \₁antē'klī₁maks\ *n* : something strikingly less important than what has preceded it — **an·ti·cli·mac·tic** \-klī'maktik\ *adj*

an·ti·dote \'anti₁dōt\ *n* : remedy for poison

an·ti·freeze \'anti₁frēz\ *n* : substance to prevent a liquid from freezing

an·ti·his·ta·mine \₁anti'histə-₁mēn\ : drug for treating allergies and colds

an·ti·mo·ny \'antə₁mōnē\ *n* : brittle white metallic chemical element

an·tip·a·thy \an'tipəthē\ *n, pl* **-thies** : strong dislike

an·ti·quar·i·an \₁antə'kwer-ēən\ *adj* : relating to antiquities or old books — **antiquarian** *n*

an·ti·quary \'antə₁kwerē\ *n, pl* **-quar·ies** : one who collects or studies antiquities

an·ti·quat·ed \'antə₁kwātəd\ *adj* : out-of-date

---

antievolution	antiglare	anti–integration
antievolutionary	antigovernment	anti–intellectual
antifamily	antiguerrilla	anti–intellectualism
antifascism	antigun	antijamming
antifascist	antihijack	anti–Jewish
antifatigue	antihomosexual	antilabor
antifemale	antihuman	antiliberal
antifeminine	antihumanism	antiliberalism
antifeminism	antihumanistic	antilitter
antifeminist	antihunting	antilittering
antifertility	anti–imperialism	antilynching
antiforeign	anti–imperialist	antimale
antiforeigner	anti–inflation	antimanagement
antifraud	anti–inflationary	antimaterialism
antigambling	anti–institutional	antimaterialist

an·tique \an'tēk\ *adj* : very old or out-of-date — **antique** *n*

an·tiq·ui·ty \an'tikwətē\ *n, pl* **-ties 1** : ancient times **2** *pl* : relics of ancient times

an·ti·sep·tic \ˌantə'septik\ *adj* : killing or checking the growth of germs — **antiseptic** *n* — **an·ti·sep·ti·cal·ly** \-tiklē\ *adv*

an·tith·e·sis \an'tithəsəs\ *n, pl* **-e·ses** \-ˌsēz\ : direct opposite

ant·ler \'antlər\ *n* : solid branched horn of a deer — **ant·lered** \-lərd\ *adj*

---

antimicrobial
antimilitarism
antimilitarist
antimilitary
antimiscegenation
antimonopolist
antimonopoly
antimosquito
antinoise
antiobesity
antiobscenity
antipapal
antipersonnel
antipolice
antipollution
antipornographic
antipornography
antipoverty
antiprofiteering
antiprogressive
antiprostitution
antirabies
antiracketeering
antiradical
antirape
antirealism

antirecession
antireform
antireligious
antirevolutionary
antiriot
antiromantic
antirust
antisegregation
antisex
antisexist
antisexual
antishoplifting
antislavery
antismoking
antismuggling
antismut
antispending
antistrike
antistudent
antisubmarine
antisubversion
antisubversive
antisuicide
antitank
antitax
antitechnological

antitechnology
antiterrorism
antiterrorist
antitheft
antitobacco
antitotalitarian
antitoxin
antitraditional
antitrust
antituberculosis
antitumor
antityphoid
antiulcer
antiunemployment
antiunion
antiuniversity
antiurban
antiviolence
antiviral
antivivisection
antiwar
anti–West
anti–Western
antiwhite
antiwoman

ant·onym \\'antə,nim\\ *n* : word of opposite meaning

anus \\'ānəs\\ *n* : the rear opening of the alimentary canal

an·vil \\'anvəl\\ *n* : heavy iron block on which metal is shaped

anx·i·ety \\aŋ'zīətē\\ *n, pl* **-eties** : uneasiness usu. over an expected misfortune

anx·ious \\'aŋkshəs\\ *adj* **1** : uneasy **2** : earnestly wishing — **anx·ious·ly** *adv*

any \\'enē\\ *adj* **1** : one chosen at random **2** : of whatever number or quantity ∼ *pron* **1** : any one or ones **2** : any amount ∼ *adv* : to any extent or degree

any·body \\-bədē, -,bäd-\\ *pron* : anyone

any·how \\-,haů\\ *adv* **1** : in any way **2** : nevertheless

any·more \\,enē'mōr\\ *adv* : at the present time

any·one \\-'enē,wən\\ *pron* : any person

any·place *adv* : anywhere

any·thing *pron* : any thing whatever

any·time *adv* : at any time whatever

any·way *adv* : anyhow

any·where *adv* : in or to any place

aor·ta \\ā'ȯrtə\\ *n, pl* **-tas** *or* **-tae** \\-ē\\ : main artery from the heart — **aor·tic** \\ā'ȯrtik\\ *adj*

apart \\ə'pärt\\ *adv* **1** : separately in place or time **2** : aside **3** : to pieces

apart·heid \\ə'pär,tāt, -,tīt\\ *n* : racial segregation

apart·ment \\ə'pärtmənt\\ *n* : set of usu. rented rooms

ap·a·thy \\'apəthē\\ *n* : lack of emotion or interest — **ap·a·thet·ic** \\,apə'thetik\\ *adj* — **ap·a·thet·i·cal·ly** \\-iklē\\ *adv*

ape \\'āp\\ *n* : large tailless primate ∼ *vb* **aped; ap·ing** : imitate

ap·er·ture \\'apər,chůr, -chər\\ *n* : opening

apex \\'ā,peks\\ *n, pl* **apex·es** *or* **api·ces** \\'āpə,sēz, 'apə-\\ : highest point

aphid \\'āfid, 'a-\\ *n* : small insect that sucks plant juices

aph·o·rism \\'afə,rizəm\\ *n* : short saying stating a general truth — **aph·oris·tic** \\,afə-'ristik\\ *adj*

aph·ro·di·si·ac \\,afrə'dēzē,ak, 'diz-\\ *n* : substance that excites sexual desire

api·a·rist \\'āpēərist\\ *n* : beekeeper — **api·ary** \\-pē,erē\\ *n*

apiece \\ə'pēs\\ *adv* : for each one

aplen·ty \\ə'plentē\\ *adj* : plentiful or abundant

aplomb \\ə'pläm, -'pləm\\ *n* : complete calmness or self= assurance

apoc·a·lypse \ə'päkə,lips\ *n* : writing prophesying a cataclysm in which evil forces are destroyed — **apoc·a·lyp·tic** \-,päkə'liptik\ *adj*

apoc·ry·pha \ə'päkrəfə\ *n* : writings of dubious authenticity — **apoc·ry·phal** \-fəl\ *adj*

apol·o·get·ic \ə,pälə'jetik\ *adj* : expressing apology — **apol·o·get·i·cal·ly** \-iklē\ *adv*

apol·o·gize \ə'pälə,jīz\ *vb* **-gized; -giz·ing** : make an apology — **apol·o·gist** \-jist\ *n*

apol·o·gy \ə'päləjē\ *n, pl* **-gies** **1** : formal justification **2** : expression of regret for a wrong

ap·o·plexy \'apə,pleksē\ *n* : sudden loss of consciousness caused by rupture or obstruction of an artery of the brain — **ap·o·plec·tic** \,apə-'plektik\ *adj*

apos·ta·sy \ə'pästəsē\ *n, pl* **-sies** : abandonment of a former loyalty — **apos·tate** \ə'päs,tāt\ *adj or n*

apos·tle \ə'päsəl\ *n* : disciple or advocate — **apos·tle·ship** *n* — **ap·os·tolic** \,apə'stälik\ *adj*

apos·tro·phe \ə'pästrə,fē\ *n* : punctuation mark ' to indicate the possessive case or the omission of a letter or figure

apoth·e·cary \ə'päthə,kerē\ *n, pl* **-car·ies** : druggist

ap·pall \ə'pȯl\ *vb* : fill with horror or dismay

ap·pa·ra·tus \,apə'ratəs, -'rāt-\ *n, pl* **-tus·es** *or* **-tus** **1** : equipment **2** : complex machine or device

ap·par·el \ə'parəl\ *n* : clothing

ap·par·ent \ə'parənt\ *adj* **1** : visible **2** : obvious **3** : seeming — **ap·par·ent·ly** *adv*

ap·pa·ri·tion \,apə'rishən\ *n* : ghost

ap·peal \ə'pēl\ *vb* **1** : try to have a court case reheard **2** : ask earnestly **3** : have an attraction — **appeal** *n*

ap·pear \ə'pir\ *vb* **1** : become visible or evident **2** : come into the presence of someone **3** : seem

ap·pear·ance \ə'pirəns\ *n* **1** : act of appearing **2** : outward aspect

ap·pease \ə'pēz\ *vb* **-peased; -peas·ing** : pacify with concessions — **ap·pease·ment** *n*

ap·pel·late \ə'pelət\ *adj* : having power to review decisions

ap·pend \ə'pend\ *vb* : attach

ap·pend·age \ə'pendij\ *n* : something attached

ap·pen·dec·to·my \,apən-'dektəmē\ *n, pl* **-mies** : surgical removal of the appendix

ap·pen·di·ci·tis \ə,pendə'sītəs\ *n* : inflammation of the appendix

ap·pen·dix \ə'pendiks\ *n, pl* **-dix·es** *or* **-di·ces** \-də,sēz\ **1** : supplementary matter **2** : narrow closed tube extending from lower right intestine

ap·pe·tite \'apə,tīt\ *n* **1** : natural desire esp. for food **2** : preference

ap·pe·tiz·er \-,tīzər\ *n* : food or drink to stimulate the appetite

ap·pe·tiz·ing \-ziŋ\ *adj* : tempting to the appetite — **ap·pe·tiz·ing·ly** *adv*

ap·plaud \ə'plȯd\ *vb* : show approval esp. by clapping

ap·plause \ə'plȯz\ *n* : a clapping in approval

ap·ple \'apəl\ *n* : rounded fruit with firm white flesh

ap·ple·jack \-,jak\ *n* : brandy made from cider

ap·pli·ance \ə'plīəns\ *n* : household machine or device

ap·pli·ca·ble \'aplikəbəl, ə'plikə-\ *adj* : capable of being applied — **ap·pli·ca·bil·i·ty** \,aplikə'bilətē, ə,plikə-\ *n*

ap·pli·cant \'aplikənt\ *n* : one who applies

ap·pli·ca·tion \,aplə'kāshən\ *n* **1** : act of applying or thing applied **2** : constant attention **3** : request **4** : computer program that performs a major task

ap·pli·ca·tor \'aplə,kātər\ *n* : device for applying a substance

ap·pli·qué \,aplə'kā\ *n* : cut-out fabric decoration — **appliqué** *vb*

ap·ply \ə'plī\ *vb* **-plied; -ply·ing** **1** : place in contact **2** : put to practical use **3** : devote (one's) attention or efforts to something **4** : submit a request **5** : have reference or a connection

ap·point \ə'pȯint\ *vb* **1** : set or assign officially **2** : equip or furnish — **ap·poin·tee** \ə,pȯin'tē, ,a-\ *n*

ap·point·ment \ə'pȯintmənt\ *n* **1** : act of appointing **2** : nonelective political job **3** : arrangement for a meeting

ap·por·tion \ə'pōrshən\ *vb* : distribute proportionately — **ap·por·tion·ment** *n*

ap·po·site \'apəzət\ *adj* : suitable — **ap·po·site·ly** *adv* — **ap·po·site·ness** *n*

ap·praise \ə'prāz\ *vb* **-praised; -prais·ing** : set value on — **ap·prais·al** \-'prāzəl\ *n* — **ap·prais·er** *n*

ap·pre·cia·ble \ə'prēshəbəl\ *adj* : considerable — **ap·pre·cia·bly** \-blē\ *adv*

ap·pre·ci·ate \ə'prēshē,āt\ *vb* **-ated; -at·ing** **1** : value justly **2** : be grateful for **3** : increase in value — **ap·pre·cia·tion** \-,prēshē'āshən\ *n*

ap·pre·cia·tive \ə'prēshətiv, -shē,āt-\ *adj* : showing appreciation

ap·pre·hend \ˌapriˈhend\ *vb* **1** : arrest **2** : look forward to in dread **3** : understand — **ap·pre·hen·sion** \-ˈhenchən\ *n*

ap·pre·hen·sive \-ˈhensiv\ *adj* : fearful — **ap·pre·hen·sive·ly** *adv* — **ap·pre·hen·sive·ness** *n*

ap·pren·tice \əˈprentəs\ *n* : person learning a craft ∼ *vb* **-ticed; -tic·ing** : employ or work as an apprentice — **ap·pren·tice·ship** *n*

ap·prise \əˈprīz\ *vb* **-prised; -pris·ing** : inform

ap·proach \əˈprōch\ *vb* **1** : move nearer or be close to **2** : make initial advances or efforts toward — **ap·proach** *n* — **ap·proach·able** *adj*

ap·pro·ba·tion \ˌaprəˈbā-shən\ *n* : approval

ap·pro·pri·ate \əˈprōprēˌāt\ *vb* **-at·ed; -at·ing** **1** : take possession of **2** : set apart for a particular use ∼ \-prēət\ *adj* : suitable — **ap·pro·pri·ate·ly** *adv* — **ap·pro·pri·ate·ness** *n* — **ap·pro·pria·tion** \əˌprōprēˈāshən\ *n*

ap·prov·al \əˈprüvəl\ *n* : act of approving

ap·prove \əˈprüv\ *vb* **-proved; -prov·ing** : accept as satisfactory

ap·prox·i·mate \əˈpräksəmət\ *adj* : nearly correct or exact ∼ \-ˌmāt\ *vb* **-mat·ed; -mat·ing** : come near — **ap·prox·i-** **mate·ly** *adv* — **ap·prox·i·ma·tion** \-ˌpräksəˈmāshən\ *n*

ap·pur·te·nance \əˈpərtnəns\ *n* : accessory — **ap·pur·te·nant** \-ˈpərtnənt\ *adj*

apri·cot \ˈaprəˌkät, ˈā-\ *n* : peachlike fruit

April \ˈāprəl\ *n* : 4th month of the year having 30 days

apron \ˈāprən\ *n* : protective garment

ap·ro·pos \ˌaprəˈpō, ˈaprəˌpō\ *adv* : suitably ∼ *adj* : being to the point

apropos of *prep* : with regard to

apt \ˈapt\ *adj* **1** : suitable **2** : likely **3** : quick to learn — **apt·ly** *adv* — **apt·ness** *n*

ap·ti·tude \ˈaptəˌtüd, -tyüd\ *n* **1** : capacity for learning **2** : natural ability

aqua \ˈakwə, ˈäk-\ *n* : light greenish blue color

aquar·i·um \əˈkwarēəm\ *n, pl* **-i·ums** *or* **-ia** \-ēə\ : glass container for aquatic animals and plants

aquat·ic \əˈkwätik, -ˈkwat-\ *adj* : of or relating to water — **aquatic** *n*

aq·ue·duct \ˈakwəˌdəkt\ *n* : conduit for carrying running water

aq·ui·line \ˈakwəˌlīn, -lən\ *adj* : curved like an eagle's beak

-ar \ər\ *adj suffix* **1** : of, relating to, or being **2** : resembling

ar·a·besque \ˌarə'besk\ *n* : intricate design

ar·a·ble \'arəbəl\ *adj* : fit for crops

ar·bi·ter \'ärbətər\ *n* : final authority

ar·bi·trary \'ärbəˌtrerē\ *adj* **1** : selected at random **2** : autocratic — **ar·bi·trari·ly** \ˌärbə'trerəlē\ *adv* — **ar·bi·trari·ness** \'ärbəˌtrerēnəs\ *n*

ar·bi·trate \'ärbəˌtrāt\ *vb* **-trat·ed; -trat·ing** : settle a dispute as arbitrator — **ar·bi·tra·tion** \ˌärbə'trāshən\ *n*

ar·bi·tra·tor \'ärbəˌtrātər\ *n* : one chosen to settle a dispute

ar·bor \'ärbər\ *n* : shelter under branches or vines

ar·bo·re·al \är'bōrēəl\ *adj* : living in trees

arc \'ärk\ *n* **1** : part of a circle **2** : bright sustained electrical discharge ∼ *vb* **arced** \'ärkt\; **arc·ing** \'ärkiŋ\ : form an arc

ar·cade \är'kād\ *n* : arched passageway between shops

ar·cane \är'kān\ *adj* : mysterious or secret

¹arch \'ärch\ *n* : curved structure spanning an opening ∼ *vb* : cover with or form into an arch

²arch *adj* **1** : chief — usu. in combination **2** : mischievous — **arch·ly** *adv* — **arch·ness** *n*

ar·chae·ol·o·gy, ar·che·ol·o·gy \ˌärkē'äləjē\ *n* : study of past human life — **ar·chae·o·log·i·cal** \-kēə'läjikəl\ *adj* — **ar·chae·ol·o·gist** \-kē'äləjist\ *n*

ar·cha·ic \är'kāik\ *adj* : belonging to an earlier time — **ar·cha·i·cal·ly** \-iklē\ *adv*

arch·an·gel \'ärkˌānjəl\ *n* : angel of high rank

arch·bish·op \ärch'bishəp\ *n* : chief bishop — **arch·bish·op·ric** \-əˌprik\ *n*

arch·di·o·cese \-'dīəsəs, -ˌsēz, -ˌsēs\ *n* : diocese of an archbishop

ar·chery \'ärchərē\ *n* : shooting with bow and arrows — **ar·cher** \-chər\ *n*

ar·che·type \'ärkiˌtīp\ *n* : original pattern or model

ar·chi·pel·a·go \ˌärkə'peləˌgō, ˌärchə-\ *n, pl* **-goes** *or* **-gos** : group of islands

ar·chi·tect \'ärkəˌtekt\ *n* : building designer

ar·chi·tec·ture \'ärkəˌtekchər\ *n* **1** : building design **2** : style of building **3** : manner of organizing elements — **ar·chi·tec·tur·al** \ˌärkə'tekchərəl, -'tekshrəl\ *adj* — **ar·chi·tec·tur·al·ly** *adv*

ar·chives \'ärˌkīvz\ *n pl* : public records or their storage place — **archi·vist** \'ärkəvist, -ˌkī-\ *n*

arch·way *n* : passageway under an arch

arc·tic \\'ärktik, 'ärt-\ *adj* **1** : relating to the region near the north pole **2** : frigid

arctic circle *n* : circle parallel to the equator approximately 23°27' from the north pole

-ard \ərd\ *n suffix* : one that is

ar·dent \\'ärd°nt\ *adj* : characterized by warmth of feeling — **ar·dent·ly** *adv*

ar·dor \\'ärdər\ *n* : warmth of feeling

ar·du·ous \\'ärjəwəs\ *adj* : difficult — **ar·du·ous·ly** *adv* — **ar·du·ous·ness** *n*

are *pres 2d sing or pres pl of* BE

ar·ea \\'ärēə\ *n* **1** : space for something **2** : amount of surface included **3** : region **4** : range covered by a thing or concept

area code *n* : 3-digit area-identifying telephone number

are·na \ə'rēnə\ *n* **1** : enclosed exhibition area **2** : sphere of activity

ar·gon \\'är₁gän\ *n* : colorless odorless gaseous chemical element

ar·got \\'ärgət, -₁gō\ *n* : special language (as of the underworld)

argu·able \\'ärgyəwəbəl\ *adj* : open to dispute

ar·gue \\'ärgyü\ *vb* **-gued; -gu·ing 1** : give reasons for or against something **2** : disagree in words

ar·gu·ment \\'ärgyəmənt\ *n* **1** : reasons given to persuade **2** : dispute with words

ar·gu·men·ta·tive \₁ärgyə-'mentətiv\ *adj* : inclined to argue

ar·gyle \\'är₁gīl\ *n* : colorful diamond pattern in knitting

aria \\'ärēə\ *n* : opera solo

ar·id \\'arəd\ *adj* : very dry — **arid·i·ty** \ə'ridətē\ *n*

arise \ə'rīz\ *vb* **arose** \-'rōz\; **aris·en** \-'riz°n\; **aris·ing** \-'rīziŋ\ **1** : get up **2** : originate

ar·is·toc·ra·cy \₁arə'stäkrəsē\ *n, pl* **-cies** : upper class — **aris·to·crat** \ə'ristə₁krat\ *n* — **aris·to·crat·ic** \ə₁ristə-'kratik\ *adj*

arith·me·tic \ə'rithmə₁tik\ *n* : mathematics that deals with numbers — **ar·ith·met·ic** \₁arith'metik\, **ar·ith·met·i·cal** \-ikəl\ *adj*

ark \\'ärk\ *n* : big boat

¹arm \\'ärm\ *n* **1** : upper limb **2** : branch — **armed** \\'ärmd\ *adj* — **arm·less** *adj*

²arm *vb* : furnish with weapons ~ *n* **1** : weapon **2** : branch of the military forces **3** *pl* : family's heraldic designs

ar·ma·da \är'mädə, -'mäd-\ *n* : naval fleet

ar·ma·dil·lo \₁ärmə'dilō\ *n, pl* **-los** : burrowing mammal covered with bony plates

ar·ma·ment \'ärməmənt\ *n* : military arms and equipment

ar·ma·ture \'ärmə,chùr, -chər\ *n* : rotating part of an electric generator or motor

armed forces *n pl* : military

ar·mi·stice \'ärməstəs\ *n* : truce

ar·mor \'ärmər\ *n* : protective covering — **ar·mored** \-mərd\ *adj*

ar·mory \'ärmərē\ *n, pl* **-mor·ies** : factory or storehouse for arms

arm·pit *n* : hollow under the junction of the arm and shoulder

ar·my \'ärmē\ *n, pl* **-mies** **1** : body of men organized for war esp. on land **2** : great number

aro·ma \ə'rōmə\ *n* : usu. pleasing odor — **ar·o·mat·ic** \,arə'matik\ *adj*

around \ə'raùnd\ *adv* **1** : in or along a circuit **2** : on all sides **3** : near **4** : in an opposite direction ~ *prep* **1** : surrounding **2** : along the circuit of **3** : to or on the other side of **4** : near

arouse \ə'raùz\ *vb* **aroused;** **arous·ing** **1** : awaken from sleep **2** : stir up — **arous·al** \-'raùzəl\ *n*

ar·raign \ə'rān\ *vb* **1** : call before a court to answer to an indictment **2** : accuse — **ar·raign·ment** *n*

ar·range \ə'rānj\ *vb* **-ranged;** **-rang·ing** **1** : put in order **2** : settle or agree on **3** : adapt (a musical composition) for voices or instruments — **ar·range·ment** *n* — **ar·rang·er** *n*

ar·ray \ə'rā\ *vb* **1** : arrange in order **2** : dress esp. splendidly ~ *n* **1** : arrangement **2** : rich clothing **3** : imposing group

ar·rears \ə'rirz\ *n pl* : state of being behind in paying debts

ar·rest \ə'rest\ *vb* **1** : stop **2** : take into legal custody — **arrest** *n*

ar·rive \ə'rīv\ *vb* **-rived; -riv·ing** **1** : reach a destination, point, or stage **2** : come near in time — **ar·riv·al** \-əl\ *n*

ar·ro·gant \'arəgənt\ *adj* : showing an offensive sense of superiority — **ar·ro·gance** \-gəns\ *n* — **ar·ro·gant·ly** *adv*

ar·ro·gate \-,gāt\ *vb* **-gat·ed;** **-gat·ing** : to claim without justification

ar·row \'arō\ *n* : slender missile shot from a bow — **ar·row·head** *n*

ar·royo \ə'ròiō, -ə\ *n, pl* **-royos** **1** : watercourse **2** : gully

ar·se·nal \'ärsᵊnəl\ *n* **1** : place where arms are made or stored **2** : store

ar·se·nic \'ärsᵊnik\ *n* : solid grayish poisonous chemical element

ar·son \'ärs°n\ *n* : willful or malicious burning of property — **ar·son·ist** \-ist\ *n*

art \'ärt\ *n* **1** : skill **2** : branch of learning **3** : creation of things of beauty or works so produced **4** : ingenuity

ar·te·rio·scle·ro·sis \ar͵tirēō-sklə'rōsəs\ *n* : hardening of the arteries — **ar·te·rio·scle-rot·ic** \-'rätik\ *adj or n*

ar·tery \'ärtərē\ *n, pl* **-ter·ies 1** : tubular vessel carrying blood from the heart **2** : thoroughfare — **ar·te·ri·al** \är-'tirēəl\ *adj*

art·ful \-fəl\ *adj* **1** : ingenious **2** : crafty — **art·ful·ly** *adv* — **art·ful·ness** *n*

ar·thri·tis \är'thrītəs\ *n, pl* **-ti·des** \-'thritə͵dēz\ : inflammation of the joints — **ar·thrit·ic** \-'thritik\ *adj or n*

ar·thro·pod \'ärthrə͵päd\ *n* : invertebrate animal (as an insect or crab) with segmented body and jointed limbs — **arthropod** *adj*

ar·ti·choke \'ärtə͵chōk\ *n* : tall thistle-like herb or its edible flower head

ar·ti·cle \'ärtikəl\ *n* **1** : distinct part of a written document **2** : nonfictional published piece of writing **3** : word (as *an, the*) used to limit a noun **4** : item or piece

ar·tic·u·late \är'tikyələt\ *adj* : able to speak effectively ~ \-͵lāt\ *vb* **-lated; -lat·ing 1** : utter distinctly **2** : unite by joints — **ar·tic·u·late·ly** *adv* — **ar·tic·u·late·ness** *n* — **ar·tic·u·la·tion** \-͵tikyə'lāshən\ *n*

ar·ti·fact \'ärtə͵fakt\ *n* : object of esp. prehistoric human workmanship

ar·ti·fice \'ärtəfəs\ *n* **1** : trick or trickery **2** : ingenious device or ingenuity

ar·ti·fi·cial \͵ärtə'fishəl\ *adj* **1** : man-made **2** : not genuine — **ar·ti·fi·ci·al·i·ty** \-͵fishē-'alətē\ *n* — **ar·ti·fi·cial·ly** *adv* — **ar·ti·fi·cial·ness** *n*

ar·til·lery \är'tilərē\ *n, pl* **-ler·ies** : large caliber firearms

ar·ti·san \'ärtəzən, -sən\ *n* : skilled craftsman

art·ist \'ärtist\ *n* : one who creates art — **ar·tis·tic** \är-'tistik\ *adj* — **ar·tis·ti·cal·ly** \-iklē\ *adv* — **ar·tis·try** \'ärtəstrē\ *n*

art·less \'ärtləs\ *adj* : sincere or natural — **art·less·ly** *adv* — **art·less·ness** *n*

arty \'ärtē\ *adj* **art·i·er; -est** : pretentiously artistic — **art·i·ly** \'ärt°lē\ *adv* — **art·i·ness** *n*

-ary \͵erē\ *adj suffix* : of, relating to, or connected with

as \əz, ˌaz\ *adv* **1** : to the same degree **2** : for example ~ *conj* **1** : in the same way or degree as **2** : while **3** : because **4** : though ~ *pron* — used after *same* or *such* ~ *prep* : in the capacity of

as·bes·tos \as'bestəs, az-\ *n* : fibrous incombustible mineral

as·cend \ə'send\ *vb* : move upward — **as·cen·sion** \-'senchən\ *n*

as·cen·dan·cy \ə'sendənsē\ *n* : domination

as·cen·dant \ə'sendənt\ *n* : dominant position ~ *adj* **1** : moving upward **2** : dominant

as·cent \ə'sent\ *n* **1** : act of moving upward **2** : degree of upward slope

as·cer·tain \ˌasər'tān\ *vb* : determine — **as·cer·tain·able** *adj*

as·cet·ic \ə'setik\ *adj* : self-denying — **ascetic** *n* — **as·cet·i·cism** \-'setəˌsizəm\ *n*

as·cribe \ə'skrīb\ *vb* **-cribed; -crib·ing** : attribute — **as·crib·able** *adj* — **as·crip·tion** \-'skripshən\ *n*

asep·tic \ā'septik\ *adj* : free of disease germs

¹ash \'ash\ *n* : tree related to the olives

²ash *n* : matter left when something is burned — **ash·tray** *n*

ashamed \ə'shāmd\ *adj* : feeling shame — **asham·ed·ly** \-'shāmədlē\ *adv*

ash·en \'ashən\ *adj* : deadly pale

ashore \ə'shōr\ *adv* : on or to the shore

aside \ə'sīd\ *adv* **1** : toward the side **2** : out of the way

aside from *prep* **1** : besides **2** : except for

as·i·nine \'asᵊnˌīn\ *adj* : foolish — **as·i·nin·i·ty** \ˌasᵊn'inətē\ *n*

ask \'ask\ *vb* **1** : call on for an answer or help **2** : utter (a question or request) **3** : invite

askance \ə'skans\ *adv* **1** : with a side glance **2** : with mistrust

askew \ə'skyü\ *adv or adj* : out of line

asleep \ə'slēp\ *adv or adj* **1** : sleeping **2** : numbed **3** : inactive

as long as *conj* **1** : on condition that **2** : because

as of *prep* : from the time of

as·par·a·gus \ə'sparəgəs\ *n* : tall herb related to the lilies or its edible stalks

as·pect \'asˌpekt\ *n* **1** : way something looks to the eye or mind **2** : phase

as·pen \'aspən\ *n* : poplar

as·per·i·ty \a'sperətē, ə-\ *n, pl* **-ties** **1** : roughness **2** : harshness

as·per·sion \ə'spərzhən\ *n* : remark that hurts someone's reputation

as·phalt \'as,fȯlt\ *n* : dark tar-like substance used in paving

as·phyx·ia \as'fiksēə\ *n* : lack of oxygen causing unconsciousness

as·phyx·i·ate \-se,āt\ *vb* **-at·ed; -at·ing** : suffocate — **as·phyx·i·a·tion** \-,fiksē'āshən\ *n*

as·pi·ra·tion \,aspə'rāshən\ *n* : strong desire to achieve a goal

as·pire \ə'spīr\ *vb* **-pired; -pir·ing** : have an ambition — **as·pir·ant** \'aspərənt, ə'spīrənt\ *n*

as·pi·rin \'asprən\ *n, pl* **aspirin** *or* **aspirins** : pain reliever

ass \'as\ *n* **1** : long-eared animal related to the horse **2** : stupid person

as·sail \ə'sāl\ *vb* : attack violently — **as·sail·able** *adj* — **as·sail·ant** *n*

as·sas·si·nate \ə'sasᵊn,āt\ *vb* **-nat·ed; -nat·ing** : murder esp. for political reasons — **as·sas·sin** \-'sasᵊn\ *n* — **as·sas·si·na·tion** \-,sasᵊn'āshən\ *n*

as·sault \ə'sȯlt\ *n or vb* : attack

as·say \'as,ā, a'sā\ *n* : analysis (as of an ore) to determine quality or properties — **as·say** \a'sā, 'as,ā\ *vb*

as·sem·ble \ə'sembəl\ *vb* **-bled; -bling 1** : collect into one place **2** : fit together the parts of

as·sem·bly \-blē\ *n, pl* **-blies 1** : meeting **2** *cap* : legislative body **3** : a fitting together of parts

as·sem·bly·man \-mən\ *n* : member of a legislative assembly

as·sem·bly·wom·an \-,wu̇-mən\ *n* : woman who is a member of a legislative assembly

as·sent \ə'sent\ *vb or n* : consent

as·sert \ə'sərt\ *vb* **1** : declare **2** : defend — **as·ser·tion** \-'sərshən\ *n* — **as·sert·ive** \-'sərtiv\ *adj* — **as·sert·ive·ness** *n*

as·sess \ə'ses\ *vb* **1** : impose (as a tax) **2** : evaluate for taxation — **as·sess·ment** *n* — **as·ses·sor** \-ər\ *n*

as·set \'as,et\ *n* **1** *pl* : individually owned property **2** : advantage or resource

as·sid·u·ous \ə'sijəwəs\ *adj* : diligent — **as·si·du·i·ty** \,asə-'düətē, -'dyü-\ *n* — **as·sid·u·ous·ly** *adv* — **as·sid·u·ous·ness** *n*

as·sign \ə'sīn\ *vb* **1** : transfer to another **2** : appoint to a duty **3** : designate as a task **4**

: attribute — **assign·able** *adj* — **as·sign·ment** *n*

as·sim·i·late \ə'simə,lāt\ *vb* -lat·ed; -lat·ing **1** : absorb as nourishment **2** : understand — **as·sim·i·la·tion** \-,simə-'lāshən\ *n*

as·sist \ə'sist\ *vb* : help — **assist** *n* — **assis·tance** \-'sistəns\ *n* — **as·sis·tant** \-tənt\ *n*

as·so·ci·ate \ə'sōshē,āt, -sē-\ *vb* -at·ed; -at·ing **1** : join in companionship or partnership **2** : connect in thought — **as·so·ci·ate** \-shēət, -sēət\ *n* — **as·so·ci·a·tion** \-,sōshē'-ā-shən, -sē-\ *n*

as soon as *conj* : when

as·sort·ed \ə'sórtəd\ *adj* : consisting of various kinds

as·sort·ment \-mənt\ *n* : assorted collection

as·suage \ə'swāj\ *vb* -suaged; -suag·ing : ease or satisfy

as·sume \ə'süm\ *vb* -sumed; -sum·ing **1** : take upon oneself **2** : pretend to have or be **3** : take as true

as·sump·tion \ə'səmpshən\ *n* : something assumed

as·sure \ə'shur\ *vb* -sured; -sur·ing **1** : give confidence or conviction to **2** : guarantee — **as·sur·ance** \-əns\ *n*

as·ter \'astər\ *n* : herb with daisylike flowers

as·ter·isk \'astə,risk\ *n* : a character * used as a reference mark or as an indication of omission of words

astern \ə'stərn\ *adv or adj* **1** : behind **2** : at or toward the stern

as·ter·oid \'astə,róid\ *n* : small planet between Mars and Jupiter

asth·ma \'azmə\ *n* : disorder marked by difficulty in breathing — **asth·mat·ic** \az'matik\ *adj or n*

astig·ma·tism \ə'stigmə,tizəm\ *n* : visual defect — **as·tig·mat·ic** \,astig'matik\ *adj*

as to *prep* **1** : concerning **2** : according to

as·ton·ish \ə'stänish\ *vb* : amaze — **as·ton·ish·ing·ly** *adv* — **as·ton·ish·ment** *n*

as·tound \ə'staund\ *vb* : fill with confused wonder — **as·tound·ing·ly** *adv*

astrad·dle \ə'strad³l\ *adv or prep* : so as to straddle

as·tral \'astrəl\ *adj* : relating to or coming from the stars

astray \ə'strā\ *adv or adj* : off the right path

astride \ə'strīd\ *adv* : with legs apart or one on each side ∼ *prep* : with one leg on each side of

as·trin·gent \ə'strinjənt\ *adj* : causing shrinking or puckering of tissues — **as·trin·gen-**

cy \-jənsē\ *n* — **as·trin·gent** *n*

as·trol·o·gy \ə'strälǝjē\ *n* : prediction of events by the stars — **as·trol·o·ger** \-ǝjǝr\ *n* — **as·tro·log·i·cal** \ˌastrǝ-'läjikǝl\ *adj*

as·tro·naut \'astrǝˌnȯt\ *n* : space traveler

as·tro·nau·tics \ˌastrǝ'nȯtiks\ *n* : construction and operation of spacecraft — **as·tro·nau·tic** \-ik\, **as·tro·nau·ti·cal** \-ikǝl\ *adj*

as·tro·nom·i·cal \ˌastrǝ'nä-mikǝl\ *adj* 1 : relating to astronomy 2 : extremely large

as·tron·o·my \ə'stränǝmē\ *n, pl* **-mies** : study of the celestial bodies — **as·tron·o·mer** \-ǝmǝr\ *n*

as·tute \ə'stüt, -'styüt\ *adj* : shrewd — **as·tute·ly** *adv* — **as·tute·ness** *n*

asun·der \ə'sǝndǝr\ *adv or adj* 1 : into separate pieces 2 : separated

asy·lum \ə'sīlǝm\ *n* 1 : refuge 2 : institution for care esp. of the insane

asym·met·ri·cal \ˌāsǝ'metri-kǝl\, **asym·met·ric** \-trik\ *adj* : not symmetrical — **asym·me·try** \ˌā'simǝtrē\ *n*

at \ǝt, 'at\ *prep* 1 — used to indicate a point in time or space 2 — used to indicate a goal 3 — used to indicate

condition, means, cause, or manner

at all *adv* : without restriction or under any circumstances

ate *past of* EAT

-ate \ǝt, ˌāt\ *n suffix* 1 : office or rank 2 : group of persons holding an office or rank ～ *adj suffix* 1 : brought into or being in a state 2 : marked by having

athe·ist \'āthēist\ *n* : one who denies the existence of God — **athe·ism** \-ˌizǝm\ *n* — **athe·is·tic** \ˌāthē'istik\ *adj*

ath·ero·scle·ro·sis \ˌathǝrōsklǝ-'rōsǝs\ *n* : arteriosclerosis with deposition of fatty substances in the arteries — **ath·ero·scle·rot·ic** \-'rätik\ *adj*

ath·lete \'athˌlēt\ *n* : one trained to compete in athletics

ath·let·ics \ath'letiks\ *n sing or pl* : exercises and games requiring physical skill — **ath·let·ic** \-ik\ *adj*

-a·tion \'āshǝn\ *n suffix* : action or process

-a·tive \ˌātiv, ǝtiv\ *adj suffix* 1 : of, relating to, or connected with 2 : tending to

atlas \'atlǝs\ *n* : book of maps

ATM \ˌāˌtē'em\ *n* : computerized machine for performing basic bank functions

at·mo·sphere \'atmǝˌsfir\ *n* 1 : mass of air surrounding the earth 2 : surrounding influence — **at·mo·spher·ic** \‚at-mə'sfirik, -'sfer-\ *adj* — **at·mo·spher·i·cal·ly** \-iklē\ *adv*

atoll \'a‚tȯl, 'ā-, -‚täl\ *n* : ring-shaped coral island

at·om \'atəm\ *n* **1** : tiny bit **2** : smallest particle of a chemical element that can exist alone or in combination

atom·ic \ə'tämik\ *adj* **1** : relating to atoms **2** : nuclear

atomic bomb *n* : bomb utilizing the energy released by splitting the atom

at·om·iz·er \'atə‚mīzər\ *n* : device for dispersing a liquid as a very fine spray

atone \ə'tōn\ *vb* **atoned; aton·ing** : make amends — **atone·ment** *n*

atop \ə'täp\ *prep* : on top of ～ *adv or adj* : on, to, or at the top

atri·um \'ātrēəm\ *n, pl* **atria** \-trēə\ *or* **atriums 1** : open central room or court **2** : heart chamber that receives blood from the veins

atro·cious \ə'trōshəs\ *adj* : appalling or abominable — **atro·cious·ly** *adv* — **atro·cious·ness** *n*

atroc·i·ty \ə'träsətē\ *n, pl* **-ties** : savage act

at·ro·phy \'atrəfē\ *n, pl* **-phies** : wasting away of a bodily part or tissue — **at·ro·phy** *vb*

at·ro·pine \'atrə‚pēn\ *n* : drug used esp. to relieve spasms

at·tach \ə'tach\ *vb* **1** : seize legally **2** : bind by personalities **3** : join — **at·tach·ment** *n*

at·ta·ché \‚atə'shā, ‚a‚ta-, ə‚ta-\ *n* : technical expert on a diplomatic staff

at·tack \ə'tak\ *vb* **1** : try to hurt or destroy with violence or words **2** : set to work on ～ *n* **1** : act of attacking **2** : fit of sickness

at·tain \ə'tān\ *vb* **1** : achieve or accomplish **2** : reach — **at·tain·abil·i·ty** \ə‚tānə'bilətē\ *n* — **at·tain·able** *adj* — **at·tain·ment** *n*

at·tempt \ə'tempt\ *vb* : make an effort toward — **attempt** *n*

at·tend \ə'tend\ *vb* **1** : handle or provide for the care of something **2** : accompany **3** : be present at **4** : pay attention — **at·ten·dance** \-'tendəns\ *n* — **at·ten·dant** \-dənt\ *adj or n*

at·ten·tion \ə'tenchən\ *n* **1** : concentration of the mind on something **2** : notice or awareness — **at·ten·tive** \-'tentiv\ *adj* — **at·ten·tive·ly** *adv* — **at·ten·tive·ness** *n*

at·ten·u·ate \ə'tenyə‚wāt\ *vb* **-at·ed; -at·ing 1** : make or become thin **2** : weaken — **at·ten·u·a·tion** \-‚tenyə'wā-shən\ *n*

at·test \ə'test\ *vb* : certify or bear witness — **at·tes·ta·tion** \‚a‚tes'tāshən\ *n*

at·tic \\'atik\ *n* : space just below the roof

at·tire \ə'tīr\ *vb* **-tired; -tiring** : dress — **attire** *n*

at·ti·tude \\'atə,tüd, -,tyüd\ *n* **1** : posture or relative position **2** : feeling, opinion, or mood

at·tor·ney \ə'tərnē\ *n, pl* **-neys** : legal agent

at·tract \ə'trakt\ *vb* **1** : draw to oneself **2** : have emotional or aesthetic appeal for — **at·trac·tion** \-'trakshən\ *n* — **at·trac·tive** \-'traktiv\ *adj* — **at·trac·tive·ly** *adv* — **at·trac·tive·ness** *n*

at·tri·bute \\'atrə,byüt\ *n* : inherent characteristic ∼ \ə'tribyət\ *vb* **-trib·ut·ed; -trib·ut·ing 1** : regard as having a specific cause or origin **2** : regard as a characteristic — **at·trib·ut·able** *adj* — **at·tri·bu·tion** \,atrə'byüshən\ *n*

at·tune \ə'tün, -'tyün\ *vb* : bring into harmony

au·burn \\'ȯbərn\ *adj* : reddish brown

auc·tion \\'ȯkshən\ *n* : public sale of property to the highest bidder — **auction** *vb* — **auc·tion·eer** \,ȯkshə'nir\ *n*

au·dac·i·ty \ȯ'dasətē\ *n* : boldness or insolence — **au·da·cious** \ȯ'dāshəs\ *adj*

au·di·ble \\'ȯdəbəl\ *adj* : capable of being heard — **au·di·bly** \-blē\ *adv*

au·di·ence \\'ȯdēəns\ *n* **1** : formal interview **2** : group of listeners or spectators

au·dio \\'ȯdē,ō\ *adj* : relating to sound or its reproduction ∼ *n* : television sound

au·dio·vi·su·al \,ȯdēō'vizhəwəl\ *adj* : relating to both hearing and sight

au·dit \\'ȯdət\ *vb* : examine financial accounts — **audit** *n* — **au·di·tor** \\'ȯdətər\ *n*

au·di·tion \ȯ'dishən\ *n* : tryout performance — **audition** *vb*

au·di·to·ri·um \,ȯdə'tōrēəm\ *n, pl* **-ri·ums** *or* **-ria** \'-rēa\ : room or building used for public performances

au·di·to·ry \\'ȯdə,tōrē\ *adj* : relating to hearing

au·ger \\'ȯgər\ *n* : tool for boring

aug·ment \ȯg'ment\ *vb* : enlarge or increase — **aug·men·ta·tion** \,ȯgmən'tāshən\ *n*

au·gur \\'ȯgər\ *n* : prophet ∼ *vb* : predict — **au·gu·ry** \\'ȯgyərē, -gər-\ *n*

au·gust \ȯ'gəst\ *adj* : majestic

Au·gust \\'ȯgəst\ *n* : 8th month of the year having 31 days

auk \\'ȯk\ *n* : stocky diving seabird

aunt \\'ant, 'ȧnt\ *n* **1** : sister of one's father or mother **2** : wife of one's uncle

au·ra \'ȯrə\ *n* **1** : distinctive atmosphere **2** : luminous radiation

au·ral \'ȯrəl\ *adj* : relating to the ear or to hearing

au·ri·cle \'ȯrikəl\ *n* : atrium or ear-shaped pouch in the atrium of the heart

au·ro·ra bo·re·al·is \ə'rōrə-ˌbōrē'aləs\ *n* : display of light in the night sky of northern latitudes

aus·pic·es \'ȯspəsəz, -ˌsēz\ *n pl* : patronage and protection

aus·pi·cious \ȯ'spishəs\ *adj* : favorable

aus·tere \ȯ'stir\ *adj* : severe — **aus·tere·ly** *adv* — **aus·ter·i·ty** \ȯ'sterətē\ *n*

au·then·tic \ə'thentik, ȯ-\ *adj* : genuine — **au·then·ti·cal·ly** \-iklē\ *adv* — **au·then·tic·i·ty** \ˌȯ,then'tisətē\ *n*

au·then·ti·cate \ə'thentiˌkāt, ȯ-\ *vb* **-cat·ed; -cat·ing** : prove genuine — **au·then·ti·ca·tion** \-ˌthenti'kāshən\ *n*

au·thor \'ȯthər\ *n* **1** : writer **2** : creator — **au·thor·ship** *n*

au·thor·i·tar·i·an \ȯˌthärə-'terēən, ə-, -ˌthȯr-\ *adj* : marked by blind obedience to authority

au·thor·i·ta·tive \ə'thärəˌtā-tiv, ȯ-, -'thȯr-\ *adj* : being an authority — **au·thor·i·ta·tive·ly** *adv* — **au·thor·i·ta·tive·ness** *n*

au·thor·i·ty \ə'thärətē, ȯ-, -'thȯr-\ *n, pl* **-ties** **1** : expert **2** : right, responsibility, or power to influence **3** *pl* : persons in official positions

au·tho·rize \'ȯthəˌrīz\ *vb* **-rized; -riz·ing** : permit or give official approval for — **au·tho·ri·za·tion** \ˌȯthərə-'zāshən\ *n*

au·tism \'ȯˌtizəm\ *n* : mental disorder marked by impaired ability to communicate and form social relationships and by repetitive behavior patterns

au·to \'ȯtō\ *n, pl* **autos** : automobile

au·to·bi·og·ra·phy \ˌȯtəbī-'ägrəfē, -bē-\ *n* : writer's own life story — **au·to·bi·og·ra·pher** \-fər\ *n* — **au·to·bio·graph·i·cal** \-ˌbīə'grafikəl\ *adj*

au·toc·ra·cy \ȯ'täkrəsē\ *n, pl* **-cies** : government by one person having unlimited power — **au·to·crat** \'ȯtəˌkrat\ *n* — **au·to·crat·ic** \ˌȯtə'kratik\ *adj* — **au·to·crat·i·cal·ly** \-iklē\ *adv*

au·to·graph \'ȯtəˌgraf\ *n* : signature ～ *vb* : write one's name on

au·to·mate \'ȯtəˌmāt\ *vb* **-mat·ed; -mat·ing** : make automatic — **au·to·ma·tion** \ˌȯtə'māshən\ *n*

au·to·mat·ic \ˌȯtə'matik\ *adj* **1** : involuntary **2** : designed to function without human intervention ~ *n* : automatic device (as a firearm) — **au·to·mat·i·cal·ly** \-iklē\ *adv*

au·tom·a·ton \ȯ'tämətən, -ˌtän\ *n, pl* **-a·tons** *or* **-a·ta** \-tə, -ˌtä\ : robot

au·to·mo·bile \ˌȯtəmō'bēl, -'mōˌbēl\ *n* : 4-wheeled passenger vehicle with its own power source

au·to·mo·tive \ˌȯtə'mōtiv\ *adj* : relating to automobiles

au·ton·o·mous \ȯ'tänəməs\ *adj* : self-governing — **au·ton·o·mous·ly** *adv* — **au·ton·o·my** \-mē\ *n*

au·top·sy \'ȯˌtäpsē, 'ȯtəp-\ *n, pl* **-sies** : medical examination of a corpse

au·tumn \'ȯtəm\ *n* : season between summer and winter — **au·tum·nal** \ȯ'təmnəl\ *adj*

aux·il·ia·ry \ȯg'zilyərē, -lərē\ *adj* **1** : being a supplement or reserve **2** : accompanying a main verb form to express person, number, mood, or tense — **auxiliary** *n*

avail \ə'vāl\ *vb* : be of use or make use ~ *n* : use

avail·able \ə'vāləbəl\ *adj* **1** : usable **2** : accessible — **avail·abil·i·ty** \-ˌvālə-'bilətē\ *n*

av·a·lanche \'avəˌlanch\ *n* : mass of sliding or falling snow or rock

av·a·rice \'avərəs\ *n* : greed — **av·a·ri·cious** \ˌavə'rishəs\ *adj*

avenge \ə'venj\ *vb* **avenged; aveng·ing** : take vengeance for — **aveng·er** *n*

av·e·nue \'avəˌnü, -ˌnyü\ *n* **1** : way of approach **2** : broad street

av·er·age \'avrij\ *adj* **1** : being about midway between extremes **2** : ordinary ~ *vb* **1** : be usually **2** : find the mean of ~ *n* : mean

averse \ə'vərs\ *adj* : feeling dislike or reluctance — **aver·sion** \-'vərzhən\ *n*

avert \ə'vərt\ *vb* : turn away

avi·ary \'āvēˌerē\ *n, pl* **-ar·ies** : place where birds are kept

avi·a·tion \ˌāvē'āshən, ˌav-\ *n* : operation or manufacture of airplanes — **avi·a·tor** \'āvēˌātər, 'av-\ *n*

av·id \'avəd\ *adj* **1** : greedy **2** : enthusiastic — **avid·i·ty** \ə'vidətē, a-\ *n* — **av·id·ly** *adv*

av·o·ca·do \ˌavə'kädō, ˌäv-\ *n, pl* **-dos** : tropical fruit with green pulp

av·o·ca·tion \ˌavə'kāshən\ *n* : hobby

avoid \ə'vȯid\ *vb* **1** : keep away from **2** : prevent the occurrence of **3** : refrain from — **avoid·able** *adj* — **avoid·ance** \-ᵊns\ *n*

av·oir·du·pois \ˌavərdəˈpȯiz\ *n* : system of weight based on the pound of 16 ounces

avow \əˈvaủ\ *vb* : declare openly — **avow·al** \-ˈvaủəl\ *n*

await \əˈwāt\ *vb* : wait for

awake \əˈwāk\ *vb* **awoke** \-ˈwōk\; **awok·en** \-ˈwōkən\ *or* **awaked; awak·ing** : wake up — **awake** *adj*

awak·en \əˈwākən\ *vb* **-ened; -en·ing** : wake up

award \əˈwȯrd\ *vb* : give (something won or deserved) ∼ *n* **1** : judgment **2** : prize

aware \əˈwar\ *adj* : having realization or consciousness — **aware·ness** *n*

awash \əˈwȯsh, -ˈwäsh\ *adv or adj* : flooded

away \əˈwā\ *adv* **1** : from this or that place or time **2** : out of the way **3** : in another direction **4** : from one's possession ∼ *adj* **1** : absent **2** : distant

awe \ˈȯ\ *n* : respectful fear or wonder ∼ *vb* **awed; aw·ing** : fill with awe — **awe·some** \-səm\ *adj* — **awe·struck** *adj*

aw·ful \ˈȯfəl\ *adj* **1** : inspiring awe **2** : extremely disagreeable **3** : very great — **aw·ful·ly** *adv*

awhile \əˈhwīl\ *adv* : for a while

awk·ward \ˈȯkwərd\ *adj* **1** : clumsy **2** : embarrassing — **awk·ward·ly** *adv* — **awk·ward·ness** *n*

awl \ˈȯl\ *n* : hole-making tool

aw·ning \ˈȯniŋ\ *n* : window cover

awry \əˈrī\ *adv or adj* : wrong

ax, axe \ˈaks\ *n* : chopping tool

ax·i·om \ˈaksēəm\ *n* : generally accepted truth — **ax·i·om·at·ic** \ˌaksēəˈmatik\ *adj*

ax·is \ˈaksəs\ *n, pl* **ax·es** \-ˌsēz\ : center of rotation — **ax·i·al** \-sēəl\ *adj* — **ax·i·al·ly** *adv*

ax·le \ˈaksəl\ *n* : shaft on which a wheel revolves

aye \ˈī\ *adv* : yes ∼ *n* : a vote of yes

aza·lea \əˈzālyə\ *n* : rhododendron with funnel-shaped blossoms

az·i·muth \ˈazəməth\ *n* : horizontal direction expressed as an angle

azure \ˈazhər\ *n* : blue of the sky — **azure** *adj*

B

b \\'bē\\ *n, pl* **b's** *or* **bs** \\'bēz\\ : 2d letter of the alphabet

bab·ble \\'babəl\\ *vb* **-bled; -bling 1** : utter meaningless sounds **2** : talk foolishly or too much — **babble** *n* — **babbler** *n*

babe \\'bāb\\ *n* : baby

ba·bel \\'bābəl, 'bab-\\ *n* : noisy confusion

ba·boon \\ba'bün\\ *n* : large Asian or African ape with a doglike muzzle

ba·by \\'bābē\\ *n, pl* **-bies** : very young child ~ *vb* **-bied; -by·ing** : pamper — **baby** *adj* — **ba·by·hood** *n* — **ba·by·ish** *adj*

ba·by–sit *vb* **-sat; -sit·ting** : care for children while parents are away — **baby–sit·ter** *n*

bac·ca·lau·re·ate \\,bakə-'lorēət\\ *n* : bachelor's degree

bac·cha·na·lia \\,bakə'nālyə\\ *n, pl* **-lia** : drunken orgy — **bac·cha·na·lian** \\-yən\\ *adj or n*

bach·e·lor \\'bachələr\\ *n* **1** : holder of lowest 4-year college degree **2** : unmarried man — **bach·e·lor·hood** *n*

ba·cil·lus \\bə'siləs\\ *n, pl* **-li** \\-,ī\\ : rod-shaped bacterium — **bac·il·lary** \\'basə,lerē\\ *adj*

back \\'bak\\ *n* **1** : part of a human or animal body nearest the spine **2** : part opposite the front **3** : player farthest from the opponent's goal ~ *adv* **1** : to or at the back **2** : ago **3** : to or in a former place or state **4** : in reply ~ *adj* **1** : located at the back **2** : not paid on time **3** : moving or working backward **4** : not current ~ *vb* **1** : support **2** : go or cause to go back **3** : form the back of — **back·ache** *n* — **back·er** *n* — **back·ing** *n* — **back·less** *adj* — **back·rest** *n*

back·bite *vb* **-bit; -bit·ten; -bit·ing** : say spiteful things about someone absent — **back·bit·er** *n*

back·bone *n* **1** : bony column in the back that encloses the spinal cord **2** : firm character

back·drop *n* : painted cloth hung across the rear of a stage

back·fire *n* : loud noise from the wrongly timed explosion of fuel in an engine ~ *vb* **1** : make or undergo a backfire **2** : have a result opposite of that intended

back·gam·mon \'bak͵gamən\ *n* : board game

back·ground *n* **1** : scenery behind something **2** : sum of a person's experience or training

back·hand *n* : stroke (as in tennis) made with the back of the hand turned forward — **back·hand** *adj or vb* — **back·hand·ed** *adj*

back·lash *n* : adverse reaction

back·log *n* : accumulation of things to be done — **backlog** *vb*

back·pack *n* : camping pack carried on the back ∼ *vb* : hike with a backpack — **back·pack·er** *n*

back·slide *vb* **-slid; -slid** *or* **-slid·den** \-͵slidᵊn\; **-slid·ing** : lapse in morals or religious practice — **back·slid·er** *n*

back·stage *adv or adj* : in or to an area behind a stage

back·up *n* : substitute

back·ward \'bakwərd\, **back·wards** *adv* **1** : toward the back **2** : with the back foremost **3** : in a reverse direction **4** : toward an earlier or worse state ∼ *adj* **1** : directed, turned, or done backward **2** : retarded in development — **back·ward·ness** *n*

back·woods *n pl* : remote or isolated place

ba·con \'bākən\ *n* : salted and smoked meat from a pig

bac·te·ri·um \bak'tirēəm\ *n, pl* **-ria** \-ēə\ : microscopic plant — **bac·te·ri·al** \-ēəl\ *adj* — **bac·te·ri·o·log·ic** \-͵tirēə-'läjik\, **bac·te·ri·o·log·i·cal** \-əl\ *adj* — **bac·te·ri·ol·o·gist** \-ē'äləjist\ *n* — **bac·te·ri·ol·o·gy** \-jē\ *n*

bad \'bad\ *adj* **worse** \'wərs\; **worst** \'wərst\ **1** : not good **2** : naughty **3** : faulty **4** : spoiled — **bad** *n or adv* — **bad·ly** *adv* — **bad·ness** *n*

bade *past of* BID

badge \'baj\ *n* : symbol of status

bad·ger \'bajər\ *n* : burrowing mammal ∼ *vb* : harass

bad·min·ton \'bad͵mintᵊn\ *n* : tennislike game played with a shuttlecock

bad–mouth \'bad͵maùth\ *vb* : criticize severely

baf·fle \'bafəl\ *vb* **-fled; -fling** : perplex ∼ *n* : device to alter flow (as of liquid or sound) — **baf·fle·ment** *n*

bag \'bag\ *n* : flexible usu. closable container ∼ *vb* **-gg-** **1** : bulge out **2** : put in a bag **3** : catch in hunting

bag·a·telle \͵bagə'tel\ *n* : trifle

ba·gel \'bāgəl\ *n* : hard doughnut-shaped roll

bag·gage \'bagij\ *n* : traveler's bags and belongings

bag·gy \'bagē\ *adj* **-gi·er; -est** : puffed out like a bag — **baggi·ness** *n*

bag·pipe *n* : musical instrument with a bag, a tube with valves, and sounding pipes — often pl.

¹**bail** \'bāl\ *n* : container for scooping water out of a boat — **bail** *vb* — **bail·er** *n*

²**bail** *n* **1** : security given to guarantee a prisoner's appearance in court **2** : release secured by bail ～ *vb* : bring about the release of by giving bail

bai·liff \'bāləf\ *n* **1** : British sheriff's aide **2** : minor officer of a U.S. court

bai·li·wick \'bāli,wik\ *n* : one's special field or domain

bail·out \'bā,laut\ *n* : rescue from financial distress

bait \'bāt\ *vb* **1** : harass with dogs usu. for sport **2** : furnish (a hook or trap) with bait ～ *n* : lure esp. for catching animals

bake \'bāk\ *vb* **baked; bak·ing** : cook in dry heat esp. in an oven ～ *n* : party featuring baked food — **bak·er** *n* — **bak·ery** \'bākərē\ *n* — **bake·shop** *n*

bal·ance \'baləns\ *n* **1** : weighing device **2** : counteracting weight, force, or influence **3** : equilibrium **4** : that which remains ～ *vb* **-anced; -anc·ing** **1** : compute the balance **2** : equalize **3**
: bring into harmony or proportion — **bal·anced** *adj*

bal·co·ny \'balkənē\ *n, pl* **-nies** : platform projecting from a wall

bald \'bȯld\ *adj* **1** : lacking a natural or usual covering (as of hair) **2** : plain — **bald·ing** *adj* — **bald·ly** *adv* — **bald·ness** *n*

bal·der·dash \'bȯldər,dash\ *n* : nonsense

bale \'bāl\ *n* : large bundle ～ *vb* **baled; bal·ing** : pack in a bale — **bal·er** *n*

bale·ful \'bālfəl\ *adj* **1** : deadly **2** : ominous

balk \'bȯk\ *n* : hindrance ～ *vb* **1** : thwart **2** : stop short and refuse to go on — **balky** *adj*

¹**ball** \'bȯl\ *n* **1** : rounded mass **2** : game played with a ball ～ *vb* : form into a ball

²**ball** *n* : large formal dance — **ballroom** *n*

bal·lad \'baləd\ *n* **1** : narrative poem **2** : slow romantic song — **bal·lad·eer** \,balə'diər\ *n*

bal·last \'baləst\ *n* : heavy material to steady a ship or balloon ～ *vb* : provide with ballast

bal·le·ri·na \,balə'rēnə\ *n* : female ballet dancer

bal·let \'ba,lā, ba'lā\ *n* : theatrical dancing

bal·lis·tics \bə'listiks\ *n sing or pl* : science of projectile motion — **ballistic** *adj*

bal·loon \bə'lün\ *n* : inflated bag ~ *vb* **1** : travel in a balloon **2** : swell out — **bal·loon·ist** *n*

bal·lot \'balət\ *n* **1** : paper used to cast a vote **2** : system of voting ~ *vb* : vote

bal·ly·hoo \'balē͵hü\ *n* : publicity — **ballyhoo** *vb*

balm \'bäm, 'bälm\ *n* **1** : fragrant healing or soothing preparation **2** : spicy fragrant herb

balmy \'bämē, 'bälmē\ *adj* **balm·i·er; -est** : gently soothing — **balm·i·ness** *n*

ba·lo·ney \bə'lōnē\ *n* : nonsense

bal·sa \'bȯlsə\ *n* : very light wood of a tropical tree

bal·sam \-səm\ *n* **1** : aromatic resinous plant substance **2** : balsam-yielding plant — **bal·sam·ic** \bȯl'samik\ *adj*

bal·us·ter \'baləstər\ *n* : upright support for a rail

bal·us·trade \-͵sträd\ *n* : row of balusters topped by a rail

bam·boo \bam'bü\ *n* : tall tropical grass with strong hollow stems

bam·boo·zle \bam'büzəl\ *vb* **-zled; -zling** : deceive

ban \'ban\ *vb* **-nn-** : prohibit ~ *n* : legal prohibition

ba·nal \bə'näl, -'nal; 'bān³l\ *adj* : ordinary and uninteresting — **ba·nal·ity** \bə'nalətē\ *n*

ba·nana \bə'nanə\ *n* : elongated fruit of a treelike tropical plant

¹band \'band\ *n* **1** : something that ties or binds **2** : strip or stripe different (as in color) from nearby matter **3** : range of radio wavelengths ~ *vb* **1** : enclose with a band **2** : unite for a common end — **band·ed** *adj* — **band·er** *n*

²band *n* **1** : group **2** : musicians playing together

ban·dage \'bandij\ *n* : material used esp. in dressing wounds ~ *vb* : dress or cover with a bandage

ban·dan·na, ban·dana \ban-'danə\ *n* : large colored figured handkerchief

ban·dit \'bandət\ *n* : outlaw or robber — **ban·dit·ry** \-dətrē\ *n*

band·stand *n* : stage for band concerts

band·wag·on *n* : candidate, side, or movement gaining support

¹ban·dy \'bandē\ *vb* **-died; -dy·ing** : exchange in rapid succession

²bandy *adj* : curved outward

bane \'bān\ *n* **1** : poison **2** : cause of woe — **bane·ful** *adj*

¹**bang** \'baŋ\ *vb* : strike, thrust, or move usu. with a loud noise ∼ *n* **1** : blow **2** : sudden loud noise ∼ *adv* : directly

²**bang** *n* : fringe of short hair over the forehead — usu. pl. ∼ *vb* : cut in bangs

ban·gle \'baŋgəl\ *n* : bracelet

ban·ish \'banish\ *vb* **1** : force by authority to leave a country **2** : expel — **ban·ish·ment** *n*

ban·is·ter \-əstər\ *n* **1** : baluster **2** : handrail

ban·jo \'ban͵jō\ *n, pl* -**jos** : stringed instrument with a drumlike body — **banjo·ist** *n*

¹**bank** \'baŋk\ *n* **1** : piled-up mass **2** : rising ground along a body of water **3** : sideways slope along a curve ∼ *vb* **1** : form a bank **2** : cover (as a fire) to keep inactive **3** : incline (an airplane) laterally

²**bank** *n* : tier of objects

³**bank** *n* **1** : money institution **2** : reserve supply ∼ *vb* : conduct business in a bank — **bank·book** *n* — **bank·er** *n* — **bank·ing** *n*

bank·rupt \'baŋ͵krəpt\ *n* : one required by law to forfeit assets to pay off debts ∼ *adj* **1** : legally a bankrupt **2** : lacking something essential — **bankrupt** *vb* — **bank·rupt·cy** \-͵krəpsē\ *n*

ban·ner \'banər\ *n* : flag ∼ *adj* : excellent

banns \'banz\ *n pl* : announcement in church of a proposed marriage

ban·quet \'baŋkwət\ *n* : ceremonial dinner — **banquet** *vb*

ban·shee \'banshē\ *n* : wailing female spirit that foretells death

ban·tam \'bantəm\ *n* : miniature domestic fowl

ban·ter \'bantər\ *n* : good-natured joking — **banter** *vb*

ban·yan \'banyən\ *n* : large tree that grows new trunks from the limbs

bap·tism \'bap͵tizəm\ *n* : Christian rite signifying spiritual cleansing — **bap·tis·mal** \bap'tizməl\ *adj*

bap·tize \bap'tīz, 'bap͵tīz\ *vb* -**tized**; -**tiz·ing** : administer baptism to

bar \'bär\ *n* **1** : long narrow object used esp. as a lever, fastening, or support **2** : barrier **3** : body of practicing lawyers **4** : wide stripe **5** : food counter **6** : place where liquor is served **7** : vertical line across the musical staff ∼ *vb* -**rr-** **1** : obstruct with a bar **2** : shut out **3** : prohibit ∼ *prep* : excluding — **barred** *adj* — **bar·room** *n* — **bar·tend·er** *n*

barb \'bärb\ *n* : sharp projection pointing backward — **barbed** *adj*

bar·bar·ian \bär'barēən\ *adj* **1** : relating to people considered backward **2** : not refined — **barbarian** *n*

bar·bar·ic \-'barik\ *adj* : barbarian

bar·ba·rous \'bärbərəs\ *adj* **1** : lacking refinement **2** : mercilessly cruel — **bar·bar·ism** \-bə₁rizəm\ *n* — **bar·bar·i·ty** \bär'barətē\ *n* — **bar·ba·rous·ly** *adv*

bar·be·cue \'bärbi₁kyü\ *n* : gathering at which barbecued food is served ~ *vb* **-cued; -cu·ing** : cook over hot coals or on a spit often with a highly seasoned sauce

bar·ber \'bärbər\ *n* : one who cuts hair

bar·bi·tu·rate \bär'bichərət\ *n* : sedative or hypnotic drug

bard \'bärd\ *n* : poet

bare \'bar\ *adj* **bar·er; bar·est** **1** : naked **2** : not concealed **3** : empty **4** : leaving nothing to spare **5** : plain ~ *vb* **bared; bar·ing** : make or lay bare — **bare·foot, bare·foot·ed** *adv or adj* — **bare–hand·ed** *adv or adj* — **bare·head·ed** *adv or adj* — **bare·ly** *adv* — **bare·ness** *n*

bare·back, bare·backed *adv or adj* : without a saddle

bare·faced *adj* : open and esp. brazen

bar·gain \'bärgən\ *n* **1** : agreement **2** : something bought for less than its value ~ *vb* **1** : negotiate **2** : barter

barge \'bärj\ *n* : broad flat=bottomed boat ~ *vb* **barged; barg·ing** : move rudely or clumsily — **barge·man** *n*

bari·tone \'barə₁tōn\ *n* : male voice between bass and tenor

bar·i·um \'barēəm\ *n* : silver=white metallic chemical element

¹**bark** \'bärk\ *vb* **1** : make the sound of a dog **2** : speak in a loud curt tone ~ *n* : sound of a barking dog

²**bark** *n* : tough corky outer covering of a woody stem or root ~ *vb* : remove bark or skin from

³**bark** *n* : sailing ship with a fore-and-aft rear sail

bark·er \'bärkər\ *n* : one who calls out to attract people to a show

bar·ley \'bärlē\ *n* : cereal grass or its seeds

barn \'bärn\ *n* : building for keeping hay or livestock — **barn·yard** *n*

bar·na·cle \'bärnikəl\ *n* : marine crustacean

barn·storm *vb* : tour through rural districts giving performances

ba·rom·e·ter \bə'rämətər\ *n* : instrument for measuring atmospheric pressure — **baro·met·ric** \₁barə'metrik\ *adj*

bar·on \'barən\ *n* : British peer — **bar·on·age** \-ij\ *n* — **ba·ro·ni·al** \bə'rōnēəl\ *adj* — **bar·ony** \'barənē\ *n*

bar·on·ess \-ənəs\ *n* **1** : baron's wife **2** : woman holding a baronial title

bar·on·et \-ənət\ *n* : man holding a rank between a baron and a knight — **bar·on·et·cy** \-sē\ *n*

ba·roque \bə'rōk, -'räk\ *adj* : elaborately ornamented

bar·racks \'barəks\ *n sing or pl* : soldiers' housing

bar·ra·cu·da \ˌbarə'küdə\ *n, pl* **-da** *or* **-das** : large predatory sea fish

bar·rage \bə'räzh, -'räj\ *n* : heavy artillery fire

bar·rel \'barəl\ *n* **1** : closed cylindrical container **2** : amount held by a barrel **3** : cylindrical part ∼ *vb* **-reled** *or* **-relled; -rel·ing** *or* **-rel·ling** **1** : pack in a barrel **2** : move at high speed

bar·ren \'barən\ *adj* **1** : unproductive of life **2** : uninteresting — **bar·ren·ness** *n*

bar·rette \bä'ret, bə-\ *n* : clasp for a woman's hair

bar·ri·cade \'barəˌkād, ˌbarə'-\ *n* : barrier — **barricade** *vb*

bar·ri·er \'barēər\ *n* : something that separates or obstructs

bar·ring \'bäriŋ\ *prep* : omitting

bar·ris·ter \'barəstər\ *n* : British trial lawyer

bar·row \'barō\ *n* : wheelbarrow

bar·ter \'bärtər\ *vb* : trade by exchange of goods — **barter** *n*

ba·salt \bə'sȯlt, 'bāˌ-\ *n* : dark fine-grained igneous rock — **ba·sal·tic** \bə'sȯltik\ *adj*

¹base \'bās\ *n, pl* **bas·es** **1** : bottom **2** : fundamental part **3** : beginning point **4** : supply source of a force **5** : compound that reacts with an acid to form a salt ∼ *vb* **based; bas·ing** : establish — **base·less** *adj*

²base *adj* **bas·er; bas·est** **1** : inferior **2** : contemptible — **base·ly** *adv* — **base·ness** *n*

base·ball *n* : game played with a bat and ball by 2 teams

base·ment \-mənt\ *n* : part of a building below ground level

bash \'bash\ *vb* : strike violently ∼ *n* : heavy blow

bash·ful \-fəl\ *adj* : self-conscious — **bash·ful·ness** *n*

ba·sic \'bāsik\ *adj* **1** : relating to or forming the base or essence **2** : relating to a chemical base — **ba·si·cally** *adv* — **ba·sic·i·ty** \bā'sisətē\ *n*

ba·sil \'bazəl, 'bās-, 'bāz-\ *n* : aromatic mint

ba·sil·i·ca \bə'silikə\ *n* : important church or cathedral

ba·sin \'bās³n\ *n* **1** : large bowl or pan **2** : region drained by a river

ba·sis \'bāsəs\ *n, pl* **ba·ses** \-₁sēz\ **1** : something that supports **2** : fundamental principle

bask \'bask\ *vb* : enjoy pleasant warmth

bas·ket \'baskət\ *n* : woven container — **bas·ket·ful** *n*

bas·ket·ball *n* : game played with a ball on a court by 2 teams

bas–re·lief \₁bäri'lēf\ *n* : flat sculpture with slightly raised design

¹bass \'bas\ *n, pl* **bass** *or* **bass·es** : spiny-finned sport and food fish

²bass \'bās\ *n* **1** : deep tone **2** : lowest choral voice

bas·set hound \'basət-\ *n* : short-legged dog with long ears

bas·si·net \₁basə'net\ *n* : baby's bed

bas·soon \bə'sün, ba-\ *n* : low-pitched wind instrument

bas·tard \'bastərd\ *n* **1** : illegitimate child **2** : offensive person ~ *adj* **1** : illegitimate **2** : inferior — **bas·tard·ize** *vb* — **bas·tardy** *n*

¹baste \'bāst\ *vb* **bast·ed; bast·ing** : sew temporarily with long stitches

²baste *vb* **bast·ed; bast·ing** : moisten at intervals while cooking

bas·tion \'baschən\ *n* : fortified position

¹bat \'bat\ *n* **1** : stick or club **2** : sharp blow ~ *vb* **-tt-** : hit with a bat

²bat *n* : small flying mammal

³bat *vb* **-tt-** : wink or blink

batch \'bach\ *n* : quantity used or produced at one time

bate \'bāt\ *vb* **bat·ed; bat·ing** : moderate or reduce

bath \'bath, 'båth\ *n, pl* **baths** \'ba<u>th</u>z, 'baths, 'bå<u>th</u>z, 'båths\ **1** : a washing of the body **2** : water for washing the body **3** : liquid in which something is immersed **4** : bathroom **5** : large financial loss — **bath·tub** *n*

bathe \'bā<u>th</u>\ *vb* **bathed; bath·ing 1** : wash in liquid **2** : flow against so as to wet **3** : shine light over **4** : take a bath or a swim — **bath·er** *n*

bath·robe *n* : robe worn around the house

bath·room *n* : room with a bathtub or shower and usu. a sink and toilet

ba·tiste \bə'tēst\ *n* : fine sheer fabric

ba·ton \bə'tän\ *n* : musical conductor's stick

bat·tal·ion \bə'talyən\ *n* : military unit composed of a headquarters and two or more companies

bat·ten \\'bat⁹n\\ *n* : strip of wood used to seal or reinforce ～ *vb* : furnish or fasten with battens

¹**bat·ter** \\'batər\\ *vb* : beat or damage with repeated blows

²**batter** *n* : mixture of flour and liquid

³**batter** *n* : player who bats

bat·tery \\'batərē\\ *n, pl* -**ter·ies** **1** : illegal beating of a person **2** : group of artillery guns **3** : group of electric cells

bat·ting \\'batiŋ\\ *n* : layers of cotton or wool for stuffing

bat·tle \\'bat⁹l\\ *n* : military fighting ～ *vb* -**tled; -tling** : engage in battle — **battle-field** *n*

bat·tle–ax *n* : long-handled ax formerly used as a weapon

bat·tle·ment \\-mənt\\ *n* : parapet on top of a wall

bat·tle·ship *n* : heavily armed warship

bat·ty \\'batē\\ *adj* -**ti·er; -est** : crazy

bau·ble \\'bȯbəl\\ *n* : trinket

bawdy \\'bȯdē\\ *adj* **bawd·i·er; -est** : obscene or lewd — **bawd·i·ly** *adv* — **bawd·i·ness** *n*

bawl \\'bȯl\\ *vb* : cry loudly ～ *n* : long loud cry

¹**bay** \\'bā\\ *adj* : reddish brown ～ *n* : bay-colored animal

²**bay** *n* : European laurel

³**bay** *n* **1** : compartment **2** : area projecting out from a building and containing a window (**bay window**)

⁴**bay** *vb* : bark with deep long tones ～ *n* **1** : position of one unable to escape danger **2** : baying of dogs

⁵**bay** *n* : body of water smaller than a gulf and nearly surrounded by land

bay·ber·ry \\-ˌberē\\ *n* : shrub bearing small waxy berries

bay·o·net \\'bāənət, ˌbāə'net\\ *n* : dagger that fits on the end of a rifle ～ *vb* -**net·ed; -net-ing** : stab with a bayonet

bay·ou \\'bīü, -ō\\ *n* : creek flowing through marshy land

ba·zaar \\bə'zär\\ *n* **1** : market **2** : fair for charity

ba·zoo·ka \\-'zükə\\ *n* : weapon that shoots armor-piercing rockets

BB *n* : small shot pellet

be \\'bē\\ *vb* **was** \\'wəz, 'wäz\\, **were** \\'wər\\; **been** \\'bin\\; **be-ing** \\'bēiŋ\\; **am** \\əm, 'am\\, **is** \\'iz, əz\\, **are** \\ər, 'är\\ **1** : equal **2** : exist **3** : occupy a certain place **4** : occur ～ *verbal auxiliary* — used to show continuous action or to form the passive voice

beach \\'bēch\\ *n* : sandy shore of a sea, lake, or river ～ *vb* : drive ashore

beach·comb·er \-ˌkōmər\ *n* : one who searches the shore for useful objects

beach·head *n* : shore area held by an attacking force in an invasion

bea·con \ˈbēkən\ *n* : guiding or warning light or signal

bead \ˈbēd\ *n* : small round body esp. strung on a thread ~ *vb* : form into a bead — **bead·ing** *n* — **beady** *adj*

bea·gle \ˈbēgəl\ *n* : small short-legged hound

beak \ˈbēk\ *n* : bill of a bird — **beaked** *adj*

bea·ker \ˈbēkər\ *n* **1** : large drinking cup **2** : laboratory vessel

beam \ˈbēm\ *n* **1** : large long piece of timber or metal **2** : ray of light **3** : directed radio signals for the guidance of pilots ~ *vb* **1** : send out light **2** : smile **3** : aim a radio broadcast

bean \ˈbēn\ *n* : edible plant seed borne in pods

¹bear \ˈbar\ *n, pl* **bears 1** *or pl* **bear** : large heavy mammal with shaggy hair **2** : gruff or sullen person — **bear·ish** *adj*

²bear *vb* **bore** \ˈbōr\; **borne** \ˈbōrn\; **bear·ing 1** : carry **2** : give birth to or produce **3** : endure **4** : press **5** : go in an indicated direction — **bear·able** *adj* — **bear·er** *n*

beard \ˈbird\ *n* **1** : facial hair on a man **2** : tuft like a beard ~ *vb* : confront boldly — **beard·ed** *adj* — **beard·less** *adj*

bear·ing *n* **1** : way of carrying oneself **2** : supporting object or purpose **3** : significance **4** : machine part in which another part turns **5** : direction with respect esp. to compass points

beast \ˈbēst\ *n* **1** : animal **2** : brutal person — **beast·li·ness** *n* — **beast·ly** *adj*

beat \ˈbēt\ *vb* **beat; beat·en** \ˈbētᵊn\ *or* **beat; beat·ing 1** : strike repeatedly **2** : defeat **3** : act or arrive before **4** : throb ~ *n* **1** : single stroke or pulsation **2** : rhythmic stress in poetry or music ~ *adj* : exhausted — **beat·er** *n*

be·atif·ic \ˌbēəˈtifik\ *adj* : blissful

be·at·i·fy \bēˈatəˌfī\ *vb* **-fied; -fy·ing** : make happy or blessed — **be·at·i·fi·ca·tion** \-ˌatəfəˈkāshən\ *n*

be·at·i·tude \-ˈatəˌtüd, -ˌtyüd\ *n* : saying in the Sermon on the Mount (Matthew 5:3-12) beginning "Blessed are"

beau \ˈbō\ *n, pl* **beaux** \ˈbōz\ *or* **beaus** : suitor

beau·ty \ˈbyütē\ *n, pl* **-ties** : qualities that please the senses or mind — **beau·te·ous** \-ēəs\ *adj* — **beau·te-**

ous·ly *adv* — **beau·ti·fi·ca·tion** \ˌbyütəfə'kāshən\ *n* — **beau·ti·fi·er** \'byütəˌfīər\ *n* — **beau·ti·ful** \-ifəl\ *adj* — **beau·ti·ful·ly** *adv* — **beau·ti·fy** \-əˌfī\ *vb*

bea·ver \'bēvər\ *n* : large fur‑bearing rodent

be·cause \bi'kȯz, -'kəz\ *conj* : for the reason that

because of *prep* : by reason of

beck \'bek\ *n* : summons

beck·on \'bekən\ *vb* : summon esp. by a nod or gesture

be·come \bi'kəm\ *vb* **-came** \-'kām\; **-come**; **-com·ing** 1 : come to be 2 : be suitable — **be·com·ing** *adj* — **be·com·ing·ly** *adv*

bed \'bed\ *n* 1 : piece of furniture to sleep on 2 : flat or level surface ∼ *vb* **-dd-** : put or go to bed — **bed·spread** *n*

bed·bug *n* : wingless blood‑sucking insect

bed·clothes *n pl* : bedding

bed·ding *n* 1 : sheets and blankets for a bed 2 : soft material (as hay) for an animal's bed

be·deck \bi'dek\ *vb* : adorn

be·dev·il \-'devəl\ *vb* : harass

bed·lam \'bedləm\ *n* : uproar and confusion

be·drag·gled \bi'dragəld\ *adj* : dirty and disordered

bed·rid·den \'bedˌridᵊn\ *adj* : kept in bed by illness

bed·rock *n* : solid subsurface rock — **bedrock** *adj*

¹**bee** \'bē\ *n* : 4‑winged honey‑producing insect — **bee·hive** *n* — **bee·keep·er** *n* — **bees·wax** *n*

²**bee** *n* : neighborly work session

beech \'bēch\ *n, pl* **beech·es** *or* **beech** : tree with smooth gray bark and edible nuts (**beech·nuts**) — **beech·en** \-ən\ *adj*

beef \'bēf\ *n, pl* **beefs** \'bēfs\ *or* **beeves** \'bēvz\ : flesh of a steer, cow, or bull ∼ *vb* : strengthen — used with *up* — **beef·steak** *n*

bee·line *n* : straight course

been *past part of* BE

beep \'bēp\ *n* : short usu. high‑pitched warning sound — **beep** *vb* — **beep·er** *n*

beer \'bir\ *n* : alcoholic drink brewed from malt and hops — **beery** *adj*

beet \'bēt\ *n* : garden root vegetable

bee·tle \'bētəl\ *n* : 4‑winged insect

be·fall \bi'fȯl\ *vb* **-fell**; **-fall·en** : happen to

be·fit \bi'fit\ *vb* : be suitable to

be·fore \bi'fōr\ *adv* 1 : in front 2 : earlier ∼ *prep* 1 : in front of 2 : earlier than ∼ *conj* : earlier than

be·fore·hand *adv or adj* : in advance

be·friend \bi'frend\ *vb* : act as friend to

be·fud·dle \-'fəd°l\ *vb* : confuse

beg \'beg\ *vb* **-gg-** : ask earnestly

be·get \bi'get\ *vb* **-got; -got-ten** *or* **-got; -get·ting** : become the father of

beg·gar \'begər\ *n* : one that begs ∼ *vb* : make poor — **beg·gar·ly** *adj* — **beg·gary** *n*

be·gin \bi'gin\ *vb* **-gan** \-'gan\; **-gun** \-'gən\; **-gin·ning** **1** : start **2** : come into being — **be·gin·ner** *n*

be·gone \bi'gȯn\ *vb* : go away

be·go·nia \-'gōnyə\ *n* : tropical herb with waxy flowers

be·grudge \-'grəj\ *vb* **1** : concede reluctantly **2** : look upon disapprovingly

be·guile \-'gīl\ *vb* **-guiled; -guil·ing** **1** : deceive **2** : amuse

be·half \-'haf, -'hȧf\ *n* : benefit

be·have \-'hāv\ *vb* **-haved; -hav·ing** : act in a certain way

be·hav·ior \-'hāvyər\ *n* : way of behaving — **be·hav·ior·al** \-əl\ *adj*

be·head \-'hed\ *vb* : cut off the head of

be·hest \-'hest\ *n* : command

be·hind \bi'hīnd\ *adv* : at the back ∼ *prep* **1** : in back of **2** : less than **3** : supporting

be·hold \-'hōld\ *vb* **-held; -hold·ing** : see — **be·hold·er** *n*

be·hold·en \-'hōldən\ *adj* : indebted

be·hoove \-'hüv\ *vb* **-hooved; -hoov·ing** : be necessary for

beige \'bāzh\ *n* : yellowish brown — **beige** *adj*

be·ing \'bēiŋ\ *n* **1** : existence **2** : living thing

be·la·bor \bi'lābər\ *vb* : carry on to absurd lengths

be·lat·ed \-'lātəd\ *adj* : delayed

belch \'belch\ *vb* **1** : expel stomach gas orally **2** : emit forcefully — **belch** *n*

be·lea·guer \bi'lēgər\ *vb* **1** : besiege **2** : harass

bel·fry \'belfrē\ *n, pl* **-fries** : bell tower

be·lie \bi'lī\ *vb* **-lied; -ly·ing** **1** : misrepresent **2** : prove false

be·lief \bə'lēf\ *n* **1** : trust **2** : something believed

be·lieve \-'lēv\ *vb* **-lieved; -liev·ing** **1** : trust in **2** : accept as true **3** : hold as an opinion — **be·liev·able** *adj* — **be·liev·ably** *adv* — **be·liev·er** *n*

be·lit·tle \bi'lit°l\ *vb* **-lit·tled; -lit·tling** **1** : disparage **2** : make seem less

bell \'bel\ *n* : hollow metallic device that rings when struck ∼ *vb* : provide with a bell

bel·la·don·na \ˌbelə'dänə\ *n* : poisonous herb yielding a drug

belle \'bel\ *n* : beautiful woman

bel·li·cose \'beliˌkōs\ *adj* : pugnacious — **bel·li·cos·i·ty** \ˌbeli'käsətē\ *n*

bel·lig·er·ent \bə'lijərənt\ *adj* **1** : waging war **2** : truculent — **bel·lig·er·ence** \-rəns\ *n* — **bel·lig·er·en·cy** \-rənsē\ *n* — **belligerent** *n*

bel·low \'belō\ *vb* : make a loud deep roar or shout — **bellow** *n*

bel·lows \-ōz, -əz\ *n sing or pl* : device with sides that can be compressed to expel air

bell·weth·er \'bel'wethər, -ˌweth-\ *n* : leader

bel·ly \'belē\ *n, pl* **-lies** : abdomen ~ *vb* **-lied; -ly·ing** : bulge

be·long \bi'lȯŋ\ *vb* **1** : be suitable **2** : be owned **3** : be a part of

be·long·ings \-iŋz\ *n pl* : possessions

be·loved \bi'ləvəd, -'ləvd\ *adj* : dearly loved — **beloved** *n*

be·low \-'lō\ *adv* : in or to a lower place ~ *prep* : lower than

belt \'belt\ *n* **1** : strip (as of leather) worn about the waist **2** : endless band to impart mo-tion **3** : distinct region ~ *vb* **1** : put a belt around **2** : thrash

be·moan \bi'mōn\ *vb* : lament

be·muse \-'myüz\ *vb* : confuse

bench \'bench\ *n* **1** : long seat **2** : judge's seat **3** : court

bend \'bend\ *vb* **bent** \'bent\; **bending 1** : curve or cause a change of shape in **2** : turn in a certain direction ~ *n* **1** : act of bending **2** : curve

be·neath \bi'nēth\ *adv or prep* : below

bene·dic·tion \ˌbenə'dik-shən\ *n* : closing blessing

bene·fac·tor \'benəˌfaktər\ *n* : one who gives esp. charitable aid

be·nef·i·cence \bə'nefəsəns\ *n* : quality of doing good — **be·nef·i·cent** \-sənt\ *adj*

ben·e·fi·cial \ˌbenə'fishəl\ *adj* : being of benefit — **ben·e·fi·cial·ly** *adv*

ben·e·fi·cia·ry \-'fishēˌerē, -'fishərē\ *n, pl* **-ries** : one who receives benefits

ben·e·fit \'benəˌfit\ *n* **1** : something that does good **2** : help **3** : fund-raising event — **benefit** *vb*

be·nev·o·lence \bə'nevələns\ *n* **1** : charitable nature **2** : act of kindness — **be·nev·o·lent** \-lənt\ *adj* — **be·nev·o·lent·ly** *adv*

be·night·ed \bi'nītəd\ *adj* : ignorant

be·nign \bi'nīn\ *adj* **1** : gentle or kindly **2** : not malignant — **be·nig·ni·ty** \-'nignətē\ *n*

be·nig·nant \-'nignənt\ *adj* : benign

bent \'bent\ *n* : aptitude or interest

be·numb \bi'nəm\ *vb* : make numb esp. by cold

ben·zene \'ben‚zēn\ *n* : colorless flammable liquid

be·queath \bi'kwēth, -'kwēth\ *vb* **1** : give by will **2** : hand down

be·quest \bi'kwest\ *n* : something bequeathed

be·rate \-'rāt\ *vb* : scold harshly

be·reaved \-'rēvd\ *adj* : suffering the death of a loved one ∼ *n, pl* **bereaved** : one who is bereaved — **be·reave·ment** *n*

be·reft \-'reft\ *adj* : deprived of or lacking something

be·ret \bə'rā\ *n* : round soft visorless cap

beri·beri \‚berē'berē\ *n* : thiamine-deficiency disease

berm \'bərm\ *n* : bank of earth

ber·ry \'berē\ *n, pl* **-ries** : small pulpy fruit

ber·serk \bər'sərk, -'zərk\ *adj* : crazed — **berserk** *adv*

berth \'bərth\ *n* **1** : place where a ship is anchored **2** : place to sit or sleep esp. on a ship **3** : job ∼ *vb* : to bring or come into a berth

ber·yl \'berəl\ *n* : light-colored silicate mineral

be·seech \bi'sēch\ *vb* **-sought** \-'sȯt\ *or* **-seeched; -seech·ing** : entreat

be·set \-'set\ *vb* **1** : harass **2** : hem in

be·side \-'sīd\ *prep* **1** : by the side of **2** : besides

be·sides \-'sīdz\ *adv* **1** : in addition **2** : moreover ∼ *prep* **1** : other than **2** : in addition to

be·siege \-'sēj\ *vb* : lay siege to — **be·sieg·er** *n*

be·smirch \-'smərch\ *vb* : soil

be·sot \-'sät\ *vb* **-tt-** : become drunk

be·speak \bi'spēk\ *vb* **-spoke; -spo·ken; -speak·ing** **1** : address **2** : indicate

best \'best\ *adj, superlative of* GOOD **1** : excelling all others **2** : most productive **3** : largest ∼ *adv superlative of* WELL **1** : in the best way **2** : most ∼ *n* : one that is best ∼ *vb* : outdo

bes·tial \'beschəl, 'bēs-\ *adj* **1** : relating to beasts **2** : brutish — **bes·ti·al·i·ty** \‚beschē'alətē, ‚bēs-\ *n*

be·stir \bi'stər\ *vb* : rouse to action

best man *n* : chief male attendant at a wedding

be·stow \bi'stō\ *vb* : give — **be·stow·al** \-əl\ *n*

bet \'bet\ *n* **1** : something risked or pledged on the outcome of a contest **2** : the making of a bet ~ *vb* **bet; betting** **1** : risk (as money) on an outcome **2** : make a bet with

be·tide \bi'tīd\ *vb* : happen to

be·to·ken \bi'tōkən\ *vb* : give an indication of

be·tray \bi'trā\ *vb* **1** : seduce **2** : report or reveal to an enemy by treachery **3** : abandon **4** : prove unfaithful to **5** : reveal unintentionally — **be·tray·al** *n* — **be·tray·er** *n*

be·troth \-'träth, -'troth, -'trōth, *or with* th\ *vb* : promise to marry — **be·troth·al** *n* — **be·trothed** *n*

bet·ter \'betər\ *adj, comparative of* GOOD **1** : more than half **2** : improved in health **3** : of higher quality ~ *adv comparative of* WELL **1** : in a superior manner **2** : more ~ *n* **1** : one that is better **2** : advantage ~ *vb* **1** : improve **2** : surpass — **bet·ter·ment** \-mənt\ *n*

bet·tor, bet·ter \'betər\ *n* : one who bets

be·tween \bi'twēn\ *prep* **1** — used to show two things considered together **2** : in the space separating **3** — used to indicate a comparison or choice ~ *adv* : in an intervening space or interval

bev·el \'bevəl\ *n* : slant on an edge ~ *vb* -eled *or* -elled; -el·ing *or* -el·ling **1** : cut or shape to a bevel **2** : incline

bev·er·age \'bevrij\ *n* : drink

bevy \'bevē\ *n, pl* **bev·ies** : large group

be·wail \bi'wāl\ *vb* : lament

be·ware \-'war\ *vb* : be cautious

be·wil·der \-'wildər\ *vb* : confuse — **be·wil·der·ment** *n*

be·witch \-'wich\ *vb* **1** : affect by witchcraft **2** : charm — **be·witch·ment** *n*

be·yond \bē'yänd\ *adv* **1** : farther **2** : besides ~ *prep* **1** : on or to the farther side of **2** : out of the reach of **3** : besides

bi- \'bī, ˌbī\ *prefix* **1** : two **2** : coming or occurring every two **3** : twice, doubly, or on both sides

bi·an·nu·al \ˌbī'anyəwəl\ *adj* : occurring twice a year — **bi·an·nu·al·ly** *adv*

List of self-explanatory words with the prefix *bi-*

bicolored	biconcavity	biconvexity
biconcave	biconvex	bicultural

bi·as \'bīəs\ *n* **1** : line diagonal to the grain of a fabric **2** : prejudice ~ *vb* **-ased** *or* **-assed; -as·ing** *or* **-as·sing** : prejudice

bib \'bib\ *n* : shield tied under the chin to protect the clothes while eating

Bi·ble \'bībəl\ *n* **1** : sacred scriptures of Christians **2** : sacred scriptures of Judaism or of some other religion — **bib·li·cal** \'biblikəl\ *adj*

bib·li·og·ra·phy \ˌbiblē'ägrəfē\ *n, pl* **-phies** : list of writings on a subject or of an author — **bib·li·og·ra·pher** \-fər\ *n* — **bib·li·o·graph·ic** \-lēə'grafik\ *adj*

bi·cam·er·al \'bī'kamərəl\ *adj* : having 2 legislative chambers

bi·car·bon·ate \-'kärbəˌnāt, -nət\ *n* : acid carbonate

bi·cen·ten·ni·al \ˌbīsen'tenēəl\ *n* : 200th anniversary — **bicentennial** *adj*

bi·ceps \'bīˌseps\ *n* : large muscle of the upper arm

bick·er \'bikər\ *vb or n* : squabble

bi·cus·pid \bī'kəspəd\ *n* : double-pointed tooth

bi·cy·cle \'bīˌsikəl\ *n* : 2-wheeled vehicle moved by pedaling ~ *vb* **-cled; -cling** : ride a bicycle — **bi·cy·cler** \-klər\ *n* — **bi·cy·clist** \-list\ *n*

bid \'bid\ *vb* **bade** \'bad, 'bād\ *or* **bid; bid·den** \'bidᵊn\ *or* **bid; bid·ding 1** : order **2** : invite **3** : express **4** : make a bid ~ *n* **1** : act of bidding **2** : buyer's proposed price — **bid·da·ble** \-əbəl\ *adj* — **bid·der** *n*

bide \'bīd\ *vb* **bode** \'bōd\ *or* **bid·ed; bided; bid·ing 1** : wait **2** : dwell

bi·en·ni·al \bī'enēəl\ *adj* **1** : occurring once in 2 years **2** : lasting 2 years — **biennial** *n* — **bi·en·ni·al·ly** *adv*

bier \'bir\ *n* : stand for a coffin

bifocals \'bīˌfōkəlz\ *n pl* : eyeglasses that correct for near and distant vision

big \'big\ *adj* **-gg-** : large in size, amount, or scope — **big·ness** *n*

big·a·my \'bigəmē\ *n* : marrying one person while still married to another — **big·a·mist** \-mist\ *n* — **big·a·mous** \-məs\ *adj*

bidirectional	**bimetallic**	**bipolar**
bifunctional	**binational**	**biracial**
bimetal	**biparental**	

big·horn *n, pl* **-horn** *or* **-horns** : wild mountain sheep

bight \'bīt\ *n* **1** : loop of a rope **2** : bay

big·ot \'bigət\ *n* : one who is intolerant of others — **big·ot·ed** \-ətəd\ *adj* — **big·ot·ry** \-ətrē\ *n*

big shot *n* : important person

big·wig *n* : big shot

bike \'bīk\ *n* : bicycle or motorcycle

bi·ki·ni \bə'kēnē\ *n* : woman's brief 2-piece bathing suit

bi·lat·er·al \bī'latərəl\ *adj* : involving 2 sides — **bi·lat·er·al·ly** *adv*

bile \'bīl\ *n* **1** : greenish liver secretion that aids digestion **2** : bad temper

bi·lin·gual \bī'liŋgwəl\ *adj* : using 2 languages

bil·ious \'bilyəs\ *adj* : irritable — **bil·ious·ness** *n*

bilk \'bilk\ *vb* : cheat

¹bill \'bil\ *n* : jaws of a bird together with their horny covering ～ *vb* : caress fondly — **billed** *adj*

²bill *n* **1** : draft of a law **2** : list of things to be paid for **3** : printed advertisement **4** : piece of paper money ～ *vb* : submit a bill or account to

bill·board *n* : surface for displaying advertising bills

bil·let \'bilət\ *n* : soldiers' quarters ～ *vb* : lodge in a billet

bill·fold *n* : wallet

bil·liards \'bilyərdz\ *n* : game of driving balls into one another or into pockets on a table

bil·lion \'bilyən\ *n, pl* **billions** *or* **billion** : 1000 millions — **billion** *adj* — **bil·lionth** \-yənth\ *adj or n*

bil·low \'bilō\ *n* **1** : great wave **2** : rolling mass ～ *vb* : swell out — **bil·lowy** \'biləwē\ *adj*

billy goat *n* : male goat

bin \'bin\ *n* : storage box

bi·na·ry \'bīnərē\ *adj* : consisting of 2 things — **binary** *n*

bind \'bīnd\ *vb* **bound** \'baůnd\; **bind·ing** **1** : tie **2** : obligate **3** : unite into a mass **4** : bandage — **bind·er** *n* — **binding** *n*

binge \'binj\ *n* : spree

bin·go \'biŋgō\ *n, pl* **-gos** : game of covering numbers on a card

bin·oc·u·lar \bī'näkyələr, bə-\ *adj* : of or relating to both eyes ～ *n* : binocular optical instrument —usu. pl.

bio·chem·is·try \ˌbīō'kem-əstrē\ *n* : chemistry dealing with organisms — **bio·chemi·cal** *adj or n* — **bio·chem·ist** *n*

bio·de·grad·able \ˌbīōdi-ˈgrādəbəl\ *adj* : able to be reduced to harmless products by organisms — **bio·de·grad·abil·i·ty** *n* — **bio·deg·ra·da·tion** *n* — **bio·de·grade** *vb*

bi·og·ra·phy \bīˈägrəfē, bē-\ *n, pl* **-phies** : written history of a person's life — **bi·og·ra·pher** \-fər\ *n* — **bi·o·graph·i·cal** \ˌbīəˈgrafikəl\ *adj*

bi·ol·o·gy \bīˈäləjē\ *n* : science of living beings and life processes — **bi·o·log·ic** \ˌbīə-ˈläjik\, **bi·o·log·i·cal** \-əl\ *adj* — **bi·ol·o·gist** \bīˈäləjist\ *n*

bi·on·ic \bīˈänik\ *adj* : having normal biological capabilities enhanced by electronic or mechanical devices

bio·phys·ics \ˌbīōˈfiziks\ *n* : application of physics to biological problems — **bio·phys·i·cal** *adj* — **bio·phys·i·cist** *n*

bi·op·sy \ˈbīˌäpsē\ *n, pl* **-sies** : removal of live bodily tissue for examination

bio·tech·nol·o·gy \ˌbīōtek-ˈnäləjē\ *n* : manufacture of products using techniques involving the manipulation of DNA

bi·par·ti·san \bīˈpärtəzən, -sən\ *adj* : involving members of 2 parties

bi·ped \ˈbīˌped\ *n* : 2-footed animal

birch \ˈbərch\ *n* : deciduous tree with close-grained wood — **birch, birch·en** \-ən\ *adj*

bird \ˈbərd\ *n* : warm-blooded egg-laying vertebrate with wings and feathers — **bird·bath** *n* — **bird·house** *n* — **bird·seed** *n*

bird's–eye \ˈbərdzˌī\ *adj* **1** : seen from above **2** : cursory

birth \ˈbərth\ *n* **1** : act or fact of being born or of producing young **2** : origin — **birth·day** *n* — **birth·place** *n* — **birth·rate** *n*

birth·mark *n* : unusual blemish on the skin at birth

birth·right *n* : something one is entitled to by birth

bis·cuit \ˈbiskət\ *n* : small bread made with leavening other than yeast

bi·sect \ˈbīˌsekt\ *vb* : divide into 2 parts — **bi·sec·tion** \ˈbīˌsekshən\ *n* — **bi·sec·tor** \-tər\ *n*

bish·op \ˈbishəp\ *n* : clergy member higher than a priest

bish·op·ric \-shəˌprik\ *n* **1** : diocese **2** : office of bishop

bis·muth \ˈbizməth\ *n* : heavy brittle metallic chemical element

bi·son \ˈbīsᵊn, ˈbīz-\ *n, pl* **-son** : large shaggy wild ox of central U.S.

bis·tro \ˈbēstrō, ˈbis-\ *n, pl* **-tros** : small restaurant or bar

¹bit \'bit\ *n* **1** : part of a bridle that goes in a horse's mouth **2** : drilling tool

²bit *n* **1** : small piece or quantity **2** : small degree

bitch \'bich\ *n* : female dog ~ *vb* : complain

bite \'bīt\ *vb* **bit** \'bit\; **bit·ten** \'bit³n\; **bit·ing** \'bītiŋ\ **1** : to grip or cut with teeth or jaws **2** : dig in or grab and hold **3** : sting **4** : take bait ~ *n* **1** : act of biting **2** : bit of food **3** : wound made by biting — **bit·ing** *adj*

bit·ter \'bitər\ *adj* **1** : having an acrid lingering taste **2** : intense or severe **3** : extremely harsh or resentful — **bit·ter·ly** *adv* — **bit·ter·ness** *n*

bit·tern \'bitərn\ *n* : small heron

bi·tu·mi·nous coal \bə'tüm-ənəs-, -'tyü-\ *n* : coal that yields volatile waste matter when heated

bi·valve \'bī,valv\ *n* : animal (as a clam) with a shell of 2 parts — **bivalve** *adj*

biv·ouac \'bivə,wak\ *n* : temporary camp ~ *vb* **-ouacked; -ouack·ing** : camp

bi·zarre \bə'zär\ *adj* : very strange — **bi·zarre·ly** *adv*

blab \'blab\ *vb* **-bb-** : talk too much

black \'blak\ *adj* **1** : of the color black **2** : dark-skinned **3** : soiled **4** : lacking light **5** : wicked or evil **6** : gloomy ~ *n* **1** : black pigment or dye **2** : something black **3** : color of least lightness **4** : person of a dark-skinned race ~ *vb* : blacken — **black·ing** *n* — **black·ish** *adj* — **black·ly** *adv* — **black·ness** *n*

black–and–blue *adj* : darkly discolored from bruising

black·ball \'blak,bȯl\ *vb* **1** : ostracize **2** : boycott — **blackball** *n*

black·ber·ry \'blak,berē\ *n* : black or purple fruit of a bramble

black·bird *n* : bird of which the male is largely or wholly black

black·board *n* : dark surface for writing on with chalk

black·en \'blakən\ *vb* **1** : make or become black **2** : defame

black·guard \'blagərd, -,ärd\ *n* : scoundrel

black·head *n* : small dark oily mass plugging the outlet of a skin gland

black hole *n* : invisible extremely massive celestial object

black·jack *n* **1** : flexible leather-covered club **2** : card game ~ *vb* : hit with a blackjack

black·list *n* : list of persons to be punished or boycotted — **blacklist** *vb*

black·mail *n* **1** : extortion by threat of exposure **2** : something extorted by blackmail — **blackmail** *vb* — **black·mail·er** *n*

black·out *n* **1** : darkness due to electrical failure **2** : brief fainting spell — **black out** *vb*

black·smith *n* : one who forges iron

black·top *n* : dark tarry material for surfacing roads — **blacktop** *vb*

blad·der \'blad**ə**r\ *n* : sac into which urine passes from the kidneys

blade \'blād\ *n* **1** : leaf esp. of grass **2** : something resembling the flat part of a leaf **3** : cutting part of an instrument or tool — **blad·ed** \'blādə**d**\ *adj*

blame \'blām\ *vb* **blamed; blam·ing 1** : find fault with **2** : hold responsible or responsible for — **blam·able** *adj* — **blame** *n* — **blame·less** *adj* — **blame·less·ly** *adv* — **blame·worthy** *adj*

blanch \'blanch\ *vb* : make or become white or pale

bland \'bland\ *adj* **1** : smooth in manner **2** : soothing **3** : tasteless — **bland·ly** *adv* — **bland·ness** *n*

blan·dish·ment \'blandish**mə**nt\ *n* : flattering or coaxing speech or act

blank \'blaŋk\ *adj* **1** : showing or causing a dazed look **2** : lacking expression **3** : empty **4** : free from writing **5** : downright ~ *n* **1** : an empty space **2** : form with spaces to write in **3** : unfinished form (as of a key) **4** : cartridge with no bullet ~ *vb* : cover or close up — **blank·ly** *adv* — **blank·ness** *n*

blan·ket \'blaŋkə**t**\ *n* **1** : heavy covering for a bed **2** : covering layer ~ *vb* : cover ~ *adj* : applying to a group

blare \'blar\ *vb* **blared; blar·ing** : make a loud harsh sound — **blare** *n*

blar·ney \'blärnē\ *n* : skillful flattery

bla·sé \blä'zā\ *adj* : indifferent to pleasure or excitement

blas·pheme \blas'fēm\ *vb* **-phemed; -phem·ing** : speak blasphemy — **blas·phem·er** *n*

blas·phe·my \'blasfə**m**ē\ *n, pl* **-mies** : irreverence toward God or anything sacred — **blas·phe·mous** *adj*

blast \'blast\ *n* **1** : violent gust of wind **2** : explosion ~ *vb* : shatter by or as if by explosive — **blast off** *vb* : take off esp. in a rocket

bla·tant \'blāt**ə**nt\ *adj* : offensively showy — **bla·tan·cy** \-**ə**nsē\ *n* — **bla·tant·ly** *adv*

¹blaze \'blāz\ *n* **1** : fire **2** : intense direct light **3** : strong display ∼ *vb* **blazed; blazing** : burn or shine brightly

²blaze *n* **1** : white stripe on an animal's face **2** : trail marker esp. on a tree ∼ *vb* **blazed; blaz·ing** : mark with blazes

blaz·er \-ər\ *n* : sports jacket

bleach \'blēch\ *vb* : whiten — **bleach** *n*

bleach·ers \-ərz\ *n sing or pl* : uncovered stand for spectators

bleak \'blēk\ *adj* **1** : desolately barren **2** : lacking cheering qualities — **bleak·ish** *adj* — **bleak·ly** *adv* — **bleak·ness** *n*

bleary \'blirē\ *adj* : dull or dimmed esp. from fatigue

bleat \'blēt\ *n* : cry of a sheep or goat or a sound like it — **bleat** *vb*

bleed \'blēd\ *vb* **bled** \'bled\; **bleed·ing** **1** : lose or shed blood **2** : feel distress **3** : flow from a wound **4** : draw fluid from **5** : extort money from — **bleed·er** *n*

blem·ish \'blemish\ *vb* : spoil by a flaw ∼ *n* : noticeable flaw

¹blench \'blench\ *vb* : flinch

²blench *vb* : grow or make pale

blend \'blend\ *vb* **1** : mix thoroughly **2** : combine into an integrated whole — **blend** *n* — **blend·er** *n*

bless \'bles\ *vb* **blessed** \'blest\; **bless·ing** **1** : consecrate by religious rite **2** : invoke divine care for **3** : make happy — **bless·ed** \'blesəd\, **blest** \'blest\ *adj* — **bless·ed·ly** \'blesədlē\ *adv* — **bless·ed·ness** \'blesədnəs\ *n* — **bless·ing** *n*

blew *past of* BLOW

blight \'blīt\ *n* **1** : plant disorder marked by withering or an organism causing it **2** : harmful influence **3** : deteriorated condition ∼ *vb* : affect with or suffer from blight

blimp \'blimp\ *n* : airship holding form by pressure of contained gas

blind \'blīnd\ *adj* **1** : lacking or quite deficient in ability to see **2** : not intelligently controlled **3** : having no way out ∼ *vb* **1** : to make blind **2** : dazzle ∼ *n* **1** : something to conceal or darken **2** : place of concealment — **blind·ly** *adv* — **blind·ness** *n*

blind·fold *vb* : cover the eyes of — **blindfold** *n*

blink \'blink\ *vb* **1** : wink **2** : shine intermittently ∼ *n* : wink

blink·er *n* : a blinking light

bliss \'blis\ *n* **1** : complete happiness **2** : heaven or paradise — **bliss·ful** *adj* — **bliss·ful·ly** *adv*

blis·ter \'blistər\ *n* **1** : raised area of skin containing watery fluid **2** : raised or swollen spot ∼ *vb* : develop or cause blisters

blithe \'blīth, 'blīth\ *adj* **blith·er; blith·est** : cheerful — **blithe·ly** *adv* — **blithe·some** \-səm\ *adj*

blitz \'blits\ *n* **1** : series of air raids **2** : fast intensive campaign — **blitz** *vb*

bliz·zard \'blizərd\ *n* : severe snowstorm

bloat \'blōt\ *vb* : swell

blob \'bläb\ *n* : small lump or drop

bloc \'bläk\ *n* : group working together

block \'bläk\ *n* **1** : solid piece **2** : frame enclosing a pulley **3** : quantity considered together **4** : large building divided into separate units **5** : a city square or the distance along one of its sides **6** : obstruction **7** : interruption of a bodily or mental function ∼ *vb* : obstruct or hinder

block·ade \blä'kād\ *n* : isolation of a place usu. by troops or ships — **block·ade** *vb* — **block·ad·er** *n*

block·head *n* : stupid person

blond, blonde \'bländ\ *adj* **1** : fair in complexion **2** : of

a light color — **blond, blonde** *n*

blood \'bləd\ *n* **1** : red liquid that circulates in the heart, arteries, and veins of animals **2** : lifeblood **3** : lineage — **blood·ed** *adj* — **blood·less** *adj* — **blood·stain** *n* — **blood·stained** *adj* — **blood·suck·er** *n* — **blood·suck·ing** *n* — **bloody** *adj*

blood·cur·dling *adj* : terrifying

blood·hound *n* : large hound with a keen sense of smell

blood·mo·bile \-mō,bēl\ *n* : truck for collecting blood from donors

blood·shed *n* : slaughter

blood·shot *adj* : inflamed to redness

blood·stream *n* : blood in a circulatory system

blood·thirsty *adj* : eager to shed blood — **blood·thirst·i·ly** *adv* — **blood·thirst·i·ness** *n*

bloom \'blüm\ *n* **1** : flower **2** : period of flowering **3** : fresh or healthy look ∼ *vb* **1** : yield flowers **2** : mature — **bloomy** *adj*

bloo·mers \'blümərz\ *n pl* : woman's underwear of short loose trousers

bloop·er \'blüpər\ *n* : public blunder

blos·som \'bläsəm\ *n or vb* : flower

blot \'blät\ *n* **1** : stain **2** : blemish ～ *vb* **-tt-** **1** : spot **2** : dry with absorbent paper — **blot·ter** *n*

blotch \'bläch\ *n* : large spot — **blotch** *vb* — **blotchy** *adj*

blouse \'blaus, 'blauz\ *n* : loose garment reaching from the neck to the waist

¹blow \'blō\ *vb* **blew** \'blü\; **blown** \'blōn\; **blow·ing** **1** : move forcibly **2** : send forth a current of air **3** : sound **4** : shape by blowing **5** : explode **6** : bungle ～ *n* **1** : gale **2** : act of blowing — **blow·er** *n* — **blowy** *adj*

²blow *n* **1** : forcible stroke **2** *pl* : fighting **3** : calamity

blow·out *n* : bursting of a tire

blow·torch *n* : small torch that uses a blast of air

¹blub·ber \'bləbər\ *n* : fat of whales

²blubber *vb* : cry noisily

blud·geon \'bləjən\ *n* : short club ～ *vb* : hit with a bludgeon

blue \'blü\ *adj* **blu·er; blu·est** **1** : of the color blue **2** : melancholy ～ *n* : color of the clear sky — **blu·ish** \-ish\ *adj*

blue·bell *n* : plant with blue bell-shaped flowers

blue·ber·ry \-ˌberē\ *n* : edible blue or blackish berry

blue·bird *n* : small bluish songbird

blue·fish *n* : bluish marine food fish

blue jay *n* : American crested jay

blue·print *n* **1** : photographic print in white on blue of a mechanical drawing **2** : plan of action — **blueprint** *vb*

blues \'blüz\ *n pl* **1** : depression **2** : music in a melancholy style

¹bluff \'bləf\ *adj* **1** : rising steeply with a broad flat front **2** : frank ～ *n* : cliff

²bluff *vb* : deceive by pretense ～ *n* : act of bluffing — **bluffer** \-ər\ *n*

blu·ing, blue·ing \'blüiŋ\ *n* : laundry preparation to keep fabrics white

blun·der \'bləndər\ *vb* **1** : move clumsily **2** : make a stupid mistake ～ *n* : bad mistake

blun·der·buss \-ˌbəs\ *n* : obsolete short-barreled firearm

blunt \'blənt\ *adj* **1** : not sharp **2** : tactless ～ *vb* : make dull — **blunt·ly** *adv* — **blunt·ness** *n*

blur \'blər\ *n* **1** : smear **2** : something perceived indistinctly ～ *vb* **-rr-** : cloud or obscure — **blur·ry** \-ē\ *adj*

blurb \'blərb\ *n* : short publicity notice

blurt \\'blərt\ *vb* : utter suddenly

blush \\'bləsh\ *n* : reddening of the face — **blush** *vb* — **blushful** *adj*

blus·ter \\'bləstər\ *vb* **1** : blow violently **2** : talk or act with boasts or threats — **blus·ter** *n* — **blus·tery** *adj*

boa \\'bōə\ *n* **1** : a large snake (as the **boa con·stric·tor** \-kən-'striktər\) that crushes its prey **2** : fluffy scarf

boar \\'bōr\ *n* : male swine

board \\'bōrd\ *n* **1** : long thin piece of sawed lumber **2** : flat thin sheet esp. for games **3** : daily meals furnished for pay **4** : official body ~ *vb* **1** : go aboard **2** : cover with boards **3** : supply meals to — **board·er** *n*

board·walk *n* : wooden walk along a beach

boast \\'bōst\ *vb* : praise oneself or one's possessions — **boast** *n* — **boast·er** *n* — **boast·ful** *adj* — **boast·ful·ly** *adv*

boat \\'bōt\ *n* : small vessel for traveling on water — **boat** *vb* — **boat·man** \-mən\ *n*

boat·swain \\'bōsᵊn\ *n* : ship's officer in charge of the hull

¹bob \\'bäb\ *vb* **-bb-** **1** : move up and down **2** : appear suddenly

²bob *n* **1** : float **2** : woman's short haircut ~ *vb* : cut hair in a bob

bob·bin \\'bäbən\ *n* : spindle for holding thread

bob·ble \\'bäbəl\ *vb* **-bled; -bling** : fumble — **bobble** *n*

bob·cat *n* : small American lynx

bob·o·link \\'bäbə₁liŋk\ *n* : American songbird

bob·sled \\'bäb₁sled\ *n* : racing sled — **bobsled** *vb*

bob·white \\'bäb'hwīt\ *n* : quail

bock \\'bäk\ *n* : dark beer

¹bode \\'bōd\ *vb* **bod·ed; bod·ing** : indicate by signs

²bode *past of* BIDE

bod·ice \\'bädəs\ *n* : close-fitting top of dress

bodi·ly \\'bädᵊlē\ *adj* : relating to the body ~ *adv* **1** : in the flesh **2** : as a whole

body \\'bädē\ *n, pl* **bod·ies** **1** : the physical whole of an organism **2** : human being **3** : main part **4** : mass of matter **5** : group — **bod·ied** *adj* — **bodi·less** \-iləs, -ᵊləs\ *adj* — **body·guard** *n*

bog \\'bäg, 'bòg\ *n* : swamp ~ *vb* **-gg-** : sink in or as if in a bog — **bog·gy** *adj*

bo·gey \\'bùgē, 'bō-\ *n, pl* **-geys** : someone or something frightening

bog·gle \\'bägəl\ *vb* **-gled; -gling** : overwhelm with amazement

bo·gus \\'bōgəs\ *adj* : fake

bo·he·mi·an \bō'hēmēən\ *n*
: one living unconventionally
— **bohemian** *adj*

¹**boil** \'bȯil\ *n* : inflamed
swelling

²**boil** *vb* **1** : heat to a temperature (**boiling point**) at which
vapor forms **2** : cook in boiling liquid **3** : be agitated —
boil *n*

boil·er \'bȯilər\ *n* : tank holding hot water or steam

bois·ter·ous \'bȯistərəs\ *adj*
: noisily turbulent — **bois·ter·
ous·ly** *adv*

bold \'bōld\ *adj* **1** : courageous **2** : insolent **3** : daring
— **bold·ly** *adv* — **bold·ness** *n*

bo·le·ro \bə'lerō\ *n, pl* **-ros 1**
: Spanish dance **2** : short
open jacket

boll \'bōl\ *n* : seed pod

boll weevil *n* : small grayish
weevil that infests the cotton
plant

bo·lo·gna \bə'lōnē\ *n* : large
smoked sausage

bol·ster \'bōlstər\ *n* : long pillow ~ *vb* **-stered; -ster·ing**
: support

bolt \'bōlt\ *n* **1** : flash of
lightning **2** : sliding bar used
to fasten a door **3** : roll of
cloth **4** : threaded pin used
with a nut ~ *vb* **1** : move
suddenly **2** : fasten with a
bolt **3** : swallow hastily

bomb \'bäm\ *n* : explosive device ~ *vb* : attack with
bombs — **bomb·proof** *adj*

bom·bard \bäm'bärd, bəm-\
vb : attack with or as if with
artillery — **bom·bard·ment** *n*

bom·bar·dier \,bämbə'dir\ *n*
: one who releases the bombs
from a bomber

bom·bast \'bäm,bast\ *n* : pretentious language — **bom-
bas·tic** \bäm'bastik\ *adj*

bomb·er *n* **1** : one that bombs
2 : airplane for dropping
bombs

bomb·shell *n* **1** : bomb **2**
: great surprise

bona fide \'bōnə,fīd, 'bän-;
,bōnə'fīdē\ *adj* **1** : made in
good faith **2** : genuine

bo·nan·za \bə'nanzə\ *n*
: something yielding a rich return

bon·bon \'bän,bän\ *n* : piece
of candy

bond \'bänd\ *n* **1** *pl* : fetters
2 : uniting force **3** : obligation made binding by money
4 : interest-bearing certificate
~ *vb* **1** : insure **2** : cause to
adhere — **bond·hold·er** *n*

bond·age \'bändij\ *n* : slavery

¹**bonds·man** \'bändzmən\ *n*
: slave

²**bondsman** *n* : surety

bone \'bōn\ *n* : skeletal material ~ *vb* **boned; bon·ing**

: to free from bones — **bone-less** *adj* — **bony** \'bōnē\ *adj*

bon·er \'bōnər\ *n* : blunder

bon·fire \'bän,fīr\ *n* : outdoor fire

bo·ni·to \bə'nētō\ *n, pl* **-tos** *or* **-to** : medium-sized tuna

bon·net \'bänət\ *n* : hat for a woman or infant

bo·nus \'bōnəs\ *n* : extra payment

boo \'bü\ *n, pl* **boos** : shout of disapproval — **boo** *vb*

boo·by \'bübē\ *n, pl* **-bies** : dunce

book \'bùk\ *n* **1** : paper sheets bound into a volume **2** : long literary work or a subdivision of one ~ *vb* : reserve — **book·case** *n* — **book·let** \-lət\ *n* — **book·mark** *n* — **book-sell·er** *n* — **book·shelf** *n*

book·end *n* : support to hold up a row of books

book·ie \-ē\ *n* : bookmaker

book·ish \-ish\ *adj* : fond of books and reading

book·keep·er *n* : one who keeps business accounts — **book·keep·ing** *n*

book·mak·er *n* : one who takes bets — **book·mak·ing** *n*

book·worm *n* : one devoted to reading

¹boom \'büm\ *n* **1** : long spar to extend the bottom of a sail **2** : beam projecting from the pole of a derrick

²boom *vb* **1** : make a deep hollow sound **2** : grow rapidly esp. in value ~ *n* **1** : booming sound **2** : rapid growth

boo·mer·ang \'bümə,raŋ\ *n* : angular club that returns to the thrower

¹boon \'bün\ *n* : benefit

²boon *adj* : congenial

boon·docks \'bün,däks\ *n pl* : rural area

boor \'bùr\ *n* : rude person — **boor·ish** *adj*

boost \'büst\ *vb* **1** : raise **2** : promote — **boost** *n* — **boost·er** *n*

boot \'büt\ *n* **1** : covering for the foot and leg **2** : kick ~ *vb* : kick

boo·tee, boo·tie \'bütē\ *n* : infant's knitted sock

booth \'büth\ *n, pl* **booths** \'bü<u>th</u>z, 'büths\ : small enclosed stall or seating area

boot·leg \'büt,leg\ *vb* : make or sell liquor illegally — **boot-leg** *adj or n* — **boot·leg·ger** *n*

boo·ty \'bütē\ *n, pl* **-ties** : plunder

booze \'büz\ *vb* **boozed; booz·ing** : drink liquor to excess ~ *n* : liquor — **booz·er** *n* — **boozy** *adj*

bo·rax \'bōr,aks\ *n* : crystalline compound of boron

bor·der \'bòrdər\ *n* **1** : edge **2** : boundary ~ *vb* **1** : put a border on **2** : be close

¹bore \'bōr\ *vb* **bored; bor·ing**
1 : pierce **2 :** make by piercing ~ *n* **:** cylindrical hole or its diameter — **bor·er** *n*

²bore *past of* BEAR

³bore *n* **:** one that is dull ~ *vb* **bored; bor·ing :** tire with dullness — **bore·dom** \'bōrdəm\ *n*

born \'bȯrn\ *adj* **1 :** brought into life **2 :** being such by birth

borne *past part of* BEAR

bo·ron \'bōr͵än\ *n* **:** dark-colored chemical element

bor·ough \'bərō\ *n* **:** incorporated town or village

bor·row \'bärō\ *vb* **1 :** take as a loan **2 :** take into use

bo·som \'bu̇zəm, 'bu̇s-\ *n* **:** breast ~ *adj* **:** intimate — **bo·somed** *adj*

boss \'bȯs\ *n* **:** employer or supervisor ~ *vb* **:** supervise — **bossy** *adj*

bot·a·ny \'bät°nē\ *n* **:** plant biology — **bo·tan·i·cal** \bə-'tanikəl\ *adj* — **bot·a·nist** \'bät°nist\ *n* — **bot·a·nize** \-°n͵īz\ *vb*

botch \'bäch\ *vb* **:** do clumsily — **botch** *n*

both \'bōth\ *adj or pron* **:** the one and the other ~ *conj* — used to show each of two is included

both·er \'bäthər\ *vb* **1 :** annoy or worry **2 :** take the trou-ble — **bother** *n* — **both·er·some** \-səm\ *adj*

bot·tle \'bät°l\ *n* **:** container with a narrow neck and no handles ~ *vb* **bot·tled; bot·tling :** put into a bottle

bot·tle·neck *n* **:** place or cause of congestion

bot·tom \'bätəm\ *n* **1 :** supporting surface **2 :** lowest part or place — **bottom** *adj* — **bot·tom·less** *adj*

bot·u·lism \'bächə͵lizəm\ *n* **:** acute food poisoning

bou·doir \'bü͵dwär, 'bu̇-, ͵bü'-, ͵bu̇'-\ *n* **:** woman's private room

bough \'bau̇\ *n* **:** large tree branch

bought *past of* BUY

bouil·lon \'bü͵yän; 'bu̇l͵yän, -yən\ *n* **:** clear soup

boul·der \'bōldər\ *n* **:** large rounded rock — **boul·dered** *adj*

bou·le·vard \'bu̇lə͵värd, 'bü-\ *n* **:** broad thoroughfare

bounce \'bau̇ns\ *vb* **bounced; bounc·ing 1 :** spring back **2 :** make bounce — **bounce** *n* — **bouncy** \'bau̇nsē\ *adj*

¹bound \'bau̇nd\ *adj* **:** intending to go

²bound *n* **:** limit or boundary ~ *vb* **:** be a boundary of — **bound·less** *adj* — **bound·less·ness** *n*

³**bound** *adj* **1** : obliged **2** : having a binding **3** : determined **4** : incapable of failing

⁴**bound** *n* : leap ∼ *vb* : move by springing

bound·ary \'baundrē\ *n, pl* **-aries** : line marking extent or separation

boun·ty \'bauntē\ *n, pl* **-ties** **1** : generosity **2** : reward — **boun·te·ous** \-ēəs\ *adj* — **boun·te·ous·ly** *adv* — **boun·ti·ful** \-ifəl\ *adj* — **boun·ti·ful·ly** *adv*

bou·quet \bō'kā, bü-\ *n* **1** : bunch of flowers **2** : fragrance

bour·bon \'bərbən\ *n* : corn whiskey

bour·geoi·sie \,burzh,wä'zē\ *n* : middle class of society — **bour·geois** \'burzh,wä, burzh'wä\ *n or adj*

bout \'baut\ *n* **1** : contest **2** : outbreak

bou·tique \bü'tēk\ *n* : specialty shop

bo·vine \'bō,vīn, -,vēn\ *adj* : relating to cattle — **bovine** *n*

¹**bow** \'bau\ *vb* **1** : submit **2** : bend the head or body ∼ *n* : act of bowing

²**bow** \'bō\ *n* **1** : bend or arch **2** : weapon for shooting arrows **3** : knot with loops **4** : rod with stretched horsehairs for playing a stringed instrument ∼ *vb* : curve or bend — **bow-man** \-mən\ *n* — **bow·string** *n*

³**bow** \'bau\ *n* : forward part of a ship — **bow** *adj*

bow·els \'bauəls\ *n pl* **1** : intestines **2** : inmost parts

bow·er \'bauər\ *n* : arbor

¹**bowl** \'bōl\ *n* : concave vessel or part — **bowl·ful** \-,ful\ *n*

²**bowl** *n* : round ball for bowling ∼ *vb* : roll a ball in bowling — **bowl·er** *n*

bowl·ing *n* : game in which balls are rolled to knock down pins

¹**box** \'bäks\ *n, pl* **box** *or* **box·es** : evergreen shrub — **box·wood** \-,wud\ *n*

²**box** *n* **1** : container usu. with 4 sides and a cover **2** : small compartment ∼ *vb* : put in a box

³**box** *n* : slap ∼ *vb* **1** : slap **2** : fight with the fists — **box·er** *n* — **box·ing** *n*

box·car *n* : roofed freight car

box office *n* : theater ticket office

boy \'bȯi\ *n* : male child — **boy·hood** *n* — **boy·ish** *adj* — **boy·ish·ly** *adv* — **boy·ish·ness** *n*

boy·cott \-,kät\ *vb* : refrain from dealing with — **boycott** *n*

boy·friend \'bȯi,frend\ *n* **1** : male friend **2** : woman's regular male companion

brace \\'brās\ *n* **1** : crank for turning a bit **2** : something that resists weight or supports **3** : punctuation mark { or } ~ *vb* **braced; brac·ing** **1** : make taut or steady **2** : invigorate **3** : strengthen

brace·let \\'brāslət\ *n* : ornamental band for the wrist or arm

brack·et \\'brakət\ *n* **1** : projecting support **2** : punctuation mark [or] **3** : class ~ *vb* **1** : furnish or fasten with brackets **2** : place within brackets **3** : group

brack·ish \-ish\ *adj* : salty

brad \\'brad\ *n* : nail with a small head

brag \\'brag\ *vb* **-gg-** : boast — **brag** *n*

brag·gart \\'bragərt\ *n* : boaster

braid \\'brād\ *vb* : interweave ~ *n* : something braided

braille \\'brāl\ *n* : system of writing for the blind using raised dots

brain \\'brān\ *n* **1** : organ of thought and nervous coordination enclosed in the skull **2** : intelligence ~ *vb* : smash the skull of — **brained** *adj* — **brain·less** *adj* — **brainy** *adj*

braise \\'brāz\ *vb* **braised; brais·ing** : cook (meat) slowly in a covered dish

brake \\'brāk\ *n* : device for slowing or stopping ~ *vb*

braked; brak·ing : slow or stop by a brake

bram·ble \\'brambəl\ *n* : prickly shrub

bran \\'bran\ *n* : edible cracked grain husks

branch \\'branch\ *n* **1** : division of a plant stem **2** : part ~ *vb* **1** : develop branches **2** : diverge — **branched** *adj*

brand \\'brand\ *n* **1** : identifying mark made by burning **2** : stigma **3** : distinctive kind (as of goods from one firm) ~ *vb* : mark with a brand

bran·dish \\'brandish\ *vb* : wave

brand–new *adj* : unused

bran·dy \\'brandē\ *n, pl* **-dies** : liquor distilled from wine

brash \\'brash\ *adj* **1** : impulsive **2** : aggressively self≠assertive

brass \\'bras\ *n* **1** : alloy of copper and zinc **2** : brazen self≠assurance **3** : high-ranking military officers — **brassy** *adj*

bras·siere \brə'zir\ *n* : woman's undergarment to support the breasts

brat \\'brat\ *n* : ill-behaved child — **brat·ti·ness** *n* — **brat·ty** *adj*

bra·va·do \brə'vädō\ *n, pl* **-does** *or* **-dos** : false bravery

¹brave \\'brāv\ *adj* **brav·er; brav·est** : showing courage ~ *vb* **braved; brav·ing**

: face with courage — **brave-ly** *adv* — **brav·ery** \-ərē\ *n*

²brave *n* : American Indian warrior

bra·vo \'brävō\ *n, pl* **-vos** : shout of approval

brawl \'brȯl\ *n* : noisy quarrel or violent fight — **brawl** *vb* — **brawl·er** *n*

brawn \'brȯn\ *n* : muscular strength — **brawny** \-ē\ *adj* — **brawn·i·ness** *n*

bray \'brā\ *n* : harsh cry of a donkey — **bray** *vb*

bra·zen \'brāz°n\ *adj* **1** : made of brass **2** : bold — **bra·zen-ly** *adv* — **bra·zen·ness** *n*

bra·zier \'brāzhər\ *n* : char-coal grill

breach \'brēch\ *n* **1** : break-ing of a law, obligation, or standard **2** : gap ~ *vb* : make a breach in

bread \'bred\ *n* : baked food made of flour ~ *vb* : cover with bread crumbs

breadth \'bredth\ *n* : width

bread·win·ner *n* : wage earner

break \'brāk\ *vb* **broke** \'brōk\; **bro·ken** \'brōkən\; **break·ing** **1** : knock into pieces **2** : transgress **3** : force a way into or out of **4** : ex-ceed **5** : interrupt **6** : fail ~ *n* **1** : act or result of breaking **2** : stroke of good luck — **break·able** *adj or n* — **break-age** \'brākij\ *n* — **break·er** *n*

— **break in** *vb* **1** : enter by force **2** : interrupt **3** : train — **break out** *vb* **1** : erupt with force **2** : develop a rash

break·down *n* : physical or mental failure — **break down** *vb*

break·fast \'brekfəst\ *n* : first meal of the day — **breakfast** *vb*

breast \'brest\ *n* **1** : milk-producing gland esp. of a woman **2** : front part of the chest

breast·bone *n* : sternum

breath \'breth\ *n* **1** : slight breeze **2** : air breathed in or out — **breath·less** *adj* — **breath·less·ly** *adv* — **breath-less·ness** *n* — **breathy** \'brethē\ *adj*

breathe \'brēth\ *vb* **breathed**; **breath·ing** **1** : draw air into the lungs and expel it **2** : live **3** : utter

breath·tak·ing *adj* : exciting

breech·es \'brichəz\ *n pl* : trousers ending near the knee

breed \'brēd\ *vb* **bred** \'bred\; **breed·ing** **1** : give birth to **2** : propagate **3** : raise ~ *n* **1** : kind of plant or animal usu. developed by humans **2** : class — **breed·er** *n*

breeze \'brēz\ *n* : light wind ~ *vb* **breezed**; **breez·ing** : move fast — **breezy** *adj*

breth·ren \'bre_th_rən, -ərn\ *pl of* BROTHER

bre·via·ry \'brēvərē, 'bre-, -vyərē, -vē͜erē\ *n, pl* **-ries** : prayer book used by Roman Catholic priests

brev·i·ty \'brevətē\ *n, pl* **-ties** : shortness or conciseness

brew \'brü\ *vb* : make by fermenting or steeping — **brew** *n* — **brew·er** *n* — **brew·ery** \'brüərē, 'brùrē\ *n*

bri·ar *var of* BRIER

bribe \'brīb\ *vb* **bribed; bribing** : corrupt or influence by gifts ∼ *n* : something offered or given in bribing — **bribable** *adj* — **brib·ery** \-ərē\ *n*

bric–a–brac \'brikə͜brak\ *n pl* : small ornamental articles

brick \'brik\ *n* : building block of baked clay — **brick** *vb* — **brick·lay·er** *n* — **brick·lay·ing** *n*

bride \'brīd\ *n* : woman just married or about to be married — **brid·al** \-əl\ *adj*

bride·groom *n* : man just married or about to be married

brides·maid *n* : woman who attends a bride at her wedding

[1]bridge \'brij\ *n* **1** : structure built for passage over a depression or obstacle **2** : upper part of the nose **3** : compartment from which a ship is navigated **4** : artificial replacement for missing teeth

∼ *vb* : build a bridge over — **bridge·able** *adj*

[2]bridge *n* : card game for 4 players

bri·dle \'brīdəl\ *n* : headgear to control a horse ∼ *vb* **-dled; -dling** **1** : put a bridle on **2** : restrain **3** : show hostility or scorn

brief \'brēf\ *adj* : short or concise ∼ *n* : concise summary (as of a legal case) ∼ *vb* : give final instructions or essential information to — **brief·ly** *adv* — **brief·ness** *n*

brief·case *n* : case for papers

[1]bri·er \'brīər\ *n* : thorny plant

[2]brier *n* : heath of southern Europe

[1]brig \'brig\ *n* : 2-masted ship

[2]brig *n* : jail on a naval ship

bri·gade \brig'ād\ *n* **1** : large military unit **2** : group organized for a special activity

brig·a·dier general \͜brigə-'dir-\ *n* : officer ranking next below a major general

brig·and \'brigənd\ *n* : bandit — **brig·and·age** \-ij\ *n*

bright \'brīt\ *adj* **1** : radiating or reflecting light **2** : cheerful **3** : intelligent — **bright·en** \-ən\ *vb* — **bright·en·er** \'brītənər\ *n* — **bright·ly** *adv* — **bright·ness** *n*

bril·liant \'brilyənt\ *adj* **1** : very bright **2** : splendid **3** : very intelligent — **bril-**

liance \-yəns\ *n* — **bril·lian-cy** \-yənsē\ *n* — **bril·liant·ly** *adv*

brim \'brim\ *n* : edge or rim ~ *vb* : be or become full — **brim·less** *adj* — **brimmed** *adj*

brim·ful \-'fůl\ *adj* : full to the brim

brim·stone *n* : sulfur

brin·dled \'brind³ld\ *adj* : gray or tawny with dark streaks or flecks

brine \'brīn\ *n* **1** : salt water **2** : ocean — **brin·i·ness** *n* — **briny** *adj*

bring \'briŋ\ *vb* **brought** \'brȯt\; **bring·ing 1** : cause to come with one **2** : persuade **3** : produce **4** : sell for — **bring·er** *n* — **bring about** *vb* : make happen — **bring up** *vb* **1** : care for and educate **2** : cause to be noticed

brink \'briŋk\ *n* : edge

bri·quette, bri·quet \bri'ket\ *n* : pressed mass (as of charcoal)

brisk \'brisk\ *adj* **1** : lively **2** : invigorating — **brisk·ly** *adv* — **brisk·ness** *n*

bris·ket \'briskət\ *n* : breast or lower chest of a quadruped

bris·tle \'brisəl\ *n* : short stiff hair ~ *vb* **-tled; -tling 1** : stand erect **2** : show angry defiance **3** : appear as if covered with bristles — **bris·tly** *adj*

brit·tle \'brit³l\ *adj* **-tler; -tlest** : easily broken — **brit·tle·ness** *n*

broach \'brōch\ *n* : pointed tool (as for opening casks) ~ *vb* **1** : pierce (as a cask) to open **2** : introduce for discussion

broad \'brȯd\ *adj* **1** : wide **2** : spacious **3** : clear or open **4** : obvious **5** : tolerant in outlook **6** : widely applicable **7** : dealing with essential points — **broad·en** \-³n\ *vb* — **broad·ly** *adv* — **broad·ness** *n*

broad·cast *n* **1** : transmission by radio waves **2** : radio or television program ~ *vb* **-cast; -cast·ing 1** : scatter or sow in all directions **2** : make widely known **3** : send out on a broadcast — **broad·cast·er** *n*

broad·cloth *n* : fine cloth

broad·loom *adj* : woven on a wide loom esp. in solid color

broad–mind·ed *adj* : tolerant of varied opinions — **broad–mind·ed·ly** *adv* — **broad–mind·ed·ness** *n*

broad·side *n* **1** : simultaneous firing of all guns on one side of a ship **2** : verbal attack

bro·cade \brō'kād\ *n* : usu. silk fabric with a raised design

broc·co·li \'bräkəlē\ *n* : green vegetable akin to cauliflower

bro·chure \brō'shůr\ *n* : pamphlet

brogue \'brōg\ *n* : Irish accent

broil \'broil\ *vb* : cook by radiant heat — **broil** *n*

broil·er *n* **1** : utensil for broiling **2** : chicken fit for broiling

¹broke \'brōk\ *past of* BREAK

²broke *adj* : out of money

bro·ken \'brōkən\ *adj* : imperfectly spoken — **bro·ken·ly** *adv*

bro·ken·heart·ed \-'härtəd\ *adj* : overcome by grief or despair

bro·ker \'brōkər\ *n* : agent who buys and sells for a fee — **broker** *vb* — **bro·ker·age** \-kərij\ *n*

bro·mine \'brō,mēn\ *n* : deep red liquid corrosive chemical element

bron·chi·tis \brän'kītəs, brän-\ *n* : inflammation of the bronchi

bron·chus \'bränkəs\ *n, pl* **-chi** \-,kī, -,kē\ : division of the windpipe leading to a lung — **bron·chi·al** \-kēəl\ *adj*

bronze \'bränz\ *vb* **bronzed; bronz·ing** : make bronze in color ∼ *n* **1** : alloy of copper and tin **2** : yellowish brown — **bronzy** \-ē\ *adj*

brooch \'brōch, 'brüch\ *n* : ornamental clasp or pin

brood \'brüd\ *n* : family of young ∼ *vb* **1** : sit on eggs to hatch them **2** : ponder ∼ *adj* : kept for breeding — **brood·er** *n* — **brood·ing·ly** *adv*

¹brook \'brůk\ *vb* : tolerate

²brook *n* : small stream

broom \'brüm, 'brům\ *n* **1** : flowering shrub **2** : implement for sweeping — **broomstick** *n*

broth \'broth\ *n, pl* **broths** \'broths, 'brothz\ : liquid in which meat has been cooked

broth·el \'bräthəl, 'broth-\ *n* : house of prostitutes

broth·er \'brəthər\ *n, pl* **brothers** *also* **breth·ren** \'brethrən, -ərn\ **1** : male sharing one or both parents with another person **2** : kinsman — **broth·er·hood** *n* — **broth·er·li·ness** *n* — **broth·er·ly** *adj*

broth·er–in–law *n, pl* **brothers–in–law** : brother of one's spouse or husband of one's sister or of one's spouse's sister

brought *past of* BRING

brow \'braů\ *n* **1** : eyebrow **2** : forehead **3** : edge of a steep place

brow·beat *vb* **-beat; -beat·en** *or* **-beat; -beat·ing** : intimidate

brown \'braůn\ *adj* **1** : of the color brown **2** : of dark or tanned complexion ∼ *n* : a color like that of coffee ∼ *vb* : make or become brown — **brown·ish** *adj*

browse \'braůz\ *vb* **browsed; brows·ing** **1** : graze **2** : look over casually — **brows·er** *n*

brows·er \\'braůzər\\ *n* : computer program for accessing Web sites

bru·in \\'brüən\\ *n* : bear

bruise \\'brüz\\ *vb* **bruised; bruis·ing 1** : make a bruise on **2** : become bruised ∼ *n* : surface injury to flesh

brunch \\'brənch\\ *n* : late breakfast, early lunch, or combination of both

bru·net, bru·nette \\brü'net\\ *adj* : having dark hair and usu. dark skin — **bru·net, brunette** *n*

brunt \\'brənt\\ *n* : main impact

¹**brush** \\'brəsh\\ *n* **1** : small cut branches **2** : coarse shrubby vegetation

²**brush** *n* **1** : bristles set in a handle used esp. for cleaning or painting **2** : light touch ∼ *vb* **1** : apply a brush to **2** : remove with or as if with a brush **3** : dismiss in an offhand way **4** : touch lightly — **brush up** *vb* : renew one's skill

³**brush** *n* : skirmish

brush–off *n* : curt dismissal

brusque \\'brəsk\\ *adj* : curt or blunt in manner — **brusque·ly** *adv*

bru·tal \\'brüt³l\\ *adj* : like a brute and esp. cruel — **bru·tal·i·ty** \\brü'talətē\\ *n* — **bru·tal·ize** \\'brüt³l,īz\\ *vb* — **bru·tal·ly** \\-³lē\\ *adv*

brute \\'brüt\\ *adj* **1** : relating to beasts **2** : unreasoning **3** : purely physical ∼ *n* **1** : beast **2** : brutal person — **brut·ish** \\-ish\\ *adj*

bub·ble \\'bəbəl\\ *vb* **-bled; -bling** : form, rise in, or give off bubbles ∼ *n* : globule of gas in or covered with a liquid — **bub·bly** \\-əlē\\ *adj*

bu·bo \\'bübō, 'byü-\\ *n, pl* **buboes** : inflammatory swelling of a lymph gland — **bu·bon·ic** \\bü'bänik, 'byü-\\ *adj*

buc·ca·neer \\,bəkə'nir\\ *n* : pirate

buck \\'bək\\ *n, pl* **buck** *or* **bucks 1** : male animal (as a deer) **2** : dollar ∼ *vb* **1** : jerk forward **2** : oppose

buck·et \\'bəkət\\ *n* : pail — **buck·et·ful** *n*

buck·le \\'bəkəl\\ *n* **1** : clasp (as on a belt) for two loose ends **2** : bend or fold ∼ *vb* **-led; -ling 1** : fasten with a buckle **2** : apply oneself **3** : bend or crumple

buck·ler \\'bəklər\\ *n* : shield

buck·shot *n* : coarse lead shot

buck·skin *n* : soft leather (as from the skin of a buck) — **buckskin** *adj*

buck·tooth *n* : large projecting front tooth — **buck–toothed** *adj*

buck·wheat *n* : herb whose seeds are used as a cereal grain or the seeds themselves

bu·col·ic \byü'kälik\ *adj* : pastoral

bud \'bəd\ *n* **1** : undeveloped plant shoot **2** : partly opened flower ~ *vb* **-dd-** **1** : form or put forth buds **2** : be or develop like a bud

Bud·dhism \'bü͵dizəm, 'bu̇-\ *n* : religion of eastern and central Asia — **Bud·dhist** \'büdist, 'bu̇d-\ *n or adj*

bud·dy \'bədē\ *n, pl* **-dies** : friend

budge \'bəj\ *vb* **budged; budg·ing** : move from a place

bud·get \'bəjət\ *n* **1** : estimate of income and expenses **2** : plan for coordinating income and expenses **3** : money available for a particular use — **budget** *vb or adj* — **bud·get·ary** \-ə͵terē\ *adj*

buff \'bəf\ *n* **1** : yellow to orange yellow color **2** : enthusiast ~ *adj* : of the color buff ~ *vb* : polish

buf·fa·lo \'bəfə͵lō\ *n, pl* **-lo** *or* **-loes** : wild ox (as a bison)

¹buff·er \'bəfər\ *n* : shield or protector

²buffer *n* : one that buffs

¹buf·fet \'bəfət\ *n* : blow or slap ~ *vb* : hit esp. repeatedly

²buf·fet \͵bə'fā, bü-\ *n* **1** : sideboard **2** : meal at which people serve themselves

buf·foon \͵bə'fün\ *n* : clown — **buf·foon·ery** \-ərē\ *n*

bug \'bəg\ *n* **1** : small usu. obnoxious crawling creature **2** : 4-winged sucking insect **3** : unexpected imperfection **4** : disease-producing germ **5** : hidden microphone ~ *vb* **-gg-** **1** : pester **2** : conceal a microphone in

bug·a·boo \'bəgə͵bü\ *n, pl* **-boos** : bogey

bug·bear *n* : source of dread

bug·gy \'bəgē\ *n, pl* **-gies** : light carriage

bu·gle \'byügəl\ *n* : trumpet-like brass instrument — **bu·gler** \-glər\ *n*

build \'bild\ *vb* **built** \'bilt\; **build·ing** **1** : put together **2** : establish **3** : increase ~ *n* : physique — **build·er** *n*

build·ing \'bildiŋ\ *n* **1** : roofed and walled structure **2** : art or business of constructing buildings

bulb \'bəlb\ *n* **1** : large underground plant bud **2** : rounded or pear-shaped object — **bul·bous** \-əs\ *adj*

bulge \'bəlj\ *n* : swelling projecting part ~ *vb* **bulged; bulg·ing** : swell out

bulk \'bəlk\ *n* **1** : magnitude **2** : indigestible food material

3 : large mass **4** : major portion ~ *vb* : cause to swell or bulge — **bulky** \-ē\ *adj*

bulk·head *n* : ship's partition

¹**bull** \'bùl\ *n* : large adult male animal (as of cattle) ~ *adj* : male

²**bull** *n* **1** : papal letter **2** : decree

bull·dog *n* : compact short-haired dog

bull·doze \-ˌdōz\ *vb* **1** : move or level with a tractor (**bull·doz·er**) having a broad blade **2** : force

bul·let \'bùlət\ *n* : missile to be shot from a gun — **bul·let-proof** *adj*

bul·le·tin \'bùlətən\ *n* **1** : brief public report **2** : periodical

bull·fight *n* : sport of taunting and killing bulls — **bull·fight-er** *n*

bull·frog *n* : large deep-voiced frog

bull·head·ed *adj* : stupidly stubborn

bul·lion \'bùlyən\ *n* : gold or silver esp. in bars

bull·ock \'bùlək\ *n* **1** : young bull **2** : steer

bull's–eye *n, pl* **bull's–eyes** : center of a target

bul·ly \'bùlē\ *n, pl* **-lies** : one who hurts or intimidates others ~ *vb* **-lied; -ly·ing** : act like a bully toward

bul·rush \'bùlˌrəsh\ *n* : tall coarse rush or sedge

bul·wark \'bùlˌwərk, -ˌwȯrk; 'bəlˌwərk\ *n* **1** : wall-like defense **2** : strong support or protection

bum \'bəm\ *vb* **-mm-** **1** : wander as a tramp **2** : get by begging ~ *n* : idle worthless person ~ *adj* : bad

bum·ble·bee \'bəmbəlˌbē\ *n* : large hairy bee

bump \'bəmp\ *vb* : strike or knock forcibly ~ *n* **1** : sudden blow **2** : small bulge or swelling — **bumpy** *adj*

¹**bum·per** \'bəmpər\ *adj* : unusually large

²**bump·er** \'bəmpər\ *n* : shock-absorbing bar at either end of a car

bump·kin \'bəmpkən\ *n* : awkward country person

bun \'bən\ *n* : sweet biscuit or roll

bunch \'bənch\ *n* : group ~ *vb* : form into a group — **bunchy** *adj*

bun·dle \'bənd³l\ *n* **1** : several items bunched together **2** : something wrapped for carrying **3** : large amount ~ *vb* **-dled; -dling** : gather into a bundle

bun·ga·low \'bəŋgəˌlō\ *n* : one-story house

bun·gle \'bəŋgəl\ *vb* **-gled; -gling** : do badly — **bungle** *n* — **bun·gler** *n*

bun·ion \'bənyən\ *n* : inflamed swelling of the first joint of the big toe

¹bunk \'bəŋk\ *n* : built-in bed that is often one of a tier ∼ *vb* : sleep

²bunk *n* : nonsense

bun·ker \-ər\ *n* **1** : storage compartment **2** : protective embankment

bun·kum, bun·combe \'bəŋkəm\ *n* : nonsense

bun·ny \'bənē\ *n, pl* **-nies** : rabbit

¹bun·ting \'bəntiŋ\ *n* : small finch

²bunting *n* : flag material

buoy \'büē, 'bȯi\ *n* : floating marker anchored in water ∼ *vb* **1** : keep afloat **2** : raise the spirits of — **buoy·an·cy** \'bȯiənsē, 'büyən-\ *n* — **buoy·ant** \-yənt\ *adj*

bur, burr \'bər\ *n* : rough or prickly covering of a fruit — **bur·ry** *adj*

bur·den \'bərdᵊn\ *n* **1** : something carried **2** : something oppressive **3** : cargo ∼ *vb* : load or oppress — **bur·den·some** \-səm\ *adj*

bur·dock \'bər‚däk\ *n* : tall coarse herb with prickly flower heads

bu·reau \'byu̇rō\ *n* **1** : chest of drawers **2** : administrative unit **3** : business office

bu·reau·cra·cy \byu̇'räkrəsē\ *n, pl* **-cies** **1** : body of government officials **2** : unwieldy administrative system — **bu·reau·crat** \'byu̇rə‚krat\ *n* — **bu·reau·crat·ic** \‚byu̇rə-'kratik\ *adj*

bur·geon \'bərjən\ *vb* : grow

bur·glary \'bərglərē\ *n, pl* **-glar·ies** : forcible entry into a building to steal — **bur·glar** \-glər\ *n* — **bur·glar·ize** \'bərglə‚rīz\ *vb*

bur·gle \'bərgəl\ *vb* **-gled; -gling** : commit burglary on or in

Bur·gun·dy \'bərgəndē\ *n, pl* **-dies** : kind of table wine

buri·al \'berēəl\ *n* : act of burying

bur·lap \'bər‚lap\ *n* : coarse fabric usu. of jute or hemp

bur·lesque \bər'lesk\ *n* **1** : witty or derisive imitation **2** : broadly humorous variety show ∼ *vb* **-lesqued; -lesqu·ing** : mock

bur·ly \'bərlē\ *adj* **-li·er; -est** : strongly and heavily built

burn \'bərn\ *vb* **burned** \'bərnd, 'bərnt\ *or* **burnt** \'bərnt\; **burn·ing** **1** : be on fire **2** : feel or look as if on fire **3** : alter or become altered by or as if by fire or heat

4 : cause or make by fire ～ *n* : injury or effect produced by burning — **burn·er** *n*

bur·nish \'bərnish\ *vb* : polish

burp \'bərp\ *n or vb* : belch

bur·ro \'bərō, 'bùr-\ *n, pl* **-os** : small donkey

bur·row \'bərō\ *n* : hole in the ground made by an animal ～ *vb* : make a burrow — **bur·row·er** *n*

bur·sar \'bərsər\ *n* : treasurer esp. of a college

bur·si·tis \bər'sītəs\ *n* : inflammation of a sac (**bur·sa** \'bərsə\) in a joint

burst \'bərst\ *vb* **burst** *or* **burst·ed; burst·ing** **1** : fly apart or into pieces **2** : enter or emerge suddenly ～ *n* : sudden outbreak or effort

bury \'berē\ *vb* **bur·ied; bury·ing** **1** : deposit in the earth **2** : hide

bus \'bəs\ *n, pl* **bus·es** *or* **bus·ses** : large motor-driven passenger vehicle ～ *vb* **bused** *or* **bussed; bus·ing** *or* **bus·sing** : travel or transport by bus

bus·boy *n* : waiter's helper

bush \'bùsh\ *n* **1** : shrub **2** : rough uncleared country **3** : a thick tuft or mat — **bushy** *adj*

bush·el \'bùshəl\ *n* : 4 pecks

bush·ing \'bùshiŋ\ *n* : metal lining used as a guide or bearing

busi·ness \'biznəs, -nəz\ *n* **1** : vocation **2** : commercial or industrial enterprise **3** : personal concerns — **busi·ness·man** \-ˌman\ *n* — **busi·ness·wom·an** \-ˌwùmən\ *n*

¹**bust** \'bəst\ *n* **1** : sculpture of the head and upper torso **2** : breasts of a woman

²**bust** *vb* **1** : burst or break **2** : tame ～ *n* **1** : punch **2** : failure

¹**bus·tle** \'bəsəl\ *vb* **-tled; -tling** : move or work briskly ～ *n* : energetic activity

²**bustle** *n* : pad or frame formerly worn under a woman's skirt

busy \'bizē\ *adj* **busi·er; -est** **1** : engaged in action **2** : being in use **3** : full of activity ～ *vb* **bus·ied; busy·ing** : make or keep busy — **busi·ly** *adv*

busy·body *n* : meddler

but \'bət\ *conj* **1** : if not for the fact **2** : that **3** : without the certainty that **4** : rather **5** : yet ～ *prep* : other than

butch·er \'bùchər\ *n* **1** : one who slaughters animals or dresses their flesh **2** : brutal killer **3** : bungler — **butcher** *vb* — **butch·ery** \-ərē\ *n*

but·ler \'bətlər\ *n* : chief male household servant

¹**butt** \'bət\ *vb* : strike with a butt ～ *n* : blow with the head or horns

²butt *n* **1 :** target **2 :** victim

³butt *vb* **:** join edge to edge

⁴butt *n* **:** large end or bottom

⁵butt *n* **:** large cask

butte \ˈbyüt\ *n* **:** isolated steep hill

but·ter \ˈbətər\ *n* **:** solid edible fat churned from cream **~** *vb* **:** spread with butter — **but·tery** *adj*

but·ter·cup *n* **:** yellow-flowered herb

but·ter·fat *n* **:** natural fat of milk and of butter

but·ter·fly *n* **:** insect with 4 broad wings

but·ter·milk *n* **:** liquid remaining after butter is churned

but·ter·nut *n* **:** edible nut of a tree related to the walnut or this tree

but·ter·scotch \-ˌskäch\ *n* **:** candy made from sugar, corn syrup, and water

but·tocks \ˈbətəks\ *n pl* **:** rear part of the hips

but·ton \ˈbətᵊn\ *n* **1 :** small knob for fastening clothing **2 :** buttonlike object **~** *vb* **:** fasten with buttons

but·ton·hole *n* **:** hole or slit for a button **~** *vb* **:** hold in talk

but·tress \ˈbətrəs\ *n* **1 :** projecting structure to support a wall **2 :** support — **buttress** *vb*

bux·om \ˈbəksəm\ *adj* **:** full-bosomed

buy \ˈbī\ *vb* **bought** \ˈbȯt\; **buy·ing :** purchase **~** *n* **:** bargain — **buy·er** *n*

buzz \ˈbəz\ *vb* **:** make a low humming sound **~** *n* **:** act or sound of buzzing

buz·zard \ˈbəzərd\ *n* **:** large bird of prey

buzz·er *n* **:** signaling device that buzzes

buzz·word \ˈbəzˌwərd\ *n* **:** word or phrase in vogue

by \ˈbī\ *prep* **1 :** near **2 :** through **3 :** beyond **4 :** throughout **5 :** no later than **~** *adv* **1 :** near **2 :** farther

by·gone \ˈbīˌgȯn\ *adj* **:** past — **by·gone** *n*

by·law, bye·law *n* **:** organization's rule

by–line *n* **:** writer's name on an article

by·pass *n* **:** alternate route **~** *vb* **:** go around

by–prod·uct *n* **:** product in addition to the main product

by·stand·er *n* **:** spectator

by·way \ˈbīˌwā\ *n* **:** side road

by·word *n* **:** proverb

C

c \'sē\ *n, pl* c's *or* cs \'sēz\ : 3d letter of the alphabet

cab \'kab\ *n* 1 : light closed horse-drawn carriage 2 : taxicab 3 : compartment for a driver — **cab·bie, cab·by** *n* — **cab·stand** *n*

ca·bal \kə'bal\ *n* : group of conspirators

ca·bana \kə'banə, -nyə\ *n* : shelter at a beach or pool

cab·a·ret \ˌkabə'rā\ *n* : nightclub

cab·bage \'kabij\ *n* : vegetable with a dense head of leaves

cab·in \-ən\ *n* 1 : private room on a ship 2 : small house 3 : airplane compartment

cab·i·net \'kabnət\ *n* 1 : display case or cupboard 2 : advisory council of a head of state — **cab·i·net·mak·er** *n* — **cab·i·net·mak·ing** *n* — **cab·i·net·work** *n*

ca·ble \'kābəl\ *n* 1 : strong rope, wire, or chain 2 : cablegram 3 : bundle of electrical wires ∼ *vb* -bled; -bling : send a cablegram to

ca·ble·gram \-ˌgram\ *n* : message sent by a submarine telegraph cable

ca·boose \kə'büs\ *n* : crew car on a train

ca·cao \kə'kaů, -'kāō\ *n, pl* cacaos : So. American tree whose seeds (**cacao beans**) yield cocoa and chocolate

cache \'kash\ *n* 1 : hiding place 2 : something hidden — **cache** *vb*

ca·chet \ka'shā\ *n* : prestige or a feature conferring this

cack·le \'kakəl\ *vb* -led; -ling : make a cry or laugh like the sound of a hen — **cackle** *n* — **cack·ler** *n*

ca·coph·o·ny \ka'käfənē\ *n, pl* -nies : harsh noise — **ca·coph·o·nous** \-nəs\ *adj*

cac·tus \'kaktəs\ *n, pl* cac·ti \-ˌtī\ *or* -tus·es : drought-resistant flowering plant with scales or prickles

cad \'kad\ *n* : ungentlemanly person — **cad·dish** \-ish\ *adj* — **cad·dish·ly** *adv*

ca·dav·er \kə'davər\ *n* : dead body — **ca·dav·er·ous** \-ərəs\ *adj*

cad·die, cad·dy \'kadē\ *n, pl* -dies : golfer's helper — **cad·die, caddy** *vb*

cad·dy \'kadē\ *n, pl* -dies : small tea chest

ca·dence \'kād³ns\ *n* : measure of a rhythmical flow — **ca·denced** \-³nst\ *adj*

ca·det \kə'det\ *n* : student in a military academy

cadge \'kaj\ *vb* **cadged; cadging** : beg — **cadg·er** *n*

cad·mi·um \'kadmēəm\ *n* : grayish metallic chemical element

cad·re \-rē\ *n* : nucleus of highly trained people

ca·fé \ka'fā, kə-\ *n* : restaurant

caf·e·te·ria \ˌkafə'tirēə\ *n* : self-service restaurant

caf·feine \ka'fēn, 'kaˌfēn\ *n* : stimulating alkaloid in coffee and tea

cage \'kāj\ *n* : box of wire or bars for confining an animal ~ *vb* **caged; cag·ing** : put or keep in a cage

ca·gey \-ē\ *adj* **-gi·er; -est** : shrewd — **ca·gi·ly** *adv* — **ca·gi·ness** *n*

cais·son \'kāˌsän, -sən\ *n* **1** : ammunition carriage **2** : watertight chamber for underwater construction

ca·jole \kə'jōl\ *vb* **-joled; -jol·ing** : persuade or coax — **ca·jol·ery** \-ərē\ *n*

cake \'kāk\ *n* **1** : food of baked or fried usu. sweet batter **2** : compacted mass ~ *vb* **caked; cak·ing** **1** : form into a cake **2** : encrust

cal·a·bash \'kaləˌbash\ *n* : gourd

cal·a·mine \'kaləˌmīn\ *n* : lotion of oxides of zinc and iron

ca·lam·i·ty \kə'lamətē\ *n, pl* **-ties** : disaster — **ca·lam·i·tous** \-ətəs\ *adj* — **ca·lam·i·tous·ly** *adv*

cal·ci·fy \'kalsəˌfī\ *vb* **-fied; -fy·ing** : harden — **cal·ci·fi·ca·tion** \ˌkalsəfə'kāshən\ *n*

cal·ci·um \'kalsēəm\ *n* : silver‑white soft metallic chemical element

cal·cu·late \'kalkyəˌlāt\ *vb* **-lat·ed; -lat·ing** **1** : determine by mathematical processes **2** : judge — **cal·cu·la·ble** \-ləbəl\ *adj* — **cal·cu·la·tion** \ˌkalkyə'lāshən\ *n* — **cal·cu·la·tor** \'kalkyəˌlātər\ *n*

cal·cu·lat·ing *adj* : shrewd

cal·cu·lus \'kalkyələs\ *n, pl* **-li** \-ˌlī\ : higher mathematics dealing with rates of change

cal·dron *var of* CAULDRON

cal·en·dar \'kaləndər\ *n* : list of days, weeks, and months

¹calf \'kaf, 'kȧf\ *n, pl* **calves** \'kavz, 'kȧvz\ : young cow or related mammal — **calfskin** *n*

²calf *n, pl* **calves** : back part of the leg below the knee

cal·i·ber, cal·i·bre \'kaləbər\ *n* **1** : diameter of a bullet or shell or of a gun bore **2** : degree of mental or moral excellence

cal·i·brate \\'kalə₁brāt\ *vb* **-brat·ed; -brat·ing** : adjust precisely — **cal·i·bra·tion** \₁kalə'brāshən\ *n*

cal·i·co \\'kali₁kō\ *n, pl* **-coes** *or* **-cos** **1** : printed cotton fabric **2** : animal with fur having patches of different colors

cal·i·pers \\'kaləpərz\ *n* : measuring instrument with two adjustable legs

ca·liph \\'kāləf, 'kal-\ *n* : title of head of Islam — **ca·liph·ate** \-₁āt, -ət\ *n*

cal·is·then·ics \₁kaləs'theniks\ *n sing or pl* : stretching and jumping exercises — **cal·is·then·ic** *adj*

calk \\'kȯk\ *var of* CAULK

call \\'kȯl\ *vb* **1** : shout **2** : summon **3** : demand **4** : telephone **5** : make a visit **6** : name — **call** *n* — **call·er** *n* — **call down** *vb* : reprimand — **call off** *vb* : cancel

call·ing *n* : vocation

cal·li·ope \kə'līə₁pē, 'kalē₁ōp\ *n* : musical instrument of steam whistles

cal·lous \\'kaləs\ *adj* **1** : thickened and hardened **2** : unfeeling ~ *vb* : make callous — **cal·los·i·ty** \ka'läsətē\ *n* — **cal·lous·ly** *adv* — **cal·lous·ness** *n*

cal·low \\'kalō\ *adj* : inexperienced or innocent — **cal·low·ness** *n*

cal·lus \\'kaləs\ *n* : callous area on skin or bark ~ *vb* : form a callus

call–waiting *n* : telephone service by which during a call in progress an incoming call is signaled

calm \\'käm, 'kälm\ *n* **1** : period or condition of peacefulness or stillness ~ *adj* : still or tranquil ~ *vb* : make calm — **calm·ly** *adv* — **calm·ness** *n*

ca·lor·ic \kə'lȯrik\ *adj* : relating to heat or calories

cal·o·rie \\'kalərē\ *n* : unit for measuring heat and energy value of food

ca·lum·ni·ate \kə'ləmnē₁āt\ *vb* **-at·ed; -at·ing** : slander — **ca·lum·ni·a·tion** \-₁ləmnē-'āshən\ *n*

cal·um·ny \\'kaləmnē\ *n, pl* **-nies** : false and malicious charge — **ca·lum·ni·ous** \kə-'ləmnēəs\ *adj*

calve \\'kav, 'kȧv\ *vb* **calved; calv·ing** : give birth to a calf

calves *pl of* CALF

ca·lyp·so \kə'lipsō\ *n, pl* **-sos** : West Indian style of music

ca·lyx \\'kāliks, 'kal-\ *n, pl* **-lyx·es** *or* **-ly·ces** \-lə₁sēz\ : sepals of a flower

cam \'kam\ *n* : machine part that slides or rotates irregularly to transmit linear motion

ca·ma·ra·de·rie \ˌkäm'rädərē, ˌkam-, -mə'-, -'rad-\ *n* : fellowship

cam·bric \'kāmbrik\ *n* : fine thin linen or cotton fabric

came *past of* COME

cam·el \'kaməl\ *n* : large hoofed mammal of desert areas

ca·mel·lia \kə'mēlyə\ *n* : shrub or tree grown for its showy roselike flowers or the flower itself

cam·eo \'kamē,ō\ *n, pl* **-eos** : gem carved in relief

cam·era \'kamrə\ *n* : box with a lens for taking pictures — **cam·era·man** \-ˌman, -mən\ *n*

cam·ou·flage \'kamə,fläzh, -ˌfläj\ *vb* : hide by disguising — **camouflage** *n*

camp \'kamp\ *n* **1** : place to stay temporarily esp. in a tent **2** : group living in a camp ∼ *vb* : make or live in a camp — **camp·er** *n* — **camp·ground** *n* — **camp·site** *n*

cam·paign \kam'pān\ *n* : series of military operations or of activities meant to gain a result — **campaign** *vb*

cam·pa·ni·le \ˌkampə'nēlē, -'nēl\ *n, pl* **-ni·les** *or* **-ni·li** \-'nēlē\ : bell tower

cam·phor \'kamfər\ *n* : gummy volatile aromatic compound from an evergreen tree (**cam·phor tree**)

cam·pus \'kampəs\ *n* : grounds and buildings of a college or school

¹can \kən, 'kan\ *vb, past* **could** \kəd, 'kud\; *pres sing & pl* **can** **1** : be able to **2** : be permitted to by conscience or feeling **3** : have permission or liberty to

²can \'kan\ *n* : metal container ∼ *vb* **-nn-** : preserve by sealing in airtight cans or jars — **can·ner** *n* — **can·nery** \-ərē\ *n*

ca·nal \kə'nal\ *n* **1** : tubular passage in the body **2** : channel filled with water

can·a·pé \'kanəpē, -ˌpā\ *n* : appetizer

ca·nard \kə'närd\ *n* : false report

ca·nary \-'nerē\ *n, pl* **-nar·ies** : yellow or greenish finch often kept as a pet

can·cel \'kansəl\ *vb* **-celed** *or* **-celled; -cel·ing** *or* **-cel·ling** **1** : cross out **2** : destroy, neutralize, or match the force or effect of — **cancel** *n* — **can·cel·la·tion** \ˌkansə'lāshən\ *n* — **can·cel·er, can·cel·ler** *n*

can·cer \'kansər\ *n* **1** : malignant tumor that tends to spread **2** : slowly destructive evil — **can·cer·ous** \-sərəs\ *adj* — **can·cer·ous·ly** *adv*

can·de·la·bra \ˌkandə'läbrə, -'lab-\ *n* : candelabrum

can·de·la·brum \-rəm\ *n, pl* **-bra** \-rə\ : ornamental branched candlestick

can·did \'kandəd\ *adj* **1** : frank **2** : unposed — **can·did·ly** *adv* — **can·did·ness** *n*

can·di·date \'kandə,dāt, -dət\ *n* : one who seeks an office or membership — **can·di·da·cy** \-dəsē\ *n*

can·dle \'kand°l\ *n* : tallow or wax molded around a wick and burned to give light — **can·dle·light** *n* — **can·dle·stick** *n*

can·dor \'kandər\ *n* : frankness

can·dy \-dē\ *n, pl* **-dies** : food made from sugar ~ *vb* **-died; -dy·ing** : encrust in sugar

cane \'kān\ *n* **1** : slender plant stem **2** : a tall woody grass or reed **3** : stick for walking or beating ~ *vb* **caned; can·ing** **1** : beat with a cane **2** : weave or make with cane — **can·er** *n*

ca·nine \'kā,nīn\ *adj* : relating to dogs ~ *n* **1** : pointed tooth next to the incisors **2** : dog

can·is·ter \'kanəstər\ *n* : cylindrical container

can·ker \'kaŋkər\ *n* : mouth ulcer — **can·ker·ous** \-kərəs\ *adj*

can·na·bis \'kanəbəs\ *n* : preparation derived from hemp

can·ni·bal \'kanəbəl\ *n* : human or animal that eats its own kind — **can·ni·bal·ism** \-bə,lizəm\ *n* — **can·ni·bal·is·tic** \ˌkanəbə'listik\ *adj*

can·ni·bal·ize \'kanəbə,līz\ *vb* **-ized; -iz·ing** **1** : take usable parts from **2** : practice cannibalism

can·non \'kanən\ *n, pl* **-nons** *or* **-non** : large heavy gun — **can·non·ball** *n* — **can·non·eer** \ˌkanə'nir\ *n*

can·non·ade \ˌkanə'nād\ *n* : heavy artillery fire ~ *vb* **-ad·ed; -ad·ing** : bombard

can·not \'kan,ät; kə'nät\ : can not — **cannot but** : be bound to

can·ny \'kanē\ *adj* **-ni·er; -est** : shrewd — **can·ni·ly** *adv* — **can·ni·ness** *n*

ca·noe \kə'nü\ *n* : narrow sharp-ended boat propelled by paddles — **canoe** *vb* — **ca·noe·ist** *n*

¹**can·on** \'kanən\ *n* **1** : regulation governing a church **2** : authoritative list **3** : an accepted principle

²**canon** *n* : clergy member in a cathedral

ca·non·i·cal \kə'nänikəl\ *adj* **1** : relating to or conforming to a canon **2** : orthodox — **ca·non·i·cal·ly** *adv*

can·on·ize \'kanə͵nīz\ *vb* **-ized** \-͵nīzd\; **-iz·ing** : recognize as a saint — **can·on·iza·tion** \͵kanənə'zāshən\ *n*

can·o·py \'kanəpē\ *n, pl* **-pies** : overhanging cover — **canopy** *vb*

¹cant \'kant\ *n* **1** : slanting surface **2** : slant ∼ *vb* **1** : tip up **2** : lean to one side

²cant *vb* : talk hypocritically ∼ *n* **1** : jargon **2** : insincere talk

can't \'kant, 'kȧnt\ : can not

can·ta·loupe \'kant°l͵ōp\ *n* : muskmelon with orange flesh

can·tan·ker·ous \kan'taŋkərəs\ *adj* : hard to deal with — **can·tan·ker·ous·ly** *adv* — **can·tan·ker·ous·ness** *n*

can·ta·ta \kən'tätə\ *n* : choral work

can·teen \kan'tēn\ *n* **1** : place of recreation for service personnel **2** : water container

can·ter \'kantər\ *n* : slow gallop — **can·ter** *vb*

can·ti·cle \'kantikəl\ *n* : liturgical song

can·ti·le·ver \'kant°l͵ēvər, -͵ev-\ *n* : beam or structure supported only at one end

can·to \'kan͵tō\ *n, pl* **-tos** : major division of a long poem

can·tor \'kantər\ *n* : synagogue official who sings liturgical music

can·vas \'kanvəs\ *n* **1** : strong cloth orig. used for making tents and sails **2** : set of sails **3** : oil painting

can·vass \-vəs\ *vb* : solicit votes, orders, or opinions from ∼ *n* : act of canvassing — **can·vass·er** *n*

can·yon \'kanyən\ *n* : deep valley with steep sides

cap \'kap\ *n* **1** : covering for the head **2** : top or cover like a cap **3** : upper limit ∼ *vb* **-pp-** **1** : provide or protect with a cap **2** : climax — **cap·ful** \-͵fu̇l\ *n*

ca·pa·ble \'kāpəbəl\ *adj* : able to do something — **ca·pa·bil·i·ty** \͵kāpə'bilətē\ *n* — **ca·pa·bly** \'kāpəblē\ *adv*

ca·pa·cious \kə'pāshəs\ *adj* : able to contain much

ca·pac·i·tance \kə'pasətəns\ *n* : ability to store electrical energy

ca·pac·i·tor \-sətər\ *n* : device for storing electrical energy

ca·pac·i·ty \-sətē\ *n, pl* **-ties** **1** : ability to contain **2** : volume **3** : ability **4** : role or job ∼ *adj* : equaling maximum capacity

¹cape \'kāp\ *n* : point of land jutting out into water

²cape *n* : garment that drapes over the shoulders

¹ca·per \'kāpər\ *n* : flower bud of a shrub pickled for use as a relish

²caper *vb* : leap or prance about ~ *n* **1** : frolicsome leap **2** : escapade

cap·il·lary \'kapə,lerē\ *adj* **1** : resembling a hair **2** : having a very small bore ~ *n, pl* **-lar·ies** : tiny thin-walled blood vessel

¹cap·i·tal \'kapət³l\ *adj* **1** : punishable by death **2** : being in the series A, B, C rather than a, b, c **3** : relating to capital **4** : excellent ~ *n* **1** : capital letter **2** : seat of government **3** : wealth **4** : total face value of a company's stock **5** : investors as a group

²capital *n* : top part of a column

cap·i·tal·ism \-,izəm\ *n* : economic system of private ownership of capital

cap·i·tal·ist \-ist\ *n* **1** : person with capital invested in business **2** : believer in capitalism ~ *adj* **1** : owning capital **2** : practicing, advocating, or marked by capitalism — **cap·i·tal·is·tic** \,kapət³l'is-tik\ *adj*

cap·i·tal·ize \-,īz\ *vb* **-ized; -iz·ing 1** : write or print with a capital letter **2** : use as capital **3** : supply capital for **4** : turn something to advantage — **cap·i·tal·iza·tion** \,kapət³lə-'zāshən\ *n*

cap·i·tol \'kapət³l\ *n* : building in which a legislature sits

ca·pit·u·late \kə'pichə,lāt\ *vb* **-lat·ed; -lat·ing** : surrender — **ca·pit·u·la·tion** \-,pichə-'lāshən\ *n*

ca·pon \'kā,pän, -pən\ *n* : castrated male chicken

ca·price \kə'prēs\ *n* : whim — **ca·pri·cious** \-'prishəs\ *adj* — **ca·pri·cious·ly** *adv* — **ca·pri·cious·ness** *n*

cap·size \'kap,sīz, kap'sīz\ *vb* **-sized; -siz·ing** : overturn

cap·stan \'kapstən, -,stan\ *n* : upright winch

cap·sule \'kapsəl, -sül\ *n* **1** : enveloping cover (as for medicine) **2** : small pressurized compartment for astronauts ~ *adj* : very brief or compact — **cap·su·lar** \-sələr\ *adj* — **cap·su·lat·ed** \-sə-,lātəd\ *adj*

cap·tain \'kaptən\ *n* **1** : commander of a body of troops **2** : officer in charge of a ship **3** : commissioned officer in the navy ranking next below a rear admiral or a commodore **4** : commissioned officer (as in the army) ranking next below a major **5** : leader ~ *vb* : be captain of — **cap·tain·cy** *n*

cap·tion \'kapshən\ *n* **1** : title **2** : explanation with an illustration — **caption** *vb*

cap·tious \'kapshəs\ *adj* : tending to find fault — **cap·tious·ly** *adv*

cap·ti·vate \'kaptə‚vāt\ *vb* **-vat·ed; -vat·ing** : attract and charm — **cap·ti·va·tion** \‚kaptə-'vāshən\ *n* — **cap·ti·va·tor** \'kaptə‚vātər\ *n*

cap·tive \-tiv\ *adj* **1** : made prisoner **2** : confined or under control — **captive** *n* — **cap·tiv·i·ty** \kap'tivətē\ *n*

cap·tor \'kaptər\ *n* : one that captures

cap·ture \-chər\ *n* : seizure by force or trickery ～ *vb* **-tured; -tur·ing** : take captive

car \'kär\ *n* **1** : vehicle moved on wheels **2** : cage of an elevator

ca·rafe \kə'raf, -'räf\ *n* : decanter

car·a·mel \'karəməl, 'kärməl\ *n* **1** : burnt sugar used for flavoring and coloring **2** : firm chewy candy

¹carat *var of* **KARAT**

²car·at \'karət\ *n* : unit of weight for precious stones

car·a·van \'karə‚van\ *n* : travelers journeying together (as in a line)

car·a·way \'karə‚wā\ *n* : aromatic herb with seeds used in seasoning

car·bine \'kär‚bēn, -‚bīn\ *n* : short-barreled rifle

car·bo·hy·drate \‚kärbō'hī-‚drāt, -drət\ *n* : compound of carbon, hydrogen, and oxygen

car·bon \'kärbən\ *n* **1** : chemical element occurring in nature esp. as diamond and graphite **2** : piece of carbon paper or a copy made with it

¹car·bon·ate \'kärbə‚nāt, -nət\ *n* : salt or ester of a carbon-containing acid

²car·bon·ate \-‚nāt\ *vb* **-at·ed; -at·ing** : impregnate with carbon dioxide — **car·bon·ation** \‚kärbə'nāshən\ *n*

carbon paper *n* : thin paper coated with a pigment for making copies

car·bun·cle \'kär‚bəŋkəl\ *n* : painful inflammation of the skin and underlying tissue

car·bu·re·tor \'kärbə‚rātər, -byə-\ *n* : device for mixing fuel and air

car·cass \'kärkəs\ *n* : dead body

car·cin·o·gen \kär'sinəjən\ *n* : agent causing cancer — **car·ci·no·gen·ic** \‚kärsᵊnō'jenik\ *adj*

car·ci·no·ma \‚kärsᵊn'ōmə\ *n, pl* **-mas** *or* **-ma·ta** \-mətə\ : malignant tumor

¹card \'kärd\ *vb* : comb (fibers) before spinning ～ *n*

: device for carding fibers — **card·er** *n*

²**card** *n* **1** : playing card **2** *pl* : game played with playing cards **3** : small flat piece of paper

card·board *n* : stiff material like paper

car·di·ac \'kärdē,ak\ *adj* : relating to the heart

car·di·gan \'kärdigən\ *n* : sweater with an opening in the front

¹**car·di·nal** \'kärdᵊnəl\ *n* **1** : official of the Roman Catholic Church **2** : bright red songbird

²**cardinal** *adj* : of basic importance

cardinal number *n* : number (as 1, 82, 357) used in counting

car·di·ol·o·gy \,kärdē'äləjē\ *n* : study of the heart — **car·di·ol·o·gist** \-jist\ *n*

car·dio·vas·cu·lar \-ō'vas-kyələr\ *adj* : relating to the heart and blood vessels

care \'ker\ *n* **1** : anxiety **2** : watchful attention **3** : supervision ~ *vb* **cared; car·ing** **1** : feel anxiety or concern **2** : like **3** : provide care — **care·free** *adj* — **care·ful** \-fəl\ *adj* — **care·ful·ly** *adv* — **care·ful·ness** *n* — **care·giv·er** \-,givər\ *n* — **care·less** *adj* — **care·less·ly** *adv* — **care·less·ness** *n*

ca·reen \kə'rēn\ *vb* **1** : sway from side to side **2** : career

ca·reer \kə'rir\ *n* : vocation ~ *vb* : go at top speed

ca·ress \kə'res\ *n* : tender touch ~ *vb* : touch lovingly or tenderly

car·et \'karət\ *n* : mark ^ showing where something is to be inserted

care·tak·er *n* : one in charge for another or temporarily

car·go \'kärgō\ *n, pl* **-goes** *or* **-gos** : transported goods

car·i·bou \'karə,bü\ *n, pl* **-bou** *or* **-bous** : large No. American deer

car·i·ca·ture \'karikə,chur\ *n* : distorted representation for humor or ridicule — **caricature** *vb* — **car·i·ca·tur·ist** \-ist\ *n*

car·ies \'karēz\ *n, pl* **caries** : tooth decay

car·il·lon \'karə,län\ *n* : set of tuned bells

car·jack·ing \'kär,jakiŋ\ *n* : theft of an automobile by force or intimidation — **car·jack·er** *n*

car·mine \'kärmən, -,mīn\ *n* : vivid red

car·nage \'kärnij\ *n* : slaughter

car·nal \'kärnᵊl\ *adj* : sensual — **car·nal·i·ty** \kär'nalətē\ *n* — **car·nal·ly** *adv*

car·na·tion \kär'nāshən\ *n* : showy flower

car·ni·val \'kärnəvəl\ *n*   **1** : festival **2** : traveling enterprise offering amusements

car·ni·vore \-ˌvōr\ *n* : flesh‐eating animal — **car·niv·o·rous** \kär'nivərəs\ *adj* — **car·niv·o·rous·ly** *adv* — **car·niv·o·rous·ness** *n*

car·ol \'karəl\ *n* : song of joy — **carol** *vb* — **car·ol·er, car·ol·ler** \-ələr\ *n*

car·om \-əm\ *n or vb* : rebound

ca·rouse \kə'rau̇z\ *vb* **-roused; -rous·ing** : drink and be boisterous — **ca·rouse** *n* — **ca·rous·er** *n*

car·ou·sel, car·rou·sel \ˌkarə-'sel, 'karəˌ-\ *n* : merry-go‐round

¹carp \'kärp\ *vb* : find fault

²carp *n, pl* **carp** *or* **carps** : freshwater fish

car·pel \'kärpəl\ *n* : modified leaf forming part of the ovary of a flower

car·pen·ter \'kärpəntər\ *n* : one who builds with wood — **carpenter** *vb* — **car·pen·try** \-trē\ *n*

car·pet \'kärpət\ *n* : fabric floor covering ∼ *vb* : cover with a carpet — **car·pet·ing** \-iŋ\ *n*

car·port *n* : open-sided automobile shelter

car·riage \'karij\ *n* **1** : conveyance **2** : manner of holding oneself **3** : wheeled vehicle

car·ri·on \'karēən\ *n* : dead and decaying flesh

car·rot \'karət\ *n* : orange root vegetable

car·ry \'karē\ *vb* **-ried; -ry·ing** **1** : move while supporting **2** : hold (oneself) in a specified way **3** : support **4** : keep in stock **5** : reach to a distance **6** : win — **car·ri·er** \-ēər\ *n* — **carry on** *vb* **1** : conduct **2** : behave excitedly — **carry out** *vb* : put into effect

cart \'kärt\ *n* : wheeled vehicle ∼ *vb* : carry in a cart — **cart·age** \-ij\ *n* — **cart·er** *n*

car·tel \kär'tel\ *n* : business combination designed to limit competition

car·ti·lage \'kärtᵊlij\ *n* : elastic skeletal tissue — **car·ti·lag·i·nous** \ˌkärtᵊl'ajənəs\ *adj*

car·tog·ra·phy \kär'tägrəfē\ *n* : making of maps — **car·tog·ra·pher** \-fər\ *n*

car·ton \'kärtᵊn\ *n* : cardboard box

car·toon \kär'tün\ *n* **1** : humorous drawing **2** : comic strip — **cartoon** *vb* — **car·toon·ist** *n*

car·tridge \'kärtrij\ *n* **1** : tube containing powder and a bullet or shot for a firearm **2**

: container of material for insertion into an apparatus

carve \\'kärv\\ *vb* **carved; carv·ing 1** : cut with care **2** : cut into pieces or slices — **carv·er** *n*

cas·cade \\kas'kād\\ *n* : small steep waterfall ∼ *vb* **-cad·ed; -cad·ing** : fall in a cascade

¹**case** \\'kās\\ *n* **1** : particular instance **2** : convincing argument **3** : inflectional form esp. of a noun or pronoun **4** : fact **5** : lawsuit **6** : instance of disease — **in case** : as a precaution — **in case of** : in the event of

²**case** *n* **1** : box **2** : outer covering ∼ *vb* **cased; cas·ing 1** : enclose **2** : inspect

case·ment \\-mənt\\ *n* : window that opens like a door

cash \\'kash\\ *n* **1** : ready money **2** : money paid at the time of purchase ∼ *vb* : give or get cash for

ca·shew \\'kashü, kə'shü\\ *n* : tropical American tree or its nut

¹**ca·shier** \\ka'shir\\ *vb* : dismiss in disgrace

²**cash·ier** *n* : person who receives and records payments

cash·mere \\'kazh,mir, 'kash-\\ *n* : fine goat's wool or a fabric of this

ca·si·no \\kə'sēnō\\ *n, pl* **-nos** : place for gambling

cask \\'kask\\ *n* : barrel-shaped container for liquids

cas·ket \\'kaskət\\ *n* : coffin

cas·se·role \\'kasə,rōl\\ *n* : baking dish or the food cooked in this

cas·sette \\kə'set, ka-\\ *n* : case containing magnetic tape

cas·sock \\'kasək\\ *n* : long clerical garment

cast \\'kast\\ *vb* **cast; cast·ing 1** : throw **2** : deposit (a ballot) **3** : assign parts in a play **4** : mold ∼ *n* **1** : throw **2** : appearance **3** : rigid surgical dressing **4** : actors in a play

cas·ta·nets \\,kastə'nets\\ *n pl* : shells clicked together in the hand

cast·away \\'kastə,wā\\ *n* : survivor of a shipwreck — **castaway** *adj*

caste \\'kast\\ *n* : social class or rank

cast·er \\'kastər\\ *n* : small wheel on furniture

cas·ti·gate \\'kastə,gāt\\ *vb* **-gat·ed; -gat·ing** : chastise severely — **cas·ti·ga·tion** \\,kastə'gāshən\\ *n* — **cas·ti·ga·tor** \\'kastə,gātər\\ *n*

cast iron *n* : hard brittle alloy of iron

cas·tle \\'kasəl\\ *n* : fortified building

cast–off *adj* : thrown away — **cast·off** *n*

cas·trate \'kas₁trāt\ *vb* **-trat·ed; -trat·ing** : remove the testes of — **cas·tra·tion** \ka-'strāshən\ *n*

ca·su·al \'kazhəwəl\ *adj* **1** : happening by chance **2** : showing little concern **3** : informal — **ca·su·al·ly** \-ē\ *adv* — **ca·su·al·ness** *n*

ca·su·al·ty \-tē\ *n, pl* **-ties** **1** : serious or fatal accident **2** : one injured, lost, or destroyed

ca·su·ist·ry \'kazhəwəstrē\ *n, pl* **-ries** : rationalization — **ca·su·ist** \-wist\ *n*

cat \'kat\ *n* **1** : small domestic mammal **2** : related animal (as a lion) — **cat·like** *adj*

cat·a·clysm \'katə₁klizəm\ *n* : violent change — **cat·a·clys·mal** \₁katə'klizməl\, **cat·a·clys·mic** \-'klizmik\ *adj*

cat·a·comb \'katə₁kōm\ *n* : underground burial place

cat·a·log, cat·a·logue \'katᵊl₁ȯg\ *n* **1** : list **2** : book containing a description of items ~ *vb* **-loged** *or* **-logued; -log·ing** *or* **-logu·ing** **1** : make a catalog of **2** : enter in a catalog — **cat·a·log·er, cat·a·logu·er** *n*

ca·tal·pa \kə'talpə\ *n* : tree with broad leaves and long pods

ca·tal·y·sis \kə'taləsəs\ *n, pl* **-y·ses** \-₁sēz\ : increase in the rate of chemical reaction caused by a substance (**cat·a·lyst** \'katᵊlist\) that is itself unchanged — **cat·a·lyt·ic** \₁katᵊl'itik\ *adj*

cat·a·ma·ran \katəmə'ran\ *n* : boat with twin hulls

cat·a·mount \'katə₁maůnt\ *n* : cougar

cat·a·pult \'katə₁pəlt, -₁půlt\ *n* : device for hurling or launching — **catapult** *vb*

cat·a·ract \'katə₁rakt\ *n* **1** : large waterfall **2** : cloudiness of the lens of the eye

ca·tarrh \kə'tär\ *n* : inflammation of the nose and throat

ca·tas·tro·phe \kə'tastrə₁fē\ *n* **1** : great disaster or misfortune **2** : utter failure — **cat·a·stroph·ic** \₁katə'sträfik\ *adj* — **cat·a·stroph·i·cal·ly** \-iklē\ *adv*

cat·bird *n* : American songbird

cat·call *n* : noise of disapproval

catch \'kach, 'kech\ *vb* **caught** \'kȯt\; **catch·ing** **1** : capture esp. after pursuit **2** : trap **3** : detect esp. by surprise **4** : grasp **5** : get entangled **6** : become affected with or by **7** : seize and hold firmly ~ *n* **1** : act of catching **2** : something caught **3** : something that fastens **4** : hidden difficulty — **catch·er** *n*

catch·ing \-iŋ\ *adj* : infectious

catch·up \'kechəp, 'kach-; 'katsəp\ *var of* **KETCHUP**

catch·word *n* : slogan

catchy \-ē\ *adj* **catch·i·er; -est** : likely to catch interest

cat·e·chism \'katə,kizəm\ *n* : set of questions and answers esp. to teach religious doctrine

cat·e·gor·i·cal \,katə'gȯrikəl\ *adj* : absolute — **cat·e·gor·i·cal·ly** \-klē\ *adv*

cat·e·go·ry \'katə,gōrē\ *n, pl* **-ries** : group or class — **cat·e·go·ri·za·tion** \,katigərə'zā-shən\ *n* — **cat·e·go·rize** \'katigə,rīz\ *vb*

ca·ter \'kātər\ *vb* **1** : provide food for **2** : supply what is wanted — **ca·ter·er** *n*

cat·er·cor·ner \,katē'kȯrnər, ,katə-, ,kitē-\, **cat·er–cornered** *adv or adj* : in a diagonal position

cat·er·pil·lar \'katər,pilər\ *n* : butterfly or moth larva

cat·er·waul \'katər,wȯl\ *vb* : make the harsh cry of a cat — **caterwaul** *n*

cat·fish *n* : big-headed fish with feelers about the mouth

cat·gut *n* : tough cord made usu. from sheep intestines

ca·thar·sis \kə'thärsəs\ *n, pl* **ca·thar·ses** \-,sēz\ : a purging — **ca·thar·tic** \kə'thärtik\ *adj or n*

ca·the·dral \-'thēdrəl\ *n* : principal church of a diocese

cath·e·ter \'kathətər\ *n* : tube for insertion into a body cavity

cath·ode \'kath,ōd\ *n* **1** : negative electrode **2** : positive battery terminal — **ca·thod·ic** \ka'thädik\ *adj*

cath·o·lic \'kathəlik\ *adj* **1** : universal **2** *cap* : relating to Roman Catholics

Cath·o·lic *n* : member of the Roman Catholic Church — **Ca·thol·i·cism** \kə'thälə,sizəm\ *n*

cat·kin \'katkən\ *n* : long dense flower cluster

cat·nap *n* : short light nap — **catnap** *vb*

cat·nip \-,nip\ *n* : aromatic mint relished by cats

cat's–paw *n, pl* **cat's–paws** : person used as if a tool

cat·sup \'kechəp, 'kach-; 'katsəp\ *var of* KETCHUP

cat·tail *n* : marsh herb with furry brown spikes

cat·tle \'katᵊl\ *n pl* : domestic bovines — **cat·tle·man** \-mən, -,man\ *n*

cat·ty \'katē\ *adj* **-ti·er; -est** : mean or spiteful — **cat·ti·ly** *adv* — **cat·ti·ness** *n*

cat·walk *n* : high narrow walk

Cau·ca·sian \kȯ'kāzhən\ *adj* : relating to the white race — **Caucasian** *n*

cau·cus \'kȯkəs\ *n* : political meeting — **caucus** *vb*

caught *past of* CATCH

cauldron \'kȯldrən\ *n* : large kettle

cau·li·flow·er \'kȯli‚flau̇ər, 'käl-\ *n* : vegetable having a compact head of usu. white undeveloped flowers

caulk \'kȯk\ *vb* : make seams watertight — **caulk** *n* — **caulk·er** *n*

caus·al \'kȯzəl\ *adj* : relating to or being a cause — **cau·sal·i·ty** \kȯ'zalətē\ *n* — **caus·al·ly** \'kȯzəlē\ *adv*

cause \'kȯz\ *n* **1** : something that brings about a result **2** : reason **3** : lawsuit **4** : principle or movement to support ∼ *vb* **caused; caus·ing** : be the cause of — **cau·sa·tion** \kȯ'zāshən\ *n* — **caus·ative** \'kȯzətiv\ *adj* — **cause·less** *adj* — **caus·er** *n*

cause·way *n* : raised road esp. over water

caus·tic \'kȯstik\ *adj* **1** : corrosive **2** : sharp or biting — **caustic** *n*

cau·ter·ize \'kȯtə‚rīz\ *vb* **-ized; -iz·ing** : burn to prevent infection or bleeding — **cau·ter·i·za·tion** \‚kȯtərə'zāshən\ *n*

cau·tion \'kȯshən\ *n* **1** : warning **2** : care or prudence ∼ *vb* : warn — **cau·tion·ary** \-shə‚nerē\ *adj*

cau·tious \'kȯshəs\ *adj* : taking caution — **cau·tious·ly** *adv* — **cau·tious·ness** *n*

cav·al·cade \‚kavəl'kād, 'kavəl‚-\ *n* **1** : procession on horseback **2** : series

cav·a·lier \‚kavə'lir\ *n* : mounted soldier ∼ *adj* : disdainful or arrogant — **cav·a·lier·ly** *adv*

cav·al·ry \'kavəlrē\ *n, pl* **-ries** : troops on horseback or in vehicles — **cav·al·ry·man** \-mən, -‚man\ *n*

cave \'kāv\ *n* : natural underground chamber — **cave in** *vb* : collapse

cav·ern \'kavərn\ *n* : large cave — **cav·ern·ous** *adj* — **cav·ern·ous·ly** *adv*

cav·i·ar, cav·i·are \'kavē‚är, 'käv-\ *n* : salted fish roe

cav·il \'kavəl\ *vb* **-iled** *or* **-illed; -il·ing** *or* **-il·ling** : raise trivial objections — **cavil** *n* — **cav·il·er, cav·il·ler** *n*

cav·i·ty \'kavətē\ *n, pl* **-ties** **1** : unfilled place within a mass **2** : decay in a tooth

ca·vort \kə'vȯrt\ *vb* : prance or caper

caw \'kȯ\ *vb* : utter the harsh call of the crow — **caw** *n*

cay·enne pepper \‚kī'en-, ‚kā-\ *n* : ground dried fruits of a hot pepper

CD \‚sē'dē\ *n* : compact disc

cease \'sēs\ *vb* **ceased; ceas·ing** : stop

cease·less \-ləs\ *adj* : continuous

ce·dar \'sēdər\ *n* : cone-bearing tree with fragrant durable wood

cede \'sēd\ *vb* **ced·ed; ced·ing** : surrender — **ced·er** *n*

ceil·ing \'sēliŋ\ *n* **1** : overhead surface of a room **2** : upper limit

cel·e·brate \'selə,brāt\ *vb* **-brat·ed; -brat·ing** **1** : perform with appropriate rites **2** : honor with ceremonies **3** : extol — **cel·e·brant** \-brənt\ *n* — **cel·e·bra·tion** \,selə-'brāshən\ *n* — **cel·e·bra·tor** \'selə,brātər\ *n*

cel·e·brat·ed \-əd\ *adj* : renowned

ce·leb·ri·ty \sə'lebrətē\ *n, pl* **-ties** **1** : renown **2** : well=known person

ce·ler·i·ty \sə'lerətē\ *n* : speed

cel·ery \'selərē\ *n, pl* **-er·ies** : herb grown for crisp edible stalks

ce·les·ta \sə'lestə\ **ce·leste** \sə'lest\ *n* : keyboard musical instrument

ce·les·tial \sə'leschəl\ *adj* **1** : relating to the sky **2** : heavenly

cel·i·ba·cy \'seləbəsē\ *n* **1** : state of being unmarried **2** : abstention from sexual intercourse — **cel·i·bate** \'seləbət\ *n or adj*

cell \'sel\ *n* **1** : small room **2** : tiny mass of protoplasm that forms the fundamental unit of living matter **3** : container holding an electrolyte for generating electricity — **celled** *adj*

cel·lar \'selər\ *n* : room or area below ground

cel·lo \'chelō\ *n, pl* **-los** : bass member of the violin family — **cel·list** \-ist\ *n*

cel·lo·phane \'selə,fān\ *n* : thin transparent cellulose wrapping

cell phone *n* : portable cordless telephone for use in a system of radio transmitters

cel·lu·lar \'selyələr\ *adj* : relating to or consisting of cells

cel·lu·lose \'selyə,lōs\ *n* : complex plant carbohydrate

Cel·sius \'selsēəs\ *adj* : relating to a thermometer scale on which the freezing point of water is 0° and the boiling point is 100°

ce·ment \si'ment\ *n* **1** : powdery mixture of clay and limestone that hardens when wetted **2** : binding agent ~ *vb* : unite or cover with cement

cem·e·tery \'semə,terē\ *n, pl* **-ter·ies** : burial ground

cen·ser \'sensər\ *n* : vessel for burning incense

cen·sor \'sensər\ *n* : one with power to suppress anything objectionable (as in printed matter) ~ *vb* : be a censor of — **cen·so·ri·al** \sen'sōrēəl\ *adj* — **cen·sor·ship** \-,ship\ *n*

cen·so·ri·ous \sen'sōrēəs\ *adj* : critical — **cen·so·ri·ous·ly** *adv* — **cen·so·ri·ous·ness** *n*

cen·sure \'senchər\ *n* : official reprimand ~ *vb* **-sured; -sur·ing** : find blameworthy — **cen·sur·able** *adj*

cen·sus \'sensəs\ *n* : periodic population count — **census** *vb*

cent \'sent\ *n* : monetary unit equal to ¹⁄₁₀₀ of a basic unit of value

cen·taur \'sen,tȯr\ *n* : mythological creature that is half man and half horse

cen·ten·ni·al \sen'tenēəl\ *n* : 100th anniversary — **centennial** *adj*

cen·ter \'sentər\ *n* **1** : middle point **2** : point of origin or greatest concentration **3** : region of concentrated population **4** : player near the middle of the team ~ *vb* **1** : place, fix, or concentrate at or around a center **2** : have a center — **cen·ter·piece** *n*

cen·ti·grade \'sentə,grād, 'sänt-\ *adj* : Celsius

cen·ti·me·ter \'sentə,mētər, 'sänt-\ *n* : ¹⁄₁₀₀ meter

cen·ti·pede \'sentə,pēd\ *n* : long flat many-legged arthropod

cen·tral \'sentrəl\ *adj* **1** : constituting or being near a center **2** : essential or principal — **cen·tral·ly** *adv*

cen·tral·ize \-trə,līz\ *vb* **-ized; -iz·ing** : bring to a central point or under central control — **cen·tral·i·za·tion** \,sentrələ-'zāshən\ *n* — **cen·tral·iz·er** *n*

cen·tre *chiefly Brit var of* CENTER

cen·trif·u·gal \sen'trifyəgəl, -'trifigəl\ *adj* : acting in a direction away from a center or axis

cen·tri·fuge \'sentrə,fyüj\ *n* : machine that separates substances by spinning

cen·trip·e·tal \sen'tripətᵊl\ *adj* : acting in a direction toward a center or axis

cen·tu·ri·on \sen'chu̇rēən, -'tu̇r-\ *n* : Roman military officer

cen·tu·ry \'senchərē\ *n, pl* **-ries** : 100 years

ce·ram·ic \sə'ramik\ *n* **1** *pl* : art or process of shaping and hardening articles from clay **2** : product of ceramics — **ceramic** *adj*

ce·re·al \'sirēəl\ *adj* : made of or relating to grain or to the plants that produce it ~ *n* **1** : grass yielding edible grain **2** : food prepared from a cereal grain

cer·e·bel·lum \,serə'beləm\ *n, pl* **-bel·lums** *or* **-bel·la** \-'belə\ : part of the brain controlling muscular coordination — **cer·e·bel·lar** \-ər\ *adj*

ce·re·bral \sə'rēbrəl, 'serə-\ *adj* **1** : relating to the brain, intellect, or cerebrum **2** : appealing to the intellect

cerebral palsy *n* : disorder caused by brain damage and marked esp. by defective muscle control

cer·e·brate \'serə,brāt\ *vb* **-brat·ed; -brat·ing** : think — **cer·e·bra·tion** \,serə'brāshən\ *n*

ce·re·brum \sə'rēbrəm, 'serə-\ *n, pl* **-brums** *or* **-bra** \-brə\ : part of the brain that contains the higher nervous centers

cer·e·mo·ny \'serə,mōnē\ *n, pl* **-nies 1** : formal act prescribed by law, ritual, or convention **2** : prescribed procedures — **cer·e·mo·ni·al** \,serə'mōnēəl\ *adj or n* — **cer·e·mo·ni·ous** \-nēəs\ *adj*

ce·rise \sə'rēs\ *n* : moderate red

cer·tain \'sərt°n\ *adj* **1** : settled **2** : true **3** : specific but not named **4** : bound **5** : assured ~ *pron* : certain ones — **cer·tain·ly** *adv* — **cer·tain·ty** \-tē\ *n*

cer·tif·i·cate \sər'tifikət\ *n* : document establishing truth or fulfillment

cer·ti·fy \'sərtə,fī\ *vb* **-fied; -fy·ing 1** : verify **2** : endorse — **cer·ti·fi·able** \-,fīəbəl\ *adj* — **cer·ti·fi·ably** \-blē\ *adv*

— **cer·ti·fi·ca·tion** \,sərtəfə-'kāshən\ *n* — **cer·ti·fi·er** *n*

cer·ti·tude \'sərtə,tüd, -,tyüd\ *n* : state of being certain

cer·vix \'sərviks\ *n, pl* **-vi·ces** \-və,sēz\ *or* **-vix·es 1** : neck **2** : narrow end of the uterus — **cer·vi·cal** \-vikəl\ *adj*

ce·sar·e·an \si'zarēən\ *n* : surgical operation to deliver a baby — **cesarean** *adj*

ce·si·um \'sēzēəm\ *n* : silver-white soft ductile chemical element

ces·sa·tion \se'sāshən\ *n* : a halting

ces·sion \'seshən\ *n* : a yielding

cess·pool \'ses,pül\ *n* : underground sewage pit

Cha·blis \'shab,lē; sha'blē\ *n, pl* **Cha·blis** \-,lēz, -'blēz\ : dry white wine

chafe \'chāf\ *vb* **chafed; chaf·ing 1** : fret **2** : make sore by rubbing

chaff \'chaf\ *n* **1** : debris separated from grain **2** : something worthless

chaf·ing dish \'chāfiŋ-\ *n* : utensil for cooking at the table

cha·grin \shə'grin\ *n* : embarrassment or humiliation ~ *vb* : cause to feel chagrin

chain \'chān\ *n* **1** : flexible series of connected links **2** *pl* : fetters **3** : linked series ~ *vb* : bind or connect with a chain

chair \'cher\ *n* **1** : seat with a back **2** : position of authority or dignity **3** : chairman ~ *vb* : act as chairman of

chair·man \-mən\ *n* : presiding officer — **chair·man·ship** *n*

chair·wom·an \-ˌwu̇mən\ *n* : woman who is a presiding officer

chaise longue \'shāz'lȯŋ\ *n, pl* **chaise longues** \-lȯŋ, -'lȯŋz\ : long chair for reclining

cha·let \sha'lā\ *n* : Swiss mountain cottage with overhanging roof

chal·ice \'chaləs\ *n* : eucharistic cup

chalk \'chȯk\ *n* **1** : soft limestone **2** : chalky material used as a crayon ~ *vb* : mark with chalk — **chalky** *adj* — **chalk up** *vb* **1** : credit **2** : achieve

chalk·board *n* : blackboard

chal·lenge \'chalənj\ *vb* **-lenged; -leng·ing 1** : dispute **2** : invite or dare to act or compete — **challenge** *n* — **chal·leng·er** *n*

cham·ber \'chāmbər\ *n* **1** : room **2** : enclosed space **3** : legislative meeting place or body **4** *pl* : judge's consultation room — **cham·bered** *adj*

cham·ber·maid *n* : bedroom maid

chamber music *n* : music by a small group for a small audience

cha·me·leon \kə'mēlyən\ *n* : small lizard whose skin changes color

cham·ois \'shamē\ *n, pl* **chamois** \-ē, -ēz\ **1** : goatlike antelope **2** : soft leather

¹**champ** \'champ, 'chämp\ *vb* : chew noisily

²**champ** \'champ\ *n* : champion

cham·pagne \sham'pān\ *n* : sparkling white wine

cham·pi·on \'champēən\ *n* **1** : advocate or defender **2** : winning contestant ~ *vb* : protect or fight for

cham·pi·on·ship \-ˌship\ *n* **1** : title of a champion **2** : contest to pick a champion

chance \'chans\ *n* **1** : unpredictable element of existence **2** : opportunity **3** : probability **4** : risk **5** : raffle ticket ~ *vb* **chanced; chanc·ing 1** : happen **2** : encounter unexpectedly **3** : risk — **chance** *adj*

chan·cel \'chansəl\ *n* : part of a church around the altar

chan·cel·lery, chan·cel·lory \'chansələrē\ *n, pl* **-ler·ies** *or* **-lor·ies 1** : position of a chancellor **2** : chancellor's office

chan·cel·lor \-ələr\ *n* **1** : chief or high state official **2** : head of a university — **chan·cel·lor·ship** *n*

chan·cre \'shaŋkər\ *n* : skin ulcer esp. from syphilis

chancy \'chansē\ *adj* **chanc·i·er; -est** : risky

chan·de·lier \,shandə'lir\ *n* : hanging lighting fixture

chan·dler \'chandlər\ *n* : provisions dealer — **chan·dlery** *n*

change \'chānj\ *vb* **changed; chang·ing 1** : make or become different **2** : exchange **3** : give or receive change for ~ *n* **1** : a changing **2** : excess from a payment **3** : money in smaller denominations **4** : coins — **change·able** *adj* — **change·less** *adj* — **chang·er** *n*

chan·nel \'chanᵊl\ *n* **1** : deeper part of a waterway **2** : means of passage or communication **3** : strait **4** : broadcast frequency ~ *vb* **-neled** *or* **-nelled; -nel·ing** *or* **-nel·ling** : make or direct through a channel

chant \'chant\ *vb* : sing or speak in one tone — **chant** *n* — **chant·er** *n*

chan·tey, chan·ty \'shantē, 'chant-\ *n, pl* **-teys** *or* **-ties** : sailors' work song

Cha·nu·kah \'ḵänəkə, 'hän-\ *var of* HANUKKAH

cha·os \'kā,äs\ *n* : complete disorder — **cha·ot·ic** \kā'ätik\ *adj* — **cha·ot·i·cal·ly** \-iklē\ *adv*

¹**chap** \'chap\ *n* : fellow

²**chap** *vb* **-pp-** : dry and crack open usu. from wind and cold

cha·pel \'chapəl\ *n* : private or small place of worship

chap·er·on, chap·er·one \'shapə,rōn\ : older person who accompanies young people at a social gathering ~ *vb* **-oned; -on·ing** : act as chaperon at or for — **chap·er·on·age** \-ij\ *n*

chap·lain \'chaplən\ *n* : clergy member in a military unit or a prison — **chap·lain·cy** \-sē\ *n*

chap·ter \'chaptər\ *n* **1** : main book division **2** : branch of a society

char \'chär\ *vb* **-rr- 1** : burn to charcoal **2** : scorch

char·ac·ter \'kariktər\ *n* **1** : letter or graphic mark **2** : trait or distinctive combination of traits **3** : peculiar person **4** : fictional person — **char·ac·ter·i·za·tion** \,kariktərə'zāshən\ *n* — **char·ac·ter·ize** \'kariktə,rīz\ *vb*

char·ac·ter·is·tic \,kariktə-'ristik\ *adj* : typical ~ *n* : distinguishing quality — **char·ac·ter·is·ti·cal·ly** \-tiklē\ *adv*

cha·rades \shə'rādz\ *n sing or pl* : pantomime guessing game

char·coal \'chär,kōl\ *n* : porous carbon prepared by partial combustion

chard \'chärd\ *n* : leafy vegetable

charge \'chärj\ *vb* **charged; charg·ing 1** : give an electric charge to **2** : impose a task or responsibility on **3** : command **4** : accuse **5** : rush forward in assault **6** : assume a debt for **7** : fix as a price ～ *n* **1** : excess or deficiency of electrons in a body **2** : tax **3** : responsibility **4** : accusation **5** : cost **6** : attack — **chargeable** *adj*

charg·er \-ər\ *n* : horse ridden in battle

char·i·ot \'charēət\ *n* : ancient 2-wheeled vehicle — **char·i·o·teer** \ˌcharēə'tir\ *n*

cha·ris·ma \kə'rizmə\ *n* : special ability to lead — **char·ismat·ic** \ˌkarəz'matik\ *adj*

char·i·ty \'charətē\ *n, pl* **-ties 1** : love for mankind **2** : generosity or leniency **3** : alms **4** : institution for relief of the needy — **char·i·ta·ble** \-əbəl\ *adj* — **char·i·ta·bleness** *n* — **char·i·ta·bly** \-blē\ *adv*

char·la·tan \'shärlətən\ *n* : impostor

charm \'chärm\ *n* **1** : something with magic power **2** : appealing trait **3** : small ornament ～ *vb* : fascinate — **charm·er** *n* — **charm·ing** *adj* — **charm·ing·ly** *adv*

char·nel house \'chärnəl-\ *n* : place for dead bodies

chart \'chärt\ *n* **1** : map **2** : diagram ～ *vb* **1** : make a chart of **2** : plan

char·ter \-ər\ *n* **1** : document granting rights **2** : constitution ～ *vb* **1** : establish by charter **2** : rent — **char·ter·er** *n*

char·treuse \shär'trüz, -'trüs\ *n* : brilliant yellow green

char·wom·an \'chärˌwümən\ *n* : cleaning woman

chary \'charē\ *adj* **chari·er; -est** : cautious — **char·i·ly** \'charəlē\ *adv*

¹**chase** \'chās\ *vb* **chased; chas·ing 1** : follow trying to catch **2** : drive away — **chase** *n* — **chas·er** *n*

²**chase** *vb* **chased; chas·ing** : decorate (metal) by embossing or engraving

chasm \'kazəm\ *n* : gorge

chas·sis \'chasē, 'shasē\ *n, pl* **chas·sis** \-ēz\ : supporting structural frame

chaste \'chāst\ *adj* **chast·er; chast·est 1** : abstaining from all or unlawful sexual relations **2** : modest or decent **3** : severely simple — **chaste·ly** *adv* — **chaste·ness** *n* — **chas·ti·ty** \'chastətē\ *n*

chas·ten \'chāsᵊn\ *vb* : discipline

chas·tise \chas'tīz\ *vb* **-tised; -tis·ing 1** : punish **2** : censure — **chas·tise·ment** \-mənt, 'chastəz-\ *n*

chat \\'chat\ *n* : informal talk — **chat** *vb* — **chat·ty** \-ē\ *adj*

châ·teau \sha'tō\ *n, pl* **-teaus** \-'tōz\ *or* **-teaux** \-'tō, -'tōz\ **1** : large country house **2** : French vineyard estate

chat·tel \\'chat⁹l\ *n* : item of tangible property other than real estate

chat·ter \\'chatər\ *vb* **1** : utter rapidly succeeding sounds **2** : talk fast or too much — **chatter** *n* — **chat·ter·er** *n*

chat·ter·box *n* : incessant talker

chauf·feur \\'shōfər, shō'fər\ *n* : hired car driver ~ *vb* : work as a chauffeur

chau·vin·ism \\'shōvə͵nizəm\ *n* : excessive patriotism — **chau·vin·ist** \-vənist\ *n* — **chau·vin·is·tic** \͵shōvə'nistik\ *adj*

cheap \\'chēp\ *adj* **1** : inexpensive **2** : shoddy — **cheap** *adv* — **cheap·en** \\'chēpən\ *vb* — **cheap·ly** *adv* — **cheap·ness** *n*

cheap·skate *n* : stingy person

cheat \\'chēt\ *n* **1** : act of deceiving **2** : one that cheats ~ *vb* **1** : deprive through fraud or deceit **2** : violate rules dishonestly — **cheat·er** *n*

check \\'chek\ *n* **1** : sudden stoppage **2** : restraint **3** : test or standard for testing **4** : written order to a bank to pay money **5** : ticket showing ownership **6** : slip showing an amount due **7** : pattern in squares or fabric in such a pattern **8** : mark placed beside an item noted ~ *vb* **1** : slow down or stop **2** : restrain **3** : compare or correspond with a source or original **4** : inspect or test for condition **5** : mark with a check **6** : leave or accept for safekeeping or shipment **7** : checker — **check in** *vb* : report one's arrival — **check out** *vb* : settle one's account and leave

¹check·er \-ər\ *n* : piece in checkers ~ *vb* : mark with different colors or into squares

²checker *n* : one that checks

check·er·board \-͵bōrd\ *n* : board of 64 squares of alternate colors

check·ers \\'chekərz\ *n* : game for 2 played on a checkerboard

check·mate *vb* : thwart completely — **checkmate** *n*

check·point *n* : place where traffic is checked

check·up *n* : physical examination

ched·dar \\'chedər\ *n* : hard smooth cheese

cheek \\'chēk\ *n* **1** : fleshy side part of the face **2** : impudence — **cheeked** \'chēkt\ *adj* — **cheeky** *adj*

cheep \'chēp\ *vb* : utter faint shrill sounds — **cheep** *n*

cheer \'chir\ *n* **1** : good spirits **2** : food and drink for a feast **3** : shout of applause or encouragement ~ *vb* **1** : give hope or courage to **2** : make or become glad **3** : urge on or applaud with shouts — **cheer·er** *n* — **cheer·ful** \-fəl\ *adj* — **cheer·ful·ly** *adv* — **cheer·ful·ness** *n* — **cheer·lead·er** *n* — **cheer·less** *adj* — **cheer·less·ly** *adv* — **cheer·less·ness** *n*

cheery \'chirē\ *adj* **cheer·i·er; -est** : cheerful — **cheer·i·ly** *adv* — **cheer·i·ness** *n*

cheese \'chēz\ *n* : curd of milk usu. pressed and cured — **cheesy** *adj*

cheese·cloth *n* : lightweight coarse cotton gauze

chee·tah \'chētə\ *n* : spotted swift-moving African cat

chef \'shef\ *n* : chief cook

chem·i·cal \'kemikəl\ *adj* **1** : relating to chemistry **2** : working or produced by chemicals ~ *n* : substance obtained by chemistry — **chem·i·cal·ly** \-klē\ *adv*

che·mise \shə'mēz\ *n* **1** : woman's one-piece undergarment **2** : loose dress

chem·ist \'kemist\ *n* **1** : one trained in chemistry **2** *Brit* : pharmacist

chem·is·try \-istrē\ *n, pl* **-tries** : science that deals with the composition and properties of substances

che·mo·ther·a·py \ˌkēmō-'therəpē, ˌkemō-\ *n* : use of chemicals in the treatment of disease — **che·mo·ther·a·peu·tic** *adj*

che·nille \shə'nēl\ *n* : yarn with protruding pile or fabric of such yarn

cheque \'chek\ *chiefly Brit var of* CHECK **4**

cher·ish \'cherish\ *vb* : hold dear

cher·ry \'cherē\ *n, pl* **-ries** : small fleshy fruit of a tree related to the roses or the tree or its wood

cher·ub \'cherəb\ *n* **1** *pl* **-u·bim** \-əˌbim, -yə-\ : angel **2** *pl* **-ubs** : chubby child — **che·ru·bic** \chə'rübik\ *adj*

chess \'ches\ *n* : game for 2 played on a checkerboard — **chess·board** *n* — **chess·man** *n*

chest \'chest\ *n* **1** : boxlike container **2** : part of the body enclosed by the ribs and breastbone — **chest·ed** *adj*

chest·nut \'chesˌnət\ *n* : nut of a tree related to the beech or the tree

chev·i·ot \'shevēət\ *n* **1** : heavy rough wool fabric **2** : soft-finished cotton fabric

chev·ron \'shevrən\ *n* : V-shaped insignia

chew \'chü\ *vb* : crush or grind with the teeth ~ *n* : something to chew — **chew·able** *adj* — **chew·er** *n* — **chewy** *adj*

chic \'shēk\ *n* : smart elegance of dress or manner ~ *adj* **1** : stylish **2** : currently fashionable

chi·ca·nery \shik'ānərē\ *n, pl* **-ner·ies** : trickery

chick \'chik\ *n* : young chicken or bird

chick·a·dee \-ə,dē\ *n* : small grayish American bird

chick·en \'chikən\ *n* **1** : common domestic fowl or its flesh used as food **2** : coward

chicken pox *n* : acute contagious virus disease esp. of children

chi·cle \'chikəl\ *n* : gum from a tropical evergreen tree

chic·o·ry \'chikərē\ *n, pl* **-ries** : herb used in salad or its dried ground root used to adulterate coffee

chide \'chīd\ *vb* **chid** \'chid\ *or* **chid·ed** \'chīdəd\; **chid** *or* **chid·den** \'chid°n\ *or* **chided; chid·ing** \'chīdiŋ\ : scold

chief \'chēf\ *n* : leader ~ *adj* **1** : highest in rank **2** : most important — **chief·dom** *n* — **chief·ly** *adv*

chief·tain \'chēftən\ *n* : chief

chif·fon \shif'än, 'shif,-\ *n* : sheer fabric

chig·ger \'chigər\ *n* : blood-sucking mite

chi·gnon \'shēn,yän\ *n* : knot of hair

chil·blain \'chil,blān\ *n* : sore or inflamed swelling caused by cold

child \'chīld\ *n, pl* **chil·dren** \'childrən\ **1** : unborn or recently born person **2** : son or daughter — **child·bear·ing** *n or adj* — **child·birth** *n* — **child·hood** *n* — **child·ish** *adj* — **child·ish·ly** *adv* — **child·ish·ness** *n* — **child·less** *adj* — **child·less·ness** *n* — **child·like** *adj* — **child·proof** \-,prüf\ *adj*

chili, chile, chil·li \'chilē\ *n, pl* **chil·ies** *or* **chil·es** *or* **chil·lies** **1** : hot pepper **2** : spicy stew of ground beef, chilies, and beans

chill \'chil\ *vb* : make or become cold or chilly ~ *adj* : moderately cold ~ *n* **1** : feeling of coldness with shivering **2** : moderate coldness

chilly \-ē\ *adj* **chill·i·er; -est** : noticeably cold — **chill·i·ness** *n*

chime \'chīm\ *n* : set of tuned bells or their sound ～ *vb* : make bell-like sounds — **chime in** *vb* : break into or join in a conversation

chi·me·ra, chi·mae·ra \kī'mirə, kə-\ *n* **1** : imaginary monster **2** : illusion — **chi·me·ri·cal** \-'merikəl\ *adj*

chim·ney \'chimnē\ *n, pl* **-neys 1** : passage for smoke **2** : glass tube around a lamp flame

chimp \'chimp, 'shimp\ *n* : chimpanzee

chim·pan·zee \ˌchimˌpan'zē, ˌshim-; chim'panzē, shim-\ *n* : small ape

chin \'chin\ *n* : part of the face below the mouth — **chin·less** *adj*

chi·na \'chīnə\ *n* **1** : porcelain ware **2** : domestic pottery

chin·chil·la \chin'chilə\ *n* : small So. American rodent with soft pearl-gray fur or this fur

chink \'chiŋk\ *n* : small crack ～ *vb* : fill chinks of

chintz \'chints\ *n* : printed cotton cloth

chip \'chip\ *n* **1** : small thin flat piece cut or broken off **2** : thin crisp morsel of food **3** : counter used in games **4** : flaw where a chip came off **5** : small slice of semiconductor containing electronic cir-cuits ～ *vb* **-pp-** : cut or break chips from — **chip in** *vb* : contribute

chip·munk \-ˌməŋk\ *n* : small striped ground-dwelling rodent

chip·per \-ər\ *adj* : lively and cheerful

chi·rop·o·dy \kə'räpədē, shə-\ *n* : podiatry — **chi·rop·o·dist** \-ədist\ *n*

chi·ro·prac·tic \'kīrəˌpraktik\ *n* : system of healing based esp. on manipulation of body structures — **chi·ro·prac·tor** \-tər\ *n*

chirp \'chərp\ *n* : short sharp sound like that of a bird or cricket — **chirp** *vb*

chis·el \'chizəl\ *n* : sharp-edged metal tool ～ *vb* **-eled** *or* **-elled; -el·ing** *or* **-el·ling 1** : work with a chisel **2** : cheat — **chis·el·er** \-ələr\ *n*

chit \'chit\ *n* : signed voucher for a small debt

chit·chat \-ˌchat\ *n* : casual conversation — **chitchat** *vb*

chiv·al·rous \'shivəlrəs\ *adj* **1** : relating to chivalry **2** : honest, courteous, or gener-ous — **chiv·al·rous·ly** *adv* — **chiv·al·rous·ness** *n*

chiv·al·ry \-rē\ *n, pl* **-ries 1** : system or practices of knighthood **2** : spirit or char-acter of the ideal knight — **chi·val·ric** \shə'valrik\ *adj*

chive \\'chīv\ *n* : herb related to the onion

chlo·ride \\'klōr‚īd\ *n* : compound of chlorine

chlo·ri·nate \-ə‚nāt\ *vb* **-nat·ed; -nat·ing** : treat or combine with chlorine — **chlo·ri·na·tion** \‚klōrə'nāshən\ *n*

chlo·rine \\'klōr‚ēn\ *n* : chemical element that is a heavy strong-smelling greenish yellow irritating gas

chlo·ro·form \\'klōrə‚fȯrm\ *n* : etherlike colorless heavy fluid ∼ *vb* : anesthetize or kill with chloroform

chlo·ro·phyll \\'klōrə‚fil\ *n* : green coloring matter of plants

chock \\'chäk\ *n* : wedge for blocking the movement of a wheel — **chock** *vb*

chock–full \\'chək'fu̇l, 'chäk-\ *adj* : full to the limit

choc·o·late \\'chäkələt, 'chȯk-\ *n* **1** : ground roasted cacao beans or a beverage made from them **2** : candy made of or with chocolate **3** : dark brown

choice \\'chȯis\ *n* **1** : act or power of choosing **2** : one selected **3** : variety offered for selection ∼ *adj* **choic·er; choic·est 1** : worthy of being chosen **2** : selected with care **3** : of high quality

choir \\'kwīr\ *n* : group of singers esp. in church — **choir·boy** *n* — **choir·mas·ter** *n*

choke \\'chōk\ *vb* **choked; chok·ing 1** : hinder breathing **2** : clog or obstruct ∼ *n* **1** : a choking or sound of choking **2** : valve for controlling air intake in a gasoline engine

chok·er \-ər\ *n* : tight necklace

cho·ler \\'kälər, 'kō-\ *n* : bad temper — **cho·ler·ic** \\'kälərik, kə'ler-\ *adj*

chol·era \\'kälərə\ *n* : disease marked by severe vomiting and dysentery

cho·les·ter·ol \kə'lestə‚rȯl, -‚rōl\ *n* : waxy substance in animal tissues

choose \\'chüz\ *vb* **chose** \\'chōz\; **cho·sen** \\'chōzᵊn\; **choos·ing 1** : select after consideration **2** : decide **3** : prefer — **choos·er** *n*

choosy, choos·ey \\'chüzē\ *adj* **choos·i·er; -est** : fussy in making choices

chop \\'chäp\ *vb* **-pp- 1** : cut by repeated blows **2** : cut into small pieces ∼ *n* **1** : sharp downward blow **2** : small cut of meat often with part of a rib

chop·per \-ər\ *n* **1** : one that chops **2** : helicopter

chop·py \-ē\ *adj* **-pi·er; -est 1** : rough with small waves **2**

: jerky or disconnected — **chop·pi·ly** *adv* — **chop·pi·ness** *n*

chops \'chäps\ *n pl* : fleshy covering of the jaws

chop·sticks *n pl* : pair of sticks used in eating in oriental countries

cho·ral \'kōrəl\ *adj* : relating to or sung by a choir or chorus or in chorus — **cho·ral·ly** *adv*

cho·rale \kə'ral, -'räl\ *n* **1** : hymn tune or harmonization of a traditional melody **2** : chorus or choir

¹**chord** \'kȯrd\ *n* : harmonious tones sounded together

²**chord** *n* **1** : cordlike anatomical structure **2** : straight line joining 2 points on a curve

chore \'chōr\ *n* **1** *pl* : daily household or farm work **2** : routine or disagreeable task

cho·re·og·ra·phy \ˌkōrē-'ägrəfē\ *n, pl* **-phies** : art of composing and arranging dances — **cho·reo·graph** \'kōrēəˌgraf\ *vb* — **cho·re·og·ra·pher** \ˌkōrē'ägrəfər\ *n* — **cho·reo·graph·ic** \-ēə-'grafik\ *adj*

cho·ris·ter \'kōrəstər\ *n* : choir singer

chor·tle \'chȯrtᵊl\ *vb* **-tled; -tling** : laugh or chuckle — **chortle** *n*

cho·rus \'kōrəs\ *n* **1** : group of singers or dancers **2** : part of a song repeated at intervals **3** : composition for a chorus ~ *vb* : sing or utter together

chose *past of* CHOOSE

cho·sen \'chōzᵊn\ *adj* : favored

¹**chow** \'chau̇\ *n* : food

²**chow** *n* : thick-coated muscular dog

chow·der \'chau̇dər\ *n* : thick soup usu. of seafood and milk

chow mein \'chau̇'mān\ *n* : thick stew of shredded vegetables and meat

chris·ten \'krisᵊn\ *vb* **1** : baptize **2** : name — **chris·ten·ing** *n*

Chris·ten·dom \-dəm\ *n* : areas where Christianity prevails

Chris·tian \'krischən\ *n* : adherent of Christianity ~ *adj* : relating to or professing a belief in Christianity or Jesus Christ — **Chris·tian·ize** \'krischəˌnīz\ *vb*

Chris·ti·an·i·ty \ˌkrischē-'anətē\ *n* : religion derived from the teachings of Jesus Christ

Christian name *n* : first name

Christ·mas \'krisməs\ *n* : December 25 celebrated as the birthday of Christ

chro·mat·ic \krō'matik\ *adj* **1** : relating to color **2** : proceeding by half steps of the musical scale

chrome \'krōm\ *n* : chromium or something plated with it

chro·mi·um \-ēəm\ *n* : a bluish white metallic element used esp. in alloys

chro·mo·some \'krōmə,sōm, -,zōm\ *n* : part of a cell nucleus that contains the genes — **chro·mo·som·al** \,krōmə-'sōməl, -'zō-\ *adj*

chron·ic \'kränik\ *adj* : frequent or persistent — **chron·i·cal·ly** \-iklē\ *adv*

chron·i·cle \'känikəl\ *n* : history ∼ *vb* -**cled; -cling** : record — **chron·i·cler** \-iklər\ *n*

chro·nol·o·gy \krə'näləjē\ *n, pl* -**gies** : list of events in order of their occurrence — **chron·o·log·i·cal** \,kränᵊl'äjikəl\ *adj* — **chron·o·log·i·cal·ly** \-iklē\ *adv*

chro·nom·e·ter \krə'nämətər\ *n* : very accurate timepiece

chrys·a·lis \'krisələs\ *n, pl* **chry·sal·i·des** \kris'alə,dēz\ *or* **chrys·a·lis·es** : insect pupa enclosed in a shell

chry·san·the·mum \kris'an-thəməm\ *n* : plant with showy flowers

chub·by \'chəbē\ *adj* -**bi·er; -est** : fat — **chub·bi·ness** *n*

¹**chuck** \'chək\ *vb* **1** : tap **2** : toss ∼ *n* **1** : light pat under the chin **2** : toss

²**chuck** *n* **1** : cut of beef **2** : machine part that holds work or another part

chuck·le \'chəkəl\ *vb* -**led; -ling** : laugh quietly — **chuckle** *n*

chug \'chəg\ *n* : sound of a laboring engine ∼ *vb* -**gg**- : work or move with chugs

chum \'chəm\ *n* : close friend ∼ *vb* -**mm**- : be chums — **chum·my** \-ē\ *adj*

chump \'chəmp\ *n* : fool

chunk \'chəŋk\ *n* **1** : short thick piece **2** : sizable amount

chunky \-ē\ *adj* **chunk·i·er; -est 1** : stocky **2** : containing chunks

church \'chərch\ *n* **1** : building esp. for Christian public worship **2** : whole body of Christians **3** : denomination **4** : congregation — **church·go·er** *n* — **church·go·ing** *adj or n*

church·yard *n* : cemetery beside a church

churl \'chərl\ *n* : rude ill-bred person — **churl·ish** *adj*

churn \'chərn\ *n* : container in which butter is made ∼ *vb* **1** : agitate in a churn **2** : shake violently

chute \'shüt\ *n* : trough or passage

chut·ney \'chətnē\ *n, pl* -**neys** : sweet and sour relish

chutz·pah \'hu̇tspə, 'ku̇t-, -ˌspä\ *n* : nerve or insolence

ci·ca·da \sə'kādə\ *n* : stout-bodied insect with transparent wings

ci·der \'sīdər\ *n* : apple juice

ci·gar \sig'är\ *n* : roll of leaf tobacco for smoking

cig·a·rette \ˌsigə'ret, 'sigəˌret\ *n* : cut tobacco rolled in paper for smoking

cinch \'sinch\ *n* **1** : strap holding a saddle or pack in place **2** : sure thing — **cinch** *vb*

cin·cho·na \siŋ'kōnə\ *n* : So. American tree that yields quinine

cinc·ture \'siŋkchər\ *n* : belt or sash

cin·der \'sindər\ *n* **1** *pl* : ashes **2** : piece of partly burned wood or coal

cin·e·ma \'sinəmə\ *n* : movies or a movie theater — **cin·e·mat·ic** \ˌsinə'matik\ *adj*

cin·na·mon \'sinəmən\ *n* : spice from an aromatic tree bark

ci·pher \'sīfər\ *n* **1** : zero **2** : code

cir·ca \'sərkə\ *prep* : about

cir·cle \'sərkəl\ *n* **1** : closed symmetrical curve **2** : cycle **3** : group with a common tie ∼ *vb* **-cled; -cling 1** : enclose in a circle **2** : move or revolve around

cir·cuit \'sərkət\ *n* **1** : boundary **2** : regular tour of a territory **3** : complete path of an electric current **4** : group of electronic components

cir·cu·itous \ˌsər'kyüətəs\ *adj* : circular or winding

cir·cuit·ry \'sərkətrē\ *n, pl* **-ries** : arrangement of an electric circuit

cir·cu·lar \'sərkyələr\ *adj* **1** : round **2** : moving in a circle ∼ *n* : advertising leaflet — **cir·cu·lar·i·ty** \ˌsərkyə'larətē\ *n*

cir·cu·late \'sərkyəˌlāt\ *vb* **-lat·ed; -lat·ing** : move or cause to move in a circle or from place to place or person to person — **cir·cu·la·tion** \ˌsərkyə'lāshən\ *n* — **cir·cu·la·to·ry** \'sərkyələˌtōrē\ *adj*

cir·cum·cise \'sərkəmˌsīz\ *vb* **-cised; -cis·ing** : cut off the foreskin of — **cir·cum·ci·sion** \ˌsərkəm'sizhən\ *n*

cir·cum·fer·ence \sər'kəmfrəns\ *n* : perimeter of a circle

cir·cum·flex \'sərkəmˌfleks\ *n* : phonetic mark (as ^)

cir·cum·lo·cu·tion \ˌsərkəmlō'kyüshən\ *n* : excessive use of words

cir·cum·nav·i·gate \ˌsərkəm'navəˌgāt\ *vb* : sail completely around — **cir·cum·nav·i·ga·tion** *n*

cir·cum·scribe \'sərkəm-ˌskrīb\ *vb* **1** : draw a line around **2** : limit

cir·cum·spect \'sərkəm-ˌspekt\ *adj* : careful — **cir·cum·spec·tion** \ˌsərkəm-'spekshən\ *n*

cir·cum·stance \'sərkəm-ˌstans\ *n* **1** : fact or event **2** *pl* : surrounding conditions **3** *pl* : financial situation — **cir·cum·stan·tial** \ˌsərkəm'stan-chəl\ *adj*

cir·cum·vent \ˌsərkəm'vent\ *vb* : get around esp. by trickery — **cir·cum·ven·tion** \-'ven-chən\ *n*

cir·cus \'sərkəs\ *n* : show with feats of skill, animal acts, and clowns

cir·rho·sis \sə'rōsəs\ *n, pl* **-rho·ses** \-ˌsēz\ : fibrosis of the liver — **cir·rhot·ic** \-'rätik\ *adj or n*

cir·rus \'sirəs\ *n, pl* **-ri** \-ˌī\ : wispy white cloud

cis·tern \'sistərn\ *n* : underground water tank

cit·a·del \'sitədᵊl, -əˌdel\ *n* : fortress

cite \'sīt\ *vb* **cit·ed; cit·ing** **1** : summon before a court **2** : quote **3** : refer to esp. in commendation — **ci·ta·tion** \sī'tāshən\ *n*

cit·i·zen \'sitəzən\ *n* : member of a country — **cit·i·zen·ry** \-rē\ *n* — **cit·i·zen·ship** *n*

cit·ron \'sitrən\ *n* : lemonlike fruit

cit·rus \'sitrəs\ *n, pl* **-rus** *or* **-rus·es** : evergreen tree or shrub grown for its fruit (as the orange or lemon)

city \'sitē\ *n, pl* **cit·ies** : place larger or more important than a town

civ·ic \'sivik\ *adj* : relating to citizenship or civil affairs

civ·ics \-iks\ *n* : study of citizenship

civ·il \'sivəl\ *adj* **1** : relating to citizens **2** : polite **3** : relating to or being a lawsuit — **civ·il·ly** *adv*

ci·vil·ian \sə'vilyən\ *n* : person not in a military, police, or fire-fighting force

ci·vil·i·ty \sə'vilətē\ *n, pl* **-ties** : courtesy

civ·i·li·za·tion \ˌsivələ'zāshən\ *n* **1** : high level of cultural development **2** : culture of a time or place

civ·i·lize \'sivəˌlīz\ *vb* **-lized; -liz·ing** : raise from a primitive stage of cultural development — **civ·i·lized** *adj*

civil liberty *n* : freedom from arbitrary governmental interference — usu. pl.

civil rights *n pl* : nonpolitical rights of a citizen

civil service *n* : government service

civil war *n* : war among citizens of one country

clack \'klak\ *vb* : make or cause a clatter — **clack** *n*

clad \'klad\ *adj* : covered

claim \'klām\ *vb* **1** : demand or take as the rightful owner **2** : maintain ~ *n* **1** : demand of right or ownership **2** : declaration **3** : something claimed — **claim·ant** \-ənt\ *n*

clair·voy·ant \klar'vȯiənt\ *adj* : able to perceive things beyond the senses — **clair·voy·ance** \-əns\ *n* — **clair·voy·ant** *n*

clam \'klam\ *n* : bivalve mollusk

clam·ber \'klambər\ *vb* : climb awkwardly

clam·my \'klamē\ *adj* **-mi·er; -est** : being damp, soft, and usu. cool — **clam·mi·ness** *n*

clam·or \-ər\ *n* **1** : uproar **2** : protest — **clamor** *vb* — **clam·or·ous** *adj*

clamp \'klamp\ *n* : device for holding things together — **clamp** *vb*

clan \'klan\ *n* : group of related families — **clan·nish** *adj* — **clan·nish·ness** *n*

clan·des·tine \klan'destən\ *adj* : secret

clang \'klaŋ\ *n* : loud metallic ringing — **clang** *vb*

clan·gor \-ər, -gər\ *n* : jumble of clangs

clank \'klaŋk\ *n* : brief sound of struck metal — **clank** *vb*

clap \'klap\ *vb* **-pp-** **1** : strike noisily **2** : applaud ~ *n* **1** : loud crash **2** : noise made by clapping the hands

clap·board \'klabərd, 'klap-, -ˌbōrd\ *n* : narrow tapered board used for siding

clap·per \'klapər\ *n* : tongue of a bell

claque \'klak\ *n* **1** : group hired to applaud at a performance **2** : group of sycophants

clar·et \'klarət\ *n* : dry red wine

clar·i·fy \'klarəˌfī\ *vb* **-fied; -fy·ing** : make or become clear — **clar·i·fi·ca·tion** \ˌklarəfə'kāshən\ *n*

clar·i·net \ˌklarə'net\ *n* : woodwind instrument shaped like a tube — **clar·i·net·ist, clar·i·net·tist** \-ist\ *n*

clar·i·on \'klarēən\ *adj* : loud and clear

clar·i·ty \'klarətē\ *n* : clearness

clash \'klash\ *vb* **1** : make or cause a clash **2** : be in opposition or disharmony ~ *n* **1** : crashing sound **2** : hostile encounter

clasp \'klasp\ *n* **1** : device for holding things together **2** : embrace or grasp ~ *vb* **1** : fasten **2** : embrace or grasp

class \'klas\ *n* **1** : group of the same status or nature **2** : social rank **3** : course of instruction **4** : group of students ∼ *vb* : classify — **class·less** *adj* — **class·mate** *n* — **class·room** *n*

clas·sic \'klasik\ *adj* **1** : serving as a standard of excellence **2** : classical ∼ *n* : work of enduring excellence and esp. of ancient Greece or Rome — **clas·si·cal** \-ikəl\ *adj* — **clas·si·cal·ly** \-klē\ *adv* — **clas·si·cism** \'klasə,sizəm\ *n* — **clas·si·cist** \-sist\ *n*

clas·si·fied \'klasə,fīd\ *adj* : restricted for security reasons

clas·si·fy \-,fī\ *vb* **-fied; -fy·ing** : arrange in or assign to classes — **clas·si·fi·ca·tion** \,klasəfə'kāshən\ *n* — **clas·si·fi·er** \'klasə,fīər\ *n*

clat·ter \'klatər\ *n* : rattling sound — **clatter** *vb*

clause \'klȯz\ *n* **1** : separate part of a document **2** : part of a sentence with a subject and predicate

claus·tro·pho·bia \,klȯstrə-'fōbēə\ *n* : fear of closed or narrow spaces — **claus·tro·pho·bic** \-bik\ *adj*

clav·i·chord \'klavə,kȯrd\ *n* : early keyboard instrument

clav·i·cle \'klavikəl\ *n* : collarbone

claw \'klȯ\ *n* : sharp curved nail or process (as on the toe of an animal) ∼ *vb* : scratch or dig — **clawed** *adj*

clay \'klā\ *n* : plastic earthy material — **clay·ey** \-ē\ *adj*

clean \'klēn\ *adj* **1** : free from dirt or disease **2** : pure or honorable **3** : thorough ∼ *vb* : make or become clean — **clean** *adv* — **clean·er** *n* — **clean·ly** \-lē\ *adv* — **clean·ness** *n*

clean·ly \'klenlē\ *adj* **-li·er; -est** : clean — **clean·li·ness** *n*

cleanse \'klenz\ *vb* **cleansed; cleans·ing** : make clean — **cleans·er** *n*

clear \'klir\ *adj* **1** : bright **2** : free from clouds **3** : transparent **4** : easily heard, seen or understood **5** : free from doubt **6** : free from restriction or obstruction ∼ *vb* **1** : make or become clear **2** : go away **3** : free from accusation or blame **4** : explain or settle **5** : net **6** : jump or pass without touching ∼ *n* : clear space or part — **clear** *adv* — **clear·ance** \'klirəns\ *n*

clear·ing \'kliriŋ\ *n* : land cleared of wood

clear·ly *adv* **1** : in a clear manner **2** : it is obvious that

cleat \'klēt\ *n* : projection that strengthens or prevents slipping

cleav·age \'klēvij\ *n* **1** : a splitting apart **2** : depression between a woman's breasts

¹**cleave** \'klēv\ *vb* **cleaved** \'klēvd\ *or* **clove** \'klōv\; **cleav·ing** : adhere

²**cleave** *vb* **cleaved** \'klēvd\; **cleav·ing** : split apart

cleav·er \'klēvər\ *n* : heavy chopping knife

clef \'klef\ *n* : sign on the staff in music to show pitch

cleft \'kleft\ *n* : crack

clem·ent \'klemənt\ *adj* **1** : merciful **2** : temperate or mild — **clem·en·cy** \-ənsē\ *n*

clench \'klench\ *vb* **1** : hold fast **2** : close tightly

cler·gy \'klərjē\ *n* : body of religious officials — **cler·gy·man** \-jimən\ *n*

cler·ic \'klerik\ *n* : member of the clergy

cler·i·cal \-ikəl\ *adj* **1** : relating to the clergy **2** : relating to a clerk or office worker

clerk \'klərk, *Brit* 'klärk\ *n* **1** : official responsible for record-keeping **2** : person doing general office work **3** : salesperson in a store — **clerk** *vb* — **clerk·ship** *n*

clev·er \'klevər\ *adj* **1** : resourceful **2** : marked by wit or ingenuity — **clev·er·ly** *adv* — **clev·er·ness** *n*

clew *var of* CLUE

cli·ché \kli'shā\ *n* : trite phrase — **cli·chéd** \-'shād\ *adj*

click \'klik\ *n* : slight sharp noise ~ *vb* : make or cause to make a click

cli·ent \'klīənt\ *n* **1** : person who engages professional services **2** : customer

cli·en·tele \ˌklīən'tel, ˌklē-\ *n* : body of customers

cliff \'klif\ *n* : high steep face of rock

cli·mate \'klīmət\ *n* : average weather conditions over a period of years — **cli·mat·ic** \klī'matik\ *adj*

cli·max \'klīˌmaks\ *n* : the highest point ~ *vb* : come to a climax — **cli·mac·tic** \klī'maktik\ *adj*

climb \'klīm\ *vb* **1** : go up or down by use of hands and feet **2** : rise ~ *n* : a climbing — **climb·er** *n*

clinch \'klinch\ *vb* **1** : fasten securely **2** : settle **3** : hold fast or firmly — **clinch** *n* — **clinch·er** *n*

cling \'kliŋ\ *vb* **clung** \'kləŋ\; **cling·ing** **1** : adhere firmly **2** : hold on tightly

clin·ic \'klinik\ *n* : facility for diagnosis and treatment of outpatients — **clin·i·cal** \-əl\ *adj* — **clin·i·cal·ly** \-klē\ *adv*

clink \'kliŋk\ *vb* : make a slight metallic sound — **clink** *n*

clin·ker \'kliŋkər\ *n* : fused stony matter esp. in a furnace

¹**clip** \'klip\ *vb* **-pp-** : fasten with a clip ～ *n* : device to hold things together

²**clip** *vb* **-pp- 1** : cut or cut off **2** : hit ～ *n* **1** : clippers **2** : sharp blow **3** : rapid pace

clip·per \'klipər\ *n* **1** *pl* : implement for clipping **2** : fast sailing ship

clique \'klēk, 'klik\ *n* : small exclusive group of people

cli·to·ris \'klitərəs, kli'tòrəs\ *n, pl* **cli·to·ri·des** \-'tòrə‚dēz\ : small organ at the front of the vulva

cloak \'klōk\ *n* **1** : loose outer garment **2** : something that conceals ～ *vb* : cover or hide with a cloak

clob·ber \'kläbər\ *vb* : hit hard

clock \'kläk\ *n* : timepiece not carried on the person ～ *vb* : record the time of

clock·wise \-‚wīz\ *adv or adj* : in the same direction as a clock's hands move

clod \'kläd\ *n* **1** : lump esp. of earth **2** : dull insensitive person

clog \'kläg\ *n* **1** : restraining weight **2** : thick-soled shoe ～ *vb* **-gg- 1** : impede with a clog **2** : obstruct passage through **3** : become plugged up

clois·ter \'klòistər\ *n* **1** : monastic establishment **2** : covered passage ～ *vb* : shut away from the world

clone \'klōn\ *n* **1** : offspring produced from a single organism **2** : copy

¹**close** \'klōz\ *vb* **closed; closing 1** : shut **2** : cease operation **3** : terminate **4** : bring or come together ～ *n* : conclusion or end

²**close** \'klōs\ *adj* **clos·er; closest 1** : confining **2** : secretive **3** : strict **4** : stuffy **5** : having little space between items **6** : fitting tightly **7** : near **8** : intimate **9** : accurate **10** : nearly even — **close** *adv* — **close·ly** *adv* — **close·ness** *n*

clos·et \'kläzət, 'klòz-\ *n* : small compartment for household utensils or clothing ～ *vb* : take into a private room for a talk

clo·sure \'klōzhər\ *n* **1** : act of closing **2** : something that closes

clot \'klät\ *n* : dried mass of a liquid — **clot** *vb*

cloth \'klòth\ *n, pl* **cloths** \'klòthz, 'klòths\ **1** : fabric **2** : tablecloth

clothe \'klōth\ *vb* **clothed** *or* **clad** \'klad\; **cloth·ing** : dress

clothes \'klōthz, 'klōz\ *n pl* **1** : clothing **2** : bedclothes

cloth·ier \'klōthyər, -thēər\ *n* : maker or seller of clothing

cloth·ing \'klōthiŋ\ *n* : covering for the human body

cloud \'klaud\ *n* **1** : visible mass of particles in the air **2** : something that darkens, hides, or threatens ~ *vb* : darken or hide — **cloud·i·ness** *n* — **cloud·less** *adj* — **cloudy** *adj*

cloud·burst *n* : sudden heavy rain

clout \'klaut\ *n* **1** : blow **2** : influence ~ *vb* : hit forcefully

¹**clove** \'klōv\ *n* : section of a bulb

²**clove** *past of* CLEAVE

³**clove** *n* : dried flower bud of an East Indian tree used as a spice

clo·ver \'klōvər\ *n* : leguminous herb with usu. 3-part leaves

clo·ver·leaf *n, pl* **-leafs** *or* **-leaves** : highway interchange

clown \'klaun\ *n* : funny costumed entertainer esp. in a circus ~ *vb* : act like a clown — **clown·ish** *adj* — **clown·ish·ly** *adv* — **clown·ish·ness** *n*

cloy \'klȯi\ *vb* : disgust with excess — **cloy·ing·ly** \-iŋlē\ *adv*

club \'kləb\ *n* **1** : heavy wooden stick **2** : playing card of a suit marked with a black figure like a clover leaf **3** : group associated for a common purpose ~ *vb* **-bb-** : hit with a club

club·foot *n* : misshapen foot twisted out of position from birth — **club·foot·ed** \-,futəd\ *adj*

cluck \'klək\ *n* : sound made by a hen — **cluck** *vb*

clue \'klü\ *n* : piece of evidence that helps solve a problem ~ *vb* **clued; clue·ing** *or* **clu·ing** : provide with a clue

clump \'kləmp\ *n* **1** : cluster **2** : heavy tramping sound ~ *vb* : tread heavily

clum·sy \'kləmzē\ *adj* **-si·er; -est** **1** : lacking dexterity, nimbleness, or grace **2** : tactless — **clum·si·ly** *adv* — **clum·si·ness** *n*

clung *past of* CLING

clunk·er \'kləŋkər\ *n* : old automobile

clus·ter \'kləstər\ *n* : group ~ *vb* : grow or gather in a cluster

clutch \'kləch\ *vb* : grasp ~ *n* **1** : grasping hand or claws **2** : control or power **3** : coupling for connecting two working parts in machinery

clut·ter \'klətər\ *vb* : fill with things that get in the way — **clutter** *n*

co- *prefix* : with, together, joint, or jointly

coach \'kōch\ *n* **1** : closed 2-door 4-wheeled carriage **2** : railroad passenger car **3** : bus **4** : 2d-class air travel **5** : one who instructs or trains performers ∼ *vb* : instruct or direct as a coach

co·ag·u·late \kō'agyə‚lāt\ *vb* **-lat·ed; -lat·ing** : clot — **co·ag·u·lant** \-lənt\ *n* — **co·ag·u·la·tion** \-‚agyə'lāshən\ *n*

coal \'kōl\ *n* **1** : ember **2** : black solid mineral used as fuel — **coal·field** *n*

co·alesce \‚kōə'les\ *vb* **-alesced; -alesc·ing** : grow together — **co·ales·cence** \-'les°ns\ *n*

co·ali·tion \-'lishən\ *n* : temporary alliance

coarse \'kōrs\ *adj* **coars·er; coars·est** **1** : composed of large particles **2** : rough or crude — **coarse·ly** *adv* — **coars·en** \-°n\ *vb* — **coarse·ness** *n*

coast \'kōst\ *n* : seashore ∼ *vb* : move without effort — **coast·al** \-°l\ *adj*

coast·er \-ər\ *n* **1** : one that coasts **2** : plate or mat to protect a surface

coast guard *n* : military force that guards or patrols a coast — **coast·guards·man** \'kōst-‚gärdzmən\ *n*

coast·line *n* : shape of a coast

coat \'kōt\ *n* **1** : outer garment for the upper body **2** : external growth of fur or feathers **3** : covering layer ∼ *vb* : cover with a coat — **coat·ed** *adj* — **coat·ing** *n*

coax \'kōks\ *vb* : move to action or achieve by gentle urging or flattery

cob \'käb\ *n* : corncob

List of self-explanatory words with the prefix *co-*

coact	codesign	coexist
coactor	codevelop	coexistence
coauthor	codeveloper	coexistent
coauthorship	codirect	cofeature
cocaptain	codirector	cofinance
cochairman	codiscoverer	cofound
cochampion	codrive	cofounder
cocomposer	codriver	coheir
coconspirator	coedit	coheiress
cocreator	coeditor	cohost
codefendant	coexecutor	cohostess

co·balt \\'kō͵bȯlt\ *n* : shiny silver-white magnetic metallic chemical element

cob·ble \\'käbəl\ *vb* **cob·bled; cob·bling** : make or put together hastily

cob·bler \\'käblər\ *n* **1** : shoemaker **2** : deep-dish fruit pie

cob·ble·stone *n* : small round paving stone

co·bra \\'kōbrə\ *n* : venomous snake

cob·web \\'käb͵web\ *n* : network spun by a spider or a similar filament

co·caine \kō'kān, 'kō͵kān\ *n* : drug obtained from the leaves of a So. American shrub (**co·ca** \\'kōkə\)

co·chlea \\'kōklēə, 'käk-\ *n, pl* **-chle·as** *or* **-chle·ae** \-lē͵ē, -͵ī\ : the usu. spiral part of the inner ear — **coch·le·ar** \-lēər\ *adj*

cock \\'käk\ *n* **1** : male fowl **2** : valve or faucet ～ *vb* **1** : draw back the hammer of a firearm **2** : tilt to one side — **cock·fight** *n*

cock·a·too \\'käkə͵tü\ *n, pl* **-toos** : large Australian crested parrot

cock·eyed \\'käk'īd\ *adj* **1** : tilted to one side **2** : slightly crazy

cock·le \\'käkəl\ *n* : edible shellfish

cock·pit \\'käk͵pit\ *n* : place for a pilot, driver, or helmsman

cock·roach *n* : nocturnal insect often infesting houses

cock·tail \\'käk͵tāl\ *n* **1** : iced drink of liquor and flavorings **2** : appetizer

cocky \\'käkē\ *adj* **cock·i·er; -est** : overconfident — **cock·i·ly** \-əlē\ *adv* — **cock·i·ness** *n*

co·coa \\'kōkō\ *n* **1** : cacao **2** : powdered chocolate or a drink made from this

co·co·nut \\'kōkə͵nət\ *n* : large nutlike fruit of a tropical palm (**coconut palm**)

co·coon \kə'kün\ *n* : case protecting an insect pupa

---

coinvent	copartnership	copublisher
coinventor	copresident	corecipient
coinvestigator	coprincipal	coresident
coleader	coprisoner	cosignatory
comanagement	coproduce	cosigner
comanager	coproducer	cosponsor
co-organizer	coproduction	costar
co-own	copromoter	cowinner
co-owner	coproprietor	coworker
copartner	copublish	cowrite

cod \'käd\ *n, pl* **cod** : food fish of the No. Atlantic

cod·dle \'käd³l\ *vb* **-dled; -dling** : pamper

code \'kōd\ *n* **1** : system of laws or rules **2** : system of signals

co·deine \'kō₁dēn\ *n* : narcotic drug used in cough remedies

cod·ger \'käjər\ *n* : odd fellow

cod·i·cil \'kädəsəl, -₁sil\ *n* : postscript to a will

cod·i·fy \'kädə₁fī, 'kōd-\ *vb* **-fied; -fy·ing** : arrange systematically — **cod·i·fi·ca·tion** \₁kädəfə'kāshən, ₁kōd-\ *n*

co·ed \'kō₁ed\ *n* : female student in a coeducational institution — **coed** *adj*

co·ed·u·ca·tion \₁kō-\ *n* : education of the sexes together — **co·ed·u·ca·tion·al** *adj*

co·ef·fi·cient \₁kōə'fishənt\ *n* **1** : number that is a multiplier of another **2** : number that serves as a measure of some property

co·erce \kō'ərs\ *vb* **-erced; -erc·ing** : force — **co·er·cion** \-'ərzhən, -shən\ *n* — **co·er·cive** \-'ərsiv\ *adj*

cof·fee \'kȯfē\ *n* : drink made from the roasted and ground seeds (**coffee beans**) of a tropical shrub — **cof·fee·house** *n* — **cof·fee·pot** *n*

cof·fer \'kȯfər\ *n* : box for valuables

cof·fin \-fən\ *n* : box for burial

cog \'käg\ *n* : tooth on the rim of a gear — **cogged** \'kägd\ *adj* — **cog·wheel** *n*

co·gent \'kōjənt\ *adj* : compelling or convincing — **co·gen·cy** \-jənsē\ *n*

cog·i·tate \'käjə₁tāt\ *vb* **-tat·ed; -tat·ing** : think over — **cog·i·ta·tion** \₁käjə'tāshən\ *n* — **cog·i·ta·tive** \'käjə₁tātiv\ *adj*

co·gnac \'kōn₁yak\ *n* : French brandy

cog·nate \'käg₁nāt\ *adj* : related — **cog·nate** *n*

cog·ni·tion \käg'nishən\ *n* : act or process of knowing — **cog·ni·tive** \'kägnətiv\ *adj*

cog·ni·zance \'kägnəzəns\ *n* : notice or awareness — **cog·ni·zant** \'kägnəzənt\ *adj*

co·hab·it \kō'habət\ *vb* : live together as husband and wife — **co·hab·i·ta·tion** \-₁habə'tāshən\ *n*

co·here \kō'hir\ *vb* **-hered; -her·ing** : stick together

co·her·ent \-'hirənt\ *adj* **1** : able to stick together **2** : logically consistent — **co·her·ence** \-əns\ *n* — **co·her·ent·ly** *adv*

co·he·sion \-'hēzhən\ *n* : a sticking together — **co·he·sive**

\-siv\ *adj* — **co·he·sive·ly** *adv* — **co·he·sive·ness** *n*

co·hort \'kō₁hȯrt\ *n* **1** : group of soldiers **2** : companion

coif·fure \kwä'fyu̇r\ *n* : hair style

coil \'kȯil\ *vb* : wind in a spiral ～ *n* : series of loops (as of rope)

coin \'kȯin\ *n* : piece of metal used as money ～ *vb* **1** : make (a coin) by stamping **2** : create — **coin·age** \-ij\ *n* — **coin·er** *n*

co·in·cide \₁kōən'sīd, 'kōən₁sīd\ *vb* **-cid·ed; -cid·ing** **1** : be in the same place **2** : happen at the same time **3** : be alike — **co·in·ci·dence** \kō'insədəns\ *n* — **co·in·ci·dent** \-dənt\ *adj* — **co·in·ci·den·tal** \-₁insə'dentᵊl\ *adj*

co·itus \'kōətəs\ *n* : sexual intercourse — **co·ital** \-ətᵊl\ *adj*

coke \'kōk\ *n* : fuel made by heating soft coal

co·la \'kōlə\ *n* : carbonated soft drink

col·an·der \'kələndər, 'käl-\ *n* : perforated utensil for draining food

cold \'kōld\ *adj* **1** : having a low or below normal temperature **2** : lacking warmth of feeling **3** : suffering from lack of warmth ～ *n* **1** : low temperature **2** : minor respiratory illness — **cold·ly** *adv*

— **cold·ness** *n* — **in cold blood** : with premeditation

cold–blood·ed *adj* **1** : cruel or merciless **2** : having a body temperature that varies with the temperature of the environment

cole·slaw \'kōl₁slȯ\ *n* : cabbage salad

col·ic \'kälik\ *n* : sharp abdominal pain — **col·icky** *adj*

col·i·se·um \₁kälə'sēəm\ *n* : arena

col·lab·o·rate \kə'labə₁rāt\ *vb* **-rat·ed; -rat·ing** **1** : work jointly with others **2** : help the enemy — **col·lab·o·ra·tion** \-₁labə'rāshən\ *n* — **col·lab·o·ra·tor** \-'labə₁rātər\ *n*

col·lapse \kə'laps\ *vb* **-lapsed; -laps·ing** **1** : fall in **2** : break down physically or mentally **3** : fold down ～ *n* : breakdown — **col·laps·ible** *adj*

col·lar \'kälər\ *n* : part of a garment around the neck ～ *vb* **1** : seize by the collar **2** : grab — **col·lar·less** *adj*

col·lar·bone *n* : bone joining the breastbone and the shoulder blade

col·lards \'kälərdz\ *n pl* : kale

col·late \kə'lāt; 'käl₁āt, 'kōl-\ *vb* **-lat·ed; -lat·ing** **1** : compare carefully **2** : assemble in order

col·lat·er·al \kə'latərəl\ *adj* **1** : secondary **2** : descended from the same ancestors but not in the same line **3** : similar ~ *n* : property used as security for a loan

col·league \'käl‚ēg\ *n* : associate

col·lect \kə'lekt\ *vb* **1** : bring, come, or gather together **2** : receive payment of ~ *adv or adj* : to be paid for by the receiver — **col·lect·ible, col·lect·able** *adj* — **col·lec·tion** \-'lekshən\ *n* — **col·lec·tor** \-'lektər\ *n*

col·lec·tive \-tiv\ *adj* : denoting or shared by a group ~ *n* : a cooperative unit — **col·lec·tive·ly** *adv*

col·lege \'kälij\ *n* : institution of higher learning granting a bachelor's degree — **col·le·gian** \kə'lējan\ *n* — **col·le·giate** \kə'lējət\ *adj*

col·lide \kə'līd\ *vb* **-lid·ed; -lid·ing** : strike together — **col·li·sion** \-'lizhən\ *n*

col·lie \'kälē\ *n* : large long-haired dog

col·loid \'käl‚ȯid\ *n* : tiny particles in suspension in a fluid — **col·loi·dal** \kə'lȯid°l\ *adj*

col·lo·qui·al \kə'lōkwēəl\ *adj* : used in informal conversation — **col·lo·qui·al·ism** \-ə‚lizəm\ *n*

col·lu·sion \kə'lüzhən\ *n* : secret cooperation for deceit — **col·lu·sive** \-'lüsiv\ *adj*

co·logne \kə'lōn\ *n* : perfumed liquid

¹co·lon \'kōlən\ *n, pl* **colons** *or* **co·la** \-lə\ : lower part of the large intestine — **co·lon·ic** \kō'länik\ *adj*

²colon *n, pl* **colons** : punctuation mark : used esp. to direct attention to following matter

col·o·nel \'kərn°l\ *n* : commissioned officer (as in the army) ranking next below a brigadier general

col·o·nize \'kälə‚nīz\ *vb* **-nized; -niz·ing** **1** : establish a colony in **2** : settle — **col·o·ni·za·tion** \‚kälənə'zāshən\ *n* — **col·o·niz·er** *n*

col·on·nade \‚kälə'nād\ *n* : row of supporting columns

col·o·ny \'kälənē\ *n, pl* **-nies** **1** : people who inhabit a new territory or the territory itself **2** : animals of one kind (as bees) living together — **co·lo·nial** \kə'lōnēəl\ *adj or n* — **col·o·nist** \'kälənist\ *n*

col·or \'kələr\ *n* **1** : quality of visible things distinct from shape that results from light reflection **2** *pl* : flag **3** : liveliness ~ *vb* **1** : give color to **2** : blush — **col·or·fast** *adj* — **col·or·ful** *adj* — **col·or·less** *adj*

col·or–blind *adj* : unable to distinguish colors — **color blindness** *n*

col·ored \\'kələrd\\ *adj* **1** : having color **2** : of a race other than the white ∼ *n, pl* **colored** *or* **coloreds** : colored person

co·los·sal \\kə'läsəl\\ *adj* : very large or great

co·los·sus \\-səs\\ *n, pl* **-si** \\-'läs,ī\\ : something of great size or scope

colt \\'kōlt\\ *n* : young male horse — **colt·ish** *adj*

col·umn \\'käləm\\ *n* **1** : vertical section of a printed page **2** : regular feature article (as in a newspaper) **3** : pillar **4** : row (as of soldiers) — **co·lum·nar** \\kə'ləmnər\\ *adj* — **col·um·nist** \\'käləmnist\\ *n*

co·ma \\'kōmə\\ *n* : deep prolonged unconsciousness — **co·ma·tose** \\-,tōs, 'kämə-\\ *adj*

comb \\'kōm\\ *n* **1** : toothed instrument for arranging the hair **2** : crest on a fowl's head — **comb** *vb* — **combed** \\'kōmd\\ *adj*

com·bat \\kəm'bat, 'käm,bat\\ *vb* **-bat·ed** *or* **-bat·ted; -bat·ing** *or* **-bat·ting** : fight — **combat** \\'käm,bat\\ *n* — **com·bat·ant** \\kəm'bat°nt\\ *n* — **com·bat·ive** \\kəm'bativ\\ *adj*

com·bi·na·tion \\,kämbə'nāshən\\ *n* **1** : process or result of combining **2** : code for opening a lock

com·bine \\kəm'bīn\\ *vb* **-bined; -bin·ing** : join together ∼ \\'käm,bīn\\ *n* **1** : association for business or political advantage **2** : harvesting machine

com·bus·ti·ble \\kəm'bəstəbəl\\ *adj* : apt to catch fire — **com·bus·ti·bil·i·ty** \\-,bəstə'bilətē\\ *n* — **combustible** *n*

com·bus·tion \\-'bəschən\\ *n* : process of burning

come \\'kəm\\ *vb* **came** \\'kām\\; **come; com·ing** **1** : move toward or arrive at something **2** : reach a state **3** : originate or exist **4** : amount — **come clean** *vb* : confess — **come into** *vb* : acquire, achieve — **come off** *vb* : succeed — **come to** *vb* : regain consciousness — **come to pass** : happen — **come to terms** : reach an agreement

come·back *n* **1** : retort **2** : return to a former position — **come back** *vb*

co·me·di·an \\kə'mēdēən\\ *n* **1** : comic actor **2** : funny person **3** : entertainer specializing in comedy

co·me·di·enne \\-,mēdē'en\\ *n* : a woman who is a comedian

com·e·dy \\'kämədē\\ *n, pl* **-dies** **1** : an amusing play **2** : humorous entertainment

come·ly \\'kəmlē\\ *adj* **-li·er; -est** : attractive — **come·li·ness** *n*

com·et \'kämət\ *n* : small bright celestial body having a tail

com·fort \'kəmfərt\ *n* **1** : consolation **2** : well-being or something that gives it ~ *vb* **1** : give hope to **2** : console — **com·fort·able** \'kəmftəbəl, 'kəmfərt-\ *adj* — **com·fort·ably** \-blē\ *adv*

com·fort·er \'kəmfərtər\ *n* **1** : one that comforts **2** : quilt

com·ic \'kämik\ *adj* **1** : relating to comedy **2** : funny ~ *n* **1** : comedian **2** : sequence of cartoons — **com·i·cal** *adj*

com·ing \'kəmiŋ\ *adj* : next

com·ma \'kämə\ *n* : punctuation mark, used esp. to separate sentence parts

com·mand \kə'mand\ *vb* **1** : order **2** : control ~ *n* **1** : act of commanding **2** : an order given **3** : mastery **4** : troops under a commander — **com·man·dant** \'kämən-ˌdant, -ˌdänt\ *n*

com·man·deer \ˌkämən'dir\ *vb* : seize by force

com·mand·er \kə'mandər\ *n* **1** : officer commanding an army or subdivision of an army **2** : commissioned officer in the navy ranking next below a captain

com·mand·ment \-'mand-mənt\ *n* : order

command sergeant major *n* : noncommissioned officer in the army ranking above a first sergeant

com·mem·o·rate \kə'memə-ˌrāt\ *vb* **-rat·ed; -rat·ing** : celebrate or honor — **com·mem·o·ra·tion** \-ˌmemə'rā-shən\ *n* — **com·mem·o·ra·tive** \-'memrətiv, -'meməˌrāt-\ *adj*

com·mence \kə'mens\ *vb* **-menced; -menc·ing** : start

com·mence·ment \-mənt\ *n* **1** : beginning **2** : graduation ceremony

com·mend \kə'mend\ *vb* **1** : entrust **2** : recommend **3** : praise — **commend·able** \-əbəl\ *adj* — **com·men·da·tion** \ˌkämən'dāshən, -ˌen-\ *n*

com·men·su·rate \kə'men-sərət, -'mench-\ *adj* : equal in measure or extent

com·ment \'kämˌent\ *n* : statement of opinion or remark — **comment** *vb*

com·men·tary \-ənˌterē\ *n, pl* **-tar·ies** : series of comments

com·men·ta·tor \-ənˌtātər\ *n* : one who discusses news

com·merce \'kämərs\ *n* : business

com·mer·cial \kə'mərshəl\ *adj* : designed for profit or for mass appeal ~ *n* : broadcast advertisement — **com·mer-**

cial·ize \-ˌīz\ vb — com·mer·cial·ly \-ē\ adv

com·min·gle \kə'miŋgəl\ vb : mix

com·mis·er·ate \kə'mizəˌrāt\ vb -at·ed; -at·ing : sympathize — com·mis·er·a·tion \-ˌmizə'rāshən\ n

com·mis·sary \'käməˌserē\ n, pl -sar·ies : store esp. for military personnel

com·mis·sion \kə'mishən\ n 1 : order granting power or rank 2 : panel to judge, approve, or act 3 : the doing of an act 4 : agent's fee ∼ vb 1 : confer rank or authority to or for 2 : request something be done

com·mis·sion·er \-shənər\ n 1 : member of a commission 2 : head of a government department

com·mit \kə'mit\ vb -tt- 1 : turn over to someone for safekeeping or confinement 2 : perform or do 3 : pledge — com·mit·ment n

com·mit·tee \kə'mitē\ n : panel that examines or acts on something

com·mo·di·ous \kə'mōdēəs\ adj : spacious

com·mod·i·ty \kə'mädətē\ n, pl -ties : article for sale

com·mo·dore \'käməˌdōr\ n 1 : former commissioned officer in the navy ranking next

below a rear admiral 2 : officer commanding a group of merchant ships

com·mon \'kämən\ adj 1 : public 2 : shared by several 3 : widely known, found, or observed 4 : ordinary ∼ n : community land — com·mon·ly adv — in common : shared together

com·mon·place \'kämənˌplās\ n : cliché ∼ adj : ordinary

common sense n : good judgment

com·mon·weal \-ˌwēl\ n : general welfare

com·mon·wealth \-ˌwelth\ n : state

com·mo·tion \kə'mōshən\ n : disturbance

¹com·mune \kə'myün\ vb -muned; -mun·ing : communicate intimately

²com·mune \'kämˌyün; kə'myün\ n : community that shares all ownership and duties — com·mu·nal \-ᵊl\ adj

com·mu·ni·cate \kə'myünəˌkāt\ vb -cat·ed; -cat·ing 1 : make known 2 : transmit 3 : exchange information or opinions — com·mu·ni·ca·ble \-'myünikəbəl\ adj — com·mu·ni·ca·tion \-ˌmyünə'kāshən\ n — com·mu·ni·ca·tive \-'myüniˌkātiv, -kət-\ adj

Com·mu·nion \kə'myünyən\ *n* : Christian sacrament of partaking of bread and wine

com·mu·ni·qué \kə'myünə-ˌkā, -ˌmyünə'kā\ *n* : official bulletin

com·mu·nism \'kämyə-ˌnizəm\ *n* **1** : social organization in which goods are held in common **2** *cap* : political doctrine based on revolutionary Marxist socialism — **com·mu·nist** \-nist\ *n or adj, often cap* — **com·mu·nis·tic** \ˌkämyə'nistik\ *adj, often cap*

com·mu·ni·ty \kə'myünətē\ *n, pl* **-ties** : body of people living in the same place under the same laws

com·mute \kə'myüt\ *vb* **-mut·ed; -mut·ing** **1** : reduce (a punishment) **2** : travel back and forth regularly ～ *n* : trip made in commuting — **com·mu·ta·tion** \ˌkämyə'tāshən\ *n* — **com·mut·er** *n*

¹**com·pact** \kəm'pakt, 'käm-ˌpakt\ *adj* **1** : hard **2** : small or brief ～ *vb* : pack together ～ \'käm,pakt\ *n* **1** : cosmetics case **2** : small car — **com·pact·ly** *adv* — **com·pact·ness** *n*

²**com·pact** \'käm,pakt\ *n* : agreement

compact disc *n* : plastic-coated disc with laser-readable recorded music

com·pan·ion \kəm'panyən\ *n* **1** : close friend **2** : one of a pair — **com·pan·ion·able** *adj* — **com·pan·ion·ship** *n*

com·pa·ny \'kəmpənē\ *n, pl* **-nies** **1** : business organization **2** : group of performers **3** : guests **4** : infantry unit

com·par·a·tive \kəm'parətiv\ *adj* **1** : relating to or being an adjective or adverb form that denotes increase **2** : relative — **comparative** *n* — **com·par·a·tive·ly** *adv*

com·pare \kəm'par\ *vb* **-pared; -par·ing** **1** : represent as similar **2** : check for likenesses or differences ～ *n* : comparison — **com·pa·ra·ble** \'kämprəbəl\ *adj*

com·par·i·son \kəm'parəsən\ *n* **1** : act of comparing **2** : change in the form and meaning of an adjective or adverb to show different levels of quality, quantity, or relation

com·part·ment \kəm'pärt-mənt\ *n* : section or room

com·pass \'kəmpəs, 'käm-\ *n* **1** : scope **2** : device for drawing circles **3** : device for determining direction

com·pas·sion \kəm'pashən\ *n* : pity — **com·pas·sion·ate** \-ənət\ *adj*

com·pat·i·ble \-'patəbəl\ *adj* : harmonious — **com·pat·i·bil·i·ty** \-ˌpatə'bilətē\ *n*

com·pa·tri·ot \kəm'pātrēət, -trē͵ät\ *n* : fellow countryman

com·pel \kəm'pel\ *vb* **-ll-** : cause through necessity

com·pen·di·ous \kam'pendēəs\ *adj* **1** : concise and comprehensive **2** : comprehensive

com·pen·di·um \-'pendēəm\ *n, pl* **-di·ums** *or* **-dia** \-dēə\ : summary

com·pen·sate \'kämpən͵sāt\ *vb* **-sat·ed; -sat·ing** **1** : offset or balance **2** : repay — **com·pen·sa·tion** \͵kämpən'sāshən\ *n* — **com·pen·sa·to·ry** \kəm'pensə͵tōrē\ *adj*

com·pete \kəm'pēt\ *vb* **-pet·ed; -pet·ing** : strive to win — **com·pe·ti·tion** \͵kämpə'tishən\ *n* — **com·pet·i·tive** \kəm'petətiv\ *adj* — **com·pet·i·tive·ness** *n* — **com·pet·i·tor** \kəm'petətər\ *n*

com·pe·tent \'kämpətənt\ *adj* : capable — **com·pe·tence** \-əns\ *n* — **com·pe·ten·cy** \-ənsē\ *n*

com·pile \kəm'pīl\ *vb* **-piled; -pil·ing** : collect or compose from several sources — **com·pi·la·tion** \͵kämpə'lāshən\ *n* — **com·pil·er** \kəm'pīlər\ *n*

com·pla·cen·cy \kəm'plā-sᵊnsē\ *n* : self-satisfaction — **com·pla·cent** \-ᵊnt\ *adj*

com·plain \kəm'plān\ *vb* **1** : express grief, pain, or discontent **2** : make an accusa-tion — **com·plain·ant** *n* — **com·plain·er** *n*

com·plaint \-'plānt\ *n* **1** : expression of grief or discontent **2** : ailment **3** : formal accusation

com·ple·ment \'kämpləmənt\ *n* **1** : something that completes **2** : full number or amount ~ \-͵ment\ *vb* : complete — **com·ple·men·ta·ry** \͵kämplə'mentərē\ *adj*

com·plete \kəm'plēt\ *adj* **-plet·er; -est** **1** : having all parts **2** : finished **3** : total ~ *vb* **-plet·ed; -plet·ing** **1** : make whole **2** : finish — **com·plete·ly** *adv* — **com·plete·ness** *n* — **com·ple·tion** \-'plēshən\ *n*

com·plex \käm'pleks, kəm-; 'käm͵pleks\ *adj* **1** : having many parts **2** : intricate ~ \'käm͵pleks\ *n* : psychological problem — **com·plex·i·ty** \kəm'pleksətē, käm-\ *n*

com·plex·ion \kəm'plekshən\ *n* : hue or appearance of the skin esp. of the face — **com·plex·ioned** *adj*

com·pli·cate \'kämplə͵kāt\ *vb* **-cat·ed; -cat·ing** : make complex or hard to understand — **com·pli·cat·ed** \-əd\ *adj* — **com·pli·ca·tion** \͵kämplə'kāshən\ *n*

com·plic·i·ty \kəm'plisətē\ *n, pl* **-ties** : participation in guilt

com·pli·ment \\'kämpləmənt\\ *n* **1** : flattering remark **2** *pl* : greeting ∼ \\-ˌment\\ *vb* : pay a compliment to

com·pli·men·ta·ry \\ˌkämplə-'mentərē\\ *adj* **1** : praising **2** : free

com·ply \\kəm'plī\\ *vb* **-plied; -ply·ing** : conform or yield — **com·pli·ance** \\-əns\\ *n* — **com·pli·ant** \\-ənt\\ *n*

com·po·nent \\kəm'pōnənt, 'kämˌpō-\\ *n* : part of something larger ∼ *adj* : serving as a component

com·port \\kəm'pōrt\\ *vb* **1** : agree **2** : behave — **com·port·ment** \\-mənt\\ *n*

com·pose \\kəm'pōz\\ *vb* **-posed; -pos·ing** **1** : create (as by writing) or put together **2** : calm **3** : set type — **com·pos·er** *n* — **com·po·si·tion** \\ˌkämpə'zishən\\ *n*

com·pos·ite \\käm'päzət, kəm-\\ *adj* : made up of diverse parts — **com·posite** *n*

com·post \\'kämˌpōst\\ *n* : decayed organic fertilizing material

com·po·sure \\kəm'pōzhər\\ *n* : calmness

com·pote \\'kämˌpōt\\ *n* : fruits cooked in syrup

¹com·pound \\'kämˌpaund, kəm'paund\\ *vb* **1** : combine or add **2** : pay (interest) on principal and accrued interest ∼ \\'kämˌpaund\\ *adj* : made up of 2 or more parts ∼ \\'kämˌpaund\\ *n* : something that is compound

²com·pound \\'kämˌpaund\\ *n* : enclosure

com·pre·hend \\ˌkämpri'hend\\ *vb* **1** : understand **2** : include — **com·pre·hen·si·ble** \\-'hensəbəl\\ *adj* — **com·pre·hen·sion** \\-'henchən\\ *n* — **com·pre·hen·sive** \\-siv\\ *adj*

com·press \\kəm'pres\\ *vb* : squeeze together ∼ \\'kämˌpres\\ *n* : pad for pressing on a wound — **com·pres·sion** \\-'preshən\\ *n* — **com·pres·sor** \\-'presər\\ *n*

compressed air *n* : air under pressure greater than that of the atmosphere

com·prise \\kəm'prīz\\ *vb* **-prised; -pris·ing** **1** : contain or cover **2** : be made up of

com·pro·mise \\'kämprəˌmīz\\ *vb* **-mised; -mis·ing** : settle differences by mutual concessions — **compromise** *n*

comp·trol·ler \\kən'trōlər, 'kämpˌtrō-\\ *n* : financial officer

com·pul·sion \\kəm'pəlshən\\ *n* **1** : coercion **2** : irresistible impulse — **com·pul·sive** \\-siv\\ *adj* — **com·pul·so·ry** \\-'pəlsərē\\ *adj*

com·punc·tion \\-'pənkshən\\ *n* : remorse

com·pute \-'pyüt\ *vb* **-put·ed; -put·ing** : calculate — **com·pu·ta·tion** \ˌkämpyu̇'tāshən\ *n*

com·put·er \kəm'pyütər\ *n* : electronic data processing machine — **com·put·er·i·za·tion** \-ˌpyütərə'zāshən\ *n* — **com·put·er·ize** \-'pyütəˌrīz\ *vb*

com·rade \'kämˌrad, -rəd\ *n* : companion — **com·rade·ship** *n*

¹**con** \'kän\ *adv* : against ∼ *n* : opposing side or person

²**con** *vb* **-nn-** : swindle

con·cave \kän'kāv, 'känˌkāv\ *adj* : curved like the inside of a sphere — **con·cav·i·ty** \kän'kavətē\ *n*

con·ceal \kən'sēl\ *vb* : hide — **con·ceal·ment** *n*

con·cede \-'sēd\ *vb* **-ced·ed; -ced·ing** : grant

con·ceit \-'sēt\ *n* : excessively high opinion of oneself — **con·ceit·ed** \-əd\ *adj*

con·ceive \-'sēv\ *vb* **-ceived; -ceiv·ing** **1** : become pregnant **2** : think of — **con·ceiv·able** \-'sēvəbəl\ *adj* — **con·ceiv·ably** \-blē\ *adv*

con·cen·trate \'känsənˌtrāt\ *vb* **-trat·ed; -trat·ing** **1** : gather together **2** : make stronger **3** : fix one's attention ∼ *n* : something concen-trated — **con·cen·tra·tion** \ˌkänsən'trāshən\ *n*

con·cen·tric \kən'sentrik\ *adj* : having a common center

con·cept \'känˌsept\ *n* : thought or idea

con·cep·tion \kən'sepshən\ *n* **1** : act of conceiving **2** : idea

con·cern \kən'sərn\ *vb* **1** : relate to **2** : involve ∼ *n* **1** : affair **2** : worry **3** : business — **con·cerned** \-'sərnd\ *adj* — **con·cern·ing** \-'sərniŋ\ *prep*

con·cert \'känˌsərt\ *n* **1** : agreement or joint action **2** : public performance of music — **con·cert·ed** \kən'sərtəd\ *adj*

con·cer·ti·na \ˌkänsər'tēnə\ *n* : accordionlike instrument

con·cer·to \kən'chertō\ *n, pl* **-ti** \-tē\ *or* **-tos** : orchestral work with solo instruments

con·ces·sion \-'seshən\ *n* **1** : act of conceding **2** : something conceded **3** : right to do business on a property

conch \'käŋk, 'känch\ *n, pl* **conchs** \'käŋks\ *or* **conch·es** \'känchəz\ : large spiral-shelled marine mollusk

con·cil·ia·to·ry \kən'silēəˌtōrē\ *adj* : mollifying

con·cise \kən'sīs\ *adj* : said in few words — **con·cise·ly** *adv* — **con·cise·ness** *n* — **con·ci·sion** \kən'sizhən\ *n*

con·clave \'kän͵klāv\ *n* : private meeting

con·clude \kən'klüd\ *vb* **-clud·ed; -clud·ing 1** : end **2** : decide — **con·clu·sion** \-'klüzhən\ *n* — **con·clu·sive** \-siv\ *adj* — **con·clu·sive·ly** *adv*

con·coct \kən'käkt, kän-\ *vb* : prepare or devise — **con·coc·tion** \-'käkshən\ *n*

con·com·i·tant \-'kämətənt\ *adj* : accompanying — **con·comitant** *n*

con·cord \'kän͵kȯrd, 'käŋ-\ *n* : agreement

con·cor·dance \kən'kȯrd°ns\ *n* **1** : agreement **2** : index of words — **con·cor·dant** \-°nt\ *adj*

con·course \'kän͵kōrs\ *n* : open space where crowds gather

con·crete \kän'krēt, 'kän͵krēt\ *adj* **1** : naming something real **2** : actual or substantial **3** : made of concrete ~ \'kän͵krēt, kän'krēt\ *n* : hard building material made of cement, sand, gravel, and water

con·cre·tion \kän'krēshən\ *n* : hard mass

con·cu·bine \'käŋkyu͵bīn\ *n* : mistress

con·cur \kən'kər\ *vb* **-rr-** : agree — **con·cur·rence** \-'kərəns\ *n*

con·cur·rent \-ənt\ *adj* : happening at the same time

con·cus·sion \kən'kəshən\ *n* **1** : shock **2** : brain injury from a blow

con·demn \-'dem\ *vb* **1** : declare to be wrong, guilty, or unfit for use **2** : sentence — **con·dem·na·tion** \͵kän͵dem-'nāshən\ *n*

con·dense \kən'dens\ *vb* **-densed; -dens·ing 1** : make or become more compact **2** : change from vapor to liquid — **con·den·sa·tion** \͵kän-͵den'sāshən, -dən-\ *n* — **con·dens·er** *n*

con·de·scend \͵kändi'send\ *vb* **1** : lower oneself **2** : act haughtily — **con·de·scen·sion** \-'senchən\ *n*

con·di·ment \'kändəmənt\ *n* : pungent seasoning

con·di·tion \kən'dishən\ *n* **1** : necessary situation or stipulation **2** *pl* : state of affairs **3** : state of being ~ *vb* : put into proper condition — **con·di·tion·al** \kən'dishənəl\ *adj* — **con·di·tion·al·ly** \-ē\ *adv*

con·do·lence \kən'dōləns\ *n* : expression of sympathy — usu. pl.

con·do·min·i·um \͵kändə-'minēəm\ *n, pl* **-ums** : individually owned apartment

con·done \kən'dōn\ *vb* **-doned; -don·ing** : overlook or forgive

con·dor \'kändər, -ˌdȯr\ *n* : large western American vulture

con·du·cive \kən'düsiv, -'dyü-\ *adj* : tending to help or promote

con·duct \'känˌdəkt\ *n* **1** : management **2** : behavior ~ \kən'dəkt\ *vb* **1** : guide **2** : manage or direct **3** : be a channel for **4** : behave — **con·duc·tion** \-'dəkshən\ *n* — **con·duc·tive** \-'dəktiv\ *adj* — **con·duc·tiv·i·ty** \ˌkänˌdək'tivətē\ *n* — **con·duc·tor** \-'dəktər\ *n*

con·duit \'känˌdüət, -ˌdyü-\ *n* : channel (as for conveying fluid)

cone \'kōn\ *n* **1** : scaly fruit of pine and related trees **2** : solid figure having a circular base and tapering sides

con·fec·tion \kən'fekshən\ *n* : sweet dish or candy — **con·fec·tion·er** \-shənər\ *n*

con·fed·er·a·cy \kən'fedərəsē\ *n, pl* **-cies** **1** : league **2** *cap* : 11 southern states that seceded from the U.S. in 1860 and 1861

con·fed·er·ate \-rət\ *adj* **1** : united in a league **2** *cap* : relating to the Confederacy ~ *n* **1** : ally **2** *cap* : adherent of the Confederacy ~ \-'fedəˌrāt\ *vb* **-at·ed; -at·ing** : unite — **con·fed·er·a·tion** \-ˌfedə'rāshən\ *n*

con·fer \kən'fər\ *vb* **-rr-** **1** : give **2** : meet to exchange views — **con·fer·ee** \ˌkänfə'rē\ *n* — **con·fer·ence** \'känfərəns\ *n*

con·fess \kən'fes\ *vb* **1** : acknowledge or disclose one's misdeed, fault, or sin **2** : declare faith in — **con·fes·sion** \-'feshən\ *n* — **con·fes·sion·al** \-'feshənəl\ *n or adj*

con·fes·sor \kən'fesər, 2 *also* 'känˌfes-\ *n* **1** : one who confesses **2** : priest who hears confessions

con·fet·ti \kən'fetē\ *n* : bits of paper or ribbon thrown in celebration

con·fi·dant \'känfəˌdant, -ˌdänt\ *n* : one to whom secrets are confided

con·fide \kən'fīd\ *vb* **-fid·ed; -fid·ing** **1** : share private thoughts **2** : reveal in confidence

con·fi·dence \'känfədəns\ *n* **1** : trust **2** : self-assurance **3** : something confided — **con·fi·dent** \-dənt\ *adj* — **con·fi·den·tial** \ˌkänfə'denchəl\ *adj* — **con·fi·den·tial·ly** \-ē\ *adv* — **con·fi·dent·ly** *adv*

con·fig·u·ra·tion \kənˌfigyə'rāshən\ *n* : arrangement

con·fine \kən'fīn\ *vb* **-fined; -fin·ing** **1** : restrain or restrict to a limited area **2** : imprison — **con·fine·ment** *n* — **con·fin·er** *n*

con·fines \'kän͵fīnz\ *n pl* : bounds

con·firm \kən'fərm\ *vb* **1** : ratify **2** : verify **3** : admit as a full member of a church or synagogue — **con·fir·ma·tion** \͵känfər'māshən\ *n*

con·fis·cate \'känfə͵skāt\ *vb* **-cat·ed; -cat·ing** : take by authority — **con·fis·ca·tion** \͵känfə'skāshən\ *n* — **con·fis·ca·to·ry** \kən'fiskə͵tōrē\ *adj*

con·fla·gra·tion \͵känflə'grā-shən\ *n* : great fire

con·flict \'kän͵flikt\ *n* **1** : war **2** : clash of ideas ~ \kən-'flikt\ *vb* : clash

con·form \kən'fòrm\ *vb* **1** : make or be like **2** : obey — **con·for·mi·ty** \kən'fòrmətē\ *n*

con·found \kən'faùnd, kän-\ *vb* : confuse

con·front \kən'frənt\ *vb* : oppose or face — **con·fron·ta·tion** \͵känfrən-'tāshən\ *n*

con·fuse \kən'fyüz\ *vb* **-fused; -fus·ing** **1** : make mentally uncertain **2** : jumble — **con·fu·sion** \-'fyüzhən\ *n*

con·fute \-'fyüt\ *vb* **-fut·ed; -fut·ing** : overwhelm by argument

con·geal \kən'jēl\ *vb* **1** : freeze **2** : become thick and solid

con·ge·nial \kən'jēnēəl\ *adj* : kindred or agreeable — **con·ge·ni·al·i·ty** *n*

con·gen·i·tal \kən'jenət³l\ *adj* : existing from birth

con·gest \kən'jest\ *vb* : overcrowd or overfill — **con·ges·tion** \-'jeschən\ *n* — **con·ges·tive** \-'jestiv\ *adj*

con·glom·er·ate \kən'gläm-ərət\ *adj* : made up of diverse parts ~ \-ə͵rāt\ *vb* **-at·ed; -at·ing** : form into a mass ~ \-ərət\ *n* : diversified corporation — **con·glom·er·a·tion** \-͵glämə'rāshən\ *n*

con·grat·u·late \kən'grachə-͵lāt, -'graj-\ *vb* **-lat·ed; -lat·ing** : express pleasure to for good fortune — **con·grat·u·la·tion** \-͵grachə'lāshən, -͵graj-\ *n* — **con·grat·u·la·to·ry** \-'grachələ͵tōrē,-'graj-\ *adj*

con·gre·gate \'kängri͵gāt\ *vb* **-gat·ed; -gat·ing** : assemble

con·gre·ga·tion \͵kängri'gā-shən\ *n* **1** : assembly of people at worship **2** : religious group — **con·gre·ga·tion·al** \-shənəl\ *adj*

con·gress \'kängrəs\ *n* : assembly of delegates or of senators and representatives — **con·gres·sio·nal** \kən'gre-shənəl, kän-\ *adj* — **con·gress·man** \'kängrəsmən\ *n* — **con·gress·wom·an** *n*

con·gru·ence \kən'grüəns, 'kängrəwəns\ *n* : likeness — **con·gru·ent** \-ənt\ *adj*

con·gru·ity \kən'grüətē, kän-\ *n* : correspondence between things — **con·gru·ous** \'käŋgrəwəs\ *adj*

con·ic \'känik\ *adj* : relating to or like a cone — **con·i·cal** \-ikəl\ *adj*

co·ni·fer \'känəfər, 'kōn-\ *n* : cone-bearing tree — **co·nif·er·ous** \kō'nifərəs\ *adj*

con·jec·ture \kən'jekchər\ *n or vb* : guess — **con·jec·tur·al** \-əl\ *adj*

con·join \kən'jȯin\ *vb* : join together — **con·joint** \-'jȯint\ *adj*

con·ju·gal \'känjigəl, kən'jü-\ *adj* : relating to marriage

con·ju·gate \'känjə,gāt\ *vb* **-gat·ed; -gat·ing** : give the inflected forms of (a verb) — **con·ju·ga·tion** \,känjə-'gā-shən\ *n*

con·junc·tion \kən'jəŋkshən\ *n* **1** : combination **2** : occurrence at the same time **3** : a word that joins other words together — **con·junc·tive** \-tiv\ *adj*

con·jure \'känjər, 'kən-\ *vb* **-jured; -jur·ing 1** : summon by sorcery **2** : practice sleight of hand **3** : entreat — **con·jur·er, con·ju·ror** \'känjərər, 'kən-\ *n*

con·nect \kə'nekt\ *vb* : join or associate — **con·nect·able** *adj* — **con·nec·tion** \-'nekshən\ *n* — **con·nec·tive** \-tiv\ *n or adj* — **con·nec·tor** *n*

con·nive \kə'nīv\ *vb* **-nived; -niv·ing 1** : pretend ignorance of wrongdoing **2** : cooperate secretly — **con·niv·ance** *n*

con·nois·seur \,känə'sər, -'sùr\ *n* : expert judge esp. of art

con·note \kə'nōt\ *vb* **-not·ed; -not·ing** : suggest additional meaning — **con·no·ta·tion** \,känə'tāshən\ *n*

con·nu·bi·al \kə'nübēəl, -'nyü-\ *adj* : relating to marriage

con·quer \'käŋkər\ *vb* : defeat or overcome — **con·quer·or** \-kərər\ *n*

con·quest \'kän,kwest, 'käŋ-\ *n* **1** : act of conquering **2** : something conquered

con·science \'känchəns\ *n* : awareness of right and wrong

con·sci·en·tious \,känchē'en-chəs\ *adj* : honest and hardworking — **con·sci·en·tious·ly** *adv*

con·scious \'känchəs\ *adj* **1** : aware **2** : mentally awake or alert **3** : intentional — **con·scious·ly** *adv* — **con·scious·ness** *n*

con·script \kən'skript\ *vb* : draft for military service — **con·script** \'kän,skript\ *n* — **con·scrip·tion** \kən'skrip-shən\ *n*

con·se·crate \'känsə,krāt\ *vb*
-crat·ed; -crat·ing **1** : declare sacred **2** : devote to a
solemn purpose — **con·se-
cra·tion** \,känə'krāshən\ *n*

con·sec·u·tive \kən'sekyətiv\
adj : following in order —
con·sec·u·tive·ly *adv*

con·sen·sus \-'sensəs\ *n* **1**
: agreement in opinion **2**
: collective opinion

con·sent \-'sent\ *vb* : give permission or approval — **consent** *n*

con·se·quence \'känsə,kwens\
n **1** : result or effect **2** : importance — **con·se·quent**
\-kwənt, -,kwent\ *adj* —
con·se·quent·ly *adv*

con·se·quen·tial \,känsə-
'kwenchəl\ *adj* : important

con·ser·va·tion \,känsər'vā-
shən\ *n* : planned management of natural resources —
con·ser·va·tion·ist \-shənist\
n

con·ser·va·tive \kən'sərvətiv\
adj **1** : disposed to maintain
the status quo **2** : cautious —
con·ser·va·tism \-və,tizəm\
n — **conservative** *n* — **con-
ser·va·tive·ly** *adv*

con·ser·va·to·ry \kən'sərvə-
,tōrē\ *n, pl* **-ries** : school for
art or music

con·serve \-'sərv\ *vb* **-served;
-serv·ing** : keep from wasting

~ \'kän,sərv\ *n* : candied
fruit or fruit preserves

con·sid·er \kən'sidər\ *vb* **1**
: think about **2** : give thoughtful attention to **3** : think that
— **con·sid·er·ate** \-'sidərət\
adj — **con·sid·er·ation** \-,sidə-
'rāshən\ *n*

con·sid·er·able \-'sidərəbəl\
adj **1** : significant **2** : noticeably large — **con·sid·er·a·bly**
\-blē\ *adv*

con·sid·er·ing *prep* : taking
notice of

con·sign \kən'sīn\ *vb* **1** : transfer **2** : send to an agent for
sale — **con·sign·ee** \,känsə-
'nē, -,sī-; kən,sī-\ *n* — **con-
sign·ment** \kən'sīnmənt\ *n*
— **con·sign·or** \,känsə'nȯr,
-,sī-; kən,sī-\ *n*

con·sist \kən'sist\ *vb* **1** : be
inherent — used with *in* **2**
: be made up — used with *of*

con·sis·ten·cy \-'sistənsē\ *n,
pl* **-cies** **1** : degree of thickness or firmness **2** : quality of
being consistent

con·sis·tent \-tənt\ *adj* : being
steady and regular — **con·sis-
tent·ly** *adv*

¹**con·sole** \kən'sōl\ *vb* **-soled;
-sol·ing** : soothe the grief of
— **con·so·la·tion** \,känsə-
'lāshən\ *n*

²**con·sole** \'kän,sōl\ *n* : cabinet
or part with controls

con·sol·i·date \kən'sälə͵dāt\ *vb* **-dat·ed; -dat·ing** : unite or compact — **con·sol·i·da·tion** \-͵sälə'dāshən\ *n*

con·som·mé \͵känsə'mā\ *n* : clear soup

con·so·nance \'känsənəns\ *n* : agreement or harmony — **con·so·nant** \-nənt\ *adj* — **con·so·nant·ly** *adv*

con·so·nant \-nənt\ *n* **1** : speech sound marked by constriction or closure in the breath channel **2** : letter other than *a, e, i, o* and *u* — **con·so·nan·tal** \͵känsə'nant³l\ *adj*

con·sort \'kän͵sȯrt\ *n* : spouse ~ \kən'sȯrt\ *vb* : keep company

con·spic·u·ous \kən'spikyəwəs\ *adj* : very noticeable — **con·spic·u·ous·ly** *adv*

con·spire \kən'spīr\ *vb* **-spired; -spir·ing** : secretly plan an unlawful act — **con·spir·a·cy** \-'spirəsē\ *n* — **con·spir·a·tor** \-'spirətər\ *n* — **con·spir·a·to·ri·al** \-͵spirə'tōrēəl\ *adj*

con·sta·ble \'känstəbəl, 'kən-\ *n* : police officer

con·stab·u·lary \kən'stabyə͵lerē\ *n, pl* **-lar·ies** : police force

con·stant \'känstənt\ *adj* **1** : steadfast or faithful **2** : not varying **3** : continually recurring ~ *n* : something un-changing — **con·stan·cy** \-stənsē\ *n* — **con·stant·ly** *adv*

con·stel·la·tion \͵känstə'lā-shən\ *n* : group of stars

con·ster·na·tion \-stər'nā-shən\ *n* : amazed dismay

con·sti·pa·tion \-stə'pāshən\ *n* : difficulty of defecation — **con·sti·pate** \'känstə͵pāt\ *vb*

con·stit·u·ent \kən'stichəwənt\ *adj* **1** : component **2** : having power to elect ~ *n* **1** : component part **2** : one who may vote for a representative — **con·stit·u·en·cy** \-wənsē\ *n*

con·sti·tute \'känstə͵tüt, -͵tyüt\ *vb* **-tut·ed; -tut·ing** **1** : establish **2** : be all or a basic part of

con·sti·tu·tion \͵känstə'tü-shən, -'tyü-\ *n* **1** : physical composition or structure **2** : the basic law of an organized body or the document containing it — **con·sti·tu·tion·al** \-əl\ *adj* — **con·sti·tu·tion·al·i·ty** \-͵tüshə'nalətē, -͵tyü-\ *n*

con·strain \kən'strān\ *vb* **1** : compel **2** : confine **3** : restrain — **con·straint** \-'strānt\ *n*

con·strict \-'strikt\ *vb* : draw or squeeze together — **con·stric·tion** \-'strikshən\ *n* — **con·stric·tive** \-'striktiv\ *adj*

con·struct \kən'strəkt\ *vb* : build or make — **con·struc·tion** \-'strəkshən\ *n* — **con·struc·tive** \-tiv\ *adj*

con·strue \kən'strü\ *vb* -strued; -stru·ing : explain or interpret

con·sul \'känsəl\ *n* 1 : Roman magistrate 2 : government commercial official in a foreign country — **con·sul·ar** \-ələr\ *adj* — **con·sul·ate** \-lət\ *n*

con·sult \kən'səlt\ *vb* 1 : ask the advice or opinion of 2 : confer — **con·sul·tant** \-ənt\ *n* — **con·sul·ta·tion** \,känsəl-'tāshən\ *n*

con·sume \kən'süm\ *vb* -sumed; -sum·ing : eat or use up — **con·sum·able** *adj* — **con·sum·er** *n*

con·sum·mate \kən'səmət\ *adj* : complete or perfect ~ \'känsə,māt\ *vb* -mat·ed; -mat·ing : make complete — **con·sum·ma·tion** \,känsə-'māshən\ *n*

con·sump·tion \kən'səmp-shən\ *n* 1 : act of consuming 2 : use of goods 3 : tuberculosis — **con·sump·tive** \-tiv\ *adj or n*

con·tact \'kän,takt\ *n* 1 : a touching 2 : association or relationship 3 : connection or communication ~ *vb* 1 : come or bring into contact 2 : communicate with

con·ta·gion \kən'tājən\ *n* 1 : spread of disease by contact 2 : disease spread by contact — **con·ta·gious** \-jəs\ *adj*

con·tain \-'tān\ *vb* 1 : enclose or include 2 : have or hold within 3 : restrain — **con·tain·er** *n* — **con·tain·ment** *n*

con·tam·i·nate \kən'tamə-,nāt\ *vb* -nat·ed; -nat·ing : soil or infect by contact or association — **con·tam·i·na·tion** \-,tamə'nāshən\ *n*

con·tem·plate \'käntəm,plāt\ *vb* -pla·ted; -plat·ing : view or consider thoughtfully — **con·tem·pla·tion** \,käntəm-'plāshən\ *n* — **con·tem·pla·tive** \kən'templətiv; 'kän-təm,plāt-\ *adj*

con·tem·po·ra·ne·ous \kən-,tempə-'rānēəs\ *adj* : contemporary

con·tem·po·rary \-'tempə,rerē\ *adj* 1 : occurring or existing at the same time 2 : of the same age — **contemporary** *n*

con·tempt \kən'tempt\ *n* 1 : feeling of scorn 2 : state of being despised 3 : disobedience to a court or legislature — **con·tempt·ible** \-'tempt-əbəl\ *adj*

con·temp·tu·ous \-'temp-chəwəs\ *adj* : feeling or expressing contempt — **con·temp·tu·ous·ly** *adv*

con·tend \-ˈtend\ *vb* **1** : strive against rivals or difficulties **2** : argue **3** : maintain or claim — **con·tend·er** *n*

¹con·tent \kənˈtent\ *adj* : satisfied ∼ *vb* : satisfy ∼ *n* : ease of mind — **con·tent·ed** *adj* — **con·tent·ed·ly** *adv* — **con·tent·ed·ness** *n* — **con·tent·ment** *n*

²con·tent \ˈkänˌtent\ *n* **1** *pl* : something contained **2** *pl* : subject matter (as of a book) **3** : essential meaning **4** : proportion contained

con·ten·tion \kənˈtenchən\ *n* : state of contending — **con·ten·tious** \-chəs\ *adj* — **con·ten·tious·ly** *adv*

con·test \kənˈtest\ *vb* : dispute or challenge ∼ \ˈkänˌtest\ *n* **1** : struggle **2** : game — **con·test·able** \kənˈtes-təbəl\ *adj* — **con·tes·tant** \-ˈtestənt\ *n*

con·text \ˈkänˌtekst\ *n* : words surrounding a word or phrase

con·tig·u·ous \kənˈtigyəwəs\ *adj* : connected to or adjoining — **con·ti·gu·i·ty** \ˌkäntə-ˈgyüətē\ *n*

con·ti·nence \ˈkäntᵊnəns\ *n* : self-restraint — **con·ti·nent** \-nənt\ *adj*

con·ti·nent \ˈkäntᵊnənt\ *n* : great division of land on the globe — **con·ti·nen·tal** \ˌkäntᵊnˈentᵊl\ *adj*

con·tin·gen·cy \kənˈtinjənsē\ *n, pl* **-cies** : possible event

con·tin·gent \-jənt\ *adj* : dependent on something else ∼ *n* : a quota from an area or group

con·tin·u·al \kənˈtinyəwəl\ *adj* **1** : continuous **2** : steadily recurring — **con·tin·u·al·ly** \-ē\ *adv*

con·tin·ue \kənˈtinyü\ *vb* **-tin-ued; -tin·u·ing** **1** : remain in a place or condition **2** : endure **3** : resume after an intermission **4** : extend — **con·tin·u·ance** \-yəwəns\ *n* — **con·tin·u·ation** \-ˌtinyəˈwā-shən\ *n*

con·tin·u·ous \-ˈtinyəwəs\ *adj* : continuing without interruption — **con·ti·nu·ity** \ˌkäntᵊn-ˈüətē, -ˈyü-\ *n* — **con·tin·u·ous·ly** *adv*

con·tort \kənˈtort\ *vb* : twist out of shape — **con·tor·tion** \-ˈtorshən\ *n*

con·tour \ˈkänˌtur\ *n* **1** : outline **2** *pl* : shape

con·tra·band \ˈkäntrəˌband\ *n* : illegal goods

con·tra·cep·tion \ˌkäntrəˈsep-shən\ *n* : prevention of conception — **con·tra·cep·tive** \-ˈseptiv\ *adj or n*

con·tract \ˈkänˌtrakt\ *n* : binding agreement ∼ \kənˈtrakt; *1 usu* ˈkänˌtrakt\ *vb* **1** : establish or undertake by contract **2** : become ill with **3** : make shorter — **con·trac·tion** \kən'trakshən\ *n* — **con·trac·tor** \'kän‚trak-tər, kən'trak-\ *n* — **con·trac·tu·al** \kən'trakchəwəl\ *adj* — **con·trac·tu·al·ly** *adv*

con·tra·dict \‚käntrə'dikt\ *vb* : state the contrary of — **con·tra·dic·tion** \-'dikshən\ *n* — **con·tra·dic·to·ry** \-'diktərē\ *adj*

con·tral·to \kən'traltō\ *n, pl* **-tos** : lowest female singing voice

con·trap·tion \kən'trapshən\ *n* : device or contrivance

con·trary \'kän‚trerē; *4 often* kən'trerē\ *adj* **1** : opposite in character, nature, or position **2** : mutually opposed **3** : unfavorable **4** : uncooperative or stubborn — **con·trari·ly** \-‚trerəlē, -'trer-\ *adv* — **con·trari·wise** \-‚wīz\ *adv* — **contrary** \'kän‚trerē\ *n*

con·trast \'kän‚trast\ *n* **1** : unlikeness shown by comparing **2** : unlike color or tone of adjacent parts ~ \kən'trast\ *vb* **1** : show differences **2** : compare so as to show differences

con·tra·vene \‚käntrə'vēn\ *vb* **-vened; -ven·ing** : go or act contrary to

con·trib·ute \kən'tribyət\ *vb* **-ut·ed; -ut·ing** : give or help along with others — **con·tri·bu·tion** \‚käntrə'byüshən\ *n* — **con·trib·u·tor** \kən'tribyətər\ *n* — **con·trib·u·to·ry** \-yə‚tōrē\ *adj*

con·trite \'kän‚trīt, kən'trīt\ *adj* : repentant — **con·tri·tion** \kən'trishən\ *n*

con·trive \kən'trīv\ *vb* **-trived; -triv·ing** **1** : devise or make with ingenuity **2** : bring about — **con·triv·ance** \-'trīvəns\ *n* — **con·triv·er** *n*

con·trol \-'trōl\ *vb* **-ll-** **1** : exercise power over **2** : dominate or rule ~ *n* **1** : power to direct or regulate **2** : restraint **3** : regulating device — **con·trol·la·ble** *adj* — **con·trol·ler** \-'trōlər, 'kän‚-\ *n*

con·tro·ver·sy \'käntrə‚vərsē\ *n, pl* **-sies** : clash of opposing views — **con·tro·ver·sial** \‚käntrə'vərshəl, -sēəl\ *adj*

con·tro·vert \'käntrə‚vərt, ‚käntrə'-\ *vb* : contradict — **con·tro·vert·ible** *adj*

con·tu·ma·cious \‚käntə'māshəs, -tyə-\ *adj* : rebellious

con·tu·me·ly \kən'tümələ, 'käntü‚mēlē, -tyü-\ *n* : rudeness

con·tu·sion \kən'tüzhən, -tyü-\ *n* : bruise — **con·tuse** \-'tüz, -'tyüz\ *vb*

co·nun·drum \kə'nəndrəm\ *n* : riddle

con·va·lesce \ˌkänvə'les\ *vb* **-lesced; -lesc·ing** : gradually recover health — **con·va·les·cence** \-ᵊns\ *n* — **con·va·les·cent** \-ᵊnt\ *adj or n*

con·vec·tion \kən'vekshən\ *n* : circulation in fluids due to warmer portions rising and colder ones sinking — **con·vec·tion·al** \-'vekshənəl\ *adj* — **con·vec·tive** \-'vektiv\ *adj*

con·vene \kən'vēn\ *vb* **-vened; -ven·ing** : assemble or meet

con·ve·nience \-'vēnyəns\ *n* **1** : personal comfort or ease **2** : device that saves work

con·ve·nient \-nyənt\ *adj* **1** : suited to one's convenience **2** : near at hand — **con·ve·nient·ly** *adv*

con·vent \'känvənt, -ˌvent\ *n* : community of nuns

con·ven·tion \kən'venchən\ *n* **1** : agreement esp. between nations **2** : large meeting **3** : body of delegates **4** : accepted usage or way of behaving — **con·ven·tion·al** \-'venchənəl\ *adj* — **con·ven·tion·al·ly** *adv*

con·verge \kən'vərj\ *vb* **-verged; -verg·ing** : approach a single point — **con·ver·gence** \-'vərjəns\ *n* — **con·ver·gent** \-jənt\ *adj*

con·ver·sant \-'vərsᵊnt\ *adj* : having knowledge and experience

con·ver·sa·tion \ˌkänvər'sā-shən\ *n* : an informal talking together — **con·ver·sa·tion·al** \-shənəl\ *adj*

¹**con·verse** \kən'vərs\ *vb* **-versed; -vers·ing** : engage in conversation — **con·verse** \'känˌvərs\ *n*

²**con·verse** \kən'vərs, 'känˌvers\ *adj* : opposite — **con·verse** \'känˌvərs\ *n* — **con·verse·ly** *adv*

con·ver·sion \kən'vərzhən\ *n* **1** : change **2** : adoption of religion

con·vert \kən'vərt\ *vb* **1** : turn from one belief or party to another **2** : change ∼ \'känˌvərt\ *n* : one who has undergone religious conversion — **con·vert·er, con·ver·tor** \kən'vərtər\ *n* — **con·vert·ible** *adj*

con·vert·ible \kən'vərtəbəl\ *n* : automobile with a removable top

con·vex \kän'veks, 'känˌ-, kən'-\ *adj* : curved or rounded like the outside of a sphere — **con·vex·i·ty** \kən'veksətē, kän-\ *n*

con·vey \kən'vā\ *vb* **-veyed; -vey·ing** : transport or transmit — **con·vey·ance** \-'vāəns\ *n* — **con·vey·or** \-ər\ *n*

con·vict \kən'vikt\ *vb* : find guilty ∼ \'känˌvikt\ *n* : person in prison

con·vic·tion \kən'vikshən\ *n* **1** : act of convicting **2** : strong belief

con·vince \-'vins\ *vb* **-vinced; -vinc·ing** : cause to believe — **con·vinc·ing·ly** *adv*

con·viv·ial \-'vivyəl, -'vivēəl\ *adj* : cheerful or festive — **con·viv·i·al·i·ty** \-,vivē'alətē\ *n*

con·voke \kən'vōk\ *vb* **-voked; -vok·ing** : call together to a meeting — **con·vo·ca·tion** \,känvə'kāshən\ *n*

con·vo·lut·ed \'känvə,lütəd\ *adj* **1** : intricately folded **2** : intricate

con·vo·lu·tion \,känvə'lüshən\ *n* : convoluted structure

con·voy \'kän,vói, kən'vói\ *vb* : accompany for protection ~ \'kän,vói\ *n* : group of vehicles or ships moving together

con·vul·sion \kən'vəlshən\ *n* : violent involuntary muscle contraction — **con·vulse** \-'vəls\ *vb* — **con·vul·sive** \-'vəlsiv\ *adj*

coo \'kü\ *n* : sound of a pigeon — **coo** *vb*

cook \'kük\ *n* : one who prepares food ~ *vb* : prepare food — **cook·book** *n* — **cook·er** *n* — **cook·ery** \-ərē\ *n* — **cook·ware** *n*

cook·ie, cooky \'kükē\ *n, pl* **-ies** : small sweet flat cake

cool \'kül\ *adj* **1** : moderately cold **2** : not excited **3** : unfriendly ~ *vb* : make or become cool ~ *n* **1** : cool time or place **2** : composure — **cool·ant** \-ənt\ *n* — **cool·er** *n* — **cool·ly** *adv* — **cool·ness** *n*

coo·lie \'külē\ *n* : unskilled laborer in or from the Far East

coop \'küp, 'kúp\ *n* : enclosure usu. for poultry ~ *vb* : confine in or as if in a coop

co–op \'kō,äp\ *n* : cooperative

coo·per \'küpər, 'kúp-\ *n* : barrel maker — **cooper** *vb*

co·op·er·ate \kō'äpə,rāt\ *vb* : act jointly — **co·op·er·a·tion** \-,äpə'rāshən\ *n*

co·op·er·a·tive \kō'äpərətiv, -'äpə,rāt-\ *adj* : willing to work with others ~ *n* : enterprise owned and run by those using its services

co–opt \kō'äpt\ *vb* **1** : elect as a colleague **2** : take over

co·or·di·nate \-'órdᵊnət\ *adj* : equal esp. in rank ~ *n* : any of a set of numbers used in specifying the location of a point on a surface or in space ~ \-ᵊn,āt\ *vb* **-nat·ed; -nat·ing** **1** : make or become coordinate **2** : work or act together harmoniously — **co·or·di·nate·ly** *adv* — **co·or·di·na·tion** \-,órdᵊn'āshən\ *n* — **co·or·di·na·tor** \-ᵊn,ātər\ *n*

coot \'küt\ *n* **1** : dark-colored ducklike bird **2** : harmless simple person

cop \'käp\ *n* : police officer

¹cope \'kōp\ *n* : cloaklike ecclesiastical vestment

²cope *vb* **coped; cop·ing** : deal with difficulties

co·pi·lot \'kō,pīlət\ *n* : assistant airplane pilot

cop·ing \'kōpiŋ\ *n* : top layer of a wall

co·pi·ous \'kōpēəs\ *adj* : very abundant — **co·pi·ous·ly** *adv* — **co·pi·ous·ness** *n*

cop·per \'käpər\ *n* **1** : malleable reddish metallic chemical element **2** : penny — **coppery** *adj*

cop·per·head *n* : largely coppery brown venomous snake

co·pra \'kōprə\ *n* : dried coconut meat

copse \'käps\ *n* : thicket

cop·u·la \'käpyələ\ *n* : verb linking subject and predicate — **cop·u·la·tive** \-,lātiv\ *adj*

cop·u·late \'käpyə,lāt\ *vb* **-lat·ed; -lat·ing** : engage in sexual intercourse — **cop·u·la·tion** \,käpyə'lāshən\ *n*

copy \'käpē\ *n, pl* **cop·ies** **1** : imitation or reproduction of an original **2** : writing to be set for printing ~ *vb* **copied; copy·ing** **1** : make a copy of **2** : imitate — **copi·er** \-ər\ *n* — **copyist** *n*

copy·right *n* : sole right to a literary or artistic work ~ *vb* : get a copyright on

co·quette \kō'ket\ *n* : flirt

cor·al \'kòrəl\ *n* **1** : skeletal material of colonies of tiny sea polyps **2** : deep pink — **coral** *adj*

cord \'kòrd\ *n* **1** : usu. heavy string **2** : long slender anatomical structure **3** : measure of firewood equal to 128 cu. ft. **4** : small electrical cable ~ *vb* **1** : tie or furnish with a cord **2** : pile (wood) in cords

cor·dial \'kòrjəl\ *adj* : warmly welcoming ~ *n* : liqueur — **cor·di·al·i·ty** \,kòrjē'alətē, kòrd'yal-\ *n* — **cor·dial·ly** \'kòrjəlē\ *adv*

cor·don \'kòrdᵊn\ *n* : encircling line of troops or police — **cordon** *vb*

cor·do·van \'kòrdəvən\ *n* : soft fine-grained leather

cor·du·roy \'kòrdə,ròi\ *n* **1** : heavy ribbed fabric **2** *pl* : trousers of corduroy

core \'kōr\ *n* **1** : central part of some fruits **2** : inmost part ~ *vb* **cored; cor·ing** : take out the core of — **cor·er** *n*

cork \'kòrk\ *n* **1** : tough elastic bark of a European oak (**cork oak**) **2** : stopper of cork ~ *vb* : stop up with a cork — **corky** *adj*

cork·screw *n* : device for drawing corks from bottles

cor·mo·rant \'kȯrmərənt, -ˌrant\ *n* : dark seabird

[1]**corn** \'kȯrn\ *n* : cereal grass or its seeds ~ *vb* : cure or preserve in brine — **corn-meal** *n* — **corn·stalk** *n* — **corn·starch** *n*

[2]**corn** *n* : local hardening and thickening of skin

corn·cob *n* : axis on which the kernels of Indian corn are arranged

cor·nea \'kȯrnēə\ *n* : transparent part of the coat of the eyeball — **cor·ne·al** *adj*

cor·ner \'kȯrnər\ *n* **1** : point or angle formed by the meeting of lines or sides **2** : place where two streets meet **3** : inescapable position **4** : control of the supply of something ~ *vb* **1** : drive into a corner **2** : get a corner on **3** : turn a corner

cor·ner·stone *n* **1** : stone at a corner of a wall **2** : something basic

cor·net \kȯr'net\ *n* : trumpet-like instrument

cor·nice \'kȯrnəs\ *n* : horizontal wall projection

cor·nu·co·pia \ˌkȯrnə'kōpēə, -nyə-\ *n* : goat's horn filled with fruits and grain emblematic of abundance

co·rol·la \kə'rälə\ *n* : petals of a flower

cor·ol·lary \'kȯrəˌlerē\ *n, pl* **-lar·ies** **1** : logical deduction **2** : consequence or result

co·ro·na \kə'rōnə\ *n* : shining ring around the sun seen during eclipses

cor·o·nary \'kȯrəˌnerē\ *adj* : relating to the heart or its blood vessels ~ *n* **1** : thrombosis of an artery supplying the heart **2** : heart attack

cor·o·na·tion \ˌkȯrə'nāshən\ *n* : crowning of a monarch

cor·o·ner \'kȯrənər\ *n* : public official who investigates causes of suspicious deaths

[1]**cor·po·ral** \'kȯrpərəl\ *adj* : bodily

[2]**corporal** *n* : noncommissioned officer ranking next below a sergeant

cor·po·ra·tion \ˌkȯrpə'rāshən\ *n* : legal creation with the rights and liabilities of a person — **cor·po·rate** \'kȯrpərət\ *adj*

cor·po·re·al \kȯr'pōrēəl\ *adj* : physical or material — **cor·po·re·al·ly** *adv*

corps \'kōr\ *n, pl* **corps** \'kōrz\ **1** : subdivision of a military force **2** : working group

corpse \'kȯrps\ *n* : dead body

cor·pu·lence \'kȯrpyələns\ *n* : obesity — **cor·pu·lent** \-lənt\ *adj*

cor·pus \'kȯrpəs\ *n, pl* **-po·ra** \-pərə\ **1** : corpse **2** : body of writings

cor·pus·cle \'kȯr͵pəsəl\ *n* : blood cell

cor·ral \kə'ral\ *n* : enclosure for animals — **corral** *vb*

cor·rect \kə'rekt\ *vb* **1** : make right **2** : chastise ∼ *adj* **1** : true or factual **2** : conforming to a standard — **cor·rec·tion** \-'rekshən\ *n* — **cor·rec·tive** \-'rektiv\ *adj* — **cor·rect·ly** *adv* — **cor·rect·ness** *n*

cor·re·late \'kȯrə͵lāt\ *vb* **-lat·ed; -lat·ing** : show a connection between — **cor·re·late** \-lət, -͵lāt\ *n* — **cor·re·la·tion** \͵kȯrə'lāshən\ *n*

cor·rel·a·tive \kə'relətiv\ *adj* : regularly used together — **correlative** *n*

cor·re·spond \͵kȯrə'spänd\ *vb* **1** : match **2** : communicate by letter — **cor·re·spon·dence** \-'spändəns\ *n* — **cor·re·spond·ing·ly** \-'spändiŋlē\ *adv*

cor·re·spon·dent \-'spändənt\ *n* **1** : person one writes to **2** : reporter

cor·ri·dor \'kȯrədər, -͵dȯr\ *n* : passageway connecting rooms

cor·rob·o·rate \kə'räbə͵rāt\ *vb* **-rat·ed; -rat·ing** : support with evidence — **cor·rob·o·ra·tion** \-͵räbə'rāshən\ *n*

cor·rode \kə'rōd\ *vb* **-rod·ed; -rod·ing** : wear away by chemical action — **cor·ro·sion** \-'rōzhən\ *n* — **cor·ro·sive** \-'rōsiv\ *adj or n*

cor·ru·gate \'kȯrə͵gāt\ *vb* **-gat·ed; -gat·ing** : form into ridges and grooves — **cor·ru·gat·ed** *adj* — **cor·ru·ga·tion** \͵kȯrə'gāshən\ *n*

cor·rupt \kə'rəpt\ *vb* **1** : change from good to bad **2** : bribe ∼ *adj* : morally debased — **cor·rupt·ible** *adj* — **cor·rup·tion** \-'rəpshən\ *n*

cor·sage \kȯr'säzh, -'säj\ *n* : bouquet worn by a woman

cor·set \'kȯrsət\ *n* : woman's stiffened undergarment

cor·tege \kȯr'tezh, 'kȯr͵-\ *n* : funeral procession

cor·tex \'kȯr͵teks\ *n, pl* **-ti·ces** \'kȯrtə͵sēz\ *or* **-tex·es** : outer or covering layer of an organism or part (as the brain) — **cor·ti·cal** \'kȯr·tikəl\ *adj*

cor·ti·sone \'kȯrtə͵sōn, -zōn\ *n* : adrenal hormone

cos·met·ic \käz'metik\ *n* : beautifying preparation ∼ *adj* : relating to beautifying

cos·mic \'käzmik\ *adj* **1** : relating to the universe **2** : vast or grand

cos·mo·naut \'käzmə‚nȯt\ *n* : Soviet or Russian astronaut

cos·mo·pol·i·tan \‚käzmə-'pälət°n\ *adj* : belonging to all the world — **cosmopolitan** *n*

cos·mos \'käzməs, -‚mōs, -‚mäs\ *n* : universe

Cos·sack \'käs‚ak, -ək\ *n* : Russian cavalryman

cost \'kȯst\ *n* **1** : amount paid for something **2** : loss or penalty ~ *vb* **cost; cost·ing 1** : require so much in payment **2** : cause to pay, suffer, or lose — **cost·li·ness** \-lēnəs\ *n* — **cost·ly** \-lē\ *adj*

cos·tume \'käs‚tüm, -‚tyüm\ *n* : clothing

co·sy \'kōzē\ *var of* COZY

cot \'kät\ *n* : small bed

cote \'kōt, 'kät\ *n* : small shed or coop

co·te·rie \'kōtə‚rē, ‚kōtə'-\ *n* : exclusive group of persons

co·til·lion \kō'tilyən\ *n* : formal ball

cot·tage \'kätij\ *n* : small house

cot·ton \'kät°n\ *n* : soft fibrous plant substance or thread or cloth made of it — **cot·ton·seed** *n* — **cot·tony** *adj*

cot·ton·mouth *n* : poisonous snake

couch \'kaůch\ *vb* **1** : lie or place on a couch **2** : phrase ~ *n* : bed or sofa

couch potato *n* : one who spends a great deal of time watching television

cou·gar \'kügər, -‚gär\ *n* : large tawny wild American cat

cough \'kȯf\ *vb* : force air from the lungs with short sharp noises — **cough** *n*

could \'kůd\ *past of* CAN

coun·cil \'kaůnsəl\ *n* **1** : assembly or meeting **2** : body of lawmakers — **coun·cil·lor, coun·cil·or** \-sələr\ *n* — **coun·cil·man** \-mən\ *n* — **coun·cil·wom·an** *n*

coun·sel \'kaůnsəl\ *n* **1** : advice **2** : deliberation together **3** *pl* **-sel** : lawyer ~ *vb* **-seled** *or* **-selled; -sel·ing** *or* **-sel·ling 1** : advise **2** : consult together — **coun·sel·or, coun·sel·lor** \-sələr\ *n*

¹count \'kaůnt\ *vb* **1** : name or indicate one by one to find the total number **2** : recite numbers in order **3** : rely **4** : be of value or account ~ *n* **1** : act of counting or the total obtained by counting **2** : charge in an indictment — **count·able** *adj*

²count *n* : European nobleman

coun·te·nance \'kaůnt°nəns\ *n* : face or facial expression ~ *vb* **-nanced; -nanc·ing** : allow or encourage

¹**count·er** \ˈkau̇ntər\ *n* **1** : piece for reckoning or games **2** : surface over which business is transacted

²**count·er** *n* : one that counts

³**coun·ter** *vb* : oppose ∼ *adv* : in an opposite direction ∼ *n* : offsetting force or move ∼ *adj* : contrary

counter- *prefix* **1** : contrary or opposite **2** : opposing **3** : retaliatory

coun·ter·act *vb* : lessen the force of — **coun·ter·ac·tive** *adj*

coun·ter·bal·ance *n* : balancing influence or weight ∼ *vb* : oppose or balance

coun·ter·clock·wise *adv or adj* : opposite to the way a clock's hands move

coun·ter·feit \ˈkau̇ntərˌfit\ *vb* **1** : copy in order to deceive **2** : pretend ∼ *adj* : spurious ∼ *n* : fraudulent copy — **coun·ter·feit·er** *n*

coun·ter·mand \-ˌmand\ *vb* : supersede with a contrary order

coun·ter·pane \-ˌpān\ *n* : bedspread

coun·ter·part *n* : one that is similar or corresponds

coun·ter·point *n* : music with interwoven melodies

List of self-explanatory words with the prefix *counter-*

counteraccusation
counteraggression
counterargue
counterassault
counterattack
counterbid
counterblockade
counterblow
countercampaign
countercharge
counterclaim
countercomplaint
countercoup
countercriticism
counterdemand

counterdemon-
    stration
counterdemon-
    strator
countereffort
counterevidence
counterguerrilla
counterinflationary
counterinfluence
countermeasure
countermove
countermovement
counteroffer
counterpetition
counterploy

counterpower
counterpressure
counterpropa-
    ganda
counterproposal
counterprotest
counterquestion
counterraid
counterrally
counterreform
counterresponse
counterretaliation
counterrevolution
counterrevolution-
    ary

coun·ter·sign *n* : secret signal ~ *vb* : add a confirming signature to

count·ess \'kaúntəs\ *n* : wife or widow of a count or an earl or a woman holding that rank in her own right

count·less \-ləs\ *adj* : too many to be numbered

coun·try \'kəntrē\ *n, pl* -tries **1** : nation **2** : rural area ~ *adj* : rural — **coun·try·man** \-mən\ *n*

coun·try·side *n* : rural area or its people

coun·ty \'kaúntē\ *n, pl* -ties : local government division esp. of a state

coup \'kü\ *n, pl* **coups** \'küz\ **1** : brilliant sudden action or plan **2** : sudden overthrow of a government

coupe \'küp\ *n* : 2-door automobile with an enclosed body

cou·ple \'kəpəl\ *vb* -pled; -pling : link together ~ *n* **1** : pair **2** : two persons closely associated or married

cou·pling \'kəpliŋ\ *n* : connecting device

cou·pon \'kü₁pän, 'kyü-\ *n* : certificate redeemable for goods or a cash discount

cour·age \'kərij\ *n* : ability to conquer fear or despair — **cou·ra·geous** \kə'rājəs\ *adj*

cou·ri·er \'kúrēər, 'kərē-\ *n* : messenger

course \'kōrs\ *n* **1** : progress **2** : ground over which something moves **3** : part of a meal served at one time **4** : method of procedure **5** : subject taught in a series of classes ~ *vb* **coursed; cours·ing 1** : hunt with dogs **2** : run speedily — **of course** : as might be expected

court \'kōrt\ *n* **1** : residence of a sovereign **2** : sovereign and his or her officials and advisers **3** : area enclosed by a building **4** : space marked for playing a game **5** : place where justice is administered ~ *vb* : woo — **court·house** *n* — **court·room** *n* — **court·ship** \-₁ship\ *n*

cour·te·ous \'kərtēəs\ *adj* : showing politeness and respect for others — **cour·te·ous·ly** *adv*

---

counterstrategy
counterstyle
countersue
countersuggestion
countersuit
countertendency
counterterror
counterterrorism
counterterrorist
counterthreat
counterthrust
countertrend

cour·te·san \'kōrtəzən, 'kərt-\ *n* : prostitute

cour·te·sy \'kərtəsē\ *n, pl* -sies : courteous behavior

court·ier \'kōrtēər, 'kōrtyər\ *n* : person in attendance at a royal court

court·ly \'kōrtlē\ *adj* -li·er; -est : polite or elegant — **court·li·ness** *n*

court–mar·tial *n, pl* **courts–martial** : military trial court — **court–martial** *vb*

court·yard *n* : enclosure open to the sky that is attached to a house

cous·in \'kəz⁰n\ *n* : child of one's uncle or aunt

cove \'kōv\ *n* : sheltered inlet or bay

co·ven \'kəvən\ *n* : group of witches

cov·e·nant \'kəvənənt\ *n* : binding agreement — **cov·e·nant** \-nənt, -ˌnant\ *vb*

cov·er \'kəvər\ *vb* **1** : place something over or upon **2** : protect or hide **3** : include or deal with ∼ *n* : something that covers — **cov·er·age** \-ərij\ *n*

cov·er·let \-lət\ *n* : bedspread

co·vert \'kōˌvərt, 'kəvərt\ *adj* : secret ∼ \'kəvərt, 'kō-\ *n* : thicket that shelters animals

cov·et \'kəvət\ *vb* : desire enviously — **cov·et·ous** *adj*

cov·ey \'kəvē\ *n, pl* -eys **1** : bird with her young **2** : small flock (as of quail)

¹cow \'kaů\ *n* : large adult female animal (as of cattle) — **cow·hide** *n*

²cow *vb* : intimidate

cow·ard \'kaůərd\ *n* : one who lacks courage — **cow·ard·ice** \-əs\ *n* — **cow·ard·ly** *adv or adj*

cow·boy *n* : a mounted ranch hand who tends cattle

cow·er \'kaůər\ *vb* : shrink from fear or cold

cow·girl *n* : woman ranch hand who tends cattle

cowl \'kaůl\ *n* : monk's hood

cow·lick \'kaůˌlik\ *n* : turned-up tuft of hair that resists control

cow·slip \-ˌslip\ *n* : yellow flower

cox·swain \'käkən, -ˌswān\ *n* : person who steers a boat

coy \'kȯi\ *adj* : shy or pretending shyness

coy·ote \'kīˌōt, kī'ōtē\ *n, pl* **coy·otes** *or* **coyote** : small No. American wolf

coz·en \'kəz⁰n\ *vb* : cheat

co·zy \'kōzē\ *adj* -zi·er; -est : snug

crab \'krab\ *n* : short broad shellfish with pincers

crab·by \'krabē\ *adj* -bi·er; -est : cross

¹**crack** \'krak\ *vb* **1** : break with a sharp sound **2** : fail in tone **3** : break without completely separating ∼ *n* **1** : sudden sharp noise **2** : witty remark **3** : narrow break **4** : sharp blow **5** : try

²**crack** *adj* : extremely proficient

crack·down *n* : disciplinary action — **crack down** *vb*

crack·er \-ər\ *n* : thin crisp bakery product

crack·le \'krakəl\ *vb* **-led; -ling** **1** : make snapping noises **2** : develop fine cracks in a surface — **crackle** *n*

crack·pot \'krak,pät\ *n* : eccentric

crack–up *n* : crash

cra·dle \'krādəl\ *n* : baby's bed ∼ *vb* **-dled; -dling** **1** : place in a cradle **2** : hold securely

craft \'kraft\ *n* **1** : occupation requiring special skill **2** : craftiness **3** *pl usu* **craft** : structure designed to provide transportation **4** *pl usu* **craft** : small boat — **crafts·man** \'kraftsmən\ *n* — **crafts·man·ship** \-,ship\ *n*

crafty \'kraftē\ *adj* **craft·i·er; -est** : sly — **craft·i·ness** *n*

crag \'krag\ *n* : steep cliff — **crag·gy** \-ē\ *adj*

cram \'kram\ *vb* **-mm-** **1** : eat greedily **2** : pack in tight **3** : study intensely for a test

cramp \'kramp\ *n* **1** : sudden painful contraction of muscle **2** *pl* : sharp abdominal pains ∼ *vb* **1** : affect with cramp **2** : restrain

cran·ber·ry \'kran,berē\ *n* : red acid berry of a trailing plant

crane \'krān\ *n* **1** : tall wading bird **2** : machine for lifting heavy objects ∼ *vb* **craned; cran·ing** : stretch one's neck to see

cra·ni·um \'krānēəm\ *n, pl* **-ni·ums** *or* **-nia** \-nēə\ : skull — **cra·ni·al** \-əl\ *adj*

crank \'kraŋk\ *n* **1** : bent lever turned to operate a machine **2** : eccentric ∼ *vb* : start or operate by turning a crank

cranky \'kraŋkē\ *adj* **crank·i·er; -est** : irritable

cran·ny \'kranē\ *n, pl* **-nies** : crevice

craps \'kraps\ *n* : dice game

crash \'krash\ *vb* **1** : break noisily **2** : fall and hit something with noise and damage ∼ *n* **1** : loud sound **2** : action of crashing **3** : failure

crass \'kras\ *adj* : crude or unfeeling

crate \'krāt\ *n* : wooden shipping container — **crate** *vb*

cra·ter \'krātər\ *n* : volcanic depression

cra·vat \krə'vat\ *n* : necktie

crave \'krāv\ *vb* **craved; craving** : long for — **craving** *n*

cra·ven \'krāvən\ *adj* : cowardly — **cra·ven** *n*

craw·fish \'krȯˌfish\ *n* : crayfish

crawl \'krȯl\ *vb* **1** : move slowly (as by drawing the body along the ground) **2** : swarm with creeping things ~ *n* : very slow pace

cray·fish \'krāˌfish\ *n* : lobsterlike freshwater crustacean

cray·on \'krāˌän, -ən\ *n* : stick of chalk or wax used for drawing or coloring — **crayon** *vb*

craze \'krāz\ *vb* **crazed; crazing** : make or become insane ~ *n* : fad

cra·zy \'krāzē\ *adj* **cra·zi·er; -est** **1** : mentally disordered **2** : wildly impractical — **cra·zi·ly** *adv* — **cra·zi·ness** *n*

creak \'krēk\ *vb or n* : squeak — **creaky** *adj*

cream \'krēm\ *n* **1** : yellowish fat-rich part of milk **2** : thick smooth sauce, confection, or cosmetic **3** : choicest part ~ *vb* : beat into creamy consistency — **creamy** *adj*

cream·ery \-ərē\ *n, pl* **-er·ies** : place where butter and cheese are made

crease \'krēs\ *n* : line made by folding — **crease** *vb*

cre·ate \krē'āt\ *vb* **-at·ed; -at·ing** : bring into being — **cre·ation** \krē'āshən\ *n* — **cre·ative** \-'ātiv\ *adj* — **cre·ativ·i·ty** \ˌkrēā'tivətē\ *n* — **cre·a·tor** \krē'ātər\ *n*

crea·ture \'krēchər\ *n* : lower animal or human being

cre·dence \'krēdᵊns\ *n* : belief

cre·den·tials \kri'denchəlz\ *n pl* : evidence of qualifications or authority

cred·i·ble \'kredəbəl\ *adj* : believable — **cred·i·bil·i·ty** \ˌkredə'bilətē\ *n*

cred·it \'kredət\ *n* **1** : balance in a person's favor **2** : time given to pay for goods **3** : belief **4** : esteem **5** : source of honor ~ *vb* **1** : believe **2** : give credit to

cred·it·able \-əbəl\ *adj* : worthy of esteem or praise — **cred·it·ably** \-əblē\ *adv*

cred·i·tor \-ər\ *n* : person to whom money is owed

cred·u·lous \'krejələs\ *adj* : easily convinced — **cre·du·li·ty** \kri'dülətē, -'dyü-\ *n*

creed \'krēd\ *n* : statement of essential beliefs

creek \'krēk, 'krik\ *n* : small stream

creel \'krēl\ *n* : basket for carrying fish

creep \'krēp\ *vb* **crept** \'krept\; **creep·ing** **1** : crawl

2 : grow over a surface like ivy — **creep** *n* — **creep·er** *n*

cre·mate \'krē͵māt\ *vb* **-mated; -mat·ing** : burn up (a corpse) — **cre·ma·tion** \kri-'māshən\ *n* — **cre·ma·to·ry** \'krēmə͵tōrē, 'krem-\ *n*

cre·o·sote \'krēə͵sōt\ *n* : oily wood preservative

crepe, crêpe \'krāp\ *n* : light crinkled fabric

cre·scen·do \krə'shendō\ *adv or adj* : growing louder — **crescendo** *n*

cres·cent \'kresᵊnt\ *n* : shape of the moon between new moon and first quarter

crest \'krest\ *n* **1** : tuft on a bird's head **2** : top of a hill or wave **3** : part of a coat of arms ∼ *vb* : rise to a crest — **crest·ed** \-təd\ *adj*

crest·fall·en *adj* : sad

cre·tin \'krētᵊn\ *n* : stupid person

cre·vasse \kri'vas\ *n* : deep fissure esp. in a glacier

crev·ice \'krevəs\ *n* : narrow fissure

crew \'krü\ *n* : body of workers (as on a ship) — **crewman** \-mən\ *n*

crib \'krib\ *n* **1** : manger **2** : grain storage bin **3** : baby's bed ∼ *vb* **-bb-** : put in a crib

crib·bage \'kribij\ *n* : card game scored by moving pegs on a board (**cribbage board**)

crick \'krik\ *n* : muscle spasm

¹**crick·et** \'krikət\ *n* : insect noted for the chirping of the male

²**cricket** *n* : bat and ball game played on a field with wickets

cri·er \'krīər\ *n* : one who calls out announcements

crime \'krīm\ *n* : serious violation of law

crim·i·nal \'krimənᵊl\ *adj* : relating to or being a crime or its punishment ∼ *n* : one who commits a crime

crimp \'krimp\ *vb* : cause to become crinkled, wavy, or bent — **crimp** *n*

crim·son \'krimzən\ *n* : deep red — **crimson** *adj*

cringe \'krinj\ *vb* **cringed; cring·ing** : shrink in fear

crin·kle \'krinkəl\ *vb* **-kled; -kling** : wrinkle — **crinkle** *n* — **crin·kly** \-klē\ *adj*

crin·o·line \'krinᵊlən\ *n* **1** : stiff cloth **2** : full stiff skirt or petticoat

crip·ple \'kripəl\ *n* : disabled person ∼ *vb* **-pled; -pling** : disable

cri·sis \'krīsəs\ *n, pl* **cri·ses** \-͵sēz\ : decisive or critical moment

crisp \'krisp\ *adj* **1** : easily crumbled **2** : firm and fresh **3** : lively **4** : invigorating — **crisp** *vb* — **crisp·ly** *adv* — **crisp·ness** *n* — **crispy** *adj*

criss·cross \'kris‚krȯs\ *n* : pattern of crossed lines ~ *vb* : mark with or follow a crisscross

cri·te·ri·on \krī'tirēən\ *n, pl* **-ria** \-ēə\ : standard

crit·ic \'kritik\ *n* : judge of literary or artistic works

crit·i·cal \-ikəl\ *adj* **1** : inclined to criticize **2** : being a crisis **3** : relating to criticism or critics — **crit·i·cal·ly** \-iklē\ *adv*

crit·i·cize \'kritə‚sīz\ *vb* **-cized; -ciz·ing 1** : judge as a critic **2** : find fault — **crit·i·cism** \-ə‚sizəm\ *n*

cri·tique \krə'tēk\ *n* : critical estimate

croak \'krōk\ *n* : hoarse harsh cry (as of a frog) — **croak** *vb*

cro·chet \krō'shā\ *n* : needlework done with a hooked needle — **crochet** *vb*

crock \'kräk\ *n* : thick earthenware pot or jar — **crock·ery** \-ərē\ *n*

croc·o·dile \'kräkə‚dīl\ *n* : large reptile of tropical waters

cro·cus \'krōkəs\ *n, pl* **-cus·es** : herb with spring flowers

crone \'krōn\ *n* : ugly old woman

cro·ny \'krōnē\ *n, pl* **-nies** : chum

crook \'krůk\ *n* **1** : bent or curved tool or part **2** : thief ~ *vb* : curve sharply

crook·ed \'krůkəd\ *adj* **1** : bent **2** : dishonest — **crook·ed·ness** *n*

croon \'krün\ *vb* : sing softly — **croon·er** *n*

crop \'kräp\ *n* **1** : pouch in the throat of a bird or insect **2** : short riding whip **3** : something that can be harvested ~ *vb* **-pp- 1** : trim **2** : appear unexpectedly — used with *up*

cro·quet \krō'kā\ *n* : lawn game of driving balls through wickets

cro·quette \-'ket\ *n* : mass of minced food deep-fried

cro·sier \'krōzhər\ *n* : bishop's staff

cross \'krȯs\ *n* **1** : figure or structure consisting of an upright and a cross piece **2** : interbreeding of unlike strains ~ *vb* **1** : intersect **2** : cancel **3** : go or extend across **4** : interbreed ~ *adj* **1** : going across **2** : contrary **3** : marked by bad temper — **cross·ing** *n* — **cross·ly** *adv*

cross·bow \-‚bō\ *n* : short bow mounted on a rifle stock

cross·breed *vb* **-bred; -breeding** : hybridize

cross–ex·am·ine *vb* : question about earlier testimony — **cross–ex·am·i·na·tion** *n*

cross–eyed *adj* : having the eye turned toward the nose

cross–re·fer *vb* : refer to another place (as in a book) — **cross–ref·er·ence** *n*

cross·roads *n* : place where 2 roads cross

cross section *n* : representative portion

cross·walk *n* : path for pedestrians crossing a street

cross·ways *adv* : crosswise

cross·wise \-ˌwīz\ *adv* : so as to cross something — **cross·wise** *adj*

crotch \'kräch\ *n* : angle formed by the parting of 2 legs or branches

crotch·ety \'krächətē\ *adj* : cranky, ill-natured

crouch \'kraüch\ *vb* : stoop over — **crouch** *n*

croup \'krüp\ *n* : laryngitis of infants

crou·ton \'krüˌtän\ *n* : bit of toast

¹**crow** \'krō\ *n* : large glossy black bird

²**crow** *vb* **1** : make the loud sound of the cock **2** : gloat ～ *n* : cry of the cock

crow·bar *n* : metal bar used as a pry or lever

crowd \'kraüd\ *vb* : collect or cram together ～ *n* : large number of people

crown \'kraün\ *n* **1** : wreath of honor or victory **2** : royal headdress **3** : top or highest part ～ *vb* **1** : place a crown on **2** : honor — **crowned** \'kraünd\ *adj*

cru·cial \'krüshəl\ *adj* : vitally important

cru·ci·ble \'krüsəbəl\ *n* : heat-resisting container

cru·ci·fix \'krüsəˌfiks\ *n* : representation of Christ on the cross

cru·ci·fix·ion \ˌkrüsə'fik-shən\ *n* : act of crucifying

cru·ci·fy \'krüsəˌfī\ *vb* **-fied; -fy·ing 1** : put to death on a cross **2** : persecute

crude \'krüd\ *adj* **crud·er; -est 1** : not refined **2** : lacking grace or elegance ～ *n* : unrefined petroleum — **crude·ly** *adv* — **cru·di·ty** \-ətē\ *n*

cru·el \'krüəl\ *adj* **-el·er** *or* **-el·ler; -el·est** *or* **-el·lest** : causing suffering to others — **cru·el·ly** \-ē\ *adv* — **cru·el·ty** \tē\ *n*

cru·et \'krüət\ *n* : bottle for salad dressings

cruise \'krüz\ *vb* **cruised; cruis·ing 1** : sail to several ports **2** : travel at the most efficient speed — **cruise** *n*

cruis·er \'krüzər\ *n* **1** : warship **2** : police car

crumb \'krəm\ *n* : small fragment

crum·ble \'krəmbəl\ *vb* **-bled; -bling** : break into small pieces — **crum·bly** \-blē\ *adj*

crum·ple \'krəmpəl\ *vb* **-pled; -pling** **1** : crush together **2** : collapse

crunch \'krənch\ *vb* : chew or press with a crushing noise ~ *n* : crunching sound — **crunchy** *adj*

cru·sade \krü'sād\ *n* **1** *cap* : medieval Christian expedition to the Holy Land **2** : reform movement — **crusade** *vb* — **cru·sad·er** *n*

crush \'krəsh\ *vb* **1** : squeeze out of shape **2** : grind or pound to bits **3** : suppress ~ *n* **1** : severe crowding **2** : infatuation

crust \'krəst\ *n* **1** : hard outer part of bread or a pie **2** : hard surface layer — **crust·al** *adj* — **crusty** *adj*

crus·ta·cean \ˌkrəs'tāshən\ *n* : aquatic arthropod having a firm shell

crutch \'krəch\ *n* : support for use by the disabled in walking

crux \'krəks, 'krüks\ *n, pl* **crux·es** **1** : hard problem **2** : crucial point

cry \'krī\ *vb* **cried; cry·ing** **1** : call out **2** : weep ~ *n, pl* **cries** **1** : shout **2** : fit of weeping **3** : characteristic sound of an animal

crypt \'kript\ *n* : underground chamber

cryp·tic \'kriptik\ *adj* : enigmatic

cryp·tog·ra·phy \krip'tägrəfē\ *n* : coding and decoding of messages — **cryp·tog·ra·pher** \-fər\ *n*

crys·tal \'kristəl\ *n* **1** : transparent quartz **2** : something (as glass) like crystal **3** : body formed by solidification that has a regular repeating atomic arrangement — **crys·tal·line** \-tələn\ *adj*

crys·tal·lize \-təˌlīz\ *vb* **-lized; -liz·ing** : form crystals or a definite shape — **crys·tal·li·za·tion** \ˌkristələ'zāshən\ *n*

cub \'kəb\ *n* : young animal

cub·by·hole \'kəbēˌhōl\ *n* : small confined space

cube \'kyüb\ *n* **1** : solid having 6 equal square sides **2** : product obtained by taking a number 3 times as a factor ~ *vb* **cubed; cub·ing** **1** : raise to the 3d power **2** : form into a cube **3** : cut into cubes — **cu·bic** \'kyübik\ *adj*

cu·bi·cle \-bikəl\ *n* : small room

cu·bit \'kyübət\ *n* : ancient unit of length equal to about 18 inches

cuck·old \'kəkəld, 'kùk-\ *n* : man whose wife is unfaithful — **cuckold** *vb*

cuck·oo \'kükü, 'kùk-\ *n, pl* **-oos** : brown European bird ~ *adj* : silly

cu·cum·ber \'kyü₁kəmbər\ *n* : fleshy fruit related to the gourds

cud \'kəd\ *n* : food chewed again by ruminating animals

cud·dle \'kəd²l\ *vb* **-dled; -dling** : lie close

cud·gel \'kəjəl\ *n or vb* : club

¹cue \'kyü\ *n* : signal — **cue** *vb*

²cue *n* : stick used in pool

¹cuff \'kəf\ *n* **1** : part of a sleeve encircling the wrist **2** : folded trouser hem

²cuff *vb or n* : slap

cui·sine \kwi'zēn\ *n* : manner of cooking

cu·li·nary \'kələ₁nerē, 'kyülə-\ *adj* : of or relating to cookery

cull \'kəl\ *vb* : select

cul·mi·nate \'kəlmə₁nāt\ *vb* **-nat·ed; -nat·ing** : rise to the highest point — **cul·mi·na·tion** \₁kəlmə'nāshən\ *n*

cul·pa·ble \'kəlpəbəl\ *adj* : deserving blame

cul·prit \'kəlprət\ *n* : guilty person

cult \'kəlt\ *n* **1** : religious system **2** : faddish devotion — **cult·ist** *n*

cul·ti·vate \'kəltə₁vāt\ *vb* **-vat·ed; -vat·ing 1** : prepare for crops **2** : foster the growth of **3** : refine — **cul·ti·va·tion** \₁kəltə'vāshən\ *n*

cul·ture \'kəlchər\ *n* **1** : cultivation **2** : refinement of in-tellectual and artistic taste **3** : particular form or stage of civilization — **cul·tur·al** \'kəlchərəl\ *adj* — **cul·tured** \'kəlchərd\ *adj*

cul·vert \'kəlvərt\ *n* : drain crossing under a road or railroad

cum·ber·some \'kəmbərsəm\ *adj* : awkward to handle due to bulk

cu·mu·la·tive \'kyümyələtiv, -₁lāt-\ *adj* : increasing by additions

cu·mu·lus \'kyümyələs\ *n, pl* **-li** \-₁lī, -₁lē\ : massive rounded cloud

cun·ning \'kəniŋ\ *adj* **1** : crafty **2** : clever **3** : appealing ∼ *n* **1** : skill **2** : craftiness

cup \'kəp\ *n* **1** : small drinking vessel **2** : contents of a cup **3** : a half pint ∼ *vb* **-pp-** : shape like a cup — **cup·ful** *n*

cup·board \'kəbərd\ *n* : small storage closet

cup·cake *n* : small cake

cu·pid·i·ty \kyu'pidətē\ *n, pl* **-ties** : excessive desire for money

cu·po·la \'kyüpələ, -₁lō\ *n* : small rooftop structure

cur \'kər\ *n* : mongrel dog

cu·rate \'kyurət\ *n* : member of the clergy — **cu·ra·cy** \-əsē\ *n*

cu·ra·tor \kyu'rātər\ *n* : one in charge of a museum or zoo

curb \'kərb\ *n* **1** : restraint **2** : raised edging along a street ～ *vb* : hold back

curd \'kərd\ *n* : coagulated milk

cur·dle \'kərd³l\ *vb* **-dled; -dling** **1** : form curds **2** : sour

cure \'kyu̇r\ *n* **1** : recovery from disease **2** : remedy ～ *vb* **cured; cur·ing** **1** : restore to health **2** : process for storage or use — **cur·able** *adj*

cur·few \'kər,fyü\ *n* : requirement to be off the streets at a set hour

cu·rio \'kyu̇rē,ō\ *n, pl* **-ri·os** : rare or unusual article

cu·ri·ous \'kyu̇rēəs\ *adj* **1** : eager to learn **2** : strange — **cu·ri·os·i·ty** \,kyu̇rē'äsətē\ *n* — **cu·ri·ous·ness** *n*

curl \'kərl\ *vb* **1** : form into ringlets **2** : curve ～ *n* **1** : ringlet of hair **2** : something with a spiral form — **curl·er** *n* — **curly** *adj*

cur·lew \'kərlü, -lyü\ *n, pl* **-lews** *or* **-lew** : long-legged brownish bird

curli·cue \'kərli,kyü\ *n* : fanciful curve

cur·rant \'kərənt\ *n* **1** : small seedless raisin **2** : berry of a shrub

cur·ren·cy \'kərənsē\ *n, pl* **-cies** **1** : general use or acceptance **2** : money

cur·rent \'kərənt\ *adj* : occurring in or belonging to the present ～ *n* **1** : swiftest part of a stream **2** : flow of electricity

cur·ric·u·lum \kə'rikyələm\ *n, pl* **-la** \-lə\ : course of study

¹**cur·ry** \'kərē\ *vb* **-ried; -ry·ing** : brush (a horse) with a wire brush (**cur·ry·comb** \-,kōm\) — **curry fa·vor** : seek favor by flattery

²**curry** *n, pl* **-ries** : blend of pungent spices or a food seasoned with this

curse \'kərs\ *n* **1** : a calling down of evil or harm upon one **2** : affliction ～ *vb* **cursed; curs·ing** **1** : call down injury upon **2** : swear at **3** : afflict

cur·sor \'kərsər\ *n* : indicator on a computer screen

cur·so·ry \'kərsərē\ *adj* : hastily done

curt \'kərt\ *adj* : rudely abrupt — **curt·ly** *adv* — **curt·ness** *n*

cur·tail \kər'tāl\ *vb* : shorten — **cur·tail·ment** *n*

cur·tain \'kərt³n\ *n* : hanging screen that can be drawn back or raised — **curtain** *vb*

curt·sy, curt·sey \'kərtsē\ *n, pl* **-sies** *or* **-seys** : courteous bow made by bending the knees — **curtsy, curtsey** *vb*

cur·va·ture \ˈkərvəˌchur\ *n*
: amount or state of curving

curve \ˈkərv\ *vb* **curved; curving** : bend from a straight line
or course ∼ *n* **1** : a bending
without angles **2** : something
curved

cush·ion \ˈkushən\ *n* **1** : soft
pillow **2** : something that eases
or protects ∼ *vb* **1** : provide
with a cushion **2** : soften the
force of

cusp \ˈkəsp\ *n* : pointed end

cus·pid \ˈkəspəd\ *n* : a canine
tooth

cus·pi·dor \ˈkəspəˌdor\ *n*
: spittoon

cus·tard \ˈkəstərd\ *n* : sweetened cooked mixture of milk
and eggs

cus·to·dy \ˈkəstədē\ *n, pl*
-dies : immediate care or
charge — **cus·to·di·al** \ˌkəs-
ˈtōdēəl\ *adj* — **cus·to·di·an**
\-dēən\ *n*

cus·tom \ˈkəstəm\ *n* **1** : habitual course of action **2** *pl*
: import taxes ∼ *adj* : made
to personal order — **cus·tom-
ar·i·ly** \ˌkəstəˈmerəlē\ *adv*
— **cus·tom·ary** \ˈkəstəˌmerē\
adj — **custom–built** *adj* —
cus·tom–made *adj*

cus·tom·er \ˈkəstəmər\ *n*
: buyer

cut \ˈkət\ *vb* **cut; cut·ting 1**
: penetrate or divide with a
sharp edge **2** : experience the

growth of (a tooth) through
the gum **3** : shorten **4** : remove by severing **5** : intersect
∼ *n* **1** : something separated
by cutting **2** : reduction —
cut in *vb* : thrust oneself between others

cu·ta·ne·ous \kyuˈtānēəs\ *adj*
: relating to the skin

cute \ˈkyüt\ *adj* **cut·er; -est**
: pretty

cu·ti·cle \ˈkyütikəl\ *n* : outer
layer (as of skin)

cut·lass \ˈkətləs\ *n* : short
heavy curved sword

cut·lery \-lərē\ *n* : cutting
utensils

cut·let \-lət\ *n* : slice of meat

cut·ter \ˈkətər\ *n* **1** : tool or
machine for cutting **2** : small
armed motorboat **3** : light
sleigh

cut·throat *n* : murderer ∼ *adj*
: ruthless

-cy \sē\ *n suffix* **1** : action or
practice **2** : rank or office **3**
: body **4** : state or quality

cy·a·nide \ˈsīəˌnīd, -nəd\ *n*
: poisonous chemical salt

cy·ber- *comb form* : computer
: computer network

cy·ber·space \ˈsībərˌspās\ *n*
: online world of the Internet

cy·cle \ˈsīkəl, *4 also* ˈsikəl\ *n*
1 : period of time for a series
of repeated events **2** : recurring round of events **3** : long
period of time **4** : bicycle

or motorcycle ∼ *vb* **-cled;
-cling** : ride a cycle — **cy·clic**
\'sīklik, 'sik-\, **cy·cli·cal**
\-əl\ *adj* — **cy·clist** \'sīklist,
'sik-\ *n*

cy·clone \'sī͟klōn\ *n* : tornado
— **cy·clon·ic** \sī'klänik\ *adj*

cy·clo·pe·dia, cy·clo·pae·dia
\͟sīklə'pēdēə\ *n* : encyclope-
dia

cyl·in·der \'siləndər\ *n* **1**
: long round body or figure **2**
: rotating chamber in a re-
volver **3** : piston chamber in
an engine — **cy·lin·dri·cal**
\sə'lindrikəl\ *adj*

cym·bal \'simbəl\ *n* : one of 2
concave brass plates clashed
together

cyn·ic \'sinik\ *n* : one who at-
tributes all actions to selfish
motives — **cyn·i·cal** \-ikəl\
adj — **cyn·i·cism** \-ə͟sizəm\
n

cy·no·sure \'sīnə͟shu̇ur, 'sin-\
n : center of attraction

cy·press \'sīprəs\ *n* : evergreen tree related to the pines

cyst \'sist\ *n* : abnormal bodily
sac — **cys·tic** \'sistik\ *adj*

czar \'zär\ *n* : ruler of Russia
until 1917 — **czar·ist** *n or adj*

D

d \'dē\ *n, pl* **d's** *or* **ds** \'dēz\
: 4th letter of the alphabet

¹dab \'dab\ *n* : gentle touch or
stroke ∼ *vb* **-bb-** : touch or
apply lightly

²dab *n* : small amount

dab·ble \'dabəl\ *vb* **-bled;
-bling 1** : splash **2** : work
without serious effort — **dab-
bler** \-blər\ *n*

dachs·hund \'däks͟hu̇nt\ *n*
: small dog with a long body
and short legs

dad \'dad\ *n* : father

dad·dy \'dadē\ *n, pl* **-dies** : father

daf·fo·dil \'dafə͟dil\ *n* : narcissus with trumpetlike flowers

daft \'daft\ *adj* : foolish —
daft·ness *n*

dag·ger \'dagər\ *n* : knife for
stabbing

dahl·ia \'dalyə, 'däl-\ *n*
: tuberous herb with showy
flowers

dai·ly \'dālē\ *adj* **1** : occurring, done, or used every day
or every weekday **2** : com-
puted in terms of one day ∼
n, pl **-lies** : daily newspaper
— **daily** *adv*

dain·ty \'dāntē\ *n, pl* **-ties** : something delicious ~ *adj* **-ti·er; -est** : delicately pretty — **dain·ti·ly** *adv* — **dain·ti·ness** *n*

dairy \'darē\ *n, pl* **-ies** : farm that produces or company that processes milk — **dairy·maid** *n* — **dairy·man** \-mən, -ˌman\ *n*

da·is \'dāəs\ *n* : raised platform (as for a speaker)

dai·sy \'dāzē\ *n, pl* **-sies** : tall leafy-stemmed plant bearing showy flowers

dale \'dāl\ *n* : valley

dal·ly \'dalē\ *vb* **-lied; -ly·ing** **1** : flirt **2** : dawdle — **dal·li·ance** \-əns\ *n*

dal·ma·tian \dal'māshən\ *n* : large dog having a spotted white coat

¹**dam** \'dam\ *n* : female parent of a domestic animal

²**dam** *n* : barrier to hold back water — **dam** *vb*

dam·age \'damij\ *n* **1** : loss or harm due to injury **2** *pl* : compensation for loss or injury ~ *vb* **-aged; -ag·ing** : do damage to

dam·ask \'daməsk\ *n* : firm lustrous figured fabric

dame \'dām\ *n* : woman of rank or authority

damn \'dam\ *vb* **1** : condemn to hell **2** : curse — **dam·na·ble** \-nəbəl\ *adj* — **dam·na-**

tion \dam'nāshən\ *n* — **damned** *adj*

damp \'damp\ *n* : moisture ~ *vb* **1** : reduce the draft in **2** : restrain **3** : moisten ~ *adj* : moist — **damp·ness** *n*

damp·en \'dampən\ *vb* **1** : diminish in activity or vigor **2** : make or become damp

damp·er \'dampər\ *n* : movable plate to regulate a flue draft

dam·sel \'damzəl\ *n* : young woman

dance \'dans\ *vb* **danced; danc·ing** : move rhythmically to music ~ *n* : act of dancing or a gathering for dancing — **danc·er** *n*

dan·de·li·on \'dandᵊlˌīən\ *n* : common yellow-flowered herb

dan·der \'dandər\ *n* : temper

dan·druff \'dandrəf\ *n* : whitish thin dry scales of skin on the scalp

dan·dy \'dandē\ *n, pl* **-dies** **1** : man too concerned with clothes **2** : something excellent ~ *adj* **-di·er; -est** : very good

dan·ger \'dānjər\ *n* **1** : exposure to injury or evil **2** : something that may cause injury — **dan·ger·ous** \'dānjərəs\ *adj*

dan·gle \'daŋgəl\ *vb* **-gled; -gling** **1** : hang and swing freely **2** : be left without support or connection **3** : allow or cause to hang **4** : offer as an inducement

dank \'daŋk\ *adj* : unpleasantly damp

dap·per \'dapər\ *adj* : neat and stylishly dressed

dap·ple \'dapəl\ *vb* **-pled; -pling** : mark with colored spots

dare \'dar\ *vb* **dared; dar·ing 1** : have sufficient courage **2** : urge or provoke to contend — **dare** *n* — **dar·ing** \'darin\ *n or adj*

dare·dev·il *n* : recklessly bold person

dark \'därk\ *adj* **1** : having little or no light **2** : not light in color **3** : gloomy ~ *n* : absence of light — **dark·en** \-ən\ *vb* — **dark·ly** *adv* — **dark·ness** *n*

dar·ling \'därlin\ *n* **1** : beloved **2** : favorite ~ *adj* **1** : dearly loved **2** : very pleasing

darn \'därn\ *vb* : mend with interlacing stitches — **darn·er** *n*

dart \'därt\ *n* **1** : small pointed missile **2** *pl* : game of throwing darts at a target **3** : tapering fold in a garment **4** : quick movement ~ *vb* : move suddenly or rapidly

dash \'dash\ *vb* **1** : smash **2** : knock or hurl violently **3** : ruin **4** : perform or finish

hastily **5** : move quickly ~ *n* **1** : sudden burst, splash, or stroke **2** : punctuation mark — **3** : tiny amount **4** : showiness or liveliness **5** : sudden rush **6** : short race **7** : dashboard

dash·board *n* : instrument panel

dash·ing \'dashin\ *adj* : dapper and charming

das·tard \'dastərd\ *n* : one who sneakingly commits malicious acts

das·tard·ly \-lē\ *adj* : base or malicious

da·ta \'dātə, 'dat-, 'dät-\ *n sing or pl* : factual information

da·ta·base \-,bās\ *n* : data organized for computer search

¹**date** \'dāt\ *n* : edible fruit of a palm

²**date** *n* **1** : day, month, or year when something is done or made **2** : historical time period **3** : social engagement or the person one goes out with ~ *vb* **dat·ed; dat·ing 1** : determine or record the date of **2** : have a date with **3** : originate — **to date** : up to now

dat·ed \-əd\ *adj* : old-fashioned

da·tum \'dātəm, 'dat-, 'dät-\ *n, pl* **-ta** \-ə\ *or* **-tums** : piece of data

daub \'dȯb\ *vb* : smear ~ *n* : something daubed on — **daub·er** *n*

daugh·ter \'dȯtər\ *n* : human female offspring

daugh·ter–in–law *n, pl* **daughters–in–law** : wife of one's son

daunt \'dȯnt\ *vb* : lessen the courage of

daunt·less \-ləs\ *adj* : fearless

dav·en·port \'davən,pōrt\ *n* : sofa

daw·dle \'dȯdᵊl\ *vb* -**dled;** -**dling** 1 : waste time 2 : loiter

dawn \'dȯn\ *vb* 1 : grow light as the sun rises 2 : begin to appear, develop, or be understood ～ *n* : first appearance (as of daylight)

day \'dā\ *n* 1 : period of light between one night and the next 2 : 24 hours 3 : specified date 4 : particular time or age 5 : period of work for a day — **day·light** *n* — **day·time** *n*

day·break *n* : dawn

day·dream *n* : fantasy of wish fulfillment — **daydream** *vb*

daylight saving time *n* : time one hour ahead of standard time

daze \'dāz\ *vb* **dazed; daz·ing** 1 : stun by a blow 2 : dazzle — **daze** *n*

daz·zle \'dazəl\ *vb* -**zled;** -**zling** 1 : overpower with light 2 : impress greatly — **dazzle** *n*

DDT \,dē,dē'tē\ *n* : long-lasting insecticide

dea·con \'dēkən\ *n* : subordinate church officer

dea·con·ess \'dēkənəs\ *n* : woman who assists in church ministry

dead \'ded\ *adj* 1 : lifeless 2 : unresponsive or inactive 3 : exhausted 4 : obsolete 5 : precise ～ *n, pl* **dead** 1 : one that is dead — usu. with *the* 2 : most lifeless time ～ *adv* 1 : completely 2 : directly — **dead·en** \'dedᵊn\ *vb*

dead·beat *n* : one who will not pay debts

dead end *n* : end of a street with no exit — **dead–end** *adj*

dead heat *n* : tie in a contest

dead·line *n* : time by which something must be finished

dead·lock *n* : struggle that neither side can win — **deadlock** *vb*

dead·ly \'dedlē\ *adj* -**li·er;** -**est** 1 : capable of causing death 2 : very accurate 3 : fatal to spiritual progress 4 : suggestive of death 5 : very great ～ *adv* : extremely — **dead·li·ness** *n*

dead·pan *adj* : expressionless — **dead·pan** *n or vb or adv*

dead·wood *n* : something useless

deaf \'def\ *adj* : unable or unwilling to hear — **deaf·en** \-ən\ *vb* — **deaf·ness** *n*

deaf–mute *n* : deaf person unable to speak

deal \'dēl\ *n* **1** : indefinite quantity **2** : distribution of playing cards **3** : negotiation or agreement **4** : treatment received **5** : bargain ~ *vb* **dealt** \'delt\; **deal·ing** \'dēliŋ\ **1** : distribute playing cards **2** : be concerned with **3** : administer or deliver **4** : take action **5** : sell **6** : reach a state of acceptance — **deal·er** *n* — **deal·ing** *n*

dean \'dēn\ *n* **1** : head of a group of clergy members **2** : university or school administrator **3** : senior member

dear \'dir\ *adj* **1** : highly valued or loved **2** : expensive ~ *n* : loved one — **dear·ly** *adv* — **dear·ness** *n*

dearth \'dərth\ *n* : scarcity

death \'deth\ *n* **1** : end of life **2** : cause of loss of life **3** : state of being dead **4** : destruction or extinction — **death·less** *adj* — **death·ly** *adj or adv*

de·ba·cle \di'bäkəl, -'bakəl\ *n* : disaster or fiasco

de·bar \di'bär\ *vb* : bar from something

de·bark \-'bärk\ *vb* : disembark — **de·bar·ka·tion** \ˌdē-ˌbär'kāshən\ *n*

de·base \di'bās\ *vb* : disparage — **de·base·ment** *n*

de·bate \-'bāt\ *vb* **-bat·ed; -bat·ing** : discuss a question by argument — **de·bat·able** *adj* — **debate** *n* — **de·bat·er** *n*

de·bauch \-'bȯch\ *vb* : seduce or corrupt — **de·bauch·ery** \-ərē\ *n*

de·bil·i·tate \-'bilə̩tāt\ *vb* **-tat·ed; -tat·ing** : make ill or weak

de·bil·i·ty \-'bilətē\ *n, pl* **-ties** : physical weakness

deb·it \'debət\ *n* : account entry of a payment or debt ~ *vb* : record as a debit

deb·o·nair \ˌdebə'nar\ *adj* : suave

de·bris \də'brē, dā-; 'dā̩brē\ *n, pl* **-bris** \-'brēz, -ˌbrēz\ : remains of something destroyed

debt \'det\ *n* **1** : sin **2** : something owed **3** : state of owing — **debt·or** \-ər\ *n*

de·bunk \dē'bəŋk\ *vb* : expose as false

de·but \'dā̩byü, dā'byü\ *n* **1** : first public appearance **2** : formal entrance into society — **debut** *vb* — **deb·u·tante** \'debyü̩tänt\ *n*

de·cade \'dek̩ād, -əd; de'kād\ *n* : 10 years

dec·a·dence \'dekədəns, di'kād³ns\ *n* : deterioration — **dec·a·dent** \-ənt, -³nt\ *adj or n*

de·cal \'dē͟,kal, di'kal, 'dekəl\ *n* : picture or design for transfer from prepared paper

de·camp \di'kamp\ *vb* : depart suddenly

de·cant \di'kant\ *vb* : pour gently

de·cant·er \-ər\ *n* : ornamental bottle

de·cap·i·tate \di'kapə͟,tāt\ *vb* -tat·ed; -tat·ing : behead — **de·cap·i·ta·tion** \-͟,kapə'tā-shən\ *n*

de·cay \di'kā\ *vb* **1** : decline in condition **2** : decompose — **decay** *n*

de·cease \-'sēs\ *n* : death — **decease** *vb*

de·ceit \-'sēt\ *n* **1** : deception **2** : dishonesty — **de·ceit·ful** \-fəl\ *adj* — **de·ceit·ful·ly** *adv* — **de·ceit·ful·ness** *n*

de·ceive \-'sēv\ *vb* -ceived; -ceiv·ing : trick or mislead — **de·ceiv·er** *n*

de·cel·er·ate \dē'selə͟,rāt\ *vb* -at·ed; -at·ing : slow down

De·cem·ber \di'sembər\ *n* : 12th month of the year having 31 days

de·cent \'dēs°nt\ *adj* **1** : good, right, or just **2** : clothed **3** : not obscene **4** : fairly good — **de·cen·cy** \-°nsē\ *n* — **de·cent·ly** *adv*

de·cep·tion \di'sepshən\ *n* **1** : act or fact of deceiving **2** : fraud — **de·cep·tive** \-'sep-tiv\ *adj* — **de·cep·tive·ly** *adv* — **de·cep·tive·ness** *n*

de·cide \di'sīd\ *vb* -cid·ed; -cid·ing **1** : make a choice or judgment **2** : bring to a conclusion **3** : cause to decide

de·cid·ed *adj* **1** : unquestionable **2** : resolute — **de·cid·ed·ly** *adv*

de·cid·u·ous \di'sijəwəs\ *adj* : having leaves that fall annually

dec·i·mal \'desəməl\ *n* : fraction in which the denominator is a power of 10 expressed by a point (**decimal point**) placed at the left of the numerator — **decimal** *adj*

de·ci·pher \di'sīfər\ *vb* : make out the meaning of — **de·ci·pher·able** *adj*

de·ci·sion \-'sizhən\ *n* **1** : act or result of deciding **2** : determination

de·ci·sive \-'sīsiv\ *adj* **1** : having the power to decide **2** : conclusive **3** : showing determination — **de·ci·sive·ly** *adv* — **de·ci·sive·ness** *n*

deck \'dek\ *n* **1** : floor of a ship **2** : pack of playing cards ~ *vb* **1** : array or dress up **2** : knock down

de·claim \di'klām\ *vb* : speak loudly or impressively — **dec·la·ma·tion** \͟,deklə'māshən\ *n*

de·clare \di'klar\ *vb* **-clared; -clar·ing** **1** : make known formally **2** : state emphatically — **dec·la·ra·tion** \ˌdeklə-'rāshən\ *n* — **de·clar·a·tive** \di'klarətiv\ *adj* — **de·clar·a·to·ry** \di'klarəˌtōrē\ *adj* — **de·clar·er** *n*

de·clen·sion \di'klenchən\ *n* : inflectional forms of a noun, pronoun, or adjective

de·cline \di'klīn\ *vb* **-clined; -clin·ing** **1** : turn or slope downward **2** : wane **3** : refuse to accept **4** : inflect ∼ *n* **1** : gradual wasting away **2** : change to a lower state or level **3** : a descending slope — **dec·li·na·tion** \ˌdeklə-'nāshən\ *n*

de·code \dē'kōd\ *vb* : decipher (a coded message) — **de·cod·er** *n*

de·com·mis·sion \ˌdēkə'mishən\ *vb* : remove from service

de·com·pose \ˌdēkəm'pōz\ *vb* **1** : separate into parts **2** : decay — **de·com·po·si·tion** \dēˌkämpə'zishən\ *n*

de·con·ges·tant \ˌdēkən'jestənt\ *n* : agent that relieves congestion

de·cor, dé·cor \dā'kȯr, 'dā-ˌkȯr\ *n* : room design or decoration

dec·o·rate \'dekəˌrāt\ *vb* **-rated; -rat·ing** **1** : add some-

thing attractive to **2** : honor with a medal — **dec·o·ra·tion** \ˌdekə'rāshən\ *n* — **dec·o·ra·tive** \'dekərətiv\ *adj* — **dec·o·ra·tor** \'dekəˌrātər\ *n*

de·co·rum \di'kōrəm\ *n* : proper behavior — **dec·o·rous** \'dekərəs, di'kōrəs\ *adj*

de·coy \'dēˌkȯi, di'-\ *n* : something that tempts or draws attention from another ∼ *vb* : tempt

de·crease \di'krēs\ *vb* **-creased; -creas·ing** : grow or cause to grow less — **de·crease** \'dēˌkrēs\ *n*

de·cree \di'krē\ *n* : official order — **de·cree** *vb*

de·crep·it \di'krepət\ *adj* : impaired by age

de·cre·scen·do \ˌdākrə-'shendō\ *adv or adj* : with a decrease in volume

de·cry \di'krī\ *vb* : express strong disapproval of

ded·i·cate \'dediˌkāt\ *vb* **-cat·ed; -cat·ing** **1** : set apart for a purpose (as honor or worship) **2** : address to someone as a compliment — **ded·i·ca·tion** \ˌdedi'kāshən\ *n* — **ded·i·ca·to·ry** \'dedikəˌtōrē\ *adj*

de·duce \di'düs, -'dyüs\ *vb* **-duced; -duc·ing** : derive by reasoning — **de·duc·ible** *adj*

de·duct \-'dəkt\ *vb* : subtract — **de·duct·ible** *adj*

de·duc·tion \-'dəkshən\ *n* **1** : subtraction **2** : reasoned conclusion — **de·duc·tive** \-'dəktiv\ *adj*

deed \'dēd\ *n* **1** : exploit **2** : document showing ownership ~ *vb* : convey by deed

deem \'dēm\ *vb* : think

deep \'dēp\ *adj* **1** : extending far or a specified distance down, back, within, or outward **2** : occupied **3** : dark and rich in color **4** : low in tone ~ *adv* **1** : deeply **2** : far along in time ~ *n* : deep place — **deep·en** \'dēpən\ *vb* — **deep·ly** *adv*

deep–seat·ed \-'sētəd\ *adj* : firmly established

deer \'dir\ *n, pl* **deer** : ruminant mammal with antlers in the male — **deer·skin** *n*

de·face \di'fās\ *vb* : mar the surface of — **de·face·ment** *n* — **de·fac·er** *n*

de·fame \di'fām\ *vb* **-famed; -fam·ing** : injure the reputation of — **def·a·ma·tion** \,defə-'māshən\ *n* — **de·fam·a·to·ry** \di'famə,tōrē\ *adj*

de·fault \di'folt\ *n* : failure in a duty — **default** *vb* — **de·fault·er** *n*

de·feat \di'fēt\ *vb* **1** : frustrate **2** : win victory over ~ *n* : loss of a battle or contest

def·e·cate \'defi,kāt\ *vb* **-cat·ed; -cat·ing** : discharge feces from the bowels — **def·e·ca·tion** \,defi'kāshən\ *n*

de·fect \'dē,fekt, di'fekt\ *n* : imperfection ~ \di'-\ *vb* : desert — **de·fec·tion** \-'fekshən\ *n* — **de·fec·tor** \-'fektər\ *n*

de·fec·tive \di'fektiv\ *adj* : faulty or deficient — **defective** *n*

de·fend \-'fend\ *vb* **1** : protect from danger or harm **2** : take the side of — **de·fend·er** *n*

de·fen·dant \-'fendənt\ *n* : person charged or sued in a court

de·fense \-'fens\ *n* **1** : act of defending **2** : something that defends **3** : party, group, or team that opposes another — **de·fense·less** *adj* — **de·fen·si·ble** *adj* — **de·fen·sive** *adj or n*

¹de·fer \di'fər\ *vb* **-rr-** : postpone — **de·fer·ment** \di'fərmənt\ *n* — **de·fer·ra·ble** \-əbəl\ *adj*

²defer *vb* **-rr-** : yield to the opinion or wishes of another — **def·er·ence** \'defrəns\ *n* — **def·er·en·tial** \,defə'renchəl\ *adj*

de·fi·ance \di'fīəns\ *n* : disposition to resist — **de·fi·ant** \-ənt\ *adj*

de·fi·cient \di'fishənt\ *adj* **1** : lacking something necessary **2** : not up to standard — **de·fi·cien·cy** \-'fishənsē\ *n*

def·i·cit \'defəsət\ *n* : shortage esp. in money

de·file \di'fīl\ *vb* **-filed; -fil·ing 1** : make filthy or corrupt **2** : profane or dishonor — **de·file·ment** *n*

de·fine \di'fīn\ *vb* **-fined; -fin·ing 1** : fix or mark the limits of **2** : clarify in outline **3** : set forth the meaning of — **de·fin·able** *adj* — **de·fin·ably** *adv* — **de·fin·er** *n* — **def·i·ni·tion** \,defə'nishən\ *n*

def·i·nite \'defənət\ *adj* **1** : having distinct limits **2** : clear in meaning, intent, or identity **3** : typically designating an identified or immediately identifiable person or thing — **def·i·nite·ly** *adv*

de·fin·i·tive \di'finətiv\ *adj* **1** : conclusive **2** : authoritative

de·flate \di'flāt\ *vb* **-flat·ed; -flat·ing 1** : release air or gas from **2** : reduce — **de·fla·tion** \-'flāshən\ *n*

de·flect \-'flekt\ *vb* : turn aside — **de·flec·tion** \-'flekshən\ *n*

de·fog \-'fȯg, -'fäg\ *vb* : remove condensed moisture from — **de·fog·ger** *n*

de·fo·li·ate \dē'fōlē,āt\ *vb* **-at·ed; -at·ing** : deprive of leaves esp. prematurely — **de·fo·li·ant** \-lēənt\ *n* — **de·fo·li·a·tion** \-,fōlē'āshən\ *n*

de·form \di'fȯrm\ *vb* **1** : distort **2** : disfigure — **de·for·ma·tion** \,dē,fȯr'māshən, ,defər-\ *n* — **de·for·mi·ty** \di'fȯrmətē\ *n*

de·fraud \di'frȯd\ *vb* : cheat

de·fray \-'frā\ *vb* : pay

de·frost \-'frȯst\ *vb* **1** : thaw out **2** : free from ice — **de·frost·er** *n*

deft \'deft\ *adj* : quick and skillful — **deft·ly** *adv* — **deft·ness** *n*

de·funct \di'fəŋkt\ *adj* : dead

de·fy \-'fī\ *vb* **-fied; -fy·ing 1** : challenge **2** : boldly refuse to obey

de·gen·er·ate \di'jenərət\ *adj* : degraded or corrupt ∼ *n* : degenerate person ∼ \-ə,rāt\ *vb* : become degenerate — **de·gen·er·a·cy** \-ərəsē\ *n* — **de·gen·er·a·tion** \-,jenə'rāshən\ *n* — **de·gen·er·a·tive** \-'jenə,rātiv\ *adj*

de·grade \di'grād\ *vb* **1** : reduce from a higher to a lower rank or degree **2** : debase **3** : decompose — **de·grad·able** \-əbəl\ *adj* — **deg·ra·da·tion** \,degrə'dāshən\ *n*

de·gree \di'grē\ *n* **1** : step in a series **2** : extent, intensity, or scope **3** : title given to a college graduate **4** : a 360th part of the circumference of a circle **5** : unit for measuring temperature

de·hy·drate \dē'hī₁drāt\ *vb* **1** : remove water from **2** : lose liquid — **de·hy·dra·tion** \₁dēhī'drāshən\ *n*

de·i·fy \'dēə₁fī, 'dā-\ *vb* **-fied; -fy·ing** : make a god of — **de·i·fi·ca·tion** \₁dēəfə'kāshən, ₁dā-\ *n*

deign \'dān\ *vb* : condescend

de·i·ty \'dēətē, 'dā-\ *n, pl* **-ties** **1** *cap* : God **2** : a god or goddess

de·ject·ed \di'jektəd\ *adj* : sad — **de·jec·tion** \-shən\ *n*

de·lay \di'lā\ *n* : a putting off of something ~ *vb* **1** : postpone **2** : stop or hinder for a time

de·lec·ta·ble \di'lektəbəl\ *adj* : delicious

del·e·gate \'deligət, -₁gāt\ *n* : representative ~ \-₁gāt\ *vb* **-gat·ed; -gat·ing** **1** : entrust to another **2** : appoint as one's delegate — **del·e·ga·tion** \₁deli'gāshən\ *n*

de·lete \di'lēt\ *vb* **-let·ed; -let·ing** : eliminate something written — **de·le·tion** \-'lēshən\ *n*

del·e·te·ri·ous \₁delə'tirēəs\ *adj* : harmful

de·lib·er·ate \di'libərət\ *adj* **1** : determined after careful thought **2** : intentional **3** : not hurried ~ \-ə₁rāt\ *vb* **-at·ed; -at·ing** : consider carefully — **de·lib·er·ate·ly** *adv* — **de·lib·er·ate·ness** *n* — **de·lib·er·a-**

tion \-₁libə'rāshən\ *n* — **de·lib·er·a·tive** \-'libə₁rātiv, -rət-\ *adj*

del·i·ca·cy \'delikəsē\ *n, pl* **-cies** **1** : something special and pleasing to eat **2** : fineness **3** : frailty

del·i·cate \'delikət\ *adj* **1** : subtly pleasing to the senses **2** : dainty and charming **3** : sensitive or fragile **4** : requiring fine skill or tact — **del·i·cate·ly** *adv*

del·i·ca·tes·sen \₁delikə'tesᵊn\ *n* : store that sells ready-to-eat food

de·li·cious \di'lishəs\ *adj* : very pleasing esp. in taste or aroma — **de·li·cious·ly** *adv* — **de·li·cious·ness** *n*

de·light \di'līt\ *n* **1** : great pleasure **2** : source of great pleasure ~ *vb* **1** : take great pleasure **2** : satisfy greatly — **de·light·ful** \-fəl\ *adj* — **de·light·ful·ly** *adv*

de·lin·eate \di'linē₁āt\ *vb* **-eat·ed; -eat·ing** : sketch or portray — **de·lin·ea·tion** \-₁linē'āshən\ *n*

de·lin·quent \-'liŋkwənt\ *n* : delinquent person ~ *adj* **1** : violating duty or law **2** : overdue in payment — **de·lin·quen·cy** \-kwənsē\ *n*

de·lir·i·um \di'lirēəm\ *n* : mental disturbance — **de·lir·i·ous** \-ēəs\ *adj*

de·liv·er \di'livər\ *vb* **1** : set free **2** : hand over **3** : assist in birth **4** : say or speak **5** : send to an intended destination — **de·liv·er·ance** \-ərəns\ *n* — **de·liv·er·er** *n* — **de·liv·ery** \-ərē\ *n*

dell \'del\ *n* : small secluded valley

del·ta \'deltə\ *n* : triangle of land at the mouth of a river

de·lude \di'lüd\ *vb* **-lud·ed; -lud·ing** : mislead or deceive

del·uge \'delyüj\ *n* **1** : flood **2** : drenching rain ~ *vb* **-uged; -ug·ing 1** : flood **2** : overwhelm

de·lu·sion \di'lüzhən\ *n* : false belief

de·luxe \di'lúks, -'ləks, -'lüks\ *adj* : very luxurious or elegant

delve \'delv\ *vb* **delved; delv·ing 1** : dig **2** : seek information in records

dem·a·gogue, dem·a·gog \'demə‚gäg\ *n* : politician who appeals to emotion and prejudice — **dem·a·gogu·ery** \-‚gägərē\ *n* — **dem·a·gogy** \-‚gägē, -‚gäjē\ *n*

de·mand \di'mand\ *n* **1** : act of demanding **2** : something claimed as due **3** : ability and desire to buy **4** : urgent need ~ *vb* **1** : ask for with authority **2** : require

de·mar·cate \di'mär‚kāt, 'dē‚mär-\ *vb* **-cat·ed; -cat-**

ing : mark the limits of — **de·mar·ca·tion** \‚dē‚mär'kā-shən\ *n*

de·mean \di'mēn\ *vb* : degrade

de·mean·or \-'mēnər\ *n* : behavior

de·ment·ed \-'mentəd\ *adj* : crazy

de·mer·it \-'merət\ *n* : mark given an offender

demi·god \'demi‚gäd\ *n* : mythological being less powerful than a god

de·mise \di'mīz\ *n* **1** : death **2** : loss of status

demi·tasse \'demi‚tas\ *n* : small cup of coffee

de·mo·bi·lize \di'mōbə‚līz, dē-\ *vb* : disband from military service — **de·mo·bi·li·za·tion** \-‚mōbələ'zāshən\ *n*

de·moc·ra·cy \di'mäkrəsē\ *n, pl* **-cies 1** : government in which the supreme power is held by the people **2** : political unit with democratic government

dem·o·crat \'demə‚krat\ *n* : adherent of democracy

dem·o·crat·ic \‚demə'kratik\ *adj* : relating to or favoring democracy — **dem·o·crat·i·cal·ly** \-tiklē\ *adv* — **de·moc·ra·tize** \di'mäkrə‚tīz\ *vb*

de·mol·ish \di'mälish\ *vb* **1** : tear down or smash **2** : put an end to — **de·mo·li·tion** \‚demə'lishən, ‚dē-\ *n*

de·mon \'dēmən\ *n* : evil spirit — **de·mon·ic** \di'mänik\ *adj*

dem·on·strate \'demən-ˌstrāt\ *vb* **-strat·ed; -strat·ing** **1** : show clearly or publicly **2** : prove **3** : explain — **de·mon·stra·ble** \di'män-strəbəl\ *adj* — **de·mon·stra·bly** \-blē\ *adv* — **dem·on·stra·tion** \ˌdemən'strāshən\ *n* — **de·mon·stra·tive** \di'mänstrətiv\ *adj or n* — **dem·on·stra·tor** \'demən-ˌstrātər\ *n*

de·mor·al·ize \di'morəˌlīz\ *vb* : destroy the enthusiasm of

de·mote \di'mōt\ *vb* **-mot·ed; -mot·ing** : reduce to a lower rank — **de·mo·tion** \-'mō-shən\ *n*

de·mur \di'mər\ *vb* **-rr-** : object — **de·mur** *n*

de·mure \di'myur\ *adj* : modest — **de·mure·ly** *adv*

den \'den\ *n* **1** : animal's shelter **2** : hiding place **3** : cozy private little room

de·na·ture \dē'nāchər\ *vb* **-tured; -tur·ing** : make (alcohol) unfit for drinking

de·ni·al \di'nīəl\ *n* : rejection of a request or of the validity of a statement

den·i·grate \'deniˌgrāt\ *vb* **-grat·ed; -grat·ing** : speak ill of

den·im \'denəm\ *n* **1** : durable twilled cotton fabric **2** *pl* : pants of denim

den·i·zen \'denəzən\ *n* : inhabitant

de·nom·i·na·tion \diˌnämə-'nāshən\ *n* **1** : religious body **2** : value or size in a series — **de·nom·i·na·tion·al** \-shənəl\ *adj*

de·nom·i·na·tor \-'nämə-ˌnātər\ *n* : part of a fraction below the line

de·note \di'nōt\ *vb* **1** : mark out plainly **2** : mean — **de·no·ta·tion** \ˌdēnō'tāshən\ *n* — **de·no·ta·tive** \'dēnōˌtātiv, di'nōtətiv\ *adj*

de·noue·ment \ˌdāˌnü'mäⁿ\ *n* : final outcome (as of a drama)

de·nounce \di'nauns\ *vb* **-nounced; -nounc·ing** **1** : pronounce blameworthy or evil **2** : inform against

dense \'dens\ *adj* **dens·er; -est** **1** : thick, compact, or crowded **2** : stupid — **dense·ly** *adv* — **dense·ness** *n* — **den·si·ty** \'densətē\ *n*

dent \'dent\ *n* : small depression — **dent** *vb*

den·tal \'dent°l\ *adj* : relating to teeth or dentistry

den·ti·frice \'dentəfrəs\ *n* : preparation for cleaning teeth

den·tin \'dent°n\, **den·tine** \'denˌtēn, ˌden'-\ *n* : bonelike component of teeth

den·tist \'dentist\ *n* : one who cares for and replaces teeth — **den·tist·ry** *n*

den·ture \ˈdenchər\ *n* : artificial teeth

de·nude \diˈnüd, -ˈnyüd\ *vb* **-nud·ed; -nud·ing** : strip of covering

de·nun·ci·a·tion \di͵nənsēˈā-shən\ *n* : act of denouncing

de·ny \-ˈnī\ *vb* **-nied; -ny·ing** **1** : declare untrue **2** : disavow **3** : refuse to grant

de·odor·ant \dēˈōdərənt\ *n* : preparation to prevent unpleasant odors — **de·odor·ize** \-͵rīz\ *vb*

de·part \diˈpärt\ *vb* **1** : go away or away from **2** : die — **de·par·ture** \-ˈpärchər\ *n*

de·part·ment \diˈpärtmənt\ *n* **1** : area of responsibility or interest **2** : functional division — **de·part·men·tal** \di-͵pärtˈmentᵊl, ͵dē-\ *adj*

de·pend \diˈpend\ *vb* **1** : rely for support **2** : be determined by or based on something else — **de·pend·abil·i·ty** \-͵pendə-ˈbilətē\ *n* — **de·pend·able** *adj* — **de·pen·dence** \diˈpen-dəns\ *n* — **de·pen·den·cy** \-dənsē\ *n* — **de·pen·dent** \-ənt\ *adj or n*

de·pict \diˈpikt\ *vb* : show by or as if by a picture — **de·pic·tion** \-ˈpikshən\ *n*

de·plete \diˈplēt\ *vb* **-plet·ed; -plet·ing** : use up resources of — **de·ple·tion** \-ˈplēshən\ *n*

de·plore \-ˈplōr\ *vb* **-plored; -plor·ing** : regret strongly — **de·plor·able** \-əbəl\ *adj*

de·ploy \-ˈplȯi\ *vb* : spread out for battle — **de·ploy·ment** \-mənt\ *n*

de·port \diˈpōrt\ *vb* **1** : behave **2** : send out of the country — **de·por·ta·tion** \͵dē͵pōr-ˈtāshən\ *n* — **de·port·ment** \diˈpōrtmənt\ *n*

de·pose \-ˈpōz\ *vb* **-posed; -pos·ing** **1** : remove (a ruler) from office **2** : testify — **de·po·si·tion** \͵depəˈzishən, ͵dē-\ *n*

de·pos·it \diˈpäzət\ *vb* **-it·ed; -it·ing** : place esp. for safekeeping ∼ *n* **1** : state of being deposited **2** : something deposited **3** : act of depositing **4** : natural accumulation — **de·pos·i·tor** \-ˈpäzətər\ *n*

de·pos·i·to·ry \diˈpäzə͵tōrē\ *n, pl* **-ries** : place for deposit

de·pot *1 usu* ˈdepō, *2 usu* ˈdēp-\ *n* **1** : place for storage **2** : bus or railroad station

de·prave \diˈprāv\ *vb* **-praved; -prav·ing** : corrupt morally — **de·praved** *adj* — **de·prav·i·ty** \-ˈpravətē\ *n*

dep·re·cate \ˈdepri͵kāt\ *vb* **-cat·ed; -cat·ing** **1** : express disapproval of **2** : belittle — **dep·re·ca·tion** \͵depriˈkā-shən\ *n* — **dep·re·ca·tory** \ˈdeprikə͵tōrē\ *adj*

de·pre·ci·ate \di'prēshē,āt\ *vb* -at·ed; -at·ing **1** : lessen in value **2** : belittle — **de·pre·ci·a·tion** \-,prēshē'āshən\ *n*

dep·re·da·tion \,deprə'dā-shən\ *n* : a laying waste or plundering — **dep·re·date** \'deprə,dāt\ *vb*

de·press \di'pres\ *vb* **1** : press down **2** : lessen the activity or force of **3** : discourage **4** : decrease the market value of — **de·pres·sant** \-ᵊnt\ *n or adj* — **de·pressed** *adj* — **de·pres·sive** \-iv\ *adj or n* — **de·pres·sor** \-ər\ *n*

de·pres·sion \di'preshən\ *n* **1** : act of depressing or state of being depressed **2** : depressed place **3** : period of low economic activity

de·prive \-'prīv\ *vb* -prived; -priv·ing : take or keep something away from — **de·pri·va·tion** \,deprə'vāshən\ *n*

depth \'depth\ *n, pl* **depths 1** : something that is deep **2** : distance down from a surface **3** : distance from front to back **4** : quality of being deep

dep·u·ta·tion \,depyə'tāshən\ *n* : delegation

dep·u·ty \'depyətē\ *n, pl* **-ties** : person appointed to act for another — **dep·u·tize** \-yə,tīz\ *vb*

de·rail \di'rāl\ *vb* : leave the rails — **de·rail·ment** *n*

de·range \-'rānj\ *vb* -ranged; -rang·ing **1** : disarrange or upset **2** : make insane — **de·range·ment** *n*

der·by \'dərbē, *Brit* 'där-\ *n, pl* **-bies 1** : horse race **2** : stiff felt hat with dome-shaped crown

de·reg·u·late \dē'regyù,lāt\ *vb* : remove restrictions on — **de·reg·u·la·tion** \-,regyù'lā-shən\ *n*

der·e·lict \'derə,likt\ *adj* **1** : abandoned **2** : negligent ~ *n* **1** : something abandoned **2** : bum — **der·e·lic·tion** \,derə-'likshən\ *n*

de·ride \di'rīd\ *vb* -rid·ed; -rid·ing : make fun of — **de·ri·sion** \-'rizhən\ *n* — **de·ri·sive** \-'rīsiv\ *adj* — **de·ri·sive·ly** *adv* — **de·ri·sive·ness** *n*

de·rive \di'rīv\ *vb* -rived; -riv·ing **1** : obtain from a source or parent **2** : come from a certain source **3** : infer or deduce — **der·i·va·tion** \,derə'vāshən\ *n* — **de·riv·a·tive** \di'rivətiv\ *adj or n*

der·ma·tol·o·gy \,dərmə'täl-əjē\ *n* : study of the skin and its disorders — **der·ma·tol·o·gist** \-jist\ *n*

de·ro·ga·tive \di'rägətiv\ *adj* : derogatory

de·rog·a·to·ry \di'rägə,tōrē\ *adj* : intended to lower the reputation

der·rick \'derik\ *n* **1** : hoisting apparatus **2** : framework over an oil well

de·scend \di'send\ *vb* **1** : move or climb down **2** : derive **3** : extend downward **4** : appear suddenly (as in an attack) — **de·scen·dant, de·scen·dent** \-ənt\ *adj or n* — **de·scent** \di'sent\ *n*

de·scribe \-'skrīb\ *vb* **-scribed; -scrib·ing** : represent in words — **de·scrib·able** *adj* — **de·scrip·tion** \-'skripshən\ *n* — **de·scrip·tive** \-'skriptiv\ *adj*

de·scry \di'skrī\ *vb* **-scried; -scry·ing** : catch sight of

des·e·crate \'desi,krāt\ *vb* **-crat·ed; -crat·ing** : treat (something sacred) with disrespect — **des·e·cra·tion** \,desi'krāshən\ *n*

de·seg·re·gate \dē'segrə,gāt\ *vb* : eliminate esp. racial segregation in — **de·seg·re·ga·tion** *n*

¹des·ert \'dezərt\ *n* : dry barren region — **desert** *adj*

²de·sert \di'zərt\ *n* : what one deserves

³de·sert \di'zərt\ *vb* : abandon — **de·sert·er** *n* — **de·ser·tion** \-'zərshən\ *n*

de·serve \-'zərv\ *vb* **-served; -serv·ing** : be worthy of

des·ic·cate \'desi,kāt\ *vb* **-cat·ed; -cat·ing** : dehydrate — **des·ic·ca·tion** \,desi'kāshən\ *n*

de·sign \di'zīn\ *vb* **1** : create and work out the details of **2** : make a pattern or sketch of ~ *n* **1** : mental project or plan **2** : purpose **3** : preliminary sketch **4** : underlying arrangement of elements **5** : decorative pattern — **de·sign·er** *n*

des·ig·nate \'dezig,nāt\ *vb* **-nat·ed; -nat·ing** **1** : indicate, specify, or name **2** : appoint — **des·ig·na·tion** \,dezig'nāshən\ *n*

de·sire \di'zīr\ *vb* **-sired; -sir·ing** **1** : feel desire for **2** : request ~ *n* **1** : strong conscious impulse to have, be, or do something **2** : something desired — **de·sir·abil·i·ty** \-,zīrə'bilətē\ *n* — **de·sir·able** \-'zīrəbəl\ *adj* — **de·sir·able·ness** *n* — **de·sir·ous** \-'zīrəs\ *adj*

de·sist \di'zist, -'sist\ *vb* : stop

desk \'desk\ *n* : table esp. for writing and reading

des·o·late \'desələt, 'dez-\ *adj* **1** : lifeless **2** : disconsolate ~ \-,lāt\ *vb* **-lat·ed; -lat·ing** : lay waste — **des·o·la·tion** \,desə'lāshən, ,dez-\ *n*

de·spair \di'spar\ *vb* : lose all hope ~ *n* : loss of hope

des·per·a·do \,despə'rädō, -'rād-\ *n, pl* **-does** *or* **-dos** : desperate criminal

des·per·ate \'desprət\ *adj* **1** : hopeless **2** : rash **3** : extremely intense — **des·per·ate·ly** *adv* — **des·per·a·tion** \ˌdespə'rāshən\ *n*

de·spi·ca·ble \di'spikəbel, 'despik-\ *adj* : deserving scorn

de·spise \di'spīz\ *vb* **-spised; -spis·ing** : feel contempt for

de·spite \-'spīt\ *prep* : in spite of

de·spoil \-'spȯil\ *vb* : strip of possessions or value

de·spon·den·cy \-'spändənsē\ *n* : dejection — **de·spon·dent** \-dənt\ *adj*

des·pot \'despət, -ˌpät\ *n* : tyrant — **des·pot·ic** \des-'pätik\ *adj* — **des·po·tism** \'despəˌtizəm\ *n*

des·sert \di'zərt\ *n* : sweet food, fruit, or cheese ending a meal

des·ti·na·tion \ˌdestə'nāshən\ *n* : place where something or someone is going

des·tine \'destən\ *vb* **-tined; -tin·ing** **1** : designate, assign, or determine in advance **2** : direct

des·ti·ny \'destənē\ *n, pl* **-nies** : that which is to happen in the future

des·ti·tute \'destəˌtüt, -ˌtyüt\ *adj* **1** : lacking something **2** : very poor — **des·ti·tu·tion** \ˌdestə'tüshən, -'tyü-\ *n*

de·stroy \di'strȯi\ *vb* : kill or put an end to

de·stroy·er \-'strȯiər\ *n* **1** : one that destroys **2** : small speedy warship

de·struc·tion \-'strəkshən\ *n* **1** : action of destroying **2** : ruin — **de·struc·ti·bil·i·ty** \-ˌstrəktə'bilətē\ *n* — **de·struc·ti·ble** \-'strəktəbəl\ *adj* — **de·struc·tive** \-'strək-tiv\ *adj*

des·ul·to·ry \'desəlˌtōrē\ *adj* : aimless

de·tach \di'tach\ *vb* : separate

de·tached \-'tacht\ *adj* **1** : separate **2** : aloof or impartial

de·tach·ment \-'tachmənt\ *n* **1** : separation **2** : troops or ships on special service **3** : aloofness **4** : impartiality

de·tail \di'tāl, 'dēˌtāl\ *n* : small item or part ~ *vb* : give details of

de·tain \di'tān\ *vb* **1** : hold in custody **2** : delay

de·tect \di'tekt\ *vb* : discover — **detect·able** *adj* — **de·tec·tion** \-'tekshən\ *n* — **de·tec·tor** \-tər\ *n*

de·tec·tive \-'tektiv\ *n* : one who investigates crime

dé·tente \dā'tänt\ *n* : relaxation of tensions between nations

de·ten·tion \di'tenchən\ *n* : confinement

de·ter \-'tər\ *vb* **-rr-** : discourage or prevent — **de·ter-**

rence \-əns\ *n* — **de·ter·rent** \-ənt\ *adj or n*

de·ter·gent \di'tərjənt\ *n* : cleansing agent

de·te·ri·o·rate \-'tirēə₁rāt\ *vb* **-rat·ed; -rat·ing** : make or become worse — **de·te·ri·o·ra·tion** \-₁tirēə'rāshən\ *n*

de·ter·mi·na·tion \di₁tərmə'nāshən\ *n* **1** : act of deciding or fixing **2** : firm purpose

de·ter·mine \-'tərmən\ *vb* **-mined; -min·ing 1** : decide on, establish, or settle **2** : find out **3** : bring about as a result

de·test \-'test\ *vb* : hate — **de·test·able** *adj* — **de·tes·ta·tion** \₁dē₁tes'tāshən\ *n*

det·o·nate \'detᵊn₁āt\ *vb* **-nat·ed; -nat·ing** : explode — **det·o·na·tion** \₁detᵊn'āshən\ *n* — **det·o·na·tor** \'detᵊn₁ātər\ *n*

de·tour \'dē₁túr\ *n* : temporary indirect route — **detour** *vb*

de·tract \di'trakt\ *vb* : take away — **de·trac·tion** \-'trakshən\ *n* — **de·trac·tor** \-'traktər\ *n*

det·ri·ment \'detrəmənt\ *n* : damage — **det·ri·men·tal** \₁detrə'mentᵊl\ *adj* — **det·ri·men·tal·ly** *adv*

deuce \'düs, 'dyüs\ *n* **1** : 2 in cards or dice **2** : tie in tennis **3** : devil — used as an oath

deut·sche mark \'dóichə-\ *n* : monetary unit of Germany

de·val·ue \dē'val₁yü\ *vb* : reduce the value of — **de·val·u·a·tion** *n*

dev·as·tate \'devə₁stāt\ *vb* **-tat·ed; -tat·ing** : ruin — **dev·as·ta·tion** \₁devə'stāshən\ *n*

de·vel·op \di'veləp\ *vb* **1** : grow, increase, or evolve gradually **2** : cause to grow, increase, or reach full potential — **de·vel·op·er** *n* — **de·vel·op·ment** *n* — **de·vel·op·men·tal** \-₁veləp'mentᵊl\ *adj*

de·vi·ate \'dēvē₁āt\ *vb* **-at·ed; -at·ing** : change esp. from a course or standard — **de·vi·ant** \-vēənt\ *adj or n* — **de·vi·ate** \-vēət, -vē₁āt\ *n* — **de·vi·a·tion** \₁dēvē'āshən\ *n*

de·vice \di'vīs\ *n* **1** : specialized piece of equipment or tool **2** : design

dev·il \'devəl\ *n* **1** : personified supreme spirit of evil **2** : demon **3** : wicked person ~ *vb* **-iled** *or* **-illed; -il·ing** *or* **-il·ling 1** : season highly **2** : pester — **dev·il·ish** \'devəlish\ *adj* — **dev·il·ry** \'devəlrē\, **dev·il·try** \-trē\ *n*

de·vi·ous \'dēvēəs\ *adj* : tricky

de·vise \di'vīz\ *vb* **-vised; -vis·ing 1** : invent **2** : plot **3** : give by will

de·void \-'vȯid\ *adj* : entirely lacking

de·vote \di'vōt\ *vb* **-vot·ed; -vot·ing** : set apart for a special purpose

de·vot·ed *adj* : faithful

dev·o·tee \ˌdevə'tē, -'tā\ *n* : ardent follower

de·vo·tion \di'vōshən\ *n* **1** : prayer — usu. pl. **2** : loyalty and dedication — **de·vo·tion·al** \-shənəl\ *adj*

de·vour \di'vaůər\ *vb* : consume ravenously — **de·vour·er** *n*

de·vout \-'vaůt\ *adj* **1** : devoted to religion **2** : serious — **de·vout·ly** *adv* — **de·vout·ness** *n*

dew \'dü, 'dyü\ *n* : moisture condensed at night — **dew·drop** *n* — **dewy** *adj*

dex·ter·ous \'dekstrəs\ *adj* : skillful with the hands — **dex·ter·i·ty** \dek'sterətē\ *n* — **dex·ter·ous·ly** *adv*

dex·trose \'dekˌstrōs\ *n* : plant or blood sugar

di·a·be·tes \ˌdīə'bētēz, -'bētəs\ *n* : disorder in which the body has too little insulin and too much sugar — **di·a·bet·ic** \-'betik\ *adj or n*

di·a·bol·ic \-'bälik\, **di·a·bol·i·cal** \-ikəl\ *adj* : fiendish

di·a·crit·ic \-'kritik\ *n* : mark accompanying a letter and indicating a specific sound value — **di·a·crit·i·cal** \-'kritikəl\ *adj*

di·a·dem \'dīəˌdem\ *n* : crown

di·ag·no·sis \ˌdīig'nōsəs, -əg-\ *n, pl* **-no·ses** \-ˌsēz\ : identifying of a disease from its symptoms — **di·ag·nose** \'dīigˌnōs, -əg-\ *vb* — **di·ag·nos·tic** \ˌdīig'nästik, -əg-\ *adj*

di·ag·o·nal \dī'agənəl\ *adj* : extending from one corner to the opposite corner ~ *n* : diagonal line, direction, or arrangement — **di·ag·o·nal·ly** *adv*

di·a·gram \'dīəˌgram\ *n* : explanatory drawing or plan ~ *vb* **-gramed** *or* **-grammed; -gram·ing** *or* **-gram·ming** : represent by a diagram — **di·a·gram·mat·ic** \ˌdīəgrə'matik\ *adj*

di·al \'dīəl\ *n* **1** : face of a clock, meter, or gauge **2** : control knob or wheel ~ *vb* **-aled** *or* **-alled; -al·ing** *or* **-al·ling** : turn a dial to call, operate, or select

di·a·lect \'dīəˌlekt\ *n* : variety of language confined to a region or group

di·a·logue \-ˌlȯg\ *n* : conversation

di·am·e·ter \dī'amətər\ *n* **1** : straight line through the center of a circle **2** : thickness

di·a·met·ric \ˌdīə'metrik\ **di·a·met·ri·cal** \-trikəl\ *adj*

: completely opposite — **di·a·met·ri·cal·ly** \-iklē\ *adv*

di·a·mond \'dīmənd, 'dīə-\ *n* **1** : hard brilliant mineral that consists of crystalline carbon **2** : flat figure having 4 equal sides, 2 acute angles, and 2 obtuse angles **3** : playing card of a suit marked with a red diamond **4** : baseball field

di·a·per \'dīpər\ *n* : baby's garment for receiving bodily wastes ∼ *vb* : put a diaper on

di·a·phragm \'dīə,fram\ *n* **1** : sheet of muscle between the chest and abdominal cavity **2** : contraceptive device

di·ar·rhea \,dīə'rēə\ *n* : abnormally watery discharge from bowels

di·a·ry \'dīərē\ *n, pl* **-ries** : daily record of personal experiences — **di·a·rist** \'dīərist\ *n*

di·a·tribe \'dīə,trīb\ *n* : biting or abusive denunciation

dice \'dīs\ *n, pl* **dice** : die or a game played with dice ∼ *vb* **diced; dic·ing** : cut into small cubes

dick·er \'dikər\ *vb* : bargain

dic·tate \'dik,tāt\ *vb* **-tat·ed; -tat·ing** **1** : speak for a person or a machine to record **2** : command ∼ *n* : order — **dic·ta·tion** \dik'tāshən\ *n*

dic·ta·tor \'dik,tātər\ *n* : person ruling absolutely and of-ten brutally — **dic·ta·to·ri·al** \,diktətōrēəl\ *adj* — **dic·ta·tor·ship** \dik'tātər,ship, 'dik,-\ *n*

dic·tion \'dikshən\ *n* **1** : choice of the best word **2** : precise pronunciation

dic·tio·nary \-shə,nerē\ *n, pl* **-nar·ies** : reference book of words with information about their meanings

dic·tum \'diktəm\ *n, pl* **-ta** \-tə\ : authoritative or formal statement

did *past of* DO

di·dac·tic \dī'daktik\ *adj* : intended to teach a moral lesson

¹**die** \'dī\ *vb* **died; dy·ing** \'dīiŋ\ **1** : stop living **2** : pass out of existence **3** : stop or subside **4** : long

²**die** \'dī\ *n* **1** *pl* **dice** \'dīs\ : small marked cube used in gambling **2** *pl* **dies** \'dīz\ : form for stamping or cutting

die·sel \'dēzəl, -səl\ *n* : engine in which high compression causes ignition of the fuel

di·et \'dīət\ *n* : food and drink regularly consumed (as by a person) ∼ *vb* : eat less or according to certain rules — **di·etary** \'dīə,terē\ *adj or n* — **di·et·er** *n*

di·etet·ics \,dīə'tetiks\ *n sing or pl* : science of nutrition — **di·etet·ic** *adj* — **di·eti·tian, di·eti·cian** \-'tishən\ *n*

dif·fer \'difər\ *vb* **1** : be unlike **2** : vary **3** : disagree — **dif·fer·ence** \'difrəns\ *n*

dif·fer·ent \-rənt\ *adj* : not the same — **dif·fer·ent·ly** *adv*

dif·fer·en·ti·ate \ˌdifə'renchē-ˌāt\ *vb* **-at·ed; -at·ing** **1** : make or become different **2** : attain a specialized adult form during development **3** : distinguish — **dif·fer·en·ti·a·tion** \-ˌrenchē'āshən\ *n*

dif·fi·cult \'difikəlt\ *adj* : hard to do, understand, or deal with

dif·fi·cul·ty \-kəltē\ *n, pl* **-ties** **1** : difficult nature **2** : great effort **3** : something hard to do, understand, or deal with

dif·fi·dent \'difədənt\ *adj* : reserved — **dif·fi·dence** \-əns\ *n*

dif·fuse \dif'yüs\ *adj* **1** : wordy **2** : not concentrated ∼ \-'yüz\ *vb* **-fused; -fus·ing** : pour out or spread widely — **dif·fu·sion** \-'yü-zhən\ *n*

dig \'dig\ *vb* **dug** \'dəg\; **dig·ging** **1** : turn up soil **2** : hollow out or form by removing earth **3** : uncover by turning up earth ∼ *n* **1** : thrust **2** : cutting remark — **dig in** *vb* **1** : establish a defensive position **2** : begin working or eating — **dig up** *vb* : discover

¹**di·gest** \'dī,jest\ *n* : body of information in shortened form

²**di·gest** \dī'jest, də-\ *vb* **1** : think over **2** : convert (food) into a form that can be absorbed **3** : summarize — **di·gest·ible** *adj* — **di·ges·tion** \-'jeschən\ *n* — **di·ges·tive** \-'jestiv\ *adj*

dig·it \'dijət\ *n* **1** : any of the figures 1 to 9 inclusive and usu. the symbol 0 **2** : finger or toe

dig·i·tal \-ᵊl\ *adj* : providing information in numerical digits — **dig·i·tal·ly** *adv*

digital camera *n* : camera that records images as digital data instead of on film

dig·ni·fy \'dignə,fī\ *vb* **-fied; -fy·ing** : give dignity or attention to

dig·ni·tary \-ˌterē\ *n, pl* **-taries** : person of high position

dig·ni·ty \'dignətē\ *n, pl* **-ties** **1** : quality or state of being worthy or honored **2** : formal reserve (as of manner)

di·gress \dī'gres, də-\ *vb* : wander from the main subject — **di·gres·sion** \-'greshən\ *n*

dike \'dīk\ *n* : earth bank or dam

di·lap·i·dat·ed \də'lapə-ˌdātəd\ *adj* : fallen into partial ruin — **di·lap·i·da·tion** \-ˌlapə'dāshən\ *n*

di·late \dī'lāt, 'dī,lāt\ *vb* **-lat·ed; -lat·ing** : swell or expand — **dil·a·ta·tion** \ˌdilə'tāshən\ *n* — **di·la·tion** \dī'lā-shən\ *n*

dil·a·to·ry \'dilə,tōrē\ *adj* **1** : delaying **2** : tardy or slow

di·lem·ma \də'lemə\ *n* **1** : undesirable choice **2** : predicament

dil·et·tante \'dilə,tänt, -,tant; ,dilə'tänt, -'tant\ *n, pl* **-tantes** *or* **-tan·ti** \-'täntē, -'tantē\ : one who dabbles in a field of interest

dil·i·gent \'diləjənt\ *adj* : attentive and busy — **dil·i·gence** \-jəns\ *n* — **dil·i·gent·ly** *adv*

dill \'dil\ *n* : herb with aromatic leaves and seeds

dil·ly·dal·ly \'dilē,dalē\ *vb* : waste time by delay

di·lute \dī'lüt, də-\ *vb* **-lut·ed; -lut·ing** : lessen the consistency or strength of by mixing with something else ~ *adj* : weak — **di·lu·tion** \-'lüshən\ *n*

dim \'dim\ *adj* **-mm- 1** : not bright or distinct **2** : having no luster **3** : not seeing or understanding clearly — **dim** *vb* — **dim·ly** *adv* — **dim·mer** *n* — **dim·ness** *n*

dime \'dīm\ *n* : U.S. coin worth ¹/₁₀ dollar

di·men·sion \də'menchən, dī-\ *n* **1** : measurement of extension (as in length, height, or breadth) **2** : extent — **di-men·sion·al** \-'menchənəl\ *adj*

di·min·ish \də'minish\ *vb* **1** : make less or cause to appear less **2** : dwindle

di·min·u·tive \də'minyətiv\ *adj* : extremely small

dim·ple \'dimpəl\ *n* : small depression esp. in the cheek or chin

din \'din\ *n* : loud noise

dine \'dīn\ *vb* **dined; din·ing** : eat dinner

din·er \'dīnər\ *n* **1** : person eating dinner **2** : railroad dining car or restaurant resembling one

din·ghy \'diŋē, -gē, -kē\ *n, pl* **-ghies** : small boat

din·gy \'dinjē\ *adj* **-gi·er; -est 1** : dirty **2** : shabby — **din·gi·ness** *n*

din·ner \'dinər\ *n* : main daily meal

di·no·saur \'dīnə,sȯr\ *n* : extinct often huge reptile

dint \'dint\ *n* : force — in the phrase *by dint of*

di·o·cese \'dīəsəs, -,sēz, -,sēs\ *n, pl* **-ces·es** \-səz, 'dīə,sēz\ : territorial jurisdiction of a bishop — **di·oc·e·san** \dī-'äsəsən, ,dīə'sēz²n\ *adj or n*

dip \'dip\ *vb* **-pp- 1** : plunge into a liquid **2** : take out with a ladle **3** : lower and quickly raise again **4** : sink or slope downward suddenly ~ *n* **1**

: plunge into water for sport **2** : sudden downward movement or incline — **dip·per** *n*

diph·the·ria \dif'thirēə\ *n* : acute contagious disease

diph·thong \'dif‚thȯŋ\ *n* : two vowel sounds joined to form one speech sound (as *ou* in *out*)

di·plo·ma \də'plōmə\ *n, pl* **-mas** : record of graduation from a school

di·plo·ma·cy \-məsē\ *n* **1** : business of conducting negotiations between nations **2** : tact — **dip·lo·mat** \'diplə‚mat\ *n* — **dip·lo·mat·ic** \‚diplə'matik\ *adj*

dire \'dīr\ *adj* **dir·er; -est 1** : very horrible **2** : extreme

di·rect \də'rekt, dī-\ *vb* **1** : address **2** : cause to move or to follow a certain course **3** : show (someone) the way **4** : regulate the activities or course of **5** : request with authority ~ *adj* **1** : leading to or coming from a point without deviation or interruption **2** : frank — **direct** *adv* — **di·rect·ly** *adv* — **di·rect·ness** *n* — **di·rec·tor** \-tər\ *n*

direct current *n* : electric current flowing in one direction only

di·rec·tion \də'rekshən, dī-\ *n* **1** : supervision **2** : order **3** : course along which some-thing moves — **di·rec·tion·al** \-shənəl\ *adj*

di·rec·tive \-tiv\ *n* : order

di·rec·to·ry \-tərē\ *n, pl* **-ries** : alphabetical list of names and addresses

dirge \'dərj\ *n* : funeral hymn

di·ri·gi·ble \'dirəjəbəl, də-'rijə-\ *n* : airship

dirt \'dərt\ *n* **1** : mud, dust, or grime that makes something unclean **2** : soil

dirty \-ē\ *adj* **dirt·i·er; -est 1** : not clean **2** : unfair **3** : indecent ~ *vb* **dirt·ied; dirty·ing** : make or become dirty — **dirt·i·ness** *n*

dis·able \dis'ābəl\ *vb* **-abled; -abling** : make unable to function — **dis·abil·i·ty** \‚disə-'bilətē\ *n*

dis·abuse \‚disə'byüz\ *vb* : free from error or misconception

dis·ad·van·tage \‚disəd'van-tij\ *n* : something that hinders success — **dis·ad·van·ta·geous** *adj*

dis·af·fect \‚disə'fekt\ *vb* : cause discontent in — **dis·af·fec·tion** *n*

dis·agree \‚disə'grē\ *vb* **1** : fail to agree **2** : differ in opinion — **dis·agree·ment** *n*

dis·agree·able \-əbəl\ *adj* : unpleasant

dis·al·low \‚disə'laủ\ *vb* : refuse to admit or recognize

dis·ap·pear \ˌdisə'pir\ *vb* **1** : pass out of sight **2** : cease to be — **dis·ap·pear·ance** *n*

dis·ap·point \ˌdisə'pȯint\ *vb* : fail to fulfill the expectation or hope of — **dis·ap·point·ment** *n*

dis·ap·prove \-ə'prüv\ *vb* **1** : condemn or reject **2** : feel or express dislike or rejection — **dis·ap·prov·al** *n* — **dis·ap·prov·ing·ly** *adv*

dis·arm \dis'ärm\ *vb* **1** : take weapons from **2** : reduce armed forces **3** : make harmless or friendly — **dis·ar·ma·ment** \-'ärməmənt\ *n*

dis·ar·range \ˌdisə'rānj\ *vb* : throw into disorder — **dis·ar·range·ment** *n*

dis·ar·ray \ˌdisə'rā\ *n* : disorder

di·sas·ter \diz'astər, dis-\ *n* : sudden great misfortune — **di·sas·trous** \-'astrəs\ *adj*

dis·avow \ˌdisə'vau̇\ *vb* : deny responsibility for — **dis·avow·al** \-'vau̇əl\ *n*

dis·band \dis'band\ *vb* : break up the organization of

dis·bar \dis'bär\ *vb* : expel from the legal profession — **dis·bar·ment** *n*

dis·be·lieve \ˌdisbi'lēv\ *vb* : hold not worthy of belief — **dis·be·lief** *n*

dis·burse \dis'bərs\ *vb* -bursed; -burs·ing : pay out — **dis·burse·ment** *n*

disc *var of* DISK

dis·card \dis'kärd, 'dis,kärd\ *vb* : get rid of as unwanted — **dis·card** \'dis,kärd\ *n*

dis·cern \dis'ərn, diz-\ *vb* : discover with the eyes or the mind — **dis·cern·ible** *adj* — **dis·cern·ment** *n*

dis·charge \dis'chärj, 'dis,chärj\ *vb* **1** : unload **2** : shoot **3** : set free **4** : dismiss from service **5** : let go or let off **6** : give forth fluid ~ \'dis,-, dis'-\ *n* **1** : act of discharging **2** : a flowing out (as of blood) **3** : dismissal

dis·ci·ple \di'sīpəl\ *n* : one who helps spread another's teachings

dis·ci·pli·nar·i·an \ˌdisəplə'nerēən\ *n* : one who enforces order

dis·ci·pline \'disəplən\ *n* **1** : field of study **2** : training that corrects, molds, or perfects **3** : punishment **4** : control gained by obedience or training ~ *vb* -plined; -plin·ing **1** : punish **2** : train in self-control — **dis·ci·plin·ary** \'disəplə,nerē\ *adj*

dis·claim \dis'klām\ *vb* : disavow

dis·close \-'klōz\ *vb* : reveal — **dis·clo·sure** \-'klōzhər\ *n*

dis·col·or \dis'kələr\ *vb* : change the color of esp. for the worse — **dis·col·or·ation** \dis,kələ'rāshən\ *n*

dis·com·fit \dis'kəmfət\ *vb* : upset — **dis·com·fi·ture** \dis'kəmfə͵chùr\ *n*

dis·com·fort \dis'kəmfərt\ *n* : uneasiness

dis·con·cert \͵diskən'sərt\ *vb* : upset

dis·con·nect \͵diskə'nekt\ *vb* : undo the connection of

dis·con·so·late \dis'känsələt\ *adj* : hopelessly sad

dis·con·tent \͵diskən'tent\ *n* : uneasiness of mind — **dis·con·tent·ed** *adj*

dis·con·tin·ue \͵diskən'tinyü\ *vb* : end — **dis·con·tin·u·ance** *n* — **dis·con·ti·nu·i·ty** \dis͵käntə'nüətē, -'nyü-\ *n* — **dis·con·tin·u·ous** \͵diskən'tinyəwəs\ *adj*

dis·cord \'dis͵kòrd\ *n* : lack of harmony — **dis·cor·dant** \dis'kòrdᵊnt\ *adj* — **dis·cor·dant·ly** *adv*

dis·count \'dis͵kaùnt\ *n* : reduction from a regular price ~ \'dis͵-, dis'-\ *vb* **1** : reduce the amount of **2** : disregard — **discount** *adj* — **dis·count·er** *n*

dis·cour·age \dis'kərij\ *vb* -aged; -ag·ing **1** : deprive of courage, confidence, or enthusiasm **2** : dissuade — **dis·cour·age·ment** *n*

dis·course \'dis͵kōrs\ *n* **1** : conversation **2** : formal treatment of a subject ~

\dis'-\ *vb* -coursed; -cours·ing : talk at length

dis·cour·te·ous \dis'kərtēəs\ *adj* : lacking courtesy — **dis·cour·te·ous·ly** *adv* — **dis·cour·te·sy** *n*

dis·cov·er \dis'kəvər\ *vb* **1** : make known **2** : obtain the first sight or knowledge of **3** : find out — **dis·cov·er·er** *n* — **dis·cov·ery** \-ərē\ *n*

dis·cred·it \dis'kredət\ *vb* **1** : disbelieve **2** : destroy confidence in ~ *n* **1** : loss of reputation **2** : disbelief — **dis·cred·it·able** *adj*

dis·creet \dis'krēt\ *adj* : capable of keeping a secret — **dis·creet·ly** *adv*

dis·crep·an·cy \dis'krepənsē\ *n, pl* -cies : difference or disagreement

dis·crete \dis'krēt, 'dis͵-\ *adj* : individually distinct

dis·cre·tion \dis'kreshən\ *n* **1** : discreet quality **2** : power of decision or choice — **dis·cre·tion·ary** *adj*

dis·crim·i·nate \dis'krimə͵nāt\ *vb* -na·ted; -nat·ing **1** : distinguish **2** : show favor or disfavor unjustly — **dis·crim·i·na·tion** \-͵krimə'nāshən\ *n* — **dis·crim·i·na·to·ry** \-'krimənə͵tōrē\ *adj*

dis·cur·sive \dis'kərsiv\ *adj* : passing from one topic to another — **dis·cur·sive·ly** *adv* — **dis·cur·sive·ness** *n*

dis·cus \'diskəs\ *n, pl* **-cus·es** : disk hurled for distance in a contest

dis·cuss \dis'kəs\ *vb* : talk about or present — **dis·cus·sion** \-'kəshən\ *n*

dis·dain \dis'dān\ *n* : feeling of contempt ～ *vb* : look upon or reject with disdain — **dis·dain·ful** \-fəl\ *adj* — **dis·dain·ful·ly** *adv*

dis·ease \di'zēz\ *n* : condition of a body that impairs its functioning — **dis·eased** \-'zēzd\ *adj*

dis·em·bark \ˌdisəm'bärk\ *vb* : get off a ship — **dis·em·bar·ka·tion** \dis͵emˌbär'kā-shən\ *n*

dis·em·bod·ied \ˌdisəm'bädēd\ *adj* : having no substance or reality

dis·en·chant \ˌdisᵊn'chant\ *vb* : to free from illusion — **dis·en·chant·ment** *n*

dis·en·chant·ed \-'chantəd\ *adj* : disappointed

dis·en·gage \-ᵊn'gāj\ *vb* : release — **dis·en·gage·ment** *n*

dis·en·tan·gle \-ᵊn'taŋgəl\ *vb* : free from entanglement

dis·fa·vor \dis'fāvər\ *n* : disapproval

dis·fig·ure \dis'figyər\ *vb* : spoil the appearance of — **dis·fig·ure·ment** *n*

dis·fran·chise \dis'franˌchīz\ *vb* : deprive of the right to vote — **dis·fran·chise·ment** *n*

dis·gorge \dis'gȯrj\ *vb* : spew forth

dis·grace \dis'grās\ *vb* : bring disgrace to ～ *n* **1** : shame **2** : cause of shame — **dis·grace·ful** \-fəl\ *adj* — **dis·grace·ful·ly** *adv*

dis·grun·tle \dis'grəntᵊl\ *vb* **-tled; -tling** : put in bad humor

dis·guise \dis'gīz\ *vb* **-guised; -guis·ing** : hide the true identity or nature of ～ *n* : something that conceals

dis·gust \dis'gəst\ *n* : strong aversion ～ *vb* : provoke disgust in — **dis·gust·ed·ly** *adv* — **dis·gust·ing·ly** *adv*

dish \'dish\ *n* **1** : vessel for serving food or the food it holds **2** : food prepared in a particular way ～ *vb* : put in a dish — **dish·cloth** *n* — **dish·rag** *n* — **dish·wash·er** *n* — **dish·wa·ter** *n*

dis·har·mo·ny \dis'härmənē\ *n* : lack of harmony — **dis·har·mo·ni·ous** \ˌdishär'mōnēəs\ *adj*

dis·heart·en \dis'härtᵊn\ *vb* : discourage

di·shev·el \di'shevəl\ *vb* **-eled** *or* **-elled; -el·ing** *or* **-el·ling** : throw into disorder — **di·shev·eled, di·shev·elled** *adj*

dishonest   **184**

dis·hon·est \dis'änəst\ *adj*
: not honest — **dis·hon·est·ly**
adv — **dis·hon·es·ty** *n*

dis·hon·or \dis'änər\ *n or vb*
: disgrace — **dis·hon·or·able**
adj — **dis·hon·or·ably** *adv*

dis·il·lu·sion \ˌdisə'lüzhən\
vb : to free from illusion —
dis·il·lu·sion·ment *n*

dis·in·cli·na·tion \disˌinklə'nā-
shən\ *n* : slight aversion —
dis·in·cline \ˌdisᵊn'klīn\ *vb*

dis·in·fect \ˌdisᵊn'fekt\ *vb*
: destroy disease germs in or
on — **dis·in·fec·tant** \-'fek-
tənt\ *adj or n* — **dis·in·fec·
tion** \-'fekshən\ *n*

dis·in·gen·u·ous \ˌdisᵊn'jen-
yəwəs\ *adj* : lacking in can-
dor

dis·in·her·it \-ᵊn'herət\ *vb*
: prevent from inheriting
property

dis·in·te·grate \dis'intəˌgrāt\
vb : break into parts or small
bits — **dis·in·te·gra·tion**
\disˌintə'grāshən\ *n*

dis·in·ter·est·ed \dis'intər-
əstəd, -ˌres-\ *adj* **1** : not interested **2** : not prejudiced —
dis·in·ter·est·ed·ness *n*

dis·joint·ed \dis'jóintəd\ *adj*
1 : separated at the joint **2**
: incoherent

disk \'disk\ *n* : something
round and flat

dis·like \dis'līk\ *vb* : regard
with dislike ～ *n* : feeling that

something is unpleasant and
to be avoided

dis·lo·cate \'dislōˌkāt, dis'-\
vb : move out of the usual or
proper place — **dis·lo·ca·tion**
\ˌdislō'kāshən\ *n*

dis·lodge \dis'läj\ *vb* : force
out of a place

dis·loy·al \dis'lóiəl\ *adj* : not
loyal — **dis·loy·al·ty** *n*

dis·mal \'dizməl\ *adj* : showing or causing gloom — **dis·
mal·ly** *adv*

dis·man·tle \dis'mantᵊl\ *vb*
-tled; -tling : take apart

dis·may \dis'mā\ *vb* **-mayed;
-may·ing** : discourage — **dis·
may** *n*

dis·mem·ber \dis'membər\
vb : cut into pieces — **dis·
mem·ber·ment** *n*

dis·miss \dis'mis\ *vb* **1** : send
away **2** : remove from service
3 : put aside or out of mind —
dis·miss·al *n*

dis·mount \dis'maůnt\ *vb* **1**
: get down from something **2**
: take apart

dis·obey \ˌdisə'bā\ *vb* : refuse
to obey — **dis·obe·di·ence**
\-'bēdēəns\ *n* — **dis·obe·di·
ent** \-ənt\ *adj*

dis·or·der \dis'órdər\ *n* **1**
: lack of order **2** : breach of
public order **3** : abnormal
state of body or mind — **dis·
order** *vb* — **dis·or·der·li·ness**
n — **dis·or·der·ly** *adj*

dis·or·ga·nize \dis'órgə‚nīz\ *vb* : throw into disorder — **dis·or·ga·ni·za·tion** *n*

dis·own \dis'ōn\ *vb* : repudiate

dis·par·age \-'parij\ *vb* **-aged; -ag·ing** : say bad things about — **dis·par·age·ment** *n*

dis·pa·rate \dis'parət, 'dis-pərət\ *adj* : different in quality or character — **dis·par·i·ty** \dis'parətē\ *n*

dis·pas·sion·ate \dis'pashənət\ *adj* : not influenced by strong feeling — **dis·pas·sion·ate·ly** *adv*

dis·patch \dis'pach\ *vb* **1** : send **2** : kill **3** : attend to rapidly **4** : defeat ~ *n* **1** : message **2** : news item from a correspondent **3** : promptness and efficiency — **dis·patch·er** *n*

dis·pel \dis'pel\ *vb* **-ll-** : clear away

dis·pen·sa·ry \-'pensərē\ *n, pl* **-ries** : place where medical or dental aid is provided

dis·pen·sa·tion \‚dispən'sā-shən\ *n* **1** : system of principles or rules **2** : exemption from a rule **3** : act of dispensing

dis·pense \dis'pens\ *vb* **-pensed; -pens·ing** **1** : portion out **2** : make up and give out (remedies) — **dis·pens·er** *n* — **dispense with** : do without

dis·perse \-'pərs\ *vb* **-persed; -pers·ing** : scatter — **dis·per·sal** \-'pərsəl\ *n* — **dis·per·sion** \-'perzhən\ *n*

dis·place \-'plās\ *vb* **1** : expel or force to flee from home or native land **2** : take the place of — **dis·place·ment** \-mənt\ *n*

dis·play \-'plā\ *vb* : present to view — **display** *n*

dis·please \-'plēz\ *vb* : arouse the dislike of — **dis·plea·sure** \-'plezhər\ *n*

dis·port \dis'pōrt\ *vb* **1** : amuse **2** : frolic

dis·pose \dis'pōz\ *vb* **-posed; -pos·ing** **1** : give a tendency to **2** : settle — **dis·pos·able** \-'pōzəbəl\ *adj* — **dis·pos·al** \-'pōzəl\ *n* — **dis·pos·er** *n* — **dispose of** **1** : determine the fate, condition, or use of **2** : get rid of

dis·po·si·tion \‚dispə'zishən\ *n* **1** : act or power of disposing of **2** : arrangement **3** : natural attitude

dis·pos·sess \‚dispə'zes\ *vb* : deprive of possession or occupancy — **dis·pos·ses·sion** \-'zeshən\ *n*

dis·pro·por·tion \‚disprə'pōr-shən\ *n* : lack of proportion — **dis·pro·por·tion·ate** \-shənət\ *adj*

dis·prove \dis'prüv\ *vb* : prove false

dis·pute \dis'pyüt\ *vb* **-put·ed; -put·ing** **1** : argue **2** : deny the truth or rightness of **3** : struggle against or over ~ *n* : debate or quarrel — **dis·put·able** \-əbəl, 'dispyət-\ *adj* — **dis·pu·ta·tion** \,dispyə-'tāshən\ *n*

dis·qual·i·fy \dis'kwälə,fī\ *vb* : make ineligible — **dis·qual·i·fi·ca·tion** *n*

dis·qui·et \dis'kwīət\ *vb* : make uneasy or restless ~ *n* : anxiety

dis·re·gard \,disri'gärd\ *vb* : pay no attention to ~ *n* : neglect

dis·re·pair \,disri'par\ *n* : need of repair

dis·rep·u·ta·ble \dis'repyə-təbəl\ *adj* : having a bad reputation

dis·re·pute \,disri'pyüt\ *n* : low regard

dis·re·spect \,disri'spekt\ *n* : lack of respect — **dis·re·spect·ful** *adj*

dis·robe \dis'rōb\ *vb* : undress

dis·rupt \dis'rəpt\ *vb* : throw into disorder — **dis·rup·tion** \-'rəpshən\ *n* — **dis·rup·tive** \-'rəptiv\ *adj*

dis·sat·is·fac·tion \dis,satəs-'fakshən\ *n* : lack of satisfaction

dis·sat·is·fy \dis'satəs,fī\ *vb* : fail to satisfy

dis·sect \di'sekt\ *vb* : cut into parts esp. to examine — **dis·sec·tion** \-'sekshən\ *n*

dis·sem·ble \di'sembəl\ *vb* **-bled; -bling** : disguise feelings or intention — **dis·sem·bler** *n*

dis·sem·i·nate \di'semə,nāt\ *vb* **-nat·ed; -nat·ing** : spread around — **dis·sem·i·na·tion** \-,semə'nāshən\ *n*

dis·sen·sion \di'senchən\ *n* : discord

dis·sent \di'sent\ *vb* : object or disagree ~ *n* : difference of opinion — **dis·sent·er** *n*

dis·ser·ta·tion \,disər'tāshən\ *n* : long written study of a subject

dis·ser·vice \dis'sərvəs\ *n* : injury

dis·si·dent \'disədənt\ *n* : one who differs openly with an establishment — **dis·si·dence** \-əns\ *n* — **dissident** *adj*

dis·sim·i·lar \di'simələr\ *adj* : different — **dis·sim·i·lar·i·ty** \di,simə'larətē\ *n*

dis·si·pate \'disə,pāt\ *vb* **-pat·ed; -pat·ing** **1** : break up and drive off **2** : squander — **dis·si·pa·tion** \,disə'pāshən\ *n*

dis·so·ci·ate \dis'ōsē,āt, -shē-\ *vb* **-at·ed; -at·ing** : separate from association — **dis·so·ci·a·tion** \dis,ōsē'āshən, -shē-\ *n*

dis·so·lute \\'disǝ‚lüt\ *adj*
: loose in morals or conduct

dis·so·lu·tion \‚disǝ'lüshǝn\ *n*
: act or process of dissolving

dis·solve \di'zälv\ *vb* **1**
: break up or bring to an end
2 : pass or cause to pass into
solution

dis·so·nance \'disǝnǝns\ *n*
: discord — **dis·so·nant**
\-nǝnt\ *adj*

dis·suade \di'swād\ *vb* **-suad-
ed; -suad·ing** : persuade not
to do something — **dis·sua-
sion** \-'swāzhǝn\ *n*

dis·tance \'distǝns\ *n* **1**
: measure of separation in
space or time **2** : reserve

dis·tant \-tǝnt\ *adj* **1** : separate in space **2** : remote in
time, space, or relationship **3**
: reserved — **dis·tant·ly** *adv*

dis·taste \dis'tāst\ *n* : dislike
— **dis·taste·ful** *adj*

dis·tem·per \dis'tempǝr\ *n*
: serious virus disease of dogs

dis·tend \dis'tend\ *vb* : swell
out — **dis·ten·sion, dis·ten-
tion** \-'tenchǝn\ *n*

dis·till \di'stil\ *vb* : obtain
by distillation — **dis·til·late**
\'distǝ‚lāt, -lǝt\ *n* — **dis-
till·er** *n* — **dis·till·ery** \di-
'stilǝrē\ *n*

dis·til·la·tion \‚distǝ'lāshǝn\
n : purification of liquid by
evaporating then condensing

dis·tinct \dis'tiŋkt\ *adj* **1**
: distinguishable from others
2 : readily discerned — **dis-
tinc·tive** \-tiv\ *adj* — **dis-
tinc·tive·ly** *adv* — **dis·tinc-
tive·ness** *n* — **dis·tinct·ly** *adv*
— **dis·tinct·ness** *n*

dis·tinc·tion \-'tiŋkshǝn\ *n* **1**
: act of distinguishing **2** : difference **3** : special recognition

dis·tin·guish \-'tiŋgwish\ *vb*
1 : perceive as different **2** : set
apart **3** : discern **4** : make
outstanding — **dis·tin·guish-
able** *adj* — **dis·tin·guished**
\-gwisht\ *adj*

dis·tort \dis'tȯrt\ *vb* : twist
out of shape, condition, or
true meaning — **dis·tor·tion**
\-'tȯrshǝn\ *n*

dis·tract \di'strakt\ *vb* : di-
vert the mind or attention of —
dis·trac·tion \-'strakshǝn\ *n*

dis·traught \dis'trȯt\ *adj* : agitated with mental conflict

dis·tress \-'tres\ *n* **1** : suffering **2** : misfortune **3** : state of
danger or great need ∼ *vb*
: subject to strain or distress
— **dis·tress·ful** *adj*

dis·trib·ute \-'tribyǝt\ *vb* **-ut-
ed; -ut·ing 1** : divide among
many **2** : spread or hand out
— **dis·tri·bu·tion** \‚distrǝ-
'byüshǝn\ *n* — **dis·trib·u-
tive** \dis'tribyǝtiv\ *adj* —
dis·trib·u·tor \-ǝr\ *n*

dis·trict \'dis‚trikt\ *n* : territorial division

dis·trust \dis'trəst\ *vb or n* : mistrust — **dis·trust·ful** \-fəl\ *adj*

dis·turb \dis'tərb\ *vb* **1** : interfere with **2** : destroy the peace, composure, or order of — **dis·tur·bance** \-'tərbəns\ *n* — **dis·turb·er** *n*

dis·use \dis'yüs\ *n* : lack of use

ditch \'dich\ *n* : trench ∼ *vb* **1** : dig a ditch in **2** : get rid of

dith·er \'dithər\ *n* : highly nervous or excited state

dit·to \'ditō\ *n, pl* **-tos** : more of the same

dit·ty \'ditē\ *n, pl* **-ties** : short simple song

di·uret·ic \‚dīyù'retik\ *adj* : tending to increase urine flow — **diuretic** *n*

di·ur·nal \dī'ərnᵊl\ *adj* **1** : daily **2** : of or occurring in the daytime

di·van \'dī‚van, di'-\ *n* : couch

dive \'dīv\ *vb* **dived** \'dīvd\ *or* **dove** \'dōv\; **dived**; **div·ing** **1** : plunge into water headfirst **2** : submerge **3** : descend quickly ∼ *n* **1** : act of diving **2** : sharp decline — **div·er** *n*

di·verge \də'vərj, dī-\ *vb* **-verged; -verg·ing** **1** : move in different directions **2** : differ — **di·ver·gence** \-'vərjəns\ *n* — **di·ver·gent** \-jənt\ *adj*

di·vers \'dīvərz\ *adj* : various

di·verse \dī'vərs, də-, 'dī‚vərs\ *adj* : involving different forms — **di·ver·si·fi·ca·tion** \də‚vərsəfə'kāshən, dī-\ *n* — **di·ver·si·fy** \-'vərsə‚fī\ *vb* — **di·ver·si·ty** \-sətē\ *n*

di·vert \də'vərt, dī-\ *vb* **1** : turn from a course or purpose **2** : distract **3** : amuse — **di·ver·sion** \-'vərzhən\ *n*

di·vest \dī'vest, də-\ *vb* : strip of clothing, possessions, or rights

di·vide \də'vīd\ *vb* **-vid·ed; -vid·ing** **1** : separate **2** : distribute **3** : share **4** : subject to mathematical division ∼ *n* : watershed — **di·vid·er** *n*

div·i·dend \'divə‚dend\ *n* **1** : individual share **2** : bonus **3** : number to be divided

div·i·na·tion \‚divə'nāshən\ *n* : practice of trying to foretell future events

di·vine \də'vīn\ *adj* **-vin·er; -est** **1** : relating to or being God or a god **2** : supremely good ∼ *n* : clergy member ∼ *vb* **-vined; -vin·ing** **1** : infer **2** : prophesy — **di·vine·ly** *adv* — **di·vin·er** *n* — **di·vin·i·ty** \də'vinətē\ *n*

di·vis·i·ble \-'vizəbəl\ *adj* : capable of being divided — **di·vis·i·bil·i·ty** \-‚vizə'bilətē\ *n*

di·vi·sion \-'vizhən\ *n* **1** : distribution **2** : part of a whole

3 : disagreement **4 :** process of finding out how many times one number is contained in another

di·vi·sive \də'vīsiv, -'vi-, -ziv\ *adj* : creating dissension

di·vi·sor \-'vīzər\ *n* : number by which a dividend is divided

di·vorce \də'vōrs\ *n* : legal breaking up of a marriage — **divorce** *vb*

di·vor·cée \-ˌvōr'sā, -'sē\ *n* : divorced woman

di·vulge \də'vəlj, dī-\ *vb* **-vulged; -vulg·ing** : reveal

diz·zy \'dizē\ *adj* **-zi·er; -est** **1 :** having a sensation of whirling **2 :** causing or caused by giddiness — **diz·zi·ly** *adv* — **diz·zi·ness** *n*

DNA \ˌdēˌen'ā\ *n* : compound in cell nuclei that is the basis of heredity

do \'dü\ *vb* **did** \'did\; **done** \'dən\; **do·ing** \'düiŋ\; **does** \'dəz\ **1 :** work to accomplish (an action or task) **2 :** behave **3 :** prepare or fix up **4 :** fare **5 :** finish **6 :** serve the needs or purpose of **7** — used as an auxiliary verb — **do·er** \'düər\ *n* — **do away with 1 :** get rid of **2 :** destroy — **do by :** deal with — **do in** *vb* **1 :** ruin **2 :** kill

doc·ile \'däsəl\ *adj* : easily managed — **do·cil·i·ty** \dä'silətē\ *n*

¹dock \'däk\ *vb* **1 :** shorten **2** : reduce

²dock *n* **1 :** berth between 2 piers to receive ships **2 :** loading wharf or platform ∼ *vb* : bring or come into dock — **dock·work·er** *n*

³dock *n* : place in a court for a prisoner

dock·et \'däkət\ *n* **1 :** record of the proceedings in a legal action **2 :** list of legal causes to be tried — **docket** *vb*

doc·tor \'däktər\ *n* **1 :** person holding one of the highest academic degrees **2 :** one (as a surgeon) skilled in healing arts ∼ *vb* **1 :** give medical treatment to **2 :** repair or alter — **doc·tor·al** \-tərəl\ *adj*

doc·trine \'däktrən\ *n* : something taught — **doc·tri·nal** \-trən°l\ *adj*

doc·u·ment \'däkyəmənt\ *n* : paper that furnishes information or legal proof — **doc·u·ment** \-ˌment\ *vb* — **doc·u·men·ta·tion** \ˌdäkyəmən'tāshən\ *n* — **doc·u·ment·er** *n*

doc·u·men·ta·ry \ˌdäkyə'mentərē\ *adj* **1 :** of or relating to documents **2 :** giving a factual presentation — **documentary** *n*

dod·der \'dädər\ *vb* : become feeble usu. from age

dodge \'däj\ *vb* **dodged; dodg·ing 1 :** move quickly aside or

out of the way of **2** : evade —
dodge *n*

do·do \'dōdō\ *n, pl* **-does** *or*
-dos **1** : heavy flightless extinct bird **2** : stupid person

doe \'dō\ *n, pl* **does** *or* **doe**
: adult female deer — **doe-
skin** \-,skin\ *n*

does *pres 3d sing of* DO

doff \'däf\ *vb* : remove

dog \'dȯg\ *n* : flesh-eating domestic mammal ~ *vb* **1**
: hunt down or track like a
hound **2** : harass — **dog-
catch·er** *n* — **dog·gy** \-ē\ *n or*
adj — **dog·house** *n*

dog–ear \'dȯg,ir\ *n* : turned-
down corner of a page —
dog–ear *vb* — **dog–eared**
\-,ird\ *adj*

dog·ged \'dȯgəd\ *adj* : stubbornly determined

dog·ma \'dȯgmə\ *n* : tenet or
code of tenets

dog·ma·tism \-,tizəm\ *n* : unwarranted stubbornness of
opinion — **dog·ma·tic** \dȯg-
'matik\ *adj*

dog·wood *n* : flowering tree

doi·ly \'dȯilē\ *n, pl* **-lies**
: small decorative mat

do·ings \'düiŋz\ *n pl* : events

dol·drums \'dōldrəmz,'däl-\
n pl : spell of listlessness, de-
spondency, or stagnation

dole \'dōl\ *n* : distribution esp.
of money to the needy or un-

employed — **dole out** *vb*
: give out esp. in small portions

dole·ful \'dōlfəl\ *adj* : sad —
dole·ful·ly *adv*

doll \'däll, 'dȯl\ *n* : small figure of a person used esp. as a
child's toy

dol·lar \'dälər\ *n* : any of various basic monetary units (as
in the U.S. and Canada)

dol·ly \'dälē\ *n, pl* **-lies** : small
cart or wheeled platform

dol·phin \'dälfən\ *n* **1** : sea
mammal related to the whales
2 : saltwater food fish

dolt \'dōlt\ *n* : stupid person
— **dolt·ish** *adj*

-dom \dəm\ *n suffix* **1** : office
or realm **2** : state or fact of
being **3** : those belonging to a
group

do·main \dō'mān, də-\ *n* **1**
: territory over which someone reigns **2** : sphere of activity or knowledge

dome \'dōm\ *n* **1** : large
hemispherical roof **2** : roofed
stadium

do·mes·tic \də'mestik\ *adj* **1**
: relating to the household or
family **2** : relating and limited to one's own country **3**
: tame ~ *n* : household
servant — **do·mes·ti·cal·ly**
\-tiklē\ *adv*

do·mes·ti·cate \-ti,kāt\ *vb*
-cat·ed; -cat·ing : tame —

do·mes·ti·ca·tion \-ˌmesti-ˈkāshən\ n

do·mi·cile \ˈdäməˌsīl, ˈdō-; ˈdäməsəl\ n : home — **domi·cile** vb

dom·i·nance \ˈdämənəns\ n : control — **dom·i·nant** \-nənt\ adj

dom·i·nate \-ˌnāt\ vb **-nat·ed; -nat·ing 1** : have control over **2** : rise high above — **dom·i·na·tion** \ˌdämə'nāshən\ n

dom·i·neer \ˌdämə'nir\ vb : exercise arbitrary control

do·min·ion \də'minyən\ n **1** : supreme authority **2** : governed territory

dom·i·no \ˈdäməˌnō\ n, pl **-noes** or **-nos** : flat rectangular block used as a piece in a game (**dominoes**)

don \ˈdän\ vb **-nn-** : put on (clothes)

do·nate \ˈdōˌnāt\ vb **-nat·ed; -nat·ing** : make a gift of — **do·na·tion** \dō'nāshən\ n

¹done \ˈdən\ past part of **DO**

²done adj **1** : finished or ended **2** : cooked sufficiently

don·key \ˈdäŋkē, ˈdəŋ-\ n, pl **-keys** : sturdy domestic ass

do·nor \ˈdōnər\ n : one that gives

doo·dle \ˈdüdᵊl\ vb **-dled; -dling** : draw or scribble aimlessly — **doodle** n

doom \ˈdüm\ n **1** : judgment **2** : fate **3** : ruin — **doom** vb

door \ˈdōr\ n : passage for entrance or a movable barrier that can open or close such a passage — **door·jamb** n — **door·knob** n — **door·mat** n — **door·step** n — **door·way** n

dope \ˈdōp\ **1** : narcotic preparation **2** : stupid person **3** : information ~ vb **doped; dop·ing** : drug

dor·mant \ˈdȯrmənt\ adj : not actively growing or functioning — **dor·man·cy** \-mənsē\ n

dor·mer \ˈdȯrmər\ n : window built upright in a sloping roof

dor·mi·to·ry \ˈdȯrməˌtōrē\ n, pl **-ries** : residence hall (as at a college)

dor·mouse \ˈdȯrˌmaủs\ n : squirrellike rodent

dor·sal \ˈdȯrsəl\ adj : relating to or on the back — **dor·sal·ly** adv

do·ry \ˈdōrē\ n, pl **-ries** : flat‗bottomed boat

dose \ˈdōs\ n : quantity (as of medicine) taken at one time ~ vb **dosed; dos·ing** : give medicine to — **dos·age** \ˈdōsij\ n

dot \ˈdät\ n **1** : small spot **2** : small round mark made with or as if with a pen ~ vb **-tt-** : mark with dots

dot·age \ˈdōtij\ n : senility

dote \\'dōt\ *vb* **dot·ed; dot·ing** **1** : act feebleminded **2** : be foolishly fond

dou·ble \\'dəbəl\ *adj* **1** : consisting of 2 members or parts **2** : being twice as great or as many **3** : folded in two ～ *n* **1** : something twice another **2** : one that resembles another ～ *adv* : doubly ～ *vb* **-bled; -bling** **1** : make or become twice as great **2** : fold or bend **3** : clench

dou·ble–cross *vb* : deceive by trickery — **dou·ble–cross·er** *n*

dou·bly \\'dəblē\ *adv* : to twice the degree

doubt \\'daut\ *vb* **1** : be uncertain about **2** : mistrust **3** : consider unlikely ～ *n* **1** : uncertainty **2** : mistrust **3** : inclination not to believe — **doubt·ful** \-fəl\ *adj* — **doubt·ful·ly** *adv* — **doubt·less** \-ləs\ *adv*

douche \\'düsh\ *n* : jet of fluid for cleaning a body part

dough \\'dō\ *n* : stiff mixture of flour and liquid — **doughy** \\'dōē\ *adj*

dough·nut \-ˌnət\ *n* : small fried ring-shaped cake

dough·ty \\'dautē\ *adj* **-ti·er; -est** : able, strong, or valiant

dour \\'dauər, 'dur\ *adj* **1** : severe **2** : gloomy or sullen — **dour·ly** *adv*

douse \\'daus, 'dauz\ *vb* **doused; dous·ing** **1** : plunge into or drench with water **2** : extinguish

¹dove \\'dəv\ *n* : small wild pigeon

²dove \\'dōv\ *past of* DIVE

dove·tail \\'dəvˌtāl\ *vb* : fit together neatly

dow·a·ger \\'dauijər\ *n* **1** : widow with wealth or a title **2** : dignified elderly woman

dowdy \\'daudē\ *adj* **dowd·i·er; -est** : lacking neatness and charm

dow·el \\'dauəl\ *n* **1** : peg used for fastening two pieces **2** : wooden rod

dow·er \\'dauər\ *n* : property given a widow for life ～ *vb* : supply with a dower

¹down \\'daun\ *adv* **1** : toward or in a lower position or state **2** : to a lying or sitting position **3** : as a cash deposit **4** : on paper ～ *adj* **1** : lying on the ground **2** : directed or going downward **3** : being at a low level ～ *prep* : toward the bottom of ～ *vb* **1** : cause to go down **2** : defeat

²down *n* : fluffy feathers

down·cast *adj* **1** : sad **2** : directed down

down·fall *n* : ruin or cause of ruin

down·grade *n* : downward slope ~ *vb* : lower in grade or position

down·heart·ed *adj* : sad

down·pour *n* : heavy rain

down·right *adv* : thoroughly ~ *adj* : absolute or thorough

downs \'daủnz\ *n pl* : rolling treeless uplands

down·size \'daủn,sīz\ *vb* : reduce in size

down·stairs *adv* : on or to a lower floor and esp. the main floor — **downstairs** *adj or n*

down–to–earth *adj* : practical

down·town *adv* : to, toward, or in the business center of a town — **downtown** *n or adj*

down·trod·den \'daủn,träd°n\ *adj* : suffering oppression

down·ward \'daủnwərd\, **down·wards** \-wərdz\ *adv* : to a lower place or condition — **downward** *adj*

down·wind *adv or adj* : in the direction the wind is blowing

downy \'daủnē\ *adj* **-i·er; -est** : resembling or covered with down

dow·ry \'daủrē\ *n, pl* **-ries** : property a woman gives her husband in marriage

dox·ol·o·gy \däk'sälǝjē\ *n, pl* **-gies** : hymn of praise to God

doze \'dōz\ *vb* **dozed; doz·ing** : sleep lightly — **doze** *n*

doz·en \'dǝz°n\ *n, pl* **-ens** or **-en** : group of 12 — **doz·enth** \-°nth\ *adj*

drab \'drab\ *adj* **-bb-** : dull — **drab·ly** *adv* — **drab·ness** *n*

dra·co·ni·an \drā'kōnēǝn, dra-\ *adj, often cap* : harsh, cruel

draft \'draft, 'dråft\ *n* **1** : act of drawing or hauling **2** : act of drinking **3** : amount drunk at once **4** : preliminary outline or rough sketch **5** : selection from a pool or the selection process **6** : order for the payment of money **7** : air current ~ *vb* **1** : select usu. on a compulsory basis **2** : make a preliminary sketch, version, or plan of ~ *adj* : drawn from a container — **draft·ee** \draf'tē, dråf-\ *n* — **drafty** \'draftē\ *adj*

drafts·man \'draftsmǝn, 'dråft-\ *n* : person who draws plans

drag \'drag\ *n* **1** : something dragged over a surface or through water **2** : something that hinders progress or is boring **3** : act or an instance of dragging ~ *vb* **-gg-** **1** : haul **2** : move or work with difficulty **3** : pass slowly **4** : search or fish with a drag — **drag·ger** *n*

drag·net \-,net\ *n* **1** : trawl **2** : planned actions for finding a criminal

dra·gon \\'dragən\ *n* : fabled winged serpent

drag·on·fly *n* : large 4-winged insect

drain \\'drān\ *vb* **1** : draw off or flow off gradually or completely **2** : exhaust ～ *n* : means or act of draining — **drain·age** \-ij\ *n* — **drain·er** *n* — **drain·pipe** *n*

drake \\'drāk\ *n* : male duck

dra·ma \\'drämə, 'dram-\ *n* **1** : composition for theatrical presentation esp. on a serious subject **2** : series of events involving conflicting forces — **dra·mat·ic** \drə'matik\ *adj* — **dra·mat·i·cal·ly** \-iklē\ *adv* — **dram·a·tist** \\'dramətist, 'dräm-\ *n* — **dram·a·ti·za·tion** \ˌdramətə'zāshən, ˌdräm-\ *n* — **dra·ma·tize** \\'draməˌtīz, 'dräm-\ *vb*

drank *past of* DRINK

drape \\'drāp\ *vb* **draped; drap·ing 1** : cover or adorn with folds of cloth **2** : cause to hang in flowing lines or folds ～ *n* : curtain

drap·ery \\'drāpərē\ *n, pl* **-er·ies** : decorative fabric hung esp. as a heavy curtain

dras·tic \\'drastik\ *adj* : extreme or harsh — **dras·ti·cal·ly** \-tiklē\ *adj*

draught \\'draft\, **draughty** \\'draftē\ *chiefly Brit var of* DRAFT, DRAFTY

draw \\'drȯ\ *vb* **drew** \\'drü\; **drawn** \\'drȯn\; **draw·ing 1** : move or cause to move (as by pulling) **2** : attract or provoke **3** : extract **4** : take or receive (as money) **5** : bend a bow in preparation for shooting **6** : leave a contest undecided **7** : sketch **8** : write out **9** : deduce ～ *n* **1** : act, process, or result of drawing **2** : tie — **draw out** : cause to speak candidly — **draw up 1** : write out **2** : pull oneself erect **3** : bring or come to a stop

draw·back *n* : disadvantage

draw·bridge *n* : bridge that can be raised

draw·er \\'drȯr, 'drȯər\ *n* **1** : one that draws **2** : sliding boxlike compartment **3** *pl* : underpants

draw·ing \\'drȯiŋ\ *n* **1** : occasion of choosing by lot **2** : act or art of making a figure, plan, or sketch with lines **3** : something drawn

drawl \\'drȯl\ *vb* : speak slowly — **drawl** *n*

dread \\'dred\ *vb* : feel extreme fear or reluctance ～ *n* : great fear ～ *adj* : causing dread — **dread·ful** \-fəl\ *adj* — **dread·ful·ly** *adv*

dream \\'drēm\ *n* **1** : series of thoughts or visions during sleep **2** : dreamlike vision **3**

: something notable **4** : ideal ~ *vb* **dreamed** \'dremt, 'drēmd\ *or* **dreamt** \'dremt\; **dream·ing 1** : have a dream **2** : imagine — **dream·er** *n* — **dream·like** *adj* — **dreamy** *adj*

drea·ry \'drirē\ *adj* **-ri·er; -est** : dismal — **drea·ri·ly** \'drirəlē\ *adv*

¹**dredge** \'drej\ *n* : machine for removing earth esp. from under water ~ *vb* **dredged; dredg·ing** : dig up or search with a dredge — **dredg·er** *n*

²**dredge** *vb* **dredged; dredg·ing** : coat (food) with flour

dregs \'dregz\ *n pl* **1** : sediment **2** : most worthless part

drench \'drench\ *vb* : wet thoroughly

dress \'dres\ *vb* **1** : put clothes on **2** : decorate **3** : prepare (as a carcass) for use **4** : apply dressings, remedies, or fertilizer to ~ *n* **1** : apparel **2** : single garment of bodice and skirt ~ *adj* : suitable for a formal event — **dress·mak·er** *n* — **dress·mak·ing** *n*

dress·er \'dresər\ *n* : bureau with a mirror

dress·ing *n* **1** : act or process of dressing **2** : sauce or a seasoned mixture **3** : material to cover an injury

dressy \'dresē\ *adj* **dress·i·er; -est 1** : showy in dress **2** : stylish

drew *past of* DRAW

drib·ble \'dribəl\ *vb* **-bled; -bling 1** : fall or flow in drops **2** : drool — **dribble** *n*

drier *comparative of* DRY

driest *superlative of* DRY

drift \'drift\ *n* **1** : motion or course of something drifting **2** : mass piled up by wind **3** : general intention or meaning ~ *vb* **1** : float or be driven along (as by a current) **2** : wander without purpose **3** : pile up under force — **drift·er** *n* — **drift·wood** *n*

¹**drill** \'dril\ *vb* **1** : bore with a drill **2** : instruct by repetition ~ *n* **1** : tool for boring holes **2** : regularly practiced exercise — **drill·er** *n*

²**drill** *n* : seed-planting implement

³**drill** *n* : twill-weave cotton fabric

drily *var of* DRYLY

drink \'driŋk\ *vb* **drank** \'draŋk\; **drunk** \'drəŋk\ *or* **drank; drink·ing 1** : swallow liquid **2** : absorb **3** : drink alcoholic beverages esp. to excess ~ *n* **1** : beverage **2** : alcoholic liquor — **drink·able** *adj* — **drink·er** *n*

drip \'drip\ *vb* **-pp-** : fall or let fall in drops ~ *n* **1** : a dripping   **2** : sound of falling drops

drive \'drīv\ *vb* **drove** \'drōv\; **driv·en** \'drivən\; **driv·ing** **1** : urge or force onward **2** : direct the movement or course of **3** : compel **4** : cause to become **5** : propel forcefully ~ *n* **1** : trip in a vehicle **2** : intensive campaign **3** : aggressive or dynamic quality **4** : basic need — **driv·er** *n*

drive–in *adj* : accommodating patrons in cars — **drive–in** *n*

driv·el \'drivəl\ *vb* **-eled** *or* **-elled; -el·ing** *or* **-el·ling 1** : drool **2** : talk stupidly ~ *n* : nonsense

drive·way *n* : usu. short private road from the street to a house

driz·zle \'drizəl\ *n* : fine misty rain — **drizzle** *vb*

droll \'drōl\ *adj* : humorous or whimsical — **droll·ery** *n* — **drol·ly** *adv*

drom·e·dary \'drämə‚derē\ *n, pl* **-dar·ies** : speedy one-humped camel

drone \'drōn\ *n* **1** : male honeybee **2** : deep hum or buzz ~ *vb* **droned; dron·ing** : make a dull monotonous sound

drool \'drül\ *vb* : let liquid run from the mouth

droop \'drüp\ *vb* **1** : hang or incline downward **2** : lose strength or spirit — **droop** *n* — **droopy** \-ē\ *adj*

drop \'dräp\ *n* **1** : quantity of fluid in one spherical mass **2** *pl* : medicine used by drops **3** : decline or fall **4** : distance something drops ~ *vb* **-pp-** **1** : fall in drops **2** : let fall **3** : convey **4** : go lower or become less strong or less active — **drop·let** \-lət\ *n* — **drop back** *vb* : move toward the rear — **drop behind** : fail to keep up — **drop in** *vb* : pay an unexpected visit

drop·per *n* : device that dispenses liquid by drops

drop·sy \'dräpsē\ *n* : edema

dross \'dräs\ *n* : waste matter

drought \'draut\ *n* : long dry spell

¹**drove** \'drōv\ *n* : crowd of moving people or animals

²**drove** *past of* **DRIVE**

drown \'draun\ *vb* **1** : suffocate in water **2** : overpower or become overpowered

drowse \'drauz\ *vb* **drowsed; drows·ing** : doze — **drowse** *n*

drowsy \'drauzē\ *adj* **drows·i·er; -est** : sleepy — **drows·i·ly** *adv* — **drows·i·ness** *n*

drub \'drəb\ *vb* **-bb-** : beat severely

drudge \'drəj\ *vb* **drudged; drudg·ing** : do hard or boring work — **drudge** *n* — **drudg·ery** \-ərē\ *n*

drug \'drəg\ *n* **1** : substance used as or in medicine **2** : narcotic ~ *vb* **-gg-** : affect with drugs — **drug·gist** \-ist\ *n* — **drug·store** *n*

dru·id \'drüəd\ *n* : ancient Celtic priest

drum \'drəm\ *n* **1** : musical instrument that is a skin‑covered cylinder beaten usu. with sticks **2** : drum-shaped object (as a container) ~ *vb* **-mm-** **1** : beat a drum **2** : drive, force, or bring about by steady effort — **drum·beat** *n* — **drum·mer** *n*

drum·stick *n* **1** : stick for beating a drum **2** : lower part of a fowl's leg

drunk \'drəŋk\ *adj* : having the faculties impaired by alcohol ~ *n* : one who is drunk — **drunk·ard** \'drəŋkərd\ *n* — **drunk·en** \-kən\ *adj* — **drunk·en·ly** *adv* — **drunk·en·ness** *n*

dry \'drī\ *adj* **dri·er** \'drīər\; **dri·est** \'drīəst\ **1** : lacking water or moisture **2** : thirsty **3** : marked by the absence of alcoholic beverages **4** : uninteresting **5** : not sweet ~ *vb* **dried; dry·ing** : make or become dry — **dry·ly** *adv* — **dry·ness** *n*

dry–clean *vb* : clean (fabrics) chiefly with solvents other than water — **dry cleaning** *n*

dry·er \'drīər\ *n* : device for drying

dry goods *n pl* : textiles, clothing, and notions

dry ice *n* : solid carbon dioxide

du·al \'düəl, 'dyü-\ *adj* : twofold — **du·al·ism** \-ə,lizəm\ *n* — **du·al·i·ty** \dü'alətē, dyü-\ *n*

dub \'dəb\ *vb* **-bb-** : name

du·bi·ous \'dübēəs, 'dyü-\ *adj* **1** : uncertain **2** : questionable — **du·bi·ous·ly** *adv* — **du·bi·ous·ness** *n*

du·cal \'dükəl, 'dyü-\ *adj* : relating to a duke or dukedom

duch·ess \'dəchəs\ *n* **1** : wife of a duke **2** : woman holding a ducal title

duchy \-ē\ *n, pl* **-ies** : territory of a duke or duchess

¹duck \'dək\ *n* : swimming bird related to the goose and swan ~ *vb* **1** : thrust or plunge under water **2** : lower the head or body suddenly **3** : evade — **duck·ling** \-liŋ\ *n*

²duck *n* : cotton fabric

duct \'dəkt\ *n* : canal for conveying a fluid — **duct·less** \-ləs\ *adj*

duc·tile \'dəkt³l\ *adj* : able to be drawn out or shaped — **duc·til·i·ty** \,dək'tilətē\ *n*

dude \'düd, 'dyüd\ *n* **1** : dandy **2** : guy

dud·geon \'dəjən\ *n* : ill humor

due \'dü, 'dyü\ *adj* **1** : owed **2** : appropriate **3** : attributable **4** : scheduled ～ *n* **1** : something due **2** *pl* : fee ～ *adv* : directly

du·el \'düəl, 'dyü-\ *n* : combat between 2 persons — **duel** *vb* — **du·el·ist** *n*

du·et \dü'et, dyü-\ *n* : musical composition for 2 performers

due to *prep* : because of

dug *past of* DIG

dug·out \'dəg,aut\ *n* **1** : boat made by hollowing out a log **2** : shelter made by digging

duke \'dük, 'dyük\ *n* : nobleman of the highest rank — **duke·dom** *n*

dull \'dəl\ *adj* **1** : mentally slow **2** : blunt **3** : not brilliant or interesting — **dull** *vb* — **dul·lard** \'dələrd\ *n* — **dull·ness** *n* — **dul·ly** *adv*

du·ly \'dülē, 'dyü-\ *adv* : in a due manner or time

dumb \'dəm\ *adj* **1** : mute **2** : stupid — **dumb·ly** *adv*

dumb·bell \'dəm,bel\ *n* **1** : short bar with weights on the ends used for exercise **2** : stupid person

dumb·found, **dum·found** \,dəm'faund\ *vb* : amaze

dum·my \'dəmē\ *n, pl* **-mies** **1** : stupid person **2** : imitative substitute

dump \'dəmp\ *vb* : let fall in a pile ～ *n* : place for dumping something (as refuse) — **in the dumps** : sad

dump·ling \'dəmpliŋ\ *n* : small mass of boiled or steamed dough

dumpy \'dəmpē\ *adj* **dump·i·er; -est** : short and thick in build

¹dun \'dən\ *adj* : brownish gray

²dun *vb* **-nn-** : hound for payment of a debt

dunce \'dəns\ *n* : stupid person

dune \'dün, 'dyün\ *n* : hill of sand

dung \'dəŋ\ *n* : manure

dun·ga·ree \,dəŋgə'rē\ *n* **1** : blue denim **2** *pl* : work clothes made of dungaree

dun·geon \'dənjən\ *n* : underground prison

dunk \'dəŋk\ *vb* : dip or submerge temporarily in liquid

duo \'düō, 'dyüō\ *n, pl* **du·os** : pair

du·o·de·num \,düə'dēnəm, ,dyü-; dü-'ädᵊnəm, dyù-\ *n, pl* **-na** \-'dēnə, -ᵊnə\ *or* **-nums** : part of the small intestine nearest the stomach — **du·o·de·nal** \-'dēnᵊl, -ᵊnəl\ *adj*

dupe \'düp, dyüp\ *n* : one easily deceived or cheated — **dupe** *vb*

du·plex \'dü,pleks, 'dyü-\ *adj* : double ～ *n* : 2-family house

du·pli·cate \'düplikət, 'dyü-\ *adj* **1** : consisting of 2 identical items **2** : being just like another ~ *n* : exact copy ~ \-ˌkāt\ *vb* **-cat·ed; -cat·ing 1** : make an exact copy of **2** : repeat or equal — **du·pli·ca·tion** \ˌdüpli'kāshən, ˌdyü-\ *n* — **du·pli·ca·tor** \'düpliˌkātər, dyü-\ *n*

du·plic·i·ty \du'plisətē, ˌdyü-\ *n, pl* **-ties** : deception

du·ra·ble \'dùrəbəl, 'dyùr-\ *adj* : lasting a long time — **du·ra·bil·i·ty** \ˌdùrə'bilətē, ˌdyùr-\ *n*

du·ra·tion \du'rāshən, dyù-\ *n* : length of time something lasts

du·ress \du'res, dyù-\ *n* : coercion

dur·ing \'dùriŋ, 'dyùr-\ *prep* **1** : throughout **2** : at some point in

dusk \'dəsk\ *n* : twilight — **dusky** *adj*

dust \'dəst\ *n* : powdered matter ~ *vb* **1** : remove dust from **2** : sprinkle with fine particles — **dust·er** *n* — **dust·pan** *n* — **dusty** *adj*

du·ty \'dütē, 'dyü-\ *n, pl* **-ties 1** : action required by one's occupation or position **2** : moral or legal obligation **3** : tax — **du·te·ous** \-əs\ *adj* — **du·ti·able** \-əbəl\ *adj* — **du·ti·ful** \'dütifəl, 'dyü-\ *adj*

DVD \ˌdēˌvē'dē\ *n* : digital video disk

dwarf \'dwȯrf\ *n, pl* **dwarfs** \'dwȯrfs\ *or* **dwarves** \'dwȯrvz\ : one that is much below normal size ~ *vb* **1** : stunt **2** : cause to seem smaller — **dwarf·ish** *adj*

dwell \'dwel\ *vb* **dwelt** \'dwelt\ *or* **dwelled** \'dweld, 'dwelt\; **dwell·ing 1** : reside **2** : keep the attention directed — **dwell·er** *n* — **dwell·ing** *n*

dwin·dle \'dwindᵊl\ *vb* **-dled; -dling** : become steadily less

dye \'dī\ *n* : coloring material ~ *vb* **dyed; dye·ing** : give a new color to

dying *pres part of* DIE

dyke *var of* DIKE

dy·nam·ic \dī'namik\ *adj* **1** : relating to physical force producing motion **2** : energetic or forceful

dy·na·mite \'dīnəˌmīt\ *n* : explosive made of nitroglycerin — **dynamite** *vb*

dy·na·mo \-ˌmō\ *n, pl* **-mos** : electrical generator

dy·nas·ty \'dīnəstē, -ˌnas-\ *n, pl* **-ties** : succession of rulers of the same family — **dy·nas·tic** \dī'nastik\ *adj*

dys·en·tery \'disᵊnˌterē\ *n, pl* **-ter·ies** : disease marked by diarrhea

dys·lex·ia \dis'leksēə\ *n* : disturbance of the ability to read — **dys·lex·ic** \-sik\ *adj*

dys·pep·sia \-'pepshə, -sēə\ *n* : indigestion — **dys·pep·tic** \-'peptik\ *adj or n*

dys·tro·phy \'distrəfē\ *n, pl* **-phies** : disorder involving nervous and muscular tissue

E

e \'ē\ *n, pl* **e's** *or* **es** \'ēz\ : 5th letter of the alphabet

e- *comb form* : electronic

each \'ēch\ *adj* : being one of the class named ~ *pron* : every individual one ~ *adv* : apiece

ea·ger \'ēgər\ *adj* : enthusiastic or anxious — **ea·ger·ly** *adv* — **ea·ger·ness** *n*

ea·gle \'ēgəl\ *n* : large bird of prey

-ean — see -AN

¹**ear** \'ir\ *n* : organ of hearing or the outer part of this — **ear·ache** *n* — **eared** *adj* — **ear·lobe** \-ˌlōb\ *n*

²**ear** *n* : fruiting head of a cereal

ear·drum *n* : thin membrane that receives and transmits sound waves in the ear

earl \'ərl\ *n* : British nobleman — **earl·dom** \-dəm\ *n*

ear·ly \'ərlē\ *adj* **-li·er; -est 1** : relating to or occurring near the beginning or before the usual time **2** : ancient — **early** *adv*

ear·mark *vb* : designate for a specific purpose

earn \'ərn\ *vb* **1** : receive as a return for service **2** : deserve

ear·nest \'ərnəst\ *n* : serious state of mind — **earnest** *adj* — **ear·nest·ly** *adv* — **ear·nest·ness** *n*

earn·ings \'ərniŋz\ *n pl* : something earned

ear·phone *n* : device that reproduces sound and is worn over or in the ear

ear·ring *n* : earlobe ornament

ear·shot *n* : range of hearing

earth \'ərth\ *n* **1** : soil or land **2** : planet inhabited by man — **earth·li·ness** *n* — **earth·ly** *adj* — **earth·ward** \-wərd\ *adv*

earth·en \'ərthən\ *adj* : made of earth or baked clay — **earth·en·ware** \-ˌwar\ *n*

earth·quake *n* : shaking or trembling of the earth

earth·worm *n* : long segmented worm

earthy \'ərthē\ *adj* **earth·i·er; -est 1** : relating to or consisting of earth **2** : practical **3** : coarse — **earth·i·ness** *n*

ease \'ēz\ *n* **1** : comfort **2** : naturalness of manner **3** : freedom from difficulty ~ *vb* **eased; eas·ing 1** : relieve from distress **2** : lessen the tension of **3** : make easier

ea·sel \'ēzəl\ *n* : frame to hold a painter's canvas

east \'ēst\ *adv* : to or toward the east ~ *adj* : situated toward or at or coming from the east ~ *n* **1** : direction of sunrise **2** *cap* : regions to the east — **east·er·ly** \'ēstərlē\ *adv or adj* — **east·ward** *adv or adj* — **east·wards** *adv*

Eas·ter \'ēstər\ *n* : church feast celebrating Christ's resurrection

east·ern \'ēstərn\ *adj* **1** *cap* : relating to a region designated East **2** : lying toward or coming from the east — **East·ern·er** *n*

easy \'ēzē\ *adj* **eas·i·er; -est 1** : marked by ease **2** : lenient — **eas·i·ly** \'ēzəlē\ *adv* — **eas·i·ness** \-ēnəs\ *n*

easy·go·ing *adj* : relaxed and casual

eat \'ēt\ *vb* **ate** \'āt\; **eat·en** \'ēt°n\; **eat·ing 1** : take in as food **2** : use up or corrode — **eat·able** *adj or n* — **eat·er** *n*

eaves \'ēvz\ *n pl* : overhanging edge of a roof

eaves·drop *vb* : listen secretly — **eaves·drop·per** *n*

ebb \'eb\ *n* **1** : outward flow of the tide **2** : decline ~ *vb* **1** : recede from the flood state **2** : wane

eb·o·ny \'ebənē\ *n, pl* **-nies** : hard heavy wood of tropical trees ~ *adj* **1** : made of ebony **2** : black

ebul·lient \i'bůlyənt, -'bəl-\ *adj* : exuberant — **ebul·lience** \-yəns\ *n*

ec·cen·tric \ik'sentrik\ *adj* **1** : odd in behavior **2** : being off center — **eccentric** *n* — **ec·cen·tri·cal·ly** \-triklē\ *adv* — **ec·cen·tric·i·ty** \ˌek-ˌsen'trisətē\ *n*

ec·cle·si·as·tic \ik,lēzē'astik\ *n* : clergyman

ec·cle·si·as·ti·cal \-tikəl\, **ec·clesiastic** *adj* : relating to a church — **ec·cle·si·as·ti·cal·ly** \-tiklē\ *adv*

ech·e·lon \'eshəˌlän\ *n* **1** : steplike arrangement **2** : level of authority

echo \'ekō\ *n, pl* **ech·oes** : repetition of a sound caused by a reflection of the sound waves — **echo** *vb*

èclair \ā'klar\ *n* : custard-filled pastry

eclec·tic \e'klektik, i-\ *adj* : drawing or drawn from varied sources

eclipse \i'klips\ *n* : total or partial obscuring of one celestial body by another — **eclipse** *vb*

ecol·o·gy \i'käləjē, e-\ *n, pl* **-gies** : science concerned with the interaction of organisms and their environment — **eco·log·i·cal** \ˌēkə'läjikəl, ˌek-\ *adj* — **eco·log·i·cal·ly** *adv* — **ecol·o·gist** \i'käləjist, e-\ *n*

eco·nom·ic \ˌekə'nämik, ˌēkə-\ *adj* : relating to the producing and the buying and selling of goods and services

eco·nom·ics \-'nämiks\ *n* : branch of knowledge dealing with goods and services — **econ·o·mist** \i'känəmist\ *n*

econ·o·mize \i'känəˌmīz\ *vb* **-mized; -miz·ing** : be thrifty — **econ·o·miz·er** *n*

econ·o·my \-əmē\ *n, pl* **-mies** **1** : thrifty use of resources **2** : economic system — **eco·nom·i·cal** \ˌekə'nämikəl, ˌēkə-\ *adj* — **ec·o·nom·i·cal·ly** *adv* — **economy** *adj*

ecru \'ekrü, 'ākrü\ *n* : beige

ec·sta·sy \'ekstəsē\ *n, pl* **-sies** : extreme emotional excitement — **ec·stat·ic** \ek'statik, ik-\ *adj* — **ec·stat·i·cal·ly** \-iklē\ *adv*

ec·u·men·i·cal \ˌekyə'menikəl\ *adj* : promoting worldwide Christian unity

ec·ze·ma \ig'zēmə, 'egzəmə, 'eksə-\ *n* : itching skin inflammation

¹**-ed** \d *after a vowel or* b, g, j, l, m, n, ŋ, r, <u>th</u>, v, z, zh; əd, id *after* d, t; t *after other sounds*\ *vb suffix or adj suffix* **1** — used to form the past participle of regular verbs **2** : having or having the characteristics of

²**-ed** *vb suffix* — used to form the past tense of regular verbs

ed·dy \'edē\ *n, pl* **-dies** : whirlpool — **eddy** *vb*

ede·ma \i'dēmə\ *n* : abnormal accumulation of fluid in the body tissues — **edem·a·tous** \-'demətəs\ *adj*

Eden \'ēdᵊn\ *n* : paradise

edge \'ej\ *n* **1** : cutting side of a blade **2** : line where something begins or ends ～ *vb* **edged; edg·ing** **1** : give or form an edge **2** : move gradually **3** : narrowly defeat — **edg·er** *n*

edge·wise \-ˌwīz\ *adv* : sideways

edgy \'ejē\ *adj* **edg·i·er; -est** : nervous — **edg·i·ness** *n*

ed·i·ble \'edəbəl\ *adj* : fit or safe to be eaten — **ed·i·bil·i·ty** \ˌedə'bilətē\ *n* — **edible** *n*

edict \'ēˌdikt\ *n* : order or decree

ed·i·fi·ca·tion \ˌedəfə'kāshən\ *n* : instruction or information — **ed·i·fy** \'edəˌfī\ *vb*

ed·i·fice \'edəfəs\ *n* : large building

ed·it \'edət\ *vb* **1** : revise and prepare for publication **2** : delete — **ed·i·tor** \-ər\ *n* — **ed·i·tor·ship** *n*

edi·tion \i'dishən\ *n* **1** : form in which a text is published **2** : total number published at one time

ed·i·to·ri·al \ˌedə'tōrēəl\ *adj* **1** : relating to an editor or editing **2** : expressing opinion ~ *n* : article (as in a newspaper) expressing the views of an editor — **ed·i·to·ri·al·ize** \-ēəˌlīz\ *vb* — **ed·i·to·ri·al·ly** *adv*

ed·u·cate \'ejəˌkāt\ *vb* **-cated; -cat·ing** **1** : give instruction to **2** : develop mentally and morally **3** : provide with information — **ed·u·ca·ble** \'ejəkəbəl\ *adj* — **ed·u·ca·tion** \ˌejə'kāshən\ *n* — **ed·u·ca·tion·al** \-shənəl\ *adj* — **ed·u·ca·tor** \-ər\ *n*

eel \'ēl\ *n* : snakelike fish

ee·rie \'irē\ *adj* **-ri·er; -est** : weird — **ee·ri·ly** \'irəlē\ *adv*

ef·face \i'fās, e-\ *vb* **-faced; -fac·ing** : obliterate by rubbing out — **ef·face·ment** *n*

ef·fect \i'fekt\ *n* **1** : result **2** : meaning **3** : influence **4** *pl* : goods or possessions ~ *vb* : cause to happen — **in ef·fect** : in substance

ef·fec·tive \i'fektiv\ *adj* **1** : producing a strong or desired effect **2** : being in operation — **ef·fec·tive·ly** *adv* — **ef·fec·tive·ness** *n*

ef·fec·tu·al \i'fekchəwəl\ *adj* : producing an intended effect — **ef·fec·tu·al·ly** *adv* — **ef·fec·tu·al·ness** *n*

ef·fem·i·nate \ə'femənət\ *adj* : having qualities more typical of women than men — **ef·fem·i·na·cy** \-nəsē\ *n*

ef·fer·vesce \ˌefər'ves\ *vb* **-vesced; -vesc·ing** **1** : bubble and hiss as gas escapes **2** : show exhilaration — **ef·fer·ves·cence** \-'vesᵊns\ *n* — **ef·fer·ves·cent** \-ᵊnt\ *adj* — **ef·fer·ves·cent·ly** *adv*

ef·fete \e'fēt\ *adj* **1** : worn out **2** : weak or decadent **3** : effeminate

ef·fi·ca·cious \ˌefə'kāshəs\ *adj* : effective — **ef·fi·ca·cy** \'efikəsē\ *n*

ef·fi·cient \i'fishənt\ *adj* : working well with little waste — **ef·fi·cien·cy** \-ənsē\ *n* — **ef·fi·cient·ly** *adv*

ef·fi·gy \'efəjē\ *n, pl* **-gies** : usu. crude image of a person

ef·flu·ent \'eˌflüənt, e'flü-\ *n* : something that flows out — **effluent** *adj*

ef·fort \'efərt\ *n* **1** : a putting forth of strength **2** : use of resources toward a goal **3**

: product of effort — **ef·fort-less** *adj* — **ef·fort·less·ly** *adv*

ef·fron·tery \i'frəntərē\ *n, pl* **-ter·ies** : insolence

ef·fu·sion \i'fyüzhən, e-\ *n* : a gushing forth — **ef·fu·sive** \-'fyüsiv\ *adj* — **ef·fu·sive·ly** *adv*

¹egg \'eg, 'āg\ *vb* : urge to action

²egg *n* **1** : rounded usu. hard= shelled reproductive body esp. of birds and reptiles from which the young hatches **2** : ovum — **egg·shell** *n*

egg·nog \-ˌnäg\ *n* : rich drink of eggs and cream

egg·plant *n* : edible purplish fruit of a plant related to the potato

ego \'ēgō\ *n, pl* **egos** : self= esteem

ego·cen·tric \ˌēgō'sentrik\ *adj* : self-centered

ego·tism \'ēgəˌtizəm\ *n* : ex-aggerated sense of self= importance — **ego·tist** \-tist\ *n* — **ego·tis·tic** \ˌēgə'tistik\, **ego·tis·ti·cal** \-tikəl\ *adj* — **ego·tis·ti·cal·ly** *adv*

egre·gious \i'grējəs\ *adj* : no-tably bad — **egre·gious·ly** *adv*

egress \'ēˌgres\ *n* : a way out

egret \'ēgrət, i'gret, 'egrət\ *n* : long-plumed heron

ei·der·down \'īdərˌdau̇n\ *n* : soft down obtained from a northern sea duck (**eider**)

eight \'āt\ *n* **1** : one more than 7 **2** : 8th in a set or series **3** : something having 8 units — **eight** *adj or pron* — **eighth** \'ātth\ *adj or adv or n*

eigh·teen \āt'tēn\ *n* : one more than 17 — **eigh·teen** *adj or pron* — **eigh·teenth** \-'tēnth\ *adj or n*

eighty \'ātē\ *n, pl* **eight·ies** : 8 times 10 — **eight·i·eth** \'ātēəth\ *adj or n* — **eighty** *adj or pron*

ei·ther \'ēthər, 'ī-\ *adj* **1** : both **2** : being the one or the other of two ~ *pron* : one of two or more ~ *conj* : one or the other

ejac·u·late \i'jakyəˌlāt\ *vb* **-lat·ed; -lat·ing** **1** : say sud-denly **2** : eject a fluid (as semen) — **ejac·u·la·tion** \-ˌjakyə'lāshən\ *n*

eject \i'jekt\ *vb* : drive or throw out — **ejec·tion** \-'jek-shən\ *n*

eke \'ēk\ *vb* **eked; ek·ing** : barely gain with effort — usu. with *out*

elab·o·rate \i'labərət\ *adj* **1** : planned in detail **2** : com-plex and ornate ~ \-əˌrāt\ *vb* **-rat·ed; -rat·ing** : work out in detail — **elab·o·rate·ly** *adv* — **elab·o·rate·ness** *n* — **elab-o·ra·tion** \-ˌlabə'rāshən\ *n*

elapse \i'laps\ *vb* **elapsed; elaps·ing** : slip by

elas·tic \i'lastik\ *adj* **1** : springy **2** : flexible ~ *n* **1** : elastic material **2** : rubber band — **elas·tic·i·ty** \-,las-'tisətē, ,ē,las-\ *n*

elate \i'lāt\ *vb* **elat·ed; elat·ing** : fill with joy — **ela·tion** \-'lāshən\ *n*

el·bow \'el,bō\ *n* **1** : joint of the arm **2** : elbow-shaped bend or joint ~ *vb* : push aside with the elbow

el·der \'eldər\ *adj* : older ~ *n* **1** : one who is older **2** : church officer

el·der·ber·ry \'eldər,berē\ *n* : edible black or red fruit or a tree or shrub bearing these

el·der·ly \'eldərlē\ *adj* : past middle age

el·dest \'eldəst\ *adj* : oldest

elect \i'lekt\ *adj* : elected but not yet in office ~ *n* **elect** *pl* : exclusive group ~ *vb* : choose esp. by vote — **elec·tion** \i'lekshən\ *n* — **elec·tive** \i'lektiv\ *n or adj* — **elec·tor** \i'lektər\ *n* — **elec·tor·al** \-tərəl\ *adj*

elec·tor·ate \i'lektərət\ *n* : body of persons entitled to vote

elec·tric \i'lektrik\ *adj* **1** *or* **elec·tri·cal** \-trikəl\ : relating to or run by electricity **2** : thrilling — **elec·tri·cal·ly** *adv*

elec·tri·cian \i,lek'trishən\ *n* : person who installs or repairs electrical equipment

elec·tric·i·ty \-'trisətē\ *n, pl* **-ties** **1** : fundamental form of energy occurring naturally (as in lightning) or produced artificially **2** : electric current

elec·tri·fy \i'lektrə,fī\ *vb* **-fied; -fy·ing** **1** : charge with electricity **2** : equip for use of electric power **3** : thrill — **elec·tri·fi·ca·tion** \-,lektrəfə-'kāshən\ *n*

elec·tro·car·dio·gram \i,lektrō-'kärdēə,gram\ *n* : tracing made by an electrocardiograph

elec·tro·car·dio·graph \-,graf\ *n* : instrument for monitoring heart function

elec·tro·cute \i'lektrə,kyüt\ *vb* **-cut·ed; -cut·ing** : kill by an electric shock — **elec·tro·cu·tion** \-,lektrə'kyüshən\ *n*

elec·trode \i'lek,trōd\ *n* : conductor at a nonmetallic part of a circuit

elec·trol·y·sis \i,lek'träləsəs\ *n* **1** : production of chemical changes by passage of an electric current through a substance **2** : destruction of hair roots with an electric current — **elec·tro·lyt·ic** \-trə'litik\ *adj*

elec·tro·lyte \i'lektrə,līt\ *n* : nonmetallic electric conductor

elec·tro·mag·net \i,lektrō-'magnət\ *n* : magnet made using electric current

elec·tro·mag·ne·tism \-nə-ˌtizəm\ *n* : natural force responsible for interactions between charged particles — **elec·tro·mag·net·ic** \-mag-ˈnetik\ *adj* — **elec·tro·mag·net·i·cal·ly** \-iklē\ *adv*

elec·tron \iˈlekˌträn\ *n* : negatively charged particle within the atom

elec·tron·ic \iˌlekˈtränik\ *adj* : relating to electrons or electronics — **elec·tron·i·cal·ly** \-iklē\ *adv*

elec·tron·ics \-iks\ *n* : physics of electrons and their use esp. in devices

elec·tro·plate \iˈlektrəˌplāt\ *vb* : coat (as with metal) by electrolysis

el·e·gance \ˈeligəns\ *n* : refined gracefulness — **el·e·gant** \-gənt\ *adj* — **el·e·gant·ly** *adv*

el·e·gy \ˈeləjē\ *n, pl* **-gies** : poem expressing grief for one who is dead — **ele·gi·ac** \ˌeləˈjīək, -ˌak\ *adj*

el·e·ment \ˈeləmənt\ *n* **1** *pl* : weather conditions **2** : natural environment **3** : constituent part **4** *pl* : simplest principles **5** : substance that has atoms of only one kind — **el·e·men·tal** \ˌeləˈmentᵊl\ *adj*

el·e·men·ta·ry \ˌeləˈmentrē\ *adj* **1** : simple **2** : relating to the basic subjects of education

el·e·phant \ˈeləfənt\ *n* : huge mammal with a trunk and 2 ivory tusks

el·e·vate \ˈeləˌvāt\ *vb* **-vat·ed; -vat·ing** **1** : lift up **2** : exalt

el·e·va·tion \ˌeləˈvāshən\ *n* : height or a high place

el·e·va·tor \ˈeləˌvātər\ *n* **1** : cage or platform for raising or lowering something **2** : grain storehouse

elev·en \iˈlevən\ *n* **1** : one more than 10 **2** : 11th in a set or series **3** : something having 11 units — **eleven** *adj or pron* — **elev·enth** \-ənth\ *adj or n*

elf \ˈelf\ *n, pl* **elves** \ˈelvz\ : mischievous fairy — **elf·in** \ˈelfən\ *adj* — **elf·ish** \ˈelfish\ *adj*

elic·it \iˈlisət\ *vb* : draw forth

el·i·gi·ble \ˈeləjəbəl\ *adj* : qualified to participate or to be chosen — **el·i·gi·bil·i·ty** \ˌeləjəˈbilətē\ *n*

elim·i·nate \iˈliməˌnāt\ *vb* **-nat·ed; -nat·ing** : get rid of — **elim·i·na·tion** \iˌliməˈnāshən\ *n*

elite \āˈlēt\ *n* : choice or select group

elix·ir \iˈliksər\ *n* : medicinal solution

elk \ˈelk\ *n* : large deer

el·lipse \iˈlips, e-\ *n* : oval

el·lip·sis \-ˈlipsəs\ *n, pl* **-lip·ses** \-ˌsēz\ **1** : omission of a word **2** : marks (as . . .) to show omission

el·lip·ti·cal \-tikəl\, **el·lip·tic** \-tik\ *adj* **1** : relating to or shaped like an ellipse **2** : relating to or marked by ellipsis

elm \'elm\ *n* : tall shade tree

el·o·cu·tion \ˌelə'kyüshən\ *n* : art of public speaking

elon·gate \i'lȯŋˌgāt\ *vb* **-gated; -gat·ing** : make or grow longer — **elon·ga·tion** \ˌē̇ˌlȯŋ-'gāshən\ *n*

elope \i'lōp\ *vb* **eloped; elop·ing** : run away esp. to be married — **elope·ment** *n* — **elop·er** *n*

el·o·quent \'eləkwənt\ *adj* : forceful and persuasive in speech — **el·o·quence** \-kwəns\ *n* — **el·o·quent·ly** *adv*

else \'els\ *adv* **1** : in a different way, time, or place **2** : otherwise ~ *adj* **1** : other **2** : more

else·where *adv* : in or to another place

elu·ci·date \i'lüsəˌdāt\ *vb* **-dat·ed; -dat·ing** : explain — **elu·ci·da·tion** \iˌlüsə'dāshən\ *n*

elude \ē'lüd\ *vb* **elud·ed; elud·ing** : evade — **elu·sive** \ē'lüsiv\ *adj* — **elu·sive·ly** *adv* — **elu·sive·ness** *n*

elves *pl of* ELF

ema·ci·ate \i'māshēˌāt\ *vb* **-at·ed; -at·ing** : become or

make very thin — **ema·ci·a·tion** \iˌmāsē'āshən, -shē-\ *n*

e–mail \'ēˌmāl\ *n* : message sent or received via computers

em·a·nate \'eməˌnāt\ *vb* **-nat·ed; -nat·ing** : come forth — **em·a·na·tion** \ˌemə'nāshən\ *n*

eman·ci·pate \i'mansəˌpāt\ *vb* **-pat·ed; -pat·ing** : set free — **eman·ci·pa·tion** \iˌmansə-'pāshən\ *n* — **eman·ci·pa·tor** \i'mansəˌpātər\ *n*

emas·cu·late \i'maskyəˌlāt\ *vb* **-lat·ed; -lat·ing** **1** : castrate **2** : weaken — **emas·cu·la·tion** \iˌmaskyə'lāshən\ *n*

em·balm \im'bäm, -'bälm\ *vb* : preserve (a corpse) — **em·balm·er** *n*

em·bank·ment \im'baŋk-mənt\ *n* : protective barrier of earth

em·bar·go \im'bärgō\ *n, pl* **-goes** : ban on trade — **em·bargo** *vb*

em·bark \-'bärk\ *vb* **1** : go on board a ship or airplane **2** : make a start — **em·bar·ka·tion** \ˌemˌbär'kāshən\ *n*

em·bar·rass \im'barəs\ *vb* : cause distress and self-consciousness — **em·bar·rass·ment** *n*

em·bas·sy \'embəsē\ *n, pl* **-sies** : residence and offices of an ambassador

em·bed \im'bed\ *vb* **-dd-** : fix firmly

em·bel·lish \-'belish\ *vb* : decorate — **em·bel·lish-ment** *n*

em·ber \'embər\ *n* : smolder-ing fragment from a fire

em·bez·zle \im'bezəl\ *vb* **-zled; -zling** : steal (money) by falsi-fying records — **em·bez·zle-ment** *n* — **em·bez·zler** \-ələr\ *n*

em·bit·ter \im'bitər\ *vb* : make bitter

em·bla·zon \-'blāzᵊn\ *vb* : dis-play conspicuously

em·blem \'embləm\ *n* : sym-bol — **em·blem·at·ic** \ˌem-blə'matik\ *adj*

em·body \im'bädē\ *vb* **-bod-ied; -body·ing** : give definite form or expression to — **em-bodi·ment** \-'bädimənt\ *n*

em·boss \-'bäs, -'bȯs\ *vb* : or-nament with raised work

em·brace \-'brās\ *vb* **-braced; -brac·ing** **1** : clasp in the arms **2** : welcome **3** : include — **embrace** *n*

em·broi·der \-'brȯidər\ *vb* : ornament with or do needle-work — **em·broi·dery** \-ərē\ *n*

em·broil \im'brȯil\ *vb* : in-volve in conflict or difficulties

em·bryo \'embrēˌō\ *n* : living being in its earliest stages of development — **em·bry·on·ic** \ˌembrē'änik\ *adj*

emend \ē'mend\ *vb* : correct — **emen·da·tion** \ˌēˌmen'dā-shən\ *n*

em·er·ald \'emrəld, 'emə-\ *n* : green gem ∼ *adj* : bright green

emerge \i'mərj\ *vb* **emerged; emerg·ing** : rise, come forth, or appear — **emer·gence** \-'mərjəns\ *n* — **emer·gent** \-jənt\ *adj*

emer·gen·cy \i'mərjənsē\ *n, pl* **-cies** : condition requiring prompt action

em·ery \'emərē\ *n, pl* **-er·ies** : dark granular mineral used for grinding

emet·ic \i'metik\ *n* : agent that induces vomiting — **emetic** *adj*

em·i·grate \'eməˌgrāt\ *vb* **-grat·ed; -grat·ing** : leave a country to settle elsewhere — **em·i·grant** \-igrənt\ *n* — **em-i·gra·tion** \ˌemə'grāshən\ *n*

em·i·nence \'emənəns\ *n* **1** : prominence or superiority **2** : person of high rank

em·i·nent \-nənt\ *adj* : promi-nent — **em·i·nent·ly** *adv*

em·is·sary \'eməˌserē\ *n, pl* **-sar·ies** : agent

emis·sion \ē'mishən\ *n* : sub-stance discharged into the air

emit \ē'mit\ *vb* **-tt-** : give off or out

emol·u·ment \i'mälyəmənt\ *n* : salary or fee

emote \i'mōt\ *vb* **emot·ed; emot·ing** : express emotion

emo·tion \i'mōshən\ *n* : intense feeling — **emo·tion·al** \-shənəl\ *adj* — **emo·tion·al·ly** *adv*

em·per·or \'empərər\ *n* : ruler of an empire

em·pha·sis \'emfəsəs\ *n, pl* **-pha·ses** \-ˌsēz\ : stress

em·pha·size \-ˌsīz\ *vb* **-sized; -siz·ing** : stress

em·phat·ic \im'fatik, em-\ *adj* : uttered with emphasis — **em·phat·i·cal·ly** \-iklē\ *adv*

em·pire \'emˌpīr\ *n* : large state or a group of states

em·pir·i·cal \im'pirikəl\ *adj* : based on observation — **em·pir·i·cal·ly** \-iklē\ *adv*

em·ploy \im'plȯi\ *vb* **1** : use **2** : occupy ～ *n* : paid occupation — **em·ploy·ee, em·ploye** \imˌplȯi'ē, -'plȯiˌē\ *n* — **em·ploy·er** *n* — **em·ploy·ment** \-mənt\ *n*

em·pow·er \im'paůər\ *vb* : give power to — **em·pow·er·ment** *n*

em·press \'emprəs\ *n* **1** : wife of an emperor **2** : woman emperor

emp·ty \'emptē\ *adj* **1** : containing nothing **2** : not occupied **3** : lacking value, sense, or purpose ～ *vb* **-tied; -ty·ing** : make or become empty — **emp·ti·ness** \-tēnəs\ *n*

emu \'ēmyü\ *n* : Australian bird related to the ostrich

em·u·late \'emyəˌlāt\ *vb* **-lat·ed; -lat·ing** : try to equal or excel — **em·u·la·tion** \ˌemyə'lāshən\ *n*

emul·si·fy \i'məlsəˌfī\ *vb* **-fied; -fy·ing** : convert into an emulsion — **emul·si·fi·ca·tion** \iˌməlsəfə'kāshən\ *n* — **emul·si·fi·er** \-'məlsəˌfīər\ *n*

emul·sion \i'məlshən\ *n* **1** : mixture of mutually insoluble liquids **2** : light-sensitive coating on photographic film

-en \ən,ᵊn\ *vb suffix* **1** : become or cause to be **2** : cause or come to have

en·able \in'ābəl\ *vb* **-abled; -abling** : give power, capacity, or ability to

en·act \in'akt\ *vb* **1** : make into law **2** : act out — **en·act·ment** *n*

enam·el \in'aməl\ *n* **1** : glasslike substance used to coat metal or pottery **2** : hard outer layer of a tooth **3** : glossy paint — **enamel** *vb*

en·am·or \in'amər\ *vb* : excite with love

en·camp \in'kamp\ *vb* : make camp — **en·camp·ment** *n*

en·case \in'kās\ *vb* : enclose in or as if in a case

-ence \əns,ᵊns\ *n suffix* **1** : action or process **2** : quality or state

en·ceph·a·li·tis \in,sefə'lītəs\ *n, pl* **-lit·i·des** \-'litə,dēz\ : inflammation of the brain

en·chant \in'chant\ *vb* **1** : bewitch **2** : fascinate — **en·chant·er** *n* — **en·chant·ment** *n* — **en·chant·ress** \-'chantrəs\ *n*

en·cir·cle \in'sərkəl\ *vb* : surround

en·close \in'klōz\ *vb* **1** : shut up or surround **2** : include — **en·clo·sure** \in'klōzhər\ *n*

en·co·mi·um \en'kōmēəm\ *n, pl* **-mi·ums** *or* **-mia** \-mēə\ : high praise

en·com·pass \in'kəmpəs, -'käm-\ *vb* : surround or include

en·core \'än,kōr\ *n* : further performance

en·coun·ter \in'kaúntər\ *vb* **1** : fight **2** : meet unexpectedly — **encounter** *n*

en·cour·age \in'kərij\ *vb* **-aged; -ag·ing** **1** : inspire with courage and hope **2** : foster — **en·cour·age·ment** *n*

en·croach \in'krōch\ *vb* : enter upon another's property or rights — **en·croach·ment** *n*

en·crust \in'krəst\ *vb* : form a crust on

en·cum·ber \in'kəmbər\ *vb* : burden — **en·cum·brance** \-brəns\ *n*

-en·cy \ənsē,ᵊn-\ *n suffix* : -ence

en·cyc·li·cal \in'siklikəl, en-\ *n* : papal letter to bishops

en·cy·clo·pe·dia \in,sīklə-'pēdēə\ *n* : reference work on many subjects — **en·cy·clo·pe·dic** \-'pēdik\ *adj*

end \'end\ *n* **1** : point at which something stops or no longer exists **2** : cessation **3** : purpose ~ *vb* **1** : stop or finish **2** : be at the end of — **end·less** *adj* — **end·less·ly** *adv*

en·dan·ger \in'dānjər\ *vb* : bring into danger

en·dear \in'dir\ *vb* : make dear — **en·dear·ment** \-mənt\ *n*

en·deav·or \in'devər\ *vb or n* : attempt

end·ing \'endiŋ\ *n* : end

en·dive \'en,dīv\ *n* : salad plant

en·do·crine \'endəkrən, -,krīn, -,krēn\ *adj* : producing secretions distributed by the bloodstream

en·dorse \in'dórs\ *vb* **-dorsed; -dors·ing** **1** : sign one's name to **2** : approve — **en·dorse·ment** *n*

en·dow \in'daú\ *vb* **1** : furnish with funds **2** : furnish naturally — **en·dow·ment** *n*

en·dure \in'dúr, -'dyúr\ *vb* **-dured; -dur·ing** **1** : last **2** : suffer patiently **3** : tolerate — **en·dur·able** *adj* — **en·dur·ance** \-əns\ *n*

en·e·ma \'enəmə\ *n* : injection of liquid into the rectum

en·e·my \-mē\ *n, pl* **-mies**
: one that attacks or tries to harm another

en·er·get·ic \ˌenərˈjetik\ *adj*
: full of energy or activity —
en·er·get·i·cal·ly \-iklē\ *adv*

en·er·gize \ˈenərˌjīz\ *vb*
-gized; -giz·ing : give energy to

en·er·gy \ˈenərjē\ *n, pl* **-gies**
1 : capacity for action **2** : vigorous action **3** : capacity for doing work

en·er·vate \ˈenərˌvāt\ *vb* **-vat·ed; -vat·ing** : make weak or listless — **en·er·va·tion** \ˌenərˈvāshən\ *n*

en·fold \inˈfōld\ *vb* : surround or embrace

en·force \-ˈfōrs\ *vb* **1** : compel **2** : carry out — **en·force·able** \-əbəl\ *adj* — **en·force·ment** *n*

en·fran·chise \-ˈfranˌchīz\ *vb* **-chised; -chis·ing** : grant voting rights to — **en·fran·chise·ment** \-ˌchīzmənt, -chəz-\ *n*

en·gage \inˈgāj\ *vb* **-gaged; -gag·ing** **1** : participate or cause to participate **2** : bring or come into working contact **3** : bind by a pledge to marry **4** : hire **5** : bring or enter into conflict — **en·gage·ment** \-mənt\ *n*

en·gag·ing *adj* : attractive

en·gen·der \inˈjendər\ *vb* **-dered; -der·ing** : create

en·gine \ˈenjən\ *n* **1** : machine that converts energy into mechanical motion **2** : locomotive

en·gi·neer \ˌenjəˈnir\ *n* **1** : one trained in engineering **2** : engine operator ～ *vb* : lay out or manage as an engineer

en·gi·neer·ing \-iŋ\ *n* : practical application of science and mathematics

en·grave \inˈgrāv\ *vb* **-graved; -gra·ving** : cut into a surface — **en·grav·er** *n* — **en·grav·ing** *n*

en·gross \-ˈgrōs\ *vb* : occupy fully

en·gulf \-ˈgəlf\ *vb* : swallow up

en·hance \-ˈhans\ *vb* **-hanced; -hanc·ing** : improve in value — **en·hance·ment** *n*

enig·ma \iˈnigmə\ *n* : puzzle or mystery — **enig·mat·ic** \ˌenigˈmatik, ˌē-\ *adj* — **enig·mat·i·cal·ly** *adv*

en·join \inˈjoin\ *vb* **1** : command **2** : forbid

en·joy \-ˈjȯi\ *vb* : take pleasure in — **en·joy·able** *adj* — **en·joy·ment** *n*

en·large \-ˈlärj\ *vb* **-larged; -larg·ing** : make or grow larger — **en·large·ment** *n* — **en·larg·er** *n*

en·light·en \-ˈlītᵊn\ *vb* : give knowledge or spiritual insight to — **en·light·en·ment** *n*

en·list \-'list\ *vb* **1** : join the armed forces **2** : get the aid of — **en·list·ee** \-ˌlis'tē\ *n* — **en·list·ment** \-'listmənt\ *n*

en·liv·en \in'līvən\ *vb* : give life or spirit to

en·mi·ty \'enmətē\ *n, pl* **-ties** : mutual hatred

en·no·ble \in'ōbəl\ *vb* **-bled; -bling** : make noble

en·nui \ˌän'wē\ *n* : boredom

enor·mi·ty \i'nȯrmətē\ *n, pl* **-ties** **1** : great wickedness **2** : huge size

enor·mous \i'nȯrməs\ *adj* : great in size, number, or degree — **enor·mous·ly** *adv* — **enor·mous·ness** *n*

enough \i'nəf\ *adj* : adequate ~ *adv* **1** : in an adequate manner **2** : in a tolerable degree ~ *pron* : adequate number, quantity, or amount

en·quire \in'kwīr\, **en·qui·ry** \'inˌkwīrē, in'-; 'inkwərē, 'iŋ-\ *var of* INQUIRE, INQUIRY

en·rage \in'rāj\ *vb* : fill with rage

en·rich \-'rich\ *vb* : make rich — **en·rich·ment** *n*

en·roll, en·rol \-'rōl\ *vb* **-rolled; -roll·ing** **1** : enter on a list **2** : become enrolled — **en·roll·ment** *n*

en route \än'rüt, en-, in-\ *adv or adj* : on or along the way

en·sconce \in'skäns\ *vb* **-sconced; -sconc·ing** : settle snugly

en·sem·ble \än'sämbəl\ *n* **1** : small group **2** : complete costume

en·shrine \in'shrīn\ *vb* **1** : put in a shrine **2** : cherish

en·sign \'ensən, *1 also* 'enˌsīn\ *n* **1** : flag **2** : lowest ranking commissioned officer in the navy

en·slave \in'slāv\ *vb* : make a slave of — **en·slave·ment** *n*

en·snare \-'snar\ *vb* : trap

en·sue \-'sü\ *vb* **-sued; -su·ing** : follow as a consequence

en·sure \-'shùr\ *vb* **-sured; -sur·ing** : guarantee

en·tail \-'tāl\ *vb* : involve as a necessary result

en·tan·gle \-'taŋgəl\ *vb* : tangle — **en·tan·gle·ment** *n*

en·ter \'entər\ *vb* **1** : go or come in or into **2** : start **3** : set down (as in a list)

en·ter·prise \'entərˌprīz\ *n* **1** : an undertaking **2** : business organization **3** : initiative

en·ter·pris·ing \-ˌprīziŋ\ *adj* : showing initiative

en·ter·tain \ˌentər'tān\ *vb* **1** : treat or receive as a guest **2** : hold in mind **3** : amuse — **en·ter·tain·er** *n* — **en·ter·tain·ment** *n*

en·thrall, en·thral \in'thról\ *vb* **-thralled; -thrall·ing** : hold spellbound

en·thu·si·asm \-'thüzē͵azəm, -'thyü-\ *n* : strong excitement of feeling or its cause — **en·thu·si·ast** \-͵ast, -əst\ *n* — **en·thu·si·as·tic** \-͵thüzē'astik, -͵thyü-\ *adj* — **en·thu·si·as·ti·cal·ly** \-tiklē\ *adv*

en·tice \-'tīs\ *vb* **-ticed; -tic·ing** : tempt — **en·tice·ment** *n*

en·tire \in'tīr\ *adj* : complete or whole — **en·tire·ly** *adv* — **en·tire·ty** \-'tīrətē, -'tīrtē\ *n*

en·ti·tle \-'tīt°l\ *vb* **-tled; -tling** **1** : name **2** : give a right to

en·ti·ty \'entətē\ *n, pl* **-ties** : something with separate existence

en·to·mol·o·gy \͵entə'mäləjē\ *n* : study of insects — **en·to·mo·log·i·cal** \-mə'läjikəl\ *adj* — **en·to·mol·o·gist** \-'mälə-jist\ *n*

en·tou·rage \͵äntù'räzh\ *n* : retinue

en·trails \'entrəlz, -͵trālz\ *n pl* : intestines

¹en·trance \'entrəns\ *n* **1** : act of entering **2** : means or place of entering — **en·trant** \'entrənt\ *n*

²en·trance \in'trans\ *vb* **-tranced; -tranc·ing** : fascinate or delight

en·trap \in'trap\ *vb* : trap — **en·trap·ment** *n*

en·treat \-'trēt\ *vb* : ask urgently — **en·treaty** \-'trētē\ *n*

en·trée, en·tree \'än͵trā\ *n* : principal dish of the meal

en·trench \in'trench\ *vb* : establish in a strong position — **en·trench·ment** *n*

en·tre·pre·neur \͵äntrəprə'nər\ *n* : organizer or promoter of an enterprise

en·trust \in'trəst\ *vb* : commit to another with confidence

en·try \'entrē\ *n, pl* **-tries** **1** : entrance **2** : an entering in a record or an item so entered

en·twine \in'twīn\ *vb* : twine together or around

enu·mer·ate \i'nümə͵rāt, -'nyü-\ *vb* **-at·ed; -at·ing** **1** : count **2** : list — **enu·mer·a·tion** \i͵nümə'rāshən, -͵nyü-\ *n*

enun·ci·ate \ē'nənsē͵āt\ *vb* **-at·ed; -at·ing** **1** : announce **2** : pronounce — **enun·ci·a·tion** \-͵nənsē'āshən\ *n*

en·vel·op \in'veləp\ *vb* : surround — **en·vel·op·ment** *n*

en·ve·lope \'envə͵lōp, 'än-\ *n* : paper container for a letter

en·vi·ron·ment \in'vīrənmənt\ *n* : surroundings — **en·vi·ron·men·tal** \-͵vīrən'ment°l\ *adj*

en·vi·ron·men·tal·ist \-°list\ *n* : person concerned about the environment

en·vi·rons \in'vīrənz\ *n pl* : vicinity

en·vis·age \in'vizij\ *vb* **-aged;**
-ag·ing : have a mental picture of

en·vi·sion \-'vizhən\ *vb* : picture to oneself

en·voy \'en,vȯi, 'än-\ *n* : diplomat

en·vy \'envē\ *n* **1** : resentful
awareness of another's advantage **2** : object of envy ∼ *vb*
-vied; -vy·ing : feel envy toward or on account of — **en-
vi·able** \-vēəbəl\ *adj* — **en-
vi·ous** \-vēəs\ *adj* — **en·vi-
ous·ly** *adv*

en·zyme \'en,zīm\ *n* : biological catalyst

eon \'ēən, ē,än\ *n* : indefinitely long time

ep·au·let \,epə'let\ *n* : shoulder ornament on a uniform

ephem·er·al \i'femərəl\ *adj*
: short-lived

ep·ic \'epik\ *n* : long poem
about a hero — **epic** *adj*

ep·i·cure \'epi,kyu̇r\ *n* : person with fastidious taste esp.
in food and wine — **ep·i·cu·re-
an** \,epikyu̇'rēən, -'kyu̇rē-\
n or adj

ep·i·dem·ic \,epə'demik\ *adj*
: affecting many persons at
one time — **epidemic** *n*

epi·der·mis \,epə'dərməs\ *n*
: outer layer of skin

ep·i·gram \'epə,gram\ *n* : short
witty poem or saying

ep·i·lep·sy \'epə,lepsē\ *n, pl*
-sies : nervous disorder
marked by convulsive attacks
— **ep·i·lep·tic** \,epə'leptik\
adj or n

epis·co·pal \i'piskəpəl\ *adj*
: governed by bishops

ep·i·sode \'epə,sōd, -,zōd\ *n*
: occurrence — **ep·i·sod·ic**
\,epə'sädik, -'zäd-\ *adj*

epis·tle \i'pisəl\ *n* : letter

ep·i·taph \'epə,taf\ *n* : inscription in memory of a dead
person

ep·i·thet \'epə,thet, -thət\ *n*
: characterizing often abusive
word or phrase

epit·o·me \i'pitəmē\ *n* **1**
: summary **2** : ideal example
— **epit·o·mize** \-,mīz\ *vb*

ep·och \'epək, 'ep,äk\ *n* : extended period — **ep·och·al**
\'epəkəl, 'ep,äkəl\ *adj*

ep·oxy \'ep,äksē, ep'äksē\ *n*
: synthetic resin used esp. in
adhesives ∼ *vb* **-ox·ied** *or*
-oxyed; -oxy·ing : glue with
epoxy

equa·ble \'ekwəbəl, 'ēkwə-\
adj : free from unpleasant
extremes — **eq·ua·bil·i·ty**
\,ekwə'bilətē, ,ē-\ *n* — **eq-
ua·bly** \-blē\ *adv*

equal \'ēkwəl\ *adj* : of the
same quantity, value, quality,
number, or status as another
∼ *n* : one that is equal ∼ *vb*
equaled *or* **equalled; equal-**

ing *or* **equal·ling** : be or become equal to — **equal·i·ty** \i'kwälətē\ *n* — **equal·ize** \'ēkwə,līz\ *vb* — **equal·ly** \'ēkwəlē\ *adv*

equa·nim·i·ty \,ēkwə'nimətē, ek-\ *n, pl* **-ties** : calmness

equate \i'kwāt\ *vb* **equat·ed; equat·ing** : treat or regard as equal

equa·tion \i'kwāzhən, -shən\ *n* : mathematical statement that two things are equal

equa·tor \i'kwātər\ *n* : imaginary circle that separates the northern and southern hemispheres — **equa·to·ri·al** \,ēkwə'tōrēəl, ,ek-\ *adj*

eques·tri·an \i'kwestrēən\ *adj* : relating to horseback riding ∼ *n* : horseback rider

equi·lat·er·al \,ēkwə'latərəl\ *adj* : having equal sides

equi·lib·ri·um \-'librēəm\ *n, pl* **-ri·ums** *or* **-ria** \-reə\ : state of balance

equine \'ē,kwīn, 'ek,wīn\ *adj* : relating to the horse — **equine** *n*

equi·nox \'ēkwə,näks, 'ek-\ *n* : time when day and night are everywhere of equal length

equip \i'kwip\ *vb* **-pp-** : furnish with needed resources — **equip·ment** \-mənt\ *n*

eq·ui·ta·ble \'ekwətəbəl\ *adj* : fair

eq·ui·ty \'ekwətē\ *n, pl* **-ties** **1** : justice **2** : value of a property less debt

equiv·a·lent \i'kwivələnt\ *adj* : equal — **equiv·a·lence** \-ləns\ *n* — **equivalent** *n*

equiv·o·cal \i'kwivəkəl\ *adj* : ambiguous or uncertain

equiv·o·cate \i'kwivə,kāt\ *vb* **-cat·ed; -cat·ing** **1** : use misleading language **2** : avoid answering definitely — **equiv·o·ca·tion** \-,kwivə'kā-shən\ *n*

[1]-er \ər\ *adj suffix or adv suffix* — used to form the comparative degree of adjectives and adverbs and esp. those of one or two syllables

[2]-er \ər\, **-ier** \ēər, yər\, **-yer** \yər\ *n suffix* **1** : one that is associated with **2** : one that performs or is the object of an action **3** : one that is

era \'irə, 'erə, 'ērə\ *n* : period of time associated with something

erad·i·cate \i'radə,kāt\ *vb* **-cat·ed; -cat·ing** : do away with

erase \i'rās\ *vb* **erased; eras·ing** : rub or scratch out — **eras·er** *n* — **era·sure** \i'rāshər\ *n*

ere \'er\ *prep or conj* : before

erect \i'rekt\ *adj* : not leaning or lying down ∼ *vb* **1** : build

2 : bring to an upright position — **erec·tion** \i'rekshən\ *n*

er·mine \'ərmən\ *n* : weasel with white winter fur or its fur

erode \i'rōd\ *vb* **erod·ed; erod·ing** : wear away gradually

ero·sion \i'rōzhən\ *n* : process of eroding

erot·ic \i'rätik\ *adj* : sexually arousing — **erot·i·cal·ly** \-iklē\ *adv* — **erot·i·cism** \i'rätə-ˌsizəm\ *n*

err \'er, 'ər\ *vb* : be or do wrong

er·rand \'erənd\ *n* : short trip taken to do something often for another

er·rant \-ənt\ *adj* **1** : traveling about **2** : going astray

er·rat·ic \ir'atik\ *adj* **1** : eccentric **2** : inconsistent — **er·rat·i·cal·ly** \-iklē\ *adv*

er·ro·ne·ous \ir'ōnēəs, e'rō-\ *adj* : wrong — **er·ro·ne·ous·ly** *adv*

er·ror \'erər\ *n* **1** : something that is not accurate **2** : state of being wrong

er·satz \'er,säts\ *adj* : phony

erst·while \'ərst,hwīl\ *adv* : in the past ~ *adj* : former

er·u·di·tion \ˌerə'dishən, ˌeryə-\ *n* : great learning — **er·u·dite** \'erə,dīt, 'eryə-\ *adj*

erupt \i'rəpt\ *vb* : burst forth esp. suddenly and violently — **erup·tion** \i'rəpshən\ *n* — **erup·tive** \-tiv\ *adj*

-ery \ərē\ *n suffix* **1** : character or condition **2** : practice **3** : place of doing

¹-es \əz, iz *after* s, z, sh, ch; z *after* v *or a vowel*\ *n pl suffix* — used to form the plural of some nouns

²-es *vb suffix* — used to form the 3d person singular present of some verbs

es·ca·late \'eskə,lāt\ *vb* **-lat·ed; -lat·ing** : become quickly larger or greater — **es·ca·la·tion** \ˌeskə'lāshən\ *n*

es·ca·la·tor \'eskə,lātər\ *n* : moving stairs

es·ca·pade \'eskə,pād\ *n* : mischievous adventure

es·cape \is'kāp\ *vb* **-caped; -cap·ing** : get away or get away from ~ *n* **1** : flight from or avoidance of something unpleasant **2** : leakage **3** : means of escape ~ *adj* : providing means of escape — **es·cap·ee** \is,kā'pē, ,es-\ *n*

es·ca·role \'eskə,rōl\ *n* : salad green

es·carp·ment \is'kärpmənt\ *n* : cliff

es·chew \is'chü\ *vb* : shun

es·cort \'es,kȯrt\ *n* : one accompanying another — **es·cort** \is'kȯrt, es-\ *vb*

es·crow \'es,krō\ *n* : deposit to be delivered upon fulfillment of a condition

esoph·a·gus \i'säfəgəs\ *n, pl* **-gi** \-ˌgī, -ˌjī\ : muscular tube connecting the mouth and stomach

es·o·ter·ic \ˌesə'terik\ *adj* : mysterious or secret

es·pe·cial·ly \is'peshəlē\ *adv* : particularly or notably

es·pi·o·nage \'espēəˌnäzh, -nij\ *n* : practice of spying

es·pous·al \is'paûzəl\ *n* **1** : betrothal **2** : wedding **3** : a taking up as a supporter — **es·pouse** \-'paûz\ *vb*

espres·so \e'spresō\ *n, pl* **-sos** : strong steam-brewed coffee

es·py \is'pī\ *vb* **-pied; -py·ing** : catch sight of

es·quire \'esˌkwīr\ *n* — used as a title of courtesy

-ess \əs, ˌes\ *n suffix* : female

es·say \'esˌā\ *n* : literary composition ～ *vb* \e'sā, 'esˌā\ : attempt — **es·say·ist** \'esˌāist\ *n*

es·sence \'esᵊns\ *n* **1** : fundamental nature or quality **2** : extract **3** : perfume

es·sen·tial \i'senchəl\ *adj* : basic or necessary — **essential** *n* — **es·sen·tial·ly** *adv*

-est \əst, ist\ *adj suffix or adv suffix* — used to form the superlative degree of adjectives and adverbs and esp. those of 1 or 2 syllables

es·tab·lish \is'tablish\ *vb* **1** : bring into existence **2** : put on a firm basis **3** : cause to be recognized

es·tab·lish·ment \-mənt\ *n* **1** : business or a place of business **2** : an establishing or being established **3** : controlling group

es·tate \is'tāt\ *n* **1** : one's possessions **2** : large piece of land with a house

es·teem \is'tēm\ *n or vb* : regard

es·ter \'estər\ *n* : organic chemical compound

esthetic *var of* AESTHETIC

es·ti·ma·ble \'estəməbəl\ *adj* : worthy of esteem

es·ti·mate \'estəˌmāt\ *vb* **-mat·ed; -mat·ing** : judge the approximate value, size, or cost ～ \-mət\ *n* **1** : rough or approximate calculation **2** : statement of the cost of a job — **es·ti·ma·tion** \ˌestə'māshən\ *n* — **es·ti·ma·tor** \'estəˌmātər\ *n*

es·trange \is'trānj\ *vb* **-tranged; -trang·ing** : make hostile — **es·trange·ment** *n*

es·tro·gen \'estrəjən\ *n* : hormone that produces female characteristics

es·tu·ary \'eschəˌwerē\ *n, pl* **-ar·ies** : arm of the sea at a river's mouth

et cet·era \et'setərə, -'setrə\ : and others esp. of the same kind

etch \'ech\ *vb* : produce by corroding parts of a surface with acid — **etch·er** *n* — **etch·ing** *n*

eter·nal \i'tərnᵊl\ *adj* : lasting forever — **eter·nal·ly** *adv*

eter·ni·ty \-nətē\ *n, pl* **-ties** : infinite duration

eth·ane \'eth‚ān\ *n* : gaseous hydrocarbon

eth·a·nol \'ethə‚nȯl, -‚nōl\ *n* : alcohol

ether \'ēthər\ *n* : light flammable liquid used as an anesthetic

ethe·re·al \i'thirēəl\ *adj* **1** : celestial **2** : exceptionally delicate

eth·i·cal \'ethikəl\ *adj* **1** : relating to ethics **2** : honorable — **eth·i·cal·ly** *adv*

eth·ics \-iks\ *n sing or pl* **1** : study of good and evil and moral duty **2** : moral principles or practice

eth·nic \'ethnik\ *adj* : relating to races or groups of people with common customs ∼ *n* : member of a minority ethnic group

eth·nol·o·gy \eth'näləjē\ *n* : study of the races of human beings — **eth·no·log·i·cal** \‚ethnə'läjikəl\ *adj* — **eth·nol·o·gist** \eth'näləjist\ *n*

et·i·quette \'etikət, -‚ket\ *n* : good manners

et·y·mol·o·gy \‚etə'mäləjē\ *n, pl* **-gies 1** : history of a word **2** : study of etymologies — **et·y·mo·log·i·cal** \-mə'läjikəl\ *adj* — **et·y·mol·o·gist** \-'mälə-jist\ *n*

eu·ca·lyp·tus \‚yükə'liptəs\ *n, pl* **-ti** \-‚tī\ *or* **-tus·es** : Australian evergreen tree

Eu·cha·rist \'yükərəst\ *n* : Communion — **eu·cha·ris·tic** \‚yükə'ristik\ *adj*

eu·lo·gy \'yüləjē\ *n, pl* **-gies** : speech in praise — **eu·lo·gis·tic** \‚yülə'jistik\ *adj* — **eu·lo·gize** \'yülə‚jīz\ *vb*

eu·nuch \'yünək\ *n* : castrated man

eu·phe·mism \'yüfə‚mizəm\ *n* : substitution of a pleasant expression for an unpleasant or offensive one — **eu·phe·mis·tic** \‚yüfə'mistik\ *adj*

eu·pho·ni·ous \yù'fōnēəs\ *adj* : pleasing to the ear — **eu·pho·ny** \'yüfənē\ *n*

eu·pho·ria \yù'fōrēə\ *n* : elation — **eu·phor·ic** \-'fȯrik\ *adj*

eu·ro \'yùrō\ *n, pl* **euros** : commmon monetary unit of most of the European Union

eu·tha·na·sia \‚yüthə'nāzhə, -zhēə\ *n* : mercy killing

evac·u·ate \i'vakyə‚wāt\ *vb* **-at·ed; -at·ing 1** : discharge wastes from the body **2** : remove or withdraw from —

evac·u·a·tion \i͵vakyə'wā-shən\ *n*

evade \i'vād\ *vb* **evad·ed; evad·ing** : manage to avoid

eval·u·ate \i'valyə͵wāt\ *vb* **-at·ed; -at·ing** : appraise — **eval·u·a·tion** \i͵valyə'wā-shən\ *n*

evan·gel·i·cal \͵ē͵van'jelikəl, ͵evən-\ *adj* : relating to the Christian gospel

evan·ge·lism \i'vanjə͵lizəm\ *n* : the winning or revival of personal commitments to Christ — **evan·ge·list** \i'vanjəlist\ *n* — **evan·ge·lis·tic** \i͵vanjə'listik\ *adj*

evap·o·rate \i'vapə͵rāt\ *vb* **-rat·ed; -rat·ing 1** : pass off in or convert into vapor **2** : disappear quickly — **evap·o·ra·tion** \i͵vapə'rāshən\ *n* — **evap·ora·tor** \i'vapə͵rātər\ *n*

eva·sion \i'vāzhən\ *n* : act or instance of evading — **eva·sive** \i'vāsiv\ *adj* — **eva·sive·ness** *n*

eve \'ēv\ *n* : evening

even \'ēvən\ *adj* **1** : smooth **2** : equal or fair **3** : fully revenged **4** : divisible by 2 ∼ *adv* **1** : already **2** — used for emphasis ∼ *vb* : make or become even — **even·ly** *adv* — **even·ness** *n*

eve·ning \'ēvniŋ\ *n* : early part of the night

event \i'vent\ *n* **1** : occurrence **2** : noteworthy happening **3** : eventuality — **event·ful** *adj*

even·tu·al \i'venchəwəl\ *adj* : later — **even·tu·al·ly** *adv*

even·tu·al·i·ty \i͵venchə'walətē\ *n, pl* **-ties** : possible occurrence or outcome

ev·er \'evər\ *adv* **1** : always **2** : at any time **3** : in any case

ev·er·green *adj* : having foliage that remains green — **evergreen** *n*

ev·er·last·ing \͵evər'lastiŋ\ *adj* : lasting forever

ev·ery \'evrē\ *adj* **1** : being each one of a group **2** : all possible

ev·ery·body \'evri͵bädē, -bəd-\ *pron* : every person

ev·ery·day *adj* : ordinary

ev·ery·one \-͵wən\ *pron* : every person

ev·ery·thing *pron* : all that exists

ev·ery·where *adv* : in every place or part

evict \i'vikt\ *vb* : force (a person) to move from a property — **evic·tion** \i'vikshən\ *n*

ev·i·dence \'evədəns\ *n* **1** : outward sign **2** : proof or testimony

ev·i·dent \-ənt\ *adj* : clear or obvious — **ev·i·dent·ly** \-ədəntlē, -ə͵dent-\ *adv*

evil \ˈēvəl\ *adj* **evil·er** *or* **evil-ler; evil·est** *or* **evil·lest** : wicked ∼ *n* **1** : sin **2** : source of sorrow or distress — **evil·do·er** \ˌēvəlˈdüər\ *n* — **evil·ly** *adv*

evince \iˈvins\ *vb* **evinced; evinc·ing** : show

evis·cer·ate \iˈvisəˌrāt\ *vb* **-at-ed; -at·ing** : remove the viscera of — **evis·cer·a·tion** \iˌvisə-ˈrāshən\ *n*

evoke \iˈvōk\ *vb* **evoked; evok-ing** : call forth or up — **evo·ca-tion** \ˌēvōˈkāshən, ˌevə-\ *n* — **evoc·a·tive** \iˈväkətiv\ *adj*

evo·lu·tion \ˌevəˈlüshən\ *n* : process of change by de-grees — **evo·lu·tion·ary** \-shə-ˌnerē\ *adj*

evolve \iˈvälv\ *vb* **evolved; evolv·ing** : develop or change by degrees

ewe \ˈyü\ *n* : female sheep

ew·er \ˈyüər\ *n* : water pitcher

ex·act \igˈzakt\ *vb* : compel to furnish ∼ *adj* : precisely cor-rect — **ex·act·ing** *adj* — **ex·ac-tion** \-ˈzakshən\ *n* — **ex·ac-ti·tude** \-ˈzaktəˌtüd, -ˌtyüd\ *n* — **ex·act·ly** *adv* — **ex·act-ness** *n*

ex·ag·ger·ate \igˈzajəˌrāt\ *vb* **-at-ed; -at·ing** : say more than is true — **ex·ag·ger·at·ed·ly** *adv* — **ex·ag·ger·a·tion** \-ˌza-jəˈrāshən\ *n* — **ex·ag·ger·a-tor** \-ˈzajərātər\ *n*

ex·alt \igˈzȯlt\ *vb* : glorify — **ex·al·ta·tion** \ˌegˌzȯlˈtāshən, ˌekˌsȯl-\ *n*

ex·am \igˈzam\ *n* : examination

ex·am·ine \-ən\ *vb* **-ined; -in-ing** **1** : inspect closely **2** : test by questioning — **ex·am·i·na-tion** \-ˌzaməˈnāshən\ *n*

ex·am·ple \igˈzampəl\ *n* **1** : representative sample **2** : model **3** : problem to be solved for teaching purposes

ex·as·per·ate \igˈzaspəˌrāt\ *vb* **-at·ed; -at·ing** : thoroughly annoy — **ex·as·per·a·tion** \-ˌzaspəˈrāshən\ *n*

ex·ca·vate \ˈekskəˌvāt\ *vb* **-vat·ed; -vat·ing** : dig or hol-low out — **ex·ca·va·tion** \ˌek-skəˈvāshən\ *n* — **ex·ca·va-tor** \ˈekskəˌvātər\ *n*

ex·ceed \ikˈsēd\ *vb* **1** : go or be beyond the limit of **2** : do better than

ex·ceed·ing·ly *adv* : extremely

ex·cel \ikˈsel\ *vb* **-ll-** : do ex-tremely well or far better than

ex·cel·lence \ˈeksələns\ *n* : quality of being excellent

ex·cel·len·cy \-lənsē\ *n, pl* **-cies** — used as a title of honor

ex·cel·lent \ˈeksələnt\ *adj* : very good — **ex·cel·lent·ly** *adv*

ex·cept \ikˈsept\ *vb* : omit ∼ *prep* : excluding ∼ *conj* : but — **ex·cep·tion** \-ˈsepshən\ *n*

ex·cep·tion·al \-'sepshənəl\ *adj* : superior — **ex·cep·tion·al·ly** *adv*

ex·cerpt \'ek,sərpt, 'eg,zərpt\ *n* : brief passage ∼ \ek'-, eg'-, 'ek,-, 'eg,-\ *vb* : select an excerpt

ex·cess \ik'ses, 'ek,ses\ *n* : amount left over — **excess** *adj* — **ex·ces·sive** \ik'sesiv\ *adj* — **ex·ces·sive·ly** *adv*

ex·change \iks'chānj, 'eks-,chānj\ *n* **1** : the giving or taking of one thing in return for another **2** : marketplace esp. for securities ∼ *vb* **-changed; -chang·ing** : transfer in return for some equivalent — **ex·change·able** \iks-'chānjəbəl\ *adj*

¹**ex·cise** \'ek,sīz, -,sīs\ *n* : tax

²**ex·cise** \ik'sīz\ *vb* **-cised; -cis·ing** : cut out — **ex·ci·sion** \-'sizhən\ *n*

ex·cite \ik'sīt\ *vb* **-cit·ed; -cit·ing** **1** : stir up **2** : kindle the emotions of — **ex·cit·abil·i·ty** \-,sītə'bilətē\ *n* — **ex·cit·able** \-'sītəbəl\ *adj* — **ex·ci·ta·tion** \,ek,sī'tāshən, -ə-\ *n* — **ex·cit·ed·ly** *adv* — **ex·cite·ment** \ik'sītmənt\ *n*

ex·claim \iks'klām\ *vb* : cry out esp. in delight — **ex·cla·ma·tion** \,eksklə'māshən\ *n* — **ex·clam·a·to·ry** \iks-'klamə,tōrē\ *adj*

exclamation point *n* : punctuation mark ! used esp. after an interjection or exclamation

ex·clude \iks'klüd\ *vb* **-clud·ed; -clud·ing** : leave out — **ex·clu·sion** \-'klüzhən\ *n*

ex·clu·sive \-'klüsiv\ *adj* **1** : reserved for particular persons **2** : stylish **3** : sole — **exclusive** *n* — **ex·clu·sive·ly** *adv* — **ex·clu·sive·ness** *n*

ex·com·mu·ni·cate \,ekskə-'myünə,kāt\ *vb* : expel from a church — **ex·com·mu·ni·ca·tion** \-,myünə'kāshən\ *n*

ex·cre·ment \'ekskrəmənt\ *n* : bodily waste

ex·crete \ik'skrēt\ *vb* **-cret·ed; -cret·ing** : eliminate wastes from the body — **ex·cre·tion** \-'skrēshən\ *n* — **ex·cre·to·ry** \'ekskrə,tōrē\ *adj*

ex·cru·ci·at·ing \ik'skrü-shē,ātiŋ\ *adj* : intensely painful — **ex·cru·ci·at·ing·ly** *adv*

ex·cul·pate \'ekskəl,pāt\ *vb* **-pat·ed; -pat·ing** : clear from alleged fault

ex·cur·sion \ik'skərzhən\ *n* : pleasure trip

ex·cuse \ik'skyüz\ *vb* **-cused; -cus·ing** **1** : pardon **2** : release from an obligation **3** : justify ∼ \-'skyüs\ *n* **1** : justification **2** : apology

ex·e·cute \'eksi,kyüt\ *vb* **-cut·ed; -cut·ing** **1** : carry out fully **2** : enforce **3** : put to death — **ex·e·cu·tion** \ˌeksi-'kyüshən\ *n* — **ex·e·cu·tion·er** \-shənər\ *n*

ex·ec·u·tive \ig'zekyətiv\ *adj* : relating to the carrying out of decisions, plans, or laws ~ *n* **1** : branch of government with executive duties **2** : administrator

ex·ec·u·tor \-yətər\ *n* : person named in a will to execute it

ex·ec·u·trix \ig'zekyə₁triks\ *n, pl* **ex·ec·u·tri·ces** \-ˌzekyə-'trī₁sēz\ *or* **ex·ec·u·trix·es** : woman executor

ex·em·pla·ry \ig'zemplərē\ *adj* : so commendable as to serve as a model

ex·em·pli·fy \-plə₁fī\ *vb* **-fied; -fy·ing** : serve as an example of — **ex·em·pli·fi·ca·tion** \-ˌzempləfə'kāshən\ *n*

ex·empt \ig'zempt\ *adj* : being free from some liability ~ *vb* : make exempt — **ex·emp·tion** \-'zempshən\ *n*

ex·er·cise \'eksər₁sīz\ *n* **1** : a putting into action **2** : exertion to develop endurance or a skill **3** *pl* : public ceremony ~ *vb* **-cised; -cis·ing 1** : exert **2** : engage in exercise — **ex·er·cis·er** *n*

ex·ert \ig'zərt\ *vb* : put into action — **ex·er·tion** \-'zərshən\ *n*

ex·hale \eks'hāl\ *vb* **-haled; -hal·ing** : breathe out — **ex·ha·la·tion** \ekshə'lāshən\ *n*

ex·haust \ig'zȯst\ *vb* **1** : draw out or develop completely **2** : use up **3** : tire or wear out ~ *n* : waste steam or gas from an engine or a system for removing it — **ex·haus·tion** \-'zȯschən\ *n* — **ex·haus·tive** \-'zȯstiv\ *adj*

ex·hib·it \ig'zibət\ *vb* : display esp. publicly ~ *n* **1** : act of exhibiting **2** : something exhibited — **ex·hi·bi·tion** \ˌeksə'bishən\ *n* — **ex·hib·i·tor** \ig'zibətər\ *n*

ex·hil·a·rate \ig'zilə₁rāt\ *vb* **-rat·ed; -rat·ing** : thrill — **ex·hil·a·ra·tion** \-ˌzilə'rāshən\ *n*

ex·hort \-'zȯrt\ *vb* : urge earnestly — **ex·hor·ta·tion** \ˌeks₁ȯr'tāshən, ˌegz-, -ər-\ *n*

ex·hume \igz'üm, -'yüm; iks-'yüm, -'hyüm\ *vb* **-humed; -hum·ing** : dig up (a buried corpse) — **ex·hu·ma·tion** \ˌeksyü'māshən, -hyü-; ˌegzü-, -zyü-\ *n*

ex·i·gen·cies \'eksəjənsēz, ig'zijən-\ *n pl* : requirements (as of a situation)

ex·ile \'eg₁zīl, 'ek₁sīl\ *n* **1** : banishment **2** : person banished from his or her country — **exile** *vb*

ex·ist \ig'zist\ *vb* **1** : have real or actual being **2** : live — **ex-**

is·tence \-əns\ *n* — **ex·is·tent** \-ənt\ *adj*

ex·it \'egzət, 'eksət\ *n* **1** : departure **2** : way out of an enclosed space **3** : way off an expressway — **exit** *vb*

ex·o·dus \'eksədəs\ *n* : mass departure

ex·on·er·ate \ig'zänə,rāt\ *vb* **-at·ed; -at·ing** : free from blame — **ex·on·er·a·tion** \-,zänə'rāshən\ *n*

ex·or·bi·tant \ig'zórbətənt\ *adj* : exceeding what is usual or proper

ex·or·cise \'ek,sór,sīz, -sər-\ *vb* **-cised; -cis·ing** : drive out (as an evil spirit) — **ex·or·cism** \-,sizəm\ *n* — **ex·or·cist** \-,sist\ *n*

ex·ot·ic \ig'zätik\ *adj* : foreign or strange — **exotic** *n* — **ex·ot·i·cal·ly** \-iklē\ *adv*

ex·pand \ik'spand\ *vb* : enlarge

ex·panse \-'spans\ *n* : very large area

ex·pan·sion \-'spanchən\ *n* **1** : act or process of expanding **2** : expanded part

ex·pan·sive \-'spansiv\ *adj* **1** : tending to expand **2** : warmly benevolent **3** : of large extent — **ex·pan·sive·ly** *adv* — **ex·pan·sive·ness** *n*

ex·pa·tri·ate \ek'spātrē,āt, -ət\ *n* : exile — **expatriate** \-,āt\ *adj or vb*

ex·pect \ik'spekt\ *vb* **1** : look forward to **2** : consider probable or one's due — **ex·pec·tan·cy** \-ənsē\ *n* — **ex·pec·tant** \-ənt\ *adj* — **ex·pec·tant·ly** *adv* — **ex·pec·ta·tion** \,ek-,spek'tāshən\ *n*

ex·pe·di·ent \ik'spēdēənt\ *adj* : convenient or advantageous rather than right or just ~ *n* : convenient often makeshift means to an end

ex·pe·dite \'ekspə,dīt\ *vb* **-dit·ed; -dit·ing** : carry out or handle promptly — **ex·pe·dit·er** *n*

ex·pe·di·tion \,ekspə'dishən\ *n* : long journey for work or research or the people making this

ex·pe·di·tious \-əs\ *adj* : prompt and efficient

ex·pel \ik'spel\ *vb* **-ll-** : force out

ex·pend \-'spend\ *vb* **1** : pay out **2** : use up — **ex·pend·able** *adj*

ex·pen·di·ture \-'spendichər, -də,chùr\ *n* : act of using or spending

ex·pense \ik'spens\ *n* : cost — **ex·pen·sive** \-'spensiv\ *adj* — **ex·pen·sive·ly** *adv*

ex·pe·ri·ence \ik'spirēəns\ *n* **1** : a participating in or living through an event **2** : an event that affects one **3** : knowledge from doing ∼ *vb* **-enced; -enc·ing** : undergo

ex·per·i·ment \ik'sperə-mənt\ *n* : test to discover something ∼ *vb* : make experiments — **ex·per·i·men·tal** \-ˌsperə'ment°l\ *adj* — **ex·per·i·men·ta·tion** \-mən'tā-shən\ *n* — **ex·per·i·men·ter** \-'sperəˌmentər\ *n*

ex·pert \'ek.spərt\ *adj* : thoroughly skilled ∼ *n* : person with special skill — **ex·pert·ly** *adv* — **ex·pert·ness** *n*

ex·per·tise \ˌekspər'tēz\ *n* : skill

ex·pi·ate \'ekspē.āt\ *vb* : make amends for — **ex·pi·a·tion** \ˌekspē'āshən\ *n*

ex·pire \ik'spīr, ek-\ *vb* **-pired; -pir·ing** 1 : breathe out 2 : die 3 : end — **ex·pi·ra·tion** \ˌekspə'rāshən\ *n*

ex·plain \ik'splān\ *vb* 1 : make clear 2 : give the reason for — **ex·plain·able** \-əbəl\ *adj* — **ex·pla·na·tion** \ˌeksplə'nāshən\ *n* — **ex·plan·a·to·ry** \ik'splanəˌtōrē\ *adj*

ex·ple·tive \'eksplətiv\ *n* : usu. profane exclamation

ex·pli·ca·ble \ek'splikəbəl, 'eksplik-\ *adj* : capable of being explained

ex·plic·it \ik'splisət\ *adj* : absolutely clear or precise — **ex-plic·it·ly** *adv* — **ex·plic·it·ness** *n*

ex·plode \ik'splōd\ *vb* **-plod·ed; -plod·ing** 1 : discredit 2 : burst or cause to burst violently 3 : increase rapidly

ex·ploit \'ekˌsplȯit\ *n* : heroic act ∼ \ik'splȯit\ *vb* 1 : utilize 2 : use unfairly — **ex·ploi·ta·tion** \ˌekˌsplȯi'tāshən\ *n*

ex·plore \ik'splōr\ *vb* **-plored; -plor·ing** : examine or range over thoroughly — **ex·plo·ra·tion** \ˌeksplə'rāshən\ *n* — **ex·plor·a·to·ry** \ik'splōrəˌtōrē\ *adj* — **ex·plor·er** *n*

ex·plo·sion \ik'splōzhən\ *n* : process or instance of exploding

ex·plo·sive \-siv\ *adj* 1 : able to cause explosion 2 : likely to explode — **explosive** *n* — **ex·plo·sive·ly** *adv*

ex·po·nent \ik'spōnənt, 'ekˌspō-\ *n* 1 : mathematical symbol showing how many times a number is to be repeated as a factor 2 : advocate — **ex·po·nen·tial** \ˌekspə'nenchəl\ *adj* — **ex·po·nen·tial·ly** *adv*

ex·port \ek'spōrt, 'ekˌspōrt\ *vb* : send to foreign countries — **export** \'ekˌ-\ *n* — **ex·por·ta·tion** \ˌekˌspōr'tāshən\ *n* — **ex·port·er** \ek'spōrtər, 'ekˌspōrt-\ *n*

ex·pose \ik'spōz\ *vb* **-posed;
-pos·ing** **1** : deprive of shelter or protection **2** : subject (film) to light **3** : make known — **ex·po·sure** \-'spōzhər\ *n*

ex·po·sé, ex·po·se \ˌekspō'zā\ *n* : exposure of something discreditable

ex·po·si·tion \ˌekspə'zishən\ *n* : public exhibition

ex·pound \ik'spaǔnd\ *vb* : set forth or explain in detail

¹ex·press \-'spres\ *adj* **1** : clear **2** : specific **3** : traveling at high speed with few stops — **express** *adv or n* — **ex·press·ly** *adv*

²express *vb* **1** : make known in words or appearance **2** : press out (as juice)

ex·pres·sion \-'spreshən\ *n* **1** : utterance **2** : mathematical symbol **3** : significant word or phrase **4** : look on one's face — **ex·pres·sive** \-'spresiv\ *adj* — **ex·pres·sive·ness** *n*

ex·press·way \ik'spres,wā\ *n* : high-speed divided highway with limited access

ex·pul·sion \ik'spəlshən\ *n* : an expelling or being expelled

ex·pur·gate \'ekspər,gāt\ *vb* **-gat·ed; -gat·ing** : censor — **ex·pur·ga·tion** \ˌekspər'gā-shən\ *n*

ex·qui·site \ek'skwizət, 'ekskwiz-\ *adj* **1** : flawlessly beautiful and delicate **2** : keenly discriminating

ex·tant \'ekstənt, ek'stant\ *adj* : existing

ex·tem·po·ra·ne·ous \ek-ˌstempə'rānēəs\ *adj* : impromptu — **ex·tem·po·ra·ne·ous·ly** *adv*

ex·tend \ik'stend\ *vb* **1** : stretch forth or out **2** : prolong **3** : enlarge — **ex·tend·able** \-'stendəbəl\ *adj*

ex·ten·sion \-'stenchən\ *n* **1** : an extending or being extended **2** : additional part **3** : extra telephone line

ex·ten·sive \-'stensiv\ *adj* : of considerable extent — **ex·ten·sive·ly** *adv*

ex·tent \-'stent\ *n* : range, space, or degree to which something extends

ex·ten·u·ate \ik'stenyə,wāt\ *vb* **-at·ed; -at·ing** : lessen the seriousness of — **ex·ten·u·a·tion** \-ˌstenyə'wāshən\ *n*

ex·te·ri·or \ek'stirēər\ *adj* : external ⁓ *n* : external part or surface

ex·ter·mi·nate \ik'stərmə-ˌnāt\ *vb* **-nat·ed; -nat·ing** : destroy utterly — **ex·ter·mi·na·tion** \-ˌstərmə'nāshən\ *n* — **ex·ter·mi·na·tor** \-'stərmə-ˌnātər\ *n*

ex·ter·nal \ek'stərnᵊl\ *adj* : relating to or on the outside — **ex·ter·nal·ly** *adv*

ex·tinct \ik'stiŋkt\ *adj* : no longer existing — **ex·tinc·tion** \-'stiŋkshən\ *n*

ex·tin·guish \-'stiŋgwish\ *vb* : cause to stop burning — **ex·tin·guish·able** *adj* — **ex·tin·guish·er** *n*

ex·tir·pate \'ekstər͵pāt\ *vb* **-pat·ed; -pat·ing** : destroy

ex·tol \ik'stōl\ *vb* **-ll-** : praise highly

ex·tort \-'stȯrt\ *vb* : obtain by force or improper pressure — **ex·tor·tion** \-'stȯrshən\ *n* — **ex·tor·tion·er** *n* — **ex·tor·tion·ist** *n*

ex·tra \'ekstrə\ *adj* **1** : additional **2** : superior — **extra** *n or adv*

extra- *prefix* : outside or beyond

ex·tract \ik'strakt\ *vb* **1** : pull out forcibly **2** : withdraw (as a juice) ~ \'ek͵-\ *n* **1** : excerpt **2** : product (as a juice) obtained by extracting — **ex·tract·able** *adj* — **ex·trac·tion** \ik'strakshən\ *n* — **ex·trac·tor** \-tər\ *n*

ex·tra·cur·ric·u·lar \͵ekstrəkə-'rikyələr\ *adj* : lying outside the regular curriculum

ex·tra·dite \'ekstrə͵dīt\ *vb* **-dit·ed; -dit·ing** : bring or deliver a suspect to a different jurisdiction for trial — **ex·tra·di·tion** \͵ekstrə'dishən\ *n*

ex·tra·mar·i·tal \͵ekstrə-'marət³l\ *adj* : relating to sex-

ual relations of a married person outside of the marriage

ex·tra·ne·ous \ek'strānēəs\ *adj* : not essential or relevant — **ex·tra·ne·ous·ly** *adv*

ex·traor·di·nary \ik'strȯrd³n͵erē, ͵ekstrə'ȯrd-\ *adj* : notably unusual or exceptional — **ex·traor·di·nari·ly** \ik͵strȯrd³n'erəlē, ͵ekstrə͵ȯrd-\ *adv*

ex·tra·sen·so·ry \͵ekstrə'sensərē\ *adj* : outside the ordinary senses

ex·tra·ter·res·tri·al \͵ekstrətə-'restrēəl\ *n* : one existing or coming from outside the earth ~ *adj* : relating to an extraterrestrial

ex·trav·a·gant \ik'stravigənt\ *adj* : wildly excessive, lavish, or costly — **ex·trav·a·gance** \-gəns\ *n* — **ex·trav·a·gant·ly** *adv*

ex·trav·a·gan·za \-͵stravə-'ganzə\ *n* : spectacular event

ex·tra·ve·hic·u·lar \͵ekstrəvē-'hikyələr\ *adj* : occurring outside a spacecraft

ex·treme \ik'strēm\ *adj* **1** : very great or intense **2** : very severe **3** : not moderate **4** : most remote ~ *n* **1** : extreme state **2** : something located at one end or the other of a range — **ex·treme·ly** *adv*

ex·trem·i·ty \-'stremətē\ *n, pl* **-ties 1** : most remote part **2**

: human hand or foot **3** : extreme degree or state (as of need)

ex·tri·cate \ˈekstrəˌkāt\ *vb* **-cat·ed; -cat·ing** : set or get free from an entanglement or difficulty — **ex·tri·ca·ble** \ikˈstrikəbəl, ek-; ˈekstrik-\ *adj* — **ex·tri·ca·tion** \ˌekstrə-ˈkāshən\ *n*

ex·tro·vert \ˈekstrəˌvərt\ *n* : gregarious person — **ex·tro·ver·sion** \ˌekstrəˈvərzhən\ *n* — **ex·tro·vert·ed** \ˈekstrə-ˌvərtəd\ *adj*

ex·trude \ikˈstrüd\ *vb* **-trud·ed; -trud·ing** : to force or push out

ex·u·ber·ant \igˈzübərənt\ *adj* : joyously unrestrained — **ex·u·ber·ance** \-rəns\ *n* — **ex·u·ber·ant·ly** *adv*

ex·ude \igˈzüd\ *vb* **-ud·ed; -ud·ing** **1** : discharge slowly through pores **2** : display conspicuously

ex·ult \igˈzəlt\ *vb* : rejoice — **ex·ul·tant** \-ˈzəltᵊnt\ *adj* — **ex·ul·tant·ly** *adv* — **ex·ul·ta·tion** \ˌeksəlˈtāshən, ˌegzəl-\ *n*

-ey — see -Y

eye \ˈī\ *n* **1** : organ of sight consisting of a globular structure (**eye·ball**) in a socket of the skull with thin movable covers (**eye·lids**) bordered with hairs (**eye·lash·es**) **2** : vision **3** : judgment **4** : something suggesting an eye ~ *vb* **eyed; eye·ing** *or* **ey·ing** : look at — **eye·brow** \-ˌbrau̇\ *n* — **eyed** \ˈīd\ *adj* — **eye·strain** *n*

eye·drop·per *n* : dropper

eye·glass·es *n pl* : glasses

eye·let \ˈīlət\ *n* : hole (as in cloth) for a lacing or rope

eye–open·er *n* : something startling — **eye–open·ing** *adj*

eye·piece *n* : lens at the eye end of an optical instrument

eye·sight *n* : sight

eye·sore *n* : unpleasant sight

eye·tooth *n* : upper canine tooth

eye·wit·ness *n* : person who actually sees something happen

ey·rie \ˈīrē, *or like* AERIE\ *var of* AERIE

F

f \'ef\ *n, pl* **f's** *or* **fs** \'efs\ **:** 6th letter of the alphabet

fa·ble \'fābəl\ *n* **1** : legendary story **2** : story that teaches a lesson — **fa·bled** \-bəld\ *adj*

fab·ric \'fabrik\ *n* **1** : structure **2** : material made usu. by weaving or knitting fibers

fab·ri·cate \'fabri,kāt\ *vb* **-cat·ed; -cat·ing 1** : construct **2** : invent — **fab·ri·cation** \,fabri'kāshən\ *n*

fab·u·lous \'fabyələs\ *adj* **1** : like, told in, or based on fable **2** : incredible or marvelous — **fab·u·lous·ly** *adv*

fa·cade \fə'säd\ *n* **1** : principal face of a building **2** : false or superficial appearance

face \'fās\ *n* **1** : front or principal surface (as of the head) **2** : presence **3** : facial expression **4** : grimace **5** : outward appearance ∼ *vb* **faced; fac·ing 1** : challenge or resist firmly or brazenly **2** : cover with different material **3** : sit or stand with the face toward **4** : have the front oriented toward — **faced** \'fāst\ *adj* — **face·less** *adj* — **fa·cial** \'fāshəl\ *adj or n*

face·down *adv* : with the face downward

face–lift \'fās,lift\ *n* **1** : cosmetic surgery on the face **2** : modernization

fac·et \'fasət\ *n* **1** : surface of a cut gem **2** : phase — **fac·et·ed** *adj*

fa·ce·tious \fə'sēshəs\ *adj* : jocular — **fa·ce·tious·ly** *adv* — **fa·ce·tious·ness** *n*

fac·ile \'fasəl\ *adj* **1** : easy **2** : fluent

fa·cil·i·tate \fə'silə,tāt\ *vb* **-tat·ed; -tat·ing** : make easier

fa·cil·i·ty \fə'silətē\ *n, pl* **-ties** **1** : ease in doing or using **2** : something built or installed to serve a purpose or facilitate an activity

fac·ing \'fāsiŋ\ *n* : lining or covering or material for this

fac·sim·i·le \fak'siməlē\ *n* : exact copy

fact \'fakt\ *n* **1** : act or action **2** : something that exists or is real **3** : piece of information — **fac·tu·al** \'fakchəwəl\ *adj* — **fac·tu·al·ly** *adv*

fac·tion \'fakshən\ *n* : part of a larger group — **fac·tion·al·ism** \-shənə,lizəm\ *n*

fac·tious \'fakshəs\ *adj* : causing discord

fac·ti·tious \fak'tishəs\ *adj* : artificial

fac·tor \'faktər\ *n* **1** : something that has an effect **2** : gene **3** : number used in multiplying

fac·to·ry \'faktərē\ *n, pl* **-ries** : place for manufacturing

fac·to·tum \fak'tōtəm\ *n* : person (as a servant) with varied duties

fac·ul·ty \'fakəltē\ *n, pl* **-ties** **1** : ability to act **2** : power of the mind or body **3** : body of teachers or department of instruction

fad \'fad\ *n* : briefly popular practice or interest — **fad·dish** *adj* — **fad·dist** *n*

fade \'fād\ *vb* **fad·ed; fad·ing** **1** : wither **2** : lose or cause to lose freshness or brilliance **3** : grow dim **4** : vanish

fag \'fag\ *vb* **-gg-** **1** : drudge **2** : tire or exhaust

fag·ot, fag·got \'fagət\ *n* : bundle of twigs

Fahr·en·heit \'farən,hīt\ *adj* : relating to a thermometer scale with the boiling point at 212 degrees and the freezing point at 32 degrees

fail \'fāl\ *vb* **1** : decline in health **2** : die away **3** : stop functioning **4** : be unsuccessful **5** : become bankrupt **6** : disappoint **7** : neglect ~ *n* : act of failing

fail·ing *n* : slight defect in character or conduct ~ *prep* : in the absence or lack of

faille \'fīl\ *n* : closely woven ribbed fabric

fail·ure \'fālyər\ *n* **1** : absence of expected action or performance **2** : bankruptcy **3** : deficiency **4** : one that has failed

faint \'fānt\ *adj* **1** : cowardly or spiritless **2** : weak and dizzy **3** : lacking vigor **4** : indistinct ~ *vb* : lose consciousness ~ *n* : act or condition of fainting — **faint·heart·ed** *adj* — **faint·ly** *adv* — **faint·ness** *n*

¹fair \'far\ *adj* **1** : pleasing in appearance **2** : not stormy or cloudy **3** : just or honest **4** : conforming with the rules **5** : open to legitimate pursuit or attack **6** : light in color **7** : adequate — **fair·ness** *n*

²fair *adv, chiefly Brit* : FAIRLY

³fair *n* : exhibition for judging or selling — **fair·ground** *n*

fair·ly \'farlē\ *adv* **1** : in a manner of speaking **2** : without bias **3** : somewhat

fairy \'farē\ *n, pl* **fair·ies** : usu. small imaginary being — **fairy tale** *n*

fairy·land \-,land\ *n* **1** : land of fairies **2** : beautiful or charming place

faith \'fāth\ *n, pl* **faiths** \'fāths, 'fāthz\ **1** : allegiance

2 : belief and trust in God **3** : confidence **4** : system of religious beliefs — **faith·ful** \-fəl\ adj — **faith·ful·ly** adv — **faith·ful·ness** n — **faith·less** adj — **faith·less·ly** adv — **faith·less·ness** n

fake \'fāk\ vb **faked; fak·ing 1** : falsify **2** : counterfeit ∼ n : copy, fraud, or impostor ∼ adj : not genuine — **fak·er** n

fa·kir \fə'kir\ n : wandering beggar of India

fal·con \'falkən, 'fȯl-\ n : small long-winged hawk used esp. for hunting — **fal·con·ry** \-rē\ n

fall \'fȯl\ vb **fell** \'fel\; **fall·en** \'fȯlən\; **fall·ing 1** : go down by gravity **2** : hang freely **3** : go lower **4** : be defeated or ruined **5** : commit a sin **6** : happen at a certain time **7** : become gradually ∼ n **1** : act of falling **2** : autumn **3** : downfall **4** pl : waterfall **5** : distance something falls

fal·la·cy \'faləsē\ n, pl **-cies 1** : false idea **2** : false reasoning — **fal·la·cious** \fə'lāshəs\ adj

fal·li·ble \'faləbəl\ adj : capable of making a mistake — **fal·li·bly** \-blē\ adv

fall·out n **1** : radioactive particles from a nuclear explosion **2** : secondary effects

fal·low \'falō\ adj **1** : plowed but not planted **2** : dormant — **fallow** n or vb

false \'fȯls\ adj **fals·er; fals·est 1** : not genuine, true, faithful, or permanent **2** : misleading — **false·ly** adv — **false·ness** n — **fal·si·fi·ca·tion** \ˌfȯlsəfə-'kāshən\ n — **fal·si·fy** \'fȯlsə-ˌfī\ vb — **fal·si·ty** \'fȯlsətē\ n

false·hood \'fȯlsˌhùd\ n : lie

fal·set·to \fȯl'setō\ n, pl **-tos** : artificially high singing voice

fal·ter \'fȯltər\ vb **-tered; -ter·ing 1** : move unsteadily **2** : hesitate — **fal·ter·ing·ly** adv

fame \'fām\ n : public reputation — **famed** \'fāmd\ adj

fa·mil·ial \fə'milyəl\ adj : relating to a family

¹**fa·mil·iar** \fə'milyər\ n **1** : companion **2** : guardian spirit

²**familiar** adj **1** : closely acquainted **2** : forward **3** : frequently seen or experienced — **fa·mil·iar·i·ty** \fəˌmil-'yarətē, -ˌmilē'yar-\ n — **fa·mil·iar·ize** \fə'milyəˌrīz\ vb — **fa·mil·iar·ly** adv

fam·i·ly \'famlē\ n, pl **-lies 1** : persons of common ancestry **2** : group living together **3** : parents and children **4** : group of related individuals

fam·ine \'famən\ n : extreme scarcity of food

fam·ish \'famish\ *vb* : starve

fa·mous \'fāməs\ *adj* : widely known or celebrated

fa·mous·ly *adv* : very well

¹**fan** \'fan\ *n* : device for producing a current of air ∼ *vb* -nn- **1** : move air with a fan **2** : direct a current of air upon **3** : stir to activity

²**fan** *n* : enthusiastic follower or admirer

fa·nat·ic \fə'natik\, **fa·nat·i·cal** \-ikəl\ *adj* : excessively enthusiastic or devoted — **fanatic** *n* — **fa·nat·i·cism** \-'natə,sizəm\ *n*

fan·ci·er \'fansēər\ *n* : one devoted to raising a particular plant or animal

fan·cy \'fansē\ *n, pl* -cies **1** : liking **2** : whim **3** : imagination ∼ *vb* -cied; -cy·ing **1** : like **2** : imagine ∼ *adj* -cier; -est **1** : not plain **2** : of superior quality — **fan·ci·ful** \-sifəl\ *adj* — **fan·ci·ful·ly** \-fəlē\ *adv* — **fan·ci·ly** *adv*

fan·dan·go \fan'daŋgō\ *n, pl* -gos : lively Spanish dance

fan·fare \'fan,far\ *n* **1** : a sounding of trumpets **2** : showy display

fang \'faŋ\ *n* : long sharp tooth

fan·light *n* : semicircular window

fan·ta·sia \fan'tāzhə, -zēə; ,fantə'zēə\ *n* : music written to fancy rather than to form

fan·tas·tic \fan'tastik\ *adj* **1** : imaginary or unrealistic **2** : exceedingly or unbelievably great — **fan·tas·ti·cal·ly** \-tiklē\ *adv*

fan·ta·sy \'fantəsē\ *n* **1** : imagination **2** : product (as a daydream) of the imagination **3** : fantasia — **fan·ta·size** \'fantə,sīz\ *vb*

FAQ *abbr* frequently asked questions

far \'fär\ *adv* **far·ther** \-thər\ *or* **fur·ther** \'fər-\; **far·thest** *or* **fur·thest** \-thəst\ **1** : at or to a distance **2** : much **3** : to a degree **4** : to an advanced point or extent ∼ *adj* **farther** *or* **further; far·thest** *or* **fur·thest 1** : remote **2** : long **3** : being more distant

far·away *adj* : distant

farce \'färs\ *n* **1** : satirical comedy with an improbable plot **2** : ridiculous display — **far·ci·cal** \-sikəl\ *adj*

¹**fare** \'far\ *vb* **fared; far·ing** : get along

²**fare** *n* **1** : price of transportation **2** : range of food

fare·well \far'wel\ *n* **1** : wish of welfare at parting **2** : departure — **farewell** *adj*

far–fetched \'fär'fecht\ *adj* : improbable

fa·ri·na \fə'rēnə\ *n* : fine meal made from cereal grains

farm \'färm\ *n* : place where something is raised for food ~ *vb* **1** : use (land) as a farm **2** : raise plants or animals for food — **farm·er** *n* — **farm·hand** \-ˌhand\ *n* — **farm·house** *n* — **farm·ing** *n* — **farm·land** \-ˌland\ *n* — **farm·yard** *n*

far–off *adj* : remote in time or space

far·ri·er \'farēər\ *n* : blacksmith who shoes horses

far·row \'farō\ *vb* : give birth to a litter of pigs — **farrow** *n*

far·sight·ed *adj* **1** : better able to see distant things than near **2** : judicious or shrewd — **far·sight·ed·ness** *n*

far·ther \'färthər\ *adv* **1** : at or to a greater distance or more advanced point **2** : to a greater degree or extent ~ *adj* : more distant

far·ther·most *adj* : most distant

far·thest \'färthəst\ *adj* : most distant ~ *adv* **1** : to or at the greatest distance **2** : to the most advanced point **3** : by the greatest extent

fas·ci·cle \'fasikəl\ *n* **1** : small bundle **2** : division of a book published in parts — **fas·ci·cled** \-kəld\ *adj*

fas·ci·nate \'fasᵊnˌāt\ *vb* -**nat·ed; -nat·ing** : transfix and hold spellbound — **fas·ci·na·tion** \ˌfasᵊn'āshən\ *n*

fas·cism \'fashˌizəm\ *n* : dictatorship that exalts nation and race — **fas·cist** \-ist\ *n or adj* — **fas·cis·tic** \fa'shistik\ *adj*

fash·ion \'fashən\ *n* **1** : manner **2** : prevailing custom or style ~ *vb* : form or construct — **fash·ion·able** \-ənəbəl\ *adj* — **fash·ion·ably** \-blē\ *adv*

¹**fast** \'fast\ *adj* **1** : firmly fixed, bound, or shut **2** : faithful **3** : moving or acting quickly **4** : indicating ahead of the correct time **5** : deep and undisturbed **6** : permanently dyed **7** : wild or promiscuous ~ *adv* **1** : so as to be secure or bound **2** : soundly or deeply **3** : swiftly

²**fast** *vb* : abstain from food or eat sparingly ~ *n* : act or time of fasting

fas·ten \'fasᵊn\ *vb* : attach esp. by pinning or tying — **fas·ten·er** *n* — **fas·ten·ing** *n*

fas·tid·i·ous \fas'tidēəs\ *adj* : hard to please — **fas·tid·i·ous·ly** *adv* — **fas·tid·i·ous·ness** *n*

fat \'fat\ *adj* -**tt-** **1** : having much fat **2** : thick ~ *n* : animal tissue rich in greasy or oily matter — **fat·ness** *n* — **fat·ten** \'fatᵊn\ *vb* — **fat·ty** *adj or n*

fa·tal \ˈfātᵊl\ *adj* : causing death or ruin — **fa·tal·i·ty** \fāˈtalətē, fə-\ *n* — **fa·tal·ly** *adv*

fa·tal·ism \ˈfātᵊlˌizəm\ *n* : belief that fate determines events — **fa·tal·ist** \-ist\ *n* — **fa·tal·is·tic** \ˌfātᵊlˈistik\ *adj* — **fa·tal·is·ti·cal·ly** \-tiklē\ *adv*

fate \ˈfāt\ *n* **1** : principle, cause, or will held to determine events **2** : end or outcome — **fat·ed** *adj* — **fate·ful** \-fəl\ *adj* — **fate·ful·ly** *adv*

fa·ther \ˈfäthər, ˈfȧth-\ *n* **1** : male parent **2** *cap* : God **3** : originator — **father** *vb* — **fa·ther·hood** \-ˌhud\ *n* — **fa·ther·land** \-ˌland\ *n* — **fa·ther·less** *adj* — **fa·ther·ly** *adj*

father–in–law *n, pl* **fa·thers–in–law** : father of one's spouse

fath·om \ˈfathəm\ *n* : nautical unit of length equal to 6 feet ~ *vb* : understand — **fath·om·able** *adj* — **fath·om·less** *adj*

fa·tigue \fəˈtēg\ *n* **1** : weariness from labor or use **2** : tendency to break under repeated stress ~ *vb* **-tigued; -tigu·ing** : tire out

fat·u·ous \ˈfachəwəs\ *adj* : foolish or stupid — **fat·u·ous·ly** *adv* — **fat·u·ous·ness** *n*

fau·cet \ˈfȯsət, ˈfäs-\ *n* : fixture for drawing off a liquid

fault \ˈfȯlt\ *n* **1** : weakness in character **2** : something wrong or imperfect **3** : responsibility for something wrong **4** : fracture in the earth's crust ~ *vb* : find fault in or with — **fault·find·er** *n* — **fault·find·ing** *n* — **fault·i·ly** \ˈfȯltəlē\ *adv* — **fault·less** *adj* — **fault·less·ly** *adv* — **faulty** *adj*

fau·na \ˈfȯnə\ *n* : animals or animal life esp. of a region — **fau·nal** \-ᵊl\ *adj*

faux pas \ˈfōˈpä\ *n, pl* **faux pas** *same or* -ˈpäz\ : social blunder

fa·vor \ˈfāvər\ *n* **1** : approval **2** : partiality **3** : act of kindness ~ *vb* : regard or treat with favor — **fa·vor·able** \ˈfāvərəbəl\ *adj* — **fa·vor·ably** \-blē\ *adv*

fa·vor·ite \ˈfāvərət\ *n* : one favored — **favorite** *adj* — **fa·vor·it·ism** \-ˌizəm\ *n*

¹**fawn** \ˈfȯn\ *vb* : seek favor by groveling

²**fawn** *n* : young deer

faze \ˈfāz\ *vb* **fazed; faz·ing** : disturb the composure of

fear \ˈfir\ *n* : unpleasant emotion caused by expectation or awareness of danger ~ *vb* : be afraid of — **fear·ful** \-fəl\ *adj* — **fear·ful·ly** *adv* — **fear·less** *adj* — **fear·less-**

ly *adv* — **fear·less·ness** *n* — **fear·some** \-səm\ *adj*

fea·si·ble \'fēzəbəl\ *adj* : capable of being done — **fea·si·bil·i·ty** \ˌfēzə'bilətē\ *n* — **fea·si·bly** \'fēzəblē\ *adv*

feast \'fēst\ *n* **1** : large or fancy meal **2** : religious festival ~ *vb* : eat plentifully

feat \'fēt\ *n* : notable deed

feath·er \'fet͟hər\ *n* : one of the light horny outgrowths that form the external covering of a bird's body — **feather** *vb* — **feath·ered** \-ərd\ *adj* — **feath·er·less** *adj* — **feath·ery** *adj*

fea·ture \'fēchər\ *n* **1** : shape or appearance of the face **2** : part of the face **3** : prominent characteristic **4** : special attraction ~ *vb* : give prominence to — **fea·ture·less** *adj*

Feb·ru·ary \'febyəˌwerē, 'fe-bə-, 'febrə-\ *n* : 2d month of the year having 28 and in leap years 29 days

fe·ces \'fēˌsēz\ *n pl* : intestinal body waste — **fe·cal** \-kəl\ *adj*

feck·less \'fekləs\ *adj* : irresponsible

fe·cund \'fekənd, 'fē-\ *adj* : prolific — **fe·cun·di·ty** \fi'kəndətē, fe-\ *n*

fed·er·al \'fedrəl, -dərəl\ *adj* : of or constituting a government with power distributed between a central authority and constituent units — **fed·er·al·ism** \-rəˌlizəm\ *n* — **fed·er·al·ist** \-list\ *n or adj* — **fed·er·al·ly** *adv*

fed·er·ate \'fedəˌrāt\ *vb* **-at·ed; -at·ing** : join in a federation

fed·er·a·tion \ˌfedə'rāshən\ *n* : union of organizations

fe·do·ra \fi'dōrə\ *n* : soft felt hat

fed up *adj* : out of patience

fee \'fē\ *n* : fixed charge

fee·ble \'fēbəl\ *adj* **-bler; -blest** : weak or ineffective — **fee·ble·mind·ed** \ˌfēbəl'mīndəd\ *adj* — **fee·ble·mind·ed·ness** *n* — **fee·ble·ness** *n* — **fee·bly** \-blē\ *adv*

feed \'fēd\ *vb* **fed** \'fed\; **feed·ing 1** : give food to **2** : eat **3** : furnish ~ *n* : food for livestock — **feed·er** *n*

feel \'fēl\ *vb* **felt** \'felt\; **feel·ing 1** : perceive or examine through physical contact **2** : think or believe **3** : be conscious of **4** : seem **5** : have sympathy ~ *n* **1** : sense of touch **2** : quality of a thing imparted through touch — **feel·er** *n*

feel·ing \'fēliŋ\ *n* **1** : sense of touch **2** : state of mind **3** *pl* : sensibilities **4** : opinion

feet *pl of* FOOT

feign \'fān\ *vb* : pretend

feint \'fānt\ *n* : mock attack intended to distract attention — **feint** *vb*

fe·lic·i·tate \fi'lisə,tāt\ *vb* -tat·ed; -tat·ing : congratulate — **fe·lic·i·ta·tion** \-,lisə-'tāshən\ *n*

fe·lic·i·tous \fi'lisətəs\ *adj* : aptly expressed — **fe·lic·i·tous·ly** *adv*

fe·lic·i·ty \-'lisətē\ *n, pl* -ties 1 : great happiness 2 : pleasing faculty esp. in art or language

fe·line \'fē,līn\ *adj* : relating to cats — **feline** *n*

¹**fell** \'fel\ *vb* : cut or knock down

²**fell** *past of* FALL

fel·low \'felō\ *n* 1 : companion or associate 2 : man or boy — **fel·low·ship** \-,ship\ *n*

fel·low·man \,felō'man\ *n* : kindred human being

fel·on \'felən\ *n* : one who has committed a felony

fel·o·ny \'felənē\ *n, pl* -nies : serious crime — **fe·lo·ni·ous** \fə'lōnēəs\ *adj*

¹**felt** \'felt\ *n* : cloth made of pressed wool and fur

²**felt** *past of* FEEL

fe·male \'fē,māl\ *adj* : relating to or being the sex that bears young — **female** *n*

fem·i·nine \'femənən\ *adj* : relating to the female sex — **fem·i·nin·i·ty** \,femə'ninətē\ *n*

fem·i·nism \'femə,nizəm\ *n* : organized activity on behalf of women's rights — **fem·i·nist** \-nist\ *n or adj*

fe·mur \'fēmər\ *n, pl* **fe·murs** *or* **fem·o·ra** \'femərə\ : long bone of the thigh — **fem·o·ral** \'femərəl\ *adj*

fence \'fens\ *n* : enclosing barrier esp. of wood or wire ∼ *vb* **fenced; fenc·ing** 1 : enclose with a fence 2 : practice fencing — **fenc·er** *n*

fenc·ing \'fensiŋ\ *n* 1 : combat with swords for sport 2 : material for building fences

fend \'fend\ *vb* : ward off

fend·er \'fendər\ *n* : guard over an automobile wheel

fen·nel \'fenᵊl\ *n* : herb related to the carrot

fer·ment \fər'ment\ *vb* : cause or undergo fermentation ∼ \'fər,ment\ *n* : agitation

fer·men·ta·tion \,fərmən'tāshən, -,men-\ *n* : chemical decomposition of an organic substance in the absence of oxygen

fern \'fərn\ *n* : flowerless seedless green plant

fe·ro·cious \fə'rōshəs\ *adj* : fierce or savage — **fe·ro·cious·ly** *adv* — **fe·ro·cious·ness** *n* — **fe·roc·i·ty** \-'räsətē\ *n*

fer·ret \'ferət\ *n* : white European polecat ~ *vb* : find out by searching

fer·ric \'ferik\, **fer·rous** \'ferəs\ *adj* : relating to or containing iron

fer·rule \'ferəl\ *n* : metal band or ring

fer·ry \'ferē\ *vb* -ried; -ry·ing : carry by boat over water ~ *n, pl* -ries : boat used in ferrying — **fer·ry·boat** *n*

fer·tile \'fərtᵊl\ *adj* 1 : producing plentifully 2 : capable of developing or reproducing — **fer·til·i·ty** \fər'tilətē\ *n*

fer·til·ize \'fərtᵊl,īz\ *vb* -ized; -iz·ing : make fertile — **fer·til·iza·tion** \,fərtᵊlə'zāshən\ *n* — **fer·til·iz·er** *n*

fer·vid \'fərvəd\ *adj* : ardent or zealous — **fer·vid·ly** *adv*

fer·vor \'fərvər\ *n* : passion — **fer·ven·cy** \-vənsē\ *n* — **fer·vent** \-vənt\ *adj* — **fer·vent·ly** *adv*

fes·ter \'festər\ *vb* 1 : form pus 2 : become more bitter or malignant

fes·ti·val \'festəvəl\ *n* : time of celebration

fes·tive \-tiv\ *adj* : joyous or happy — **fes·tive·ly** *adv* — **fes·tiv·i·ty** \fes'tivətē\ *n*

fes·toon \fes'tün\ *n* : decorative chain or strip hanging in a curve — **festoon** *vb*

fe·tal \'fētᵊl\ *adj* : of, relating to, or being a fetus

fetch \'fech\ *vb* 1 : go or come after and bring or take back 2 : sell for

fetch·ing \'fechiŋ\ *adj* : attractive — **fetch·ing·ly** *adv*

fête \'fāt, 'fet\ *n* : lavish party ~ *vb* **fêt·ed; fêt·ing** : honor or commemorate with a fête

fet·id \'fetəd\ *adj* : having an offensive smell

fe·tish \'fetish\ *n* 1 : object believed to have magical powers 2 : object of unreasoning devotion or concern

fet·lock \'fet,läk\ *n* : projection on the back of a horse's leg above the hoof

fet·ter \'fetər\ *n* : chain or shackle for the feet — **fetter** *vb*

fet·tle \'fetᵊl\ *n* : state of fitness

fe·tus \'fētəs\ *n* : vertebrate not yet born or hatched

feud \'fyüd\ *n* : prolonged quarrel — **feud** *vb*

feu·dal \'fyüdᵊl\ *adj* : of or relating to feudalism

feu·dal·ism \-,izəm\ *n* : medieval political order in which land is granted in return for service — **feu·dal·is·tic** \,fyüdᵊl'istik\ *adj*

fe·ver \'fēvər\ *n* 1 : abnormal rise in body temperature 2 : state of heightened emotion — **fe·ver·ish** *adj* — **fe·ver·ish·ly** *adv*

few \\'fyü\ *pron* : not many ∼ *adj* : some but not many — often with *a* ∼ *n* : small number — often with *a*

few·er \-ər\ *pron* : smaller number of things

fez \\'fez\ *n, pl* **fez·zes** : round flat-crowned hat

fi·an·cé \ˌfēˌän'sā\ *n* : man one is engaged to

fi·an·cée \ˌfēˌän'sā\ *n* : woman one is engaged to

fi·as·co \fē'askō\ *n, pl* **-coes** : ridiculous failure

fi·at \\'fēət, -ˌat, -ˌät; 'fīət, -ˌat\ *n* : decree

fib \\'fib\ *n* : trivial lie — **fib** *vb* — **fib·ber** *n*

fi·ber, fi·bre \\'fībər\ *n* **1** : threadlike substance or structure (as a muscle cell or fine root) **2** : indigestible material in food **3** : element that gives texture or substance — **fi·brous** \-brəs\ *adj*

fi·ber·board *n* : construction material made of compressed fibers

fi·ber·glass *n* : glass in fibrous form in various products (as insulation)

fi·bril·la·tion \ˌfibrə'lāshən, ˌfīb-\ *n* : rapid irregular contractions of heart muscle — **fib·ril·late** \\'fibrəˌlāt, 'fīb-\ *vb*

fib·u·la \\'fibyələ\ *n, pl* **-lae** \-lē, -lī\ *or* **-las** : outer of the two leg bones below the knee — **fib·u·lar** \-lər\ *adj*

fick·le \\'fikəl\ *adj* : unpredictably changeable — **fick·le·ness** *n*

fic·tion \\'fikshən\ *n* : a made-up story or literature consisting of these — **fic·tion·al** \-shənəl\ *adj*

fic·ti·tious \fik'tishəs\ *adj* : made up or pretended

fid·dle \\'fidᵊl\ *n* : violin ∼ *vb* **-dled; -dling** **1** : play on the fiddle **2** : move the hands restlessly — **fid·dler** \\'fidlər, -ᵊlər\ *n*

fid·dle·sticks *n* : nonsense — used as an interjection

fi·del·i·ty \fə'delətē, fī-\ *n, pl* **-ties** **1** : quality or state of being faithful **2** : quality of reproduction

fid·get \\'fijət\ *n* **1** *pl* : restlessness **2** : one that fidgets ∼ *vb* : move restlessly — **fid·gety** *adj*

fi·du·cia·ry \fə'düshēˌerē, -'dyü-, -shərē\ *adj* : held or holding in trust — **fiduciary** *n*

field \\'fēld\ *n* **1** : open country **2** : cleared land **3** : land yielding some special product **4** : sphere of activity **5** : area for sports **6** : region or space in which a given effect (as magnetism) exists ∼ *vb* : put into the field — **field** *adj* — **field·er** *n*

fiend \'fēnd\ *n* **1** : devil **2** : extremely wicked person — **fiend·ish** *adj* — **fiend·ish·ly** *adv*

fierce \'firs\ *adj* **fierc·er; -est 1** : violently hostile or aggressive **2** : intense **3** : menacing looking — **fierce·ly** *adv* — **fierce·ness** *n*

fi·ery \'fīərē\ *adj* **fi·er·i·er; -est 1** : burning **2** : hot or passionate — **fi·eri·ness** \'fīərēnəs\ *n*

fi·es·ta \fē'estə\ *n* : festival

fife \'fīf\ *n* : small flute

fif·teen \fif'tēn\ *n* : one more than 14 — **fifteen** *adj or pron* — **fif·teenth** \-'tēnth\ *adj or n*

fifth \'fifth\ *n* **1** : one that is number 5 in a countable series **2** : one of 5 equal parts of something — **fifth** *adj or adv*

fif·ty \'fiftē\ *n, pl* **-ties** : 5 times 10 — **fif·ti·eth** \-tēəth\ *adj or n* — **fifty** *adj or pron*

fif·ty–fif·ty *adv or adj* : shared equally

fig \'fig\ *n* : pear-shaped edible fruit

fight \'fīt\ *vb* **fought** \'fȯt\; **fight·ing 1** : contend against another in battle **2** : box **3** : struggle ~ *n* **1** : hostile encounter **2** : boxing match **3** : verbal disagreement — **fight·er** *n*

fig·ment \'figmənt\ *n* : something imagined or made up

fig·u·ra·tive \'figyərətiv, -gə-\ *adj* : metaphorical — **fig·u·ra·tive·ly** *adv*

fig·ure \'figyər, -gər\ *n* **1** : symbol representing a number **2** *pl* : arithmetical calculations **3** : price **4** : shape or outline **5** : illustration **6** : pattern or design **7** : prominent person ~ *vb* **-ured; -uring 1** : be important **2** : calculate — **fig·ured** *adj*

fig·u·rine \ˌfigyə'rēn\ *n* : small statue

fil·a·ment \'filəmənt\ *n* : fine thread or threadlike part — **fil·a·men·tous** \ˌfilə'mentəs\ *adj*

fil·bert \'filbərt\ *n* : edible nut of a European hazel

filch \'filch\ *vb* : steal furtively

¹file \'fīl\ *n* : tool for smoothing or sharpening ~ *vb* **filed; fil·ing** : rub or smooth with a file

²file *vb* **filed; fil·ing 1** : arrange in order **2** : enter or record officially ~ *n* : device for keeping papers in order

³file *n* : row of persons or things one behind the other ~ *vb* **filed; fil·ing** : march in file

fil·ial \'filēəl, 'filyəl\ *adj* : relating to a son or daughter

fil·i·bus·ter \'filəˌbəstər\ *n* : long speeches to delay a legislative vote — **filibuster** *vb* — **fil·i·bus·ter·er** *n*

fil·i·gree \'filə,grē\ *n* : ornamental designs of fine wire — **fil·i·greed** \-,grēd\ *adj*

fill \'fil\ *vb* **1** : make or become full **2** : stop up **3** : feed **4** : satisfy **5** : occupy fully **6** : spread through ∼ *n* **1** : full supply **2** : material for filling — **fill·er** *n* — **fill in** *vb* **1** : provide information to or for **2** : substitute

fil·let \'filət, fi'lā, 'fil,ā\ *n* : piece of boneless meat or fish ∼ *vb* : cut into fillets

fill·ing *n* : material used to fill something

fil·ly \'filē\ *n, pl* -lies : young female horse

film \'film\ *n* **1** : thin skin or membrane **2** : thin coating or layer **3** : strip of material used in taking pictures **4** : movie ∼ *vb* : make a movie of — **filmy** *adj*

film·strip *n* : strip of film with photographs for still projection

fil·ter \'filtər\ *n* **1** : device for separating matter from a fluid **2** : device (as on a camera lens) that absorbs light ∼ *vb* **1** : pass through a filter **2** : remove by means of a filter — **fil·ter·able** *adj* — **fil·tra·tion** \fil'trāshən\ *n*

filth \'filth\ *n* : repulsive dirt or refuse — **filth·i·ness** *n* — **filthy** \'filthē\ *adj*

fin \'fin\ *n* **1** : thin external process controlling movement in an aquatic animal **2** : fin-shaped part (as on an airplane) **3** : flipper — **finned** \'find\ *adj*

fi·na·gle \fə'nāgəl\ *vb* -gled; -gling : get by clever or tricky means — **fi·na·gler** *n*

fi·nal \'fīnᵊl\ *adj* **1** : not to be changed **2** : ultimate **3** : coming at the end — **final** *n* — **fi·nal·ist** \'fīnᵊlist\ *n* — **fi·nal·i·ty** \fī'nalətē, fə-\ *n* — **fi·nal·ize** \-,īz\ *vb* — **fi·nal·ly** *adv*

fi·na·le \fə'nalē, fi'näl-\ *n* : last or climactic part

fi·nance \fə'nans, 'fī,nans\ *n* **1** *pl* : money resources **2** : management of money affairs ∼ *vb* -nanced; -nancing **1** : raise funds for **2** : give necessary funds to **3** : sell on credit

fi·nan·cial \fə'nanchəl, fī-\ *adj* : relating to finance — **fi·nan·cial·ly** *adv*

fi·nan·cier \,finən'sir, ,fī,nan-\ *n* : person who invests large sums of money

finch \'finch\ *n* : songbird (as a sparrow or linnet) with a strong bill

find \'fīnd\ *vb* **found** \'faůnd\; **find·ing** **1** : discover or encounter **2** : obtain by effort **3** : experience or feel **4** : gain or regain the use of **5** : decide on (a verdict) ∼ *n* **1** : act or instance of finding **2** : something found — **find·er** *n* — **find·ing** *n* — **find out** *vb* : learn, discover, or verify something

fine \'fīn\ *n* : money paid as a penalty ∼ *vb* **fined; fin·ing** : impose a fine on ∼ *adj* **fin·er; -est 1** : free from impurity **2** : small or thin **3** : not coarse **4** : superior in quality or appearance ∼ *adv* : finely — **fine·ly** *adv* — **fine·ness** *n*

fin·ery \'fīnərē\ *n, pl* **-er·ies** : showy clothing and jewels

fi·nesse \fə'nes\ *n* **1** : delicate skill **2** : craftiness — **finesse** *vb*

fin·ger \'fiŋgər\ *n* **1** : one of the 5 divisions at the end of the hand and esp. one other than the thumb **2** : something like a finger **3** : part of a glove for a finger ∼ *vb* **1** : touch with the fingers **2** : identify as if by pointing — **fin·gered** *adj* — **fin·ger·nail** *n* — **fin·ger·tip** *n*

fin·ger·ling \-gərliŋ\ *n* : small fish

fin·ger·print *n* : impression of the pattern of marks on the tip of a finger — **fingerprint** *vb*

fin·icky \'finikē\ *adj* : excessively particular in taste or standards

fin·ish \'finish\ *vb* **1** : come or bring to an end **2** : use or dispose of entirely **3** : put a final coat or surface on ∼ *n* **1** : end **2** : final treatment given a surface — **fin·ish·er** *n*

fi·nite \'fī,nīt\ *adj* : having definite limits

fink \'fiŋk\ *n* : contemptible person

fiord *var of* **FJORD**

fir \'fər\ *n* : evergreen tree or its wood

fire \'fīr\ *n* **1** : light or heat and esp. the flame of something burning **2** : destructive burning (as of a house) **3** : enthusiasm **4** : the shooting of weapons ∼ *vb* **fired; fir·ing 1** : kindle **2** : stir up or enliven **3** : dismiss from employment **4** : shoot **5** : bake — **fire·bomb** *n or vb* — **fire·fight·er** *n* — **fire·less** *adj* — **fire·proof** *adj or vb* — **fire·wood** *n*

fire·arm *n* : weapon (as a rifle) that works by an explosion of gunpowder

fire·ball *n* **1** : ball of fire **2** : brilliant meteor

fire·boat *n* : boat equipped for fighting fire

fire·box *n* **1** : chamber (as of a furnace) that contains a fire **2** : fire-alarm box

fire·break *n* : cleared land for checking a forest fire

fire·bug *n* : person who deliberately sets destructive fires

fire·crack·er *n* : small firework that makes noise

fire·fight·er \'fīr,fītər\ *n* : a person who fights fires

fire·fly *n* : night-flying beetle that produces a soft light

fire·place *n* : opening made in a chimney to hold an open fire

fire·plug *n* : hydrant

fire·side *n* **1** : place near the fire or hearth **2** : home ∼ *adj* : having an informal quality

fire·trap *n* : place apt to catch on fire

fire·work *n* : device that explodes to produce noise or a display of light

¹**firm** \'fərm\ *adj* **1** : securely fixed in place **2** : strong or vigorous **3** : not subject to change **4** : resolute ∼ *vb* : make or become firm — **firm·ly** *adv* — **firm·ness** *n*

²**firm** *n* : business enterprise

fir·ma·ment \'fərməmənt\ *n* : sky

first \'fərst\ *adj* **1** : being number one **2** : foremost ∼ *adv* **1** : before any other **2** : for the first time ∼ *n* **1** : number one **2** : one that is first — **first class** *n* — **first–class** *adj or adv* — **first·ly** *adv* — **first–rate** *adj or adv*

first aid *n* : emergency care

first lieutenant *n* : commissioned officer ranking next below a captain

first sergeant *n* **1** : noncommissioned officer serving as the chief assistant to the commander of a military unit **2** : rank in the army below a sergeant major and in the marine corps below a master gunnery sergeant

firth \'fərth\ *n* : estuary

fis·cal \'fiskəl\ *adj* : relating to money — **fis·cal·ly** *adv*

fish \'fish\ *n, pl* **fish** *or* **fish·es** : water animal with fins, gills, and usu. scales ∼ *vb* **1** : try to catch fish **2** : grope — **fish·er** *n* — **fish·hook** *n* — **fish·ing** *n*

fish·er·man \-mən\ *n* : one who fishes

fish·ery \'fishərē\ *n, pl* **-er·ies** : fishing business or a place for this

fishy \'fishē\ *adj* **fish·i·er; -est** **1** : relating to or like fish **2** : questionable

fis·sion \'fishən, 'fizh-\ *n* : splitting of an atomic nucleus — **fis·sion·able** \-ən-əbəl\ *adj*

fis·sure \'fishər\ *n* : crack

fist \'fist\ *n* : hand doubled up — **fist·ed** \'fistəd\ *adj* — **fist·ful** \-,fùl\ *n*

fist·i·cuffs \'fisti,kəfs\ *n pl* : fist fight

¹fit \'fit\ *n* : sudden attack of illness or emotion

²fit *adj* **-tt-** **1** : suitable **2** : qualified **3** : sound in body ～ *vb* **-tt-** **1** : be suitable to **2** : insert or adjust correctly **3** : make room for **4** : supply or equip **5** : belong ～ *n* : state of fitting or being fitted — **fit·ly** *adv* — **fit·ness** *n* — **fit·ter** *n*

fit·ful \'fitfəl\ *adj* : restless — **fit·ful·ly** *adv*

fit·ting *adj* : suitable ～ *n* : a small part

five \'fīv\ *n* **1** : one more than 4 **2** : 5th in a set or series **3** : something having 5 units — **five** *adj or pron*

fix \'fiks\ *vb* **1** : attach **2** : establish **3** : make right **4** : prepare **5** : improperly influence ～ *n* **1** : predicament **2** : determination of location — **fix·er** *n*

fix·a·tion \fik'sāshən\ *n* : obsessive attachment — **fix·ate** \'fik,sāt\ *vb*

fixed \'fikst\ *adj* **1** : stationary **2** : settled — **fixed·ly** \'fikədlē\ *adv* — **fixed·ness** \-nəs\ *n*

fix·ture \'fikschər\ *n* : permanent part of something

fizz \'fiz\ *vb* : make a hissing sound ～ *n* : effervescence

fiz·zle \'fizəl\ *vb* **-zled; -zling** **1** : fizz **2** : fail ～ *n* : failure

fjord \fē'ȯrd\ *n* : inlet of the sea between cliffs

flab \'flab\ *n* : flabby flesh

flab·ber·gast \'flabər,gast\ *vb* : astound

flab·by \'flabē\ *adj* **-bi·er; -est** : not firm — **flab·bi·ness** *n*

flac·cid \'flaksəd, 'flasəd\ *adj* : not firm

¹flag \'flag\ *n* : flat stone

²flag *n* **1** : fabric that is a symbol (as of a country) **2** : something used to signal ～ *vb* **-gg-** : signal with a flag — **flag·pole** *n* — **flag·staff** *n*

³flag *vb* **-gg-** : lose strength or spirit

flag·el·late \'flajə,lāt\ *vb* **-lated; -lat·ing** : whip — **flag·el·la·tion** \,flajə'lāshən\ *n*

flag·on \'flagən\ *n* : container for liquids

fla·grant \'flāgrənt\ *adj* : conspicuously bad — **fla·grant·ly** *adv*

flag·ship *n* : ship carrying a commander

flag·stone *n* : flag

flail \'flāl\ *n* : tool for threshing grain ～ *vb* : beat with or as if with a flail

flair \'flar\ *n* : natural aptitude

flak \'flak\ *n, pl* **flak** **1** : antiaircraft fire **2** : criticism

flake \'flāk\ *n* : small flat piece ～ *vb* **flaked; flak·ing** : separate or form into flakes

flam·boy·ant \flam'bȯiənt\ *adj* : showy — **flam·boy·ance** \-əns\ *n* — **flam·boy·ant·ly** *adv*

flame \'flām\ *n* **1** : glowing part of a fire **2** : state of combustion **3** : burning passion — **flame** *vb* — **flam·ing** *adj*

fla·min·go \flə'miŋgō\ *n, pl* **-gos** : long-legged long-necked tropical water bird

flam·ma·ble \'flaməbəl\ *adj* : easily ignited

flange \'flanj\ *n* : rim

flank \'flaŋk\ *n* : side of something ∼ *vb* **1** : attack or go around the side of **2** : be at the side of

flan·nel \'flanəl\ *n* : soft napped fabric

flap \'flap\ *n* **1** : slap **2** : something flat that hangs loose ∼ *vb* **-pp-** **1** : move (wings) up and down **2** : swing back and forth noisily

flap·jack \-ˌjak\ *n* : pancake

flare \'flar\ *vb* **flared; flar·ing** : become suddenly bright or excited ∼ *n* : blaze of light

flash \'flash\ *vb* **1** : give off a sudden flame or burst of light **2** : appear or pass suddenly ∼ *n* **1** : sudden burst of light or inspiration **2** : instant ∼ *adj* : coming suddenly

flash·light *n* : small battery-operated light

flashy \'flashē\ *adj* **flash·i·er; -est** : showy — **flash·i·ly** *adv* — **flash·i·ness** *n*

flask \'flask\ *n* : flattened bottle

flat \'flat\ *adj* **-tt-** **1** : smooth **2** : broad and thin **3** : definite **4** : uninteresting **5** : deflated **6** : below the true pitch ∼ *n* **1** : level surface of land **2** : flat note in music **3** : apartment **4** : deflated tire ∼ *adv* **-tt-** **1** : exactly **2** : below the true pitch ∼ *vb* **-tt-** : make flat — **flat·ly** *adv* — **flat·ness** *n* — **flat·ten** \-ᵊn\ *vb*

flat·car *n* : railroad car without sides

flat·fish *n* : flattened fish with both eyes on the upper side

flat·foot *n, pl* **flat·feet** : foot condition in which the arch is flattened — **flat–foot·ed** *adj*

flat–out *adj* **1** : being maximum effort or speed **2** : downright

flat·ter \'flatər\ *vb* **1** : praise insincerely **2** : judge or represent too favorably — **flat·ter·er** *n* — **flat·tery** \'flatərē\ *n*

flat·u·lent \'flachələnt\ *adj* : full of gas — **flat·u·lence** \-ləns\ *n*

flat·ware *n* : eating utensils

flaunt \'flȯnt\ *vb* : display ostentatiously — **flaunt** *n*

fla·vor \'flāvər\ *n* **1** : quality that affects the sense of taste **2** : something that adds flavor

~ *vb* : give flavor to — **fla-vor-ful** *adj* — **fla-vor-ing** *n* — **fla-vor-less** *adj*

flaw \'flȯ\ *n* : fault — **flaw-less** *adj* — **flaw-less-ly** *adv* — **flaw-less-ness** *n*

flax \'flaks\ *n* : plant from which linen is made

flax-en \'flaksən\ *adj* : made of or like flax

flay \'flā\ *vb* **1** : strip off the skin of **2** : criticize harshly

flea \'flē\ *n* : leaping blood-sucking insect

fleck \'flek\ *vb or n* : streak or spot

fledg-ling \'flejliŋ\ *n* : young bird

flee \'flē\ *vb* **fled** \'fled\; **flee-ing** : run away

fleece \'flēs\ *n* : sheep's wool ~ *vb* **fleeced; fleec-ing 1** : shear **2** : get money from dishonestly — **fleecy** *adj*

¹fleet \'flēt\ *vb* : pass rapidly ~ *adj* : swift — **fleet-ing** *adj* — **fleet-ness** *n*

²fleet *n* : group of ships

fleet admiral *n* : commissioned officer of the highest rank in the navy

flesh \'flesh\ *n* **1** : soft parts of an animal's body **2** : soft plant tissue (as fruit pulp) — **fleshed** \'flesht\ *adj* — **fleshy** *adj* — **flesh out** *vb* : make fuller

flesh-ly \'fleshlē\ *adj* : sensual

flew *past of* FLY

flex \'fleks\ *vb* : bend

flex-i-ble \'fleksəbəl\ *adj* **1** : capable of being flexed **2** : adaptable — **flex-i-bil-i-ty** \ˌfleksə'bilətē\ *n* — **flex-i-bly** \-səblē\ *adv*

flick \'flik\ *n* : light jerky stroke ~ *vb* **1** : strike lightly **2** : flutter

flick-er \'flikər\ *vb* **1** : waver **2** : burn unsteadily ~ *n* **1** : sudden movement **2** : wavering light

fli-er \'flīər\ *n* **1** : aviator **2** : advertising circular

¹flight \'flīt\ *n* **1** : act or instance of flying **2** : ability to fly **3** : a passing through air or space **4** : series of stairs — **flight-less** *adj*

²flight *n* : act or instance of running away

flighty \-ē\ *adj* **flight-i-er; -est** : capricious or silly — **flight-i-ness** *n*

flim-flam \'flimˌflam\ *n* : trickery

flim-sy \-zē\ *adj* **-si-er; -est 1** : not strong or well made **2** : not believable — **flim-si-ly** *adv* — **flim-si-ness** *n*

flinch \'flinch\ *vb* : shrink from pain

fling \'fliŋ\ *vb* **flung** \'fləŋ\; **fling-ing 1** : move brusquely **2** : throw ~ *n* **1** : act or instance of flinging **2** : attempt **3** : period of self-indulgence

flint \\'flint\ *n* : hard quartz that gives off sparks when struck with steel — **flinty** *adj*

flip \\'flip\ *vb* **-pp-** **1** : cause to turn over quickly or many times **2** : move with a quick push ~ *adj* : insolent — **flip** *n*

flip·pant \\'flipənt\ *adj* : not serious enough — **flip·pan·cy** \-ənsē\ *n*

flip·per \\'flipər\ *n* : paddlelike limb (as of a seal) for swimming

flirt \\'flərt\ *vb* **1** : be playfully romantic **2** : show casual interest ~ *n* : one who flirts — **flir·ta·tion** \ˌflər'tāshən\ *n* — **flir·ta·tious** \-shəs\ *adj*

flit \\'flit\ *vb* **-tt-** : dart

float \\'flōt\ *n* **1** : something that floats **2** : vehicle carrying an exhibit ~ *vb* **1** : rest on or in a fluid without sinking **2** : wander **3** : finance by issuing stock or bonds — **float·er** *n*

flock \\'fläk\ *n* : group of animals (as birds) or people ~ *vb* : gather or move as a group

floe \\'flō\ *n* : mass of floating ice

flog \\'fläg\ *vb* **-gg-** : beat with a rod or whip — **flog·ger** *n*

flood \\'fləd\ *n* **1** : great flow of water over the land **2** : overwhelming volume ~ *vb* : cover or fill esp. with water — **flood·wa·ter** *n*

floor \\'flōr\ *n* **1** : bottom of a room on which one stands **2** : story of a building **3** : lower limit ~ *vb* **1** : furnish with a floor **2** : knock down **3** : amaze — **floor·board** *n* — **floor·ing** \-iŋ\ *n*

floo·zy, floo·zie \\'flüzē\ *n, pl* **-zies** : promiscuous young woman

flop \\'fläp\ *vb* **-pp-** **1** : flap **2** : slump heavily **3** : fail — **flop** *n*

flop·py \\'fläpē\ *adj* **-pi·er; -est** : soft and flexible

flo·ra \\'flōrə\ *n* : plants or plant life of a region

flo·ral \\'flōrəl\ *adj* : relating to flowers

flor·id \\'flōrəd\ *adj* **1** : very flowery in style **2** : reddish

flo·rist \\'flōrist\ *n* : flower dealer

floss \\'fläs\ *n* **1** : soft thread for embroidery **2** : thread used to clean between teeth — **floss** *vb*

flo·ta·tion \flō'tāshən\ *n* : process or instance of floating

flo·til·la \flō'tilə\ *n* : small fleet

flot·sam \\'flätsəm\ *n* : floating wreckage

¹**flounce** \\'flaůns\ *vb* **flounced; flounc·ing** : move with exag-

gerated jerky motions — **flounce** *n*

²**flounce** *n* : fabric border or wide ruffle

¹**floun·der** \'flaundər\ *n, pl* **flounder** *or* **flounders** : flatfish

²**flounder** *vb* **1** : struggle for footing **2** : proceed clumsily

flour \'flauər\ *n* : finely ground meal ~ *vb* : coat with flour — **floury** *adj*

flour·ish \'flərish\ *vb* **1** : thrive **2** : wave threateningly ~ *n* **1** : embellishment **2** : fanfare **3** : wave **4** : showiness of action

flout \'flaut\ *vb* : treat with disdain

flow \'flō\ *vb* **1** : move in a stream **2** : proceed smoothly and readily ~ *n* : uninterrupted stream

flow·er \'flauər\ *n* **1** : showy plant shoot that bears seeds **2** : state of flourishing ~ *vb* **1** : produce flowers **2** : flourish — **flow·ered** *adj* — **flow·er·less** *adj* — **flow·er·pot** *n* — **flow·ery** \-ē\ *adj*

flown *past part of* FLY

flu \'flü\ *n* **1** : influenza **2** : minor virus ailment

flub \'fləb\ *vb* **-bb-** : bungle — **flub** *n*

fluc·tu·ate \'fləkchə,wāt\ *vb* **-at·ed; -at·ing** : change rapidly esp. up and down — **fluc-**

tu·a·tion \,fləkchə'wāshən\ *n*

flue \'flü\ *n* : smoke duct

flu·ent \'flüənt\ *adj* : speaking with ease — **flu·en·cy** \-ənsē\ *n* — **flu·ent·ly** *adv*

fluff \'fləf\ *n* **1** : something soft and light **2** : blunder ~ *vb* **1** : make fluffy **2** : make a mistake — **fluffy** \-ē\ *adj*

flu·id \'flüəd\ *adj* : flowing ~ *n* : substance that can flow — **flu·id·i·ty** \flü'idətē\ *n* — **flu·id·ly** *adv*

fluid ounce *n* : unit of liquid measure equal to ¹⁄₁₆ pint

fluke \'flük\ *n* : stroke of luck

flume \'flüm\ *n* : channel for water

flung *past of* FLING

flunk \'fləŋk\ *vb* : fail in school work

flun·ky, flun·key \'fləŋkē\ *n, pl* **-kies** *or* **-keys** : lackey

flu·o·res·cence \,flur'es°ns, ,flor-\ *n* : emission of light after initial absorption — **flu·o·resce** \-'es\ *vb* — **flu·o·res·cent** \-'es°nt\ *adj*

flu·o·ri·date \'florə,dāt, 'flur-\ *vb* **-dat·ed; -dat·ing** : add fluoride to — **flu·o·ri·da·tion** \,florə'dāshən, ,flur-\ *n*

flu·o·ride \'flor,īd, 'flur-\ *n* : compound of fluorine

flu·o·rine \'flur,ēn, -ən\ *n* : toxic gaseous chemical element

flu·o·ro·car·bon \ˌflȯrō'kär-bən, ˌflu̇r-\ *n* : compound containing fluorine and carbon

flu·o·ro·scope \'flu̇rəˌskōp\ *n* : instrument for internal examination — **flu·o·ro·scop·ic** \ˌflu̇rə'skäpik\ *adj* — **flu·o·ros·co·py** \ˌflu̇r'äskəpē\ *n*

flur·ry \'flərē\ *n, pl* **-ries** **1** : light snowfall **2** : bustle **3** : brief burst of activity — **flurry** *vb*

¹**flush** \'fləsh\ *vb* : cause (a bird) to fly from cover

²**flush** *n* **1** : sudden flow (as of water) **2** : surge of emotion **3** : blush ~ *vb* **1** : blush **2** : wash out with a rush of liquid ~ *adj* **1** : filled to overflowing **2** : of a reddish healthy color **3** : smooth or level **4** : abutting — **flush** *adv*

³**flush** *n* : cards of the same suit

flus·ter \'fləstər\ *vb* : upset — **fluster** *n*

flute \'flüt\ *n* **1** : pipelike musical instrument **2** : groove — **flut·ed** *adj* — **flut·ing** *n* — **flut·ist** \-ist\ *n*

flut·ter \'flətər\ *vb* **1** : flap the wings rapidly **2** : move with quick wavering or flapping motions **3** : behave in an agitated manner ~ *n* **1** : a fluttering **2** : state of confusion — **flut·tery** \-ərē\ *adj*

flux \'fləks\ *n* : state of continuous change

¹**fly** \'flī\ *vb* **flew** \'flü\; **flown** \'flōn\; **fly·ing** **1** : move through the air with wings **2** : float or soar **3** : flee **4** : move or pass swiftly **5** : operate an airplane

²**fly** *n, pl* **flies** : garment closure

³**fly** *n, pl* **flies** : winged insect

fly·er *var of* FLIER

fly·pa·per *n* : sticky paper for catching flies

fly·speck *n* **1** : speck of fly dung **2** : something tiny

fly·wheel *n* : rotating wheel that regulates the speed of machinery

foal \'fōl\ *n* : young horse — **foal** *vb*

foam \'fōm\ *n* **1** : mass of bubbles on top of a liquid **2** : material of cellular form ~ *vb* : form foam — **foamy** *adj*

fob \'fäb\ *n* : short chain for a pocket watch

fo'·c'sle *var of* FORECASTLE

fo·cus \'fōkəs\ *n, pl* **-ci** \-ˌsī\ **1** : point at which reflected or refracted rays meet **2** : adjustment (as of eyeglasses) for clear vision **3** : central point ~ *vb* : bring to a focus — **fo·cal** \-kəl\ *adj* — **fo·cal·ly** *adv*

fod·der \'fädər\ *n* : food for livestock

foe \'fō\ *n* : enemy

fog \'fȯg, 'fäg\ *n* **1** : fine particles of water suspended near the ground **2** : mental confusion ~ *vb* **-gg-** : obscure or be obscured with fog — **fog·gy** *adj*

fog·horn *n* : warning horn sounded in a fog

fo·gy \\'fōgē\\ *n, pl* **-gies** : person with old-fashioned ideas

foi·ble \\'fȯibəl\\ *n* : minor character fault

¹**foil** \\'fȯil\\ *vb* : defeat ~ *n* : light fencing sword

²**foil** *n* **1** : thin sheet of metal **2** : one that sets off another by contrast

foist \\'fȯist\\ *vb* : force another to accept

¹**fold** \\'fōld\\ *n* **1** : enclosure for sheep **2** : group with a common interest

²**fold** *vb* **1** : lay one part over another **2** : embrace ~ *n* : part folded

fold·er \\'fōldər\\ *n* **1** : one that folds **2** : circular **3** : folded cover or envelope for papers

fol·de·rol \\'fäldə,räl\\ *n* : nonsense

fo·liage \\'fōlēij, -lij\\ *n* : plant leaves

fo·lio \\'fōlē,ō\\ *n, pl* **-li·os** : sheet of paper folded once

folk \\'fōk\\ *n, pl* **folk** *or* **folks** **1** : people in general **2** *folks pl* : one's family ~ *adj* : relating to the common people

folk·lore *n* : customs and traditions of a people — **folk·lor·ist** *n*

folksy \\'fōksē\\ *adj* **folks·i·er; -est** : friendly and informal

fol·li·cle \\'fälikəl\\ *n* : small anatomical cavity or gland

fol·low \\'fälō\\ *vb* **1** : go or come after **2** : pursue **3** : obey **4** : proceed along **5** : keep one's attention fixed on **6** : result from — **fol·low·er** *n*

fol·low·ing \\'fäləwiŋ\\ *adj* : next ~ *n* : group of followers ~ *prep* : after

fol·ly \\'fälē\\ *n, pl* **-lies** : foolishness

fo·ment \\fō'ment\\ *vb* : incite

fond \\'fänd\\ *adj* **1** : strongly attracted **2** : affectionate **3** : dear — **fond·ly** *adv* — **fond·ness** *n*

fon·dle \\'fändᵊl\\ *vb* **-dled; -dling** : touch lovingly

fon·due \\fän'dü, -'dyü\\ *n* : preparation of melted cheese

font \\'fänt\\ *n* **1** : baptismal basin **2** : fountain

food \\'füd\\ *n* : material eaten to sustain life

fool \\'fül\\ *n* **1** : stupid person **2** : jester ~ *vb* **1** : waste time **2** : meddle **3** : deceive — **fool·ery** \\'fülərē\\ *n* — **fool·ish** \\'fülish\\ *adj* — **fool·ish·ly** *adv* — **fool·ish·ness** *n* — **fool·proof** *adj*

fool·har·dy \\'fül,härdē\\ *adj* : rash — **fool·har·di·ness** *n*

foot \\'fu̇t\\ *n, pl* **feet** \\'fēt\\ **1** : end part of a leg **2** : unit of

length equal to ⅓ yard **3** : unit of verse meter **4** : bottom —
foot·age \-ij\ *n* — **foot·ed** *adj* — **foot·path** *n* — **foot·print** *n* — **foot·race** *n* — **foot·rest** *n* — **foot·wear** *n*

foot·ball *n* : ball game played by 2 teams on a rectangular field

foot·bridge *n* : bridge for pedestrians

foot·hill *n* : hill at the foot of higher hills

foot·hold *n* : support for the feet

foot·ing *n* **1** : foothold **2** : basis

foot·lights *n pl* : stage lights along the floor

foot·lock·er *n* : small trunk

foot·loose *adj* : having no ties

foot·man \'fu̇tmən\ *n* : male servant

foot·note *n* : note at the bottom of a page

foot·step *n* **1** : step **2** : distance covered by a step **3** : footprint

foot·stool *n* : stool to support the feet

foot·work *n* : skillful movement of the feet (as in boxing)

fop \'fäp\ *n* : dandy — **fop·pery** \-ərē\ *n* — **fop·pish** *adj*

for \'fȯr\ *prep* **1** — used to show preparation or purpose **2** : because of **3** — used to show a recipient **4** : in support of **5** : so as to support or help cure **6** : so as to be equal to **7** : concerning **8** : through the period of ~ *conj* : because

for·age \'fȯrij\ *n* : food for animals ~ *vb* **-aged; -ag·ing 1** : hunt food **2** : search for provisions

for·ay \'fȯr͵ā\ *n or vb* : raid

¹**for·bear** \fȯr'bar\ *vb* **-bore** \-'bōr\; **-borne** \-'bōrn\; **-bear·ing 1** : refrain from **2** : be patient — **for·bear·ance** \-'barəns\ *n*

²**forbear** *var of* FOREBEAR

for·bid \fər'bid\ *vb* **-bade** \-'bad, -'bād\ *or* **-bad** \-'bad\; **-bid·den** \-'bid°n\; **-bid·ding 1** : prohibit **2** : order not to do something

for·bid·ding *adj* : tending to discourage

force \'fōrs\ *n* **1** : exceptional strength or energy **2** : military strength **3** : body (as of persons) available for a purpose **4** : violence **5** : influence (as a push or pull) that causes motion ~ *vb* **forced; forc·ing 1** : compel **2** : gain against resistance **3** : break open — **force·ful** \-fəl\ *adj* — **force·ful·ly** *adv* — **in force 1** : in great numbers **2** : valid

for·ceps \'fȯrsəps\ *n, pl* **forceps** : surgical instrument for grasping objects

forc·ible \'fōrsəbəl\ *adj* **1** : done by force **2** : showing force — **forc·i·bly** \-blē\ *adv*

ford \'fōrd\ *n* : place to wade across a stream ~ *vb* : wade across

fore \'fōr\ *adv* : in or toward the front ~ *adj* : being or coming before in time, place, or order ~ *n* : front

fore–and–aft *adj* : lengthwise

fore·arm \'fōr,ärm\ *n* : part of the arm between the elbow and the wrist

fore·bear \'fōr,bar\ *n* : ancestor

fore·bod·ing \fōr'bōdiŋ\ *n* : premonition of disaster — **fore·bod·ing** *adj*

fore·cast \'fōr,kast\ *vb* **-cast; -cast·ing** : predict — **forecast** *n* — **fore·cast·er** *n*

fore·cas·tle \'fōksəl\ *n* : forward part of a ship

fore·close \fōr'klōz\ *vb* : take legal measures to terminate a mortgage — **fore·clo·sure** \-'klōzhər\ *n*

fore·fa·ther \'fōr,fäthər\ *n* : ancestor

fore·fin·ger \'fōr,fiŋgər\ *n* : finger next to the thumb

fore·foot \'fōr,fut\ *n* : front foot of a quadruped

fore·front \'fōr,frənt\ *n* : foremost position or place

¹fore·go \fōr'gō\ *vb* **-went; -gone; -go·ing** : precede

²forego *var of* FORGO

fore·go·ing *adj* : preceding

fore·gone *adj* : determined in advance

fore·ground \'fōr,graund\ *n* : part of a scene nearest the viewer

fore·hand \'fōr,hand\ *n* : stroke (as in tennis) made with the palm of the hand turned forward — **forehand** *adj*

fore·head \'fōrəd, 'fōr,hed\ *n* : part of the face above the eyes

for·eign \'fōrən\ *adj* **1** : situated outside a place or country and esp. one's own country **2** : belonging to a different place or country **3** : not pertinent **4** : related to or dealing with other nations — **for·eign·er** \-ər\ *n*

fore·know \fōr'nō\ *vb* **-knew; -known; -know·ing** : know beforehand — **fore·knowl·edge** *n*

fore·leg \'fōr,leg\ *n* : front leg

fore·lock \'fōr,läk\ *n* : front lock of hair

fore·man \'fōrmən\ *n* **1** : spokesman of a jury **2** : workman in charge

fore·most \'fōr,mōst\ *adj* : first in time, place, or order — **foremost** *adv*

fore·noon \'fōr,nün\ *n* : morning

fo·ren·sic \fə'rensik\ *adj* : relating to courts or public speaking or debate

fo·ren·sics \-siks\ *n pl* : art or study of speaking or debating

fore·or·dain \ˌfōrȯr'dān\ *vb* : decree beforehand

fore·quar·ter \'fōrˌkwȯrtər\ *n* : front half on one side of the body of a quadruped

fore·run·ner \'fōrˌrənər\ *n* : one that goes before

fore·see \fōr'sē\ *vb* **-saw; -seen; -see·ing** : see or realize beforehand — **fore·see·able** *adj*

fore·shad·ow \fōrˌshadō\ *vb* : hint or suggest beforehand

fore·sight \'fōrˌsīt\ *n* : care or provision for the future — **fore·sight·ed** *adj* — **fore·sight·ed·ness** *n*

for·est \'fȯrəst\ *n* : large thick growth of trees and underbrush — **for·est·ed** \'fȯrəstəd\ *adj* — **for·est·er** \-əstər\ *n* — **for·est·land** \-ˌland\ *n* — **for·est·ry** \-əstrē\ *n*

fore·stall \fōr'stȯl, fȯr-\ *vb* : prevent by acting in advance

foreswear *var of* FORSWEAR

fore·taste \'fōrˌtāst\ *n* : advance indication or notion ~ *vb* : anticipate

fore·tell \fōr'tel\ *vb* **-told; -tell·ing** : predict

fore·thought \'fōrˌthȯt\ *n* : foresight

for·ev·er \fȯr'evər\ *adv* **1** : for a limitless time **2** : always

for·ev·er·more \-ˌevər'mōr\ *adv* : forever

fore·warn \fōr'wȯrn\ *vb* : warn beforehand

fore·word \'fōrwərd\ *n* : preface

for·feit \'fȯrfət\ *n* : something forfeited ~ *vb* : lose or lose the right to by an error or crime — **for·fei·ture** \-fəˌchȯr\ *n*

¹forge \'fōrj\ *n* : smithy ~ *vb* **forged; forg·ing** **1** : form (metal) by heating and hammering **2** : imitate falsely esp. to defraud — **forg·er** *n* — **forg·ery** \-ərē\ *n*

²forge *vb* **forged; forg·ing** : move ahead steadily

for·get \fər'get\ *vb* **-got** \-'gät\; **-got·ten** \-'gät°n\ *or* **-got; -get·ting** **1** : be unable to think of or recall **2** : fail to think of at the proper time — **for·get·ta·ble** *adj* — **for·get·ful** \-fəl\ *adj* — **for·get·ful·ly** *adv*

forget–me–not *n* : small herb with blue or white flowers

for·give \fər'giv\ *vb* **-gave** \-'gāv\; **-giv·en** \-'givən\; **-giv·ing** : pardon — **for·giv·able** *adj* — **for·give·ness** *n*

for·giv·ing *adj* **1** : able to forgive **2** : allowing room for error or weakness

for·go, fore·go \fōr'gō\ *vb* **-went; -gone; -go·ing** : do without

fork \'fȯrk\ *n* **1** : implement with prongs for lifting, holding, or digging **2** : forked part **3** : a dividing into branches or a place where something branches ~ *vb* **1** : divide into branches **2** : move with a fork — **forked** \'fȯrkt, 'fȯrkəd\ *adj*

fork·lift *n* : machine for lifting with steel fingers

for·lorn \fər'lȯrn\ *adj* **1** : deserted **2** : wretched — **for·lorn·ly** *adv*

form \'fȯrm\ *n* **1** : shape **2** : set way of doing or saying something **3** : document with blanks to be filled in **4** : manner of performing with respect to what is expected **5** : mold **6** : kind or variety **7** : one of the ways in which a word is changed to show difference in use ~ *vb* **1** : give form or shape to **2** : train **3** : develop **4** : constitute — **for·ma·tive** \'fȯrmətiv\ *adj* — **form·less** \-ləs\ *adj*

for·mal \'fȯrməl\ *adj* : following established custom ~ *n* : formal social event — **for·mal·i·ty** \fȯr'malətē\ *n* — **for·mal·ize** \'fȯrmə‚līz\ *vb* — **for·mal·ly** *adv*

form·al·de·hyde \fȯr'maldə‚hīd\ *n* : colorless pungent gas used as a preservative and disinfectant

for·mat \'fȯr‚mat\ *n* : general style or arrangement of something — **format** *vb*

for·ma·tion \fȯr'māshən\ *n* **1** : a giving form to something **2** : something formed **3** : arrangement

for·mer \'fȯrmər\ *adj* : coming before in time — **for·mer·ly** *adv*

for·mi·da·ble \'fȯrmədəbəl, fȯr'mid-\ *adj* **1** : causing fear or dread **2** : very difficult — **for·mi·da·bly** \-blē\ *adv*

for·mu·la \'fȯrmyələ\ *n, pl* **-las** *or* **-lae** \-‚lē, -‚lī\ **1** : set form of words for ceremonial use **2** : recipe **3** : milk mixture for a baby **4** : group of symbols or figures briefly expressing information **5** : set form or method

for·mu·late \-‚lāt\ *vb* **-lat·ed; -lat·ing** : design, devise — **for·mu·la·tion** \‚fȯrmyə'lāshən\ *n*

for·ni·ca·tion \‚fȯrnə'kāshən\ *n* : illicit sexual intercourse — **for·ni·cate** \'fȯrnə‚kāt\ *vb* — **for·ni·ca·tor** \-‚kātər\ *n*

for·sake \fər'sāk\ *vb* **-sook** \-'sùk\; **-sak·en** \-'sākən\; **-sak·ing** : renounce completely

for·swear \fȯr'swar\ *vb* **-swore; -sworn; -swear·ing**

1 : renounce under oath **2** : perjure

for·syth·ia \fər'sithēə\ *n* : shrub grown for its yellow flowers

fort \'fōrt\ *n* **1** : fortified place **2** : permanent army post

forte \'fōrt, 'fȯr‚tā\ *n* : something at which a person excels

forth \'fōrth\ *adv* : forward

forth·com·ing *adj* **1** : coming or available soon **2** : open and direct

forth·right *adj* : direct — **forth·right·ly** *adv* — **forth·right·ness** *n*

forth·with *adv* : immediately

for·ti·fy \'fȯrtə‚fī\ *vb* **-fied; -fy·ing** : make strong — **for·ti·fi·ca·tion** \‚fȯrtəfə'kāshən\ *n*

for·ti·tude \'fȯrtə‚tüd, -‚tyüd\ *n* : ability to endure

fort·night \'fōrt‚nīt\ *n* : 2 weeks — **fort·night·ly** *adj or adv*

for·tress \'fȯrtrəs\ *n* : strong fort

for·tu·itous \fȯr'tüətəs, -'tyü-\ *adj* : accidental

for·tu·nate \'fȯrchənət\ *adj* **1** : coming by good luck **2** : lucky — **for·tu·nate·ly** *adv*

for·tune \'fȯrchən\ *n* **1** : prosperity attained partly through luck **2** : good or bad luck **3** : destiny **4** : wealth

for·tune–tel·ler \-‚telər\ *n* : one who foretells a person's future — **for·tune–tell·ing** \-iŋ\ *n or adj*

for·ty \'fȯrtē\ *n, pl* **forties** : 4 times 10 — **for·ti·eth** \-ēəth\ *adj or n* — **forty** *adj or pron*

fo·rum \'fōrəm\ *n, pl* **-rums 1** : Roman marketplace **2** : medium for open discussion

for·ward \'fȯrwərd\ *adj* **1** : being near or at or belonging to the front **2** : brash ~ *adv* : toward what is in front ~ *n* : player near the front of his team ~ *vb* **1** : help onward **2** : send on — **for·ward·er** \-wərdər\ *n* — **for·ward·ness** *n*

for·wards \'fȯrwərdz\ *adv* : forward

fos·sil \'fäsəl\ *n* : preserved trace of an ancient plant or animal ~ *adj* : being or originating from a fossil — **fos·sil·ize** *vb*

fos·ter \'fȯstər\ *adj* : being, having, or relating to substitute parents ~ *vb* : help to grow or develop

fought *past of* FIGHT

foul \'faůl\ *adj* **1** : offensive **2** : clogged with dirt **3** : abusive **4** : wet and stormy **5** : unfair ~ *n* : a breaking of the rules in a game ~ *adv* : foully ~ *vb* **1** : make or become foul or filthy **2** : tangle — **foul·ly** *adv* —

foul·mouthed \-'maüth̲d, -'maütht\ *adj* — **foul·ness** *n*

fou·lard \fu̇'lärd\ *n* : light-weight silk

foul–up *n* : error or state of confusion — **foul up** *vb* : bungle

¹**found** \'fau̇nd\ *past of* FIND

²**found** *vb* : establish — **found·er** *n*

foun·da·tion \faun'dāshən\ *n* **1** : act of founding **2** : basis for something **3** : endowed institution **4** : supporting structure — **foun·da·tion·al** \-shənəl\ *adj*

foun·der \'fau̇ndər\ *vb* : sink

found·ling \'faundliŋ\ *n* : abandoned infant that is found

found·ry \'faundrē\ *n, pl* **-dries** : place where metal is cast

fount \'faunt\ *n* : fountain

foun·tain \'fauntᵊn\ *n* **1** : spring of water **2** : source **3** : artificial jet of water

four \'fōr\ *n* **1** : one more than 3 **2** : 4th in a set or series **3** : something having 4 units — **four** *adj or pron*

four·fold *adj* : quadruple — **four·fold** *adv*

four·score *adj* : 80

four·some \'fōrsəm\ *n* : group of 4

four·teen \fōr'tēn\ *n* : one more than 13 — **fourteen** *adj or pron* — **four·teenth** \-'tēnth\ *adj or n*

fourth \'fōrth\ *n* **1** : one that is 4th **2** : one of 4 equal parts of something — **fourth** *adj or adv*

fowl \'faul\ *n, pl* **fowl** *or* **fowls** **1** : bird **2** : chicken

fox \'fäks\ *n, pl* **fox·es** **1** : small mammal related to wolves **2** : clever person ～ *vb* : trick — **foxy** \'fäksē\ *adj*

fox·glove *n* : flowering plant that provides digitalis

fox·hole \'fäks,hōl\ *n* : pit for protection against enemy fire

foy·er \'fȯiər, 'fȯi,yā\ *n* : entrance hallway

fra·cas \'frākəs, 'frak-\ *n, pl* **-cas·es** \-əsəz\ : brawl

frac·tion \'frakshən\ *n* **1** : number indicating one or more equal parts of a whole **2** : portion — **frac·tion·al** \-shənəl\ *adj* — **frac·tion·al·ly** *adv*

frac·tious \'frakshəs\ *adj* : hard to control

frac·ture \'frakchər\ *n* : a breaking of something — **fracture** *vb*

frag·ile \'frajəl, -,īl\ *adj* : easily broken — **fra·gil·i·ty** \frə-'jilətē\ *n*

frag·ment \'fragmənt\ *n* : part broken off ～ \-,ment\ *vb* : break into parts — **frag·men·tary** \'fragmən,terē\ *adj* —

frag·men·ta·tion \ˌfragmən-ˈtāshən, -ˌmen-\ *n*

fra·grant \ˈfrāgrənt\ *adj* : sweet-smelling — **fra·grance** \-grəns\ *n* — **fra·grant·ly** *adv*

frail \ˈfrāl\ *adj* : weak or delicate — **frail·ty** \-tē\ *n*

frame \ˈfrām\ *vb* **framed; fram·ing 1** : plan **2** : formulate **3** : construct or arrange **4** : enclose in a frame **5** : make appear guilty ∼ *n* **1** : makeup of the body **2** : supporting or enclosing structure **3** : state or disposition (as of mind) — **frame·work** *n*

franc \ˈfraŋk\ *n* : monetary unit (as of France)

fran·chise \ˈfranˌchīz\ *n* **1** : special privilege **2** : the right to vote — **fran·chi·see** \ˌfranˌchīˈzē, -chə-\ *n*

fran·gi·ble \ˈfranjəbəl\ *adj* : breakable — **fran·gi·bil·i·ty** \ˌfranjəˈbilətē\ *n*

¹frank \ˈfraŋk\ *adj* : direct and sincere — **frank·ly** *adv* — **frank·ness** *n*

²frank *vb* : mark (mail) with a sign showing it can be mailed free ∼ *n* : sign on franked mail

frank·furt·er \ˈfraŋkfərtər, -ˌfərt-\, **frank·furt** \-fərt\ *n* : cooked sausage

frank·in·cense \ˈfraŋkənˌsens\ *n* : incense resin

fran·tic \ˈfrantik\ *adj* : wildly excited — **fran·ti·cal·ly** \-iklē\ *adv*

fra·ter·nal \frəˈtərnᵊl\ *adj* **1** : brotherly **2** : of a fraternity — **fra·ter·nal·ly** *adv*

fra·ter·ni·ty \frəˈtərnətē\ *n, pl* **-ties** : men's student social group

frat·er·nize \ˈfratərˌnīz\ *vb* **-nized; -niz·ing 1** : mingle as friends **2** : associate with members of a hostile group — **frat·er·ni·za·tion** \ˌfratərnəˈzāshən\ *n*

frat·ri·cide \ˈfratrəˌsīd\ *n* : killing of a sibling — **frat·ri·cid·al** \ˌfratrəˈsīdᵊl\ *adj*

fraud \ˈfrȯd\ *n* : trickery — **fraud·u·lent** \ˈfrȯjələnt\ *adj* — **fraud·u·lent·ly** *adv*

fraught \ˈfrȯt\ *adj* : full of or accompanied by something specified

¹fray \ˈfrā\ *n* : fight

²fray *vb* **1** : wear by rubbing **2** : separate the threads of **3** : irritate

fraz·zle \ˈfrazəl\ *vb* **-zled; -zling** : wear out ∼ *n* : exhaustion

freak \ˈfrēk\ *n* **1** : something abnormal or unusual **2** : enthusiast — **freak·ish** *adj* —

freak out *vb* **1** : experience nightmarish hallucinations from drugs **2** : distress or become distressed

freck·le \\'frekəl\ *n* : brown spot on the skin — **freckle** *vb*

free \\'frē\ *adj* **fre·er; fre·est 1** : having liberty or independence **2** : not taxed **3** : given without charge **4** : voluntary **5** : not in use **6** : not fastened ~ *adv* : without charge ~ *vb* **freed; free·ing** : set free — **free** *adv* — **free·born** *adj* — **free·dom** \\'frēdəm\ *n* — **free·ly** *adv*

free·boo·ter \-ˌbütər\ *n* : pirate

free–for–all *n* : fight with no rules

free·load *vb* : live off another's generosity — **free·load·er** *n*

free·stand·ing *adj* : standing without support

free·way \\'frēˌwā\ *n* : expressway

free will *n* : independent power to choose — **free·will** *adj*

freeze \\'frēz\ *vb* **froze** \\'frōz\; **fro·zen** \\'frōzᵊn\; **freez·ing 1** : harden into ice **2** : become chilled **3** : damage by frost **4** : stick fast **5** : become motionless **6** : fix at one stage or level ~ *n* **1** : very cold weather **2** : state of being frozen — **freez·er** *n*

freeze–dry *vb* : preserve by freezing then drying — **freeze–dried** *adj*

freight \\'frāt\ *n* **1** : carrying of goods or payment for this **2** : shipped goods ~ *vb* : load or ship goods — **freigh·ter** *n*

french fry *vb* : fry in deep fat — **french fry** *n*

fre·net·ic \fri'netik\ *adj* : frantic — **fre·net·i·cal·ly** \-iklē\ *adv*

fren·zy \\'frenzē\ *n, pl* **-zies** : violent agitation — **fren·zied** \-zēd\ *adj*

fre·quen·cy \\'frēkwənsē\ *n, pl* **-cies 1** : frequent or regular occurrence **2** : number of cycles or sound waves per second

fre·quent \\'frēkwənt\ *adj* : happening often ~ \frē-'kwent, 'frēkwənt\ *vb* : go to habitually — **fre·quent·er** *n* — **fre·quent·ly** *adv*

fres·co \\'freskō\ *n, pl* **-coes** : painting on fresh plaster

fresh \\'fresh\ *adj* **1** : not salt **2** : pure **3** : not preserved **4** : not stale **5** : like new **6** : insolent — **fres·hen** \-ən\ *vb* — **fresh·ly** *adv* — **fresh·ness** *n*

fresh·et \-ət\ *n* : overflowing stream

fresh·man \-mən\ *n* : first-year student

fresh·wa·ter *n* : water that is not salty

fret \\'fret\ *vb* **-tt- 1** : worry or become irritated **2** : fray **3** : agitate ~ *n* **1** : worn spot **2** : irritation — **fret·ful** \-fəl\ *adj* — **fret·ful·ly** *adv*

fri·a·ble \'frīəbəl\ *adj* : easily pulverized

fri·ar \'frīər\ *n* : member of a religious order

fri·ary \-ē\ *n, pl* **-ar·ies** : monastery of friars

fric·as·see \'frikə‚sē, ‚frikə'-\ *n* : meat stewed in a gravy ∼ *vb* **-seed; -see·ing** : stew in gravy

fric·tion \'frikshən\ *n* **1** : a rubbing between 2 surfaces **2** : clash of opinions — **fric·tion·al** *adj*

Fri·day \'frīdā\ *n* : 6th day of the week

friend \'frend\ *n* : person one likes — **friend·less** \-ləs\ *adj* — **friend·li·ness** \-lēnəs\ *n* — **friend·ly** *adj* — **friend·ship** \-‚ship\ *n*

frieze \'frēz\ *n* : ornamental band around a room

frig·ate \'frigət\ *n* : warship smaller than a destroyer

fright \'frīt\ *n* : sudden fear — **frigh·ten** \-ᵊn\ *vb* — **fright·ful** \-fəl\ *adj* — **fright·ful·ly** *adv* — **fright·ful·ness** *n*

frig·id \'frijəd\ *adj* : intensely cold — **fri·gid·i·ty** \frij'idətē\ *n*

frill \'fril\ *n* **1** : ruffle **2** : pleasing but nonessential addition — **frilly** *adj*

fringe \'frinj\ *n* **1** : ornamental border of short hanging threads or strips **2** : edge — **fringe** *vb*

frisk \'frisk\ *vb* **1** : leap about **2** : search (a person) esp. for weapons

frisky \'friskē\ *adj* **frisk·i·er; -est** : playful — **frisk·i·ly** *adv* — **frisk·i·ness** *n*

¹frit·ter \'fritər\ *n* : fried batter containing fruit or meat

²fritter *vb* : waste little by little

friv·o·lous \'frivələs\ *adj* : not important or serious — **fri·vol·i·ty** \friv'älətē\ *n* — **friv·o·lous·ly** *adv*

frizz \'friz\ *vb* : curl tightly — **frizz** *n* — **frizzy** *adj*

fro \'frō\ *adv* : away

frock \'fräk\ *n* **1** : loose outer garment **2** : dress

frog \'fròg, 'fräg\ *n* **1** : leaping amphibian **2** : hoarseness **3** : ornamental braid fastener **4** : small holder for flowers

frog·man \-‚man, -mən\ *n* : underwater swimmer

frol·ic \'frälik\ *vb* **-icked; -ick·ing** : romp ∼ *n* : fun — **frol·ic·some** \-səm\ *adj*

from \'frəm, 'främ\ *prep* — used to show a starting point

frond \'fränd\ *n* : fern or palm leaf

front \'frənt\ *n* **1** : face **2** : behavior **3** : main side of a building **4** : forward part **5** : boundary between air masses ~ *vb* **1** : have the main side adjacent to something **2** : serve as a front — **fron·tal** \-ᵊl\ *adj*

front·age \'frəntij\ *n* : length of boundary line on a street

fron·tier \ˌfrən'tir\ *n* : outer edge of settled territory — **fron·tiers·man** \-'tirzmən\ *n*

fron·tis·piece \'frəntəˌspēs\ *n* : illustration facing a title page

frost \'frȯst\ *n* **1** : freezing temperature **2** : ice crystals on a surface ~ *vb* **1** : cover with frost **2** : put icing on (a cake) — **frosty** *adj*

frost·bite \-ˌbīt\ *n* : partial freezing of part of the body — **frost·bit·ten** \-ˌbitᵊn\ *adj*

frost·ing *n* : icing

froth \'frȯth\ *n, pl* **froths** \'frȯths, 'frȯthz\ : bubbles on a liquid — **frothy** *adj*

fro·ward \'frōwərd\ *adj* : willful

frown \'fraun\ *vb or n* : scowl

frow·sy, frow·zy \'frauzē\ *adj* **-si·er** *or* **-zi·er; -est** : untidy

froze *past of* FREEZE

frozen *past part of* FREEZE

fru·gal \'frügəl\ *adj* : thrifty — **fru·gal·i·ty** \frü'galətē\ *n* — **fru·gal·ly** *adv*

fruit \'früt\ *n* **1** : usu. edible and sweet part of a seed plant **2** : result ~ *vb* : bear fruit —

fruit·cake *n* — **fruit·ed** \-əd\ *adj* — **fruit·ful** *adj* — **fruit·ful·ness** *n* — **fruit·less** *adj* — **fruit·less·ly** *adv* — **fruity** *adj*

fru·ition \frü'ishən\ *n* : completion

frumpy \'frəmpē\ *adj* **frump·i·er; -est** : dowdy

frus·trate \'frəsˌtrāt\ *vb* **-trat·ed; -trat·ing** **1** : block **2** : cause to fail — **frus·trat·ing·ly** *adv* — **frus·tra·tion** \ˌfrəs'trāshən\ *n*

¹**fry** \'frī\ *vb* **fried; fry·ing** **1** : cook esp. with fat or oil **2** : be cooked by frying ~ *n, pl* **fries** **1** : something fried **2** : social gathering with fried food

²**fry** *n, pl* **fry** : recently hatched fish

fud·dle \'fədᵊl\ *vb* **-dled; -dling** : muddle

fud·dy–dud·dy \'fədēˌdədē\ *n, pl* **-dies** : one who is old-fashioned or unimaginative

fudge \'fəj\ *vb* **fudged; fudg·ing** : cheat or exaggerate ~ *n* : creamy candy

fu·el \'fyüəl\ *n* : material burned to produce heat or power ~ *vb* **-eled** *or* **-elled; -el·ing** *or* **-el·ling** : provide with or take in fuel

fu·gi·tive \'fyüjətiv\ *adj* **1** : running away or trying to escape **2** : not lasting — **fugitive** *n*

-ful \'fəl\ *adj suffix* **1** : full of **2** : having the qualities of **3** : -able ∼ *n suffix* : quantity that fills

ful·crum \'fùlkrəm, 'fəl-\ *n, pl* **-crums** *or* **-cra** \-krə\ : support on which a lever turns

ful·fill, ful·fil \fùl'fil\ *vb* **-filled; -fill·ing 1** : perform **2** : satisfy — **ful·fill·ment** *n*

¹full \'fùl\ *adj* **1** : filled **2** : complete **3** : rounded **4** : having an abundance of something ∼ *adv* : entirely ∼ *n* : utmost degree — **full-ness** *n* — **ful·ly** *adv*

²full *vb* : shrink and thicken woolen cloth — **full·er** *n*

full–fledged \'fùl'flejd\ *adj* : fully developed

ful·some \'fùlsəm\ *adj* : copious verging on excessive

fum·ble \'fəmbəl\ *vb* **-bled; -bling** : fail to hold something properly — **fumble** *n*

fume \'fyüm\ *n* : irritating gas ∼ *vb* **fumed; fum·ing 1** : give off fumes **2** : show annoyance

fu·mi·gate \'fyümə,gāt\ *vb* **-gat·ed; -gat·ing** : treat with pest-killing fumes — **fu·mi·gant** \'fyümigənt\ *n* — **fu·mi·ga·tion** \,fyümə'gāshən\ *n*

fun \'fən\ *n* **1** : something providing amusement or en-joyment **2** : enjoyment ∼ *adj* : full of fun

func·tion \'fəŋkshən\ *n* **1** : special purpose **2** : formal ceremony or social affair ∼ *vb* : have or carry on a func-tion — **func·tion·al** \-shənəl\ *adj* — **func·tion·al·ly** *adv*

func·tion·ary \-shə,nerē\ *n, pl* **-ar·ies** : official

fund \'fənd\ *n* **1** : store **2** : sum of money intended for a special purpose **3** *pl* : avail-able money ∼ *vb* : provide funds for

fun·da·men·tal \,fəndə-'ment°l\ *adj* **1** : basic **2** : of central importance or neces-sity — **fundamental** *n* — **fun·da·men·tal·ly** *adv*

fu·ner·al \'fyünərəl\ *n* : cere-mony for a dead person — **fu-neral** *adj* — **fu·ne·re·al** \fyü'nirēəl\ *adj*

fun·gi·cide \'fənjə,sīd, 'fəŋgə-\ *n* : agent that kills fungi — **fun·gi·cid·al** \,fənjə'sīd°l, ,fəŋgə-\ *adj*

fun·gus \'fəŋgəs\ *n, pl* **fun·gi** \'fən,jī, 'fəŋ,gī\ : lower plant that lacks chlorophyll — **fun-gal** \'fəŋgəl\ *adj* — **fun·gous** \-gəs\ *adj*

funk \'fəŋk\ *n* : state of de-pression

funky \'fəŋkē\ *adj* **funk·i·er; -est** : unconventional and un-sophisticated

fun·nel \'fən⁹l\ *n* **1** : cone-shaped utensil with a tube for directing the flow of a liquid **2** : ship's smokestack ∼ *vb* **-neled; -nel·ing** : move to a central point or into a central channel

fun·nies \'fənēz\ *n pl* : section of comic strips

fun·ny \'fənē\ *adj* **-ni·er; -est** **1** : amusing **2** : strange

fur \'fər\ *n* **1** : hairy coat of a mammal **2** : article of clothing made with fur — **fur** *adj* — **furred** \'fərd\ *adj* — **fur·ry** \-ē\ *adj*

fur·bish \'fərbish\ *vb* : make lustrous or new looking

fu·ri·ous \'fyu̇rēəs\ *adj* : fierce or angry — **fu·ri·ous·ly** *adv*

fur·long \'fər,lȯŋ\ *n* : a unit of distance equal to 220 yards

fur·lough \'fərlō\ *n* : authorized absence from duty — **furlough** *vb*

fur·nace \'fərnəs\ *n* : enclosed structure in which heat is produced

fur·nish \'fərnish\ *vb* **1** : provide with what is needed **2** : make available for use

fur·nish·ings \-iŋs\ *n pl* **1** : articles or accessories of dress **2** : furniture

fur·ni·ture \'fərnichər\ *n* : movable articles for a room

fu·ror \'fyu̇r,ȯr\ *n* **1** : anger **2** : sensational craze

fur·ri·er \'fərēər\ *n* : dealer in furs

fur·row \'fərō\ *n* **1** : trench made by a plow **2** : wrinkle or groove — **furrow** *vb*

fur·ther \'fərthər\ *adv* **1** : at or to a more advanced point **2** : more ∼ *adj* : additional ∼ *vb* : promote — **fur·ther·ance** \-ərəns\ *n*

fur·ther·more \'fərthər,mōr\ *adv* : in addition

fur·ther·most \-,mōst\ *adj* : most distant

fur·thest \'fərthəst\ *adv or adj* : farthest

fur·tive \'fərtiv\ *adj* : slyly or secretly done — **fur·tive·ly** *adv* — **fur·tive·ness** *n*

fu·ry \'fyu̇rē\ *n, pl* **-ries** **1** : intense rage **2** : violence

¹**fuse** \'fyüz\ *n* **1** : cord lighted to transmit fire to an explosive **2** *usu* **fuze** : device for exploding a charge ∼ *or* **fuze** *vb* **fused** *or* **fuzed; fus·ing** *or* **fuz·ing** : equip with a fuse

²**fuse** *vb* **fused; fus·ing** **1** : melt and run together **2** : unite ∼ *n* : electrical safety device — **fus·ible** *adj*

fu·se·lage \'fyüsə,läzh, -zə-\ *n* : main body of an aircraft

fu·sil·lade \'fyüsə,läd, -,lād, ,fyüsə'-, -zə-\ *n* : volley of fire

fu·sion \'fyüzhən\ *n* **1** : process of merging by melting **2** : union of atomic nuclei

fuss \\'fəs\ *n* **1** : needless bustle or excitement **2** : show of attention **3** : objection or protest ~ *vb* : make a fuss

fuss·bud·get \-ˌbəjət\ *n* : one who fusses or is fussy about trifles

fussy \\'fəsē\ *adj* **fuss·i·er; -est 1** : irritable **2** : paying very close attention to details — **fuss·i·ly** *adv* — **fuss·i·ness** *n*

fu·tile \\'fyütᵊl, 'fyüˌtīl\ *adj* : useless or vain — **fu·til·i·ty** \fyü'tilətē\ *n*

fu·ton \\'füˌtän\ *n* : a cotton-filled mattress

fu·ture \\'fyüchər\ *adj* : coming after the present ~ *n* **1** : time yet to come **2** : what will happen — **fu·tur·is·tic** \ˌfyüchə'ristik\ *adj*

fuze *var of* FUSE

fuzz \\'fəz\ *n* : fine particles or fluff

fuzzy \-ē\ *adj* **fuzz·i·er; -est 1** : covered with or like fuzz **2** : indistinct — **fuzz·i·ness** *n*

-fy \ˌfī\ *vb suffix* : make — **-fi·er** \ˌfīər\ *n suffix*

G

g \\'jē\ *n, pl* **g's** *or* **gs** \\'jēz\ **1** : 7th letter of the alphabet **2** : unit of gravitational force

gab \\'gab\ *vb* **-bb-** : chatter — **gab** *n* — **gab·by** \\'gabē\ *adj*

gab·ar·dine \\'gabərˌdēn\ *n* : durable twilled fabric

ga·ble \\'gābəl\ *n* : triangular part of the end of a building — **ga·bled** \-bəld\ *adj*

gad \\'gad\ *vb* **-dd-** : roam about

gad·fly *n* : persistently critical person

gad·get \\'gajət\ *n* : device — **gad·get·ry** \\'gajətrē\ *n*

gaff \\'gaf\ *n* : metal hook for lifting fish — **gaff** *vb*

gaffe \\'gaf\ *n* : social blunder

gag \\'gag\ *vb* **-gg- 1** : prevent from speaking or crying out by stopping up the mouth **2** : retch or cause to retch ~ *n* **1** : something that stops up the mouth **2** : laugh-provoking remark or act

gage *var of* GAUGE

gag·gle \\'gagəl\ *n* : flock of geese

gai·ety \\'gāətē\ *n, pl* **-eties** : high spirits

gai·ly \\'gālē\ *adv* : in a gay manner

gain \\'gān\ *n* **1** : profit **2** : obtaining of profit or possessions **3** : increase ∼ *vb* **1** : get possession of **2** : win **3** : arrive at **4** : increase or increase in **5** : profit — **gain·er** *n* — **gain·ful** *adj* — **gain·ful·ly** *adv*

gain·say \gān'sā\ *vb* -**said** \-'sād, -'sed\; -**say·ing**; -**says** \-'sāz, -'sez\ : deny or dispute — **gain·say·er** *n*

gait \'gāt\ *n* : manner of walking or running — **gait·ed** *adj*

gal \'gal\ *n* : girl

ga·la \'gālə, 'galə, 'gälə\ *n* : festive celebration — **gala** *adj*

gal·axy \'galəksē\ *n, pl* -**ax·ies** : very large group of stars — **ga·lac·tic** \gə'laktik\ *adj*

gale \'gāl\ *n* **1** : strong wind **2** : outburst

¹**gall** \'gȯl\ *n* **1** : bile **2** : insolence

²**gall** *n* **1** : skin sore caused by chafing **2** : swelling of plant tissue caused by parasites ∼ *vb* **1** : chafe **2** : irritate or vex

gal·lant \gə'lant, -'länt; 'galənt\ *n* : man very attentive to women ∼ \'galənt; gə'lant, -'länt\ *adj* **1** : splendid **2** : brave **3** : polite and attentive to women — **gal·lant·ly** *adv* — **gal·lant·ry** \'galəntrē\ *n*

gall·blad·der *n* : pouch attached to the liver in which bile is stored

gal·le·on \'galyən\ *n* : large sailing ship formerly used esp. by the Spanish

gal·lery \'galərē\ *n, pl* -**ler·ies** **1** : outdoor balcony **2** : long narrow passage or hall **3** : room or building for exhibiting art **4** : spectators — **gal·ler·ied** \-rēd\ *adj*

gal·ley \'galē\ *n, pl* -**leys** **1** : old ship propelled esp. by oars **2** : kitchen of a ship or airplane

gal·li·um \'galēəm\ *n* : bluish white metallic chemical element

gal·li·vant \'galə,vant\ *vb* : travel or roam about for pleasure

gal·lon \'galən\ *n* : unit of liquid measure equal to 4 quarts

gal·lop \'galəp\ *n* : fast 3-beat gait of a horse — **gallop** *vb* — **gal·lop·er** *n*

gal·lows \'galōz\ *n, pl* -**lows** *or* -**lows·es** : upright frame for hanging criminals

gall·stone *n* : abnormal concretion in the gallbladder or bile passages

ga·lore \gə'lōr\ *adj* : in abundance

ga·losh \gə'läsh\ *n* : overshoe — usu. pl.

gal·va·nize \'galvə,nīz\ *vb* -**nized**; -**niz·ing** **1** : shock into action **2** : coat (iron or steel) with zinc — **gal·va·ni-**

za·tion \ˌgalvənəˈzāshən\ *n* — **gal·va·niz·er** *n*

gam·bit \ˈgambit\ *n* **1** : opening tactic in chess **2** : stratagem

gam·ble \ˈgambəl\ *vb* **-bled; -bling 1** : play a game for stakes **2** : bet **3** : take a chance ~ *n* : risky undertaking — **gam·bler** \-blər\ *n*

gam·bol \ˈgambəl\ *vb* **-boled** *or* **-bolled; -bol·ing** *or* **-bol·ling** : skip about in play — **gambol** *n*

game \ˈgām\ *n* **1** : playing activity **2** : competition according to rules **3** : animals hunted for sport or food ~ *vb* **gamed; gam·ing** : gamble ~ *adj* **1** : plucky **2** : lame — **game·ly** *adv* — **game·ness** *n*

game·cock *n* : fighting cock

game·keep·er *n* : person in charge of game animals or birds

gam·ete \gəˈmēt, ˈgamˌēt\ *n* : mature germ cell — **ga·met·ic** \gəˈmetik\ *adj*

ga·mine \gaˈmēn\ *n* : charming tomboy

gam·ut \ˈgamət\ *n* : entire range or series

gamy *or* **gam·ey** \ˈgāmē\ *adj* **gam·i·er; -est** : having the flavor of game esp. when slightly tainted — **gam·i·ness** *n*

¹**gan·der** \ˈgandər\ *n* : male goose

²**gander** *n* : glance

gang \ˈgaŋ\ *n* **1** : group of persons working together **2** : group of criminals ~ *vb* : attack in a gang — with *up*

gan·gling \ˈgaŋgliŋ\ *adj* : lanky

gan·gli·on \ˈgaŋglēən\ *n, pl* **-glia** \-glēə\ : mass of nerve cells

gang·plank *n* : platform used in boarding or leaving a ship

gan·grene \ˈgaŋˌgrēn, gaŋˈ-, ˈgan-, gan-\ *n* : local death of body tissue — **gangrene** *vb* — **gan·gre·nous** \ˈgaŋgrənəs\ *adj*

gang·ster \ˈgaŋstər\ *n* : member of criminal gang

gang·way \-ˌwā\ *n* : passage in or out

gan·net \ˈganət\ *n* : large fish-eating marine bird

gan·try \ˈgantrē\ *n, pl* **-tries** : frame structure supported over or around something

gap \ˈgap\ *n* **1** : break in a barrier **2** : mountain pass **3** : empty space

gape \ˈgāp\ *vb* **gaped; gaping 1** : open widely **2** : stare with mouth open — **gape** *n*

ga·rage \gəˈräzh, -ˈräj\ *n* : shelter or repair shop for automobiles ~ *vb* **-raged; -rag·ing** : put or keep in a garage

garb \ˈgärb\ *n* : clothing ~ *vb* : dress

gar·bage \\'gärbij\ *n* **1** : food waste **2** : trash — **gar·bage-man** *n*

gar·ble \\'gärbəl\ *vb* **-bled; -bling** : distort the meaning of

gar·den \\'gärdᵊn\ *n* **1** : plot for growing fruits, flowers, or vegetables **2** : public recreation area ∼ *vb* : work in a garden — **gar·den·er** \\'gärdᵊnər\ *n*

gar·de·nia \gär'dēnyə\ *n* : tree or shrub with fragrant white or yellow flowers or the flower

gar·gan·tuan \gär'ganchə-wən\ *adj* : having tremendous size or volume

gar·gle \\'gärgəl\ *vb* **-gled; -gling** : rinse the throat with liquid — **gargle** *n*

gar·goyle \\'gär‚gȯil\ *n* : waterspout in the form of a grotesque human or animal

gar·ish \\'garish\ *adj* : offensively bright or gaudy

gar·land \\'gärlənd\ *n* : wreath ∼ *vb* : form into or deck with a garland

gar·lic \\'gärlik\ *n* : herb with pungent bulbs used in cooking — **gar·licky** \-likē\ *adj*

gar·ment \\'gärmənt\ *n* : article of clothing

gar·ner \\'gärnər\ *vb* : acquire by effort

gar·net \\'gärnət\ *n* : deep red mineral

gar·nish \\'gärnish\ *vb* : add decoration to (as food) — **garnish** *n*

gar·nish·ee \‚gärnə'shē\ *vb* **-eed; -ee·ing** : take (as a debtor's wages) by legal authority

gar·nish·ment \\'gärnishmənt\ *n* : attachment of property to satisfy a creditor

gar·ret \\'garət\ *n* : attic

gar·ri·son \\'garəsən\ *n* : military post or the troops stationed there — **garrison** *vb*

gar·ru·lous \\'garələs\ *adj* : talkative — **gar·ru·li·ty** \gə'rülətē\ *n* — **gar·ru·lous·ly** *adv* — **gar·ru·lous·ness** *n*

gar·ter \\'gärtər\ *n* : band to hold up a stocking or sock

gas \\'gas\ *n, pl* **gas·es** **1** : fluid (as hydrogen or air) that tends to expand indefinitely **2** : gasoline ∼ *vb* **gassed; gas·sing** **1** : treat with gas **2** : fill with gasoline — **gas·eous** \\'gasēəs, 'gashəs\ *adj*

gash \\'gash\ *n* : deep long cut — **gash** *vb*

gas·ket \\'gaskət\ *n* : material or a part used to seal a joint

gas·light *n* : light of burning illuminating gas

gas·o·line \\'gasə‚lēn, ‚gasə'-\ *n* : flammable liquid from petroleum

gasp \'gasp\ *vb* **1** : catch the breath audibly **2** : breathe laboriously — **gasp** *n*

gas·tric \'gastrik\ *adj* : relating to or located near the stomach

gas·tron·o·my \gas'tränəmē\ *n* : art of good eating — **gas·tro·nom·ic** \ˌgastrə'nämik\ *adj*

gate \'gāt\ *n* : an opening for passage in a wall or fence — **gate·keep·er** *n* — **gate·post** *n*

gate·way *n* : way in or out

gath·er \'gathər\ *vb* **1** : bring or come together **2** : harvest **3** : pick up little by little **4** : deduce — **gath·er·er** *n* — **gath·er·ing** *n*

gauche \'gōsh\ *adj* : crude or tactless

gaudy \'gȯdē\ *adj* **gaud·i·er; -est** : tastelessly showy — **gaud·i·ly** \'gȯdᵊlē\ *adv* — **gaud·i·ness** *n*

gauge \'gāj\ *n* : instrument for measuring ∼ *vb* **gauged; gaug·ing** : measure

gaunt \'gȯnt\ *adj* : thin or emaciated — **gaunt·ness** *n*

¹**gaunt·let** \-lət\ *n* **1** : protective glove **2** : challenge to combat

²**gauntlet** *n* : ordeal

gauze \'gȯz\ *n* : thin often transparent fabric — **gauzy** *adj*

gave *past of* GIVE

gav·el \'gavəl\ *n* : mallet of a presiding officer, auctioneer, or judge

gawk \'gȯk\ *vb* : stare stupidly

gawky \-ē\ *adj* **gawk·i·er; -est** : clumsy

gay \'gā\ *adj* **1** : merry **2** : bright and lively **3** : homosexual — **gay** *n*

gaze \'gāz\ *vb* **gazed; gaz·ing** : fix the eyes in a steady intent look — **gaze** *n* — **gaz·er** *n*

ga·zelle \gə'zel\ *n* : small swift antelope

ga·zette \-'zet\ *n* : newspaper

gaz·et·teer \ˌgazə'tir\ *n* : geographical dictionary

gear \'gir\ *n* **1** : clothing **2** : equipment **3** : toothed wheel — **gear** *vb*

gear·shift *n* : mechanism by which automobile gears are shifted

geek \'gēk\ *n* : socially inept person

geese *pl of* GOOSE

gei·sha \'gāshə, 'gē-\ *n, pl* **-sha** *or* **-shas** : Japanese girl or woman trained to entertain men

gel·a·tin \'jelətᵊn\ *n* : sticky substance obtained from animal tissues by boiling — **ge·lat·i·nous** \jə'latᵊnəs\ *adj*

geld \'geld\ *vb* : castrate

geld·ing \-iŋ\ *n* : castrated horse

gem \'jem\ *n* : cut and polished valuable stone — **gemstone** *n*

gen·der \'jendər\ *n* **1** : sex **2** : division of a class of words (as nouns) that determines agreement of other words

gene \'jēn\ *n* : segment of DNA that controls inheritance of a trait

ge·ne·al·o·gy \‚jēnē'äləjē, ‚jen-, -'al-\ *n, pl* **-gies** : study of family pedigrees — **ge·ne·a·log·i·cal** \-ēə'läjikəl\ *adj* — **ge·ne·a·log·i·cal·ly** *adv* — **ge·ne·al·o·gist** \-ē'äləjist, -'al-\ *n*

genera *pl of* GENUS

gen·er·al \'jenrəl, 'jenə-\ *adj* **1** : relating to the whole **2** : applicable to all of a group **3** : common or widespread ~ *n* **1** : something that involves or is applicable to the whole **2** : commissioned officer in the army, air force, or marine corps ranking above a lieutenant general — **gen·er·al·ly** *adv* — **in general** : for the most part

gen·er·al·i·ty \‚jenə'ralətē\ *n, pl* **-ties** : general statement

gen·er·al·ize \'jenrə‚līz, 'jenə-\ *vb* **-ized; -iz·ing** : reach a general conclusion esp. on the basis of particular instances — **gen·er·al·iza·tion** \‚jenrələ-'zāshən, ‚jenə-\ *n*

general of the air force : commissioned officer of the highest rank in the air force

general of the army : commissioned officer of the highest rank in the army

gen·er·ate \'jenə‚rāt\ *vb* **-at·ed; -at·ing** : create or produce

gen·er·a·tion \‚jenə'rāshən\ *n* **1** : living beings constituting a single step in a line of descent **2** : production — **gen·er·a·tive** \'jenə‚rātiv, -rət-\ *adj*

gen·er·a·tor \'jenə‚rātər\ *n* **1** : one that generates **2** : machine that turns mechanical into electrical energy

ge·ner·ic \jə'nerik\ *adj* **1** : general **2** : not protected by a trademark **3** : relating to a genus — **generic** *n*

gen·er·ous \'jenərəs\ *adj* : freely giving or sharing — **gen·er·os·i·ty** \‚jenə'räsətē\ *n* — **gen·er·ous·ly** *adv* — **gen·er·ous·ness** *n*

ge·net·ics \jə'netiks\ *n* : biology dealing with heredity and variation — **ge·net·ic** \-ik\ *adj* — **ge·net·i·cal·ly** *adv* — **ge·net·i·cist** \-'netəsist\ *n*

ge·nial \'jēnēəl\ *adj* : cheerful — **ge·nial·i·ty** \‚jēnē'alətē\ *n* — **ge·nial·ly** *adv*

ge·nie \'jēnē\ *n* : supernatural spirit that often takes human form

gen·i·tal \\'jenət³l\\ *adj* : concerned with reproduction — **gen·i·tal·ly** \\-təlē\\ *adv*

gen·i·ta·lia \\ˌjenəˈtālyə\\ *n pl* : external genital organs

gen·i·tals \\'jenət³lz\\ *n pl* : genitalia

ge·nius \\'jēnyəs\\ *n* **1** : single strongly marked capacity **2** : extraordinary intellectual power or a person having such power

geno·cide \\'jenəˌsīd\\ *n* : systematic destruction of a racial or cultural group

genre \\'zhänrə, 'zhäⁿrə\\ *n* : category esp. of literary composition

gen·teel \\jenˈtēl\\ *adj* : polite or refined

gen·tile \\'jenˌtīl\\ *n* : person who is not Jewish — **gentile** *adj*

gen·til·i·ty \\jenˈtilətē\\ *n, pl* **-ties** **1** : good birth and family **2** : good manners

gen·tle \\'jent³l\\ *adj* **-tler; -tlest** **1** : of a family of high social station **2** : not harsh, stern, or violent **3** : soft or delicate ∼ *vb* **-tled; -tling** : make gentle — **gen·tle·ness** *n* — **gen·tly** *adv*

gen·tle·man \\-mən\\ *n* : man of good family or manners — **gen·tle·man·ly** *adv*

gen·tle·wom·an \\-ˌwu̇mən\\ *n* : woman of good family or breeding

gen·try \\'jentrē\\ *n, pl* **-tries** : people of good birth or breeding

gen·u·flect \\'jenyəˌflekt\\ *vb* : bend the knee in worship — **gen·u·flec·tion** \\ˌjenyəˈflek-shən\\ *n*

gen·u·ine \\'jenyəwən\\ *adj* : being the same in fact as in appearance — **gen·u·ine·ly** *adv* — **gen·u·ine·ness** *n*

ge·nus \\'jēnəs\\ *n, pl* **gen·era** \\'jenərə\\ : category of biological classification

ge·ode \\'jēˌōd\\ *n* : stone having a mineral-lined cavity

geo·de·sic \\ˌjēəˈdesik, -ˈdēs-\\ *adj* : made of a framework of linked polygons

ge·og·ra·phy \\jēˈägrəfē\\ *n* **1** : study of the earth and its climate, products, and inhabitants **2** : natural features of a region — **ge·og·ra·pher** \\-fər\\ *n* — **geo·graph·ic** \\ˌjēə-ˈgrafik\\, **geo·graph·i·cal** \\-ikəl\\ *adj* — **geo·graph·i·cal·ly** *adv*

ge·ol·o·gy \\jēˈäləjē\\ *n* : study of the history of the earth and its life esp. as recorded in rocks — **geo·log·ic** \\ˌjēə-ˈläjik\\, **geo·log·i·cal** \\-ikəl\\ *adj* — **geo·log·i·cal·ly** *adv* — **ge·ol·o·gist** \\jēˈäləjist\\ *n*

ge·om·e·try \\jēˈämətrē\\ *n, pl* **-tries** : mathematics of the relations, properties, and measurements of solids, surfaces, lines, and angles — **geo·met·ric** \ˌjēə'metrik\, **geo·met·ri·cal** \-rikəl\ *adj*

geo·ther·mal \ˌjēo'thərməl\ *adj* : relating to or derived from the heat of the earth's interior

ge·ra·ni·um \jə'rānēəm\ *n* : garden plant with clusters of white, pink, or scarlet flowers

ger·bil \'jərbəl\ *n* : burrowing desert rodent

ge·ri·at·ric \ˌjerē'atrik\ *adj* **1** : relating to aging or the aged **2** : old

ge·ri·at·rics \-triks\ *n* : medicine dealing with the aged and aging

germ \'jərm\ *n* **1** : microorganism **2** : source or rudiment

ger·mane \jər'mān\ *adj* : relevant

ger·ma·ni·um \-'mānēəm\ *n* : grayish white hard chemical element

ger·mi·cide \'jərmə,sīd\ *n* : agent that destroys germs — **ger·mi·cid·al** \ˌjərmə'sīdᵊl\ *adj*

ger·mi·nate \'jərmə,nāt\ *vb* **-nat·ed; -nat·ing** : begin to develop — **ger·mi·na·tion** \ˌjərmə'nāshən\ *n*

ger·ry·man·der \ˌjerē-'mandər, 'jerē,-, ˌgerē'-, 'gerē,-\ *vb* : divide into election districts so as to give one political party an advantage — **gerrymander** *n*

ger·und \'jerənd\ *n* : word having the characteristics of both verb and noun

ge·sta·po \gə'stäpō\ *n, pl* **-pos** : secret police

ges·ta·tion \je'stāshən\ *n* : pregnancy or incubation — **ges·tate** \'jes,tāt\ *vb*

ges·ture \'jeschər\ *n* **1** : movement of the body or limbs that expresses something **2** : something said or done for its effect on the attitudes of others — **ges·tur·al** \-chərəl\ *adj* — **gesture** *vb*

ge·sund·heit \gə'zünt,hīt\ *interj* — used to wish good health to one who has just sneezed

get \'get\ *vb* **got** \'gät\; **got** *or* **got·ten** \'gätᵊn\; **get·ting** **1** : gain or be in possession of **2** : succeed in coming or going **3** : cause to come or go or to be in a certain condition or position **4** : become **5** : be subjected to **6** : understand **7** : be obliged — **get along** *vb* **1** : get by **2** : be on friendly terms — **get by** *vb* : meet one's needs

get·away \'getə,wā\ *n* **1** : escape **2** : a starting or getting under way

gey·ser \'gīzər\ *n* : spring that intermittently shoots up hot water and steam

ghast·ly \'gastlē\ *adj* **-li·er; -est** : horrible or shocking

gher·kin \'gərkən\ *n* : small pickle

ghet·to \'getō\ *n, pl* **-tos** *or* **-toes** : part of a city in which members of a minority group live

ghost \'gōst\ *n* : disembodied soul — **ghost·ly** *adv*

ghost·write *vb* **-wrote; -writ-ten** : write for and in the name of another — **ghost·writ·er** *n*

ghoul \'gül\ *n* : legendary evil being that feeds on corpses — **ghoul·ish** *adj*

GI \ˌjē'ī\ *n, pl* **GI's** *or* **GIs** : member of the U.S. armed forces

gi·ant \'jīənt\ *n* **1** : huge leg-endary being **2** : something very large or very powerful — **giant** *adj*

gib·ber \'jibər\ *vb* **-bered; -ber·ing** : speak rapidly and foolishly

gib·ber·ish \'jibərish\ *n* : un-intelligible speech or language

gib·bon \'gibən\ *n* : manlike ape

gibe \'jīb\ *vb* **gibed; gib·ing** : jeer at — **gibe** *n*

gib·lets \'jibləts\ *n pl* : edible fowl viscera

gid·dy \'gidē\ *adj* **-di·er; -est** **1** : silly **2** : dizzy — **gid·di-ness** *n*

gift \'gift\ *n* **1** : something given **2** : talent — **gift·ed** *adj*

gi·gan·tic \jī'gantik\ *adj* : very big

gig·gle \'gigəl\ *vb* **-gled; -gling** : laugh in a silly man-ner — **giggle** *n* — **gig·gly** \-əlē\ *adj*

gig·o·lo \'jigəˌlō\ *n, pl* **-los** : man living on the earnings of a woman

Gi·la monster \'hēlə-\ *n* : large venomous lizard

gild \'gild\ *vb* **gild·ed** \'gildəd\ *or* **gilt** \'gilt\; **gild·ing** : cover with or as if with gold

gill \'gil\ *n* : organ of a fish for obtaining oxygen from water

gilt \'gilt\ *adj* : gold-colored ∼ *n* : gold or goldlike sub-stance on the surface of an object

gim·bal \'gimbəl, 'jim-\ *n* : device that allows something to incline freely

gim·let \'gimlət\ *n* : small tool for boring holes

gim·mick \'gimik\ *n* : new and ingenious scheme, fea-ture, or device — **gim·mick-ry** *n* — **gim·micky** \-ikē\ *adj*

gimpy \'gimpē\ *adj* : lame

¹**gin** \'jin\ *n* : machine to sepa-rate seeds from cotton — **gin** *vb*

²**gin** *n* : clear liquor flavored with juniper berries

gin·ger \'jinjər\ *n* : pungent aromatic spice from a tropical plant — **gin·ger·bread** *n*

gin·ger·ly *adv* : very cautiously

ging·ham \'giŋəm\ *n* : cotton clothing fabric

gin·gi·vi·tis \ˌjinjə'vītəs\ *n* : inflammation of the gums

gink·go \'giŋkō\ *n, pl* **-goes** *or* **-gos** : tree of eastern China

gin·seng \'jinˌsiŋ, -ˌseŋ, -saŋ\ *n* : aromatic root of a Chinese herb

gi·raffe \jə'raf\ *n* : African mammal with a very long neck

gird \'gərd\ *vb* **gird·ed** \'gərdəd\ *or* **girt** \'gərt\; **gird·ing** 1 : encircle or fasten with or as if with a belt 2 : prepare

gird·er \'gərdər\ *n* : horizontal supporting beam

gir·dle \'gərd°l\ *n* : woman's supporting undergarment ∼ *vb* : surround

girl \'gərl\ *n* 1 : female child 2 : young woman 3 : sweetheart — **girl·hood** \-ˌhu̇d\ *n* — **girl·ish** *adj*

girl·friend *n* : frequent or regular female companion of a boy or man

girth \'gərth\ *n* : measure around something

gist \'jist\ *n* : main point or part

give \'giv\ *vb* **gave** \'gāv\; **giv·en** \'givən\; **giv·ing** 1 : put into the possession or keeping of another 2 : pay 3 : perform 4 : contribute or donate 5 : produce 6 : utter 7 : yield to force, strain, or pressure ∼ *n* : capacity or tendency to yield to force or strain — **give in** *vb* : surrender — **give out** *vb* : become used up or exhausted — **give up** *vb* 1 : let out of one's control 2 : cease from trying, doing, or hoping

give·away *n* 1 : unintentional betrayal 2 : something given free

giv·en \'givən\ *adj* 1 : prone or disposed 2 : having been specified

giz·zard \'gizərd\ *n* : muscular usu. horny-lined enlargement following the crop of a bird

gla·cial \'glāshəl\ *adj* 1 : relating to glaciers 2 : very slow — **gla·cial·ly** *adv*

gla·cier \'glāshər\ *n* : large body of ice moving slowly

glad \'glad\ *adj* **-dd-** 1 : experiencing or causing pleasure, joy, or delight 2 : very willing — **glad·den** \-°n\ *vb* — **glad·ly** *adv* — **glad·ness** *n*

glade \'glād\ *n* : grassy open space in a forest

glad·i·a·tor \'gladēˌātər\ *n* : one who fought to the death for the entertainment of ancient Romans — **glad·i·a·to·ri·al** \ˌgladēə'tōrēəl\ *adj*

glad·i·o·lus \ˌgladē'ōləs\ *n, pl* **-li** \-lē, -ˌlī\ : plant related to the irises

glam·our, glam·or \'glamər\ *n* : romantic or exciting attractiveness — **glam·or·ize** \-əˌrīz\ *vb* — **glam·or·ous** \-ərəs\ *adj*

glance \'glans\ *vb* **glanced; glanc·ing** 1 : strike and fly off to one side 2 : give a quick look ～ *n* : quick look

gland \'gland\ *n* : group of cells that secretes a substance — **glan·du·lar** \'glanjələr\ *adj*

glans \'glanz\ *n, pl* **glan·des** \'glanˌdēz\ : conical vascular body forming the end of the penis or clitoris

glare \'glar\ *vb* **glared; glar·ing** 1 : shine with a harsh dazzling light 2 : stare angrily ～ *n* 1 : harsh dazzling light 2 : angry stare

glar·ing \'glariŋ\ *adj* : painfully obvious — **glar·ing·ly** *adv*

glass \'glas\ *n* 1 : hard usu. transparent material made by melting sand and other materials 2 : something made of glass 3 *pl* : lenses used to correct defects of vision — **glass** *adj* — **glass·ful** \-ˌfül\ *n* — **glass·ware** \-ˌwar\ *n* — **glassy** *adj*

glass·blow·ing *n* : art of shaping a mass of molten glass by blowing air into it — **glass·blow·er** *n*

glau·co·ma \glau'kōmə, glo-\ *n* : state of increased pressure within the eyeball

glaze \'glāz\ *vb* **glazed; glaz·ing** 1 : furnish with glass 2 : apply glaze to ～ *n* : glassy surface or coating

gla·zier \'glāzhər\ *n* : one who sets glass in window frames

gleam \'glēm\ *n* 1 : transient or partly obscured light 2 : faint trace ～ *vb* : send out gleams

glean \'glēn\ *vb* : collect little by little — **glean·able** *adj* — **glean·er** *n*

glee \'glē\ *n* : joy — **glee·ful** *adj*

glen \'glen\ *n* : narrow hidden valley

glib \'glib\ *adj* **-bb-** : speaking or spoken with ease — **glib·ly** *adv*

glide \'glīd\ *vb* **glid·ed; glid·ing** : move or descend smoothly and effortlessly — **glide** *n*

glid·er \'glīdər\ *n* 1 : winged aircraft having no engine 2 : swinging porch seat

glim·mer \'glimər\ *vb* : shine faintly or unsteadily ～ *n* 1 : faint light 2 : small amount

glimpse \'glimps\ *vb* **glimpsed; glimps·ing** : take a brief look at — **glimpse** *n*

glint \'glint\ *vb* : gleam or sparkle — **glint** *n*

glis·ten \'glisᵊn\ *vb* : shine or sparkle by reflection — **glisten** *n*

glit·ter \'glitər\ *vb* : shine with brilliant or metallic luster ～ *n* : small glittering ornaments — **glit·tery** *adj*

glitz \'glits\ *n* : extravagant showiness — **glitzy** \'glitsē\ *adj*

gloat \'glōt\ *vb* : think of something with triumphant delight

glob \'gläb\ *n* : large rounded lump

glob·al \'glōbəl\ *adj* : worldwide — **glob·al·ly** *adv*

globe \'glōb\ *n* **1** : sphere **2** : the earth or a model of it

glob·u·lar \'gläbyələr\ *adj* **1** : round **2** : made up of globules

glob·ule \'gläbyül\ *n* : tiny ball

glock·en·spiel \'gläkən-ˌshpēl\ *n* : portable musical instrument consisting of tuned metal bars

gloom \'glüm\ *n* **1** : darkness **2** : sadness — **gloom·i·ly** *adv* — **gloom·i·ness** *n* — **gloomy** *adj*

glop \'gläp\ *n* : messy mass or mixture

glo·ri·fy \'glōrəˌfī\ *vb* **-fied;** **-fy·ing** **1** : make to seem glo-rious **2** : worship — **glo·ri·fi·ca·tion** \ˌglōrəfə'kāshən\ *n*

glo·ry \'glōrē\ *n, pl* **-ries** **1** : praise or honor offered in worship **2** : cause for praise or renown **3** : magnificence **4** : heavenly bliss ～ *vb* **-ried;** **-ry·ing** : rejoice proudly — **glo·ri·ous** \'glōrēəs\ *adj* — **glo·ri·ous·ly** *adv*

¹**gloss** \'gläs, 'glȯs\ *n* : luster — **gloss·i·ly** \-əlē\ *adv* — **gloss·i·ness** \-ēnəs\ *n* — **glossy** \-ē\ *adj* — **gloss over** *vb* **1** : mask the true nature of **2** : deal with only superficially

²**gloss** *n* : brief explanation or translation ～ *vb* : translate or explain

glos·sa·ry \'gläsərē, 'glȯs-\ *n, pl* **-ries** : dictionary — **glos·sar·i·al** \glä- 'sarēəl, glȯ-\ *adj*

glove \'gləv\ *n* : hand covering with sections for each finger

glow \'glō\ *vb* **1** : shine with or as if with intense heat **2** : show exuberance ～ *n* : brightness or warmth of color or feeling

glow·er \'glau̇ər\ *vb* : stare angrily — **glower** *n*

glow·worm *n* : insect or insect larva that emits light

glu·cose \'glüˌkōs\ *n* : sugar found esp. in blood, plant sap, and fruits

glue \'glü\ *n* : substance used for sticking things together — **glue** *vb* — **glu·ey** \'glüē\ *adj*

glum \'gləm\ *adj* **-mm-** **1** : sullen **2** : dismal

glut \'glət\ *vb* **-tt-** : fill to excess — **glut** *n*

glu·ten \'glüt⁀n\ *n* : gluey protein substance in flour

glu·ti·nous \'glüt⁀nəs\ *adj* : sticky

glut·ton \'glət⁀n\ *n* : one who eats to excess — **glut·ton·ous** \'glət⁀nəs\ *adj* — **glut·tony** \'glət⁀nē\ *n*

gnarled \'närld\ *adj* **1** : knotty **2** : gloomy or sullen

gnash \'nash\ *vb* : grind (as teeth) together

gnat \'nat\ *n* : small biting fly

gnaw \'nȯ\ *vb* : bite or chew on

gnome \'nōm\ *n* : dwarf of folklore — **gnom·ish** *adj*

gnu \'nü, 'nyü\ *n, pl* **gnu** *or* **gnus** : large African antelope

go \'gō\ *vb* **went** \'went\; **gone** \'gȯn, 'gän\; **go·ing** \'goiŋ\; **goes** \'gōz\ **1** : move, proceed, run, or pass **2** : leave **3** : extend or lead **4** : sell or amount — with *for* **5** : happen **6** — used in present participle to show intent or imminent action **7** : become **8** : fit or harmonize **9** : belong ~ *n, pl* **goes 1** : act or manner of going **2** : vigor **3** : attempt — **go back on** : betray — **go by the board** : be discarded — **go for** : favor — **go off** : explode — **go one better**

: outdo — **go over 1** : examine **2** : study — **go to town** : be very successful — **on the go** : constantly active

goad \'gōd\ *n* : something that urges — **goad** *vb*

goal \'gōl\ *n* **1** : mark to reach in a race **2** : purpose **3** : object in a game through which a ball is propelled

goal·ie \'gōlē\ *n* : player who defends the goal

goal·keep·er *n* : goalie

goat \'gōt\ *n* : horned ruminant mammal related to the sheep — **goat·skin** *n*

goa·tee \gō'tē\ *n* : small pointed beard

gob \'gäb\ *n* : lump

¹**gob·ble** \'gäbəl\ *vb* **-bled; -bling** : eat greedily

²**gobble** *vb* **-bled; -bling** : make the noise of a turkey (**gobbler**)

gob·ble·dy·gook \'gäbəldē-ˌgúk, -'gük\ *n* : nonsense

gob·let \'gäblət\ *n* : large stemmed drinking glass

gob·lin \'gäblən\ *n* : ugly mischievous sprite

god \'gäd, 'gȯd\ *n* **1** *cap* : supreme being **2** : being with supernatural powers — **god·like** *adj* — **god·ly** *adj*

god·child *n* : person one sponsors at baptism — **god·daughter** *n* — **god·son** *n*

god·dess \\'gädəs, 'gȯd-\ *n* : female god

god·less \-ləs\ *adj* : not believing in God — **god·less·ness** *n*

god·par·ent *n* : sponsor at baptism — **god·fa·ther** *n* — **god·moth·er** *n*

god·send \-ˌsend\ *n* : something needed that comes unexpectedly

goes *pres 3d sing of* GO

go–get·ter \\'gōˌgetər\ *n* : enterprising person — **go–get·ting** \-iŋ\ *adj or n*

gog·gle \\'gägəl\ *vb* **-gled; -gling** : stare wide-eyed

gog·gles \-əlz\ *n pl* : protective glasses

go·ings–on \ˌgōiŋz'ȯn, -'än\ *n pl* : events

goi·ter \\'gȯitər\ *n* : abnormally enlarged thyroid gland

gold \\'gōld\ *n* : malleable yellow metallic chemical element — **gold·smith** \-ˌsmith\ *n*

gold·brick \-ˌbrik\ *n* : person who shirks duty — **goldbrick** *vb*

gold·en \\'gōldən\ *adj* **1** : made of, containing, or relating to gold **2** : having the color of gold **3** : precious or favorable

gold·en·rod \\'gōldənˌräd\ *n* : herb having tall stalks with tiny yellow flowers

gold·finch \\'gōldˌfinch\ *n* : yellow American finch

gold·fish \-ˌfish\ *n* : small usu. orange or golden carp

golf \\'gälf, 'gȯlf\ *n* : game played by hitting a small ball (**golf ball**) with clubs (**golf clubs**) into holes placed in a field (**golf course**) — **golf** *vb* — **golf·er** *n*

go·nad \\'gōˌnad\ *n* : sex gland

gon·do·la \\'gändələ (*usual for* 1), gän'dō-\ *n* **1** : long narrow boat used on the canals of Venice **2** : car suspended from a cable

gon·do·lier \ˌgändə'lir\ *n* : person who propels a gondola

gone \\'gȯn\ *adj* **1** : past **2** : involved

gon·er \\'gȯnər\ *n* : hopeless case

gong \\'gäŋ, 'gȯŋ\ *n* : metallic disk that makes a deep sound when struck

gon·or·rhea \ˌgänə'rēə\ *n* : bacterial inflammatory venereal disease of the genital tract

goo \\'gü\ *n* : thick or sticky substance — **goo·ey** \-ē\ *adj*

good \\'gu̇d\ *adj* **bet·ter** \\'betər\; **best** \\'best\ **1** : satisfactory **2** : salutary **3** : considerable **4** : desirable **5** : well-behaved, kind, or virtuous ~ *n* **1** : something good **2** : benefit **3** *pl* : personal property **4** *pl* : wares ~ *adv* : well — **good–heart·ed** \-'härtəd\ *adj* — **good–look·ing** *adj* —

good–na·tured *adj* — **good-ness** *n* — **for good** : forever

good–bye, good–by \gùd'bī\ *n* : parting remark

good–for–noth·ing *n* : idle worthless person

Good Friday *n* : Friday before Easter observed as the anniversary of the crucifixion of Christ

good·ly *adj* **-li·er; -est** : considerable

good·will *n* **1** : good intention **2** : kindly feeling

goody \'gùdē\ *n, pl* **good·ies** : something that is good esp. to eat

goody–goody *adj* : affectedly or annoyingly sweet or self-righteous — **goody–goody** *n*

goof \'güf\ *vb* **1** : blunder **2** : waste time — usu. with *off* or *around* — **goof** *n* — **goof–off** *n*

goofy \'güfē\ *adj* **goof·i·er; -est** : crazy — **goof·i·ness** *n*

goose \'güs\ *n, pl* **geese** \'gēs\ : large bird with webbed feet

goose·ber·ry \'güs,berē, 'güz-\ *n* : berry of a shrub related to the currant

goose bumps *n pl* : roughening of the skin caused by fear, excitement, or cold

goose·flesh *n* : goose bumps

goose pimples *n pl* : goose bumps

go·pher \'gōfər\ *n* : burrowing rodent

¹**gore** \'gōr\ *n* : blood

²**gore** *vb* **gored; gor·ing** : pierce or wound with a horn or tusk

¹**gorge** \'gȯrj\ *n* : narrow ravine

²**gorge** *vb* **gorged; gorg·ing** : eat greedily

gor·geous \'gȯrjəs\ *adj* : supremely beautiful

go·ril·la \gə'rilə\ *n* : African manlike ape

gory \'gōrē\ *adj* **gor·i·er; -est** : bloody

gos·hawk \'gäs,hȯk\ *n* : long-tailed hawk with short rounded wings

gos·ling \'gäzliŋ, 'gȯz-\ *n* : young goose

gos·pel \'gäspəl\ *n* **1** : teachings of Christ and the apostles **2** : something accepted as infallible truth — **gospel** *adj*

gos·sa·mer \'gäsəmər, gäz-\ *n* **1** : film of cobweb **2** : light filmy substance

gos·sip \'gäsəp\ *n* **1** : person who reveals personal information **2** : rumor or report of an intimate nature ~ *vb* : spread gossip — **gos·sipy** \-ē\ *adj*

got *past of* GET

Goth·ic \'gäthik\ *adj* : relating to a medieval style of architecture

gotten *past part of* GET

gouge \'gaùj\ *n* **1** : rounded chisel **2** : cavity or groove

scooped out ~ *vb* **gouged;
goug·ing 1** : cut or scratch a groove in **2** : overcharge

gou·lash \'gü₁läsh, -₁lash\ *n* : beef stew with vegetables and paprika

gourd \'gōrd, 'gùrd\ *n* **1** : any of a group of vines including the cucumber, squash, and melon **2** : inedible hard-shelled fruit of a gourd

gour·mand \'gùr₁mänd\ *n* : person who loves good food and drink

gour·met \'gùr₁mā, gùr'mā\ *n* : connoisseur of food and drink

gout \'gaùt\ *n* : disease marked by painful inflammation and swelling of the joints — **gouty** *adj*

gov·ern \'gəvərn\ *vb* **1** : control and direct policy in **2** : guide or influence strongly **3** : restrain — **gov·ern·ment** \-ərmənt\ *n* — **gov·ern·men·tal** \₁gəvər'ment³l\ *adj*

gov·ern·ess \'gəvərnəs\ *n* : female teacher in a private home

gov·er·nor \'gəvənər, 'gəvər-\ *n* **1** : head of a political unit **2** : automatic speed-control device — **gov·er·nor·ship** *n*

gown \'gaùn\ *n* **1** : loose flowing outer garment **2** : woman's formal evening dress — **gown** *vb*

grab \'grab\ *vb* **-bb-** : take by sudden grasp — **grab** *n*

grace \'grās\ *n* **1** : unmerited divine assistance **2** : short prayer before or after a meal **3** : respite **4** : ease of movement or bearing ~ *vb* **graced; grac·ing 1** : honor **2** : adorn — **graceful** \-fəl\ *adj* — **grace·ful·ly** *adv* — **grace·ful·ness** *n* — **grace·less** *adj*

gra·cious \'grāshəs\ *adj* : marked by kindness and courtesy or charm and taste — **gra·cious·ly** *adv* — **gra·cious·ness** *n*

grack·le \'grakəl\ *n* : American blackbird

gra·da·tion \grā'dāshən, grə-\ *n* : step, degree, or stage in a series

grade \'grād\ *n* **1** : stage in a series, order, or ranking **2** : division of school representing one year's work **3** : mark of accomplishment in school **4** : degree of slope ~ *vb* **grad·ed; grad·ing 1** : arrange in grades **2** : make level or evenly sloping **3** : give a grade to — **grad·er** *n*

grade school *n* : school including the first 4 or 8 grades

gra·di·ent \'grādēənt\ *n* : slope

grad·u·al \'grajəwəl\ *adj* : going by steps or degrees — **grad·u·al·ly** *adv*

grad·u·ate \'grajəwət\ *n* : holder of a diploma ~ *adj* : of or relating to studies beyond the bachelor's degree ~ \-ə‚wāt\ *vb* **-at·ed; -at·ing** **1** : grant or receive a diploma **2** : mark with degrees of measurement — **grad·u·a·tion** \‚grajə'wāshən\ *n*

graf·fi·to \gra'fētō, grə-\ *n, pl* **-ti** \-ē\ : inscription on a wall

graft \'graft\ *vb* : join one thing to another so that they grow together ~ *n* **1** : grafted plant **2** : the getting of money dishonestly or the money so gained — **graft·er** *n*

grain \'grān\ *n* **1** : seeds or fruits of cereal grasses **2** : small hard particle **3** : arrangement of fibers in wood — **grained** \'grānd\ *adj* — **grainy** *adj*

gram \'gram\ *n* : metric unit of weight equal to 1/1000 kilogram

gram·mar \'gramər\ *n* : study of words and their functions and relations in the sentence — **gram·mar·i·an** \grə'marēən\ *n* — **gram·mat·i·cal** \-'matikəl\ *adj* — **gram·mat·i·cal·ly** *adv*

grammar school *n* : grade school

gra·na·ry \'grānərē, 'gran-\ *n, pl* **-ries** : storehouse for grain

grand \'grand\ *adj* **1** : large or striking in size or scope **2** : fine and imposing **3** : very good — **grand·ly** *adv* — **grand·ness** *n*

grand·child \-‚chīld\ *n* : child of one's son or daughter — **grand·daugh·ter** *n* — **grand·son** *n*

gran·deur \'granjər\ *n* : quality or state of being grand

gran·dil·o·quence \gran'diləkwəns\ *n* : pompous speaking — **gran·dil·o·quent** \-kwənt\ *adj*

gran·di·ose \'grandē‚ōs, ‚grandē'-\ *adj* **1** : impressive **2** : affectedly splendid — **gran·di·ose·ly** *adv*

grand·par·ent \'grand‚parənt\ *n* : parent of one's father or mother — **grand·fa·ther** \-‚fäthər, -‚fàth-\ *n* — **grand·moth·er** \-‚məthər\ *n*

grand·stand \-‚stand\ *n* : usu. roofed stand for spectators

grange \'grānj\ *n* : farmers association

gran·ite \'granət\ *n* : hard igneous rock

grant \'grant\ *vb* **1** : consent to **2** : give **3** : admit as true ~ *n* **1** : act of granting **2** : something granted — **grant·ee** \grant'ē\ *n* — **grant·er** \'grantər\ *n* — **grant·or** \-ər, -‚òr\ *n*

gran·u·late \'granyə,lāt\ *vb* **-lat·ed; -lat·ing** : form into grains or crystals — **gran·u·la·tion** \,granyə'lāshən\ *n*

gran·ule \'granyül\ *n* : small particle — **gran·u·lar** \-yələr\ *adj* — **gran·u·lar·i·ty** \,granyə'larətē\ *n*

grape \'grāp\ *n* : smooth juicy edible berry of a woody vine (**grape·vine**)

grape·fruit *n* : large edible yellow-skinned citrus fruit

graph \'graf\ *n* : diagram that shows relationships between things — **graph** *vb*

graph·ic \'grafik\ *adj* **1** : vividly described **2** : relating to the arts (**graphic arts**) of representation and printing on flat surfaces ∼ *n* **1** : picture used for illustration **2** *pl* : computer screen display — **graph·i·cal·ly** \-iklē\ *adv*

graph·ite \'graf,īt\ *n* : soft carbon used for lead pencils and lubricants

grap·nel \'grapnəl\ *n* : small anchor with several claws

grap·ple \'grapəl\ *vb* **-pled; -pling 1** : seize or hold with or as if with a hooked implement **2** : wrestle

grasp \'grasp\ *vb* **1** : take or seize firmly **2** : understand ∼ *n* **1** : one's hold or control **2** : one's reach **3** : comprehension

grass \'gras\ *n* : plant with jointed stem and narrow leaves — **grassy** *adj*

grass·hop·per \-,häpər\ *n* : leaping plant-eating insect

grass·land *n* : land covered with grasses

¹grate \'grāt\ *n* **1** : grating **2** : frame of iron bars to hold burning fuel

²grate *vb* **grat·ed; -ing 1** : pulverize by rubbing against something rough **2** : irritate — **grat·er** *n* — **grat·ing·ly** *adv*

grate·ful \'grātfəl\ *adj* : thankful or appreciative — **grate·ful·ly** *adv* — **grate·ful·ness** *n*

grat·i·fy \'gratə,fī\ *vb* **-fied; -fy·ing** : give pleasure to — **grat·i·fi·ca·tion** \,gratəfə'kā-shən\ *n*

grat·ing \'grātiŋ\ *n* : framework with bars across it

gra·tis \'gratəs, 'grāt-\ *adv or adj* : free

grat·i·tude \'gratə,tüd, -,tyüd\ *n* : state of being grateful

gra·tu·itous \grə'tüətəs, -'tyü-\ *adj* **1** : free **2** : uncalled-for

gra·tu·ity \-ətē\ *n, pl* **-ities** : tip

¹grave \'grāv\ *n* : place of burial — **grave·stone** *n* — **grave·yard** *n*

²grave *adj* **grav·er; grav·est 1** : threatening great harm or danger **2** : solemn — **grave-ly** *adv* — **grave·ness** *n*

grav·el \'gravəl\ *n* : loose rounded fragments of rock — **grav·el·ly** *adj*

grav·i·tate \'gravə,tāt\ *vb* **-tat·ed; -tat·ing** : move toward something

grav·i·ta·tion \,gravə'tāshən\ *n* : natural force of attraction that tends to draw bodies together — **grav·i·ta·tion·al** \-shənəl\ *adj*

grav·i·ty \'gravətē\ *n, pl* **-ties** **1** : serious importance **2** : gravitation

gra·vy \'grāvē\ *n, pl* **-vies** : sauce made from thickened juices of cooked meat

gray \'grā\ *adj* **1** : of the color gray **2** : having gray hair ～ *n* : neutral color between black and white ～ *vb* : make or become gray — **gray·ish** \-ish\ *adj* — **gray·ness** *n*

¹graze \'grāz\ *vb* **grazed; graz·ing** : feed on herbage or pasture — **graz·er** *n*

²graze *vb* **grazed; graz·ing** : touch lightly in passing

grease \'grēs\ *n* : thick oily material or fat ～ \'grēs, 'grēz\ *vb* **greased; greas·ing** : smear or lubricate with grease — **greasy** \'grēsē, -zē\ *adj*

great \'grāt\ *adj* **1** : large in size or number **2** : larger than

usual — **great·ly** *adv* — **great·ness** *n*

grebe \'grēb\ *n* : diving bird related to the loon

greed \'grēd\ *n* : selfish desire beyond reason — **greed·i·ly** \-ᵊlē\ *adv* — **greed·i·ness** \-ēnəs\ *n* — **greedy** \'grēdē\ *adj*

green \'grēn\ *adj* **1** : of the color green **2** : unripe **3** : inexperienced ～ *vb* : become green ～ *n* **1** : color between blue and yellow **2** *pl* : leafy parts of plants — **green·ish** *adj* — **green·ness** *n*

green·ery \'grēnərē\ *n, pl* **-er-ies** : green foliage or plants

green·horn *n* : inexperienced person

green·house *n* : glass structure for the growing of plants

greet \'grēt\ *vb* **1** : address with expressions of kind wishes **2** : react to — **greet·er** *n*

greet·ing *n* **1** : friendly address on meeting **2** *pl* : best wishes

gre·gar·i·ous \gri'garēəs\ *adj* : social or companionable — **gre·gar·i·ous·ly** *adv* — **gre·gar·i·ous·ness** *n*

grem·lin \'gremlən\ *n* : small mischievous gnome

gre·nade \grə'nād\ *n* : small missile filled with explosive or chemicals

grew *past of* **GROW**

grey *var of* GRAY

grey·hound \\'grā͵hauṅd\ *n* : tall slender dog noted for speed

grid \\'grid\ *n* **1** : grating **2** : evenly spaced horizontal and vertical lines (as on a map)

grid·dle \\'grid°l\ *n* : flat metal surface for cooking

grid·iron \\'grid͵īərn\ *n* **1** : grate for broiling **2** : football field

grief \\'grēf\ *n* **1** : emotional suffering caused by or as if by bereavement **2** : disaster

griev·ance \\'grēvəns\ *n* : complaint

grieve \\'grēv\ *vb* **grieved; griev·ing** : feel or cause to feel grief or sorrow

griev·ous \\'grēvəs\ *adj* **1** : oppressive **2** : causing grief or sorrow — **griev·ous·ly** *adv*

grill \\'gril\ *vb* **1** : cook on a grill **2** : question intensely ~ *n* **1** : griddle **2** : informal restaurant

grille, grill \\'gril\ *n* : grating forming a barrier or screen — **grill·work** *n*

grim \\'grim\ *adj* **-mm-** **1** : harsh and forbidding in appearance **2** : relentless — **grim·ly** *adv* — **grim·ness** *n*

gri·mace \\'griməs, grim'ās\ *n* : facial expression of disgust — **grimace** *vb*

grime \\'grīm\ *n* : embedded or accumulated dirt — **grimy** *adj*

grin \\'grin\ *vb* **-nn-** : smile so as to show the teeth — **grin** *n*

grind \\'grīnd\ *vb* **ground** \\'grauṅd\; **grind·ing** **1** : reduce to powder **2** : wear down or sharpen by friction **3** : operate or produce by turning a crank ~ *n* : monotonous labor or routine — **grind·er** *n* — **grind·stone** \\'grīn͵stōn\ *n*

grip \\'grip\ *vb* **-pp-** : seize or hold firmly ~ *n* **1** : grasp **2** : control **3** : device for holding

gripe \\'grīp\ *vb* **griped; grip·ing** **1** : cause pains in the bowels **2** : complain — **gripe** *n*

grippe \\'grip\ *n* : influenza

gris·ly \\'grizlē\ *adj* **-li·er; -est** : horrible or gruesome

grist \\'grist\ *n* : grain to be ground or already ground — **grist·mill** *n*

gris·tle \\'grisəl\ *n* : cartilage — **gris·tly** \-lē\ *adj*

grit \\'grit\ *n* **1** : hard sharp granule **2** : material composed of granules **3** : unyielding courage ~ *vb* **-tt-** : press with a grating noise — **grit·ty** *adj*

grits \\'grits\ *n pl* : coarsely ground hulled grain

griz·zled \\'grizəld\ *adj* : streaked with gray

groan \\'grōn\ *vb* **1** : moan **2** : creak under a strain — **groan** *n*

gro·cer \\'grōsər\ *n* : food dealer — **gro·cery** \\'grōsrē, 'grōsh-, -ərē\ *n*

grog \\'gräg\ *n* : rum diluted with water

grog·gy \-ē\ *adj* **-gi·er; -est** : dazed and unsteady on the feet — **grog·gi·ly** *adv* — **grog·gi·ness** *n*

groin \\'groin\ *n* : juncture of the lower abdomen and inner thigh

grom·met \\'grämət, 'grəm-\ *n* : eyelet

groom \\'grüm, 'grum\ *n* **1** : one who cares for horses **2** : bridegroom ∼ *vb* **1** : clean and care for (as a horse) **2** : make neat or attractive **3** : prepare

groove \\'grüv\ *n* **1** : long narrow channel **2** : fixed routine — **groove** *vb*

grope \\'grōp\ *vb* **groped; grop·ing** : search for by feeling

gros·beak \\'grōs,bēk\ *n* : finch with large conical bill

¹gross \\'grōs\ *adj* **1** : glaringly noticeable **2** : bulky **3** : consisting of an overall total exclusive of deductions **4** : vulgar ∼ *n* : the whole before any deductions ∼ *vb* : earn as a total — **gross·ly** *adv* — **gross·ness** *n*

²gross *n, pl* **gross** : 12 dozen

gro·tesque \grō'tesk\ *adj* **1** : absurdly distorted or repulsive **2** : ridiculous — **gro·tesque·ly** *adv*

grot·to \\'grätō\ *n, pl* **-toes** : cave

grouch \\'graùch\ *n* : complaining person — **grouch** *vb* — **grouchy** *adj*

¹ground \\'graùnd\ *n* **1** : bottom of a body of water **2** *pl* : sediment **3** : basis for something **4** : surface of the earth **5** : conductor that makes electrical connection with the earth or a framework ∼ *vb* **1** : force or bring down to the ground **2** : give basic knowledge to **3** : connect with an electrical ground — **ground·less** *adj*

²ground *past of* GRIND

ground·hog *n* : woodchuck

ground·wa·ter *n* : underground water

ground·work *n* : foundation

group \\'grüp\ *n* : number of associated individuals ∼ *vb* : gather or collect into groups

grou·per \\'grüpər\ *n* : large fish of warm seas

grouse \\'graùs\ *n, pl* **grouse** *or* **grouses** : ground-dwelling game bird

grout \\'graùt\ *n* : mortar for filling cracks — **grout** *vb*

grove \'grōv\ *n* : small group of trees

grov·el \'grävəl, 'grəv-\ *vb* **-eled** *or* **-elled; -el·ing** *or* **-el·ling** : abase oneself

grow \'grō\ *vb* **grew** \'grü\; **grown** \'grōn\; **grow·ing** **1** : come into existence and develop to maturity **2** : be able to grow **3** : advance or increase **4** : become **5** : cultivate — **grow·er** *n*

growl \'graùl\ *vb* : utter a deep threatening sound — **growl** *n*

grown–up \'grōn,əp\ *n* : adult — **grown–up** *adj*

growth \'grōth\ *n* **1** : stage in growing **2** : process of growing **3** : result of something growing

grub \'grəb\ *vb* **-bb-** **1** : root out by digging **2** : search about ~ *n* **1** : thick wormlike larva **2** : food

grub·by \'grəbē\ *adj* **-bi·er; -est** : dirty — **grub·bi·ness** *n*

grub·stake *n* : supplies for a prospector

grudge \'grəj\ *vb* **grudged; grudg·ing** : be reluctant to give ~ *n* : feeling of ill will

gru·el \'grüəl\ *n* : thin porridge

gru·el·ing, gru·el·ling \-əliŋ\ *adj* : requiring extreme effort

grue·some \'grüsəm\ *adj* : horribly repulsive

gruff \'grəf\ *adj* : rough in speech or manner — **gruff·ly** *adv*

grum·ble \'grəmbəl\ *vb* **-bled; -bling** : mutter in discontent — **grum·bler** \-blər\ *n*

grumpy \-pē\ *adj* **grump·i·er; -est** : cross — **grump·i·ly** *adv* — **grump·i·ness** *n*

grunge \'grənj\ *n* **1** : something shabby, tattered, or dirty **2** rock music expressing alienation and discontent — **grun·gy** \'grənjē\ *adj*

grun·ion \'grənyən\ *n* : fish of the California coast

grunt \'grənt\ *n* : deep guttural sound — **grunt** *vb*

gua·no \'gwänō\ *n* : excrement of seabirds used as fertilizer

guar·an·tee \,garən'tē\ *n* **1** : assurance of the fulfillment of a condition **2** : something given or held as a security ~ *vb* **-teed; -tee·ing** **1** : promise to be responsible for **2** : state with certainty — **guar·an·tor** \,garən'tòr\ *n*

guar·an·ty \'garəntē\ *n, pl* **-ties 1** : promise to answer for another's failure to pay a debt **2** : guarantee **3** : pledge ~ *vb* **-tied; -ty·ing** : guarantee

guard \'gärd\ *n* **1** : defensive position **2** : act of protecting **3** : an individual or group that guards against danger **4** : pro-

tective or safety device ~ *vb*
1 : protect or watch over **2**
: take precautions — **guard-house** *n* — **guard-room** *n*

guard-ian \'gärdēən\ *n* **:** one who has responsibility for the care of the person or property of another — **guard-ian-ship** *n*

gua-va \'gwävə\ *n* **:** shrubby tropical tree or its mildly acid fruit

gu-ber-na-to-ri-al \ˌgübənə-'tōrēəl, ˌgyü-\ *adj* **:** relating to a governor

guer-ril-la, gue-ril-la \gə'rilə\ *n* **:** soldier engaged in small-scale harassing tactics

guess \'ges\ *vb* **1 :** form an opinion from little evidence **2 :** state correctly solely by chance **3 :** think or believe — **guess** *n*

guest \'gest\ *n* **1 :** person to whom hospitality (as of a house) is extended **2 :** patron of a commercial establishment (as a hotel) **3 :** person not a regular cast member who appears on a program

guf-faw \gə'fȯ, 'gəfˌȯ\ *n* **:** loud burst of laughter — **guf-faw** \gə'fȯ\ *vb*

guide \'gīd\ *n* **1 :** one that leads or gives direction to another **2 :** device on a machine to direct motion ~ *vb* **guid-ed; guid-ing 1 :** show the way

to **2 :** direct — **guid-able** *adj* — **guid-ance** \'gīdᵊns\ *n* — **guide-book** *n*

guide-line \-ˌlīn\ *n* **:** summary of procedures regarding policy or conduct

guild \'gild\ *n* **:** association

guile \'gīl\ *n* **:** craftiness — **guile-ful** *adj* — **guile-less** *adj* — **guile-less-ness** *n*

guil-lo-tine \'gilə,tēn, ˌgēyə-'tēn, 'gēyə,-\ *n* **:** machine for beheading persons — **guillo-tine** *vb*

guilt \'gilt\ *n* **1 :** fact of having committed an offense **2 :** feeling of responsibility for offenses — **guilt-i-ly** *adv* — **guilt-i-ness** *n* — **guilty** \'giltē\ *adj*

guin-ea \'ginē\ *n* **1 :** old gold coin of United Kingdom **2 :** 21 shillings

guinea pig *n* **:** small So. American rodent

guise \'gīz\ *n* **:** external appearance

gui-tar \gə'tär, gi-\ *n* **:** 6-stringed musical instrument played by plucking

gulch \'gəlch\ *n* **:** ravine

gulf \'gəlf\ *n* **1 :** extension of an ocean or a sea into the land **2 :** wide gap

¹gull \'gəl\ *n* **:** seabird with webbed feet

²gull *vb* **:** make a dupe of ~ *n* **:** dupe — **gull-ible** *adj*

gul·let \\'gələt\ *n* : throat

gul·ly \\'gəlē\ *n, pl* **-lies** : trench worn by running water

gulp \\'gəlp\ *vb* : swallow hurriedly or greedily — **gulp** *n*

¹**gum** \\'gəm\ *n* : tissue along the jaw at the base of the teeth

²**gum** *n* **1** : sticky plant substance **2** : gum usu. of sweetened chicle prepared for chewing — **gum·my** *adj*

gum·bo \\'gəmbō\ *n* : thick soup

gum·drop *n* : gumlike candy

gump·tion \\'gəmpshən\ *n* : initiative

gun \\'gən\ *n* **1** : cannon **2** : portable firearm **3** : discharge of a gun **4** : something like a gun ∼ *vb* **-nn-** : hunt with a gun — **gun·fight** *n* — **gun·fight·er** *n* — **gun·fire** *n* — **gunman** \-mən\ *n* — **gun·pow·der** *n* — **gun·shot** *n* — **gun·smith** *n*

gun·boat *n* : small armed ship

gun·ner \\'gənər\ *n* : person who uses a gun

gun·nery sergeant \\'gənərē-\ *n* : noncommissioned officer in the marine corps ranking next below a master sergeant

gun·ny·sack \\'gənē,sak\ *n* : burlap sack

gun·sling·er \\'gən,sliŋər\ *n* : skilled gunman in the old West

gun·wale \\'gənᵊl\ *n* : upper edge of a boat's side

gup·py \\'gəpē\ *n, pl* **-pies** : tiny tropical fish

gur·gle \\'gərgəl\ *vb* **-gled; -gling** : make a sound like that of a flowing and gently splashing liquid — **gurgle** *n*

gu·ru \\'gü,rü\ *n, pl* **-rus** **1** : personal religious teacher in Hinduism **2** : expert

gush \\'gəsh\ *vb* : pour forth violently or enthusiastically — **gush·er** \\'gəshər\ *n*

gushy \-ē\ *adj* **gush·i·er; -est** : effusively sentimental

gust \\'gəst\ *n* **1** : sudden brief rush of wind **2** : sudden outburst — **gust** *vb* — **gusty** *adj*

gus·ta·to·ry \\'gəstə,tōrē\ *adj* : relating to the sense of taste

gus·to \\'gəstō\ *n* : zest

gut \\'gət\ *n* **1** *pl* : intestines **2** : digestive canal **3** *pl* : courage ∼ *vb* **-tt-** : eviscerate

gut·ter \\'gətər\ *n* : channel for carrying off rainwater

gut·tur·al \\'gətərəl\ *adj* : sounded in the throat — **guttural** *n*

¹**guy** \\'gī\ *n* : rope, chain, or rod attached to something to steady it — **guy** *vb*

²**guy** *n* : person

guz·zle \\'gəzəl\ *vb* **-zled; -zling** : drink greedily

gym \\'jim\ *n* : gymnasium

gym·na·si·um \jim'nāzēəm, -zhəm\ *n, pl* **-si·ums** *or* **-sia** \-zēə, -zhə\ : place for indoor sports

gym·nas·tics \jim'nastiks\ *n* : physical exercises performed in a gymnasium — **gym·nast** \'jim͵nast\ *n* — **gym·nas·tic** *adj*

gy·ne·col·o·gy \͵gīnə'käləjē, ͵jin-\ *n* : branch of medicine dealing with the diseases of women — **gy·ne·co·log·ic** \-ikə'läjik\, **gy·ne·co·log·i-** **cal** \-ikəl\ *adj* — **gy·ne·col·o·gist** \-ə'käləjist\ *n*

gyp \'jip\ *n* **1** : cheat **2** : trickery — **gyp** *vb*

gyp·sum \'jipsəm\ *n* : calcium-containing mineral

gy·rate \'jī͵rāt\ *vb* **-rat·ed; -rat·ing** : revolve around a center — **gy·ra·tion** \jī'rāshən\ *n*

gy·ro·scope \'jīro͵skōp\ *n* : wheel mounted to spin rapidly about an axis that is free to turn in various directions

H

h \'āch\ *n, pl* **h's** *or* **hs** \'āchəz\ : 8th letter of the alphabet

hab·er·dash·er \'habər͵dashər\ *n* : men's clothier — **hab·er·dash·ery** \-ərē\ *n*

hab·it \'habət\ *n* **1** : monk's or nun's clothing **2** : usual behavior **3** : addiction — **hab-it–form·ing** *adj*

hab·it·able \-əbəl\ *adj* : capable of being lived in

hab·i·tat \'habə͵tat\ *n* : place where a plant or animal naturally occurs

hab·i·ta·tion \͵habə'tāshən\ *n* **1** : occupancy **2** : dwelling place

ha·bit·u·al \hə'bichəwəl\ *adj* **1** : commonly practiced or observed **2** : doing, practicing, or acting by habit — **ha·bit·u-al·ly** *adv*

ha·bit·u·ate \hə'bichə͵wāt\ *vb* **-at·ed; -at·ing** : accustom

ha·ci·en·da \͵häsē'endə\ *n* : ranch house

¹hack \'hak\ *vb* **1** : cut with repeated irregular blows **2** : cough in a short dry manner **3** : manage successfully — **hack** *n* — **hack·er** *n*

²hack *n* **1** : horse or vehicle for hire **2** : saddle horse **3** : writer for hire — **hack** *adj* — **hack·man** \-mən\ *n*

hack·le \\'hakəl\\ *n* **1** : long feather on the neck or back of a bird **2** *pl* : hairs that can be erected **3** *pl* : temper

hack·ney \\-nē\\ *n, pl* **-neys** **1** : horse for riding or driving **2** : carriage for hire

hack·neyed \\-nēd\\ *adj* : trite

hack·saw *n* : saw for metal

had *past of* HAVE

had·dock \\'hadək\\ *n, pl* **haddock** : Atlantic food fish

Ha·des \\'hādēz\\ *n* **1** : mythological abode of the dead **2** *often not cap* : hell

haft \\'haft\\ *n* : handle of a weapon or tool

hag \\'hag\\ *n* **1** : witch **2** : ugly old woman

hag·gard \\'hagərd\\ *adj* : worn or emaciated — **hag·gard·ly** *adv*

hag·gle \\'hagəl\\ *vb* **-gled; -gling** : argue in bargaining — **hag·gler** *n*

¹**hail** \\'hāl\\ *n* **1** : precipitation in small lumps of ice **2** : something like a rain of hail ~ *vb* : rain hail — **hail·stone** *n* — **hail·storm** *n*

²**hail** *vb* **1** : greet or salute **2** : summon ~ *n* : expression of greeting or praise — often used as an interjection

hair \\'har\\ *n* : threadlike growth from the skin — **hair·brush** *n* — **hair·cut** *n* — **hair·dress·er** *n* — **haired** *adj* — **hair·i·ness** *n* — **hair·less** *adj* — **hair·pin** *n* — **hair·style** *n* — **hair·styl·ing** *n* — **hair·styl·ist** *n* — **hairy** *adj*

hair·breadth \\-ˌbredth\\, **hairs·breadth** \\'harz-\\ *n* : tiny distance or margin

hair·do \\-ˌdü\\ *n, pl* **-dos** : style of wearing hair

hair·line *n* **1** : thin line **2** : outline of the hair on the head

hair·piece *n* : toupee

hair–rais·ing *adj* : causing terror or astonishment

hake \\'hāk\\ *n* : marine food fish

hal·cy·on \\'halsēən\\ *adj* : prosperous or most pleasant

¹**hale** \\'hāl\\ *adj* : healthy or robust

²**hale** *vb* **haled; hal·ing** **1** : haul **2** : compel to go

half \\'haf, 'haf\\ *n, pl* **halves** \\'havz, 'havz\\ : either of 2 equal parts ~ *adj* **1** : being a half or nearly a half **2** : partial — **half** *adv*

half brother *n* : brother related through one parent only

half·heart·ed \\-'härtəd\\ *adj* : without enthusiasm — **half·heart·ed·ly** *adv*

half–life *n* : time for half of something to undergo a process

half sister *n* : sister related through one parent only

half·way *adj* : midway between 2 points — **half·way** *adv*

half–wit \-ˌwit\ *n* : foolish person — **half–wit·ted** \-ˌwitəd\ *adj*

hal·i·but \'haləbət\ *n, pl* **halibut** : large edible marine flatfish

hal·i·to·sis \ˌhalə'tōsəs\ *n* : bad breath

hall \'hȯl\ *n* **1** : large public or college or university building **2** : lobby **3** : auditorium

hal·le·lu·jah \ˌhalə'lüyə\ *interj* — used to express praise, joy, or thanks

hall·mark \'hȯlˌmärk\ *n* : distinguishing characteristic

hal·low \'halō\ *vb* : consecrate — **hal·lowed** \-ōd, -əwəd\ *adj*

Hal·low·een \ˌhalə'wēn, ˌhäl-\ *n* : evening of October 31 observed esp. by children in merrymaking and masquerading

hal·lu·ci·na·tion \həˌlüs°n-'āshən\ *n* : perception of objects that are not real — **hal·lu·ci·nate** \ha'lüs°nˌāt\ *vb* — **hal·lu·ci·na·to·ry** \-'lüs°nəˌtōrē\ *adj*

hal·lu·ci·no·gen \hə'lüs°nəjən\ *n* : substance that induces hallucinations — **hal·lu·ci·no·gen·ic** \-ˌlüs°nə'jenik\ *adj*

hall·way *n* : entrance hall

ha·lo \'hālō\ *n, pl* **-los** *or* **-loes** : circle of light appearing to surround a shining body

¹halt \'hȯlt\ *adj* : lame

²halt *vb* : stop or cause to stop — **halt** *n*

hal·ter \'hȯltər\ *n* **1** : rope or strap for leading or tying an animal **2** : brief blouse held up by straps ∼ *vb* : catch (an animal) with a halter

halt·ing \'hȯltiŋ\ *adj* : uncertain — **halt·ing·ly** *adv*

halve \'hav, 'håv\ *vb* **halved**; **halv·ing** **1** : divide into halves **2** : reduce to half

halves *pl of* HALF

ham \'ham\ *n* **1** : thigh — usu. pl. **2** : cut esp. of pork from the thigh **3** : showy actor **4** : amateur radio operator ∼ *vb* **-mm-** : overplay a part — **ham** *adj*

ham·burg·er \'hamˌbərgər\, **ham·burg** \-ˌbərg\ *n* : ground beef or a sandwich made with this

ham·let \'hamlət\ *n* : small village

ham·mer \'hamər\ *n* **1** : hand tool for pounding **2** : gun part whose striking explodes the charge ∼ *vb* : beat, drive, or shape with a hammer — **hammer out** *vb* : produce with effort

ham·mer·head *n* **1** : striking part of a hammer **2** : shark with a hammerlike head

ham·mock \'hamək\ *n* : swinging bed hung by cords at each end

¹**ham·per** \'hampər\ *vb* : impede

²**hamper** *n* : large covered basket

ham·ster \'hamstər\ *n* : stocky shorttailed rodent

ham·string \'ham,striŋ\ *vb* -strung \-,strəŋ\; -string·ing \-,striŋiŋ\ 1 : cripple by cutting the leg tendons 2 : make ineffective or powerless

hand \'hand\ *n* 1 : end of a front limb adapted for grasping 2 : side 3 : promise of marriage 4 : handwriting 5 : assistance or participation 6 : applause 7 : cards held by a player 8 : worker ~ *vb* : lead, assist, give, or pass with the hand — **hand·clasp** *n* — **hand·craft** *vb* — **hand·ful** *n* — **hand·gun** *n* — **hand·less** *adj* — **hand·made** *adj* — **hand·rail** *n* — **hand·saw** *n* — **hand·wo·ven** *adj* — **hand·writ·ing** *n* — **hand·writ·ten** *adj*

hand·bag *n* : woman's purse

hand·ball *n* : game played by striking a ball with the hand

hand·bill *n* : printed advertisement or notice distributed by hand

hand·book *n* : concise reference book

hand·cuffs *n pl* : locking bracelets that bind the wrists together — **handcuff** *vb*

hand·i·cap \'handē,kap\ *n* 1 : advantage given or disad-vantage imposed to equalize a competition 2 : disadvantage — **handicap** *vb* — **hand·i·capped** *adj* — **hand·i·cap·per** *n*

hand·i·craft \'handē,kraft\ *n* 1 : manual skill 2 : article made by hand — **hand·i·craft·er** *n*

hand·i·work \-,wərk\ *n* : work done personally or by the hands

hand·ker·chief \'haŋkərchəf, -,chēf\ *n, pl* -chiefs \-chəfs, -,chēfs\ : small piece of cloth carried for personal use

han·dle \'handᵊl\ *n* : part to be grasped ~ *vb* -dled; -dling 1 : touch, hold, or manage with the hands 2 : deal with 3 : deal or trade in — **han·dle·bar** *n* — **han·dled** \-dᵊld\ *adj* — **han·dler** \'handlər\ *n*

hand·maid·en *n* : female attendant

hand·out *n* : something given out

hand·pick *vb* : select personally

hand·shake *n* : clasping of hands (as in greeting)

hand·some \'hansəm\ *adj* -som·er; -est 1 : sizable 2 : generous 3 : nice-looking — **hand·some·ly** *adv* — **hand·some·ness** *n*

hand·spring *n* : somersault on the hands

hand·stand *n* : a balancing upside down on the hands

handy \'handē\ *adj* **hand·i·er; -est 1** : conveniently near **2** : easily used **3** : dexterous — **hand·i·ly** *adv* — **hand·i·ness** *n*

handy·man \-ˌman\ *n* : one who does odd jobs

hang \'haŋ\ *vb* **hung** \'həŋ\; **hang·ing 1** : fasten or remain fastened to an elevated point without support from below **2** : suspend by the neck until dead — past tense often *hanged* **3** : droop ~ *n* **1** : way a thing hangs **2** : an understanding of something — **hang·er** *n* — **hang·ing** *n*

han·gar \'haŋər\ *n* : airplane shelter

hang·dog \'haŋˌdȯg\ *adj* : ashamed or guilty

hang·man \-mən\ *n* : public executioner

hang·nail *n* : loose skin near a fingernail

hang·out *n* : place where one likes to spend time

hang·over *n* : sick feeling following heavy drinking

hank \'haŋk\ *n* : coil or loop

han·ker \'haŋkər\ *vb* : desire strongly — **han·ker·ing** *n*

han·ky–pan·ky \ˌhaŋkē-ˈpaŋkē\ *n* : questionable or underhanded activity

han·som \'hansəm\ *n* : 2-wheeled covered carriage

Ha·nuk·kah \'k͟änəkə, 'hän-\ *n* : 8-day Jewish holiday commemorating the rededication of the Temple of Jerusalem after its defilement by Antiochus of Syria

hap·haz·ard \hap'hazərd\ *adj* : having no plan or order — **hap·haz·ard·ly** *adv*

hap·less \'hapləs\ *adj* : unfortunate — **hap·less·ly** *adv* — **hap·less·ness** *n*

hap·pen \'hapən\ *vb* **1** : take place **2** : be fortunate to encounter something unexpectedly — often used with infinitive

hap·pen·ing \-əniŋ\ *n* : occurrence

hap·py \'hapē\ *adj* **-pi·er; -est 1** : fortunate **2** : content, pleased, or joyous — **hap·pi·ly** \'hapəlē\ *adv* — **hap·pi·ness** *n*

ha·rangue \hə'raŋ\ *n* : ranting or scolding speech — **ha·rangue** *vb* — **ha·rangu·er** \-'raŋər\ *n*

ha·rass \hə'ras, 'harəs\ *vb* **1** : disturb and impede by repeated raids **2** : annoy continually — **ha·rass·ment** *n*

har·bin·ger \'härbənjər\ *n* : one that announces or foreshadows what is coming

har·bor \-bər\ *n* : protected body of water suitable for anchorage ~ *vb* **1** : give refuge to **2** : hold as a thought or feeling

hard \'härd\ *adj* **1** : not easily penetrated **2** : firm or definite **3** : close or searching **4** : severe or unfeeling **5** : strenuous or difficult **6** : physically strong or intense — **hard** *adv* — **hard·ness** *n*

hard·en \'härdᵊn\ *vb* : make or become hard or harder — **hard·en·er** *n*

hard·head·ed \ˌhärd'hedəd\ *adj* **1** : stubborn **2** : realistic — **hard·head·ed·ly** *adv* — **hard·head·ed·ness** *n*

hard–heart·ed \-'härtəd\ *adj* : lacking sympathy — **hard–heart·ed·ly** *adv* — **hard–heart·ed·ness** *n*

hard·ly \'härdlē\ *adv* **1** : only just **2** : certainly not

hard–nosed \-ˌnōzd\ *adj* : tough or uncompromising

hard·ship \-ˌship\ *n* : suffering or privation

hard·tack \-ˌtak\ *n* : hard biscuit

hard·ware *n* **1** : cutlery or tools made of metal **2** : physical components of a vehicle or apparatus

hard·wood *n* : wood of a broad-leaved usu. deciduous tree — **hardwood** *adj*

har·dy \'härdē\ *adj* **-di·er; -est** : able to withstand adverse conditions — **har·di·ly** *adv* — **har·di·ness** *n*

hare \'har\ *n, pl* **hare** *or* **hares** : long-eared mammal related to the rabbit

hare·brained \-ˌbrānd\ *adj* : foolish

hare·lip *n* : deformity in which the upper lip is vertically split — **hare·lipped** \-ˌlipt\ *adj*

ha·rem \'harəm\ *n* : house or part of a house allotted to women in a Muslim household or the women and servants occupying it

hark \'härk\ *vb* : listen

har·le·quin \'härlikən, -kwən\ *n* : clown

har·lot \'härlət\ *n* : prostitute

harm \'härm\ *n* **1** : physical or mental damage **2** : mischief ~ *vb* : cause harm — **harm·ful** \-fəl\ *adj* — **harm·ful·ly** *adv* — **harm·ful·ness** *n* — **harm·less** *adj* — **harm·less·ly** *adv* — **harm·less·ness** *n*

har·mon·ic \här'mänik\ *adj* **1** : of or relating to musical harmony **2** : pleasing to hear — **har·mon·i·cal·ly** \-iklē\ *adv*

har·mon·i·ca \här'mänikə\ *n* : small wind instrument with metallic reeds

har·mo·ny \'härmənē\ *n, pl* **-nies** **1** : musical combination of sounds **2** : pleasing arrangement of parts **3** : lack of conflict **4** : internal calm — **har·mo·ni·ous** \här'mōnēəs\ *adj* — **har·mo·ni·ous·ly** *adv* — **har·mo·ni·ous·ness** *n* — **har·mo·ni·za·tion** \ˌhärmənə-'zāshən\ *n* — **har·mo·nize** \'härməˌnīz\ *vb*

har·ness \'härnəs\ *n* : gear of a draft animal ∼ *vb* **1** : put a harness on **2** : put to use

harp \'härp\ *n* : musical instrument with many strings plucked by the fingers ∼ *vb* **1** : play on a harp **2** : dwell on a subject tiresomely — **harp·er** *n* — **harp·ist** *n*

har·poon \här'pün\ *n* : barbed spear used in hunting whales — **harpoon** *vb* — **har·poon·er** *n*

harp·si·chord \'härpsiˌkȯrd\ *n* : keyboard instrument with strings that are plucked

har·py \'härpē\ *n, pl* **-pies** : shrewish woman

har·row \'harō\ *n* : implement used to break up soil ∼ *vb* **1** : cultivate with a harrow **2** : distress

har·ry \'harē\ *vb* **-ried; -ry·ing** : torment by or as if by constant attack

harsh \'härsh\ *adj* **1** : disagreeably rough **2** : severe — **harsh·ly** *adv* — **harsh·ness** *n*

har·um–scar·um \ˌharəm-'skarəm\ *adv* : recklessly

har·vest \'härvəst\ *n* **1** : act or time of gathering in a crop **2** : mature crop — **harvest** *vb* — **har·vest·er** *n*

has *pres 3d sing of* HAVE

hash \'hash\ *vb* : chop into small pieces ∼ *n* : chopped meat mixed with potatoes and browned

hasp \'hasp\ *n* : hinged strap fastener esp. for a door

has·sle \'hasəl\ *n* **1** : quarrel **2** : struggle **3** : cause of annoyance — **hassle** *vb*

has·sock \'hasək\ *n* : cushion used as a seat or leg rest

haste \'hāst\ *n* **1** : rapidity of motion **2** : rash action **3** : excessive eagerness — **hast·i·ly** \'hāstəlē\ *adv* — **hast·i·ness** \-stēnəs\ *n* — **hasty** \-stē\ *adj*

has·ten \'hāsᵊn\ *vb* : hurry

hat \'hat\ *n* : covering for the head

¹hatch \'hach\ *n* : small door or opening — **hatch·way** *n*

²hatch *vb* : emerge from an egg — **hatch·ery** \-ərē\ *n*

hatch·et \'hachət\ *n* : short⸗handled ax

hate \'hāt\ *n* : intense hostility and aversion ∼ *vb* **hat·ed; hat·ing** **1** : express or feel hate **2** : dislike — **hate·ful**

\-fəl\ *adj* — **hate·ful·ly** *adv* — **hate·ful·ness** *n* — **hat·er** *n*

ha·tred \'hātrəd\ *n* : hate

hat·ter \'hatər\ *n* : one that makes or sells hats

haugh·ty \'hȯtē\ *adj* **-ti·er; -est** : disdainfully proud — **haugh·ti·ly** *adv* — **haugh·ti·ness** *n*

haul \'hȯl\ *vb* **1** : draw or pull **2** : transport or carry ∼ *n* **1** : amount collected **2** : load or the distance it is transported — **haul·er** *n*

haunch \'hȯnch\ *n* : hip or hindquarter — usu. pl.

haunt \'hȯnt\ *vb* **1** : visit often **2** : visit or inhabit as a ghost ∼ *n* : place frequented — **haunt·er** *n* — **haunt·ing·ly** *adv*

have \'hav, *in sense 2 before* "to" *usu* 'haf\ *vb* **had** \'had\; **hav·ing** \'haviŋ\; **has** \'haz, *in sense 2 before* "to" *usu* 'has\ **1** : hold in possession, service, or affection **2** : be compelled or forced to **3** — used as an auxiliary with the past participle to form the present perfect, past perfect, or future perfect **4** : obtain or receive **5** : undergo **6** : cause to **7** : bear — **have to do with** : have in the way of connection or relation with or effect on

ha·ven \'hāvən\ *n* : place of safety

hav·oc \'havək\ *n* **1** : wide destruction **2** : great confusion

¹hawk \'hȯk\ *n* : bird of prey with a strong hooked bill and sharp talons

²hawk *vb* : offer for sale by calling out in the street — **hawk·er** *n*

haw·ser \'hȯzər\ *n* : large rope

haw·thorn \'hȯ͵thȯrn\ *n* : spiny shrub or tree with pink or white fragrant flowers

hay \'hā\ *n* : herbs (as grass) cut and dried for use as fodder — **hay** *vb* — **hay·loft** *n* — **hay·mow** \-͵maů\ *n* — **hay·stack** *n*

hay·cock \'hā͵käk\ *n* : small pile of hay

hay·rick \-͵rik\ *n* : large outdoor stack of hay

hay·seed \'hā͵sēd\ *n* : bumpkin

hay·wire *adj* : being out of order

haz·ard \'hazərd\ *n* **1** : source of danger **2** : chance ∼ *vb* : venture or risk — **haz·ard·ous** *adj*

¹haze \'hāz\ *n* : fine dust, smoke, or light vapor in the air that reduces visibility

²haze *vb* **hazed; haz·ing** : harass by abusive and humiliating tricks

ha·zel \'hāzəl\ *n* **1** : shrub or small tree bearing edible nuts (**ha·zel·nuts**) **2** : light brown color

hazy \\'hāzē\ *adj* **haz·i·er; -est**
1 : obscured by haze **2 :** vague
or indefinite — **haz·i·ly** *adv*
— **haz·i·ness** *n*

he \\'hē\ *pron* **1 :** that male one
2 : a or the person

head \\'hed\ *n* **1 :** front or upper part of the body **2 :** mind
3 : upper or higher end **4 :** director or leader **5 :** place of
leadership or honor ~ *adj*
: principal or chief ~ *vb* **1**
: provide with or form a head
2 : put, stand, or be at the head
3 : point or proceed in a certain direction — **head·ache** *n*
— **head·band** *n* — **headdress** *n* — **head·ed** *adj* —
head·first *adv or adj* — **headgear** *n* — **head·less** *adj* —
head·rest *n* — **head·ship** *n*
— **head·wait·er** *n*

head·ing \-iŋ\ *n* **1 :** direction
in which a plane or ship heads
2 : something (as a title) standing at the top or beginning

head·land \\'hedlənd, -ˌland\
n **:** promontory

head·light *n* **:** light on the front
of a vehicle

head·line *n* **:** introductory line
of a newspaper story printed
in large type

head·long \-ˈlȯŋ\ *adv* **1 :** head
foremost **2 :** in a rash or reckless manner — **head·long**
\-ˌlȯŋ\ *adj*

head·mas·ter *n* **:** man who is
head of a private school

head·mis·tress *n* **:** woman who
is head of a private school

head–on *adj* **:** having the front
facing in the direction of initial contact — **head–on** *adv*

head·phone *n* **:** an earphone
held on by a band over the
head — usu. pl.

head·quar·ters *n sing or pl*
: command or administrative
center

head·stone *n* **:** stone at the
head of a grave

head·strong *adj* **:** stubborn or
willful

head·wa·ters *n pl* **:** source of a
stream

head·way *n* **:** forward motion

heady \\'hedē\ *adj* **head·i·er;
-est 1 :** intoxicating **2 :** shrewd

heal \\'hēl\ *vb* **:** make or become sound or whole — **heal-
er** *n*

health \\'helth\ *n* **:** sound
physical or mental condition

health·ful \-fəl\ *adj* **:** beneficial to health — **health·ful·ly**
adv — **health·ful·ness** *n*

healthy \\'helthē\ *adj* **health·i-
er; -est :** enjoying or typical
of good health — **health·i·ly**
adv — **health·i·ness** *n*

heap \\'hēp\ *n* **:** pile ~ *vb*
: throw or lay in a heap

hear \\'hir\ *vb* **heard** \\'hərd\; **hear·ing** \\'hiriŋ\ **1** : perceive by the ear **2** : heed **3** : learn

hear·ing *n* **1** : process or power of perceiving sound **2** : earshot **3** : session in which witnesses are heard

hear·ken \\'härkən\ *vb* : give attention

hear·say *n* : rumor

hearse \\'hərs\ *n* : vehicle for carrying the dead to the grave

heart \\'härt\ *n* **1** : hollow muscular organ that keeps up the circulation of the blood **2** : playing card of a suit marked with a red heart **3** : whole personality or the emotional or moral part of it **4** : courage **5** : essential part — **heart·beat** *n* — **heart·ed** *adj*

heart·ache *n* : anguish of mind

heart·break *n* : crushing grief — **heart·break·er** *n* — **heart·break·ing** *adj* — **heart·bro·ken** *adj*

heart·burn *n* : burning distress in the heart area after eating

heart·en \\'härtᵊn\ *vb* : encourage

hearth \\'härth\ *n* **1** : area in front of a fireplace **2** : home — **hearth·stone** *n*

heart·less \\'härtləs\ *adj* : cruel

heart·rend·ing \-ˌrendiŋ\ *adj* : causing intense grief or anguish

heart·sick *adj* : very despondent

heart·strings *n pl* : deepest emotions

heart·throb *n* : sweetheart

heart·warm·ing *adj* : inspiring sympathetic feeling

heart·wood *n* : central portion of wood

hearty \\'härtē\ *adj* **heart·i·er; -est** **1** : vigorously healthy **2** : nourishing — **heart·i·ly** *adv* — **heart·i·ness** *n*

heat \\'hēt\ *vb* : make or become warm or hot ~ *n* **1** : condition of being hot **2** : form of energy that causes a body to rise in temperature **3** : intensity of feeling — **heat·ed·ly** *adv* — **heat·er** *n*

heath \\'hēth\ *n* **1** : often evergreen shrubby plant of wet acid soils **2** : tract of wasteland — **heathy** *adj*

hea·then \\'hēthən\ *n, pl* **-thens** *or* **-then** : uncivilized or godless person — **heathen** *adj*

heath·er \\'hethər\ *n* : evergreen heath with lavender flowers — **heath·ery** *adj*

heat·stroke *n* : disorder that follows prolonged exposure to excessive heat

heave \\'hēv\ *vb* **heaved** *or* **hove** \\'hōv\; **heav·ing** **1** : rise or lift upward **2** : throw **3** : rise and fall ~ *n* **1** : an effort to lift or raise **2** : throw

heav·en \'hevən\ *n* **1** *pl* : sky **2** : abode of the Deity and of the blessed dead **3** : place of supreme happiness — **heav·en·ly** *adj* — **heav·en·ward** *adv or adj*

heavy \'hevē\ *adj* **heavi·er; -est** **1** : having great weight **2** : hard to bear **3** : greater than the average — **heav·i·ly** *adv* — **heavi·ness** *n* — **heavy·weight** *n*

heavy–du·ty *adj* : able to withstand unusual strain

heavy·set *adj* : stocky and compact in build

heck·le \'hekəl\ *vb* **-led; -ling** : harass with gibes — **heck·ler** \'heklər\ *n*

hec·tic \'hektik\ *adj* : filled with excitement, activity, or confusion — **hec·ti·cal·ly** \-tiklē\ *adv*

hedge \'hej\ *n* **1** : fence or boundary of shrubs or small trees **2** : means of protection ~ *vb* **hedged; hedg·ing** **1** : protect oneself against loss **2** : evade the risk of commitment — **hedg·er** *n*

hedge·hog *n* : spiny mammal (as a porcupine)

he·do·nism \'hēd³n͜izəm\ *n* : way of life devoted to pleasure — **he·do·nist** \-³nist\ *n* — **he·do·nis·tic** \͜hēd³n'istik\ *adj*

heed \'hēd\ *vb* : pay attention ~ *n* : attention — **heed·ful** \-fəl\ *adj* — **heed·ful·ly** *adv* — **heed·ful·ness** *n* — **heed·less** *adj* — **heed·less·ly** *adv* — **heed·less·ness** *n*

¹**heel** \'hēl\ *n* **1** : back of the foot **2** : crusty end of a loaf of bread **3** : solid piece forming the back of the sole of a shoe — **heel·less** \'hēlləs\ *adj*

²**heel** *vb* : tilt to one side

heft \'heft\ *n* : weight ~ *vb* : judge the weight of by lifting

hefty \'heftē\ *adj* **heft·i·er; -est** : big and bulky

he·ge·mo·ny \hi'jemənē\ *n* : preponderant influence over others

heif·er \'hefər\ *n* : young cow

height \'hīt, 'hītth\ *n* **1** : highest part or point **2** : distance from bottom to top **3** : altitude

height·en \'hīt³n\ *vb* : increase in amount or degree

hei·nous \'hānəs\ *adj* : shockingly evil — **hei·nous·ly** *adv* — **hei·nous·ness** *n*

heir \'ar\ *n* : one who inherits or is entitled to inherit property

heir·ess \'arəs\ *n* : female heir esp. to great wealth

heir·loom \'ar͜lüm\ *n* : something handed on from one generation to another

held *past of* HOLD

he·li·cal \'helikəl, 'hē-\ *adj* : spiral

he·li·cop·ter \'helə̩käptər, 'hē-\ *n* : aircraft supported in the air by rotors

he·lio·trope \'hēlyə̩trōp\ *n* : garden herb with small fragrant white or purple flowers

he·li·um \'hēlēəm\ *n* : very light nonflammable gaseous chemical element

he·lix \'hēliks\ *n, pl* **-li·ces** \'helə̩sēz, 'hē-\ : something spiral

hell \'hel\ *n* **1** : nether world in which the dead continue to exist **2** : realm of the devil **3** : place or state of torment or destruction — **hell·ish** *adj*

hell·gram·mite \'helgrə̩mīt\ *n* : aquatic insect larva

hel·lion \'helyən\ *n* : troublesome person

hel·lo \hə'lō, he-\ *n, pl* **-los** : expression of greeting

helm \'helm\ *n* : lever or wheel for steering a ship — **helms·man** \'helmzmən\ *n*

hel·met \'helmət\ *n* : protective covering for the head

help \'help\ *vb* **1** : supply what is needed **2** : be of use **3** : refrain from or prevent ～ *n* **1** : something that helps or a source of help **2** : one who helps another — **help·er** *n* — **help·ful** \-fəl\ *adj* — **help·ful·ly** *adv* — **help·ful·ness** *n* — **help·less** *adj* — **help·less·ly** *adv* — **help·less·ness** *n*

help·ing \'helpiŋ\ *n* : portion of food

help·mate *n* **1** : helper **2** : wife

help·meet \-̩mēt\ *n* : helpmate

hel·ter–skel·ter \̩heltər-'skeltər\ *adv* : in total disorder

hem \'hem\ *n* : border of an article of cloth doubled back and stitched down ～ *vb* **-mm-** **1** : sew a hem **2** : surround restrictively — **hem·line** *n*

he·ma·tol·o·gy \̩hēmə'täləjē\ *n* : study of the blood and blood-forming organs — **hema·to·log·ic** \-mətᵊl'äjik\ *adj* — **he·ma·tol·o·gist** \-'täləjist\ *n*

hemi·sphere \'hemə̩sfir\ *n* : one of the halves of the earth divided by the equator into northern and southern parts (**northern hemisphere, southern hemisphere**) or by a meridian into eastern and western parts (**eastern hemisphere, western hemisphere**) — **hemi·spher·ic** \̩hemə-'sfirik, -'sfer-\, **hemi·spher·i·cal** \-'sfirikəl, -'sfer-\ *adj*

hem·lock \'hem̩läk\ *n* **1** : poisonous herb related to the carrot **2** : evergreen tree related to the pines

he·mo·glo·bin \'hēmə̩glōbən\ *n* : iron-containing compound found in red blood cells

he·mo·phil·ia \ˌhēmə'filēə\ *n* : hereditary tendency to severe prolonged bleeding — **he·mo·phil·i·ac** \-ē̩ak\ *adj or n*

hem·or·rhage \'hemərij\ *n* : large discharge of blood — **hemorrhage** *vb* — **hem·or·rhag·ic** \ˌhemə'rajik\ *adj*

hem·or·rhoids \'hemə̩ròidz\ *n pl* : swollen mass of dilated veins at or just within the anus

hemp \'hemp\ *n* : tall Asian herb grown for its tough fiber

hen \'hen\ *n* : female domestic fowl

hence \'hens\ *adv* **1** : away **2** : therefore **3** : from this source or origin

hence·forth *adv* : from this point on

hence·for·ward *adv* : henceforth

hench·man \'henchmən\ *n* : trusted follower

hen·na \'henə\ *n* : reddish brown dye from a tropical shrub used esp. on hair

hen·peck \'hen̩pek\ *vb* : subject (one's husband) to persistent nagging

he·pat·ic \hi'patik\ *adj* : relating to or resembling the liver

hep·a·ti·tis \ˌhepə'tītəs\ *n, pl* **-tit·i·des** \-'titə̩dēz\ : disease in which the liver becomes inflamed

her \'hər\ *adj* : of or relating to her or herself ∼ \ər, (')hər\ *pron objective case of* SHE

her·ald \'herəld\ *n* **1** : official crier or messenger **2** : harbinger ∼ *vb* : give notice

her·ald·ry \'herəldrē\ *n, pl* **-ries** : practice of devising and granting stylized emblems (as for a family) — **he·ral·dic** \he'raldik, hə-\ *adj*

herb \'ərb, 'hərb\ *n* **1** : seed plant that lacks woody tissue **2** : plant or plant part valued for medicinal or savory qualities — **her·ba·ceous** \ˌər'bāshəs, ̩hər-\ *adj* — **herb·age** \'ərbij, 'hər-\ *n* — **herb·al** \-bəl\ *n or adj* — **herb·al·ist** \-bəlist\ *n*

her·bi·cide \'ərbə̩sīd, 'hər-\ *n* : agent that destroys plants — **her·bi·cid·al** \ˌərbə'sīdᵊl, ̩hər-\ *adj*

her·biv·o·rous \ər'bivərəs, ̩hər-\ *adj* : feeding on plants — **her·bi·vore** \'ərbə̩vōr, 'hər-\ *n*

her·cu·le·an \ˌhərkyə'lēən, ̩hər'kyülēən\ *adj* : of extraordinary power, size, or difficulty

herd \'hərd\ *n* : group of animals of one kind ∼ *vb* : assemble or move in a herd — **herd·er** *n* — **herds·man** \'hərdzmən\ *n*

here \'hir\ *adv* **1** : in, at, or to this place **2** : now **3** : at or in this point or particular **4** : in the present life or state ∼ *n* : this place — **here·abouts** \'hirəˌbau̇ts\, **here·about** \-ˌbau̇t\ *adv*

here·af·ter *adv* : in some future time or state ∼ *n* : existence beyond earthly life

here·by *adv* : by means of this

he·red·i·tary \hə'redəˌterē\ *adj* **1** : genetically passed or passable from parent to offspring **2** : passing by inheritance

he·red·i·ty \-ətē\ *n* : the passing of characteristics from parent to offspring

here·in *adv* : in this

here·of *adv* : of this

here·on *adv* : on this

her·e·sy \'herəsē\ *n, pl* **-sies** : opinion or doctrine contrary to church dogma — **her·e·tic** \-ˌtik\ *n* — **he·re·ti·cal** \hə-'retikəl\ *adj*

here·to *adv* : to this document

here·to·fore \'hirtüˌfōr\ *adv* : up to this time

here·un·der *adv* : under this

here·un·to *adv* : to this

here·upon *adv* : on this

here·with *adv* **1** : with this **2** : hereby

her·i·tage \'herətij\ *n* **1** : inheritance **2** : birthright

her·maph·ro·dite \hər'mafrə-ˌdīt\ *n* : animal or plant hav-ing both male and female reproductive organs — **her-maphrodite** *adj* — **her-maph·ro·dit·ic** \-ˌmafrə-'ditik\ *adj*

her·met·ic \hər'metik\ *adj* : sealed airtight — **her·met·i·cal·ly** \-iklē\ *adv*

her·mit \'hərmət\ *n* : one who lives in solitude

her·nia \'hərnēə\ *n, pl* **-ni·as** *or* **-ni·ae** \-nēˌ ē, -nēˌ ī\ : protrusion of a bodily part through the weakened wall of its enclosure — **her·ni·ate** \-nēˌ āt\ *vb*

he·ro \'hērō, 'hirō\ *n, pl* **-roes** : one that is much admired or shows great courage — **he·ro·ic** \hi'rōik\ *adj* — **he·ro·i·cal·ly** \-iklē\ *adv* — **he·ro·ics** \-iks\ *n pl* — **her·o·ism** \'herəˌwizəm\ *n*

her·o·in \'herəwən\ *n* : strongly addictive narcotic

her·o·ine \'herəwən\ *n* : woman of heroic achievements or qualities

her·on \'herən\ *n* : long-legged long-billed wading bird

her·pes \'hərpēz\ *n* : virus disease characterized by the formation of blisters

her·pe·tol·o·gy \ˌhərpə'täləjē\ *n* : study of reptiles and amphibians — **her·pe·tol·o·gist** \-pə'täləjist\ *n*

her·ring \\'heriŋ\ *n, pl* **-ring** *or* **-rings** : narrow-bodied Atlantic food fish

hers \\'hərz\ *pron* : one or the ones belonging to her

her·self \hər'self\ *pron* : she, her — used reflexively or for emphasis

hertz \\'herts, 'hərts\ *n, pl* **hertz** : unit of frequency equal to one cycle per second

hes·i·tant \\'hezətənt\ *adj* : tending to hesitate — **hes·i·tance** \-tens\ *n* — **hes·i·tan·cy** \-tənsē\ *n* — **hes·i·tant·ly** *adv*

hes·i·tate \\'hezə,tāt\ *vb* **-tat·ed; -tat·ing** **1** : hold back esp. in doubt **2** : pause — **hes·i·ta·tion** \,hezə'tāshən\ *n*

het·er·o·ge·neous \,hetərə-'jēnēəs, -nyəs\ *adj* : consisting of dissimilar ingredients or constituents — **het·er·o·ge·ne·ity** \-jə'nēətē\ *n* — **het·ero·ge·neous·ly** *adv*

het·ero·sex·u·al \,hetərō'sek-shəwəl\ *adj* : oriented toward the opposite sex — **heterosexual** *n* — **het·ero·sex·u·al·i·ty** \-,sekshə'walətē\ *n*

hew \\'hyü\ *vb* **hewed; hewed** *or* **hewn** \\'hyün\; **hew·ing** **1** : cut or shape with or as if with an ax **2** : conform strictly — **hew·er** *n*

hex \\'heks\ *vb* : put an evil spell on — **hex** *n*

hexa·gon \\'heksə,gän\ *n* : 6-sided polygon — **hex·ag·o·nal** \hek'sagən³l\ *adj*

hey·day \\'hā,dā\ *n* : time of flourishing

hi·a·tus \hī'ātəs\ *n* : lapse in continuity

hi·ba·chi \hi'bächē\ *n* : brazier

hi·ber·nate \\'hībər,nāt\ *vb* **-nat·ed; -nat·ing** : pass the winter in a torpid or resting state — **hi·ber·na·tion** \,hībər-'nāshən\ *n* — **hi·ber·na·tor** \\'hībər,nātər\ *n*

hic·cup \\'hikəp\ *vb* **-cuped; -cup·ing** : to inhale spasmodically and make a peculiar sound ∼ *n pl* : attack of hiccuping

hick \\'hik\ *n* : awkward provincial person — **hick** *adj*

hick·o·ry \\'hikərē\ *n, pl* **-ries** : No. American hardwood tree — **hickory** *adj*

¹hide \\'hīd\ *vb* **hid** \\'hid\; **hidden** \\'hid³n\ *or* **hid; hid·ing** : put or remain out of sight — **hid·er** *n*

²hide *n* : animal skin

hide·bound \\'hīd,baůnd\ *adj* : inflexible or conservative

hid·eous \\'hidēəs\ *adj* : very ugly — **hid·eous·ly** *adv* — **hid·eous·ness** *n*

hie \\'hī\ *vb* **hied; hy·ing** *or* **hie·ing** : hurry

hi·er·ar·chy \\'hīə,rärkē\ *n, pl* **-chies** : persons or things

arranged in a graded series —
hi·er·ar·chi·cal \ˌhīə'rärkikəl\
adj

hi·er·o·glyph·ic \ˌhīərə'glifik\
n : character in the picture
writing of the ancient Egyp-
tians

high \'hī\ *adj* **1** : having large
extension upward **2** : elevated
in pitch **3** : exalted in character **4** : of greater degree or
amount than average **5** : expensive **6** : excited or stupe-
fied by alcohol or a drug ∼
adv : at or to a high place or
degree ∼ *n* **1** : elevated point
or level **2** : automobile gear
giving the highest speed —
high·ly *adv*

high·boy *n* : high chest of
drawers on legs

high·brow \-ˌbrau̇\ *n* : person
of superior learning or culture
— **highbrow** *adj*

high–definition *adj* : being or
relating to a television system
with twice as many scan lines
per frame as a conventional
system

high–flown *adj* : pretentious

high–hand·ed *adj* : willful and
arrogant — **high–hand·ed·ly**
adv — **high–hand·ed·ness** *n*

high·land \'hīlənd\ *n* : hilly
country — **high·land·er**
\-ləndər\ *n*

high·light *n* : event or detail of
major importance ∼ *vb* **1**

: emphasize **2** : be a highlight
of

high·ness \-nəs\ *n* **1** : quality
or degree of being high **2** —
used as a title (as for kings)

high–rise *adj* : having several
stories

high school *n* : school usu. including grades 9 to 12 or 10
to 12

high–spir·it·ed *adj* : lively

high–strung \ˌhī'strəŋ\ *adj*
: very nervous or sensitive

high·way *n* : public road

high·way·man \-mən\ *n* : one
who robs travelers on a road

hi·jack \'hīˌjak\ *vb* : steal esp.
by commandeering a vehicle
— **hijack** *n* — **hi·jack·er** *n*

hike \'hīk\ *vb* **hiked; hik·ing**
1 : raise quickly **2** : take a
long walk ∼ *n* **1** : long walk
2 : increase — **hik·er** *n*

hi·lar·i·ous \hi'larēəs, hī'-\
adj : extremely funny — **hi-
lar·i·ous·ly** *adv* — **hi·lar·i·ty**
\-ətē\ *n*

hill \'hil\ *n* : place where the
land rises — **hill·side** *n* —
hill·top *n* — **hilly** *adj*

hill·bil·ly \'hilˌbilē\ *n, pl* **-lies**
: person from a backwoods
area

hill·ock \'hilək\ *n* : small hill

hilt \'hilt\ *n* : handle of a sword

him \'him\ *pron, objective
case of* HE

him·self \him'self\ *pron* : he, him — used reflexively or for emphasis

¹**hind** \'hīnd\ *n* : female deer

²**hind** *adj* : back

hin·der \'hindər\ *vb* : obstruct or hold back

hind·most *adj* : farthest to the rear

hind·quar·ter *n* : back half of a complete side of a carcass

hin·drance \'hindrəns\ *n* : something that hinders

hind·sight *n* : understanding of an event after it has happened

Hin·du·ism \'hindü,izəm\ *n* : body of religious beliefs and practices native to India — **Hin·du** *n or adj*

hinge \'hinj\ *n* : jointed piece on which a swinging part (as a door) turns ~ *vb* **hinged; hing·ing 1** : attach by or furnish with hinges **2** : depend

hint \'hint\ *n* **1** : indirect suggestion **2** : clue **3** : very small amount — **hint** *vb*

hin·ter·land \'hintər,land\ *n* : remote region

hip \'hip\ *n* : part of the body on either side just below the waist — **hip·bone** *n*

hip·po·pot·a·mus \,hipə-'pätəməs\ *n, pl* **-mus·es** *or* **-mi** \-,mī\ : large thick-skinned African river animal

hire \'hīr\ *n* **1** : payment for labor **2** : employment **3** : one who is hired ~ *vb* **hired; hir·ing** : employ for pay

hire·ling \-liŋ\ *n* : one who serves another only for gain

hir·sute \'hər,süt, 'hir-\ *adj* : hairy

his \'hiz\ *adj* : of or belonging to him ~ *pron* : ones belonging to him

hiss \'his\ *vb* **1** : make a sibilant sound **2** : show dislike by hissing — **hiss** *n*

his·to·ri·an \his'tōrēən\ *n* : writer of history

his·to·ry \'histərē\ *n, pl* **-ries 1** : chronological record of significant events **2** : study of past events **3** : an established record — **his·tor·ic** \his'tȯrik\, **his·tor·i·cal** \-ikəl\ *adj* — **his·tor·i·cal·ly** \-klē\ *adv*

his·tri·on·ics \,histrē'äniks\ *n pl* : exaggerated display of emotion

hit \'hit\ *vb* **hit; hit·ting 1** : reach with a blow **2** : come or cause to come in contact **3** : affect detrimentally ~ *n* **1** : blow **2** : great success — **hit·ter** *n*

hitch \'hich\ *vb* **1** : move by jerks **2** : catch by a hook **3** : hitchhike ~ *n* **1** : jerk **2** : sudden halt

hitch·hike \'hich,hīk\ *vb* : travel by securing free rides from passing vehicles — **hitch·hik·er** *n*

hith·er \'hithər\ *adv* : to this place

hith·er·to \-ˌtü\ *adv* : up to this time

hive \'hīv\ *n* **1** : container housing honeybees **2** : colony of bees — **hive** *vb*

hives \'hīvz\ *n sing or pl* : allergic disorder with itchy skin patches

HMO \ˌāchˌem'ō\ *n* : comprehensive health-care organization financed by clients

hoard \'hōrd\ *n* : hidden accumulation — **hoard** *vb* — **hoard·er** *n*

hoar·frost \'hōrˌfrȯst\ *n* : frost

hoarse \'hōrs\ *adj* **hoars·er; -est 1** : harsh in sound **2** : speaking in a harsh strained voice — **hoarse·ly** *adv* — **hoarse·ness** *n*

hoary \'hōrē\ *adj* **hoar·i·er; -est** : gray or white with age — **hoar·i·ness** *n*

hoax \'hōks\ *n* : act intended to trick or dupe — **hoax** *vb* — **hoax·er** *n*

hob·ble \'häbəl\ *vb* **-bled; -bling** : limp along ~ *n* : hobbling movement

hob·by \'häbē\ *n, pl* **-bies** : interest engaged in for relaxation — **hob·by·ist** \-ēist\ *n*

hob·gob·lin \'häbˌgäblən\ *n* **1** : mischievous goblin **2** : bogey

hob·nail \-ˌnāl\ *n* : short nail for studding shoe soles — **hob·nailed** \-ˌnāld\ *adj*

hob·nob \-ˌnäb\ *vb* **-bb-** : associate socially

ho·bo \'hōbō\ *n, pl* **-boes** : tramp

¹hock \'häk\ *n* : joint or region in the hind limb of a quadruped corresponding to the human ankle

²hock *n or vb* : pawn

hock·ey \'häkē\ *n* : game played on ice or a field by 2 teams

hod \'häd\ *n* : carrier for bricks or mortar

hodge·podge \'häjˌpäj\ *n* : heterogeneous mixture

hoe \'hō\ *n* : long-handled tool for cultivating or weeding — **hoe** *vb*

hog \'hȯg, 'häg\ *n* **1** : domestic adult swine **2** : glutton ~ *vb* : take selfishly — **hog·gish** *adj*

hogs·head \'hȯgzˌhed, 'hägz-\ *n* : large cask or barrel

hog·wash *n* : nonsense

hoist \'hȯist\ *vb* : lift ~ *n* **1** : lift **2** : apparatus for hoisting

hok·ey \'hōkē\ *adj* **hok·i·er; -est 1** : tiresomely simple or sentimental **2** : phony

¹hold \'hōld\ *vb* **held** \'held\; **hold·ing 1** : possess **2** : restrain **3** : have a grasp on **4**

: remain or keep in a particular situation or position **5** : contain **6** : regard **7** : cause to occur **8** : occupy esp. by appointment or election ~ *n* **1** : act or manner of holding **2** : restraining or controlling influence — **hold·er** *n* — **hold forth** : speak at length — **hold to** : adhere to — **hold with** : agree with

²**hold** *n* : cargo area of a ship

hold·ing \'hōldiŋ\ *n* : property owned — usu. pl.

hold·up *n* **1** : robbery at the point of a gun **2** : delay

hole \'hōl\ *n* **1** : opening into or through something **2** : hollow place (as a pit) **3** : den — **hole** *vb*

hol·i·day \'hälə,dā\ *n* **1** : day of freedom from work **2** : vacation — **holiday** *vb*

ho·li·ness \'hōlēnəs\ *n* : quality or state of being holy — used as a title for a high religious official

ho·lis·tic \hō'listik\ *adj* : relating to a whole (as the body)

hol·ler \'hälər\ *vb* : cry out — **holler** *n*

hol·low \'hälō\ *adj* **-low·er** \-əwər\; **-est** **1** : sunken **2** : having a cavity within **3** : sounding like a noise made in an empty place **4** : empty of value or meaning ~ *vb* : make or become hollow ~

n **1** : surface depression **2** : cavity — **hol·low·ness** *n*

hol·ly \'hälē\ *n, pl* **-lies** : evergreen tree or shrub with glossy leaves

hol·ly·hock \-,häk, -,hȯk\ *n* : tall perennial herb with showy flowers

ho·lo·caust \'hälə,kȯst, 'hō-, 'hȯ-\ *n* : thorough destruction esp. by fire

hol·stein \'hōl,stēn, -,stīn\ *n* : large black-and-white dairy cow

hol·ster \'hōlstər\ *n* : case for a pistol

ho·ly \'hōlē\ *adj* **-li·er; -est** **1** : sacred **2** : spiritually pure

hom·age \'ämij, 'hä-\ *n* : reverent regard

home \'hōm\ *n* **1** : residence **2** : congenial environment **3** : place of origin or refuge ~ *vb* **homed; hom·ing** : go or return home — **home·bred** *adj* — **home·com·ing** *n* — **home·grown** *adj* — **home·land** \-,land\ *n* — **home·less** *adj* — **home·made** \-'mād\ *adj*

home·ly \-lē\ *adj* **-li·er; -est** : plain or unattractive — **home·li·ness** *n*

home·mak·er *n* : one who manages a household — **home·mak·ing** *n*

home·sick *adj* : longing for home — **home·sick·ness** *n*

home·spun \-ˌspən\ *adj* : simple

home·stead \-ˌsted\ *n* : home and land occupied and worked by a family — **home·stead·er** \-ər\ *n*

home·stretch *n* **1** : last part of a racetrack **2** : final stage

home·ward \-wərd\, **home·wards** \-wərdz\ *adv* : toward home — **homeward** *adj*

home·work *n* : school lessons to be done outside the classroom

hom·ey \ˈhōmē\ *adj* **hom·i·er; -est** : characteristic of home

ho·mi·cide \ˈhäməˌsīd, ˈhō-\ *n* : the killing of one human being by another — **hom·i·cid·al** \ˌhäməˈsīdᵊl, ˌhō-\ *adj*

hom·i·ly \ˈhäməlē\ *n, pl* **-lies** : sermon

hom·i·ny \ˈhämənē\ *n* : type of processed hulled corn

ho·mo·ge·neous \ˌhōməˈjēnēəs, -nyəs\ *adj* : of the same or a similar kind — **ho·mo·ge·ne·i·ty** \-jəˈnēətē\ *n* — **ho·mo·ge·neous·ly** *adv*

ho·mog·e·nize \hōˈmäjəˌnīz, hə-\ *vb* **-nized; -niz·ing** : make the particles in (as milk) of uniform size and even distribution — **ho·mog·e·ni·za·tion** \-ˌmäjənəˈzāshən\ *n* — **ho·mog·e·niz·er** *n*

ho·mo·graph \ˈhäməˌgraf, ˈhō-\ *n* : one of 2 or more words (as the noun *conduct* and the verb *conduct*) spelled alike but different in origin or meaning or pronunciation

hom·onym \ˈhäməˌnim, ˈhō-\ *n* **1** : homophone **2** : homograph **3** : one of 2 or more words (as *pool* of water and *pool* the game) spelled and pronounced alike but different in meaning

ho·mo·phone \ˈhäməˌfōn, ˈhō-\ *n* : one of 2 or more words (as *to, too,* and *two*) pronounced alike but different in origin or meaning or spelling

Ho·mo sa·pi·ens \ˌhōmōˈsapēənz, -ˈsā-\ *n* : humankind

ho·mo·sex·u·al \ˌhōməˈsekshəwəl\ *adj* : oriented toward one's own sex — **homosexual** *n* — **ho·mo·sex·u·al·i·ty** \-ˌsekshəˈwalətē\ *n*

hone \ˈhōn\ *vb* : sharpen with or as if with an abrasive stone

hon·est \ˈänəst\ *adj* **1** : free from deception **2** : trustworthy **3** : frank — **hon·est·ly** *adv* — **hon·esty** \-əstē\ *n*

hon·ey \ˈhənē\ *n, pl* **-eys** : sweet sticky substance made by bees (**hon·ey·bees**) from the nectar of flowers

hon·ey·comb *n* : mass of 6-sided wax cells built by honeybees or something like it ∼ *vb* : make or become full of holes like a honeycomb

hon·ey·moon *n* : holiday taken by a newly married couple — **honeymoon** *vb*

hon·ey·suck·le \-ˌsəkəl\ *n* : shrub or vine with flowers rich in nectar

honk \'häŋk, 'hȯŋk\ *n* : cry of a goose or a similar sound — **honk** *vb* — **honk·er** *n*

hon·or \'änər\ *n* **1** : good name **2** : outward respect or symbol of this **3** : privilege **4** : person of superior rank or position — used esp. as a title **5** : something or someone worthy of respect **6** : integrity ∼ *vb* **1** : regard with honor **2** : confer honor on **3** : fulfill the terms of — **hon·or·able** \'änərəbəl\ *adj* — **hon·or·ably** \-blē\ *adv* — **hon·or·ari·ly** \ˌänə'rerəlē\ *adv* — **hon·or·ary** \'änəˌrerē\ *adj* — **hon·or·ee** \ˌänə'rē\ *n*

hood \'hu̇d\ *n* **1** : part of a garment that covers the head **2** : covering over an automobile engine compartment — **hood·ed** *adj*

-hood \ˌhu̇d\ *n suffix* **1** : state, condition, or quality **2** : individuals sharing a state or character

hood·lum \'hu̇dləm, 'hüd-\ *n* : thug

hood·wink \'hu̇dˌwiŋk\ *vb* : deceive

hoof \'hu̇f, 'hüf\ *n, pl* **hooves** \'hu̇vz, 'hüvz\ *or* **hoofs** : horny covering of the toes of some mammals (as horses or cattle) — **hoofed** \'hu̇ft, 'hüft\ *adj*

hook \'hu̇k\ *n* : curved or bent device for catching, holding, or pulling ∼ *vb* : seize or make fast with a hook — **hook·er** *n*

hook·worm *n* : parasitic intestinal worm

hoo·li·gan \'hüligən\ *n* : thug

hoop \'hüp\ *n* : circular strip, figure, or object

hoot \'hüt\ *vb* **1** : shout in contempt **2** : make the cry of an owl — **hoot** *n* — **hoot·er** *n*

¹hop \'häp\ *vb* **-pp-** : move by quick springy leaps — **hop** *n*

²hop *n* : vine whose ripe dried flowers are used to flavor malt liquors

hope \'hōp\ *vb* **hoped; hoping** : desire with expectation of fulfillment ∼ *n* **1** : act of hoping **2** : something hoped for — **hope·ful** \-fəl\ *adj* — **hope·ful·ly** *adv* — **hope·ful·ness** *n* — **hope·less** *adj* — **hope·less·ly** *adv* — **hope·less·ness** *n*

hop·per \'häpər\ *n* : container that releases its contents through the bottom

horde \'hōrd\ *n* : throng or swarm

ho·ri·zon \hə'rīzᵊn\ *n* : apparent junction of earth and sky

hor·i·zon·tal \ˌhȯrəˈzäntᵊl\ *adj* : parallel to the horizon — **hor·i·zon·tal·ly** *adv*

hor·mone \ˈhȯrˌmōn\ *n* : cell product in body fluids that has a specific effect on other cells — **hor·mon·al** \hȯrˈmōnᵊl\ *adj*

horn \ˈhȯrn\ *n* **1** : hard bony projection on the head of a hoofed animal **2** : brass wind instrument — **horned** *adj* — **horn·less** *adj*

hor·net \ˈhȯrnət\ *n* : large social wasp

horny \ˈhȯrnē\ *adj* **horn·i·er; -est** **1** : made of horn **2** : hard or callous **3** : sexually aroused

horo·scope \ˈhȯrəˌskōp\ *n* : astrological forecast

hor·ren·dous \hȯˈrendəs\ *adj* : horrible

hor·ri·ble \ˈhȯrəbəl\ *adj* **1** : having or causing horror **2** : highly disagreeable — **hor·ri·ble·ness** *n* — **hor·ri·bly** \-blē\ *adv*

hor·rid \ˈhȯrəd\ *adj* : horrible — **hor·rid·ly** *adv*

hor·ri·fy \ˈhȯrəˌfī\ *vb* **-fied; -fy·ing** : cause to feel horror

hor·ror \ˈhȯrər\ *n* **1** : intense fear, dread, or dismay **2** : intense repugnance **3** : something horrible

hors d'oeuvre \ȯrˈdərv\ *n, pl* **hors d'oeuvres** \-ˈdərvz\ : appetizer

horse \ˈhȯrs\ *n* : large solid-hoofed domesticated mammal — **horse·back** *n or adv* — **horse·hair** *n* — **horse·hide** *n* — **horse·less** *adj* — **horse·man** \-mən\ *n* — **horse·man·ship** *n* — **horse·wom·an** *n* — **hors·ey, horsy** *adj*

horse·fly *n* : large fly with bloodsucking female

horse·play *n* : rough boisterous play

horse·pow·er *n* : unit of mechanical power

horse·rad·ish *n* : herb with a pungent root used as a condiment

horse·shoe *n* : U-shaped protective metal plate fitted to the rim of a horse's hoof

hor·ti·cul·ture \ˈhȯrtəˌkəlchər\ *n* : science of growing fruits, vegetables, and flowers — **hor·ti·cul·tur·al** \ˌhȯrtəˈkəlchərəl\ *adj* — **hor·ti·cul·tur·ist** \-rist\ *n*

ho·san·na \hōˈzanə, -ˈzän-\ *interj* — used as a cry of acclamation and adoration — **hosanna** *n*

hose \ˈhōz\ *n* **1** *pl* **hose** : stocking or sock **2** *pl* **hos·es** : flexible tube for conveying fluids ∼ *vb* **hosed; hos·ing** : spray, water, or wash with a hose

ho·siery \ˈhōzhərē, ˈhōzə-\ *n* : stockings or socks

hos·pice \'häspəs\ *n* **1** : lodging (as for travelers) maintained by a religious order **2** : facility or program for caring for dying persons

hos·pi·ta·ble \hä'spitəbəl, 'häs₁pit-\ *adj* : given to generous and cordial reception of guests — **hos·pi·ta·bly** \-blē\ *adv*

hos·pi·tal \'häs₁pit³l\ *n* : institution where the sick or injured receive medical care — **hos·pi·tal·i·za·tion** \₁häs₁pit³lə-'zāshən\ *n* — **hos·pi·tal·ize** \'häs₁pit³l₁īz\ *vb*

hos·pi·tal·i·ty \₁häspə'talətē\ *n, pl* **-ties** : hospitable treatment, reception, or disposition

¹**host** \'hōst\ *n* **1** : army **2** : multitude

²**host** *n* : one who receives or entertains guests — **host** *vb*

³**host** *n* : eucharistic bread

hos·tage \'hästij\ *n* : person held to guarantee that promises be kept or demands met

hos·tel \'häst³l\ *n* : lodging for youth — **hos·tel·er** *n*

hos·tel·ry \-rē\ *n, pl* **-ries** : hotel

host·ess \'hōstəs\ *n* : woman who is host

hos·tile \'häst³l, -₁tīl\ *adj* : openly or actively unfriendly or opposed to someone or something — **hostile** *n*

— **hos·tile·ly** *adv* — **hos·til·i·ty** \häs'tilətē\ *n*

hot \'hät\ *adj* **-tt-** **1** : having a high temperature **2** : giving a sensation of heat or burning **3** : ardent **4** : pungent — **hot** *adv* — **hot·ly** *adv* — **hot·ness** *n*

hot·bed *n* : environment that favors rapid growth

hot dog *n* : frankfurter

ho·tel \hō'tel\ *n* : building where lodging and personal services are provided

hot·head·ed *adj* : impetuous — **hot·head** *n* — **hot·head·ed·ly** *adv* — **hot·head·ed·ness** *n*

hot·house *n* : greenhouse

hound \'haůnd\ *n* : long-eared hunting dog ~ *vb* : pursue relentlessly

hour \'aůər\ *n* **1** : 24th part of a day **2** : time of day — **hour·ly** *adv or adj*

hour·glass *n* : glass vessel for measuring time

house \'haůs\ *n, pl* **hous·es** \'haůzəz\ **1** : building to live in **2** : household **3** : legislative body **4** : business firm ~ \'haůz\ *vb* **housed; hous·ing** : provide with or take shelter — **house·boat** \'haůs₁bōt\ *n* — **house·clean** \'haůs₁klēn\ *vb* — **house·clean·ing** *n* — **house·ful** \-₁fůl\ *n* — **house·maid** *n* — **house·wares** *n pl* — **house·work** *n*

house·bro·ken \-ˌbrōkən\ *adj* : trained in excretory habits acceptable in indoor living

house·fly *n* : two-winged fly common about human habitations

house·hold \-ˌhōld\ *n* : those who dwell as a family under the same roof ~ *adj* **1** : domestic **2** : common or familiar — **house·hold·er** *n*

house·keep·ing \-ˌkēpiŋ\ *n* : care and management of a house or institution — **house-keep·er** *n*

house·warm·ing *n* : party to celebrate moving into a house

house·wife \'haůsˌwīf\ *n* : married woman in charge of a household — **house-wife·ly** *adj* — **house·wif·ery** \-ˌwīfərē\ *n*

hous·ing \'haůziŋ\ *n* **1** : dwellings for people **2** : protective covering

hove *past of* HEAVE

hov·el \'həvəl, 'häv-\ *n* : small wretched house

hov·er \'həvər, 'häv-\ *vb* **1** : remain suspended in the air **2** : move about in the vicinity

how \'haů\ *adv* **1** : in what way or condition **2** : for what reason **3** : to what extent ~ *conj* : the way or manner in which

how·ev·er \haů'evər\ *conj* : in whatever manner ~ *adv*

1 : to whatever degree or in whatever manner **2** : in spite of that

how·it·zer \'haůətsər\ *n* : short cannon

howl \'haůl\ *vb* : emit a loud long doleful sound like a dog — **howl** *n* — **howl·er** *n*

hoy·den \'hȯidᵊn\ *n* : girl or woman of saucy or carefree behavior

hub \'həb\ *n* : central part of a circular object (as of a wheel) — **hub·cap** *n*

hub·bub \'həbˌəb\ *n* : uproar

hu·bris \'hyübrəs\ *n* : excessive pride

huck·le·ber·ry \'həkəlˌberē\ *n* **1** : shrub related to the blueberry or its berry **2** : blueberry

huck·ster \'həkstər\ *n* : peddler

hud·dle \'hədᵊl\ *vb* **-dled; -dling** **1** : crowd together **2** : confer — **huddle** *n*

hue \'hyü\ *n* : color or gradation of color — **hued** \'hyüd\ *adj*

huff \'həf\ *n* : fit of pique — **huffy** *adj*

hug \'həg\ *vb* **-gg-** **1** : press tightly in the arms **2** : stay close to — **hug** *n*

huge \'hyüj\ *adj* **hug·er; hug·est** : very large or extensive — **huge·ly** *adv* — **huge·ness** *n*

hu·la \'hülə\ *n* : Polynesian dance

hulk \'həlk\ *n* **1** : bulky or unwieldy person or thing **2** : old ship unfit for service — **hulking** *adj*

hull \'həl\ *n* **1** : outer covering of a fruit or seed **2** : frame or body of a ship or boat ~ *vb* : remove the hulls of — **huller** *n*

hul·la·ba·loo \'hələbə‚lü\ *n, pl* **-loos** : uproar

hum \'həm\ *vb* **-mm-** **1** : make a prolonged sound like that of the speech sound \m\ **2** : be busily active **3** : run smoothly **4** : sing with closed lips — **hum** *n* — **hum·mer** *n*

hu·man \'hyümən, 'yü-\ *adj* **1** : of or relating to the species people belong to **2** : by, for, or like people — **human** *n* — **hu·man·kind** *n* — **hu·man·ly** *adv* — **hu·man·ness** *n*

hu·mane \hyü'mān, ‚yü-\ *adj* : showing compassion or consideration for others — **hu·mane·ly** *adv* — **hu·mane·ness** *n*

hu·man·ism \'hyümə‚nizəm, 'yü-\ *n* : doctrine or way of life centered on human interests or values — **hu·man·ist** \-nist\ *n or adj* — **hu·man·is·tic** \‚hyümə'nistik, ‚yü-\ *adj*

hu·man·i·tar·i·an \hyü‚manə'terēən, yü-\ *n* : person promoting human welfare — **hu·manitarian** *adj* — **hu·man·i·tari·an·ism** *n*

hu·man·i·ty \hyü'manətē, yü-\ *n, pl* **-ties** **1** : human or humane quality or state **2** : the human race

hu·man·ize \'hyümə‚nīz, 'yü-\ *vb* **-ized; -iz·ing** : make human or humane — **hu·man·iza·tion** \‚hyümənə'zāshən, ‚yü-\ *n* — **hu·man·iz·er** *n*

hu·man·oid \'hyümə‚noid, 'yü-\ *adj* : having human form — **humanoid** *n*

hum·ble \'həmbəl\ *adj* **-bler; -blest** **1** : not proud or haughty **2** : not pretentious ~ *vb* **-bled; -bling** : make humble — **hum·ble·ness** *n* — **hum·bler** *n* — **hum·bly** \-blē\ *adv*

hum·bug \'həm‚bəg\ *n* : nonsense

hum·drum \-‚drəm\ *adj* : monotonous

hu·mid \'hyüməd, 'yü-\ *adj* : containing or characterized by moisture — **hu·mid·i·fi·ca·tion** \hyü‚midəfɔ'kāshən\ *n* — **hu·mid·i·fi·er** \-'midə‚fīər\ *n* — **hu·mid·i·fy** \-‚fī\ *vb* — **hu·mid·ly** *adv*

hu·mid·i·ty \hyü'midətē, yü-\ *n, pl* **-ties** : atmospheric moisture

hu·mi·dor \'hyümə‚dȯr, 'yü-\ *n* : humidified storage case (as for cigars)

hu·mil·i·ate \hyü'milē͵āt, yü-\ *vb* **-at·ed; -at·ing** : injure the self-respect of — **hu·mil·i·at·ing·ly** *adv* — **hu·mil·i·ation** \-͵milē'āshən\ *n*

hu·mil·i·ty \hyü'milətē, yü-\ *n* : humble quality or state

hum·ming·bird \'həmiŋ͵bərd\ *n* : tiny American bird that can hover

hum·mock \'həmək\ *n* : mound or knoll — **hum·mocky** \-məkē\ *adj*

hu·mor \'hyümər, 'yü-\ *n* **1** : mood **2** : quality of being laughably ludicrous or incongruous **3** : appreciation of what is ludicrous or incongruous **4** : something intended to be funny ∼ *vb* : comply with the wishes or mood of — **hu·mor·ist** \-ərist\ *n* — **hu·mor·less** *adj* — **hu·mor·less·ly** *adv* — **hu·mor·less·ness** *n* — **hu·mor·ous** \'hyümərəs, 'yü-\ *adj* — **hu·mor·ous·ly** *adv* — **hu·mor·ous·ness** *n*

hump \'həmp\ *n* : rounded protuberance — **humped** *adj*

hump·back *n* : hunchback — **hump·backed** *adj*

hu·mus \'hyüməs, 'yü-\ *n* : dark organic part of soil

hunch \'hənch\ *vb* : assume or cause to assume a bent or crooked posture ∼ *n* : strong intuitive feeling

hunch·back *n* **1** : back with a hump **2** : person with a crooked back — **hunch·backed** *adj*

hun·dred \'həndrəd\ *n, pl* **-dreds** *or* **-dred** : 10 times 10 — **hundred** *adj* — **hun·dredth** \-drədth\ *adj or n*

¹hung *past of* HANG

²hung *adj* : unable to reach a verdict

hun·ger \'həŋgər\ *n* **1** : craving or urgent need for food **2** : strong desire — **hunger** *vb* — **hun·gri·ly** \-grəlē\ *adv* — **hun·gry** *adj*

hunk \'həŋk\ *n* : large piece

hun·ker \'həŋkər\ *vb* : settle in for a sustained period — used with *down*

hunt \'hənt\ *vb* **1** : pursue for food or sport **2** : try to find ∼ *n* : act or instance of hunting — **hunt·er** *n*

hur·dle \'hərd³l\ *n* **1** : barrier to leap over in a race **2** : obstacle — **hurdle** *vb* — **hur·dler** *n*

hurl \'hərl\ *vb* : throw with violence — **hurl** *n* — **hurl·er** *n*

hur·rah \hu̇'rä, -'rȯ\ *interj* — used to express joy or approval

hur·ri·cane \'hərə͵kān\ *n* : tropical storm with winds of 74 miles per hour or greater

hur·ry \'hərē\ *vb* **-ried; -ry·ing** : go or cause to go with haste ∼ *n* : extreme haste — **hur·ried·ly** *adv* — **hur·ried·ness** *n*

hurt \'hərt\ *vb* **hurt; hurt·ing 1** : feel or cause pain **2** : do harm to ~ *n* **1** : bodily injury **2** : harm — **hurt·ful** \-fəl\ *adj* — **hurt·ful·ness** *n*

hur·tle \'hərtᵊl\ *vb* **-tled; -tling** : move rapidly or forcefully

hus·band \'həzbənd\ *n* : married man ~ *vb* : manage prudently

hus·band·ry \-bəndrē\ *n* **1** : careful use **2** : agriculture

hush \'həsh\ *vb* : make or become quiet ~ *n* : silence

husk \'həsk\ *n* : outer covering of a seed or fruit ~ *vb* : strip the husk from — **husk·er** *n*

¹**hus·ky** \'həskē\ *adj* **-ki·er; -est** : hoarse — **hus·ki·ly** *adv* — **hus·ki·ness** *n*

²**husky** *adj* **-ki·er; -est** : burly — **husk·i·ness** *n*

³**husky** *n, pl* **-kies** : working dog of the arctic

hus·sy \'həsē, -zē\ *n, pl* **-sies 1** : brazen woman **2** : mischievous girl

hus·tle \'həsəl\ *vb* **-tled; -tling 1** : hurry **2** : work energetically — **hustle** *n* — **hus·tler** \'həslər\ *n*

hut \'hət\ *n* : small often temporary dwelling

hutch \'həch\ *n* **1** : cupboard with open shelves **2** : pen for an animal

hy·a·cinth \'hīə,sinth\ *n* : bulbous herb grown for bell-shaped flowers

hy·brid \'hībrəd\ *n* : offspring of genetically differing parents — **hybrid** *adj* — **hy·brid·iza·tion** \,hībrədə-'zāshən\ *n* — **hy·brid·ize** \'hībrəd,īz\ *vb* — **hy·brid·iz·er** *n*

hy·drant \'hīdrənt\ *n* : pipe from which water may be drawn to fight fires

hy·drau·lic \hī'drȯlik\ *adj* : operated by liquid forced through a small hole — **hy·drau·lics** \-liks\ *n*

hy·dro·car·bon \,hīdrə'kär-bən\ *n* : organic compound of carbon and hydrogen

hy·dro·elec·tric \,hīdrōi'lek-trik\ *adj* : producing electricity by waterpower — **hy·dro·elec·tric·i·ty** \-,lek'trisətē\ *n*

hy·dro·gen \'hīdrəjən\ *n* : very light gaseous colorless odorless flammable chemical element

hydrogen bomb *n* : powerful bomb that derives its energy from the union of atomic nuclei

hy·dro·pho·bia \,hīdrə'fōbēə\ *n* : rabies

hy·dro·plane \'hīdrə,plān\ *n* : speedboat that skims the water

hy·drous \'hīdrəs\ *adj* : containing water

hy·e·na \hī'ēnə\ *n* : nocturnal carnivorous mammal of Asia and Africa

hy·giene \'hī͜jēn\ *n* : conditions or practices conducive to health — **hy·gien·ic** \hī-'jenik, -'jēn-; ͵hījē'enik\ *adj* — **hy·gien·i·cal·ly** \-iklē\ *adv* — **hy·gien·ist** \hī'jēnist, -'jen-; 'hī͜jēn-\ *n*

hy·grom·e·ter \hī'grämətər\ *n* : instrument for measuring atmospheric humidity

hying *pres part of* HIE

hymn \'him\ *n* : song of praise esp. to God — **hymn** *vb*

hym·nal \'himnəl\ *n* : book of hymns

hype \'hīp\ *vb* **hyped; hyping** : publicize extravagantly — **hype** *n*

hyper- *prefix* **1** : above or beyond **2** : excessively or excessive

hy·per·bo·le \hī'pərbəlē\ *n* : extravagant exaggeration

hy·per·ten·sion \'hīpər͵tenchən\ *n* : high blood pressure — **hy·per·ten·sive** \͵hīpər-'tensiv\ *adj or n*

hy·phen \'hīfən\ *n* : punctuation mark - used to divide or compound words — **hyphen** *vb*

hy·phen·ate \'hīfə͵nāt\ *vb* **-at·ed; -at·ing** : connect or divide with a hyphen — **hyphen·ation** \͵hīfə'nāshən\ *n*

hyp·no·sis \hip'nōsəs\ *n, pl* **-no·ses** \-͵sēz\ : induced state like sleep in which the subject is responsive to suggestions of the inducer (**hyp·no·tist** \'hipnətist\) — **hyp·no·tism** \'hipnə͵tizəm\ *n* — **hyp·no-**

List of self-explanatory words with the prefix *hyper-*

hyperacid	hyperenergetic	hypersensitive
hyperacidity	hyperexcitable	hypersensitiveness
hyperactive	hyperfastidious	hypersensitivity
hyperacute	hyperintense	hypersexual
hyperaggressive	hypermasculine	hypersusceptible
hypercautious	hypernationalistic	hypertense
hypercorrect	hyperreactive	hypervigilant
hypercritical	hyperrealistic	
hyperemotional	hyperromantic	

tiz·able \ˌhipnə'tīzəbəl\ *adj* — **hyp·no·tize** \'hipnə,tīz\ *vb*

hyp·not·ic \hip'nätik\ *adj* : relating to hypnosis — **hyp-notic** *n* — **hyp·not·i·cal·ly** \-iklē\ *adv*

hy·po·chon·dria \ˌhīpə'kän-drēə\ *n* : morbid concern for one's health — **hy·po·chon-dri·ac** \-drē,ak\ *adj or n*

hy·poc·ri·sy \hip'äkrəsē\ *n, pl* **-sies** : a feigning to be what one is not — **hyp·o·crite** \'hipə,krit\ *n* — **hyp·o·crit·i-cal** \ˌhipə'kritikəl\ *adj* — **hyp·o·crit·i·cal·ly** *adv*

hy·po·der·mic \ˌhīpə'dərmik\ *adj* : administered or used in making an injection beneath the skin ~ *n* : hypodermic syringe

hy·pot·e·nuse \hī'pätə,nüs, -,nüz, -,nyüs, -,nyüz\ *n* : side of a right-angled triangle opposite the right angle

hy·poth·e·sis \hī'päthəsəs\ *n, pl* **-e·ses** \-,sēz\ : assumption made in order to test its conse-quences — **hy·poth·e·size** \-,sīz\ *vb* — **hy·po·thet·i·cal** \ˌhīpə'thetikəl\ *adj* — **hy-po·thet·i·cal·ly** *adv*

hys·ter·ec·to·my \ˌhistə'rek-təmē\ *n, pl* **-mies** : surgical removal of the uterus

hys·te·ria \his'terēə, -tir-\ *n* : uncontrollable fear or out-burst of emotion — **hys·ter·i-cal** \-'terikəl\ *adj* — **hys·ter-i·cal·ly** *adv*

hys·ter·ics \-'teriks\ *n pl* : un-controllable laughter or crying

I

i \'ī\ *n, pl* **i's** *or* **is** \'īz\ : 9th letter of the alphabet

I \'ī\ *pron* : the speaker

-ial *adj suffix* : of, relating to, or characterized by

-ian — see -AN

ibis \'ībəs\ *n, pl* **ibis** *or* **ibis·es** : wading bird with a down-curved bill

-ible — see -ABLE

ibu·pro·fen \ˌībyù'prōfən\ *n* : drug used to relieve inflam-mation, pain, and fever

-ic \ik\ *adj suffix* **1** : of, relat-ing to, or being **2** : contain-ing **3** : characteristic of **4** : marked by **5** : caused by

-i·cal \ikəl\ *adj suffix* : -ic — **-i·cal·ly** \iklē, -kəlē\ *adv suf-fix*

ice \'īs\ *n* **1** : frozen water **2** : flavored frozen dessert ~ *vb* **iced; ic·ing 1** : freeze **2** : chill **3** : cover with icing

ice·berg \'īs,bərg\ *n* : large floating mass of ice

ice·box *n* : refrigerator

ice·break·er *n* : ship equipped to cut through ice

ice cream *n* : sweet frozen food

ice–skate *vb* : skate on ice — **ice skater** *n*

ich·thy·ol·o·gy \,ikthē'äləjē\ *n* : study of fishes — **ich·thy·ol·o·gist** \-jist\ *n*

ici·cle \'ī,sikəl\ *n* : hanging mass of ice

ic·ing \'īsiŋ\ *n* : sweet usu. creamy coating for baked goods

icon \'ī,kän\ *n* **1** : religious image **2** : small picture on a computer screen identified with an available function

icon·o·clast \ī'känə,klast\ *n* : attacker of cherished beliefs or institutions — **icon·o·clasm** \-,klazəm\ *n*

icy \'īsē\ *adj* **ic·i·er; -est 1** : covered with or consisting of ice **2** : very cold — **ic·i·ly** *adv* — **ic·i·ness** *n*

id \'id\ *n* : unconscious instinctual part of the mind

idea \ī'dēə\ *n* **1** : something imagined in the mind **2** : purpose or plan

ide·al \ī'dēəl\ *adj* **1** : imaginary **2** : perfect ~ *n* **1** : standard of excellence **2** : model **3** : aim — **ide·al·ly** *adv*

ide·al·ism \ī'dēə,lizəm\ *n* : adherence to ideals — **ide·al·ist** \-list\ *n* — **ide·al·is·tic** \ī,dēə'listik\ *adj* — **ide·al·is·ti·cal·ly** \-tiklē\ *adv*

ide·al·ize \ī'dēə,līz\ *vb* **-ized; -iz·ing** : think of or represent as ideal — **ide·al·i·za·tion** \-,dēələ'zāshən\ *n*

iden·ti·cal \ī'dentikəl\ *adj* **1** : being the same **2** : exactly or essentially alike

iden·ti·fi·ca·tion \ī,dentəfə'kāshən\ *n* **1** : act of identifying **2** : evidence of identity

iden·ti·fy \ī'dentə,fī\ *vb* **-fied; -fy·ing 1** : associate **2** : establish the identity of — **iden·ti·fi·able** \ī,dentə'fīəbəl\ *adj* — **iden·ti·fi·er** \ī'dentə,fīər\ *n*

iden·ti·ty \ī'dentətē\ *n, pl* **-ties 1** : sameness of essential character **2** : individuality **3** : fact of being what is supposed

ide·ol·o·gy \,īdē'äləjē, ,id-\ *n, pl* **-gies** : body of beliefs — **ide·o·log·i·cal** \,īdēə'läjikəl, ,id-\ *adj*

id·i·om \'idēəm\ *n* **1** : language peculiar to a person or group **2** : expression with a special meaning — **id·i·om·at·ic** \ˌidēəˈmatik\ *adj* — **id·i·om·at·i·cal·ly** \-iklē\ *adv*

id·io·syn·cra·sy \ˌidēōˈsiŋkrəsē\ *n, pl* **-sies** : personal peculiarity — **id·io·syn·crat·ic** \-sinˈkratik\ *adj* — **id·io·syn·crat·i·cal·ly** \-ˈkratiklē\ *adv*

id·i·ot \ˈidēət\ *n* : mentally retarded or foolish person — **id·i·o·cy** \-əsē\ *n* — **id·i·ot·ic** \ˌidēˈätik\ *adj* — **id·i·ot·i·cal·ly** \-iklē\ *adv*

idle \ˈīdᵊl\ *adj* **idler; idlest 1** : worthless **2** : inactive **3** : lazy ~ *vb* **idled; idling** : spend time doing nothing — **idle·ness** *n* — **idler** *n* — **idly** \ˈīdlē\ *adv*

idol \ˈīdᵊl\ *n* **1** : image of a god **2** : object of devotion — **idol·iza·tion** \ˌīdᵊləˈzāshən\ *n* — **idol·ize** \ˈīdᵊlīz\ *vb*

idol·a·ter, idol·a·tor \īˈdälətər\ *n* : worshiper of idols — **idol·a·trous** \-trəs\ *adj* — **idol·a·try** \-trē\ *n*

idyll \ˈīdᵊl\ *n* : period of peace and contentment — **idyl·lic** \īˈdilik\ *adj*

-ier — see **-ER**

if \ˈif\ *conj* **1** : in the event that **2** : whether **3** : even though

-i·fy \əˌfī\ *vb suffix* : -fy

ig·loo \ˈiglü\ *n, pl* **-loos** : hut made of snow blocks

ig·nite \igˈnīt\ *vb* **-nit·ed; -nit·ing** : set afire or catch fire — **ig·nit·able** \-ˈnītəbəl\ *adj*

ig·ni·tion \igˈnishən\ *n* **1** : a setting on fire **2** : process or means of igniting fuel

ig·no·ble \igˈnōbəl\ *adj* : not honorable — **ig·no·bly** \-blē\ *adv*

ig·no·min·i·ous \ˌignəˈminēəs\ *adj* **1** : dishonorable **2** : humiliating — **ig·no·min·i·ous·ly** *adv* — **ig·no·mi·ny** \ˈignəˌminē, igˈnämənē\ *n*

ig·no·ra·mus \ˌignəˈrāməs\ *n* : ignorant person

ig·no·rant \ˈignərənt\ *adj* **1** : lacking knowledge **2** : showing a lack of knowledge or intelligence **3** : unaware — **ig·no·rance** \-rəns\ *n* — **ig·no·rant·ly** *adv*

ig·nore \igˈnōr\ *vb* **-nored; -nor·ing** : refuse to notice

igua·na \iˈgwänə\ *n* : large tropical American lizard

ilk \ˈilk\ *n* : kind

ill \ˈil\ *adj* **worse** \ˈwərs\; **worst** \ˈwərst\ **1** : sick **2** : bad **3** : rude or unacceptable **4** : hostile ~ *adv* **worse; worst 1** : with displeasure **2** : harshly **3** : scarcely **4** : badly ~ *n* **1** : evil **2** : misfortune **3** : sickness

il·le·gal \ilˈlēgəl\ *adj* : not lawful — **il·le·gal·i·ty** \iliˈgalətē\

n — **il·le·gal·ly** \il'lēgəlē\ *adv*

il·leg·i·ble \il'lejəbəl\ *adj* : not legible — **il·leg·i·bil·i·ty** \il-ˌlejə'bilətē\ *n* — **il·leg·i·bly** \il'lejəblē\ *adv*

il·le·git·i·mate \ˌili'jitəmət\ *adj* **1** : born of unmarried parents **2** : illegal — **il·le·git·i·ma·cy** \-əməsē\ *n* — **il·le·git·i·mate·ly** *adv*

il·lic·it \il'lisət\ *adj* : not lawful — **il·lic·it·ly** *adv*

il·lim·it·able \il'limətəbəl\ *adj* : boundless — **il·lim·it·ably** \-blē\ *adv*

il·lit·er·ate \il'litərət\ *adj* : unable to read or write — **il·lit·er·a·cy** \-ərəsē\ *n* — **illiterate** *n*

ill–na·tured \-'nāchərd\ *adj* : cross — **ill–na·tured·ly** *adv*

ill·ness \'ilnəs\ *n* : sickness

il·log·i·cal \il'läjikəl\ *adj* : contrary to sound reasoning — **il·log·i·cal·ly** *adv*

ill–starred \'il'stärd\ *adj* : unlucky

il·lu·mi·nate \il'üməˌnāt\ *vb* **-nat·ed; -nat·ing 1** : light up **2** : make clear — **il·lu·mi·nat·ing·ly** \-ˌnātiŋlē\ *adv* — **il·lu·mi·na·tion** \-ˌümə'nāshən\ *n*

ill–use \-'yüz\ *vb* : abuse — **ill–use** \-'yüs\ *n*

il·lu·sion \il'üzhən\ *n* **1** : mistaken idea **2** : misleading visual image

il·lu·so·ry \il'üsərē, -'üz-\ *adj* : based on or producing illusion

il·lus·trate \'iləsˌtrāt\ *vb* **-trat·ed; -trat·ing 1** : explain by example **2** : provide with pictures or figures — **il·lus·tra·tor** \-ər\ *n*

il·lus·tra·tion \ˌiləs'trāshən\ *n* **1** : example that explains **2** : pictorial explanation

il·lus·tra·tive \il'əstrətiv\ *adj* : designed to illustrate — **il·lus·tra·tive·ly** *adv*

il·lus·tri·ous \-trēəs\ *adj* : notably or brilliantly outstanding — **il·lus·tri·ous·ness** *n*

ill will *n* : unfriendly feeling

im·age \'imij\ *n* **1** : likeness **2** : visual counterpart of an object formed by a lens or mirror **3** : mental picture ∼ *vb* **-aged; -ag·ing** : create a representation of

im·ag·ery \'imijrē\ *n* **1** : images **2** : figurative language

imag·i·nary \im'ajəˌnerē\ *adj* : existing only in the imagination

imag·i·na·tion \imˌajə'nāshən\ *n* **1** : act or power of forming a mental image **2** : creative ability — **imag·i·na·tive** \im'ajənətiv, -əˌnātiv\ *adj* — **imag·i·na·tive·ly** *adv*

imag·ine \im'ajən\ *vb* **-ined; -in·ing** : form a mental picture of something not present

— **imag·in·able** \-'ajənəbəl\ *adj* — **imag·in·ably** \-blē\ *adv*

im·bal·ance \im'baləns\ *n* : lack of balance

im·be·cile \'imbəsəl, -ˌsil\ *n* : idiot — **imbecile, im·be·cil·ic** \ˌimbə'silik\ *adj* — **im·be·cil·i·ty** \-'silətē\ *n*

im·bibe \im'bīb\ *vb* **-bibed; -bib·ing** : drink — **im·bib·er** *n*

im·bro·glio \im'brōlyō\ *n, pl* **-glios** : complicated situation

im·bue \-'byü\ *vb* **-bued; -bu·ing** : fill (as with color or a feeling)

im·i·tate \'iməˌtāt\ *vb* **-tat·ed; -tat·ing 1** : follow as a model **2** : mimic — **im·i·ta·tive** \-ˌtātiv\ *adj* — **im·i·ta·tor** \-ər\ *n*

im·i·ta·tion \ˌimə'tāshən\ *n* **1** : act of imitating **2** : copy — **imitation** *adj*

im·mac·u·late \im'akyələt\ *adj* : without stain or blemish — **im·mac·u·late·ly** *adv*

im·ma·te·ri·al \ˌimə'tirēəl\ *adj* **1** : spiritual **2** : not relevant — **im·ma·te·ri·al·i·ty** \-ˌtirē'alətē\ *n*

im·ma·ture \ˌimə'tùr, -'tyùr\ *adj* : not yet mature — **im·ma·tu·ri·ty** \-ətē\ *n*

im·mea·sur·able \im'ezhər-əbəl\ *adj* : indefinitely ex-tensive — **im·mea·sur·ably** \-blē\ *adv*

im·me·di·a·cy \im'ēdēəsē\ *n, pl* **-cies** : quality or state of being urgent

im·me·di·ate \-ēət\ *adj* **1** : direct **2** : being next in line **3** : made or done at once **4** : not distant — **im·me·di·ate·ly** *adv*

im·me·mo·ri·al \ˌimə'mōrēəl\ *adj* : old beyond memory

im·mense \im'ens\ *adj* : vast — **immense·ly** *adv* — **im·men·si·ty** \-'ensətē\ *n*

im·merse \im'ərs\ *vb* **-mersed; -mers·ing 1** : plunge or dip esp. into liquid **2** : engross — **im·mer·sion** \-'ərzhən\ *n*

im·mi·grant \'imigrənt\ *n* : one that immigrates

im·mi·grate \'iməˌgrāt\ *vb* **-grat·ed; -grat·ing** : come into a place and take up residence — **im·mi·gra·tion** \ˌimə'grā-shən\ *n*

im·mi·nent \'imənənt\ *adj* : ready to take place — **im·mi·nence** \-nəns\ *n* — **im·mi·nent·ly** *adv*

im·mo·bile \im'ōbəl\ *adj* : incapable of being moved — **im·mo·bil·i·ty** \ˌimō'bilətē\ *n* — **im·mo·bi·lize** \im-'ōbəlīz\ *vb*

im·mod·er·ate \im'ädərət\ *adj* : not moderate — **im·mod·er·a·cy** \-ərəsē\ *n* — **im·mod·er·ate·ly** *adv*

im·mod·est \im'ädəst\ *adj* : not modest — **im·mod·est·ly** *adv* — **im·mod·es·ty** \-əstē\ *n*

im·mo·late \'imə‚lāt\ *vb* **-lated; -lat·ing** : offer in sacrifice — **im·mo·la·tion** \‚imə'lā-shən\ *n*

im·mor·al \im'òrəl\ *adj* : not moral — **im·mo·ral·i·ty** \‚imò-'ralətē, ‚imə-\ *n* — **im·mor·al·ly** *adv*

im·mor·tal \im'òrt°l\ *adj* **1** : not mortal **2** : having lasting fame ～ *n* : one exempt from death or oblivion — **im·mor·tal·i·ty** \‚im‚òr'talətē\ *n* — **im·mor·tal·ize** \im'òrt°l‚īz\ *vb*

im·mov·able \im'üvəbəl\ *adj* **1** : stationary **2** : unyielding — **im·mov·abil·ity** \‚im‚üvə-'bilətē\ *n* — **im·mov·ably** *adv*

im·mune \im'yün\ *adj* : not liable esp. to disease — **im·mu·ni·ty** \im'yünətē\ *n* — **im·mu·ni·za·tion** \‚imyənə-'zāshən\ *n* — **im·mu·nize** \'imyə‚nīz\ *vb*

im·mu·nol·o·gy \‚imyə'näləjē\ *n* : science of immunity to disease — **im·mu·no·log·ic** \-yən°l'äjik\, **im·mu·no·log·i·cal** \-ikəl\ *adj* — **im·mu·nol·o·gist** \‚imyə'näləjist\ *n*

im·mu·ta·ble \im'yütəbəl\ *adj* : unchangeable — **im·mu·ta·bil·i·ty** \im‚yütə'bilətē\ *n* — **im·mu·ta·bly** *adv*

imp \'imp\ *n* **1** : demon **2** : mischievous child

im·pact \im'pakt\ *vb* **1** : press close **2** : have an effect on ～ \'im‚pakt\ *n* **1** : forceful contact **2** : influence

im·pact·ed \im'paktəd\ *adj* : wedged between the jawbone and another tooth

im·pair \im'par\ *vb* : diminish in quantity, value, or ability — **im·pair·ment** *n*

im·pa·la \im'palə\ *n, pl* **impalas** *or* **impala** : large African antelope

im·pale \im'pāl\ *vb* **-paled; -pal·ing** : pierce with something pointed

im·pal·pa·ble \im'palpəbəl\ *adj* : incapable of being felt — **im·pal·pa·bly** *adv*

im·pan·el \im'pan°l\ *vb* : enter in or on a panel

im·part \-'pärt\ *vb* : give from or as if from a store

im·par·tial \im'pärshəl\ *adj* : not partial — **im·par·tial·i·ty** \im‚pärshē'alətē\ *n* — **im·par·tial·ly** *adv*

im·pass·able \im'pasəbəl\ *adj* : not passable — **im·pass·ably** \-'pasəblē\ *adv*

im·passe \'im‚pas\ *n* : inescapable predicament

im·pas·sioned \im'pashənd\ *adj* : filled with passion

im·pas·sive \im'pasiv\ *adj* : showing no feeling or interest — **im·pas·sive·ly** *adv* — **im·pas·siv·i·ty** \ˌimˌpas'ivətē\ *n*

im·pa·tiens \im'pāshənz, -shəns\ *n* : annual herb with showy flowers

im·pa·tient \im'pāshənt\ *adj* : not patient — **im·pa·tience** \-shəns\ *n* — **im·pa·tient·ly** *adv*

im·peach \im'pēch\ *vb* **1** : charge (an official) with misconduct **2** : cast doubt on **3** : remove from office for misconduct — **im·peach·ment** *n*

im·pec·ca·ble \im'pekəbəl\ *adj* : faultless — **im·pec·ca·bly** *adv*

im·pe·cu·nious \ˌimpi'kyünēəs\ *adj* : broke — **im·pe·cu·nious·ness** *n*

im·pede \im'pēd\ *vb* **-ped·ed; -ped·ing** : interfere with

im·ped·i·ment \-'pedəmənt\ *n* **1** : hindrance **2** : speech defect

im·pel \-'pel\ *vb* **-pelled; -pel·ling** : urge forward

im·pend \-'pend\ *vb* : be about to occur

im·pen·e·tra·ble \im'penətrəbəl\ *adj* : incapable of being penetrated or understood — **im·pen·e·tra·bil·i·ty** \imˌpenətrə'bilətē\ *n* — **im·pen·e·tra·bly** *adv*

im·pen·i·tent \im'penətənt\ *adj* : not penitent — **im·pen·i·tence** \-təns\ *n*

im·per·a·tive \im'perətiv\ *adj* **1** : expressing a command **2** : urgent ∼ *n* **1** : imperative mood or verb form **2** : unavoidable fact, need, or obligation — **im·per·a·tive·ly** *adv*

im·per·cep·ti·ble \ˌimpər'septəbəl\ *adj* : not perceptible — **im·per·cep·ti·bly** *adv*

im·per·fect \im'pərfikt\ *adj* : not perfect — **im·per·fec·tion** *n* — **im·per·fect·ly** *adv*

im·pe·ri·al \im'pirēəl\ *adj* **1** : relating to an empire or an emperor **2** : royal

im·pe·ri·al·ism \im'pirēəˌlizəm\ *n* : policy of controlling other nations — **im·pe·ri·al·ist** \-list\ *n or adj* — **im·pe·ri·al·is·tic** \-ˌpirēə'listik\ *adj* — **im·pe·ri·al·is·ti·cal·ly** \-tiklē\ *adv*

im·per·il \im'perəl\ *vb* **-iled** *or* **-illed; -il·ing** *or* **-il·ling** : endanger

im·pe·ri·ous \im'pirēəs\ *adj* : arrogant or domineering — **im·pe·ri·ous·ly** *adv*

im·per·ish·able \im'perishəbəl\ *adj* : not perishable

im·per·ma·nent \-'pərmənənt\ *adj* : not permanent — **im·per·ma·nent·ly** *adv*

im·per·me·able \-'pərmēəbəl\ *adj* : not permeable

im·per·mis·si·ble \ˌimpər'misəbəl\ *adj* : not permissible

im·per·son·al \im'pərsᵊnəl\ *adj* : not involving human personality or emotion — **im·per·son·al·i·ty** \im,pərsᵊn-'alətē\ *n* — **im·per·son·al·ly** *adv*

im·per·son·ate \im'pərsᵊn,āt\ *vb* **-at·ed; -at·ing** : assume the character of — **im·per·son·a·tion** \-,pərsᵊn'āshən\ *n* — **im·per·son·a·tor** \-'pərsᵊn-,ātər\ *n*

im·per·ti·nent \im'pərtᵊnənt\ *adj* **1** : irrelevant **2** : insolent — **im·per·ti·nence** \-ᵊnəns\ *n* — **im·per·ti·nent·ly** *adv*

im·per·turb·able \,impər'tərb-əbəl\ *adj* : calm and steady

im·per·vi·ous \im'pərvēəs\ *adj* : incapable of being penetrated or affected

im·pet·u·ous \im'pechəwəs\ *adj* : impulsive — **im·pet·u·os·i·ty** \im,pechə'wäsətē\ *n* — **im·pet·u·ous·ly** *adv*

im·pe·tus \'impətəs\ *n* : driving force

im·pi·ety \im'pīətē\ *n* : quality or state of being impious

im·pinge \im'pinj\ *vb* **-pinged; -ping·ing** : encroach — **im·pinge·ment** \-mənt\ *n*

im·pi·ous \'impēəs, im'pī-\ *adj* : not pious

imp·ish \'impish\ *adj* : mischievous — **imp·ish·ly** *adv* — **imp·ish·ness** *n*

im·pla·ca·ble \im'plakəbəl, -'plā-\ *adj* : not capable of being appeased or changed — **im·pla·ca·bil·i·ty** \im,plakə-'bilətē, -,plā-\ *n* — **im·pla·ca·bly** \im'plakəblē\ *adv*

im·plant \im'plant\ *vb* **1** : set firmly or deeply **2** : fix in the mind or spirit ∼ \'im,plant\ *n* : something implanted in tissue — **im·plan·ta·tion** \,im-,plan'tāshən\ *n*

im·plau·si·ble \im'plȯzəbəl\ *adj* : not plausible — **im·plau·si·bil·i·ty** \im,plȯzə'bilətē\ *n*

im·ple·ment \'impləmənt\ *n* : tool, utensil ∼ \-,ment\ *vb* : put into practice — **im·ple·men·ta·tion** \,impləmən'tā-shən\ *n*

im·pli·cate \'implə,kāt\ *vb* **-cat·ed; -cat·ing** : involve

im·pli·ca·tion \,implə'kāshən\ *n* **1** : an implying **2** : something implied

im·plic·it \im'plisət\ *adj* **1** : understood though only implied **2** : complete and unquestioning — **im·plic·it·ly** *adv*

im·plode \im'plōd\ *vb* **-plod·ed; -plod·ing** : burst inward — **im·plo·sion** \-'plōzhən\ *n* — **im·plo·sive** \-'plōsiv\ *adj*

im·plore \im'plōr\ *vb* **-plored; -plor·ing** : entreat

im·ply \-'plī\ *vb* **-plied; -ply-ing** : express indirectly

im·po·lite \ˌimpə'līt\ *adj* : not polite

im·pol·i·tic \im'päləˌtik\ *adj* : not politic

im·pon·der·a·ble \im'pändər-əbəl\ *adj* : incapable of being precisely evaluated — **im-ponderable** *n*

im·port \im'pōrt\ *vb* **1** : mean **2** : bring in from an external source ~ \'imˌpōrt\ *n* **1** : meaning **2** : importance **3** : something imported — **im-por·ta·tion** \ˌimˌpȯr'tāshən\ *n* — **im·port·er** *n*

im·por·tant \im'pȯrtənt\ *adj* : having great worth, significance, or influence — **im·por-tance** \-°ns\ *n* — **im·por-tant·ly** *adv*

im·por·tu·nate \im'pȯrchə-nət\ *adj* : troublesomely persistent or urgent

im·por·tune \ˌimpər'tün, -'tyün; im'pȯrchən\ *vb* **-tuned; -tun·ing** : urge or beg persistently — **im·por·tu·ni-ty** \ˌimpər'tünətē, -'tyü-\ *n*

im·pose \im'pōz\ *vb* **-posed; -pos·ing 1** : establish as compulsory **2** : take unwarranted advantage of — **im·po·si·tion** \ˌimpə'zishən\ *n*

im·pos·ing \im'pōziŋ\ *adj* : impressive — **im·pos·ing·ly** *adv*

im·pos·si·ble \im'päsəbəl\ *adj* **1** : incapable of occurring **2** : enormously difficult — **im-pos·si·bil·i·ty** \imˌpäsə'bilətē\ *n* — **im·pos·si·bly** \im-'päsəblē\ *adv*

im·post \'imˌpōst\ *n* : tax

im·pos·tor, im·pos·ter \im-'pästər\ *n* : one who assumes an identity or title to deceive — **im·pos·ture** \-'päschər\ *n*

im·po·tent \'impətənt\ *adj* **1** : lacking power **2** : sterile — **im·po·tence** \-pətəns\ *n* — **im·po·ten·cy** \-ənsē\ *n* — **im·po·tent·ly** *adv*

im·pound \im'paünd\ *vb* : seize and hold in legal custody — **im·pound·ment** *n*

im·pov·er·ish \im'pävərish\ *vb* : make poor — **im·pov·er-ish·ment** *n*

im·prac·ti·ca·ble \im'prak-tikəbəl\ *adj* : not practicable

im·prac·ti·cal \-'praktikəl\ *adj* : not practical

im·pre·cise \ˌimpri'sīs\ *adj* : not precise — **im·pre·cise·ly** *adv* — **im·pre·cise·ness** *n* — **im·pre·ci·sion** \-'sizhən\ *n*

im·preg·na·ble \im'preg-nəbəl\ *adj* : able to resist attack — **im·preg·na·bil·i·ty** \imˌpregnə'bilətē\ *n*

im·preg·nate \im'pregˌnāt\ *vb* **-nat·ed; -nat·ing 1** : make pregnant **2** : cause to be filled, permeated, or saturated —

im·preg·na·tion \ˌimˌpreg-ˈnāshən\ n

im·pre·sa·rio \ˌimprəˈsärēˌō\ n, pl **-ri·os** : one who sponsors an entertainment

¹**im·press** \imˈpres\ vb **1** : apply with or produce by pressure **2** : press, stamp, or print in or upon **3** : produce a vivid impression of **4** : affect (as the mind) forcibly

²**im·press** \imˈpres\ vb : force into naval service — **im·press·ment** n

im·pres·sion \imˈpreshən\ n **1** : mark made by impressing **2** : marked influence or effect **3** : printed copy **4** : vague notion or recollection — **im·pres·sion·able** \-ˈpreshənəbəl\ adj

im·pres·sive \imˈpresiv\ adj : making a marked impression — **im·pres·sive·ly** adv — **im·pres·sive·ness** n

im·pri·ma·tur \ˌimprəˈmäˌtu̇r\ n : official approval (as of a publication by a censor)

im·print \imˈprint, ˈimˌ-\ vb : stamp or mark by or as if by pressure ~ \ˈimˌ-\ n : something imprinted or printed

im·pris·on \imˈprizᵊn\ vb : put in prison — **im·pris·on·ment** \-mənt\ n

im·prob·a·ble \imˈpräbəbəl\ adj : unlikely to be true or to occur — **im·prob·a·bil·i·ty** \imˌpräbəˈbilətē\ n — **im·prob·a·bly** adv

im·promp·tu \imˈprämptü, -tyü\ adj : not planned beforehand — **impromptu** adv or n

im·prop·er \imˈpräpər\ adj : not proper — **im·prop·er·ly** adv

im·pro·pri·ety \ˌimprəˈprīətē\ n, pl **-eties** : state or instance of being improper

im·prove \imˈprüv\ vb **-proved; -proving** : grow or make better — **im·prov·able** \-ˈprüvəbəl\ adj — **im·prove·ment** n

im·prov·i·dent \imˈprävədənt\ adj : not providing for the future — **im·prov·i·dence** \-əns\ n

im·pro·vise \ˈimprəˌvīz\ vb **-vised; -vis·ing** : make, invent, or arrange offhand — **im·pro·vi·sa·tion** \imˌprävəˈzāshən, ˌimprəvə-\ n — **im·pro·vis·er, im·pro·vi·sor** \ˈimprəˌvīzər\ n

im·pru·dent \imˈprüdᵊnt\ adj : not prudent — **im·pru·dence** \-ᵊns\ n

im·pu·dent \ˈimpyədənt\ adj : insolent — **im·pu·dence** \-əns\ n — **im·pu·dent·ly** adv

im·pugn \imˈpyün\ vb : attack as false

im·pulse \ˈimˌpəls\ n **1** : moving force **2** : sudden inclination

im·pul·sive \im'pəlsiv\ *adj* : acting on impulse — **im·pul·sive·ly** *adv* — **im·pul·sive·ness** *n*

im·pu·ni·ty \im'pyünətē\ *n* : exemption from punishment or harm

im·pure \im'pyùr\ *adj* : not pure — **im·pu·ri·ty** \-'pyù-rətē\ *n*

im·pute \im'pyüt\ *vb* **-put·ed; -put·ing** : credit to or blame on a person or cause — **im·pu·ta·tion** \,impyə'tā-shən\ *n*

in \'in\ *prep* **1** — used to indicate location, inclusion, situation, or manner **2** : into **3** : during ~ *adv* : to or toward the inside ~ *adj* : located inside

in- \in\ *prefix* **1** : not **2** : lack of

in·ad·ver·tent \,inəd'vərt°nt\ *adj* : unintentional — **in·ad·ver·tence** \-°ns\ *n* — **in·ad·ver·ten·cy** \-°nsē\ *n* — **in·ad·ver·tent·ly** *adv*

in·alien·able \in'ālyənəbəl, -'ālēənə-\ *adj* : incapable of being transferred or given up — **in·alien·abil·i·ty** \in-,ālyənə'bilətē, -'ālēənə-\ *n* — **in·alien·ably** *adv*

inane \in'ān\ *adj* **inan·er; -est** : silly or stupid — **inan·i·ty** \in'anətē\ *n*

in·an·i·mate \in'anəmət\ *adj* : not animate or animated — **in·an·i·mate·ly** *adv* — **in·an·i·mate·ness** *n*

in·ap·pre·cia·ble \,inə'prē-shəbəl\ *adj* : too small to be perceived — **in·ap·pre·cia·bly** *adv*

in·ar·tic·u·late \,inär'tikyələt\ *adj* : without the power of speech or effective expression — **in·ar·tic·u·late·ly** *adv*

in·as·much as \,inaz'məchaz\ *conj* : because

in·at·ten·tion \,inə'tenchən\ *n* : failure to pay attention

in·au·gu·ral \in'ògyərəl, -gərəl\ *adj* : relating to an inauguration ~ *n* **1** : inaugural speech **2** : inauguration

in·au·gu·rate \in'ògyə,rāt, -gə-\ *vb* **-rat·ed; -rat·ing 1** : install in office **2** : start — **in·au·gu·ra·tion** \-,ògyə'rā-shən, -gə-\ *n*

List of self-explanatory words with the prefix *in-*

inability	inaccuracy	inactive
inaccessibility	inaccurate	inactivity
inaccessible	inaction	inadequacy

in·board \ˌinˌbōrd\ *adv* : inside a vehicle or craft — **inboard** *adj*

in·born \ˈinˌbȯrn\ *adj* : present from birth

in·bred \ˈinˌbred\ *adj* : deeply ingrained in one's nature

in·breed·ing \ˈinˌbrēdiŋ\ *n* : interbreeding of closely related individuals — **in·breed** \-ˌbred\ *vb*

in·cal·cu·la·ble \inˈkalkyələbəl\ *adj* : too large to be calculated — **in·cal·cu·la·bly** *adv*

in·can·des·cent \ˌinkənˈdesᵊnt\ *adj* **1** : glowing with heat **2** : brilliant — **in·can·des·cence** \-ᵊns\ *n*

in·can·ta·tion \ˌinˌkanˈtāshən\ *n* : use of spoken or sung charms or spells as a magic ritual

in·ca·pac·i·tate \ˌinkəˈpasəˌtāt\ *vb* **-tat·ed; -tat·ing** : disable

in·ca·pac·i·ty \ˌinkəˈpasətē\ *n, pl* **-ties** : quality or state of being incapable

in·car·cer·ate \inˈkärsəˌrāt\ *vb* **-at·ed; -at·ing** : imprison — **in·car·cer·a·tion** \inˌkärsəˈrāshən\ *n*

in·car·nate \inˈkärnət, -ˌnāt\ *adj* : having bodily form and substance — **in·car·nate** \-ˌnāt\ *vb* — **in·car·na·tion** \-ˌkärˈnāshən\ *n*

in·cen·di·ary \inˈsendēˌerē\ *adj* **1** : pertaining to or used to ignite fire **2** : tending to excite — **incendiary** *n*

in·cense \ˈinˌsens\ *n* : material burned to produce a fragrant odor or its smoke ∼ \inˈsens\ *vb* **-censed; -cens·ing** : make very angry

in·cen·tive \inˈsentive\ *n* : inducement to do something

in·cep·tion \inˈsepshən\ *n* : beginning

in·ces·sant \inˈsesᵊnt\ *adj* : continuing without interruption — **in·ces·sant·ly** *adv*

in·cest \ˈinˌsest\ *n* : sexual intercourse between close relatives — **in·ces·tu·ous** \inˈseschəwəs\ *adj*

inch \ˈinch\ *n* : unit of length equal to ¹/₁₂ foot ∼ *vb* : move by small degrees

in·cho·ate \inˈkōət, ˈinkəˌwāt\ *adj* : new and not fully formed or ordered

in·ci·dent \ˈinsədənt\ *n* : occurrence — **in·ci·dence** \-əns\ *n* — **incident** *adj*

---

inadequate   inadmissible   inapparent
inadequately   inadvisability   inapplicable
inadmissibility   inadvisable   inapposite

in·ci·den·tal \ˌinsə'dent³l\ *adj* **1** : subordinate, non-essential, or attendant **2** : met by chance ~ *n* **1** : something incidental **2** *pl* : minor expenses that are not itemized — **in·ci·den·tal·ly** *adv*

in·cin·er·ate \in'sinə͵rāt\ *vb* **-at·ed; -at·ing** : burn to ashes — **in·cin·er·a·tor** \-͵rātər\ *n*

in·cip·i·ent \in'sipēənt\ *adj* : beginning to be or appear

in·cise \in'sīz\ *vb* **-cised; -cis·ing** : carve into

in·ci·sion \in'sizhən\ *n* : surgical cut

in·ci·sive \in'sīsiv\ *adj* : keen and discerning — **in·ci·sive·ly** *adv*

in·ci·sor \in'sīzər\ *n* : tooth for cutting

in·cite \in'sīt\ *vb* **-cit·ed; -cit·ing** : arouse to action — **in·cite·ment** *n*

in·ci·vil·i·ty \ˌinsə'vilətē\ *n* : rudeness

in·clem·ent \in'klemənt\ *adj* : stormy — **in·clem·en·cy** \-ənsē\ *n*

in·cline \in'klīn\ *vb* **-clined; -clin·ing** **1** : bow **2** : tend toward an opinion **3** : slope ~ *n* : slope — **in·cli·na·tion** \ˌinklə'nāshən\ *n* — **in·clin·er** *n*

inclose, inclosure *var of* EN-CLOSE, ENCLOSURE

in·clude \in'klüd\ *vb* **-clud·ed; -clud·ing** : take in or comprise — **in·clu·sion** \in'klüzhən\ *n* — **in·clu·sive** \-'klüsiv\ *adj*

in·cog·ni·to \ˌin͵käg'nētō, in'kägnə͵tō\ *adv or adj* : with one's identity concealed

in·come \'in͵kəm\ *n* : money gained (as from work or investment)

in·com·ing \'in͵kəmiŋ\ *adj* : coming in

in·com·mu·ni·ca·do \ˌinkə͵myünə'kädō\ *adv or adj* : without means of communication

in·com·pa·ra·ble \in'kämpərəbəl\ *adj* : eminent beyond comparison

in·com·pe·tent \in'kämpətənt\ *adj* : lacking sufficient knowledge or skill — **in·com·pe·tence** \-pətəns\ *n* — **in·com·pe·ten·cy** \-ənsē\ *n* — **incompetent** *n*

in·con·ceiv·able \ˌinkən'sēvəbəl\ *adj* **1** : impossible to comprehend **2** : unbeliev-

---

inappositely	inapproachable	inappropriateness
inappositeness	inappropriate	inapt
inappreciative	inappropriately	inarguable

able — **in·con·ceiv·ably** \-blē\ *adv*

in·con·gru·ous \in'käŋgrəwəs\ *adj* : inappropriate or out of place — **in·con·gru·i·ty** \ˌinkən'grüətē, -ˌkän-\ *n* — **in·con·gru·ous·ly** *adv*

in·con·se·quen·tial \ˌin,känsə'kwenchəl\ *adj* : unimportant — **in·con·se·quence** \in'känsə,kwens\ *n* — **in·con·se·quen·tial·ly** *adv*

in·con·sid·er·able \ˌinkən-'sidərəbəl\ *adj* : trivial

in·con·sol·able \ˌinkən'sōl-əbəl\ *adj* : incapable of being consoled — **in·con·sol·ably** *adv*

in·con·ve·nience \ˌinkən-'vēnyəns\ *n* **1** : discomfort **2** : something that causes trouble or annoyance ∼ *vb* : cause inconvenience to — **in·con·ve·nient** \ˌinkən-'vēnyənt\ *adj* — **in·con·ve·nient·ly** *adv*

in·cor·po·rate \in'kȯrpə,rāt\ *vb* -rat·ed; -rat·ing **1** : blend **2** : form into a legal body — **in·cor·po·rat·ed** *adj* — **in·cor·po·ra·tion** \-ˌkȯrpə'rā-shən\ *n*

in·cor·ri·gi·ble \in'kȯrəjəbəl\ *adj* : incapable of being cor-

rected or reformed — **in·cor·ri·gi·bil·i·ty** \inˌkȯrəjə'bilətē\ *n*

in·crease \in'krēs, 'in,krēs\ *vb* -creased; -creas·ing : make or become greater ∼ \'in,-, in'-\ *n* **1** : enlargement in size **2** : something added — **in·creas·ing·ly** \-'krēsiŋlē\ *adv*

in·cred·i·ble \in'kredəbəl\ *adj* : too extraordinary to be believed — **in·cred·ibil·i·ty** \inˌkredə'bilətē\ *n* — **in·cred·i·bly** \in'kredəblē\ *adv*

in·cred·u·lous \in'krejələs\ *adj* : skeptical — **in·cre·du·li·ty** \ˌinkri'dülətē, -'dyü-\ *n* — **in·cred·u·lous·ly** *adv*

in·cre·ment \'iŋkrəmənt, 'in-\ *n* : increase or amount of increase — **in·cre·men·tal** \ˌiŋkrə'mentᵊl, ˌin-\ *adj*

in·crim·i·nate \in'krimə,nāt\ *vb* -nat·ed; -nat·ing : show to be guilty of a crime — **in·crim·i·na·tion** \-ˌkrimə'nā-shən\ *n* — **in·crim·i·na·to·ry** \-'krimənə,tōrē\ *adj*

in·cu·bate \'iŋkyə,bāt, 'in-\ *vb* -bat·ed; -bat·ing : keep (as eggs) under conditions favorable for development — **in·cu·ba·tion** \ˌiŋkyə'bāshən, ˌin-\ *n* — **in·cu·ba·tor** \'iŋkyə,bātər, 'in-\ *n*

---

inartistic
inartistically
inattentive
inattentively
inattentiveness
inaudible
inaudibly
inauspicious
inauthentic

in·cul·cate \in'kəl‚kāt, 'in-‚kəl-\ *vb* **-cat·ed; -cat·ing** : instill by repeated teaching — **in·cul·ca·tion** \‚in‚kəl'kā-shən\ *n*

in·cum·bent \in'kəmbənt\ *n* : holder of an office ∼ *adj* : obligatory — **in·cum·ben·cy** \-bənsē\ *n*

in·cur \in'kər\ *vb* **-rr-** : become liable or subject to

in·cur·sion \in'kərzhən\ *n* : invasion

in·debt·ed \in'detəd\ *adj* : owing something — **in·debt·ed·ness** *n*

in·de·ci·sion \‚indi'sizhən\ *n* : inability to decide

in·deed \in'dēd\ *adv* : without question

in·de·fat·i·ga·ble \‚indi'fati-gəbəl\ *adj* : not tiring — **in·de·fat·i·ga·bly** \-blē\ *adv*

in·def·i·nite \in'defənət\ *adj* **1** : not defining or identifying **2** : not precise **3** : having no fixed limit — **in·def·i·nite·ly** *adv*

in·del·i·ble \in'deləbəl\ *adj* : not capable of being removed or erased — **in·del·i·bly** *adv*

in·del·i·cate \in'delikət\ *adj* : improper — **in·del·i·ca·cy** \in'deləkəsē\ *n*

in·dem·ni·fy \in'demnə‚fī\ *vb* **-fied; -fy·ing** : repay for a loss — **in·dem·ni·fi·ca·tion** \-‚demnəfə'kāshən\ *n*

in·dem·ni·ty \in'demnətē\ *n, pl* **-ties** : security against loss or damage

¹in·dent \in'dent\ *vb* : leave a space at the beginning of a paragraph

²indent *vb* : force inward so as to form a depression or dent

in·den·ta·tion \‚in‚den'tashən\ *n* **1** : notch, recess, or dent **2** : action of indenting **3** : space at the beginning of a paragraph

in·den·ture \in'denchər\ *n* : contract binding one person to work for another for a given period — usu. in pl. ∼ *vb* **-tured; -tur·ing** : bind by indentures

Independence Day *n* : July 4 observed as a legal holiday in commemoration of the adoption of the Declaration of Independence in 1776

in·de·pen·dent \‚ində'pendənt\ *adj* **1** : not governed by another **2** : not requiring or relying on something or somebody else **3** : not easily influenced — **in·de·pen·dence** \-dəns\ *n* — **inde-**

---

incapability	**incoherence**	**incombustible**
incapable	**incoherent**	**incommensurate**
incautious	**incoherently**	**incommodious**

pendent *n* — **in·de·pen·dent·ly** *adv*

in·de·ter·mi·nate \ˌindiˈtər-mənət\ *adj* : not definitely determined — **in·de·ter·mi·na·cy** \-nəsē\ *n* — **in·de·ter·mi·nate·ly** *adv*

in·dex \ˈinˌdeks\ *n, pl* **-dex·es** *or* **-di·ces** \-dəˌsēz\ **1** : alphabetical list of items (as topics in a book) **2** : a number that serves as a measure or indicator of something ∼ *vb* **1** : provide with an index **2** : serve as an index of

index finger *n* : forefinger

in·di·cate \ˈindəˌkāt\ *vb* **-cat·ed; -cat·ing 1** : point out or to **2** : show indirectly **3** : state briefly — **in·di·ca·tion** \ˌindəˈkāshən\ *n* — **in·di·ca·tor** \ˈindəˌkātər\ *n*

in·dic·a·tive \inˈdikətiv\ *adj* : serving to indicate

in·dict \inˈdīt\ *vb* : charge with a crime — **in·dict·able** *adj* — **in·dict·ment** *n*

in·dif·fer·ent \inˈdifrənt\ *adj* **1** : having no preference **2** : showing neither interest nor dislike **3** : mediocre — **in·dif·fer·ence** \-ˈdifrəns\ *n* — **in·dif·fer·ent·ly** *adv*

in·dig·e·nous \inˈdijənəs\ *adj* : native to a particular region

in·di·gent \ˈindijənt\ *adj* : needy — **in·di·gence** \-jəns\ *n*

in·di·ges·tion \ˌindīˈjeschən, -də-\ *n* : discomfort from inability to digest food

in·dig·na·tion \ˌindigˈnāshən\ *n* : anger aroused by something unjust or unworthy — **in·dig·nant** \inˈdignənt\ *adj* — **in·dig·nant·ly** *adv*

in·dig·ni·ty \inˈdignətē\ *n, pl* **-ties 1** : offense against self-respect **2** : humiliating treatment

in·di·go \ˈindiˌgō\ *n, pl* **-gos** *or* **-goes 1** : blue dye **2** : deep reddish blue color

in·di·rect \ˌindəˈrekt, -dī-\ *adj* : not straight or straightforward — **in·di·rec·tion** \-ˈrekshən\ *n* — **in·di·rect·ly** *adv* — **in·di·rect·ness** *n*

in·dis·crim·i·nate \ˌindisˈkrimənət\ *adj* **1** : not careful or discriminating **2** : haphazard — **in·dis·crim·i·nate·ly** *adv*

in·dis·pens·able \ˌindisˈpensəbəl\ *adj* : absolutely essential — **in·dis·pens·abil·i·ty** \-ˌpensəˈbilətē\ *n* — **indispensable** *n* — **in·dis·pens·ably** \-ˈpensəblē\ *adv*

---

incommunicable   incomplete   incomprehensible
incompatibility   incompletely   inconclusive
incompatible   incompleteness   incongruent

in·dis·posed \-'pōzd\ *adj* : slightly ill — **in·dis·po·si·tion** \in͵dispə'zishən\ *n*

in·dis·sol·u·ble \͵indis'älyəbəl\ *adj* : not capable of being dissolved or broken

in·di·vid·u·al \͵ində'vijəwəl\ *n* **1** : single member of a category **2** : person — **individual** *adj* — **in·di·vid·u·al·ly** *adv*

in·di·vid·u·al·ist \-əwəlist\ *n* : person who is markedly independent in thought or action

in·di·vid·u·al·i·ty \-͵vijə'walətē\ *n* : special quality that distinguishes an individual

in·di·vid·u·al·ize \-'vijəwə͵līz\ *vb* **-ized; -iz·ing 1** : make individual **2** : treat individually

in·doc·tri·nate \in'däktrə͵nāt\ *vb* **-nat·ed; -nat·ing** : instruct in fundamentals (as of a doctrine) — **in·doc·tri·na·tion** \in͵däktrə'nāshən\ *n*

in·do·lent \'indələnt\ *adj* : lazy — **in·do·lence** \-ləns\ *n*

in·dom·i·ta·ble \in'dämətəbəl\ *adj* : invincible — **in·dom·i·ta·bly** \-blē\ *adv*

in·door \'in͵dōr\ *adj* : relating to the inside of a building

in·doors \in'dōrz\ *adv* : in or into a building

in·du·bi·ta·ble \in'dübətəbəl, -'dyü-\ *adj* : being beyond question — **in·du·bi·ta·bly** \-blē\ *adv*

in·duce \in'düs, -'dyüs\ *vb* **-duced; -duc·ing 1** : persuade **2** : bring about — **in·duce·ment** *n* — **in·duc·er** *n*

in·duct \in'dəkt\ *vb* **1** : put in office **2** : admit as a member **3** : enroll (as for military service) — **in·duct·ee** \in͵dək'tē\ *n*

in·duc·tion \in'dəkshən\ *n* **1** : act or instance of inducting **2** : reasoning from particular instances to a general conclusion

in·duc·tive \in'dəktiv\ *adj* : reasoning by induction

in·dulge \in'dəlj\ *vb* **-dulged; -dulg·ing** : yield to the desire of or for — **in·dul·gence** \-'dəljəns\ *n* — **in·dul·gent** \-jənt\ *adj* — **in·dul·gent·ly** *adv*

in·dus·tri·al \in'dəstrēəl\ *adj* **1** : relating to industry **2** : heavy-duty — **in·dus·tri·al·ist** \-əlist\ *n* — **in·dus·tri·al·iza·tion** \-͵dəstrēələ'zāshən\ *n* — **in·dus·tri·al·ize** \-'dəs-

---

inconsecutive

inconsiderate

inconsiderately

inconsiderateness

inconsistency

inconsistent

inconsistently

inconspicuous

inconspicuously

trē₁līz\ *vb* — **in·dus·tri·al·ly** *adv*

in·dus·tri·ous \in'dəstrēəs\ *adj* : diligent or busy — **in·dus·tri·ous·ly** *adv* — **in·dus·tri·ous·ness** *n*

in·dus·try \'indəstrē\ *n, pl* **-tries 1** : diligence **2** : manufacturing enterprises or activity

in·ebri·at·ed \i'nēbrē₁ātəd\ *adj* : drunk — **in·ebri·a·tion** \-₁ēbrē'āshən\ *n*

in·ef·fa·ble \in'efəbəl\ *adj* : incapable of being expressed in words — **in·ef·fa·bly** \-blē\ *adv*

in·ept \in'ept\ *adj* **1** : inappropriate or foolish **2** : generally incompetent — **in·ep·ti·tude** \in'eptə₁tüd, -₁tyüd\ *n* — **in·ept·ly** *adv* — **in·ept·ness** *n*

in·equal·i·ty \₁ini'kwälətē\ *n* : quality of being unequal or uneven

in·ert \in'ərt\ *adj* **1** : powerless to move or act **2** : sluggish — **in·ert·ly** *adv* — **in·ert·ness** *n*

in·er·tia \in'ərshə\ *n* : tendency of matter to remain at rest or in motion — **in·er·tial** \-shəl\ *adj*

in·es·cap·able \₁inə'skāpəbəl\ *adj* : inevitable — **in·es·cap·ably** \-blē\ *adv*

in·es·ti·ma·ble \in'estəməbəl\ *adj* : incapable of being estimated — **in·es·ti·ma·bly** \-blē\ *adv*

in·ev·i·ta·ble \in'evətəbəl\ *adj* : incapable of being avoided or escaped — **in·ev·i·ta·bil·i·ty** \in₁evətə'bilətē\ *n* — **in·ev·i·ta·bly** \in'evətəblē\ *adv*

in·ex·cus·able \₁inik'skyüzəbəl\ *adj* : being without excuse or justification — **in·ex·cus·ably** \-blē\ *adv*

in·ex·haust·ible \₁inig'zostəbəl\ *adj* : incapable of being used up or tired out — **in·ex·haust·ibly** \-blē\ *adv*

in·ex·o·ra·ble \in'eksərəbəl\ *adj* : unyielding or relentless — **in·ex·o·ra·bly** *adv*

in·fal·li·ble \in'faləbəl\ *adj* : incapable of error — **in·fal·li·bil·i·ty** \in₁falə'bilətē\ *n* — **in·fal·li·bly** *adv*

in·fa·mous \'infəməs\ *adj* : having the worst kind of reputation — **in·fa·mous·ly** *adv*

in·fa·my \-mē\ *n, pl* **-mies** : evil reputation

inconstancy	inconsumable	incorporeal
inconstant	incontestable	incorporeally
inconstantly	incontestably	incorrect

in·fan·cy \'infənsē\ *n, pl* **-cies** 1 : early childhood 2 : early period of existence

in·fant \'infənt\ *n* : baby

in·fan·tile \'infən,tīl, -t^əl, -,tēl\ *adj* 1 : relating to infants 2 : childish

in·fan·try \'infəntrē\ *n, pl* **-tries** : soldiers that fight on foot

in·fat·u·ate \in'fachə,wāt\ *vb* **-at·ed; -at·ing** : inspire with foolish love or admiration — **in·fat·u·a·tion** \-,fachə'wā-shən\ *n*

in·fect \in'fekt\ *vb* : contaminate with disease-producing matter — **in·fec·tion** \-'fek-shən\ *n* — **in·fec·tious** \-shəs\ *adj* — **in·fec·tive** \-'fektiv\ *adj*

in·fer \in'fər\ *vb* **-rr-** : deduce — **in·fer·ence** \'infərəns\ *n* — **in·fer·en·tial** \,infə'ren-chəl\ *adj*

in·fe·ri·or \in'firēər\ *adj* 1 : being lower in position, degree, rank, or merit 2 : of lesser quality — **inferior** *n* — **in·fe·ri·or·i·ty** \in,firē'òrətē\ *n*

in·fer·nal \in'fərn^əl\ *adj* : of or like hell — often used as a general expression of disapproval — **in·fer·nal·ly** *adv*

in·fer·no \in'fərnō\ *n, pl* **-nos** : place or condition suggesting hell

in·fest \in'fest\ *vb* : swarm or grow in or over — **in·fes·ta·tion** \,in,fes'tāshən\ *n*

in·fi·del \'infəd^əl, -fə,del\ *n* : one who does not believe in a particular religion

in·fi·del·i·ty \,infə'delətē, -fī-\ *n, pl* **-ties** : lack of faithfulness

in·field \'in,fēld\ *n* : baseball field inside the base lines — **in·field·er** *n*

in·fil·trate \in'fil,trāt, 'infil-\ *vb* **-trat·ed; -trat·ing** : enter or become established in without being noticed — **in·fil·tra·tion** \,infil'trāshən\ *n*

in·fi·nite \'infənət\ *adj* 1 : having no limit or extending indefinitely 2 : vast — **infinite** *n* — **in·fi·nite·ly** *adv* — **in·fin·i·tude** \in'finə,tüd, -tyüd\ *n*

in·fin·i·tes·i·mal \in,finə-'tesəməl\ *adj* : immeasurably small — **in·fin·i·tes·i·mal·ly** *adv*

in·fin·i·tive \in'finətiv\ *n* : verb form in English usu. used with *to*

in·fin·i·ty \in'finətē\ *n, pl* **-ties** 1 : quality or state of be-

incorrectly   inculpable   indecency
incorrectness   incurable   indecent
incorruptible   incurious   indecently

ing **infinite** **2** : indefinitely great number or amount

in·firm \in'fərm\ *adj* : feeble from age — **in·fir·mi·ty** \-'fərmətē\ *n*

in·fir·ma·ry \in'fərmərē\ *n, pl* -ries : place for the care of the sick

in·flame \in'flām\ *vb* -flamed; -flam·ing **1** : excite to intense action or feeling **2** : affect or become affected with inflammation — **in·flam·ma·to·ry** \-'flamə̩tōrē\ *adj*

in·flam·ma·ble \in'flaməbəl\ *adj* : flammable

in·flam·ma·tion \̩inflə'mā-shən\ *n* : response to injury in which an affected area becomes red and painful and congested with blood

in·flate \in'flāt\ *vb* -flat·ed; -flat·ing **1** : swell or puff up (as with gas) **2** : expand or increase abnormally — **in·flat·able** *adj*

in·fla·tion \in'flāshən\ *n* **1** : act of inflating **2** : continual rise in prices — **in·fla·tion·ary** \-shə̩nerē\ *adj*

in·flec·tion \in'flekshən\ *n* **1** : change in pitch or loudness of the voice **2** : change in form of a word — **in·flect** \-'flekt\ *vb* — **in·flec·tion·al** \-'flekshənəl\ *adj*

in·flict \in'flikt\ *vb* : give by or as if by hitting — **in·flic·tion** \-'flikshən\ *n*

in·flu·ence \'in̩flüəns\ *n* **1** : power or capacity of causing an effect in indirect or intangible ways **2** : one that exerts influence ~ *vb* -enced; -enc·ing : affect or alter by influence — **in·flu·en·tial** \̩inflü-'enchəl\ *adj*

in·flu·en·za \̩inflü'enzə\ *n* : acute very contagious virus disease

in·flux \'in̩fləks\ *n* : a flowing in

in·form \in'fȯrm\ *vb* : give information or knowledge to — **in·for·mant** \-ənt\ *n* — **in·form·er** *n*

in·for·mal \in'fȯrməl\ *adj* **1** : without formality or ceremony **2** : for ordinary or familiar use — **in·for·mal·i·ty** \̩infȯr'malətē, -fər-\ *n* — **in·for·mal·ly** *adv*

in·for·ma·tion \̩infər'mā-shən\ *n* : knowledge obtained from investigation, study, or instruction — **in·for·ma·tion·al** \-shənəl\ *adj*

in·for·ma·tive \in'fȯrmətiv\ *adj* : giving knowledge

---

indecipherable   **indecisiveness**   **indecorousness**
indecisive   **indecorous**   **indefensible**
indecisively   **indecorously**   **indefinable**

in·frac·tion \in'frakshən\ *n* : violation

in·fra·red \ˌinfrə'red\ *adj* : being, relating to, or using radiation of wavelengths longer than those of red light — **infrared** *n*

in·fra·struc·ture \'infrəˌstrək-chər\ *n* : foundation of a system or organization

in·fringe \in'frinj\ *vb* **-fringed; -fring·ing** : violate another's right or privilege — **in·fringe-ment** *n*

in·fu·ri·ate \in'fyurēˌāt\ *vb* **-at·ed; -at·ing** : make furious — **in·fu·ri·at·ing·ly** \-ˌātiŋlē\ *adv*

in·fuse \in'fyüz\ *vb* **-fused; -fus·ing 1** : instill a principle or quality in **2** : steep in liquid without boiling — **in·fu-sion** \-'fyüzhən\ *n*

¹-ing \iŋ\ *vb suffix or adj suffix* — used to form the present participle and sometimes an adjective resembling a present participle

²-ing *n suffix* **1** : action or process **2** : something connected with or resulting from an action or process

in·ge·nious \in'jēnyəs\ *adj* : very clever — **in·ge·nious·ly** *adv* — **in·ge·nious·ness** *n*

in·ge·nue, in·gé·nue \'anjə-ˌnü, 'än-; 'aⁿzhə-, 'äⁿ-\ *n* : naive young woman

in·ge·nu·ity \ˌinjə'nüətē, -'nyü-\ *n, pl* **-ities** : skill or cleverness in planning or inventing

in·gen·u·ous \in'jenyəwəs\ *adj* : innocent and candid — **in·gen·u·ous·ly** *adv* — **in·gen·u·ous·ness** *n*

in·gest \in'jest\ *vb* : eat — **in·ges·tion** \-'jeschən\ *n*

in·gle·nook \'iŋgəlˌnuk\ *n* : corner by the fireplace

in·got \'iŋgət\ *n* : block of metal

in·grained \in'grānd\ *adj* : deep-seated

in·grate \'inˌgrāt\ *n* : ungrateful person

in·gra·ti·ate \in'grāshēˌāt\ *vb* **-at·ed; -at·ing** : gain favor for (oneself) — **in·gra·ti·at·ing** *adj*

in·gre·di·ent \in'grēdēənt\ *n* : one of the substances that make up a mixture

in·grown \'inˌgrōn\ *adj* : grown in and esp. into the flesh

in·hab·it \in'habət\ *vb* : live or dwell in — **in·hab·it·able** *adj* — **in·hab·it·ant** \-ətənt\ *n*

indefinably
indescribable
indescribably

indestructibility
indestructible
indigestible

indiscernible
indiscreet
indiscreetly

in·hale \in'hāl\ *vb* **-haled; -hal·ing** : breathe in — **in·hal·ant** \-ənt\ *n* — **in·ha·la·tion** \ˌinhə'lāshən, ˌinə-\ *n* — **in·hal·er** *n*

in·here \in'hir\ *vb* **-hered; -her·ing** : be inherent

in·her·ent \in'hirənt, -'her-\ *adj* : being an essential part of something — **in·her·ent·ly** *adv*

in·her·it \in'herət\ *vb* : receive from one's ancestors — **in·her·it·able** \-əbəl\ *adj* — **in·her·i·tance** \-ətəns\ *n* — **in·her·i·tor** \-ətər\ *n*

in·hib·it \in'hibət\ *vb* : hold in check — **in·hi·bi·tion** \ˌinhə'bishən, ˌinə-\ *n*

in·hu·man \in'hyümən, -'yü-\ *adj* : cruel or impersonal — **in·hu·man·i·ty** \-hyü'manətē, -yü-\ *n* — **in·hu·man·ly** *adv* — **in·hu·man·ness** *n*

in·im·i·cal \in'imikəl\ *adj* : hostile or harmful — **in·im·i·cal·ly** *adv*

in·im·i·ta·ble \in'imətəbəl\ *adj* : not capable of being imitated

in·iq·ui·ty \in'ikwətē\ *n, pl* **-ties** : wickedness — **in·iq·ui·tous** \-wətəs\ *adj*

ini·tial \in'ishəl\ *adj* **1** : of or relating to the beginning **2** : first ~ *n* : 1st letter of a word or name ~ *vb* **-tialed** *or* **-tialled; -tial·ing** *or* **-tial·ling** : put initials on — **ini·tial·ly** *adv*

ini·ti·ate \in'ishē̱ˌāt\ *vb* **-at·ed; -at·ing** **1** : start **2** : induct into membership **3** : instruct in the rudiments of something — **initiate** \-'ishēət\ *n* — **ini·ti·a·tion** \-ˌishē'āshən\ *n* — **ini·tia·to·ry** \-'ishēəˌtōrē\ *adj*

ini·tia·tive \in'ishətiv\ *n* **1** : first step **2** : readiness to undertake something on one's own

in·ject \in'jekt\ *vb* : force or introduce into something — **in·jec·tion** \-'jekshən\ *n*

in·junc·tion \in'jəŋkshən\ *n* : court writ requiring one to do or to refrain from doing a specified act

in·jure \'injər\ *vb* **-jured; -jur·ing** : do damage, hurt, or a wrong to

in·ju·ry \'injərē\ *n, pl* **-ries** **1** : act that injures **2** : hurt, damage, or loss sustained — **in·ju·ri·ous** \in'jùrēəs\ *adj*

in·jus·tice \in'jəstəs\ *n* : unjust act

ink \'iŋk\ *n* : usu. liquid and colored material for writing and printing ~ *vb* : put ink

---

on — **ink·well** \-ˌwel\ *n* — **inky** *adj*

in·kling \ˈiŋkliŋ\ *n* : hint or idea

in·land \ˈinˌland, -lənd\ *n* : interior of a country — **inland** *adj or adv*

in–law \ˈinˌlȯ\ *n* : relative by marriage

in·lay \inˈlā, ˈinˌlā\ *vb* **-laid** \-ˈlād\; **-lay·ing** : set into a surface for decoration ∼ \ˈinˌlā\ *n* **1** : inlaid work **2** : shaped filling cemented into a tooth

in·let \ˈinˌlet, -lət\ *n* : small bay

in·mate \ˈinˌmāt\ *n* : person confined to an asylum or prison

in me·mo·ri·am \ˌinməˈmōrēəm\ *prep* : in memory of

in·most \ˈinˌmōst\ *adj* : deepest within

inn \ˈin\ *n* : hotel

in·nards \ˈinərdz\ *n pl* : internal parts

in·nate \inˈāt\ *adj* **1** : inborn **2** : inherent — **in·nate·ly** *adv*

in·ner \ˈinər\ *adj* : being on the inside

in·ner·most \ˈinərˌmōst\ *adj* : farthest inward

in·ner·sole \ˌinərˈsōl\ *n* : insole

in·ning \ˈiniŋ\ *n* : baseball team's turn at bat

inn·keep·er \ˈinˌkēpər\ *n* : owner of an inn

in·no·cent \ˈinəsənt\ *adj* **1** : free from guilt **2** : harmless **3** : not sophisticated — **in·no·cence** \-səns\ *n* — **innocent** *n* — **in·no·cent·ly** *adv*

in·noc·u·ous \inˈäkyəwəs\ *adj* **1** : harmless **2** : inoffensive

in·no·va·tion \ˌinəˈvāshən\ *n* : new idea or method — **in·no·vate** \ˈinəˌvāt\ *vb* — **in·no·va·tive** \ˈinəˌvātiv\ *adj* — **in·no·va·tor** \-ˌvātər\ *n*

in·nu·en·do \ˌinyəˈwendō\ *n, pl* **-dos** *or* **-does** : insinuation

in·nu·mer·a·ble \inˈümərəbəl, -ˈyüm-\ *adj* : countless

in·oc·u·late \inˈäkyəˌlāt\ *vb* **-lat·ed**; **-lat·ing** : treat with something esp. to establish immunity — **in·oc·u·la·tion** \-ˌäkyəˈlāshən\ *n*

in·op·por·tune \inˌäpərˈtün, -ˈtyün\ *adj* : inconvenient — **in·op·por·tune·ly** *adv*

in·or·di·nate \inˈȯrdᵊnət\ *adj* : unusual or excessive — **in·or·di·nate·ly** *adv*

in·or·gan·ic \ˌinȯrˈganik\ *adj* : made of mineral matter

---

ineffective

ineffectively

ineffectiveness

ineffectual

ineffectually

ineffectualness

inefficiency

inefficient

inefficiently

in·pa·tient \'in͵pāshənt\ *n* : patient who stays in a hospital

in·put \'in͵pu̇t\ *n* : something put in — **input** *vb*

in·quest \'in͵kwest\ *n* : inquiry esp. before a jury

in·quire \in'kwīr\ *vb* -**quired**; -**quir·ing** 1 : ask 2 : investigate — **in·quir·er** *n* — **in·quir·ing·ly** *adv* — **in·qui·ry** \'in͵kwīrē, in'kwīrē; 'inkwərē, 'iŋ-\ *n*

in·qui·si·tion \͵inkwə'zishən, ͵iŋ-\ *n* 1 : official inquiry 2 : severe questioning — **in·quis·i·tor** \in'kwizətər\ *n* — **in·quis·i·to·ri·al** \-͵kwizə'tōrēəl\ *adj*

in·quis·i·tive \in'kwizətiv\ *adj* : curious — **in·quis·i·tive·ly** *adv* — **in·quis·i·tive·ness** *n*

in·road \'in͵rōd\ *n* : encroachment

in·rush \'in͵rəsh\ *n* : influx

in·sane \in'sān\ *adj* 1 : not sane 2 : absurd — **in·sane·ly** *adv* — **in·san·i·ty** \in'sanətē\ *n*

in·sa·tia·ble \in'sāshəbəl\ *adj* : incapable of being satisfied — **in·sa·tia·bil·i·ty** \in͵sāshə'bilətē\ *n* — **in·sa·tia·bly** *adv*

in·scribe \in'skrīb\ *vb* 1 : write 2 : engrave 3 : dedi-cate (a book) to someone — **in·scrip·tion** \-'skripshən\ *n*

in·scru·ta·ble \in'skrütəbəl\ *adj* : mysterious — **in·scru·ta·bly** *adv*

in·seam \'in͵sēm\ *n* : inner seam (of a garment)

in·sect \'in͵sekt\ *n* : small usu. winged animal with 6 legs

in·sec·ti·cide \in'sektə͵sīd\ *n* : insect poison — **in·sec·ti·cid·al** \in͵sektə'sīdᵊl\ *adj*

in·se·cure \͵insi'kyu̇r\ *adj* 1 : uncertain 2 : unsafe 3 : fearful — **in·se·cure·ly** *adv* — **in·se·cu·ri·ty** \-'kyu̇rətē\ *n*

in·sem·i·nate \in'semə͵nāt\ *vb* -**nat·ed**; -**nat·ing** : introduce semen into — **in·sem·i·na·tion** \-͵semə'nāshən\ *n*

in·sen·si·ble \in'sensəbəl\ *adj* 1 : unconscious 2 : unable to feel 3 : unaware — **in·sen·si·bil·i·ty** \in͵sensə'bilətē\ *n* — **in·sen·si·bly** *adv*

in·sen·tient \in'senchənt\ *adj* : lacking feeling — **in·sen·tience** \-chəns\ *n*

in·sert \in'sərt\ *vb* : put in — **insert** \'in͵sərt\ *n* — **in·ser·tion** \in'sərshən\ *n*

in·set \'in͵set\ *vb* **inset** *or* **in·set·ted**; **in·set·ting** : set in — **inset** *n*

---

inelastic	inelegant	ineradicable
inelasticity	ineligibility	inessential
inelegance	ineligible	inexact

in·shore \'in'shōr\ *adj* **1** : situated near shore **2** : moving toward shore ~ *adv* : toward shore

in·side \in'sīd, 'in,sīd\ *n* **1** : inner side **2** *pl* : innards ~ *prep* **1** : in or into the inside of **2** : within ~ *adv* **1** : on the inner side **2** : into the interior — **inside** *adj* — **in·sid·er** \in'sīdər\ *n*

inside of *prep* : inside

in·sid·i·ous \in'sidēəs\ *adj* **1** : treacherous **2** : seductive — **in·sid·i·ous·ly** *adv* — **in·sid·i·ous·ness** *n*

in·sight \'in,sīt\ *n* : understanding — **in·sight·ful** \in'sītfəl-\ *adj*

in·sig·nia \in'signēə\, **in·sig·ne** \-,nē\ *n, pl* **-nia** *or* **-ni·as** : badge of authority or office

in·sin·u·ate \in'sinyə,wāt\ *vb* **-at·ed; -at·ing 1** : imply **2** : bring in artfully — **in·sin·u·a·tion** \in,sinyə'wāshən\ *n*

in·sip·id \in'sipəd\ *adj* **1** : tasteless **2** : not stimulating — **in·si·pid·i·ty** \,insə'pidətē\ *n*

in·sist \in'sist\ *vb* : be firmly demanding — **in·sis·tence** \in'sistəns\ *n* — **in·sis·tent** \-tənt\ *adj* — **in·sis·tent·ly** *adv*

insofar as \,insō'färaz\ *conj* : to the extent that

in·sole \'in,sōl\ *n* : inside sole of a shoe

in·so·lent \'insələnt\ *adj* : contemptuously rude — **in·so·lence** \-ləns\ *n*

in·sol·vent \in'sälvənt\ *adj* : unable or insufficient to pay debts — **in·sol·ven·cy** \-vənsē\ *n*

in·som·nia \in'sämnēə\ *n* : inability to sleep — **in·som·ni·ac** \-nē-,ak\ *n*

in·so·much as \,insō'məchaz\ *conj* : inasmuch as

insomuch that *conj* : to such a degree that

in·sou·ci·ance \in'süsēəns, aⁿsü'syäⁿs\ *n* : lighthearted indifference — **in·sou·ci·ant** \in'süsēənt, aⁿsü'syäⁿ\ *adj*

in·spect \in'spekt\ *vb* : view closely and critically — **in·spec·tion** \-'spekshən\ *n* — **in·spec·tor** \-tər\ *n*

in·spire \in'spīr\ *vb* **-spired; -spir·ing 1** : inhale **2** : influence by example **3** : bring about **4** : stir to action — **in·spi·ra·tion** \,inspə'rāshən\ *n* — **in·spi·ra·tion·al** \-'rāshənəl\ *adj* — **in·spir·er** *n*

---

in·stall, in·stal \in'stȯl\ *vb* -stalled; -stall·ing 1 : induct into office 2 : set up for use — **in·stal·la·tion** \ˌinstə'lā-shən\ *n*

in·stall·ment \in'stȯlmənt\ *n* : partial payment

in·stance \'instəns\ *n* 1 : request or instigation 2 : example

in·stant \'instənt\ *n* : moment ~ *adj* 1 : immediate 2 : ready to mix — **in·stan·ta·neous** \ˌinstən'tānēəs\ *adj* — **in·stan·ta·neous·ly** *adv* — **in·stant·ly** *adv*

in·stead \in'sted\ *adv* : as a substitute or alternative

instead of *prep* : as a substitute for or alternative to

in·step \'inˌstep\ *n* : part of the foot in front of the ankle

in·sti·gate \'instəˌgāt\ *vb* -gat·ed; -gat·ing : incite — **in·sti·ga·tion** \ˌinstə'gāshən\ *n* — **in·sti·ga·tor** \'instəˌgātər\ *n*

in·still \in'stil\ *vb* -stilled; -still·ing : impart gradually

in·stinct \'inˌstiŋkt\ *n* 1 : natural talent 2 : natural inherited or subconsciously motivated behavior — **in·stinc·tive** \in'stiŋktiv\ *adj* — **in·stinc·tive·ly** *adv* — **in·stinc·tu·al** \in'stiŋkchəwəl\ *adj*

in·sti·tute \'instəˌtüt, -ˌtyüt\ *vb* -tut·ed; -tut·ing : establish, start, or organize ~ *n* 1 : organization promoting a cause 2 : school

in·sti·tu·tion \ˌinstə'tüshən, -'tyü-\ *n* 1 : act of instituting 2 : custom 3 : corporation or society of a public character — **in·sti·tu·tion·al** \-shənəl\ *adj* — **in·sti·tu·tion·al·ize** \-ˌīz\ *vb* — **in·sti·tu·tion·al·ly** *adv*

in·struct \in'strəkt\ *vb* 1 : teach 2 : give an order to — **in·struc·tion** \in'strəkshən\ *n* — **in·struc·tion·al** \-shənəl\ *adj* — **in·struc·tive** \in'strək-tiv\ *adj* — **in·struc·tor** \in'strəktər\ *n* — **in·struc·tor·ship** *n*

in·stru·ment \'instrəmənt\ *n* 1 : something that produces music 2 : means 3 : device for doing work and esp. precision work 4 : legal document — **in·stru·men·tal** \ˌinstrə-'mentᵊl\ *adj* — **in·stru·men·tal·ist** \-ist\ *n* — **in·stru·men·tal·i·ty** \ˌinstrəmən'talətē,

---

inexplicably	inexpressibly	infeasibility
inexplicit	inextinguishable	infeasible
inexpressible	inextricable	infelicitous

-ˌmen-\ *n* — **in·stru·men·ta·tion** \ˌinstrəmən'tāshən, -ˌmen-\ *n*

in·sub·or·di·nate \ˌinsə'bȯrdᵊnət\ *adj* : not obeying — **in·sub·or·di·na·tion** \-ˌbȯrdᵊn'āshən\ *n*

in·suf·fer·able \in'səfərəbəl\ *adj* : unbearable — **in·suf·fer·ably** \-blē\ *adv*

in·su·lar \'insülər, -syü-\ *adj* **1** : relating to or residing on an island **2** : narrow-minded — **in·su·lar·i·ty** \ˌinsü-'larətē, -syü-\ *n*

in·su·late \'insəˌlāt\ *vb* **-lat·ed; -lat·ing** : protect from heat loss or electricity — **in·su·la·tion** \ˌinsə'lāshən\ *n* — **in·su·la·tor** \'insəˌlātər\ *n*

in·su·lin \'insələn\ *n* : hormone used by diabetics

in·sult \in'səlt\ *vb* : treat with contempt ~ \'inˌsəlt\ *n* : insulting act or remark — **in·sult·ing·ly** \-iŋlē\ *adv*

in·su·per·a·ble \in'süpərəbəl\ *adj* : too difficult — **in·su·per·a·bly** \-blē\ *adv*

in·sure \in'shür\ *vb* **-sured; -sur·ing** **1** : guarantee against loss **2** : make certain — **in·sur·able** \-əbəl\ *adj* — **in-**

sur·ance \-əns\ *n* — **in·sured** \in'shürd\ *n* — **in·sur·er** *n*

in·sur·gent \in'sərjənt\ *n* : rebel — **in·sur·gence** \-jəns\ *n* — **in·sur·gen·cy** \-jənsē\ *n* — **in·sur·gent** *adj*

in·sur·mount·able \ˌinsər-'maúntəbəl\ *adj* : too great to be overcome — **in·sur·mount·ably** \-blē\ *adv*

in·sur·rec·tion \ˌinsə'rekshən\ *n* : revolution — **in·sur·rec·tion·ist** *n*

in·tact \in'takt\ *adj* : undamaged

in·take \'inˌtāk\ *n* **1** : opening through which something enters **2** : act of taking in **3** : amount taken in

in·te·ger \'intijər\ *n* : number that is not a fraction and does not include a fraction

in·te·gral \'intigrəl\ *adj* : essential

in·te·grate \'intəˌgrāt\ *vb* **-grat·ed; -grat·ing** **1** : unite **2** : end segregation of or at — **in·te·gra·tion** \ˌintə'grāshən\ *n*

in·teg·ri·ty \in'tegrətē\ *n* **1** : soundness **2** : adherence to a code of values **3** : completeness

---

infelicity   inflexibility   infrequent
infertile   inflexible   infrequently
infertility   inflexibly   inglorious

in·tel·lect \'int⁺l,ekt\ *n* : power of knowing or thinking — **in·tel·lec·tu·al** \,int⁺l-'ekchəwəl\ *adj or n* — **in·tel·lec·tu·al·ism** \-chəwə,li-zəm\ *n* — **in·tel·lec·tu·al·ly** *adv*

in·tel·li·gence \in'teləjəns\ *n* **1** : ability to learn and understand **2** : mental acuteness **3** : information

in·tel·li·gent \in'teləjənt\ *adj* : having or showing intelligence — **in·tel·li·gent·ly** *adv*

in·tel·li·gi·ble \in'teləjəbəl\ *adj* : understandable — **in·tel·li·gi·bil·i·ty** \-,teləjə'bilətē\ *n* — **in·tel·li·gi·bly** *adv*

in·tem·per·ance \in'tempər-əns\ *n* : lack of moderation — **in·tem·per·ate** \-pərət\ *adj* — **in·tem·per·ate·ness** *n*

in·tend \in'tend\ *vb* : have as a purpose

in·tend·ed \-'tendəd\ *n* : engaged person — **intended** *adj*

in·tense \in'tens\ *adj* **1** : extreme **2** : deeply felt — **in·tense·ly** *adv* — **in·ten·si·fi·ca·tion** \-,tensəfə'kāshən\ *n* — **in·ten·si·fy** \-'tensə,fī\ *vb* — **in·ten·si·ty** \in'tensətē\ *n* — **in·ten·sive** \in'tensiv\ *adj* — **in·ten·sive·ly** *adv*

¹in·tent \in'tent\ *n* : purpose — **in·ten·tion** \-'tenchən\ *n* — **in·ten·tion·al** \-'tenchənəl\ *adj* — **in·ten·tion·al·ly** *adv*

²intent *adj* : concentrated — **in·tent·ly** *adv* — **in·tent·ness** *n*

in·ter \in'tər\ *vb* **-rr-** : bury

ingloriously
ingratitude
inhumane
inhumanely
injudicious
injudiciously
injudiciousness
inoffensive
inoperable
inoperative
insalubrious
insensitive
insensitivity
inseparable
insignificant
insincere
insincerely
insincerity
insolubility
insoluble
instability
insubstantial
insufficiency
insufficient
insufficiently
insupportable
intangibility
intangible
intangibly
intolerable
intolerably
intolerance
intolerant
intractable
invariable
invariably
inviable
invisibility
invisible
invisibly
involuntarily
involuntary
invulnerability
invulnerable
invulnerably

inter- *prefix* : between or among

in·ter·ac·tion \ˌintər'akshən\ *n* : mutual influence — **in·ter·act** \-'akt\ *vb* — **in·ter·ac·tive** *adj*

in·ter·breed \ˌintər'brēd\ *vb* **-bred** \-'bred\; **-breed·ing** : breed together

in·ter·ca·late \in'tərkəˌlāt\ *vb* **-lat·ed; -lat·ing** : insert — **in·ter·ca·la·tion** \-ˌtərkə'lāshən\ *n*

in·ter·cede \ˌintər'sēd\ *vb* **-ced·ed; -ced·ing** : act to reconcile — **in·ter·ces·sion** \-'seshən\ *n* — **in·ter·ces·sor** \-'sesər\ *n*

in·ter·cept \ˌintər'sept\ *vb* : interrupt the progress of — **intercept** \'intərˌsept\ *n* — **in·ter·cep·tion** \ˌintər'sepshən\ *n* — **in·ter·cep·tor** \-'septər\ *n*

in·ter·change \ˌintər'chānj\ *vb* **1** : exchange **2** : change places ∼ \'intərˌchānj\ *n* **1** : exchange **2** : junction of highways — **in·ter·change·able** \ˌintər'chānjəbəl\ *adj*

in·ter·course \'intərˌkōrs\ *n* **1** : relations between persons or nations **2** : copulation

in·ter·de·pen·dent \ˌintərdi'pendənt\ *adj* : mutually dependent — **in·ter·de·pen·dence** \-dəns\ *n*

in·ter·dict \ˌintər'dikt\ *vb* **1** : prohibit **2** : destroy or cut (an enemy supply line) — **in·ter·dic·tion** \-'dikshən\ *n*

in·ter·est \'intrəst, -təˌrest\ *n* **1** : right **2** : benefit **3** : charge for borrowed money **4** : readiness to pay special attention **5** : quality that causes interest ∼ *vb* **1** : concern **2** : get the attention of — **in·ter·est·ing** *adj* — **in·ter·est·ing·ly** *adv*

in·ter·face \'intərˌfās\ *n* : common boundary — **in·ter·fa·cial** \ˌintər'fāshəl\ *adj*

in·ter·fere \ˌintər'fir\ *vb* **-fered; -fer·ing** **1** : collide or be in opposition **2** : try to run the affairs of others — **in·ter·fer·ence** \-'firəns\ *n*

in·ter·im \'intərəm\ *n* : time between — **interim** *adj*

List of self-explanatory words with the prefix *inter-*

interagency	intercity	intercommunity
interatomic	interclass	intercompany
interbank	intercoastal	intercontinental
interborough	intercollegiate	intercounty
intercampus	intercolonial	intercultural
interchurch	intercommunal	

in·te·ri·or \in'tirēər\ *adj* : being on the inside ~ *n* **1** : inside **2** : inland area

in·ter·ject \ˌintər'jekt\ *vb* : stick in between

in·ter·jec·tion \-'jekshən\ *n* : an exclamatory word — **in·ter·jec·tion·al·ly** \-shənəlē\ *adv*

in·ter·lace \ˌintər'lās\ *vb* : cross or cause to cross one over another

in·ter·lin·ear \ˌintər'linēər\ *adj* : between written or printed lines

in·ter·lock \ˌintər'läk\ *vb* **1** : interlace **2** : connect for mutual effect — **interlock** \'intərˌläk\ *n*

in·ter·lop·er \ˌintər'lōpər\ *n* : intruder or meddler

in·ter·lude \'intərˌlüd\ *n* : intervening period

in·ter·mar·ry \ˌintər'marē\ *vb* **1** : marry each other **2** : marry within a group — **in·ter·mar·riage** \-'marij\ *n*

in·ter·me·di·ary \ˌintər'mēdēˌerē\ *n, pl* **-ar·ies** : agent between individuals or groups — **intermediary** *adj*

in·ter·me·di·ate \ˌintər'mēdēət\ *adj* : between extremes — **intermediate** *n*

in·ter·ment \in'tərmənt\ *n* : burial

in·ter·mi·na·ble \in'tərmənəbəl\ *adj* : endless — **in·ter·mi·na·bly** *adv*

in·ter·min·gle \ˌintər'miŋgəl\ *vb* : mingle

in·ter·mis·sion \ˌintər'mishən\ *n* : break in a performance

in·ter·mit·tent \-'mitᵊnt\ *adj* : coming at intervals — **in·ter·mit·tent·ly** *adv*

in·ter·mix \ˌintər'miks\ *vb* : mix together — **in·ter·mix·ture** \-'mikschər\ *n*

¹in·tern \'inˌtərn, in'tərn\ *vb* : confine esp. during a war — **in·tern·ee** \ˌinˌtər'nē\ *n* — **in·tern·ment** *n*

²in·tern \'inˌtərn\ *n* : advanced student (as in medicine) gaining supervised experience ~ *vb* : act as an intern — **in·tern·ship** *n*

in·ter·nal \in'tərnᵊl\ *adj* **1** : inward **2** : inside of the body **3** : relating to or existing in the mind — **in·ter·nal·ly** *adv*

---

interdenomina- tional	interfaculty	intergovernmental
interdepartmental	interfamily	intergroup
interdivisional	interfiber	interhemispheric
interelectronic	interfraternity	interindustry
interethnic	intergalactic	interinstitutional
	intergang	interisland

in·ter·na·tion·al \ˌintər'na-shənəl\ *adj* : affecting 2 or more nations ∼ *n* : something having international scope — **in·ter·na·tion·al·ism** \-ˌizəm\ *n* — **in·ter·na·tion·al·ize** \-ˌīz\ *vb* — **in·ter·na·tion·al·ly** *adv*

In·ter·net \'intər,net\ *n* : network that connects computer networks worldwide

in·ter·nist \'in,tərnist\ *n* : specialist in nonsurgical medicine

in·ter·play \'intər,plā\ *n* : interaction

in·ter·po·late \in'tərpə,lāt\ *vb* -**lat·ed**; -**lat·ing** : insert — **in·ter·po·la·tion** \-ˌtərpə'lāshən\ *n*

in·ter·pose \ˌintər'pōz\ *vb* -**posed**; -**pos·ing** **1** : place between **2** : intrude — **in·ter·po·si·tion** \-pə'zishən\ *n*

in·ter·pret \in'tərprət\ *vb* : explain the meaning of — **in·ter·pre·ta·tion** \in,tərprə'tāshən\ *n* — **in·ter·pre·ta·tive** \-'tərprə,tātiv\ *adj* — **in·ter·pret·er** *n* — **in·ter·pre·tive** \-'tərprətiv\ *adj*

in·ter·re·late \ˌintəri'lāt\ *vb* : have a mutual relationship

— **in·ter·re·lat·ed·ness** \-'lāt-ədnəs\ *n* — **in·ter·re·la·tion** \-'lāshən\ *n* — **in·ter·re·la·tion·ship** *n*

in·ter·ro·gate \in'terə,gāt\ *vb* -**gat·ed**; -**gat·ing** : question — **in·ter·ro·ga·tion** \-ˌterə'gāshən\ *n* — **in·ter·rog·a·tive** \ˌintə'rägətiv\ *adj or n* — **in·ter·ro·ga·tor** \-'terə,gātər\ *n* — **in·ter·rog·a·to·ry** \ˌintə'rägə,tōrē\ *adj*

in·ter·rupt \ˌintə'rəpt\ *vb* : intrude so as to hinder or end continuity — **in·ter·rupt·er** *n* — **in·ter·rup·tion** \-'rəpshən\ *n* — **in·ter·rup·tive** \-'rəptiv\ *adv*

in·ter·sect \ˌintər'sekt\ *vb* **1** : cut across or divide **2** : cross — **in·ter·sec·tion** \-'sekshən\ *n*

in·ter·sperse \ˌintər'spərs\ *vb* -**spersed**; -**spers·ing** : insert at intervals — **in·ter·per·sion** \-'spərzhən\ *n*

in·ter·stice \in'tərstəs\ *n, pl* -**stic·es** \-stə,sēz, -stəsəz\ : space between — **in·ter·sti·tial** \ˌintər'stishəl\ *adj*

interlibrary	interparty	interregional
intermolecular	interpersonal	interreligious
intermountain	interplanetary	interscholastic
interoceanic	interpopulation	intersectional
interoffice	interprovincial	interstate
interparticle	interracial	interstellar

in·ter·twine \ˌintər'twīn\ *vb* : twist together — **in·ter·twine·ment** *n*

in·ter·val \'intərvəl\ *n* **1** : time between **2** : space between

in·ter·vene \ˌintər'vēn\ *vb* **-vened; -ven·ing 1** : happen between events **2** : intercede — **in·ter·ven·tion** \-'ven-chən\ *n*

in·ter·view \'intər,vyü\ *n* : a meeting to get information — **interview** *vb* — **in·ter·view·er** *n*

in·ter·weave \ˌintər'wēv\ *vb* **-wove** \-'wōv\; **-wo·ven** \-'wōvən\; **-weav·ing** : weave together — **in·ter·wo·ven** \-'wōvən\ *adj*

in·tes·tate \in'tes,tāt, -tət\ *adj* : not leaving a will

in·tes·tine \in'testən\ *n* : tubular part of the digestive system after the stomach including a long narrow upper part (**small intestine**) followed by a broader shorter lower part (**large intestine**) — **in·tes·ti·nal** \-tən³l\ *adj*

in·ti·mate \'intə,māt\ *vb* **-mat·ed; -mat·ing** : hint ∼ \'in-təmət\ *adj* **1** : very friendly **2** : suggesting privacy **3** : very personal ∼ *n* : close friend — **in·ti·ma·cy** \'intəməsē\ *n* — **in·ti·mate·ly** *adv* — **in·ti·ma·tion** \ˌintə'māshən\ *n*

in·tim·i·date \in'timə,dāt\ *vb* **-dat·ed; -dat·ing** : make fearful — **in·tim·i·da·tion** \-ˌtimə-'dāshən\ *n*

in·to \'intü\ *prep* **1** : to the inside of **2** : to the condition of **3** : against

in·to·na·tion \ˌintō'nāshən\ *n* : way of singing or speaking

in·tone \in'tōn\ *vb* **-toned; -ton·ing** : chant

in·tox·i·cate \in'täkə,kāt\ *vb* **-cat·ed; -cat·ing** : make drunk — **in·tox·i·cant** \-sikənt\ *n or adj* — **in·tox·i·ca·tion** \-ˌtäkə-'kāshən\ *n*

in·tra·mu·ral \ˌintrə'myùrəl\ *adj* : within a school

in·tran·si·gent \in'transəjənt\ *adj* : uncompromising — **in·tran·si·gence** \-jəns\ *n* — **intransigent** *n*

in·tra·ve·nous \ˌintrə'vēnəs\ *adj* : by way of the veins — **in·tra·ve·nous·ly** *adv*

---

intersystem	intertropical	intervillage
interterm	interuniversity	interwar
interterminal	interurban	interzonal
intertribal	intervalley	interzone
intertroop		

in·trep·id \in'trepəd\ *adj* : fearless — **in·tre·pid·i·ty** \ˌintrə'pidətē\ *n*

in·tri·cate \'intrikət\ *adj* : very complex and delicate — **in·tri·ca·cy** \-trikəsē\ *n* — **in·tri·cate·ly** *adv*

in·trigue \in'trēg\ *vb* **-trigued; -trigu·ing** **1** : scheme **2** : arouse curiosity of ~ *n* : secret scheme — **in·trigu·ing·ly** \-iŋlē\ *adv*

in·trin·sic \in'trinzik, -sik\ *adj* : essential — **in·trin·si·cal·ly** \-ziklē, -si-\ *adv*

in·tro·duce \ˌintrə'düs, -'dyüs\ *vb* **-duced; -duc·ing** **1** : bring in esp. for the 1st time **2** : cause to be acquainted **3** : bring to notice **4** : put in — **in·tro·duc·tion** \'dəkshən\ *n* — **in·tro·duc·to·ry** \-'dəktərē\ *adj*

in·tro·spec·tion \ˌintrə'spekshən\ *n* : examination of one's own thoughts or feelings — **in·tro·spec·tive** \-'spektiv\ *adj* — **in·tro·spec·tive·ly** *adv*

in·tro·vert \'intrəˌvərt\ *n* : shy or reserved person — **in·tro·ver·sion** \ˌintrə'vərzhən\ *n* — **introvert** *adj* — **in·tro·vert·ed** \'intrəˌvərtəd\ *adj*

in·trude \in'trüd\ *vb* **-trud·ed; -trud·ing** **1** : thrust in **2** : encroach — **in·trud·er** *n* — **in·tru·sion** \-'trüzhən\ *n* —

in·tru·sive \-'trüsiv\ *adj* — **in·tru·sive·ness** *n*

in·tu·i·tion \ˌintü'ishən, -tyü-\ *n* : quick and ready insight — **in·tu·it** \in'tüət, -'tyü-\ *vb* — **in·tu·i·tive** \-ətiv\ *adj* — **in·tu·i·tive·ly** *adv*

in·un·date \'inənˌdāt\ *vb* **-dat·ed; -dat·ing** : flood — **in·un·da·tion** \ˌinən'dāshən\ *n*

in·ure \in'ùr, -'yùr\ *vb* **-ured; -ur·ing** : accustom to accept something undesirable

in·vade \in'vād\ *vb* **-vad·ed; -vad·ing** : enter for conquest — **in·vad·er** *n* — **in·va·sion** \-'vāzhən\ *n*

¹in·val·id \in'valəd\ *adj* : not true or legal — **in·va·lid·i·ty** \ˌinvə'lidətē\ *n* — **in·val·id·ly** *adv*

²in·va·lid \'invələd\ *adj* : sickly ~ *n* : one chronically ill

in·val·i·date \in'valəˌdāt\ *vb* : make invalid — **in·val·i·da·tion** \inˌvalə'dāshən\ *n*

in·valu·able \in'valyəwəbəl\ *adj* : extremely valuable

in·va·sive \in'vāsiv\ *adj* : involving entry into the body

in·vec·tive \in'vektiv\ *n* : abusive language — **invective** *adj*

in·veigh \in'vā\ *vb* : protest or complain forcefully

in·vei·gle \in'vāgəl, -'vē-\ *vb* **-gled; -gling** : win over or get by flattery

in·vent \in'vent\ *vb* **1** : think up **2** : create for the 1st time — **in·ven·tion** \-'venchən\ *n* — **in·ven·tive** \-'ventiv\ *adj* — **in·ven·tive·ness** *n* — **in·ven·tor** \-'ventər\ *n*

in·ven·to·ry \'invən,tōrē\ *n, pl* **-ries** **1** : list of goods **2** : stock — **inventory** *vb*

in·verse \in'vərs, 'in,vərs\ *adj or n* : opposite — **in·verse·ly** *adv*

in·vert \in'vərt\ *vb* **1** : turn upside down or inside out **2** : reverse — **in·ver·sion** \-'verzhən\ *n*

in·ver·te·brate \in'vərtəbrət, -,brāt\ *adj* : lacking a backbone ～ *n* : invertebrate animal

in·vest \in'vest\ *vb* **1** : give power or authority to **2** : endow with a quality **3** : commit money to someone else's use in hope of profit — **in·vest·ment** \-mənt\ *n* — **in·ves·tor** \-'vestər\ *n*

in·ves·ti·gate \in'vestə,gāt\ *vb* **-gat·ed; -gat·ing** : study closely and systematically — **in·ves·ti·ga·tion** \-,vestə'gā-shən\ *n* — **in·ves·ti·ga·tive** \-'vestə,gātiv\ *adj* — **in·ves·ti·ga·tor** \-'vestə,gātər\ *n*

in·ves·ti·ture \in'vestə,chùr, -chər\ *n* : act of establishing in office

in·vet·er·ate \in'vetərət\ *adj* : acting out of habit

in·vid·i·ous \in'vidēəs\ *adj* : harmful or obnoxious — **in·vid·i·ous·ly** *adv*

in·vig·o·rate \in'vigə,rāt\ *vb* **-rat·ed; -rat·ing** : give life and energy to — **in·vig·o·ra·tion** \-,vigə'rāshən\ *n*

in·vin·ci·ble \in'vinsəbəl\ *adj* : incapable of being conquered — **in·vin·ci·bil·i·ty** \in,vinsə-'bilətē\ *n* — **in·vin·ci·bly** \in-'vinsəblē\ *adv*

in·vi·o·la·ble \in'vīələbəl\ *adj* : safe from violation or desecration — **in·vi·o·la·bil·i·ty** \in,vīələ'bilətē\ *n*

in·vi·o·late \in'vīələt\ *adj* : not violated or profaned

in·vite \in'vīt\ *vb* **-vit·ed; -vit·ing** **1** : entice **2** : increase the likelihood of **3** : request the presence or participation of **4** : encourage — **in·vi·ta·tion** \,invə'tāshən\ *n* — **in·vit·ing** \in'vītiŋ\ *adj*

in·vo·ca·tion \,invə'kāshən\ *n* **1** : prayer **2** : incantation

in·voice \'in,vòis\ *n* : itemized bill for goods shipped ～ *vb* **-voiced; -voic·ing** : bill

in·voke \in'vōk\ *vb* **-voked; -vok·ing** **1** : call on for help **2** : cite as authority **3** : conjure **4** : carry out

in·volve \in'välv\ *vb* **-volved; -volv·ing** **1** : draw in as a participant **2** : relate closely **3** : require as a necessary part **4**

: occupy fully — **in·volve·ment** *n*

in·volved \-ˈvälvd\ *adj* : intricate

¹**in·ward** \ˈinwərd\ *adj* : inside

²**inward, in·wards** \-wərdz\ *adv* : toward the inside, center, or inner being

in·ward·ly *adv* **1** : mentally or spiritually **2** : internally **3** : to oneself

io·dide \ˈīə,dīd\ *n* : compound of iodine

io·dine \ˈīə,dīn, -əd°n\ *n* **1** : nonmetallic chemical element **2** : solution of iodine used as an antiseptic

io·dize \ˈīə,dīz\ *vb* **-dized; -diz·ing** : treat with iodine or an iodide

ion \īən, ˈī,än\ *n* : electrically charged particle — **ion·ic** \īänik\ *adj* — **ion·iz·able** \ˈīə,nīzəbəl\ *adj* — **ion·iza·tion** \,īənəˈzāshən\ *n* — **ion·ize** \ˈīə,nīz\ *vb* — **ion·iz·er** \ˈīə,nīzər\ *n*

-ion *n suffix* **1** : act or process **2** : state or condition

ion·o·sphere \īˈänə,sfir\ *n* : layer of the upper atmosphere containing ionized gases — **ion·o·spher·ic** \ī,änəˈsfirik, -ˈsfer-\ *adj*

io·ta \īˈōtə\ *n* : small quantity

IOU \,ī,ōˈyü\ *n* : acknowledgment of a debt

IRA \,ī,ärˈā\ *n* : individual retirement savings account

iras·ci·ble \irˈasəbəl, īˈras-\ *adj* : marked by hot temper — **iras·ci·bil·i·ty** \-,asəˈbilətē, -,ras-\ *n*

irate \īˈrāt\ *adj* : roused to intense anger — **irate·ly** *adv*

ire \ˈīr\ *n* : anger

ir·i·des·cence \,irəˈdes°ns\ *n* : rainbowlike play of colors — **ir·i·des·cent** \-°nt\ *adj*

iris \ˈīrəs\ *n, pl* **iris·es** *or* **iri·des** \ˈīrə,dēz, ˈir-\ **1** : colored part around the pupil of the eye **2** : plant with long leaves and large showy flowers

irk \ˈərk\ *vb* : annoy — **irk·some** \-əm\ *adj* — **irk·some·ly** *adv*

iron \ˈīərn\ *n* **1** : heavy metallic chemical element **2** : something made of iron **3** : heated device for pressing clothes **4** : hardness, determination ~ *vb* : press or smooth out with an iron — **iron·ware** *n* — **iron·work** *n* — **iron·work·er** *n* — **iron·works** *n pl*

iron·clad \-ˈklad\ *adj* **1** : sheathed in iron armor **2** : strict or exacting

iron·ing \ˈīərniŋ\ *n* : clothes to be ironed

iron·wood \-,wu̇d\ *n* : tree or shrub with very hard wood or this wood

iro·ny \\'īrənē\ *n, pl* **-nies 1** : use of words to express the opposite of the literal meaning **2** : incongruity between the actual and expected result of events — **iron·ic** \ī'ränik\, **iron·i·cal** \-ikəl\ *adj* — **iron·i·cal·ly** \-iklē\ *adv*

ir·ra·di·ate \ir'ādē,āt\ *vb* **-at·ed; -at·ing** : treat with radiation — **ir·ra·di·a·tion** \-,ādē'āshən\ *n*

ir·ra·tio·nal \ir'ashənəl\ *adj* **1** : incapable of reasoning **2** : not based on reason — **ir·ra·tio·nal·i·ty** \ir,ashə'nalətē\ *n* — **ir·ra·tio·nal·ly** *adv*

ir·rec·on·cil·able \ir,ekən'sīləbəl\ *adj* : impossible to reconcile — **ir·rec·on·cil·abil·i·ty** \-,sīlə'bilətē\ *n*

ir·re·cov·er·able \,iri'kəvərəbəl\ *adj* : not capable of being recovered — **ir·re·cov·er·ably** \-blē\ *adv*

ir·re·deem·able \,iri'dēməbəl\ *adj* : not redeemable

ir·re·duc·ible \,iri'düsəbəl, -'dyü-\ *adj* : not reducible — **ir·re·duc·ibly** \-blē\ *adv*

ir·re·fut·able \,iri'fyütəbəl, ir'refyət-\ *adj* : impossible to refute

ir·reg·u·lar \ir'egyələr\ *adj* : not regular or normal — **irregular** *n* — **ir·reg·u·lar·i·ty** \ir,egyə'larətē\ *n* — **ir·reg·u·lar·ly** *adv*

ir·rel·e·vant \ir'eləvənt\ *adj* : not relevant — **ir·rel·e·vance** \-vəns\ *n*

ir·re·li·gious \,iri'lijəs\ *adj* : not following religious practices

ir·rep·a·ra·ble \ir'epərəbəl\ *adj* : impossible to make good, undo, or remedy

ir·re·place·able \,iri'plāsəbəl\ *adj* : not replaceable

ir·re·press·ible \-'presəbəl\ *adj* : impossible to repress or control

ir·re·proach·able \-'prōchəbəl\ *adj* : blameless

ir·re·sist·ible \-'zistəbəl\ *adj* : impossible to successfully resist — **ir·re·sist·ibly** \-blē\ *adv*

ir·res·o·lute \ir'ezəlüt\ *adj* : uncertain — **ir·res·o·lute·ly** *adv* — **ir·res·o·lu·tion** \-,ezə'lüshən\ *n*

ir·re·spec·tive of \,iri'spektiv-\ *prep* : without regard to

ir·re·spon·si·ble \,iri'spänsəbəl\ *adj* : not responsible — **ir·re·spon·si·bil·i·ty** \-,spänsə'bilətē\ *n* — **ir·re·spon·si·bly** *adv*

ir·re·triev·able \,iri'trēvəbəl\ *adj* : not retrievable

ir·rev·er·ence \ir'evərəns\ *n* **1** : lack of reverence **2** : irreverent act or utterance — **ir·rev·er·ent** \-rənt\ *adj*

ir·re·vers·ible \ˌiri'vsərəbəl\ *adj* : incapable of being reversed

ir·rev·o·ca·ble \ir'evəkəbəl\ *adj* : incapable of being revoked — **ir·rev·o·ca·bly** \-blē\ *adv*

ir·ri·gate \'irəˌgāt\ *vb* **-gat·ed; -gat·ing** : supply with water by artificial means — **ir·ri·ga·tion** \ˌirə'gāshən\ *n*

ir·ri·tate \'irəˌtāt\ *vb* **-tat·ed; -tat·ing** **1** : excite to anger **2** : make sore or inflamed — **ir·ri·ta·bil·i·ty** \ˌirətə'bilətē\ *n* — **ir·ri·ta·ble** \'irətəbəl\ *adj* — **ir·ri·ta·bly** \'irətəblē\ *adv* — **ir·ri·tant** \'irətənt\ *adj or n* — **ir·ri·tat·ing·ly** *adv* — **ir·ri·ta·tion** \ˌirə'tāshən\ *n*

is *pres 3d sing of* BE

-ish \ish\ *adj suffix* **1** : characteristic of **2** : somewhat

Is·lam \is'läm, iz-, -'lam\ *n* : religious faith of Muslims — **Is·lam·ic** \-ik\ *adj*

is·land \'īlənd\ *n* : body of land surrounded by water — **is·land·er** \'īləndər\ *n*

isle \'īl\ *n* : small island

is·let \'īlət\ *n* : small island

-ism \ˌizəm\ *n suffix* **1** : act or practice **2** : characteristic manner **3** : condition **4** : doctrine

iso·late \'īsəˌlāt\ *vb* **-lat·ed; -lat·ing** : place or keep by itself — **iso·la·tion** \ˌīsə'lāshən\ *n*

iso·met·rics \ˌīsə'metriks\ *n sing or pl* : exercise against unmoving resistance — **iso·metric** *adj*

isos·ce·les \ī'säsəˌlēz\ *adj* : having 2 equal sides

iso·tope \'īsəˌtōp\ *n* : species of atom of a chemical element — **iso·to·pic** \ˌīsə'täpik, -'tō-\ *adj*

is·sue \'ishü\ *vb* **-sued; -su·ing** **1** : go, come, or flow out **2** : descend from a specified ancestor **3** : emanate or result **4** : put forth or distribute officially ~ *n* **1** : action of issuing **2** : offspring **3** : result **4** : point of controversy **5** : act of giving out or printing **6** : quantity given out or printed — **is·su·ance** \'ishəwəns\ *n* — **is·su·er** *n*

-ist \ist\ *n suffix* **1** : one that does **2** : one that plays **3** : one that specializes in **4** : follower of a doctrine

isth·mus \'isməs\ *n* : narrow strip of land connecting 2 larger portions

it \'it\ *pron* **1** : that one — used of a lifeless thing or an abstract entity **2** — used as an anticipatory subject or object ~ *n* : player who tries to catch others (as in a game of tag)

ital·ic \ə'talik, i-, ī-\ *n* : style of type with slanting letters

— **italic** *adj* — **ital·i·ci·za·tion** \ə,taləsə'zāshən, i-, ī-\ *n* — **ital·i·cize** \ə'talə,sīz, i-, ī-\ *vb*

itch \'ich\ *n* **1** : uneasy irritating skin sensation **2** : skin disorder **3** : persistent desire — **itch** *vb* — **itchy** *adj*

item \'ītəm\ *n* **1** : particular in a list, account, or series **2** : piece of news — **item·iza·tion** \,ītəmə'zāshən\ *n* — **item·ize** \'ītə,mīz\ *vb*

itin·er·ant \ī'tinərənt, ə-\ *adj* : traveling from place to place

itin·er·ary \ī'tinə,rerē, ə-\ *n, pl* **-ar·ies** : route or outline of a journey

its \'its\ *adj* : relating to it

it·self \it'self\ *pron* : it — used reflexively or for emphasis

-ity \ətē\ *n suffix* : quality, state, or degree

-ive \iv\ *adj suffix* : that performs or tends toward an action

ivo·ry \'īvərē\ *n, pl* **-ries** **1** : hard creamy-white material of elephants' tusks **2** : pale yellow color

ivy \'īvē\ *n, pl* **ivies** : trailing woody vine with evergreen leaves

-ize \,īz\ *vb suffix* **1** : cause to be, become, or resemble **2** : subject to an action **3** : treat or combine with **4** : engage in an activity

J

j \'jā\ *n, pl* **j's** *or* **js** \'jāz\ : 10th letter of the alphabet

jab \'jab\ *vb* **-bb-** : thrust quickly or abruptly ～ *n* : short straight punch

jab·ber \'jabər\ *vb* : talk rapidly or unintelligibly — **jabber** *n*

jack \'jak\ *n* **1** : mechanical device to raise a heavy body **2** : small flag **3** : small 6-pointed metal object used in a game (**jacks**) **4** : electrical

socket ～ *vb* **1** : raise with a jack **2** : increase

jack·al \'jakəl, -,ȯl\ *n* : wild dog

jack·ass *n* **1** : male ass **2** : stupid person

jack·et \'jakət\ *n* : garment for the upper body

jack·ham·mer \'jak,hamər\ *n* : pneumatic tool for drilling

jack·knife \'jak,nīf\ *n* : pocketknife ～ *vb* : fold like a jackknife

jack–o'–lan·tern \'jakə₁lan-tərn\ *n* : lantern made of a carved pumpkin

jack·pot \'jak₁pät\ *n* : sum of money won

jack·rab·bit \-₁rabət\ *n* : large hare of western No. America

jade \'jād\ *n* : usu. green gem-stone

jad·ed \'jādəd\ *adj* : dulled or bored by having too much

jag·ged \'jagəd\ *adj* : sharply notched

jag·uar \'jag₁wär, 'jagyə-\ *n* : black-spotted tropical American cat

jai alai \'hī₁lī\ *n* : game with a ball propelled by a basket on the hand

jail \'jāl\ *n* : prison — **jail** *vb* — **jail·break** *n* — **jail·er, jail·or** *n*

ja·la·pe·ño \₁hälə'pān₁yō, -₁pēnō\ *n* : Mexican hot pepper

ja·lopy \jə'läpē\ *n, pl* **-lopies** : dilapidated vehicle

jal·ou·sie \'jaləsē\ *n* : door or window with louvers

jam \'jam\ *vb* **-mm-** **1** : press into a tight position **2** : cause to become wedged and un-workable ∼ *n* **1** : crowded mass that blocks or impedes **2** : difficult situation **3** : thick sweet food made of cooked fruit

jamb \'jam\ *n* : upright fram-ing piece of a door

jam·bo·ree \₁jambə'rē\ *n* : large festive gathering

jan·gle \'jaŋgəl\ *vb* **-gled; -gling** : make a harsh ringing sound — **jangle** *n*

jan·i·tor \'janətər\ *n* : person who has the care of a building — **jan·i·to·ri·al** \₁janə'tō-rēəl\ *adj*

Jan·u·ary \'janyə₁werē\ *n* : 1st month of the year having 31 days

¹jar \'jär\ *vb* **-rr-** **1** : have a harsh or disagreeable effect **2** : vibrate or shake ∼ *n* **1** : jolt **2** : painful effect

²jar *n* : wide-mouthed container

jar·gon \'järgən, -₁gän\ *n* : spe-cial vocabulary of a group

jas·mine \'jazmən\ *n* : climb-ing shrub with fragrant flowers

jas·per \'jaspər\ *n* : red, yel-low, or brown opaque quartz

jaun·dice \'jȯndəs\ *n* : yel-lowish discoloration of skin, tissues, and body fluids

jaun·diced \-dəst\ *adj* : ex-hibiting envy or hostility

jaunt \'jȯnt\ *n* : short pleasure trip

jaun·ty \'jȯntē\ *adj* **-ti·er; -est** : lively in manner or appear-ance — **jaun·ti·ly** \'jȯntᵊlē\ *adv* — **jaun·ti·ness** *n*

jav·e·lin \\'javələn\ *n* : light spear

jaw \\'jȯ\ *n* **1** : either of the bony or cartilaginous structures that support the mouth **2** : one of 2 movable parts for holding or crushing ∼ *vb* : talk indignantly or at length — **jaw·bone** \-,bōn\ *n* — **jawed** \\'jȯd\ *adj*

jay \\'jā\ *n* : noisy brightly colored bird

jay·bird *n* : jay

jay·walk *vb* : cross a street carelessly — **jay·walk·er** *n*

jazz \\'jaz\ *vb* : enliven ∼ *n* **1** : kind of American music involving improvisation **2** : empty talk — **jazzy** *adj*

jeal·ous \\'jeləs\ *adj* : suspicious of a rival or of one believed to enjoy an advantage — **jeal·ous·ly** *adv* — **jeal·ou·sy** \-əsē\ *n*

jeans \\'jēnz\ *n pl* : pants made of durable twilled cotton cloth

jeep \\'jēp\ *n* : 4-wheel army vehicle

jeer \\'jir\ *vb* **1** : speak or cry out in derision **2** : ridicule ∼ *n* : taunt

Je·ho·vah \ji'hōvə\ *n* : God

je·june \ji'jün\ *adj* : dull or childish

jell \\'jel\ *vb* **1** : come to the consistency of jelly **2** : take shape

jel·ly \\'jelē\ *n, pl* **-lies** : a substance (as food) with a soft somewhat elastic consistency — **jelly** *vb*

jel·ly·fish *n* : sea animal with a saucer-shaped jellylike body

jen·ny \\'jenē\ *n, pl* **-nies** : female bird or donkey

jeop·ar·dy \\'jepərdē\ *n* : exposure to death, loss, or injury — **jeop·ar·dize** \-ər,dīz\ *vb*

jerk \\'jərk\ *vb* **1** : give a sharp quick push, pull, or twist **2** : move in short abrupt motions ∼ *n* **1** : short quick pull or twist **2** : stupid or foolish person — **jerk·i·ly** *adv* — **jerky** *adj*

jer·kin \\'jərkən\ *n* : close-fitting sleeveless jacket

jer·ry–built \\'jerē,bilt\ *adj* : built cheaply and flimsily

jer·sey \\'jərzē\ *n, pl* **-seys** **1** : plain knit fabric **2** : knitted shirt

jest \\'jest\ *n* : witty remark — **jest** *vb*

jest·er \\'jestər\ *n* : one employed to entertain a court

¹jet \\'jet\ *n* : velvet-black coal used for jewelry

²jet *vb* **-tt-** **1** : spout or emit in a stream **2** : travel by jet ∼ *n* **1** : forceful rush of fluid through a narrow opening **2** : jet-propelled airplane

jet–propelled *adj* : driven by an engine (**jet engine**) that produces propulsion (**jet propulsion**) by the rearward discharge of a jet of fluid

jet·sam \\'jetsəm\ *n* : jettisoned goods

jet·ti·son \\'jetəsən\ *vb* **1** : throw (goods) overboard **2** : discard — **jettison** *n*

jet·ty \\'jetē\ *n, pl* **-ties** : pier or wharf

Jew \\'jü\ *n* : one whose religion is Judaism — **Jew·ish** *adj*

jew·el \\'jüəl\ *n* **1** : ornament of precious metal **2** : gem ~ *vb* **-eled** *or* **-elled; -el·ing** *or* **-el·ling** : adorn with jewels — **jew·el·er, jew·el·ler** \-ər\ *n* — **jew·el·ry** \-rē\ *n*

jib \\'jib\ *n* : triangular sail

jibe \\'jīb\ *vb* **jibed; jib·ing** : be in agreement

jif·fy \\'jifē\ *n, pl* **-fies** : short time

jig \\'jig\ *n* : lively dance ~ *vb* **-gg-** : dance a jig

jig·ger \\'jigər\ *n* : measure used in mixing drinks

jig·gle \\'jigəl\ *vb* **-gled; -gling** : move with quick little jerks — **jiggle** *n*

jig·saw *n* : machine saw with a narrow blade that moves up and down

jilt \\'jilt\ *vb* : drop (a lover) unfeelingly

jim·my \\'jimē\ *n, pl* **-mies** : small crowbar ~ *vb* **-mied; -my·ing** : pry open

jim·son·weed \\'jimsən‚wēd\ *n* : coarse poisonous weed

jin·gle \\'jiŋgəl\ *vb* **-gled; -gling** : make a light tinkling sound ~ *n* **1** : light tinkling sound **2** : short verse or song

jin·go·ism \\'jiŋgō‚izəm\ *n* : extreme chauvinism or nationalism — **jin·go·ist** \-ist\ *n* — **jin·go·is·tic** \‚jiŋgō'istik\ *adj*

jinx \\'jiŋks\ *n* : one that brings bad luck — **jinx** *vb*

jit·ney \\'jitnē\ *n, pl* **-neys** : small bus

jit·ters \\'jitərz\ *n pl* : extreme nervousness — **jit·tery** \-ərē\ *adj*

job \\'jäb\ *n* **1** : something that has to be done **2** : regular employment — **job·hold·er** *n* — **job·less** *adj*

job·ber \\'jäbər\ *n* : middleman

jock·ey \\'jäkē\ *n, pl* **-eys** : one who rides a horse in a race ~ *vb* **-eyed; -ey·ing** : manipulate or maneuver adroitly

jo·cose \jō'kōs\ *adj* : jocular

joc·u·lar \\'jäkyələr\ *adj* : marked by jesting — **joc·u·lar·i·ty** \‚jäkyə'larətē\ *n* — **joc·u·lar·ly** *adv*

jo·cund \\'jäkənd\ *adj* : full of mirth or gaiety

jodh·purs \\'jädpərz\ *n pl* : riding breeches

¹jog \\'jäg\ *vb* **-gg-** **1** : give a slight shake or push to **2** : run or ride at a slow pace ~ *n* **1** : slight shake **2** : slow pace — **jog·ger** *n*

²**jog** *n* : brief abrupt change in direction or line

join \'jȯin\ *vb* **1** : come or bring together **2** : become a member of — **join·er** *n*

joint \'jȯint\ *n* **1** : point of contact between bones **2** : place where 2 parts connect **3** : often disreputable place ~ *adj* : common to 2 or more — **joint·ed** *adj* — **joint·ly** *adv*

joist \'jȯist\ *n* : beam supporting a floor or ceiling

joke \'jōk\ *n* : something said or done to provoke laughter ~ *vb* **joked; jok·ing** : make jokes — **jok·er** *n* — **jok·ing·ly** \'jōkiŋlē\ *adv*

jol·li·ty \'jälətē\ *n, pl* **-ties** : gaiety or merriment

jol·ly \'jälē\ *adj* **-li·er; -est** : full of high spirits

jolt \'jōlt\ *vb* **1** : move with a sudden jerky motion **2** : give a jolt to ~ *n* **1** : abrupt jerky blow or movement **2** : sudden shock — **jolt·er** *n*

jon·quil \'jänkwəl\ *n* : narcissus with white or yellow flowers

josh \'jäsh\ *vb* : tease or joke

jos·tle \'jäsəl\ *vb* **-tled; -tling** : push or shove

jot \'jät\ *n* : least bit ~ *vb* **-tt-** : write briefly and hurriedly

jounce \'jau̇ns\ *vb* **jounced; jounc·ing** : jolt — **jounce** *n*

jour·nal \'jərnᵊl\ *n* **1** : brief account of daily events **2** : periodical (as a newspaper)

jour·nal·ism \'jərnᵊl,izəm\ *n* : business of reporting or printing news — **jour·nal·ist** \-ist\ *n* — **jour·nal·is·tic** \,jərnᵊl'istik\ *adj*

jour·ney \'jərnē\ *n, pl* **-neys** : a going from one place to another ~ *vb* **-neyed; -ney·ing** : make a journey

jour·ney·man \-mən\ *n* : worker who has learned a trade and works for another person

joust \'jau̇st\ *n* : combat on horseback between 2 knights with lances — **joust** *vb*

jo·vial \'jōvēəl\ *adj* : marked by good humor — **jo·vi·al·i·ty** \,jōvē'alətē\ *n* — **jo·vi·al·ly** \'jōvēəlē\ *adv*

¹**jowl** \'jau̇l\ *n* : loose flesh about the lower jaw or throat

²**jowl** *n* **1** : lower jaw **2** : cheek

joy \'jȯi\ *n* **1** : feeling of happiness **2** : source of happiness — **joy** *vb* — **joy·ful** *adj* — **joy·ful·ly** *adv* — **joy·less** *adj* — **joy·ous** \'jȯiəs\ *adj* — **joy·ous·ly** *adv* — **joy·ous·ness** *n*

joy·ride *n* : reckless ride for pleasure — **joy·rid·er** *n* — **joy·rid·ing** *n*

ju·bi·lant \'jübələnt\ *adj* : expressing great joy — **ju·bi·lant·ly** *adv* — **ju·bi·la·tion** \ˌjübə'lāshən\ *n*

ju·bi·lee \'jübəˌlē\ *n* **1** : 50th anniversary **2** : season or occasion of celebration

Ju·da·ism \'jüdəˌizəm\ *n* : religion developed among the ancient Hebrews — **Ju·da·ic** \ju'dāik\ *adj*

judge \'jəj\ *vb* **judged; judging** **1** : form an opinion **2** : decide as a judge ∼ *n* **1** : public official authorized to decide questions brought before a court **2** : one who gives an authoritative opinion — **judge·ship** *n*

judg·ment, judge·ment \'jəjmənt\ *n* **1** : decision or opinion given after judging **2** : capacity for judging — **judg·men·tal** \ˌjəj'mentəl\ *adj* — **judg·men·tal·ly** *adv*

ju·di·ca·ture \'jüdikəˌchủr\ *n* : administration of justice

ju·di·cial \ju'dishəl\ *adj* : relating to judicature or the judiciary — **ju·di·cial·ly** *adv*

ju·di·cia·ry \ju'dishēˌerē, -'dishərē\ *n* : system of courts of law or the judges of them — **judiciary** *adj*

ju·di·cious \ju'dishəs\ *adj* : having or characterized by sound judgment — **ju·di·cious·ly** *adv*

ju·do \'jüdō\ *n* : form of wrestling — **judo·ist** *n*

jug \'jəg\ *n* : large deep container with a narrow mouth and a handle

jug·ger·naut \'jəgərˌnȯt\ *n* : massive inexorable force or object

jug·gle \'jəgəl\ *vb* **-gled; -gling** **1** : keep several objects in motion in the air at the same time **2** : manipulate for an often tricky purpose — **jug·gler** \'jəglər\ *n*

jug·u·lar \'jəgyələr\ *adj* : in or on the throat or neck

juice \'jüs\ *n* **1** : extractable fluid contents of cells or tissues **2** : electricity — **juic·er** *n* — **juic·i·ly** \'jüsəlē\ *adv* — **juic·i·ness** \-sēnəs\ *n* — **juicy** \'jüsē\ *adj*

ju·jube \'jüˌjüb, 'jüjủˌbē\ *n* : gummy candy

juke·box \'jükˌbäks\ *n* : coin‗operated machine for playing music recordings

ju·lep \'jüləp\ *n* : mint-flavored bourbon drink

Ju·ly \ju'lī\ *n* : 7th month of the year having 31 days

jum·ble \'jəmbəl\ *vb* **-bled; -bling** : mix in a confused mass — **jumble** *n*

jum·bo \'jəmbō\ *n, pl* **-bos** : very large version — **jumbo** *adj*

jump \ˈjəmp\ *vb* **1** : rise into or through the air esp. by muscular effort **2** : pass over **3** : give a start **4** : rise or increase sharply ~ *n* **1** : a jumping **2** : sharp sudden increase **3** : initial advantage

¹**jump·er** \ˈjəmpər\ *n* : one that jumps

²**jumper** *n* : sleeveless one-piece dress

jumpy \ˈjəmpē\ *adj* **jump·i·er; -est** : nervous or jittery

junc·tion \ˈjəŋkshən\ *n* **1** : a joining **2** : place or point of meeting

junc·ture \ˈjəŋkchər\ *n* **1** : joint or connection **2** : critical time or state of affairs

June \ˈjün\ *n* : 6th month of the year having 30 days

jun·gle \ˈjəŋgəl\ *n* : thick tangled mass of tropical vegetation

ju·nior \ˈjünyər\ *n* **1** : person who is younger or of lower rank than another **2** : student in the next-to-last year ~ *adj* : younger or lower in rank

ju·ni·per \ˈjünəpər\ *n* : evergreen shrub or tree

¹**junk** \ˈjəŋk\ *n* **1** : discarded articles **2** : shoddy product ~ *vb* : discard or scrap — **junky** *adj*

²**junk** *n* : flat-bottomed ship of Chinese waters

jun·ket \ˈjəŋkət\ *n* : trip made by an official at public expense

jun·ta \ˈhu̇ntə, ˈjəntə, ˈhəntə\ *n* : group of persons controlling a government

ju·ris·dic·tion \ˌju̇rəsˈdikshən\ *n* **1** : right or authority to interpret and apply the law **2** : limits within which authority may be exercised — **ju·ris·dic·tion·al** \-shənəl\ *adj*

ju·ris·pru·dence \-ˈprüdᵊns\ *n* **1** : system of laws **2** : science or philosophy of law

ju·rist \ˈju̇rist\ *n* : judge

ju·ror \ˈju̇rər\ *n* : member of a jury

ju·ry \ˈju̇rē\ *n, pl* **-ries** : body of persons sworn to give a verdict on a matter

just \ˈjəst\ *adj* **1** : reasonable **2** : correct or proper **3** : morally or legally right **4** : deserved ~ *adv* **1** : exactly **2** : very recently **3** : barely **4** : only **5** : quite **6** : possibly — **just·ly** *adv* — **just·ness** *n*

jus·tice \ˈjəstəs\ *n* **1** : administration of what is just **2** : judge **3** : administration of law **4** : fairness

jus·ti·fy \ˈjəstəˌfī\ *vb* **-fied; -fy·ing** : prove to be just, right, or reasonable — **jus·ti·fi·able** *adj* — **jus·ti·fi·ca·tion** \ˌjəstəfəˈkāshən\ *n*

jut \ˈjət\ *vb* **-tt- :** stick out

jute \ˈjüt\ *n* : strong glossy fiber from a tropical plant

ju·ve·nile \'jüvə‚nīl, -vənᵊl\ *adj* : relating to children or young people ∼ *n* : young person

jux·ta·pose \'jəkstə‚pōz\ *vb* **-posed; -pos·ing** : place side by side — **jux·ta·po·si·tion** \‚jəkstəpə'zishən\ *n*

K

k \'kā\ *n, pl* **k's** *or* **ks** \'kāz\ : 11th letter of the alphabet

kai·ser \'kīzər\ *n* : German ruler

kale \'kāl\ *n* : curly cabbage

ka·lei·do·scope \kə'līdə‚skōp\ *n* : device containing loose bits of colored material reflecting in many patterns — **ka·lei·do·scop·ic** \-‚līdə'skäpik\ *adj* — **ka·lei·do·scop·i·cal·ly** \-iklē\ *adv*

kan·ga·roo \‚kaŋgə'rü\ *n, pl* **-roos** : large leaping Australian mammal

ka·o·lin \'kāələn\ *n* : fine white clay

kar·a·o·ke \‚karē'ōkē\ *n* : device that plays accompaniments for singers

kar·at \'karət\ *n* : unit of gold content

ka·ra·te \kə'rätē\ *n* : art of self-defense by crippling kicks and punches

ka·ty·did \'kātē‚did\ *n* : large American grasshopper

kay·ak \'kī‚ak\ *n* : Eskimo canoe

ka·zoo \kə'zü\ *n, pl* **-zoos** : toy musical instrument

keel \'kēl\ *n* : central lengthwise strip on the bottom of a ship — **keeled** \'kēld\ *adj*

keen \'kēn\ *adj* **1** : sharp **2** : severe **3** : enthusiastic **4** : mentally alert — **keen·ly** *adv* — **keen·ness** *n*

keep \'kēp\ *vb* **kept** \'kept\; **keep·ing** **1** : perform **2** : guard **3** : maintain **4** : retain in one's possession **5** : detain **6** : continue in good condition **7** : refrain ∼ *n* **1** : fortress **2** : means by which one is kept — **keep·er** *n*

keep·ing \'kēpiŋ\ *n* : conformity

keep·sake \'kēp‚sāk\ *n* : souvenir

keg \'keg\ *n* : small cask or barrel

kelp \'kelp\ *n* : coarse brown seaweed

ken \'ken\ *n* : range of sight or understanding

ken·nel \'ken°l\ *n* : dog shelter — **ken·nel** *vb*

ker·chief \'kərchəf, -ˌchēf\ *n* : square of cloth worn as a head covering

ker·nel \'kərn°l\ *n* **1** : inner softer part of a seed or nut **2** : whole seed of a cereal **3** : central part

ker·o·sene, ker·o·sine \'kerə-ˌsēn, ˌkerə'-\ *n* : thin flammable oil from petroleum

ketch·up \'kechəp, 'ka-\ *n* : spicy tomato sauce

ket·tle \'ket°l\ *n* : vessel for boiling liquids

ket·tle·drum \-ˌdrum\ *n* : brass or copper kettle-shaped drum

¹**key** \'kē\ *n* **1** : usu. metal piece to open a lock **2** : explanation **3** : lever pressed by a finger in playing an instrument or operating a machine **4** : leading individual or principle **5** : system of musical tones or pitch ∼ *vb* : attune ∼ *adj* : basic — **key·hole** *n* — **key up** *vb* : make nervous

²**key** *n* : low island or reef

key·board *n* : arrangement of keys

key·note \-ˌnōt\ *n* **1** : 1st note of a scale **2** : central fact, idea, or mood ∼ *vb* **1** : set the keynote of **2** : deliver the major speech

key·stone *n* : wedge-shaped piece at the crown of an arch

kha·ki \'kakē, 'käk-\ *n* : light yellowish brown color

khan \'kän, 'kan\ *n* : Mongol leader

kib·butz \kib'üts, -'üts\ *n, pl* **-but·zim** \-ˌüt'sēm, -ˌüt-\ : Israeli communal farm or settlement

ki·bitz·er \'kibətsər, kə'bit-\ *n* : one who offers unwanted advice — **kib·itz** \'kibəts\ *vb*

kick \'kik\ *vb* **1** : strike out or hit with the foot **2** : object strongly **3** : recoil ∼ *n* **1** : thrust with the foot **2** : recoil of a gun **3** : stimulating effect — **kick·er** *n*

kid \'kid\ *n* **1** : young goat **2** : child ∼ *vb* **-dd-** **1** : deceive as a joke **2** : tease — **kid·der** *n* — **kid·ding·ly** *adv*

kid·nap \'kidˌnap\ *vb* **-napped** *or* **-naped** \-ˌnapt\; **-nap·ping** *or* **-nap·ing** : carry a person away by illegal force — **kid·nap·per, kid·nap·er** *n*

kid·ney \'kidnē\ *n, pl* **-neys** : either of a pair of organs that excrete urine

kill \'kil\ *vb* **1** : deprive of life **2** : finish **3** : use up (time) ∼ *n* : act of killing — **kill·er** *n*

kiln \'kil, 'kiln\ *n* : heated enclosure for burning, firing, or drying — **kiln** *vb*

ki·lo \'kēlō\ *n, pl* **-los** : kilogram

kilo·cy·cle \'kilə₁sīkəl\ *n* : kilohertz

ki·lo·gram \'kēlə₁gram, 'kilə-\ *n* : metric unit of weight equal to 2.2 pounds

ki·lo·hertz \'kilə₁hərts, 'kēlə-, -₁herts\ *n* : 1000 hertz

ki·lo·me·ter \kil'ämətər, 'kilə-₁mēt-\ *n* : 1000 meters

ki·lo·volt \'kilə₁vōlt\ *n* : 1000 volts

kilo·watt \'kilə₁wät\ *n* : 1000 watts

kilt \'kilt\ *n* : knee-length pleated skirt

kil·ter \'kiltər\ *n* : proper condition

ki·mo·no \kə'mōnō\ *n, pl* **-nos** : loose robe

kin \'kin\ *n* **1** : one's relatives **2** : kinsman

kind \'kīnd\ *n* **1** : essential quality **2** : group with common traits **3** : variety ~ *adj* **1** : of a sympathetic nature **2** : arising from sympathy — **kind·heart·ed** *adj* — **kind·ness** *n*

kin·der·gar·ten \'kindər-₁gärt⁹n\ *n* : class for young children — **kin·der·gart·ner** \-₁gärtnər\ *n*

kin·dle \'kind⁹l\ *vb* **-dled; -dling 1** : set on fire or start burning **2** : stir up

kin·dling \'kindliŋ, 'kinlən\ *n* : material for starting a fire

kind·ly \'kīndlē\ *adj* **-li·er; -est** : of a sympathetic nature ~ *adv* **1** : sympathetically **2** : courteously — **kind·li·ness** *n*

kin·dred \'kindrəd\ *n* **1** : related individuals **2** : kin ~ *adj* : of a like nature

kin·folk \'kin₁fōk\, **kinfolks** *n pl* : kin

king \'kiŋ\ *n* : male sovereign — **king·dom** \-dəm\ *n* — **king·less** *adj* — **king·ly** *adj* — **king·ship** *n*

king·fish·er \-₁fishər\ *n* : bright-colored crested bird

kink \'kiŋk\ *n* **1** : short tight twist or curl **2** : cramp — **kinky** *adj*

kin·ship *n* : relationship

kins·man \'kinzmən\ *n* : male relative

kins·wom·an \-₁wùmən\ *n* : female relative

kip·per \'kipər\ *n* : dried or smoked fish — **kipper** *vb*

kiss \'kis\ *vb* : touch with the lips as a mark of affection — **kiss** *n*

kit \'kit\ *n* : set of articles (as tools or parts)

kitch·en \'kichən\ *n* : room with cooking facilities

kite \'kīt\ *n* **1** : small hawk **2** : covered framework flown at the end of a string

kith \'kith\ *n* : familiar friends

kit·ten \'kit³n\ *n* : young cat — **kit·ten·ish** *adj*

¹kit·ty \'kitē\ *n, pl* **-ties** : kitten

²kitty *n, pl* **-ties** : fund or pool (as in a card game)

kit·ty–cor·ner, kit·ty–cor·nered *var of* CATERCORNER

ki·wi \'kē,wē\ *n* **1** : small flightless New Zealand bird **2** : brownish egg-shaped subtropical fruit

klep·to·ma·nia \,kleptə'mā-nēə\ *n* : neurotic impulse to steal — **klep·to·ma·ni·ac** \-nē-,ak\ *n*

knack \'nak\ *n* **1** : clever way of doing something **2** : natural aptitude

knap·sack \'nap,sak\ *n* : bag for carrying supplies on one's back

knave \'nāv\ *n* : rogue — **knav·ery** \'nāvərē\ *n* — **knav·ish** \'nāvish\ *adj*

knead \'nēd\ *vb* **1** : work and press with the hands **2** : massage — **knead·er** *n*

knee \'nē\ *n* : joint in the middle part of the leg — **kneed** \'nēd\ *adj*

knee·cap \'nē,kap\ *n* : bone forming the front of the knee

kneel \'nēl\ *vb* **knelt** \'nelt\ *or* **kneeled; kneel·ing** : rest on one's knees

knell \'nel\ *n* : stroke of a bell

knew *past of* KNOW

knick·ers \'nikərz\ *n pl* : pants gathered at the knee

knick·knack \'nik,nak\ *n* : small decorative object

knife \'nīf\ *n, pl* **knives** \'nīvz\ : sharp blade with a handle ~ *vb* **knifed; knif·ing** : stab or cut with a knife

knight \'nīt\ *n* **1** : mounted warrior of feudal times **2** : man honored by a sovereign ~ *vb* : make a knight of — **knight·hood** *n* — **knight·ly** *adv*

knit \'nit\ *vb* **knit** *or* **knit·ted; knit·ting** **1** : link firmly or closely **2** : form a fabric by interlacing yarn or thread ~ *n* : knitted garment — **knit·ter** *n*

knob \'näb\ *n* : rounded protuberance or handle — **knobbed** \'näbd\ *adj* — **knob·by** \'näbē\ *adj*

knock \'näk\ *vb* **1** : strike with a sharp blow **2** : collide **3** : find fault with ~ *n* : sharp blow — **knock out** *vb* : make unconscious

knock·er *n* : device hinged to a door to knock with

knoll \'nōl\ *n* : small round hill

knot \'nät\ *n* **1** : interlacing (as of string) that forms a lump **2** : base of a woody branch in the stem **3** : group **4** : one nautical mile per hour ~ *vb* **-tt-** : tie in or with a knot — **knot·ty** *adj*

know \'nō\ *vb* **knew** \'nü, 'nyü\; **known** \'nōn\; **know·ing** **1** : perceive directly or understand **2** : be familiar with — **know·able** *adj* — **know·er** *n*

know·ing \'nōiŋ\ *adj* : shrewdly and keenly alert — **know·ing·ly** *adv*

knowl·edge \'nälij\ *n* **1** : understanding gained by experience **2** : range of information — **knowl·edge·able** *adj*

knuck·le \'nəkəl\ *n* : rounded knob at a finger joint

ko·ala \kō'älə\ *n* : gray furry Australian animal

kohl·ra·bi \kōl'rabē, -'räb-\ *n, pl* **-bies** : cabbage that forms no head

Ko·ran \kə'ran, -'rän\ *n* : book of Islam containing revelations made to Muhammad by Allah

ko·sher \'kōshər\ *adj* : ritually fit for use according to Jewish law

kow·tow \kau'tau, 'kau̩tau\ *vb* : show excessive deference

kryp·ton \'krip̩tän\ *n* : gaseous chemical element used in lamps

ku·dos \'kyü̩däs, 'kü-, -̩dōz\ *n* : fame and renown

kum·quat \'kəm̩kwät\ *n* : small citrus fruit

Kwan·zaa, Kwan·za \'kwänzə\ *n* : African-American festival held from December 26 to January 1 ~

L

l \'el\ *n, pl* **l's** *or* **ls** \'elz\ : 12th letter of the alphabet

lab \'lab\ *n* : laboratory

la·bel \'lābəl\ *n* **1** : identification slip **2** : identifying word or phrase ~ *vb* **-beled** *or* **-belled; -bel·ing** *or* **-bel·ling** : put a label on

la·bi·al \'lābēəl\ *adj* : of or relating to the lips

la·bor \'lābər\ *n* **1** : physical or mental effort **2** : physical efforts of childbirth **3** : task **4** : people who work manually ~ *vb* : work esp. with great effort — **la·bor·er** *n*

lab·o·ra·to·ry \\'labrə,tōrē\ *n,* *pl* **-ries** : place for experimental testing

Labor Day *n* : 1st Monday in September observed as a legal holiday in recognition of working people

la·bo·ri·ous \lə'bōrēəs\ *adj* : requiring great effort — **la·bo·ri·ous·ly** *adv*

lab·y·rinth \\'labə,rinth\ *n* : maze — **lab·y·rin·thine** \,labə'rinthən\ *adj*

lace \\'lās\ *n* **1** : cord or string for tying **2** : fine net usu. figured fabric ~ *vb* **laced; lac·ing 1** : tie **2** : adorn with lace — **lacy** \\'lāsē\ *adj*

lac·er·ate \\'lasə,rāt\ *vb* **-at·ed; -at·ing** : tear roughly — **lac·er·a·tion** \,lasə'rāshən\ *n*

lach·ry·mose \\'lakrə,mōs\ *adj* : tearful

lack \\'lak\ *vb* : be missing or deficient in ~ *n* : deficiency

lack·a·dai·si·cal \,lakə'dāzikəl\ *adj* : lacking spirit — **lack·a·dai·si·cal·ly** \-klē\ *adv*

lack·ey \\'lakē\ *n, pl* **-eys 1** : footman or servant **2** : toady

lack·lus·ter \\'lak,ləstər\ *adj* : dull

la·con·ic \lə'känik\ *adj* : sparing of words — **la·con·i·cal·ly** \-iklē\ *adv*

lac·quer \\'lakər\ *n* : glossy surface coating — **lacquer** *vb*

la·crosse \lə'kròs\ *n* : ball game played with long-handled rackets

lac·tate \\'lak,tāt\ *vb* **-tat·ed; -tat·ing** : secrete milk — **lac·ta·tion** \lak'tāshən\ *n*

lac·tic \\'laktik\ *adj* : relating to milk

la·cu·na \lə'künə, -'kyü-\ *n, pl* **-nae** \-,nē\ *or* **-nas** : blank space or missing part

lad \\'lad\ *n* : boy

lad·der \\'ladər\ *n* : device with steps or rungs for climbing

lad·en \\'lādᵊn\ *adj* : loaded

la·dle \\'lādᵊl\ *n* : spoon with a deep bowl **-ladle** *vb*

la·dy \\'lādē\ *n, pl* **-dies 1** : woman of rank or authority **2** : woman

la·dy·bird \\'lādē,bərd\ *n* : ladybug

la·dy·bug \-,bəg\ *n* : brightly colored beetle

lag \\'lag\ *vb* **-gg-** : fail to keep up ~ *n* **1** : a falling behind **2** : interval

la·ger \\'lägər\ *n* : beer

lag·gard \\'lagərd\ *adj* : slow ~ *n* : one that lags — **lag·gard·ly** *adv*

la·gniappe \\'lan,yap\ *n* : bonus

la·goon \lə'gün\ *n* : shallow sound, channel, or pond near or connecting with a larger body of water

laid *past of* **LAY**

lain *past part of* LIE

lair \'lar\ *n* : den

lais·sez–faire \ˌlesˌā'far\ *n* : doctrine opposing government interference in business

la·ity \'lāətē\ *n* : people of a religious faith who are not clergy members

lake \'lāk\ *n* : inland body of water

la·ma \'lämə\ *n* : Buddhist monk

lamb \'lam\ *n* : young sheep or its flesh used as food

lam·baste, lam·bast \lam-'bāst, -'bast\ *vb* **1** : beat **2** : censure

lam·bent \'lambənt\ *adj* : light or bright — **lam·bent·ly** *adv*

lame \'lām\ *adj* **lam·er; lam·est** **1** : having a limb disabled **2** : weak ~ *vb* **lamed; lam·ing** : make lame — **lame·ly** *adv* **-lame·ness** *n*

la·mé \lä'mā, la-\ *n* : cloth with tinsel threads

lame·brain \'lāmˌbrān\ *n* : fool

la·ment \lə'ment\ *vb* **1** : mourn **2** : express sorrow for ~ *n* **1** : mourning **2** : complaint — **lam·en·ta·ble** \'laməntəbəl, lə'mentə-\ *adj* — **lam·en·ta·bly** \-blē\ *adv* — **lam·en·ta·tion** \ˌlamən-'tāshən\ *n*

lam·i·nat·ed \'laməˌnātəd\ *adj* : made of thin layers of material — **lam·i·nate** \-ˌnāt\ *vb* —

lam·i·nate \-nət\ *n or adj* — **lam·i·na·tion** \ˌlamə'nā-shən\ *n*

lamp \'lamp\ *n* : device for producing light or heat

lam·poon \lam'pün\ *n* : satire — **lam·poon** *vb*

lam·prey \'lamprē\ *n, pl* **-preys** : sucking eellike fish

lance \'lans\ *n* : spear ~ *vb* **lanced; lanc·ing** : pierce or open with a lancet

lance corporal *n* : enlisted man in the marine corps ranking above a private first class and below a corporal

lan·cet \'lansət\ *n* : pointed surgical instrument

land \'land\ *n* **1** : solid part of the surface of the earth **2** : country ~ *vb* **1** : go ashore **2** : catch or gain **3** : touch the ground or a surface — **land·less** *adj* — **land·own·er** *n*

land·fill *n* : dump

land·ing \'landiŋ\ *n* **1** : action of one that lands **2** : place for loading passengers and cargo **3** : level part of a staircase

land·la·dy \'landˌlādē\ *n* : woman landlord

land·locked *adj* : enclosed by land

land·lord *n* : owner of property

land·lub·ber \-ˌləbər\ *n* : one with little sea experience

land·mark \-ˌmärk\ *n* **1** : object that marks a boundary or serves as a guide **2** : event that marks a turning point

land·scape \-ˌskāp\ *n* : view of natural scenery ∼ *vb* **-scaped; -scap·ing** : beautify a piece of land (as by decorative planting)

land·slide *n* **1** : slipping down of a mass of earth **2** : overwhelming victory

land·ward \ˈlandwərd\ *adj* : toward the land — **landward** *adv*

lane \ˈlān\ *n* : narrow way

lan·guage \ˈlaŋgwij\ *n* : words and the methods of combining them for communication

lan·guid \ˈlaŋgwəd\ *adj* **1** : weak **2** : sluggish — **lan·guid·ly** *adv* — **lan·guid·ness** *n*

lan·guish \ˈlaŋgwish\ *vb* : become languid or discouraged

lan·guor \ˈlaŋgər\ *n* : listless indolence — **lan·guor·ous** *adj* — **lan·guor·ous·ly** *adv*

lank \ˈlaŋk\ *adj* **1** : thin **2** : limp

lanky *adj* **lank·i·er; -est** : tall and thin

lan·o·lin \ˈlanᵊlən\ *n* : fatty wax from sheep's wool used in ointments

lan·tern \ˈlantərn\ *n* : enclosed portable light

¹lap \ˈlap\ *n* **1** : front part of the lower trunk and thighs of a seated person **2** : overlapping part **3** : one complete circuit completing a course (as around a track or pool) ∼ *vb* **-pp-** : fold over

²lap *vb* **-pp- 1** : scoop up with the tongue **2** : splash gently

lap·dog *n* : small dog

la·pel \ləˈpel\ *n* : fold of the front of a coat

lap·i·dary \ˈlapəˌderē\ *n* : one who cuts and polishes gems ∼ *adj* : relating to gems

lapse \ˈlaps\ *n* **1** : slight error **2** : termination of a right or privilege **3** : interval ∼ *vb* **lapsed; laps·ing 1** : slip **2** : subside **3** : cease

lap·top \ˈlapˌtäp\ *adj* : of a size that may be used on one's lap

lar·board \ˈlärbərd\ *n* : port side

lar·ce·ny \ˈlärsᵊnē\ *n, pl* **-nies** : theft — **lar·ce·nous** \ˈlärsᵊnəs\ *adj*

larch \ˈlärch\ *n* : tree like a pine that loses its needles

lard \ˈlärd\ *n* : pork fat

lar·der \ˈlärdər\ *n* : pantry

large \ˈlärj\ *adj* **larg·er; larg·est** : greater than average — **large·ly** *adv* — **large·ness** *n*

lar·gesse, lar·gess \lärˈzhes, -ˈjes; ˈlärˌ-\ *n* : liberal giving

lar·i·at \ˈlarēət\ *n* : lasso

¹lark \ˈlärk\ *n* : small songbird

²lark *vb or n* : romp

lar·va \'lärvə\ *n, pl* **-vae** \-ˌvē\ : wormlike form of an insect — **lar·val** \-vəl\ *adj*

lar·yn·gi·tis \ˌlarən'jītəs\ *n* : inflammation of the larynx

lar·ynx \'lariŋks\ *n, pl* **-ryn·ges** \lə'rinˌjēz\ *or* **-ynx·es** : upper part of the trachea — **la·ryn·ge·al** \ˌlarən'jēəl, lə'rinjēəl\ *adj*

la·sa·gna \lə'zänyə\ *n* : flat noodles baked usu. with tomato sauce, meat, and cheese

las·civ·i·ous \lə'sivēəs\ *adj* : lewd — **las·civ·i·ous·ness** *n*

la·ser \'lāzər\ *n* : device that produces an intense light beam

¹**lash** \'lash\ *vb* : whip ~ *n* **1** : stroke esp. of a whip **2** : eyelash

²**lash** *vb* : bind with a rope or cord

lass \'las\ *n* : girl

lass·ie \'lasē\ *n* : girl

las·si·tude \'lasəˌtüd, -ˌtyüd\ *n* **1** : fatigue **2** : listlessness

las·so \'lasō, la'sü\ *n, pl* **-sos** *or* **-soes** : rope with a noose for catching livestock — **lasso** *vb*

¹**last** \'last\ *vb* : continue in existence or operation

²**last** *adj* **1** : final **2** : previous **3** : least likely ~ *adv* **1** : at the end **2** : most recently **3** : in conclusion ~ *n* : something that is last — **last·ly** *adv* — **at last** : finally

³**last** *n* : form on which a shoe is shaped

latch \'lach\ *vb* : catch or get hold ~ *n* : catch that holds a door closed

late \'lāt\ *adj* **lat·er; lat·est 1** : coming or staying after the proper time **2** : advanced toward the end **3** : recently deceased **4** : recent — **late** *adv* — **late·com·er** \-ˌkəmər\ *n* — **late·ly** *adv* — **late·ness** *n*

la·tent \'lāt°nt\ *adj* : present but not visible or expressed — **la·ten·cy** \-°nsē\ *n*

lat·er·al \'latərəl\ *adj* : on or toward the side — **lat·er·al·ly** *adv*

la·tex \'lāˌteks\ *n, pl* **-ti·ces** \'lātəˌsēz, 'lat-\ *or* **-tex·es** : emulsion of synthetic rubber or plastic

lath \'lath, 'la͟th\ *n, pl* **laths** *or* **lath** : building material (as a thin strip of wood) used as a base for plaster — **lath** *vb* — **lath·ing** \-iŋ\ *n*

lathe \'lā͟th\ *n* : machine that rotates material for shaping

lath·er \'la͟thər\ *n* : foam ~ *vb* : form or spread lather

lat·i·tude \'latəˌtüd, -ˌtyüd\ *n* **1** : distance north or south from the earth's equator **2** : freedom of action

la·trine \lə'trēn\ *n* : toilet

lat·ter \\'latər\\ *adj* **1** : more recent **2** : being the second of 2 — **lat·ter·ly** *adv*

lat·tice \\'latəs\\ *n* : framework of crossed strips

laud *vb or n* : praise — **laud·able** *adj* — **laud·ably** *adv*

laugh \\'laf, 'làf\\ *vb* : show mirth, joy, or scorn with a smile and explosive sound — **laugh** *n* — **laugh·able** *adj* — **laugh·ing·ly** \\-iŋlē\\ *adv*

laugh·ing·stock \\'lafiŋ,stäk, 'làf-\\ *n* : object of ridicule

laugh·ter \\'laftər, 'làf-\\ *n* : action or sound of laughing

¹launch \\'lònch\\ *vb* **1** : hurl or send off **2** : set afloat **3** : start — **launch** *n* — **launch·er** *n*

²launch *n* : small open boat

laun·der \\'lòndər\\ *vb* : wash or iron fabrics — **laun·der·er** *n* — **laun·dress** \\-drəs\\ *n* — **laun·dry** \\-drē\\ *n*

lau·re·ate \\'lòrēət\\ *n* : recipient of honors — **laureate** *adj*

lau·rel \\'lòrəl\\ *n* **1** : small evergreen tree **2** : honor

la·va \\'lävə, 'lav-\\ *n* : volcanic molten rock

lav·a·to·ry \\'lavə,tōrē\\ *n, pl* **-ries** : bathroom

lav·en·der \\'lavəndər\\ *n* **1** : aromatic plant used for perfume **2** : pale purple color

lav·ish \\'lavish\\ *adj* : expended profusely ∼ *vb* : expend or give freely — **lav·ish·ly** *adv* — **lav·ish·ness** *n*

law \\'lò\\ *n* **1** : established rule of conduct **2** : body of such rules **3** : principle of construction or procedure **4** : rule stating uniform behavior under uniform conditions **5** : lawyer's profession — **law·break·er** *n* — **law·giv·er** *n* — **law·less** *adj* — **law·less·ly** *adv* — **law·less·ness** *n* — **law·mak·er** *n* — **law·man** \\-mən\\ *n* — **law·suit** *n*

law·ful \\'lòfəl\\ *adj* : permitted by law — **law·ful·ly** *adv*

lawn \\'lòn\\ *n* : grass-covered yard

law·yer \\'lòyər\\ *n* : legal practitioner

lax \\'laks\\ *adj* : not strict or tense — **lax·i·ty** \\'laksətē\\ *n* — **lax·ly** *adv*

lax·a·tive \\'lakətiv\\ *n* : drug relieving constipation

¹lay \\'lā\\ *vb* **laid** \\'lād\\; **lay·ing** **1** : put or set down **2** : produce eggs **3** : bet **4** : impose as a duty or burden **5** : put forward ∼ *n* : way something lies or is laid

²lay *past of* LIE

³lay *n* : song

⁴lay *adj* : of the laity — **lay·man** \\-mən\\ *n* — **lay·wom·an** \\-,wùmən\\ *n*

lay·er \\'lāər\\ *n* **1** : one that lays **2** : one thickness over or under another

lay·off \\'lā͵ȯf\ *n* : temporary dismissal of a worker

lay·out \\'lā͵aủt\ *n* : arrangement

la·zy \\'lāzē\ *adj* **-zi·er; -est** : disliking activity or exertion — **la·zi·ly** \\'lāzəlē\ *adv* **-la·zi·ness** *n*

lea \\'lē, 'lā\ *n* : meadow

leach \\'lēch\ *vb* : remove (a soluble part) with a solvent

¹lead \\'lēd\ *vb* **led** \\'led\; **lead·ing** **1** : guide on a way **2** : direct the activity of **3** : go at the head of **4** : tend to a definite result ~ *n* : position in front — **lead·er** *n* — **lead·er·less** *adj* — **lead·er·ship** *n*

²lead \\'led\ *n* **1** : heavy bluish white chemical element **2** : marking substance in a pencil — **lead·en** \\'led³n\ *adj*

leaf \\'lēf\ *n, pl* **leaves** \\'lēvz\ **1** : green outgrowth of a plant stem **2** : leaflike thing ~ *vb* **1** : produce leaves **2** : turn book pages — **leaf·age** \\'lēfij\ *n* — **leafed** \\'lēft\ *adj* — **leaf·less** *adj* — **leafy** *adj* — **leaved** \\'lēfd\ *adj*

leaf·let \\'lēflət\ *n* : pamphlet

¹league \\'lēg\ *n* : unit of distance equal to about 3 miles

²league *n* : association for a common purpose — **league** *vb* — **leagu·er** *n*

leak \\'lēk\ *vb* **1** : enter or escape through a leak **2** : become or make known ~ *n* : opening that accidentally admits or lets out a substance — **leak·age** \\'lēkij\ *n* — **leaky** *adj*

¹lean \\'lēn\ *vb* **1** : bend from a vertical position **2** : rely on for support **3** : incline in opinion — **lean** *n*

²lean *adj* **1** : lacking in flesh **2** : lacking richness — **lean·ness** \\'lēnnəs\ *n*

leap \\'lēp\ *vb* **leapt** *or* **leaped** \\'lēpt, 'lept\; **leap·ing** : jump — **leap** *n*

leap year *n* : 366-day year

learn \\'lərn\ *vb* **1** : gain understanding or skill by study or experience **2** : memorize **3** : find out — **learn·er** *n*

learn·ed \-əd\ *adj* : having great learning — **learn·ed·ness** *n*

learn·ing \-iŋ\ *n* : knowledge

lease \\'lēs\ *n* : contract transferring real estate for a term and usu. for rent ~ *vb* **leased; leas·ing** : grant by or hold under a lease

leash \\'lēsh\ *n* : line to hold an animal — **leash** *vb*

least \\'lēst\ *adj* **1** : lowest in importance or position **2** : smallest **3** : scantiest ~ *n* : one that is least ~ *adv* : in the smallest or lowest degree

leath·er \\'lethər\ *n* : dressed animal skin — **leath·ern** \-ərn\ *adj* — **leath·ery** *adj*

¹**leave** \'lēv\ *vb* **left** \'left\; **leav·ing 1** : bequeath **2** : allow or cause to remain **3** : have as a remainder **4** : go away ~ *n* **1** : permission **2** : authorized absence **3** : departure

²**leave** *vb* **leaved; leav·ing** : leaf

leav·en \'levən\ *n* : substance for producing fermentation ~ *vb* : raise dough with a leaven

leaves *pl of* LEAF

lech·ery \'lechərē\ *n* : inordinate indulgence in sex — **lech·er** \'lechər\ *n* — **lech·er·ous** \-chərəs\ *adj* — **lech·er·ous·ly** *adv* — **lech·er·ous·ness** *n*

lec·ture \'lekchər\ *n* **1** : instructive talk **2** : reprimand — **lecture** *vb* — **lec·tur·er** *n* — **lec·ture·ship** *n*

led *past of* LEAD

ledge \'lej\ *n* : shelflike projection

led·ger \'lejər\ *n* : account book

lee \'lē\ *n* : side sheltered from the wind — **lee** *adj*

leech \'lēch\ *n* : segmented freshwater worm that feeds on blood

leek \'lēk\ *n* : onionlike herb

leer \'lir\ *n* : suggestive or malicious look — **leer** *vb*

leery \'lirē\ *adj* : suspicious or wary

lees \'lēz\ *n pl* : dregs

lee·ward \'lēwərd, 'lüərd\ *adj* : situated away from the wind ~ *n* : the lee side

lee·way \'lē,wā\ *n* : allowable margin

¹**left** \'left\ *adj* : on the same side of the body as the heart ~ *n* : left hand — **left** *adv*

²**left** *past of* LEAVE

leg \'leg\ *n* **1** : limb of an animal that supports the body **2** : something like a leg **3** : clothing to cover the leg ~ *vb* **-gg-** : walk or run — **leg·ged** \'legəd\ *adj* — **leg·less** *adj*

leg·a·cy \'legəsē\ *n, pl* **-cies** : inheritance

le·gal \'lēgəl\ *adj* **1** : relating to law or lawyers **2** : lawful — **le·gal·is·tic** \,lēgə'listik\ *adj* — **le·gal·i·ty** \li'galətē\ *n* — **le·gal·ize** \'lēgə,līz\ *vb* — **le·gal·ly** \-gəlē\ *adv*

leg·ate \'legət\ *n* : official representative

le·ga·tion \li'gāshən\ *n* **1** : diplomatic mission **2** : official residence and office of a diplomat

leg·end \'lejənd\ *n* **1** : story handed down from the past **2** : inscription **3** : explanation of map symbols — **leg·end·ary** \-ən,derē\ *adj*

leg·er·de·main \,lejərdə'mān\ *n* : sleight of hand

leg·ging, leg·gin \'legən, -iŋ\ *n* : leg covering

leg·i·ble \'lejəbəl\ *adj* : capable of being read — **leg·i·bil·i·ty** \ˌlejə'bilətē\ *n* — **leg·i·bly** \'lejəblē\ *adv*

le·gion \'lējən\ *n* **1** : large army unit **2** : multitude **3** : association of former servicemen — **le·gion·ary** \-ˌerē\ *n* — **le·gion·naire** \ˌlējən'ar\ *n*

leg·is·late \'lejəˌslāt\ *vb* **-lat·ed; -lat·ing** : enact or bring about with laws — **leg·is·la·tion** \ˌlejə'slāshən\ *n* — **leg·is·la·tive** \'lejəˌslātiv\ *adj* — **leg·is·la·tor** \-ər\ *n*

leg·is·la·ture \'lejəˌslāchər\ *n* : organization with authority to make laws

le·git·i·mate \li'jitəmət\ *adj* **1** : lawfully begotten **2** : genuine **3** : conforming with law or accepted standards — **le·git·i·ma·cy** \-məsē\ *n* — **le·git·i·mate·ly** *adv* — **le·git·i·mize** \-mīz\ *vb*

le·gume \'legˌyüm, li'gyüm\ *n* : plant bearing pods — **le·gu·mi·nous** \li'gyümənəs\ *adj*

lei \'lā\ *n* : necklace of flowers

lei·sure \'lēzhər, 'lezh-, 'lāzh-\ *n* **1** : free time **2** : ease **3** : convenience — **lei·sure·ly** *adj or adv*

lem·ming \'lemiŋ\ *n* : short-tailed rodent

lem·on \'lemən\ *n* : yellow citrus fruit — **lem·ony** *adj*

lem·on·ade \ˌlemə'nād\ *n* : sweetened lemon beverage

lend \'lend\ *vb* **lent** \'lent\; **lend·ing 1** : give for temporary use **2** : furnish — **lend·er** *n*

length \'leŋth\ *n* **1** : longest dimension **2** : duration in time **3** : piece to be joined to others — **length·en** \'leŋthən\ *vb* — **length·wise** *adv or adj* — **lengthy** *adj*

le·nient \'lēnēənt, -nyənt\ *adj* : of mild and tolerant disposition or effect — **le·ni·en·cy** \'lēnēənsē -nyənsē\ *n* — **le·ni·ent·ly** *adv*

len·i·ty \'lenətē\ *n* : leniency

lens \'lenz\ *n* **1** : curved piece for forming an image in an optical instrument **2** : transparent body in the eye that focuses light rays

Lent \'lent\ *n* : 40-day period of penitence and fasting from Ash Wednesday to Easter — **Lent·en** \-ᵊn\ *adj*

len·til \'lentᵊl\ *n* : legume with flat edible seeds

le·o·nine \'lēəˌnīn\ *adj* : like a lion

leop·ard \'lepərd\ *n* : large tawny black-spotted cat

le·o·tard \'lēəˌtärd\ *n* : close-fitting garment

lep·er \'lepər\ *n* : person with leprosy

lep·re·chaun \\'leprə͵kän\ *n* : mischievous Irish elf

lep·ro·sy \\'leprəsē\ *n* : chronic bacterial disease — **lep·rous** \-rəs\ *adj*

les·bi·an \\'lezbēən\ *n* : female homosexual — **lesbian** *adj* — **les·bi·an·ism** \-͵izəm\ *n*

le·sion \\'lēzhən\ *n* : abnormal area in the body due to injury or disease

less \\'les\ *adj* **1** : fewer **2** : of lower rank, degree, or importance **3** : smaller ~ *adv* : to a lesser degree ~ *n, pl* **less** : smaller portion ~ *prep* : minus — **less·en** \-ᵊn\ *vb*

-less \ləs\ *adj suffix* **1** : not having **2** : unable to act or be acted on

les·see \le'sē\ *n* : tenant under a lease

less·er \\'lesər\ *adj* : of less size, quality, or significance

les·son \\'lesᵊn\ *n* **1** : reading or exercise to be studied by a pupil **2** : something learned

les·sor \\'les͵or, le'sor\ *n* : one who transfers property by a lease

lest \͵lest\ *conj* : for fear that

¹let \\'let\ *n* : hindrance or obstacle

²let *vb* **let; let·ting 1** : cause to **2** : rent **3** : permit

-let \lət\ *n suffix* : small one

le·thal \\'lēthəl\ *adj* : deadly — **le·thal·ly** *adv*

leth·ar·gy \\'lethərjē\ *n* **1** : drowsiness **2** : state of being lazy or indifferent — **le·thar·gic** \li'thärjik\ *adj*

let·ter \\'letər\ *n* **1** : unit of an alphabet **2** : written or printed communication **3** *pl* : literature or learning **4** : literal meaning ~ *vb* : mark with letters — **let·ter·er** *n*

let·tuce \\'letəs\ *n* : garden plant with crisp leaves

leu·ke·mia \lü'kēmēə\ *n* : cancerous blood disease — **leu·ke·mic** \-mik\ *adj or n*

lev·ee \\'levē\ *n* : embankment to prevent flooding

lev·el \\'levəl\ *n* **1** : device for establishing a flat surface **2** : horizontal surface **3** : position in a scale ~ *vb* **-eled** *or* **-elled; -el·ing** *or* **-el·ling 1** : make flat or level **2** : aim **3** : raze ~ *adj* **1** : having an even surface **2** : of the same height or rank — **lev·el·er** *n* — **lev·el·ly** *adv* — **lev·el·ness** *n*

le·ver \\'levər, 'lē-\ *n* : bar for prying or dislodging something — **le·ver·age** \\'levərij, 'lēv-\ *n*

le·vi·a·than \li'vīəthən\ *n* **1** : large sea animal **2** : enormous thing

lev·i·ty \\'levətē\ *n* : unseemly frivolity

levy \'levē\ *n, pl* **lev·ies** : imposition or collection of a tax ~ *vb* **lev·ied; levy·ing 1** : impose or collect legally **2** : enlist for military service **3** : wage

lewd \'lüd\ *adj* **1** : sexually unchaste **2** : vulgar — **lewd·ly** *adv* — **lewd·ness** *n*

lex·i·cog·ra·phy \ˌleksə'kägrəfē\ *n* : dictionary making — **lex·i·cog·ra·pher** \-fər\ *n* — **lex·i·co·graph·i·cal** \-kō'grafikəl\, **lex·i·co·graph·ic** \-ik\ *adj*

lex·i·con \'leksəˌkän\ *n, pl* **-i·ca** \-sikə\ *or* **-icons** : dictionary

li·a·ble \'līəbəl\ *adj* **1** : legally obligated **2** : probable **3** : susceptible — **li·a·bil·i·ty** \ˌlīə'bilətē\ *n*

li·ai·son \'lēəˌzän, lē'ā-\ *n* **1** : close bond **2** : communication between groups

li·ar \'līər\ *n* : one who lies

li·bel \'lībəl\ *n* : action, crime, or an instance of injuring a person's reputation esp. by something written ~ *vb* **-beled** *or* **-belled; -bel·ing** *or* **-bel·ling** : make or publish a libel — **li·bel·er** *n* — **li·bel·ist** *n* — **li·bel·ous, li·bel·lous** \-bələs\ *adj*

lib·er·al \'librəl, 'libə-\ *adj* : not stingy, narrow, or conservative — **liberal** *n* — **lib·er·al·ism** \-ˌizəm\ *n* — **lib·er·al·i·ty** \ˌlibə'ralətē\ *n* — **lib·er·al·ize** \'librəˌlīz, 'libə-\ *vb* — **lib·er·al·ly** \-rəlē\ *adv*

lib·er·ate \'libəˌrāt\ *vb* **-at·ed; -at·ing** : set free — **lib·er·a·tion** \ˌlibə'rāshən\ *n* — **lib·er·a·tor** \'libəˌrātər\ *n*

lib·er·tine \'libərˌtēn\ *n* : one who leads a dissolute life

lib·er·ty \'libərtē\ *n, pl* **-ties 1** : quality or state of being free **2** : action going beyond normal limits

li·bi·do \lə'bēdō, -'bīd-\ *n, pl* **-dos** : sexual drive — **li·bid·i·nal** \lə'bidᵊnəl\ *adj* — **li·bid·i·nous** \-əs\ *adj*

li·brary \'līˌbrerē\ *n, pl* **-brar·ies 1** : place where books are kept for use **2** : collection of books — **li·brar·i·an** \līˈbrerēən\ *n*

li·bret·to \lə'bretō\ *n, pl* **-tos** *or* **-ti** \-ē\ : text of an opera — **li·bret·tist** \-ist\ *n*

lice *pl of* LOUSE

li·cense, li·cence \'līsᵊns\ *n* **1** : legal permission to engage in some activity **2** : document or tag providing proof of a license **3** : irresponsible use of freedom — **license** *vb* — **li·cens·ee** \ˌlīsᵊn'sē\ *n*

li·cen·tious \lī'senchəs\ *adj* : disregarding sexual restraints — **li·cen·tious·ly** *adv* — **li·cen·tious·ness** *n*

li·chen \'līkən\ *n* : complex lower plant made up of an alga and a fungus

lic·it \'lisət\ *adj* : lawful

lick \'lik\ *vb* **1** : draw the tongue over **2** : beat ∼ *n* **1** : stroke of the tongue **2** : small amount

lic·o·rice \'likərish, -rəs\ *n* : dried root of a European legume or candy flavored by it

lid \'lid\ *n* **1** : movable cover **2** : eyelid

¹lie \'lī\ *vb* **lay** \'lā\; **lain** \'lān\; **ly·ing** \'līiŋ\ **1** : be in, rest in, or assume a horizontal position **2** : occupy a certain relative position ∼ *n* : position in which something lies

²lie *vb* **lied; ly·ing** \'līiŋ\ : tell a lie ∼ *n* : untrue statement

liege \'lēj\ *n* : feudal superior or vassal

lien \'lēn, 'lēən\ *n* : legal claim on the property of another

lieu·ten·ant \lü'tenənt\ *n* **1** : representative **2** : first lieutenant or second lieutenant **3** : commissioned officer in the navy ranking next below a lieutenant commander — **lieu·ten·an·cy** \-ənsē\ *n*

lieutenant colonel *n* : commissioned officer (as in the army) ranking next below a colonel

lieutenant commander *n* : commissioned officer in the navy ranking next below a commander

lieutenant general *n* : commissioned officer (as in the army) ranking next below a general

lieutenant junior grade *n, pl* **lieutenants junior grade** : commissioned officer in the navy ranking next below a lieutenant

life \'līf\ *n, pl* **lives** \'līvz\ **1** : quality that distinguishes a vital and functional being from a dead body or inanimate matter **2** : physical and mental experiences of an individual **3** : biography **4** : period of existence **5** : way of living **6** : liveliness — **life·less** *adj* — **life·like** *adj*

life·blood *n* : basic source of strength and vitality

life·boat *n* : boat for saving lives at sea

life·guard *n* : one employed to safeguard bathers

life·long *adj* : continuing through life

life·sav·ing *n* : art or practice of saving lives — **life·sav·er** \-ˌsāvər\ *n*

life·style \'līfˌstīl\ *n* : a way of life

life·time *n* : duration of an individual's existence

lift \'lift\ *vb* **1** : move upward or cause to move upward **2**

: put an end to — **lift** *n* — **lift-er** *n*

lift·off \'lift‚óf\ *n* : vertical takeoff by a rocket

lig·a·ment \'ligəmənt\ *n* : band of tough tissue that holds bones together

lig·a·ture \'ligə‚chùr, -chər\ *n* : something that binds or ties

¹**light** \'līt\ *n* **1** : radiation that makes vision possible **2** : daylight **3** : source of light **4** : public knowledge **5** : aspect **6** : celebrity **7** : flame for lighting ∼ *adj* **1** : bright **2** : weak in color ∼ *vb* **lit** \'lit\ *or* **light·ed; light·ing 1** : make or become light **2** : cause to burn — **light·er** *n* — **light·ness** *n* — **light·proof** *adj*

²**light** *adj* : not heavy, serious, or abundant — **light** *adv* — **light·ly** *adv* — **light·ness** *n* — **light·weight** *adj*

³**light** *vb* **light·ed** *or* **lit** \'lit\; **light·ing** : settle or dismount

¹**light·en** \'lītᵊn\ *vb* **1** : make light or bright **2** : give out flashes of lightning

²**lighten** *vb* **1** : relieve of a burden **2** : become lighter

light·heart·ed \-'härtəd\ *adj* : free from worry — **light-heart·ed·ly** *adv* — **light-heart·ed·ness** *n*

light·house *n* : structure with a powerful light for guiding sailors

light·ning \'lītniŋ\ *n* : flashing discharge of atmospheric electricity

light–year \'līt‚yir\ *n* : distance traveled by light in one year equal to about 5.88 trillion miles

lig·nite \'lig‚nīt\ *n* : brownish black soft coal

¹**like** \'līk\ *vb* **liked; lik·ing 1** : enjoy **2** : desire ∼ *n* : preference — **lik·able, like·able** \'līkəbəl\ *adj*

²**like** *adj* : similar ∼ *prep* **1** : similar or similarly to **2** : typical of **3** : such as ∼ *n* : counterpart ∼ *conj* : as or as if — **like·ness** *n* — **like-wise** *adv*

-like \‚līk\ *adj comb form* : resembling or characteristic of

like·li·hood \'līklē‚hùd\ *n* : probability

like·ly \'līklē\ *adj* **-li·er; -est 1** : probable **2** : believable ∼ *adv* : in all probability

lik·en \'līkən\ *vb* : compare

lik·ing \'līkiŋ\ *n* : favorable regard

li·lac \'līlək, -‚lak, -‚läk\ *n* : shrub with clusters of fragrant pink, purple, or white flowers

lilt \'lilt\ *n* : rhythmical swing or flow

lily \'lilē\ *n, pl* **lil·ies** : tall bulbous herb with funnel-shaped flowers

lima bean \\'līmə-\ *n* : flat edible seed of a plant or the plant itself

limb \\'lim\ *n* **1** : projecting appendage used in moving or grasping **2** : tree branch — **limb·less** *adj*

lim·ber \\'limbər\ *adj* : supple or agile ~ *vb* : make or become limber

lim·bo \\'limbō\ *n, pl* **-bos** : place or state of confinement or oblivion

¹lime \\'līm\ *n* : caustic white oxide of calcium

²lime *n* : small green lemonlike citrus fruit — **lime·ade** \-,ād\ *n*

lime·light *n* : center of public attention

lim·er·ick \\'limərik\ *n* : light poem of 5 lines

lime·stone *n* : rock that yields lime when burned

lim·it \\'limət\ *n* **1** : boundary **2** : something that restrains or confines ~ *vb* : set limits on — **lim·i·ta·tion** \,limə-'tāshən\ *n* — **lim·it·less** *adj*

lim·ou·sine \\'limə,zēn, ,limə'-\ *n* : large luxurious sedan

limp \\'limp\ *vb* : walk lamely ~ *n* : limping movement or gait ~ *adj* : lacking firmness and body — **limp·ly** *adv* — **limp·ness** *n*

lim·pid \\'limpəd\ *adj* : clear or transparent

lin·den \\'lindən\ *n* : tree with large heart-shaped leaves

¹line \\'līn\ *vb* **lined; lin·ing** : cover the inner surface of — **lin·ing** *n*

²line *n* **1** : cord, rope, or wire **2** : row or something like a row **3** : note **4** : course of action or thought **5** : state of agreement **6** : occupation **7** : limit **8** : transportation system **9** : long narrow mark ~ *vb* **lined; lin·ing 1** : mark with a line **2** : place in a line **3** : form a line

lin·e·age \\'linēij\ *n* : descent from a common ancestor

lin·e·al \\'linēəl\ *adj* **1** : linear **2** : in a direct line of ancestry

lin·ea·ments \\'linēəmənts\ *n pl* : features or contours esp. of a face

lin·e·ar \\'linēər\ *adj* **1** : straight **2** : long and narrow

lin·en \\'linən\ *n* **1** : cloth or thread made of flax **2** : household articles made of linen cloth

lin·er \\'līnər\ *n* **1** : one that lines **2** : ship or airplane belonging to a line

line·up \\'līn,əp\ *n* **1** : line of persons for inspection or identification **2** : list of players in a game

-ling \liŋ\ *n suffix* **1** : one linked with **2** : young, small, or minor one

lin·ger \'liŋgər\ *vb* : be slow to leave or act — **lin·ger·er** *n*

lin·ge·rie \ˌlänjə'rā, ˌlaⁿzhə-, -'rē\ *n* : women's underwear

lin·go \'liŋgō\ *n, pl* **-goes** : usu. strange language

lin·guist \'liŋgwist\ *n* **1** : person skilled in speech or languages **2** : student of language — **lin·guis·tic** \liŋ'gwistik\ *adj* — **lin·guis·tics** *n pl*

lin·i·ment \'linəmənt\ *n* : liquid medication rubbed on the skin

link \'liŋk\ *n* **1** : connecting structure (as a ring of a chain) **2** : bond — **link** *vb* — **link·age** \-ij\ *n* — **link·er** *n*

li·no·leum \lə'nōlēəm\ *n* : floor covering with hard surface

lin·seed \'lin,sēd\ *n* : seeds of flax yielding an oil (**linseed oil**)

lint \'lint\ *n* : fine fluff or loose short fibers from fabric

lin·tel \'lintᵊl\ *n* : horizontal piece over a door or window

li·on \'līən\ *n* : large cat of Africa and Asia — **li·on·ess** \'līənəs\ *n*

li·on·ize \'līə,nīz\ *vb* **-ized; -iz·ing** : treat as very important — **li·on·iza·tion** \ˌlīənə'zāshən\ *n*

lip \'lip\ *n* **1** : either of the 2 fleshy folds surrounding the mouth **2** : edge of something hollow — **lipped** \'lipt\ *adj* — **lip·read·ing** *n*

li·po·suc·tion \'lipə,səkshən, 'lī-\ *n* : surgical removal of fat deposits (as from the thighs)

lip·stick \'lip,stik\ *n* : stick of cosmetic to color lips

liq·ue·fy \'likwə,fī\ *vb* **-fied; -fy·ing** : make or become liquid — **liq·ue·fi·er** \'likwə,fīər\ *n*

li·queur \li'kər\ *n* : sweet or aromatic alcoholic liquor

liq·uid \'likwəd\ *adj* **1** : flowing freely like water **2** : neither solid nor gaseous **3** : of or convertible to cash — **liquid** *n* — **li·quid·i·ty** \lik'widətē\ *n*

liq·ui·date \'likwə,dāt\ *vb* **-dat·ed; -dat·ing 1** : pay off **2** : dispose of — **liq·ui·da·tion** \ˌlikwə'dāshən\ *n*

li·quor \'likər\ *n* : liquid substance and esp. a distilled alcoholic beverage

lisp \'lisp\ *vb* : pronounce *s* and *z* imperfectly — **lisp** *n*

lis·some \'lisəm\ *adj* : supple or agile

¹list \'list\ *n* **1** : series of names or items ~ *vb* **1** : make a list of **2** : put on a list

²list *vb* : tilt or lean over ~ *n* : slant

lis·ten \'lisᵊn\ *vb* **1** : pay attention in order to hear **2** : heed — **lis·ten·er** \'lisᵊnər\ *n*

list·less \'listləs\ *adj* : having no desire to act — **list·less·ly** *adv* — **list·less·ness** *n*

lit \'lit\ *past of* LIGHT

lit·a·ny \'lit³nē\ *n, pl* **-nies** **1** : prayer said as a series of responses to a leader **2** : long recitation

li·ter \'lētər\ *n* : unit of liquid measure equal to about 1.06 quarts

lit·er·al \'litərəl\ *adj* : being exactly as stated — **lit·er·al·ly** *adv*

lit·er·ary \'litə‚rerē\ *adj* : relating to literature

lit·er·ate \'litərət\ *adj* : able to read and write — **lit·er·a·cy** \'litərəsē\ *n*

lit·er·a·ture \'litərə‚chùr, -chər\ *n* : writings of enduring interest

lithe \'līth, 'līth\ *adj* **1** : supple **2** : graceful — **lithe·some** \-səm\ *adj*

lith·o·graph \'lithə‚graf\ *n* : print from a drawing on metal or stone — **li·thog·ra·pher** \lith'ägrəfər, 'lithə‚grafər\ *n* — **lith·o·graph·ic** \‚lithə'grafik\ *adj* — **li·thog·ra·phy** \lith'ägrəfē\ *n*

lit·i·gate \'litə‚gāt\ *vb* **-gat·ed; -gat·ing** : carry on a lawsuit — **lit·i·gant** \'litigənt\ *n* — **lit·i·ga·tion** \‚litə'gāshən\ *n* — **li·ti·gious** \lə'tijəs, li-\ *adj* — **li·ti·gious·ness** *n*

lit·mus \'litməs\ *n* : coloring matter that turns red in acid solutions and blue in alkaline

lit·ter \'litər\ *n* **1** : animal offspring of one birth **2** : stretcher **3** : rubbish **4** : material to absorb animal waste ~ *vb* **1** : give birth to young **2** : strew with litter

lit·tle \'lit³l\ *adj* **lit·tler** *or* **less** \'les\ *or* **less·er** \'lesər\; **lit·tlest** *or* **least** \'lēst\ **1** : not big **2** : not much **3** : not important ~ *adv* **less** \'les\; **least** \'lēst\ **1** : slightly **2** : not often ~ *n* : small amount — **lit·tle·ness** *n*

lit·ur·gy \'litərjē\ *n, pl* **-gies** : rite of worship — **li·tur·gi·cal** \lə'tərjikəl\ *adj* — **li·tur·gi·cal·ly** \-klē\ *adv* — **lit·ur·gist** \'litərjist\ *n*

liv·able \'livəbəl\ *adj* : suitable for living in or with — **liv·a·bil·i·ty** \‚livə'bilətē\ *n*

¹**live** \'liv\ *vb* **lived; liv·ing** **1** : be alive **2** : conduct one's life **3** : subsist **4** : reside

²**live** \'līv\ *adj* **1** : having life **2** : burning **3** : connected to electric power **4** : not exploded **5** : of continuing interest **6** : involving the actual presence of real people

live·li·hood \'līvlē‚hùd\ *n* : means of subsistence

live·long \'liv'lòŋ\ *adj* : whole

live·ly \'līvlē\ *adj* **-li·er; -est** : full of life and vigor — **live·li·ness** *n*

liv·en \'līvən\ *vb* : enliven

liv·er \'livər\ *n* : organ that se-cretes bile

liv·ery \'livərē\ *n, pl* **-er·ies 1** : servant's uniform **2** : care of horses for pay — **liv·er·ied** \-rēd\ *adj* — **liv·ery·man** \-mən\ *n*

lives *pl of* LIFE

live·stock \'līv,stäk\ *n* : farm animals

liv·id \'livəd\ *adj* **1** : discol-ored by bruising **2** : pale **3** : enraged

liv·ing \'liviŋ\ *adj* : having life ~ *n* : livelihood

liz·ard \'lizərd\ *n* : reptile with 4 legs and a long tapering tail

lla·ma \'lämə\ *n* : So. American mammal related to the camel

load \'lōd\ *n* **1** : cargo **2** : supported weight **3** : burden **4** : a large quantity — usu. pl. ~ *vb* **1** : put a load on **2** : burden **3** : put ammunition in

¹loaf \'lōf\ *n, pl* **loaves** \'lōvz\ : mass of bread

²loaf *vb* : waste time — **loaf·er** *n*

loam \'lōm, 'lüm\ *n* : soil — **loamy** *adj*

loan \'lōn\ *n* **1** : money bor-rowed at interest **2** : something lent temporarily **3** : grant of use ~ *vb* : lend

loath \'lōth, 'lōth\ *adj* : very reluctant

loathe \'lōth\ *vb* **loathed; loath·ing** : hate

loath·ing \'lōthiŋ\ *n* : extreme disgust

loath·some \'lōthsəm, 'lōth-\ *adj* : repulsive

lob \'läb\ *vb* **-bb-** : throw or hit in a high arc **-lob** *n*

lob·by \'läbē\ *n, pl* **-bies 1** : public waiting room at the entrance of a building **2** : persons lobbying ~ *vb* **-bied; -by·ing** : try to influ-ence legislators — **lob·by·ist** *n*

lobe \'lōb\ *n* : rounded part — **lo·bar** \'lōbər\ *adj* — **lobed** \'lōbd\ *adj*

lo·bot·o·my \lō'bätəmē\ *n, pl* **-mies** : surgical severance of nerve fibers in the brain

lob·ster \'läbstər\ *n* : marine crustacean with 2 large pin-cerlike claws

lo·cal \'lōkəl\ *adj* : confined to or serving a limited area — **local** *n* — **lo·cal·ly** *adv*

lo·cale \lō'kal\ *n* : setting for an event

lo·cal·i·ty \lō'kalətē\ *n, pl* **-ties** : particular place

lo·cal·ize \'lōkə,līz\ *vb* **-ized; -iz·ing** : confine to a definite place — **lo·cal·i·za·tion** \,lōkələ'zāshən\ *n*

lo·cate \'lō,kāt, lō'kāt\ *vb* **-cat·ed; -cat·ing 1** : settle **2** : find a site for **3** : discover the place of — **lo·ca·tion** \lō-'kāshən\ *n*

¹**lock** \'läk\ *n* : tuft or strand of hair

²**lock** *n* **1** : fastener using a bolt **2** : enclosure in a canal to raise or lower boats ～ *vb* **1** : make fast with a lock **2** : confine **3** : interlock

lock·er \'läkər\ *n* : storage compartment

lock·et \'läkət\ *n* : small case worn on a necklace

lock·jaw *n* : tetanus

lock·out *n* : closing of a plant by an employer during a labor dispute

lock·smith \-ˌsmith\ *n* : one who makes or repairs locks

lo·co·mo·tion \ˌlōkə'mōshən\ *n* : power of moving — **lo·co·mo·tive** \-'mōtiv\ *adj*

lo·co·mo·tive \-'mōtiv\ *n* : vehicle that moves railroad cars

lo·co·weed \'lōkōˌwēd\ *n* : western plant poisonous to livestock

lo·cust \'lōkəst\ *n* **1** : migratory grasshopper **2** : cicada **3** : tree with hard wood or this wood

lo·cu·tion \lō'kyüshən\ *n* : way of saying something

lode \'lōd\ *n* : ore deposit

lode·stone *n* : magnetic rock

lodge \'läj\ *vb* **lodged; lodg·ing** **1** : provide quarters for **2** : come to rest **3** : file ～ *n* **1** : special house (as for hunters) **2** : animal's den **3** : branch of a fraternal organization — **lodg·er** \'läjər\ *n* — **lodg·ing** *n* — **lodg·ment, lodge·ment** \-mənt\ *n*

loft \'lȯft\ *n* **1** : attic **2** : upper floor (as of a warehouse)

lofty \'lȯftē\ *adj* **loft·i·er; -est** **1** : noble **2** : proud **3** : tall or high — **loft·i·ly** *adv* — **loft·i·ness** *n*

log \'lȯg, 'läg\ *n* **1** : unshaped timber **2** : daily record of a ship's or plane's progress ～ *vb* **-gg-** **1** : cut (trees) for lumber **2** : enter in a log — **log·ger** \-ər\ *n*

log·a·rithm \'lȯgəˌrithəm, 'läg-\ *n* : exponent to which a base number is raised to produce a given number

loge \'lōzh\ *n* : box in a theater

log·ger·head \'lȯgərˌhed, 'läg-\ *n* : large Atlantic sea turtle — **at loggerheads** : in disagreement

log·ic \'läjik\ *n* **1** : science of reasoning **2** : sound reasoning — **log·i·cal** \-ikəl\ *adj* — **log·i·cal·ly** *adv* — **lo·gi·cian** \lō'jishən\ *n*

lo·gis·tics \lō'jistiks\ *n sing or pl* : procurement and movement of people and supplies — **lo·gis·tic** *adj*

logo \'lōgō, 'lȯg-, 'läg-\ *n, pl* **log·os** \-ōz\ : advertising symbol

loin \'lȯin\ *n* **1** : part of the body on each side of the spine between the hip and lower ribs **2** *pl* : pubic regions

loi·ter \'lȯitər\ *vb* : remain around a place idly — **loi·ter·er** *n*

loll \'läl\ *vb* : lounge

lol·li·pop, lol·ly·pop \'läli,päp\ *n* : hard candy on a stick

lone \'lōn\ *adj* **1** : alone or isolated **2** : only — **lone·li·ness** *n* — **lone·ly** *adj* — **lon·er** \'lōnər\ *n*

lone·some \-səm\ *adj* : sad from lack of company — **lone·some·ly** *adv* — **lone·some·ness** *n*

long \'lȯŋ\ *adj* **lon·ger** \'lȯŋgər\; **long·est** \'lȯŋgəst\ **1** : extending far or for a considerable time **2** : having a specified length **3** : tedious **4** : well supplied — used with *on* ~ *adv* : for a long time ~ *n* : long period ~ *vb* : feel a strong desire — **long·ing** \'lȯŋiŋ\ *n* — **long·ing·ly** *adv*

lon·gev·i·ty \län'jevətē\ *n* : long life

long·hand *n* : handwriting

long·horn *n* : cattle with long horns

lon·gi·tude \'länjə,tüd, -,tyüd\ *n* : angular distance east or west from a meridian

lon·gi·tu·di·nal \,länjə'tüd°nəl, -'tyüd-\ *adj* : lengthwise — **lon·gi·tu·di·nal·ly** *adv*

long·shore·man \'lȯŋ'shōr-mən\ *n* : one who loads and unloads ships

look \'lu̇k\ *vb* **1** : see **2** : seem **3** : direct one's attention **4** : face ~ *n* **1** : action of looking **2** : appearance of the face **3** : aspect — **look after** : take care of — **look for** **1** : expect **2** : search for

look·out *n* **1** : one who watches **2** : careful watch

¹**loom** \'lüm\ *n* : frame or machine for weaving

²**loom** *vb* : appear large and indistinct or impressive

loon \'lün\ *n* : black-and-white diving bird

loo·ny, loo·ney \'lünē\ *adj* **-ni·er; -est** : crazy

loop \'lüp\ *n* **1** : doubling of a line that leaves an opening **2** : something like a loop **loop** *vb*

loop·hole \'lüp,hōl\ *n* : means of evading

loose \'lüs\ *adj* **loos·er; -est** **1** : not fixed tight **2** : not restrained **3** : not dense **4** : slack **5** : not exact ~ *vb* **loosed; loos·ing** **1** : release **2** : untie or relax — **loose** *adv* — **loose·ly** *adv* — **loos·en** \'lüs°n\ *vb* — **loose·ness** *n*

loot \'lüt\ *n or vb* : plunder — **loot·er** *n*

lop \'läp\ *vb* **-pp-** : cut off

lope \'lōp\ *n* : bounding gait — **lope** *vb*

lop·sid·ed \'läp'sīdəd\ *adj* **1** : leaning to one side **2** : not symmetrical — **lop·sid·ed·ly** *adv* — **lop·sid·ed·ness** *n*

lo·qua·cious \lō'kwāshəs\ *adj* : very talkative — **lo·quac·i·ty** \-'kwasətē\ *n*

lord \'lȯrd\ *n* **1** : one with authority over others **2** : British nobleman

lord·ly \-lē\ *adj* **-li·er; -est** : haughty

lord·ship \-ˌship\ *n* : rank of a lord

Lord's Supper *n* : Communion

lore \'lōr\ *n* : traditional knowledge

lose \'lüz\ *vb* **lost** \'lȯst\; **losing** \'lüziŋ\ **1** : have pass from one's possession **2** : be deprived of **3** : waste **4** : be defeated in **5** : fail to keep to or hold **6** : get rid of — **los·er** *n*

loss \'lȯs\ *n* **1** : something lost **2** *pl* : killed, wounded, or captured soldiers **3** : failure to win

lost \'lȯst\ *adj* **1** : not used, won, or claimed **2** : unable to find the way

lot \'lät\ *n* **1** : object used in deciding something by chance **2** : share **3** : fate **4** : plot of land **5** : much

loth \'lōth, 'lōth\ *var of* LOATH

lo·tion \'lōshən\ *n* : liquid to rub on the skin

lot·tery \'lätərē\ *n, pl* **-ter·ies** : drawing of lots with prizes going to winners

lo·tus \'lōtəs\ *n* **1** : legendary fruit that causes forgetfulness **2** : water lily

loud \'laud\ *adj* **1** : high in volume of sound **2** : noisy **3** : obtrusive in color or pattern — **loud** *adv* — **loud·ly** *adv* — **loud·ness** *n*

loud·speak·er *n* : device that amplifies sound

lounge \'launj\ *vb* **lounged; loung·ing** : act or move lazily ∼ *n* : room with comfortable furniture

lour \'lauər\ *var of* LOWER

louse \'laus\ *n, pl* **lice** \'līs\ : parasitic wingless usu. flat insect

lousy \'lauzē\ *adj* **lous·i·er; -est** **1** : infested with lice **2** : not good — **lous·i·ly** *adv* — **lous·i·ness** *n*

lout \'laut\ *n* : stupid awkward person — **lout·ish** *adj* — **lout·ish·ly** *adv*

lou·ver, lou·vre \'lüvər\ *n* : opening having parallel slanted slats for ventilation or such a slat

love \\'ləv\\ *n* **1** : strong affection **2** : warm attachment **3** : beloved person ∼ *vb* **loved; lov·ing 1** : feel affection for **2** : enjoy greatly — **lov·able** \\-əbəl\\ *adj* — **love·less** *adj* — **lov·er** *n* — **lov·ing·ly** *adv*

love·lorn \\-ˌlȯrn\\ *adj* : deprived of love or of a lover

love·ly \\'ləvlē\\ *adj* **-li·er; -est** : beautiful — **love·li·ness** *n* — **lovely** *adv*

¹**low** \\'lō\\ *vb or n* : moo

²**low** *adj* **low·er; low·est 1** : not high or tall **2** : below normal level **3** : not loud **4** : humble **5** : sad **6** : less than usual **7** : falling short of a standard **8** : unfavorable ∼ *n* **1** : something low **2** : automobile gear giving the slowest speed — **low** *adv* — **low·ness** *n*

low·brow \\'lō,brau̇\\ *n* : person with little taste or intellectual interest

¹**low·er** \\'lau̇ər\\ *vb* **1** : scowl **2** : become dark and threatening

²**low·er** \\'lōər\\ *adj* : relatively low (as in rank)

³**low·er** \\'lōər\\ *vb* **1** : drop **2** : let descend **3** : reduce in amount

low·land \\'lōlənd, -ˌland\\ *n* : low flat country

low·ly \\'lōlē\\ *adj* — **li·er; -est 1** : humble **2** : low in rank — **low·li·ness** *n*

loy·al \\'lȯiəl\\ *adj* : faithful to a country, cause, or friend — **loy·al·ist** *n* — **loy·al·ly** *adv* — **loy·al·ty** \\'lȯiəltē\\ *n*

loz·enge \\'läzᵊnj\\ *n* : small medicated candy

lu·bri·cant \\'lübrikənt\\ *n* : material (as grease) to reduce friction

lu·bri·cate \\-ˌkāt\\ *vb* **-cat·ed; -cat·ing** : apply a lubricant to — **lu·bri·ca·tion** \\ˌlübrə-'kāshən\\ *n* — **lu·bri·ca·tor** \\'lübrəˌkātər\\ *n*

lu·cid \\'lüsəd\\ *adj* **1** : mentally sound **2** : easily understood — **lu·cid·i·ty** \\lü'sidətē\\ *n* — **lu·cid·ly** *adv* — **lu·cid·ness** *n*

luck \\'lək\\ *n* **1** : chance **2** : good fortune — **luck·i·ly** *adv* — **luck·i·ness** *n* — **luck·less** *adj* — **lucky** *adj*

lu·cra·tive \\'lükrətiv\\ *adj* : profitable — **lu·cra·tive·ly** *adv* — **lu·cra·tive·ness** *n*

Ludd·ite \\'lə,dīt\\ *n* : one who opposes technological change

lu·di·crous \\'lüdəkrəs\\ *adj* : comically ridiculous — **lu·di·crous·ly** *adv* — **lu·di·crous·ness** *n*

lug \\'ləg\\ *vb* **-gg-** : drag or carry laboriously

lug·gage \\'ləgij\\ *n* : baggage

lu·gu·bri·ous \\lu̇'gübrēəs\\ *adj* : mournful often to an exaggerated degree — **lu·gu·bri-**

ous·ly *adv* — **lu·gu·bri·ous·ness** *n*

luke·warm \'lük'wȯrm\ *adj* **1** : moderately warm **2** : not enthusiastic

lull \'ləl\ *vb* : make or become quiet or relaxed ~ *n* : temporary calm

lul·la·by \'lələ‚bī\ *n, pl* **-bies** : song to lull children to sleep

lum·ba·go \‚ləm'bāgō\ *n* : rheumatic back pain

lum·ber \'ləmbər\ *n* : timber dressed for use ~ *vb* : cut logs — **lum·ber·man** *n* — **lumber·yard** *n*

lum·ber·jack \-‚jak\ *n* : logger

lu·mi·nary \'lümə‚nerē\ *n, pl* **-nar·ies** : very famous person

lu·mi·nes·cence \‚lümə'nesᵊns\ *n* : low-temperature emission of light — **lu·mi·nes·cent** \-ᵊnt\ *adj*

lu·mi·nous \'lümənəs\ *adj* : emitting light — **lu·mi·nance** \-nəns\ *n* — **lu·mi·nos·i·ty** \‚lümə'näsətē\ *n* — **lu·mi·nous·ly** *adv*

lump \'ləmp\ *n* **1** : mass of irregular shape **2** : abnormal swelling ~ *vb* : heap together — **lump·ish** *adj* — **lumpy** *adj*

lu·na·cy \'lünəsē\ *n, pl* **-cies** : state of insanity

lu·nar \'lünər\ *adj* : of the moon

lu·na·tic \'lünə‚tik\ *adj* : insane — **lunatic** *n*

lunch \'lənch\ *n* : noon meal ~ *vb* : eat lunch

lun·cheon \'lənchən\ *n* : usu. formal lunch

lung \'ləŋ\ *n* : breathing organ in the chest — **lunged** \'ləŋd\ *adj*

lunge \'lənj\ *n* **1** : sudden thrust **2** : sudden move forward — **lunge** *vb*

lurch \'lərch\ *n* : sudden swaying — **lurch** *vb*

lure \'lu̇r\ *n* **1** : something that attracts **2** : artificial fish bait ~ *vb* **lured; lur·ing** : attract

lu·rid \'lu̇rəd\ *adj* **1** : gruesome **2** : sensational — **lu·rid·ly** *adv*

lurk \'lərk\ *vb* : lie in wait

lus·cious \'ləshəs\ *adj* **1** : pleasingly sweet in taste or smell **2** : sensually appealing — **lus·cious·ly** *adv* — **luscious·ness** *n*

lush \'ləsh\ *adj* : covered with abundant growth

lust \'ləst\ *n* **1** : intense sexual desire **2** : intense longing — **lust** *vb* — **lust·ful** *adj*

lus·ter, lus·tre \'ləstər\ *n* **1** : brightness from reflected light **2** : magnificence — **luster·less** *adj* — **lus·trous** \-trəs\ *adj*

lusty \'ləstē\ *adj* **lust·i·er; -est** : full of vitality — **lust·i·ly** *adv* — **lust·i·ness** *n*

lute \\'lüt\ *n* : pear-shaped stringed instrument — **lutenist, lu·ta·nist** \\'lüt⁼nist\ *n*

lux·u·ri·ant \ˌləg'zhu̇rēənt, ˌlək'shu̇r-\ *adj* **1** : growing plentifully **2** : rich and varied — **lux·u·ri·ance** \-ēəns\ *n* — **lux·u·ri·ant·ly** *adv*

lux·u·ri·ate \-ē-ˌāt\ *vb* **-at·ed; -at·ing** : revel

lux·u·ry \\'ləkshərē, 'ləgzh-\ *n, pl* **-ries** **1** : great comfort **2** : something adding to pleasure or comfort — **lux·u·ri·ous** \ˌləg'zhu̇rēəs, ˌlək'shu̇r-\ *adj* — **lux·u·ri·ous·ly** *adv*

-ly \lē\ *adv suffix* **1** : in a specified way **2** : from a specified point of view

ly·ce·um \lī'sēəm, 'līsē-\ *n* : hall for public lectures

lye \\'lī\ *n* : caustic alkaline substance

lying *pres part of* LIE

lymph \\'limf\ *n* : bodily liquid consisting chiefly of blood plasma and white blood cells — **lym·phat·ic** \lim'fatik\ *adj*

lynch \\'linch\ *vb* : put to death by mob action — **lyncher** *n*

lynx \\'liŋks\ *n, pl* **lynx** *or* **lynx·es** : wildcat

lyre \\'līr\ *n* : ancient Greek stringed instrument

lyr·ic \\'lirik\ *adj* **1** : suitable for singing **2** : expressing direct personal emotion ~ *n* **1** : lyric poem **2** *pl* : words of a song — **lyr·i·cal** \-ikəl\ *adj*

M

m \\'em\ *n, pl* **m's** *or* **ms** \\'emz\ : 13th letter of the alphabet

ma'am \\'mam\ *n* : madam

ma·ca·bre \mə'käb, -'käbər, -'käbrə\ *adj* : gruesome

mac·ad·am \mə'kadəm\ *n* : pavement of cemented broken stone — **mac·ad·am·ize** \-ˌīz\ *vb*

mac·a·ro·ni \ˌmakə'rōnē\ *n* : tube-shaped pasta

mac·a·roon \ˌmakə'rün\ *n* : cookie of ground almonds or coconut

ma·caw \mə'kȯ\ *n* : large long-tailed parrot

¹**mace** \\'mās\ *n* **1** : heavy spiked club **2** : ornamental staff as a symbol of authority

²**mace** *n* : spice from the fibrous coating of the nutmeg

ma·chete \mə'shetē\ *n* : large heavy knife

mach·i·na·tion \ˌmakə'nā-shən, ˌmashə-\ *n* : plot or scheme — **mach·i·nate** \'makəˌnāt, 'mash-\ *vb*

ma·chine \mə'shēn\ *n* : combination of mechanical or electrical parts ~ *vb* **-chined; -chin·ing** : modify by machine-operated tools — **ma·chin·able** *adj* — **ma·chin·ery** \-ərē\ *n* — **ma·chin·ist** *n*

mack·er·el \'makərəl\ *n, pl* **-el** *or* **-els** : No. Atlantic food fish

mack·i·naw \'makəˌnȯ\ *n* : short heavy plaid coat

mac·ra·mé \ˌmakrə'mā\ *n* : coarse lace or fringe made by knotting

mac·ro \'makrō\ *adj* : very large

mac·ro·cosm \'makrəˌkäzəm\ *n* : universe

mad \'mad\ *adj* **-dd-** **1** : insane or rabid **2** : rash and foolish **3** : angry **4** : carried away by enthusiasm — **mad·den** \'madᵊn\ *vb* — **mad·den·ing·ly** \'madᵊniŋlē\ *adv* — **mad·ly** *adv* — **mad·ness** *n*

mad·am \'madəm\ *n, pl* **mes·dames** \mā'däm\ — used in polite address to a woman

ma·dame \mə'dam, *before a surname also* 'madəm\ *n, pl* **mes·dames** \mā'däm\ — used as a title for a woman not of English-speaking nationality

mad·cap \'madˌkap\ *adj* : wild or zany — **madcap** *n*

made *past of* MAKE

Ma·dei·ra \mə'dirə\ *n* : amber-colored dessert wine

ma·de·moi·selle \ˌmadmwə-'zel, -mə'zel\ *n, pl* **ma·de·moi·selles** \-'zelz\ *or* **mes·de·moi·selles** \ˌmādmwə'zel\ : an unmarried girl or woman — used as a title for a woman esp. of French nationality

mad·house *n* **1** : insane asylum **2** : place of great uproar or confusion

mad·man \-ˌman, -mən\ *n* : lunatic

mad·ri·gal \'madrigəl\ *n* : elaborate song for several voice parts

mad·wom·an \'madˌwu̇mən\ *n* : woman who is insane

mael·strom \'mālstrəm\ *n* **1** : whirlpool **2** : tumult

mae·stro \'mīstrō\ *n, pl* **-stros** *or* **-stri** \-ˌstrē\ : eminent composer or conductor

Ma·fia \'mäfēə\ *n* : secret criminal organization

ma·fi·o·so \ˌmäfē'ōsō\ *n, pl* **-si** \-sē\ : member of the Mafia

mag·a·zine \'magəˌzēn\ *n* **1** : storehouse **2** : publication issued at regular intervals **3** : cartridge container in a gun

ma·gen·ta \mə'jentə\ *n* : deep purplish red color

mag·got \'magət\ *n* : worm-like fly larva — **mag·goty** *adj*

mag·ic \'majik\ *n* **1** : art of using supernatural powers **2** : extraordinary power or influence **3** : sleight of hand — **magic, mag·i·cal** \-ikəl\ *adj* — **mag·i·cal·ly** *adv* — **ma·gi·cian** \mə'jishən\ *n*

mag·is·te·ri·al \ˌmajə'stirēəl\ *adj* **1** : authoritative **2** : relating to a magistrate

mag·is·trate \'majəˌstrāt\ *n* : judge — **mag·is·tra·cy** \-strəsē\ *n*

mag·ma \'magmə\ *n* : molten rock

mag·nan·i·mous \mag'nan-əməs\ *adj* : noble or generous — **mag·na·nim·i·ty** \ˌmagnə-'nimətē\ *n* — **mag·nan·i·mous·ly** *adv*

mag·ne·sia \mag'nēzhə, -shə\ *n* : oxide of magnesium used as a laxative

mag·ne·sium \mag'nēzēəm, -zhəm\ *n* : silver-white metallic chemical element

mag·net \'magnət\ *n* **1** : body that attracts iron **2** : something that attracts — **mag·net·ic** \mag'netik\ *adj* — **mag·net·i·cal·ly** \-iklē\ *adv* — **mag·ne·tism** \'magnəˌtizəm\ *n*

mag·ne·tite \'magnəˌtīt\ *n* : black iron ore

mag·ne·tize \'magnəˌtīz\ *vb* **-tized; -tiz·ing 1** : attract like a magnet **2** : give magnetic properties to — **mag·ne·tiz·able** *adj* — **mag·ne·ti·za·tion** \ˌmagnətə'zāshən\ *n* — **mag·ne·tiz·er** *n*

mag·nif·i·cent \mag'nifəsənt\ *adj* : splendid — **mag·nif·i·cence** \-səns\ *n* — **mag·nif·i·cent·ly** *adv*

mag·ni·fy \'magnəˌfī\ *vb* **-fied; -fy·ing 1** : intensify **2** : enlarge — **mag·ni·fi·ca·tion** \ˌmagnəfə'kāshən\ *n* — **mag·ni·fi·er** \'magnəˌfīər\ *n*

mag·ni·tude \'magnəˌtüd, -ˌtyüd\ *n* **1** : greatness of size or extent **2** : quantity

mag·no·lia \mag'nōlyə\ *n* : shrub with large fragrant flowers

mag·pie \'magˌpī\ *n* : long-tailed black-and-white bird

ma·hog·a·ny \mə'hägənē\ *n, pl* **-nies** : tropical evergreen tree or its reddish brown wood

maid \'mād\ *n* **1** : unmarried young woman **2** : female servant

maid·en \'mād°n\ *n* : unmarried young woman ~ *adj* **1** : unmarried **2** : first — **maid·en·hood** \-ˌhud\ *n* — **maid·en·ly** *adj*

maid·en·hair \-ˌhar\ *n* : fern with delicate feathery fronds

¹mail \'māl\ *n* **1** : something sent or carried in the postal system **2** : postal system ~ *vb* : send by mail — **mail·box** *n* — **mail·man** \-ₘman, -mən\ *n*

²mail *n* : armor of metal links or plates

maim \'mām\ *vb* : seriously wound or disfigure

main \'mān\ *n* **1** : force **2** : ocean **3** : principal pipe, duct, or circuit of a utility system ~ *adj* : chief — **main·ly** *adv*

main·frame \'mān₁frām\ *n* : large fast computer

main·land \'mān₁land, -lənd\ *n* : part of a country on a continent

main·stay *n* : chief support

main·stream *n* : prevailing current or direction of activity or influence — **mainstream** *adj*

main·tain \mān'tān\ *vb* **1** : keep in an existing state (as of repair) **2** : sustain **3** : declare — **main·tain·abil·i·ty** \-ₜānə'bilətē\ *n* — **main·tain·able** \-'tānəbəl\ *adj* — **main·te·nance** \'mānt³nəns\ *n*

mai·tre d'hô·tel \ₘmātrədō-'tel, ₘme-\ *n* : head of a dining room staff

maize \'māz\ *n* : corn

maj·es·ty \'majəstē\ *n, pl* **-ties** **1** : sovereign power or dignity — used as a title **2** : grandeur or splendor — **ma·jes·tic** \mə'jestik\ *adj* — **ma·jes·ti·cal·ly** \-tiklē\ *adv*

ma·jor \'mājər\ *adj* **1** : larger or greater **2** : noteworthy or conspicuous ~ *n* **1** : commissioned officer (as in the army) ranking next below a lieutenant colonel **2** : main field of study ~ *vb* **-jored; -jor·ing** : pursue an academic major

ma·jor·do·mo \ₘmājər'dōmō\ *n, pl* **-mos** : head steward

major general *n* : commissioned officer (as in the army) ranking next below a lieutenant general

ma·jor·i·ty \mə'jȯrətē\ *n, pl* **-ties** **1** : age of full civil rights **2** : quantity more than half

make \'māk\ *vb* **made** \'mād\; **mak·ing** **1** : cause to exist, occur, or appear **2** : fashion or manufacture **3** : formulate in the mind **4** : constitute **5** : prepare **6** : cause to be or become **7** : carry out or perform **8** : compel **9** : gain **10** : have an effect — used with *for* ~ *n* : brand — **mak·er** *n* — **make do** *vb* : get along with what is available — **make good** *vb* **1** : repay **2** : succeed — **make out** *vb* **1** : draw up or write **2** : discern or understand **3** : fare — **make**

up *vb* **1** : invent **2** : become reconciled **3** : compensate for

make–be·lieve *n* : a pretending to believe ~ *adj* : imagined or pretended

make·shift *n* : temporary substitute — **makeshift** *adj*

make·up \-ˌəp\ *n* **1** : way in which something is constituted **2** : cosmetics

mal·ad·just·ed \ˌmalə'jəstəd\ *adj* : poorly adjusted (as to one's environment) — **mal·ad·just·ment** \-'jəstmənt\ *n*

mal·adroit \ˌmalə'drȯit\ *adj* : clumsy or inept

mal·a·dy \'malədē\ *n, pl* **-dies** : disease or disorder

mal·aise \mə'lāz, ma-\ *n* : sense of being unwell

mal·a·mute \'maləˌmyüt\ *n* : powerful heavy-coated dog

mal·a·prop·ism \'maləˌpräp-ˌizəm\ *n* : humorous misuse of a word

ma·lar·ia \mə'lerēə\ *n* : disease transmitted by a mosquito — **ma·lar·i·al** \-əl\ *adj*

ma·lar·key \mə'lärkē\ *n* : foolishness

mal·con·tent \ˌmalkən'tent\ *n* : discontented person — **malcontent** *adj*

male \'māl\ *adj* **1** : relating to the sex that performs a fertilizing function **2** : masculine ~ *n* : male individual — **male·ness** *n*

mal·e·dic·tion \ˌmalə'dik-shən\ *n* : curse

mal·e·fac·tor \'maləˌfaktər\ *n* : one who commits an offense esp. against the law

ma·lef·i·cent \mə'lefəsənt\ *adj* : harmful

ma·lev·o·lent \mə'levələnt\ *adj* : malicious or spiteful — **ma·lev·o·lence** \-ləns\ *n*

mal·fea·sance \mal'fēzⁿns\ *n* : misconduct by a public official

mal·for·ma·tion \ˌmalfȯr'mā-shən\ *n* : distortion or faulty formation — **mal·formed** \mal'fȯrmd\ *adj*

mal·func·tion \mal'fəŋkshən\ *vb* : fail to operate properly — **malfunction** *n*

mal·ice \'maləs\ *n* : desire to cause pain or injury to another — **ma·li·cious** \mə'lishəs\ *adj* — **ma·li·cious·ly** *adv*

ma·lign \mə'līn\ *adj* **1** : wicked **2** : malignant ~ *vb* : speak evil of

ma·lig·nant \mə'lignənt\ *adj* **1** : harmful **2** : likely to cause death — **ma·lig·nan·cy** \-nənsē\ *n* — **ma·lig·nant·ly** *adv* — **ma·lig·ni·ty** \-nətē\ *n*

ma·lin·ger \mə'liŋgər\ *vb* : pretend illness to avoid duty — **ma·lin·ger·er** *n*

mall \'mȯl\ *n* **1** : shaded promenade **2** : concourse providing access to rows of shops

mal·lard \\'malərd\ *n, pl* **-lard** *or* **-lards** : common wild duck

mal·lea·ble \\'malēəbəl\ *adj* **1** : easily shaped **2** : adaptable — **mal·le·a·bil·i·ty** \\,malēə-'bilətē\ *n*

mal·let \\'malət\ *n* : hammer-like tool

mal·nour·ished \mal'nərisht\ *adj* : poorly nourished

mal·nu·tri·tion \\,malnu̇'tri-shən, -nyu̇-\ *n* : inadequate nutrition

mal·odor·ous \mal'ōdərəs\ *adj* : foul-smelling — **mal·odor·ous·ly** *adv* — **mal·odor·ous·ness** *n*

mal·prac·tice \-'praktəs\ *n* : failure of professional duty

malt \\'mȯlt\ *n* : sprouted grain used in brewing

mal·treat \mal'trēt\ *vb* : treat badly — **mal·treat·ment** *n*

ma·ma, mam·ma \\'mämə\ *n* : mother

mam·mal \\'maməl\ *n* : warm-blooded vertebrate animal that nourishes its young with milk — **mam·ma·li·an** \mə-'mālēən, ma-\ *adj or n*

mam·ma·ry \\'mamərē\ *adj* : relating to the milk-secreting glands (**mammary glands**) of mammals

mam·mo·gram \\'mamə-,gram\ *n* : X-ray photograph of the breasts

mam·moth \\'maməth\ *n* : large hairy extinct elephant ~ *adj* : enormous

man \\'man\ *n, pl* **men** \\'men\ **1** : human being **2** : adult male **3** : mankind ~ *vb* **-nn-** : supply with people for working — **man·hood** *n* — **man·hunt** *n* — **man·like** *adj* — **man·li·ness** *n* — **man·ly** *adj or adv* — **man–made** *adj* — **man·nish** *adj* — **man·nish·ly** *adv* — **man·nish·ness** *n* — **man–size, man–sized** *adj*

man·a·cle \\'manikəl\ *n* : shackle for the hands or wrists — **manacle** *vb*

man·age \\'manij\ *vb* **-aged; -ag·ing** **1** : control **2** : direct or carry on business or affairs **3** : cope — **man·age·abil·i·ty** \\,manijə'bilətē\ *n* — **man·age·able** \\'manijəbəl\ *adj* — **man·age·able·ness** *n* — **man·age·ably** \-blē\ *adv* — **man·age·ment** \\'manijmənt\ *n* — **man·ag·er** \\'manijər\ *n* — **man·a·ge·ri·al** \\,manə'jirēəl\ *adj*

man·da·rin \\'mandərən\ *n* : Chinese imperial official

man·date \\'man,dāt\ *n* : authoritative command

man·da·to·ry \\'mandə,tōrē\ *adj* : obligatory

man·di·ble \\'mandəbəl\ *n* : lower jaw — **man·dib·u·lar** \man'dibyələr\ *adj*

man·do·lin \,mandə'lin, 'mand³lən\ *n* : stringed musical instrument

man·drake \'man,drāk\ *n* : herb with a large forked root

mane \'mān\ *n* : animal's neck hair — **maned** \'mānd\ *adj*

ma·neu·ver \mə'nüvər, -'nyü-\ *n* **1** : planned movement of troops or ships **2** : military training exercise **3** : clever or skillful move or action — **maneuver** *vb* — **ma·neu·ver·abil·i·ty** \-,nüvərə-'bilətē, -,nyü-\ *n*

man·ful \'manfəl\ *adj* : courageous — **man·ful·ly** *adv*

man·ga·nese \'maŋgə,nēz, -,nēs\ *n* : gray metallic chemical element

mange \'mānj\ *n* : skin disease of domestic animals — **mangy** \'mānjē\ *adj*

man·ger \'mānjər\ *n* : feeding trough for livestock

man·gle \'maŋgəl\ *vb* **-gled; -gling** **1** : mutilate **2** : bungle — **man·gler** *n*

man·go \'maŋgō\ *n, pl* **-goes** : juicy yellowish red tropical fruit

man·grove \'man,grōv, 'maŋ-\ *n* : tropical tree growing in salt water

man·han·dle *vb* : handle roughly

man·hole *n* : entry to a sewer

ma·nia \'mānēə, -nyə\ *n* **1** : insanity marked by uncontrollable emotion or excitement **2** : excessive enthusiasm — **ma·ni·ac** \-nē,ak\ *n* — **ma·ni·a·cal** \mə'nīəkəl\ *adj* — **man·ic** \'manik\ *adj or n*

man·i·cure \'manə,kyúr\ *n* : treatment for the fingernails ~ *vb* **-cured; -cur·ing** **1** : do manicure work on **2** : trim precisely — **man·i·cur·ist** \-,kyúrist\ *n*

¹man·i·fest \'manə,fest\ *adj* : clear to the senses or to the mind ~ *vb* : make evident — **man·i·fes·ta·tion** \,manəfə-'stāshən\ *n* — **man·i·fest·ly** *adv*

²manifest *n* : invoice of cargo or list of passengers

man·i·fes·to \,manə'festō\ *n, pl* **-tos** *or* **-toes** : public declaration of policy or views

man·i·fold \'manə,fōld\ *adj* : marked by diversity or variety ~ *n* : pipe fitting with several outlets for connections

ma·nila paper \mə'nilə-\ *n* : durable brownish paper

ma·nip·u·late \mə'nipyə,lāt\ *vb* **-lat·ed; -lat·ing** **1** : treat or operate manually or mechanically **2** : influence esp. by cunning — **ma·nip·u·la·tion** \mə,nipyə'lāshən\ *n* — **ma·nip·u·la·tive** \-'nipyə,lātiv,

-lətiv\ *adj* — **ma·nip·u·la·tor** \-ˌlātər\ *n*

man·kind \'man'kīnd\ *n* : human race

man·na \'manə\ *n* : something valuable that comes unexpectedly

manned \'mand\ *adj* : carrying or performed by a man

man·ne·quin \'manikən\ *n* : dummy used to display clothes

man·ner \'manər\ *n* **1** : kind **2** : usual way of acting **3** : artistic method **4** *pl* : social conduct

man·nered \-ərd\ *adj* **1** : having manners of a specified kind **2** : artificial

man·ner·ism \'manəˌrizəm\ *n* : individual peculiarity of action

man·ner·ly \-lē\ *adj* : polite — **man·ner·li·ness** *n* — **man·nerly** *adv*

man–of–war \ˌmanə'wȯr, -əv'wȯr\ *n, pl* **men–of–war** \ˌmen-\ : warship

man·or \'manər\ *n* : country estate — **ma·no·ri·al** \mə'nȯrēəl\ *adj*

man·pow·er *n* : supply of people available for service

man·sard \'manˌsärd\ *n* : roof with two slopes on all sides and the lower slope the steeper

manse \'mans\ *n* : parsonage

man·ser·vant *n, pl* **men·ser·vants** : a male servant

man·sion \'manchən\ *n* : very big house

man·slaugh·ter *n* : unintentional killing of a person

man·tel \'mantᵊl\ *n* : shelf above a fireplace

man·tis \'mantəs\ *n, pl* **-tis·es** *or* **-tes** \'manˌtēz\ : large green insect-eating insect with stout forelegs

man·tle \'mantᵊl\ *n* **1** : sleeveless cloak **2** : something that covers, enfolds, or envelops — **mantle** *vb*

man·tra \'mantrə\ *n* : mystical chant

man·u·al \'manyəwəl\ *adj* : involving the hands or physical force ∼ *n* : handbook — **man·u·al·ly** *adv*

man·u·fac·ture \ˌmanyə'fakchər, ˌmanə-\ *n* : process of making wares by hand or by machinery ∼ *vb* **-tured; -turing** : make from raw materials — **man·u·fac·tur·er** *n*

ma·nure \mə'nu̇r, -'nyu̇r\ *n* : animal excrement used as fertilizer

manu·script \'manyəˌskript\ *n* **1** : something written or typed **2** : document submitted for publication

many \'menē\ *adj* **more** \'mȯr\; **most** \'mōst\ : consisting of a large number — **many** *n or pron*

map \'map\ *n* : representation of a geographical area ~ *vb* **-pp-** **1** : make a map of **2** : plan in detail — **map·pa·ble** \-əbəl\ *adj* — **map·per** *n*

ma·ple \'māpəl\ *n* : tree with hard light-colored wood

mar \'mär\ *vb* **-rr-** : damage

mar·a·schi·no \ˌmarə'skēnō, -'shē-\ *n, pl* **-nos** : preserved cherry

mar·a·thon \'marəˌthän\ *n* **1** : long-distance race **2** : test of endurance — **mar·a·thon·er** \-ˌthänər\ *n*

ma·raud \mə'ròd\ *vb* : roam about in search of plunder — **ma·raud·er** *n*

mar·ble \'märbəl\ *n* **1** : crystallized limestone **2** : small glass ball used in a children's game (**marbles**)

mar·bling \-bəliŋ\ *n* : intermixture of fat and lean in meat

march \'märch\ *vb* : move with regular steps or in a purposeful manner ~ *n* **1** : distance covered in a march **2** : measured stride **3** : forward movement **4** : music for marching — **march·er** *n*

March *n* : 3d month of the year having 31 days

mar·chio·ness \'märshənəs\ *n* : woman holding the rank of a marquess

Mar·di Gras \'märdēˌgrä\ *n* : Tuesday before the beginning of Lent often observed with parades and merrymaking

mare \'mar\ *n* : female horse

mar·ga·rine \'märjərən\ *n* : butter substitute made usu. from vegetable oils

mar·gin \'märjən\ *n* **1** : edge **2** : spare amount, measure, or degree

mar·gin·al \-jənəl\ *adj* **1** : relating to or situated at a border or margin **2** : close to the lower limit of acceptability — **mar·gin·al·ly** *adv*

mari·gold \'marəˌgōld\ *n* : garden plant with showy flower heads

mar·i·jua·na \ˌmarə'wänə, -'hwä-\ *n* : intoxicating drug obtained from the hemp plant

ma·ri·na \mə'rēnə\ *n* : place for mooring pleasure boats

mar·i·nate \'marəˌnāt\ *vb* **-nat·ed; -nat·ing** : soak in a savory sauce

ma·rine \mə'rēn\ *adj* **1** : relating to the sea **2** : relating to marines ~ *n* : infantry soldier associated with a navy

mar·i·ner \'marənər\ *n* : sailor

mar·i·o·nette \ˌmarēə'net\ *n* : puppet

mar·i·tal \'marət³l\ *adj* : relating to marriage

mar·i·time \'marə‚tīm\ *adj* : relating to the sea or commerce on the sea

mar·jo·ram \'märjərəm\ *n* : aromatic mint used as a seasoning

mark \'märk\ *n* **1** : something aimed at **2** : something (as a line) designed to record position **3** : visible sign **4** : written symbol **5** : grade **6** : lasting impression **7** : blemish ~ *vb* **1** : designate or set apart by a mark or make a mark on **2** : characterize **3** : remark — **mark·er** *n*

marked \'märkt\ *adj* : noticeable — **mark·ed·ly** \'märk-ədlē\ *adv*

mar·ket \'märkət\ *n* **1** : buying and selling of goods or the place this happens **2** : demand for commodities **3** : store ~ *vb* : sell — **mar·ket·able** *adj*

mar·ket·place *n* **1** : market **2** : world of trade or economic activity

marks·man \'märksmən\ *n* : good shooter — **marks·man·ship** *n*

mar·lin \'märlən\ *n* : large oceanic fish

mar·ma·lade \'märmə‚lād\ *n* : jam with pieces of fruit and rind

mar·mo·set \'märmə‚set\ *n* : small bushy-tailed monkey

mar·mot \'märmət\ *n* : burrowing rodent

¹ma·roon \mə'rün\ *vb* : isolate without hope of escape

²maroon *n* : dark red color

mar·quee \mär'kē\ *n* : canopy over an entrance

mar·quess \'märkwəs\, **mar·quis** \'märkwəs, mär'kē\ *n, pl* **-quess·es** *or* **-quis·es** *or* **-quis** : British noble ranking next below a duke

mar·quise \mär'kēz\ *n, pl* **mar·quises** \-'kēz, -'kēzəz\ : marchioness

mar·riage \'marij\ *n* **1** : state of being married **2** : wedding ceremony — **mar·riage·able** *adj*

mar·row \'marō\ *n* : soft tissue in the cavity of bone

mar·ry \'marē\ *vb* **-ried; -ry·ing** **1** : join as husband and wife **2** : take or give in marriage — **mar·ried** *adj or n*

marsh \'märsh\ *n* : soft wet land — **marshy** *adj*

mar·shal \'märshəl\ *n* **1** : leader of ceremony **2** : usu. high military or administrative officer ~ *vb* **-shaled** *or* **-shalled; -shal·ing** *or* **-shal·ling** **1** : arrange in order, rank, or position **2** : lead with ceremony

marsh·mal·low \'märsh‚melō, -‚malō\ *n* : spongy candy

mar·su·pi·al \mär'süpēəl\ *n* : mammal that nourishes young in an abdominal pouch — **marsupial** *adj*

mart \\'märt\\ *n* : market

mar·ten \\'märt⁰n\\ *n, pl* **-ten** *or* **-tens** : weasellike mammal with soft fur

mar·tial \\'märshəl\\ *adj* **1** : relating to war or an army **2** : warlike

mar·tin \\'märt⁰n\\ *n* : small swallow

mar·ti·net \\ˌmärt⁰n'et\\ *n* : strict disciplinarian

mar·tyr \\'märtər\\ *n* : one who dies or makes a great sacrifice for a cause ∼ *vb* : make a martyr of — **mar·tyr·dom** \\-dəm\\ *n*

mar·vel \\'märvəl\\ *vb* **-veled** *or* **-velled; -vel·ing** *or* **-vel·ling** : feel surprise or wonder ∼ *n* : something amazing — **mar·vel·ous,** **mar·vel·lous** \\'märvələs\\ *adj* — **mar·vel·ous·ly** *adv* — **mar·vel·ous·ness** *n*

Marx·ism \\'märkˌsizəm\\ *n* : political and social principles of Karl Marx — **Marx·ist** \\-sist\\ *n or adj*

mas·cara \\mas'karə\\ *n* : eye cosmetic

mas·cot \\'masˌkät, -kət\\ *n* : one believed to bring good luck

mas·cu·line \\'maskyələn\\ *adj* : relating to the male sex — **mas·cu·lin·i·ty** \\ˌmaskyə'lin-ətē\\ *n*

mash \\'mash\\ *n* **1** : crushed steeped grain for fermenting **2** : soft pulpy mass ∼ *vb* **1** : reduce to a pulpy mass **2** : smash — **mash·er** *n*

mask \\'mask\\ *n* : disguise for the face ∼ *vb* **1** : disguise **2** : cover to protect — **mask·er** *n*

mas·och·ism \\'masəˌkizəm, 'maz-\\ *n* : pleasure in being abused — **mas·och·ist** \\-kist\\ *n* — **mas·och·is·tic** \\ˌmasə-'kistik, ˌmaz-\\ *adj*

ma·son \\'mās⁰n\\ *n* : workman who builds with stone or brick — **ma·son·ry** \\-rē\\ *n*

mas·quer·ade \\ˌmaskə'rād\\ *n* **1** : costume party **2** : disguise ∼ *vb* **-ad·ed; -ad·ing** **1** : disguise oneself **2** : take part in a costume party — **mas·quer·ad·er** *n*

mass \\'mas\\ *n* **1** : large amount of matter or number of things **2** : expanse or magnitude **3** : great body of people — usu. pl. ∼ *vb* : form into a mass — **mass·less** \\-ləs\\ *adj* — **massy** *adj*

Mass *n* : worship service of the Roman Catholic Church

mas·sa·cre \\'masikər\\ *n* : wholesale slaughter — **mas·sacre** *vb*

mas·sage \\mə'säzh, -'säj\\ *n* : a rubbing of the body — **massage** *vb*

mas·seur \\ma'sər\\ *n* : man who massages

mas·seuse \-'sœz, -'süz\ *n* : woman who massages

mas·sive \'masiv\ *adj* **1** : being a large mass **2** : large in scope — **mas·sive·ly** *adv* — **mas·sive·ness** *n*

mast \'mast\ *n* : tall pole esp. for supporting sails — **masted** *adj*

mas·ter \'mastər\ *n* **1** : male teacher **2** : holder of an academic degree between a bachelor's and a doctor's **3** : one highly skilled **4** : one in authority ∼ *vb* **1** : subdue **2** : become proficient in — **mas·ter·ful** \-fəl\ *adj* — **mas·ter·ful·ly** *adv* — **mas·ter·ly** *adj* — **mas·tery** \'mastərē\ *n*

master chief petty officer *n* : petty officer of the highest rank in the navy

master gunnery sergeant *n* : noncommissioned officer in the marine corps ranking above a master sergeant

mas·ter·piece \'mastər,pēs\ *n* : great piece of work

master sergeant *n* **1** : noncommissioned officer in the army ranking next below a sergeant major **2** : noncommissioned officer in the air force ranking next below a senior master sergeant **3** : noncommissioned officer in the marine corps ranking next

below a master gunnery sergeant

mas·ter·work *n* : masterpiece

mas·tic \'mastik\ *n* : pasty glue

mas·ti·cate \'mastə,kāt\ *vb* -cat·ed; -cat·ing : chew — **mas·ti·ca·tion** \,mastə'kāshən\ *n*

mas·tiff \'mastəf\ *n* : large dog

mas·to·don \'mastə,dän\ *n* : extinct elephantlike animal

mas·toid \'mas,tȯid\ *n* : bone behind the ear — **mastoid** *adj*

mas·tur·ba·tion \,mastər'bāshən\ *n* : stimulation of sex organs by hand — **mas·tur·bate** \'mastər,bāt\ *vb*

¹mat \'mat\ *n* **1** : coarse woven or plaited fabric **2** : mass of tangled strands **3** : thick pad ∼ *vb* -tt- : form into a mat

²mat *vb* -tt- **1** : make matte **2** : provide (a picture) with a mat ∼ *or* **matt** *or* **matte** *n* : border around a picture

³mat *var of* MATTE

mat·a·dor \'matə,dȯr\ *n* : bullfighter

¹match \'mach\ *n* **1** : one equal to another **2** : one able to cope with another **3** : suitable pairing **4** : game **5** : marriage ∼ *vb* **1** : set in competition **2** : marry **3** : be or provide the equal of **4** : fit or go together — **match·less** *adj* — **match·mak·er** *n*

²**match** *n* : piece of wood or paper material with a combustible tip

mate \'māt\ *n* **1** : companion **2** : subordinate officer on a ship **3** : one of a pair ~ *vb* **mat·ed; mat·ing 1** : fit together **2** : come together as a pair **3** : copulate

ma·te·ri·al \mə'tirēəl\ *adj* **1** : natural **2** : relating to matter **3** : important **4** : of a physical or worldly nature ~ *n* : stuff something is made of — **ma·te·ri·al·ly** *adv*

ma·te·ri·al·ism \mə'tirēə‚lizəm\ *n* **1** : theory that matter is the only reality **2** : preoccupation with material and not spiritual things — **ma·te·ri·al·ist** \-list\ *n or adj* — **ma·te·ri·al·is·tic** \-‚tirēə'listik\ *adj*

ma·te·ri·al·ize \mə'tirēə‚līz\ *vb* **-ized; -iz·ing** : take or cause to take bodily form — **ma·te·ri·al·i·za·tion** \mə‚tirēələ'zāshən\ *n*

ma·té·ri·el, ma·te·ri·el \mə‚tirē'el\ *n* : military supplies

ma·ter·nal \mə'tərnᵊl\ *adj* : motherly — **ma·ter·nal·ly** *adv*

ma·ter·ni·ty \mə'tərnətē\ *n, pl* **-ties 1** : state of being a mother **2** : hospital's childbirth facility ~ *adj* **1** : worn during pregnancy **2** : relating to the period close to childbirth

math \'math\ *n* : mathematics

math·e·mat·ics \‚mathə'matiks\ *n pl* : science of numbers and of shapes in space — **math·e·mat·i·cal** \-ikəl\ *adj* — **math·e·mat·i·cal·ly** *adv* — **math·e·ma·ti·cian** \‚mathəmə'tishən\ *n*

mat·i·nee, mat·i·née \‚matᵊn'ā\ *n* : afternoon performance

mat·ins \'matᵊnz\ *n* : morning prayers

ma·tri·arch \'mātrē‚ärk\ *n* : woman who rules a family — **ma·tri·ar·chal** \‚mātrē'ärkəl\ *adj* — **ma·tri·ar·chy** \'mātrē‚ärkē\ *n*

ma·tri·cide \'matrə‚sīd, 'mā-\ *n* : murder of one's mother — **ma·tri·cid·al** \‚matrə'sīdᵊl, ‚mā-\ *adj*

ma·tric·u·late \mə'trikyə‚lāt\ *vb* **-lat·ed; -lat·ing** : enroll in school — **ma·tric·u·la·tion** \-‚trikyə'lāshən\ *n*

mat·ri·mo·ny \'matrə‚mōnē\ *n* : marriage — **mat·ri·mo·ni·al** \‚matrə'mōnēəl\ *adj* — **mat·ri·mo·ni·al·ly** *adv*

ma·trix \'mātriks\ *n, pl* **-tri·ces** \'mātrə‚sēz, 'ma-\ *or* **-trix·es** \'mātriksəz\ : something (as a mold) that gives form, foundation, or origin to something else enclosed in it

ma·tron \'mātrən\ *n* **1** : dignified mature woman **2** : woman supervisor — **ma·tron·ly** *adj*

matte \'mat\ *adj* : not shiny

mat·ter \'matər\ *n* **1** : subject of interest **2** *pl* : circumstances **3** : trouble **4** : physical substance ~ *vb* : be important

mat·tock \'matək\ *n* : a digging tool

mat·tress \'matrəs\ *n* : pad to sleep on

ma·ture \mə'tùr, -'tyùr, -'chùr\ *adj* **-tur·er; -est** **1** : carefully considered **2** : fully grown or developed **3** : due for payment ~ *vb* **-tured; -tur·ing** : become mature — **mat·u·ra·tion** \ˌmachə'rāshən\ *n* — **ma·ture·ly** *adv* — **ma·tu·ri·ty** \-ətē\ *n*

maud·lin \'mȯdlən\ *adj* : excessively sentimental

maul \'mȯl\ *n* : heavy hammer ~ *vb* **1** : beat **2** : handle roughly

mau·so·le·um \ˌmȯsə'lēəm, ˌmȯzə-\ *n, pl* **-leums** *or* **-lea** \-'lēə\ : large above-ground tomb

mauve \'mōv, 'mȯv\ *n* : lilac color

ma·ven, ma·vin \'māvən\ *n* : expert

mav·er·ick \'mavrik\ *n* **1** : unbranded range animal **2** : nonconformist

maw \'mȯ\ *n* **1** : stomach **2** : throat, esophagus, or jaws

mawk·ish \'mȯkish\ *adj* : sickly sentimental — **mawk·ish·ly** *adv* — **mawk·ish·ness** *n*

max·im \'maksəm\ *n* : proverb

max·i·mum \'maksəməm\ *n, pl* **-ma** \-səmə\ *or* **-mums** **1** : greatest quantity **2** : upper limit **3** : largest number — **maximum** *adj* — **max·i·mize** \-səˌmīz\ *vb*

may \'mā\ *verbal auxiliary, past* **might** \'mīt\; *pres sing & pl* **may** **1** : have permission **2** : be likely to **3** — used to express desire, purpose, or contingency

May \'mā\ *n* : 5th month of the year having 31 days

may·ap·ple *n* : woodland herb having edible fruit

may·be \'mābē\ *adv* : perhaps

may·flow·er *n* : spring-blooming herb

may·fly *n* : fly with an aquatic larva

may·hem \'māˌhem, 'māəm\ *n* **1** : crippling or mutilation of a person **2** : needless damage

may·on·naise \'māəˌnāz\ *n* : creamy white sandwich spread

may·or \'māər, 'mer\ *n* : chief city official — **may·or·al** \-əl\ *adj* — **may·or·al·ty** \-əltē\ *n*

maze \'māz\ *n* : confusing network of passages — **mazy** *adj*

ma·zur·ka \mə'zərkə\ *n* : Polish dance

me \'mē\ *pron, objective case of* I

mead \'mēd\ *n* : alcoholic beverage brewed from honey

mead·ow \'medō\ *n* : low-lying usu. level grassland — **mead·ow·land** \-ˌland\ *n*

mead·ow·lark *n* : songbird with a yellow breast

mea·ger, mea·gre \'mēgər\ *adj* **1** : thin **2** : lacking richness or strength — **mea·ger·ly** *adv* — **mea·ger·ness** *n*

¹meal \'mēl\ *n* **1** : food to be eaten at one time **2** : act of eating — **meal·time** *n*

²meal *n* : ground grain — **mealy** *adj*

¹mean \'mēn\ *adj* **1** : humble **2** : worthy of or showing little regard **3** : stingy **4** : malicious — **mean·ly** *adv* — **mean·ness** *n*

²mean \'mēn\ *vb* **meant** \'ment\; **mean·ing** \'mēniŋ\ **1** : intend **2** : serve to convey, show, or indicate **3** : be important

³mean *n* **1** : middle point **2** *pl* : something that helps gain an end **3** *pl* : material resources **4** : sum of several quantities divided by the number of quantities ~ *adj* : being a mean

me·an·der \mē'andər\ *vb* **-dered; -der·ing 1** : follow a winding course **2** : wander aimlessly — **meander** *n*

mean·ing \'mēniŋ\ *n* **1** : idea conveyed or intended to be conveyed **2** : aim — **mean·ing·ful** \-fəl\ *adj* — **mean·ing·ful·ly** *adv* — **mean·ing·less** *adj*

mean·time \'mēnˌtīm\ *n* : intervening time — **meantime** *adv*

mean·while \-ˌhwīl\ *n* : meantime ~ *adv* **1** : meantime **2** : at the same time

mea·sles \'mēzəlz\ *n pl* : disease that is marked by red spots on the skin

mea·sly \'mēzlē\ *adj* **-sli·er; -est** : contemptibly small in amount

mea·sure \'mezhər, 'māzh-\ *n* **1** : moderate amount **2** : dimensions or amount **3** : something to show amount **4** : unit or system of measurement **5** : act of measuring **6** : means to an end ~ *vb* **-sured; -sur·ing 1** : find out or mark off size or amount of **2** : have a specified measurement — **mea·sur·able** \'mezhərəbəl, 'māzh-\ *adj* — **mea·sur·ably**

\-blē\ *adv* — **mea·sure·less** *adj* — **mea·sure·ment** *n* — **mea·sur·er** *n*

meat \'mēt\ *n* **1** : food **2** : animal flesh used as food — **meat·ball** *n* — **meaty** *adj*

me·chan·ic \mi'kanik\ *n* : worker who repairs cars

me·chan·i·cal \mi'kanikəl\ *adj* **1** : relating to machines or mechanics **2** : involuntary — **me·chan·i·cal·ly** *adv*

me·chan·ics \-iks\ *n sing or pl* **1** : branch of physics dealing with energy and forces in relation to bodies **2** : mechanical details

mech·a·nism \'mekə,nizəm\ *n* **1** : piece of machinery **2** : technique for gaining a result **3** : basic processes producing a phenomenon — **mech·a·nis·tic** \,mekə'nistik\ *adj* — **mech·a·ni·za·tion** \,mekənə'zāshən\ *n* — **mech·a·nize** \'mekə,nīz\ *vb* — **mech·a·niz·er** *n*

med·al \'med³l\ *n* **1** : religious pin or pendant **2** : coin-like commemorative metal piece

med·al·ist, med·al·list \'med³l-ist\ *n* : person awarded a medal

me·dal·lion \mə'dalyən\ *n* : large medal

med·dle \'med³l\ *vb* **-dled; -dling** : interfere — **med·dler**

\'med³lər\ *n* — **med·dle·some** \'med³lsəm\ *adj*

me·dia \'mēdēə\ *n pl* : communications organizations

me·di·an \'mēdēən\ *n* : middle value in a range — **median** *adj*

me·di·ate \'mēdē,āt\ *vb* **-at·ed; -at·ing** : help settle a dispute — **me·di·a·tion** \,mēdē-'āshən\ *n* — **me·di·a·tor** \'mēdē,ātər\ *n*

med·ic \'medik\ *n* : medical worker esp. in the military

med·i·ca·ble \'medikəbəl\ *adj* : curable

med·ic·aid \'medi,kād\ *n* : government program of medical aid for the poor

med·i·cal \'medikəl\ *adj* : relating to medicine — **med·i·cal·ly** \-klē\ *adv*

medi·care \'medi,ker\ *n* : government program of medical care for the aged

med·i·cate \'medə,kāt\ *vb* **-cat·ed; -cat·ing** : treat with medicine

med·i·ca·tion \,medə'kāshən\ *n* **1** : act of medicating **2** : medicine

med·i·cine \'medəsən\ *n* **1** : preparation used to treat disease **2** : science dealing with the cure of disease — **me·dic·i·nal** \mə'dis³nəl\ *adj* — **me·dic·i·nal·ly** *adv*

me·di·e·val, me·di·ae·val \,mē-dē'ēval, ,med-, ,mid-; ,mē-

'dē-, ˌme-, ˌmi-\ *adj* : of or relating to the Middle Ages — **me·di·eval·ist** \-ist\ *n*

me·di·o·cre \ˌmēdē'ōkər\ *adj* : not very good — **me·di·oc·ri·ty** \-'äkrətē\ *n*

med·i·tate \'medəˌtāt\ *vb* **-tat·ed; -tat·ing** : contemplate — **med·i·ta·tion** \ˌmedə'tāshən\ *n* — **med·i·ta·tive** \'medəˌtātiv\ *adj* — **med·i·ta·tive·ly** *adv*

me·di·um \'mēdēəm\ *n, pl* **-diums** *or* **-dia** \-ēə\ **1** : middle position or degree **2** : means of effecting or conveying something **3** : surrounding substance **4** : means of communication **5** : mode of artistic expression — **medium** *adj*

med·ley \'medlē\ *n, pl* **-leys** : series of songs performed as one

meek \'mēk\ *adj* **1** : mild-mannered **2** : lacking spirit — **meek·ly** *adv* — **meek·ness** *n*

meer·schaum \'mirshəm, -ˌshȯm\ *n* : claylike tobacco pipe

¹meet \'mēt\ *vb* **met** \'met\; **meet·ing 1** : run into **2** : join **3** : oppose **4** : assemble **5** : satisfy **6** : be introduced to ∼ *n* : sports team competition

²meet *adj* : proper

meet·ing \'mētiŋ\ *n* : a getting together — **meet·ing·house** *n*

mega·byte \'megəbīt\ *n* : unit of computer storage capacity

mega·hertz \-ˌhərts, -ˌherts\ *n* : one million hertz

mega·phone \'megəˌfōn\ *n* : cone-shaped device to intensify or direct the voice

mel·an·choly \'melənˌkälē\ *n* : depression — **mel·an·chol·ic** \ˌmelən'kälik\ *adj* — **melan·choly** *adj*

mel·a·no·ma \ˌmelə'nōmə\ *n, pl* **-mas** : usu. malignant skin tumor

me·lee \'māˌlā, mā'lā\ *n* : brawl

me·lio·rate \'mēlyəˌrāt, 'mēlēə-\ *vb* **-rat·ed; -rat·ing** : improve — **me·lio·ra·tion** \ˌmēlyə'rāshən, ˌmēlēə-\ *n* — **me·lio·ra·tive** \'mēlyəˌrātiv, 'mēlēə-\ *adj*

mel·lif·lu·ous \me'lifləwəs, mə-\ *adj* : sweetly flowing — **mel·lif·lu·ous·ly** *adv* — **mel·lif·lu·ous·ness** *n*

mel·low \'melō\ *adj* **1** : grown gentle or mild **2** : rich and full — **mellow** *vb* — **mel·low·ness** *n*

melo·dra·ma \'meləˌdrämə, -ˌdram-\ *n* : overly theatrical play — **melo·dra·mat·ic** \ˌmelədrə'matik\ *adj* — **melo·dra·mat·i·cal·ly** \-tiklē\ *adv*

mel·o·dy \'melədē\ *n, pl* **-dies 1** : agreeable sound **2** : succession of musical notes — **me·lod·ic** \mə'lädik\ *adj* — **me·lod·i·cal·ly** \-iklē\ *adv* — **me·lo·di·ous** \mə'lōdēəs\ *adj* — **me·lo·di·ous·ly** *adv* — **me·lo·di·ous·ness** *n*

mel·on \'melən\ *n* : gourdlike fruit

melt \'melt\ *vb* **1** : change from solid to liquid usu. by heat **2** : dissolve or disappear gradually **3** : move or be moved emotionally

mem·ber \'membər\ *n* **1** : part of a person, animal, or plant **2** : one of a group **3** : part of a whole — **mem·ber·ship** \-ˌship\ *n*

mem·brane \'memˌbrān\ *n* : thin layer esp. in an organism — **mem·bra·nous** \-brənəs\ *adj*

me·men·to \mi'mentō\ *n, pl* **-tos** *or* **-toes** : souvenir

memo \'memō\ *n, pl* **mem·os** : memorandum

mem·oirs \'memˌwärz\ *n pl* : autobiography

mem·o·ra·bil·ia \ˌmemərə-'bilēə, -'bilyə\ *n pl* **1** : memorable things **2** : mementos

mem·o·ra·ble \'memərəbəl\ *adj* : worth remembering — **mem·o·ra·bil·i·ty** \ˌmemərə-'bilətē\ *n* — **mem·o·ra·ble·ness** *n* — **mem·o·ra·bly** \-blē\ *adv*

mem·o·ran·dum \ˌmemə-'randəm\ *n, pl* **-dums** *or* **-da** \-də\ : informal note

me·mo·ri·al \mə'mōrēəl\ *n* : something (as a monument) meant to keep remembrance alive — **memorial** *adj* — **me·mo·ri·al·ize** *vb*

Memorial Day *n* : last Monday in May or formerly May 30 observed as a legal holiday in commemoration of dead servicemen

mem·o·ry \'memrē, 'memə-\ *n, pl* **-ries** **1** : power of remembering **2** : something remembered **3** : commemoration **4** : time within which past events are remembered — **mem·o·ri·za·tion** \ˌmem-ərə'zāshən\ *n* — **mem·o·rize** \'meməˌrīz\ *vb* — **mem·o·riz·er** *n*

men *pl of* MAN

men·ace \'menəs\ *n* : threat of danger ~ *vb* **-aced; -ac·ing** **1** : threaten **2** : endanger — **men·ac·ing·ly** *adv*

me·nag·er·ie \mə'najərē\ *n* : collection of wild animals

mend \'mend\ *vb* **1** : improve **2** : repair **3** : heal — **mend** *n* — **mend·er** *n*

men·da·cious \men'dāshəs\ *adj* : dishonest — **men·da·cious·ly** *adv* — **men·dac·i·ty** \-'dasətē\ *n*

men·di·cant \'mendikənt\ *n* : beggar — **men·di·can·cy** \-kənsē\ *n* — **mendicant** *adj*

men·ha·den \men'hād³n, mən-\ *n, pl* **-den** : fish related to the herring

me·nial \'mēnēəl, -nyəl\ *adj* **1** : relating to servants **2** : humble ~ *n* : domestic servant — **me·ni·al·ly** *adv*

men·in·gi·tis \‚menən'jītəs\ *n, pl* **-git·i·des** \-'jitə‚dēz\ : disease of the brain and spinal cord

meno·pause \'menə‚pȯz\ *n* : time when menstruation ends — **meno·paus·al** \‚menə-'pȯzəl\ *adj*

me·no·rah \mə'nōrə\ *n* : candelabrum used in Jewish worship

men·stru·a·tion \‚menstrə'wā-shən, men'strā-\ *n* : monthly discharge of blood from the uterus — **men·stru·al** \'men-strəwəl\ *adj* — **men·stru·ate** \'menstrə‚wāt, -‚strāt\ *vb*

-ment \mənt\ *n suffix* **1** : result or means of an action **2** : action or process **3** : place of an action **4** : state or condition

men·tal \'ment³l\ *adj* : relating to the mind or its disorders — **men·tal·i·ty** \men'talətē\ *n* — **men·tal·ly** *adv*

men·thol \'men‚thȯl, -‚thōl\ *n* : soothing substance from oil of peppermint — **men·tho·lat·ed** \-thə‚lātəd\ *adj*

men·tion \'menchən\ *vb* : refer to — **mention** *n*

men·tor \'men‚tȯr, 'mentər\ *n* : instructor

menu \'menyü\ *n* **1** : restaurant's list of food **2** : list of offerings

me·ow \mē'aủ\ *n* : characteristic cry of a cat — **meow** *vb*

mer·can·tile \'mərkən‚tēl, -‚tīl\ *adj* : relating to merchants or trade

mer·ce·nary \'mərs³n‚erē\ *n, pl* **-nar·ies** : hired soldier ~ *adj* : serving only for money

mer·chan·dise \'mərchən‚dīz, -‚dīs\ *n* : goods bought and sold ~ *vb* **-dised; -dis·ing** : buy and sell — **mer·chan·dis·er** *n*

mer·chant \'mərchənt\ *n* : one who buys and sells

merchant marine *n* : commercial ships

mer·cu·ri·al \‚mər'kyủrēəl\ *adj* : unpredictable — **mer·cu·ri·al·ly** *adv* — **mer·cu·ri·al·ness** *n*

mer·cu·ry \'mərkyərē\ *n* : heavy liquid metallic chemical element

mer·cy \'mərsē\ *n, pl* **-cies** **1** : show of pity or leniency **2** : divine blessing — **mer·ci·ful** \-sifəl\ *adj* — **mer·ci·ful·ly** *adv* — **mer·ci·less** \-siləs\

adj — **mer·ci·less·ly** *adv* — **mercy** *adj*

mere \'mir\ *adj, superlative* **mer·est** : nothing more than — **mere·ly** *adv*

merge \'mərj\ *vb* **merged; merg·ing** 1 : unite 2 : blend — **merg·er** \'mərjər\ *n*

me·rid·i·an \mə'ridēən\ *n* : imaginary circle on the earth's surface passing through the poles — **meridian** *adj*

me·ringue \mə'raŋ\ *n* : baked dessert topping of beaten egg whites

me·ri·no \mə'rēnō\ *n, pl* **-nos** 1 : kind of sheep 2 : fine soft woolen yarn

mer·it \'merət\ *n* 1 : praise-worthy quality 2 *pl* : rights and wrongs of a legal case ~ *vb* : deserve — **mer·i·to·ri·ous** \,merə'tōrēəs\ *adj* — **mer·i·to·ri·ous·ly** *adv* — **mer·i·to·ri·ous·ness** *n*

mer·lot \mer'lō\ *n* : dry red wine

mer·maid \'mər,mād\ *n* : legendary female sea creature

mer·ry \'merē\ *adj* **-ri·er; -est** : full of high spirits — **mer·ri·ly** *adv* — **mer·ri·ment** \'merimənt\ *n* — **mer·ry·mak·er** \'merē,mākər\ *n* — **mer·ry·mak·ing** \'merē,mākiŋ\ *n*

merry–go–round *n* : revolving amusement ride

me·sa \'māsə\ *n* : steep flat-topped hill

mesdames *pl of* MADAM *or of* MADAME *or of* MRS.

mesdemoiselles *pl of* MADE-MOISELLE

mesh \'mesh\ *n* 1 : one of the openings in a net 2 : net fabric 3 : working contact ~ *vb* : fit together properly — **meshed** \'mesht\ *adj*

mes·mer·ize \'mezmə,rīz\ *vb* **-ized; -iz·ing** : hypnotize

mess \'mes\ *n* 1 : meal eaten by a group 2 : confused, dirty, or offensive state ~ *vb* 1 : make dirty or untidy 2 : put-ter 3 : interfere — **messy** *adj*

mes·sage \'mesij\ *n* : news, in-formation, or a command sent by one person to another

mes·sen·ger \'mesᵊnjər\ *n* : one who carries a message or does an errand

Mes·si·ah \mə'sīə\ *n* 1 : ex-pected deliverer of the Jews 2 : Jesus Christ 3 *not cap* : great leader

messieurs *pl of* MONSIEUR

Messrs. *pl of* MR.

mes·ti·zo \me'stēzō\ *n, pl* **-zos** : person of mixed blood

met *past of* MEET

me·tab·o·lism \mə'tabə,lizəm\ *n* : biochemical processes necessary to life — **met·a·bol·ic** \,metə'bälik\

adj — **me·tab·o·lize** \mə-ˈtabə͵līz\ *vb*

met·al \ˈmetᵊl\ *n* : shiny substance that can be melted and shaped and conducts heat and electricity — **me·tal·lic** \mə-ˈtalik\ *adj* — **met·al·ware** *n* — **met·al·work** *n* — **met·al·work·er** *n* — **met·al·work·ing** *n*

met·al·lur·gy \ˈmetᵊl͵ərjē\ *n* : science of metals — **met·al·lur·gi·cal** \͵metᵊlˈərjikəl\ *adj* — **met·al·lur·gist** \ˈmetᵊl͵ərjist\ *n*

meta·mor·pho·sis \͵metəˈmȯr-fəsəs\ *n, pl* **-pho·ses** \-͵sēz\ : sudden and drastic change (as of form) — **meta·mor·phose** \-͵fōz, -͵fōs\ *vb*

met·a·phor \ˈmetə͵fȯr, -fər\ *n* : use of a word denoting one kind of object or idea in place of another to suggest a likeness between them — **met·a·phor·i·cal** \͵metəˈfȯrikəl\ *adj*

meta·phys·ics \͵metəˈfiziks\ *n* : study of the causes and nature of things — **meta·phys·i·cal** \-ˈfizəkəl\ *adj*

mete \ˈmēt\ *vb* **met·ed; met·ing** : allot

me·te·or \ˈmētēər, -ē͵ȯr\ *n* : small body that produces a streak of light as it burns up in the atmosphere

me·te·or·ic \͵mētēˈȯrik\ *adj* **1** : relating to a meteor **2** : sudden and spectacular — **me·te·or·i·cal·ly** \-iklē\ *adv*

me·te·or·ite \ˈmētēə͵rīt\ *n* : meteor that reaches the earth

me·te·o·rol·o·gy \͵mētēə-ˈräləjē\ *n* : science of weather — **me·te·o·ro·log·ic** \͵mētē-͵ȯrəˈläjik\, **me·te·o·ro·log·i·cal** \-ˈläjikəl\ *adj* — **me·te·o·rol·o·gist** \-ēəˈräləjist\ *n*

¹me·ter \ˈmētər\ *n* : rhythm in verse or music

²meter *n* : unit of length equal to 39.37 inches

³meter *n* : measuring instrument

meth·a·done \ˈmethə͵dōn\ *n* : synthetic addictive narcotic

meth·ane \ˈmeth͵ān\ *n* : colorless odorless flammable gas

meth·a·nol \ˈmethə͵nȯl, -͵nōl\ *n* : volatile flammable poisonous liquid

meth·od \ˈmethəd\ *n* **1** : procedure for achieving an end **2** : orderly arrangement or plan — **me·thod·i·cal** \mə-ˈthädikəl\ *adj* — **me·thod·i·cal·ly** \-klē\ *adv* — **me·thod·i·cal·ness** *n*

me·tic·u·lous \məˈtikyələs\ *adj* : extremely careful in attending to details — **me·tic·u·lous·ly** *adv* — **me·tic·u·lous·ness** *n*

met·ric \ˈmetrik\, **met·ri·cal** \-trikəl\ *adj* : relating to meter or the metric system — **met·ri·cal·ly** *adv*

metric system *n* : system of weights and measures using the meter and kilogram

met·ro·nome \'metrə,nōm\ *n* : instrument that ticks regularly to mark a beat in music

me·trop·o·lis \mə'träpələs\ *n* : major city — **met·ro·pol·i·tan** \,metrə'pälət^ən\ *adj*

met·tle \'met^əl\ *n* : spirit or courage — **met·tle·some** \-səm\ *adj*

mez·za·nine \'mez^ən,ēn, ,mez^ən'ēn\ *n* **1** : intermediate level between 2 main floors **2** : lowest balcony

mez·zo–so·pra·no \,metsōsə'pranō, ,medz-\ *n* : voice between soprano and contralto

mi·as·ma \mī'azmə\ *n* **1** : noxious vapor **2** : harmful influence — **mi·as·mic** \-mik\ *adj*

mi·ca \'mīkə\ *n* : mineral separable into thin transparent sheets

mice *pl of* MOUSE

mi·cro \'mīkrō\ *adj* : very small

mi·crobe \'mī,krōb\ *n* : disease-causing microorganism — **mi·cro·bi·al** \mī'krōbēəl\ *adj*

mi·cro·bi·ol·o·gy \,mīkrōbī'äləjē\ *n* : biology dealing with microscopic life — **mi·cro·bi·o·log·i·cal** \'mīkrō,bīə'läjikəl\ *adj* — **mi·cro·bi·ol·o·gist** \,mīkrōbī'äləjist\ *n*

mi·cro·com·put·er \'mīkrōkəm,pyütər\ *n* : small computer that uses a microprocessor

mi·cro·cosm \'mīkrə,käzəm\ *n* : one thought of as a miniature universe

mi·cro·film \-,film\ *n* : small film recording printed matter — **microfilm** *vb*

mi·crom·e·ter \mī'krämətər\ *n* : instrument for measuring minute distances

mi·cro·min·i·a·tur·ized \,mīkrō'minēəchə,rīzd, -'minichə-\ *adj* : reduced to a very small size — **mi·cro·min·i·a·tur·iza·tion** \-,minēə,chùrə'zāshən, -,mini,chùr-, -chər-\ *n*

mi·cron \'mī,krän\ *n* : one millionth of a meter

mi·cro·or·gan·ism \,mīkrō'ôrgə,nizəm\ *n* : very tiny living thing

mi·cro·phone \'mīkrə,fōn\ *n* : instrument for changing sound waves into variations of an electric current

mi·cro·pro·ces·sor \'mīkrō,präsesər\ *n* : miniaturized computer processing unit on a single chip

mi·cro·scope \-,skōp\ *n* : optical device for magnifying tiny objects — **mi·cro·scop·ic**

\ˌmīkrə'skäpik\ *adj* — **mi·cro·scop·i·cal·ly** *adv* — **mi·cros·copy** \mī'kräskəpē\ *n*

mi·cro·wave \'mīkrə͵wāv\ *n* **1** : short radio wave **2** : oven that cooks food using microwaves ∼ *vb* : heat or cook in a microwave oven — **mi·cro·wav·able, mi·cro·wave·able** \ˌmīkrə'wāvəbəl\ *adj*

mid \'mid\ *adj* : middle — **mid·point** *n* — **mid·stream** *n* — **mid·sum·mer** *n* — **mid·town** *n or adj* — **mid·week** *n* — **mid·win·ter** *n* — **mid·year** *n*

mid·air *n* : a point in the air well above the ground

mid·day *n* : noon

mid·dle \'mid°l\ *adj* **1** : equally distant from the extremes **2** : being at neither extreme ∼ *n* : middle part or point

Middle Ages *n pl* : period from about A.D. 500 to about 1500

mid·dle·man \-͵man\ *n* : dealer or agent between the producer and consumer

mid·dling \'midliŋ, -lən\ *adj* **1** : of middle or medium size, degree, or quality **2** : mediocre

midge \'mij\ *n* : very tiny fly

midg·et \'mijət\ *n* : very small person or thing

mid·land \'midlənd, -͵land\ *n* : interior of a country

mid·most *adj* : being nearest the middle — **midmost** *adv*

mid·night *n* : 12 o'clock at night

mid·riff \'mid͵rif\ *n* : mid= region of the torso

mid·ship·man \'mid͵ship-mən, ͵mid'ship-\ *n* : student naval officer

midst \'midst\ *n* : position close to or surrounded by others — **midst** *prep*

mid·way \'mid͵wā\ *n* : concessions and amusements at a carnival ∼ *adv* : in the middle

mid·wife \'mid͵wīf\ *n* : person who aids at childbirth — **mid·wife·ry** \mid'wifərē, -'wīf-\ *n*

mien \'mēn\ *n* : appearance

miff \'mif\ *vb* : upset or peeve

¹might \'mīt\ *past of* MAY — used to express permission or possibility or as a polite alternative to *may*

²might *n* : power or resources

mighty \'mītē\ *adj* **might·i·er; -est 1** : very strong **2** : great — **might·i·ly** *adv* — **might·i·ness** *n* — **mighty** *adv*

mi·graine \'mī͵grān\ *n* : severe headache often with nausea

mi·grant \'mīgrənt\ *n* : one who moves frequently to find work

mi·grate \\'mī͵grāt\\ *vb* **-grat-ed; -grat·ing 1** : move from one place to another **2** : pass periodically from one region or climate to another — **mi-gra·tion** \\mī'grāshən\\ *n* — **mi·gra·to·ry** \\'mīgrə͵tōrē\\ *adj*

mild \\'mīld\\ *adj* **1** : gentle in nature or behavior **2** : moderate in action or effect — **mild-ly** *adv* — **mild·ness** *n*

mil·dew \\'mil͵dü, -͵dyü\\ *n* : whitish fungal growth — **mildew** *vb*

mile \\'mīl\\ *n* : unit of length equal to 5280 feet

mile·age \\'mīlij\\ *n* **1** : allowance per mile for traveling expenses **2** : amount or rate of use expressed in miles

mile·stone *n* : significant point in development

mi·lieu \\mēl'yü, -'yœ̄\\ *n, pl* **-lieus** *or* **-lieux** \\-'yüz, -'yœ̄\\ : surroundings or setting

mil·i·tant \\'milətənt\\ *adj* : aggressively active or hostile — **mil·i·tan·cy** \\-tənsē\\ *n* — **militant** *n* — **mil·i·tant·ly** *adv*

mil·i·tar·ism \\'milətə͵rizəm\\ *n* : dominance of military ideals or of a policy of aggressive readiness for war — **mil·i·ta·rist** \\-rist\\ *n* — **mil·i·tar·is·tic** \\͵milətə'ristik\\ *adj*

mil·i·tary \\'milə͵terē\\ *adj* **1** : relating to soldiers, arms, or war **2** : relating to or performed by armed forces ～ *n* : armed forces or the people in them — **mil·i·tar·i·ly** \\͵milə-'terəlē\\ *adv*

mil·i·tate \\-͵tāt\\ *vb* **-tat-ed; -tat·ing** : have an effect

mi·li·tia \\mə'lishə\\ *n* : civilian soldiers — **mi·li·tia·man** \\-mən\\ *n*

milk \\'milk\\ *n* : white nutritive fluid secreted by female mammals for feeding their young ～ *vb* **1** : draw off the milk of **2** : draw something from as if by milking — **milk-er** *n* — **milk·i·ness** \\-ēnəs\\ *n* — **milky** *adj*

milk·man \\-͵man, -mən\\ *n* : man who sells or delivers milk

milk·weed *n* : herb with milky juice

¹mill \\'mil\\ *n* **1** : building in which grain is ground into flour **2** : manufacturing plant **3** : machine used esp. for forming or processing ～ *vb* **1** : subject to a process in a mill **2** : move in a circle — **mill·er** *n*

²mill *n* : ¹/₁₀ cent

mil·len·ni·um \\mə'lenēəm\\ *n, pl* **-nia** \\-ēə\\ *or* **-niums** : a period of 1000 years

mil·let \\'milət\\ *n* : cereal and forage grass with small seeds

mil·li·gram \\'milə͵gram\\ *n* : ¹/₁₀₀₀ gram

mil·li·li·ter \-ˌlētər\ *n* : ¹⁄₁₀₀₀ liter

mil·li·me·ter \-ˌmētər\ : ¹⁄₁₀₀₀ meter

mil·li·ner \ˈmilənər\ *n* : person who makes or sells women's hats — **mil·li·nery** \ˈmiləˌnerē\ *n*

mil·lion \ˈmilyən\ *n, pl* **millions** *or* **million** : 1000 thousands — **million** *adj* — **millionth** \-yənth\ *adj or n*

mil·lion·aire \ˌmilyəˈnar, ˈmilyəˌnar\ *n* : person worth a million or more (as of dollars)

mil·li·pede \ˈmiləˌpēd\ *n* : longbodied arthropod with 2 pairs of legs on most segments

mill·stone *n* : either of 2 round flat stones used for grinding grain

mime \ˈmīm\ *n* **1** : mimic **2** : pantomime — **mime** *vb*

mim·eo·graph \ˈmimēəˌgraf\ *n* : machine for making many stencil copies — **mimeograph** *vb*

mim·ic \ˈmimik\ *n* : one that mimics ∼ *vb* **-icked; -ick·ing** **1** : imitate closely **2** : ridicule by imitation — **mim·ic·ry** \ˈmimikrē\ *n*

min·a·ret \ˌminəˈret\ *n* : tower attached to a mosque

mince \ˈmins\ *vb* **minced; minc·ing** **1** : cut into small pieces **2** : choose (one's words) carefully **3** : walk in a prim affected manner

mind \ˈmīnd\ *n* **1** : memory **2** : the part of an individual that feels, perceives, and esp. reasons **3** : intention **4** : normal mental condition **5** : opinion **6** : intellectual ability ∼ *vb* **1** : attend to **2** : obey **3** : be concerned about **4** : be careful — **mind·ed** *adj* — **mind·less** \ˈmīndləs\ *adj* — **mind·less·ly** *adv* — **mind·less·ness** *n*

mind·ful \-fəl\ *adj* : aware or attentive — **mind·ful·ly** *adv* — **mind·ful·ness** *n*

¹mine \ˈmīn\ *pron* : that which belongs to me

²mine \ˈmīn\ *n* **1** : excavation from which minerals are taken **2** : explosive device placed in the ground or water for destroying enemy vehicles or vessels that later pass ∼ *vb* **mined; min·ing** **1** : get ore from **2** : place military mines in — **mine·field** *n* — **min·er** *n*

min·er·al \ˈminərəl\ *n* **1** : crystalline substance not of organic origin **2** : useful natural substance (as coal) obtained from the ground — **mineral** *adj*

min·er·al·o·gy \ˌminəˈrāləjē, -ˈral-\ *n* : science dealing with minerals — **min·er·al·og·i·cal** \ˌminərəˈläjikəl\ *adj* —

min·er·al·o·gist \ˌminəˈrälə-jist, -ˈral-\ *n*

min·gle \ˈmiŋgəl\ *vb* **-gled; -gling** : bring together or mix

mini- *comb form* : miniature or of small dimensions

min·ia·ture \ˈminēəˌchùr, ˈminiˌchùr, -chər\ *n* : tiny copy or very small version — **miniature** *adj* — **min·ia·tur·ist** \-ˌchùrist, -chər-\ *n* — **min·ia·tur·ize** \-ēəchəˌrīz, -ichə-\ *vb*

mini·bike \ˈminēˌbīk\ *n* : small motorcycle

mini·bus \-ˌbəs\ *n* : small bus

mini·com·put·er \-kəmˌpyütər\ *n* : computer intermediate between a mainframe and a microcomputer in size and speed

mini·course \-ˌkōrs\ *n* : short course of study

min·i·mal \ˈminəməl\ *adj* : relating to or being a minimum — **min·i·mal·ly** *adv*

min·i·mize \ˈminəˌmīz\ *vb* **-mized; -miz·ing 1** : reduce to a minimum **2** : underestimate intentionally

min·i·mum \ˈminəməm\ *n, pl* **-ma** \-mə\ *or* **-mums** : lowest quantity or amount — **minimum** *adj*

min·ion \ˈminyən\ *n* **1** : servile dependent **2** : subordinate official

mini·se·ries \ˈminēˌsirēz\ *n* : television story in several parts

mini·skirt \-ˌskərt\ *n* : very short skirt

min·is·ter \ˈminəstər\ *n* **1** : Protestant member of the clergy **2** : high officer of state **3** : diplomatic representative ～ *vb* : give aid or service — **min·is·te·ri·al** \ˌminəˈstirēəl\ *adj* — **min·is·tra·tion** *n*

min·is·try \ˈminəstrē\ *n, pl* **-tries 1** : office or duties of a minister **2** : body of ministers **3** : government department headed by a minister

mini·van \ˈminēˌvan\ *n* : small van

mink \ˈmiŋk\ *n, pl* **mink** *or* **minks** : weasellike mammal or its soft brown fur

min·now \ˈminō\ *n, pl* **-nows** : small freshwater fish

mi·nor \ˈmīnər\ *adj* **1** : less in size, importance, or value **2** : not serious ～ *n* **1** : person not yet of legal age **2** : secondary field of academic specialization

mi·nor·i·ty \məˈnȯrətē, mī-\ *n, pl* **-ties 1** : time or state of being a minor **2** : smaller number (as of votes) **3** : part of a population differing from others (as in race or religion)

min·strel \ˈminstrəl\ *n* **1** : medieval singer of verses **2**

: performer in a program usu. of black American songs and jokes — **min·strel·sy** \-sē\ *n*

¹mint \'mint\ *n* **1** : fragrant herb that yields a flavoring oil **2** : mint-flavored piece of candy — **minty** *adj*

²mint *n* **1** : place where coins are made **2** : vast sum ~ *adj* : unused — **mint** *vb* — **mint·er** *n*

min·u·et \ˌminyə'wet\ *n* : slow graceful dance

mi·nus \'mīnəs\ *prep* **1** : diminished by **2** : lacking ~ *n* : negative quantity or quality

mi·nus·cule \'minəsˌkyül, min'əs-\, **min·is·cule** \'minəs-\ *adj* : very small

¹min·ute \'minət\ *n* **1** : 60th part of an hour or of a degree **2** : short time **3** *pl* : official record of a meeting

²mi·nute \mī'nüt, mə-, -'nyüt\ *adj* **-nut·er; -est** **1** : very small **2** : marked by close attention to details — **mi·nute·ly** *adv* — **mi·nute·ness** *n*

mir·a·cle \'mirikəl\ *n* **1** : extraordinary event taken as a sign of divine intervention in human affairs **2** : marvel — **mi·rac·u·lous** \mə'rakyələs\ *adj* — **mi·rac·u·lous·ly** *adv*

mi·rage \mə'räzh\ *n* : distant illusion caused by atmospheric conditions (as in the desert)

mire \'mīr\ *n* : heavy deep mud ~ *vb* **mired; mir·ing** : stick or sink in mire — **miry** *adj*

mir·ror \'mirər\ *n* : smooth surface (as of glass) that reflects images ~ *vb* : reflect in or as if in a mirror

mirth \'mərth\ *n* : gladness and laughter — **mirth·ful** \-fəl\ *adj* — **mirth·ful·ly** *adv* — **mirth·ful·ness** *n* — **mirth·less** *adj*

mis·an·thrope \'misᵊnˌthrōp\ *n* : one who hates mankind — **mis·an·throp·ic** \ˌmisᵊn'thräpik\ *adj* — **mis·an·thro·py** \mis'anthrəpē\ *n*

mis·ap·pre·hend \ˌmisˌaprə'hend\ *vb* : misunderstand — **mis·ap·pre·hen·sion** *n*

mis·ap·pro·pri·ate \ˌmisə'prōprēˌāt\ *vb* : take dishonestly for one's own use — **mis·ap·pro·pri·a·tion** *n*

mis·be·got·ten \-bi'gätᵊn\ *adj* **1** : illegitimate **2** : ill-conceived

mis·be·have \ˌmisbi'hāv\ *vb* : behave improperly — **mis·be·hav·er** *n* — **mis·be·hav·ior** *n*

mis·cal·cu·late \mis'kalkyəˌlāt\ *vb* : calculate wrongly — **mis·cal·cu·la·tion** *n*

mis·car·ry \ˌmis'karē, 'misˌkarē\ *vb* **1** : give birth prematurely before the fetus can survive **2** : go wrong or be unsuccessful — **mis·car·riage** \-rij\ *n*

mis·ce·ge·na·tion \mis‚ejə'nā-shən, ‚misijə'nā-\ *n* : marriage between persons of different races

mis·cel·la·neous \‚misə'lānēəs\ *adj* : consisting of many things of different kinds — **mis·cel·la·neous·ly** *adv* — **mis·cel·la·neous·ness** *n*

mis·cel·la·ny \'misə‚lānē\ *n, pl* **-nies** : collection of various things

mis·chance \mis'chans\ *n* : bad luck

mis·chief \'mischəf\ *n* : conduct esp. of a child that annoys or causes minor damage

mis·chie·vous \'mischəvəs\ *adj* **1** : causing annoyance or minor injury **2** : irresponsibly playful — **mis·chie·vous·ly** *adv* — **mis·chie·vous·ness** *n*

mis·con·ceive \‚miskən'sēv\ *vb* : interpret incorrectly — **mis·con·cep·tion** *n*

mis·con·duct \mis'kändəkt\ *n* **1** : mismanagement **2** : bad behavior

mis·con·strue \‚miskən'strü\ *vb* : misinterpret — **mis·con·struc·tion** *n*

mis·cre·ant \'miskrēənt\ *n* : one who behaves criminally or viciously — **miscreant** *adj*

mis·deed \mis'dēd\ *n* : wrong deed

mis·de·mean·or \‚misdi'mēnər\ *n* : crime less serious than a felony

mi·ser \'mīzər\ *n* : person who hoards and is stingy with money — **mi·ser·li·ness** \-lēnəs\ *n* — **mi·ser·ly** *adj*

mis·er·a·ble \'mizərəbəl\ *adj* **1** : wretchedly deficient **2** : causing extreme discomfort **3** : shameful — **mis·er·a·ble·ness** *n* — **mis·er·a·bly** \-blē\ *adv*

mis·ery \'mizərē\ *n, pl* **-er·ies** : suffering and want caused by distress or poverty

mis·fire \mis'fīr\ *vb* **1** : fail to fire **2** : miss an intended effect — **mis·fire** \'mis‚fīr\ *n*

mis·fit \'mis‚fit, mis'fit\ *n* : person poorly adjusted to his environment

mis·for·tune \mis'fȯrchən\ *n* **1** : bad luck **2** : unfortunate condition or event

mis·giv·ing \mis'giviŋ\ *n* : doubt or concern

mis·guid·ed \mis'gīdəd\ *adj* : mistaken, uninformed, or deceived

mis·hap \'mis‚hap\ *n* : accident

mis·in·form \‚misᵊn'fȯrm\ *vb* : give wrong information to — **mis·in·for·ma·tion** \‚mis‚infər'māshən\ *n*

mis·in·ter·pret \‚misᵊn'tər-prət\ *vb* : understand or explain wrongly — **mis·in·ter-**

pre·ta·tion \-ˌtərprə'tāshən\ *n*

mis·judge \mis'jəj\ *vb* : judge incorrectly or unjustly — **mis·judg·ment** *n*

mis·lay \mis'lā\ *vb* **-laid; -lay·ing** : misplace

mis·lead \mis'lēd\ *vb* **-led; -lead·ing** : lead in a wrong direction or into error — **mis·lead·ing·ly** *adv*

mis·man·age \mis'manij\ *vb* : manage badly — **mis·man·age·ment** *n*

mis·no·mer \mis'nōmər\ *n* : wrong name

mi·sog·y·nist \mə'säjənist\ *n* : one who hates or distrusts women — **mi·sog·y·nis·tic** \mə,säjə'nistik\ *adj* — **mi·sog·y·ny** \-nē\ *n*

mis·place \mis'plās\ *vb* : put in a wrong or unremembered place

mis·print \'mis,print, mis'-\ *n* : error in printed matter

mis·pro·nounce \ˌmisprə'naùns\ *vb* : pronounce incorrectly — **mis·pro·nun·ci·a·tion** *n*

mis·quote \mis'kwōt\ *vb* : quote incorrectly — **mis·quo·ta·tion** \ˌmiskwō'tāshən\ *n*

mis·read \mis'rēd\ *vb* **-read; -read·ing** : read or interpret incorrectly

mis·rep·re·sent \ˌmis,repri'zent\ *vb* : represent falsely or unfairly — **mis·rep·re·sen·ta·tion** *n*

mis·rule \mis'rül\ *vb* : govern badly ∼ *n* **1** : bad or corrupt government **2** : disorder

¹**miss** \'mis\ *vb* **1** : fail to hit, reach, or contact **2** : notice the absence of **3** : fail to obtain **4** : avoid **5** : omit — **miss** *n*

²**miss** *n* : young unmarried woman or girl — often used as a title

mis·sal \'misəl\ *n* : book containing what is said at mass during the year

mis·shap·en \mis'shāpən\ *adj* : distorted

mis·sile \'misəl\ *n* : object (as a stone or rocket) thrown or shot

miss·ing \'misiŋ\ *adj* : absent or lost

mis·sion \'mishən\ *n* **1** : ministry sent by a church to spread its teaching **2** : group of diplomats sent to a foreign country **3** : task

mis·sion·ary \'mishə,nerē\ *adj* : relating to religious missions ∼ *n, pl* **-ar·ies** : person sent to spread religious faith

mis·sive \'misiv\ *n* : letter

mis·spell \mis'spel\ *vb* : spell incorrectly — **mis·spell·ing** *n*

mis·state \mis'stāt\ *vb* : state incorrectly — **mis·state·ment** *n*

mis·step \'mis,step\ *n* **1** : wrong step **2** : mistake

mist \'mist\ *n* : particles of water falling as fine rain

mis·take \mə'stāk\ *n* **1** : misunderstanding or wrong belief **2** : wrong action or statement — **mistake** *vb*

mis·tak·en \-'stākən\ *adj* : having a wrong opinion or incorrect information — **mis·tak·en·ly** *adv*

mis·ter \'mistər\ *n* : sir — used without a name in addressing a man

mis·tle·toe \'misəl,tō\ *n* : parasitic green shrub with waxy white berries

mis·treat \mis'trēt\ *vb* : treat badly — **mis·treat·ment** *n*

mis·tress \'mistrəs\ *n* **1** : woman in control **2** : a woman not his wife with whom a married man has recurrent sexual relations

mis·tri·al \mis'trīəl\ *n* : trial that has no legal effect

mis·trust \-'trəst\ *n* : lack of confidence ~ *vb* : have no confidence in — **mis·trust·ful** \-fəl\ *adj* — **mis·trust·ful·ly** *adv* — **mis·trust·ful·ness** *n*

misty \'mistē\ *adj* **mist·i·er; -est 1** : obscured by mist **2**

: tearful — **mist·i·ly** *adv* — **mist·i·ness** *n*

mis·un·der·stand \,mis,əndər-'stand\ *vb* **1** : fail to understand **2** : interpret incorrectly

mis·un·der·stand·ing \-'standiŋ\ *n* **1** : wrong interpretation **2** : disagreement

mis·use \mis'yüz\ *vb* **1** : use incorrectly **2** : mistreat — **misuse** \-'yüs\ *n*

mite \'mīt\ *n* **1** : tiny spiderlike animal **2** : small amount

mi·ter, mi·tre \'mītər\ *n* **1** : bishop's headdress **2** : angular joint in wood ~ *vb* **-tered** *or* **-tred; -ter·ing** *or* **-tring** \'mītəriŋ\ : bevel the ends of for a miter joint

mit·i·gate \'mitə,gāt\ *vb* **-gated; -gat·ing** : make less severe — **mit·i·ga·tion** \,mitə-'gāshən\ *n* — **mit·i·ga·tive** \'mitə,gātiv\ *adj*

mi·to·sis \mī'tōsəs\ *n, pl* **-to·ses** \-,sēz\ : process of forming 2 cell nuclei from one — **mi·tot·ic** \-'tätik\ *adj*

mitt \'mit\ *n* : mittenlike baseball glove

mit·ten \'mitᵊn\ *n* : hand covering without finger sections

mix \'miks\ *vb* : combine or join into one mass or group ~ *n* : commercially prepared food mixture — **mix·able** *adj* — **mix·er** *n* — **mix up** *vb* : confuse

mix·ture \'mikschər\ *n* : act or product of mixing

mix–up *n* : instance of confusion

mne·mon·ic \ni'mänik\ *adj* : relating to or assisting memory

moan \'mōn\ *n* : low prolonged sound of pain or grief — **moan** *vb*

moat \'mōt\ *n* : deep wide trench around a castle

mob \'mäb\ *n* **1** : large disorderly crowd **2** : criminal gang ∼ *vb* **-bb-** : crowd around and attack or annoy

mo·bile \'mōbəl, -ˌbēl, -ˌbīl\ *adj* : capable of moving or being moved ∼ \'mō̇ˌbēl\ *n* : suspended art construction with freely moving parts — **mo·bil·i·ty** \mō'bilətē\ *n*

mo·bi·lize \'mōbəˌlīz\ *vb* **-lized; -liz·ing** : assemble and make ready for war duty — **mo·bi·li·za·tion** \ˌmōbələ-'zāshən\ *n*

moc·ca·sin \'mäkəsən\ *n* **1** : heelless shoe **2** : venomous U.S. snake

mo·cha \'mōkə\ *n* **1** : mixture of coffee and chocolate **2** : dark brown color

mock \'mäk, 'mȯk\ *vb* **1** : ridicule **2** : mimic in derision ∼ *adj* **1** : simulated **2** : phony — **mock·er** *n* —

mock·ery \-ərē\ *n* — **mock·ing·ly** *adv*

mock·ing·bird \'mäkiŋˌbərd, 'mȯk-\ *n* : songbird that mimics other birds

mode \'mōd\ *n* **1** : particular form or variety **2** : style — **mod·al** \-ᵊl\ *adj* — **mod·ish** \'mōdish\ *adj*

mod·el \'mädᵊl\ *n* **1** : structural design **2** : miniature representation **3** : something worthy of copying **4** : one who poses for an artist or displays clothes **5** : type or design ∼ *vb* **-eled** *or* **-elled; -el·ing** *or* **-el·ling 1** : shape **2** : work as a model ∼ *adj* **1** : serving as a pattern **2** : being a miniature representation of

mo·dem \'mōdəm, -ˌdem\ *n* : device by which a computer communicates with another computer over telephone lines

mod·er·ate \'mädərət\ *adj* : avoiding extremes ∼ \'mädəˌrāt\ *vb* **-at·ed; -at·ing 1** : lessen the intensity of **2** : act as a moderator — **moderate** *n* — **mod·er·ate·ly** *adv* — **mod·er·ate·ness** *n* — **mod·er·a·tion** \ˌmädə'rā-shən\ *n*

mod·er·a·tor \'mädəˌrātər\ *n* : one who presides

mod·ern \'mädərn\ *adj* : relating to or characteristic of the present — **modern** *n* — **mo·der·ni·ty** \mə'dərnətē\ *n* — **mod·ern·i·za·tion** \ˌmädərnə-'zāshən\ *n* — **mod·ern·ize** \'mädərˌnīz\ *vb* — **mod·ern·iz·er** \'mädərˌnīzər\ *n* — **mod·ern·ly** *adv* — **mod·ern·ness** *n*

mod·est \'mädəst\ *adj* **1** : having a moderate estimate of oneself **2** : reserved or decent in thoughts or actions **3** : limited in size, amount, or aim — **mod·est·ly** *adv* — **mod·es·ty** \-əstē\ *n*

mod·i·cum \'mädikəm\ *n* : small amount

mod·i·fy \'mädəˌfī\ *vb* **-fied; -fy·ing 1** : limit the meaning of **2** : change — **mod·i·fi·ca·tion** \ˌmädəfə'kāshən\ *n* — **mod·i·fi·er** \'mädəˌfīər\ *n*

mod·u·lar \'mäjələr\ *adj* : built with standardized units — **mod·u·lar·ized** \-ləˌrīzd\ *adj*

mod·u·late \'mäjəˌlāt\ *vb* **-lat·ed; -lat·ing 1** : keep in proper measure or proportion **2** : vary a radio wave — **mod·u·la·tion** \ˌmäjə'lāshən\ *n* — **mod·u·la·tor** \'mäjəˌlātər\ *n* — **mod·u·la·to·ry** \-ləˌtōrē\ *adj*

mod·ule \'mäjül\ *n* : standardized unit

mo·gul \'mōgəl\ *n* : important person

mo·hair \'mōˌhar\ *n* : fabric made from the hair of the Angora goat

moist \'mȯist\ *adj* : slightly or moderately wet — **moist·en** \'mȯisᵊn\ *vb* — **moist·en·er** \'mȯisᵊnər\ *n* — **moist·ly** *adv* — **moist·ness** *n*

mois·ture \'mȯischər\ *n* : small amount of liquid that causes dampness — **mois·tur·ize** \-chəˌrīz\ *vb* — **mois·tur·iz·er** *n*

mo·lar \'mōlər\ *n* : grinding tooth — **molar** *adj*

mo·las·ses \mə'lasəz\ *n* : thick brown syrup from raw sugar

¹mold \'mōld\ *n* : crumbly organic soil

²mold *n* : frame or cavity for forming ∼ *vb* : shape in or as if in a mold — **mold·er** *n*

³mold *n* : surface growth of fungus ∼ *vb* : become moldy — **mold·i·ness** \'mōldēnəs\ *n* — **moldy** *adj*

mold·er \'mōldər\ *vb* : crumble

mold·ing \'mōldiŋ\ *n* : decorative surface, plane, or strip

¹mole \'mōl\ *n* : spot on the skin

²mole *n* : small burrowing mammal — **mole·hill** *n*

mol·e·cule \'mäliˌkyül\ *n* : small particle of matter — **mo·lec·u·lar** \mə'lekyələr\ *adj*

mole·skin \-ˌskin\ *n* : heavy cotton fabric

mo·lest \mə'lest\ *vb* **1** : annoy or disturb **2** : force physical and usu. sexual contact on — **mo·les·ta·tion** \ˌmōlˌes-ˈtāshən, ˌmäl-\ *n* — **mo·lest·er** *n*

mol·li·fy \ˈmäləˌfī\ *vb* -**fied**; -**fy·ing** : soothe in temper — **mol·li·fi·ca·tion** \ˌmäləfəˈkāshən\ *n*

mol·lusk, mol·lusc \ˈmäləsk\ *n* : shelled aquatic invertebrate — **mol·lus·can** \məˈləskən\ *adj*

mol·ly·cod·dle \ˈmäleˌkädᵊl\ *vb* -**dled**; -**dling** : pamper

molt \ˈmōlt\ *vb* : shed hair, feathers, outer skin, or horns periodically — **molt** *n* — **molt·er** *n*

mol·ten \ˈmōltᵊn\ *adj* : fused or liquefied by heat

mom \ˈmäm, ˈməm\ *n* : mother

mo·ment \ˈmōmənt\ *n* **1** : tiny portion of time **2** : time of excellence **3** : importance

mo·men·tar·i·ly \ˌmōmən-ˈterəlē\ *adv* **1** : for a moment **2** : at any moment

mo·men·tary \ˈmōmənˌterē\ *adj* : continuing only a moment — **mo·men·tar·i·ness** *n*

mo·men·tous \mōˈmentəs\ *adj* : very important — **mo·men·tous·ly** *adv* — **mo·men·tous·ness** *n*

mo·men·tum \-əm\ *n, pl* -**ta** \-ə\ *or* -**tums** : force of a moving body

mon·arch \ˈmänərk, -ˌärk\ *n* : ruler of a kingdom or empire — **mo·nar·chi·cal** \məˈnärkikəl\ *adj*

mon·ar·chist \ˈmänərkist\ *n* : believer in monarchical government — **mon·ar·chism** \-ˌkizəm\ *n*

mon·ar·chy \ˈmänərkē\ *n, pl* -**chies** : realm of a monarch

mon·as·tery \ˈmänəˌsterē\ *n, pl* -**ter·ies** : house for monks

mo·nas·tic \məˈnastik\ *adj* : relating to monasteries, monks, or nuns — **monastic** *n* — **mo·nas·ti·cal·ly** \-tiklē\ *adv* — **mo·nas·ti·cism** \-tə-ˌsizəm\ *n*

Mon·day \ˈməndā, -dē\ *n* : 2d day of the week

mon·e·tary \ˈmänəˌterē, ˈmən-\ *adj* : relating to money

mon·ey \ˈmənē\ *n, pl* -**eys** *or* -**ies** \ˈmənēz\ **1** : something (as coins or paper currency) used in buying **2** : wealth — **mon·eyed** \-ēd\ *adj* — **mon·ey·lend·er** *n*

mon·ger \ˈməngər, ˈmäŋ-\ *n* : dealer

mon·gol·ism \ˈmäŋgəˌlizəm\ *n* : congenital mental retardation — **Mon·gol·oid** \-gəˌlȯid\ *adj or n*

mon·goose \ˈmänˌgüs, ˈmäŋ-\ *n, pl* -**goos·es** : small agile mammal esp. of India

mon·grel \'mäŋgrəl, 'məŋ-\ *n* : offspring of mixed breed

mon·i·tor \'mänətər\ *n* **1** : student assistant **2** : television screen ~ *vb* : watch or observe esp. for quality

monk \'məŋk\ *n* : member of a religious order living in a monastery — **monk·ish** *adj*

mon·key \'məŋkē\ *n, pl* **-keys** : small long-tailed arboreal primate ~ *vb* **1** : fool **2** : tamper

mon·key·shines \-ˌshīnz\ *n pl* : pranks

monks·hood \'məŋksˌhúd\ *n* : poisonous herb with showy flowers

mon·o·cle \'mänikəl\ *n* : eyeglass for one eye

mo·nog·a·my \mə'nägəmē\ *n* **1** : marriage with one person at a time **2** : practice of having a single mate for a period of time — **mo·nog·a·mist** \mə'nägəmist\ *n* — **mo·nog·a·mous** \-məs\ *adj*

mono·gram \'mänəˌgram\ *n* : sign of identity made of initials — **monogram** *vb*

mono·graph \-ˌgraf\ *n* : learned treatise

mono·lin·gual \ˌmänə'liŋgwəl\ *adj* : using only one language

mono·lith \'mänᵊlˌith\ *n* **1** : single great stone **2** : single uniform massive whole —

mono·lith·ic \ˌmänᵊl'ithik\ *adj*

mono·logue \'mänᵊlˌóg\ *n* : long speech — **mono·logu·ist** \-ˌógist\, **mo·no·lo·gist** \mə'näləjist, 'mänᵊlˌógist\ *n*

mono·nu·cle·o·sis \ˌmänōˌnüklē'ōsəs, -ˌnyü-\ *n* : acute infectious disease

mo·nop·o·ly \mə'näpəlē\ *n, pl* **-lies** **1** : exclusive ownership or control of a commodity **2** : one controlling a monopoly — **mo·nop·o·list** \-list\ *n* — **mo·nop·o·lis·tic** \mə̯näpə'listik\ *adj* — **mo·nop·o·li·za·tion** \-lə'zāshən\ *n* — **mo·nop·o·lize** \mə'näpəˌlīz\ *vb*

mono·rail \'mänəˌrāl\ *n* : single rail for a vehicle or a vehicle or system using it

mono·syl·lab·ic \ˌmänəsə'labik\ *adj* : consisting of or using words of only one syllable — **mono·syl·la·ble** \'mänəˌsiləbəl\ *n*

mono·the·ism \'mänōthēˌizəm\ *n* : doctrine or belief that there is only one deity — **mono·the·ist** \-ˌthēist\ *n* — **mono·the·is·tic** \ˌmänōthē'istik\ *adj*

mono·tone \'mänəˌtōn\ *n* : succession of words in one unvarying tone

mo·not·o·nous \mə'nätᵊnəs\ *adj* **1** : sounded in one unvarying tone **2** : tediously uniform — **mo·not·o·nous·ly** *adv* — **mo·not·o·nous·ness** *n* — **mo·not·o·ny** \-ᵊnē\ *n*

mon·ox·ide \mə'näk‚sīd\ *n* : oxide containing one atom of oxygen in a molecule

mon·sieur \məs'yər, məsh-\ *n, pl* **mes·sieurs** \-yərz, mā-'syərz\ : man of high rank or station — used as a title for a man esp. of French nationality

mon·si·gnor \män'sēnyər\ *n, pl* **mon·si·gnors** *or* **mon·si·gno·ri** \‚män‚sēn'yōrē\ : Roman Catholic prelate — used as a title

mon·soon \män'sün\ *n* : periodic rainy season

mon·ster \'mänstər\ *n* **1** : abnormal or terrifying animal **2** : ugly, wicked, or cruel person — **mon·stros·i·ty** \män-'sträsətē\ *n* — **mon·strous** \'mänstrəs\ *adj* — **mon·strous·ly** *adv*

mon·tage \män'täzh\ *n* : artistic composition of several different elements

month \'mənth\ *n* : 12th part of a year — **month·ly** *adv or adj or n*

mon·u·ment \'mänyəmənt\ *n* : structure erected in remembrance

mon·u·men·tal \‚mänyə-'mentᵊl\ *adj* **1** : serving as a monument **2** : outstanding **3**

: very great — **mon·u·men·tal·ly** *adv*

moo \'mü\ *vb* : make the noise of a cow — **moo** *n*

mood \'müd\ *n* : state of mind or emotion

moody \'müdē\ *adj* **mood·i·er; -est 1** : sad **2** : subject to changing moods and esp. to bad moods — **mood·i·ly** \'müdᵊlē\ *adv* — **mood·i·ness** \-ēnəs\ *n*

moon \'mün\ *n* : natural satellite (as of earth) — **moon·beam** *n* — **moon·light** *n* — **moon·lit** *adj*

moon·light \-‚līt\ *vb* **-ed; -ing** : hold a 2d job — **moon·light·er** *n*

moon·shine *n* **1** : moonlight **2** : meaningless talk **3** : illegally distilled liquor

¹**moor** \'mu̇r\ *n* : open usu. swampy wasteland — **moor·land** \-lənd, -‚land\ *n*

²**moor** *vb* : fasten with line or anchor

moor·ing \-iŋ\ *n* : place where boat can be moored

moose \'müs\ *n, pl* **moose** : large heavy-antlered deer

moot \'müt\ *adj* : open to question

mop \'mäp\ *n* : floor-cleaning implement ~ *vb* **-pp-** : use a mop on

mope \'mōp\ *vb* **moped; mop·ing** : be sad or listless

mo·ped \\'mō͵ped\ *n* : low=powered motorbike

mo·raine \mə'rān\ *n* : glacial deposit of earth and stones

mor·al \\'mȯrəl\ *adj* **1** : relating to principles of right and wrong **2** : conforming to a standard of right behavior **3** : relating to or acting on the mind, character, or will ∼ *n* **1** : point of a story **2** *pl* : moral practices or teachings — **mor·al·ist** \\'mȯrəlist\ *n* — **mor·al·is·tic** \͵mȯrə'listik\ *adj* — **mor·al·i·ty** \mə'ralətē\ *n* — **mor·al·ize** \\'mȯrə͵līz\ *vb* — **mor·al·ly** *adv*

mo·rale \mə'ral\ *n* : emotional attitude

mo·rass \mə'ras\ *n* : swamp

mor·a·to·ri·um \͵mȯrə'tō-rēəm\ *n, pl* **-ri·ums** *or* **-ria** \-ēə\ : suspension of activity

mo·ray \\'mȯr͵ā, mə'rā\ *n* : savage eel

mor·bid \\'mȯrbəd\ *adj* **1** : relating to disease **2** : gruesome — **mor·bid·i·ty** \mȯr'bidətē\ *n* — **mor·bid·ly** *adv* — **mor·bid·ness** *n*

mor·dant \\'mȯrdᵊnt\ *adj* : sarcastic — **mor·dant·ly** *adv*

more \\'mōr\ *adj* **1** : greater **2** : additional ∼ *adv* **1** : in addition **2** : to a greater degree ∼ *n* **1** : greater quantity **2** : additional amount ∼ *pron* : additional ones

mo·rel \mə'rel\ *n* : pitted edible mushroom

more·over \mōr'ōvər\ *adv* : in addition

mo·res \\'mȯr͵āz, -ēz\ *n pl* : customs

morgue \\'mȯrg\ *n* : temporary holding place for dead bodies

mor·i·bund \\'mȯrə͵bənd\ *adj* : dying

morn \\'mȯrn\ *n* : morning

morn·ing \\'mȯrniŋ\ *n* : time from sunrise to noon

mo·ron \\'mōr͵än\ *n* **1** : mentally retarded person **2** : very stupid person — **mo·ron·ic** \mə'ränik\ *adj* — **mo·ron·i·cal·ly** *adv*

mo·rose \mə'rōs\ *adj* : sullen — **mo·rose·ly** *adv* — **mo·rose·ness** *n*

mor·phine \\'mȯr͵fēn\ *n* : addictive painkilling drug

mor·row \\'märō\ *n* : next day

Morse code \\'mȯrs-\ *n* : code of dots and dashes or long and short sounds used for transmitting messages

mor·sel \\'mȯrsəl\ *n* : small piece or quantity

mor·tal \\'mȯrtᵊl\ *adj* **1** : causing or subject to death **2** : extreme — **mortal** *n* — **mor·tal·i·ty** \mȯr'talətē\ *n* — **mor·tal·ly** \\'mȯrtᵊlē\ *adv*

mor·tar \\'mȯrtər\ *n* **1** : strong bowl **2** : short-barreled cannon

3 : masonry material used to cement bricks or stones in place — **mortar** *vb*

mort·gage \\'mȯrgij\\ *n* **:** transfer of property rights as security for a loan — **mortgage** *vb* — **mort·gag·ee** \\ˌmȯrgi'jē\\ *n* — **mort·ga·gor** \\ˌmȯrgi'jȯr\\ *n*

mor·ti·fy \\'mȯrtəˌfī\\ *vb* **-fied; -fy·ing 1 :** subdue by abstinence or self-inflicted pain **2 :** humiliate — **mor·ti·fi·ca·tion** \\ˌmȯrtəfə'kāshən\\ *n*

mor·tu·ary \\'mȯrchəˌwerē\\ *n, pl* **-ar·ies :** place where dead bodies are kept until burial

mo·sa·ic \\mō'zāik\\ *n* **:** inlaid stone decoration — **mosaic** *adj*

Mos·lem \\'mäzləm\\ *var of* MUSLIM

mosque \\'mäsk\\ *n* **:** building where Muslims worship

mos·qui·to \\mə'skētō\\ *n, pl* **-toes :** biting bloodsucking insect

moss \\'mȯs\\ *n* **:** green seedless plant — **mossy** *adj*

most \\'mōst\\ *adj* **1 :** majority of **2 :** greatest ~ *adv* **:** to the greatest or a very great degree ~ *n* **:** greatest amount ~ *pron* **:** greatest number or part

-most \\ˌmōst\\ *adj suffix* **:** most **:** most toward

most·ly \\'mōstlē\\ *adv* **:** mainly

mote \\'mōt\\ *n* **:** small particle

mo·tel \\mō'tel\\ *n* **:** hotel with rooms accessible from the parking lot

moth \\'mȯth\\ *n* **:** small pale insect related to the butterflies

moth·er \\'məthər\\ *n* **1 :** female parent **2 :** source ~ *vb* **1 :** give birth to **2 :** cherish or protect — **moth·er·hood** \\-ˌhu̇d\\ *n* — **moth·er·land** \\-ˌland\\ *n* — **moth·er·less** *adj* — **moth·er·ly** *adj*

moth·er–in–law *n, pl* **mothers–in–law :** spouse's mother

mo·tif \\mō'tēf\\ *n* **:** dominant theme

mo·tion \\'mōshən\\ *n* **1 :** act or instance of moving **2 :** proposal for action ~ *vb* **:** direct by a movement — **mo·tion·less** *adj* — **mo·tion·less·ly** *adv* — **mo·tion·less·ness** *n*

motion picture *n* **:** movie

mo·ti·vate \\'mōtəˌvāt\\ *vb* **-vat·ed; -vat·ing :** provide with a motive — **mo·ti·va·tion** \\ˌmōtə'vāshən\\ *n* — **mo·ti·va·tor** \\'mōtəˌvātər\\ *n*

mo·tive \\'mōtiv\\ *n* **:** cause of a person's action ~ *adj* **1 :** moving to action **2 :** relating to motion — **mo·tive·less** *adj*

mot·ley \\'mätlē\\ *adj* **:** of diverse colors or elements

mo·tor \\'mōtər\\ *n* **:** unit that supplies power or motion ~ *vb* **:** travel by automobile —

mo·tor·ist \-ist\ *n* — **mo·tor·ize** \'mōtə,rīz\ *vb*

mo·tor·bike *n* : lightweight motorcycle

mo·tor·boat *n* : engine-driven boat

mo·tor·car *n* : automobile

mo·tor·cy·cle *n* : 2-wheeled automotive vehicle — **mo·tor·cy·clist** *n*

mo·tor·truck *n* : automotive truck

mot·tle \'mät³l\ *vb* **-tled; -tling** : mark with spots of different color

mot·to \'mätō\ *n, pl* **-toes** : brief guiding rule

mould \'mōld\ *var of* MOLD

mound \'maund\ *n* : pile (as of earth)

¹**mount** \'maunt\ *n* : mountain

²**mount** *vb* **1** : increase in amount **2** : get up on **3** : put in position ∼ *n* **1** : frame or support **2** : horse to ride — **mount·able** *adj* — **mount·er** *n*

moun·tain \'maunt³n\ *n* : elevated land higher than a hill — **moun·tain·ous** \'maunt³nəs\ *adj* — **moun·tain·top** *n*

moun·tain·eer \,maunt³n'ir\ *n* : mountain resident or climber

moun·te·bank \'maunti,baŋk\ *n* : impostor

mourn \'mōrn\ *vb* : feel or express grief — **mourn·er** *n* — **mourn·ful** \-fəl\ *adj* — **mourn·ful·ly** *adv* — **mourn·ful·ness** *n* — **mourn·ing** *n*

mouse \'maus\ *n, pl* **mice** \'mīs\ **1** : small rodent **2** : device for controlling cursor movement on a computer display — **mouse·trap** *n or vb* — **mousy, mous·ey** \'mausē, -zē\ *adj*

mousse \'müs\ *n* **1** : light chilled dessert **2** : foamy hair-styling preparation

mous·tache \'məs,tash, məs-'tash\ *var of* MUSTACHE

mouth \'mauth\ *n* : opening through which an animal takes in food ∼ \'mauth\ *vb* **1** : speak **2** : repeat without comprehension or sincerity **3** : form soundlessly with the lips — **mouthed** \'mauthd, 'mautht\ *adj* — **mouth·ful** \-,ful\ *n*

mouth·piece *n* **1** : part (as of a musical instrument) held in or to the mouth **2** : spokesman

mou·ton \'mü,tän\ *n* : processed sheepskin

move \'müv\ *vb* **moved; moving** **1** : go or cause to go to another point **2** : change residence **3** : change or cause to change position **4** : take or cause to take action **5** : make a formal request **6** : stir the emotions ∼ *n* **1** : act or instance of moving **2** : step taken to achieve a goal — **mov-able, move·able** \-əbəl\ *adj* — **move·ment** *n* — **mov·er** *n*

mov·ie \'müvē\ *n* : projected picture in which persons and objects seem to move

¹**mow** \'maů\ *n* : part of a barn where hay or straw is stored

²**mow** \'mō\ *vb* **mowed; mowed** *or* **mown** \'mōn\; **mow·ing** : cut with a machine — **mow-er** *n*

Mr. \'mistər\ *n, pl* **Messrs.** \'mesərz\ — conventional title for a man

Mrs. \'misəz, -səs, *esp South* 'mizəz, -əs\ *n, pl* **Mes·dames** \mā'däm, -'dam\ — conventional title for a married woman

Ms. \'miz\ *n* — conventional title for a woman

much \'məch\ *adj* **more** \'mōr\; **most** \'mōst\ : great in quantity, extent, or degree ∼ *adv* **more; most** : to a great degree or extent ∼ *n* : great quantity, extent, or degree

mu·ci·lage \'myüsəlij\ *n* : weak glue

muck \'mək\ *n* : manure, dirt, or mud — **mucky** *adj*

mu·cus \'myükəs\ *n* : slippery protective secretion of membranes (**mucous membranes**) lining body cavities — **mu·cous** \-kəs\ *adj*

mud \'məd\ *n* : soft wet earth — **mud·di·ly** \'məd³lē\ *adv* — **mud·di·ness** \-ēnəs\ *n* — **mud·dy** *adj or vb*

mud·dle \'məd³l\ *vb* **-dled; -dling** **1** : make, be, or act confused **2** : make a mess of — **muddle** *n* — **mud·dle-head·ed** \,məd³l'hedəd\ *adj*

mu·ez·zin \mü'ez³n, myü-\ *n* : Muslim who calls the hour of daily prayer

¹**muff** \'məf\ *n* : tubular hand covering

²**muff** *vb* : bungle — **muff** *n*

muf·fin \'məfən\ *n* : soft cake baked in a cup-shaped container

muf·fle \'məfəl\ *vb* **-fled; -fling** **1** : wrap up **2** : dull the sound of — **muf·fler** \'məflər\ *n*

muf·ti \'məftē\ *n* : civilian clothes

¹**mug** \'məg\ *n* : drinking cup ∼ *vb* **-gg-** : make faces

²**mug** *vb* **-gg-** : assault with intent to rob — **mug·ger** *n*

mug·gy \'məgē\ *adj* **-gi·er; -est** : hot and humid — **mug·gi·ness** *n*

Mu·ham·mad·an \mō'haməd·ən, -'häm-; mü-\ *n* : Muslim — **Mu·ham·mad·an·ism** \-,izəm\ *n*

mu·lat·to \mů'lätō, -'lat-\ *n, pl* **-toes** *or* **-tos** : person of mixed black and white ancestry

mul·ber·ry \'məl‚berē\ *n* : tree with small edible fruit

mulch \'məlch\ *n* : protective ground covering — **mulch** *vb*

mulct \'məlkt\ *n or vb* : fine

¹**mule** \'myül\ *n* **1** : offspring of a male ass and a female horse **2** : stubborn person — **mul·ish** \'myülish\ *adj* — **mul·ish·ly** *adv* — **mu·lish·ness** *n*

²**mule** *n* : backless shoe

mull \'məl\ *vb* : ponder

mul·let \'mələt\ *n, pl* **-let** *or* **-lets** : marine food fish

multi- *comb form* **1** : many or multiple **2** : many times over

mul·ti·far·i·ous \‚məltə'far-ēəs\ *adj* : diverse

mul·ti·lat·er·al \‚məlti'latərəl, -‚tī-\ *adj* : having many sides or participants

mul·ti·lin·gual \-'liŋgwəl\ *adj* : knowing or using several languages — **mul·ti·lin·gual·ism** \-gwə‚lizəm\ *n*

mul·ti·na·tion·al \-'nashənəl\ *adj* **1** : relating to several nations or nationalities **2** : having divisions in several countries — **multinational** *n*

mul·ti·ple \'məltəpəl\ *adj* **1** : several or many **2** : various ~ *n* : product of one number by another

multiple sclerosis \-sklə'rōsəs\ *n* : brain or spinal disease affecting muscle control

mul·ti·pli·ca·tion \‚məltəplə-'kāshən\ *n* **1** : increase **2** : short method of repeated addition

mul·ti·plic·i·ty \‚məltə'plisətē\ *n, pl* **-ties** : great number or variety

mul·ti·ply \'məltə‚plī\ *vb* **-plied; -ply·ing 1** : increase in number **2** : perform multiplication — **mul·ti·pli·er** \-‚plīər\ *n*

mul·ti·tude \'məltə‚tüd, -‚tyüd\ *n* : great number —

List of self-explanatory words with the prefix *multi-*

multiarmed	multicultural	multifunctional
multibarreled	multidimensional	multigrade
multibillion	multidirectional	multiheaded
multibranched	multidisciplinary	multihospital
multibuilding	multidiscipline	multihued
multicenter	multidivisional	multilane
multichambered	multifaceted	multilevel
multichannel	multifamily	multimedia
multicolored	multifilament	multimember
multicounty	multifunction	multimillion

mul·ti·tu·di·nous \ˌməltə-ˈtüdᵊnəs, -ˈtyü-\ adj

¹**mum** \ˈməm\ adj : silent

²**mum** n : chrysanthemum

mum·ble \ˈməmbəl\ vb -**bled**; -**bling** : speak indistinctly — **mumble** n — **mum·bler** n

mum·mer \ˈməmər\ n **1** : actor esp. in a pantomime **2** : disguised merrymaker — **mum·mery** n

mum·my \ˈməmē\ n, pl -**mies** : embalmed body — **mum·mi·fi·ca·tion** \ˌməmifəˈkā-shən\ n — **mum·mi·fy** \ˈməmiˌfī\ vb

mumps \ˈməmps\ n sing or pl : virus disease with swelling esp. of the salivary glands

munch \ˈmənch\ vb : chew

mun·dane \ˌmənˈdān, ˈmənˌ-\ adj **1** : relating to the world **2** : lacking concern for the ideal or spiritual — **mun·dane·ly** adv

mu·nic·i·pal \myuˈnisəpəl\ adj : of or relating to a town or city — **mu·nic·i·pal·i·ty** \myu-ˌnisəˈpalətē\ n

mu·nif·i·cent \myuˈnifəsənt\ adj : generous — **mu·nif·i·cence** \-səns\ n

mu·ni·tion \myuˈnishən\ n : armaments

mu·ral \ˈmyurəl\ adj : relating to a wall ～ n : wall painting — **mu·ra·list** n

mur·der \ˈmərdər\ n : unlawful killing of a person ～ vb : commit a murder — **mur·der·er** n — **mur·der·ess** \-əs\ n — **mur·der·ous** \-əs\ adj — **mur·der·ous·ly** adv

murk \ˈmərk\ n : darkness — **murk·i·ly** \ˈmərkəlē\ adv — **murk·i·ness** \-kēnəs\ n — **murky** adj

mur·mur \ˈmərmər\ n **1** : muttered complaint **2** : low indistinct sound — **murmur** vb — **mur·mur·er** n — **mur·mur·ous** adj

mus·ca·tel \ˌməskəˈtel\ n : sweet wine

---

multimillionaire	multiracial	multisyllabic
multipart	multiroom	multitalented
multipartite	multisense	multitrack
multiparty	multiservice	multiunion
multiplant	multisided	multiunit
multipolar	multispeed	multiuse
multiproblem	multistage	multivitamin
multiproduct	multistep	multiwarhead
multipurpose	multistory	multiyear

mus·cle \'məsəl\ *n* **1** : body tissue capable of contracting to produce motion **2** : strength ~ *vb* **-cled; -cling** : force one's way — **mus·cled** *adj* — **mus·cu·lar** \'məskyələr\ *adj* — **mus·cu·lar·i·ty** \,məskyə-'larətē\ *n*

muscular dystrophy *n* : disease marked by progressive wasting of muscles

mus·cu·la·ture \'məskyələ-,chùr\ *n* : bodily muscles

¹**muse** \'myüz\ *vb* **mused; mus·ing** : ponder — **mus·ing·ly** *adv*

²**muse** *n* : source of inspiration

mu·se·um \myù'zēəm\ *n* : institution displaying objects of interest

mush \'məsh\ *n* **1** : corn meal boiled in water or something of similar consistency **2** : sentimental nonsense — **mushy** *adj*

mush·room \'məsh,rüm, -,rùm\ *n* : caplike organ of a fungus ~ *vb* : grow rapidly

mu·sic \'myüzik\ *n* : vocal or instrumental sounds — **mu·si·cal** \-zikəl\ *adj or n* — **mu·si·cal·ly** *adv*

mu·si·cian \myù'zishən\ *n* : composer or performer of music — **mu·si·cian·ly** *adj* — **mu·si·cian·ship** *n*

musk \'məsk\ *n* : strong-smelling substance from an Asiatic deer used in perfume

— **musk·i·ness** \'məskēnəs\ *n* — **musky** *adj*

mus·kel·lunge \'məskə,lənj\ *n, pl* **-lunge** : large No. American pike

mus·ket \'məskət\ *n* : former shoulder firearm — **mus·ke·teer** \,məskə'tir\ *n*

musk·mel·on \'məsk,melən\ *n* : small edible melon

musk–ox \'məsk,äks\ *n* : shaggy-coated wild ox of the arctic

musk·rat \-,rat\ *n, pl* **-rat** *or* **-rats** : No. American aquatic rodent

Mus·lim \'məzləm, 'mùs-, 'mùz-\ *n* : adherent of Islam — **Muslim** *adj*

mus·lin \'məzlən\ *n* : cotton fabric

muss \'məs\ *n* : untidy state ~ *vb* : disarrange — **muss·i·ly** \'məsəlē\ *adv* — **muss·i·ness** \-ēnəs\ *n* — **mussy** *adj*

mus·sel \'məsəl\ *n* : edible mollusk

must \'məst\ *vb* — used as an auxiliary esp. to express a command, obligation, or necessity ~ \'məst\ *n* : something necessary

mus·tache \'məs,tash, məs'-\ *n* : hair of the human upper lip

mus·tang \'məs,taŋ\ *n* : wild horse of Western America

mus·tard \'məstərd\ *n* : pungent yellow seasoning

mus·ter \\'məstər\ *vb* **1** : assemble **2** : rouse ~ *n* : assembled group

musty \\'məstē\ *adj* **mus·ti·er; -est** : stale — **must·i·ly** *adv* — **must·i·ness** *n*

mu·ta·ble \\'myütəbəl\ *adj* : changeable — **mu·ta·bil·i·ty** \\,myütə'bilətē\ *n*

mu·tant \\'myüt°nt\ *adj* : relating to or produced by mutation — **mutant** *n*

mu·tate \\'myü,tāt\ *vb* **-tat·ed; -tat·ing** : undergo mutation — **mu·ta·tive** \\'myü,tātiv, 'myütət-\ *adj*

mu·ta·tion \\myü'tāshən\ *n* : change in a hereditary character — **mu·ta·tion·al** *adj*

mute \\'myüt\ *adj* **mut·er; mut·est** **1** : unable to speak **2** : silent ~ *n* **1** : one who is mute **2** : muffling device ~ *vb* **mut·ed; mut·ing** : muffle — **mute·ly** *adv* — **mute·ness** *n*

mu·ti·late \\'myüt°l,āt\ *vb* **-lat·ed; -lat·ing** : damage seriously (as by cutting off or altering an essential part) — **mu·ti·la·tion** \\,myüt°l'āshən\ *n* — **mu·ti·la·tor** \\'myüt°l-,ātər\ *n*

mu·ti·ny \\'myütənē\ *n, pl* **-nies** : rebellion — **mu·ti·neer** \\,myüt°n'ir\ *n* — **mu·ti·nous** \\'myüt°nəs\ *adj* —

mu·ti·nous·ly *adv* — **mutiny** *vb*

mutt \\'mət\ *n* : mongrel

mut·ter \\'mətər\ *vb* **1** : speak indistinctly or softly **2** : grumble — **mutter** *n*

mut·ton \\'mət°n\ *n* : flesh of a mature sheep — **mut·tony** *adj*

mu·tu·al \\'myüchəwəl\ *adj* **1** : given or felt by one another in equal amount **2** : common — **mu·tu·al·ly** *adv*

muz·zle \\'məzəl\ *n* **1** : nose and jaws of an animal **2** : muzzle covering to immobilize an animal's jaws **3** : discharge end of a gun ~ *vb* **-zled; -zling** : restrain with or as if with a muzzle

my \\'mī\ *adj* **1** : relating to me or myself **2** — used interjectionally esp. to express surprise

my·nah, my·na \\'mīnə\ *n* : dark crested Asian bird

my·o·pia \\mī'ōpēə\ *n* : nearsightedness — **my·o·pic** \\-'ōpik, -'äpik\ *adj* — **my·o·pi·cal·ly** *adv*

myr·i·ad \\'mirēəd\ *n* : indefinitely large number — **myr·iad** *adj*

myrrh \\'mər\ *n* : aromatic plant gum

myr·tle \\'mərt°l\ *n* : shiny evergreen

my·self \mī'self\ *pron* **:** I, me — used reflexively or for emphasis

mys·tery \'mistərē\ *n, pl* **-ter·ies 1 :** religious truth **2 :** something not understood **3 :** puzzling or secret quality or state — **mys·te·ri·ous** \mis'tirēəs\ *adj* — **mys·te·ri·ous·ly** *adv* — **mys·te·ri·ous·ness** *n*

mys·tic \'mistik\ *adj* **:** mystical or mysterious ∼ *n* **:** one who has mystical experiences — **mys·ti·cism** \-tə-ˌsizəm\ *n*

mys·ti·cal \'mistikəl\ *adj* **1 :** spiritual **2 :** relating to direct communion with God — **mys·ti·cal·ly** *adj*

mys·ti·fy \'mistəˌfī\ *vb* **-fied; -fy·ing :** perplex — **mys·ti·fi·ca·tion** \ˌmistəfə'kāshən\ *n*

mys·tique \mis'tēk\ *n* **:** aura of mystery surrounding something

myth \'mith\ *n* **1 :** legendary narrative explaining a belief or phenomenon **2 :** imaginary person or thing — **myth·i·cal** \-ikəl\ *adj*

my·thol·o·gy \mith'äləjē\ *n, pl* **-gies :** body of myths — **myth·o·log·i·cal** \ˌmithə'läjikəl\ *adj* — **my·thol·o·gist** \mith'äləjist\ *n*

N

n \'en\ *n, pl* **n's** *or* **ns** \'enz\ **:** 14th letter of the alphabet

nab \'nab\ *vb* **-bb- :** seize or arrest

na·cho \'nächō\ *n* **:** tortilla chip topped with a savory mixture and cheese and broiled

na·dir \'nāˌdir, 'nādər\ *n* **:** lowest point

¹nag \'nag\ *n* **:** old or decrepit horse

²nag *vb* **-gg- 1 :** complain **2 :** scold or urge continually **3 :** be persistently annoying ∼ *n* **:** one who nags habitually

na·iad \'nāəd, 'nī-, -ˌad\ *n, pl* **-iads** *or* **-ia·des** \-ə,dēz\ **:** mythological water nymph

nail \'nāl\ *n* **1 :** horny sheath at the end of each finger and toe **2 :** pointed metal fastener ∼ *vb* **:** fasten with a nail — **nail·er** *n*

na·ive, na·ïve \nä'ēv\ *adj* **-iv·er; -est 1 :** innocent and unsophisticated **2 :** easily deceived — **na·ive·ly** *adv* — **na·ive·ness** *n*

na·ive·té \ˌnäˌēvə'tā, nä'ēvə,-\ *n* **:** quality or state of being naive

na·ked \'nākəd, 'nekəd\ *adj*
1 : having no clothes on **2**
: uncovered **3** : plain or obvious **4** : unaided — **na·ked·ly**
adv — **na·ked·ness** *n*

nam·by–pam·by \ˌnambē-
'pambē\ *adj* : weak or indecisive

name \'nām\ *n* **1** : word by
which a person or thing is
known **2** : disparaging word
for someone **3** : distinguished
reputation ~ *vb* **named;**
nam·ing 1 : give a name to **2**
: mention or identify by name
3 : nominate or appoint ~
adj **1** : relating to a name **2**
: prominent — **name·able** *adj*
— **name·less** *adj* — **name-**
less·ly *adv*

name·ly \'nāmlē\ *adv* : that is
to say

name·sake \-ˌsāk\ *n* : one
named after another

nano·tech·nol·o·gy \ˌnanōtek-
'näləjē\ *n* : manipulation of
materials on an atomic or molecular scale

¹nap \'nap\ *vb* **-pp- 1** : sleep
briefly **2** : be off guard ~ *n*
: short sleep

²nap *n* : soft downy surface —
nap·less *adj* — **napped**
\'napt\ *adj*

na·palm \'näˌpälm, -ˌpäm\ *n*
: gasoline in the form of a jelly

nape \'nāp, 'nap\ *n* : back of
the neck

naph·tha \'nafthə\ *n* : flammable solvent

nap·kin \'napkən\ *n* : small
cloth for use at the table

nar·cis·sism \'närsəˌsizəm\ *n*
: self-love — **nar·cis·sist**
\-sist\ *n or adj* — **nar·cis·sis-**
tic \ˌnärsə'sistik\ *adj*

nar·cis·sus \när'sisəs\ *n, pl*
-cis·sus *or* **-cis·sus·es** *or* **-cis-**
si \-'sisˌī, -ˌē\ : plant with flowers usu. borne separately

nar·cot·ic \när'kätik\ *n*
: painkilling addictive drug —
narcotic *adj*

nar·rate \'narˌāt\ *vb* **nar·rat-**
ed; nar·rat·ing : tell (a story)
— **nar·ra·tion** \na'rāshən\ *n*
— **nar·ra·tive** \'narətiv\ *n or*
adj — **nar·ra·tor** \'narˌātər\
n

nar·row \'narō\ *adj* **1** : of less
than standard width **2** : limited **3** : not liberal **4** : barely
successful ~ *vb* : make narrow — **nar·row·ly** *adv* —
nar·row·ness *n*

nar·row–mind·ed \ˌnarō-
'mīndəd\ *adj* : shallow,
provincial, or bigoted

nar·rows \'narōz\ *n pl* : narrow passage

nar·whal \'närˌhwäl, 'närwəl\
n : sea mammal with a tusk

nasal \'nāzəl\ *adj* : relating to
or uttered through the nose —
na·sal·ly *adv*

nas·tur·tium \nə'stərshəm, na-\ *n* : herb with showy flowers

nas·ty \'nastē\ *adj* **nas·ti·er; -est 1** : filthy **2** : indecent **3** : malicious or spiteful **4** : difficult or disagreeable **5** : unfair — **nas·ti·ly** \'nastəlē\ *adv* — **nas·ti·ness** \-tēnəs\ *n*

na·tal \'nāt³l\ *adj* : relating to birth

na·tion \'nāshən\ *n* **1** : people of similar characteristics **2** : community with its own territory and government — **na·tion·al** \'nashənəl\ *adj or n* — **na·tion·al·ly** *adv* — **na·tion·hood** *n* — **na·tion·wide** *adj*

na·tion·al·ism \'nashənəl-ˌizəm\ *n* : devotion to national interests, unity, and independence — **na·tion·al·ist** \-ist\ *n or adj* — **na·tion·al·is·tic** \ˌnashənəl'istik\ *adj*

na·tion·al·i·ty \ˌnashə'nalətē\ *n, pl* **-ties 1** : national character **2** : membership in a nation **3** : political independence **4** : ethnic group

na·tion·al·ize \'nashənəlˌīz\ *vb* **-ized; -iz·ing 1** : make national **2** : place under government control — **na·tion·al·i·za·tion** \ˌnashənələ'zāshən\ *n*

na·tive \'nātiv\ *adj* **1** : belonging to a person at or by way of birth **2** : born or produced in a particular place ~ *n* : one who belongs to a country by birth

Na·tiv·i·ty \nə'tivətē, nā-\ *n, pl* **-ties 1** : birth of Christ **2** *not cap* : birth

nat·ty \'natē\ *adj* **-ti·er; -est** : smartly dressed — **nat·ti·ly** \'nat³lē\ *adv*

nat·u·ral \'nachərəl\ *adj* **1** : relating to or determined by nature **2** : not artificial **3** : simple and sincere **4** : lifelike ~ *n* : one having an innate talent — **nat·u·ral·ness** *n*

nat·u·ral·ism \'nachərə-ˌlizəm\ *n* : realism in art and literature — **nat·u·ral·is·tic** \ˌnachərə'listik\ *adj*

nat·u·ral·ist \-list\ *n* **1** : one who practices naturalism **2** : student of animals or plants

nat·u·ral·ize \-ˌlīz\ *vb* **-ized; -iz·ing 1** : become or cause to become established **2** : confer citizenship on — **nat·u·ral·i·za·tion** \ˌnachərələ'zāshən\ *n*

nat·u·ral·ly \'nachərəlē\ *adv* **1** : in a natural way **2** : as might be expected

na·ture \'nāchər\ *n* **1** : basic quality of something **2** : kind **3** : disposition **4** : physical universe **5** : natural environment

naught \'nȯt, 'nät\ *n* **1** : nothing **2** : zero

naugh·ty \\'nȯtē, 'nät-\ *adj* **-ti·er; -est 1 :** disobedient or misbehaving **2 :** improper — **naught·i·ly** \\'nȯt°lē, 'nät-\ *adv* — **naught·i·ness** \-ēnəs\ *n*

nau·sea \\'nȯzēə, -shə\ *n* **1 :** sickness of the stomach with a desire to vomit **2 :** extreme disgust — **nau·seous** \-shəs, -zēəs\ *adj*

nau·se·ate \\'nȯzē̩āt, -zhē-, -sē-, -shē-\ *vb* **-at·ed; -at·ing :** affect or become affected with nausea — **nau·se·at·ing·ly** \-̩ātiŋlē\ *adv*

nau·ti·cal \\'nȯtikəl\ *adj* **:** relating to ships and sailing — **nau·ti·cal·ly** *adv*

nau·ti·lus \\'nȯt°ləs\ *n, pl* **-lus·es** *or* **-li** \-°l̩ī, -̩ē\ **:** sea mollusk with a spiral shell

na·val \\'nāvəl\ *adj* **:** relating to a navy

nave \\'nāv\ *n* **:** central part of a church

na·vel \\'nāvəl\ *n* **:** depression in the abdomen

nav·i·ga·ble \\'navigəbəl\ *adj* **:** capable of being navigated — **nav·i·ga·bil·i·ty** \̩navigə-'bilətē\ *n*

nav·i·gate \\'navə̩gāt\ *vb* **-gat·ed; -gat·ing 1 :** sail on or through **2 :** direct the course of — **nav·i·ga·tion** \̩navə-'gāshən\ *n* — **nav·i·ga·tor** \\'navə̩gātər\ *n*

na·vy \\'nāvē\ *n, pl* **-vies 1 :** fleet **2 :** nation's organization for sea warfare

nay \\'nā\ *adv* **:** no — used in oral voting ∼ *n* **:** negative vote

Na·zi \\'nätsē, 'nat-\ *n* **:** member of a German fascist party from 1933 to 1945 — **Nazi** *adj* — **Na·zism** \\'nät̩sizəm, 'nat-\, **Na·zi·ism** \-sē̩izəm\ *n*

near \\'nir\ *adv* **:** at or close to ∼ *prep* **:** close to ∼ *adj* **1 :** not far away **2 :** very much like ∼ *vb* **:** approach — **near·ly** *adv* — **near·ness** *n*

near·by \nir'bī, 'nir̩bī\ *adv or adj* **:** near

near·sight·ed \\'nir'sītəd\ *adj* **:** seeing well at short distances only — **near·sight·ed·ly** *adv* — **near·sight·ed·ness** *n*

neat \\'nēt\ *adj* **1 :** not diluted **2 :** tastefully simple **3 :** orderly and clean — **neat** *adv* — **neat·ly** *adv* — **neat·ness** *n*

neb·u·la \\'nebyələ\ *n, pl* **-lae** \-̩lē, -̩lī\ **:** large cloud of interstellar gas — **neb·u·lar** \-lər\ *adj*

neb·u·lous \-ləs\ *adj* **:** indistinct

nec·es·sary \\'nesə̩serē\ *n, pl* **-saries :** indispensable item ∼ *adj* **1 :** inevitable **2 :** compulsory **3 :** positively needed — **nec·es·sar·i·ly** \̩nesə'serəlē\ *adv*

ne·ces·si·tate \ni'sesə‚tāt\ *vb* -**tat·ed; -tat·ing** : make necessary

ne·ces·si·ty \ni'sesətē\ *n, pl* -**ties** **1** : very great need **2** : something that is necessary **3** : poverty **4** : circumstances that cannot be changed

neck \'nek\ *n* **1** : body part connecting the head and trunk **2** : part of a garment at the neck **3** : narrow part ~ *vb* : kiss and caress — **necked** \'nekt\ *adj*

neck·er·chief \'nekərchəf, -‚chēf\ *n, pl* -**chiefs** \-chəfs, -‚chēfs\ : cloth worn tied about the neck

neck·lace \'nekləs\ *n* : ornament worn around the neck

neck·tie *n* : ornamental cloth tied under a collar

nec·ro·man·cy \'nekrə‚man-sē\ *n* : art of conjuring up the spirits of the dead — **nec·ro·man·cer** \-sər\ *n*

ne·cro·sis \nə'krōsəs, ne-\ *n, pl* -**cro·ses** \-‚sēz\ : death of body tissue

nec·tar \'nektər\ *n* : sweet plant secretion

nec·tar·ine \‚nektə'rēn\ *n* : smooth-skinned peach

née, nee \'nā\ *adj* — used to identify a married woman by maiden name

need \'nēd\ *n* **1** : obligation **2** : lack of something or what is lacking **3** : poverty ~ *vb* **1** : be in want **2** : have cause for **3** : be under obligation — **need·ful** \-fəl\ *adj* — **need·less** *adj* — **need·less·ly** *adv* — **needy** *adj*

nee·dle \'nēdᵊl\ *n* **1** : pointed sewing implement or something like it **2** : movable bar in a compass **3** : hollow instrument for injecting or withdrawing material ~ *vb* -**dled; -dling** : incite to action by repeated gibes — **nee·dle·work** \-‚wərk\ *n*

nee·dle·point \'nēdᵊl‚pȯint\ *n* **1** : lace fabric **2** : embroidery on canvas — **needlepoint** *adj*

ne·far·i·ous \ni'farēəs\ *adj* : very wicked — **ne·far·i·ous·ly** *adv*

ne·gate \ni'gāt\ *vb* -**gat·ed; -gat·ing** **1** : deny **2** : nullify — **ne·ga·tion** \-'gāshən\ *n*

neg·a·tive \'negətiv\ *adj* **1** : marked by denial or refusal **2** : showing a lack of something suspected or desirable **3** : less than zero **4** : having more electrons than protons **5** : having light and shadow images reversed ~ *n* **1** : negative word or vote **2** : a negative number **3** : negative photographic image — **neg·a·tive·ly** *adv* — **neg·a·tive·ness** *n* — **neg·a·tiv·i·ty** \‚negə'tivətē\ *n*

ne·glect \ni'glekt\ *vb* **1** : disregard **2** : leave unattended to

~ *n* **1** : act of neglecting **2** : condition of being neglected — **ne·glect·ful** *adj*

neg·li·gee \ˌneglə'zhā\ *n* : woman's loose robe

neg·li·gent \'neglijənt\ *adj* : marked by neglect — **neg·li·gence** \-jəns\ *n* — **neg·li·gent·ly** *adv*

neg·li·gi·ble \'neglijəbəl\ *adj* : insignificant

ne·go·ti·ate \ni'gōshē,āt\ *vb* **-at·ed; -at·ing** **1** : confer with another to settle a matter **2** : obtain cash for **3** : get through successfully — **ne·go·tia·ble** \-shəbəl, -shēə-\ *adj* — **ne·go·ti·a·tion** \-ˌgōshē'āshən, -shē'ā-\ *n* — **ne·go·ti·a·tor** \-'gōshē,ātər\ *n*

Ne·gro \'nēgrō\ *n, pl* **-groes** *sometimes offensive* : member of the dark-skinned race native to Africa — **Negro** *adj* — **Ne·groid** \'nē,gròid\ *n or adj, often not cap*

neigh \'nā\ *n* : cry of a horse — **neigh** *vb*

neigh·bor \'nābər\ *n* **1** : one living nearby **2** : fellowman **~** *vb* : be near or next to — **neigh·bor·hood** \-ˌhùd\ *n* — **neigh·bor·li·ness** *n* — **neigh·bor·ly** *adv*

nei·ther \'nēthər, 'nī-\ *pron or adj* : not the one or the other **~** *conj* **1** : not either **2** : nor

nem·e·sis \'neməsəs\ *n, pl* **-e·ses** \-əˌsēz\ **1** : old and usu. frustrating rival **2** : retaliation

ne·ol·o·gism \nē'älə,jizəm\ *n* : new word

ne·on \'nē,än\ *n* : gaseous colorless chemical element that emits a reddish glow in electric lamps — **neon** *adj*

neo·phyte \'nēə,fīt\ *n* : beginner

neph·ew \'nefyü, *chiefly Brit* 'nev-\ *n* : a son of one's brother, sister, brother-in-law, or sister-in-law

nep·o·tism \'nepə,tizəm\ *n* : favoritism shown in hiring a relative

nerd \'nərd\ *n* : one who is not stylish or socially at ease — **nerdy** *adj*

nerve \'nərv\ *n* **1** : strand of body tissue that connects the brain with other parts of the body **2** : self-control **3** : daring **4** *pl* : nervousness — **nerved** \'nərvd\ *adj* — **nerve·less** *adj*

ner·vous \'nərvəs\ *adj* **1** : relating to or made up of nerves **2** : easily excited **3** : timid or fearful — **ner·vous·ly** *adv* — **ner·vous·ness** *n*

nervy \'nərvē\ *adj* **nerv·i·er; -est** : insolent or presumptuous

-ness \nəs\ *n suffix* : condition or quality

nest \'nest\ *n* **1** : shelter prepared by a bird for its eggs **2** : place where eggs (as of insects or fish) are laid and hatched **3** : snug retreat **4** : set of objects fitting one inside or under another ∼ *vb* : build or occupy a nest

nes·tle \'nesəl\ *vb* **-tled; -tling** : settle snugly (as in a nest)

¹**net** \'net\ *n* : fabric with spaces between strands or something made of this ∼ *vb* **-tt-** : cover with or catch in a net

²**net** *adj* : remaining after deductions ∼ *vb* **-tt-** : have as profit

neth·er \'neth̲ər\ *adj* : situated below

net·tle \'net³l\ *n* : coarse herb with stinging hairs ∼ *vb* **-tled; -tling** : provoke or vex — **net·tle·some** *adj*

net·work *n* : system of crossing or connected elements

neu·ral \'nu̇rəl, 'nyu̇r-\ *adj* : relating to a nerve

neu·ral·gia \nu̇'raljə, nyu̇-\ *n* : pain along a nerve — **neu·ral·gic** \-jik\ *adj*

neu·ri·tis \nu̇'rītəs, nyu̇-\ *n, pl* **-rit·i·des** \-'ritə‚dēz\ *or* **-ri·tis·es** : inflammation of a nerve

neu·rol·o·gy \nu̇'räləjē, nyu̇-\ *n* : study of the nervous system — **neu·ro·log·i·cal** \‚nu̇rə-'läjikəl, ‚nyu̇r-\, **neu·ro·log-**

ic \-ik\ *adj* — **neu·rol·o·gist** \nu̇'räləjist, nyu̇-\ *n*

neu·ro·sis \nu̇'rōsəs, nyu̇-\ *n, pl* **-ro·ses** \-‚sēz\ : nervous disorder

neu·rot·ic \nu̇'rätik, nyu̇-\ *adj* : relating to neurosis ∼ *n* : unstable person — **neu·rot·i·cal·ly** *adv*

neu·ter \'nütər, 'nyü-\ *adj* : neither masculine nor feminine ∼ *vb* : castrate or spay

neu·tral \-trəl\ *adj* **1** : not favoring either side **2** : being neither one thing nor the other **3** : not decided in color **4** : not electrically charged ∼ *n* **1** : one that is neutral **2** : position of gears that are not engaged — **neu·tral·i·za·tion** \‚nütrələ'zāshən, ‚nyü-\ *n* — **neu·tral·ize** \'nütrə‚līz, 'nyü-\ *vb*

neu·tral·i·ty \nü'tralətē, nyü-\ *n* : state of being neutral

neu·tron \'nü‚trän, 'nyü-\ *n* : uncharged atomic particle

nev·er \'nevər\ *adv* **1** : not ever **2** : not in any degree, way, or condition

nev·er·more *adv* : never again

nev·er·the·less *adv* : in spite of that

new \'nü, 'nyü\ *adj* **1** : not old or familiar **2** : different from the former **3** : recently discovered or learned **4** : not accustomed **5** : refreshed or regenerated **6** : being such for the first time ~ *adv* : newly — **new·ish** *adj* — **new·ness** *n*

new·born *adj* **1** : recently born **2** : born anew ~ *n, pl* **-born** *or* **-borns** : newborn individual

new·ly \-lē\ *adv* : recently

news \'nüz, 'nyüz\ *n* : report of recent events — **news·let·ter** *n* — **news·mag·a·zine** *n* — **news·man** \-mən, -ˌman\ *n* — **news·pa·per** *n* — **news·pa·per·man** \-ˌman\ *n* — **news·stand** *n* — **news·wom·an** \-ˌwümən\ *n* — **news·wor·thy** *adj*

news·cast \-ˌkast\ *n* : broadcast of news — **news·cast·er** \-ˌkastər\ *n*

news·print *n* : paper made from wood pulp

newsy \'nüzē, 'nyü-\ *adj* **news·i·er; -est** : filled with news

newt \'nüt, 'nyüt\ *n* : small salamander

New Year *n* : New Year's Day

New Year's Day *n* : January 1 observed as a legal holiday

next \'nekst\ *adj* : immediately preceding or following ~ *adv* **1** : in the time or place nearest **2** : at the first time yet to come ~ *prep* : nearest to

nex·us \'neksəs\ *n, pl* **-us·es** \-səsəz\ *or* **-us** \-səs, -ˌsüs\ : connection

nib \'nib\ *n* : pen point

nib·ble \'nibəl\ *vb* **-bled; -bling** : bite gently or bit by bit ~ *n* : small bite

nice \'nīs\ *adj* **nic·er; nic·est** **1** : fastidious **2** : very precise or delicate **3** : pleasing **4** : respectable — **nice·ly** *adv* — **nice·ness** *n*

nice·ty \'nīsətē\ *n, pl* **-ties** **1** : dainty or elegant thing **2** : fine detail **3** : exactness

niche \'nich\ *n* **1** : recess in a wall **2** : fitting place, work, or use

nick \'nik\ *n* **1** : small broken area or chip **2** : critical moment ~ *vb* : make a nick in

nick·el \'nikəl\ *n* **1** : hard silver-white metallic chemical element used in alloys **2** : U.S. 5-cent piece

nick·name \'nikˌnām\ *n* : informal substitute name — **nickname** *vb*

nic·o·tine \'nikəˌtēn\ *n* : poisonous and addictive substance in tobacco

niece \'nēs\ *n* : a daughter of one's brother, sister, brother-in-law, or sister-in-law

nig·gard·ly \'nigərdlē\ *adj* : stingy — **nig·gard** *n* — **nig·gard·li·ness** *n*

nig·gling \'nigəliŋ\ *adj* : petty and annoying

nigh \'nī\ *adv or adj or prep* : near

night \'nīt\ *n* **1** : period between dusk and dawn **2** : the coming of night — **night** *adj* — **night·ly** *adj or adv* — **night·time** *n*

night·clothes *n pl* : garments worn in bed

night·club \-ˌkləb\ *n* : place for drinking and entertainment open at night

night crawler *n* : earthworm

night·fall *n* : the coming of night

night·gown *n* : gown worn for sleeping

night·in·gale \'nītᵊnˌgāl, -iŋ-\ *n* : Old World thrush that sings at night

night·mare \'nītˌmar\ *n* : frightening dream — **nightmare** *adj* — **night·mar·ish** \-ˌmarish\ *adj*

night·shade \'nītˌshād\ *n* : group of plants that include poisonous forms and food plants (as the potato and eggplant)

nil \'nil\ *n* : nothing

nim·ble \'nimbəl\ *adj* **-bler; -blest** **1** : agile **2** : clever — **nim·ble·ness** *n* — **nim·bly** \-blē\ *adv*

nine \'nīn\ *n* **1** : one more than 8 **2** : 9th in a set or series — **nine** *adj or pron* — **ninth** \'nīnth\ *adj or adv or n*

nine·pins *n* : bowling game using 9 pins

nine·teen \nīn'tēn\ *n* : one more than 18 — **nineteen** *adj or pron* — **nine·teenth** \-'tēnth\ *adj or n*

nine·ty \'nīntē\ *n, pl* **-ties** : 9 times 10 — **nine·ti·eth** \-ēəth\ *adj or n* — **ninety** *adj or pron*

nin·ny \'ninē\ *n, pl* **nin·nies** : fool

¹**nip** \'nip\ *vb* **-pp-** **1** : catch hold of and squeeze tightly **2** : pinch or bite off **3** : destroy the growth or fulfillment of ∼ *n* **1** : biting cold **2** : tang **3** : pinch or bite

²**nip** *n* : small quantity of liquor ∼ *vb* **-pp-** : take liquor in nips

nip·per \'nipər\ *n* **1** : one that nips **2** *pl* : pincers **3** : small boy

nip·ple \'nipəl\ *n* : tip of the breast or something resembling it

nip·py \'nipē\ *adj* **-pi·er; -est** **1** : pungent **2** : chilly

nir·va·na \nir'vänə\ *n* : state of blissful oblivion

nit \'nit\ *n* : egg of a parasitic insect

ni·ter \'nītər\ *n* : potassium nitrate used in gunpowder or fertilizer or in curing meat

ni·trate \'nīˌtrāt, -trət\ *n* : chemical salt used esp. in curing meat

ni·tric acid \'nītrik-\ *n* : liquid acid used in making dyes, explosives, and fertilizers

ni·trite \-ˌtrīt\ *n* : chemical salt used in curing meat

ni·tro·gen \'nītrəjən\ *n* : tasteless odorless gaseous chemical element

ni·tro·glyc·er·in, ni·tro·glyc·er·ine \ˌnītrō'glisərən\ *n* : heavy oily liquid used as an explosive and as a blood-vessel relaxer

nit·wit \'nitˌwit\ *n* : stupid person

no \'nō\ *adv* **1** — used to express the negative **2** : in no respect or degree **3** : not so **4** — used as an interjection of surprise or doubt ∼ *adj* **1** : not any **2** : not a ∼ *n, pl* **noes** *or* **nos** \'nōz\ **1** : refusal **2** : negative vote

no·bil·i·ty \nō'bilətē\ *n* **1** : quality or state of being noble **2** : class of people of noble rank

no·ble \'nōbəl\ *adj* **-bler; -blest 1** : illustrious **2** : aristocratic **3** : stately **4** : of outstanding character ∼ *n* : nobleman — **no·ble·ness** *n* — **no·bly** *adv*

no·ble·man \-mən\ *n* : member of the nobility

no·ble·wom·an \-ˌwu̇mən\ *n* : a woman of noble rank

no·body \'nōbədē, -ˌbädē\ *pron* : no person ∼ *n, pl* **-bod·ies** : person of no influence or importance

no–brain·er \'nō'brānər\ : something that requires a minimum of thought

noc·tur·nal \näk'tərnᵊl\ *adj* : relating to, occurring at, or active at night

noc·turne \'näkˌtərn\ *n* : dreamy musical composition

nod \'näd\ *vb* **-dd- 1** : bend the head downward or forward (as in bowing or going to sleep or as a sign of assent) **2** : move up and down **3** : show by a nod of the head — **nod** *n*

node \'nōd\ *n* : stem part from which a leaf arises — **nod·al** \-ᵊl\ *adj*

nod·ule \'näjül\ *n* : small lump or swelling — **nod·u·lar** \'näjələr\ *adj*

no·el \nō'el\ *n* **1** : Christmas carol **2** *cap* : Christmas season

noes *pl of* NO

nog·gin \'nägən\ *n* **1** : small mug **2** : person's head

no·how \'nōˌhau̇\ *adv* : in no manner

noise \'nȯiz\ *n* : loud or unpleasant sound ∼ *vb* **noised; nois·ing** : spread by rumor — **noise·less** *adj* — **noise·less·ly** *adv* — **noise·mak·er** *n* — **nois·i·ly** \'nȯizəlē\ *adv* — **nois·i·ness** \-zēnəs\ *n* — **noisy** \'nȯizē\ *adj*

noi·some \'nȯisəm\ *adj* : harmful or offensive

no·mad \'nōˌmad\ *n* : one who has no permanent home

— **nomad** *adj* — **no·mad·ic** \nō'madik\ *adj*

no·men·cla·ture \'nōmən-ˌklāchər\ *n* : system of names

nom·i·nal \'nämən³l\ *adj* **1** : being something in name only **2** : small or negligible — **nom·i·nal·ly** *adv*

nom·i·nate \'nämə,nāt\ *vb* **-nat·ed; -nat·ing** : propose or choose as a candidate — **nom·i·na·tion** \,nämə'nāshən\ *n*

nom·i·na·tive \'nämənətiv\ *adj* : relating to or being a grammatical case marking typically the subject of a verb — **nominative** *n*

nom·i·nee \,nämə'nē\ *n* : person nominated

non- \'nän, ,nän\ *prefix* **1** : not, reverse of, or absence of **2** : not important

non·age \'nänij, 'nōnij\ *n* : period of youth and esp. legal minority

nonce \'näns\ *n* : present occasion ∼ *adj* : occurring, used, or made only once

non·cha·lant \,nänshə'länt\ *adj* : showing indifference —

List of self-explanatory words with the prefix *non-*

nonabrasive	non-Catholic	noncriminal
nonabsorbent	non-Christian	noncritical
nonacademic	nonchurchgoer	noncumulative
nonaccredited	noncitizen	noncurrent
nonacid	nonclassical	nondeductible
nonaddictive	nonclassified	nondeferrable
nonadhesive	noncombat	nondegradable
nonadjacent	noncombatant	nondelivery
nonadjustable	noncombustible	nondemocratic
nonaffiliated	noncommercial	nondenomina-
nonaggression	noncommunist	tional
nonalcoholic	noncompliance	nondestructive
nonaligned	nonconflicting	nondiscrimination
nonappearance	nonconforming	nondiscriminatory
nonautomatic	nonconsecutive	noneducational
nonbeliever	nonconstructive	nonelastic
nonbinding	noncontagious	nonelected
nonbreakable	noncontrollable	nonelective
noncancerous	noncontroversial	nonelectric
noncandidate	noncorrosive	nonelectronic

non·cha·lance \-'läns\ *n* — **non·cha·lant·ly** *adv*

non·com·mis·sioned officer \ˌnänkə'mishənd-\ *n* : subordinate officer in the armed forces appointed from enlisted personnel

non·com·mit·tal \ˌnänkə-'mit³l\ *adj* : indicating neither consent nor dissent

non·con·duc·tor *n* : substance that is a very poor conductor

non·con·form·ist *n* : one who does not conform to an established belief or mode of behavior — **non·con·for·mi·ty** *n*

non·de·script \ˌnändi'skript\ *adj* : lacking distinctive qualities

none \'nən\ *pron* : not any ∼ *adv* : not at all

non·en·ti·ty *n* : one of no consequence

none·the·less \ˌnənthə'les\ *adv* : nevertheless

non·pa·reil \ˌnänpə'rel\ *adj* : having no equal ∼ *n* **1** : one who has no equal **2** : chocolate candy disk

---

nonemotional
nonenforcement
nonessential
nonexclusive
nonexistence
nonexistent
nonexplosive
nonfat
nonfatal
nonfattening
nonfictional
nonflammable
nonflowering
nonfunctional
nongovernmental
nongraded
nonhazardous
nonhereditary
nonindustrial
nonindustrialized
noninfectious

noninflationary
nonintegrated
nonintellectual
noninterference
nonintoxicating
noninvasive
non-Jewish
nonlegal
nonlethal
nonliterary
nonliving
nonmagnetic
nonmalignant
nonmedical
nonmember
nonmetal
nonmetallic
nonmilitary
nonmusical
nonnative
nonnegotiable

nonobjective
nonobservance
nonorthodox
nonparallel
nonparticipant
nonparticipating
nonpaying
nonpayment
nonperformance
nonperishable
nonphysical
nonpoisonous
nonpolitical
nonpolluting
nonporous
nonpregnant
nonproductive
nonprofessional
nonprofit
nonracial
nonradioactive

non·par·ti·san *adj* : not influenced by political party bias

non·per·son *n* : person without social or legal status

non·plus \ˌnän'pləs\ *vb* **-ss-** : perplex

non·pre·scrip·tion *adj* : available without a doctor's prescription

non·pro·lif·er·a·tion *adj* : aimed at ending increased use of nuclear arms

non·sched·uled *adj* : licensed to carry by air without a regular schedule

non·sense \'nän,sens, -səns\ *n* : foolish or meaningless words or actions — **non·sen·si·cal** \nän'sensikəl\ *adj* — **non·sen·si·cal·ly** *adv*

non·sup·port *n* : failure in a legal obligation to provide for someone's needs

non·vi·o·lence *n* : avoidance of violence esp. in political demonstrations — **non·vi·o·lent** *adj*

noo·dle \'nüdᵊl\ *n* : ribbon-shaped food paste

nook \'nuk\ *n* **1** : inside corner **2** : private place

noon \'nün\ *n* : middle of the day — **noon** *adj*

noon·day \-,dā\ *n* : noon

no one *pron* : no person

noon·time *n* : noon

noose \'nüs\ *n* : rope loop that slips down tight

nor \nȯr\ *conj* : and not — used esp. after *neither* to intro-

---

nonrated	nonsexist	nontaxable
nonrealistic	nonsexual	nonteaching
nonrecurring	nonsignificant	nontechnical
nonrefillable	nonskier	nontoxic
nonrefundable	nonsmoker	nontraditional
nonreligious	nonsmoking	nontransferable
nonrenewable	nonspeaking	nontropical
nonrepresentative	nonspecialist	nontypical
nonresident	nonspecific	nonunion
nonresponsive	nonstandard	nonuser
nonrestricted	nonstick	nonvenomous
nonreversible	nonstop	nonverbal
nonsalable	nonstrategic	nonvoter
nonscientific	nonstudent	nonwhite
nonscientist	nonsugar	nonworker
nonsegregated	nonsurgical	
non–self–governing	nonswimmer	

duce and negate the 2d member of a series

norm \'nȯrm\ *n* **1** : standard usu. derived from an average **2** : typical widespread practice or custom

nor·mal \'nȯrməl\ *adj* : average, regular, or standard — **nor·mal·cy** \-sē\ *n* — **nor·mal·i·ty** \nȯr'malətē\ *n* — **nor·mal·i·za·tion** \ˌnȯrmələ-'zāshən\ *n* — **nor·mal·ize** \'nȯrmə͟līz\ *vb* — **nor·mal·ly** *adv*

north \'nȯrth\ *adv* : to or toward the north ∼ *adj* : situated toward, at, or coming from the north ∼ *n* **1** : direction to the left of one facing east **2** *cap* : regions to the north — **north·er·ly** \'nȯrthərlē\ *adv or adj* — **north·ern** \-ərn\ *adj* **North·ern·er** *n* — **north·ern·most** \-ˌmōst\ *adj* — **north·ward** \-wərd\ *adv or adj* — **north·wards** \-wərdz\ *adv*

north·east \nȯrth'ēst\ *n* **1** : direction between north and east **2** *cap* : regions to the northeast — **northeast** *adj or adv* — **north·east·er·ly** \-ərlē\ *adv or adj* — **north·east·ern** \-ərn\ *adj*

northern lights *n pl* : aurora borealis

north pole *n* : northernmost point of the earth

north·west \-'west\ *n* **1** : direction between north and west **2** *cap* : regions to the northwest — **northwest** *adj or adv* — **north·west·er·ly** \-ərlē\ *adv or adj* — **north·west·ern** \-ərn\ *adj*

nose \'nōz\ *n* **1** : part of the face containing the nostrils **2** : sense of smell **3** : front part ∼ *vb* **nosed; nos·ing** **1** : detect by smell **2** : push aside with the nose **3** : pry **4** : inch ahead — **nose·bleed** *n* — **nosed** \'nōzd\ *adj* — **nose out** *vb* : narrowly defeat

nose·gay \-ˌgā\ *n* : small bunch of flowers

nos·tal·gia \nä'staljə, nə-\ *n* : wistful yearning for something past — **nos·tal·gic** \-jik\ *adj*

nos·tril \'nästrəl\ *n* : opening of the nose

nos·trum \-trəm\ *n* : questionable remedy

nosy, nos·ey \'nōzē\ *adj* **nos·i·er; -est** : tending to pry

not \'nät\ *adv* — used to make a statement negative

no·ta·ble \'nōtəbəl\ *adj* **1** : noteworthy **2** : distinguished ∼ *n* : notable person — **no·ta·bil·i·ty** \nōtə'bilətē\ *n* — **no·ta·bly** \'nōtəblē\ *adv*

no·ta·rize \'nōtəˌrīz\ *vb* **-rized; -riz·ing** : attest as a notary public

no·ta·ry public \\'nōtərē-\\ *n, pl* **-ries public** *or* **-ry publics** : public official who attests writings to make them legally authentic

no·ta·tion \\nō'tāshən\\ *n* **1** : note **2** : act, process, or method of marking things down

notch \\'näch\\ *n* : V-shaped hollow — **notch** *vb*

note \\'nōt\\ *vb* **not·ed; not·ing** **1** : notice **2** : write down ~ *n* **1** : musical tone **2** : written comment or record **3** : short informal letter **4** : notice or heed — **note·book** *n*

not·ed \\'nōtəd\\ *adj* : famous

note·wor·thy \\-ˌwərthē\\ *adj* : worthy of special mention

noth·ing \\'nəthiŋ\\ *pron* **1** : no thing **2** : no part **3** : one of no value or importance ~ *adv* : not at all ~ *n* **1** : something that does not exist **2** : zero **3** : one of little or no importance — **noth·ing·ness** *n*

no·tice \\'nōtəs\\ *n* **1** : warning or announcement **2** : attention ~ *vb* **-ticed; -tic·ing** : take notice of — **no·tice·able** *adj* — **no·tice·ably** *adv*

no·ti·fy \\'nōtəˌfī\\ *vb* **-fied; -fy·ing** : give notice of or to — **no·ti·fi·ca·tion** \\ˌnōtəfə-'kāshən\\ *n*

no·tion \\'nōshən\\ *n* **1** : idea or opinion **2** : whim

no·to·ri·ous \\nō'tōrēəs\\ *adj* : widely and unfavorably known — **no·to·ri·e·ty** \\ˌnōtə-'rīətē\\ *n* — **no·to·ri·ous·ly** *adv*

not·with·stand·ing \\ˌnätwith-'standiŋ, -with-\\ *prep* : in spite of ~ *adv* : nevertheless ~ *conj* : although

nou·gat \\'nügət\\ *n* : nuts or fruit pieces in a sugar paste

nought \\'nȯt, 'nät\\ *var of* NAUGHT

noun \\'naün\\ *n* : word that is the name of a person, place, or thing

nour·ish \\'nərish\\ *vb* : promote the growth of — **nour·ish·ing** *adj* — **nour·ish·ment** *n*

no·va \\'nōvə\\ *n, pl* **-vas** *or* **-vae** \\-ˌvē, -ˌvī\\ : star that suddenly brightens and then fades gradually

nov·el \\'nävəl\\ *adj* : new or strange ~ *n* : long invented prose story — **nov·el·ist** \\-əlist\\ *n*

nov·el·ty \\'nävəltē\\ *n, pl* **-ties** **1** : something new or unusual **2** : newness **3** : small manufactured article — usu. pl.

No·vem·ber \\nō'vembər\\ *n* : 11th month of the year having 30 days

nov·ice \\'nävəs\\ *n* **1** : one preparing to take vows in a religious order **2** : one who is inexperienced or untrained

no·vi·tiate \nō'vishət, nə-\ *n* : period or state of being a novice

now \'naù\ *adv* **1** : at the present time or moment **2** : forthwith **3** : under these circumstances ~ *conj* : in view of the fact ~ *n* : present time

now·a·days \'naùə,dāz\ *adv* : now

no·where \-,hwer\ *adv* : not anywhere — **no·where** *n*

nox·ious \'näkshəs\ *adj* : harmful

noz·zle \'näzəl\ *n* : device to direct or control a flow of fluid

nu·ance \'nü,äns, 'nyü-\ *n* : subtle distinction or variation

nub \'nəb\ *n* **1** : knob or lump **2** : gist

nu·bile \'nü,bīl, 'nyü-, -bəl\ *adj* **1** : of marriageable condition or age **2** : sexually attractive

nu·cle·ar \'nüklēər, 'nyü-\ *adj* **1** : relating to the atomic nucleus or atomic energy **2** : relating to a weapon whose power is from a nuclear reaction

nu·cle·us \'nüklēəs, 'nyü-\ *n, pl* **-clei** \-klē,ī\ : central mass or part (as of a cell or an atom)

nude \'nüd, 'nyüd\ *adj* **nuder; nud·est** : naked ~ *n* : nude human figure — **nu·di·ty** \'nüdətē, 'nyü-\ *n*

nudge \'nəj\ *vb* **nudged; nudg·ing** : touch or push gently — **nudge** *n*

nud·ism \'nüd,izəm, 'nyü-\ *n* : practice of going nude — **nud·ist** \'nüdist, 'nyü-\ *n*

nug·get \'nəgət\ *n* : lump of gold

nui·sance \'nüsᵊns, 'nyü-\ *n* : something annoying

null \'nəl\ *adj* : having no legal or binding force — **nul·li·ty** \'nələtē\ *n*

nul·li·fy \'nələ,fī\ *vb* **-fied; -fy·ing** : make null or valueless — **nul·li·fi·ca·tion** \,nələfə-'kāshən\ *n*

numb \'nəm\ *adj* : lacking feeling — **numb** *vb* — **numb·ly** *adv* — **numbness** *n*

num·ber \'nəmbər\ *n* **1** : total of individuals taken together **2** : indefinite total **3** : unit of a mathematical system **4** : numeral **5** : one in a sequence ~ *vb* **1** : count **2** : assign a number to **3** : comprise in number — **num·ber·less** *adj*

nu·mer·al \'nümərəl, 'nyü-\ *n* : conventional symbol representing a number

nu·mer·a·tor \'nümə,rātər, 'nyü-\ *n* : part of a fraction above the line

nu·mer·i·cal \nù'merikəl, nyü-\, **nu·mer·ic** \-'merik\ *adj* **1** : relating to numbers **2** : expressed in or involving numbers — **nu·mer·i·cal·ly** *adv*

nu·mer·ol·o·gy \ˌnümə'räləjē, ˌnyü-\ *n* : occult study of numbers — **nu·mer·ol·o·gist** \-jist\ *n*

nu·mer·ous \'nümərəs, 'nyü-\ *adj* : consisting of a great number

nu·mis·mat·ics \ˌnüməz'matiks, ˌnyü-\ *n* : study or collection of monetary objects — **nu·mis·mat·ic** \-ik\ *adj* — **nu·mis·ma·tist** \nü'mizmətist, nyü-\ *n*

num·skull \'nəmˌskəl\ *n* : stupid person

nun \'nən\ *n* : woman belonging to a religious order — **nun·nery** \-ərē\ *n*

nup·tial \'nəpshəl\ *adj* : relating to marriage or a wedding ~ *n* : marriage or wedding — usu. pl.

nurse \'nərs\ *n* **1** : one hired to care for children **2** : person trained to care for sick people ~ *vb* **nursed; nurs·ing 1** : suckle **2** : care for

nurs·ery \'nərsərē\ *n, pl* -er·ies **1** : place where children are cared for **2** : place where young plants are grown

nursing home *n* : private establishment providing care for persons who are unable to care for themselves

nur·ture \'nərchər\ *n* **1** : training or upbringing **2** : food or nourishment ~ *vb* -tured; -tur·ing **1** : care for or feed **2** : educate

nut \'nət\ *n* **1** : dry hard-shelled fruit or seed with a firm inner kernel **2** : metal block with a screw hole through it **3** : foolish, eccentric, or crazy person **4** : enthusiast — **nut·crack·er** *n* — **nut·shell** *n* — **nut·ty** *adj*

nut·hatch \'nətˌhach\ *n* : small bird

nut·meg \'nətˌmeg, -ˌmāg\ *n* : nutlike aromatic seed of a tropical tree

nu·tri·ent \'nütrēənt, 'nyü-\ *n* : something giving nourishment — **nutrient** *adj*

nu·tri·ment \-trəmənt\ *n* : nutrient

nu·tri·tion \nu'trishən, nyü-\ *n* : act or process of nourishing esp. with food — **nu·tri·tion·al** \-'trishənəl\ *adj* — **nu·tri·tious** \-'trishəs\ *adj* — **nu·tri·tive** \'nütrətiv, 'nyü-\ *adj*

nuts \'nəts\ *adj* **1** : enthusiastic **2** : crazy

nuz·zle \'nəzəl\ *vb* -zled; -zling **1** : touch with or as if with the nose **2** : snuggle

ny·lon \'nīˌlän\ *n* **1** : tough synthetic material used esp. in textiles **2** *pl* : stockings made of nylon

nymph \'nimf\ *n* **1** : lesser goddess in ancient mythology **2** : girl **3** : immature insect

O

o \'ō\ *n, pl* **o's** *or* **os** \'ōz\ **1** : 15th letter of the alphabet **2** : zero

O *var of* OH

oaf \'ōf\ *n* : stupid or awkward person — **oaf·ish** \'ōfish\ *adj*

oak \'ōk\ *n, pl* **oaks** *or* **oak** : tree bearing a thin-shelled nut or its wood — **oak·en** \'ōkən\ *adj*

oar \'ōr\ *n* : pole with a blade at the end used to propel a boat

oar·lock \-,läk\ *n* : U-shaped device for holding an oar

oa·sis \ō'āsəs\ *n, pl* **oa·ses** \-,sēz\ : fertile area in a desert

oat \'ōt\ *n* : cereal grass or its edible seed — **oat·cake** *n* — **oat·en** \-ᵊn\ *adj* — **oat·meal** *n*

oath \'ōth\ *n, pl* **oaths** \'ōthz, 'ōths\ **1** : solemn appeal to God as a pledge of sincerity **2** : profane utterance

ob·du·rate \'äbdùret, -dyù-\ *adj* : stubbornly resistant — **ob·du·ra·cy** \-rəsē\ *n*

obe·di·ent \ō'bēdēənt\ *adj* : willing to obey — **obe·di·ence** \-əns\ *n* — **obe·di·ent·ly** *adv*

obei·sance \ō'bēsəns, -'bās-\ *n* : bow of respect or submission

obe·lisk \'äbə,lisk\ *n* : 4-sided tapering pillar

obese \ōbēs\ *adj* : extremely fat — **obe·si·ty** \-'bēsətē\ *n*

obey \ō'bā\ *vb* **obeyed; obey·ing 1** : follow the commands or guidance of **2** : behave in accordance with

ob·fus·cate \'äbfə,skāt\ *vb* **-cat·ed; -cat·ing** : confuse — **ob·fus·ca·tion** \,äbfəs'kā-shən\ *n*

obit·u·ary \ə'bichə,werē\ *n, pl* **-ar·ies** : death notice

¹ob·ject \'äbjikt\ *n* **1** : something that may be seen or felt **2** : purpose **3** : noun or equivalent toward which the action of a verb is directed or which follows a preposition

²object \əb'jekt\ *vb* : offer opposition or disapproval — **ob·jec·tion** \-'jekshən\ *n* — **ob·jec·tion·able** \-shən-əbəl\ *adj* — **ob·jec·tion·ably** \-blē\ *adv* — **ob·jec·tor** \-'jektər\ *n*

ob·jec·tive \əb'jektiv\ *adj* **1** : relating to an object or end **2** : existing outside an individual's thoughts or feelings **3** : treating facts without distortion **4** : relating to or being a grammatical case marking objects ~ *n* : aim or end of action — **ob·jec·tive·ly** *adv*

— **ob·jec·tive·ness** *n* — **ob·jec·tiv·i·ty** \ˌäbˌjek'tivətē\ *n*

ob·li·gate \'äbləˌgāt\ *vb* -**gat·ed; -gat·ing** : bind legally or morally — **ob·li·ga·tion** \ˌäblə'gāshən\ *n* — **oblig·a·to·ry** \ə'bligəˌtōrē, 'äbligə-\ *adj*

oblige \ə'blīj\ *vb* **obliged; oblig·ing 1** : compel **2** : do a favor for — **oblig·ing** *adj* — **oblig·ing·ly** *adv*

oblique \ō'blēk, -'blīk\ *adj* **1** : lying at a slanting angle **2** : indirect — **oblique·ly** *adv* — **oblique·ness** *n* — **obliq·ui·ty** \-'blikwətē\ *n*

oblit·er·ate \ə'blitəˌrāt\ *vb* -**at·ed; -at·ing** : completely remove or destroy — **oblit·er·a·tion** \-ˌblitə'rāshən\ *n*

obliv·i·on \ə'blivēən\ *n* **1** : state of having lost conscious awareness **2** : state of being forgotten

obliv·i·ous \-ēəs\ *adj* : not aware or mindful — with *to* or *of* — **obliv·i·ous·ly** *adv* — **obliv·i·ous·ness** *n*

ob·long \'äbˌlȯŋ\ *adj* : longer in one direction than in the other with opposite sides parallel — **oblong** *n*

ob·lo·quy \'äbləkwē\ *n, pl* -**quies 1** : strongly condemning utterance **2** : bad repute

ob·nox·ious \äb'näkshəs, əb-\ *adj* : repugnant — **ob·nox-**

ious·ly *adv* — **ob·nox·ious·ness** *n*

oboe \'ōbō\ *n* : slender woodwind instrument with a reed mouthpiece — **obo·ist** \'oˌbō·ist\ *n*

ob·scene \äb'sēn, əb-\ *adj* : repugnantly indecent — **ob·scene·ly** *adv* — **ob·scen·i·ty** \-'senətē\ *n*

ob·scure \äb'skyu̇r, əb-\ *adj* **1** : dim or hazy **2** : not well known **3** : vague ~ *vb* : make indistinct or unclear — **ob·scure·ly** *adv* — **ob·scu·ri·ty** \-'skyu̇rətē\ *n*

ob·se·quies \'äbsəkwēz\ *n pl* : funeral or burial rites

ob·se·qui·ous \əb'sēkwēəs\ *adj* : excessively attentive or flattering — **ob·se·qui·ous·ly** *adv* — **ob·se·qui·ous·ness** *n*

ob·ser·va·to·ry \əb'zərvəˌtōrē\ *n, pl* -**ries** : place for observing astronomical phenomena

ob·serve \əb'zərv\ *vb* -**served; -serv·ing 1** : conform to **2** : celebrate **3** : see, watch, or notice **4** : remark — **ob·serv·able** *adj* — **ob·ser·vance** \-'zərvəns\ *n* — **ob·ser·vant** \-vənt\ *adj* — **ob·ser·va·tion** \ˌäbsər'vāshən, -zər-\ *n*

ob·sess \əb'ses\ *vb* : preoccupy intensely or abnormally — **ob·ses·sion** \äb'seshən, əb-\ *n* — **ob·ses·sive** \-'sesiv\ *adj* — **ob·ses·sive·ly** *adv*

ob·so·les·cent \ˌäbsə'les°nt\ *adj* : going out of use — **ob·so·les·cence** \-°ns\ *n*

ob·so·lete \ˌäbsə'lēt, 'äbsəˌ-\ *adj* : no longer in use

ob·sta·cle \'äbstikəl\ *n* : something that stands in the way or opposes

ob·stet·rics \əb'stetriks\ *n sing or pl* : branch of medicine that deals with childbirth — **ob·stet·ric** \-rik\, **ob·stet·ri·cal** \-rikəl\ *adj* — **ob·ste·tri·cian** \ˌäbstə'trishən\ *n*

ob·sti·nate \'äbstənət\ *adj* : stubborn — **ob·sti·na·cy** \-nəsē\ *n* — **ob·sti·nate·ly** *adv*

ob·strep·er·ous \əb'strepərəs\ *adj* : uncontrollably noisy or defiant — **ob·strep·er·ous·ness** *n*

ob·struct \əb'strəkt\ *vb* : block or impede — **ob·struc·tion** \-'strəkshən\ *n* — **ob·struc·tive** \-'strəktiv\ *adj* — **ob·struc·tor** \-tər\ *n*

ob·tain \əb'tān\ *vb* **1** : gain by effort **2** : be generally recognized — **ob·tain·able** *adj*

ob·trude \əb'trüd\ *vb* **-trud·ed; -trud·ing 1** : thrust out **2** : intrude — **ob·tru·sion** \-'trüzhən\ *n* — **ob·tru·sive** \-'trüsiv\ *adj* — **ob·tru·sive·ly** *adv* — **ob·tru·sive·ness** *n*

ob·tuse \äb'tüs, əb-, -'tyüs\ *adj* **1** : slow-witted **2** : ex-ceeding 90 but less than 180 degrees — **ob·tuse·ly** *adv* — **ob·tuse·ness** *n*

ob·verse \'äbˌvərs, äb'-\ *n* : principal side (as of a coin)

ob·vi·ate \'äbvēˌāt\ *vb* **-at·ed; -at·ing** : make unnecessary

ob·vi·ous \'äbvēəs\ *adj* : plain or unmistakable — **ob·vi·ous·ly** *adv* — **ob·vi·ous·ness** *n*

oc·ca·sion \ə'kāzhən\ *n* **1** : favorable opportunity **2** : cause **3** : time of an event **4** : special event ∼ *vb* : cause — **oc·ca·sion·al** \-'kāzhənəl\ *adj* — **oc·ca·sion·al·ly** *adv*

oc·ci·den·tal \ˌäksə'dent°l\ *adj* : western — **Occidental** *n*

oc·cult \ə'kəlt, 'äkˌəlt\ *adj* **1** : secret or mysterious **2** : relating to supernatural agencies — **oc·cult·ism** \-'kəlˌtizəm\ *n* — **oc·cult·ist** \-tist\ *n*

oc·cu·pan·cy \'äkyəpənsē\ *n, pl* **-cies** : an occupying

oc·cu·pant \-pənt\ *n* : one who occupies

oc·cu·pa·tion \ˌäkyə'pāshən\ *n* **1** : vocation **2** : action or state of occupying — **oc·cu·pa·tion·al** \-shənəl\ *adj* — **oc·cu·pa·tion·al·ly** *adv*

oc·cu·py \'äkyəˌpī\ *vb* **-pied; -py·ing 1** : engage the attention of **2** : fill up **3** : take or hold possession of **4** : reside in — **oc·cu·pi·er** \-ˌpīər\ *n*

oc·cur \ə'kər\ *vb* **-rr-** **1** : be found or met with **2** : take place **3** : come to mind

oc·cur·rence \ə'kərəns\ *n* : something that takes place

ocean \'ōshən\ *n* **1** : whole body of salt water **2** : very large body of water — **ocean-front** *n* — **ocean·go·ing** *adj* — **oce·an·ic** \ˌōshē'anik\ *adj*

ocean·og·ra·phy \ˌōshə'nägrəfē\ *n* : science dealing with the ocean — **ocean·og·ra·pher** \-fər\ *n* — **ocean·o·graph·ic** \-nə'grafik\ *adj*

oce·lot \'äsəˌlät, 'ōsə-\ *n* : medium-sized American wildcat

ocher, ochre \'ōkər\ *n* : red or yellow pigment

o'·clock \ə'kläk\ *adv* : according to the clock

oc·ta·gon \'äktəˌgän\ *n* : 8-sided polygon — **oc·tag·o·nal** \äk'tagənᵊl\ *adj*

oc·tave \'äktiv\ *n* : musical interval of 8 steps or the notes within this interval

Oc·to·ber \äk'tōbər\ *n* : 10th month of the year having 31 days

oc·to·pus \'äktəpəs\ *n, pl* **-pus-es** *or* **-pi** \-ˌpī\ : sea mollusk with 8 arms

oc·u·lar \'äkyələr\ *adj* : relating to the eye

oc·u·list \'äkyəlist\ *n* **1** : oph-thalmologist **2** : optometrist

odd \'äd\ *adj* **1** : being only one of a pair or set **2** : not divisible by two without a remainder **3** : additional to what is usual or to the number mentioned **4** : queer — **odd-ly** *adv* — **odd·ness** *n*

odd·i·ty \'ädətē\ *n, pl* **-ties** : something odd

odds \'ädz\ *n pl* **1** : difference by which one thing is favored **2** : disagreement **3** : ratio between winnings and the amount of the bet

ode \'ōd\ *n* : solemn lyric poem

odi·ous \'ōdēəs\ *adj* : hated — **odi·ous·ly** *adv* — **odi·ous·ness** *n*

odi·um \'ōdēəm\ *n* **1** : merited loathing **2** : disgrace

odor \'ōdər\ *n* : quality that affects the sense of smell — **odor·less** *adj* — **odor·ous** *adj*

od·ys·sey \'ädəsē\ *n, pl* **-seys** : long wandering

o'er \'ōr\ *adv or prep* : OVER

of \'əv, 'äv\ *prep* **1** : from **2** : distinguished by **3** : because of **4** : made or written by **5** : made with, being, or containing **6** : belonging to or connected with **7** : about **8** : that is **9** : concerning **10** : before

off \'öf\ *adv* **1** : from a place **2** : unattached or removed **3** : to a state of being no longer in use **4** : away from work **5**

: at a distance in time or space ~ *prep* **1** : away from **2** : at the expense of **3** : not engaged in or abstaining from **4** : below the usual level of ~ *adj* **1** : not operating, up to standard, or correct **2** : remote **3** : provided for

of·fal \'òfəl\ *n* **1** : waste **2** : viscera and trimmings of a butchered animal

of·fend \ə'fend\ *vb* **1** : sin or act in violation **2** : hurt, annoy, or insult — **of·fend·er** *n*

of·fense, of·fence \ə'fens, 'äfˌ ens\ *n* : attack, misdeed, or insult

of·fen·sive \ə'fensiv, 'äfˌen-\ *adj* : causing offense ~ *n* : attack — **of·fen·sive·ly** *adv* — **of·fen·sive·ness** *n*

of·fer \'òfər\ *vb* **1** : present for acceptance **2** : propose **3** : put up (an effort) ~ *n* **1** : proposal **2** : bid — **of·fer·ing** *n*

of·fer·to·ry \'òfərˌtōrē\ *n, pl* **-ries** : presentation of offerings or its musical accompaniment

off·hand *adv or adj* : without previous thought or preparation

of·fice \'òfəs\ *n* **1** : position of authority (as in government) **2** : rite **3** : place where a business is transacted — **of·fice·hold·er** *n*

of·fi·cer \'òfəsər\ *n* **1** : one charged with law enforcement **2** : one who holds an office of trust or authority **3** : one who holds a commission in the armed forces

of·fi·cial \ə'fishəl\ *n* : one in office ~ *adj* : authorized or authoritative — **of·fi·cial·dom** \-dəm\ *n* — **of·fi·cial·ly** *adv*

of·fi·ci·ant \ə'fishēənt\ *n* : clergy member who officiates at a religious rite

of·fi·ci·ate \ə'fishēˌāt\ *vb* **-at·ed; -at·ing** : perform a ceremony or function

of·fi·cious \ə'fishəs\ *adj* : volunteering one's services unnecessarily — **of·fi·cious·ly** *adv* — **of·fi·cious·ness** *n*

off·ing \'òfiŋ\ *n* : future

off·set \'òfˌset\ *vb* **-set; -set·ting** : provide an opposite or equaling effect to

off·shoot \'òfˌshüt\ *n* : outgrowth

off·shore *adv* : at a distance from the shore ~ *adj* : moving away from or situated off the shore

off·spring \'òfˌspriŋ\ *n, pl* **offspring** : one coming into being through animal or plant reproduction

of·ten \'òfən, 'òft-\ *adv* : many times — **of·ten·times, oft·times** *adv*

ogle \'ōgəl\ *vb* **ogled; ogling** : stare at lustily — **ogle** *n* — **ogler** \-ələr\ *n*

ogre \'ōgər\ *n* **1** : monster **2** : dreaded person

oh \'ō\ *interj* **1** — used to express an emotion **2** — used in direct address

ohm \'ōm\ *n* : unit of electrical resistance — **ohm·me·ter** \'ōm₁mētər\ *n*

oil \'òil\ *n* **1** : greasy liquid substance **2** : petroleum ～ *vb* : put oil in or on — **oil·er** *n* — **oil·i·ness** \'òilēnəs\ *n* — **oily** \'òilē\ *adj*

oil·cloth *n* : cloth treated with oil or paint and used for coverings

oil·skin *n* : oiled waterproof cloth

oink \'òiŋk\ *n* : natural noise of a hog — **oink** *vb*

oint·ment \'òintmənt\ *n* : oily medicinal preparation

OK *or* **okay** \ō'kā\ *adv or adj* : all right ～ *vb* **OK'd** *or* **okayed; OK'·ing** *or* **okay·ing** : approve ～ *n* : approval

okra \'ōkrə, *South also* -krē\ *n* : leafy vegetable with edible green pods

old \'ōld\ *adj* **1** : of long standing **2** : of a specified age **3** : relating to a past era **4** : having existed a long time — **old·ish** \'ōldish\ *adj*

old·en \'ōldən\ *adj* : of or relating to a bygone era

old–fash·ioned \-'fashənd\ *adj* **1** : out-of-date **2** : conservative

old maid *n* : spinster

old–tim·er \ōld'tīmər\ *n* **1** : veteran **2** : one who is old

ole·an·der \'ōlē₁andər\ *n* : poisonous evergreen shrub

oleo·mar·ga·rine \₁ōlēō'mär-jərən\ *n* : margarine

ol·fac·to·ry \äl'faktərē, ōl-\ *adj* : relating to the sense of smell

oli·gar·chy \'älə₁gärkē, 'ōlə-\ *n, pl* **-chies 1** : government by a few people **2** : those holding power in an oligarchy — **oli·garch** \-₁gärk\ *n* — **oli·gar·chic** \₁älə'gärkik, ₁ōlə-\, **oli·gar·chi·cal** \-kikəl\ *adj*

ol·ive \'äliv, -əv\ *n* **1** : evergreen tree bearing small edible fruit or the fruit **2** : dull yellowish green color

om·buds·man \'äm₁bùdzmən, äm'bùdz-\ *n, pl* **-men** \-mən\ : complaint investigator

om·e·let, om·e·lette \'ämələt\ *n* : beaten eggs lightly fried and folded

omen \'ōmən\ *n* : sign or warning of the future

om·i·nous \'ämənəs\ *adj* : presaging evil — **om·i·nous·ly** *adv* — **om·i·nous·ness** *n*

omit \ō'mit\ *vb* **-tt- 1 :** leave out **2 :** fail to perform — **omis·si·ble** \ō'misəbəl\ *adj* — **omis·sion** \-'mishən\ *n*

om·nip·o·tent \äm'nipətənt\ *adj* **:** almighty — **om·nip·o·tence** \-əns\ *n* — **om·nip·o·tent·ly** *adv*

om·ni·pres·ent \‚ämni'prez³nt\ *adj* **:** ever-present — **om·ni·pres·ence** \-³ns\ *n*

om·ni·scient \äm'nishənt\ *adj* **:** all-knowing — **om·ni·sci·ence** \-əns\ *n* — **om·ni·sci·ent·ly** *adv*

om·niv·o·rous \äm'nivərəs\ *adj* **1 :** eating both meat and vegetables **2 :** avid — **om·niv·o·rous·ly** *adv*

on \'ȯn, 'än\ *prep* **1 :** in or to a position over and in contact with **2 :** at or to **3 :** about **4 :** from **5 :** with regard to **6 :** in a state or process **7 :** during the time of ~ *adv* **1 :** in or into contact with **2 :** forward **3 :** into operation

once \'wəns\ *adv* **1 :** one time only **2 :** at any one time **3 :** formerly ~ *n* **:** one time ~ *conj* **:** as soon as ~ *adj* **:** former — **at once 1 :** simultaneously **2 :** immediately

once–over *n* **:** swift examination

on·com·ing *adj* **:** approaching

one \'wən\ *adj* **1 :** being a single thing **2 :** being one in particular **3 :** being the same in kind ~ *pron* **1 :** certain indefinitely indicated person or thing **2 :** a person in general ~ *n* **1 :** 1st in a series **2 :** single person or thing — **one·ness** *n*

oner·ous \'änərəs, 'ōnə-\ *adj* **:** imposing a burden

one·self \‚wən'self\ *pron* **:** one's own self — usu. used reflexively or for emphasis

one–sid·ed \-'sīdəd\ *adj* **1 :** occurring on one side only **2 :** partial

one·time *adj* **:** former

one–way *adj* **:** made or for use in only one direction

on·go·ing *adj* **:** continuing

on·ion \'ənyən\ *n* **:** plant grown for its pungent edible bulb or this bulb

on·ly \'ōnlē\ *adj* **:** alone in its class ~ *adv* **1 :** merely or exactly **2 :** solely **3 :** at the very least **4 :** as a result ~ *conj* **:** but

on·set *n* **:** start

on·shore *adj* **1 :** moving toward shore **2 :** lying on or near the shore — **onshore** *adv*

on·slaught \'än‚slȯt, 'ȯn-\ *n* **:** attack

on·to \'ȯntü, 'än-\ *prep* **:** to a position or point on

onus \'ōnəs\ *n* **:** burden (as of obligation or blame)

on·ward \'ȯnwərd, 'än-\ *adv or adj* **:** forward

on·yx \'äniks\ *n* : quartz used as a gem

ooze \'üz\ *n* : soft mud ∼ *vb* **oozed; ooz·ing** : flow or leak out slowly — **oozy** \'üzē\ *adj*

opac·i·ty \ō'pasətē\ *n* : quality or state of being opaque or an opaque spot

opal \'ōpəl\ *n* : gem with delicate colors

opaque \ō'pāk\ *adj* **1** : blocking light **2** : not easily understood **3** : dull-witted — **opaque·ly** *adv*

open \'ōpən\ *adj* **1** : not shut or shut up **2** : not secret or hidden **3** : frank or generous **4** : extended **5** : free from controls **6** : not decided ∼ *vb* **1** : make or become open **2** : make or become functional **3** : start ∼ *n* : outdoors — **open·er** \-ər\ *n* — **open·ly** *adv* — **open·ness** *n*

open·hand·ed \-'handəd\ *adj* : generous — **open·hand·ed·ly** *adv*

open·ing \'ōpəniŋ\ *n* **1** : act or instance of making open **2** : something that is open **3** : opportunity

op·era \'äpərə, 'äprə\ *n* : drama set to music — **op·er·at·ic** \ˌäpə'ratik\ *adj*

op·er·a·ble \'äpərəbəl\ *adj* **1** : usable or in working condition **2** : suitable for surgical treatment

op·er·ate \'äpəˌrāt\ *vb* **-at·ed; -at·ing 1** : perform work **2** : perform an operation **3** : manage — **op·er·a·tor** \-ˌrātər\ *n*

op·er·a·tion \ˌäpə'rāshən\ *n* **1** : act or process of operating **2** : surgical work on a living body **3** : military action or mission — **op·er·a·tion·al** \-shənəl\ *adj*

op·er·a·tive \'äpərətiv, -ˌrāt-\ *adj* : working or having an effect

op·er·et·ta \ˌäpə'retə\ *n* : light opera

oph·thal·mol·o·gy \ˌäfˌthal-'mäləjē\ *n* : branch of medicine dealing with the eye — **oph·thal·mol·o·gist** \-jist\ *n*

opi·ate \'ōpēət, -pēˌāt\ *n* : preparation or derivative of opium

opine \ō'pīn\ *vb* **opined; opin·ing** : express an opinion

opin·ion \ə'pinyən\ *n* **1** : belief **2** : judgment **3** : formal statement by an expert

opin·ion·at·ed \-yəˌnātəd\ *adj* : stubborn in one's opinions

opi·um \'ōpēəm\ *n* : addictive narcotic drug that is the dried juice of a poppy

opos·sum \ə'päsəm\ *n* : common tree-dwelling nocturnal mammal

op·po·nent \ə'pōnənt\ *n* : one that opposes

op·por·tune \ˌäpər'tün, -'tyün\ *adj* : suitable or timely — **op·por·tune·ly** *adv*

op·por·tun·ism \-'tü͟ˌnizəm, -'tyü-\ *n* : a taking advantage of opportunities — **op·por·tun·ist** \-nist\ *n* — **op·por·tu·nis·tic** \-tü'nistik, -tyü-\ *adj*

op·por·tu·ni·ty \-'tünətē, -'tyü-\ *n, pl* **-ties** : favorable time

op·pose \ə'pōz\ *vb* **-posed; -pos·ing** **1** : place opposite or against something **2** : resist — **op·po·si·tion** \ˌäpə'zishən\ *n*

op·po·site \'äpəzət\ *n* : one that is opposed ~ *adj* **1** : set facing something that is at the other side or end **2** : opposed or contrary ~ *adv* : on opposite sides ~ *prep* : across from — **op·po·site·ly** *adv*

op·press \ə'pres\ *vb* **1** : persecute **2** : weigh down — **op·pres·sion** \ə'preshən\ *n* — **op·pres·sive** \-'presiv\ *adj* — **op·pres·sive·ly** *adv* — **op·pres·sor** \-'presər\ *n*

op·pro·bri·ous \ə'prōbrēəs\ *adj* : expressing or deserving opprobrium — **op·pro·bri·ous·ly** *adv*

op·pro·bri·um \-brēəm\ *n* **1** : something that brings disgrace **2** : infamy

opt \'äpt\ *vb* : choose

op·tic \'äptik\ *adj* : relating to vision or the eye

op·ti·cal \'äptikəl\ *adj* : relating to optics, vision, or the eye

op·ti·cian \äp'tishən\ *n* : maker of or dealer in eyeglasses

op·tics \'äptiks\ *n pl* : science of light and vision

op·ti·mal \'äptəməl\ *adj* : most favorable — **op·ti·mal·ly** *adv*

op·ti·mism \'äptəˌmizəm\ *n* : tendency to hope for the best — **op·ti·mist** \-mist\ *n* — **op·ti·mis·tic** \ˌäptə'mistik\ *adj* — **op·ti·mis·ti·cal·ly** *adv*

op·ti·mum \'äptəməm\ *n, pl* **-ma** \-mə\ : amount or degree of something most favorable to an end — **optimum** *adj*

op·tion \'äpshən\ *n* **1** : ability to choose **2** : right to buy or sell a stock **3** : alternative — **op·tion·al** \-shənəl\ *adj*

op·tom·e·try \äp'tämətrē\ *n* : profession of examining the eyes — **op·tom·e·trist** \-trist\ *n*

op·u·lent \'äpyələnt\ *adj* : lavish — **op·u·lence** \-ləns\ *n* — **op·u·lent·ly** *adv*

opus \'ōpəs\ *n, pl* **opera** \'ōpərə, 'äpə-\ : work esp. of music

or \'ȯr\ *conj* — used to indicate an alternative

-or \ər\ *n suffix* : one that performs an action

or·a·cle \\'orəkəl\\ *n* **1** : one held to give divinely inspired answers or revelations **2** : wise person or an utterance of such a person — **orac·u·lar** \o'rakyələr\ *adj*

oral \\'ōrəl\\ *adj* **1** : spoken **2** : relating to the mouth — **oral·ly** *adv*

or·ange \\'orinj\\ *n* **1** : reddish yellow citrus fruit **2** : color between red and yellow — **or·ange·ade** \ˌorinj'ād\ *n*

orang·u·tan \ə'raŋəˌtaŋ, -ˌtan\ *n* : large reddish brown ape

ora·tion \ə'rāshən\ *n* : elaborate formal speech

or·a·tor \\'orətər\\ *n* : one noted as a public speaker

or·a·to·rio \ˌorə'tōrēˌō\ *n, pl* **-ri·os** : major choral work

or·a·to·ry \\'orəˌtōrē\\ *n* : art of public speaking — **or·a·tor·i·cal** \ˌorə'torikəl\ *adj*

orb \\'orb\\ *n* : spherical body

or·bit \\'orbət\\ *n* : path made by one body revolving around another ~ *vb* : revolve around — **or·bit·al** \-ᵊl\ *adj* — **or·bit·er** *n*

or·chard \\'orchərd\\ *n* : place where fruit or nut trees are grown — **or·chard·ist** \-ist\ *n*

or·ches·tra \\'orkəstrə\\ *n* **1** : group of musicians **2** : front seats of a theater's main floor — **or·ches·tral** \or'kestrəl\ *adj* — **or·ches·tral·ly** *adv*

or·ches·trate \\'orkəˌstrāt\\ *vb* **-trat·ed; -trat·ing** **1** : compose or arrange for an orchestra **2** : arrange or combine for best effect — **or·ches·tra·tion** \ˌorkə'strāshən\ *n*

or·chid \\'orkəd\\ *n* : plant with showy 3-petal flowers or its flower

or·dain \or'dān\ *vb* **1** : admit to the clergy **2** : decree

or·deal \or'dēl, 'orˌdēl\ *n* : severely trying experience

or·der \\'ordər\\ *n* **1** : rank, class, or special group **2** : arrangement **3** : rule of law **4** : authoritative regulation or instruction **5** : working condition **6** : special request for a purchase or what is purchased ~ *vb* **1** : arrange **2** : give an order to **3** : place an order for

or·der·ly \-lē\ *adj* **1** : being in order or tidy **2** : well behaved ~ *n, pl* **-lies** **1** : officer's attendant **2** : hospital attendant — **or·der·li·ness** *n*

or·di·nal \\'ordᵊnəl\\ *n* : number indicating order in a series

or·di·nance \-ᵊnəns\ *n* : municipal law

or·di·nary \\'ordᵊnˌerē\\ *adj* : of common occurrence, quality, or ability — **or·di·nar·i·ly** \ˌordᵊn'erəlē\ *adv*

or·di·na·tion \ˌordᵊn'āshən\ *n* : act of ordaining

ord·nance \ˈȯrdnəns\ *n* : military supplies

ore \ˈōr\ *n* : mineral containing a valuable constituent

oreg·a·no \əˈregəˌnō\ *n* : mint used as a seasoning and source of oil

or·gan \ˈȯrgən\ *n* **1** : air-powered or electronic keyboard instrument **2** : animal or plant structure with special function **3** : periodical

or·gan·ic \ȯrˈganik\ *adj* **1** : relating to a bodily organ **2** : relating to living things **3** : relating to or containing carbon or its compounds **4** : relating to foods produced without the use of laboratory-made products — **or·gan·i·cal·ly** *adv*

or·gan·ism \ˈȯrgəˌnizəm\ *n* : a living thing

or·gan·ist \ˈȯrgənist\ *n* : organ player

or·ga·nize \ˈȯrgəˌnīz\ *vb* **-nized; -niz·ing** : form parts into a functioning whole — **or·ga·ni·za·tion** \ˌȯrgənəˈzāshən\ *n* — **or·ga·ni·za·tion·al** \-shənəl\ *adj* — **or·ga·niz·er** *n*

or·gasm \ˈȯrˌgazəm\ *n* : climax of sexual excitement — **or·gas·mic** \ȯrˈgazmik\ *adj*

or·gy \ˈȯrjē\ *n, pl* **-gies** : unrestrained indulgence (as in sexual activity)

ori·ent \ˈōrēˌent\ *vb* **1** : set in a definite position **2** : acquaint with a situation — **ori·en·ta·tion** \ˌōrēənˈtāshən\ *n*

ori·en·tal \ˌōrēˈentᵊl\ *adj* : Eastern — **Oriental** *n*

or·i·fice \ˈȯrəfəs\ *n* : opening

or·i·gin \ˈȯrəjən\ *n* **1** : ancestry **2** : rise, beginning, or derivation from a source — **orig·i·nate** \əˈrijəˌnāt\ *vb* — **orig·i·na·tor** \-ər\ *n*

orig·i·nal \əˈrijənəl\ *n* : something from which a copy is made ∼ *adj* **1** : first **2** : not copied from something else **3** : inventive — **orig·i·nal·i·ty** *n* — **orig·i·nal·ly** *adv*

ori·ole \ˈōrēˌōl, -ēəl\ *n* : American songbird

or·na·ment \ˈȯrnəmənt\ *n* : something that adorns ∼ *vb* : provide with ornament — **or·na·men·tal** \ˌȯrnəˈmentᵊl\ *adj* — **or·na·men·ta·tion** \-mənˈtāshən\ *n*

or·nate \ȯrˈnāt\ *adj* : elaborately decorated — **or·nate·ly** *adv* — **or·nate·ness** *n*

or·nery \ˈȯrnərē, ˈän-\ *adj* : irritable

or·ni·thol·o·gy \ˌȯrnəˈthäləjē\ *n, pl* **-gies** : study of birds — **or·ni·tho·log·i·cal** \-thəˈläjikəl\ *adj* — **or·ni·thol·o·gist** \-ˈthäləjist\ *n*

or·phan \ˈȯrfən\ *n* : child whose parents are dead —

orphan *vb* — **or·phan·age** \-ənij\ *n*

or·tho·don·tics \ˌȯrthə'dän-tiks\ *n* : dentistry dealing with straightening teeth — **or·tho·don·tist** \-'däntist\ *n*

or·tho·dox \'ȯrthəˌdäks\ *adj* **1** : conforming to established doctrine **2** *cap* : of or relating to a Christian church originating in the Eastern Roman Empire — **or·tho·doxy** \-ˌdäksē\ *n*

or·thog·ra·phy \ȯr'thägrəfē\ *n* : spelling — **or·tho·graph·ic** \ˌȯrthə'grafik\ *adj*

or·tho·pe·dics \ˌȯrthə'pēdiks\ *n sing or pl* : correction or prevention of skeletal deformities — **or·tho·pe·dic** \-ik\ *adj* — **or·tho·pe·dist** \-'pēdist\ *n*

-o·ry \ˌōrē, ˌȯrē, ərē\ *adj suffix* **1** : of, relating to, or characterized by **2** : serving for, producing, or maintaining

os·cil·late \'äsəˌlāt\ *vb* **-lat·ed; -lat·ing** : swing back and forth — **os·cil·la·tion** \ˌäsə'lāshən\ *n*

os·mo·sis \äz'mōsəs, äs-\ *n* : diffusion esp. of water through a membrane — **os·mot·ic** \-'mätik\ *adj*

os·prey \'äsprē, -ˌprā\ *n, pl* **-preys** : large fish-eating hawk

os·si·fy \'äsəˌfī\ *vb* **-fied; -fy·ing** : make or become hardened or set in one's ways

os·ten·si·ble \ä'stensəbəl\ *adj* : seeming — **os·ten·si·bly** \-blē\ *adv*

os·ten·ta·tion \ˌästən'tāshən\ *n* : pretentious display — **os·ten·ta·tious** \-shəs\ *adj* — **os·ten·ta·tious·ly** *adv*

os·te·op·a·thy \ˌästē'äpəthē\ *n* : system of healing that emphasizes manipulation (as of joints) — **os·te·o·path** \'ästēəˌpath\ *n* — **os·te·o·path·ic** \ˌästēə'pathik\ *adj*

os·te·o·po·ro·sis \ˌästēōpə'rōsəs\ *n, pl* **-ro·ses** \-ˌsēz\ : condition characterized by fragile and porous bones

os·tra·cize \'ästrəˌsīz\ *vb* **-cized; -ciz·ing** : exclude by common consent — **os·tra·cism** \-ˌsizəm\ *n*

os·trich \'ästrich, 'ȯs-\ *n* : very large flightless bird

oth·er \'əthər\ *adj* **1** : being the one left **2** : alternate **3** : additional ∼ *pron* **1** : remaining one **2** : different one

oth·er·wise *adv* **1** : in a different way **2** : in different circumstances **3** : in other respects — **otherwise** *adj*

ot·ter \'ätər\ *n* : fish-eating mammal with webbed feet

ot·to·man \'ätəmən\ *n* : upholstered footstool

ought \'ȯt\ *verbal auxiliary* — used to express obligation, advisability, or expectation

ounce \'aůns\ *n* **1** : unit of weight equal to about 28.3 grams **2** : unit of capacity equal to about 29.6 milliliters

our \'är, 'aůr\ *adj* : of or relating to us

ours \'aůrz, 'ärz\ *pron* : that which belongs to us

our·selves \är'selvz, aůr-\ *pron* : we, us — used reflexively or for emphasis

-ous \əs\ *adj suffix* : having or having the qualities of

oust \'aůst\ *vb* : expel or eject

oust·er \'aůstər\ *n* : expulsion

out \'aůt\ *adv* **1** : away from the inside or center **2** : beyond control **3** : to extinction, exhaustion, or completion **4** : in or into the open ~ *vb* : become known ~ *adj* **1** : situated outside **2** : absent ~ *prep* **1** : out through **2** : outward on or along — **out·bound** *adj* — **out·build·ing** *n*

out·age \'aůtij\ *n* : period of no electricity

out·board \'aůt‚bōrd\ *adv* : outside a boat or ship — **outboard** *adj*

out·break \'aůt‚brāk\ *n* : sudden occurrence

out·burst \-‚bərst\ *n* : violent expression of feeling

out·cast \-‚kast\ *n* : person cast out by society

out·come \-‚kəm\ *n* : result

out·crop \'aůt‚kräp\ *n* : part of a rock stratum that appears above the ground — **outcrop** *vb*

out·cry \-‚krī\ *n* : loud cry

out·dat·ed \aůt'dātəd\ *adj* : out-of-date

out·dis·tance *vb* : go far ahead of

out·do \aůt'dü\ *vb* **-did** \-'did\; **-done** \-'dən\; **-do·ing** \-'düiŋ\; **-does** \-'dəz\ : do better than

out·doors \aůt'dōrz\ *adv* : in or into the open air ~ *n* : open air — **out·door** *adj*

out·er \'aůtər\ *adj* **1** : external **2** : farther out — **out·er·most** *adj*

out·field \'aůt‚fēld\ *n* : baseball field beyond the infield — **out·field·er** \-‚fēldər\ *n*

out·fit \'aůt‚fit\ *n* **1** : equipment for a special purpose **2** : group ~ *vb* **-tt-** : equip — **out·fit·ter** *n*

out·go \'aůt‚gō\ *n, pl* **outgoes** : expenditure

out·go·ing \'aůt‚gōiŋ\ *adj* **1** : retiring from a position **2** : friendly

out·grow \aůt'grō\ *vb* **-grew** \-'grü\; **-grown** \-'grōn\; **-grow·ing** **1** : grow faster than **2** : grow too large for

out·growth \'aůt‚grōth\ *n* **1** : product of growing out **2** : consequence

out·ing \'aȯtiŋ\ *n* : excursion

out·land·ish \aȯt'landish\ *adj* : very strange — **out·land·ish·ly** *adv*

outlast *vb* : last longer than

out·law \'aȯt,lȯ\ *n* : lawless person ～ *vb* : make illegal

out·lay \'aȯt,lā\ *n* : expenditure

out·let \'aȯt,let, -lət\ *n* **1** : exit **2** : means of release **3** : market for goods **4** : electrical device that gives access to wiring

out·line \'aȯt,līn\ *n* **1** : line marking the outer limits **2** : summary ～ *vb* **1** : draw the outline of **2** : indicate the chief parts of

out·live \aȯt'liv\ *vb* : live longer than

out·look \'aȯt,lu̇k\ *n* **1** : viewpoint **2** : prospect for the future

out·ly·ing \'aȯt,līiŋ\ *adj* : far from a central point

out·ma·neu·ver \,aȯtmə'nüvər, -'nyü,-\ *vb* : defeat by more skillful maneuvering

out·mod·ed \aȯt'mōdəd\ *adj* : out-of-date

out·num·ber \-'nəmbər\ *vb* : exceed in number

out of *prep* **1** : out from within **2** : beyond the limits of **3** : among **4** — used to indicate absence or loss **5** : because of **6** : from or with

out–of–date *adj* : no longer in fashion or in use

out·pa·tient *n* : person treated at a hospital who does not stay overnight

out·post *n* : remote military post

out·put *n* : amount produced ～ *vb* **-put·ted** *or* **-put; -put·ting** : produce

out·rage \'aȯt,rāj\ *n* **1** : violent or shameful act **2** : injury or insult **3** : extreme anger ～ *vb* **-raged; -rag·ing** **1** : subject to violent injury **2** : make very angry

out·ra·geous \aȯt'rājəs\ *adj* : extremely offensive or shameful — **out·ra·geous·ly** *adv* — **out·ra·geous·ness** *n*

out·right *adv* **1** : completely **2** : instantly ～ *adj* **1** : complete **2** : given without reservation

out·set *n* : beginning

out·side \aȯt'sīd, 'aȯt,-\ *n* **1** : place beyond a boundary **2** : exterior **3** : utmost limit ～ *adj* **1** : outer **2** : coming from without **3** : remote ～ *adv* : on or to the outside ～ *prep* **1** : on or to the outside of **2** : beyond the limits of

outside of *prep* **1** : outside **2** : besides

out·sid·er \-'sīdər\ *n* : one who does not belong to a group

out·skirts *n pl* : outlying parts (as of a city)

out·smart \aȯt'smärt\ *vb* : outwit

out·source \'aut͵sȯrs\ *vb* **-sourced; -sourc·ing :** obtain from an outside supplier

out·spo·ken *adj* **:** direct and open in speech — **out·spo·ken·ness** *n*

out·stand·ing *adj* **1 :** unpaid **2 :** very good — **out·stand·ing·ly** *adv*

out·strip \aut'strip\ *vb* **1 :** go faster than **2 :** surpass

¹**out·ward** \'autwərd\ *adj* **1 :** being toward the outside **2 :** showing outwardly

²**outward, out·wards** \-wərdz\ *adv* **:** toward the outside — **out·ward·ly** *adv*

out·wit \aut'wit\ *vb* **:** get the better of by superior cleverness

ova *pl of* OVUM

oval \'ōvəl\ *adj* **:** egg-shaped — **oval** *n*

ova·ry \'ōvərē\ *n, pl* **-ries 1 :** egg-producing organ **2 :** seed-producing part of a flower — **ovar·i·an** \ō'varēən\ *adj*

ova·tion \ō'vāshən\ *n* **:** enthusiastic applause

ov·en \'əvən\ *n* **:** chamber (as in a stove) for baking

over \'ōvər\ *adv* **1 :** across **2 :** upside down **3 :** in excess or addition **4 :** above **5 :** at an end

---

List of self-explanatory words with the prefix *over-*

overabundance	overbroad	overconfident
overabundant	overbuild	overconscientious
overachiever	overburden	overconsume
overactive	overbusy	overconsumption
overaggressive	overbuy	overcontrol
overambitious	overcapacity	overcook
overanalyze	overcapitalize	overcorrect
overanxiety	overcareful	overcritical
overanxious	overcautious	overcrowd
overarousal	overcharge	overdecorate
overassertive	overcivilized	overdependence
overbake	overclean	overdependent
overbid	overcommit	overdevelop
overbill	overcompensate	overdose
overbold	overcomplicate	overdramatic
overborrow	overconcern	overdramatize
overbright	overconfidence	overdress

6 : again ~ *prep* **1** : above in position or authority **2** : more than **3** : along, through, or across **4** : because of ~ *adj* **1** : upper **2** : remaining **3** : ended

over- *prefix* **1** : so as to exceed or surpass **2** : excessive or excessively

¹**over·age** \ˌōvərˈāj\ *adj* : too old

²**overage** \ˈōvərij\ *n* : surplus

over·all \ˌōvərˈȯl\ *adj* : including everything

over·alls \ˈōvərˌȯlz\ *n pl* : pants with an extra piece covering the chest

over·awe *vb* : subdue by awe

over·bear·ing \-ˈbariŋ\ *adj* : arrogant

over·blown \-ˈblōn\ *adj* : pretentious

over·board *adv* : over the side into the water

over·cast *adj* : clouded over ~ *n* : cloud covering

over·coat *n* : outer coat

over·come *vb* **-came** \-ˈkām\; **-come**; **-com·ing** **1** : defeat **2** : make helpless or exhausted

over·do *vb* **-did**; **-done**; **-do·ing**; **-does** : do too much

over·draft *n* : overdrawn sum

over·draw *vb* **-drew**; **-drawn**; **-draw·ing** : write checks for more than one's bank balance

overdrink	overexpand	overharvest
overdue	overexpansion	overhasty
overeager	overexplain	overheat
overeat	overexploit	overidealize
overeducated	overexpose	overimaginative
overelaborate	overextend	overimpress
overemotional	overextension	overindebtedness
overemphasis	overexuberant	overindulge
overemphasize	overfamiliar	overindulgence
overenergetic	overfatigued	overindulgent
overenthusiastic	overfeed	overinflate
overestimate	overfertilize	overinsistent
overexaggerate	overfill	overintense
overexaggeration	overfond	overintensity
overexcite	overgeneralization	overinvestment
overexcited	overgeneralize	overladen
overexercise	overgenerous	overlarge
overexert	overglamorize	overlend
overexertion	overgraze	overload

over·flow \ˌōvər'flō\ *vb* **1** : flood **2** : flow over — **over·flow** \'ōvərˌflō\ *n*

over·grow *vb* **-grew; -grown; -grow·ing** : grow over

over·hand *adj* : made with the hand brought down from above — **overhand** *adv* — **over·hand·ed** \-ˌhandəd\ *adv or adj*

over·hang *vb* **-hung; -hang·ing** : jut out over ∼ *n* : something that overhangs

over·haul *vb* **1** : repair **2** : overtake

over·head \ˌōvər'hed\ *adv* : aloft ∼ \'ōvərˌ-\ *adj* : situated above ∼ \'ōvərˌ-\ *n* : general business expenses

over·hear *vb* **-heard; -hear·ing** : hear without the speaker's knowledge

over·joyed *adj* : filled with joy

over·kill \'ōvərˌkil\ *n* : large excess

over·land \-ˌland, -lənd\ *adv or adj* : by, on, or across land

over·lap *vb* : lap over — **over·lap** \'ōvərˌlap\ *n*

over·lay \ˌōvər'lā\ *vb* **-laid; -lay·ing** : lay over or across — **over·lay** \'ōvərˌlā\ *n*

over·look \ˌōvər'lùk\ *vb* **1** : look down on **2** : fail to see **3** : ignore **4** : pardon **5** : supervise ∼ \'ōvərˌ-\ *n* : observation point

overlong	overproduction	oversexed
overloud	overpromise	oversimple
overmedicate	overprotect	oversimplify
overmodest	overprotective	oversolicitous
overmuch	overqualified	overspecialize
overobvious	overrate	overspend
overoptimistic	overreact	overstaff
overorganize	overreaction	overstimulation
overparticular	overrefined	overstock
overpay	overregulate	overstrain
overpayment	overregulation	overstress
overplay	overreliance	overstretch
overpopulated	overrepresented	oversubtle
overpraise	overrespond	oversupply
overprescribe	overripe	oversuspicious
overpressure	oversaturate	oversweeten
overprice	oversell	overtax
overprivileged	oversensitive	overtighten
overproduce	overserious	overtip

over·ly \\'ōvərlē\ *adv* : excessively

over·night *adv* **1** : through the night **2** : suddenly — **overnight** *adj*

over·pass *n* : bridge over a road

over·pow·er *vb* : conquer

over·reach \\ˌōvər'rēch\ *vb* : try or seek too much

over·ride *vb* **-rode; -rid·den; -rid·ing** : neutralize action of

over·rule *vb* : rule against or set aside

over·run *vb* **-ran; -run·ning 1** : swarm or flow over **2** : go beyond ~ *n* : an exceeding of estimated costs

over·seas *adv or adj* : beyond or across the sea

over·see \\ˌōvər'sē\ *vb* **-saw; -seen; -seeing** : supervise — **over·seer** \\'ōvərˌsiər\ *n*

over·shad·ow *vb* : exceed in importance

over·shoe *n* : protective outer shoe

over·shoot *vb* **-shot; -shooting** : shoot or pass beyond

over·sight *n* : inadvertent omission or error

over·sleep *vb* **-slept; -sleeping** : sleep longer than intended

over·spread *vb* **-spread; -spread·ing** : spread over or above

over·state *vb* : exaggerate — **over·state·ment** *n*

over·stay *vb* : stay too long

over·step *vb* : exceed

overt \\ō'vərt, 'ōˌvərt\ *adj* : not secret — **overt·ly** *adv*

over·take *vb* **-took; -tak·en; -tak·ing** : catch up with

over·throw \\ˌōvər'thrō\ *vb* **-threw; -thrown; -throw·ing 1** : upset **2** : defeat — **over·throw** \\'ōvərˌ-\ *n*

over·time *n* : extra working time — **overtime** *adv*

over·tone *n* **1** : higher tone in a complex musical tone **2** : suggestion

over·ture \\'ōvərˌchủr, -chər\ *n* **1** : opening offer **2** : musical introduction

over·turn *vb* **1** : turn over **2** : nullify

over·view *n* : brief survey

over·ween·ing \\ˌōvər'wēniŋ\ *adj* **1** : arrogant **2** : excessive

over·whelm \\ˌōvər'hwelm\ *vb* : overcome completely — **over·whelm·ing·ly** \\-'hwelmiŋlē\ *adv*

over·wrought \\ˌōvər'rȯt\ *adj* : extremely excited

ovoid \\'ōˌvȯid\, **ovoi·dal** \\ō'vȯidᵊl\ *adj* : egg-shaped

ovu·late \\'ävyəˌlāt, 'ōv-\ *vb* **-lat·ed; -lat·ing** : produce eggs

overtired	overuse	overweight
overtrain	overutilize	overwork
overtreat	overvalue	overzealous

from an ovary — **ovu·la·tion** \ˌävyə'lāshən, ˌōv-\ *n*

ovum \'ōvəm\ *n, pl* **ova** \-və\ : female germ cell

owe \'ō\ *vb* **owed; ow·ing 1** : have an obligation to pay **2** : be indebted to or for

owing to *prep* : because of

owl \'aül\ *n* : nocturnal bird of prey — **owl·ish** *adj* — **owl·ish·ly** *adv*

own \'ōn\ *adj* : belonging to oneself ~ *vb* **1** : have as property **2** : acknowledge ~ *pron* : one or ones belonging to oneself — **own·er** *n* — **own·er·ship** *n*

ox \'äks\ *n, pl* **ox·en** \'äksən\ : bovine mammal and esp. a castrated bull

ox·ide \'äkˌsīd\ *n* : compound of oxygen

ox·i·dize \'äksəˌdīz\ *vb* **-dized; -diz·ing** : combine with oxygen — **ox·i·da·tion** \ˌäksə'dāshən\ *n* — **ox·i·diz·er** *n*

ox·y·gen \'äksijən\ *n* : gaseous chemical element essential for life

oys·ter \'öistər\ *n* : bivalve mollusk — **oys·ter·ing** \-riŋ\ *n*

ozone \'ōˌzōn\ *n* : very reactive bluish form of oxygen

P

p \'pē\ *n, pl* **p's** *or* **ps** \'pēz\ : 16th letter of the alphabet

pace \'pās\ *n* **1** : walking step **2** : rate of progress ~ *vb* **paced; pac·ing 1** : go at a pace **2** : cover with slow steps **3** : set the pace of

pace·mak·er *n* : electrical device to regulate heartbeat

pachy·derm \'pakiˌdərm\ *n* : elephant

pa·cif·ic \pə'sifik\ *adj* : calm or peaceful

pac·i·fism \'pasəˌfizəm\ *n* : opposition to war or violence — **pac·i·fist** \-fist\ *n or*

adj — **pac·i·fis·tic** \ˌpasə'fistik\ *adj*

pac·i·fy \'pasəˌfī\ *vb* **-fied; -fy·ing** : make calm — **pac·i·fi·ca·tion** \ˌpasəfə'kāshən\ *n* — **pac·i·fi·er** \'pasəˌfīər\ *n*

pack \'pak\ *n* **1** : compact bundle **2** : group of animals ~ *vb* **1** : put into a container **2** : fill tightly or completely **3** : send without ceremony — **pack·er** *n*

pack·age \'pakij\ *n* : items bundled together ~ *vb* **-aged; -ag·ing** : enclose in a package

pack·et \'pakət\ *n* : small package

pact \'pakt\ *n* : agreement

pad \'pad\ *n* **1** : cushioning part or thing **2** : floating leaf of a water plant **3** : tablet of paper ∼ *vb* **-dd-** **1** : furnish with a pad **2** : expand with needless matter — **pad·ding** *n*

pad·dle \'pad³l\ *n* : implement with a flat blade ∼ *vb* **-dled; -dling** : move, beat, or stir with a paddle

pad·dock \'padək\ *n* : enclosed area for racehorses

pad·dy \'padē\ *n, pl* **-dies** : wet land where rice is grown

pad·lock *n* : lock with a U-shaped catch — **padlock** *vb*

pae·an \'pēən\ *n* : song of praise

pa·gan \'pāgən\ *n or adj* : heathen — **pa·gan·ism** \-ˌizəm\ *n*

¹page \'pāj\ *n* : messenger ∼ *vb* **paged; pag·ing** : summon by repeated calls — **pag·er** *n*

²page *n* **1** : single leaf (as of a book) or one side of the leaf **2** : information at a single World Wide Web address

pag·eant \'pajənt\ *n* : elaborate spectacle or procession — **pag·eant·ry** \-əntrē\ *n*

pa·go·da \pə'gōdə\ *n* : tower with roofs curving upward

paid *past of* PAY

pail \'pāl\ *n* : cylindrical container with a handle — **pail·ful** \-ˌfùl\ *n*

pain \'pān\ *n* **1** : punishment or penalty **2** : suffering of body or mind **3** *pl* : great care ∼ *vb* : cause or experience pain — **pain·ful** \-fəl\ *adj* — **pain·ful·ly** *adv* — **pain·kill·er** *n* — **pain·kill·ing** *adj* — **pain·less** *adj* — **pain·less·ly** *adv*

pains·tak·ing \'pānˌstākiŋ\ *adj* : taking pains — **pain·staking** *n* — **pains·tak·ing·ly** *adv*

paint \'pānt\ *vb* **1** : apply color or paint to **2** : portray esp. in color ∼ *n* : mixture of pigment and liquid — **paint·brush** *n* — **paint·er** *n* — **paint·ing** *n*

pair \'par\ *n* : a set of two ∼ *vb* : put or go together as a pair

pa·ja·mas \pə'jäməz, -'jam-\ *n pl* : loose suit for sleeping

pal \'pal\ *n* : close friend

pal·ace \'paləs\ *n* **1** : residence of a chief of state **2** : mansion — **pa·la·tial** \pə'lāshəl\ *adj*

pal·at·able \'palətəbəl\ *adj* : agreeable to the taste

pal·ate \'palət\ *n* **1** : roof of the mouth **2** : taste — **pal·a·tal** \-ət³l\ *adj*

pa·la·ver \pə'lavər, -'läv-\ *n* : talk — **palaver** *vb*

¹pale \'pāl\ *adj* **pal·er; pal·est** **1** : lacking in color or brightness **2** : light in color or shade ~ *vb* **paled; pal·ing** : make or become pale — **pale·ness** *n*

²**pale** *n* **1** : fence stake **2** : enclosed place

pa·le·on·tol·o·gy \ˌpālēˌän-'täləjē\ *n* : branch of biology dealing with ancient forms of life known from fossils — **pa·le·on·tol·o·gist** \-ˌän'täləjist, -ən-\ *n*

pal·ette \'palət\ *n* : board on which paints are laid and mixed

pal·i·sade \ˌpalə'sād\ *n* **1** : high fence **2** : line of cliffs

¹**pall** \'pȯl\ *n* **1** : cloth draped over a coffin **2** : something that produces gloom

²**pall** *vb* : lose in interest or attraction

pall·bear·er *n* : one who attends the coffin at a funeral

¹**pal·let** \'palət\ *n* : makeshift bed

²**pallet** *n* : portable storage platform

pal·li·ate \'palēˌāt\ *vb* **-at·ed; -at·ing** **1** : ease without curing **2** : cover or conceal by excusing — **pal·li·a·tion** \ˌpalē-'āshən\ *n* — **pal·li·a·tive** \'palēˌātiv\ *adj or n*

pal·lid \'paləd\ *adj* : pale

pal·lor \'palər\ *n* : paleness

¹**palm** \'päm, 'pälm\ *n* **1** : tall tropical tree crowned with large leaves **2** : symbol of victory

²**palm** *n* : underside of the hand ~ *vb* **1** : conceal in the hand **2** : impose by fraud

palm·ist·ry \'päməstrē, 'pälmə-\ *n* : reading a person's character or future in his palms — **palm·ist** \'pämist, 'pälm-\ *n*

palmy \'pämē, 'pälmē\ *adj* **palm·i·er; -est** : flourishing

pal·o·mi·no \ˌpalə'mēnō\ *n, pl* **-nos** : light-colored horse

pal·pa·ble \'palpəbəl\ *adj* **1** : capable of being touched **2** : obvious — **pal·pa·bly** \-blē\ *adv*

pal·pi·tate \'palpəˌtāt\ *vb* **-tat·ed; -tat·ing** : beat rapidly — **pal·pi·ta·tion** \ˌpalpə'tā-shən\ *n*

pal·sy \'pȯlzē\ *n, pl* **-sies** **1** : paralysis **2** : condition marked by tremor — **pal·sied** \-zēd\ *adj*

pal·try \'pȯltrē\ *adj* **-tri·er; -est** : trivial

pam·per \'pampər\ *vb* : spoil or indulge

pam·phlet \'pamflət\ *n* : unbound publication — **pam·phle·teer** \ˌpamflə'tir\ *n*

pan \'pan\ *n* : broad, shallow, and open container ~ *vb* **1** : wash gravel in a pan to search for gold **2** : criticize severely

pan·a·cea \ˌpanə'sēə\ *n* : remedy for all ills or difficulties

pan·cake *n* : fried flat cake

pan·cre·as \'paŋkrēəs, 'pan-\ *n* : gland that produces insulin — **pan·cre·at·ic** \ˌpaŋkrē-'atik, ˌpan-\ *adj*

pan·da \'pandə\ *n* : black=and-white bearlike animal

pan·de·mo·ni·um \ˌpandə-'mōnēəm\ *n* : wild uproar

pan·der \'pandər\ *n* **1** : pimp **2** : one who caters to others' desires or weaknesses ∼ *vb* : act as a pander

pane \'pān\ *n* : sheet of glass

pan·e·gy·ric \ˌpanə'jirik\ *n* : eulogistic oration — **pan·e·gyr·ist** \-'jirist\ *n*

pan·el \'panəl\ *n* **1** : list of persons (as jurors) **2** : discussion group **3** : flat piece of construction material **4** : board with instruments or controls ∼ *vb* **-eled** *or* **-elled; -el·ing** *or* **-el·ling** : decorate with panels — **pan·el·ing** *n* — **pan·el·ist** \-ist\ *n*

pang \'paŋ\ *n* : sudden sharp pain

pan·han·dle \'panˌhandəl\ *vb* **-dled; -dling** : ask for money on the street — **pan·han·dler** \-ər\ *n*

pan·ic \'panik\ *n* : sudden overpowering fright ∼ *vb* **-icked; -ick·ing** : affect or be affected with panic — **pan·icky** \-ikē\ *adj*

pan·o·ply \'panəplē\ *n, pl* **-plies 1** : full suit of armor **2** : impressive array

pan·o·ra·ma \ˌpanə'ramə, -'räm-\ *n* : view in every direction — **pan·o·ram·ic** \-'ramik\ *adj*

pan·sy \'panzē\ *n, pl* **-sies** : low-growing garden herb with showy flowers

pant \'pant\ *vb* **1** : breathe with great effort **2** : yearn ∼ *n* : panting sound

pan·ta·loons \ˌpantəl'ünz\ *n pl* : pants

pan·the·on \'panthēˌän, -ən\ *n* **1** : the gods of a people **2** : group of famous people

pan·ther \'panthər\ *n* : large wild cat

pant·ies \'pantēz\ *n pl* : woman's or child's short underpants

pan·to·mime \'pantəˌmīm\ *n* **1** : play without words **2** : expression by bodily or facial movements ∼ *vb* : represent by pantomime

pan·try \'pantrē\ *n, pl* **-tries** : storage room for food and dishes

pants \'pants\ *n pl* **1** : 2-legged outer garment **2** : panties

pap \'pap\ *n* : soft food

pa·pa·cy \'pāpəsē\ *n, pl* **-cies 1** : office of pope **2** : reign of a pope

pa·pal \'pāpəl\ *adj* : relating to the pope

pa·pa·ya \pə'pīə\ *n* : tropical tree with large yellow edible fruit

pa·per \'pāpər\ *n* **1** : pliable substance used to write or print on, to wrap things in, or to cover walls **2** : printed or written document **3** : newspaper — **paper** *adj or vb* — **pa·per·hang·er** *n* — **pa·per·weight** *n* — **pa·pery** \'pāpərē\ *adj*

pa·per·board *n* : cardboard

pa·pier–mâ·ché \ˌpāpərmə-'shā, ˌpap ˌyāmə-, -ma-\ *n* : molding material of waste paper

pa·poose \pa'püs, pə-\ *n* : young child of American Indian parents

pa·pri·ka \pə'prēkə, pa-\ *n* : mild red spice from sweet peppers

pa·py·rus \pə'pīrəs\ *n, pl* **-rus·es** *or* **-ri** \-ˌrē, -ˌrī\ **1** : tall grasslike plant **2** : paper from papyrus

par \'pär\ *n* **1** : stated value **2** : common level **3** : accepted standard or normal condition — **par** *adj*

par·a·ble \'parəbəl\ *n* : simple story illustrating a moral truth

para·chute \'parəˌshüt\ *n* : large umbrella-shaped device for making a descent through air — **parachute** *vb* — **para·chut·ist** \-ˌshütist\ *n*

pa·rade \pə'rād\ *n* **1** : pompous display **2** : ceremonial formation and march ~ *vb* **-rad·ed; -rad·ing** **1** : march in a parade **2** : show off

par·a·digm \'parəˌdīm, -ˌdim\ *n* : model

par·a·dise \'parəˌdīs, -ˌdīz\ *n* : place of bliss

par·a·dox \'parəˌdäks\ *n* : statement that seems contrary to common sense yet is perhaps true — **par·a·dox·i·cal** \ˌparə'däksikəl\ *adj* — **par·a·dox·i·cal·ly** *adv*

par·af·fin \'parəfən\ *n* : white waxy substance used esp. for making candles and sealing foods

par·a·gon \'parəˌgän, -gən\ *n* : model of perfection

para·graph \'parəˌgraf\ *n* : unified division of a piece of writing ~ *vb* : divide into paragraphs

par·a·keet \'parəˌkēt\ *n* : small slender parrot

par·al·lel \'parəˌlel\ *adj* **1** : lying or moving in the same direction but always the same distance apart **2** : similar ~ *n* **1** : parallel line, curve, or surface **2** : line of latitude **3** : similarity ~ *vb* **1** : compare **2**

: correspond to — **par·al·lel·ism** \-ͺizəm\ *n*

par·al·lel·o·gram \ͺparə'leləͺgram\ *n* : 4-sided polygon with opposite sides equal and parallel

pa·ral·y·sis \pə'raləsəs\ *n, pl* **-y·ses** \-ͺsēz\ : loss of function and esp. of voluntary motion — **par·a·lyt·ic** \ͺparə'litik\ *adj or n*

par·a·lyze \'parəͺlīz\ *vb* **-lyzed; -lyz·ing** : affect with paralysis — **par·a·lyz·ing·ly** *adv*

para·med·ic \ͺparə'medik\ *n* : person trained to provide initial emergency medical treatment

pa·ram·e·ter \pə'ramətər\ *n* : characteristic element — **para·met·ric** \ͺparə'metrik\ *adj*

par·a·mount \'parəͺmaunt\ *adj* : superior to all others

par·amour \'parəͺmur\ *n* : illicit lover

para·noia \ͺparə'nóiə\ *n* : mental disorder marked by irrational suspicion — **para·noid** \'parəͺnóid\ *adj or n*

par·a·pet \'parəpət, -ͺpet\ *n* : protecting rampart in a fort

par·a·pher·na·lia \ͺparəfə'nālyə, -fər-\ *n sing or pl* : equipment

para·phrase \'parəͺfrāz\ *n* : restatement of a text giving the meaning in different words — **paraphrase** *vb*

para·ple·gia \ͺparə'plējə, -jēə\ *n* : paralysis of the lower trunk and legs — **para·ple·gic** \-jik\ *adj or n*

par·a·site \'parəͺsīt\ *n* : organism living on another — **par·a·sit·ic** \ͺparə'sitik\ *adj* — **par·a·sit·ism** \'parəseͺtizəm, -ͺsītͺiz-\ *n*

para·sol \'parəͺsól\ *n* : umbrella used to keep off the sun

para·troops \-ͺtrüps\ *n pl* : troops trained to parachute from an airplane — **para·troop·er** \-ͺtrüpər\ *n*

par·boil \'pärͺbóil\ *vb* : boil briefly

par·cel \'pärsəl\ *n* **1** : lot **2** : package ∼ *vb* **-celed** *or* **-celled; -cel·ing** *or* **-cel·ling** : divide into portions

parch \'pärch\ *vb* : toast or shrivel with dry heat

parch·ment \'pärchmənt\ *n* : animal skin prepared to write on

par·don \'pärdᵊn\ *n* : excusing of an offense ∼ *vb* : free from penalty — **par·don·able** \'pärdᵊnəbəl\ *adj* — **par·don·er** \-ᵊnər\ *n*

pare \'par\ *vb* **pared; par·ing** **1** : trim off an outside part **2** : reduce as if by paring — **par·er** *n*

par·e·go·ric \ˌparə'gȯrik\ *n* : tincture of opium and camphor

par·ent \'parənt\ *n* : one that begets or brings up offspring — **par·ent·age** \-ij\ *n* — **pa·ren·tal** \pə'rent³l\ *adj* — **par·ent·hood** *n*

pa·ren·the·sis \pə'renthəsəs\ *n, pl* **-the·ses** \-ˌsēz\ **1** : word or phrase inserted in a passage **2** : one of a pair of punctuation marks ( ) — **par·en·thet·ic** \ˌparən'thetik\, **par·en·thet·i·cal** \-ikəl\ *adj* — **par·en·thet·i·cal·ly** *adv*

par·fait \pär'fā\ *n* : layered cold dessert

pa·ri·ah \pə'rīə\ *n* : outcast

par·ish \'parish\ *n* : local church community

pa·rish·io·ner \pə'rishənər\ *n* : member of a parish

par·i·ty \'parətē\ *n, pl* **-ties** : equality

park \'pärk\ *n* : land set aside for recreation or for its beauty ~ *vb* : leave a vehicle standing

par·ka \'pärkə\ *n* : usu. hooded heavy jacket

park·way \'pärkˌwā\ *n* : broad landscaped thoroughfare

par·lance \'pärləns\ *n* : manner of speaking

par·lay \'pärˌlā\ *n* : the risking of a stake plus its winnings — **parlay** *vb*

par·ley \'pärlē\ *n, pl* **-leys** : conference about a dispute — **parley** *vb*

par·lia·ment \'pärləmənt\ *n* : legislative assembly — **par·lia·men·tar·i·an** *n* — **par·lia·men·ta·ry** \ˌpärlə'mentərē\ *adj*

par·lor \'pärlər\ *n* **1** : reception room **2** : place of business

pa·ro·chi·al \pə'rōkēəl\ *adj* **1** : relating to a church parish **2** : provincial — **pa·ro·chi·al·ism** \-əˌlizəm\ *n*

par·o·dy \'parədē\ *n, pl* **-dies** : humorous or satirical imitation — **parody** *vb*

pa·role \pə'rōl\ *n* : conditional release of a prisoner — **parole** *vb* — **pa·rol·ee** \-ˌrō'lē, -'rōˌlē\ *n*

par·ox·ysm \'parəkˌsizəm, pə'räk-\ *n* : convulsion

par·quet \'pärˌkā, pär'kā\ *n* : flooring of patterned wood inlay

par·ra·keet *var of* PARAKEET

par·rot \'parət\ *n* : bright=colored tropical bird

par·ry \'parē\ *vb* **-ried; -ry·ing** **1** : ward off a blow **2** : evade adroitly — **parry** *n*

parse \'pärs\ *vb* **parsed; pars·ing** : analyze grammatically

par·si·mo·ny \'pärsəˌmōnē\ *n* : extreme frugality — **par·si·mo·ni·ous**

\ˌpärsə'mōnēəs\ *adj* — **par·si·mo·ni·ous·ly** *adv*

pars·ley \'pärslē\ *n* : garden plant used as a seasoning or garnish

pars·nip \'pärsnəp\ *n* : carrotlike vegetable with a white edible root

par·son \'pärs°n\ *n* : minister

par·son·age \'pärs°nij\ *n* : parson's house

part \'pärt\ *n* **1** : one of the units into which a larger whole is divided **2** : function or role ～ *vb* **1** : take leave **2** : separate **3** : go away **4** : give up

par·take \pär'tāk, pər-\ *vb* **-took; -tak·en; -tak·ing** : have or take a share — **par·tak·er** *n*

par·tial \'pärshəl\ *adj* **1** : favoring one over another **2** : affecting a part only — **par·tial·i·ty** \ˌpärshē'alətē\ *n* — **par·tial·ly** \'pärshəlē\ *adv*

par·tic·i·pate \pər'tisəˌpāt, pär-\ *vb* **-pat·ed; -pat·ing** : take part in something — **par·tic·i·pant** \-pənt\ *adj or n* — **par·tic·i·pa·tion** \-ˌtisə'pāshən\ *n* — **par·tic·i·pa·to·ry** \-'tisəpəˌtōrē\ *adj*

par·ti·ci·ple \'pärtəˌsipəl\ *n* : verb form with functions of both verb and adjective — **par·ti·cip·i·al** \ˌpärtə'sipēəl\ *adj*

par·ti·cle \'pärtikəl\ *n* : small bit

par·tic·u·lar \pär'tikyələr\ *adj* **1** : relating to a specific person or thing **2** : individual **3** : hard to please ～ *n* : detail — **par·tic·u·lar·ly** *adv*

par·ti·san \'pärtəzen, -sən\ *n* **1** : adherent **2** : guerrilla — **partisan** *adj* — **par·ti·san·ship** *n*

par·tite \'pärˌtīt\ *adj* : divided into parts

par·ti·tion \pər'tishən, pär-\ *n* **1** : distribution **2** : something that divides — **partition** *vb*

part·ly \'pärtlē\ *adv* : in some degree

part·ner \'pärtnər\ *n* **1** : associate **2** : companion **3** : business associate — **part·ner·ship** *n*

part of speech : class of words distinguished esp. according to function

par·tridge \'pärtrij\ *n, pl* **-tridge** *or* **-tridg·es** : stout‚bodied game bird

par·ty \'pärtē\ *n, pl* **-ties** **1** : political organization **2** : participant **3** : company of persons esp. with a purpose **4** : social gathering

par·ve·nu \'pärvəˌnü, -ˌnyü\ *n* : social upstart

pass \'pas\ *vb* **1** : move past, over, or through **2** : go away or die **3** : allow to elapse **4** : go unchallenged **5** : transfer or undergo transfer **6** : render a judgment **7** : occur **8** : enact **9** : undergo testing successfully **10** : be regarded **11** : decline ~ *n* **1** : low place in a mountain range **2** : act of passing **3** : accomplishment **4** : permission to leave, enter, or move about — **pass·able** *adj* — **pass·ably** *adv* — **pass-er** *n* — **pass·er·by** *n*

pas·sage \\'pasij\ *n* **1** : process of passing **2** : means of passing **3** : voyage **4** : right to pass **5** : literary selection — **pas·sage·way** *n*

pass·book *n* : bankbook

pas·sé \pa'sā\ *adj* : out-of= date

pas·sen·ger \pasᵊnjər\ *n* : traveler in a conveyance

pass·ing \\'pasiŋ\ *n* : death

pas·sion \\'pashən\ *n* **1** : strong feeling esp. of anger, love, or desire **2** : object of affection or enthusiasm — **pas·sion·ate** \\'pashənət\ *adj* — **pas·sion·ate·ly** *adv* — **pas·sion·less** *adj*

pas·sive \\'pasiv\ *adj* **1** : not active but acted upon **2** : submissive — **passive** *n* — **pas·sive·ly** *adv* — **pas·siv·i·ty** \pa'sivətē\ *n*

Pass·over \\'pas,ōvər\ *n* : Jewish holiday celebrated in March or April in commemoration of the Hebrews' liberation from slavery in Egypt

pass·port \\'pas,pōrt\ *n* : government document needed for travel abroad

pass·word *n* **1** : word or phrase spoken to pass a guard **2** : sequence of characters needed to get into a computer system

past \\'past\ *adj* **1** : ago **2** : just gone by **3** : having existed before the present **4** : expressing past time ~ *prep or adv* : beyond ~ *n* **1** : time gone by **2** : verb tense expressing time gone by **3** : past life

pas·ta \\'pästə\ *n* : fresh or dried shaped dough

paste \\'pāst\ *n* **1** : smooth ground food **2** : moist adhesive ~ *vb* **past·ed; past·ing** : attach with paste — **pasty** *adj*

paste·board *n* : cardboard

pas·tel \pas'tel\ *n* : light color — **pastel** *adj*

pas·teur·ize \\'paschə,rīz, 'pastə-\ *vb* **-ized; -iz·ing** : heat (as milk) so as to kill germs — **pas·teur·i·za·tion** \,paschərə'zāshən, ,pastə-\ *n*

pas·time \\'pas,tīm\ *n* : amusement

pas·tor \\'pastər\ *n* : priest or minister serving a church or parish — **pas·tor·ate** \-tərət\ *n*

pas·to·ral \'pastərəl\ *adj* **1** : relating to rural life **2** : of or relating to spiritual guidance or a pastor ~ *n* : literary work dealing with rural life

past·ry \'pāstrē\ *n, pl* **-ries** : sweet baked goods

pas·ture \'paschər\ *n* : land used for grazing ~ *vb* **-tured; -tur·ing** : graze

pat \'pat\ *n* **1** : light tap **2** : small mass ~ *vb* **-tt-** : tap gently ~ *adj or adv* **1** : apt or glib **2** : unyielding

patch \'pach\ *n* **1** : piece used for mending **2** : small area distinct from surrounding area ~ *vb* **1** : mend with a patch **2** : make of fragments **3** : repair hastily — **patchy** \-ē\ *adj*

patch·work *n* : something made of pieces of different materials, shapes, or colors

pate \'pāt\ *n* : crown of the head

pa·tel·la \pə'telə\ *n, pl* **-lae** \-'tel‚ē, -‚ī\ *or* **-las** : kneecap

pa·tent *adj* **1** \'pat°nt, 'pāt-\ : obvious **2** \'pat-\ : protected by a patent ~ \'pat-\ *n* : document conferring or securing a right ~ \'pat-\ *vb* : secure by patent — **pat·ent·ly** *adv*

pa·ter·nal \pə'tərn°l\ *adj* **1** : fatherly **2** : related through or inherited from a father — **pa·ter·nal·ly** *adv*

pa·ter·ni·ty \pə'tərnətē\ *n* : fatherhood

path \'path, 'pàth\ *n* **1** : trodden way **2** : route or course — **path·find·er** *n* — **path·way** *n* — **path·less** *adj*

pa·thet·ic \pə'thetik\ *adj* : pitiful — **pa·thet·i·cal·ly** *adv*

pa·thol·o·gy \pə'thäləjē\ *n, pl* **-gies** **1** : study of disease **2** : physical abnormality — **path·o·log·i·cal** \‚pathə'läjikəl\ *adj* — **pa·thol·o·gist** \pə-'thälə-jist\ *n*

pa·thos \'pā‚thäs\ *n* : element evoking pity

pa·tience \'pāshəns\ *n* : habit or fact of being patient

pa·tient \'pāshənt\ *adj* : bearing pain or trials without complaint ~ *n* : one under medical care — **pa·tient·ly** *adv*

pa·ti·na \pə'tēnə, 'patənə\ *n, pl* **-nas** \-nəz\ *or* **-nae** \-‚nē, -‚nī\ : green film formed on copper and bronze

pa·tio \'patē‚ō, 'pät-\ *n, pl* **-ti·os** **1** : courtyard **2** : paved recreation area near a house

pa·tri·arch \'pātrē‚ärk\ *n* **1** : man revered as father or founder **2** : venerable old man — **pa·tri·ar·chal** \‚pātrē-'ärkəl\ *adj* — **pa·tri·ar·chy** \-‚ärkē\ *n*

pa·tri·cian \pə'trishən\ *n* : person of high birth — **patrician** *adj*

pat·ri·mo·ny \'patrə,mōnē\ *n* : something inherited — **pat·ri·mo·ni·al** \,patrə'mōnēəl\ *adj*

pa·tri·ot \'pātrēət, -,ät\ *n* : one who loves his or her country — **pa·tri·ot·ic** \,pātrē'ätik\ *adj* — **pa·tri·ot·i·cal·ly** *adv* — **pa·tri·o·tism** \'pātrēə,tizəm\ *n*

pa·trol \pə'trōl\ *n* **1** : a going around for observation or security **2** : group on patrol ∼ *vb* **-ll-** : carry out a patrol

pa·trol·man \-mən\ *n* : police officer

pa·tron \'pātrən\ *n* **1** : special protector **2** : wealthy supporter **3** : customer

pa·tron·age \'patrənij, 'pā-\ *n* **1** : support or influence of a patron **2** : trade of customers **3** : control of government appointments

pa·tron·ess \'pātrənəs\ *n* : woman who is a patron

pa·tron·ize \'pātrə,nīz, 'pa-\ *vb* **-ized; -iz·ing** **1** : be a customer of **2** : treat with condescension

¹pat·ter \'patər\ *vb* : talk glibly or mechanically ∼ *n* : rapid talk

²patter *vb* : pat or tap rapidly ∼ *n* : quick succession of pats or taps

pat·tern \'patərn\ *n* **1** : model for imitation or for making things **2** : artistic design **3** : noticeable formation or set of characteristics ∼ *vb* : form according to a pattern

pat·ty \'patē\ *n, pl* **-ties** : small flat cake

pau·ci·ty \'pȯsətē\ *n* : shortage

paunch \'pȯnch\ *n* : large belly — **paunchy** *adj*

pau·per \'pȯpər\ *n* : poor person — **pau·per·ism** \-pə,rizəm\ *n* — **pau·per·ize** \-pə,rīz\ *vb*

pause \'pȯz\ *n* : temporary stop ∼ *vb* **paused; paus·ing** : stop briefly

pave \'pāv\ *vb* **paved; pav·ing** : cover to smooth or firm the surface — **pave·ment** \-mənt\ *n* — **pav·ing** *n*

pa·vil·ion \pə'vilyən\ *n* **1** : large tent **2** : light structure used for entertainment or shelter

paw \'pȯ\ *n* : foot of a 4-legged clawed animal ∼ *vb* **1** : handle clumsily or rudely **2** : touch or strike with a paw

pawn \'pȯn\ *n* **1** : goods deposited as security for a loan **2** : state of being pledged ∼ *vb* : deposit as a pledge — **pawn·bro·ker** *n* — **pawn·shop** *n*

pay \'pā\ *vb* **paid** \'pād\; **pay·ing** **1** : make due return for goods or services **2** : discharge indebtedness for **3** : requite **4**

payable

: give freely or as fitting **5** : be profitable ∼ *n* **1** : status of being paid **2** : something paid — **pay·able** *adj* — **pay-check** *n* — **pay·ee** \pā'ē\ *n* — **pay·er** *n* — **pay·ment** *n*

PC \ˌpē'sē\ *n, pl* **PCs** *or* **PC's** : microcomputer

pea \'pē\ *n* : round edible seed of a leguminous vine

peace \'pēs\ *n* **1** : state of calm and quiet **2** : absence of war or strife — **peace·able** \-əbəl\ *adj* — **peace·ably** \-blē\ *adv* — **peace·ful** \-fəl\ *adj* — **peace·ful·ly** *adv* — **peace-keep·er** *n* — **peace·keep·ing** *n* — **peace·mak·er** *n* — **peace-time** *n*

peach \'pēch\ *n* : sweet juicy fruit of a flowering tree or this tree

pea·cock \'pē,käk\ *n* : brilliantly colored male pheasant

peak \'pēk\ *n* **1** : pointed or projecting part **2** : top of a hill **3** : highest level ∼ *vb* : reach a maximum — **peak** *adj*

peak·ed \'pēkəd\ *adj* : sickly

peal \'pēl\ *n* : loud sound (as of ringing bells) ∼ *vb* : give out peals

pea·nut \'pē,nət\ *n* : annual herb that bears underground pods or the pod or the edible seed inside

pear \'par\ *n* : fleshy fruit of a tree related to the apple

pearl \'pərl\ *n* : gem formed within an oyster — **pearly** \'pərlē\ *adj*

peas·ant \'pezᵊnt\ *n* : tiller of the soil — **peas·ant·ry** \-ᵊntrē\ *n*

peat \'pēt\ *n* : decayed organic deposit often dried for fuel — **peaty** *adj*

peb·ble \'pebəl\ *n* : small stone — **peb·bly** *adj*

pe·can \pi'kän, -'kan\ *n* : hickory tree bearing a smooth-shelled nut or the nut

pec·ca·dil·lo \ˌpekə'dilō\ *n, pl* **-loes** *or* **-los** : slight offense

¹peck \'pek\ *n* : unit of dry measure equal to 8 quarts

²peck *vb* : strike or pick up with the bill ∼ *n* : quick sharp stroke

pec·tin \'pektən\ *n* : water-soluble plant substance that causes fruit jellies to set — **pec·tic** \-tik\ *adj*

pec·to·ral \'pektərəl\ *adj* : relating to the breast or chest

pe·cu·liar \pi'kyülyər\ *adj* **1** : characteristic of only one **2** : strange — **pe·cu·liar·i·ty** \-ˌkyül'yarətē, -ē'ar-\ *n* — **pe·cu·liar·ly** *adv*

pe·cu·ni·ary \pi'kyünē,erē\ *adj* : relating to money

ped·a·go·gy \'pedə,gōjē, -ˌgäj-\ *n* : art or profession of teaching — **ped·a·gog·ic** \ˌpedə'gäjik, -'gōj-\, **ped·a-**

gog·i·cal \-ikəl\ *adj* — **ped·a·gogue** \'pedə‚gäg\ *n*

ped·al \'pedᵊl\ *n* : lever worked by the foot ~ *adj* : relating to the foot ~ *vb* : use a pedal

ped·ant \'pedᵊnt\ *n* : learned bore — **pe·dan·tic** \pi'dantik\ *adj* — **ped·ant·ry** \'pedᵊntrē\ *n*

ped·dle \'pedᵊl\ *vb* **-dled; -dling** : offer for sale — **ped·dler** \'pedlər\ *n*

ped·es·tal \'pedəstᵊl\ *n* : support or foot of something upright

pe·des·tri·an \pə'destrēən\ *adj* **1** : ordinary **2** : walking ~ *n* : person who walks

pe·di·at·rics \‚pēdē'atriks\ *n* : branch of medicine dealing with children — **pe·di·at·ric** \-trik\ *adj* — **pe·di·a·tri·cian** \‚pēdēə'trishən\ *n*

ped·i·gree \'pedə‚grē\ *n* : line of ancestors or a record of it

ped·i·ment \'pedəmənt\ *n* : triangular gablelike decoration on a building

peek \'pēk\ *vb* **1** : look furtively **2** : glance — **peek** *n*

peel \'pēl\ *vb* **1** : strip the skin or rind from **2** : lose the outer layer ~ *n* : skin or rind — **peel·ing** *n*

¹peep \'pēp\ *vb or n* : cheep

²peep *vb* **1** : look slyly **2** : begin to emerge ~ *n* : brief look — **peep·er** *n* — **peep·hole** *n*

¹peer \'pir\ *n* **1** : one's equal **2** : nobleman — **peer·age** \-ij\ *n*

²peer *vb* : look intently or curiously

peer·less \-ləs\ *adj* : having no equal

peeve \'pēv\ *vb* **peeved; peeving** : make resentful ~ *n* : complaint — **peev·ish** \-ish\ *adj* — **peev·ish·ly** *adv* — **peev·ish·ness** *n*

peg \'peg\ *n* : small pinlike piece ~ *vb* **-gg- 1** : put a peg into **2** : fix or mark with or as if with pegs

pei·gnoir \pān'wär, pen-\ *n* : negligee

pe·jo·ra·tive \pi'jòrətiv\ *adj* : having a negative or degrading effect ~ *n* : a degrading word or phrase — **pe·jo·ra·tive·ly** *adv*

pel·i·can \'pelikən\ *n* : large-billed seabird

pel·la·gra \pə'lagrə, -'lāg-\ *n* : protein-deficiency disease

pel·let \'pelət\ *n* : little ball — **pel·let·al** \-ᵊl\ *adj* — **pel·let·ize** \-‚īz\ *vb*

pell–mell \'pel'mel\ *adv* : in confusion or haste

pel·lu·cid \pə'lüsəd\ *adj* : very clear

¹pelt \'pelt\ *n* : skin of a fur-bearing animal

²**pelt** *vb* : strike with blows or missiles

pel·vis \'pelvəs\ *n, pl* **-vis·es** \-vəsəz\ *or* **-ves** \-ˌvēz\ : cavity formed by the hip bones — **pel·vic** \-vik\ *adj*

¹**pen** \'pen\ *n* : enclosure for animals ∼ *vb* **-nn-** : shut in a pen

²**pen** *n* : tool for writing with ink ∼ *vb* **-nn-** : write

pe·nal \'pēnᵊl\ *adj* : relating to punishment

pe·nal·ize \'pēnᵊlˌīz, 'pen-\ *vb* **-ized; -iz·ing** : put a penalty on

pen·al·ty \'penᵊltē\ *n, pl* **-ties** **1** : punishment for crime **2** : disadvantage, loss, or hardship due to an action

pen·ance \'penəns\ *n* : act performed to show repentance

pence \'pens\ *pl of* PENNY

pen·chant \'penchənt\ *n* : strong inclination

pen·cil \'pensəl\ *n* : writing or drawing tool with a solid marking substance (as graphite) as its core ∼ *vb* **-ciled** *or* **-cilled; -cil·ing** *or* **-cil·ling** : draw or write with a pencil

pen·dant \'pendənt\ *n* : hanging ornament

pen·dent, pen·dant \'pendənt\ *adj* : hanging

pend·ing \'pendiŋ\ *prep* : while awaiting ∼ *adj* : not yet decided

pen·du·lous \'penjələs, -dyùləs\ *adj* : hanging loosely

pen·du·lum \-ləm\ *n* : a hanging weight that is free to swing

pen·e·trate \'penəˌtrāt\ *vb* **-trat·ed; -trat·ing** **1** : enter into **2** : permeate **3** : see into — **pen·e·tra·ble** \-trəbəl\ *adj* — **pen·e·tra·tion** \ˌpenə-'trāshən\ *n* — **pen·e·tra·tive** \'penəˌtrātiv\ *adj*

pen·guin \'pengwən, 'peŋ-\ *n* : short-legged flightless seabird

pen·i·cil·lin \ˌpenə'silən\ *n* : antibiotic usu. produced by a mold

pen·in·su·la \pə'ninsələ, -'ninchə-\ *n* : land extending out into the water — **pen·in·su·lar** \-lər\ *adj*

pe·nis \'pēnəs\ *n, pl* **-nes** \-ˌnēz\ *or* **-nis·es** : male organ of copulation

pen·i·tent \'penətənt\ *adj* : feeling sorrow for sins or offenses ∼ *n* : penitent person — **pen·i·tence** \-təns\ *n* — **pen·i·ten·tial** \ˌpenə'tenchəl\ *adj*

pen·i·ten·tia·ry \ˌpenə'tenchərē\ *n, pl* **-ries** : state or federal prison

pen·man·ship \'penmənˌship\ *n* : art or practice of writing

pen·nant \'penənt\ *n* : nautical or championship flag

pen·ny \'penē\ *n, pl* **-nies** \-ēz\ *or* **pence** \'pens\ **1** : monetary unit equal to 1/100 pound **2** *pl* **-nies** : cent — **pen·ni·less** \'peniləs\ *adj*

pen·sion \'penchən\ *n* : retirement income ~ *vb* : pay a pension to — **pen·sion·er** *n*

pen·sive \'pensiv\ *adj* : thoughtful — **pen·sive·ly** *adv*

pent \'pent\ *adj* : confined

pent·a·gon \'pentə₁gän\ *n* : 5-sided polygon — **pen·tag·o·nal** \pen'tagənᵊl\ *adj*

pen·tam·e·ter \pen'tamətər\ *n* : line of verse containing 5 metrical feet

pent·house \'pent₁haủs\ *n* : rooftop apartment

pen·u·ry \'penyərē\ *n* **1** : poverty **2** : thrifty or stingy manner — **pe·nu·ri·ous** \pə-'nủrēəs, -'nyủr-\ *adj*

pe·on \'pē₁än, -ən\ *n, pl* **-ons** *or* **-o·nes** \pā'ōnēz\ : landless laborer in Spanish America — **pe·on·age** \-ənij\ *n*

pe·o·ny \'pēənē\ *n, pl* **-nies** : garden plant having large flowers

peo·ple \'pēpəl\ *n, pl* **people** **1** *pl* : human beings in general **2** *pl* : human beings in a certain group (as a family) or community **3** *pl* **peoples** : tribe, nation, or race ~ *vb* **-pled; -pling** : constitute the population of

pep \'pep\ *n* : brisk energy ~ *vb* **pepped; pep·ping** : put pep into — **pep·py** *adj*

pep·per \'pepər\ *n* **1** : pungent seasoning from the berry (**peppercorn**) of a shrub **2** : vegetable grown for its hot or sweet fruit ~ *vb* : season with pepper — **pep·pery** \-ərē\ *adj*

pep·per·mint \-₁mint, -mənt\ *n* : pungent aromatic mint

pep·per·o·ni \₁pepə'rōnē\ *n* : spicy beef and pork sausage

pep·tic \'peptik\ *adj* : relating to digestion or the effect of digestive juices

per \'pər\ *prep* **1** : by means of **2** : for each **3** : according to

per·am·bu·late \pə'rambyə-₁lāt\ *vb* **-lat·ed; -lat·ing** : walk — **per·am·bu·la·tion** \-₁ram-byə'lāshən\ *n*

per·cale \₁pər'kāl, 'pər-₁; ₁pər-'kal\ *n* : fine woven cotton cloth

per·ceive \pər'sēv\ *vb* **-ceived; -ceiv·ing** **1** : realize **2** : become aware of through the senses — **per·ceiv·able** *adj*

per·cent \pər'sent\ *adv* : in each hundred ~ *n, pl* **-cent** *or* **-cents** **1** : one part in a hundred **2** : percentage

per·cent·age \pər'sentij\ *n* : part expressed in hundredths

per·cen·tile \pər'sen₁tīl\ *n* : a standing on a scale of 0–100

per·cep·ti·ble \pər'septəbəl\ *adj* : capable of being perceived — **per·cep·ti·bly** \-blē\ *adv*

per·cep·tion \pər'sepshən\ *n* **1** : act or result of perceiving **2** : ability to understand

per·cep·tive \pər'septiv\ *adj* : showing keen perception — **per·cep·tive·ly** *adv*

[1]**perch** \'pərch\ *n* : roost for birds ∼ *vb* : roost

[2]**perch** *n, pl* **perch** *or* **perch·es** : freshwater spiny-finned food fish

per·co·late \'pərkə,lāt\ *vb* **-lat·ed; -lat·ing** : trickle or filter down through a substance — **per·co·la·tor** \-,lātər\ *n*

per·cus·sion \pər'kəshən\ *n* **1** : sharp blow **2** : musical instrument sounded by striking

pe·remp·to·ry \pə'remptərē\ *adj* **1** : imperative **2** : domineering — **pe·remp·to·ri·ly** \-tərəlē\ *adv*

pe·ren·ni·al \pə'renēəl\ *adj* **1** : present at all seasons **2** : continuing from year to year **3** : recurring regularly ∼ *n* : perennial plant — **pe·ren·ni·al·ly** *adv*

per·fect \'pərfikt\ *adj* **1** : being without fault or defect **2** : exact **3** : complete ∼ \pər'fekt\ *vb* : make perfect — **per·fect·ibil·i·ty** \pər,fektə'bilətē\ *n* — **per·fect·ible**

\pər'fektəbəl\ *adj* — **per·fect·ly** *adv* — **per·fect·ness** *n*

per·fec·tion \pər'fekshən\ *n* **1** : quality or state of being perfect **2** : highest degree of excellence — **per·fec·tion·ist** \-shənist\ *n*

per·fid·i·ous \pər'fidēəs\ *adj* : treacherous — **per·fid·i·ous·ly** *adv*

per·fo·rate \'pərfə,rāt\ *vb* **-rat·ed; -rat·ing** : make a hole in — **per·fo·ra·tion** \,pərfə'rāshən\ *n*

per·force \pər'fōrs\ *adv* : of necessity

per·form \pər'fórm\ *vb* **1** : carry out **2** : do in a set manner **3** : give a performance — **per·form·er** *n*

per·for·mance \pər'fór,məns\ *n* **1** : act or process of performing **2** : public presentation

per·fume \'pər,fyüm, pər'-\ *n* **1** : pleasant odor **2** : something that gives a scent ∼ \pər'-, 'pər,-\ *vb* **-fumed; -fum·ing** : add scent to

per·func·to·ry \pər'fəŋktərē\ *adj* : done merely as a duty — **per·func·to·ri·ly** \-tərəlē\ *adv*

per·haps \pər'haps\ *adv* : possibly but not certainly

per·il \'perəl\ *n* : danger — **per·il·ous** *adj* — **per·il·ous·ly** *adv*

pe·rim·e·ter \pə'rimətər\ *n* : outer boundary of a body or figure

pe·ri·od \'pirēəd\ *n* **1** : punctuation mark . used esp. to mark the end of a declarative sentence or an abbreviation **2** : division of time **3** : stage in a process or development

pe·ri·od·ic \,pirē'ädik\ *adj* : occurring at regular intervals — **pe·ri·od·i·cal·ly** *adv*

pe·ri·od·i·cal \,pirē'ädikəl\ *n* : newspaper or magazine

pe·riph·ery \pə'rifərē\ *n, pl* **-er·ies** : outer boundary — **pe·riph·er·al** \-ərəl\ *adj*

peri·scope \'perə,skōp\ *n* : optical instrument for viewing from a submarine

per·ish \'perish\ *vb* : die or spoil — **per·ish·able** \-əbəl\ *adj or n*

per·ju·ry \'pərjərē\ *n* : lying under oath — **per·jure** \'pərjər\ *vb* — **per·jur·er** *n*

¹perk \'pərk\ *vb* **1** : thrust (as the head) up jauntily **2** : freshen **3** : gain vigor or spirit — **perky** *adj*

²perk *vb* : percolate

³perk *n* : privilege or benefit in addition to regular pay

per·ma·nent \'pərmənənt\ *adj* : lasting ~ *n* : hair wave — **per·ma·nence** \-nəns\ *n* — **per·ma·nent·ly** *adv*

per·me·able \'pərmēəbəl\ *adj* : permitting fluids to seep through — **per·me·a·bil·i·ty** \,pərmēə'bilətē\ *n*

per·me·ate \'pərmē,āt\ *vb* **-at·ed; -at·ing** **1** : seep through **2** : pervade — **per·me·ation** \,pərmē'āshən\ *n*

per·mis·si·ble \pər'misəbəl\ *adj* : that may be permitted

per·mis·sion \pər'mishən\ *n* : formal consent

per·mis·sive \pər'misiv\ *adj* : granting freedom esp. to excess — **per·miss·ive·ly** *adv* — **per·mis·sive·ness** *n*

per·mit \pər'mit\ *vb* **-tt-** **1** : approve **2** : make possible ~ \'pər,-, pər'-\ *n* : license

per·ni·cious \pər'nishəs\ *adj* : very harmful — **per·ni·cious·ly** *adv*

per·ox·ide \pə'räk,sīd\ *n* : compound (as hydrogen peroxide) in which oxygen is joined to oxygen

per·pen·dic·u·lar \,pərpən'dikyələr\ *adj* **1** : vertical **2** : meeting at a right angle — **perpendicular** *n* — **per·pen·dic·u·lar·i·ty** \-,dikyə'larətē\ *n* — **per·pen·dic·u·lar·ly** *adv*

per·pe·trate \'pərpə,trāt\ *vb* **-trat·ed; -trat·ing** : be guilty of doing — **per·pe·tra·tion** \,pərpə'trāshən\ *n* — **per·pe·tra·tor** \'pərpə,trātər\ *n*

per·pet·u·al \pər'pechəwəl\ *adj* **1** : continuing forever **2** : occurring continually — **per·pet·u·al·ly** *adv* — **per·pe·tu·ity** \ˌpərpə'tüətē, -'tyü-\ *n*

per·pet·u·ate \pər'pechəˌwāt\ *vb* **-at·ed; -at·ing** : make perpetual — **per·pet·u·a·tion** \-ˌpechə'wāshən\ *n*

per·plex \pər'pleks\ *vb* : confuse — **per·plex·i·ty** \-ətē\ *n*

per·se·cute \'pərsiˌkyüt\ *vb* **-cut·ed; -cut·ing** : harass, afflict — **per·se·cu·tion** \ˌpərsi'kyüshən\ *n* — **per·se·cu·tor** \'pərsiˌkyütər\ *n*

per·se·vere \ˌpərsə'vir\ *vb* **-vered; -ver·ing** : persist — **per·se·ver·ance** \-'virəns\ *n*

per·sist \pər'sist, -'zist\ *vb* **1** : go on resolutely in spite of difficulties **2** : continue to exist — **per·sis·tence** \-'sistəns, -'zis-\ *n* — **per·sis·ten·cy** \-tənsē\ *n* — **per·sis·tent** \-tənt\ *adj* — **per·sis·tent·ly** *adv*

per·son \'pərsᵊn\ *n* **1** : human being **2** : human being's body or individuality **3** : reference to the speaker, one spoken to, or one spoken of

per·son·able \'pərsᵊnəbəl\ *adj* : having a pleasing personality

per·son·age \'pərsᵊnij\ *n* : person of rank or distinction

per·son·al \'pərsᵊnəl\ *adj* **1** : relating to a particular person **2** : done in person **3** : affecting one's body **4** : offensive to a certain individual — **per·son·al·ly** *adv*

per·son·al·i·ty \ˌpərsᵊn'alətē\ *n, pl* **-ties** **1** : manner and disposition of an individual **2** : distinctive or well-known person

per·son·al·ize \'pərsᵊnəˌlīz\ *vb* **-ized; -iz·ing** : mark as belonging to a particular person

per·son·i·fy \pər'sänəˌfī\ *vb* **-fied; -fy·ing** **1** : represent as a human being **2** : be the embodiment of — **per·son·i·fi·ca·tion** \-ˌsänəfə'kāshən\ *n*

per·son·nel \ˌpərsᵊn'el\ *n* : body of persons employed

per·spec·tive \pər'spektiv\ *n* **1** : apparent depth and distance in painting **2** : view of things in their true relationship or importance

per·spi·ca·cious \ˌpərspə'kā-shəs\ *adj* : showing keen understanding or discernment — **per·spi·cac·i·ty** \-'kasətē\ *n*

per·spire \pər'spīr\ *vb* **-spired; -spir·ing** : sweat — **per·spi·ra·tion** \ˌpərspə'rāshən\ *n*

per·suade \pər'swād\ *vb* **-suad·ed; -suad·ing** : win over to a belief or course of action by argument or entreaty — **per·sua·sion** \pər'swāzhən\ *n* — **per·sua·sive** \-'swāsiv,

-ziv\ *adj* — **per·sua·sive·ly** *adv* — **per·sua·sive·ness** *n*

pert \'pərt\ *adj* : flippant or irreverent

per·tain \pər'tān\ *vb* **1** : belong **2** : relate

per·ti·nent \'pərt⁹nənt\ *adj* : relevant — **per·ti·nence** \-əns\ *n*

per·turb \pər'tərb\ *vb* : make uneasy — **per·tur·ba·tion** \ˌpərtər'bāshən\ *n*

pe·ruse \pə'rüz\ *vb* **-rused; -rus·ing** : read attentively — **pe·rus·al** \-'rüzəl\ *n*

per·vade \pər'vād\ *vb* **-vaded; -vad·ing** : spread through every part of — **per·va·sive** \-'vāsiv, -ziv\ *adj*

per·verse \pər'vərs\ *adj* **1** : corrupt **2** : unreasonably contrary — **per·verse·ly** *adv* — **per·verse·ness** *n* — **per·ver·sion** \pər'vərzhən\ *n* — **per·ver·si·ty** \-'vərsətē\ *n*

per·vert \pər'vərt\ *vb* : corrupt or distort ~ \'pərˌ-\ *n* : one that is perverted

pe·so \'pāsō\ *n, pl* **-sos** : monetary unit (as of Mexico)

pes·si·mism \'pesəˌmizəm\ *n* : inclination to expect the worst — **pes·si·mist** \-mist\ *n* — **pes·si·mis·tic** \ˌpesə-'mistik\ *adj*

pest \'pest\ *n* **1** : nuisance **2** : plant or animal detrimental

to humans or their crops — **pes·ti·cide** \'pestəˌsīd\ *n*

pes·ter \'pestər\ *vb* **-tered; -ter·ing** : harass with petty matters

pes·ti·lence \'pestələns\ *n* : plague — **pes·ti·lent** \-lənt\ *adj*

pes·tle \'pesəl, 'pest⁹l\ *n* : implement for grinding substances in a mortar

pet \'pet\ *n* **1** : domesticated animal kept for pleasure **2** : favorite ~ *vb* **-tt-** : stroke gently or lovingly

pet·al \'pet⁹l\ *n* : modified leaf of a flower head

pe·tite \pə'tēt\ *adj* : having a small trim figure

pe·ti·tion \pə'tishən\ *n* : formal written request ~ *vb* : make a request — **pe·ti·tion·er** *n*

pet·ri·fy \'petrəˌfī\ *vb* **-fied; -fy·ing** **1** : change into stony material **2** : make rigid or inactive (as from fear) — **pet·ri·fac·tion** \ˌpetrə'fakshən\ *n*

pe·tro·leum \pə'trōlēəm\ *n* : raw oil obtained from the ground

pet·ti·coat \'petēˌkōt\ *n* : skirt worn under a dress

pet·ty \'petē\ *adj* **-ti·er; -est** **1** : minor **2** : of no importance **3** : narrow-minded or mean — **pet·ti·ly** \'pet⁹lē\ *adv* — **pet·ti·ness** *n*

petty officer *n* : subordinate officer in the navy or coast guard

pet·u·lant \\'pechələnt\\ *adj* : irritable — **pet·u·lance** \\-ləns\\ *n* — **pet·u·lant·ly** *adv*

pe·tu·nia \\pi'tünyə, -'tyü-\\ *n* : tropical herb with bright flowers

pew \\'pyü\\ *n* : bench with a back used in a church

pew·ter \\'pyütər\\ *n* : alloy of tin used for household utensils

pH \\ˌpē'āch\\ *n* : number expressing relative acidity and alkalinity

pha·lanx \\'fāˌlaŋks\\ *n, pl* **-lanx·es** *or* **-lan·ges** \\fə'lanˌjēz\\ **1** : body (as of troops) in compact formation **2** *pl* *phalanges* : digital bone of the hand or foot

phal·lus \\'faləs\\ *n, pl* **-li** \\'falˌī\\ *or* **-lus·es** : penis — **phal·lic** *adj*

phantasy *var of* FANTASY

phan·tom \\'fantəm\\ *n* : something that only appears to be real — **phantom** *adj*

pha·raoh \\'ferō, 'fārō\\ *n* : ruler of ancient Egypt

phar·ma·ceu·ti·cal \\ˌfärmə'sütikəl\\ *adj* : relating to pharmacy or the making and selling of medicinal drugs — **pharmaceutical** *n*

phar·ma·col·o·gy \\ˌfärmə'käləjē\\ *n* : science of drugs esp. as related to medicinal uses — **phar·ma·co·log·i·cal** \\-ikəl\\ *adj* — **phar·ma·col·o·gist** \\-'käləjist\\ *n*

phar·ma·cy \\'färməsē\\ *n, pl* **-cies 1** : art or practice of preparing and dispensing medical drugs **2** : drugstore — **phar·ma·cist** \\-sist\\ *n*

phar·ynx \\'fariŋks\\ *n, pl* **pha·ryn·ges** \\fə'rinˌjēz\\ : space behind the mouth into which the nostrils, esophagus, and windpipe open — **pha·ryn·ge·al** \\fə'rinjəl, ˌfarən'jēəl\\ *adj*

phase \\'fāz\\ *n* **1** : particular appearance or stage in a recurring series of changes **2** : stage in a process —**phase in** *vb* : introduce in stages — **phase out** *vb* : discontinue gradually

pheas·ant \\'fezᵊnt\\ *n, pl* **-ant** *or* **-ants** : long-tailed brilliantly colored game bird

phe·nom·e·non \\fi'näməˌnän, -nən\\ *n, pl* **-na** \\-nə\\ *or* **-nons 1** : observable fact or event **2** *pl* **-nons** : prodigy — **phe·nom·e·nal** \\-'nämənᵊl\\ *adj*

phi·lan·der·er \\fə'landərər\\ *n* : one who makes love without serious intent

phi·lan·thro·py \\fə'lanthrəpē\\ *n, pl* **-pies** : charitable act or gift or an organization that distributes such gifts — **phil·an·throp·ic** \ˌfilən'thräpik\ *adj* — **phi·lan·thro·pist** \fə-'lanthrəpist\ *n*

phi·lat·e·ly \fə'latᵊlē\ *n* : collection and study of postage stamps — **phi·lat·e·list** \-ᵊlist\ *n*

phi·lis·tine \'filəˌstēn, fə'lis-tən\ *n* : one who is smugly indifferent to intellectual or artistic values — **philistine** *adj*

philo·den·dron \ˌfilə'dendrən\ *n, pl* **-drons** *or* **-dra** \-drə\ : plant grown for its showy leaves

phi·los·o·pher \fə'läsəfər\ *n* **1** : reflective thinker **2** : student of philosophy

phi·los·o·phy \fə'läsəfē\ *n, pl* **-phies** **1** : critical study of fundamental beliefs **2** : sciences and liberal arts exclusive of medicine, law, and theology **3** : system of ideas **4** : sum of personal convictions — **phil·o·sóph·ic** \ˌfilə'säfik\, **phil·o·soph·i·cal** \-ikəl\ *adj* — **phil·o·soph·i·cal·ly** \-klē\ *adv* — **phi·los·o·phize** \fə'läsəˌfīz\ *vb*

phle·bi·tis \fli'bītəs\ *n* : inflammation of a vein

phlegm \'flem\ *n* : thick mucus in the nose and throat

phlox \'fläks\ *n, pl* **phlox** *or* **phlox·es** : herb grown for its flower clusters

pho·bia \'fōbēə\ *n* : irrational persistent fear

phoe·nix \'fēniks\ *n* : legendary bird held to burn itself to death and rise fresh and young from its ashes

phone \'fōn\ *n* : telephone ∼ *vb* **phoned; phon·ing** : call on a telephone

pho·neme \'fōˌnēm\ *n* : basic distinguishable unit of speech — **pho·ne·mic** \fō'nēmik\ *adj*

pho·net·ics \fə'netiks\ *n* : study of speech sounds — **pho·net·ic** \-ik\ *adj* — **pho·ne·ti·cian** \ˌfōnə'tishən\ *n*

pho·nics \'fäniks\ *n* : method of teaching reading by stressing sound values of syllables and words

pho·no·graph \'fōnəˌgraf\ *n* : instrument that reproduces sounds from a grooved disc

pho·ny, pho·ney \'fōnē\ *adj* **-ni·er; -est** : not sincere or genuine — **phony** *n*

phos·phate \'fäsˌfāt\ *n* : chemical salt used in fertilizers — **phos·phat·ic** \fäs'fatik\ *adj*

phos·phor \'fäsfər\ *n* : phosphorescent substance

phos·pho·res·cence \ˌfäsfə-'resᵊns\ *n* : luminescence from absorbed radiation — **phos·pho·res·cent** \-ᵊnt\ *adj*

phos·pho·rus \'fäsfərəs\ *n* : poisonous waxy chemical element — **phos·phor·ic** \fäs-

photo 482

'fȯrik, -'fär-\ *adj* — **phos·pho·rous** \'fäsfərəs, fäs'fōrəs\ *adj*

pho·to \'fōtō\ *n, pl* **-tos** : photograph — **photo** *vb or adj*

pho·to·copy \'fōtə,käpē\ *n* : photographic copy (as of a printed page) — **photocopy** *vb*

pho·to·elec·tric \,fōtōi'lek-trik\ *adj* : relating to an electrical effect due to the interaction of light with matter

pho·to·ge·nic \,fōtə'jenik\ *adj* : suitable for being photographed

pho·to·graph \'fōtə,graf\ *n* : picture taken by photography — **photograph** *vb* — **pho·tog·ra·pher** \fə'tägrəfər\ *n*

pho·tog·ra·phy \fə'tägrəfē\ *n* : process of using light to produce images on a sensitized surface — **pho·to·graph·ic** \,fōtə'grafik\ *adj* — **pho·to·graph·i·cal·ly** *adv*

pho·to·syn·the·sis \,fōtō'sin-thəsəs\ *n* : formation of carbohydrates by chlorophyll-containing plants exposed to sunlight — **pho·to·syn·the·size** \-,sīz\ *vb* — **pho·to·syn·thet·ic** \-sin'thetik\ *adj*

phrase \'frāz\ *n* **1** : brief expression **2** : group of related words that express a thought ~ *vb* **phrased; phras·ing** : express in a particular manner

phrase·ol·o·gy \,frāzē'äləjē\ *n, pl* **-gies** : manner of phrasing

phy·lum \'fīləm\ *n, pl* **-la** \-lə\ : major division of the plant or animal kingdom

phys·i·cal \'fizikəl\ *adj* **1** : relating to nature **2** : material as opposed to mental or spiritual **3** : relating to the body ~ *n* : medical examination — **phys·i·cal·ly** \-klē\ *adv*

phy·si·cian \fə'zishən\ *n* : doctor of medicine

physician's assistant *n* : person certified to provide basic medical care under a physician's supervision

phys·i·cist \'fizəsist\ *n* : specialist in physics

phys·ics \'fiziks\ *n* : science that deals with matter and motion

phys·i·og·no·my \,fizē'ägnəmē\ *n, pl* **-mies** : facial appearance esp. as a reflection of inner character

phys·i·ol·o·gy \,fizē'äləjē\ *n* : functional processes in an organism — **phys·i·o·log·i·cal** \-ēə'läjikəl\, **phys·i·o·log·ic** \-ik\ *adj* — **phys·i·ol·o·gist** \-ē'äləjist\ *n*

phy·sique \fə'zēk\ *n* : build of a person's body

pi \'pī\ *n, pl* **pis** \'pīz\ : symbol π denoting the ratio of the circumference of a circle to its diameter or the ratio itself

pi·a·nist \pē'anist, 'pēənist\ *n* : one who plays the piano

pi·ano \pē'anō\ *n, pl* **-anos** : musical instrument with strings sounded by hammers operated from a keyboard

pi·az·za \pē'azə, -'äz-, -tsə\ *n, pl* **-zas** *or* **-ze** \-tsā\ : public square in a town

pic·a·yune \ˌpikē'yün\ *adj* : trivial or petty

pic·co·lo \'pikəˌlō\ *n, pl* **-los** : small shrill flute

¹pick \'pik\ *vb* **1** : break up with a pointed instrument **2** : remove bit by bit **3** : gather by plucking **4** : select **5** : rob **6** : provoke **7** : unlock with a wire **8** : eat sparingly ~ *n* **1** : act of choosing **2** : choicest one — **pick·er** *n* — **pick up** *vb* **1** : improve **2** : put in order

²pick *n* : pointed digging tool

pick·ax *n* : pick

pick·er·el \'pikərəl\ *n, pl* **-el** *or* **-els** : small pike

pick·et \'pikət\ *n* **1** : pointed stake (as for a fence) **2** : worker demonstrating on strike ~ *vb* : demonstrate as a picket

pick·le \'pikəl\ *n* **1** : brine or vinegar solution for preserving foods or a food preserved in a pickle **2** : bad state — **pickle** *vb*

pick·pock·et *n* : one who steals from pockets

pick·up \'pikˌəp\ *n* **1** : revival or acceleration **2** : light truck with an open body

pic·nic \'pikˌnik\ *n* : outing with food usu. eaten in the open ~ *vb* **-nicked; -nick·ing** : go on a picnic

pic·to·ri·al \pik'tōrēəl\ *adj* : relating to pictures

pic·ture \'pikchər\ *n* **1** : representation by painting, drawing, or photography **2** : vivid description **3** : copy **4** : movie ~ *vb* **-tured; -tur·ing** : form a mental image of

pic·tur·esque \ˌpikchə'resk\ *adj* : attractive enough for a picture

pie \'pī\ *n* : pastry crust and a filling

pie·bald \'pīˌbȯld\ *adj* : blotched with white and black

piece \'pēs\ *n* **1** : part of a whole **2** : one of a group or set **3** : single item **4** : product of creative work ~ *vb* **pieced; piec·ing** : join into a whole

piece·meal \'pēsˌmēl\ *adv or adj* : gradually

pied \'pīd\ *adj* : colored in blotches

pier \'pir\ *n* **1** : support for a bridge span **2** : deck or wharf built out over water **3** : pillar

pierce \'pirs\ *vb* **pierced; pierc·ing** **1** : enter or thrust into or through **2** : penetrate **3** : see through

pi·ety \'pīətē\ *n, pl* **-eties** : devotion to religion

pig \'pig\ *n* **1** : young swine **2** : dirty or greedy individual **3** : iron casting — **pig·gish** \-ish\ *adj* — **pig·let** \-lət\ *n* — **pig·pen** *n* — **pig·sty** *n*

pi·geon \'pijən\ *n* : stout-bodied short-legged bird

pi·geon·hole *n* : small open compartment for letters or documents ~ *vb* **1** : place in a pigeonhole **2** : classify

pig·gy·back \'pigē‚bak\ *adv or adj* : up on the back and shoulders

pig·head·ed \-'hedəd\ *adj* : stubborn

pig·ment \'pigmənt\ *n* : coloring matter — **pig·men·ta·tion** *n*

pigmy *var of* PYGMY

pig·tail *n* : tight braid of hair

¹**pike** \'pīk\ *n, pl* **pike** *or* **pikes** : large freshwater fish

²**pike** *n* : former weapon consisting of a long wooden staff with a steel point

³**pike** *n* : turnpike

pi·laf, pi·laff \pi'läf, 'pē‚läf\, **pi·lau** \pi'lō, -'lȯ; 'pēlō, -lȯ\ *n* : dish of seasoned rice

¹**pile** \'pīl\ *n* : supporting pillar driven into the ground

²**pile** *n* : quantity of things thrown on one another ~ *vb* **piled; pil·ing** : heap up, accumulate

³**pile** *n* : surface of fine hairs or threads — **piled** *adj*

piles \'pīls\ *n pl* : hemorrhoids

pil·fer \'pilfər\ *vb* : steal in small quantities

pil·grim \'pilgrəm\ *n* **1** : one who travels to a shrine or holy place in devotion **2** *cap* : one of the English settlers in America in 1620

pil·grim·age \-grəmij\ *n* : pilgrim's journey

pill \'pil\ *n* : small rounded mass of medicine — **pill·box** *n*

pil·lage \'pilij\ *vb* **-laged; -laging** : loot and plunder — **pillage** *n*

pil·lar \'pilər\ *n* : upright usu. supporting column — **pil·lared** *adj*

pil·lo·ry \'pilərē\ *n, pl* **-ries** : wooden frame for public punishment with holes for the head and hands ~ *vb* **-ried; -ry·ing** **1** : set in a pillory **2** : expose to public scorn

pil·low \'pilō\ *n* : soft cushion for the head — **pil·low·case** *n*

pi·lot \'pīlət\ *n* **1** : helmsman **2** : person licensed to take ships into and out of a port **3** : guide **4** : one that flies an aircraft or spacecraft ~ *vb* : act as pilot of — **pi·lot·less** *adj*

pi·men·to \pə'mentō\ *n, pl* **-tos** *or* **-to** **1** : allspice **2** : pimiento

pi·mien·to \pə'mentō, -'myen-\ *n, pl* **-tos** : mild red sweet pepper

pimp \\'pimp\ *n* : man who so-licits clients for a prostitute — **pimp** *vb*

pim·ple \\'pimpəl\ *n* : small inflamed swelling on the skin — **pim·ply** \-pəlē\ *adj*

pin \\'pin\ *n* **1** : fastener made of a small pointed piece of wire **2** : ornament or emblem fastened to clothing with a pin **3** : wooden object used as a target in bowling ∼ *vb* **-nn-** **1** : fasten with a pin **2** : hold fast or immobile — **pin·hole** *n*

pin·a·fore \\'pinə‚fōr\ *n* : sleeveless dress or apron fas-tened at the back

pin·cer \\'pinsər\ *n* **1** *pl* : grip-ping tool with 2 jaws **2** : pin-cerlike claw

pinch \\'pinch\ *vb* **1** : squeeze between the finger and thumb or between the jaws of a tool **2** : compress painfully **3** : re-strict **4** : steal ∼ *n* **1** : emer-gency **2** : painful effect **3** : act of pinching **4** : very small quantity

pin·cush·ion *n* : cushion for storing pins

¹**pine** \\'pīn\ *n* : evergreen cone-bearing tree or its wood

²**pine** *vb* **pined; pin·ing 1** : lose health through distress **2** : yearn for intensely

pine·ap·ple *n* : tropical plant bearing an edible juicy fruit

pin·feath·er *n* : new feather just coming through the skin

¹**pin·ion** \\'pinyən\ *vb* : restrain by binding the arms

²**pinion** *n* : small gear

¹**pink** \\'piŋk\ *n* **1** : plant with narrow leaves and showy flowers **2** : highest degree

²**pink** *n* : light red color — **pink** *adj* — **pink·ish** *adj*

pink·eye *n* : contagious eye in-flammation

pin·na·cle \\'pinikəl\ *n* : high-est point

pi·noch·le \\'pē‚nəkəl\ *n* : card game played with a 48-card deck

pin·point *vb* : locate, hit, or aim with great precision

pint \\'pīnt\ *n* : ½ quart

pin·to \\'pin‚tō\ *n, pl* **pintos** : spotted horse or pony

pin·worm *n* : small parasitic intestinal worm

pi·o·neer \‚pīə'nir\ *n* **1** : one that originates or helps open up a new line of thought or activity **2** : early settler ∼ *vb* : act as a pioneer

pi·ous \\'pīəs\ *adj* **1** : consci-entious in religious practices **2** : affectedly religious — **pi-ous·ly** *adv*

pipe \\'pīp\ *n* **1** : tube that pro-duces music when air is forced through **2** : bagpipe **3** : long tube for conducting a

fluid **4** : smoking tool ∼ *vb*
piped; pip·ing 1 : play on a
pipe **2** : speak in a high voice
3 : convey by pipes — **pip·er** *n*

pipe·line *n* **1** : line of pipe **2**
: channel for information

pip·ing \\'pīpiŋ\\ *n* **1** : music of
pipes **2** : narrow fold of material used to decorate edges
or seams

pi·quant \\'pēkənt\\ *adj* **1**
: tangy **2** : provocative or
charming — **pi·quan·cy**
\\-kənsē\\ *n*

pique \\'pēk\\ *n* : resentment
∼ *vb* **piqued; piqu·ing 1**
: offend **2** : arouse by provo-
cation

pi·qué, pi·que \\pi'kā\\ *n*
: durable ribbed clothing fabric

pi·ra·cy \\'pīrəsē\\ *n, pl* **-cies 1**
: robbery on the seas **2** : unauthorized use of another's production or invention

pi·ra·nha \\pə'ranyə, -'ränə\\
n : small So. American fish
with sharp teeth

pi·rate \\'pīrət\\ *n* : one who
commits piracy — **pirate** *vb*
— **pi·rat·i·cal** \\pə'ratikəl,
pī-\\ *adj*

pir·ou·ette \\ˌpirə'wet\\ *n* : ballet turn on the toe or ball of
one foot — **pirouette** *vb*

pis *pl of* PI

pis·ta·chio \\pə'stashēˌō,
-'stäsh-\\ *n, pl* **-chios** : small

tree bearing a greenish edible
seed or its seed

pis·til \\'pistəl\\ *n* : female reproductive organ in a flower
— **pis·til·late** \\'pistəˌlāt\\ *adj*

pis·tol \\'pistəl\\ *n* : firearm held
with one hand

pis·ton \\'pistən\\ *n* : sliding
piece that receives and transmits motion usu. inside a cylinder

[1]pit \\'pit\\ *n* **1** : hole or shaft in
the ground **2** : sunken or en-
closed place for a special purpose **3** : hell **4** : hollow or
indentation ∼ *vb* -tt- **1** : form
pits in **2** : become marred
with pits

[2]pit *n* : stony seed of some
fruits ∼ *vb* -tt- : remove the
pit from

pit bull *n* : powerful compact
dog bred for fighting

[1]pitch \\'pich\\ *n* : resin from
conifers — **pitchy** *adj*

[2]pitch *vb* **1** : erect and fix
firmly in place **2** : throw **3**
: set at a particular tone level
4 : fall headlong ∼ *n* **1** : action or manner of pitching **2**
: degree of slope **3** : relative
highness of a tone **4** : sales
talk — **pitched** *adj*

[1]pitch·er \\'pichər\\ *n* : container for liquids

[2]pitcher *n* : one that pitches (as
in baseball)

pitch·fork *n* : long-handled fork for pitching hay

pit·e·ous \\'pitēəs\\ *adj* : arousing pity — **pit·e·ous·ly** *adv*

pit·fall \\'pit͵fȯl\\ *n* : hidden danger

pith \\'pith\\ *n* **1** : spongy plant tissue **2** : essential or meaningful part — **pithy** *adj*

piti·able \\'pitēəbəl\\ *adj* : pitiful

piti·ful \\'pitifəl\\ *adj* **1** : arousing or deserving pity **2** : contemptible — **piti·ful·ly** *adv*

pit·tance \\'pitᵊns\\ *n* : small portion or amount

pi·tu·i·tary \\pə'tüə͵terē, -'tyü-\\ *adj* : relating to or being a small gland attached to the brain

pity \\'pitē\\ *n, pl* **pi·ties** **1** : sympathetic sorrow **2** : something to be regretted ~ *vb* **pit·ied; pity·ing** : feel pity for — **piti·less** *adj* — **piti·less·ly** *adv*

piv·ot \\'pivət\\ *n* : fixed pin on which something turns ~ *vb* : turn on or as if on a pivot — **piv·ot·al** *adj*

pix·ie, pixy \\'piksē\\ *n, pl* **pix·ies** : mischievous sprite

piz·za \\'pētsə\\ *n* : thin pie of bread dough spread with a spiced mixture (as of tomatoes, cheese, and meat)

piz·zazz, pi·zazz \\pə'zaz\\ *n* : glamour

piz·ze·ria \\͵pētsə'rēə\\ *n* : pizza restaurant

plac·ard \\'plakərd, -͵ärd\\ *n* : poster ~ *vb* : display placards in or on

pla·cate \\'plā͵kāt, 'plak͵āt\\ *vb* **-cat·ed; -cat·ing** : appease — **pla·ca·ble** \\'plakəbəl, 'plākə-\\ *adj*

place \\'plās\\ *n* **1** : space or room **2** : indefinite area **3** : a particular building, locality, area, or part **4** : relative position in a scale or sequence **5** : seat **6** : job ~ *vb* **placed; plac·ing** **1** : put in a place **2** : identify — **place·ment** *n*

pla·ce·bo \\plə'sēbō\\ *n, pl* **-bos** : something inactive prescribed as a remedy for its psychological effect

pla·cen·ta \\plə'sentə\\ *n, pl* **-tas** *or* **-tae** \\-͵ē\\ : structure in a uterus by which a fetus is nourished — **pla·cen·tal** \\-'sentᵊl\\ *adj*

plac·id \\'plasəd\\ *adj* : undisturbed or peaceful — **pla·cid·i·ty** \\pla'sidətē\\ *n* — **plac·id·ly** *adv*

pla·gia·rize \\'plājə͵rīz\\ *vb* **-rized; -riz·ing** : use (words or ideas) of another as if your own — **pla·gia·rism** \\-͵rizəm\\ *n* — **pla·gia·rist** \\-rist\\ *n*

plague \\'plāg\\ *n* **1** : disastrous evil **2** : destructive contagious bacterial disease ~ *vb*

plagued; plagu·ing 1 : afflict with disease or disaster **2** : harass

plaid \'plad\ *n* : woolen fabric with a pattern of crossing stripes or the pattern itself — **plaid** *adj*

plain \'plān\ *n* : expanse of relatively level treeless country ~ *adj* **1** : lacking ornament **2** : not concealed or disguised **3** : easily understood **4** : frank **5** : not fancy or pretty — **plain·ly** *adv* — **plain·ness** \'plānnəs\ *n*

plain·tiff \'plāntəf\ *n* : complaining party in a lawsuit

plain·tive \'plāntiv\ *adj* : expressive of suffering or woe — **plain·tive·ly** *adv*

plait \'plāt, 'plat\ *n* **1** : pleat **2** : braid of hair or straw — **plait** *vb*

plan \'plan\ *n* **1** : drawing or diagram **2** : method for accomplishing something ~ *vb* **-nn- 1** : form a plan of **2** : intend — **plan·less** *adj* — **plan·ner** *n*

[1]**plane** \'plān\ *vb* **planed; plan·ing** : smooth or level off with a plane ~ *n* : smoothing or shaping tool — **plan·er** *n*

[2]**plane** *n* **1** : level surface **2** : level of existence, consciousness, or development **3** : airplane ~ *adj* **1** : flat **2** : dealing with flat surfaces or figures

plan·et \'planət\ *n* : celestial body that revolves around the sun — **plan·e·tary** \-ə,terē\ *adj*

plan·e·tar·i·um \,planə'ter-ēəm\ *n, pl* **-iums** *or* **-ia** \-ēə\ : building or room housing a device to project images of celestial bodies

plank \'plaŋk\ *n* **1** : heavy thick board **2** : article in the platform of a political party — **plank·ing** *n*

plank·ton \'plaŋktən\ *n* : tiny aquatic animal and plant life — **plank·ton·ic** \plaŋk'tänik\ *adj*

plant \'plant\ *vb* **1** : set in the ground to grow **2** : place firmly or forcibly ~ *n* **1** : living thing without sense organs that cannot move about **2** : land, buildings, and machinery used esp. in manufacture

[1]**plan·tain** \'plantᵊn\ *n* : short-stemmed herb with tiny greenish flowers

[2]**plantain** *n* : banana plant with starchy greenish fruit

plan·ta·tion \plan'tāshən\ *n* : agricultural estate usu. worked by resident laborers

plant·er \'plantər\ *n* **1** : plantation owner **2** : plant container

plaque \'plak\ *n* **1** : commemorative tablet **2** : film layer on a tooth

plas·ma \'plazmə\ *n* **1** : watery part of blood **2** : highly ionized gas — **plas·mat·ic** \plaz'matik\ *adj*

plasma TV *n* : television screen in which cells of plasma emit light upon receiving an electric current

plas·ter \'plastər\ *n* **1** : medicated dressing **2** : hardening paste for coating walls and ceilings ~ *vb* : cover with plaster — **plas·ter·er** *n*

plas·tic \'plastik\ *adj* : capable of being molded ~ *n* : material that can be formed into rigid objects, films, or filaments — **plas·tic·i·ty** \plas'tisətē\ *n*

plate \'plāt\ *n* **1** : flat thin piece **2** : plated metalware **3** : shallow usu. circular dish **4** : denture or the part of it that fits to the mouth **5** : something printed from an engraving ~ *vb* **plat·ed; plat·ing** : overlay with metal — **plat·ing** *n*

pla·teau \pla'tō\ *n, pl* **-teaus** *or* **-teaux** \-'tōz\ : large level area of high land

plat·form \'plat,fȯrm\ *n* **1** : raised flooring or stage **2** : declaration of principles for a political party

plat·i·num \'platᵊnəm\ *n* : heavy grayish-white metallic chemical element

plat·i·tude \'platə,tüd, -,tyüd\ *n* : trite remark — **plat·i·tu-**di·nous \,platə'tüdᵊnəs, -'tyüd-\ *adj*

pla·toon \plə'tün\ *n* : small military unit

platoon sergeant *n* : noncommissioned officer in the army ranking below a first sergeant

plat·ter \'platər\ *n* : large serving plate

platy·pus \'platipəs\ *n* : small aquatic egg-laying mammal

plau·dit \'plȯdət\ *n* : act of applause

plau·si·ble \'plȯzəbəl\ *adj* : reasonable or believeable — **plau·si·bil·i·ty** \,plȯzə'bilətē\ *n* — **plau·si·bly** \-blē\ *adv*

play \'plā\ *n* **1** : action in a game **2** : recreational activity **3** : light or fitful movement **4** : free movement **5** : stage representation of a drama ~ *vb* **1** : engage in recreation **2** : move or toy with aimlessly **3** : perform music **4** : act in a drama — **play·act·ing** *n* — **play·er** *n* — **play·ful** \-fəl\ *adj* — **play·ful·ly** *adv* — **play·ful·ness** *n* — **play·pen** *n* — **play·suit** *n* — **play·thing** *n*

play·ground *n* : place for children to play

play·house *n* **1** : theater **2** : small house for children to play in

playing card *n* : one of a set of 24 to 78 cards marked to show its rank and suit and used to play a game of cards

play·mate *n* : companion in play

play·off *n* : contest or series of contests to determine a champion

play·wright \-ˌrīt\ *n* : writer of plays

pla·za \'plazə, 'pläz-\ *n* **1** : public square **2** : shopping mall

plea \'plē\ *n* **1** : defendant's answer to charges **2** : urgent request

plead \'plēd\ *vb* **plead·ed** \'plēdəd\ *or* **pled** \'pled\; **plead·ing** **1** : argue for or against in court **2** : answer to a charge or indictment **3** : appeal earnestly — **plead·er** *n*

pleas·ant \'plezᵊnt\ *adj* **1** : giving pleasure **2** : marked by pleasing behavior or appearance — **pleas·ant·ly** *adv* — **pleas·ant·ness** *n*

pleas·ant·ries \-ᵊntrēz\ *n pl* : pleasant and casual conversation

please \'plēz\ *vb* **pleased**; **pleas·ing** **1** : give pleasure or satisfaction to **2** : desire or intend

pleas·ing \'plēziŋ\ *adj* : giving pleasure — **pleas·ing·ly** *adv*

plea·sur·able \'plezhərəbəl\ *adj* : pleasant — **plea·sur·ably** \-blē\ *adv*

plea·sure \'plezhər\ *n* **1** : desire or inclination **2** : enjoyment **3** : source of delight

pleat \'plēt\ *vb* : arrange in pleats ~ *n* : fold in cloth

ple·be·ian \pli'bēən\ *n* : one of the common people ~ *adj* : ordinary

pledge \'plej\ *n* **1** : something given as security **2** : promise or vow ~ *vb* **pledged; pledging** **1** : offer as or bind by a pledge **2** : promise

ple·na·ry \'plēnərē, 'plen-\ *adj* : full

pleni·po·ten·tia·ry \ˌplenəpə-'tenchərē, -'tenchēˌerē\ *n* : diplomatic agent having full authority — **plenipotentiary** *adj*

plen·i·tude \'plenəˌtüd, -ˌtyüd\ *n* **1** : completeness **2** : abundance

plen·te·ous \'plentēəs\ *adj* : existing in plenty

plen·ty \'plentē\ *n* : more than adequate number or amount — **plen·ti·ful** \'plentifəl\ *adj* — **plen·ti·ful·ly** *adv*

pleth·o·ra \'plethərə\ *n* : excess

pleu·ri·sy \'plu̇rəsē\ *n* : inflammation of the chest membrane

pli·able \'plīəbəl\ *adj* : flexible

pli·ant \'plīənt\ *adj* : flexible — **pli·an·cy** \-ənsē\ *n*

pli·ers \\'plīərz\\ *n pl* : pinching or gripping tool

¹plight \\'plīt\\ *vb* : pledge

²plight *n* : bad state

plod \\'pläd\\ *vb* **-dd-** **1** : walk heavily or slowly **2** : work laboriously and monotonously — **plod·der** *n* — **plod·ding·ly** \\-iŋlē\\ *adv*

plot \\'plät\\ *n* **1** : small area of ground **2** : ground plan **3** : main story development (as of a book or movie) **4** : secret plan for doing something ~ *vb* **-tt-** **1** : make a plot or plan of **2** : plan or contrive — **plot·ter** *n*

plo·ver \\'pləvər, 'plōvər\\ *n, pl* **-ver** *or* **-vers** : shorebird related to the sandpiper

plow, plough \\'plau̇\\ *n* **1** : tool used to turn soil **2** : device for pushing material aside ~ *vb* **1** : break up with a plow **2** : cleave or move through like a plow — **plow·man** \\-mən, -ˌman\\ *n*

plow·share \\-ˌsher\\ *n* : plow part that cuts the earth

ploy \\'plȯi\\ *n* : clever maneuver

pluck \\'plək\\ *vb* **1** : pull off or out **2** : tug or twitch ~ *n* **1** : act or instance of plucking **2** : spirit or courage

plucky \\'pləkē\\ *adj* **pluck·i·er; -est** : courageous or spirited

plug \\'pləg\\ *n* **1** : something for sealing an opening **2** : electrical connector at the end of a cord **3** : piece of favorable publicity ~ *vb* **-gg-** **1** : stop or make tight or secure by inserting a plug **2** : publicize

plum \\'pləm\\ *n* **1** : smooth-skinned juicy fruit **2** : fine reward

plum·age \\'plümij\\ *n* : feathers of a bird — **plum·aged** \\-mijd\\ *adj*

plumb \\'pləm\\ *n* : weight on the end of a line (**plumb line**) to show vertical direction ~ *adv* **1** : vertically **2** : completely ~ *vb* : sound or test with a plumb ~ *adj* : vertical

plumb·er \\'pləmər\\ *n* : one who repairs usu. water pipes and fixtures

plumb·ing \\'pləmiŋ\\ *n* : system of water pipes in a building

plume \\'plüm\\ *n* : large, conspicuous, or showy feather ~ *vb* **plumed; plum·ing** **1** : provide or deck with feathers **2** : indulge in pride — **plumed** \\'plümd\\ *adj*

plum·met \\'pləmət\\ *vb* : drop straight down

¹plump \\'pləmp\\ *vb* : drop suddenly or heavily ~ *adv* **1** : straight down **2** : in a direct manner

²plump *adj* : having a full rounded form — **plump·ness** *n*

plun·der \'pləndər\ *vb* : rob or take goods by force (as in war) ~ *n* : something taken in plundering — **plun·der·er** *n*

plunge \'plənj\ *vb* **plunged; plung·ing** **1** : thrust or drive with force **2** : leap or dive into water **3** : begin an action suddenly **4** : dip or move suddenly forward or down ~ *n* : act or instance of plunging — **plung·er** *n*

plu·ral \'plùrəl\ *adj* : relating to a word form denoting more than one — **plural** *n*

plu·ral·i·ty \plù'ralətē\ *n, pl* **-ties** : greatest number of votes cast when not a majority

plu·ral·ize \'plùrə,līz\ *vb* **-ized; -iz·ing** : make plural — **plu·ral·i·za·tion** \,plùrələ'zā-shən\ *n*

plus \'pləs\ *prep* : with the addition of ~ *n* **1** : sign + (**plus sign**) in mathematics to indicate addition **2** : added or positive quantity **3** : advantage ~ *adj* : being more or in addition ~ *conj* : and

plush \'pləsh\ *n* : fabric with a long pile ~ *adj* : luxurious — **plush·ly** *adv* — **plushy** *adj* — **plush·ness** *n*

plu·toc·ra·cy \plü'täkrəsē\ *n, pl* **-cies** **1** : government by the wealthy **2** : a controlling class of the wealthy — **plu·to·crat** \'plütə,krat\ *n* — **plu·to·crat·ic** \,plütə'kratik\ *adj*

plu·to·ni·um \plü'tōnēəm\ *n* : radioactive chemical element

¹ply \'plī\ *n, pl* **plies** : fold, thickness, or strand of which something is made

²ply *vb* **plied; ply·ing** **1** : use or work at **2** : keep supplying something to **3** : travel regularly usu. by sea

ply·wood *n* : sheets of wood glued and pressed together

pneu·mat·ic \nù'matik, nyù-\ *adj* **1** : moved by air pressure **2** : filled with compressed air — **pneu·mat·i·cal·ly** *adv*

pneu·mo·nia \nù'mōnyə, nyù-\ *n* : inflammatory lung disease

¹poach \'pōch\ *vb* : cook in simmering liquid

²poach *vb* : hunt or fish illegally — **poach·er** *n*

pock \'päk\ *n* : small swelling on the skin or its scar — **pock·mark** *n* — **pock·marked** *adj*

pock·et \'päkət\ *n* **1** : small open bag sewn into a garment **2** : container or receptacle **3** : isolated area or group ~ *vb* : put in a pocket — **pock·et·ful** \-,fùl\ *n*

pock·et·book *n* **1** : purse **2** : financial resources

pock·et·knife *n* : knife with a folding blade carried in the pocket

pod \'päd\ *n* **1** : dry fruit that splits open when ripe **2** : compartment on a ship or craft

po·di·a·try \pə'dīətrē, pō-\ *n* : branch of medicine dealing with the foot — **po·di·a·trist** \pə'dīətrist, pō-\ *n*

po·di·um \'pōdēəm\ *n, pl* **-di·ums** *or* **-dia** \-ēə\ : dais

po·em \'pōəm\ *n* : composition in verse

po·et \'pōət\ *n* : writer of poetry

po·et·ry \'pōətrē\ *n* **1** : metrical writing **2** : poems — **po·et·ic** \pō'etik\, **po·et·i·cal** \-ikəl\ *adj*

po·grom \'pōgrəm, pə'gräm, 'pägrəm\ *n* : organized massacre

poi·gnant \'pȯinyənt\ *adj* **1** : emotionally painful **2** : deeply moving — **poi·gnan·cy** \-nyənsē\ *n*

poin·set·tia \pȯin'setēə, -'setə\ *n* : showy tropical American plant

point \'pȯint\ *n* **1** : individual often essential detail **2** : purpose **3** : particular place, time, or stage **4** : sharp end **5** : projecting piece of land **6** : dot or period **7** : division of the compass **8** : unit of counting ~ *vb* **1** : sharpen **2** : indicate direction by extending a finger **3** : direct attention to **4** : aim — **point·ed·ly** \-ədlē\ *adv* — **point·less** *adj*

point-blank *adj* **1** : so close to a target that a missile fired goes straight to it **2** : direct — **point-blank** *adv*

point·er \'pȯintər\ *n* **1** : one that points out **2** : large short-haired hunting dog **3** : hint or tip

poise \'pȯiz\ *vb* **poised; pois·ing** : balance ~ *n* : self-possessed calmness

poi·son \'pȯiz³n\ *n* : chemical that can injure or kill ~ *vb* **1** : injure or kill with poison **2** : apply poison to **3** : affect destructively — **poi·son·er** *n* — **poi·son·ous** \'pȯiz³nəs\ *adj*

poke \'pōk\ *vb* **poked; pok·ing** **1** : prod **2** : dawdle ~ *n* : quick thrust

¹**pok·er** \'pōkər\ *n* : rod for stirring a fire

²**poker** *n* : card game for gambling

po·lar \'pōlər\ *adj* : relating to a geographical or magnetic pole

po·lar·ize \'pōlə,rīz\ *vb* **-ized; -iz·ing** **1** : cause to have magnetic poles **2** : break up into opposing groups — **po·lar·i·za·tion** \,pōlərə'zāshən\ *n*

¹**pole** \'pōl\ *n* : long slender piece of wood or metal

²**pole** *n* **1** : either end of the earth's axis **2** : battery terminal **3** : either end of a magnet

pole·cat \'pōl,kat\ *n, pl* **pole·cats** *or* **polecat** **1** : European carnivorous mammal **2** : skunk

po·lem·ics \pə'lemiks\ *n sing or pl* : practice of disputation

— **po·lem·i·cal** \-ikəl\ *adj* — **po·lem·i·cist** \-əsist\ *n*

po·lice \pə'lēs\ *n, pl* **police** **1** : department of government that keeps public order and enforces the laws **2** : members of the police ~ *vb* **-liced; -lic·ing** : regulate and keep in order — **po·lice·man** \-mən\ *n* — **po·lice·wom·an** *n*

police officer *n* : member of the police

¹**pol·i·cy** \'päləsē\ *n, pl* **-cies** : course of action selected to guide decisions

²**policy** *n, pl* **-cies** : insurance contract — **pol·i·cy·hold·er** *n*

po·lio \'pōlē,ō\ *n* : poliomyelitis — **polio** *adj*

po·lio·my·eli·tis \-,mīə'lītəs\ *n* : acute virus disease of the spinal cord

pol·ish \'pälish\ *vb* **1** : make smooth and glossy **2** : develop or refine ~ *n* **1** : shiny surface **2** : refinement

po·lite \pə'līt\ *adj* **-lit·er; -est** : marked by courteous social conduct — **po·lite·ly** *adv* — **po·lite·ness** *n*

pol·i·tic \'pälə,tik\ *adj* : shrewdly tactful

politically correct *adj* : seeking to avoid offending members of a different group

pol·i·tics \'pälə,tiks\ *n sing or pl* : practice of government and managing of public affairs —

po·lit·i·cal \pə'litikəl\ *adj* — **po·lit·i·cal·ly** *adv* — **pol·i·ti·cian** \,pälə'tishən\ *n*

pol·ka \'pōlkə\ *n* : lively couple dance — **polka** *vb*

pol·ka dot \'pōkə,dät\ *n* : one of a series of regular dots in a pattern

poll \'pōl\ *n* **1** : head **2** : place where votes are cast — usu. pl. **3** : a sampling of opinion ~ *vb* **1** : cut off **2** : receive or record votes **3** : question in a poll — **poll·ster** \-stər\ *n*

pol·len \'pälən\ *n* : spores of a seed plant

pol·li·na·tion \,pälə'nāshən\ *n* : the carrying of pollen to fertilize the seed — **pol·li·nate** \'pälə,nāt\ *vb* — **pol·li·na·tor** \-ər\ *n*

pol·lute \pə'lüt\ *vb* **-lut·ed; -lut·ing** : contaminating with waste products — **pol·lut·ant** \-'lütᵊnt\ *n* — **pol·lut·er** *n* — **pol·lu·tion** \-'lüshən\ *n*

pol·ly·wog, pol·li·wog \'pälē,wäg\ *n* : tadpole

po·lo \'pōlō\ *n* : game played by 2 teams on horseback using long-handled mallets to drive a wooden ball

pol·ter·geist \'pōltər,gīst\ *n* : mischievous ghost

pol·troon \päl'trün\ *n* : coward

poly·es·ter \'pälē,estər\ *n* : synthetic fiber

po·lyg·a·my \pə'ligəmē\ *n* : marriage to several spouses at the same time — **po·lyg·a·mist** \-mist\ *n* — **po·lyg·a·mous** \-məs\ *adj*

poly·gon \'päli͵gän\ *n* : closed plane figure with straight sides

poly·mer \'päləmər\ *n* : chemical compound of molecules joined in long strings — **po·lym·er·i·za·tion** \pə͵limərə-'zāshən\ *n* — **po·lym·er·ize** \pə'limə͵rīz\ *vb*

poly·tech·nic \͵päli'teknik\ *adj* : relating to many technical arts or applied sciences

poly·the·ism \'pälithē͵izəm\ *n* : worship of many gods — **poly·the·ist** \-͵thēist\ *adj or n*

poly·un·sat·u·rat·ed \͵päle-͵ən'sachə͵rātəd\ *adj* : having many double or triple bonds in a molecule

pome·gran·ate \'päm͵granət, 'pämə-\ *n* : tropical reddish fruit with many seeds

pom·mel \'pəməl, 'päm-\ *n* **1** : knob on the hilt of a sword **2** : knob at the front of a saddle ∼ \'pəməl\ *vb* **-meled** *or* **-melled; -mel·ing** *or* **-mel·ling** : pummel

pomp \'pämp\ *n* **1** : brilliant display **2** : ostentation

pomp·ous \'pämpəs\ *adj* : pretentiously dignified — **pom·pos·i·ty** \päm'päsətē\ *n* — **pomp·ous·ly** *adv*

pon·cho \'pänchō\ *n, pl* **-chos** : blanketlike cloak

pond \'pänd\ *n* : small body of water

pon·der \'pändər\ *vb* : consider

pon·der·ous \'pändərəs\ *adj* **1** : very heavy **2** : clumsy **3** : oppressively dull

pon·tiff \'päntəf\ *n* : pope — **pon·tif·i·cal** \pän'tifikəl\ *adj*

pon·tif·i·cate \pän'tifə͵kāt\ *vb* **-cat·ed; -cat·ing** : talk pompously

pon·toon \pän'tün\ *n* : flat-bottomed boat or float

po·ny \'pōnē\ *n, pl* **-nies** : small horse

po·ny·tail \-͵tāl\ *n* : hair arrangement like the tail of a pony

poo·dle \'püd³l\ *n* : dog with a curly coat

¹pool \'pül\ *n* **1** : small body of water **2** : puddle

²pool *n* **1** : amount contributed by participants in a joint venture **2** : game of pocket billiards ∼ *vb* : combine in a common fund

poor \'pu̇r, 'pōr\ *adj* **1** : lacking material possessions **2** : less than adequate **3** : arousing pity **4** : unfavorable — **poor·ly** *adv*

¹pop \'päp\ *vb* **-pp-** **1** : move suddenly **2** : burst with or make a sharp sound **3** : protrude ∼ *n* **1** : sharp explosive sound **2** : flavored soft drink

²pop *adj* : popular

pop·corn \'päp,kȯrn\ *n* : corn whose kernels burst open into a light mass when heated

pope \'pōp\ *n, often cap* : head of the Roman Catholic Church

pop·lar \'päplər\ *n* : slender quick-growing tree

pop·lin \'päplən\ *n* : strong plain-woven fabric with crosswise ribs

pop·over \'päp,ōvər\ *n* : hollow muffin made from egg‑rich batter

pop·py \'päpē\ *n, pl* **-pies** : herb with showy flowers

pop·u·lace \'päpyələs\ *n* **1** : common people **2** : population

pop·u·lar \'päpyələr\ *adj* **1** : relating to the general public **2** : widely accepted **3** : commonly liked — **pop·u·lar·i·ty** \,päpyə'larətē\ *n* — **pop·u·lar·ize** \'päpyələ,rīz\ *vb* — **pop·u·lar·ly** \-lərlē\ *adv*

pop·u·late \'päpyə,lāt\ *vb* **-lat·ed; -lat·ing** : inhabit or occupy

pop·u·la·tion \,päpyə'lāshən\ *n* : people or number of people in an area

pop·u·list \'päpyəlist\ *n* : advocate of the rights of the common people — **pop·u·lism** \-,lizəm\ *n*

pop·u·lous \'päpyələs\ *adj* : densely populated — **pop·u·lous·ness** *n*

por·ce·lain \'pōrsələn\ *n* : fine-grained ceramic ware

porch \'pōrch\ *n* : covered entrance

por·cu·pine \'pȯrkyə,pīn\ *n* : mammal with sharp quills

¹pore \'pōr\ *vb* **pored; por·ing** : read attentively

²pore *n* : tiny hole (as in the skin) — **pored** *adj*

pork \'pȯrk\ *n* : pig meat

pork barrel *n* : government projects benefiting political patrons

por·nog·ra·phy \pȯr'nägrəfē\ *n* : depiction of erotic behavior intended to cause sexual excitement — **por·no·graph·ic** \,pȯrnə'grafik\ *adj*

po·rous \'pōrəs\ *adj* : permeable to fluids — **po·ros·i·ty** \pə'räsətē\ *n*

por·poise \'pȯrpəs\ *n* **1** : small whale with a blunt snout **2** : dolphin

por·ridge \'pȯrij\ *n* : soft boiled cereal

por·rin·ger \'pȯrənjər\ *n* : low one-handled metal bowl or cup

¹port \'pōrt\ *n* **1** : harbor **2** : city with a harbor

²port *n* **1** : inlet or outlet (as in an engine) for a fluid **2** : porthole

³**port** *n* : left side of a ship or airplane looking forward — **port** *adj*

⁴**port** *n* : sweet wine

por·ta·ble \'pōrtəbəl\ *adj* : capable of being carried — **portable** *n*

por·tage \'pōrtij, pȯr'täzh\ *n* : carrying of boats overland between navigable bodies of water or the route where this is done — **portage** *vb*

por·tal \'pōrtᵊl\ *n* : entrance

por·tend \pȯr'tend\ *vb* : give a warning of beforehand

por·tent \'pȯr,tent\ *n* : something that foreshadows a coming event — **por·ten·tous** \pȯr'tentəs\ *adj*

por·ter \'pōrtər\ *n* : baggage carrier

por·ter·house \-,haus\ *n* : choice cut of steak

port·fo·lio \pōrt'fōlē,ō\ *n, pl* **-lios** 1 : portable case for papers 2 : office or function of a diplomat 3 : investor's securities

port·hole \'pōrt,hōl\ *n* : window in the side of a ship or aircraft

por·ti·co \'pōrti,kō\ *n, pl* **-coes** *or* **-cos** : colonnade forming a porch

por·tion \'pōrshən\ *n* : part or share of a whole ~ *vb* : divide into or allot portions

port·ly \'pōrtlē\ *adj* **-li·er; -est** : somewhat stout

por·trait \'pōrtrət, -,trāt\ *n* : picture of a person — **por·trait·ist** \-ist\ *n* — **por·trai·ture** \'pōrtrə,chur\ *n*

por·tray \pōr'trā\ *vb* 1 : make a picture of 2 : describe in words 3 : play the role of — **por·tray·al** *n*

por·tu·laca \,pōrchə'lakə\ *n* : tropical herb with showy flowers

pose \'pōz\ *vb* **posed; pos·ing** 1 : assume a posture or attitude 2 : propose 3 : pretend to be what one is not ~ *n* 1 : sustained posture 2 : pretense — **pos·er** *n*

posh \'päsh\ *adj* : elegant

po·si·tion \pə'zishən\ *n* 1 : stand taken on a question 2 : place or location 3 : status 4 : job — **position** *vb*

pos·i·tive \'päzətiv\ *adj* 1 : definite 2 : confident 3 : relating to or being an adjective or adverb form that denotes no increase 4 : greater than zero 5 : having a deficiency of electrons 6 : affirmative — **pos·i·tive·ly** *adv* — **pos·i·tive·ness** *n*

pos·se \'päsē\ *n* : emergency assistants of a sheriff

pos·sess \pə'zes\ *vb* 1 : have as property or as a quality 2 : control — **pos·ses·sion**

\-'zeshən\ *n* — **pos·ses·sor** \-'zesər\ *n*

pos·ses·sive \pə'zesiv\ *adj* **1** : relating to a grammatical case denoting ownership **2** : jealous — **possessive** *n* — **pos·ses·sive·ness** *n*

pos·si·ble \'päsəbəl\ *adj* **1** : that can be done **2** : potential — **pos·si·bil·i·ty** \ˌpäsə-'bilətē\ *n* — **pos·si·bly** *adv*

pos·sum \'päsəm\ *n* : opossum

¹**post** \'pōst\ *n* : upright stake serving to support or mark ~ *vb* : put up or announce by a notice

²**post** *vb* **1** : mail **2** : inform

³**post** *n* **1** : sentry's station **2** : assigned task **3** : army camp ~ *vb* : station

post- *prefix* : after or subsequent to

post·age \'pōstij\ *n* : fee for mail

post·al \'pōst³l\ *adj* : relating to the mail

post·card *n* : card for mailing a message

post·date \ˌpōst'dāt\ *vb* : assign a date to that is later than the actual date of execution

post·er \'pōstər\ *n* : large usu. printed notice

pos·te·ri·or \pō'stirēər, pä-\ *adj* **1** : later **2** : situated behind ~ *n* : buttocks

pos·ter·i·ty \pä'sterətē\ *n* : all future generations

post·haste \'pōst'hāst\ *adv* : speedily

post·hu·mous \'päschəməs\ *adj* : occurring after one's death — **post·hu·mous·ly** *adv*

post·man \'pōstmən, -ˌman\ *n* : mail carrier

post·mark *n* : official mark on mail — **postmark** *vb*

post·mas·ter *n* : chief of a post office

post me·ri·di·em \'pōstmə-'ridēəm, -ēˌem\ *adj* : being after noon

post·mor·tem \ˌpōst'mȯrtəm\ *adj* : occurring or done after death ~ *n* **1** : medical exam-

---

List of self-explanatory words with the prefix *post-*

postadolescent	postelection	postharvest
postattack	postexercise	posthospital
postbaccalaureate	postflight	postimperial
postbiblical	postgame	postinaugural
postcollege	postgraduate	postindustrial
postcolonial	postgraduation	postinoculation

ination of a corpse **2** : analysis after an event

post office *n* : agency or building for mail service

post·op·er·a·tive \ˌpōstˈäpərə-tiv, -ˈäpəˌrāt-\ *adj* : following surgery

post·paid *adv* : with postage paid by the sender

post·par·tum \-ˈpärtəm\ *adj* : following childbirth — **post-partum** *adv*

post·pone \-ˈpōn\ *vb* **-poned; -pon·ing** : put off to a later time — **post·pone·ment** *n*

post·script \ˈpōstˌskript\ *n* : added note

pos·tu·lant \ˈpäschələnt\ *n* : candidate for a religious order

pos·tu·late \ˈpäschəˌlāt\ *vb* **-lat·ed; -lat·ing** : assume as true ∼ *n* : assumption

pos·ture \ˈpäschər\ *n* : bearing of the body ∼ *vb* **-tured; -tur·ing** : strike a pose

po·sy \ˈpōzē\ *n, pl* **-sies** : flower or bunch of flowers

pot \ˈpät\ *n* : rounded container ∼ *vb* **-tt-** : place in a pot — **pot·ful** *n*

po·ta·ble \ˈpōtəbəl\ *adj* : drinkable

pot·ash \ˈpätˌash\ *n* : white chemical salt of potassium used esp. in agriculture

po·tas·si·um \pəˈtasēəm\ *n* : silver-white metallic chemical element

po·ta·to \pəˈtātō\ *n, pl* **-toes** : edible plant tuber

pot·bel·ly *n* : paunch — **pot-bel·lied** *adj*

po·tent \ˈpōtᵊnt\ *adj* : powerful or effective — **po·ten·cy** \-ᵊnsē\ *n*

po·ten·tate \ˈpōtᵊnˌtāt\ *n* : powerful ruler

po·ten·tial \pəˈtenchəl\ *adj* : capable of becoming actual ∼ *n* **1** : something that can become actual **2** : degree of electrification with reference to a standard — **po·ten·ti·al·i·ty** \pəˌtenchēˈalətē\ *n* — **po·ten·tial·ly** *adv*

poth·er \ˈpäthər\ *n* : fuss

pot·hole \ˈpätˌhōl\ *n* : large hole in a road surface

po·tion \ˈpōshən\ *n* : liquid medicine or poison

---

postmarital
postmenopausal
postnatal
postnuptial
postproduction
postpuberty
postrecession
postretirement
postrevolutionary
postseason
postsecondary
postsurgical
posttreatment
posttrial
postvaccination
postwar

pot·luck *n* : whatever food is available

pot·pour·ri \ˌpōpu̇'rē\ *n* **1** : mix of flowers, herbs, and spices used for scent **2** : miscellaneous collection

pot·shot *n* **1** : casual or easy shot **2** : random critical remark

pot·ter \'pätər\ *n* : pottery maker

pot·tery \'pätərē\ *n, pl* **-ter·ies** : objects (as dishes) made from clay

pouch \'pau̇ch\ *n* **1** : small bag **2** : bodily sac

poul·tice \'pōltəs\ *n* : warm medicated dressing — **poultice** *vb*

poul·try \'pōltrē\ *n* : domesticated fowl

pounce \'pau̇ns\ *vb* **pounced; pounc·ing** : spring or swoop upon and seize

¹pound \'pau̇nd\ *n* **1** : unit of weight equal to 16 ounces **2** : monetary unit (as of the United Kingdom) — **pound·age** \-ij\ *n*

²pound *n* : shelter for stray animals

³pound *vb* **1** : crush by beating **2** : strike heavily **3** : drill **4** : move along heavily

pour \'pōr\ *vb* **1** : flow or supply esp. copiously **2** : rain hard

pout \'pau̇t\ *vb* : look sullen — **pout** *n*

pov·er·ty \'pävərtē\ *n* **1** : lack of money or possessions **2** : poor quality

pow·der \'pau̇dər\ *n* : dry material of fine particles ∼ *vb* : sprinkle or cover with powder — **pow·dery** *adj*

pow·er \'pau̇ər\ *n* **1** : position of authority **2** : ability to act **3** : one that has power **4** : physical might **5** : force or energy used to do work ∼ *vb* : supply with power — **pow·er·ful** \-fəl\ *adj* — **pow·er·ful·ly** *adv* — **pow·er·less** *adj*

pow·er·house *n* : dynamic or energetic person

pow·wow \'pau̇ˌwau̇\ *n* : conference

pox \'päks\ *n, pl* **pox** *or* **pox·es** : disease marked by skin rash

prac·ti·ca·ble \'praktikəbəl\ *adj* : feasible — **prac·ti·ca·bil·i·ty** \ˌpraktikə'bilətē\ *n*

prac·ti·cal \'praktikəl\ *adj* **1** : relating to practice **2** : virtual **3** : capable of being put to use **4** : inclined to action as opposed to speculation — **prac·ti·cal·i·ty** \ˌprakti'kalətē\ *n* — **prac·ti·cal·ly** \'praktiklē\ *adv*

prac·tice, prac·tise \'praktəs\ *vb* **-ticed** *or* **-tised; -tic·ing** *or* **-tis·ing** **1** : perform repeatedly to become proficient **2** : do or perform customarily **3** : be professionally engaged in

~ *n* **1** : actual performance **2** : habit **3** : exercise for proficiency **4** : exercise of a profession

prac·ti·tio·ner \prak'tishənər\ *n* : one who practices a profession

prag·ma·tism \'pragmə-ˌtizəm\ *n* : practical approach to problems — **prag·mat·ic** \prag'matik\ *adj* — **prag·mat·i·cal·ly** *adv*

prai·rie \'prerē\ *n* : broad grassy rolling tract of land

praise \'prāz\ *vb* **praised; prais·ing** **1** : express approval of **2** : glorify — **praise** *n* — **praise·wor·thy** *adj*

prance \'prans\ *vb* **pranced; pranc·ing** **1** : spring from the hind legs **2** : swagger — **prance** *n* — **pranc·er** *n*

prank \'praŋk\ *n* : playful or mischievous act — **prank·ster** \-stər\ *n*

prate \'prāt\ *vb* **prat·ed; prat·ing** : talk long and foolishly

prat·fall \'pratˌfȯl\ *n* : fall on the buttocks

prat·tle \'pratᵊl\ *vb* **-tled; -tling** : babble — **prattle** *n*

prawn \'prȯn\ *n* : shrimplike crustacean

pray \'prā\ *vb* **1** : entreat **2** : ask earnestly for something **3** : address God or a god

prayer \'prer\ *n* **1** : earnest request **2** : an addressing of God or a god **3** : words used in praying — **prayer·ful** *adj* — **prayer·ful·ly** *adv*

praying mantis *n* : mantis

pre- *prefix* : before, prior to, or in advance

preach \'prēch\ *vb* **1** : deliver a sermon **2** : advocate earnestly — **preach·er** *n* — **preach·ment** *n*

pre·am·ble \'prēˌambəl\ *n* : introduction

pre·can·cer·ous \ˌprē'kan-sərəs\ *adj* : likely to become cancerous

pre·car·i·ous \pri'karēəs\ *adj* : dangerously insecure — **pre·car·i·ous·ly** *adv* — **pre·car·i·ous·ness** *n*

pre·cau·tion \pri'kȯshən\ *n* : care taken beforehand — **pre·cau·tion·ary** \-shəˌnerē\ *adj*

pre·cede \pri'sēd\ *vb* **-ced·ed; -ced·ing** : be, go, or come

---

List of self-explanatory words with the prefix *pre-*

preadmission	preanesthetic	preassign
preadolescence	prearrange	prebattle
preadolescent	prearrangement	prebiblical
preadult	preassembled	prebreakfast

ahead of — **pre·ce·dence** \\'presədəns, pri'sēd°ns\ *n*

prec·e·dent \\'presədənt\ *n* : something said or done earlier that serves as an example

pre·cept \\'prē,sept\ *n* : rule of action or conduct

pre·cinct \\'prē,siŋkt\ *n* **1** : district of a city **2** *pl* : vicinity

pre·cious \\'preshəs\ *adj* **1** : of great value **2** : greatly cherished **3** : affected

prec·i·pice \\'presəpəs\ *n* : steep cliff

pre·cip·i·tate \pri'sipə,tāt\ *vb* **-tat·ed; -tat·ing** **1** : cause to happen quickly or abruptly **2** : cause to separate out of a liquid **3** : fall as rain, snow, or hail ∼ *n* : solid matter precipitated from a liquid ∼ \-'sipətət, -ə,tāt\ *adj* : unduly hasty — **pre·cip·i·tate·ly** *adv* — **pre·cip·i·tate·ness** *n* — **pre·cip·i·tous** \pri'sipətəs\ *adj* — **pre·cip·i·tous·ly** *adv*

pre·cip·i·ta·tion \pri,sipə'tā-shən\ *n* **1** : rash haste **2** : rain, snow, or hail

pré·cis \prā'sē\ *n, pl* **pré·cis** \-'sēz\ : concise summary of essentials

pre·cise \pri'sīs\ *adj* **1** : definite **2** : highly accurate — **pre·cise·ly** *adv* — **pre·cise·ness** *n*

pre·ci·sion \pri'sizhən\ *n* : quality or state of being precise

pre·clude \pri'klüd\ *vb* **-clud·ed; -clud·ing** : make impossible

pre·co·cious \pri'kōshəs\ *adj* : exceptionally advanced — **pre·co·cious·ly** *adv* — **pre·coc·i·ty** \pri-'käsətē\ *n*

pre·cur·sor \pri'kərsər\ *n* : harbinger

pred·a·to·ry \\'predə,tōrē\ *adj* : preying upon others — **pred·a·tor** \\'predətər\ *n*

pre·de·ces·sor \\'predə,sesər, 'prēd-\ *n* : a previous holder of a position

pre·des·tine \prē'destən\ *vb* : settle beforehand — **pre·des·ti·na·tion** \-,destə'nāshən\ *n*

pre·dic·a·ment \pri'dikəmənt\ *n* : difficult situation

pred·i·cate \\'predikət\ *n* : part of a sentence that states something about the subject ∼ \\'predə,kāt\ *vb* **-cat·ed; -cat·ing** **1** : affirm **2** : establish — **pred·i·ca·tion** \,predə'kā-shən\ *n*

---

precalculus   preclearance   precompute
precancel   precollege   preconceive
precancellation   precolonial   preconception
preclear   precombustion   preconcert

pre·dict \pri'dikt\ *vb* : declare in advance — **pre·dict·abil·i·ty** \-ˌdikte'bilətē\ *n* — **pre·dict·able** \-'diktəbəl\ *adj* — **pre·dict·ably** \-blē\ *adv* — **pre·dic·tion** \-'dikshən\ *n*

pre·di·lec·tion \ˌpredᵊl'ek-shən, ˌprēd-\ *n* : established preference

pre·dis·pose \ˌprēdis'pōz\ *vb* : cause to be favorable or susceptible to something beforehand — **pre·dis·po·si·tion** \ˌprē,dispə'zishən\ *n*

pre·dom·i·nate \pri'dämə,nāt\ *vb* : be superior — **pre·dom·i·nance** \-nəns\ *n* — **pre·dom·i·nant** \-nənt\ *adj* — **pre·dom·i·nant·ly** *adv*

pre·em·i·nent \prē'emənənt\ *adj* : having highest rank — **pre·em·i·nence** \-nəns\ *n* — **pre·em·i·nent·ly** *adv*

pre·empt \prē'empt\ *vb* **1** : seize for oneself **2** : take the place of — **pre·emp·tion** \-'empshən\ *n* — **pre·emp·tive** \-'emptiv\ *adj*

preen \'prēn\ *vb* : dress or smooth up (as feathers)

pre·fab·ri·cat·ed \'prē'fabrə,kātəd\ *adj* : manufactured for rapid assembly elsewhere — **pre·fab·ri·ca·tion** \ˌprē-ˌfabri'kāshən\ *n*

pref·ace \'prefəs\ *n* : introductory comments ~ *vb* -aced; -ac·ing : introduce with a preface — **pref·a·to·ry** \'prefe-ˌtōrē\ *adj*

pre·fect \'prē,fekt\ *n* : chief officer or judge — **pre·fec·ture** \-ˌfekchər\ *n*

pre·fer \pri'fər\ *vb* -rr- **1** : like better **2** : bring (as a charge) against a person — **pref·er·a·ble** \'prefərəbəl\ *adj* — **pref·er·a·bly** *adv* — **pref·er·ence** \-ərəns\ *n* — **pref·er·en·tial** \ˌprefə'renchəl\ *adj*

pre·fer·ment \pri'fərmənt\ *n* : promotion

pre·fig·ure \prē'figyər\ *vb* : foreshadow

¹**pre·fix** \'prē,fiks, prē'fiks\ *vb* : place before

²**pre·fix** \'prē,fiks\ *n* : affix at the beginning of a word

preg·nant \'pregnənt\ *adj* **1** : containing unborn young **2** : meaningful — **preg·nan·cy** \-nənsē\ *n*

pre·hen·sile \prē'hensəl, -ˌsīl\ *adj* : adapted for grasping

pre·his·tor·ic \ˌprēhis'tȯrik\, **pre·his·tor·i·cal** \-ikəl\ *adj*

---

precondition	precool	predeparture
preconstructed	precut	predesignate
preconvention	predawn	predetermine
precook	predefine	predischarge

: relating to the period before written history

prej·u·dice \\'prejədəs\\ *n* **1** : damage esp. to one's rights **2** : unreasonable attitude for or against something ∼ *vb* **-diced; -dic·ing 1** : damage **2** : cause to have prejudice — **prej·u·di·cial** \\ˌprejə'dishəl\\ *adj*

prel·ate \\'prelət\\ *n* : clergy member of high rank — **prel·a·cy** \\-əsē\\ *n*

pre·lim·i·nary \\pri'limə ˌnerē\\ *n, pl* **-nar·ies** : something that precedes or introduces — **preliminary** *adj*

pre·lude \\'prel ˌüd, -ˌyüd; 'prā-ˌlüd\\ *n* : introductory performance, event, or musical piece

pre·ma·ture \\ˌprēmə'tüər, -'tyùr, -'chùr\\ *adj* : coming before the usual or proper time — **pre·ma·ture·ly** *adv*

pre·med·i·tate \\pri'medə ˌtāt\\ *vb* : plan beforehand — **pre·med·i·ta·tion** \\-ˌmedə'tā-shən\\ *n*

pre·mier \\pri'mir, -'myir; 'prēmēər\\ *adj* : first in rank or importance ∼ *n* : prime minister — **pre·mier·ship** *n*

pre·miere \\pri'myer, -'mir\\ *n* : 1st performance ∼ *vb*

-miered; -mier·ing : give a 1st performance of

prem·ise \\'preməs\\ *n* **1** : statement made or implied as a basis of argument **2** *pl* : piece of land with the structures on it

pre·mi·um \\'prēmēəm\\ *n* **1** : bonus **2** : sum over the stated value **3** : sum paid for insurance **4** : high value

pre·mo·ni·tion \\ˌprēmə'ni-shən, ˌpremə-\\ *n* : feeling that something is about to happen — **pre·mon·i·to·ry** \\pri'mänə ˌtōrē\\ *adj*

pre·oc·cu·pied \\prē'äkyə ˌpīd\\ *adj* : lost in thought

pre·oc·cu·py \\-ˌpī\\ *vb* : occupy the attention of — **pre·oc·cu·pa·tion** \\prē ˌäkyə'päshən\\ *n*

pre·pare \\pri'par\\ *vb* **-pared; -par·ing 1** : make or get ready often beforehand **2** : put together or compound — **prep·a·ra·tion** \\ˌprepə'rāshən\\ *n* — **pre·pa·ra·to·ry** \\pri'parə ˌtōrē\\ *adj* — **pre·pared·ness** \\-'parədnəs\\ *n*

pre·pon·der·ant \\pri'pändər-ənt\\ *adj* : having great weight, power, importance, or numbers — **pre·pon·der·ance** \\-rəns\\ *n* — **pre·pon·der·ant·ly** *adv*

predrill	**preestablish**	**prefight**
preelection	**preexist**	**preform**
preelectric	**preexistence**	**pregame**
preemployment	**preexistent**	**preheat**

prep·o·si·tion \ˌprepə'zishən\ *n* : word that combines with a noun or pronoun to form a phrase — **prep·o·si·tion·al** \-'zishənəl\ *adj*

pre·pos·sess·ing \ˌprēpə'zesiŋ\ *adj* : tending to create a favorable impression

pre·pos·ter·ous \pri'pästərəs\ *adj* : absurd

pre·req·ui·site \prē'rekwəzət\ *n* : something required beforehand — **prerequisite** *adj*

pre·rog·a·tive \pri'rägətiv\ *n* : special right or power

pre·sage \'presij, pri'sāj\ *vb* **-saged; -sag·ing 1** : give a warning of **2** : predict — **pres·age** \'presij\ *n*

pres·by·ter \'prezbətər\ *n* : priest or minister

pre·science \'prēshəns, 'presh-\ *n* : foreknowledge of events — **pre·scient** \-ənt\ *adj*

pre·scribe \pri'skrīb\ *vb* **-scribed; -scrib·ing 1** : lay down as a guide **2** : direct the use of as a remedy

pre·scrip·tion \pri'skripshən\ *n* : written direction for the preparation and use of a medicine or the medicine prescribed

pres·ence \'prez°ns\ *n* **1** : fact or condition of being present **2** : appearance or bearing

¹**pres·ent** \'prez°nt\ *n* : gift

²**pre·sent** \pri'zent\ *vb* **1** : introduce **2** : bring before the public **3** : make a gift to or of **4** : bring before a court for inquiry — **pre·sent·able** *adj* — **pre·sen·ta·tion** \ˌprē,zen'tā-shən, ˌprez°n-\ *n* — **pre·sent·ment** \pri'zentmənt\ *n*

³**pres·ent** \'prez°nt\ *adj* : now existing, in progress, or attending ~ *n* : present time

pre·sen·ti·ment \pri'zentə-mənt\ *n* : premonition

pres·ent·ly \'prez°ntlē\ *adv* **1** : soon **2** : now

present participle *n* : participle that typically expresses present action

pre·serve \pri'zərv\ *vb* **-served; -serv·ing 1** : keep safe from danger or spoilage **2** : maintain ~ *n* **1** : preserved fruit — often in pl. **2** : area for protection of natural resources — **pres·er·va·tion** \ˌprezər'vāshən\ *n* — **pre·ser·va·tive** \pri'zərvətiv\ *adj or n* — **pre·serv·er** \-'zərvər\ *n*

---

preinaugural	prekindergarten	premenopausal
preindustrial	prelaunch	premenstrual
preinterview	prelife	premix
prejudge	premarital	premodern

pre·side \pri'zīd\ *vb* **-sid·ed; -sid·ing 1** : act as chairman **2** : exercise control

pres·i·dent \'prezədənt\ *n* **1** : one chosen to preside **2** : chief official (as of a company or nation) — **pres·i·den·cy** \-ənsē\ *n* — **pres·i·den·tial** \ˌprezə'denchəl\ *adj*

press \'pres\ *n* **1** : crowded condition **2** : machine or device for exerting pressure and esp. for printing **3** : pressure **4** : printing or publishing establishment **5** : news media and esp. newspapers ~ *vb* **1** : lie against and exert pressure on **2** : smooth with an iron or squeeze with something heavy **3** : urge **4** : crowd **5** : force one's way — **press·er** *n*

press·ing *adj* : urgent

pres·sure \'preshər\ *n* **1** : burden of distress or urgent business **2** : direct application of force — **pressure** *vb* — **pres·sur·i·za·tion** \ˌpreshərə'zāshən\ *n* — **pres·sur·ize** \-ˌīz\ *vb*

pres·ti·dig·i·ta·tion \ˌprestəˌdijə'-tāshən\ *n* : sleight of hand

pres·tige \pres'tēzh, -'tēj\ *n* : estimation in the eyes of peo-ple — **pres·ti·gious** \-'tijəs\ *adj*

pres·to \'prestō\ *adv or adj* : quickly

pre·sume \pri'züm\ *vb* **-sumed; -sum·ing 1** : assume authority without right to do so **2** : take for granted — **pre·sum·able** \-'züməbəl\ *adj* — **pre·sum·ably** \-blē\ *adv*

pre·sump·tion \pri'zəmp-shən\ *n* **1** : presumptuous attitude or conduct **2** : belief supported by probability — **pre·sump·tive** \-tiv\ *adj*

pre·sump·tu·ous \pri'zəmp-chəwəs\ *adj* : too bold or forward — **pre·sump·tu·ous·ly** *adv*

pre·sup·pose \ˌprēsə'pōz\ *vb* : take for granted — **pre·sup·po·si·tion** \ˌprēˌsəpə'zishən\ *n*

pre·tend \pri'tend\ *vb* **1** : act as if something is real or true when it is not **2** : act in a way that is false **3** : lay claim — **pre·tend·er** *n*

pre·tense, pre·tence \'prēˌtens, pri'tens\ *n* **1** : insincere effort **2** : deception — **pre·ten·sion** \pri'tenchən\ *n*

pre·ten·tious \pri'tenchəs\ *adj* : overly showy or self-important

premodify	**prenotification**	**preoperational**
premoisten	**prenotify**	**preoperative**
premold	**prenuptial**	**preordain**
prenatal	**preopening**	**prepackage**

— **pre·ten·tious·ly** *adv* — **pre·ten·tious·ness** *n*

pre·ter·nat·u·ral \ˌprētər-ˈnachərəl\ *adj* **1** : exceeding what is natural **2** : inexplicable by ordinary means — **pre·ter·nat·u·ral·ly** *adv*

pre·text \ˈprē₁tekst\ *n* : falsely stated purpose

pret·ty \ˈpritē, ˈpu̇rt-\ *adj* **-ti·er; -est** : pleasing by delicacy or attractiveness ∼ *adv* : in some degree ∼ *vb* **-tied; -ty·ing** : make pretty — **pret·ti·ly** \ˈpritᵊlē\ *adv* — **pret·ti·ness** *n*

pret·zel \ˈpretsəl\ *n* : twisted thin bread that is glazed and salted

pre·vail \priˈvāl\ *vb* **1** : triumph **2** : urge successfully **3** : be frequent, widespread, or dominant

prev·a·lent \ˈprevələnt\ *adj* : widespread — **prev·a·lence** \-ləns\ *n*

pre·var·i·cate \priˈvarə₁kāt\ *vb* **-cat·ed; -cat·ing** : deviate from the truth — **pre·var·i·ca·tion** \-ˌvarə-ˈkāshən\ *n* — **pre·var·i·ca·tor** \-ˈvarə-ˌkā-tər\ *n*

pre·vent \priˈvent\ *vb* : keep from happening or acting — **pre·vent·able** *adj* — **pre·ven·tion** \-ˈvenchən\ *n* — **pre·ven·tive** \-ˈventiv\ *adj or n* — **pre·ven·ta·tive** \-ˈ ventə-tiv\ *adj or n*

pre·view \ˈprē₁vyü\ *vb* : view or show beforehand — **pre·view** *n*

pre·vi·ous \ˈprēvēəs\ *adj* : having gone, happened, or existed before — **pre·vi·ous·ly** *adv*

prepay	prerelease	presterilize
preplan	preretirement	prestrike
preprocess	prerevolutionary	presurgery
preproduction	prerinse	presweeten
preprofessional	presale	pretape
preprogram	preschool	pretelevision
prepubertal	preseason	pretournament
prepublication	preselect	pretreat
prepunch	preset	pretreatment
prepurchase	preshrink	pretrial
prerecorded	preshrunk	prewar
preregister	presoak	prewash
preregistration	presort	prewrap
prerehearsal	prestamp	

prey

prey \'prā\ *n, pl* **preys** **1** : animal taken for food by another **2** : victim ~ *vb* **1** : seize and devour animals as prey **2** : have a harmful effect on

price \'prīs\ *n* : cost ~ *vb* **priced; pric·ing** : set a price on

price·less \-ləs\ *adj* : too precious to have a price

pric·ey \'prīsē\ *adj* **pric·i·er; -est** : expensive

prick \'prik\ *n* **1** : tear or small wound made by a point **2** : something sharp or pointed ~ *vb* : pierce slightly with a sharp point — **prick·er** *n*

prick·le \'prikəl\ *n* **1** : small sharp spine or thorn **2** : slight stinging pain ~ *vb* **-led; -ling** : tingle — **prick·ly** \'priklē\ *adj*

pride \'prīd\ *n* : quality or state of being proud ~ *vb* **prid·ed; prid·ing** : indulge in pride — **pride·ful** *adj*

priest \'prēst\ *n* : person having authority to perform the sacred rites of a religion — **priest·hood** *n* — **priest·li·ness** \-lēnəs\ *n* — **priest·ly** *adj*

priest·ess \'prēstəs\ *n* : woman who is a priest

prig \'prig\ *n* : one who irritates by rigid or pointed observance of proprieties — **prig·gish** \-ish\ *adj* — **prig·gish·ly** *adv*

prim \'prim\ *adj* **-mm-** : stiffly formal and proper — **prim·ly** *adv* — **prim·ness** *n*

pri·mal \'prīməl\ *adj* **1** : original or primitive **2** : most important

pri·ma·ry \'prī,merē, 'prīm-ərē\ *adj* : first in order of time, rank, or importance ~ *n, pl* **-ries** : preliminary election — **pri·mar·i·ly** \prī-'merəlē\ *adv*

primary school *n* : elementary school

pri·mate *n* **1** \'prī,māt, -mət\ : highest-ranking bishop **2** \-,māt\ : mammal of the group that includes humans and monkeys

prime \'prīm\ *n* : earliest or best part or period ~ *adj* : standing first (as in significance or quality) ~ *vb* **primed; prim·ing** **1** : fill or load **2** : lay a preparatory coating on

prime minister *n* : chief executive of a parliamentary government

¹**prim·er** \'primər\ *n* : small introductory book

²**prim·er** \'prīmər\ *n* **1** : device for igniting an explosive **2** : material for priming a surface

pri·me·val \prī'mēvəl\ *adj* : relating to the earliest ages

prim·i·tive \\'primətiv\ *adj* **1** : relating to or characteristic of an early stage of development **2** : of or relating to a tribal people or culture ∼ *n* : one that is primitive — **prim·i·tive·ly** *adv* — **prim·i·tive·ness** *n*

pri·mor·di·al \prī'mȯrdēəl\ *adj* : primeval

primp \'primp\ *vb* : dress or groom in a finicky manner

prim·rose \'prim,rōz\ *n* : low herb with clusters of showy flowers

prince \'prins\ *n* **1** : ruler **2** : son of a king or queen — **prince·ly** *adj*

prin·cess \'prinsəs, -,ses\ *n* **1** : daughter of a king or queen **2** : wife of a prince

prin·ci·pal \'prinsəpəl\ *adj* : most important ∼ *n* **1** : leading person **2** : head of a school **3** : sum lent at interest — **prin·ci·pal·ly** *adv*

prin·ci·pal·i·ty \,prinsə'pal-ətē\ *n, pl* **-ties** : territory of a prince

prin·ci·ple \'prinsəpəl\ *n* **1** : general or fundamental law **2** : rule or code of conduct or devotion to such a code

print \'print\ *n* **1** : mark or impression made by pressure **2** : printed state or form **3** : printed matter **4** : copy made by printing **5** : cloth with a figure stamped on it ∼ *vb* **1** : produce impressions of (as from type) **2** : write in letters like those of printer's type — **print·able** *adj* — **print·er** *n*

print·ing \'printiŋ\ *n* : art or business of a printer

print·out \'print,aút\ *n* : printed output produced by a computer — **print out** *vb*

¹**pri·or** \'prīər\ *n* : head of a religious house — **pri·o·ry** \'prīərē\ *n*

²**prior** *adj* : coming before in time, order, or importance — **pri·or·i·ty** \prī'ȯrətē\ *n*

pri·or·ess \'prīərəs\ *n* : nun who is head of a religious house

prism \'prizəm\ *n* : transparent 3-sided object that separates light into colors — **pris·mat·ic** \priz'matik\ *adj*

pris·on \'prizᵊn\ *n* : place where criminals are confined

pris·on·er \'prizᵊnər\ *n* : person on trial or in prison

pris·sy \'prisē\ *adj* **-si·er; -est** : overly prim — **pris·si·ness** *n*

pris·tine \'pris,tēn, pris'-\ *adj* : pure

pri·va·cy \'prīvəsē\ *n, pl* **-cies** : quality or state of being apart from others

pri·vate \'prīvət\ *adj* **1** : belonging to a particular individual or group **2** : carried on independently **3** : withdrawn from company or observation ~ *n* : enlisted person of the lowest rank in the marine corps or of one of the two lowest ranks in the army — **pri·vate·ly** *adv*

pri·va·teer \ˌprīvə'tir\ *n* : private ship armed to attack enemy ships and commerce

private first class *n* : enlisted person ranking next below a corporal in the army and next below a lance corporal in the marine corps

pri·va·tion \prī'vāshən\ *n* : lack of what is needed for existence

priv·i·lege \'privəlij\ *n* : right granted as an advantage or favor — **priv·i·leged** *adj*

privy \'privē\ *adj* **1** : private or secret **2** : having access to private or secret information ~ *n, pl* **priv·ies** : outdoor toilet — **priv·i·ly** \'privəlē\ *adv*

¹**prize** \'prīz\ *n* **1** : something offered or striven for in competition or in contests of chance **2** : something very desirable — **prize** *adj* — **prize·win·ner** *n* — **prize·win·ning** *adj*

²**prize** *vb* **prized; priz·ing** : value highly

³**prize** *vb* **prized; priz·ing** : pry

prize·fight *n* : professional boxing match — **prize·fight·er** *n* — **prize·fight·ing** *n*

¹**pro** \'prō\ *n* : favorable argument or person ~ *adv* : in favor

²**pro** *n or adj* : professional

prob·a·ble \'präbəbəl\ *adj* : seeming true or real or to have a good chance of happening — **prob·a·bil·i·ty** \ˌpräbə'bilətē\ *n* — **prob·a·bly** \'präbəblē\ *adv*

pro·bate \'prō,bāt\ *n* : judicial determination of the validity of a will ~ *vb* **-bat·ed; -bat·ing** : establish by probate

pro·ba·tion \prō'bāshən\ *n* **1** : period of testing and trial **2** : freedom for a convict during good behavior under supervision — **pro·ba·tion·ary** \-shə,nerē\ *adj* — **pro·ba·tion·er** *n*

probe \'prōb\ *n* **1** : slender instrument for examining a cavity **2** : investigation ~ *vb* **probed; prob·ing 1** : examine with a probe **2** : investigate

pro·bi·ty \'prōbətē\ *n* : honest behavior

prob·lem \'präbləm\ *n* **1** : question to be solved **2** : source of perplexity or vexation — **problem** *adj* — **prob·lem·at·ic** \ˌpräblə'matik\ *adj* — **prob·lem·at·i·cal** \-ikəl\ *adj*

pro·bos·cis \prə'bäsəs\ *n, pl* **-cis·es** *also* **-ci·des** \-ə,dēz\ : long flexible snout

pro·ce·dure \prə'sējər\ *n* **1** : way of doing something **2** : series of steps in regular order — **pro·ce·dur·al** \-'sēj-ərəl\ *adj*

pro·ceed \prō'sēd\ *vb* **1** : come forth **2** : go on in an orderly way **3** : begin and carry on an action **4** : advance

pro·ceed·ing *n* **1** : procedure **2** *pl* : something said or done or its official record

pro·ceeds \'prō‚sēdz\ *n pl* : total money taken in

pro·cess \'präs‚es, 'prōs-\ *n, pl* **-cess·es** \-‚esəz, -əsəz, -ə‚sēz\ **1** : something going on **2** : natural phenomenon marked by gradual changes **3** : series of actions or operations directed toward a result **4** : summons **5** : projecting part ~ *vb* : subject to a process — **pro·ces·sor** \-ər\ *n*

pro·ces·sion \prə'seshən\ *n* : group moving along in an orderly way

pro·ces·sion·al \-'seshənəl\ *n* : music for a procession

pro·claim \prō'klām\ *vb* : announce publicly or with conviction — **proc·la·ma·tion** \‚präklə'māshən\ *n*

pro·cliv·i·ty \prō'klivətē\ *n, pl* **-ties** : inclination

pro·cras·ti·nate \prə'krastə‚nāt\ *vb* **-nat·ed; -nat·ing** : put something off until later —

pro·cras·ti·na·tion \-‚krastə'nāshən\ *n* — **pro·cras·ti·na·tor** \-'krastə‚nātər\ *n*

pro·cre·ate \'prōkrē‚āt\ *vb* **-at·ed; -at·ing** : produce offspring — **pro·cre·ation** \‚prōkrē'āshən\ *n* — **pro·cre·ative** \'prōkrē‚ātiv\ *adj* — **pro·cre·ator** \-‚ātər\ *n*

proc·tor \'präktər\ *n* : supervisor of students (as at an examination) — **proctor** *vb*

pro·cure \prə'kyùr\ *vb* **-cured; -cur·ing** : get possession of — **pro·cur·able** \-'kyùrəbəl\ *adj* — **pro·cure·ment** *n* — **pro·cur·er** *n*

prod \'präd\ *vb* **-dd-** : push with or as if with a pointed instrument — **prod** *n*

prod·i·gal \'prädigəl\ *adj* : recklessly extravagant or wasteful — **prodigal** *n* — **prod·i·gal·i·ty** \‚prädə'galətē\ *n*

pro·di·gious \prə'dijəs\ *adj* : extraordinary in size or degree — **pro·di·gious·ly** *adv*

prod·i·gy \'prädəjē\ *n, pl* **-gies** : extraordinary person or thing

pro·duce \prə'düs, -'dyüs\ *vb* **-duced; -duc·ing** **1** : present to view **2** : give birth to **3** : bring into existence ~ \'präd‚üs, 'prōd-, -‚yüs\ *n* **1** : product **2** : agricultural products — **pro·duc·er** \prə'düsər, -'dyü-\ *n*

prod·uct \\'präd₁əkt\\ *n* **1** : number resulting from multiplication **2** : something produced

pro·duc·tion \\prə'dəkshən\\ *n* : act, process, or result of producing — **pro·duc·tive** \\-'dəktiv\\ *adj* — **pro·duc·tive·ness** *n* — **pro·duc·tiv·i·ty** \\₁prō₁dək'tivətē, ₁prä-\\ *n*

prof \\'präf\\ *n* : professor

pro·fane \\prō'fān\\ *vb* **-faned; -fan·ing** : treat with irreverence ~ *adj* **1** : not concerned with religion **2** : serving to debase what is holy — **pro·fane·ly** *adv* — **pro·fane·ness** *n* — **pro·fan·i·ty** \\prō'fanətē\\ *n*

pro·fess \\prə'fes\\ *vb* **1** : declare openly **2** : confess one's faith in — **pro·fessed·ly** \\-ədlē\\ *adv*

pro·fes·sion \\prə'feshən\\ *n* **1** : open declaration of belief **2** : occupation requiring specialized knowledge and academic training

pro·fes·sion·al \\prə'feshənəl\\ *adj* **1** : of, relating to, or engaged in a profession **2** : playing sport for pay — **professional** *n* — **pro·fes·sion·al·ism** *n* — **pro·fes·sion·al·ize** *vb* — **pro·fes·sion·al·ly** *adv*

pro·fes·sor \\prə'fesər\\ *n* : university or college teacher — **pro·fes·so·ri·al** \\₁prōfə'sōrēəl, ₁präfə-\\ *adj* — **pro·fes·sor·ship** *n*

prof·fer \\'präfər\\ *vb* **-fered; -fer·ing** : offer — **proffer** *n*

pro·fi·cient \\prə'fishənt\\ *adj* : very good at something — **pro·fi·cien·cy** \\-ənsē\\ *n* — **proficient** *n* — **pro·fi·cient·ly** *adv*

pro·file \\'prō₁fīl\\ *n* : picture in outline — **profile** *vb*

prof·it \\'präfət\\ *n* **1** : valuable return **2** : excess of the selling price of goods over cost ~ *vb* : gain a profit — **prof·it·able** \\'präfətəbəl\\ *adj* — **prof·it·ably** *adv* — **prof·it·less** *adj*

prof·i·teer \\₁präfə'tir\\ *n* : one who makes an unreasonable profit — **profiteer** *vb*

prof·li·gate \\'präfligət, -lə₁gāt\\ *adj* **1** : shamelessly immoral **2** : wildly extravagant — **prof·li·ga·cy** \\-gəsē\\ *n* — **profligate** *n* — **prof·li·gate·ly** *adv*

pro·found \\prə'faund\\ *adj* **1** : marked by intellectual depth or insight **2** : deeply felt — **pro·found·ly** *adv* — **pro·fun·di·ty** \\-'fəndətē\\ *n*

pro·fuse \\prə'fyüs\\ *adj* : pouring forth liberally — **pro·fuse·ly** *adv* — **pro·fu·sion** \\-'fyüzhən\\ *n*

pro·gen·i·tor \\prō'jenətər\\ *n* : direct ancestor

prog·e·ny \'präjənē\ *n, pl* **-nies** : offspring

pro·ges·ter·one \prō'jestə-ˌrōn\ *n* : female hormone

prog·no·sis \präg'nōsəs\ *n, pl* **-no·ses** \-ˌsēz\ : prospect of recovery from disease

prog·nos·ti·cate \präg'nästə-ˌkāt\ *vb* **-cat·ed; -cat·ing** : predict from signs or symptoms — **prog·nos·ti·ca·tion** \-ˌnästə'kāshən\ *n* — **prog·nos·ti·ca·tor** \-'nästəˌkātər\ *n*

pro·gram \'prōˌgram, -grəm\ *n* **1** : outline of the order to be pursued or the subjects included (as in a performance) **2** : plan of procedure **3** : coded instructions for a computer ~ *vb* **-grammed** *or* **-gramed; -gram·ming** *or* **-gram·ing** **1** : enter in a program **2** : provide a computer with a program — **pro·gram·ma·bil·i·ty** \ˌprōˌgramə'bilətē\ *n* — **pro·gram·ma·ble** \'prōˌgraməbəl\ *adj* — **pro·gram·mer** \'prōˌgramər\ *n*

prog·ress \'prägrəs, -ˌres\ *n* : movement forward or to a better condition ~ \prō'gres\ *vb* **1** : move forward **2** : improve — **pro·gres·sive** \-'gresiv\ *adj* — **pro·gres·sive·ly** *adv*

pro·gres·sion \prə'greshən\ *n* **1** : act of progressing **2** : continuous connected series

pro·hib·it \prō'hibət\ *vb* : prevent by authority

pro·hi·bi·tion \ˌprōə'bishən\ *n* **1** : act of prohibiting **2** : legal restriction on sale or manufacture of alcoholic beverages — **pro·hi·bi·tion·ist** \-'bishənist\ *n* — **pro·hib·i·tive** \prō'hibətiv\ *adj* — **pro·hib·i·tive·ly** *adv* — **pro·hib·i·to·ry** \-'hibəˌtōrē\ *adj*

proj·ect \'präjˌekt, -ikt\ *n* : planned undertaking ~ \prə'jekt\ *vb* **1** : design or plan **2** : protrude **3** : throw forward — **pro·jec·tion** \-'jekshən\ *n*

pro·jec·tile \prə'jektᵊl\ *n* : missile hurled by external force

pro·jec·tor \-'jektər\ *n* : device for projecting pictures on a screen

pro·le·tar·i·an \ˌprōlə'terēən\ *n* : member of the proletariat — **proletarian** *adj*

pro·le·tar·i·at \-ēət\ *n* : laboring class

pro·lif·er·ate \prə'lifəˌrāt\ *vb* **-at·ed; -at·ing** : grow or increase in number rapidly — **pro·lif·er·a·tion** \-ˌlifə'rāshən\ *n*

pro·lif·ic \prə'lifik\ *adj* : producing abundantly — **pro·lif·i·cal·ly** *adv*

pro·logue \'prōˌlȯg, -ˌläg\ *n* : preface

pro·long \prə'lȯŋ\ *vb* : lengthen in time or extent — **pro·lon·ga·tion** \ˌprō͟ˌlȯŋ'gā-shən\ *n*

prom \'präm\ *n* : formal school dance

prom·e·nade \ˌprämə'nād, -'näd\ *n* **1** : leisurely walk **2** : place for strolling — **promenade** *vb*

prom·i·nence \'prämənəns\ *n* **1** : quality, state, or fact of being readily noticeable or distinguished **2** : something that stands out — **prom·i·nent** \-nənt\ *adj* — **prom·i·nent·ly** *adv*

pro·mis·cu·ous \prə'miskyə-wəs\ *adj* : having a number of sexual partners — **prom·is·cu·ity** \ˌprämis'kyüətē, ˌprō-ˌmis-\ *n* — **pro·mis·cu·ous·ly** *adv* — **pro·mis·cu·ous·ness** *n*

prom·ise \'präməs\ *n* **1** : statement that one will do or not do something **2** : basis for expectation — **promise** *vb* — **prom·is·so·ry** \-əˌsōrē\ *adj*

prom·is·ing \'präməsiŋ\ *adj* : likely to succeed — **prom·is·ing·ly** *adv*

prom·on·to·ry \'prämənˌtōrē\ *n, pl* **-ries** : point of land jutting into the sea

pro·mote \prə'mōt\ *vb* **-mot·ed; -mot·ing** **1** : advance in rank **2** : contribute to the growth, development, or pros-

perity of — **pro·mot·er** *n* — **pro·mo·tion** \-'mōshən\ *n* — **pro·mo·tion·al** \-'mōshənəl\ *adj*

¹prompt \'prämpt\ *vb* **1** : incite **2** : give a cue to (an actor or singer) — **prompt·er** *n*

²prompt *adj* : ready and quick — **prompt·ly** *adv* — **prompt·ness** *n*

prone \'prōn\ *adj* **1** : having a tendency **2** : lying face downward — **prone·ness** \'prōn-nəs\ *n*

prong \'prȯŋ\ *n* : sharp point of a fork — **pronged** \'prȯŋd\ *adj*

pro·noun \'prōˌnau̇n\ *n* : word used as a substitute for a noun

pro·nounce \prə'nau̇ns\ *vb* **-nounced; -nounc·ing** **1** : utter officially or as an opinion **2** : say or speak esp. correctly — **pro·nounce·able** *adj* — **pro·nounce·ment** *n* — **pro·nun·ci·a·tion** \-ˌnənsē'āshən\ *n*

pro·nounced \-'nau̇nst\ *adj* : decided

¹proof \'prüf\ *n* **1** : evidence of a truth or fact **2** : trial impression or print

²proof *adj* : designed for or successful in resisting or repelling

proof·read *vb* : read and mark corrections in — **proof·read·er** *n*

prop \'präp\ *vb* **-pp-** **1** : support **2** : sustain — **prop** *n*

pro·pa·gan·da \ˌpräpə'gandə, ˌprōpə-\ *n* : the spreading of ideas or information to further or damage a cause — **pro·pa·gan·dist** \-dist\ *n* — **pro·pa·gan·dize** \-ˌdīz\ *vb*

prop·a·gate \'präpəˌgāt\ *vb* **-gat·ed; -gat·ing** **1** : reproduce biologically **2** : cause to spread — **prop·a·ga·tion** \ˌpräpə'gāshən\ *n*

pro·pane \'prōˌpān\ *n* : heavy flammable gaseous fuel

pro·pel \prə'pel\ *vb* **-ll-** : drive forward — **pro·pel·lant, pro·pel·lent** *n or adj*

pro·pel·ler \prə'pelər\ *n* : hub with revolving blades that propels a craft

pro·pen·si·ty \prə'pensətē\ *n, pl* **-ties** : particular interest or inclination

prop·er \'präpər\ *adj* **1** : suitable or right **2** : limited to a specified thing **3** : correct **4** : strictly adhering to standards of social manners, dignity, or good taste — **prop·er·ly** *adv*

prop·er·ty \'präpərtē\ *n, pl* **-ties** **1** : quality peculiar to an individual **2** : something owned **3** : piece of real estate **4** : ownership

proph·e·cy \'präfəsē\ *n, pl* **-cies** : prediction

proph·e·sy \-ˌsī\ *vb* **-sied; -sy·ing** : predict — **proph·e·si·er** \-ˌsīər\ *n*

proph·et \'präfət\ *n* : one who utters revelations or predicts events — **proph·et·ess** \-əs\ *n* — **pro·phet·ic** \prə'fetik\ *adj* — **pro·phet·i·cal·ly** *adv*

pro·pin·qui·ty \prə'piŋkwətē\ *n* : nearness

pro·pi·ti·ate \prō'pishēˌāt\ *vb* **-at·ed; -at·ing** : gain or regain the favor of — **pro·pi·ti·a·tion** \-ˌpishē'āshən\ *n* — **pro·pi·tia·to·ry** \-'pishēəˌtōrē\ *adj*

pro·pi·tious \prə'pishəs\ *adj* : favorable

pro·po·nent \prə'pōnənt\ *n* : one who argues in favor of something

pro·por·tion \prə'pōrshən\ *n* **1** : relation of one part to another or to the whole with respect to magnitude, quantity, or degree **2** : symmetry **3** : share ∼ *vb* : adjust in size in relation to others — **pro·por·tion·al** \-shənəl\ *adj* — **pro·por·tion·al·ly** *adv* — **pro·por·tion·ate** \-shənət\ *adj* — **pro·por·tion·ate·ly** *adv*

pro·pose \prə'pōz\ *vb* **-posed; -pos·ing** **1** : plan or intend **2** : make an offer of marriage **3** : present for consideration — **pro·pos·al** \-'pōzəl\ *n*

prop·o·si·tion \ˌpräpə'zishən\ *n* : something proposed ~ *vb* : suggest sexual intercourse to

pro·pound \prə'paůnd\ *vb* : set forth for consideration

pro·pri·etor \prə'prīətər\ *n* : owner — **pro·pri·etary** \prə-'prīəˌterē\ *adj* — **pro·pri·etor·ship** *n* — **pro·pri·etress** \-'prīətrəs\ *n*

pro·pri·ety \prə'prīətē\ *n, pl* **-eties** : standard of accept-ability in social conduct

pro·pul·sion \prə'pəlshən\ *n* **1** : action of propelling **2** : driving power — **pro·pul·sive** \-siv\ *adj*

pro·sa·ic \prō'zāik\ *adj* : dull

pro·scribe \prō'skrīb\ *vb* **-scribed; -scrib·ing** : prohibit — **pro·scrip·tion** \-'skrip-shən\ *n*

prose \'prōz\ *n* : ordinary lan-guage

pros·e·cute \'präsiˌkyüt\ *vb* **-cut·ed; -cut·ing** **1** : follow to the end **2** : seek legal pun-ishment of — **pros·e·cu·tion** \ˌpräsi'kyüshən\ *n* — **pros·e·cu·tor** \'präsiˌkyütər\ *n*

pros·e·lyte \'präsəˌlīt\ *n* : new convert — **pros·e·ly·tize** \'präsələˌtīz\ *vb*

pros·pect \'präsˌpekt\ *n* **1** : extensive view **2** : some-thing awaited **3** : potential buyer ~ *vb* : look for mineral deposits — **pro·spec·tive**

\prə'spektiv, 'präsˌpek-\ *adj* — **pro·spec·tive·ly** *adv* — **pros·pec·tor** \-ˌpektər, -'pek-\ *n*

pro·spec·tus \prə'spektəs\ *n* : introductory description of an enterprise

pros·per \'präspər\ *vb* : thrive or succeed — **pros·per·ous** \-pərəs\ *adj*

pros·per·i·ty \präs'perətē\ *n* : economic well-being

pros·tate \'präsˌtāt\ *n* : glandu-lar body about the base of the male urethra — **prostate** *adj*

pros·the·sis \präs'thēsəs, 'prästhə-\ *n, pl* **-the·ses** \-ˌsēz\ : artificial replacement for a body part — **pros·thet·ic** \präs'thetik\ *adj*

pros·ti·tute \'prästəˌtüt, -ˌtyüt\ *vb* **-tut·ed; -tut·ing** **1** : offer sexual activity for money **2** : put to corrupt or unworthy purposes ~ *n* : one who engages in sexual activi-ties for money — **pros·ti·tu·tion** \ˌprästə'tüshən, -'tyü-\ *n*

pros·trate \'präsˌtrāt\ *adj* : stretched out with face on the ground ~ *vb* **-trat·ed; -trat·ing** **1** : fall or throw (oneself) into a prostrate position **2** : reduce to helplessness — **pros·tra·tion** \präs'trāshən\ *n*

pro·tag·o·nist \prō'tagənist\ *n* : main character in a drama or story

pro·tect \prə'tekt\ *vb* : shield from injury — **pro·tec·tor** \-tər\ *n*

pro·tec·tion \prə'tekshən\ *n* **1** : act of protecting **2** : one that protects — **pro·tec·tive** \-'tektiv\ *adj*

pro·tec·tor·ate \-tərət\ *n* : state dependent upon the authority of another state

pro·té·gé \'prōtə‚zhā\ *n* : one under the care and protection of an influential person

pro·tein \'prō‚tēn\ *n* : complex combination of amino acids present in living matter

pro·test \'prō‚test\ *n* **1** : organized public demonstration of disapproval **2** : strong objection ∼ \prə'test\ *vb* **1** : assert positively **2** : object strongly — **pro·tes·ta·tion** \‚prätəs'tāshən\ *n* — **pro·test·er, pro·tes·tor** \'prō‚testər\ *n*

Prot·es·tant \'prätəstənt\ *n* : Christian not of a Catholic or Orthodox church — **Prot·es·tant·ism** \'prätəstənt‚izəm\ *n*

pro·to·col \'prōtə‚kȯl\ *n* : diplomatic etiquette

pro·ton \'prō‚tän\ *n* : positively charged atomic particle

pro·to·plasm \'prōtə‚plazəm\ *n* : complex colloidal living substance of plant and animal cells — **pro·to·plas·mic** \‚prōtə'plazmik\ *adj*

pro·to·type \'prōtə‚tīp\ *n* : original model

pro·to·zo·an \‚prōtə'zōən\ *n* : single-celled lower invertebrate animal

pro·tract \prō'trakt\ *vb* : prolong

pro·trac·tor \-'traktər\ *n* : instrument for drawing and measuring angles

pro·trude \prō'trüd\ *vb* **-trud·ed; -trud·ing** : stick out or cause to stick out — **pro·tru·sion** \-'trüzhən\ *n*

pro·tu·ber·ance \prō'tübərəns, -'tyü-\ *n* : something that protrudes — **pro·tu·ber·ant** *adj*

proud \'praùd\ *adj* **1** : having or showing excessive self‑esteem **2** : highly pleased **3** : having proper self-respect **4** : glorious — **proud·ly** *adv*

prove \'prüv\ *vb* **proved; proved** *or* **prov·en** \'prüvən\; **prov·ing 1** : test by experiment or by a standard **2** : establish the truth of by argument or evidence **3** : turn out esp. after trial or test — **prov·able** \'prüvəbəl\ *adj*

prov·en·der \'prävəndər\ *n* : dry food for domestic animals

prov·erb \'präv‚ərb\ *n* : short meaningful popular saying —

pro·ver·bi·al \prə'vərbēəl\ *adj*

pro·vide \prə'vīd\ *vb* **-vid·ed; -vid·ing 1 :** take measures beforehand **2 :** make a stipulation **3 :** supply what is needed — **pro·vid·er** *n*

pro·vid·ed *conj* **:** if

prov·i·dence \'prävədəns\ *n* **1** *often cap* **:** divine guidance **2** *cap* **:** God **3 :** quality of being provident

prov·i·dent \-ədənt\ *adj* **1 :** making provision for the future **2 :** thrifty — **prov·i·dent·ly** *adv*

prov·i·den·tial \ˌprävə'denchəl\ *adj* **1 :** relating to Providence **2 :** opportune

pro·vid·ing *conj* **:** provided

prov·ince \'prävəns\ *n* **1 :** administrative district **2** *pl* **:** all of a country outside the metropolis **3 :** sphere

pro·vin·cial \prə'vinchəl\ *adj* **1 :** relating to a province **2 :** limited in outlook — **pro·vin·cial·ism** \-ˌizəm\ *n*

pro·vi·sion \prə'vizhən\ *n* **1 :** act of providing **2 :** stock of food — usu. in pl. **3 :** stipulation ~ *vb* **:** supply with provisions

pro·vi·sion·al \-'vizhənəl\ *adj* **:** provided for a temporary need — **pro·vi·sion·al·ly** *adv*

pro·vi·so \prə'vīzō\ *n, pl* **-sos** *or* **-soes :** stipulation

pro·voke \prə'vōk\ *vb* **-voked; -vok·ing 1 :** incite to anger **2 :** stir up on purpose — **prov·o·ca·tion** \ˌprävə'kāshən\ *n* — **pro·voc·a·tive** \prə'väkətiv\ *adj*

prow \'praù\ *n* **:** bow of a ship

prow·ess \'praùəs\ *n* **1 :** valor **2 :** extraordinary ability

prowl \'praùl\ *vb* **:** roam about stealthily — **prowl** *n* — **prowl·er** *n*

prox·i·mate \'präksəmət\ *adj* **:** very near

prox·im·i·ty \präk'simətē\ *n* **:** nearness

proxy \'präksē\ *n, pl* **prox·ies :** authority to act for another — **proxy** *adj*

prude \'prüd\ *n* **:** one who shows extreme modesty — **prud·ery** \'prüdərē\ *n* — **prud·ish** \'prüdish\ *adj*

pru·dent \'prüdᵊnt\ *adj* **1 :** shrewd **2 :** cautious **3 :** thrifty — **pru·dence** \-ᵊns\ *n* — **pru·den·tial** \prü'denchəl\ *adj* — **pru·dent·ly** *adv*

¹prune \'prün\ *n* **:** dried plum

²prune *vb* **pruned; prun·ing :** cut off unwanted parts

pru·ri·ent \'prùrēənt\ *adj* **:** lewd — **pru·ri·ence** \-ēəns\ *n*

¹pry \'prī\ *vb* **pried; pry·ing :** look closely or inquisitively

²pry *vb* **pried; pry·ing :** raise, move, or pull apart with a lever

psalm \'säm, 'sälm\ *n* : sacred song or poem — **psalm·ist** *n*

pseu·do·nym \'südᵊnˌim\ *n* : fictitious name — **pseu·don·y·mous** \sü'dänəməs\ *adj*

pso·ri·a·sis \sə'rīəsəs\ *n* : chronic skin disease

psy·che \'sīkē\ *n* : soul or mind

psy·chi·a·try \sə'kīətrē, sī-\ *n* : branch of medicine dealing with mental, emotional, and behavioral disorders — **psy·chi·at·ric** \ˌsīkē'atrik\ *adj* — **psy·chi·a·trist** \sə'kīətrist, sī-\ *n*

psy·chic \'sīkik\ *adj* **1** : relating to the psyche **2** : sensitive to supernatural forces ∼ *n* : person sensitive to supernatural forces — **psy·chi·cal·ly** *adv*

psy·cho·anal·y·sis \ˌsīkōə'naləsəs\ *n* : study of the normally hidden content of the mind esp. to resolve conflicts — **psy·cho·an·a·lyst** \-'anᵊlist\ *n* — **psy·cho·an·al·yt·ic** \-ˌanᵊl'itik\ *adj* — **psy·cho·an·a·lyze** \-'anᵊlˌīz\ *vb*

psy·chol·o·gy \sī'käləjē\ *n, pl* **-gies** **1** : science of mind and behavior **2** : mental and behavioral aspect (as of an individual) — **psy·cho·log·i·cal** \ˌsīkə'läjikəl\ *adj* — **psy·cho·log·i·cal·ly** *adv* — **psy·chol·o·gist** \sī'käləjist\ *n*

psy·cho·path \'sīkəˌpath\ *n* : mentally ill or unstable per-

son — **psy·cho·path·ic** \ˌsīkə'pathik\ *adj*

psy·cho·sis \sī'kōsəs\ *n, pl* **-cho·ses** \-ˌsēz\ : mental derangement (as paranoia) — **psy·chot·ic** \-'kätik\ *adj or n*

psy·cho·so·mat·ic \ˌsīkəsə'matik\ *adj* : relating to bodily symptoms caused by mental or emotional disturbance

psy·cho·ther·a·py \ˌsīkō'therəpē\ *n* : treatment of mental disorder by psychological means — **psy·cho·ther·a·pist** \-pist\ *n*

pto·maine \'tōˌmān\ *n* : bacterial decay product

pu·ber·ty \'pyübərtē\ *n* : time of sexual maturity

pu·bic \'pyübik\ *adj* : relating to the lower abdominal region

pub·lic \'pəblik\ *adj* **1** : relating to the people as a whole **2** : civic **3** : not private **4** : open to all **5** : well-known ∼ *n* : people as a whole — **pub·lic·ly** *adv*

pub·li·ca·tion \ˌpəblə'kāshən\ *n* **1** : process of publishing **2** : published work

pub·lic·i·ty \pə'blisətē\ *n* **1** : news information given out to gain public attention **2** : public attention

pub·li·cize \'pəbləˌsīz\ *vb* **-cized; -ciz·ing** : bring to public attention — **pub·li·cist** \-sist\ *n*

pub·lish \'pəblish\ *vb* **1** : announce publicly **2** : reproduce for sale esp. by printing — **pub·lish·er** *n*

puck·er \'pəkər\ *vb* : pull together into folds or wrinkles ~ *n* : wrinkle

pud·ding \'pùdiŋ\ *n* : creamy dessert

pud·dle \'pədᵊl\ *n* : very small pool of water

pudgy \'pəjē\ *adj* **pudg·i·er; -est** : short and plump

pu·er·ile \'pyùrəl\ *adj* : childish

puff \'pəf\ *vb* **1** : blow in short gusts **2** : pant **3** : enlarge ~ *n* **1** : short discharge (as of air) **2** : slight swelling **3** : something light and fluffy — **puffy** *adj*

pug \'pəg\ *n* : small stocky dog

pu·gi·lism \'pyüjə,lizəm\ *n* : boxing — **pu·gi·list** \-list\ *n* — **pu·gi·lis·tic** \,pyüjə'listik\ *adj*

pug·na·cious \,pəg'nāshəs\ *adj* : prone to fighting — **pug·nac·i·ty** \-'nasətē\ *n*

puke \'pyük\ *vb* **puked; puk·ing** : vomit — **puke** *n*

pul·chri·tude \'pəlkrə,tüd, -,tyüd\ *n* : beauty — **pul·chri·tu·di·nous** \,pəlkrə-'tüdᵊnəs, -'tyüd-\ *adj*

pull \'pùl\ *vb* **1** : exert force so as to draw (something) to-ward or out **2** : move **3** : stretch or tear ~ *n* **1** : act of pulling **2** : influence **3** : device for pulling something — **pull·er** *n*

pul·let \'pùlət\ *n* : young hen

pul·ley \'pùlē\ *n, pl* **-leys** : wheel with a grooved rim

Pull·man \'pùlmən\ *n* : railroad car with berths

pull·over \'pùl,ōvər\ *adj* : put on by being pulled over the head — **pullover** *n*

pul·mo·nary \'pùlmə,nerē, 'pəl-\ *adj* : relating to the lungs

pulp \'pəlp\ *n* **1** : soft part of a fruit or vegetable **2** : soft moist mass (as of mashed wood) — **pulpy** *adj*

pul·pit \'pùl,pit\ *n* : raised desk used in preaching

pul·sate \'pəl,sāt\ *vb* **-sat·ed; -sat·ing** : expand and contract rhythmically — **pul·sa·tion** \,pəl'sāshən\ *n*

pulse \'pəls\ *n* : arterial throbbing caused by heart contractions — **pulse** *vb*

pul·ver·ize \'pəlvə,rīz\ *vb* **-ized; -iz·ing** : beat or grind into a powder

pu·ma \'pümə, 'pyü-\ *n* : cougar

pum·ice \'pəməs\ *n* : light porous volcanic glass used in polishing

pum·mel \'pəməl\ *vb* **-meled; -mel·ing** : beat

¹pump \'pəmp\ *n* : device for moving or compressing fluids ~ *vb* **1** : raise (as water) with a pump **2** : fill by means of a pump — with *up* **3** : move like a pump — **pump·er** *n*

²pump *n* : woman's low shoe

pum·per·nick·el \'pəmpər-ˌnikəl\ *n* : dark rye bread

pump·kin \'pəŋkən, 'pəmp-kən\ *n* : large usu. orange fruit of a vine related to the gourd

pun \'pən\ *n* : humorous use of a word in a way that suggests two or more interpretations — **pun** *vb*

¹punch \'pənch\ *vb* **1** : strike with the fist **2** : perforate with a punch ~ *n* : quick blow with the fist — **punch·er** *n*

²punch *n* : tool for piercing or stamping

³punch *n* : mixed beverage often including fruit juice

punc·til·i·ous \pəŋk'tiləs\ *adj* : marked by precise accordance with conventions

punc·tu·al \'pəŋkchəwəl\ *adj* : prompt — **punc·tu·al·i·ty** \ˌpəŋkchə'walətē\ *n* — **punc·tu·al·ly** *adv*

punc·tu·ate \'peŋkchəˌwāt\ *vb* **-at·ed; -at·ing** : mark with punctuation

punc·tu·a·tion \ˌpəŋkchə'wā-shən\ *n* : standardized marks in written matter to clarify the meaning and separate parts

punc·ture \'pəŋkchər\ *n* : act or result of puncturing ~ *vb* **-tured; -tur·ing** : make a hole in

pun·dit \'pəndət\ *n* **1** : learned person **2** : expert or critic

pun·gent \'pənjənt\ *adj* : having a sharp or stinging odor or taste — **pun·gen·cy** \-jənsē\ *n* — **pun·gent·ly** *adv*

pun·ish \'pənish\ *vb* : impose a penalty on or for — **pun·ish·able** *adj* — **pun·ish·ment** *n*

pu·ni·tive \'pyünətiv\ *adj* : inflicting punishment

pun·kin *var of* PUMPKIN

¹punt \'pənt\ *n* : long narrow flat-bottomed boat ~ *vb* : propel (a boat) by pushing with a pole

²punt *vb* : kick a ball dropped from the hands ~ *n* : act of punting a ball

pu·ny \'pyünē\ *adj* **-ni·er; -est** : slight in power or size

pup \'pəp\ *n* : young dog

pu·pa \'pyüpə\ *n, pl* **-pae** \-ˌpē, -ˌpī\ *or* **-pas** : insect (as a moth) when it is in a cocoon — **pu·pal** \-pəl\ *adj*

¹pu·pil \'pyüpəl\ *n* : young person in school

²pupil *n* : dark central opening of the iris of the eye

pup·pet \'pəpət\ *n* : small doll moved by hand or by strings — **pup·pe·teer** \ˌpəpə'tir\ *n*

pup·py \'pəpē\ *n, pl* **-pies** : young dog

pur·chase \'pərchəs\ *vb* **-chased; -chas·ing** : obtain in exchange for money ～ *n* **1** : act of purchasing **2** : something purchased **3** : secure grasp — **pur·chas·er** *n*

pure \'pyu̇r\ *adj* **pur·er; pur·est** : free of foreign matter, contamination, or corruption — **pure·ly** *adv*

pu·ree \pyu̇'rā, -'rē\ *n* : thick liquid mass of food — **puree** *vb*

pur·ga·to·ry \'pərgə,tōrē\ *n, pl* **-ries** : intermediate state after death for purification by expiating sins — **pur·ga·tor·i·al** \,pərgə'tōrēəl\ *adj*

purge \'pərj\ *vb* **purged; purg·ing** **1** : purify esp. from sin **2** : have or cause emptying of the bowels **3** : get rid of ～ *n* **1** : act or result of purging **2** : something that purges — **pur·ga·tive** \'pərgə·tiv\ *adj or n*

pu·ri·fy \'pyu̇rə,fī\ *vb* **-fied; -fy·ing** : make or become pure — **pu·ri·fi·ca·tion** \,pyu̇rəfə'kāshən\ *n* — **pu·ri·fi·er** \-,fīər\ *n*

Pu·rim \'pu̇rim\ *n* : Jewish holiday celebrated in February or March in commemoration of the deliverance of the Jews from the massacre plotted by Haman

pu·ri·tan \'pyu̇rət°n\ *n* : one who practices or preaches a very strict moral code — **pu·ri·tan·i·cal** \,pyu̇rə'tanikəl\ *adj* — **pu·ri·tan·i·cal·ly** *adv*

pu·ri·ty \'pyu̇rətē\ *n* : quality or state of being pure

purl \'pərl\ *n* : stitch in knitting ～ *vb* : knit in purl stitch

pur·loin \pər'lȯin, 'pər,lȯin\ *vb* : steal

pur·ple \'pərpəl\ *n* : bluish red color — **pur·plish** \'pərpəlish\ *adj*

pur·port \pər'pōrt\ *vb* : convey outwardly as the meaning ～ \'pər,pōrt\ *n* : meaning — **pur·port·ed·ly** \-ədlē\ *adv*

pur·pose \'pərpəs\ *n* **1** : something (as a result) aimed at **2** : resolution ～ *vb* **-posed; -pos·ing** : intend — **pur·pose·ful** \-fəl\ *adj* — **pur·pose·ful·ly** *adv* — **pur·pose·less** *adj* — **pur·pose·ly** *adv*

purr \'pər\ *n* : low murmur typical of a contented cat — **purr** *vb*

¹**purse** \'pərs\ *n* **1** : bag or pouch for money and small objects **2** : financial resource **3** : prize money

²**purse** *vb* **pursed; purs·ing** : pucker

pur·su·ance \pər'süəns\ *n* : act of carrying out or into effect

pur·suant to \-'süənt-\ *prep* : according to

pur·sue \pər'sü\ *vb* **-sued; -su-ing 1 :** follow in order to overtake **2 :** seek to accomplish **3 :** proceed along **4 :** engage in — **pur·su·er** *n*

pur·suit \pər'süt\ *n* **1 :** act of pursuing **2 :** occupation

pur·vey \pər'vā\ *vb* **-veyed; -vey·ing :** supply (as provisions) usu. as a business — **pur·vey·or** \-ər\ *n*

pus \'pəs\ *n* **:** thick yellowish fluid (as in a boil)

push \'pùsh\ *vb* **1 :** press against to move forward **2 :** urge on or provoke ~ *n* **1 :** vigorous effort **2 :** act of pushing — **push·cart** *n* — **push·er** \'pùshər\ *n*

pushy \'pùshē\ *adj* **push·i·er; -est :** objectionably aggressive

pu·sil·lan·i·mous \pyüsə-'lanəməs\ *adj* **:** cowardly

pussy \'pùsē\ *n, pl* **puss·ies :** cat

pus·tule \'pəschül\ *n* **:** pus-filled pimple

put \'pùt\ *vb* **put; put·ting 1 :** bring to a specified position or condition **2 :** subject to pain, suffering, or death **3 :** impose or cause to exist **4 :** express **5 :** cause to be used or employed — **put off** *vb* **:** postpone or delay — **put out** *vb* **:** bother or inconvenience — **put up** *vb* **1 :** prepare for stor-age **2 :** lodge **3 :** contribute or pay — **put up with :** endure

pu·tre·fy \'pyütrə,fī\ *vb* **-fied; -fy·ing :** make or become putrid — **pu·tre·fac·tion** \,pyütrə'fakshən\ *n*

pu·trid \'pyütrəd\ *adj* **:** rotten — **pu·trid·i·ty** \pyü'tridətē\ *n*

put·ty \'pətē\ *n, pl* **-ties :** doughlike cement — **putty** *vb*

puz·zle \'pəzəl\ *vb* **-zled; -zling 1 :** confuse **2 :** attempt to solve — with *out* or *over* ~ *n* **:** something that confuses or tests ingenuity — **puz·zle·ment** *n* — **puz·zler** \-ələr\ *n*

pyg·my \'pigmē\ *n, pl* **-mies :** dwarf — **pygmy** *adj*

py·lon \'pī,län, -lən\ *n* **:** tower or tall post

pyr·a·mid \'pirə,mid\ *n* **:** structure with a square base and 4 triangular sides meeting at a point

pyre \'pīr\ *n* **:** material heaped for a funeral fire

py·ro·ma·nia \,pīrō'mānēə\ *n* **:** irresistible impulse to start fires — **py·ro·ma·ni·ac** \-nē-,ak\ *n*

py·ro·tech·nics \,pīrə'tekniks\ *n pl* **:** spectacular display (as of fireworks) — **py·ro·tech·nic** \-nik\ *adj*

Pyr·rhic \'pirik\ *adj* **:** achieved at excessive cost

py·thon \'pī,thän, -thən\ *n* **:** very large constricting snake

Q

q \'kyü\ *n, pl* **q's** *or* **qs** \'kyüz\ : 17th letter of the alphabet

¹quack \'kwak\ *vb* : make a cry like that of a duck — **quack** *n*

²quack *n* : one who pretends to have medical or healing skill — **quack** *adj* — **quack·ery** \-ərē\ *n*

quad·ran·gle \'kwäd,raŋgəl\ *n* : rectangular courtyard

quad·rant \'kwädrənt\ *n* : 1/4 of a circle

quad·ri·lat·er·al \,kwädrə-'latərəl\ *n* : 4-sided polygon

qua·drille \kwä'dril, kə-\ *n* : square dance for 4 couples

quad·ru·ped \'kwädrə,ped\ *n* : animal having 4 feet

qua·dru·ple \kwä'drüpəl, -'drəp-; 'kwädrəp-\ *vb* **-pled; -pling** \-pliŋ\ : multiply by 4 ~ *adj* : being 4 times as great or as many

qua·dru·plet \kwä'drəplət, -'drüp-; 'kwädrəp-\ *n* : one of 4 offspring born at one birth

quaff \'kwäf, 'kwaf\ *vb* : drink deeply or repeatedly — **quaff** *n*

quag·mire \'kwag,mīr, 'kwäg-\ *n* : soft land or bog

qua·hog \'kō,hȯg, 'kwȯ-, 'kwō-, -,häg\ *n* : thick-shelled clam

¹quail \'kwāl\ *n, pl* **quail** *or* **quails** : short-winged plump game bird

²quail *vb* : cower in fear

quaint \'kwānt\ *adj* : pleasingly old-fashioned or odd — **quaint·ly** *adv* — **quaint·ness** *n*

quake \'kwāk\ *vb* **quaked; quak·ing** : shake or tremble ~ *n* : earthquake

qual·i·fi·ca·tion \,kwäləfə-'kāshən\ *n* **1** : limitation or stipulation **2** : special skill or experience for a job

qual·i·fy \'kwälə,fī\ *vb* **-fied; -fy·ing 1** : modify or limit **2** : fit by skill or training for some purpose **3** : become eligible — **qual·i·fied** *adj* — **qual·i·fi·er** \-,fīər\ *n*

qual·i·ty \'kwälətē\ *n, pl* **-ties 1** : peculiar and essential character, nature, or feature **2** : excellence or distinction

qualm \'kwäm, 'kwälm, 'kwȯm\ *n* : sudden feeling of doubt or uneasiness

quan·da·ry \'kwändrē\ *n, pl* **-ries** : state of perplexity or doubt

quan·ti·ty \\'kwäntətē\ *n, pl* **-ties** **1** : something that can be measured or numbered **2** : considerable amount

quan·tum theory \\'kwäntəm-\ *n* : theory in physics that radiant energy (as light) is composed of separate packets of energy

quar·an·tine \\'kwȯrən‚tēn\ *n* **1** : restraint on the movements of persons or goods to prevent the spread of pests or disease **2** : place or period of quarantine — **quarantine** *vb*

quar·rel \\'kwȯrəl\ *n* : basis of conflict — **quarrel** *vb* — **quar·rel·some** \-səm\ *adj*

¹quar·ry \\'kwȯrē\ *n, pl* **-ries** : prey

²quarry *n, pl* **-ries** : excavation for obtaining stone — **quarry** *vb*

quart \\'kwȯrt\ *n* : unit of liquid measure equal to .95 liter or of dry measure equal to 1.10 liters

quar·ter \\'kwȯrtər\ *n* **1** : 1/4 part **2** : 1/4 of a dollar **3** : city district **4** *pl* : place to live esp. for a time **5** : mercy ~ *vb* : divide into 4 equal parts

quar·ter·ly \\'kwȯrtərlē\ *adv or adj* : at 3-month intervals ~ *n, pl* **-lies** : periodical published 4 times a year

quar·ter·mas·ter *n* **1** : ship's helmsman **2** : army supply officer

quar·tet \kwȯr'tet\ *n* **1** : music for 4 performers **2** : group of 4

quar·to \\'kwȯrtō\ *n, pl* **-tos** : book printed on pages cut 4 from a sheet

quartz \\'kwȯrts\ *n* : transparent crystalline mineral

quash \\'kwäsh, 'kwȯsh\ *vb* **1** : set aside by judicial action **2** : suppress summarily and completely

qua·si \\'kwā‚zī, -sī; 'kwäzē, 'kwäs-; 'kwāzē\ *adj* : similar or nearly identical

qua·train \\'kwä‚trān\ *n* : unit of 4 lines of verse

qua·ver \\'kwāvər\ *vb* : tremble or trill — **quaver** *n*

quay \\'kē, 'kā, 'kwā\ *n* : wharf

quea·sy \\'kwēzē\ *adj* **-si·er; -est** : nauseated — **quea·si·ly** \-zəlē\ *adv* — **quea·si·ness** \-zēnəs\ *n*

queen \\'kwēn\ *n* **1** : wife or widow of a king **2** : female monarch **3** : woman of rank, power, or attractiveness **4** : fertile female of a social insect — **queen·ly** *adj*

queer \\'kwir\ *adj* : differing from the usual or normal — **queer·ly** *adv* — **queer·ness** *n*

quell \\'kwel\ *vb* : put down by force

quench \\'kwench\ *vb* **1** : put out **2** : satisfy (a thirst) —

quench·able *adj* — **quench-er** *n*

quer·u·lous \'kwerələs, -yələs\ *adj* : fretful or whining — **quer·u·lous·ly** *adv* — **quer-u·lous·ness** *n*

que·ry \'kwirē, 'kwer-\ *n, pl* **-ries** : question — **query** *vb*

quest \'kwest\ *n or vb* : search

ques·tion \'kweschən\ *n* **1** : something asked **2** : subject for debate **3** : dispute ∼ *vb* **1** : ask questions **2** : doubt or dispute **3** : subject to analysis — **ques·tion·er** *n*

ques·tion·able \'kweschən-əbəl\ *adj* **1** : not certain **2** : of doubtful truth or morality — **ques·tion·ably** \-blē\ *adv*

question mark *n* : a punctuation mark ? used esp. at the end of a sentence to indicate a direct question

ques·tion·naire \,kweschə-'nar\ *n* : set of questions

queue \'kyü\ *n* **1** : braid of hair **2** : a waiting line ∼ *vb* **queued; queu·ing** *or* **queue-ing** : line up

quib·ble \'kwibəl\ *n* : minor objection — **quibble** *vb* — **quib·bler** *n*

quick \'kwik\ *adj* **1** : rapid **2** : alert or perceptive ∼ *n* : sensitive area of living flesh — **quick** *adv* — **quick·ly** *adv* — **quick·ness** *n*

quick·en \'kwikən\ *vb* **1** : come to life **2** : increase in speed

quick·sand *n* : deep mass of sand and water

quick·sil·ver *n* : mercury

qui·es·cent \kwī'es°nt\ *adj* : being at rest — **qui·es·cence** \-əns\ *n*

qui·et \'kwīət\ *adj* **1** : marked by little motion or activity **2** : gentle **3** : free from noise **4** : not showy **5** : secluded ∼ *vb* : pacify — **quiet** *adv or n* — **qui·et·ly** *adv* — **qui·et-ness** *n*

qui·etude \'kwīə,tüd, -,tyüd\ *n* : quietness or repose

quill \'kwil\ *n* **1** : a large stiff feather **2** : porcupine's spine

quilt \'kwilt\ *n* : padded bed-spread ∼ *vb* : stitch or sew in layers with padding in between

quince \'kwins\ *n* : hard yellow applelike fruit

qui·nine \'kwī,nīn\ *n* : bitter drug used against malaria

quin·tes·sence \kwin'tes°ns\ *n* **1** : purest essence of something **2** : most typical example — **quin·tes·sen·tial** \,kwintə-'senchəl\ *adj* — **quin·tes-sen·tial·ly** *adv*

quin·tet \kwin'tet\ *n* **1** : music for 5 performers **2** : group of 5

quin·tu·ple \kwin'tüpəl, -'tyüp-, -'təp-; 'kwintəp-\ *adj* **1** : having 5 units or members **2** : being 5 times as great or as many — **quintuple** *n or vb*

quin·tu·plet \-plət\ *n* : one of 5 offspring at one birth

quip \ˈkwip\ *vb* **-pp-** : make a clever remark — **quip** *n*

quire \ˈkwīr\ *n* : 24 or 25 sheets of paper of the same size and quality

quirk \ˈkwərk\ *n* : peculiarity of action or behavior — **quirky** *adj*

quit \ˈkwit\ *vb* **quit; quit·ting** **1** : stop **2** : leave — **quit·ter** *n*

quite \ˈkwīt\ *adv* **1** : completely **2** : to a considerable extent

quits \ˈkwits\ *adj* : even or equal with another (as by repaying a debt)

¹**quiv·er** \ˈkwivər\ *n* : case for arrows

²**quiver** *vb* : shake or tremble — **quiver** *n*

quix·ot·ic \kwikˈsätik\ *adj* : idealistic to an impractical degree — **quix·ot·i·cal·ly** \-tiklē\ *adv*

quiz \ˈkwiz\ *n, pl* **quiz·zes** : short test ∼ *vb* **-zz-** : question closely

quiz·zi·cal \ˈkwizikəl\ *adj* **1** : teasing **2** : curious

quoit \ˈkȯit, ˈkwȯit, ˈkwāt\ *n* : ring thrown at a peg in a game (**quoits**)

quon·dam \ˈkwändəm, -ˌdam\ *adj* : former

quo·rum \ˈkwȯrəm\ *n* : required number of members present

quo·ta \ˈkwōtə\ *n* : proportional part or share

quotation mark *n* : one of a pair of punctuation marks " " or ' ' used esp. to indicate the beginning and the end of a quotation

quote \ˈkwōt\ *vb* **quot·ed; quot·ing** **1** : repeat (another's words) exactly **2** : state (a price) — **quot·able** *adj* — **quo·ta·tion** \kwōˈtāshən\ *n* — **quote** *n*

quo·tient \ˈkwōshənt\ *n* : number obtained from division

R

r \ˈär\ *n, pl* **r's** *or* **rs** \ˈärz\ : 18th letter of the alphabet

rab·bet \ˈrabət\ *n* : groove in a board

rab·bi \ˈrabˌī\ *n* : Jewish religious leader — **rab·bin·ic** \rəˈbinik\, **rab·bin·i·cal** \-ikəl\ *adj*

rab·bin·ate \\'rabənət, -ˌnāt\\ *n* : office of a rabbi

rab·bit \\'rabət\\ *n, pl* **-bit** *or* **-bits** : long-eared burrowing mammal

rab·ble \\'rabəl\\ *n* : mob

ra·bid \\'rabəd\\ *adj* **1** : violent **2** : fanatical **3** : affected with rabies — **ra·bid·ly** *adv*

ra·bies \\'rābēz\\ *n, pl* **rabies** : acute deadly virus disease

rac·coon \\ra'kün\\ *n, pl* **-coon** *or* **-coons** : tree-dwelling mammal with a black mask and a bushy ringed tail

¹race \\'rās\\ *n* **1** : strong current of water **2** : contest of speed **3** : election campaign ∼ *vb* **raced; rac·ing** **1** : run in a race **2** : rush — **race·course** *n* — **rac·er** *n* — **race·track** *n*

²race *n* **1** : family, tribe, people, or nation of the same stock **2** : division of mankind based on hereditary traits — **ra·cial** \\'rāshəl\\ *adj* — **ra·cial·ly** *adv*

race·horse *n* : horse used for racing

rac·ism \\'rāsˌizəm\\ *n* : discrimination based on the belief that some races are by nature superior — **rac·ist** \\-ist\\ *n*

rack \\'rak\\ *n* **1** : framework for display or storage **2** : instrument that stretches the body for torture ∼ *vb* : torture with or as if with a rack

¹rack·et \\'rakət\\ *n* : bat with a tight netting across an open frame

²racket *n* **1** : confused noise **2** : fraudulent scheme — **rack·e·teer** \\ˌrakə'tir\\ *n* — **rack·e·teer·ing** *n*

ra·con·teur \\ˌrakˌän'tər\\ *n* : storyteller

racy \\'rāsē\\ *adj* **rac·i·er; -est** : risqué — **rac·i·ly** *adv* — **rac·i·ness** *n*

ra·dar \\'rāˌdär\\ *n* : radio device for determining distance and direction of distant objects

ra·di·al \\'rādēəl\\ *adj* : having parts arranged like rays coming from a common center — **ra·di·al·ly** *adv*

ra·di·ant \\'rādēənt\\ *adj* **1** : glowing **2** : beaming with happiness **3** : transmitted by radiation — **ra·di·ance** \\-əns\\ *n* — **ra·di·ant·ly** *adv*

ra·di·ate \\'rādēˌāt\\ *vb* **-at·ed; -at·ing** **1** : issue rays or in rays **2** : spread from a center — **ra·di·a·tion** \\ˌrādē'āshən\\ *n*

ra·di·a·tor \\'rādēˌātər\\ *n* : cooling or heating device

rad·i·cal \\'radikəl\\ *adj* **1** : fundamental **2** : extreme ∼ *n* : person favoring extreme changes — **rad·i·cal·ism** \\-ˌizəm\\ *n* — **rad·i·cal·ly** *adv*

radii *pl of* **RADIUS**

ra·dio \'rādē͟ˌō\ *n, pl* **-di·os** **1** : wireless transmission or reception of sound by means of electric waves **2** : radio receiving set ~ *vb* : send a message to by radio — **radio** *adj*

ra·dio·ac·tiv·i·ty \ˌrādēō͟ˌak-'tivətē\ *n* : property of an element that emits energy through nuclear disintegration — **ra·dio·ac·tive** \-'aktiv\ *adj*

ra·di·ol·o·gy \ˌrādē'äləjē\ *n* : medical use of radiation — **ra·di·ol·o·gist** \-jist\ *n*

rad·ish \'radish\ *n* : pungent fleshy root usu. eaten raw

ra·di·um \'rādēəm\ *n* : metallic radioactive chemical element

ra·di·us \'rādēəs\ *n, pl* **-dii** \-ē͟ˌī\ **1** : line from the center of a circle or sphere to the circumference or surface **2** : area defined by a radius

ra·don \'rā͟ˌdän\ *n* : gaseous radioactive chemical element

raff·ish \'rafish\ *adj* : flashily vulgar — **raff·ish·ly** *adv* — **raff·ish·ness** *n*

raf·fle \'rafəl\ *n* : lottery among people who have bought tickets ~ *vb* **-fled; -fling** : offer in a raffle

¹raft \'raft\ *n* : flat floating platform ~ *vb* : travel or transport by raft

²raft *n* : large amount or number

raf·ter \'raftər\ *n* : beam supporting a roof

¹rag \'rag\ *n* : waste piece of cloth

²rag *n* : composition in ragtime

rag·a·muf·fin \'ragə͟ˌməfən\ *n* : ragged dirty person

rage \'rāj\ *n* **1** : violent anger **2** : vogue ~ *vb* **raged; raging** **1** : be extremely angry or violent **2** : be out of control

rag·ged \'ragəd\ *adj* : torn — **rag·ged·ly** *adv* — **rag·ged·ness** *n*

ra·gout \ra'gü\ *n* : meat stew

rag·time *n* : syncopated music

rag·weed *n* : coarse weedy herb with allergenic pollen

raid \'rād\ *n* : sudden usu. surprise attack — **raid** *vb* — **raid·er** *n*

¹rail \'rāl\ *n* **1** : bar serving as a guard or barrier **2** : bar forming a track for wheeled vehicles **3** : railroad

²rail *vb* : scold someone vehemently — **rail·er** *n*

rail·ing \'rāliŋ\ *n* : rail or a barrier of rails

rail·lery \'rālərē\ *n, pl* **-ler·ies** : good-natured ridicule

rail·road \'rāl͟ˌrōd\ *n* : road for a train laid with iron rails and wooden ties ~ *vb* : force something hastily — **rail·road·er** *n* — **rail·road·ing** *n*

rail·way \-͟ˌwā\ *n* : railroad

rai·ment \'rāmənt\ *n* : clothing

rain \'rān\ **1** : water falling in drops from the clouds **2** : shower of objects ～ *vb* : fall as or like rain — **rain·coat** *n* — **rain·drop** *n* — **rain·fall** *n* — **rain·mak·er** *n* — **rain·mak·ing** *n* — **rain·storm** *n* — **rain·water** *n* — **rainy** *adj*

rain·bow \-ˌbō\ *n* : arc of colors formed by the sun shining through moisture

raise \'rāz\ *vb* **raised; rais·ing** **1** : lift **2** : arouse **3** : erect **4** : collect **5** : breed, grow, or bring up **6** : increase **7** : make light ～ *n* : increase esp. in pay — **rais·er** *n*

rai·sin \'rāzᵊn\ *n* : dried grape

ra·ja, ra·jah \'räjə\ *n* : Indian prince

¹**rake** \'rāk\ *n* : garden tool for smoothing or sweeping ～ *vb* **raked; rak·ing** **1** : gather, loosen, or smooth with or as if with a rake **2** : sweep with gunfire

²**rake** *n* : dissolute man

rak·ish \'rākish\ *adj* : smart or jaunty — **rak·ish·ly** *adv* — **rak·ish·ness** *n*

ral·ly \'ralē\ *vb* **-lied; -ly·ing** **1** : bring or come together **2** : revive or recover **3** : make a comeback ～ *n, pl* **-lies** **1** : act of rallying **2** : mass meeting

ram \'ram\ *n* **1** : male sheep **2** : beam used in battering down walls or doors ～ *vb* **-mm-** **1** : force or drive in or through **2** : strike against violently

RAM \'ram\ *n* : main internal storage area in a computer

ram·ble \'rambəl\ *vb* **-bled; -bling** : wander — **ramble** *n* — **ram·bler** \-blər\ *n*

ram·bunc·tious \ram'bəŋk-shəs\ *adj* : unruly

ram·i·fi·ca·tion \ˌraməfə'kā-shən\ *n* : consequence

ram·i·fy \'raməˌfī\ *vb* **-fied; -fy·ing** : branch out

ramp \'ramp\ *n* : sloping passage or connecting roadway

ram·page \'ramˌpāj, ram'pāj\ *vb* **-paged; -pag·ing** : rush about wildly ～ \'ramˌ-\ *n* : violent or riotous action or behavior

ram·pant \'rampənt\ *adj* : widespread — **ram·pant·ly** *adv*

ram·part \'ramˌpärt\ *n* : embankment of a fortification

ram·rod *n* : rod used to load or clean a gun ～ *adj* : strict or inflexible

ram·shack·le \'ramˌshakəl\ *adj* : shaky

ran *past of* RUN

ranch \'ranch\ *n* **1** : establishment for the raising of cattle, sheep, or horses **2** : specialized farm ～ *vb* : operate a ranch — **ranch·er** *n*

ran·cid \'ransəd\ *adj* : smelling or tasting as if spoiled — **ran·cid·i·ty** \ran'sidətē\ *n*

ran·cor \'raŋkər\ *n* : bitter deep-seated ill will — **ran·cor·ous** *adj*

ran·dom \'randəm\ *adj* : occurring by chance — **ran·dom·ly** *adv* — **ran·dom·ness** *n* — **at random** : without definite aim or method

ran·dom·ize \'randə,mīz\ *vb* **-ized; -izing** : select, assign, or arrange in a random way

rang *past of* RING

range \'rānj\ *n* **1** : series of things in a row **2** : open land for grazing **3** : cooking stove **4** : variation within limits **5** : place for target practice **6** : extent ~ *vb* **ranged; ranging 1** : arrange **2** : roam at large, freely, or over **3** : vary within limits

rang·er \'rānjər\ *n* : officer who manages and protects public lands

rangy \'rānjē\ *adj* **rang·i·er; -est** : being slender with long limbs — **rang·i·ness** *n*

¹rank \'raŋk\ *adj* **1** : vigorous in growth **2** : unpleasantly strong-smelling — **rank·ly** *adv* — **rank·ness** *n*

²rank *n* **1** : line of soldiers **2** : orderly arrangement **3** : grade of official standing **4** : position within a group ~ *vb* **1** : arrange in formation or according to class **2** : take or have a relative position

rank and file *n* : general membership

ran·kle \'raŋkəl\ *vb* **-kled; -kling** : cause anger, irritation, or bitterness

ran·sack \'ran,sak\ *vb* : search through and rob

ran·som \'ransəm\ *n* : something demanded for the freedom of a captive ~ *vb* : gain the freedom of by paying a price — **ran·som·er** *n*

rant \'rant\ *vb* : talk or scold violently — **rant·er** *n* — **rant·ing·ly** *adv*

¹rap \'rap\ *n* : sharp blow or rebuke ~ *vb* **-pp-** : strike or criticize sharply

²rap *vb* **-pp-** : talk freely

ra·pa·cious \rə'pāshəs\ *adj* **1** : excessively greedy **2** : ravenous — **ra·pa·cious·ly** *adv* — **ra·pa·cious·ness** *n* — **ra·pac·i·ty** \-'pasətē\ *n*

¹rape \'rāp\ *n* : herb grown as a forage crop and for its seeds (**rape·seed**)

²rape *vb* **raped; rap·ing** : force to have sexual intercourse — **rape** *n* — **rap·er** *n* — **rap·ist** \'rāpist\ *n*

rap·id \'rapəd\ *adj* : very fast — **ra·pid·i·ty** \rə'pidətē\ *n* — **rap·id·ly** *adv*

rap·ids \-ədz\ *n pl* : place in a stream where the current is swift

ra·pi·er \'rāpēər\ *n* : narrow 2-edged sword

rap·ine \'rapən, -ˌīn\ *n* : plunder

rap·port \ra'pōr\ *n* : harmonious relationship

rapt \'rapt\ *adj* : engrossed — **rapt·ly** *adv* — **rapt·ness** *n*

rap·ture \'rapchər\ *n* : spiritual or emotional ecstasy — **rap·tur·ous** \-chərəs\ *adj* — **rap·tur·ous·ly** *adv*

¹**rare** \'rar\ *adj* **rar·er; rar·est** : having a portion relatively uncooked

²**rare** *adj* **rar·er; rar·est 1** : not dense **2** : unusually fine **3** : seldom met with — **rare·ly** *adv* — **rare·ness** *n* — **rar·i·ty** \'rarətē\ *n*

rar·e·fy \'rarəˌfī\ *vb* **-fied; -fy·ing** : make or become rare, thin, or less dense — **rar·e·fac·tion** \ˌrarə'fakshən\ *n*

rar·ing \'rarən, -iŋ\ *adj* : full of enthusiasm

ras·cal \'raskəl\ *n* : mean, dishonest, or mischievous person — **ras·cal·i·ty** \ras'kalətē\ *n* — **ras·cal·ly** \'raskəlē\ *adj*

¹**rash** \'rash\ *adj* : too hasty in decision or action — **rash·ly** *adv* — **rash·ness** *n*

²**rash** *n* : a breaking out of the skin with red spots

rasp \'rasp\ *vb* **1** : rub with or as if with a rough file **2** : speak in a grating tone ∼ *n* : coarse file

rasp·ber·ry \'razˌberē\ *n* : edible red or black berry

rat \'rat\ *n* : destructive rodent larger than the mouse ∼ *vb* : betray or inform on

ratch·et \'rachət\ *n* : notched device for allowing motion in one direction

rate \'rāt\ *n* **1** : quantity, amount, or degree measured in relation to some other quantity **2** : rank ∼ *vb* **rat·ed; rat·ing 1** : estimate or determine the rank or quality of **2** : deserve

rath·er \'rathər, 'rəth-, 'räth-\ *adv* **1** : preferably **2** : on the other hand **3** : more properly **4** : somewhat

rat·i·fy \'ratəˌfī\ *vb* **-fied; -fy·ing** : approve and accept formally — **rat·i·fi·ca·tion** \ˌratəfə'kāshən\ *n*

rat·ing \'rātiŋ\ *n* : classification according to grade

ra·tio \'rāshēō\ *n, pl* **-tios** : relation in number, quantity, or degree between things

ra·tion \'rashən, 'rāshən\ *n* : share or allotment (as of food) ∼ *vb* : use or allot sparingly

ra·tio·nal \'rashənəl\ *adj* **1** : having reason or sanity **2** : relating to reason — **ra·tio·nal·ly** *adv*

ra·tio·nale \ˌrashə'nal\ *n* **1** : explanation of principles of belief or practice **2** : underlying reason

ra·tio·nal·ize \'rashənəˌlīz\ *vb* **-ized; -iz·ing** : justify (as one's behavior or weaknesses) esp. to oneself — **ra·tio·nal·i·za·tion** \ˌrashənələ'zāshən\ *n*

rat·tan \ra'tan, rə-\ *n* : palm with long stems used esp. for canes and wickerwork

rat·tle \'ratᵊl\ *vb* **-tled; -tling** **1** : make a series of clattering sounds **2** : say briskly **3** : confuse or upset ~ *n* **1** : series of clattering sounds **2** : something (as a toy) that rattles

rat·tler \'ratlər\ *n* : rattlesnake

rat·tle·snake *n* : American venomous snake with a rattle at the end of the tail

rat·ty \'ratē\ *adj* **rat·ti·er; -est** : shabby

rau·cous \'rȯkəs\ *adj* : harsh or boisterous — **rau·cous·ly** *adv* — **rau·cous·ness** *n*

rav·age \'ravij\ *n* : destructive effect ~ *vb* **-aged; -ag·ing** : lay waste — **rav·ag·er** *n*

rave \'rāv\ *vb* **raved; rav·ing** **1** : talk wildly in or as if in delirium **2** : talk with extreme enthusiasm ~ *n* **1** : act of raving **2** : enthusiastic praise

rav·el \'ravəl\ *vb* **-eled** *or* **-elled; -el·ing** *or* **-el·ling** **1** : unravel **2** : tangle ~ *n* **1** : something tangled **2** : loose thread

ra·ven \'rāvən\ *n* : large black bird ~ *adj* : black and shiny

rav·en·ous \'ravənəs\ *adj* : very hungry — **rav·en·ous·ly** *adv* — **rav·en·ous·ness** *n*

ra·vine \rə'vēn\ *n* : narrow steep-sided valley

rav·ish \'ravish\ *vb* **1** : seize and take away by violence **2** : overcome with joy or delight **3** : rape — **rav·ish·er** *n* — **rav·ish·ment** *n*

raw \'rȯ\ *adj* **raw·er** \'rȯər\; **raw·est** \'rȯəst\ **1** : not cooked **2** : not processed **3** : not trained **4** : having the surface rubbed off **5** : cold and damp **6** : vulgar — **raw·ness** *n*

raw·hide \'rȯˌhīd\ *n* : untanned skin of cattle

ray \'rā\ *n* **1** : thin beam of radiant energy (as light) **2** : tiny bit

ray·on \'rāˌän\ *n* : fabric made from cellulose fiber

raze \'rāz\ *vb* **razed; raz·ing** : destroy or tear down

ra·zor \'rāzər\ *n* : sharp cutting instrument used to shave off hair

re- \rē, ˌrē, ˈrē\ *prefix* **1** : again or anew **2** : back or backward

reach \ˈrēch\ *vb* **1** : stretch out **2** : touch or try to touch or grasp **3** : extend to or arrive at **4** : communicate with ~ *n* **1** : act of reaching **2** : distance one can reach **3** : ability to reach — **reach·able** *adj* — **reach·er** *n*

re·act \rēˈakt\ *vb* **1** : act in response to some influence or stimulus **2** : undergo chemical change — **re·ac·tive** \-ˈaktiv\ *adj*

re·ac·tion \rēˈakshən\ *n* **1** : action or emotion caused by and directly related or counter to another action **2** : chemical change

re·ac·tion·ary \-shəˌnerē\ *adj* : relating to or favoring return to an earlier political order or policy — **reactionary** *n*

re·ac·tor \rēˈaktər\ *n* **1** : one that reacts **2** : device for the controlled release of nuclear energy

read \ˈrēd\ *vb* **read** \ˈred\; **read·ing** \ˈrēdiŋ\ **1** : understand written language **2** : utter aloud printed words **3** : interpret **4** : study **5** : indi-cate ~ \ˈred\ *adj* : informed by reading — **read·a·bil·i·ty** \ˌrēdəˈbilətē\ *n* — **read·able** *adj* — **read·ably** *adv* — **read·er** *n* — **read·er·ship** *n*

read·ing \ˈrēdiŋ\ *n* **1** : something read or for reading **2** : particular version, interpretation, or performance **3** : data indicated by an instrument

ready \ˈredē\ *adj* **read·i·er; -est** **1** : prepared or available for use or action **2** : willing to do something ~ *vb* **read·ied; ready·ing** : make ready ~ *n* : state of being ready — **read·i·ly** *adv* — **read·i·ness** *n*

re·al \ˈrēl\ *adj* **1** : relating to fixed or immovable things (as land) **2** : genuine **3** : not imaginary ~ *adv* : very — **re·al·ness** *n* — **for real** **1** : in earnest **2** : genuine

real estate *n* : property in houses and land

re·al·ism \ˈrēəˌlizəm\ *n* **1** : disposition to deal with facts practically **2** : faithful portrayal of reality — **re·al·ist** \-list\ *adj or n* — **re·al·is·tic** \ˌrēəˈlistik\ *adj* — **re·al·is·ti·cal·ly** \-tiklē\ *adv*

List of self-explanatory words with the prefix *re-*

reaccelerate	**reaccredit**	**reactivate**
reaccept	**reacquaint**	**reactivation**
reacclimatize	**reacquire**	**readdress**

re·al·i·ty \rē'alətē\ *n, pl* **-ties** **1** : quality or state of being real **2** : something real

re·al·ize \'rēə‚līz\ *vb* **-ized; -iz-ing** **1** : make actual **2** : obtain **3** : be aware of — **re·al·iz·able** *adj* — **re·al·i·za·tion** \‚rēələ-'zāshən\ *n*

re·al·ly \'rēlē, 'ril-\ *adv* : in truth

realm \'relm\ *n* **1** : kingdom **2** : sphere

¹ream \'rēm\ *n* : quantity of paper that is 480, 500, or 516 sheets

²ream *vb* : enlarge, shape, or clean with a specially shaped tool (**reamer**)

reap \'rēp\ *vb* : cut or clear (as a crop) with a scythe or machine — **reap·er** *n*

¹rear \'rir\ *vb* **1** : raise upright **2** : breed or bring up **3** : rise on the hind legs

²rear *n* **1** : back **2** : position at the back of something ~ *adj* : being at the back — **rear-ward** \-wərd\ *adj or adv*

rear admiral *n* : commissioned officer in the navy or coast guard ranking next below a vice admiral

rea·son \'rēzᵊn\ *n* **1** : explanation or justification **2** : mo-tive for action or belief **3** : power or process of thinking ~ *vb* **1** : use the faculty of reason **2** : try to persuade another — **rea·son·er** *n* — **rea·son·ing** \'rēzᵊniŋ\ *n*

rea·son·able \'rēzᵊnəbəl\ *adj* **1** : being within the bounds of reason **2** : inexpensive — **rea·son·able·ness** *n* — **rea·son·ably** \-blē\ *adv*

re·as·sure \‚rēə'shu̇r\ *vb* : restore one's confidence — **re·as·sur·ance** \-'shu̇rəns\ *n* — **re·as·sur·ing·ly** *adv*

re·bate \'rē‚bāt\ *n* : return of part of a payment — **rebate** *vb*

reb·el \'rebəl\ *n* : one that resists authority ~ \ri'bel\ *vb* **-belled; -bel·ling** **1** : resist authority **2** : feel or exhibit anger — **rebel** \'rebəl\ *adj*

re·bel·lion \ri'belyən\ *n* : resistance to authority and esp. to one's government

re·bel·lious \-yəs\ *adj* **1** : engaged in rebellion **2** : inclined to resist authority — **re·bel·lious·ly** *adv* — **re·bel·lious·ness** *n*

re·birth \'rē'bərth\ *n* **1** : new or second birth **2** : revival

readjust readopt realignment
readjustment reaffirm reallocate
readmit realign reanalysis

re·bound \'rē'baůnd, ri-\ *vb* **1** : spring back on striking something **2** : recover from a reverse ~ \'rē͜-\ *n* **1** : action of rebounding **2** : reaction to a reverse

re·buff \ri'bəf\ *vb* : refuse or repulse rudely — **rebuff** *n*

re·buke \-'byük\ *vb* **-buked; -buk·ing** : reprimand sharply — **rebuke** *n*

re·bus \'rēbəs\ *n* : riddle representing syllables or words with pictures

re·but \ri'bət\ *vb* **-but·ted; -but·ting** : refute — **re·but·ter** *n*

re·but·tal \-ᵊl\ *n* : opposing argument

re·cal·ci·trant \ri'kalsətrənt\ *adj* **1** : stubbornly resisting authority **2** : resistant to handling or treatment — **re·cal·ci·trance** \-trəns\ *n*

re·call \ri'kȯl\ *vb* **1** : call back **2** : remember **3** : revoke ~ \ri'-, 'rē͜-\ *n* **1** : a summons to return **2** : remembrance **3** : act of revoking

re·cant \ri'kant\ *vb* : take back (something said) publicly

re·ca·pit·u·late \͜rēkə'pichə͜lāt\ *vb* : summarize — **re·ca·pit·u·la·tion** \-͜pichə'lāshən\ *n*

re·cede \ri'sēd\ *vb* **-ced·ed; -ced·ing** **1** : move back or away **2** : slant backward

re·ceipt \-'sēt\ *n* **1** : act of receiving **2** : something (as payment) received — usu. in pl. **3** : writing acknowledging something received

re·ceive \ri'sēv\ *vb* **-ceived; -ceiv·ing** **1** : take in or accept **2** : greet or entertain (visitors) **3** : pick up radio waves and convert into sounds or pictures — **re·ceiv·able** *adj*

re·ceiv·er \ri'sēvər\ *n* **1** : one that receives **2** : one having charge of property or money involved in a lawsuit **3** : apparatus for receiving radio waves — **re·ceiv·er·ship** *n*

re·cent \'rēsᵊnt\ *adj* **1** : having lately come into existence **2** : of the present time or time just past — **re·cent·ly** *adv* — **re·cent·ness** *n*

re·cep·ta·cle \ri'septikəl\ *n* : container

re·cep·tion \ri'sepshən\ *n* **1** : act of receiving **2** : social gathering at which guests are formally welcomed

reanalyze   reapply   reappraisal
reappear   reappoint   reappraise
reappearance   reapportion   reapprove

re·cep·tion·ist \-shənist\ *n*
: person employed to greet callers

re·cep·tive \ri'septiv\ *adj*
: open and responsive to ideas, impressions, or suggestions — **re·cep·tive·ly** *adv* — **re·cep·tive·ness** *n* — **re·cep·tiv·i·ty** \ˌrēˌsep'tivətē\ *n*

re·cess \'rēˌses, ri'ses\ *n* **1** : indentation in a line or surface **2** : suspension of a session for rest ∼ *vb* **1** : make a recess in or put into a recess **2** : interrupt a session for a recess

re·ces·sion \ri'seshən\ *n* **1** : departing procession **2** : period of reduced economic activity

rec·i·pe \'resəˌpē\ *n* : instructions for making something

re·cip·i·ent \ri'sipēənt\ *n* : one that receives

re·cip·ro·cal \ri'siprəkəl\ *adj* **1** : affecting each in the same way **2** : so related that one is equivalent to the other — **re·cip·ro·cal·ly** *adv* — **re·ci·proc·i·ty** \ˌresə'präsətē\ *n*

re·cip·ro·cate \-ˌkāt\ *vb* : make a return for something done or given — **re·cip·ro·ca·tion** \-ˌsiprə'kāshən\ *n*

re·cit·al \ri'sītᵊl\ *n* **1** : public reading or recitation **2** : music or dance concert or exhibition by pupils — **re·cit·al·ist** \-ᵊlist\ *n*

rec·i·ta·tion \ˌresə'tāshən\ *n* : a reciting or recital

re·cite \ri'sīt\ *vb* **-cit·ed; -cit·ing** **1** : repeat verbatim **2** : recount — **re·cit·er** *n*

reck·less \'rekləs\ *adj* : lacking caution — **reck·less·ly** *adv* — **reck·less·ness** *n*

reck·on \'rekən\ *vb* **1** : count or calculate **2** : consider

reck·on·ing *n* **1** : act or instance of reckoning **2** : settling of accounts

re·claim \ri'klām\ *vb* **1** : change to a desirable condition **2** : obtain from a waste product or by-product **3** : demand or obtain the return of — **re·claim·able** *adj* — **rec·la·ma·tion** \ˌreklə'māshən\ *n*

re·cline \ri'klīn\ *vb* **-clined; -clin·ing** : lean backward or lie down

rec·luse \'rekˌlüs, ri'klüs\ *n* : one who leads a secluded or solitary life

rec·og·ni·tion \ˌrekig'nishən\ *n* : act of recognizing or state of being recognized

---

reargue	**reassemble**	**reassessment**
rearrange	**reassert**	**reassign**
rearrest	**reassess**	**reassignment**

re·cog·ni·zance \ri'känəzəns, -'käg-\ *n* : promise recorded before a court

rec·og·nize \'rekig,nīz\ *vb* **1** : identify as previously known **2** : take notice of **3** : acknowledge esp. with appreciation — **rec·og·niz·able** \'rekəg,nīz-əbəl\ *adj* — **rec·og·niz·ably** \-blē\ *adv*

re·coil \ri'kȯil\ *vb* : draw or spring back ~ \'rē,-, ri'-\ *n* : action of recoiling

rec·ol·lect \,rekə'lekt\ *vb* : remember

rec·ol·lec·tion \,rekə'lekshən\ *n* **1** : act or power of recollecting **2** : something recollected

rec·om·mend \,rekə'mend\ *vb* **1** : present as deserving of acceptance or trial **2** : advise — **rec·om·mend·able** \-'mendəbəl\ *adj*

rec·om·men·da·tion \,rek-əmən'dāshən\ *n* **1** : act of recommending **2** : something recommended or that recommends

rec·om·pense \'rekəm,pens\ *n* : compensation — **recompense** *vb*

rec·on·cile \'rekən,sīl\ *vb* **-ciled; -cil·ing 1** : cause to be friendly again **2** : adjust or settle **3** : bring to acceptance — **rec·on·cil·able** *adj* — **rec·on·cile·ment** *n* — **rec·on·cil·er** *n* — **rec·on·cil·i·a·tion** \,rekən-,silē-'āshən\ *n*

re·con·dite \'rekən,dīt, ri-'kän-\ *adj* **1** : hard to understand **2** : little known

re·con·di·tion \,rēkən,dishən\ *vb* : restore to good condition

re·con·nais·sance \ri'känə-zəns, -səns\ *n* : exploratory survey of enemy territory

re·con·noi·ter, re·con·noi·tre \,rēkə'nȯitər, ,rekə-\ *vb* **-tered** *or* **-tred; -ter·ing** *or* **-tring** : make a reconnaissance of

re·cord \ri'kȯrd\ *vb* **1** : set down in writing **2** : register permanently **3** : indicate **4** : preserve (as sound or images) for later reproduction ~ \'rekərd\ *n* **1** : something recorded **2** : best performance

re·cord·er \ri'kȯrdər\ *n* **1** : person or device that records **2** : wind instrument with finger holes

¹**re·count** \ri'kaunt\ *vb* : relate in detail

---

reattach   rebalance   rebind
reattain   rebaptize   reborn
reawaken   rebid   rebroadcast

²**re·count** \ˌrē'-\ *vb* : count again — **recount** \'rē͵-, ͵rē'-\ *n*

re·coup \ri'küp\ *vb* : make up for (an expense or loss)

re·course \'rē͵kōrs, ri'-\ *n* : source of aid or a turning to such a source

re·cov·er \ri'kəvər\ *vb* **1** : regain position, poise, or health **2** : recoup — **re·cov·er·able** *adj* — **re·cov·ery** \-'kəvərē\ *n*

rec·re·a·tion \ˌrekrē'āshən\ *n* : a refreshing of strength or spirits as a change from work or study — **rec·re·a·tion·al** \-shənəl\ *adj*

re·crim·i·na·tion \ri͵krimə-'nāshən\ *n* : retaliatory accusation — **re·crim·i·nate** *vb*

re·cruit \ri'krüt\ *n* : newly enlisted member ∼ *vb* : enlist the membership or services of — **re·cruit·er** *n* — **re·cruit·ment** *n*

rect·an·gle \'rek͵taŋgəl\ *n* : 4-sided figure with 4 right angles — **rect·an·gu·lar** \rek-'taŋgyələr\ *adj*

rec·ti·fy \'rektə͵fī\ *vb* **-fied; -fy·ing** : make or set right — **rec·ti·fi·ca·tion** \ˌrektəfə'kā-shən\ *n*

rec·ti·tude \'rektə͵tüd, -͵tyüd\ *n* : moral integrity

rec·tor \'rektər\ *n* : pastor

rec·to·ry \'rektərē\ *n, pl* **-ries** : rector's residence

rec·tum \'rektəm\ *n, pl* **-tums** *or* **-ta** \-tə\ : last part of the intestine joining the colon and anus — **rec·tal** \-t°l\ *adj*

re·cum·bent \ri'kəmbənt\ *adj* : lying down

re·cu·per·ate \ri'küpə͵rāt, -'kyü-\ *vb* **-at·ed; -at·ing** : recover (as from illness) — **re·cu·per·a·tion** \-͵küpə'rāshən, -͵kyü-\ *n* — **re·cu·per·a·tive** \-'küpərātiv, -'kyü-\ *adj*

re·cur \ri'kər\ *vb* **-rr- 1** : return in thought or talk **2** : occur again — **re·cur·rence** \-'kərəns\ *n* — **re·cur·rent** \-ənt\ *adj*

re·cy·cle \rē'sīkəl\ *vb* : process (as glass or cans) in order to regain a material for human use — **re·cy·cla·ble** \-kələbəl\ *adj*

red \'red\ *n* **1** : color of blood or of the ruby **2** *cap* : communist — **red** *adj* — **red·dish** *adj* — **red·ness** *n*

red·den \'red°n\ *vb* : make or become red or reddish

---

rebuild	**recapture**	**recertify**
rebury	**recast**	**rechannel**
recalculate	**recertification**	**recharge**

re·deem \ri'dēm\ *vb* **1** : regain, free, or rescue by paying a price **2** : atone for **3** : free from sin **4** : convert into something of value — **re·deem·able** *adj* — **re·deem·er** *n*

re·demp·tion \-'dempshən\ *n* : act of redeeming — **re·demp·tive** \-tiv\ *adj* — **re·demp·to·ry** \-tərē\ *adj*

red·head \-ˌhed\ *n* : one having red hair — **red·head·ed** \-'hedəd\ *adj*

red·o·lent \'redᵊlənt\ *adj* **1** : having a fragrance **2** : suggestive — **red·o·lence** \-əns\ *n* — **red·o·lent·ly** *adv*

re·dou·ble \rē'dəbəl\ *vb* **1** : make twice as great in size or amount **2** : intensify

re·doubt \ri'daut\ *n* : small fortification

re·doubt·able \-əbəl\ *adj* : arousing dread

re·dound \ri'daund\ *vb* : have an effect

re·dress \ri'dres\ *vb* : set right ~ *n* **1** : relief or remedy **2** : compensation

red tape *n* : complex obstructive official routine

re·duce \ri'düs, -'dyüs\ *vb* **1** : lessen **2** : put in a lower rank **3** : lose weight — **re·duc·er** *n* — **re·duc·ible** \-'düsəbəl, -'dyü-\ *adj*

re·duc·tion \ri'dəkshən\ *n* **1** : act of reducing **2** : amount lost in reducing **3** : something made by reducing

re·dun·dant \ri'dəndənt\ *adj* : using more words than necessary — **re·dun·dan·cy** \-dənsē\ *n* — **re·dun·dant·ly** *adv*

red·wood *n* : tall coniferous timber tree

reed \'rēd\ *n* **1** : tall slender grass of wet areas **2** : elastic strip that vibrates to produce tones in certain wind instruments — **reedy** *adj*

reef \'rēf\ *n* : ridge of rocks or sand at or near the surface of the water

reek \'rēk\ *n* : strong or disagreeable fume or odor ~ *vb* : give off a reek

¹**reel** \'rēl\ *n* : revolvable device on which something flexible is wound or a quantity of something wound on it ~ *vb* **1** : wind on a reel **2** : pull in by reeling — **reel·able** *adj* — **reel·er** *n*

---

rechargeable	**recirculate**	**reclassify**
recheck	**recirculation**	**recolonize**
rechristen	**reclassification**	**recombine**

²**reel** *vb* **1** : whirl or waver as from a blow **2** : walk or move unsteadily ∼ *n* : reeling motion

³**reel** *n* : lively dance

re·fer \ri'fər\ *vb* **-rr- 1** : direct or send to some person or place **2** : submit for consideration or action **3** : have connection **4** : mention or allude to something — **re·fer·able** \'refərəbəl, ri'fərə-\ *adj* — **re·fer·ral** \ri'fərəl\ *n*

ref·er·ee \ˌrefə'rē\ *n* **1** : one to whom an issue is referred for settlement **2** : sports official ∼ *vb* **-eed; -ee·ing** : act as referee

ref·er·ence \'refərəns\ *n* **1** : act of referring **2** : a bearing on a matter **3** : consultation for information **4** : person who can speak for one's character or ability or a recommendation given by such a person

ref·er·en·dum \ˌrefə'rendəm\ *n, pl* **-da** \-də\ *or* **-dums** : a submitting of legislative measures for voters' approval or rejection

re·fill \ˌrē'fil\ *vb* : fill again — **re·fill** \'rē,-\ *n* — **re·fill·able** *adj*

re·fine \ri'fīn\ *vb* **-fined; -fin·ing 1** : free from impurities or waste matter **2** : improve or perfect **3** : free or become free of what is coarse or uncouth — **re·fine·ment** \-mənt\ *n* — **re·fin·er** *n*

re·fin·ery \ri'fīnərē\ *n, pl* **-er·ies** : place for refining (as oil or sugar)

re·flect \ri'flekt\ *vb* **1** : bend or cast back (as light or heat) **2** : bring as a result **3** : cast reproach or blame **4** : ponder — **re·flec·tion** \-'flekshən\ *n* — **re·flec·tive** \-tiv\ *adj* — **re·flec·tor** \ri'flektər\ *n*

re·flex \'rē,fleks\ *n* : automatic response to a stimulus ∼ *adj* **1** : bent back **2** : relating to a reflex — **re·flex·ly** *adv*

re·flex·ive \ri'fleksiv\ *adj* : of or relating to an action directed back upon the doer or the grammatical subject — **reflexive** *n* — **re·flex·ive·ly** *adv* — **re·flex·ive·ness** *n*

re·form \ri'fȯrm\ *vb* : make or become better esp. by correcting bad habits — **reform** *n* — **re·form·able** *adj* — **re·for·ma·tive** \-'fȯrmətiv\ *adj* — **re·form·er** *n*

recompute
reconceive
reconnect
reconquer
reconquest
reconsider
reconsideration
reconsolidate
reconstruct

re·for·ma·to·ry \ri'förmə-,törē\ *n, pl* **-ries** : penal institution for reforming young offenders

re·fract \ri'frakt\ *vb* : subject to refraction

re·frac·tion \-'frakshən\ *n* : the bending of a ray (as of light) when it passes from one medium into another — **re·frac·tive** \-tiv\ *adj*

re·frac·to·ry \ri'fraktərē\ *adj* : obstinate or unmanageable

re·frain \ri'frān\ *vb* : hold oneself back ～ *n* : verse recurring regularly in a song — **re·frain·ment** *n*

re·fresh \ri'fresh\ *vb* **1** : make or become fresh or fresher **2** : supply or take refreshment — **re·fresh·er** *n* — **re·fresh·ing·ly** *adv*

re·fresh·ment \-mənt\ *n* **1** : act of refreshing **2** *pl* : light meal

re·frig·er·ate \ri'frijə,rāt\ *vb* **-at·ed; -at·ing** : chill or freeze (food) for preservation — **re·frig·er·ant** \-ərənt\ *adj or n* — **re·frig·er·a·tion** \-,frijə-'rāshən\ *n* — **re·frig·er·a·tor** \-'frijə,rātər\ *n*

ref·uge \'ref,yüj\ *n* **1** : protection from danger **2** : place that provides protection

ref·u·gee \,refyù'jē\ *n* : person who flees for safety

re·fund \ri'fənd, 'rē,fənd\ *vb* : give or put back (money) ～ \'rē,-\ *n* **1** : act of refunding **2** : sum refunded — **re·fund·able** *adj*

re·fur·bish \ri'fərbish\ *vb* : renovate

¹re·fuse \ri'fyüz\ *vb* **-fused; -fus·ing** : decline to accept, do, or give — **re·fus·al** \-'fyüzəl\ *n*

²ref·use \'ref,yüs, -,yüz\ *n* : worthless matter

re·fute \ri'fyüt\ *vb* **-fut·ed; -fut·ing** : prove to be false — **ref·u·ta·tion** \,refyù'tāshən\ *n* — **re·fut·er** \ri'fyùtər\ *n*

re·gal \'rēgəl\ *adj* **1** : befitting a king **2** : stately — **re·gal·ly** *adv*

re·gale \ri'gāl\ *vb* **-galed; -gal·ing** **1** : entertain richly or agreeably **2** : delight

re·ga·lia \ri'gālyə\ *n pl* **1** : symbols of royalty **2** : insignia of an office or order **3** : finery

re·gard \ri'gärd\ *n* **1** : consideration **2** : feeling of ap-

recontaminate	recopy	redecorate
reconvene	re-create	rededicate
reconvict	recross	rededication

543

: friendly greetings **4** : relation ∼ *vb* **1** : pay attention to **2** : show respect for **3** : have an opinion of **4** : look at **5** : relate to — **re·gard·ful** *adj* — **re·gard·less** *adj*

re·gard·ing *prep* : concerning

regardless of \ri'gärdləs-\ *prep* : in spite of

re·gen·er·ate \ri'jenərət\ *adj* **1** : formed or created again **2** : spiritually reborn ∼ \-'jenə,rāt\ *vb* **1** : reform completely **2** : replace (a lost body part) by new tissue growth **3** : give new life to — **re·gen·er·a·tion** \-,jenə'rāshən\ *n* — **re·gen·er·a·tive** \-'jenə,rātiv\ *adj* — **re·gen·er·a·tor** \-,rātər\ *n*

re·gent \'rējənt\ *n* **1** : person who rules during the childhood, absence, or incapacity of the sovereign **2** : member of a governing board — **re·gen·cy** \-jənsē\ *n*

re·gime \rā'zhēm, ri-\ *n* : government in power

reg·i·men \'rejəmən\ *n* : systematic course of treatment or training

reg·i·ment \'rejəmənt\ *n* : military unit ∼ \-,ment\ *vb* **1**

: organize rigidly for control **2** : make orderly — **reg·i·men·tal** \,rejə'ment³l\ *adj* — **reg·i·men·ta·tion** \-mən'tāshən\ *n*

re·gion \'rējən\ *n* : indefinitely defined area — **re·gion·al** \'rejənəl\ *adj* — **re·gion·al·ly** *adv*

reg·is·ter \'rejəstər\ *n* **1** : record of items or details or a book for keeping such a record **2** : device to regulate ventilation **3** : counting or recording device **4** : range of a voice or instrument ∼ *vb* **1** : enter in a register **2** : record automatically **3** : get special care for mail by paying more postage

reg·is·trar \-,strär\ *n* : official keeper of records

reg·is·tra·tion \,rejə'strāshən\ *n* **1** : act of registering **2** : entry in a register

reg·is·try \'rejəstrē\ *n, pl* **-tries 1** : enrollment **2** : place of registration **3** : official record book

re·gress \ri'gres\ *vb* : go or cause to go back or to a lower level — **re·gres·sion** \-'greshən\ *n* — **re·gres·sive** *adj*

redefine	**redevelop**	**redissolve**
redeposit	**rediscover**	**redistribute**
redesign	**rediscovery**	**redraft**

re·gret \ri'gret\ *vb* **-tt-** **1** : mourn the loss or death of **2** : be very sorry for ～ *n* **1** : sorrow or the expression of sorrow **2** *pl* : message declining an invitation — **re·gret·ful** \-fəl\ *adj* — **re·gret·ful·ly** *adv* — **re·gret·ta·ble** \-əbəl\ *adj* — **re·gret·ta·bly** \-blē\ *adv* — **re·gret·ter** *n*

reg·u·lar \'regyələr\ *adj* **1** : conforming to what is usual, normal, or average **2** : steady, uniform, or unvarying — **regular** *n* — **reg·u·lar·i·ty** \ˌregyə'larətē\ *n* — **reg·u·lar·ize** \'regyələˌrīz\ *vb* — **reg·u·lar·ly** *adv*

reg·u·late \'regyəˌlāt\ *vb* **-lat·ed; -lat·ing** **1** : govern according to rule **2** : adjust to a standard — **reg·u·la·tive** \-ˌlātiv\ *adj* — **reg·u·la·tor** \-ˌlātər\ *n* — **reg·u·la·to·ry** \-ləˌtōrē\ *adj*

reg·u·la·tion \ˌregyə'lāshən\ *n* **1** : act of regulating **2** : rule dealing with details of procedure

re·gur·gi·tate \rē'gərjəˌtāt\ *vb* **-tat·ed; -tat·ing** : vomit — **re·gur·gi·ta·tion** \-ˌgərjə'tāshən\ *n*

re·ha·bil·i·tate \ˌrēhə'biləˌtāt\ *vb* **-tat·ed; -tat·ing** **1** : rein-state **2** : make good or usable again — **re·ha·bil·i·ta·tion** \-ˌbilə'tāshən\ *n*

re·hears·al \ri'hərsəl\ *n* : practice session or performance

re·hearse \-'hərs\ *vb* **-hearsed; -hearsing** **1** : repeat or recount **2** : engage in a rehearsal of — **re·hears·er** *n*

reign \'rān\ *n* : sovereign's authority or rule ～ *vb* : rule as a sovereign

re·im·burse \ˌrēəm'bərs\ *vb* **-bursed; -burs·ing** : repay — **re·im·burs·able** *adj* — **re·im·burse·ment** *n*

rein \'rān\ *n* **1** : strap fastened to a bit to control an animal **2** : restraining influence ～ *vb* : direct by reins

re·in·car·na·tion \ˌrēˌin·kär'nāshən\ *n* : rebirth of the soul — **re·in·car·nate** \ˌrēin'kärˌnāt\ *vb*

rein·deer \'rānˌdir\ *n* : caribou

re·in·force \ˌrēən'fōrs\ *vb* : strengthen or support — **re·in·force·ment** *n* — **re·in·forc·er** *n*

re·in·state \ˌrēən'stāt\ *vb* : restore to a former position — **re·in·state·ment** *n*

redraw	reemphasize	reenlist
reemerge	reenergize	reenlistment
reemergence	reengage	reenroll

re·it·er·ate \rē'itə‚rāt\ *vb* : say again — **re·it·er·a·tion** \-‚itə-'rāshən\ *n*

re·ject \ri'jekt\ *vb* **1** : refuse to grant or consider **2** : refuse to admit, believe, or receive **3** : throw out as useless or unsatisfactory ~ \'rē‚-\ *n* : rejected person or thing — **re·jec·tion** \-'jekshən\ *n*

re·joice \ri'jȯis\ *vb* **-joiced; -joic·ing** : feel joy — **re·joic·er** *n*

re·join *vb* **1** \‚rē'jȯin\ : join again **2** \ri'-\ : say in answer

re·join·der \ri'jȯindər\ *n* : answer

re·ju·ve·nate \ri'jüvə‚nāt\ *vb* **-nat·ed; -nat·ing** : make young again — **re·ju·ve·na·tion** \-‚jüvə'nāshən\ *n*

re·lapse \ri'laps, 'rē‚laps\ *n* : recurrence of illness after a period of improvement ~ \ri'-\ *vb* : suffer a relapse

re·late \ri'lāt\ *vb* **-lat·ed; -lat·ing** **1** : give a report of **2** : show a connection between **3** : have a relationship — **re·lat·able** *adj* — **re·lat·er, re·la·tor** *n*

re·la·tion \-'lāshən\ *n* **1** : account **2** : connection **3** : rela-tionship **4** : reference **5** *pl* : dealings

re·la·tion·ship \-‚ship\ *n* : state of being related or interrelated

rel·a·tive \'relətiv\ *n* : person connected with another by blood or marriage ~ *adj* : considered in comparison with something else — **rel·a·tive·ly** *adv* — **rel·a·tive·ness** *n*

re·lax \ri'laks\ *vb* **1** : make or become less tense or rigid **2** : make less severe **3** : seek rest or recreation — **re·lax·er** *n*

re·lax·a·tion \‚rē‚lak'sāshən\ *n* **1** : lessening of tension **2** : recreation

re·lay \'rē‚lā\ *n* : fresh supply (as of horses or people) arranged to relieve others ~ \'rē‚-, ri'-\ *vb* **-layed; -lay·ing** : pass along in stages

re·lease \ri'lēs\ *vb* **-leased; -leas·ing** **1** : free from confinement or oppression **2** : relinquish **3** : permit publication, performance, exhibition, or sale ~ *n* **1** : relief from trouble **2** : discharge from an obligation **3** : act of releasing or what is released

rel·e·gate \'relə‚gāt\ *vb* **-gat·ed; -gat·ing** **1** : remove to

reenter	reestablishment	reevaluation
reequip	reestimate	reexamination
reestablish	reevaluate	reexamine

some less prominent position **2** : assign to a particular class or sphere — **rel·e·ga·tion** \ˌreləˈgāshən\ n

re·lent \riˈlent\ vb : become less severe

re·lent·less \-ləs\ adj : mercilessly severe or persistent — **re·lent·less·ly** adv — **re·lent·less·ness** n

rel·e·vance \ˈreləvəns\ n : relation to the matter at hand — **rel·e·vant** \-vənt\ adj — **rel·e·vant·ly** adv

re·li·able \riˈlīəbəl\ adj : fit to be trusted — **re·li·abil·i·ty** \-ˌlīəˈbilətē\ n — **re·li·able·ness** n — **re·li·ably** \-ˈlīəblē\ adv

re·li·ance \riˈlīəns\ n : act or result of relying

re·li·ant \riˈlīənt\ adj : dependent

rel·ic \ˈrelik\ n **1** : object venerated because of its association with a saint or martyr **2** : remaining trace

re·lief \riˈlēf\ n **1** : lightening of something oppressive **2** : welfare

re·lieve \riˈlēv\ vb -lieved; -liev·ing **1** : free from a burden or distress **2** : release from

a post or duty **3** : break the monotony of — **re·liev·er** n

re·li·gion \riˈlijən\ n **1** : service and worship of God **2** : set or system of religious beliefs — **re·li·gion·ist** n

re·li·gious \-ˈlijəs\ adj **1** : relating or devoted to an ultimate reality or deity **2** : relating to religious beliefs or observances **3** : faithful, fervent, or zealous — **re·li·gious·ly** adv

re·lin·quish \-ˈliŋkwish, -ˈlin-\ vb **1** : renounce **2** : let go of — **re·lin·quish·ment** n

rel·ish \ˈrelish\ n **1** : keen enjoyment **2** : highly seasoned sauce (as of pickles) ~ vb : enjoy — **rel·ish·able** adj

re·live \ˌrēˈliv\ vb : live over again (as in the imagination)

re·lo·cate \ˌrēˈlō̱ˌkāt, ˌrēlōˈkāt\ vb : move to a new location — **re·lo·ca·tion** \ˌrēlōˈkāshən\ n

re·luc·tant \riˈləktənt\ adj : feeling or showing doubt or unwillingness — **re·luc·tance** \riˈləktəns\ n — **re·luc·tant·ly** adv

re·ly \riˈlī\ vb -lied; -ly·ing : place faith or confidence — often with on

refinance	refocus	refreeze
refire	refold	refuel
refloat	reformulate	regain

re·main \ri'mān\ *vb* **1** : be left after others have been removed **2** : be something yet to be done **3** : stay behind **4** : continue unchanged

re·main·der \-'māndər\ *n* : that which is left over

re·mains \-'mānz\ *n pl* **1** : remaining part or trace **2** : dead body

re·mark \ri'märk\ *vb* : express as an observation ⁓ *n* : passing comment

re·mark·able \-'märkəbəl\ *adj* : extraordinary — **re·mark·able·ness** *n* — **re·mark·ably** \-blē\ *adv*

re·me·di·al \ri'mēdēəl\ *adj* : intended to remedy or improve

rem·e·dy \'remədē\ *n, pl* **-dies** **1** : medicine that cures **2** : something that corrects an evil or compensates for a loss ⁓ *vb* **-died; -dy·ing** : provide or serve as a remedy for

re·mem·ber \ri'membər\ *vb* **1** : think of again **2** : keep from forgetting **3** : convey greetings from

re·mem·brance \-brəns\ *n* **1** : act of remembering **2** : something that serves to bring to mind

re·mind \ri'mīnd\ *vb* : cause to remember — **re·mind·er** *n*

rem·i·nisce \remə'nis\ *vb* **-nisced; -nisc·ing** : indulge in reminiscence

rem·i·nis·cence \-'nisᵊns\ *n* **1** : recalling of a past experience **2** : account of a memorable experience

rem·i·nis·cent \-ᵊnt\ *adj* **1** : relating to reminiscence **2** : serving to remind — **rem·i·nis·cent·ly** *adv*

re·miss \ri'mis\ *adj* : negligent or careless in performance of duty — **re·miss·ly** *adv* — **re·miss·ness** *n*

re·mis·sion \ri'mishən\ *n* **1** : act of forgiving **2** : period of relief from or easing of symptoms of a disease

re·mit \ri'mit\ *vb* **-tt-** **1** : pardon **2** : send money in payment

re·mit·tance \ri'mitᵊns\ *n* : sum of money remitted

rem·nant \'remnənt\ *n* : small part or trace remaining

re·mod·el \rē'mädᵊl\ *vb* : alter the structure of

re·mon·strance \ri'mänstrəns\ *n* : act or instance of remonstrating

regrow	reheat	rehospitalize
regrowth	rehire	reidentify
rehear	rehospitalization	reignite

re·mon·strate \ri'män₁strāt\ *vb* **-strat·ed; -strat·ing** : speak in protest, reproof, or opposition — **re·mon·stra·tion** \ri₁män'strāshən, ₁remən-\ *n*

re·morse \ri'mȯrs\ *n* : distress arising from a sense of guilt — **re·morse·ful** *adj* — **re·morse·less** *adj*

re·mote \ri'mōt\ *adj* **-mot·er; -est** **1** : far off in place or time **2** : hard to reach or find **3** : acting, acted on, or controlled indirectly or from afar **4** : slight **5** : distant in manner — **re·mote·ly** *adv* — **re·mote·ness** *n*

re·move \ri'müv\ *vb* **-moved; -mov·ing** **1** : move by lifting or taking off or away **2** : get rid of — **re·mov·able** *adj* — **re·mov·al** \-vəl\ *n* — **re·mov·er** *n*

re·mu·ner·ate \ri'myünə₁rāt\ *vb* **-at·ed; -at·ing** : pay — **re·mu·ner·a·tion** *n* — **re·mu·ner·a·tor** \-₁rātər\ *n*

re·mu·ner·a·tive \ri'myünər-ətiv, -₁rāt-\ *adj* : gainful

re·nais·sance \₁renə'säns, -'zäns\ *n* : rebirth or revival

re·nal \'rēnᵊl\ *adj* : relating to the kidneys

rend \'rend\ *vb* **rent** \'rent\; **rend·ing** : tear apart forcibly

ren·der \'rendər\ *vb* **1** : extract by heating **2** : hand over or give up **3** : do (a service) for another **4** : cause to be or become

ren·dez·vous \'rändi₁vü, -dā-\ *n, pl* **ren·dez·vous** \-₁vüz\ **1** : place appointed for a meeting **2** : meeting at an appointed place ~ *vb* **-voused; -vous·ing** : meet at a rendezvous

ren·di·tion \ren'dishən\ *n* : version

ren·e·gade \'reni₁gād\ *n* : deserter of one faith or cause for another

re·nege \ri'nig, -'neg, -'nēg, -'nāg\ *vb* **-neged; -neg·ing** : go back on a promise — **re·neg·er** *n*

re·new \ri'nü, -'nyü\ *vb* **1** : make or become new, fresh, or strong again **2** : begin again **3** : grant or obtain an extension of — **re·new·able** *adj* — **re·new·al** *n* — **re·new·er** *n*

re·nounce \ri'naùns\ *vb* **-nounced; -nounc·ing** : give up, refuse, or resign — **re·nounce·ment** *n*

reimplant
reimpose
reincorporate

reindict
reinfection
reinflate

reinject
reinjection
reinoculate

ren·o·vate \\'renə‚vāt\ *vb* **-vat-ed; -vat·ing** : make like new again — **ren·o·va·tion** \‚renə-'vāshən\ *n* — **ren·o·va·tor** \\'renə‚vātər\ *n*

re·nown \ri'naùn\ *n* : state of being widely known and honored — **renowned** \-'naùnd\ *adj*

¹rent \\'rent\ *n* : money paid or due periodically for the use of another's property ∼ *vb* : hold or give possession and use of for rent — **rent·al** *n or adj* — **rent·er** *n*

²rent *n* : a tear in cloth

re·nun·ci·a·tion \ri‚nənsē'ā-shən\ *n* : act of renouncing

¹re·pair \ri'par\ *vb* : go

²repair *vb* : restore to good condition ∼ *n* **1** : act or instance of repairing **2** : condition — **re·pair·er** *n* — **re·pair·man** \-‚man\ *n*

rep·a·ra·tion \‚repə'rāshən\ *n* : money paid for redress — usu. pl.

rep·ar·tee \‚repər'tē\ *n* : clever replies

re·past \ri'past, 'rē‚past\ *n* : meal

re·pa·tri·ate \rē'pātrē‚āt\ *vb* **-at·ed; -at·ing** : send back to one's own country — **re·pa·tri·ate** \-trēət, -trē‚āt\ *n* — **re·pa·tri·a·tion** \-‚pātrē'ā-shən\ *n*

re·pay \rē'pā\ *vb* **-paid; -pay·ing** : pay back — **re·pay·able** *adj* — **re·pay·ment** *n*

re·peal \ri'pēl\ *vb* : annul by legislative action — **repeal** *n* — **re·peal·er** *n*

re·peat \ri'pēt\ *vb* : say or do again ∼ *n* **1** : act of repeating **2** : something repeated — **re·peat·able** *adj* — **re·peat·ed·ly** *adv* — **re·peat·er** *n*

re·pel \ri'pel\ *vb* **-pelled; -pel·ling** **1** : drive away **2** : disgust — **re·pel·lent** \-'pelənt\ *adj or n*

re·pent \ri'pent\ *vb* **1** : turn from sin **2** : regret — **re·pen·tance** \ri'pentᵊns\ *n* — **re·pen·tant** \-ᵊnt\ *adj*

re·per·cus·sion \‚rēpər'kə-shən, ‚rep-\ *n* : effect of something done or said

rep·er·toire \\'repər‚twär\ *n* : pieces a company or performer can present

rep·er·to·ry \\'repər‚tōrē\ *n, pl* **-ries** **1** : repertoire **2** : theater with a resident company doing several plays

---

reinsert	**reinstall**	**reintegration**
reinsertion	**reinstitute**	**reinter**
reinspect	**reintegrate**	**reintroduce**

rep·e·ti·tion \ˌrepə'tishən\ *n* : act or instance of repeating

rep·e·ti·tious \-'tishəs\ *adj* : tediously repeating — **rep·e·ti·tious·ly** *adv* — **rep·e·ti·tious·ness** *n*

re·pet·i·tive \ri'petətiv\ *adj* : repetitious — **re·pet·i·tive·ly** *adv* — **re·pet·i·tive·ness** *n*

re·pine \ri'pīn\ *vb* **re·pined; re·pin·ing** : feel or express discontent

re·place \ri'plās\ *vb* **1** : restore to a former position **2** : take the place of **3** : put something new in the place of — **re·place·able** *adj* — **re·place·ment** *n* — **re·plac·er** *n*

re·plen·ish \ri'plenish\ *vb* : stock or supply anew — **re·plen·ish·ment** *n*

re·plete \ri'plēt\ *adj* : full — **re·plete·ness** *n* — **re·ple·tion** \-'plēshən\ *n*

rep·li·ca \'replikə\ *n* : exact copy

rep·li·cate \'replə,kāt\ *vb* **-cat·ed; -cat·ing** : duplicate or repeat — **rep·li·cate** \-likət\ *n* — **rep·li·ca·tion** \-lə'kā-shən\ *n*

re·ply \ri'plī\ *vb* **-plied; -ply·ing** : say or do in answer ~ *n, pl* **-plies** : answer

re·port \ri'pōrt\ *n* **1** : rumor **2** : statement of information (as events or causes) **3** : explosive noise ~ *vb* **1** : give an account of **2** : present an account of (an event) as news **3** : present oneself **4** : make known to authorities — **re·port·age** \ri'pōrtij, ˌrepər-'täzh, ˌrep,ȯr'-\ *n* — **re·port·ed·ly** *adv* — **re·port·er** *n* — **re·por·to·ri·al** \ˌrepər-'tōrēəl\ *adj*

re·pose \ri'pōz\ *vb* **-posed; -pos·ing** : lay or lie at rest ~ *n* **1** : state of resting **2** : calm or peace — **re·pose·ful** *adj*

re·pos·i·to·ry \ri'päzə,tōrē\ *n, pl* **-ries** : place where something is stored

re·pos·sess \ˌrēpə'zes\ *vb* : regain possession and legal ownership of — **re·pos·ses·sion** \-'zeshən\ *n*

rep·re·hend \ˌrepri'hend\ *vb* : censure — **rep·re·hen·sion** \-'henchən\ *n*

rep·re·hen·si·ble \-'hensəbəl\ *adj* : deserving condemnation — **rep·re·hen·si·bly** *adv*

rep·re·sent \ˌrepri'zent\ *vb* **1** : serve as a sign or symbol of **2** : act or speak for **3** : describe

reinvent	reinvigorate	reknit
reinvestigate	rejudge	relabel
reinvestigation	rekindle	relandscape

as having a specified quality or character — **rep·re·sen·ta·tion** \ˌrepriˌzen'tāshən\ *n*

rep·re·sen·ta·tive \ˌrepri'zen-tətiv\ *adj* **1** : standing or acting for another **2** : carried on by elected representatives ∼ *n* **1** : typical example **2** : one that represents another **3** : member of usu. the lower house of a legislature — **rep·re·sen·ta·tive·ly** *adv* — **rep·re·sen·ta·tive·ness** *n*

re·press \ri'pres\ *vb* : restrain or suppress — **re·pres·sion** \-'preshən\ *n* — **re·pres·sive** \-'presiv\ *adj*

re·prieve \ri'prēv\ *n* **1** : a delay in punishment **2** : temporary respite — **reprieve** *vb*

rep·ri·mand \'reprəˌmand\ *n* : formal or severe criticism — **reprimand** *vb*

re·pri·sal \ri'prīzəl\ *n* : act in retaliation

re·prise \ri'prēz\ *n* : musical repetition

re·proach \ri'prōch\ *n* **1** : disgrace **2** : rebuke ∼ *vb* : express disapproval to — **re·proach·ful** *adj* — **re·proach·ful·ly** *adv* — **re·proach·ful·ness** *n*

rep·ro·bate \'reprəˌbāt\ *n* : scoundrel — **reprobate** *adj*

rep·ro·ba·tion \ˌreprə'bāshən\ *n* : strong disapproval

re·pro·duce \ˌrēprə'düs, -'dyüs\ *vb* **1** : produce again or anew **2** : produce offspring — **re·pro·duc·ible** \-'dü-səbəl, -'dyü-\ *adj* — **re·pro·duc·tion** \-'dəkshən\ *n* — **re·pro·duc·tive** \-'dəktiv\ *adj*

re·proof \ri'prüf\ *n* : blame or censure for a fault

re·prove \ri'prüv\ *vb* **-proved; -prov·ing** : express disapproval to or of

rep·tile \'reptᵊl, -ˌtīl\ *n* : air-breathing scaly vertebrate — **rep·til·ian** \rep'tilēən\ *adj or n*

re·pub·lic \ri'pəblik\ *n* : country with representative government

re·pub·li·can \-likən\ *adj* **1** : relating to or resembling a republic **2** : supporting a republic — **republican** *n* — **re·pub·li·can·ism** *n*

re·pu·di·ate \ri'pyüdēˌāt\ *vb* **-at·ed; -at·ing** : refuse to have anything to do with — **re·pu·di·a·tion** \-ˌpyüdē'āshən\ *n*

---

relaunch	reline	remarry
relearn	reload	rematch
relight	remarriage	remelt

re·pug·nant \ri'pəgnənt\ *adj* : contrary to one's tastes or principles — **re·pug·nance** \-nəns\ *n* — **re·pug·nant·ly** *adv*

re·pulse \ri'pəls\ *vb* **-pulsed; -puls·ing** 1 : drive or beat back 2 : rebuff 3 : be repugnant to — **repulse** *n* — **re·pul·sion** \-'pəlshən\ *n*

re·pul·sive \-siv\ *adj* : arousing aversion or disgust — **re·pul·sive·ly** *adv* — **re·pul·sive·ness** *n*

rep·u·ta·ble \'repyətəbəl\ *adj* : having a good reputation — **rep·u·ta·bly** \-blē\ *adv*

rep·u·ta·tion \,repyə'tāshən\ *n* : one's character or public esteem

re·pute \ri'pyüt\ *vb* **-put·ed; -put·ing** : think of as being ~ *n* : reputation — **re·put·ed** *adj* — **re·put·ed·ly** *adv*

re·quest \ri'kwest\ *n* : act or instance of asking for something or a thing asked for ~ *vb* 1 : make a request of 2 : ask for — **re·quest·er** *n*

re·qui·em \'rekwēəm, 'rāk-\ *n* : Mass for a dead person or a musical setting for this

re·quire \ri'kwīr\ *vb* **-quired; -quir·ing** 1 : insist on 2 : call for as essential — **re·quire·ment** *n*

req·ui·site \'rekwəzət\ *adj* : necessary — **requisite** *n*

req·ui·si·tion \,rekwə'zishən\ *n* : formal application or demand — **requisition** *vb*

re·quite \ri'kwīt\ *vb* **-quit·ed; -quit·ing** : make return for or to — **re·quit·al** \-'kwīt°l\ *n*

re·scind \ri'sind\ *vb* : repeal or cancel — **re·scis·sion** \-'sizhən\ *n*

res·cue \'reskyü\ *vb* **-cued; -cu·ing** : set free from danger or confinement — **rescue** *n* — **res·cu·er** *n*

re·search \ri'sərch, 'rē,sərch\ *n* : careful or diligent search esp. for new knowledge — **research** *vb* — **re·search·er** *n*

re·sem·ble \ri'zembəl\ *vb* **-sem·bled; -sem·bling** : be like or similar to — **re·sem·blance** \-'zembləns\ *n*

re·sent \ri'zent\ *vb* : feel or show annoyance at — **re·sent·ful** *adj* — **re·sent·ful·ly** *adv* — **re·sent·ment** *n*

res·er·va·tion \,rezər'vāshən\ *n* 1 : act of reserving or

remobilize	**remotivate**	**reoccupy**
remoisten	**rename**	**reoccur**
remold	**renegotiate**	**reoccurrence**

something reserved **2** : limiting condition

re·serve \ri'zərv\ *vb* **-served; -serv·ing 1** : store for future use **2** : set aside for special use ~ *n* **1** : something reserved **2** : restraint in words or bearing **3** : military forces withheld from action or not part of the regular services — **re·served** *adj*

res·er·voir \'rezər‚vwär, -‚vwȯr, -‚vȯr, -‚vȯi\ *n* : place where something (as water) is kept in store

re·side \ri'zīd\ *vb* **-sid·ed; -sid·ing 1** : make one's home **2** : be present

res·i·dence \'rezədəns\ *n* **1** : act or fact of residing in a place **2** : place where one lives — **res·i·dent** \-ənt\ *adj or n* — **res·i·den·tial** \‚rezə-'denchəl\ *adj*

res·i·due \'rezə‚dü, -‚dyü\ *n* : part remaining — **re·sid·u·al** \ri'zijəwəl\ *adj*

re·sign \ri'zīn\ *vb* **1** : give up deliberately **2** : give (oneself) over without resistance — **res-ig·na·tion** \‚rezig'nāshən\ *n* — **re·sign·ed·ly** \-'zīnədlē\ *adv*

re·sil·ience \ri'zilyəns\ *n* : ability to recover or adjust easily

re·sil·ien·cy \-yənsē\ *n* : resilience

re·sil·ient \-yənt\ *adj* : elastic

res·in \'rez°n\ *n* : substance from the gum or sap of trees — **res·in·ous** *adj*

re·sist \ri'zist\ *vb* **1** : withstand the force or effect of **2** : fight against — **re·sist·ible** \-'zistəbəl\ *adj* — **re·sist·less** *adj*

re·sis·tance \ri'zistəns\ *n* **1** : act of resisting **2** : ability of an organism to resist disease **3** : opposition to electric current

re·sis·tant \-tənt\ *adj* : giving resistance

res·o·lute \'rezə‚lüt\ *adj* : having a fixed purpose — **res·o·lute·ly** *adv* — **res·o·lute·ness** *n*

res·o·lu·tion \‚rezə'lüshən\ *n* **1** : process of resolving **2** : firmness of purpose **3** : statement of the opinion, will, or intent of a body

re·solve \ri'zälv\ *vb* **-solved; -solv·ing 1** : find an answer to **2** : make a formal resolution ~ *n* **1** : something resolved

---

reoperate reorganize repave
reorchestrate reorient   rephotograph
reorganization repack   replan

2 : steadfast purpose — **re·solv·able** *adj*

res·o·nant \'rezᵊnənt\ *adj* **1** : continuing to sound **2** : relating to intensification or prolongation of sound (as by a vibrating body) — **res·o·nance** \-əns\ *n* — **res·o·nant·ly** *adv*

re·sort \ri'zȯrt\ *n* **1** : source of help **2** : place to go for vacation ∼ *vb* **1** : go often or habitually **2** : have recourse

re·sound \ri'zaùnd\ *vb* : become filled with sound

re·sound·ing \-iŋ\ *adj* : impressive — **re·sound·ing·ly** *adv*

re·source \'rē₌sōrs, ri'sōrs\ *n* **1** : new or reserve source **2** *pl* : available funds **3** : ability to handle situations — **re·source·ful** *adj* — **re·source·ful·ness** *n*

re·spect \ri'spekt\ *n* **1** : relation to something **2** : high or special regard **3** : detail ∼ *vb* : consider deserving of high regard — **re·spect·er** *n* — **re·spect·ful** *adj* — **re·spect·ful·ly** *adv* — **re·spect·ful·ness** *n*

re·spect·able \ri'spektəbəl\ *adj* **1** : worthy of respect **2** : fair in size, quantity, or quality — **re·spect·abil·i·ty** \-₌spektə-'bilətē\ *n* — **re·spect·ably** \-'spektəblē\ *adv*

re·spec·tive \-tiv\ *adj* : individual and specific

re·spec·tive·ly \-lē\ *adv* **1** : as relating to each **2** : each in the order given

res·pi·ra·tion \₌respə'rāshən\ *n* : act or process of breathing — **re·spi·ra·to·ry** \'respərə₌tōrē, ri'spīrə-\ *adj* — **re·spire** \ri'spīr\ *vb*

res·pi·ra·tor \'respə₌rātər\ *n* : device for artificial respiration

re·spite \'respət\ *n* : temporary delay or rest

re·splen·dent \ri'splendənt\ *adj* : shining brilliantly — **re·splen·dence** \-dəns\ *n* — **re·splen·dent·ly** *adv*

re·spond \ri'spänd\ *vb* **1** : answer **2** : react — **re·spon·dent** \-'spändənt\ *n or adj* — **re·spond·er** *n*

re·sponse \ri'späns\ *n* **1** : act of responding **2** : answer

re·spon·si·ble \ri'spänsəbəl\ *adj* **1** : answerable for acts or decisions **2** : able to fulfill obligations **3** : having important duties — **re·spon·si·bil·i·ty** \ri₌spänsə'bilətē\ *n* — **re-**

replaster   repolish   reprice
replay   repopulate   reprint
replot   repressurize   reprocess

spon·si·ble·ness *n* — **re·spon·si·bly** \-blē\ *adv*

re·spon·sive \-siv\ *adj* : quick to respond — **re·spon·sive·ly** *adv* — **re·spon·sive·ness** *n*

¹**rest** \'rest\ *n* **1** : sleep **2** : freedom from work or activity **3** : state of inactivity **4** : something used as a support ~ *vb* **1** : get rest **2** : cease action or motion **3** : give rest to **4** : sit or lie fixed or supported **5** : depend — **rest·ful** *adj* — **rest·ful·ly** *adv*

²**rest** *n* : remainder

res·tau·rant \'restərənt, -tə-ränt\ *n* : public eating place

res·ti·tu·tion \restə'tüshən, -'tyü-\ *n* : act or fact of restoring something or repaying someone

res·tive \'restiv\ *adj* : uneasy or fidgety — **res·tive·ly** *adv* — **res·tive·ness** *n*

rest·less \'restləs\ *adj* **1** : lacking or giving no rest **2** : always moving **3** : uneasy — **rest·less·ly** *adv* — **rest·less·ness** *n*

re·store \ri'stōr\ *vb* **-stored; -stor·ing** **1** : give back **2** : put back into use or into a former state — **re·stor·able**

adj — **res·to·ra·tion** \restə'rāshən\ *n* — **re·stor·ative** \ri'stōrətiv\ *n or adj* — **re·stor·er** *n*

re·strain \ri'strān\ *vb* : limit or keep under control — **re·strain·able** *adj* — **re·strained** \-'strānd\ *adj* — **re·strain·ed·ly** \-'strānədlē\ *adv* — **re·strain·er** *n*

restraining order *n* : legal order directing one person to stay away from another

re·straint \-'strānt\ *n* **1** : act of restraining **2** : restraining force **3** : control over feelings

re·strict \ri'strikt\ *vb* **1** : confine within bounds **2** : limit use of — **re·stric·tion** \-'strikshən\ *n* — **re·stric·tive** *adj* — **re·stric·tive·ly** *adv*

re·sult \ri'zəlt\ *vb* : come about because of something else ~ *n* **1** : thing that results **2** : something obtained by calculation or investigation — **re·sul·tant** \-'zəltᵊnt\ *adj or n*

re·sume \ri'züm\ *vb* **-sumed; -sum·ing** : return to or take up again after interruption — **re·sump·tion** \-'zəmpshən\ *n*

ré·su·mé, re·su·me, re·su·mé \'rezə,mā, rezə'-\ *n* : sum-

---

reprogram	rerecord	reroute
reread	reregister	resalable
rereading	reroof	resale

mary of one's career and qualifications

re·sur·gence \ri'sərjəns\ *n* : a rising again — **re·sur·gent** \-jənt\ *adj*

res·ur·rect \ˌrezə'rekt\ *vb* **1** : raise from the dead **2** : bring to attention or use again — **res·ur·rec·tion** \-'rekshən\ *n*

re·sus·ci·tate \ri'səsəˌtāt\ *vb* **-tat·ed; -tat·ing** : bring back from apparent death — **re·sus·ci·ta·tion** \riˌsəsə'tāshən, ˌrē-\ *n* — **re·sus·ci·ta·tor** \-ˌtātər\ *n*

re·tail \'rēˌtāl\ *vb* : sell in small quantities directly to the consumer ∼ *n* : business of selling to consumers — **retail** *adj or adv* — **re·tail·er** *n*

re·tain \ri'tān\ *vb* **1** : keep or hold onto **2** : engage the services of

re·tain·er *n* **1** : household servant **2** : retaining fee

re·tal·i·ate \ri'talēˌāt\ *vb* **-at·ed; -at·ing** : return (as an injury) in kind — **re·tal·i·a·tion** \-ˌtalē'āshən\ *n* — **re·tal·ia·to·ry** \-'talyəˌtōrē\ *adj*

re·tard \ri'tärd\ *vb* : hold back — **re·tar·da·tion** \ˌrē-ˌtär'dāshən, ri-\ *n*

re·tard·ed \ri'tärdəd\ *adj* : slow or limited in intellectual development

retch \'rech\ *vb* : try to vomit

re·ten·tion \ri'tenchən\ *n* **1** : state of being retained **2** : ability to retain — **re·ten·tive** \-'tentiv\ *adj*

ret·i·cent \'retəsənt\ *adj* : tending not to talk — **ret·i·cence** \-səns\ *n* — **ret·i·cent·ly** *adv*

ret·i·na \'ret³nə\ *n, pl* **-nas** *or* **-nae** \-³nˌē\ : sensory membrane lining the eye — **ret·i·nal** \'ret³nəl\ *adj*

ret·i·nue \'ret³nˌü, -ˌyü\ *n* : attendants or followers of a distinguished person

re·tire \ri'tīr\ *vb* **-tired; -tir·ing** **1** : withdraw for privacy **2** : end a career **3** : go to bed — **re·tir·ee** \riˌtī'rē\ *n* — **re·tire·ment** *n*

re·tir·ing \ri'tīriŋ\ *adj* : shy

re·tort \ri'tȯrt\ *vb* : say in reply ∼ *n* : quick, witty, or cutting answer

re·trace \ˌrē'trās\ *vb* : go over again or in reverse

re·tract \ri'trakt\ *vb* **1** : draw back or in **2** : withdraw a charge or promise — **re·tract-**

---

reschedule	**resell**	**resettle**
reseal	**resentence**	**resew**
resegregate	**reset**	**reshoot**

able *adj* — **re·trac·tion** \-'trakshən\ *n*

re·treat \ri'trēt\ *n* **1** : act of withdrawing **2** : place of privacy or safety or meditation and study ∼ *vb* : make a retreat

re·trench \ri'trench\ *vb* : cut down (as expenses) — **re·trench·ment** *n*

ret·ri·bu·tion \ˌretrə'byushən\ *n* : retaliation — **re·trib·u·tive** \ri'tribyətiv\ *adj* — **re·trib·u·to·ry** \-yəˌtōrē\ *adj*

re·trieve \ri'trēv\ *vb* **-trieved; -triev·ing** **1** : search for and bring in game **2** : recover — **re·triev·able** *adj* — **re·triev·al** \-'trēvəl\ *n*

re·triev·er \-'trēvər\ *n* : dog for retrieving game

ret·ro·ac·tive \ˌretrō'aktiv\ *adj* : made effective as of a prior date — **ret·ro·ac·tive·ly** *adv*

ret·ro·grade \'retrəˌgrād\ *adj* **1** : moving backward **2** : becoming worse

ret·ro·gress \ˌretrə'gres\ *vb* : move backward — **ret·ro·gres·sion** \-'greshən\ *n*

ret·ro·spect \'retrəˌspekt\ *n* : review of past events — **ret-**

ro·spec·tion \ˌretrə'spekshən\ *n* — **ret·ro·spec·tive** \-'spektiv\ *adj* — **ret·ro·spec·tive·ly** *adv*

re·turn \ri'tərn\ *vb* **1** : go or come back **2** : pass, give, or send back to an earlier possessor **3** : answer **4** : bring in as a profit **5** : give or do in return ∼ *n* **1** : act of returning or something returned **2** *pl* : report of balloting results **3** : statement of taxable income **4** : profit — **return** *adj* — **re·turn·able** *adj or n* — **re·turn·er** *n*

re·union \rē'yünyən\ *n* **1** : act of reuniting **2** : a meeting of persons after a separation

re·vamp \ˌrē'vamp\ *vb* : renovate or revise

re·veal \ri'vēl\ *vb* **1** : make known **2** : show plainly

rev·eil·le \'revəlē\ *n* : military signal sounded about sunrise

rev·el \'revəl\ *vb* **-eled** *or* **-elled; -el·ing** *or* **-el·ling** **1** : take part in a revel **2** : take great pleasure ∼ *n* : wild party or celebration — **rev·el·er, rev·el·ler** \-ər\ *n* — **rev·el·ry** \-rē\ *n*

---

reshow	resolidify	restate
resocialization	restage	restatement
resod	restart	restimulate

rev·e·la·tion \ˌrevəˈlāshən\ n
1 : act of revealing 2 : something enlightening or astonishing

re·venge \riˈvenj\ vb : avenge ∼ n 1 : desire for retaliation 2 : act of retaliation — **re·venge·ful** adj — **re·veng·er** n

rev·e·nue \ˈrevəˌnü, -ˌnyü\ n : money collected by a government

re·ver·ber·ate \riˈvərbəˌrāt\ vb -at·ed; -at·ing : resound in a series of echoes — **re·ver·ber·a·tion** \-ˌvərbəˈrāshən\ n

re·vere \riˈvir\ vb -vered; -ver·ing : show honor and devotion to — **rev·er·ence** \ˈrevərəns\ n — **rev·er·ent** \-rənt\ adj — **rev·er·ent·ly** adv

rev·er·end \ˈrevərənd\ adj : worthy of reverence ∼ n : clergy member

rev·er·ie \ˈrevərē\ n, pl -er·ies : daydream

re·verse \riˈvərs\ adj 1 : opposite to a previous or normal condition 2 : acting in an opposite way ∼ vb -versed; -vers·ing 1 : turn upside down or completely around 2 : change to the contrary or in the opposite direction ∼ n 1 : something contrary 2 : change for the worse 3 : back of something — **re·ver·sal** \-səl\ n — **re·verse·ly** adv — **re·vers·ible** \-ˈvərs-əbəl\ adj

re·vert \riˈvərt\ vb : return to an original type or condition — **re·ver·sion** \-ˈvərzhən\ n

re·view \riˈvyü\ n 1 : formal inspection 2 : general survey 3 : critical evaluation 4 : second or repeated study or examination ∼ vb 1 : examine or study again 2 : reexamine judicially 3 : look back over 4 : examine critically 5 : inspect — **re·view·er** n

re·vile \riˈvīl\ vb -viled; -vil·ing : abuse verbally — **re·vile·ment** n — **re·vil·er** n

re·vise \-ˈvīz\ vb -vised; -vis·ing 1 : look over something written to correct or improve 2 : make a new version of — **re·vis·able** adj — **revise** n — **re·vis·er, re·vi·sor** \-ˈvīzər\ n — **re·vi·sion** \-ˈvizhən\ n

re·viv·al \-ˈvīvəl\ n 1 : act of reviving or state of being revived 2 : evangelistic meeting

restock   restyle   resurface
restructure   resubmit   resurvey
restudy   resupply   resynthesis

re·vive \-'vīv\ *vb* **-vived; -viv-ing** : bring back to life or consciousness or into use — **re·viv·er** *n*

re·vo·ca·tion \ˌrevə'kāshən\ *n* : act or instance of revoking

re·voke \ri'vōk\ *vb* **-voked; -vok·ing** : annul by recalling — **re·vok·er** *n*

re·volt \-'vōlt\ *vb* **1** : throw off allegiance **2** : cause or experience disgust or shock ~ *n* : rebellion or revolution — **re·volt·er** *n*

re·volt·ing \-iŋ\ *adj* : extremely offensive — **re·volt·ing·ly** *adv*

rev·o·lu·tion \ˌrevə'lüshən\ *n* **1** : rotation **2** : progress in an orbit **3** : sudden, radical, or complete change (as overthrow of a government) — **rev·o·lu·tion·ary** \-shəˌnerē\ *adj or n*

rev·o·lu·tion·ize \-shəˌnīz\ *vb* **-ized; -iz·ing** : change radically — **rev·o·lu·tion·iz·er** *n*

re·volve \ri'välv\ *vb* **-volved; -volv·ing** **1** : ponder **2** : move in an orbit **3** : rotate — **re·volv·able** *adj*

re·volv·er \ri'välvər\ *n* : pistol with a revolving cylinder

re·vue \ri'vyü\ *n* : theatrical production of brief numbers

re·vul·sion \ri'vəlshən\ *n* : complete dislike or repugnance

re·ward \ri'wȯrd\ *vb* : give a reward to or for ~ *n* : something offered for service or achievement

re·write \ˌrē'rīt\ *vb* **-wrote; -writ·ten; -writ·ing** : revise — **rewrite** *n*

rhap·so·dy \'rapsədē\ *n, pl* **-dies** **1** : expression of extravagant praise **2** : flowing free-form musical composition — **rhap·sod·ic** \rap-'sädik\ *adj* — **rhap·sod·i·cal·ly** \-iklē\ *adv* — **rhap·so·dize** \'rapsəˌdīz\ *vb*

resynthesize	retransmit	revaccination
retarget	retry	revisit
reteach	retune	rewash
retell	retype	reweave
retest	reupholster	rewind
rethink	reusable	rewire
retighten	reuse	rewrap
retrain	reutilize	
retranslate	revaccinate	

rhet·o·ric \'retərik\ *n* : art of speaking or writing effectively — **rhe·tor·i·cal** \ri'tȯrikəl\ *adj* — **rhet·o·ri·cian** \ˌretə'rishən\ *n*

rheu·ma·tism \'rümə̇ˌtizəm, 'rùm-\ *n* : disorder marked by inflammation or pain in muscles or joints — **rheu·mat·ic** \rù'matik\ *adj*

rhine·stone \'rīnˌstōn\ *n* : a colorless imitation gem

rhi·no \'rīnō\ *n, pl* **-no** *or* **-nos** : rhinoceros

rhi·noc·er·os \rī'näsərəs\ *n, pl* **-noc·er·os·es** *or* **-noc·er·os** *or* **-noc·eri** \-'näsəˌrī\ : large thick-skinned mammal with 1 or 2 horns on the snout

rho·do·den·dron \ˌrōdə'dendrən\ *n* : flowering evergreen shrub

rhom·bus \'rämbəs\ *n, pl* **-bus·es** *or* **-bi** \-ˌbī\ : parallelogram with equal sides

rhu·barb \'rüˌbärb\ *n* : garden plant with edible stalks

rhyme \'rīm\ *n* **1** : correspondence in terminal sounds **2** : verse that rhymes ~ *vb* **rhymed; rhym·ing** : make or have rhymes

rhythm \'rithəm\ *n* : regular succession of sounds or motions — **rhyth·mic** \'rithmik\, **rhyth·mi·cal** \-mikəl\ *adj* — **rhyth·mi·cal·ly** *adv*

rhythm and blues *n* : popular music based on blues and black folk music

rib \'rib\ *n* **1** : curved bone joined to the spine **2** : riblike thing ~ *vb* **-bb-** **1** : furnish or mark with ribs **2** : tease — **rib·ber** *n*

rib·ald \'ribəld\ *adj* : coarse or vulgar — **rib·ald·ry** \-əldrē\ *n*

rib·bon \'ribən\ *n* **1** : narrow strip of fabric used esp. for decoration **2** : strip of inked cloth (as in a typewriter)

ri·bo·fla·vin \ˌrībə'flāvən, 'rībəˌ-\ *n* : growth-promoting vitamin

rice \'rīs\ *n, pl* **rice** : starchy edible seeds of an annual cereal grass

rich \'rich\ *adj* **1** : having a lot of money or possessions **2** : valuable **3** : containing much sugar, fat, or seasoning **4** : abundant **5** : deep and pleasing in color or tone **6** : fertile — **rich·ly** *adv* — **rich·ness** *n*

rich·es \'richəz\ *n pl* : wealth

rick·ets \'rikəts\ *n* : childhood bone disease

rick·ety \'rikətē\ *adj* : shaky

rick·sha, rick·shaw \'rikˌshȯ\ *n* : small covered 2-wheeled carriage pulled by one person

ric·o·chet \'rikəˌshā, *Brit also* -ˌshet\ *vb* **-cheted** \-ˌshād\ *or* **-chet·ted** \-ˌshetəd\; **-chet-**

ing \-ˌshāiŋ\ *or* **-chet·ting** \-ˌshetiŋ\ : bounce off at an angle — **ricochet** *n*

rid \ˈrid\ *vb* **rid; rid·ding** : make free of something unwanted — **rid·dance** \ˈridᵊns\ *n*

rid·den \ˈridᵊn\ *adj* : overburdened with — used in combination

¹**rid·dle** \ˈridᵊl\ *n* : puzzling question ∼ *vb* **-dled; -dling** : speak in riddles

²**riddle** *vb* **-dled; -dling** : fill full of holes

ride \ˈrīd\ *vb* **rode** \ˈrōd\; **rid·den** \ˈridᵊn\; **rid·ing** \ˈrīdiŋ\ **1** : be carried along **2** : sit on and cause to move **3** : travel over a surface **4** : tease or nag ∼ *n* **1** : trip on an animal or in a vehicle **2** : mechanical device ridden for amusement

rid·er *n* **1** : one that rides **2** : attached clause or document — **rid·er·less** *adj*

ridge \ˈrij\ *n* **1** : range of hills **2** : raised line or strip **3** : line of intersection of 2 sloping surfaces — **ridgy** *adj*

rid·i·cule \ˈridəˌkyül\ *vb* : laugh at or make fun of — **ridicule** *n*

ri·dic·u·lous \rəˈdikyələs\ *adj* : arousing ridicule — **ri·dic·u·lous·ly** *adv* — **ri·dic·u·lous·ness** *n*

rife \ˈrīf\ *adj* : abounding — **rife** *adv*

riff·raff \ˈrifˌraf\ *n* : mob

¹**ri·fle** \ˈrīfəl\ *vb* **-fled; -fling** : ransack esp. with intent to steal — **ri·fler** \-flər\ *n*

²**rifle** *n* : long shoulder weapon with spiral grooves in the bore — **ri·fle·man** \-mən\ *n* — **ri·fling** *n*

rift \ˈrift\ *n* : separation — **rift** *vb*

¹**rig** \ˈrig\ *vb* **-gg-** **1** : fit out with rigging **2** : set up esp. as a makeshift ∼ *n* **1** : distinctive shape, number, and arrangement of sails and masts of a sailing ship **2** : equipment **3** : carriage with its horse

²**rig** *vb* **-gg-** : manipulate esp. by deceptive or dishonest means

rig·ging \ˈrigiŋ, -ən\ *n* : lines that hold and move the masts, sails, and spars of a sailing ship

right \ˈrīt\ *adj* **1** : meeting a standard of conduct **2** : correct **3** : genuine **4** : normal **5** : opposite of left ∼ *n* **1** : something that is correct, just, proper, or honorable **2** : something to which one has a just claim **3** : something that is on the right side ∼ *adv* **1** : according to what is right **2** : immediately **3** : completely **4** : on or to the right ∼ *vb* **1** : restore to a proper state **2** : bring or become upright again — **right·er** *n* — **right·ness** *n* — **right·ward** \-wərd\ *adj*

right angle *n* : angle whose sides are perpendicular to each other — **right–an·gled** \'rīt-'aŋgəld\, **right–an·gle** \-gəl\ *adj*

righ·teous \'rīchəs\ *adj* : acting or being in accordance with what is just or moral — **righ·teous·ly** *adv* — **righ·teous·ness** *n*

right·ful \'rītfəl\ *adj* : lawful — **right·ful·ly** \-ē\ *adv* — **right·ful·ness** *n*

right·ly \'rītlē\ *adv* **1** : justly **2** : properly **3** : correctly

rig·id \'rijəd\ *adj* : lacking flexibility — **ri·gid·i·ty** \rə-'jidətē\ *n* — **rig·id·ly** *adv*

rig·ma·role \'rigmə‚rōl, 'rigə-\ *n* **1** : meaningless talk **2** : complicated often unnecessary procedure

rig·or \'rigər\ *n* : severity — **rig·or·ous** *adj* — **rig·or·ous·ly** *adv*

rig·or mor·tis \‚rigər'mȯrtəs\ *n* : temporary stiffness of muscles occurring after death

rile \'rīl\ *vb* **riled; ril·ing** : anger

rill \'ril\ *n* : small brook

rim \'rim\ *n* : edge esp. of something curved ∼ *vb* -mm- : border

¹rime \'rīm\ *n* : frost — **rimy** \'rīmē\ *adj*

²rime *var of* **RHYME**

rind \'rīnd\ *n* : usu. hard or tough outer layer

¹ring \'riŋ\ *n* **1** : circular band used as an ornament or for holding or fastening **2** : something circular **3** : place for contest or display **4** : group with a selfish or dishonest aim ∼ *vb* : surround — **ringed** \'riŋd\ *adj* — **ring·like** *adj*

²ring *vb* **rang** \'raŋ\; **rung** \'rəŋ\; **ringing 1** : sound resonantly when struck **2** : cause to make a metallic sound by striking **3** : resound **4** : call esp. by a bell ∼ *n* **1** : resonant sound or tone **2** : act or instance of ringing

ring·er \'riŋər\ *n* **1** : one that sounds by ringing **2** : illegal substitute **3** : one that closely resembles another

ring·lead·er \'riŋ‚lēdər\ *n* : leader esp. of troublemakers

ring·let *n* : long curl

ring·worm *n* : contagious skin disease caused by fungi

rink \'riŋk\ *n* : enclosed place for skating

rinse \'rins\ *vb* **rinsed; rinsing 1** : cleanse usu. with water only **2** : treat (hair) with a rinse ∼ *n* : liquid used for rinsing — **rins·er** *n*

ri·ot \'rīət\ *n* **1** : violent public disorder **2** : random or disorderly profusion — **riot** *vb* — **ri·ot·er** *n* — **ri·ot·ous** *adj*

rip \'rip\ *vb* **-pp-** : cut or tear open ∼ *n* : rent made by ripping — **rip·per** *n*

ripe \'rīp\ *adj* **rip·er; rip·est** : fully grown, developed, or prepared — **ripe·ly** *adv* — **rip·en** \'rīpən\ *vb* — **ripe·ness** *n*

rip–off *n* : theft — **rip off** *vb*

rip·ple \'ripəl\ *vb* **-pled; -pling** **1** : become lightly ruffled on the surface **2** : sound like rippling water — **ripple** *n*

rise \'rīz\ *vb* **rose** \'rōz\; **ris·en** \'riz³n\; **ris·ing** \'rīziŋ\ **1** : get up from sitting, kneeling, or lying **2** : take arms **3** : appear above the horizon **4** : ascend **5** : gain a higher position or rank **6** : increase ∼ *n* **1** : act of rising **2** : origin **3** : elevation **4** : increase **5** : upward slope **6** : area of high ground — **ris·er** \'rīzər\ *n*

risk \'risk\ *n* : exposure to loss or injury — **risk** *vb* — **risk·i·ness** *n* — **risky** *adj*

ris·qué \ris'kā\ *adj* : nearly indecent

rite \'rīt\ *n* **1** : set form for conducting a ceremony **2** : liturgy of a church **3** : ceremonial action

rit·u·al \'richəwəl\ *n* : rite — **ritual** *adj* — **rit·u·al·ism** \-ˌizəm\ *n* — **rit·u·al·is·tic** \ˌrichəwəl'istik\ *adj* — **rit·u·al·is·ti·cal·ly** \-tiklē\ *adv* — **rit·u·al·ly** \'richəwəlē\ *adv*

ri·val \'rīvəl\ *n* **1** : competitor **2** : peer ∼ *vb* **-valed** *or* **-valled; -val·ing** *or* **-val·ling 1** : be in competition with **2** : equal — **rival** *adj* — **ri·val·ry** \-rē\ *n*

riv·er \'rivər\ *n* : large natural stream of water — **riv·er·bank** *n* — **riv·er·bed** *n* — **riv·er·boat** *n* — **riv·er·side** *n*

riv·et \'rivət\ *n* : headed metal bolt ∼ *vb* : fasten with a rivet — **riv·et·er** *n*

riv·u·let \'rivyələt\ *n* : small stream

roach \'rōch\ *n* : cockroach

road \'rōd\ *n* : open way for vehicles, persons, and animals — **road·bed** *n* — **road·side** *n* *or adj* — **road·way** *n*

road·block *n* : obstruction on a road

road·run·ner *n* : large fast-running bird

roam \'rōm\ *vb* : wander

roan \'rōn\ *adj* : of a dark color sprinkled with white ∼ *n* : animal with a roan coat

roar \'rōr\ *vb* : utter a full loud prolonged sound — **roar** *n* — **roar·er** *n*

roast \'rōst\ *vb* **1** : cook by dry heat **2** : criticize severely ∼ *n* : piece of meat suitable for roasting — **roast** *adj* — **roast·er** *n*

rob \'räb\ *vb* **-bb- 1** : steal from **2** : commit robbery — **rob·ber** *n*

rob·bery \'räbərē\ *n, pl* **-ber·ies** : theft of something from a person by use of violence or threat

robe \'rōb\ *n* **1** : long flowing outer garment **2** : covering for the lower body ~ *vb* **robed; rob·ing** : clothe with or as if with a robe

rob·in \'räbən\ *n* : No. American thrush with a reddish breast

ro·bot \'rō,bät, -bət\ *n* **1** : machine that looks and acts like a human being **2** : efficient but insensitive person — **ro·bot·ic** \rō'bätik\ *adj*

ro·bust \rō'bəst, 'rō,bəst\ *adj* : strong and vigorously healthy — **ro·bust·ly** *adv* — **ro·bust·ness** *n*

¹rock \'räk\ *vb* : sway or cause to sway back and forth ~ *n* **1** : rocking movement **2** : popular music marked by repetition and a strong beat

²rock *n* : mass of hard mineral material — **rock** *adj* — **rocky** *adj*

rock·er *n* **1** : curved piece on which a chair rocks **2** : chair that rocks

rock·et \'räkət\ *n* **1** : self=propelled firework or missile **2** : jet engine that carries its own oxygen ~ *vb* : rise abruptly and rapidly — **rock·et·ry** \-ətrē\ *n*

rod \'räd\ *n* **1** : straight slender stick **2** : unit of length equal to 5 yards

rode *past of* RIDE

ro·dent \'rōdᵊnt\ *n* : usu. small gnawing mammal

ro·deo \'rōdē,ō, rō'dāō\ *n, pl* **-de·os** : contest of cowboy skills

roe \'rō\ *n* : fish eggs

rogue \'rōg\ *n* : dishonest or mischievous person — **rogu·ery** \'rōgərē\ *n* — **rogu·ish** \'rōgish\ *adj* — **rogu·ish·ly** *adv* — **rogu·ish·ness** *n*

roil \'ròil\ *vb* **1** : make cloudy or muddy by stirring up **2** : make angry

role \'rōl\ *n* **1** : part to play **2** : function

roll \'rōl\ *n* **1** : official record or list of names **2** : something rolled up or rounded **3** : bread baked in a small rounded mass **4** : sound of rapid drum strokes **5** : heavy reverberating sound **6** : rolling movement ~ *vb* **1** : move by turning over **2** : move on wheels **3** : flow in a continuous stream **4** : swing from side to side **5** : shape or be shaped in rounded form **6** : press with a roller

roll·er *n* **1** : revolving cylinder **2** : rod on which something is rolled up **3** : long heavy ocean wave

roller skate *n* : a skate with wheels instead of a runner — **roller–skate** *vb*

rol·lick·ing \'rälikiŋ\ *adj* : full of good spirits

Ro·man Catholic \'rōmən-\ *n* : member of a Christian church led by a pope — **Roman Catholic** *adj* — **Roman Catholicism** *n*

ro·mance \rō'mans, 'rō-ˌmans\ *n* **1** : medieval tale of knightly adventure **2** : love story **3** : love affair ∼ *vb* **-manced; -manc·ing 1** : have romantic fancies **2** : have a love affair with — **ro·manc·er** *n*

ro·man·tic \rō'mantik\ *adj* **1** : visionary or imaginative **2** : appealing to one's emotions — **ro·man·ti·cal·ly** \-iklē\ *adv*

romp \'rämp\ *vb* : play actively and noisily — **romp** *n*

roof \'rüf, 'rùf\ *n, pl* **roofs** \'rüfs, 'rùfs; 'rüvz, 'rùvz\ : upper covering part of a building ∼ *vb* : cover with a roof — **roofed** \'rüft, 'rùft\ *adj* — **roof·ing** *n* — **roof·less** *adj* — **roof·top** *n*

¹rook \'rùk\ *n* : crowlike bird

²rook *vb* : cheat

rook·ie \'rùkē\ *n* : novice

room \'rüm, 'rùm\ *n* **1** : sufficient space **2** : partitioned part of a building ∼ *vb* : occupy lodgings — **room·er** *n* — **room·ful** *n* — **roomy** *adj*

room·mate *n* : one sharing the same lodgings

roost \'rüst\ *n* : support on which birds perch ∼ *vb* : settle on a roost

roost·er \'rüstər, 'rùs-\ *n* : adult male domestic chicken

¹root \'rüt, 'rùt\ *n* **1** : leafless underground part of a seed plant **2** : rootlike thing or part **3** : source **4** : essential core ∼ *vb* : form, fix, or become fixed by roots — **root·less** *adj* — **root·let** \-lət\ *n* — **root·like** *adj*

²root *vb* : turn up with the snout

³root \'rüt, 'rùt\ *vb* : applaud or encourage noisily — **root·er** *n*

rope \'rōp\ *n* : large strong cord of strands of fiber ∼ *vb* **roped; rop·ing 1** : tie with a rope **2** : lasso

ro·sa·ry \'rōzərē\ *n, pl* **-ries 1** : string of beads used in praying **2** : Roman Catholic devotion

¹rose *past of* RISE

²rose \'rōz\ *n* **1** : prickly shrub with bright flowers **2** : purplish red — **rose** *adj* — **rose·bud** *n* — **rose·bush** *n*

rose·mary \'rōzˌmerē\ *n, pl* **-mar·ies** : fragrant shrubby mint

ro·sette \rō'zet\ *n* : rose-shaped ornament

Rosh Ha·sha·nah \ˌräshhä-'shänə, ˌrōsh-\ *n* : Jewish

New Year observed as a religious holiday in September or October

ros·in \\'räzᵊn\\ *n* : brittle resin

ros·ter \\'rästər\\ *n* : list of names

ros·trum \\'rästrəm\\ *n, pl* **-trums** *or* **-tra** \\-trə\\ : speaker's platform

rosy \\'rōzē\\ *adj* **ros·i·er; -est** **1** : of the color rose **2** : hopeful — **ros·i·ly** *adv* — **ros·i·ness** *n*

rot \\'rät\\ *vb* **-tt-** : undergo decomposition ∼ *n* **1** : decay **2** : disease in which tissue breaks down

ro·ta·ry \\'rōtərē\\ *adj* **1** : turning on an axis **2** : having a rotating part

ro·tate \\'rō₁tāt\\ *vb* **-tat·ed; -tat·ing** **1** : turn about an axis or a center **2** : alternate in a series — **ro·ta·tion** \\rō'tāshən\\ *n* — **ro·ta·tor** \\'rō₁tātər\\ *n*

rote \\'rōt\\ *n* : repetition from memory

ro·tor \\'rōtər\\ *n* **1** : part that rotates **2** : system of rotating horizontal blades for supporting a helicopter

rot·ten \\'rätᵊn\\ *adj* **1** : having rotted **2** : corrupt **3** : extremely unpleasant or inferior — **rot·ten·ness** *n*

ro·tund \\rō'tənd\\ *adj* : rounded — **ro·tun·di·ty** \\-'təndətē\\ *n*

ro·tun·da \\rō'təndə\\ *n* : building or room with a dome

roué \\rù'ā\\ *n* : man given to debauched living

rouge \\'rüzh, 'rüj\\ *n* : cosmetic for the cheeks — **rouge** *vb*

rough \\'rəf\\ *adj* **1** : not smooth **2** : not calm **3** : harsh, violent, or rugged **4** : crudely or hastily done ∼ *n* : rough state or something in that state ∼ *vb* **1** : roughen **2** : manhandle **3** : make roughly — **rough·ly** *adv* — **rough·ness** *n*

rough·age \\'rəfij\\ *n* : coarse bulky food

rough·en \\'rəfən\\ *vb* : make or become rough

rough·neck \\'rəf₁nek\\ *n* : rowdy

rou·lette \\rü'let\\ *n* : gambling game using a whirling numbered wheel

¹round \\'raùnd\\ *adj* **1** : having every part the same distance from the center **2** : cylindrical **3** : complete **4** : approximate **5** : blunt **6** : moving in or forming a circle ∼ *n* **1** : round or curved thing **2** : series of recurring actions or events **3** : period of time or a unit of action **4** : fired shot **5** : cut of beef ∼ *vb* **1** : make or become round **2** : go around **3** : finish **4** : express as an approximation — **round-**

ish *adj* — **round·ly** *adv* — **round·ness** *n*

²**round** *prep or adv* : around

round·about *adj* : indirect

round·up \'raùnd,əp\ *n*   **1** : gathering together of range cattle   **2** : summary — **round up** *vb*

rouse \'raùz\ *vb* **roused; rous·ing**   **1** : wake from sleep   **2** : stir up

rout \'raùt\ *n*   **1** : state of wild confusion   **2** : disastrous defeat ~ *vb* : defeat decisively

route \'rüt, 'raùt\ *n* : line of travel ~ *vb* **rout·ed; rout·ing** : send by a selected route

rou·tine \rü'tēn\ *n*   **1** : regular course of procedure   **2** : an often repeated speech, formula, or part — **routine** *adj* — **rou·tine·ly** *adv*

rove \'rōv\ *vb* **roved; rov·ing** : wander or roam — **rov·er** *n*

¹**row** \'rō\ *vb*   **1** : propel a boat with oars   **2** : carry in a rowboat ~ *n* : act of rowing — **row·boat** *n* — **row·er** \'rōər\ *n*

²**row** *n* : number of objects in a line

³**row** \'raù\ *n* : noisy quarrel — **row** *vb*

row·dy \'raùdē\ *adj* **-di·er; -est** : coarse or boisterous in behavior — **row·di·ness** *n* — **rowdy** *n*

roy·al \'rȯiəl\ *adj* : relating to or befitting a king ~ *n* : person of royal blood — **roy·al·ly** *adv*

roy·al·ty \'rȯiəltē\ *n, pl* **-ties**   **1** : state of being royal   **2** : royal persons   **3** : payment for use of property

rub \'rəb\ *vb* **-bb-**   **1** : use pressure and friction on a body   **2** : scour, polish, erase, or smear by pressure and friction   **3** : chafe with friction ~ *n* : difficulty

rub·ber \'rəbər\ *n*   **1** : one that rubs   **2** : waterproof elastic substance or something made of it — **rubber** *adj* — **rub·ber·ize** \-,īz\ *vb* — **rub·bery** *adj*

rub·bish \'rəbish\ *n* : waste or trash

rub·ble \'rəbəl\ *n* : broken fragments esp. of a destroyed building

ru·ble \'rübəl\ *n* : monetary unit of Russia

ru·by \'rübē\ *n, pl* **-bies** : precious red stone or its color — **ruby** *adj*

rud·der \'rədər\ *n* : steering device at the rear of a ship or aircraft

rud·dy \'rədē\ *adj* **-di·er; -est** : reddish — **rud·di·ness** *n*

rude \'rüd\ *adj* **rud·er; rud·est**   **1** : roughly made   **2** : impolite — **rude·ly** *adv* — **rude·ness** *n*

ru·di·ment \'rüdəmənt\ *n* **1** : something not fully developed **2** : elementary principle — **ru·di·men·ta·ry** \,rüdə-'mentərē\ *adj*

rue \'rü\ *vb* **rued; ru·ing** : feel regret for ~ *n* : regret — **rue·ful** \-fəl\ *adj* — **rue·ful·ly** *adv* — **rue·ful·ness** *n*

ruf·fi·an \'rəfēən\ *n* : brutal person

ruf·fle \'rəfəl\ *vb* **-fled; -fling** **1** : draw into or provide with pleats **2** : roughen the surface of **3** : irritate ~ *n* : strip of fabric pleated on one edge — **ruf·fly** \'rəfəlē, -flē\ *adj*

rug \'rəg\ *n* : piece of heavy fabric used as a floor covering

rug·ged \'rəgəd\ *adj* **1** : having a rough uneven surface **2** : severe **3** : strong — **rug·ged·ly** *adv* — **rug·ged·ness** *n*

ru·in \'rüən\ *n* **1** : complete collapse or destruction **2** : remains of something destroyed — usu. in pl. **3** : cause of destruction ~ *vb* **1** : destroy **2** : damage beyond repair **3** : bankrupt

ru·in·ous \'rüənəs\ *adj* : causing ruin — **ruin·ous·ly** *adv*

rule \'rül\ *n* **1** : guide or principle for governing action **2** : usual way of doing something **3** : government **4** : straight strip (as of wood or metal) marked off in units for mea-suring ~ *vb* **ruled; rul·ing** **1** : govern **2** : give as a decision — **rul·er** *n*

rum \'rəm\ *n* : liquor made from molasses or sugarcane

rum·ble \'rəmbəl\ *vb* **-bled; -bling** : make a low heavy rolling sound — **rumble** *n*

ru·mi·nant \'rümənənt\ *n* : hoofed mammal (as a cow or deer) that chews the cud — **ru·minant** *adj*

ru·mi·nate \'rümə,nāt\ *vb* **-nat·ed; -nat·ing** : contemplate — **ru·mi·na·tion** \,rümə-'nāshən\ *n*

rum·mage \'rəmij\ *vb* **-maged; -maging** : search thoroughly

rum·my \'rəmē\ *n* : card game

ru·mor \'rümər\ *n* **1** : common talk **2** : widespread statement not authenticated — **rumor** *vb*

rump \'rəmp\ *n* : rear part of an animal

rum·ple \'rəmpəl\ *vb* **-pled; -pling** : tousle or wrinkle — **rumple** *n*

rum·pus \'rəmpəs\ *n* : disturbance

run \'rən\ *vb* **ran** \'ran\; **run; run·ning** **1** : go rapidly or hurriedly **2** : enter a race or election **3** : operate **4** : continue in force **5** : flow rapidly **6** : take a certain direction **7** : manage **8** : incur ~ *n* **1** : act of running **2** : brook

3 : continuous series **4** : usual kind **5** : freedom of movement **6** : lengthwise ravel

run·around *n* : evasive or delaying action esp. in response to a request

run·away \'rənə₁wā\ *n* : fugitive ∼ *adj* **1** : fugitive **2** : out of control

run–down *adj* : being in poor condition

¹**rung** *past part of* RING

²**rung** \'rəŋ\ *n* : horizontal piece of a chair or ladder

run·ner \'rənər\ *n* **1** : one that runs **2** : thin piece or part on which something slides **3** : slender creeping branch of a plant

run·ner–up *n, pl* **run·ners–up** : competitor who finishes second

run·ning \'rəniŋ\ *adj* **1** : flowing **2** : continuous

runt \'rənt\ *n* : small person or animal — **runty** *adj*

run·way \'rən₁wā\ *n* : strip on which aircraft land and take off

ru·pee \rü'pē, 'rü₁-\ *n* : monetary unit (as of India)

rup·ture \'rəpchər\ *n* **1** : breaking or tearing apart **2** : hernia ∼ *vb* **-tured; -turing** : cause or undergo rupture

ru·ral \'rùrəl\ *adj* : relating to the country or agriculture

ruse \'rüs, 'rüz\ *n* : trick

¹**rush** \'rəsh\ *n* : grasslike marsh plant

²**rush** *vb* **1** : move forward or act with too great haste **2** : perform in a short time ∼ *n* : violent forward motion ∼ *adj* : requiring speed — **rush·er** *n*

rus·set \'rəsət\ *n* **1** : reddish brown color **2** : a baking potato — **russet** *adj*

rust \'rəst\ *n* **1** : reddish coating on exposed iron **2** : reddish brown color — **rust** *vb* — **rusty** *adj*

rus·tic \'rəstik\ *adj* : relating to or suitable for the country or country dwellers ∼ *n* : rustic person — **rus·ti·cal·ly** *adv*

rus·tle \'rəsəl\ *vb* **-tled; -tling** **1** : make or cause a rustle **2** : forage food **3** : steal cattle from the range ∼ *n* : series of small sounds — **rus·tler** \-ələr\ *n*

rut \'rət\ *n* **1** : track worn by wheels or feet **2** : set routine — **rut·ted** *adj*

ruth·less \'rüthləs\ *adj* : having no pity — **ruth·less·ly** *adv* — **ruth·less·ness** *n*

RV \₁är-'vē\ *n* recreational vehicle

-ry \rē\ *n suffix* : -ery

rye \'rī\ *n* **1** : cereal grass grown for grain **2** : whiskey from rye

S

s \'es\ *n, pl* **s's** *or* **ss** \'esəz\ : 19th letter of the alphabet

¹-s \s *after sounds* f, k, k̲, p, t, th; əz *after sounds* ch, j, s, sh, z, zh; z *after other sounds*\ — used to form the plural of most nouns

²-s *vb suffix* — used to form the 3d person singular present of most verbs

Sab·bath \'sabəth\ *n* **1** : Saturday observed as a day of worship by Jews and some Christians **2** : Sunday observed as a day of worship by Christians

sa·ber, sa·bre \'sābər\ *n* : curved cavalry sword

sa·ble \'sābəl\ *n* **1** : black **2** : dark brown mammal or its fur

sab·o·tage \'sabə,täzh\ *n* : deliberate destruction or hampering ~ *vb* **-taged; -tag·ing** : wreck through sabotage

sab·o·teur \,sabə'tər\ *n* : person who sabotages

sac \'sak\ *n* : anatomical pouch

sac·cha·rin \'sakərən\ *n* : low-calorie artificial sweetener

sac·cha·rine \-ərən\ *adj* : nauseatingly sweet

sa·chet \sa'shā\ *n* : small bag with perfumed powder (**sachet powder**)

¹sack \'sak\ *n* : bag ~ *vb* : fire

²sack *vb* : plunder a captured place

sack·cloth *n* : rough garment worn as a sign of penitence

sac·ra·ment \'sakrəmənt\ *n* : formal religious act or rite — **sac·ra·men·tal** \,sakrə'mentᵊl\ *adj*

sa·cred \'sākrəd\ *adj* **1** : set apart for or worthy of worship **2** : worthy of reverence **3** : relating to religion — **sa·cred·ly** *adv* — **sa·cred·ness** *n*

sac·ri·fice \'sakrə,fīs\ *n* **1** : the offering of something precious to a deity or the thing offered **2** : loss or deprivation ~ *vb* **-ficed; -fic·ing** : offer or give up as a sacrifice — **sac·ri·fi·cial** \,sakrə'fishəl\ *adj*

sac·ri·lege \'sakrəlij\ *n* : violation of something sacred — **sac·ri·le·gious** \,sakrə'lijəs, -'lējəs\ *adj*

sac·ro·sanct \'sakrō,saŋkt\ *adj* : sacred

sad \'sad\ *adj* **-dd-** **1** : affected with grief or sorrow **2** : causing sorrow — **sad·den** \'sad°n\ *vb* — **sad·ly** *adv* — **sad·ness** *n*

sad·dle \'sad°l\ *n* : seat for riding on horseback ～ *vb* **-dled; -dling** : put a saddle on

sa·dism \'sā‚dizəm, 'sad‚iz-\ *n* : delight in cruelty — **sa·dist** \'sādist, 'sad-\ *n* — **sa·dis·tic** \sə'distik\ *adj* — **sa·dis·ti·cal·ly** *adv*

sa·fa·ri \sə'färē, -'far-\ *n* : hunting expedition in Africa

safe \'sāf\ *adj* **saf·er; saf·est 1** : free from harm **2** : providing safety ～ *n* : container to keep valuables safe — **safe·keep·ing** *n* — **safe·ly** *adv*

safe·guard *n* : measure or device for preventing accidents — **safeguard** *vb*

safe·ty \'sāftē\ *n, pl* **-ties 1** : freedom from danger **2** : protective device

saf·flow·er \'saf‚laůər\ *n* : herb with seeds rich in edible oil

saf·fron \'safrən\ *n* : orange powder from a crocus flower used in cooking

sag \'sag\ *vb* **-gg-** : droop, sink, or settle — **sag** *n*

sa·ga \'sägə\ *n* : story of heroic deeds

sa·ga·cious \sə'gāshəs\ *adj* : shrewd — **sa·gac·i·ty** \-'gasətē\ *n*

¹sage \'sāj\ *adj* : wise or prudent ～ *n* : wise man — **sage·ly** *adv*

²sage *n* : mint used in flavoring

sage·brush *n* : low shrub of the western U.S.

said *past of* SAY

sail \'sāl\ *n* **1** : fabric used to catch the wind and move a boat or ship **2** : trip on a sailboat ～ *vb* **1** : travel on a ship or sailboat **2** : move with ease or grace — **sail·boat** *n* — **sail·or** \'sālər\ *n*

sail·fish *n* : large fish with a very large dorsal fin

saint \'sānt, *before a name* ‚sānt *or* sənt\ *n* : holy or godly person — **saint·ed** \-əd\ *adj* — **saint·hood** \-‚hůd\ *n* — **saint·li·ness** *n* — **saint·ly** *adj*

¹sake \'sāk\ *n* **1** : purpose or reason **2** : one's good or benefit

²sa·ke, sa·ki \'säkē\ *n* : Japanese rice wine

sa·la·cious \sə'lāshəs\ *adj* : sexually suggestive — **sa·la·cious·ly** *adv*

sal·ad \'saləd\ *n* : dish usu. of raw lettuce, vegetables, or fruit

sal·a·man·der \'salə‚mandər\ *n* : lizardlike amphibian

sa·la·mi \sə'lämē\ *n* : highly seasoned dried sausage

sal·a·ry \'salərē\ *n, pl* **-ries** : regular payment for services

sale \'sāl\ *n* **1** : transfer of ownership of property for money **2** : selling at bargain prices **3 sales** *pl* : activities involved in selling — **sal·able, sale·able** \'sāləbəl\ *adj* — **sales·man** \-mən\ *n* — **sales·per·son** *n* — **sales·wom·an** *n*

sa·lient \'sālyənt\ *adj* : standing out conspicuously

sa·line \'sā͵lēn, -͵līn\ *adj* : containing salt — **sa·lin·i·ty** \sā'linətē, sə-\ *n*

sa·li·va \sə'līvə\ *n* : liquid secreted into the mouth — **sal·i·vary** \'salə͵verē\ *adj* — **sal·i·vate** \-͵vāt\ *vb* — **sal·i·va·tion** \͵salə'vāshən\ *n*

sal·low \'salō\ *adj* : of a yellowish sickly color

sal·ly \'salē\ *n, pl* **-lies** **1** : quick attack on besiegers **2** : witty remark — **sally** *vb*

salm·on \'samən\ *n, pl* **salmon** **1** : food fish with pink or red flesh **2** : deep yellowish pink color

sa·lon \sə'län, 'sal͵än, sa'lōⁿ\ *n* : elegant room or shop

sa·loon \sə'lün\ *n* **1** : public cabin on a passenger ship **2** : barroom

sal·sa \'solsə, 'säl-\ *n* : spicy sauce of tomatoes, onions, and hot peppers

salt \'solt\ *n* **1** : white crystalline substance that consists of sodium and chlorine **2** : compound formed usu. from acid and metal — **salt** *vb or adj* — **salt·i·ness** *n* — **salty** *adj*

salt·wa·ter *adj* : relating to or living in salt water

sa·lu·bri·ous \sə'lübrēəs\ *adj* : good for health

sal·u·tary \'salyə͵terē\ *adj* : health-giving or beneficial

sal·u·ta·tion \͵salyə'tāshən\ *n* : greeting

sa·lute \sə'lüt\ *vb* **-lut·ed; -lut·ing** : honor by ceremony or formal movement — **salute** *n*

sal·vage \'salvij\ *n* : something saved from destruction ∼ *vb* **-vaged; -vag·ing** : rescue or save

sal·va·tion \sal'vāshən\ *n* : saving of a person from sin or danger

salve \'sav, 'såv\ *n* : medicinal ointment ∼ *vb* **salved; salv·ing** : soothe

sal·ver \'salvər\ *n* : small tray

sal·vo \'salvō\ *n, pl* **-vos** *or* **-voes** : simultaneous discharge of guns

same \'sām\ *adj* : being the one referred to ∼ *pron* : the same one or ones ∼ *adv* : in the same manner — **same·ness** *n*

sam·ple \'sampəl\ *n* : piece or part that shows the quality of a whole ∼ *vb* **-pled; -pling** : judge by a sample

sam·pler \'samplər\ *n* : piece of needlework testing skill in embroidering

san·a·to·ri·um \ˌsanəˈtōrēəm\ *n, pl* **-riums** *or* **-ria** \-ēə\ : hospital for the chronically ill

sanc·ti·fy \ˈsaŋktəˌfī\ *vb* **-fied; -fy·ing** : make holy — **sanc·ti·fi·ca·tion** \ˌsaŋktəfəˈkāshən\ *n*

sanc·ti·mo·nious \ˌsaŋktəˈmō-nēəs\ *adj* : hypocritically pious — **sanc·ti·mo·nious·ly** *adv*

sanc·tion \ˈsaŋkshən\ *n* **1** : authoritative approval **2** : coercive measure — usu. pl ∼ *vb* : approve

sanc·ti·ty \ˈsaŋktətē\ *n, pl* **-ties** : quality or state of being holy or sacred

sanc·tu·ary \ˈsaŋkchəˌwerē\ *n, pl* **-ar·ies** **1** : consecrated place **2** : place of refuge

sand \ˈsand\ *n* : loose granular particles of rock ∼ *vb* : smooth with an abrasive — **sand·bank** *n* — **sand·er** *n* — **sand·storm** *n* — **sandy** *adj*

san·dal \ˈsandᵊl\ *n* : shoe consisting of a sole strapped to the foot

sand·pa·per *n* : abrasive paper — **sandpaper** *vb*

sand·pip·er \-ˌpīpər\ *n* : long-billed shorebird

sand·stone *n* : rock made of naturally cemented sand

sand·wich \ˈsandˌwich\ *n* : 2 or more slices of bread with a filling between them ∼ *vb* : squeeze or crowd in

sane \ˈsān\ *adj* **san·er; san·est** **1** : mentally healthy **2** : sensible — **sane·ly** *adv*

sang *past of* SING

san·gui·nary \ˈsaŋgwəˌnerē\ *adj* : bloody

san·guine \ˈsaŋgwən\ *adj* **1** : reddish **2** : cheerful

san·i·tar·i·um \ˌsanəˈterēəm\ *n, pl* **-i·ums** *or* **-ia** \-ēə\ : sanatorium

san·i·tary \ˈsanəterē\ *adj* **1** : relating to health **2** : free from filth or infective matter

san·i·ta·tion \ˌsanəˈtāshən\ *n* : protection of health by maintenance of sanitary conditions

san·i·ty \ˈsanətē\ *n* : soundness of mind

sank *past of* SINK

¹sap \ˈsap\ *n* **1** : fluid that circulates through a plant **2** : gullible person

²sap *vb* **-pp-** **1** : undermine **2** : weaken or exhaust gradually

sa·pi·ent \ˈsāpēənt, ˈsapē-\ *adj* : wise — **sa·pi·ence** \-əns\ *n*

sap·ling \ˈsapliŋ\ *n* : young tree

sap·phire \ˈsafˌīr\ *n* : hard transparent blue gem

sap·py \ˈsapē\ *adj* **-pi·er; -est** **1** : full of sap **2** : overly sentimental

sap·suck·er \ˈsapˌsəkər\ *n* : small No. American woodpecker

sar·casm \'sär,kazəm\ *n* **1** : cutting remark **2** : ironical criticism or reproach — **sar·cas·tic** \sär'kastik\ *adj* — **sar·cas·ti·cal·ly** *adv*

sar·coph·a·gus \sär'käfəgəs\ *n, pl* **-gi** \-,gī, -,jī\ : large stone coffin

sar·dine \sär'dēn\ *n* : small fish preserved for use as food

sar·don·ic \sär'dänik\ *adj* : disdainfully humorous — **sar·don·i·cal·ly** *adv*

sa·rong \sə'röŋ, -'räŋ\ *n* : loose garment worn esp. by Pacific islanders

sar·sa·pa·ril·la \,saspə'rilə, ,särs-\ *n* : dried roots of a tropical American plant used esp. for flavoring or a carbonated drink flavored with this

sar·to·ri·al \sär'tōrēəl\ *adj* : relating to a tailor or men's clothes

¹**sash** \'sash\ *n* : broad band worn around the waist or over the shoulder

²**sash** *n, pl* **sash** **1** : frame for a pane of glass in a door or window **2** : movable part of a window

sas·sa·fras \'sasə,fras\ *n* : No. American tree or its dried root bark

sassy \'sasē\ *adj* **sass·i·er; -est** : saucy

sat *past of* SIT

Sa·tan \'sāt²n\ *n* : devil — **sa·tan·ic** \sə'tanik, sā-\ *adj* — **sa·tan·i·cal·ly** *adv*

satch·el \'sachəl\ *n* : small bag

sate \'sāt\ *vb* **sat·ed; sat·ing** : satisfy fully

sat·el·lite \'sat²l,īt\ *n* **1** : toady **2** : body or object that revolves around a larger celestial body

sa·ti·ate \'sāshē,āt\ *vb* **-at·ed; -at·ing** : sate — **sa·ti·ety** \sə'tīətē\ *n*

sat·in \'sat²n\ *n* : glossy fabric — **sat·iny** *adj*

sat·ire \'sa,tīr\ *n* : literary ridicule done with humor — **sa·tir·ic** \sə'tirik\, **sa·tir·i·cal** \-ikəl\ *adj* — **sa·tir·i·cal·ly** *adv* — **sat·i·rist** \'satərist\ *n* — **sat·i·rize** \-ə,rīz\ *vb*

sat·is·fac·tion \,satəs'fakshən\ *n* : state of being satisfied — **sat·is·fac·to·ri·ly** \-'faktərəlē\ *adv* — **sat·is·fac·to·ry** \-'faktərē\ *adj*

sat·is·fy \'satəs,fī\ *vb* **-fied; -fy·ing** **1** : make happy **2** : pay what is due to or on — **sat·is·fy·ing·ly** *adv*

sat·u·rate \'sachə,rāt\ *vb* **-rat·ed; -rat·ing** : soak or charge thoroughly — **sat·u·ra·tion** \,sachə'rāshən\ *n*

Sat·ur·day \'satərdā, -dē\ *n* : 7th day of the week

sat·ur·nine \'satər,nīn\ *adj* : sullen

sa·tyr \'sātər, 'sat-\ *n* : pleasure-loving forest god of ancient Greece

sauce \'sȯs\ *n* : fluid dressing or topping for food — **sauce-pan** *n*

sau·cer \'sȯsər\ *n* : small shallow dish under a cup

saucy \'sasē, 'sȯsē\ *adj* **sauc·i·er; -est** : insolent — **sauc·i·ly** *adv* — **sauc·i·ness** *n*

sau·er·kraut \'saủər,kraủt\ *n* : finely cut and fermented cabbage

sau·na \'saủnə\ *n* : steam or dry heat bath or a room or cabinet used for such a bath

saun·ter \'sȯntər, 'sänt-\ *vb* : stroll

sau·sage \'sȯsij\ *n* : minced and highly seasoned meat

sau·té \sȯ'tā, sō-\ *vb* **-téed** *or* **-téd; -té·ing** : fry in a little fat — **sauté** *n*

sav·age \'savij\ *adj* **1** : wild **2** : cruel ～ *n* : person belonging to a primitive society — **sav·age·ly** *adv* — **sav·age·ness** *n* — **sav·age·ry** *n*

¹**save** \'sāv\ *vb* **saved; sav·ing 1** : rescue from danger **2** : guard from destruction **3** : redeem from sin **4** : put aside as a reserve — **sav·er** *n*

²**save** *prep* : except

sav·ior, sav·iour \'sāvyər\ *n* **1** : one who saves **2** *cap* : Jesus Christ

sa·vor \'sāvər\ *n* : special flavor ～ *vb* : taste with pleasure — **sa·vory** *adj*

¹**saw** *past of* SEE

²**saw** \'sȯ\ *n* : cutting tool with teeth ～ *vb* **sawed; sawed** *or* **sawn; saw·ing** : cut with a saw — **saw·dust** \-,dəst\ *n* — **saw·mill** *n* — **saw·yer** \-yər\ *n*

saw·horse *n* : support for wood being sawed

sax·o·phone \'saksə,fōn\ *n* : wind instrument with a reed mouthpiece and usu. a bent metal body

say \'sā\ *vb* **said** \'sed\; **say·ing** \'sāiŋ\; **says** \'sez\ **1** : express in words **2** : state positively ～ *n, pl* **says** \'sāz\ **1** : expression of opinion **2** : power of decision

say·ing \'sāiŋ\ *n* : commonly repeated statement

scab \'skab\ *n* **1** : protective crust over a sore or wound **2** : worker taking a striker's job ～ *vb* **-bb- 1** : become covered with a scab **2** : work as a scab — **scab·by** *adj*

scab·bard \'skabərd\ *n* : sheath for the blade of a weapon

scaf·fold \'skafəld, -,ōld\ *n* **1** : raised platform for workmen **2** : platform on which a criminal is executed

scald \'skȯld\ *vb* **1** : burn with hot liquid or steam **2** : heat to the boiling point

¹scale \'skāl\ *n* : weighing device ~ *vb* **scaled; scal·ing** : weigh

²scale *n* **1** : thin plate esp. on the body of a fish or reptile **2** : thin coating or layer ~ *vb* **scaled; scal·ing** : strip of scales — **scaled** \'skāld\ *adj* — **scaleless** *adj* — **scaly** *adj*

³scale *n* **1** : graduated series **2** : size of a sample (as a model) in proportion to the size of the actual thing **3** : standard of estimation or judgment **4** : series of musical tones ~ *vb* **scaled; scal·ing 1** : climb by a ladder **2** : arrange in a graded series

scal·lion \'skalyən\ *n* : bulbless onion

scal·lop \'skäləp, 'skal-\ *n* **1** : marine mollusk **2** : rounded projection on a border

scalp \'skalp\ *n* : skin and flesh of the head ~ *vb* **1** : remove the scalp from **2** : resell at a greatly increased price — **scalp·er** *n*

scal·pel \'skalpəl\ *n* : surgical knife

scamp \'skamp\ *n* : rascal

scam·per \'skampər\ *vb* : run nimbly — **scamper** *n*

scan \'skan\ *vb* **-nn- 1** : read (verses) so as to show meter **2** : examine closely or hastily **3** : examine with a sensing device — **scan** *n* — **scan·ner** *n*

scan·dal \'skand³l\ *n* **1** : disgraceful situation **2** : mali-

cious gossip — **scan·dal·ize** *vb* — **scan·dal·ous** *adj*

scant \'skant\ *adj* : barely sufficient ~ *vb* : stint — **scant·i·ly** *adv* — **scanty** *adj*

scape·goat \'skāp,gōt\ *n* : one that bears the blame for others

scap·u·la \'skapyələ\ *n, pl* **-lae** \-,lē\ *or* **-las** : shoulder blade

scar \'skär\ *n* : mark where a wound has healed — **scar** *vb*

scar·ab \'skarəb\ *n* : large dark beetle or an ornament representing one

scarce \'skers\ *adj* **scarc·er; scarc·est** : lacking in quantity or number — **scar·ci·ty** \'skersətē\ *n*

scarce·ly \'skerslē\ *adv* **1** : barely **2** : almost not

scare \'sker\ *vb* **scared; scaring** : frighten ~ *n* : fright — **scary** *adj*

scare·crow \'sker,krō\ *n* : figure for scaring birds from crops

scarf \'skärf\ *n, pl* **scarves** \'skärvz\ *or* **scarfs** : cloth worn about the shoulders or the neck

scar·let \'skärlət\ *n* : bright red color — **scarlet** *adj*

scarlet fever *n* : acute contagious disease marked by fever, sore throat, and red rash

scath·ing \'skā<u>th</u>iŋ\ *adj* : bitterly severe

scat·ter \'skatər\ *vb* **1** : spread about irregularly **2** : disperse

scav·en·ger \\'skavənjər\\ *n* **1** : person that collects refuse or waste **2** : animal that feeds on decayed matter — **scav·enge** \\'skavənj\\ *vb*

sce·nar·io \\sə'narē͵ō, -'när-\\ *n, pl* **-i·os 1** : plot of a play or movie **2** : possible sequence of events

scene \\'sēn\\ *n* **1** : single situation in a play or movie **2** : stage setting **3** : view **4** : display of emotion — **sce·nic** \\'sēnik\\ *adj*

scen·ery \\'sēnərē\\ *n, pl* **-er·ies 1** : painted setting for a stage **2** : picturesque view

scent \\'sent\\ *vb* **1** : smell **2** : fill with odor ∼ *n* **1** : odor **2** : sense of smell **3** : perfume — **scent·ed** \\'sentəd\\ *adj*

scep·ter \\'septər\\ *n* : staff signifying authority

scep·tic \\'skeptik\\ *var of* SKEPTIC

sched·ule \\'skejül, *esp Brit* 'shedyül\\ *n* : list showing sequence of events ∼ *vb* **-uled; -ul·ing** : make a schedule of

scheme \\'skēm\\ *n* **1** : crafty plot **2** : systematic design ∼ *vb* **schemed; schem·ing** : form a plot — **sche·mat·ic** \\ski'matik\\ *adj* — **schem·er** *n*

schism \\'sizəm, 'skiz-\\ *n* : split — **schis·mat·ic** \\siz'matik, skiz-\\ *n or adj*

schizo·phre·nia \\͵skitsə'frē-nēə\\ *n* : severe mental illness

— **schiz·oid** \\'skit͵sȯid\\ *adj or n* — **schizo·phren·ic** \\͵skitsə-'frenik\\ *adj or n*

schol·ar \\'skälər\\ *n* : student or learned person — **schol·ar·ly** *adj*

schol·ar·ship \\-͵ship\\ *n* **1** : qualities or learning of a scholar **2** : money given to a student to pay for education

scho·las·tic \\skə'lastik\\ *adj* : relating to schools, scholars, or scholarship

¹**school** \\'skül\\ *n* **1** : institution for learning **2** : pupils in a school **3** : group with shared beliefs ∼ *vb* : teach — **school·boy** *n* — **school·girl** *n* — **school·house** *n* — **school·mate** *n* — **school·room** *n* — **school·teach·er** *n*

²**school** *n* : large number of fish swimming together

schoo·ner \\'skünər\\ *n* : sailing ship

sci·ence \\'sīəns\\ *n* : branch of systematic study esp. of the physical world — **sci·en·tif·ic** \\͵sīən'tifik\\ *adj* — **sci·en·tif·i·cal·ly** *adv* — **sci·en·tist** \\'sīəntist\\ *n*

scin·til·late \\'sint³l͵āt\\ *vb* **-lat·ed; -lat·ing** : flash — **scin·til·la·tion** \\͵sint³l'āshən\\ *n*

scin·til·lat·ing *adj* : brilliantly lively or witty

sci·on \\'sīən\\ *n* : descendant

scis·sors \\'sizərz\ *n pl* : small shears

scoff \\'skäf\ *vb* : mock — **scoff·er** *n*

scold \\'skōld\ *n* : person who scolds ~ *vb* : criticize severely

scoop \\'sküp\ *n* : shovellike utensil ~ *vb* **1** : take out with a scoop **2** : dig out

scoot \\'süt\ *vb* : move swiftly

scoot·er \\'skütər\ *n* : child's foot-propelled vehicle

¹scope \\'skōp\ *n* **1** : extent **2** : room for development

²scope *n* : viewing device (as a microscope)

scorch \\'skȯrch\ *vb* : burn the surface of

score \\'skōr\ *n, pl* **scores 1** *or pl* **score** : twenty **2** : cut **3** : record of points made (as in a game) **4** : debt **5** : music of a composition ~ *vb* **scored; scor·ing 1** : record **2** : mark with lines **3** : gain in a game **4** : assign a grade to **5** : compose a score for — **score·less** *adj* — **scor·er** *n*

scorn \\'skȯrn\ *n* : emotion involving both anger and disgust ~ *vb* : hold in contempt — **scorn·er** *n* — **scorn·ful** \-fəl\ *adj* — **scorn·ful·ly** *adv*

scor·pi·on \\'skȯrpēən\ *n* : poisonous long-tailed animal

scoun·drel \\'skaündrəl\ *n* : villain

¹scour \\'skaůər\ *vb* : examine thoroughly

²scour *vb* : rub in order to clean

scourge \\'skərj\ *n* **1** : whip **2** : punishment ~ *vb* **scourged; scourg·ing 1** : lash **2** : punish severely

scout \\'skaůt\ *vb* : inspect or observe to get information ~ *n* : person sent out to get information

scow \\'skaů\ *n* : large flat‐bottomed boat with square ends

scowl \\'skaůl\ *vb* : make a frowning expression of displeasure — **scowl** *n*

scrag·gly \\'skraglē\ *adj* : irregular or unkempt

scram \\'skram\ *vb* **-mm-** : go away at once

scram·ble \\'skrambəl\ *vb* **-bled; -bling 1** : clamber clumsily around **2** : struggle for possession of something **3** : mix together **4** : cook (eggs) by stirring during frying — **scramble** *n*

¹scrap \\'skrap\ *n* **1** : fragment **2** : discarded material ~ *vb* **-pp-** : get rid of as useless

²scrap *vb* **-pp-** : fight — **scrap** *n* — **scrap·per** *n*

scrap·book *n* : blank book in which mementos are kept

scrape \\'skrāp\ *vb* **scraped; scrap·ing 1** : remove by drawing a knife over **2** : clean or smooth by rubbing **3** : draw across a surface with a grating sound **4 :** damage by contact with a rough surface **5 :** gather or proceed with difficulty **∼** *n* **1 :** act of scraping **2 :** predicament — **scrap·er** *n*

scratch \\'skrach\\ *vb* **1 :** scrape or dig with or as if with claws or nails **2 :** cause to move gratingly **3 :** delete by or as if by drawing a line through **∼** *n* **:** mark or sound made in scratching — **scratchy** *adj*

scrawl \\'skrȯl\\ *vb* **:** write hastily and carelessly — **scrawl** *n*

scraw·ny \\'skrȯnē\\ *adj* **-ni·er; -est :** very thin

scream \\'skrēm\\ *vb* **:** cry out loudly and shrilly **∼** *n* **:** loud shrill cry

screech \\'skrēch\\ *vb or n* **:** shriek

screen \\'skrēn\\ *n* **1 :** device or partition used to protect or decorate **2 :** surface on which pictures appear (as in movies) **∼** *vb* **:** shield or separate with or as if with a screen

screw \\'skrü\\ *n* **1 :** grooved fastening device **2 :** propeller **∼** *vb* **1 :** fasten by means of a screw **2 :** move spirally

screw·driv·er \\'skrü,drīvər\\ *n* **:** tool for turning screws

scrib·ble \\'skribəl\\ *vb* **-bled; -bling :** write hastily or carelessly — **scribble** *n* — **scrib·bler** \\-ələr\\ *n*

scribe \\'skrīb\\ *n* **:** one who writes or copies writing

scrimp \\'skrimp\\ *vb* **:** economize greatly

scrip \\'skrip\\ *n* **1 :** paper money for less than a dollar **2 :** certificate entitling one to something (as stock)

script \\'skript\\ *n* **:** text (as of a play)

scrip·ture \\'skripchər\\ *n* **:** sacred writings of a religion — **scrip·tur·al** \\'skripchərəl\\ *adj*

scroll \\'skrōl\\ *n* **1 :** roll of paper for writing a document **2 :** spiral or coiled design

scro·tum \\'skrōtəm\\ *n, pl* **-ta** \\-ə\\ *or* **-tums :** pouch containing the testes

scrounge \\'skraunj\\ *vb* **scrounged; scroung·ing :** collect by or as if by foraging

¹scrub \\'skrəb\\ *n* **:** stunted tree or shrub or a growth of these — **scrub** *adj* — **scrub·by** *adj*

²scrub *vb* **-bb- :** clean or wash by rubbing — **scrub** *n*

scruff \\'skrəf\\ *n* **:** loose skin of the back of the neck

scrump·tious \\'skrəmpshəs\\ *adj* **:** delicious

scru·ple \\'skrüpəl\\ *n* **:** reluctance due to ethical considerations — **scruple** *vb* — **scru·pu·lous** \\-pyələs\\ *adj* — **scru·pu·lous·ly** *adv*

scru·ti·ny \\'skrüt°nē\\ *n, pl* **-nies** : careful inspection — **scru·ti·nize** \\-°n‚īz\\ *vb*

scud \\'skəd\\ *vb* **-dd-** : move speedily

scuff \\'skəf\\ *vb* : scratch, scrape, or wear away — **scuff** *n*

scuf·fle \\'skəfəl\\ *vb* **-fled; -fling** **1** : struggle at close quarters **2** : shuffle one's feet — **scuffle** *n*

scull \\'skəl\\ *n* **1** : oar **2** : racing shell propelled with sculls ∼ *vb* : propel a boat by an oar over the stern

scul·lery \\'skələrē\\ *n, pl* **-leries** : room for cleaning dishes and cookware

sculpt \\'skəlpt\\ *vb* : sculpture

sculp·ture \\'skəlpchər\\ *n* : work of art carved or molded ∼ *vb* **-tured; -tur·ing** : form as sculpture — **sculp·tor** \\-tər\\ *n* — **sculp·tur·al** \\-chərəl\\ *adj*

scum \\'skəm\\ *n* : slimy film on a liquid

scur·ri·lous \\'skərələs\\ *adj* : vulgar or abusive

scur·ry \\'skərē\\ *vb* **-ried; -ry·ing** : scamper

scur·vy \\'skərvē\\ *n* : vitamin‑deficiency disease

¹scut·tle \\'skət°l\\ *n* : pail for coal

²scuttle *vb* **-tled; -tling** : sink (a ship) by cutting holes in its bottom

³scuttle *vb* **-tled; -tling** : scamper

scythe \\'sīth\\ *n* : tool for mowing by hand — **scythe** *vb*

sea \\'sē\\ *n* **1** : large body of salt water **2** : ocean **3** : rough water — **sea** *adj* — **sea·coast** *n* — **sea·food** *n* — **sea·port** *n* — **sea·shore** *n* — **sea·wa·ter** *n*

sea·bird *n* : bird frequenting the open ocean

sea·board *n* : country's seacoast

sea·far·er \\-‚farər\\ *n* : seaman — **sea·far·ing** \\-‚fariŋ\\ *adj or n*

sea horse *n* : small fish with a horselike head

¹seal \\'sēl\\ *n* : large sea mammal of cold regions — **seal·skin** *n*

²seal *n* **1** : device for stamping a design **2** : something that closes ∼ *vb* **1** : affix a seal to **2** : close up securely **3** : determine finally — **seal·ant** \\-ənt\\ *n* — **seal·er** *n*

sea lion *n* : large Pacific seal with external ears

seam \\'sēm\\ *n* **1** : line of junction of 2 edges **2** : layer of a mineral ∼ *vb* : join by sewing — **seam·less** *adj*

sea·man \\'sēmən\\ *n* **1** : one who helps to handle a ship **2** : naval enlisted man ranking next below a petty officer third class — **sea·man·ship** *n*

seaman apprentice *n* : naval enlisted man ranking next below a seaman

seaman recruit *n* : naval enlisted man of the lowest rank

seam·stress \\'sēmstrəs\\ *n* : woman who sews

seamy \'sēmē\ *adj* **seam·i·er; -est** : unpleasant or sordid

sé·ance \'sā,äns\ *n* : meeting for communicating with spirits

sea·plane *n* : airplane that can take off from and land on the water

sear \'sir\ *vb* : scorch — **sear** *n*

search \'sərch\ *vb* **1** : look through **2** : seek — **search** *n* — **search·er** *n* — **search·light** *n*

search engine *n* : computer software used to search for specified information on the World Wide Web

sea·sick *adj* : nauseated by the motion of a ship — **sea·sick·ness** *n*

¹sea·son \'sēz°n\ *n* **1** : division of the year **2** : customary time for something — **sea·son·al** \'sēz°nəl\ *adj* — **sea·son·al·ly** *adv*

²season *vb* **1** : add spice to (food) **2** : make strong or fit for use — **sea·son·ing** \-°niŋ\ *n*

sea·son·able \'sēznəbəl\ *adj* : occurring at a suitable time — **sea·son·ably** \-blē\ *adv*

seat \'sēt\ *n* **1** : place to sit **2** : chair, bench, or stool for sitting on **3** : place that serves as a capital or center ∼ *vb* **1** : place in or on a seat **2** : provide seats for

sea·weed *n* : marine alga

sea·wor·thy *adj* : strong enough to hold up to a sea voyage

se·cede \si'sēd\ *vb* **-ced·ed; -ced·ing** : withdraw from a body (as a nation)

se·clude \si'klüd\ *vb* **-clud·ed; -clud·ing** : shut off alone — **se·clu·sion** \si'klüzhən\ *n*

¹sec·ond \'sekənd\ *adj* : next after the 1st ∼ *n* **1** : one that is second **2** : one who assists (as in a duel) — **second, sec·ond·ly** *adv*

²second *n* **1** : 60th part of a minute **2** : moment

sec·ond·ary \'sekən,derē\ *adj* **1** : second in rank or importance **2** : coming after the primary or elementary

sec·ond·hand *adj* **1** : not original **2** : used before

second lieutenant *n* : lowest ranking commissioned officer of the army, air force, or marines

se·cret \'sēkrət\ *adj* **1** : hidden **2** : kept from general knowledge — **se·cre·cy** \-krəsē\ *n* — **secret** *n* — **se·cre·tive** \'sēkrətiv, si'krēt-\ *adj* — **se·cret·ly** *adv*

sec·re·tar·i·at \,sekrə'terēət\ *n* : administrative department

sec·re·tary \'sekrə,terē\ *n, pl* **-tar·ies 1** : one hired to handle correspondence and other tasks for a superior **2** : official in charge of correspondence or records **3** : head of a government department — **sec·re·tari·al** \ˌsekrə'terēəl\ *adj*

¹**se·crete** \si'krēt\ *vb* **-cret·ed; -cret·ing** : produce as a secretion

²**se·crete** \si'krēt, 'sēkrət\ *vb* **-cret·ed; -cret·ing** : hide

se·cre·tion \si'krēshən\ *n* **1** : process of secreting **2** : product of glandular activity

sect \'sekt\ *n* : religious group

sec·tar·i·an \sek'terēən\ *adj* **1** : relating to a sect **2** : limited in character or scope ~ *n* : member of a sect

sec·tion \'sekshən\ *n* : distinct part — **sec·tion·al** \-shənəl\ *adj*

sec·tor \'sektər\ *n* **1** : part of a circle between 2 radii **2** : distinctive part

sec·u·lar \'sekyələr\ *adj* **1** : not sacred **2** : not monastic

se·cure \si'kyùr\ *adj* **-cur·er; -est** : free from danger or loss ~ *vb* **1** : fasten safely **2** : get — **se·cure·ly** *adv*

se·cu·ri·ty \si'kyùrətē\ *n, pl* **-ties** **1** : safety **2** : something given to guarantee payment **3** *pl* : bond or stock certificates

se·dan \si'dan\ *n* **1** : chair carried by 2 men **2** : enclosed automobile

¹**se·date** \si'dāt\ *adj* : quiet and dignified — **se·date·ly** *adv*

²**sedate** *vb* **-dat·ed; -dat·ing** : dose with sedatives — **se·da·tion** \si'dāshən\ *n*

sed·a·tive \'sedətiv\ *adj* : serving to relieve tension ~ *n* : sedative drug

sed·en·tary \'sedᵊnˌterē\ *adj* : characterized by much sitting

sedge \'sej\ *n* : grasslike marsh plant

sed·i·ment \'sedəmənt\ *n* : material that settles to the bottom of a liquid or is deposited by water or a glacier — **sed·i·men·ta·ry** \ˌsedə'mentərē\ *adj* — **sed·i·men·ta·tion** \-mən'tāshən, -ˌmen-\ *n*

se·di·tion \si'dishən\ *n* : revolution against a government — **se·di·tious** \-əs\ *adj*

se·duce \si'düs, -'dyüs\ *vb* **-duced; -duc·ing** **1** : lead astray **2** : entice to sexual intercourse — **se·duc·er** *n* — **se·duc·tion** \-'dəkshən\ *n* — **se·duc·tive** \-tiv\ *adj*

sed·u·lous \'sejələs\ *adj* : diligent

¹**see** \'sē\ *vb* **saw** \'sȯ\; **seen** \'sēn\; **see·ing** **1** : perceive by the eye **2** : have experience of **3** : understand **4** : make sure **5** : meet with or escort

²**see** *n* : jurisdiction of a bishop

seed \'sēd\ *n, pl* **seed** *or* **seeds** **1** : part by which a plant is propagated **2** : source ~ *vb* **1** : sow **2** : remove seeds from — **seed·less** *adj*

seed·ling \-liŋ\ *n* : young plant grown from seed

seedy \-ē\ *adj* **seed·i·er; -est 1** : full of seeds **2** : shabby

seek \'sēk\ *vb* **sought** \'sȯt\; **seek·ing 1** : search for **2** : try to reach or obtain — **seek·er** *n*

seem \'sēm\ *vb* : give the impression of being — **seem·ing·ly** *adv*

seem·ly \-lē\ *adj* **seem·li·er; -est** : proper or fit

seep \'sēp\ *vb* : leak through fine pores or cracks — **seep·age** \'sēpij\ *n*

seer \'sēər\ *n* : one who foresees or predicts events

seer·suck·er \'sir,səkər\ *n* : light puckered fabric

see·saw \'sē,sȯ\ *n* : board balanced in the middle — **seesaw** *vb*

seethe \'sēth\ *vb* **seethed; seething** : become violently agitated

seg·ment \'segmənt\ *n* : division of a thing — **seg·ment·ed** \-,mentəd\ *adj*

seg·re·gate \'segri,gāt\ *vb* **-gat·ed; -gat·ing 1** : cut off from others **2** : separate by races — **seg·re·ga·tion** \,segri'gā-shən\ *n*

seine \'sān\ *n* : large weighted fishing net ~ *vb* : fish with a seine

seis·mic \'sīzmik, 'sīs-\ *adj* : relating to an earthquake

seis·mo·graph \-mə,graf\ *n* : apparatus for detecting earthquakes

seize \'sēz\ *vb* **seized; seiz·ing** : take by force — **sei·zure** \'sēzhər\ *n*

sel·dom \'seldəm\ *adv* : not often

se·lect \sə'lekt\ *adj* **1** : favored **2** : discriminating ~ *vb* : take by preference — **se·lec·tive** \-'lektiv\ *adj*

se·lec·tion \sə'lekshən\ *n* : act of selecting or thing selected

se·lect·man \si'lekt,man, -mən\ *n* : New England town official

self \'self\ *n, pl* **selves** \'selvz\ : essential person distinct from others

self- *comb form* **1** : oneself or itself **2** : of oneself or itself **3** : by oneself or automatic **4** : to, for, or toward oneself

self–cen·tered *adj* : concerned only with one's own self

List of self-explanatory words with the prefix *self-*

self–addressed	self–assertive	self–cleaning
self–administered	self–assurance	self–closing
self–analysis	self–assured	self–complacent
self–appointed	self–awareness	self–conceit

self·con·scious *adj* : uncomfortably aware of oneself as an object of observation — **self·con·scious·ly** *adv* — **self·conscious·ness** *n*

self·ish \'selfish\ *adj* : excessively or exclusively concerned with one's own well-being — **self·ish·ly** *adv* — **self·ish·ness** *n*

self·less \'selfləs\ *adj* : unselfish — **self·less·ness** *n*

self–made *adj* : having succeeded by one's own efforts

self–righ·teous *adj* : strongly convinced of one's own righteousness

self·same \'self₁sām\ *adj* : precisely the same

sell \'sel\ *vb* **sold** \'sōld\; **sell·ing 1** : transfer (property) esp. for money **2** : deal in as a business **3** : be sold — **sell·er** *n*

selves *pl of* SELF

se·man·tic \si'mantik\ *adj* : relating to meaning in language — **se·man·tics** \-iks\ *n sing or pl*

self–confessed	self–esteem	self–possession
self–confidence	self–evident	self–preservation
self–confident	self–explanatory	self–proclaimed
self–contained	self–expression	self–propelled
self–contempt	self–fulfilling	self–propelling
self–contradiction	self–fulfillment	self–protection
self–contradictory	self–governing	self–reliance
self–control	self–government	self–reliant
self–created	self–help	self–respect
self–criticism	self–image	self–respecting
self–defeating	self–importance	self–restraint
self–defense	self–important	self–sacrifice
self–denial	self–imposed	self–satisfaction
self–denying	self–improvement	self–satisfied
self–destruction	self–indulgence	self–service
self–destructive	self–indulgent	self–serving
self–determination	self–inflicted	self–starting
self–determined	self–interest	self–styled
self–discipline	self–love	self–sufficiency
self–doubt	self–operating	self–sufficient
self–educated	self–pity	self–supporting
self–employed	self–portrait	self–taught
self–employment	self–possessed	self–winding

sem·a·phore \\'semə₁fōr\ *n* **1** : visual signaling apparatus **2** : signaling by flags

sem·blance \\'sembləns\ *n* : appearance

se·men \\'sēmən\ *n* : male reproductive fluid

se·mes·ter \sə'mestər\ *n* : half a school year

semi- \₁semi, 'sem-, -₁ī\ *prefix* **1** : half **2** : partial

semi·co·lon \\'semi₁kōlən\ *n* : punctuation mark ;

semi·con·duc·tor *n* : substance between a conductor and a nonconductor in ability to conduct electricity — **semi·con·duct·ing** *adj*

semi·fi·nal *adj* : being next to the final — **semifinal** *n*

semi·for·mal *adj* : being or suitable for an occasion of moderate formality

sem·i·nal \\'semən⁽ə⁾l\ *adj* **1** : relating to seed or semen **2** : causing or influencing later development

sem·i·nar \\'semə₁när\ *n* : conference or conferencelike study

sem·i·nary \\'semə₁nerē\ *n, pl* **-nar·ies** : school and esp. a theological school — **sem·i·nar·i·an** \₁semə'nerēən\ *n*

sen·ate \\'senət\ *n* : upper branch of a legislature — **sen·a·tor** \-ər\ *n* — **sen·a·to·rial** \₁senə'tōrēəl\ *adj*

send \\'send\ *vb* **sent** \\'sent\; **send·ing** **1** : cause to go **2** : propel — **send·er** *n*

se·nile \\'sēn₁īl, 'sen-\ *adj* : mentally deficient through old age — **se·nil·i·ty** \si'nilətē\ *n*

se·nior \\'sēnyər\ *adj* : older or higher ranking — **senior** *n* — **se·nior·i·ty** \₁sēn'yòrətē\ *n*

senior chief petty officer *n* : petty officer in the navy or coast guard ranking next below a master chief petty officer

senior master sergeant *n* : noncommissioned officer in the air force ranking next below a chief master sergeant

sen·sa·tion \sen'sāshən\ *n* **1** : bodily feeling **2** : condition of excitement or the cause of it — **sen·sa·tion·al** \-shənəl\ *adj*

sense \\'sens\ *n* **1** : meaning **2** : faculty of perceiving something physical **3** : sound mental capacity ∼ *vb* **sensed**; **sens·ing** **1** : perceive by the senses **2** : detect automatically — **sense·less** *adj* — **sense·less·ly** *adv*

sen·si·bil·i·ty \₁sensə'bilətē\ *n, pl* **-ties** : delicacy of feeling

sen·si·ble \\'sensəbəl\ *adj* **1** : capable of sensing or being sensed **2** : aware or conscious **3** : reasonable — **sen·si·bly** \-blē\ *adv*

sen·si·tive \\'sensətiv\ *adj* **1** : subject to excitation by or responsive to stimuli **2** : having power of feeling **3** : easily affected — **sen·si·tive·ness** *n* — **sen·si·tiv·i·ty** \ˌsensəˈtivətē\ *n*

sen·si·tize \ˈsensəˌtīz\ *vb* **-tized; -tiz·ing** : make or become sensitive

sen·sor \ˈsenˌsȯr, -sər\ *n* : device that responds to a physical stimulus

sen·so·ry \ˈsensərē\ *adj* : relating to sensation or the senses

sen·su·al \ˈsenchəwəl, -shəwəl\ *adj* **1** : pleasing the senses **2** : devoted to the pleasures of the senses — **sen·su·al·ist** *n* — **sen·su·al·i·ty** \ˌsenchəˈwalətē\ *n* — **sen·su·al·ly** *adv*

sen·su·ous \ˈsenchəwəs\ *adj* : having strong appeal to the senses

sent *past of* SEND

sen·tence \ˈsentᵊns, -ᵊnz\ *n* **1** : judgment of a court **2** : grammatically self-contained speech unit ∼ *vb* **-tenced; -tenc·ing** : impose a sentence on

sen·ten·tious \senˈtenchəs\ *adj* : using pompous language

sen·tient \ˈsenchēənt\ *adj* : capable of feeling

sen·ti·ment \ˈsentəmənt\ *n* **1** : belief **2** : feeling

sen·ti·men·tal \ˌsentəˈmentᵊl\ *adj* : influenced by tender feelings — **sen·ti·men·tal·ism** *n*

— **sen·ti·men·tal·ist** *n* — **sen·ti·men·tal·i·ty** \-ˌmenˈtalətē, -mən-\ *n* — **sen·ti·men·tal·ize** \-ˈmentᵊlˌīz\ *vb* — **sen·ti·men·tal·ly** *adv*

sen·ti·nel \ˈsentᵊnəl\ *n* : sentry

sen·try \ˈsentrē\ *n, pl* **-tries** : one who stands guard

se·pal \ˈsēpəl, ˈsep-\ *n* : modified leaf in a flower calyx

sep·a·rate \ˈsepəˌrāt\ *vb* **-rat·ed; -rat·ing** **1** : set or keep apart **2** : become divided or detached ∼ \ˈseprət, ˈsepə-\ *adj* **1** : not connected or shared **2** : distinct from each other — **sep·a·ra·ble** \ˈsepərəbəl\ *adj* — **sep·a·rate·ly** *adv* — **sep·a·ra·tion** \ˌsepəˈrāshən\ *n* — **sep·a·ra·tor** \ˈsepəˌrātər\ *n*

se·pia \ˈsēpēə\ *n* : brownish gray

Sep·tem·ber \sepˈtembər\ *n* : 9th month of the year having 30 days

sep·ul·chre, sep·ul·cher \ˈsepəlkər\ *n* : burial vault — **se·pul·chral** \səˈpəlkrəl\ *adj*

se·quel \ˈsēkwəl\ *n* **1** : consequence or result **2** : continuation of a story

se·quence \ˈsēkwəns\ *n* : continuous or connected series — **se·quen·tial** \siˈkwenchəl\ *adj* — **se·quen·tial·ly** *adv*

se·ques·ter \siˈkwestər\ *vb* : segregate

se·quin \ˈsēkwən\ *n* : spangle

se·quoia \si'kwȯiə\ *n* : huge California coniferous tree

sera *pl of* SERUM

ser·aph \'serəf\ *n, pl* **-a·phim** \-ə‚fim\ *or* **-aphs** : angel — **se·raph·ic** \sə'rafik\ *adj*

sere \'sir\ *adj* : dried up or withered

ser·e·nade \‚serə'nād\ *n* : music sung or played esp. to a woman being courted — **serenade** *vb*

ser·en·dip·i·ty \‚serən'dipətē\ *n* : good luck in finding things not sought for — **ser·en·dip·i·tous** \-əs\ *adj*

se·rene \sə'rēn\ *adj* : tranquil — **se·rene·ly** *adv* — **se·ren·i·ty** \sə'renətē\ *n*

serf \'sərf\ *n* : peasant obligated to work the land — **serf·dom** \-dəm\ *n*

serge \'sərj\ *n* : twilled woolen cloth

ser·geant \'särjənt\ *n* : noncommissioned officer (as in the army) ranking next below a staff sergeant

sergeant first class *n* : noncommissioned officer in the army ranking next below a master sergeant

sergeant major *n, pl* **sergeants major** *or* **sergeant majors** **1** : noncommissioned officer serving as an enlisted adviser in a headquarters **2** : noncommissioned officer in the ma-

rine corps ranking above a first sergeant

se·ri·al \'sirēəl\ *adj* : being or relating to a series or sequence ~ *n* : story appearing in parts — **se·ri·al·ly** *adv*

se·ries \'sirēz\ *n, pl* **series** : number of things in order

se·ri·ous \'sirēəs\ *adj* **1** : subdued in appearance or manner **2** : sincere **3** : of great importance — **se·ri·ous·ly** *adv* — **se·ri·ous·ness** *n*

ser·mon \'sərmən\ *n* : lecture on religion or behavior

ser·pent \'sərpənt\ *n* : snake — **ser·pen·tine** \-pən‚tēn, -‚tīn\ *adj*

ser·rated \'ser‚ātəd\ *adj* : saw-toothed

se·rum \'sirəm\ *n, pl* **-rums** *or* **-ra** \-ə\ : watery part of blood

ser·vant \'sərvənt\ *n* : person employed for domestic work

serve \'sərv\ *vb* **served; serving** **1** : work through or perform a term of service **2** : be of use **3** : prove adequate **4** : hand out (food or drink) **5** : be of service to — **serv·er** *n*

ser·vice \'sərvəs\ *n* **1** : act or means of serving **2** : meeting for worship **3** : branch of public employment or the persons in it **4** : set of dishes or silverware **5** : benefit ~ *vb* **-viced; -vic·ing** : repair — **ser·vice·able** *adj* — **ser·vice·man**

\-ˌman, -mən\ *n* — **ser·vice·wom·an** *n*

ser·vile \'sərvəl, -ˌvīl\ *adj* : behaving like a slave — **ser·vil·i·ty** \ˌsər'vilətē\ *n*

serv·ing \'sərviŋ\ *n* : helping

ser·vi·tude \'sərvəˌtüd, -ˌtyüd\ *n* : slavery

ses·a·me \'sesəmē\ *n* : annual herb or its seeds that are used in flavoring

ses·sion \'seshən\ *n* : meeting

set \'set\ *vb* **set; set·ting 1** : cause to sit **2** : place **3** : settle, arrange, or adjust **4** : cause to be or do **5** : become fixed or solid **6** : sink below the horizon ~ *adj* : settled ~ *n* **1** : group classed together **2** : setting for the scene of a play or film **3** : electronic apparatus **4** : collection of mathematical elements — **set forth** : begin a trip — **set off** *vb* : set forth — **set out** *vb* : begin a trip or undertaking — **set up** *vb* **1** : assemble or erect **2** : cause

set·back *n* : reverse

set·tee \se'tē\ *n* : bench or sofa

set·ter \'setər\ *n* : large long-coated hunting dog

set·ting \'setiŋ\ *n* : the time, place, and circumstances in which something occurs

set·tle \'set°l\ *vb* **-tled; -tling 1** : come to rest **2** : sink gradually **3** : establish in residence **4** : adjust or arrange **5** : calm **6** : dispose of (as by paying) **7** : decide or agree on — **set·tle·ment** \-mənt\ *n* — **set·tler** \'set°lər\ *n*

sev·en \'sevən\ *n* : one more than 6 — **seven** *adj or pron* — **sev·enth** \-ənth\ *adj or adv or n*

sev·en·teen \ˌsevən'tēn\ *n* : one more than 16 — **seventeen** *adj or pron* — **sev·en·teenth** \-'tēnth\ *adj or n*

sev·en·ty \'sevəntē\ *n, pl* **-ties** : 7 times 10 — **sev·en·ti·eth** \-tēəth\ *adj or n* — **seventy** *adj or pron*

sev·er \'sevər\ *vb* **-ered; -er·ing** : cut off or apart — **sev·er·ance** \'sevrəns, -vərəns\ *n*

sev·er·al \'sevrəl, 'sevə-\ *adj* **1** : distinct **2** : consisting of an indefinite but not large number — **sev·er·al·ly** *adv*

se·vere \sə'vir\ *adj* **-ver·er; -est 1** : strict **2** : restrained or unadorned **3** : painful or distressing **4** : hard to endure — **se·vere·ly** *adv* — **se·ver·i·ty** \-'verətē\ *n*

sew \'sō\ *vb* **sewed; sewn** \'sōn\ *or* **sewed; sew·ing** : join or fasten by stitches — **sew·ing** *n*

sew·age \'süij\ *n* : liquid household waste

¹sew·er \'sōər\ *n* : one that sews

²**sew·er** \'süər\ *n* : pipe or channel to carry off waste matter

sex \'seks\ *n* **1** : either of 2 divisions into which organisms are grouped according to their reproductive roles or the qualities which differentiate them **2** : copulation — **sexed** \'sekst\ *adj* — **sex·less** *adj* — **sex·u·al** \'sekshəwəl\ *adj* — **sex·u·al·i·ty** \ˌsekshə'walətē\ *n* — **sex·u·al·ly** *adv* — **sexy** *adj*

sex·ism \'sek,sizəm\ *n* : discrimination based on sex and esp. against women — **sex·ist** \'seksist\ *adj or n*

sex·tant \'sekstənt\ *n* : instrument for navigation

sex·tet \sek'stet\ *n* **1** : music for 6 performers **2** : group of 6

sex·ton \'sekstən\ *n* : church caretaker

shab·by \'shabē\ *adj* -**bi·er**; -**est** **1** : worn and faded **2** : dressed in worn clothes **3** : not generous or fair — **shab·bi·ly** *adv* — **shab·bi·ness** *n*

shack \'shak\ *n* : hut

shack·le \'shakəl\ *n* : metal device to bind legs or arms ~ *vb* -**led**; -**ling** : bind or fasten with shackles

shad \'shad\ *n* : Atlantic food fish

shade \'shād\ *n* **1** : space sheltered from the light esp. of the sun **2** : gradation of color **3** : small difference **4** : something that shades ~ *vb* **shad·ed**; **shad·ing** **1** : shelter from light and heat **2** : add shades of color to **3** : show slight differences esp. in color or meaning

shad·ow \'shadō\ *n* **1** : shade cast upon a surface by something blocking light **2** : trace **3** : gloomy influence ~ *vb* **1** : cast a shadow **2** : follow closely — **shad·owy** *adj*

shady \'shādē\ *adj* **shad·i·er**; -**est** **1** : giving shade **2** : of dubious honesty

shaft \'shaft\ *n* **1** : long slender cylindrical part **2** : deep vertical opening (as of a mine)

shag \'shag\ *n* : shaggy tangled mat

shag·gy \'shagē\ *adj* -**gi·er**; -**est** **1** : covered with long hair or wool **2** : not neat and combed

shake \'shāk\ *vb* **shook** \'shuk\; **shak·en** \'shākən\; **shak·ing** **1** : move or cause to move quickly back and forth **2** : distress **3** : clasp (hands) as friendly gesture — **shake** *n* — **shak·er** \-ər\ *n*

shake–up *n* : reorganization

shaky \'shākē\ *adj* **shak·i·er**; -**est** : not sound, stable, or reliable — **shak·i·ly** *adv* — **shak·i·ness** *n*

shale \'shāl\ *n* : stratified rock

shall \'shal\ *vb, past* **should** \'shud\; *pres sing & pl* **shall**

— used as an auxiliary to express a command, futurity, or determination

shal·low \'shalō\ *adj* **1** : not deep **2** : not intellectually profound

shal·lows \-ōz\ *n pl* : area of shallow water

sham \'sham\ *adj or n or vb* : fake

sham·ble \'shambəl\ *vb* **-bled; -bling** : shuffle along — **sham·ble** *n*

sham·bles \'shambəlz\ *n* : state of disorder

shame \'shām\ *n* **1** : distress over guilt or disgrace **2** : cause of shame or regret ~ *vb* **shamed; sham·ing 1** : make ashamed **2** : disgrace — **shame·ful** \-fəl\ *adj* — **shame·ful·ly** \-ē\ *adv* — **shame·less** *adj* — **shame·less·ly** *adv*

shame·faced \'shām'fāst\ *adj* : ashamed

sham·poo \sham'pü\ *vb* : wash one's hair ~ *n, pl* **-poos** : act of or preparation used in shampooing

sham·rock \'sham,räk\ *n* : plant of legend with 3-lobed leaves

shank \'shaŋk\ *n* : part of the leg between the knee and ankle

shan·ty \'shantē\ *n, pl* **-ties** : hut

shape \'shāp\ *vb* **shaped; shap·ing** : form esp. in a particular structure or appearance ~ *n* **1** : distinctive appearance or arrangement of parts **2** : condition — **shape·less** \-ləs\ *adj* — **shape·li·ness** *n* — **shape·ly** *adj*

shard \'shärd\ *n* : broken piece

share \'sher\ *n* **1** : portion belonging to one **2** : interest in a company's stock ~ *vb* **shared; shar·ing** : divide or use with others — **share·hold·er** *n* — **shar·er** *n*

share·crop·per \-,kräpər\ *n* : farmer who works another's land in return for a share of the crop — **share·crop** *vb*

shark \'shärk\ *n* : voracious sea fish

sharp \'shärp\ *adj* **1** : having a good point or cutting edge **2** : alert, clever, or sarcastic **3** : vigorous or fierce **4** : having prominent angles or a sudden change in direction **5** : distinct **6** : higher than the true pitch ~ *adv* : exactly ~ *n* : sharp note — **sharp·ly** *adv* — **sharp·ness** *n*

shar·pen \'shärpən\ *vb* : make sharp — **sharp·en·er** \-ənər\ *n*

sharp·shoot·er *n* : expert marksman — **sharp·shoot·ing** *n*

shat·ter \'shatər\ *vb* : smash or burst into fragments — **shat·ter·proof** \-,prüf\ *adj*

shave \'shāv\ *vb* **shaved; shaved** *or* **shav·en** \'shāvən\; **shav·ing 1** : cut off with a razor **2** : make bare by cutting the hair from **3** : slice very thin ~ *n* : act or instance of shaving — **shav·er** *n*

shawl \'shȯl\ *n* : loose covering for the head or shoulders

she \'shē\ *pron* : that female one

sheaf \'shēf\ *n, pl* **sheaves** \'shēvz\ : bundle esp. of grain stalks

shear \'shir\ *vb* **sheared; sheared** *or* **shorn** \'shōrn\; **shear·ing 1** : trim wool from **2** : cut off with scissorlike action

shears \'shirz\ *n pl* : cutting tool with 2 blades fastened so that the edges slide by each other

sheath \'shēth\ *n, pl* **sheaths** \'shēthz, 'shēths\ : covering (as for a blade)

sheathe \'shēth\ *vb* **sheathed; sheath·ing** : put into a sheath

shed \'shed\ *vb* **shed; shedding 1** : give off (as tears or hair) **2** : cause to flow or diffuse ~ *n* : small storage building

sheen \'shēn\ *n* : subdued luster

sheep \'shēp\ *n, pl* **sheep** : domesticated mammal covered with wool — **sheep·skin** *n*

sheep·ish \'shēpish\ *adj* : embarrassed by awareness of a fault

sheer \'shir\ *adj* **1** : pure **2** : very steep **3** : very thin or transparent

sheet \'shēt\ *n* : broad flat piece (as of cloth or paper)

sheikh, sheik \'shēk, 'shāk\ *n* : Arab chief — **sheikh·dom, sheik·dom** \-dəm\ *n*

shelf \'shelf\ *n, pl* **shelves** \'shelvz\ **1** : flat narrow structure used for storage or display **2** : sandbank or rock ledge

shell \'shel\ *n* **1** : hard or tough outer covering **2** : case holding explosive powder and projectile for a weapon **3** : light racing boat with oars ~ *vb* **1** : remove the shell of **2** : bombard — **shelled** \'sheld\ *adj* — **shell·er** *n*

shel·lac \shə'lak\ *n* : varnish ~ *vb* **-lacked; -lack·ing 1** : coat with shellac **2** : defeat — **shel·lack·ing** *n*

shell·fish *n* : water animal with a shell

shel·ter \'sheltər\ *n* : something that gives protection ~ *vb* : give refuge to

shelve \'shelv\ *vb* **shelved; shelv·ing 1** : place or store on shelves **2** : dismiss or put aside

she·nan·i·gans \shə'nanigənz\ *n pl* : mischievous or deceitful conduct

shep·herd \'shepərd\ *n* : one that tends sheep ~ *vb* : act as a shepherd or guardian

shep·herd·ess \'shepərdəs\ *n* : woman who tends sheep

sher·bet \'shərbət\, **sher·bert** \-bərt\ *n* : fruit-flavored frozen dessert

sher·iff \'sherəf\ *n* : county law officer

sher·ry \'sherē\ *n, pl* **-ries** : type of wine

shield \'shēld\ *n* **1** : broad piece of armor carried on the arm **2** : something that pro-tects — **shield** *vb*

shier *comparative of* **SHY**

shiest *superlative of* **SHY**

shift \'shift\ *vb* **1** : change place, position, or direction **2** : get by ~ *n* **1** : loose-fitting dress **2** : an act or instance of shifting **3** : scheduled work period

shift·less \-ləs\ *adj* : lazy

shifty \'shiftē\ *adj* **shift·i·er; -est** : tricky or untrustworthy

shil·le·lagh \shə'lālē\ *n* : club or stick

shil·ling \'shiliŋ\ *n* : former British coin

shilly–shally \'shilē,shalē\ *vb* **-shall·ied; -shally·ing 1** : hes-itate **2** : dawdle

shim·mer \'shimər\ *vb or n* : glimmer

shin \'shin\ *n* : front part of the leg below the knee ~ *vb* **-nn-** : climb by sliding the body close along

shine \'shīn\ *vb* **shone** \-shōn\ *or* **shined; shin·ing 1** : give off or cause to give off light **2** : be outstanding **3** : polish ~ *n* : brilliance

shin·gle \'shiŋgəl\ *n* **1** : small thin piece used in covering roofs or exterior walls — **shin-gle** *vb*

shin·gles \'shiŋgəlz\ *n pl* : acute inflammation of spinal nerves

shin·ny \'shinē\ *vb* **-nied; -ny-ing** : shin

shiny \'shīnē\ *adj* **shin·i·er; -est** : bright or polished

ship \'ship\ *n* **1** : large ocean-going vessel **2** : aircraft or spacecraft ~ *vb* **-pp- 1** : put on a ship **2** : transport by car-rier — **ship·board** *n* — **ship-build·er** *n* — **ship·per** *n* — **ship·wreck** *n or vb* — **ship-yard** *n*

–ship \,ship\ *n suffix* **1** : state, condition, or quality **2** : rank or profession **3** : skill **4** : some-thing showing a state or quality

ship·ment \-mənt\ *n* : an act of shipping or the goods shipped

ship·ping \'shipiŋ\ *n* **1** : ships **2** : transportation of goods

ship·shape *adj* : tidy

shire \'shīr, *in place-name com-pounds* ,shir, shər\ *n* : British county

shirk \'shərk\ *vb* : evade — **shirk·er** *n*

shirr \'shər\ *vb* **1** : gather (cloth) by drawing up parallel lines of stitches **2** : bake (eggs) in a dish

shirt \\'shərt\\ *n* : garment for covering the torso — **shirt-less** *adj*

shiv·er \\'shivər\\ *vb* : tremble — **shiver** *n* — **shiv·ery** *adj*

shoal \\'shōl\\ *n* : shallow place (as in a river)

¹shock \\'shäk\\ *n* : pile of sheaves set up in a field

²shock *n* **1** : forceful impact **2** : violent mental or emotional disturbance **3** : effect of a charge of electricity **4** : depression of the vital bodily processes ~ *vb* **1** : strike with surprise, horror, or disgust **2** : subject to an electrical shock — **shock·proof** *adj*

³shock *n* : bushy mass (as of hair)

shod·dy \\'shädē\\ *adj* **-di·er; -est** : poorly made or done — **shod·di·ly** \\'shädᵊlē\\ *adv* — **shod·di·ness** *n*

shoe \\'shü\\ *n* **1** : covering for the human foot **2** : horseshoe ~ *vb* **shod** \\'shäd\\; **shoe·ing** : put horseshoes on — **shoe-lace** *n* — **shoe·ma·ker** *n*

shone *past of* SHINE

shook *past of* SHAKE

shoot \\'shüt\\ *vb* **shot** \\'shät\\; **shoot·ing** **1** : propel (as an arrow or bullet) **2** : wound or kill with a missile **3** : discharge (a weapon) **4** : drive (as a ball) at a goal **5** : photograph **6** : move

swiftly ~ *n* : new plant growth — **shoot·er** *n*

shop \\'shäp\\ *n* : place where things are made or sold ~ *vb* **-pp-** : visit stores — **shop-keep·er** *n* — **shop·per** *n*

shop·lift *vb* : steal goods from a store — **shop·lift·er** \\-ˌliftər\\ *n*

¹shore \\'shōr\\ *n* : land along the edge of water — **shore·line** *n*

²shore *vb* **shored; shor·ing** : prop up ~ *n* : something that props

shore·bird *n* : bird of the seashore

shorn *past part of* SHEAR

short \\'shȯrt\\ *adj* **1** : not long or tall or extending far **2** : brief in time **3** : curt **4** : not having or being enough ~ *adv* : curtly ~ *n* **1** *pl* : short drawers or trousers **2** : short circuit — **short·en** \\-ᵊn\\ *vb* — **short·ly** *adv* — **short·ness** *n*

short·age \\'shȯrtij\\ *n* : deficiency

short·cake *n* : dessert of biscuit with sweetened fruit

short·change *vb* : cheat esp. by giving too little change

short circuit *n* : abnormal electric connection — **short–circuit** *vb*

short·com·ing *n* : fault or failing

short·cut \\-ˌkət\\ *n* **1** : more direct route than that usu. taken **2** : quicker way of doing something

short·hand *n* : method of speed writing

short–lived \'shȯrt'līvd, -ˌlivd\ *adj* : of short life or duration

short·sight·ed *adj* : lacking foresight

shot \'shät\ *n* **1** : act of shooting **2** : attempt (as at making a goal) **3** : small pellets forming a charge **4** : range or reach **5** : photograph **6** : injection of medicine **7** : small serving of liquor — **shot·gun** *n*

should \'shu̇d\ *past of* SHALL — used as an auxiliary to express condition, obligation, or probability

shoul·der \'shōldər\ *n* **1** : part of the body where the arm joins the trunk **2** : part that projects or lies to the side ∼ *vb* : push with or bear on the shoulder

shoulder blade *n* : flat triangular bone at the back of the shoulder

shout \'shau̇t\ *vb* : give voice loudly — **shout** *n*

shove \'shəv\ *vb* **shoved; shov-ing** : push along or away — **shove** *n*

shov·el \'shəvəl\ *n* : broad tool for digging or lifting ∼ *vb* **-eled** *or* **-elled; -el·ing** *or* **-el·ling** : take up or dig with a shovel

show \'shō\ *vb* **showed** \'shōd\; **shown** \'shōn\ *or*

showed; show·ing 1 : present to view **2** : reveal or demonstrate **3** : teach **4** : prove **5** : conduct or escort **6** : appear or be noticeable ∼ *n* **1** : demonstrative display **2** : spectacle **3** : theatrical, radio, or television program — **show·case** *n* — **show off** *vb* **1** : display proudly **2** : act so as to attract attention — **show up** *vb* : arrive

show·down *n* : decisive confrontation

show·er \'shau̇ər\ *n* **1** : brief fall of rain **2** : bath in which water sprinkles down on the person or a facility for such a bath **3** : party at which someone gets gifts ∼ *vb* **1** : rain or fall in a shower **2** : bathe in a shower — **show·ery** *adj*

showy \'shōē\ *adj* **show·i·er; -est** : very noticeable or overly elaborate — **show·i·ly** *adv* — **show·i·ness** *n*

shrap·nel \'shrapnᵊl\ *n, pl* **shrapnel** : metal fragments of a bomb

shred \'shred\ *n* : narrow strip cut or torn off ∼ *vb* **-dd-** : cut or tear into shreds

shrew \'shrü\ *n* **1** : scolding woman **2** : mouselike mammal — **shrew·ish** \-ish\ *adj*

shrewd \'shrüd\ *adj* : clever — **shrewd·ly** *adv* — **shrewd-ness** *n*

shriek \'shrēk\ *n* : shrill cry — **shriek** *vb*

shrill \'shril\ *adj* : piercing and high-pitched — **shril·ly** *adv*

shrimp \'shrimp\ *n* : small sea crustacean

shrine \'shrīn\ *n* **1** : tomb of a saint **2** : hallowed place

shrink \'shriŋk\ *vb* **shrank** \'shraŋk\; **shrunk** \'shrəŋk\ *or* **shrunk·en** \'shrəŋkən\; **shrink·ing 1** : draw back or away **2** : become smaller — **shrink·able** *adj*

shrink·age \'shriŋkij\ *n* : amount lost by shrinking

shriv·el \'shrivəl\ *vb* **-eled** *or* **-elled; -el·ing** *or* **-el·ling** : shrink or wither into wrinkles

shroud \'shraúd\ *n* **1** : cloth put over a corpse **2** : cover or screen ~ *vb* : veil or screen from view

shrub \'shrəb\ *n* : low woody plant — **shrub·by** *adj*

shrub·bery \'shrəbərē\ *n, pl* **-ber·ies** : growth of shrubs

shrug \'shrəg\ *vb* **-gg-** : hunch the shoulders up in doubt, indifference, or uncertainty — **shrug** *n*

shuck \'shək\ *vb* : strip of a shell or husk — **shuck** *n*

shud·der \'shədər\ *vb* : tremble — **shudder** *n*

shuf·fle \'shəfəl\ *vb* **-fled; -fling 1** : mix together **2** : walk with a sliding movement — **shuffle** *n*

shuf·fle·board \'shəfəl,bōrd\ *n* : game of sliding disks into a scoring area

shun \'shən\ *vb* **-nn-** : keep away from

shunt \'shənt\ *vb* : turn off to one side

shut \'shət\ *vb* **shut; shut·ting 1** : bar passage into or through (as by moving a lid or door) **2** : suspend activity — **shut out** *vb* : exclude — **shut up** *vb* : stop or cause to stop talking

shut–in *n* : invalid

shut·ter \'shətər\ *n* **1** : movable cover for a window **2** : camera part that exposes film

shut·tle \'shət³l\ *n* **1** : part of a weaving machine that carries thread back and forth **2** : vehicle traveling back and forth over a short route ~ *vb* **-tled; -tling** : move back and forth frequently

shut·tle·cock \'shət³l,käk\ *n* : light conical object used in badminton

shy \'shī\ *adj* **shi·er** *or* **shy·er** \'shīər\; **shi·est** *or* **shy·est** \'shīəst\ **1** : sensitive and hesitant in dealing with others **2** : wary **3** : lacking ~ *vb* **shied; shy·ing** : draw back (as in fright) — **shy·ly** *adv* — **shyness** *n*

sib·i·lant \'sibələnt\ *adj* : having the sound of the *s* or the *sh* in *sash* — **sibilant** *n*

sib·ling \'siblin\ *n* : brother or sister

sick \'sik\ *adj* **1** : not in good health **2** : nauseated **3** : relating to or meant for the sick — **sick·bed** *n* — **sick·en** \-ən\ *vb* — **sick·ly** *adj* — **sick·ness** *n*

sick·le \'sikəl\ *n* : curved short‑handled blade

side \'sīd\ *n* **1** : part to left or right of an object or the torso **2** : edge or surface away from the center or at an angle to top and bottom or ends **3** : contrasting or opposing position or group — **sid·ed** *adj*

side·board *n* : piece of dining‑room furniture for table service

side·burns \-ˌbərnz\ *n pl* : whiskers in front of the ears

side·long \'sīdˌlȯŋ\ *adv or adj* : to or along the side

side·show *n* : minor show at a circus

side·step *vb* **1** : step aside **2** : avoid

side·swipe \-ˌswīp\ *vb* : strike with a glancing blow — **side·swipe** *n*

side·track *vb* : lead aside or astray

side·walk *n* : paved walk at the side of a road

side·ways \-ˌwāz\ *adv or adj* **1** : to or from the side **2** : with one side to the front

sid·ing \'sīdiŋ\ *n* **1** : short rail‑road track **2** : material for covering the outside of a building

si·dle \'sīdᵊl\ *vb* **-dled; -dling** : move sideways or unobtrusively

siege \'sēj\ *n* : persistent attack (as on a fortified place)

si·es·ta \sē'estə\ *n* : midday nap

sieve \'siv\ *n* : utensil with holes to separate particles

sift \'sift\ *vb* **1** : pass through a sieve **2** : examine carefully — **sift·er** *n*

sigh \'sī\ *n* : audible release of the breath (as to express weariness) — **sigh** *vb*

sight \'sīt\ *n* **1** : something seen or worth seeing **2** : process, power, or range of seeing **3** : device used in aiming **4** : view or glimpse ~ *vb* : get sight of — **sight·ed** *adj* — **sight·less** *adj* — **sight–see·ing** *adj* — **sight·seer** \-ˌsēər\ *n*

sign \'sīn\ *n* **1** : symbol **2** : gesture expressing a command or thought **3** : public notice to advertise or warn **4** : trace ~ *vb* **1** : mark with or make a sign **2** : write one's name on — **sign·er** *n*

sig·nal \'signᵊl\ *n* **1** : sign of command or warning **2** : electronic transmission ~ *vb* **-naled** *or* **-nalled; -nal·ing** *or* **-nal·ling** : communicate or notify by signals ~ *adj* : distinguished

sig·na·to·ry \'signəˌtōrē\ *n, pl* **-ries** : person or government that signs jointly with others

sig·na·ture \\'signə,chur\ *n* : one's name written by oneself

sig·net \\'signət\ *n* : small seal

sig·nif·i·cance \sig'nifikəns\ *n* **1** : meaning **2** : importance — **sig·nif·i·cant** \-kənt\ *adj* — **sig·nif·i·cant·ly** *adv*

sig·ni·fy \\'signə,fī\ *vb* **-fied; -fy·ing** **1** : show by a sign **2** : mean — **sig·ni·fi·ca·tion** \,signəfə'kāshən\ *n*

si·lence \\'sīləns\ *n* : state of being without sound ~ *vb* **-lenced; -lenc·ing** : keep from making noise or sound — **si·lenc·er** *n*

si·lent \\'sīlənt\ *adj* : having or producing no sound — **si·lent·ly** *adv*

sil·hou·ette \,silə'wet\ *n* : outline filled in usu. with black ~ *vb* **-ett·ed; -ett·ing** : represent by a silhouette

sil·i·ca \\'silikə\ *n* : mineral found as quartz and opal

sil·i·con \\'silikən, -,kän\ *n* : nonmetallic chemical element

silk \\'silk\ *n* **1** : fine strong lustrous protein fiber from moth larvae (**silkworms** \-,wərmz\) **2** : thread or cloth made from silk — **silk·en** \\'silkən\ *adj* **silky** *adj*

sill \\'sil\ *n* : bottom part of a window frame or a doorway

sil·ly \\'silē\ *adj* **sil·li·er; -est** : foolish or stupid — **sil·li·ness** *n*

si·lo \\'sīlō\ *n, pl* **-los** : tall building for storing animal feed

silt \\'silt\ *n* : fine earth carried by rivers ~ *vb* : obstruct or cover with silt

sil·ver \\'silvər\ *n* **1** : white ductile metallic chemical element **2** : silverware ~ *adj* : having the color of silver — **sil·very** *adj*

sil·ver·ware \-,war\ *n* : eating and serving utensils esp. of silver

sim·i·lar \\'simələr\ *adj* : resembling each other in some ways — **sim·i·lar·i·ty** \,simə'larətē\ *n* — **sim·i·lar·ly** \\'simələrlē\ *adv*

sim·i·le \\'simə,lē\ *n* : comparison of unlike things using *like* or *as*

sim·mer \\'simər\ *vb* : stew gently

sim·per \\'simpər\ *vb* : give a silly smile — **simper** *n*

sim·ple \\'simpəl\ *adj* **-pler; -plest** **1** : free from dishonesty, vanity, or pretense **2** : of humble origin or modest position **3** : not complex **4** : lacking education, experience, or intelligence — **sim·ple·ness** *n* — **sim·ply** \-plē\ *adv*

sim·ple·ton \\'simpəltən\ *n* : fool

sim·plic·i·ty \sim'plisətē\ *n* : state or fact of being simple

sim·pli·fy \'simplə,fī\ *vb* **-fied; -fy·ing** : make easier — **sim·pli·fi·ca·tion** \,simpləfə'kā-shən\ *n*

sim·u·late \'simyə,lāt\ *vb* **-lat·ed; -lat·ing** : create the effect or appearance of — **sim·u·la·tion** \,simyə'lāshən\ *n* — **sim·u·la·tor** \'simyə,lātər\ *n*

si·mul·ta·ne·ous \,sīməl'tā-nēəs\ *adj* : occurring or operating at the same time — **si·mul·ta·ne·ous·ly** *adv* — **simul·ta·ne·ous·ness** *n*

sin \'sin\ *n* : offense against God ~ *vb* **-nn-** : commit a sin — **sin·ful** \-fəl\ *adj* — **sin·less** *adj* — **sin·ner** *n*

since \'sins\ *adv* **1** : from a past time until now **2** : backward in time ~ *prep* **1** : in the period after **2** : continuously from ~ *conj* **1** : from the time when **2** : because

sin·cere \sin'sir\ *adj* **-cer·er; -cer·est** : genuine or honest — **sin·cere·ly** *adv* — **sin·cer·i·ty** \-'serətē\ *n*

si·ne·cure \'sīni,kyùr, 'sini-\ *n* : well-paid job that requires little work

sin·ew \'sinyü\ *n* **1** : tendon **2** : physical strength — **sin·ewy** *adj*

sing \'siŋ\ *vb* **sang** \'saŋ\ *or* **sung** \'səŋ\; **sung; sing·ing** : produce musical tones with the voice — **sing·er** *n*

singe \'sinj\ *vb* **singed; singe·ing** : scorch lightly

sin·gle \'siŋgəl\ *adj* **1** : one only **2** : unmarried ~ *n* : separate one — **single·ness** *n* — **sin·gly** \-glē\ *adv* — **single out** *vb* : select or set aside

sin·gu·lar \'siŋgyələr\ *adj* **1** : relating to a word form denoting one **2** : outstanding or superior **3** : queer — **singular** *n* — **sin·gu·lar·i·ty** \,siŋgyə-'larətē\ *n* — **sin·gu·lar·ly** \'siŋgyələrlē\ *adv*

sin·is·ter \'sinəstər\ *adj* : threatening evil

sink \'siŋk\ *vb* **sank** \'saŋk\ *or* **sunk** \'səŋk\; **sunk; sink·ing** **1** : submerge or descend **2** : grow worse **3** : make by digging or boring **4** : invest ~ *n* : basin with a drain

sink·er \'siŋkər\ *n* : weight to sink a fishing line

sin·u·ous \'sinyəwəs\ *adj* : winding in and out — **sin·u·os·i·ty** \,sinyə-'wäsətē\ *n* — **sin·u·ous·ly** *adv*

si·nus \'sīnəs\ *n* : skull cavity usu. connecting with the nostrils

sip \'sip\ *vb* **-pp-** : drink in small quantities — **sip** *n*

si·phon \'sīfən\ *n* : tube that draws liquid by suction — **siphon** *vb*

sir \'sər\ *n* **1** — used before the first name of a knight or baronet **2** — used as a respect-ful form of address

sire \'sīr\ *n* : father ~ *vb* **sired; sir·ing** : beget

si·ren \'sīrən\ *n* **1** : seductive woman **2** : wailing warning whistle

sir·loin \'sər‚lȯin\ *n* : cut of beef

sirup *var of* SYRUP

si·sal \'sīsəl, -zəl\ *n* : strong rope fiber

sis·sy \'sisē\ *n, pl* **-sies** : timid or effeminate boy

sis·ter \'sistər\ *n* : female shar-ing one or both parents with another person — **sis·ter·hood** \-‚hu̇d\ *n* — **sis·ter·ly** *adj*

sis·ter–in–law *n, pl* **sis·ters–in–law** : sister of one's spouse or wife of one's brother

sit \'sit\ *vb* **sat** \'sat\; **sit·ting 1** : rest on the buttocks or haunches **2** : roost **3** : hold a session **4** : pose for a portrait **5** : have a location **6** : rest or fix in place — **sit·ter** *n*

site \'sīt\ *n* **1** : place **2** : Web site

sit·u·at·ed \'sichə‚wātəd\ *adj* : located

sit·u·a·tion \‚sichə'wāshən\ *n* **1** : location **2** : condition **3** : job

six \'siks\ *n* : one more than 5 — **six** *adj or pron* — **sixth** \'siksth\ *adj or adv or n*

six·teen \siks'tēn\ *n* : one more than 15 — **sixteen** *adj or pron* — **six·teenth** \-'tēnth\ *adj or n*

six·ty \'sikstē\ *n, pl* **-ties** : 6 times 10 — **six·ti·eth** \-əth\ *adj or n* — **sixty** *adj or pron*

siz·able, size·able \'sīzəbəl\ *adj* : quite large — **siz·ably** \-blē\ *adv*

size \'sīz\ *n* : measurement of the amount of space some-thing takes up ~ *vb* : grade according to size

siz·zle \'sizəl\ *vb* **-zled; -zling** : fry with a hissing sound — **sizzle** *n*

skate \'skāt\ *n* **1** : metal run-ner on a shoe for gliding over ice **2** : roller skate — **skate** *vb* — **skat·er** *n*

skein \'skān\ *n* : loosely twisted quantity of yarn or thread

skel·e·ton \'skelətᵊn\ *n* : bony framework — **skel·e·tal** \-ətᵊl\ *adj*

skep·tic \'skeptik\ *n* : one who is critical or doubting — **skep·ti·cal** \-tikəl\ *adj* — **skep·ti·cism** \-tə‚sizəm\ *n*

sketch \'skech\ *n* **1** : rough drawing **2** : short story or essay — **sketch** *vb* — **sketchy** *adj*

skew·er \'skyu̇ər\ *n* : long pin for holding roasting meat — **skewer** *vb*

ski \'skē\ *n, pl* **skis** : long strip for gliding over snow or water — **ski** *vb* — **ski·er** *n*

skid \'skid\ *n* **1** : plank for supporting something or on which it slides **2** : act of skidding ∼ *vb* **-dd-** : slide sideways

skiff \'skif\ *n* : small boat

skill \'skil\ *n* : developed or learned ability — **skilled** \'skild\ *adj* — **skill·ful** \-fəl\ *adj* — **skill·ful·ly** *adv*

skil·let \'skilət\ *n* : pan for frying

skim \'skim\ *vb* **-mm-** **1** : take off from the top of a liquid **2** : read or move over swiftly ∼ *adj* : having the cream removed — **skim·mer** *n*

skimp \'skimp\ *vb* : give too little of something — **skimpy** *adj*

skin \'skin\ *n* **1** : outer layer of an animal body **2** : rind ∼ *vb* **-nn-** : take the skin from — **skin·less** *adj* — **skinned** *adj* — **skin·tight** *adj*

skin diving *n* : sport of swimming under water with a face mask and flippers

skin·flint \'skin,flint\ *n* : stingy person

skin·ny \'skinē\ *adj* **-ni·er; -est** : very thin

skip \'skip\ *vb* **-pp-** **1** : move with leaps **2** : read past or ignore — **skip** *n*

skip·per \'skipər\ *n* : ship's master — **skipper** *vb*

skir·mish \'skərmish\ *n* : minor combat — **skirmish** *vb*

skirt \'skərt\ *n* : garment or part of a garment that hangs below the waist ∼ *vb* : pass around the edge of

skit \'skit\ *n* : brief usu. humorous play

skit·tish \'skitish\ *adj* : easily frightened

skulk \'skəlk\ *vb* : move furtively

skull \'skəl\ *n* : bony case that protects the brain

skunk \'skəŋk\ *n* : mammal that can forcibly eject an ill= smelling fluid

sky \'skī\ *n, pl* **skies** **1** : upper air **2** : heaven — **sky·line** *n* — **sky·ward** \-wərd\ *adv or adj*

sky·lark \'skī,lärk\ *n* : European lark noted for its song

sky·light *n* : window in a roof or ceiling

sky·rock·et *n* : shooting firework ∼ *vb* : rise suddenly

sky·scrap·er \-,skrāpər\ *n* : very tall building

slab \'slab\ *n* : thick slice

slack \'slak\ *adj* **1** : careless **2** : not taut **3** : not busy ∼ *n* **1** : part hanging loose **2** *pl* : casual trousers — **slack·en** *vb* — **slack·ly** *adv* — **slack·ness** *n*

slag \'slag\ *n* : waste from melting of ores

slain *past part of* SLAY

slake \'slāk\ *vb* **slaked; slak-ing** : quench

slam \'slam\ *n* : heavy jarring impact ~ *vb* **-mm-** : shut, strike, or throw violently and loudly

slan·der \'slandər\ *n* : malicious gossip ~ *vb* : hurt (someone) with slander — **slan·der·er** *n* — **slan·der·ous** *adj*

slang \'slaŋ\ *n* : informal non-standard vocabulary — **slangy** *adj*

slant \'slant\ *vb* **1** : slope **2** : present with a special viewpoint ~ *n* : sloping direction, line, or plane

slap \'slap\ *vb* **-pp-** : strike sharply with the open hand — **slap** *n*

slash \'slash\ *vb* **1** : cut with sweeping strokes **2** : reduce sharply ~ *n* : gash

slat \'slat\ *n* : thin narrow flat strip

slate \'slāt\ *n* **1** : dense fine-grained layered rock **2** : roofing tile or writing tablet of slate **3** : list of candidates ~ *vb* **slat·ed; slat·ing** : designate

slat·tern \'slatərn\ *n* : untidy woman — **slat·tern·ly** *adj*

slaugh·ter \'slȯtər\ *n* **1** : butchering of livestock for market **2** : great and cruel destruction of lives ~ *vb*

: commit slaughter upon — **slaughter·house** *n*

slave \'slāv\ *n* : one owned and forced into service by another ~ *vb* **slaved; slav·ing** : work as or like a slave — **slave** *adj* — **slav·ery** \'slāvərē\ *n*

sla·ver \'slavər, 'slāv-\ *vb or n* : slobber

slav·ish \'slāvish\ *adj* : of or like a slave — **slav·ish·ly** *adv*

slay \'slā\ *vb* **slew** \'slü\; **slain** \'slān\; **slay·ing** : kill — **slay·er** *n*

slea·zy \'slēzē, 'slā-\ *adj* **-zi·er; -est** : shabby or shoddy

sled \'sled\ *n* : vehicle on runners — **sled** *vb*

¹sledge \'slej\ *n* : sledgehammer

²sledge *n* : heavy sled

sledge·ham·mer *n* : heavy long-handled hammer — **sledgehammer** *adj or vb*

sleek \'slēk\ *adj* : smooth or glossy — **sleek** *vb*

sleep \'slēp\ *n* : natural suspension of consciousness ~ *vb* **slept** \'slept\; **sleep·ing** : rest in a state of sleep — **sleep·er** *n* — **sleep·less** *adj* — **sleep·walk·er** *n*

sleepy \'slēpē\ *adj* **sleep·i·er; -est** **1** : ready for sleep **2** : quietly inactive — **sleep·i·ly** \'slēpəlē\ *adv* — **sleep·i·ness** \-pēnəs\ *n*

sleet \'slēt\ *n* : frozen rain — **sleet** *vb* — **sleety** *adj*

sleeve \ˈslēv\ *n* : part of a garment for the arm — **sleeve·less** *adj*

sleigh \ˈslā\ *n* : horse-drawn sled with seats ～ *vb* : drive or ride in a sleigh

sleight of hand \ˈslīt-\ : skillful manual manipulation or a trick requiring it

slen·der \ˈslendər\ *adj* **1** : thin esp. in physique **2** : scanty

sleuth \ˈslüth\ *n* : detective

slew \ˈslü\ *past of* SLAY

slice \ˈslīs\ *n* : thin flat piece ～ *vb* **sliced; slic·ing** : cut a slice from

slick \ˈslik\ *adj* **1** : very smooth **2** : clever — **slick** *vb*

slick·er \ˈslikər\ *n* : raincoat

slide \ˈslīd\ *vb* **slid** \ˈslid\; **slid·ing** \ˈslīdiŋ\ : move smoothly along a surface ～ *n* **1** : act of sliding **2** : surface on which something slides **3** : transparent picture for projection

slier *comparative of* SLY

sliest *superlative of* SLY

slight \ˈslīt\ *adj* **1** : slender **2** : frail **3** : small in degree ～ *vb* **1** : ignore or treat as unimportant — **slight** *n* — **slight·ly** *adv*

slim \ˈslim\ *adj* **-mm-** **1** : slender **2** : scanty ～ *vb* **-mm-** : make or become slender

slime \ˈslīm\ *n* : dirty slippery film (as on water) — **slimy** *adj*

sling \ˈsliŋ\ *vb* **slung** \ˈsləŋ\; **sling·ing** : hurl with or as if with a sling ～ *n* **1** : strap for swinging and hurling stones **2** : looped strap or bandage to lift or support

sling·shot *n* : forked stick with elastic bands for shooting pebbles

slink \ˈsliŋk\ *vb* **slunk** \ˈsləŋk\; **slink·ing** : move stealthily or sinuously — **slinky** *adj*

¹**slip** \ˈslip\ *vb* **-pp-** **1** : escape quietly or secretly **2** : slide along smoothly **3** : make a mistake **4** : to pass without being noticed or done **5** : fall off from a standard ～ *n* **1** : ship's berth **2** : sudden mishap **3** : mistake **4** : woman's undergarment

²**slip** *n* **1** : plant shoot **2** : small strip (as of paper)

slip·per \ˈslipər\ *n* : shoe that slips on easily

slip·pery \ˈslipərē\ *adj* **-peri·er; -est** **1** : slick enough to slide on **2** : tricky — **slip·peri·ness** *n*

slip·shod \ˈslip₁shäd\ *adj* : careless

slit \ˈslit\ *vb* **slit; slit·ting** : make a slit in ～ *n* : long narrow cut

slith·er \ˈslithər\ *vb* : glide along like a snake — **slith·ery** *adj*

sliv·er \ˈslivər\ *n* : splinter

slob \ˈsläb\ *n* : untidy person

slob·ber \ˈsläbər\ *vb* : dribble saliva — **slobber** *n*

slo·gan \\'slōgən\ *n* : word or phrase expressing the aim of a cause

sloop \\'slüp\ *n* : one-masted sailboat

slop \\'släp\ *n* : food waste for animal feed ~ *vb* **-pp-** : spill

slope \\'slōp\ *vb* **sloped; slop-ing** : deviate from the vertical or horizontal ~ *n* : upward or downward slant

slop·py \\'släpē\ *adj* **-pi·er; -est** **1** : muddy **2** : untidy

slot \\'slät\ *n* : narrow opening

sloth \\'slȯth, 'slōth\ *n, pl* **sloths** *with* ths *or* thz\ **1** : laziness **2** : slow-moving mammal — **sloth·ful** *adj*

slouch \\'slauch\ *n* **1** : drooping posture **2** : lazy or incompetent person ~ *vb* : walk or stand with a slouch

¹slough \\'slü, 'slau\ *n* : swamp

²slough, sluff \\'sləf\ *vb* : cast off (old skin)

slov·en·ly \\'sləvənlē\ *adj* : untidy

slow \\'slō\ *adj* **1** : sluggish or stupid **2** : moving, working, or happening at less than the usual speed ~ *vb* **1** : make slow **2** : go slower — **slow** *adv* — **slow·ly** *adv* — **slow·ness** *n*

sludge \\'sləj\ *n* : slushy mass (as of treated sewage)

slug \\'sləg\ *n* **1** : mollusk related to the snails **2** : bullet **3** : metal disk ~ *vb* **-gg-** : strike forcibly — **slug·ger** *n*

slug·gish \\'sləgish\ *adj* : slow in movement or flow — **slug-gish·ly** *adv* — **slug·gish·ness** *n*

sluice \\'slüs\ *n* : channel for water ~ *vb* **sluiced; sluic·ing** : wash in running water

slum \\'sləm\ *n* : thickly populated area marked by poverty

slum·ber \\'sləmbər\ *vb or n* : sleep

slump \\'sləmp\ *vb* **1** : sink suddenly **2** : slouch — **slump** *n*

slung *past of* SLING

slunk *past of* SLINK

¹slur \\'slər\ *vb* **-rr-** : run (words or notes) together — **slur** *n*

²slur *n* : malicious or insulting remark

slurp \\'slərp\ *vb* : eat or drink noisily — **slurp** *n*

slush \\'sləsh\ *n* : partly melted snow — **slushy** *adj*

slut \\'slət\ *n* **1** : untidy woman **2** : lewd woman — **slut·tish** *adj*

sly \\'slī\ *adj* **sli·er** \\'slīər\; **sli-est** \\'slīəst\ : given to or showing secrecy and deception — **sly·ly** *adv* — **sly·ness** *n*

¹smack \\'smak\ *n* : characteristic flavor ~ *vb* : have a taste or hint

²smack *vb* **1** : move (the lips) so as to make a sharp noise **2** : kiss or slap with a loud noise smack

~ *n* **1** : sharp noise made by the lips **2** : noisy slap

³**smack** *adv* : squarely and sharply

⁴**smack** *n* : fishing boat

small \'smȯl\ *adj* **1** : little in size or amount **2** : few in number **3** : trivial — **small·ish** *adj* — **small·ness** *n*

small·pox \'smȯl͵päks\ *n* : contagious virus disease

smart \'smärt\ *vb* **1** : cause or feel stinging pain **2** : endure distress ~ *adj* **1** : intelligent or resourceful **2** : stylish — **smart** *n* — **smart·ly** *adv* — **smart·ness** *n*

smash \'smash\ *vb* : break or be broken into pieces ~ *n* **1** : smashing blow **2** : act or sound of smashing

smat·ter·ing \'smatəriŋ\ *n* **1** : superficial knowledge **2** : small scattered number or amount

smear \'smir\ *n* : greasy stain ~ *vb* **1** : spread (something sticky) **2** : smudge **3** : slander

smell \'smel\ *vb* **smelled** \'smeld\ *or* **smelt** \'smelt\; **smell·ing** **1** : perceive the odor of **2** : have or give off an odor ~ *n* **1** : sense by which one perceives odor **2** : odor — **smelly** *adj*

¹**smelt** \'smelt\ *n, pl* **smelts** *or* **smelt** : small food fish

²**smelt** *vb* : melt or fuse (ore) in order to separate the metal — **smelt·er** *n*

smile \'smīl\ *n* : facial expression with the mouth turned up usu. to show pleasure — **smile** *vb*

smirk \'smərk\ *vb* : wear a conceited smile — **smirk** *n*

smite \'smīt\ *vb* **smote** \'smōt\; **smit·ten** \'smitᵊn\ *or* **smote**; **smit·ing** \'smītiŋ\ **1** : strike heavily or kill **2** : affect strongly

smith \'smith\ *n* : worker in metals and esp. a blacksmith

smithy \'smithē\ *n, pl* **smith·ies** : a smith's workshop

smock \'smäk\ *n* : loose dress or protective coat

smog \'smäg, 'smȯg\ *n* : fog and smoke — **smog·gy** *adj*

smoke \'smōk\ *n* : sooty gas from burning ~ *vb* **smoked**; **smok·ing** **1** : give off smoke **2** : inhale the fumes of burning tobacco **3** : cure (as meat) with smoke — **smoke·less** *adj* — **smok·er** *n* — **smoky** *adj*

smoke·stack *n* : chimney through which smoke is discharged

smol·der, smoul·der \'smōldər\ *vb* **1** : burn and smoke without flame **2** : be suppressed but active — **smolder** *n*

smooth \'smüth\ *adj* **1** : having a surface without irregularities **2** : not jarring or jolting ~ *vb* : make smooth

— **smooth·ly** *adv* — **smooth-
ness** *n*

smor·gas·bord \'smȯrgəs-
ˌbōrd\ *n* : buffet consisting of
many foods

smoth·er \'sməthər\ *vb* **1**
: kill by depriving of air **2**
: cover thickly

smudge \'sməj\ *vb* **smudged;
smudg·ing** : soil or blur by
rubbing ∼ *n* **1** : thick smoke
2 : dirty spot

smug \'sməg\ *adj* **-gg-** : content in one's own virtue or accomplishment — **smug·ly** *adv*
— **smug·ness** *n*

smug·gle \'sməgəl\ *vb* **-gled;
-gling** : import or export secretly or illegally — **smug-
gler** \'sməglər\ *n*

smut \'smət\ *n* **1** : something
that soils **2** : indecent language or matter **3** : disease of
plants caused by fungi —
smut·ty *adj*

snack \'snak\ *n* : light meal

snag \'snag\ *n* : unexpected
difficulty ∼ *vb* **-gg-** : become
caught on something that
sticks out

snail \'snāl\ *n* : small mollusk
with a spiral shell

snake \'snāk\ *n* : long-bodied
limbless reptile — **snake·bite**
n

snap \'snap\ *vb* **-pp-** **1** : bite at
something **2** : utter angry
words **3** : break suddenly with
a sharp sound ∼ *n* **1** : act or
sound of snapping **2** : fastening that closes with a click **3**
: something easy to do —
snap·per *n* — **snap·pish** *adj*
— **snap·py** *adj*

snap·drag·on *n* : garden plant
with spikes of showy flowers

snap·shot \'snap·shät\ *n* : casual photograph

snare \'snar\ *n* : trap for catching game ∼ *vb* : capture or
hold with or as if with a snare

¹**snarl** \'snärl\ *n* : tangle ∼ *vb*
: cause to become knotted

²**snarl** *vb or n* : growl

snatch \'snach\ *vb* **1** : try to
grab something suddenly **2**
: seize or take away suddenly
∼ *n* **1** : act of snatching **2**
: something brief or frag-
mentary

sneak \'snēk\ *vb* : move or take
in a furtive manner ∼ *n* : one
who acts in a furtive manner
— **sneak·i·ly** \'snēkəlē\ *adv*
— **sneak·ing·ly** *adv* — **sneaky**
adj

sneak·er \'snēkər\ *n* : sports
shoe

sneer \'snir\ *vb* : smile scorn-
fully — **sneer** *n*

sneeze \'snēz\ *vb* **sneezed;
sneez·ing** : force the breath out
with sudden and involuntary
violence — **sneeze** *n*

snick·er \'snikər\ *n* : partly suppressed laugh — **snicker** *vb*

snide \'snīd\ *adj* : subtly ridiculing

sniff \'snif\ *vb* **1** : draw air audibly up the nose **2** : detect by smelling — **sniff** *n*

snip \'snip\ *n* : fragment snipped off ~ *vb* **-pp-** : cut off by bits

¹snipe \'snīp\ *n, pl* **snipes** *or* **snipe** : game bird of marshy areas

²snipe *vb* **sniped; snip·ing** : shoot at an enemy from a concealed position — **snip·er** *n*

snips \'snips\ *n pl* : scissorslike tool

sniv·el \'snivəl\ *vb* **-eled** *or* **-elled; -el·ing** *or* **-el·ling** **1** : have a running nose **2** : whine

snob \'snäb\ *n* : one who acts superior to others — **snob·bery** \-ərē\ *n* — **snob·bish** *adj* — **snob·bish·ly** *adv* — **snob·bish·ness** *n*

snoop \'snüp\ *vb* : pry in a furtive way ~ *n* : prying person

snooze \'snüz\ *vb* **snoozed; snooz·ing** : take a nap — **snooze** *n*

snore \'snōr\ *vb* **snored; snor·ing** : breathe with a hoarse noise while sleeping — **snore** *n*

snort \'snȯrt\ *vb* : force air noisily through the nose — **snort** *n*

snout \'snaut\ *n* : long projecting muzzle (as of a swine)

snow \'snō\ *n* : crystals formed from water vapor ~ *vb* : fall as snow — **snow·ball** *n* — **snow·bank** *n* — **snow·drift** *n* — **snow·fall** *n* — **snow·plow** *n* — **snow·storm** *n* — **snowy** *adj*

snow·shoe *n* : frame of wood strung with thongs for walking on snow

snub \'snəb\ *vb* **-bb-** : ignore or avoid through disdain — **snub** *n*

¹snuff \'snəf\ *vb* : put out (a candle) — **snuff·er** *n*

²snuff *vb* : draw forcibly into the nose ~ *n* : pulverized tobacco

snug \'snəg\ *adj* **-gg-** **1** : warm, secure, and comfortable **2** : fitting closely — **snug·ly** *adv* — **snug·ness** *n*

snug·gle \'snəgəl\ *vb* **-gled; -gling** : curl up comfortably

so \'sō\ *adv* **1** : in the manner or to the extent indicated **2** : in the same way **3** : therefore **4** : finally **5** : thus ~ *conj* : for that reason

soak \'sōk\ *vb* **1** : lie in a liquid **2** : absorb ~ *n* : act of soaking

soap \'sōp\ *n* : cleaning substance — **soap** *vb* — **soapy** *adj*

soar \'sōr\ *vb* : fly upward on or as if on wings

sob \'säb\ *vb* **-bb-** : weep with convulsive heavings of the chest — **sob** *n*

so·ber \'sōbər\ *adj* **1** : not drunk **2** : serious or solemn — **so·ber·ly** *adv*

so·bri·ety \sə'brīətē, sō-\ *n* : quality or state of being sober

soc·cer \'säkər\ *n* : game played by kicking a ball

so·cia·ble \'sōshəbəl\ *adj* : friendly — **so·cia·bil·i·ty** \,sōshə'bilətē\ *n* — **so·cia·bly** \'sōshəblē\ *adv*

so·cial \'sōshəl\ *adj* **1** : relating to pleasant companionship **2** : naturally living or growing in groups **3** : relating to human society ～ *n* : social gathering — **so·cial·ly** *adv*

so·cial·ism \'sōshə,lizəm\ *n* : social system based on government control of the production and distribution of goods — **so·cial·ist** \'sōshəlist\ *n or adj* — **so·cial·is·tic** \,sōshə-'listik\ *adj*

so·cial·ize \'sōshə,līz\ *vb* **-ized; -iz·ing 1** : regulate by socialism **2** : adapt to social needs **3** : participate in a social gathering — **so·cial·i·za·tion** \,sōshələ'zāshən\ *n*

social work *n* : services concerned with aiding the poor and socially maladjusted — **social worker** *n*

so·ci·ety \sə'sīətē\ *n, pl* **-et·ies 1** : companionship **2** : community life **3** : rich or fash-

ionable class **4** : voluntary group

so·ci·ol·o·gy \,sōsē'äləjē\ *n* : study of social relationships — **so·ci·o·log·i·cal** \-ə'läjikəl\ *adj* — **so·ci·ol·o·gist** \-'älə-jist\ *n*

¹sock \'säk\ *n, pl* **socks** *or* **sox** : short stocking

²sock *vb or n* : punch

sock·et \'säkət\ *n* : hollow part that holds something

sod \'säd\ *n* : turf ～ *vb* **-dd-** : cover with sod

so·da \'sōdə\ *n* **1** : carbonated water or a soft drink **2** : ice cream drink made with soda

sod·den \'sädᵊn\ *adj* **1** : lacking spirit **2** : soaked or soggy

so·di·um \'sōdēəm\ *n* : soft waxy silver white metallic chemical element

so·fa \'sōfə\ *n* : wide padded chair

soft \'sȯft\ *adj* **1** : not hard, rough, or harsh **2** : nonalcoholic — **soft·en** \'sȯfən\ *vb* — **soft·en·er** \-ənər\ *n* — **soft·ly** *adv* — **soft·ness** *n*

soft·ball *n* : game like baseball

soft·ware \'sȯft,war\ *n* : computer programs

sog·gy \'sägē\ *adj* **-gi·er; -est** : heavy with moisture — **sog·gi·ness** \-ēnəs\ *n*

¹soil \'sȯil\ *vb* : make or become dirty ～ *n* : embedded dirt

²**soil** *n* : loose surface material of the earth

so·journ \\'sō͟,jərn, sō'jərn\\ *n* : temporary stay ~ *vb* : reside temporarily

so·lace \\'säləs\\ *n or vb* : comfort

so·lar \\'sōlər\\ *adj* : relating to the sun or the energy in sunlight

sold *past of* SELL

sol·der \\'sädər, 'sȯd-\\ *n* : metallic alloy melted to join metallic surfaces ~ *vb* : cement with solder

sol·dier \\'sōljər\\ *n* : person in military service ~ *vb* : serve as a soldier — **sol·dier·ly** *adj or adv*

¹**sole** \\'sōl\\ *n* : bottom of the foot or a shoe — **soled** *adj*

²**sole** *n* : flatfish caught for food

³**sole** *adj* : single or only — **sole·ly** *adv*

sol·emn \\'säləm\\ *adj* **1** : dignified and ceremonial **2** : highly serious — **so·lem·ni·ty** \\sə'lemnətē\\ *n* — **sol·emn·ly** *adv*

so·lic·it \\sə'lisət\\ *vb* : ask for — **so·lic·i·ta·tion** \\-,lisə'tā-shən\\ *n*

so·lic·i·tor \\sə'lisətər\\ *n* **1** : one that solicits **2** : lawyer

so·lic·i·tous \\sə'lisətəs\\ *adj* : showing or expressing concern — **so·lic·i·tous·ly** *adv* — **so·lic·i·tude** \\sə'lisə,tüd, -,tyüd\\ *n*

sol·id \\'säləd\\ *adj* **1** : not hollow **2** : having 3 dimensions **3** : hard **4** : of good quality **5** : of one character ~ *n* **1** : 3-dimensional figure **2** : substance in solid form — **solid** *adv* — **so·lid·i·ty** \\sə'lidətē\\ *n* — **sol·id·ly** *adv* — **sol·id·ness** *n*

sol·i·dar·i·ty \\,sälə'darətē\\ *n* : unity of purpose

so·lid·i·fy \\sə'lidə,fī\\ *vb* **-fied; -fy·ing** : make or become solid — **so·lid·i·fi·ca·tion** \\-,lidəfə'kāshən\\ *n*

so·lil·o·quy \\sə'liləkwē\\ *n, pl* **-quies** : dramatic monologue — **so·lil·o·quize** \\-,kwīz\\ *vb*

sol·i·taire \\'sälə,tar\\ *n* **1** : solitary gem **2** : card game for one person

sol·i·tary \\-,terē\\ *adj* **1** : alone **2** : secluded **3** : single

sol·i·tude \\-,tüd, -,tyüd\\ *n* : state of being alone

so·lo \\'sōlō\\ *n, pl* **-los** : performance by only one person ~ *adv* : alone — **solo** *adj or vb* — **so·lo·ist** *n*

sol·stice \\'sälstəs\\ *n* : time of the year when the sun is farthest north or south of the equator

sol·u·ble \\'sälyəbəl\\ *adj* **1** : capable of being dissolved **2** : capable of being solved — **sol·u·bil·i·ty** \\,sälyə'bilətē\\ *n*

so·lu·tion \\sə'lüshən\\ *n* **1** : answer to a problem **2** : homogeneous liquid mixture

solve \'sälv\ *vb* **solved; solv-ing** : find a solution for — **solv·able** *adj*

sol·vent \'sälvənt\ *adj* **1** : able to pay all debts **2** : dissolving or able to dissolve ∼ *n* : substance that dissolves or disperses another substance — **sol·ven·cy** \-vənsē\ *n*

som·ber, som·bre \'sämbər\ *adj* **1** : dark **2** : grave — **som·ber·ly** *adv*

som·bre·ro \səm'brerō\ *n, pl* **-ros** : broad-brimmed hat

some \'səm\ *adj* **1** : one unspecified **2** : unspecified or indefinite number of **3** : at least a few or a little ∼ *pron* : a certain number or amount

-some \səm\ *adj suffix* : characterized by a thing, quality, state, or action

some·body \'səmbədē, -ˌbäd-\ *pron* : some person

some·day \'səmˌdā\ *adv* : at some future time

some·how \-ˌhaů\ *adv* : by some means

some·one \-ˌwən\ *pron* : some person

som·er·sault \'səmərˌsȯlt\ *n* : body flip — **somersault** *vb*

some·thing \'səmthiŋ\ *pron* : some undetermined or unspecified thing

some·time \'səmˌtīm\ *adv* : at a future, unknown, or unnamed time

some·times \-ˌtīmz\ *adv* : occasionally

some·what \-ˌhwət, -ˌhwät\ *adv* : in some degree

some·where \-ˌhwer\ *adv* : in, at, or to an unknown or unnamed place

som·no·lent \'sämnələnt\ *adj* : sleepy — **som·no·lence** \-ləns\ *n*

son \'sən\ *n* : male offspring

so·nar \'sōˌnär\ *n* : device that detects and locates underwater objects using sound waves

so·na·ta \sə'nätə\ *n* : instrumental composition

song \'sȯŋ\ *n* : music and words to be sung

song·bird *n* : bird with musical tones

son·ic \'sänik\ *adj* : relating to sound waves or the speed of sound

son–in–law *n, pl* **sons–in–law** : husband of one's daughter

son·net \'sänət\ *n* : poem of 14 lines

so·no·rous \sə'nōrəs, 'sänərəs\ *adj* **1** : loud, deep, or rich in sound **2** : impressive — **so·nor·i·ty** \sə'nȯrətē\ *n*

soon \'sün\ *adv* **1** : before long **2** : promptly **3** : early

soot \'sůt, 'sət, 'süt\ *n* : fine black substance formed by combustion — **sooty** *adj*

soothe \'sü<u>th</u>\ *vb* **soothed; sooth·ing** : calm or comfort — **sooth·er** *n*

sooth·say·er \'sü<u>th</u>ˌsāər\ *n* : prophet — **sooth·say·ing** \-iŋ\ *n*

sop \'säp\ *n* : conciliatory bribe, gift, or concession ∼ *vb* **-pp-** **1** : dip in a liquid **2** : soak **3** : mop up

so·phis·ti·cat·ed \səˈfistəˌkātəd\ *adj* **1** : complex **2** : wise, cultured, or shrewd in human affairs — **so·phis·ti·ca·tion** \-ˌfistəˈkāshən\ *n*

soph·ist·ry \'säfəstrē\ *n* : subtly fallacious reasoning or argument — **sophist** \'säfist\ *n*

soph·o·more \'säfᵊmˌōr, 'säfˌmōr\ *n* : 2d-year student

so·po·rif·ic \ˌsäpəˈrifik, ˌsōp-\ *adj* : causing sleep or drowsiness

so·pra·no \səˈpranō\ *n, pl* **-nos** : highest singing voice

sor·cery \'sȯrsərē\ *n* : witchcraft — **sor·cer·er** \-rər\ *n* — **sor·cer·ess** \-rəs\ *n*

sor·did \'sȯrdəd\ *adj* : filthy or vile — **sor·did·ly** *adv* — **sor·did·ness** *n*

sore \'sōr\ *adj* **sor·er; sor·est** **1** : causing pain or distress **2** : severe or intense **3** : angry ∼ *n* : sore usu. infected spot on the body — **sore·ly** *adv* — **sore·ness** *n*

sor·ghum \'sȯrgəm\ *n* : forage grass

so·ror·i·ty \səˈrȯrətē\ *n, pl* **-ties** : women's student social group

¹**sor·rel** \'sȯrəl\ *n* : brownish orange to light brown color or an animal of this color

²**sorrel** *n* : herb with sour juice

sor·row \'särō\ *n* : deep distress, sadness, or regret or a cause of this — **sor·row·ful** \-fəl\ *adj* — **sor·row·ful·ly** *adv*

sor·ry \'särē\ *adj* **-ri·er; -est** **1** : feeling sorrow, regret, or penitence **2** : dismal

sort \'sȯrt\ *n* **1** : kind **2** : nature ∼ *vb* : classify — **out of sorts** : grouchy

sor·tie \'sȯrtē, sȯr'tē\ *n* : military attack esp. against besiegers

SOS \ˌesˌōˈes\ *n* : call for help

so–so \'sōˈsō\ *adj or adv* : barely acceptable

sot \'sät\ *n* : drunkard — **sot·tish** *adj*

souf·flé \süˈflā\ *n* : baked dish made light with beaten egg whites

sought *past of* SEEK

soul \'sōl\ *n* **1** : immaterial essence of an individual life **2** : essential part **3** : person

soul·ful \'sōlfəl\ *adj* : full of or expressing deep feeling — **soul·ful·ly** *adv*

¹**sound** \'saund\ *adj* **1** : free from fault, error, or illness **2** : firm or hard **3** : showing good judgment — **sound·ly** *adv* — **sound·ness** *n*

²**sound** *n* **1** : sensation of hearing **2** : energy of vibration sensed in hearing **3** : something heard ∼ *vb* **1** : make or cause to make a sound **2** : seem — **sound·less** *adj* — **sound·less·ly** *adv* — **sound·proof** *adj or vb*

³**sound** *n* : wide strait ∼ *vb* **1** : measure the depth of (water) **2** : investigate

soup \'süp\ *n* : broth usu. containing pieces of solid food — **soupy** *adj*

sour \'saur\ *adj* **1** : having an acid or tart taste **2** : disagreeable ∼ *vb* : become or make sour — **sour·ish** *adj* — **sour·ly** *adv* — **sour·ness** *n*

source \'sōrs\ *n* **1** : point of origin **2** : one that provides something needed

souse \'saus\ *vb* **soused; sousing** **1** : pickle **2** : immerse **3** : intoxicate ∼ *n* **1** : something pickled **2** : drunkard

south \'sauth\ *adv* : to or toward the south ∼ *adj* : situated toward, at, or coming from the south ∼ *n* **1** : direction to the right of sunrise **2** *cap* : regions to the south — **south·er·ly** \'səthərlē\ *adv or adj* — **south·ern** \'səthərn\ *adj* — **South·ern·er** *n* — **south·ern·most** \-,mōst\ *adj* — **southward** \'sauthwərd\ *adv or adj* — **south·wards** \-wərdz\ *adv*

south·east \sauth'ēst, *naut* saȯ'ēst\ *n* **1** : direction between south and east **2** *cap* : regions to the southeast — **southeast** *adj or adv* — **south·east·er·ly** *adv or adj* — **south·east·ern** \-ərn\ *adj*

south pole *n* : the southernmost point of the earth

south·west \sauth'west, *naut* saȯ'west\ *n* **1** : direction between south and west **2** *cap* : regions to the southwest — **southwest** *adj or adv* — **south·west·er·ly** *adv or adj* — **south·west·ern** \-ərn\ *adj*

sou·ve·nir \'süvə,nir\ *n* : something that is a reminder of a place or event

sov·er·eign \'sävərən\ *n* **1** : supreme ruler **2** : gold coin of the United Kingdom ∼ *adj* **1** : supreme **2** : independent — **sov·er·eign·ty** \-tē\ *n*

¹**sow** \'sau\ *n* : female swine

²**sow** \'sō\ *vb* **sowed; sown** \'sōn\ *or* **sowed; sow·ing** **1** : plant or strew with seed **2** : scatter abroad — **sow·er** \'sōər\ *n*

sox *pl of* SOCK

soy·bean \'sȯi,bēn\ *n* : legume with edible seeds

spa \'spä\ *n* : resort at a mineral spring

space \'spās\ *n* **1** : period of time **2** : area in, around, or between **3** : region beyond earth's atmosphere **4** : accommodations ~ *vb* **spaced; spac·ing** : place at intervals — **space·craft** *n* — **space·flight** *n* — **space·man** *n* — **space·ship** *n*

spa·cious \'spāshəs\ *adj* : large or roomy — **spa·cious·ly** *adv* — **spa·cious·ness** *n*

¹spade \'spād\ *n or vb* : shovel — **spade·ful** *n*

²spade *n* : playing card marked with a black figure like an inverted heart

spa·ghet·ti \spə'getē\ *n* : pasta strings

spam \'spam\ *n* : unsolicited commercial e-mail

span \'span\ *n* **1** : amount of time **2** : distance between supports ~ *vb* **-nn-** : extend across

span·gle \'spaŋgəl\ *n* : small disk of shining metal or plastic — **spangle** *vb*

span·iel \'spanyəl\ *n* : small or medium-sized dog with drooping ears and long wavy hair

spank \'spaŋk\ *vb* : hit on the buttocks with an open hand

¹spar \'spär\ *n* : pole or boom

²spar *vb* **-rr-** : practice boxing

spare \'spar\ *adj* **1** : held in reserve **2** : thin or scanty ~ *vb* **spared; spar·ing** **1** : reserve or avoid using **2** : avoid punishing or killing — **spare** *n*

spar·ing \'spariŋ\ *adj* : thrifty — **spar·ing·ly** *adv*

spark \'spärk\ *n* **1** : tiny hot and glowing particle **2** : smallest beginning or germ **3** : visible electrical discharge ~ *vb* **1** : emit or produce sparks **2** : stir to activity

spar·kle \'spärkəl\ *vb* **-kled; -kling** **1** : flash **2** : effervesce ~ *n* : gleam — **spark·ler** \-klər\ *n*

spar·row \'sparō\ *n* : small singing bird

sparse \'spärs\ *adj* **spars·er; spars·est** : thinly scattered — **sparse·ly** *adv*

spasm \'spazəm\ *n* **1** : involuntary muscular contraction **2** : sudden, violent, and temporary effort or feeling — **spas·mod·ic** \spaz'mädik\ *adj* — **spas·mod·i·cal·ly** *adv*

spas·tic \'spastik\ *adj* : relating to, marked by, or affected with muscular spasm — **spas·tic** *n*

¹spat \'spat\ *past of* SPIT

²spat *n* : petty dispute

spa·tial \'spāshəl\ *adj* : relating to space — **spa·tial·ly** *adv*

spat·ter \'spatər\ *vb* : splash with drops of liquid — **spatter** *n*

spat·u·la \'spachələ\ *n* : flexible knifelike utensil

spawn \\'spȯn\ *vb* **1** : produce eggs or offspring **2** : bring forth ~ *n* : egg cluster — **spawn·er** *n*

spay \\'spā\ *vb* : remove the ovaries of (a female)

speak \\'spēk\ *vb* **spoke** \\'spōk\; **spo·ken** \\'spōkən\; **speak·ing** **1** : utter words **2** : express orally **3** : address an audience **4** : use (a language) in talking — **speak·er** *n*

spear \\'spir\ *n* : long pointed weapon ~ *vb* : strike or pierce with a spear

spear·head *n* : leading force, element, or influence — **spear·head** *vb*

spear·mint *n* : aromatic garden mint

spe·cial \\'speshəl\ *adj* **1** : unusual or unique **2** : particularly favored **3** : set aside for a particular use — **special** *n* — **spe·cial·ly** *adv*

spe·cial·ist \\'speshəlist\ *n* **1** : person who specializes in a particular branch of learning or activity **2** : any of four enlisted ranks in the army corresponding to the grades of corporal through sergeant first class

spe·cial·ize \\'speshə,līz\ *vb* **-ized; -iz·ing** : concentrate one's efforts — **spe·cial·i·za·tion** \,speshələ'zāshən\ *n*

spe·cial·ty \\'speshəltē\ *n, pl* **-ties** : area or field in which one specializes

spe·cie \\'spēshē, -sē\ *n* : money in coin

spe·cies \\'spēshēz, -sēz\ *n, pl* **spe·cies** : biological grouping of closely related organisms

spe·cif·ic \spi'sifik\ *adj* : definite or exact — **spe·cif·i·cal·ly** *adv*

spec·i·fi·ca·tion \,spesəfə'kā-shən\ *n* **1** : act or process of specifying **2** : detailed description of work to be done — usu. pl.

spec·i·fy \\'spesə,fī\ *vb* **-fied; -fy·ing** : mention precisely or by name

spec·i·men \-əmən\ *n* : typical example

spe·cious \\'spēshəs\ *adj* : apparently but not really genuine or correct

speck \\'spek\ *n* : tiny particle or blemish — **speck** *vb*

speck·led \\'spekəld\ *adj* : marked with spots

spec·ta·cle \\'spektikəl\ *n* **1** : impressive public display **2** *pl* : eyeglasses

spec·tac·u·lar \spek'takyələr\ *adj* : sensational or showy

spec·ta·tor \\'spek,tātər\ *n* : person who looks on

spec·ter, spec·tre \\'spektər\ *n* **1** : ghost **2** : haunting vision

spec·tral \'spektrəl\ *adj* : relating to or resembling a specter or spectrum

spec·trum \'spektrəm\ *n, pl* **-tra** \-trə\ *or* **-trums** : series of colors formed when white light is dispersed into its components

spec·u·late \'spekyə‚lāt\ *vb* **-lat·ed; -lat·ing** **1** : think about things yet unknown **2** : risk money in a business deal in hope of high profit — **spec·u·la·tion** \‚spekyə'lāshən\ *n* — **spec·u·la·tive** \'spekyə‚lātiv\ *adj* — **spec·u·la·tor** \-‚lātər\ *n*

speech \'spēch\ *n* **1** : power, act, or manner of speaking **2** : talk given to an audience — **speech·less** *adj*

speed \'spēd\ *n* **1** : quality of being fast **2** : rate of motion or performance ∼ *vb* **sped** \'sped\ *or* **speed·ed; speed·ing** : go at a great or excessive rate of speed — **speed·boat** *n* — **speed·er** *n* — **speed·i·ly** \'spēd³lē\ *adv* — **speed·up** \-‚əp\ *n* — **speedy** *adj*

speed·om·e·ter \spi'dämətər\ *n* : instrument for indicating speed

¹spell \'spel\ *n* : influence of or like magic

²spell *vb* **1** : name, write, or print the letters of **2** : mean — **spell·er** *n*

³spell *vb* : substitute for or relieve (someone) ∼ *n* **1** : turn at work **2** : period of time

spell·bound *adj* : held by a spell

spend \'spend\ *vb* **spent** \'spent\; **spend·ing** **1** : pay out **2** : cause or allow to pass — **spend·er** *n*

spend·thrift \'spend‚thrift\ *n* : wasteful person

sperm \'spərm\ *n, pl* **sperm** *or* **sperms** : semen or a germ cell in it

spew \'spyü\ *vb* : gush out in a stream

sphere \'sfir\ *n* **1** : figure with every point on its surface at an equal distance from the center **2** : round body **3** : range of action or influence — **spher·i·cal** \'sfirikəl, 'sfer-\ *adj*

spher·oid \'sfir-\ *n* : spherelike figure

spice \'spīs\ *n* **1** : aromatic plant product for seasoning food **2** : interesting quality — **spice** *vb* — **spicy** *adj*

spi·der \'spīdər\ *n* : small insectlike animal with 8 legs — **spi·dery** *adj*

spig·ot \'spigət, 'spikət\ *n* : faucet

spike \'spīk\ *n* : very large nail ∼ *vb* **spiked; spik·ing** : fasten or pierce with a spike — **spiked** \'spīkt\ *adj*

spill \'spil\ *vb* **1** : fall, flow, or run out unintentionally **2** : divulge ~ *n* **1** : act of spilling **2** : something spilled — **spill-able** *adj*

spill·way *n* : passage for surplus water

spin \\'spin\\ *vb* **spun** \\'spən\\; **spin·ning** **1** : draw out fiber and twist into thread **2** : form thread from a sticky body fluid **3** : revolve or cause to revolve extremely fast ~ *n* : rapid rotating motion — **spin·ner** *n*

spin·ach \\'spinich\\ *n* : garden herb with edible leaves

spi·nal \\'spīn³l\\ *adj* : relating to the backbone — **spi·nal·ly** *adv*

spinal cord *n* : thick strand of nervous tissue that extends from the brain along the back within the backbone

spin·dle \\'spind³l\\ *n* **1** : stick used for spinning thread **2** : shaft around which something turns

spin·dly \\'spindlē\\ *adj* : tall and slender

spine \\'spīn\\ *n* **1** : backbone **2** : stiff sharp projection on a plant or animal — **spine·less** *adj* — **spiny** *adj*

spin·et \\'spinət\\ *n* : small piano

spin·ster \\'spinstər\\ *n* : woman who has never married

spi·ral \\'spīrəl\\ *adj* : circling or winding around a single point or line — **spiral** *n or vb* — **spi·ral·ly** *adv*

spire \\'spīr\\ *n* : steeple — **spiry** *adj*

spir·it \\'spirət\\ *n* **1** : life-giving force **2** *cap* : presence of God **3** : ghost **4** : mood **5** : vivacity or enthusiasm **6** *pl* : alcoholic liquor ~ *vb* : carry off secretly — **spir·it·ed** *adj* — **spir·it·less** *adj*

spir·i·tu·al \\'spirichəwəl\\ *adj* **1** : relating to the spirit or sacred matters **2** : deeply religious ~ *n* : religious folk song — **spir·i·tu·al·i·ty** \\ˌspirichə-'walətē\\ *n* — **spir·i·tu·al·ly** *adv*

spir·i·tu·al·ism \\'spirichəwə-ˌlizəm\\ *n* : belief that spirits communicate with the living — **spir·i·tu·al·ist** \\-list\\ *n or adj*

¹spit \\'spit\\ *n* **1** : rod for holding and turning meat over a fire **2** : point of land that runs into the water

²spit *vb* **spit** *or* **spat** \\'spat\\; **spit·ting** : eject saliva from the mouth ~ *n* **1** : saliva **2** : perfect likeness

spite \\'spīt\\ *n* : petty ill will ~ *vb* **spit·ed; spit·ing** : annoy or offend — **spite·ful** \\-fəl\\ *adj* — **spite·ful·ly** *adv* — **in spite of** : in defiance or contempt of

spit·tle \\'spit³l\\ *n* : saliva

spit·toon \\spi'tün\\ *n* : receptacle for spit

splash \\'splash\\ *vb* : scatter a liquid on — **splash** *n*

splat·ter \'splatər\ *vb* : spatter
— **splatter** *n*

splay \'splā\ *vb* : spread out or
apart — **splay** *n or adj*

spleen \'splēn\ *n* **1** : organ for
maintenance of the blood **2**
: spite or anger

splen·did \'splendəd\ *adj* **1**
: impressive in beauty or brilliance **2** : outstanding —
splen·did·ly *adv*

splen·dor \'splendər\ *n* **1**
: brilliance **2** : magnificence

splice \'splīs\ *vb* **spliced; splic-
ing** : join (2 things) end to end
— **splice** *n*

splint \'splint\ *n* **1** : thin strip
of wood **2** : something that
keeps an injured body part in
place

splin·ter \'splintər\ *n* : thin
needlelike piece ~ *vb* : break
into splinters

split \'split\ *vb* **split; split·ting**
: divide lengthwise or along a
grain — **split** *n*

splotch \'spläch\ *n* : blotch

splurge \'splərj\ *vb* **splurged;
splurg·ing** : indulge oneself
— **splurge** *n*

splut·ter \'splətər\ *n* : sputter
— **splutter** *vb*

spoil \'spȯil\ *n* : plunder ~ *vb*
spoiled \'spȯild, 'spȯilt\ *or*
spoilt \'spȯilt\; **spoil·ing 1**
: pillage **2** : ruin **3** : rot —
spoil·age \'spȯilij\ *n* — **spoil-
er** *n*

¹**spoke** \'spōk\ *past of* SPEAK

²**spoke** *n* : rod from the hub to
the rim of a wheel

spo·ken *past part of* SPEAK

spokes·man \'spōksmən\ *n*
: person who speaks for others

spokes·wom·an \-ˌwümən\ *n*
: woman who speaks for others

sponge \'spənj\ *n* **1** : porous
water-absorbing mass that
forms the skeleton of some
marine animals **2** : spongelike
material used for wiping ~
vb **sponged; spong·ing 1**
: wipe with a sponge **2** : live
at another's expense — **spongy**
\'spənjē\ *adj*

spon·sor \'spänsər\ *n* : one
who assumes responsibility for
another or who provides financial support — **sponsor** *vb* —
spon·sor·ship *n*

spon·ta·ne·ous \spän'tānēəs\
adj : done, produced, or occurring naturally or without
planning — **spon·ta·ne·i·ty**
\ˌspäntən'ēətē\ *n* — **spon·ta-
ne·ous·ly** \spän'tānēəslē\ *adv*

spoof \'spüf\ *vb* : make good-
natured fun of — **spoof** *n*

spook \'spük\ *n* : ghost ~ *vb*
: frighten — **spooky** *adj*

spool \'spül\ *n* : cylinder on
which something is wound

spoon \'spün\ *n* : utensil consisting of a small shallow bowl
with a handle — **spoon** *vb* —
spoon·ful \-ˌfül\ *n*

spoor \\'spu̇r, 'spōr\ *n* : track or trail esp. of a wild animal

spo·rad·ic \spə'radik\ *adj* : occasional — **spo·rad·i·cal·ly** *adv*

spore \spōr\ *n* : primitive usu. one-celled reproductive body

sport \\'spōrt\ *vb* **1** : frolic **2** : show off ～ *n* **1** : physical activity engaged in for pleasure **2** : jest **3** : person who shows good sportsmanship — **sport·ive** \-iv\ *adj* — **sporty** *adj*

sports·cast \\'spōrts,kast\ *n* : broadcast of a sports event — **sports·cast·er** \-,kastər\ *n*

sports·man \-mən\ *n* : one who enjoys hunting and fishing

sports·man·ship \-mən,ship\ *n* : ability to be gracious in winning or losing

spot \\'spät\ *n* **1** : blemish **2** : distinctive small part **3** : location ～ *vb* **-tt-** **1** : mark with spots **2** : see or recognize ～ *adj* : made at random or in limited numbers — **spot·less** *adj* — **spot·less·ly** *adv*

spot·light *n* **1** : intense beam of light **2** : center of public interest — **spotlight** *vb*

spot·ty \\'spätē\ *adj* **-ti·er; -est** : uneven in quality

spouse \\'spau̇s\ *n* : one's husband or wife

spout \\'spau̇t\ *vb* **1** : shoot forth in a stream **2** : say pompously ～ *n* **1** : opening through which liquid spouts **2** : jet of liquid

sprain \\'sprān\ *n* : twisting injury to a joint ～ *vb* : injure with a sprain

sprat \\'sprat\ *n* : small or young herring

sprawl \\'sprȯl\ *vb* : lie or sit with limbs spread out — **sprawl** *n*

¹spray \\'sprā\ *n* : branch or arrangement of flowers

²spray *n* **1** : mist **2** : device that discharges liquid as a mist — **spray** *vb* — **spray·er** *n*

spread \\'spred\ *vb* **spread; spread·ing** **1** : open up or unfold **2** : scatter or smear over a surface **3** : cause to be known or to exist over a wide area ～ *n* **1** : extent to which something is spread **2** : cloth cover **3** : something intended to be spread — **spread·er** *n*

spread·sheet \\'spred,shēt\ *n* : accounting program for a computer

spree \\'sprē\ *n* : burst of indulging in something

sprig \\'sprig\ *n* : small shoot or twig

spright·ly \\'sprītlē\ *adj* **-li·er; -est** : lively — **spright·li·ness** *n*

spring \sprin\ *vb* **sprang** \\'spran\ *or* **sprung** \\'sprən\; **sprung; spring·ing** **1** : move or grow quickly or by elastic force **2** : come from by descent **3** : make known suddenly ∼ *n* **1** : source **2** : flow of water from underground **3** : season between winter and summer **4** : elastic body or device (as a coil of wire) **5** : leap **6** : elastic power — **springy** *adj*

sprin·kle \'spriŋkəl\ *vb* **-kled; -kling** : scatter in small drops or particles ∼ *n* : light rainfall — **sprin·kler** *n*

sprint \'sprint\ *n* : short run at top speed — **sprint** *vb* — **sprint·er** *n*

sprite \'sprīt\ *n* : elf or elfish person

sprock·et \'spräkət\ *n* : toothed wheel whose teeth engage the links of a chain

sprout \'spraut\ *vb* : send out new growth ∼ *n* : plant shoot

¹**spruce** \'sprüs\ *n* : conical evergreen tree

²**spruce** *adj* **spruc·er; spruc·est** : neat and stylish in appearance ∼ *vb* **spruced; sprucing** : make or become neat

spry \'sprī\ *adj* **spri·er** *or* **spry·er** \'sprīər\; **spri·est** *or* **spry·est** \'sprīəst\ : agile and active

spume \'spyüm\ *n* : froth

spun *past of* SPIN

spunk \'spəŋk\ *n* : courage — **spunky** *adj*

spur \'spər\ *n* **1** : pointed device used to urge on a horse **2** : something that urges to action **3** : projecting part ∼ *vb* **-rr-** : urge on — **spurred** *adj*

spu·ri·ous \'spyurēəs\ *adj* : not genuine

spurn \'spərn\ *vb* : reject

¹**spurt** \'spərt\ *n* : burst of effort, speed, or activity ∼ *vb* : make a spurt

²**spurt** *vb* : gush out ∼ *n* : sudden gush

sput·ter \'spətər\ *vb* **1** : talk hastily and indistinctly in excitement **2** : make popping sounds — **sputter** *n*

spy \'spī\ *vb* **spied; spy·ing** : watch or try to gather information secretly — **spy** *n*

squab \'skwäb\ *n, pl* **squabs** *or* **squab** : young pigeon

squab·ble \'skwäbəl\ *n or vb* : dispute

squad \'skwäd\ *n* : small group

squad·ron \'skwädrən\ *n* : small military unit

squal·id \'skwäləd\ *adj* : filthy or wretched

squall \'skwol\ *n* : sudden violent brief storm — **squally** *adj*

squa·lor \'skwälər\ *n* : quality or state of being squalid

squan·der \'skwändər\ *vb* : waste

square \'skwar\ *n* **1** : instrument for measuring right angles **2** : flat figure that has 4

equal sides and 4 right angles
3 : open area in a city **4** : product of number multiplied by itself ~ *adj* **squar·er; squar-
est 1** : being a square in form
2 : having sides meet at right
angles **3** : multiplied by itself **4** : being a square unit of
area **5** : honest ~ *vb* **squared;
squar·ing 1** : form into a
square **2** : multiply (a number)
by itself **3** : conform **4** : settle — **square·ly** *adv*

¹**squash** \'skwäsh, 'skwȯsh\
vb **1** : press flat **2** : suppress

²**squash** *n, pl* **squash·es** *or*
squash : garden vegetable

squat \'skwät\ *vb* **-tt-** **1**
: stoop or sit on one's heels **2**
: settle on land one does not
own ~ *n* : act or posture of
squatting ~ *adj* **squat·ter;
squat·test** : short and thick —
squat·ter *n*

squawk \'skwȯk\ *n* : harsh
loud cry — **squawk** *vb*

squeak \'skwēk\ *vb* : make a
thin high-pitched sound —
squeak *n* — **squeaky** *adj*

squeal \'skwēl\ *vb* **1** : make a
shrill sound or cry **2** : protest
— **squeal** *n*

squea·mish \'skwēmish\ *adj*
: easily nauseated or disgusted

squeeze \'skwēz\ *vb* **squeezed;
squeez·ing 1** : apply pressure
to **2** : extract by pressure —
squeeze *n* — **squeez·er** *n*

squelch \'skwelch\ *vb* : suppress (as with a retort) —
squelch *n*

squid \'skwid\ *n, pl* **squid** *or*
squids : 10-armed long-
bodied sea mollusk

squint \'skwint\ *vb* : look with
the eyes partly closed — **squint**
n or adj

squire \'skwīr\ *n* **1** : knight's
aide **2** : country landholder **3**
: lady's devoted escort ~ *vb*
squired; squir·ing : escort

squirm \'skwərm\ *vb* : wriggle

squir·rel \'skwərəl\ *n* : rodent
with a long bushy tail

squirt \'skwərt\ *vb* : eject liquid in a spurt — **squirt** *n*

stab \stab\ *n* **1** : wound made
by a pointed weapon **2** : quick
thrust **3** : attempt ~ *vb* **-bb-**
: pierce or wound with or as if
with a pointed weapon

¹**sta·ble** \'stābəl\ *n* : building
for domestic animals ~ *vb*
-bled; -bling : keep in a stable

²**stable** *adj* **sta·bler; sta·blest 1**
: firmly established **2** : mentally and emotionally healthy
3 : steady — **sta·bil·i·ty** \stə-
'bilətē\ *n* — **sta·bil·iza·tion**
\ˌstābələ'zāshən\ *n* — **sta·bi-
lize** \'stābəˌlīz\ *vb* — **sta·bi-
liz·er** *n*

stac·ca·to \stə'kätō\ *adj* : disconnected

stack \'stak\ *n* : large pile ~
vb : pile up

sta·di·um \'stādēəm\ *n* : outdoor sports arena

staff \'staf\ *n, pl* **staffs** \'stafs, stavz\ *or* **staves** \'stāvz, 'stāvz\ 1 : rod or supporting cane 2 : people assisting a leader 3 : 5 horizontal lines on which music is written ~ *vb* : supply with workers — **staffer** *n*

staff sergeant *n* : noncommissioned officer ranking next above a sergeant in the army, air force, or marine corps

stag \'stag\ *n, pl* **stags** *or* **stag** : male deer ~ *adj* : only for men ~ *adv* : without a date

stage \'stāj\ *n* 1 : raised platform for a speaker or performers 2 : theater 3 : step in a process ~ *vb* **staged; staging** : produce (a play)

stage·coach *n* : passenger coach

stag·ger \'stagər\ *vb* 1 : reel or cause to reel from side to side 2 : overlap or alternate — **stagger** *n* — **stag·ger·ing·ly** *adv*

stag·nant \'stagnənt\ *adj* : not moving or active — **stag·nate** \-ˌnāt\ *vb* — **stag·na·tion** \stag'nāshən\ *n*

¹**staid** \'stād\ *adj* : sedate

²**staid** *past of* STAY

stain \'stān\ *vb* 1 : discolor 2 : dye (as wood) 3 : disgrace ~ *n* 1 : discolored area 2 : mark of guilt 3 : coloring preparation — **stain·less** *adj*

stair \'star\ *n* 1 : step in a series for going from one level to another 2 *pl* : flight of steps — **stair·way** *n*

stair·case *n* : series of steps with their framework

stake \'stāk\ *n* 1 : usu. small post driven into the ground 2 : bet 3 : prize in a contest ~ *vb* **staked; stak·ing** 1 : mark or secure with a stake 2 : bet

sta·lac·tite \stə'lakˌtīt\ *n* : icicle-shaped deposit hanging in a cavern

sta·lag·mite \stə'lagˌmīt\ *n* : icicle-shaped deposit on a cavern floor

stale \'stāl\ *adj* **stal·er; stal·est** 1 : having lost good taste and quality from age 2 : no longer new, strong, or effective — **stale·ness** *n*

stale·mate \'stālˌmāt\ *n* : deadlock — **stalemate** *vb*

¹**stalk** \'stȯk\ *vb* 1 : walk stiffly or proudly 2 : pursue stealthily

²**stalk** *n* : plant stem — **stalked** \'stȯkt\ *adj*

¹**stall** \'stȯl\ *n* 1 : compartment in a stable 2 : booth where articles are sold

²**stall** *vb* : bring or come to a standstill unintentionally

³**stall** *vb* : delay, evade, or keep a situation going to gain advantage or time

stal·lion \'stalyən\ *n* : male horse

stal·wart \'stȯlwərt\ *adj* : strong or brave

sta·men \'stāmən\ *n* : flower organ that produces pollen

stam·i·na \'stamənə\ *n* : endurance

stam·mer \'stamər\ *vb* : hesitate in speaking — **stammer** *n*

stamp \'stamp\ *vb* **1** : pound with the sole of the foot or a heavy implement **2** : impress or imprint **3** : cut out with a die **4** : attach a postage stamp to ~ *n* **1** : device for stamping **2** : act of stamping **3** : government seal showing a tax or fee has been paid

stam·pede \stam'pēd\ *n* : headlong rush of frightened animals ~ *vb* **-ped·ed; -ped·ing** : flee in panic

stance \'stans\ *n* : way of standing

¹**stanch** \'stȯnch, 'stänch\ *vb* : stop the flow of (as blood)

²**stanch** *var of* STAUNCH

stan·chion \'stanchən\ *n* : upright support

stand \'stand\ *vb* **stood** \'stu̇d\; **stand·ing 1** : be at rest in or assume an upright position **2** : remain unchanged **3** : be steadfast **4** : maintain a relative position or rank **5** : set upright **6** : undergo or endure ~ *n* **1** : act or place of standing, staying, or resisting **2** : sales

booth **3** : structure for holding something upright **4** : group of plants growing together **5** *pl* : tiered seats **6** : opinion or viewpoint

stan·dard \'standərd\ *n* **1** : symbolic figure or flag **2** : model, rule, or guide **3** : upright support — **standard** *adj* — **stan·dard·i·za·tion** \ˌstandərdə'zāshən\ *n* — **stan·dard·ize** \'standərdˌīz\ *vb*

standard time *n* : time established over a region or country

stand·ing \'standiŋ\ *n* **1** : relative position or rank **2** : duration

stand·still *n* : state of rest

stank *past of* STINK

stan·za \'stanzə\ *n* : division of a poem

¹**sta·ple** \'stāpəl\ *n* : U-shaped wire fastener — **staple** *vb* — **sta·pler** \-plər\ *n*

²**staple** *n* : chief commodity or item — **staple** *adj*

star \'stär\ *n* **1** : celestial body visible as a point of light **2** : 5- or 6-pointed figure representing a star **3** : leading performer ~ *vb* **-rr- 1** : mark with a star **2** : play the leading role — **stardom** \'stärdəm\ *n* — **star·less** *adj* — **star·light** *n* — **star·ry** *adj*

star·board \'stärbərd\ *n* : right side of a ship or airplane looking forward — **starboard** *adj*

starch \'stärch\ *n* : nourishing carbohydrate from plants also used in adhesives and laundering ~ *vb* : stiffen with starch — **starchy** *adj*

stare \'star\ *vb* **stared; star·ing** : look intently with wide-open eyes — **stare** *n* — **star·er** *n*

stark \'stärk\ *adj* **1** : absolute **2** : severe or bleak ~ *adv* : completely — **stark·ly** *adv*

star·ling \'stärliŋ\ *n* : bird related to the crows

start \'stärt\ *vb* **1** : twitch or jerk (as from surprise) **2** : perform or show performance of the first part of an action or process ~ *n* **1** : sudden involuntary motion **2** : beginning — **start·er** *n*

star·tle \'stärt⁰l\ *vb* **-tled; -tling** : frighten or surprise suddenly

starve \'stärv\ *vb* **starved; starv·ing** **1** : suffer or die from hunger **2** : kill with hunger — **star·va·tion** \stär'vāshən\ *n*

stash \'stash\ *vb* : store in a secret place for future use — **stash** *n*

state \'stāt\ *n* **1** : condition of being **2** : condition of mind **3** : nation or a political unit within it ~ *vb* **stat·ed; stat·ing** **1** : express in words **2** : establish — **state·hood** \-ˌhùd\ *n*

state·ly \'stātlē\ *adj* **-li·er; -est** : having impressive dignity — **state·li·ness** *n*

state·ment \'stātmənt\ *n* **1** : something stated **2** : financial summary

state·room *n* : private room on a ship

states·man \'stātsmən\ *n* : one skilled in government or diplomacy — **states·man·like** *adj* — **states·man·ship** *n*

stat·ic \'statik\ *adj* **1** : relating to bodies at rest or forces in equilibrium **2** : not moving **3** : relating to stationary charges of electricity ~ *n* : noise on radio or television from electrical disturbances

sta·tion \'stāshən\ *n* **1** : place of duty **2** : regular stop on a bus or train route **3** : social standing **4** : place where radio or television programs originate ~ *vb* : assign to a station

sta·tion·ary \'stāshəˌnerē\ *adj* **1** : not moving or not movable **2** : not changing

sta·tio·nery \'stāshəˌnerē\ *n* : letter paper with envelopes

sta·tis·tic \stə'tistik\ *n* : single item of statistics

sta·tis·tics \-tiks\ *n pl* : numerical facts collected for study — **sta·tis·ti·cal** \-tikəl\ *adj* — **sta·tis·ti·cal·ly** *adv* — **stat·is·ti·cian** \ˌstatə'stishən\ *n*

stat·u·ary \'stachəˌwerē\ *n, pl* **-ar·ies** : collection of statues

stat·ue \'stachü\ *n* : solid 3-dimensional likeness — **stat·u·ette** \ˌstachə'wet\ *n*

stat·u·esque \ˌstachə'wesk\ *adj* : tall and shapely

stat·ure \'stachər\ *n* **1** : height **2** : status gained by achievement

sta·tus \'stātəs, 'stat-\ *n* : relative situation or condition

sta·tus quo \-'kwō\ *n* : existing state of affairs

stat·ute \'stachüt\ *n* : law — **stat·u·to·ry** \'stachəˌtōrē\ *adj*

staunch \'stȯnch\ *adj* : steadfast — **staunch·ly** *adv*

stave \'stāv\ *n* : narrow strip of wood ~ *vb* **staved** *or* **stove** \'stōv\; **stav·ing** **1** : break a hole in **2** : drive away

staves *pl of* STAFF

¹**stay** \'stā\ *n* : support ~ *vb* **stayed; stay·ing** : prop up

²**stay** *vb* **stayed** \'stād\ *or* **staid** \'stād\; **stay·ing** **1** : pause **2** : remain **3** : reside **4** : stop or postpone **5** : satisfy for a time ~ *n* : a staying

stead \'sted\ *n* : one's place, job, or function — **in good stead** : to advantage

stead·fast \-ˌfast\ *adj* : faithful or determined — **stead·fast·ly** *adv*

steady \'stedē\ *adj* **steadi·er; -est** **1** : firm in position or sure in movement **2** : calm or reliable **3** : constant **4** : regular ~ *vb* **stead·ied; steady·ing** : make or become steady —

steadi·ly \'sted³lē\ *adv* — **steadi·ness** *n* — **steady** *adv*

steak \'stāk\ *n* : thick slice of meat

steal \'stēl\ *vb* **stole** \'stōl\; **sto·len** \'stōlən\; **steal·ing** **1** : take and carry away wrongfully and with intent to keep **2** : move secretly or slowly

stealth \'stelth\ *n* : secret or unobtrusive procedure — **stealth·i·ly** \-thəlē\ *adv* — **stealthy** *adj*

steam \'stēm\ *n* : vapor of boiling water ~ *vb* : give off steam — **steam·boat** *n* — **steam·ship** *n* — **steamy** *adj*

steed \'stēd\ *n* : horse

steel \'stēl\ *n* : tough carbon-containing iron ~ *vb* : fill with courage — **steel** *adj* — **steely** *adj*

¹**steep** \'stēp\ *adj* : having a very sharp slope or great elevation — **steep·ly** *adv* — **steep·ness** *n*

²**steep** *vb* : soak in a liquid

stee·ple \'stēpəl\ *n* : usu. tapering church tower

stee·ple·chase *n* : race over hurdles

¹**steer** \'stir\ *n* : castrated ox

²**steer** *vb* **1** : direct the course of (as a ship or car) **2** : guide

steer·age \'stirij\ *n* : section in a ship for people paying the lowest fares

stein \'stīn\ *n* : mug

stel·lar \'stelər\ *adj* : relating to stars or resembling a star

¹**stem** \'stem\ *n* : main upright part of a plant ~ *vb* **-mm-** **1** : derive **2** : make progress against — **stem·less** *adj* — **stemmed** *adj*

²**stem** *vb* **-mm-** : stop the flow of

stem cell *n* : undifferentiated cell that may give rise to many different types of cells

stench \'stench\ *n* : stink

sten·cil \'stensəl\ *n* : printing sheet cut with letters to let ink pass through — **stencil** *vb*

ste·nog·ra·phy \stə'nägrəfē\ *n* : art or process of writing in shorthand — **ste·nog·ra·pher** \-fər\ *n* — **steno·graph·ic** \ˌstenə'grafik\ *adj*

sten·to·ri·an \sten'tōrēən\ *adj* : extremely loud and powerful

step \'step\ *n* **1** : single action of a leg in walking or running **2** : rest for the foot in going up or down **3** : degree, rank, or stage **4** : way of walking ~ *vb* **-pp-** **1** : move by steps **2** : press with the foot

step- \'step-\ *comb form* : related by a remarriage and not by blood

step·lad·der *n* : light portable set of steps in a hinged frame

steppe \'step\ *n* : dry grassy treeless land esp. of Asia

-ster \stər\ *n suffix* **1** : one that does, makes, or uses **2** : one that is associated with or takes part in **3** : one that is

ste·reo \'sterēˌō, 'stir-\ *n, pl* **-reos** : stereophonic sound system — **stereo** *adj*

ste·reo·phon·ic \ˌsterēə'fänik, ˌstir-\ *adj* : relating to a 3-dimensional effect of reproduced sound

ste·reo·type \'sterēəˌtīp, 'stir-\ *n* : gross often mistaken generalization — **stereotype** *vb* — **ste·reo·typ·i·cal** \ˌsterēə-tipikəl\ *adj* — **ste·reo·typi·cal·ly** *adv*

ste·reo·typed \'sterēəˌtīpt, 'stir-\ *adj* : lacking originality or individuality

ster·ile \'sterəl\ *adj* **1** : unable to bear fruit, crops, or offspring **2** : free from disease germs — **ste·ril·i·ty** \stə-'rilətē\ *n* — **ster·il·i·za·tion** \ˌsterələ'zāshən\ *n* — **ster·il·ize** \-əˌlīz\ *vb* — **ster·il·iz·er** *n*

ster·ling \'stərliŋ\ *adj* **1** : being or made of an alloy of 925 parts of silver with 75 parts of copper **2** : excellent

¹**stern** \'stərn\ *adj* : severe — **stern·ly** *adv* — **stern·ness** *n*

²**stern** *n* : back end of a boat

ster·num \'stərnəm\ *n, pl* **-nums** *or* **-na** \-nə\ : long flat chest bone joining the 2 sets of ribs

stetho·scope \'stethəˌskōp\ *n* : instrument used for listening to sounds in the chest

ste·ve·dore \\'stēvə‚dōr\ *n* : worker who loads and unloads ships

stew \\'stü, 'styü\ *n* **1** : dish of boiled meat and vegetables **2** : state of worry or agitation — **stew** *vb*

stew·ard \\'stüərd, 'styü-\ *n* **1** : manager of an estate or an organization **2** : person on a ship or airliner who looks after passenger comfort — **steward-ship** *n*

stew·ard·ess \-əs\ *n* : woman who is a steward (as on an airplane)

¹**stick** \\'stik\ *n* **1** : cut or broken branch **2** : long thin piece of wood or something resembling it

²**stick** *vb* **stuck** \\'stək\; **sticking 1** : stab **2** : thrust or project **3** : hold fast to something **4** : attach **5** : become jammed or fixed

stick·er \\'stikər\ *n* : adhesive label

stick·ler \\'stiklər\ *n* : one who insists on exactness or completeness

sticky \\'stikē\ *adj* **stick·i·er; -est 1** : adhesive or gluey **2** : muggy **3** : difficult

stiff \\'stif\ *adj* **1** : not bending easily **2** : tense **3** : formal **4** : strong **5** : severe — **stiff·en** \\'stifən\ *vb* — **stiff·en·er** \-ənər\ *n* — **stiff·ly** *adv* — **stiff·ness** *n*

sti·fle \\'stīfəl\ *vb* **-fled; -fling 1** : smother or suffocate **2** : suppress

stig·ma \\'stigmə\ *n, pl* **-ma·ta** \stig'mätə, 'stigmətə\ *or* **-mas** : mark of disgrace — **stig·ma·tize** \\'stigmə‚tīz\ *vb*

stile \\'stīl\ *n* : steps for crossing a fence

sti·let·to \stə'letō\ *n, pl* **-tos** *or* **-toes** : slender dagger

¹**still** \\'stil\ *adj* **1** : motionless **2** : silent ~ *vb* : make or become still ~ *adv* **1** : without motion **2** : up to and during this time **3** : in spite of that ~ *n* : silence — **still·ness** *n*

²**still** *n* : apparatus used in distillation

still·born *adj* : born dead — **still·birth** *n*

stilt \\'stilt\ *n* : one of a pair of poles for walking

stilt·ed \\'stiltəd\ *adj* : not easy and natural

stim·u·lant \\'stimyələnt\ *n* : substance that temporarily increases the activity of an organism — **stimulant** *adj*

stim·u·late \-‚lāt\ *vb* **-lat·ed; -lat·ing** : make active — **stim·u·la·tion** \‚stimyə'lāshən\ *n*

stim·u·lus \\'stimyələs\ *n, pl* **-li** \-‚lī\ : something that stimulates

sting \\'stiŋ\ *vb* **stung** \\'stəŋ\; **sting·ing 1** : prick painfully **2** : cause to suffer acutely ~ *n*

: act of stinging or a resulting wound — **sting·er** n

stin·gy \'stinjē\ adj **stin·gi·er; -est** : not generous — **stin·gi·ness** n

stink \'stiŋk\ vb **stank** \'staŋk\ or **stunk** \'stəŋk\; **stunk; stink·ing** : have a strong offensive odor — **stink** n — **stink·er** n

stint \'stint\ vb : be sparing or stingy ~ n 1 : restraint 2 : quantity or period of work

sti·pend \'stī‚pend, -pənd\ n : money paid periodically

stip·ple \'stipəl\ vb **-pled; -pling** : engrave, paint, or draw with dots instead of lines — **stipple** n

stip·u·late \'stipyə‚lāt\ vb **-lat·ed; -lat·ing** : demand as a condition — **stip·u·la·tion** \‚stipyə'lāshən\ n

stir \'stər\ vb **-rr-** 1 : move slightly 2 : prod or push into activity 3 : mix by continued circular movement ~ n : act or result of stirring

stir·rup \'stərəp\ n : saddle loop for the foot

stitch \'stich\ n 1 : loop formed by a needle in sewing 2 : sudden sharp pain ~ vb 1 : fasten or decorate with stitches 2 : sew

stock \'stäk\ n 1 : block or part of wood 2 : original from which others derive 3 : farm animals 4 : supply of goods 5 : money invested in a large business 6 pl : instrument of punishment like a pillory with holes for the feet or feet and hands ~ vb : provide with stock

stock·ade \stä'kād\ n : defensive or confining enclosure

stock·ing \'stäkiŋ\ n : close-fitting covering for the foot and leg

stock·pile n : reserve supply — **stockpile** vb

stocky \'stäkē\ adj **stock·i·er; -est** : short and relatively thick

stock·yard n : yard for livestock to be slaughtered or shipped

stodgy \'stäjē\ adj **stodg·i·er; -est** 1 : dull 2 : old-fashioned

sto·ic \'stōik\, **sto·i·cal** \-ikəl\ adj : showing indifference to pain — **stoic** n — **sto·i·cal·ly** adv — **sto·i·cism** \'stōə‚sizəm\ n

stoke \'stōk\ vb **stoked; stok·ing** : stir up a fire or supply fuel to a furnace — **stok·er** n

¹**stole** \'stōl\ past of STEAL

²**stole** n : long wide scarf

stolen past part of STEAL

stol·id \'stäləd\ adj : having or showing little or no emotion — **stol·id·ly** \'stälədlē\ adv

stom·ach \'stəmək, -ik\ n 1 : saclike digestive organ 2 : abdomen 3 : appetite or de-

sire ~ *vb* : put up with —
stom·ach·ache *n*

stomp \'stämp, 'stȯmp\ *vb*
: stamp

stone \'stōn\ *n* **1** : hardened earth or mineral matter **2** : small piece of rock **3** : seed that is hard or has a hard covering ~ *vb* **stoned; ston·ing** : pelt or kill with stones — **stony** *adj*

stood *past of* STAND

stool \'stül\ *n* **1** : seat usu. without back or arms **2** : footstool **3** : discharge of feces

¹**stoop** \'stüp\ *vb* **1** : bend over **2** : lower oneself ~ *n* **1** : act of bending over **2** : bent position of shoulders

²**stoop** *n* : small porch at a house door

stop \'stäp\ *vb* **-pp- 1** : block an opening **2** : end or cause to end **3** : pause for rest or a visit in a journey ~ *n* **1** : plug **2** : act or place of stopping **3** : delay in a journey — **stoplight** *n* — **stop·page** \-ij\ *n* — **stop·per** *n*

stop·gap *n* : temporary measure or thing

stor·age \'stōrij\ *n* : safekeeping of goods (as in a warehouse)

store \'stōr\ *vb* **stored; storing** : put aside for future use ~ *n* **1** : something stored **2** : retail business establishment — **store·house** *n* — **store·keep·er** *n* — **store·room** *n*

stork \'stȯrk\ *n* : large wading bird

storm \'stȯrm\ *n* **1** : heavy fall of rain or snow **2** : violent outbreak ~ *vb* **1** : rain or snow heavily **2** : rage **3** : make an attack against — **stormy** *adj*

¹**sto·ry** \'stōrē\ *n, pl* **-ries 1** : narrative **2** : report — **sto·ry·tell·er** *n*

²**story** *n, pl* **-ries** : floor of a building

stout \'staȯt\ *adj* **1** : firm or strong **2** : thick or bulky — **stout·ly** *adv* — **stout·ness** *n*

¹**stove** \'stōv\ *n* : apparatus for providing heat (as for cooking or heating)

²**stove** *past of* STAVE

stow \'stō\ *vb* **1** : pack in a compact mass **2** : put or hide away

strad·dle \'stradᵊl\ *vb* **-dled; -dling** : stand over or sit on with legs on opposite sides — **straddle** *n*

strafe \'strāf\ *vb* **strafed; straf·ing** : fire upon with machine guns from a low-flying airplane

strag·gle \'stragəl\ *vb* **-gled; -gling** : wander or become separated from others — **straggler** \-ələr\ *n*

straight \'strāt\ *adj* **1** : having no bends, turns, or twists **2**

: just, proper, or honest **3** : neat and orderly ～ *adv* : in a straight manner — **straight·en** \'strāt³n\ *vb*

straight·for·ward \strāt'fȯr-wərd\ *adj* : frank or honest

straight·way *adv* : immediately

¹**strain** \'strān\ *n* **1** : lineage **2** : trace

²**strain** *vb* **1** : exert to the utmost **2** : filter or remove by filtering **3** : injure by improper use ～ *n* **1** : excessive tension or exertion **2** : bodily injury from excessive effort — **strain·er** *n*

strait \'strāt\ *n* **1** : narrow channel connecting 2 bodies of water **2** *pl* : distress

strait·en \'strāt³n\ *vb* **1** : hem in **2** : make distressing or difficult

¹**strand** \'strand\ *vb* **1** : drive or cast upon the shore **2** : leave helpless

²**strand** *n* **1** : twisted fiber of a rope **2** : length of something ropelike

strange \'strānj\ *adj* **strang·er; strang·est 1** : unusual or queer **2** : new — **strange·ly** *adv* — **strange·ness** *n*

strang·er \'strānjər\ *n* : person with whom one is not acquainted

stran·gle \'straŋgəl\ *vb* **-gled; -gling** : choke to death — **stran·gler** \-glər\ *n*

stran·gu·la·tion \ˌstraŋgyə'lā-shən\ *n* : act or process of strangling

strap \'strap\ *n* : narrow strip of flexible material used esp. for fastening ～ *vb* **1** : secure with a strap **2** : beat with a strap — **strap·less** *n*

strap·ping \'strapiŋ\ *adj* : robust

strat·a·gem \'stratəjəm, -ˌjem\ *n* : deceptive scheme or maneuver

strat·e·gy \'stratəjē\ *n, pl* **-gies** : carefully worked out plan of action — **stra·te·gic** \strə'tējik\ *adj* — **strat·e·gist** \'stratəjist\ *n*

strat·i·fy \'stratəˌfī\ *vb* **-fied; -fy·ing** : form or arrange in layers — **strat·i·fi·ca·tion** \ˌstratəfə'kāshən\ *n*

strato·sphere \'stratəˌsfir\ *n* : earth's atmosphere from about 7 to 31 miles above the surface

stra·tum \'strātəm, 'strat-\ *n, pl* **-ta** \'strātə, 'strat-\ : layer

straw \'strȯ\ *n* **1** : grass stems after grain is removed **2** : tube for drinking ～ *adj* : made of straw

straw·ber·ry \'strȯˌberē\ *n* : juicy red pulpy fruit

stray \'strā\ *vb* : wander or deviate ～ *n* : person or animal that strays ～ *adj* : separated from or not related to anything close by

streak \\'strēk\ *n* **1** : mark of a different color **2** : narrow band of light **3** : trace **4** : run (as of luck) or series ~ *vb* **1** : form streaks in or on **2** : move fast

stream \\'strēm\ *n* **1** : flow of water on land **2** : steady flow (as of water or air) ~ *vb* **1** : flow in a stream **2** : pour out streams

stream·er \\'strēmər\ *n* : long ribbon or ribbonlike flag

stream·lined \-ₚlīnd, -'līnd\ *adj* **1** : made with contours to reduce air or water resistance **2** : simplified **3** : modernized — **streamline** *vb*

street \\'strēt\ *n* : thoroughfare esp. in a city or town

street·car *n* : passenger vehicle running on rails in the streets

strength \\'streŋth\ *n* **1** : quality of being strong **2** : toughness **3** : intensity

strength·en \\'streŋthən\ *vb* : make, grow, or become stronger — **strength·en·er** \\'streŋthənər\ *n*

stren·u·ous \\'strenyəwəs\ *adj* **1** : vigorous **2** : requiring or showing energy — **stren·u·ous·ly** *adv*

stress \\'stres\ *n* **1** : pressure or strain that tends to distort a body **2** : relative prominence given to one thing among others **3** : state of physical or mental tension or something inducing it ~ *vb* : put stress on — **stress·ful** \\'stresfəl\ *adj*

stretch \\'strech\ *vb* **1** : spread or reach out **2** : draw out in length or breadth **3** : make taut **4** : exaggerate **5** : become extended without breaking ~ *n* : act of extending beyond normal limits

stretch·er \\'strechər\ *n* : device for carrying a sick or injured person

strew \\'strü\ *vb* **strewed; strewed** *or* **strewn** \\'strün\; **strew·ing** **1** : scatter **2** : cover by scattering something over

strick·en \\'strikən\ *adj* : afflicted with disease

strict \\'strikt\ *adj* **1** : allowing no escape or evasion **2** : precise — **strict·ly** *adv* — **strict·ness** *n*

stric·ture \\'strikchər\ *n* : hostile criticism

stride \\'strīd\ *vb* **strode** \\'strōd\; **strid·den** \\'strid°n\; **strid·ing** : walk or run with long steps ~ *n* **1** : long step **2** : manner of striding

stri·dent \\'strīd°nt\ *adj* : loud and harsh

strife \\'strīf\ *n* : conflict

strike \\'strīk\ *vb* **struck** \\'strək\; **struck; strik·ing** \\'strīkiŋ\ **1** : hit sharply **2** : delete **3** : produce by impressing **4** : cause to sound **5**

: afflict **6** : occur to or impress **7** : cause (a match) to ignite by rubbing **8** : refrain from working **9** : find **10** : take on (as a pose) ~ *n* **1** : act or instance of striking **2** : work stoppage **3** : military attack — **strik·er** *n* — **strike out** *vb* : start out vigorously — **strike up** *vb* : start

strik·ing \'strīkiŋ\ *adj* : very noticeable — **strik·ing·ly** *adv*

string \'striŋ\ *n* **1** : line usu. of twisted threads **2** : series **3** *pl* : stringed instruments ~ *vb* **strung** \'strəŋ\; **string·ing 1** : thread on or with a string **2** : hang or fasten by a string

stringed \'striŋd\ *adj* : having strings

strin·gent \'strinjənt\ *adj* : severe

stringy \'striŋē\ *adj* **string·i·er; -est** : tough or fibrous

¹**strip** \'strip\ *vb* **-pp- 1** : take the covering or clothing from **2** : undress — **strip·per** *n*

²**strip** *n* : long narrow flat piece

stripe \'strīp\ *n* : distinctive line or long narrow section ~ *vb* **striped** \'strīpt\; **strip·ing** : make stripes on — **striped** \'strīpt, 'strīpəd\ *adj*

strive \'strīv\ *vb* **strove** \'strōv\; **stri·ven** \'strivən\ *or* **strived; striv·ing** \'strīviŋ\ **1** : struggle **2** : try hard

strode *past of* STRIDE

stroke \'strōk\ *vb* **stroked; strok·ing** : rub gently ~ *n* **1** : act of swinging or striking **2** : sudden action

stroll \'strōl\ *vb* : walk leisurely — **stroll** *n* — **stroll·er** *n*

strong \'stroŋ\ *adj* **1** : capable of exerting great force or of withstanding stress or violence **2** : healthy **3** : zealous — **strong·ly** *adv*

strong·hold *n* : fortified place

struck *past of* STRIKE

struc·ture \'strəkchər\ *n* **1** : building **2** : arrangement of elements ~ *vb* **-tured; -tur·ing** : make into a structure — **struc·tur·al** \-chərəl\ *adj*

strug·gle \'strəgəl\ *vb* **-gled; -gling 1** : make strenuous efforts to overcome an adversary **2** : proceed with great effort ~ *n* **1** : strenuous effort **2** : intense competition for superiority

strum \'strəm\ *vb* **-mm-** : play (a musical instrument) by brushing the strings with the fingers

strum·pet \'strəmpət\ *n* : prostitute

strung *past of* STRING

strut \'strət\ *vb* **-tt-** : walk in a proud or showy manner ~ *n* **1** : proud walk **2** : supporting bar or rod

strych·nine \'strik‚nīn, -nən, -‚nēn\ *n* : bitter poisonous substance

stub \\'stəb\ *n* : short end or section ~ *vb* **-bb-** : strike against something

stub·ble \\'stəbəl\ *n* : short growth left after cutting — **stub·bly** *adj*

stub·born \\'stəbərn\ *adj* **1** : determined not to yield **2** : hard to control — **stub·born·ly** *adv* — **stub·born·ness** *n*

stub·by \\'stəbē\ *adj* : short, blunt, and thick

stuc·co \\'stəkō\ *n, pl* **-cos** *or* **-coes** : plaster for coating outside walls — **stuc·coed** \\'stəkōd\ *adj*

stuck *past of* STICK

stuck–up \\'stək'əp\ *adj* : conceited

¹stud \\'stəd\ *n* : male horse kept for breeding

²stud *n* **1** : upright beam for holding wall material **2** : projecting nail, pin, or rod ~ *vb* **-dd-** : supply or dot with studs

stu·dent \\'stüd²nt, 'styü-\ *n* : one who studies

stud·ied \\'stədēd\ *adj* : premeditated

stu·dio \\'stüdē₁ō, 'styü-\ *n, pl* **-dios** **1** : artist's workroom **2** : place where movies are made or television or radio shows are broadcast

stu·di·ous \\'stüdēəs, 'styü-\ *adj* : devoted to study — **stu·di·ous·ly** *adv*

study \\'stədē\ *n, pl* **stud·ies** **1** : act or process of learning about something **2** : branch of learning **3** : careful examination **4** : room for reading or studying ~ *vb* **stud·ied; study·ing** : apply the attention and mind to a subject

stuff \\'stəf\ *n* **1** : personal property **2** : raw or fundamental material **3** : unspecified material or things ~ *vb* : fill by packing things in — **stuff·ing** *n*

stuffy \\'stəfē\ *adj* **stuff·i·er; -est** **1** : lacking fresh air **2** : unimaginative or pompous

stul·ti·fy \\'stəltə₁fī\ *vb* **-fied; -fy·ing** **1** : cause to appear foolish **2** : impair or make ineffective **3** : have a dulling effect on

stum·ble \\'stəmbəl\ *vb* **-bled; -bling** **1** : lose one's balance or fall in walking or running **2** : speak or act clumsily **3** : happen by chance — **stumble** *n*

stump \\'stəmp\ *n* : part left when something is cut off ~ *vb* : confuse — **stumpy** *adj*

stun \\'stən\ *vb* **-nn-** **1** : make senseless or dizzy by or as if by a blow **2** : bewilder

stung *past of* STING

stunk *past of* STINK

stun·ning \\'stəniŋ\ *adj* **1** : astonishing or incredible **2** : strikingly beautiful — **stun·ning·ly** *adv*

¹stunt \\'stənt\ *vb* : hinder the normal growth or progress of

²stunt *n* : spectacular feat

stu·pe·fy \'stüpə‚fī, 'styü-\ *vb* **-fied; -fy·ing 1** : make insensible by or as if by drugs **2** : amaze

stu·pen·dous \stú'pendəs, styù-\ *adj* : very big or impressive — **stu·pendous·ly** *adv*

stu·pid \'stüpəd, 'styü-\ *adj* : not sensible or intelligent — **stu·pid·i·ty** \stù'pidətē, styù-\ *n* — **stu·pid·ly** *adv*

stu·por \'stüpər, 'styü-\ *n* : state of being conscious but not aware or sensible

stur·dy \'stərdē\ *adj* **-di·er; -est** : strong — **stur·di·ly** \'stərdᵊlē\ *adv* — **stur·di·ness** *n*

stur·geon \'stərjən\ *n* : fish whose roe is caviar

stut·ter \'stətər\ *vb or n* : stammer

¹sty \'stī\ *n, pl* **sties** : pig pen

²sty, stye \'stī\ *n, pl* **sties** *or* **styes** : inflamed swelling on the edge of an eyelid

style \'stīl\ *n* **1** : distinctive way of speaking, writing, or acting **2** : elegant or fashionable way of living ∼ *vb* **styled; styl·ing 1** : name **2** : give a particular design or style to — **stylish** \'stīlish\ *adj* — **styl·ish·ly** *adv* — **styl·ish·ness** *n* — **styl·ist** \-ist\ *n* — **styl·ize** \'stīəl‚īz\ *vb*

sty·lus \'stīləs\ *n, pl* **-li** \'stīl‚ī\ **1** : pointed writing tool **2** : phonograph needle

sty·mie \'stīmē\ *vb* **-mied; -mie·ing** : block or frustrate

suave \'swäv\ *adj* : well=mannered and gracious — **suave·ly** *adv*

¹sub \'səb\ *n or vb* : substitute

²sub *n* : submarine

sub- \‚səb, 'səb\ *prefix* **1** : under or beneath **2** : subordinate or secondary **3** : subordinate portion of **4** : with repetition of a process so as to form, stress, or deal with subordinate parts or relations **5** : somewhat **6** : nearly

sub·con·scious \‚səb'känchəs\ *adj* : existing without conscious awareness ∼ *n* : part of the mind concerned with sub-

---

List of self-explanatory words with the prefix *sub-*

subacute	subaverage	subclass
subagency	subbase	subclassification
subagent	subbasement	subclassify
subarctic	subbranch	subcommission
subarea	subcabinet	subcommittee
subatmospheric	subcategory	subcommunity

conscious activities — **sub-con·scious·ly** adv

sub·di·vide \ˌsəbdə'vīd, 'səb-dəˌvīd\ vb **1** : divide into several parts **2** : divide (land) into building lots — **sub·di·vi·sion** \-'vizhən, -ˌvizh-\ n

sub·due \səb'dü, -'dyü\ vb **-dued; -du·ing 1** : bring under control **2** : reduce the intensity of

sub·ject \'səbjikt\ n **1** : person under the authority of another **2** : something being discussed or studied **3** : word or word group about which something is said in a sentence ~ adj **1** : being under one's authority **2** : prone **3** : dependent on some condition or act ~ \səb'jekt\ vb **1** : bring under control **2** : cause to undergo — **sub·jec·tion** \-'jek-shən\ n

sub·jec·tive \ˌsəb'jektiv\ adj : deriving from an individual viewpoint or bias — **sub·jec·tive·ly** adv — **sub·jec·tiv·i·ty** \-ˌjek'tivətē\ n

sub·ju·gate \'səbjiˌgāt\ vb **-gat·ed; -gat·ing** : bring under one's control — **sub·ju·ga·tion** \ˌsəbji'gāshən\ n

sub·junc·tive \səb'jənktiv\ adj : relating to a verb form which expresses possibility or contingency — **subjunctive** n

sub·let \'səbˌlet\ vb **-let; -let-ting** : rent (a property) from a lessee

sub·lime \sə'blīm\ adj : splendid — **sub·lime·ly** adv

sub·ma·rine \'səbməˌrēn, ˌsəbmə'-\ adj : existing, acting, or growing under the sea ~ n : underwater boat

sub·merge \səb'mərj\ vb **-merged; -merg·ing** : put or plunge under the surface of water — **sub·mer·gence** \-'mərjəns\ n — **sub·mers·ible** \səb'mərsəbəl\ adj or n — **sub·mer·sion** \-'mərzhən\ n

sub·mit \səb'mit\ vb **-tt- 1** : yield **2** : give or offer — **sub·mis·sion** \-'mishən\ n — **sub·mis·sive** \-'misiv\ adj

subcomponent	subentry	subindex
subcontract	subfamily	subindustry
subcontractor	subfreezing	sublease
subculture	subgroup	sublethal
subdean	subhead	sublevel
subdepartment	subheading	subliterate
subdistrict	subhuman	subnetwork

sub·nor·mal \ˌsəb'nȯrməl\ *adj* : falling below what is normal

sub·or·di·nate \sə'bȯrd°nət\ *adj* : lower in rank ～ *n* : one that is subordinate ～ \sə'bȯrd°n₋ˌāt\ *vb* **-nat·ed; -nat·ing** : place in a lower rank or class — **sub·or·di·na·tion** \-ˌbȯrd°n'āshən\ *n*

sub·poe·na \sə'pēnə\ *n* : summons to appear in court ～ *vb* **-naed; -na·ing** : summon with a subpoena

sub·scribe \səb'skrīb\ *vb* **-scribed; -scrib·ing 1** : give consent or approval **2** : agree to support or to receive and pay for — **sub·scrib·er** *n*

sub·scrip·tion \səb'skripshən\ *n* : order for regular receipt of a publication

sub·se·quent \'səbsikwənt, -səˌkwent\ *adj* : following after — **sub·se·quent·ly** \-ˌkwentlē, -kwənt-\ *adv*

sub·ser·vi·ence \səb'sərvēəns\ *n* : obsequious submission — **sub·ser·vi·ent** \-ənt\ *adj*

sub·side \səb'sīd\ *vb* **-sid·ed; -sid·ing** : die down in intensity

sub·sid·iary \səb'sidēˌerē\ *adj* **1** : furnishing support **2** : of secondary importance ～ *n* : company controlled by another company

sub·si·dize \'səbsəˌdīz\ *vb* **-dized; -diz·ing** : aid with a subsidy

sub·si·dy \'səbsədē\ *n, pl* **-dies** : gift of supporting funds

sub·sist \səb'sist\ *vb* : acquire the necessities of life — **sub·sis·tence** \-'sistəns\ *n*

sub·stance \'səbstəns\ *n* **1** : essence or essential part **2** : physical material **3** : wealth

sub·stan·dard \ˌsəb'standərd\ *adj* : falling short of a standard or norm

sub·stan·tial \səb'stanchəl\ *adj* **1** : plentiful **2** : considerable — **sub·stan·tial·ly** *adv*

sub·stan·ti·ate \səb'stanchēˌāt\ *vb* **-at·ed; -at·ing** : verify — **sub·stan·ti·a·tion** \-ˌstanchē'āshən\ *n*

suboceanic	subprocess	subspecialty
suborder	subprogram	subspecies
subpar	subproject	substage
subpart	subregion	subsurface
subplot	subsea	subsystem
subpolar	subsection	subtemperate
subprincipal	subsense	subtheme

sub·sti·tute \'səbstəˌtüt, -ˌtyüt\ *n* : replacement ∼ *vb* **-tut·ed; -tut·ing** : put or serve in place of another — **substitute** *adj* — **sub·sti·tu·tion** \ˌsəbstə'tüshən, -'tyü-\ *n*

sub·ter·fuge \'səbtərˌfyüj\ *n* : deceptive trick

sub·ter·ra·nean \ˌsəbtə'rā-nēən\ *adj* : lying or being underground

sub·ti·tle \'səbˌtīt³l\ *n* : movie caption

sub·tle \'sət³l\ *adj* **-tler** \-ər\; **-tlest** \-ist\ **1** : hardly noticeable **2** : clever — **sub·tle·ty** \-tē\ *n* — **sub·tly** \-³lē\ *adv*

sub·tract \səb'trakt\ *vb* : take away (as one number from another) — **sub·trac·tion** \-'trak-shən\ *n*

sub·urb \'səbˌərb\ *n* : residential area adjacent to a city — **sub·ur·ban** \sə'bərbən\ *adj or n* — **sub·ur·ban·ite** \-bə-ˌnīt\ *n*

sub·vert \səb'vərt\ *vb* : overthrow or ruin — **sub·ver·sion** \-'vərzhən\ *n* — **sub·ver·sive** \-'vərsiv\ *adj*

sub·way \'səbˌwā\ *n* : underground electric railway

suc·ceed \sək'sēd\ *vb* **1** : follow (someone) in a job, role, or title **2** : attain a desired object or end

suc·cess \-'ses\ *n* **1** : favorable outcome **2** : gaining of wealth and fame **3** : one that succeeds — **suc·cess·ful** \-fəl\ *adj* — **suc·cess·ful·ly** *adv*

suc·ces·sion \sək'seshən\ *n* **1** : order, act, or right of succeeding **2** : series

suc·ces·sive \-'sesiv\ *adj* : following in order — **suc·ces·sive·ly** *adv*

suc·ces·sor \-'sesər\ *n* : one that succeeds another

suc·cinct \sək'siŋkt, sə'siŋkt\ *adj* : brief — **suc·cinct·ly** *adv* — **suc·cinct·ness** *n*

suc·cor \'səkər\ *n or vb* : help

suc·co·tash \'səkəˌtash\ *n* : beans and corn cooked together

suc·cu·lent \'səkyələnt\ *adj* : juicy — **suc·cu·lence** \-ləns\ *n* — **succulent** *n*

suc·cumb \sə'kəm\ *vb* **1** : yield **2** : die

such \'səch\ *adj* **1** : of this or that kind **2** : having a specified quality — **such** *pron or adv*

suck \'sək\ *vb* **1** : draw in liquid with the mouth **2** : draw liquid from by or as if by mouth — **suck** *n*

---

subtopic	subtreasury	subunit
subtotal	subtype	subvariety

suck·er \\'səkər\\ *n* **1** : one that sucks or clings **2** : easily deceived person

suck·le \\'səkəl\\ *vb* **-led; -ling** : give or draw milk from the breast or udder

suck·ling \\'səkliŋ\\ *n* : young unweaned mammal

su·crose \\'sü‚krōs, -‚krōz\\ *n* : cane or beet sugar

suc·tion \\'səkshən\\ *n* **1** : act of sucking **2** : act or process of drawing in by partially exhausting the air

sud·den \\'səd³n\\ *adj* **1** : happening unexpectedly **2** : steep **3** : hasty — **sud·den·ly** *adv* — **sud·den·ness** *n*

suds \\'sədz\\ *n pl* : soapy water esp. when frothy — **sudsy** \\'sədzē\\ *adj*

sue \\'sü\\ *vb* **sued; su·ing 1** : petition **2** : bring legal action against

suede, suède \\'swād\\ *n* : leather with a napped surface

su·et \\'süət\\ *n* : hard beef fat

suf·fer \\'səfər\\ *vb* **1** : experience pain, loss, or hardship **2** : permit — **suf·fer·er** *n*

suf·fer·ing \\-əriŋ\\ *n* : pain or hardship

suf·fice \\sə'fīs\\ *vb* **-ficed; -fic·ing** : be sufficient

suf·fi·cient \\sə'fishənt\\ *adj* : adequate — **suf·fi·cien·cy** \\-ənsē\\ *n* — **suf·ficient·ly** *adv*

suf·fix \\'səf‚iks\\ *n* : letters added at the end of a word — **suffix** \\'səfiks, sə'fiks\\ *vb* — **suf·fix·a·tion** \\‚səf‚ik'sāshən\\ *n*

suf·fo·cate \\'səfə‚kāt\\ *vb* **-cated; -cat·ing** : suffer or die or cause to die from lack of air — **suf·fo·cat·ing·ly** *adv* — **suf·fo·ca·tion** \\‚səfə'kāshən\\ *n*

suf·frage \\'səfrij\\ *n* : right to vote

suf·fuse \\sə'fyüz\\ *vb* **-fused; -fus·ing** : spread over or through

sug·ar \\'shu̇gər\\ *n* : sweet substance ∼ *vb* : mix, cover, or sprinkle with sugar — **sug·ar·cane** *n* — **sug·ary** *adj*

sug·gest \\sə'jest, səg-\\ *vb* **1** : put into someone's mind **2** : remind one by association of ideas — **sug·gest·ible** \\-'jestəbəl\\ *adj* — **sug·ges·tion** \\-'jeschən\\ *n*

sug·ges·tive \\-'jestiv\\ *adj* : suggesting something improper — **sug·ges·tive·ly** *adv* — **sug·ges·tive·ness** *n*

sui·cide \\'süə‚sīd\\ *n* **1** : act of killing oneself purposely **2** : one who commits suicide — **sui·cid·al** \\‚süə'sīd³l\\ *adj*

suit \\'süt\\ *n* **1** : action in court to recover a right or claim **2** : number of things used or worn together **3** : one of the 4 sets of playing cards ∼ *vb* **1** : be appropriate or becoming

to **2** : meet the needs of —
suit·abil·i·ty \ˌsütəˈbilətē\ *n*
— **suit·able** \ˈsütəbəl\ *adj* —
suit·ably *adv*

suit·case *n* : case for a traveler's clothing

suite \ˈswēt, *for 2 also* ˈsüt\ *n*
1 : group of rooms **2** : set of matched furniture

suit·or \ˈsütər\ *n* : one who seeks to marry a woman

sul·fur \ˈsəlfər\ *n* : nonmetallic yellow chemical element —
sul·fu·ric \ˌsəlˈfyu̇rik\ *adj* —
sul·fu·rous \-ˈfyu̇rəs, ˈsəlfərəs, ˈsəlfyə-\ *adj*

sulk \ˈsəlk\ *vb* : be moodily silent or irritable — **sulk** *n*

sulky \ˈsəlkē\ *adj* : inclined to sulk ～ *n* : light 2-wheeled horse-drawn cart — **sulk·i·ly** \ˈsəlkəlē\ *adv* — **sulk·i·ness** \-kēnəs\ *n*

sul·len \ˈsələn\ *adj* **1** : gloomily silent **2** : dismal — **sul·len·ly** *adv* — **sul·len·ness** *n*

sul·ly \ˈsəlē\ *vb* **-lied; -ly·ing** : cast doubt or disgrace on

sul·tan \ˈsəltᵊn\ *n* : sovereign of a Muslim state — **sul·tan·ate** \-ˌāt\ *n*

sul·try \ˈsəltrē\ *adj* **-tri·er; -est 1** : very hot and moist **2** : sexually arousing

sum \ˈsəm\ *n* **1** : amount **2** : gist **3** : result of addition ～ *vb* **-mm-** : find the sum of

su·mac \ˈshu̇ˌmak, ˈsü-\ *n* : shrub with spikes of berries

sum·ma·ry \ˈsəmərē\ *adj* **1** : concise **2** : done without delay or formality ～ *n, pl* **-ries** : concise statement — **sum·mar·i·ly** \səˈmerəlē, ˈsəmərəlē\ *adv* — **sum·ma·rize** \ˈsəməˌrīz\ *vb*

sum·ma·tion \səˈmāshən\ *n* : a summing up esp. in court

sum·mer \ˈsəmər\ *n* : season in which the sun shines most directly — **summery** *adj*

sum·mit \ˈsəmət\ *n* **1** : highest point **2** : high-level conference

sum·mon \ˈsəmən\ *vb* **1** : send for or call together **2** : order to appear in court — **sum·mon·er** *n*

sum·mons \ˈsəmənz\ *n, pl* **sum·mons·es** : an order to answer charges in court

sump·tu·ous \ˈsəmpchəwəs\ *adj* : lavish

sun \ˈsən\ *n* **1** : shining celestial body around which the planets revolve **2** : light of the sun ～ *vb* **-nn-** : expose to the sun — **sun·beam** *n* — **sun·block** *n* — **sun·burn** *n or vb* — **sun·glass·es** *n pl* — **sunlight** *n* — **sun·ny** *adj* — **sunrise** *n* — **sun·set** *n* — **sun·shine** *n* — **sun·tan** *n*

sun·dae \ˈsəndē\ *n* : ice cream with topping

Sun·day \\'səndā, -dē\\ *n* : 1st day of the week

sun·di·al \\-ˌdīəl\\ *n* : device for showing time by the sun's shadow

sun·dries \\'səndrēz\\ *n pl* : various small articles

sun·dry \\-drē\\ *adj* : several

sun·fish *n* : perchlike freshwater fish

sun·flow·er *n* : tall plant grown for its oil-rich seeds

sung *past of* SING

sunk *past of* SINK

sunk·en \\'səŋkən\\ *adj* **1** : submerged **2** : fallen in

sun·spot *n* : dark spot on the sun

sun·stroke *n* : heatstroke from the sun

sup \\'səp\\ *vb* **-pp-** : eat the evening meal

super \\'süpər\\ *adj* : very fine

super- \\ˌsüpər, 'sü-\\ *prefix* **1** : higher in quantity, quality, or degree than **2** : in addition **3** : exceeding a norm **4** : in excessive degree or intensity **5** : surpassing others of its kind **6** : situated above, on, or at the top of **7** : more inclusive than **8** : superior in status or position

su·perb \\su'pərb\\ *adj* : outstanding — **su·perb·ly** *adv*

su·per·cil·ious \\ˌsüpər'silēəs\\ *adj* : haughtily contemptuous

su·per·fi·cial \\ˌsüpər'fishəl\\ *adj* : relating to what is only apparent — **su·per·fi·ci·al·i·ty** \\-ˌfishē'alətē\\ *n* — **su·per·fi·cial·ly** *adv*

su·per·flu·ous \\su'pərfləwəs\\ *adj* : more than necessary — **su·per·flu·i·ty** \\ˌsüpər'flüətē\\ *n*

su·per·im·pose \\ˌsüpərim'pōz\\ *vb* : lay over or above something

su·per·in·tend \\ˌsüpərin'tend\\ *vb* : have charge and oversight of — **su·per·in·ten·dence**

List of self-explanatory words with the prefix *super-*

superabundance	superdense	superheroine
superabundant	supereffective	superhuman
superambitious	superefficiency	superintellectual
superathlete	superefficient	superintelligence
superbomb	superfast	superintelligent
superclean	supergood	superman
supercolossal	supergovernment	supermodern
superconvenient	supergroup	superpatriot
supercop	superhero	superpatriotic

\-'tendəns\ *n* — **su·per·in·ten·den·cy** \-dənsē\ *n* — **su·per·in·ten·dent** \-dənt\ *n*

su·pe·ri·or \sù'pirēər\ *adj* **1** : higher, better, or more important **2** : haughty — **superior** *n* — **su·pe·ri·or·i·ty** \-ˌpirē'ȯrətē\ *n*

su·per·la·tive \sù'pərlətiv\ *adj* **1** : relating to or being an adjective or adverb form that denotes an extreme level **2** : surpassing others — **superlative** *n* — **su·per·la·tive·ly** *adv*

su·per·mar·ket \'süpərˌmärkət\ *n* : self-service grocery store

su·per·nat·u·ral \ˌsüpər'nachərəl\ *adj* : beyond the observable physical world — **su·per·nat·u·ral·ly** *adv*

su·per·pow·er \'süpərˌpaủər\ *n* : politically and militarily dominant nation

su·per·sede \ˌsüpər'sēd\ *vb* **-sed·ed; sed·ing** : take the place of

su·per·son·ic \-'sänik\ *adj* : faster than the speed of sound

su·per·sti·tion \ˌsüpər'stishən\ *n* : beliefs based on ignorance, fear of the unknown, or trust in magic — **su·per·sti·tious** \-əs\ *adj*

su·per·struc·ture \'süpərˌstrəkchər\ *n* : something built on a base or as a vertical extension

su·per·vise \'süpərˌvīz\ *vb* **-vised; -vis·ing** : have charge of — **su·per·vi·sion** \ˌsüpər'vizhən\ *n* — **su·per·vi·sor** \'süpərˌvīzər\ *n* — **su·per·vi·so·ry** \ˌsüpər'vīzərē\ *adj*

su·pine \sù'pīn\ *adj* **1** : lying on the back **2** : indifferent or abject

sup·per \'səpər\ *n* : evening meal

sup·plant \sə'plant\ *vb* : take the place of

sup·ple \'səpəl\ *adj* **-pler; -plest** : able to bend easily

superpatriotism	supersensitive	superstate
superplane	supersize	superstrength
superpolite	supersized	superstrong
superport	superslick	supersystem
superpowerful	supersmooth	supertanker
superrich	supersoft	superthick
supersalesman	superspecial	superthin
superscout	superspecialist	supertight
supersecrecy	superspy	superweapon
supersecret	superstar	superwoman

sup·ple·ment \\'səpləmənt\ *n* : something that adds to or makes up for a lack — **supplement** *vb* — **sup·ple·men·tal** \\,səplə'ment³l\ *adj* — **sup·ple·men·ta·ry** \\-'mentərē\ *adj*

sup·pli·ant \\'səplēənt\ *n* : one who supplicates

sup·pli·cate \\'səplə,kāt\ *vb* **-cat·ed; -cat·ing** **1** : pray to God **2** : ask earnestly and humbly — **sup·pli·cant** \\-likənt\ *n* — **sup·pli·ca·tion** \\,səplə'kāshən\ *n*

sup·ply \sə'plī\ *vb* **-plied; -ply·ing** : furnish ~ *n, pl* **-plies** **1** : amount needed or available **2** *pl* : provisions — **sup·pli·er** \\-'plīər\ *n*

sup·port \sə'pōrt\ *vb* **1** : take sides with **2** : provide with food, clothing, and shelter **3** : hold up or serve as a foundation for — **support** *n* — **sup·port·able** *adj* — **sup·port·er** *n*

sup·pose \sə'pōz\ *vb* **-posed; -pos·ing** **1** : assume to be true **2** : expect **3** : think probable — **sup·po·si·tion** \\,səpə'zishən\ *n*

sup·pos·i·to·ry \sə'päzə,tōrē\ *n, pl* **-ries** : medicated material for insertion (as into the rectum)

sup·press \sə'pres\ *vb* **1** : put an end to by authority **2** : keep from being known **3** : hold back — **sup·pres·sant** \sə'pres³nt\ *n* — **sup·pres·sion** \\-'preshən\ *n*

su·prem·a·cy \sù'preməsē\ *n, pl* **-cies** : supreme power or authority

su·preme \sù'prēm\ *adj* **1** : highest in rank or authority **2** : greatest possible — **su·preme·ly** *adv*

Supreme Being *n* : God

sur·charge \\'sər,chärj\ *n* **1** : excessive load or burden **2** : extra fee or cost

sure \\'shùr\ *adj* **sur·er; sur·est** **1** : confident **2** : reliable **3** : not to be disputed **4** : bound to happen ~ *adv* : surely — **sure·ness** *n*

sure·ly \\'shùrlē\ *adv* **1** : in a sure manner **2** : without doubt **3** : indeed

sure·ty \\'shùrətē\ *n, pl* **-ties** **1** : guarantee **2** : one who gives a guarantee for another person

surf \\'sərf\ *n* : waves that break on the shore ~ *vb* : ride the surf — **surf·board** *n* — **surf·er** *n* — **surf·ing** *n*

sur·face \\'sərfəs\ *n* **1** : the outside of an object **2** : outward aspect ~ *vb* **-faced; -fac·ing** : rise to the surface

sur·feit \\'sərfət\ *n* **1** : excess **2** : excessive indulgence (as in food or drink) **3** : disgust caused by excess ~ *vb* : feed, supply, or indulge to the point of surfeit

surge \\'sərj\\ *vb* **surged; surg-ing** : rise and fall in or as if in waves ~ *n* : sudden increase

sur·geon \\'sərjən\\ *n* : physician who specializes in surgery

sur·gery \\'sərjərē\\ *n, pl* **-ger-ies** : medical treatment involving cutting open the body

sur·gi·cal \\'sərjikəl\\ *adj* : relating to surgeons or surgery — **sur·gi·cal·ly** *adv*

sur·ly \\'sərlē\\ *adj* **-li·er; -est** : having a rude nature — **sur-li·ness** *n*

sur·mise \\sər'mīz\\ *vb* **-mised; -mis·ing** : guess — **surmise** *n*

sur·mount \\-'maůnt\\ *vb* **1** : prevail over **2** : get to or be the top of

sur·name \\'sər,nām\\ *n* : family name

sur·pass \\sər'pas\\ *vb* : go beyond or exceed — **sur·pass-ing·ly** *adv*

sur·plice \\'sərpləs\\ *n* : loose white outer ecclesiastical vestment

sur·plus \\'sər,pləs\\ *n* : quantity left over

sur·prise \\sə'prīz, sər-\\ *vb* **-prised; -pris·ing** **1** : come upon or affect unexpectedly **2** : amaze — **surprise** *n* — **sur-pris·ing** *adj* — **sur·pris·ing·ly** *adv*

sur·ren·der \\sə'rendər\\ *vb* : give up oneself or a posses-sion to another ~ *n* : act of surrendering

sur·rep·ti·tious \\,sərəp'tishəs\\ *adj* : done, made, or acquired by stealth — **sur·rep·ti·tious·ly** *adv*

sur·rey \\'sərē\\ *n, pl* **-reys** : horse-drawn carriage

sur·ro·gate \\'sərəgāt, -gət\\ *n* : substitute

sur·round \\sə'raůnd\\ *vb* : enclose on all sides

sur·round·ings \\sə'raůndiŋz\\ *n pl* : objects, conditions, or area around something

sur·veil·lance \\sər'vāləns, -'vālyəns, -'vāəns\\ *n* : careful watch

sur·vey \\sər'vā\\ *vb* **-veyed; -vey·ing** **1** : look over and examine closely **2** : make a survey of (as a tract of land) ~ \\'sər,-\\ *n, pl* **-veys** **1** : inspection **2** : process of measuring (as land) — **sur·vey·or** \\-ər\\ *n*

sur·vive \\sər'vīv\\ *vb* **-vived; -viv·ing** **1** : remain alive or in existence **2** : outlive or outlast — **sur·viv·al** *n* — **sur·vi·vor** \\-'vīvər\\ *n*

sus·cep·ti·ble \\sə'septəbəl\\ *adj* : likely to allow or be affected by something — **sus-cep·ti·bil·i·ty** \\-,septə'bilətē\\ *n*

sus·pect \\'səs,pekt, sə'spekt\\ *adj* **1** : regarded with suspicion **2** : questionable ~ \\'səs,pekt\\ *n* : one who is suspected (as of a crime) ∼ \sə'spekt\ *vb* **1** : have doubts of **2** : believe guilty without proof **3** : guess

sus·pend \sə'spend\ *vb* **1** : temporarily stop or keep from a function or job **2** : withhold (judgment) temporarily **3** : hang

sus·pend·er \sə'spendər\ *n* : one of 2 supporting straps holding up trousers and passing over the shoulders

sus·pense \sə'spens\ *n* : excitement and uncertainty as to outcome — **suspense·ful** *adj*

sus·pen·sion \sə'spenchən\ *n* : act of suspending or the state or period of being suspended

sus·pi·cion \sə'spishən\ *n* **1** : act of suspecting something **2** : trace

sus·pi·cious \-əs\ *adj* **1** : arousing suspicion **2** : inclined to suspect — **sus·pi·cious·ly** *adv*

sus·tain \sə'stān\ *vb* **1** : provide with nourishment **2** : keep going **3** : hold up **4** : suffer **5** : support or prove

sus·te·nance \'səstənəns\ *n* **1** : nourishment **2** : something that sustains or supports

svelte \'sfelt\ *adj* : slender and graceful

swab \'swäb\ *n* **1** : mop **2** : wad of absorbent material for applying medicine ∼ *vb* **-bb-** : use a swab on

swad·dle \'swäd³l\ *vb* **-dled; -dling** \'swäd³liŋ\ : bind (an infant) in bands of cloth

swag·ger \'swagər\ *vb* **-gered; -ger·ing** **1** : walk with a conceited swing **2** : boast — **swagger** *n*

¹**swal·low** \'swälō\ *n* : small migratory bird

²**swallow** *vb* **1** : take into the stomach through the throat **2** : envelop or take in **3** : accept too easily — **swallow** *n*

swam *past of* SWIM

swamp \'swämp\ *n* : wet spongy land ∼ *vb* : deluge (as with water) — **swampy** *adj*

swan \'swän\ *n* : white long-necked swimming bird

swap \'swäp\ *vb* **-pp-** : trade — **swap** *n*

swarm \'sworm\ *n* **1** : mass of honeybees leaving a hive to start a new colony **2** : large crowd ∼ *vb* : gather in a swarm

swar·thy \'sworthē, -thē\ *adj* **-thi·er; -est** : dark in complexion

swash·buck·ler \'swäsh,bək-lər\ *n* : swaggering or daring soldier or adventurer — **swash-buck·ling** \-,bəkliŋ\ *adj*

swat \'swät\ *vb* **-tt-** : hit sharply — **swat** *n* — **swat·ter** *n*

swatch \'swäch\ *n* : sample piece (as of fabric)

swath \'swäth, 'swȯth\, **swathe** \'swäth, 'swȯth, 'swāth\ *n* : row or path cut (as through grass)

swathe \'swäth, 'swȯth, 'swāth\ *vb* **swathed; swathing** : wrap with or as if with a bandage

sway \'swā\ *vb* **1** : swing gently from side to side **2** : influence ∼ *n* **1** : gentle swinging from side to side **2** : controlling power or influence

swear \'swar\ *vb* **swore** \'swōr\; **sworn** \'swōrn\; **swear·ing 1** : make or cause to make a solemn statement under oath **2** : use profane language — **swear·er** *n* — **swearing** *n*

sweat \'swet\ *vb* **sweat** *or* **sweat·ed; sweat·ing 1** : excrete salty moisture from skin glands **2** : form drops of moisture on the surface **3** : work or cause to work hard — **sweat** *n* — **sweaty** *adj*

sweat·er \'swetǝr\ *n* : knitted jacket or pullover

sweat·shirt \'swet,shǝrt\ *n* : loose collarless heavy cotton jersey pullover

sweep \'swēp\ *vb* **swept** \'swept\; **sweep·ing 1** : remove or clean by a brush or a single forceful wipe (as of the hand) **2** : move over with speed and force (as of the hand) **3**

: move or extend in a wide curve ∼ *n* **1** : a clearing off or away **2** : single forceful wipe or swinging movement **3** : scope — **sweep·er** *n* — **sweep·ing** *adj*

sweep·stakes \'swēp,stāks\ *n, pl* **sweep·stakes** : contest in which the entire prize may go to the winner

sweet \'swēt\ *adj* **1** : being or causing the pleasing taste typical of sugar **2** : not stale or spoiled **3** : not salted **4** : pleasant **5** : much loved ∼ *n* : something sweet — **sweet·en** \'swēt°n\ *vb* — **sweet·ly** *adv* — **sweet·ness** *n* — **sweet·en·er** \-°nǝr\ *n*

sweet·heart *n* : person one loves

sweet potato *n* : sweet yellow edible root of a tropical vine

swell \'swel\ *vb* **swelled; swelled** *or* **swol·len** \'swōlǝn\; **swell·ing 1** : enlarge **2** : bulge **3** : fill or be filled with emotion ∼ *n* **1** : long rolling ocean wave **2** : condition of bulging — **swell·ing** *n*

swel·ter \'sweltǝr\ *vb* : be uncomfortable from excessive heat

swept *past of* SWEEP

swerve \'swǝrv\ *vb* **swerved; swerv·ing** : move abruptly aside from a course — **swerve** *n*

¹**swift** \'swift\ *adj* **1** : moving with great speed **2** : occurring

suddenly — **swift·ly** *adv* — **swift·ness** *n*

²**swift** *n* : small insect-eating bird

swig \'swig\ *vb* **-gg-** : drink in gulps — **swig** *n*

swill \'swil\ *vb* : swallow greedily ∼ *n* **1** : animal food of refuse and liquid **2** : garbage

swim \'swim\ *vb* **swam** \'swam\; **swum** \'swəm\; **swim·ming** **1** : propel oneself in water **2** : float in or be surrounded with a liquid **3** : be dizzy ∼ *n* : act or period of swimming — **swim·mer** *n*

swin·dle \'swind²l\ *vb* **-dled; -dling** \-iŋ\ : cheat (someone) of money or property — **swin·dle** *n* — **swin·dler** \-ər\ *n*

swine \'swīn\ *n, pl* **swine** : short-legged hoofed mammal with a snout — **swinish** \'swīnish\ *adj*

swing \'swiŋ\ *vb* **swung** \'swəŋ\; **swing·ing** **1** : move or cause to move rapidly in an arc **2** : sway or cause to sway back and forth **3** : hang so as to sway or sag **4** : turn on a hinge or pivot **5** : manage or handle successfully ∼ *n* **1** : act or instance of swinging **2** : swinging movement (as in trying to hit something) **3** : suspended seat for swinging — **swing** *adj* — **swing·er** *n*

swipe \'swīp\ *n* : strong sweeping blow ∼ *vb* **swiped; swip-** ing **1** : strike or wipe with a sweeping motion **2** : steal esp. with a quick movement

swirl \'swərl\ *vb* : move or cause to move in a circle — **swirl** *n*

swish \'swish\ *n* : hissing, sweeping, or brushing sound — **swish** *vb*

switch \'swich\ *n* **1** : slender flexible whip or twig **2** : blow with a switch **3** : shift, change, or reversal **4** : device that opens or closes an electrical circuit ∼ *vb* **1** : punish or urge on with a switch **2** : change or reverse roles, positions, or subjects **3** : operate a switch of

switch·board *n* : panel of switches to make and break telephone connections

swiv·el \'swivəl\ *vb* **-eled** *or* **-elled; -eling** *or* **-el·ling** : swing or turn on a pivot — **swivel** *n*

swollen *past part of* SWELL

swoon \'swün\ *n* : faint — **swoon** *vb*

swoop \'swüp\ *vb* : make a swift diving attack — **swoop** *n*

sword \'sord\ *n* : thrusting or cutting weapon with a long blade

sword·fish *n* : large ocean fish with a long swordlike projection

swore *past of* SWEAR

sworn *past part of* SWEAR

swum *past part of* SWIM

swung *past of* SWING

syc·a·more \'sikə₁mōr\ *n* : shade tree

sy·co·phant \'sikəfənt\ *n* : servile flatterer — **syc·o·phan·tic** \₁sikə'fantik\ *adj*

syl·la·ble \'siləbəl\ *n* : unit of a spoken word — **syl·lab·ic** \sə'labik\ *adj*

syl·la·bus \'siləbəs\ *n, pl* **-bi** \-₁bī\ *or* **-bus·es** : summary of main topics (as of a course of study)

syl·van \'silvən\ *adj* **1** : living or located in a wooded area **2** : abounding in woods

sym·bol \'simbəl\ *n* : something that represents or suggests another thing — **sym·bol·ic** \sim-'bälik\ *adj* — **sym·bol·i·cal·ly** *adv*

sym·bol·ism \'simbə₁lizəm\ *n* : representation of meanings with symbols

sym·bol·ize \'simbə₁līz\ *vb* **-ized; -izing** : serve as a symbol of — **sym·bol·i·za·tion** \₁simbələ'zāshən\ *n*

sym·me·try \'simətrē\ *n, pl* **-tries** : regularity and balance in the arrangement of parts — **sym·met·ri·cal** \sə'metrikəl\ *adj* — **sym·met·ri·cal·ly** *adv*

sym·pa·thize \'simpə₁thīz\ *vb* **-thized; -thiz·ing** : feel or show sympathy — **sym·pa·thiz·er** *n*

sym·pa·thy \'simpəthē\ *n, pl* **-thies** **1** : ability to understand or share the feelings of another **2** : expression of sorrow for another's misfortune — **sym·pa·thet·ic** \₁simpə'thetik\ *adj* — **sym·pa·thet·i·cal·ly** *adv*

sym·pho·ny \'simfənē\ *n, pl* **-nies** : composition for an orchestra or the orchestra itself — **sym·phon·ic** \sim'fänik\ *adj*

sym·po·sium \sim'pōzēəm\ *n, pl* **-sia** \-zēə\ *or* **-siums** : conference at which a topic is discussed

symp·tom \'simptəm\ *n* : unusual feeling or reaction that is a sign of disease — **symp·tom·at·ic** \₁simptə'matik\ *adj*

syn·a·gogue, syn·a·gog \'sinə₁gäg, -₁gȯg\ *n* : Jewish house of worship

syn·chro·nize \'siŋkrə₁nīz, 'sin-\ *vb* **-nized; -niz·ing** **1** : occur or cause to occur at the same instant **2** : cause to agree in time — **syn·chro·ni·za·tion** \₁siŋkrənə'zāshən, ₁sin-\ *n*

syn·co·pa·tion \₁siŋkə'pāshən, ₁sin-\ *n* : shifting of the regular musical accent to the weak beat — **syn·co·pate** \'siŋkə₁pāt, 'sin-\ *vb*

syn·di·cate \'sindikət\ *n* : business association ∼ \-də₁kāt\ *vb* **-cat·ed; -cat·ing** **1** : form a syndicate **2** : publish through a syndicate — **syn·di·ca·tion** \ˌsindəˈkāshən\ *n*

syn·drome \ˈsinˌdrōm\ *n* : particular group of symptoms

syn·onym \ˈsinəˌnim\ *n* : word with the same meaning as another — **syn·on·y·mous** \səˈnänəməs\ *adj* — **syn·on·y·my** \-mē\ *n*

syn·op·sis \səˈnäpsəs\ *n, pl* **-op·ses** \-ˌsēz\ : condensed statement or outline

syn·tax \ˈsinˌtaks\ *n* : way in which words are put together — **syn·tac·tic** \sinˈtaktik\, **syn·tac·ti·cal** \-tikəl\ *adj*

syn·the·sis \ˈsinthəsəs\ *n, pl* **-the·ses** \-ˌsēz\ : combination of parts or elements into a whole — **syn·the·size** \-ˌsīz\ *vb*

syn·thet·ic \sinˈthetik\ *adj* : artificially made — **synthetic** *n* — **syn·thet·i·cal·ly** *adv*

syph·i·lis \ˈsifələs\ *n* : venereal disease

sy·ringe \səˈrinj, ˈsirinj\ *n* : plunger device for injecting or withdrawing liquids

syr·up \ˈsərəp, ˈsirəp\ *n* : thick sticky sweet liquid — **syr·upy** *adj*

sys·tem \ˈsistəm\ *n* **1** : arrangement of units that function together **2** : regular order — **sys·tem·at·ic** \ˌsistəˈmatik\ *adj* — **sys·tem·at·i·cal·ly** *adv* — **sys·tem·a·tize** \ˈsistəməˌtīz\ *vb*

sys·tem·ic \sisˈtemik\ *adj* : relating to the whole body

T

t \ˈtē\ *n, pl* **t's** *or* **ts** \ˈtēz\ : 20th letter of the alphabet

tab \ˈtab\ *n* **1** : short projecting flap **2** *pl* : careful watch

tab·by \ˈtabē\ *n, pl* **-bies** : domestic cat

tab·er·na·cle \ˈtabərˌnakəl\ *n* : house of worship

ta·ble \ˈtābəl\ *n* **1** : piece of furniture having a smooth slab fixed on legs **2** : supply of food **3** : arrangement of data in columns **4** : short list — **ta·**ble·cloth *n* — **ta·ble·top** *n* — **ta·ble·ware** *n* — **tab·u·lar** \ˈtabyələr\ *adj*

tab·leau \ˈtabˌlō\ *n, pl* **-leaux** \-ˌlōz\ **1** : graphic description **2** : depiction of a scene by people in costume

ta·ble·spoon *n* **1** : large serving spoon **2** : measuring spoon holding 1/2 fluid ounce — **ta·ble·spoon·ful** \-ˌful\ *n*

tab·let \ˈtablət\ *n* **1** : flat slab suited for an inscription **2**

: collection of sheets of paper glued together at one edge **3** : disk-shaped pill

tab·loid \'tab,lȯid\ *n* : newspaper of small page size

ta·boo \tə'bü, ta-\ *adj* : banned esp. as immoral or dangerous — **taboo** *n or vb*

tab·u·late \'tabyə,lāt\ *vb* **-lat·ed; -lat·ing** : put in the form of a table — **tab·u·la·tion** \,tabyə'lāshən\ *n* — **tab·u·la·tor** \'tabyə,lātər\ *n*

tac·it \'tasət\ *adj* : implied but not expressed — **tac·it·ly** *adv* — **tac·it·ness** *n*

tac·i·turn \'tasə,tərn\ *adj* : not inclined to talk

tack \'tak\ *n* **1** : small sharp nail **2** : course of action ∼ *vb* **1** : fasten with tacks **2** : add on

tack·le \'takəl, *naut often* 'tāk-\ *n* **1** : equipment **2** : arrangement of ropes and pulleys **3** : act of tackling ∼ *vb* **-led; -ling** **1** : seize or throw down **2** : start dealing with

¹tacky \'takē\ *adj* **tack·i·er; -est** : sticky to the touch

²tacky *adj* **tack·i·er; -est** : cheap or gaudy

tact \'takt\ *n* : sense of the proper thing to say or do — **tact·ful** \-fəl\ *adj* — **tact·ful·ly** *adv* — **tact·less** *adj* — **tact·less·ly** *adv*

tac·tic \'taktik\ *n* : action as part of a plan

tac·tics \'taktiks\ *n sing or pl* **1** : science of maneuvering forces in combat **2** : skill of using available means to reach an end — **tac·ti·cal** \-tikəl\ *adj* — **tac·ti·cian** \tak'tishən\ *n*

tac·tile \'takt³l, -,tīl\ *adj* : relating to or perceptible through the sense of touch

tad·pole \'tad,pōl\ *n* : larval frog or toad with tail and gills

taf·fe·ta \'tafətə\ *n* : crisp lustrous fabric (as of silk)

taf·fy \'tafē\ *n, pl* **-fies** : candy stretched until porous

¹tag \'tag\ *n* : piece of hanging or attached material ∼ *vb* **-gg-** **1** : provide or mark with a tag **2** : follow closely

²tag *n* : children's game of trying to catch one another ∼ *vb* : touch a person in tag

tail \'tāl\ *n* **1** : rear end or a growth extending from the rear end of an animal **2** : back or last part **3** : the reverse of a coin ∼ *vb* : follow — **tailed** \'tāld\ *adj* — **tail·less** *adj*

tail·gate \-,gāt\ *n* : hinged gate on the back of a vehicle that can be lowered for loading ∼ *vb* **-gat·ed; -gat·ing** : drive too close behind another vehicle

tail·light *n* : red warning light at the back of a vehicle

tai·lor \'tālər\ *n* : one who makes or alters garments ∼

tailspin 648

vb **1** : fashion or alter (clothes) **2** : make or adapt for a special purpose

tail·spin *n* : spiral dive by an airplane

taint \'tānt\ *vb* : affect or become affected with something bad and esp. decay ～ *n* : trace of decay or corruption

take \'tāk\ *vb* **took** \'tůk\; **tak·en** \'tākən\; **tak·ing** **1** : get into one's possession **2** : become affected by **3** : receive into one's body (as by eating) **4** : pick out or remove **5** : use for transportation **6** : need or make use of **7** : lead, carry, or cause to go to another place **8** : undertake and do, make, or perform ～ *n* : amount taken — **take·over** *n* — **tak·er** *n* — **take advantage of** : profit by — **take exception** : object — **take off** *vb* **1** : remove **2** : go away **3** : mimic **4** : begin flight — **take over** *vb* : assume control or possession of or responsibility for — **take place** : happen

take·off *n* : act or instance of taking off

talc \'talk\ *n* : soft mineral used in making toilet powder (**tal·cum powder** \'talkəm-\)

tale \'tāl\ *n* **1** : story or anecdote **2** : falsehood

tal·ent \'talənt\ *n* : natural mental or creative ability — **tal·ent·ed** *adj*

tal·is·man \'taləsmən, -əz-\ *n*, *pl* **-mans** : object thought to act as a charm

talk \'tòk\ *vb* **1** : express one's thoughts in speech **2** : discuss **3** : influence to a position or course of action by talking ～ *n* **1** : act of talking **2** : formal discussion **3** : rumor **4** : informal lecture — **talk·a·tive** \-ətiv\ *adj* — **talk·er** *n*

tall \'tòl\ *adj* : extending to a great or specified height — **tall·ness** *n*

tal·low \'talō\ *n* : hard white animal fat used esp. in candles

tal·ly \'talē\ *n*, *pl* **-lies** : recorded amount ～ *vb* **-lied; -ly·ing** **1** : add or count up **2** : match

tal·on \'talən\ *n* : bird's claw

tam \'tam\ *n* : tam-o'-shanter

tam·bou·rine \ˌtambə'rēn\ *n* : small drum with loose disks at the sides

tame \'tām\ *adj* **tam·er; tam·est** **1** : changed from being wild to being controllable by man **2** : docile **3** : dull ～ *vb* **tamed; tam·ing** : make or become tame — **tam·able, tame·able** *adj* — **tame·ly** *adv* — **tam·er** *n*

tam–o'–shan·ter \'taməˌshantər\ *n* : Scottish woolen cap with a wide flat circular crown

tamp \'tamp\ *vb* : drive down or in by a series of light blows

tam·per \'tampər\ *vb* : interfere so as to change for the worse

tan \'tan\ *vb* **-nn-** **1** : change (hide) into leather esp. by soaking in a liquid containing tannin **2** : make or become brown (as by exposure to the sun) ～ *n* **1** : brown skin color induced by the sun **2** : light yellowish brown — **tan·ner** *n* — **tan·nery** \'tanərē\ *n*

tan·dem \'tandəm\ *adv* : one behind another

tang \'taŋ\ *n* : sharp distinctive flavor — **tangy** *adj*

tan·gent \'tanjənt\ *adj* : touching a curve or surface at only one point ～ *n* **1** : tangent line, curve, or surface **2** : abrupt change of course — **tan·gen·tial** \tan'jenchəl\ *adj*

tan·ger·ine \'tanjə,rēn, ,tanjə'-\ *n* : deep orange citrus fruit

tan·gi·ble \'tanjəbəl\ *adj* **1** : able to be touched **2** : substantially real — **tan·gi·bly** *adv*

tan·gle \'taŋgəl\ *vb* **-gled; -gling** : unite in intricate confusion ～ *n* : tangled twisted mass

tan·go \'taŋgō\ *n, pl* **-gos** : dance of Latin-American origin — **tango** *vb*

tank \'taŋk\ *n* **1** : large artificial receptacle for liquids **2** : armored military vehicle — **tank·ful** *n*

tan·kard \'taŋkərd\ *n* : tall one-handled drinking vessel

tank·er \'taŋkər\ *n* : vehicle or vessel with tanks for transporting a liquid

tan·nin \'tanən\ *n* : substance of plant origin used in tanning and dyeing

tan·ta·lize \'tant³l,īz\ *vb* **-lized; -liz·ing** : tease or torment by keeping something desirable just out of reach — **tan·ta·liz·er** *n* — **tan·ta·liz·ing·ly** *adv*

tan·ta·mount \'tantə,maùnt\ *adj* : equivalent in value or meaning

tan·trum \'tantrəm\ *n* : fit of bad temper

¹tap \'tap\ *n* **1** : faucet **2** : act of tapping ～ *vb* **-pp-** **1** : pierce so as to draw off fluid **2** : connect into — **tap·per** *n*

²tap *vb* **-pp-** : rap lightly ～ *n* : light stroke or its sound

tape \'tāp\ *n* **1** : narrow flexible strip (as of cloth, plastic, or metal) **2** : tape measure ～ *vb* **taped; tap·ing** **1** : fasten with tape **2** : record on tape

tape measure *n* : strip of tape marked in units for use in measuring

ta·per \'tāpər\ *n* **1** : slender wax candle **2** : gradual lessening of width in a long object ～ *vb* **1** : make or become smaller toward one end **2** : diminish gradually

tap·es·try \'tapəstrē\ *n, pl* **-tries** : heavy handwoven rug-like wall hanging

tape·worm *n* : long flat intestinal worm

tap·i·o·ca \ˌtapē'ōkə\ *n* : a granular starch used esp. in puddings

tar \'tär\ *n* : thick dark sticky liquid distilled (as from coal) ~ *vb* **-rr-** : treat or smear with tar

ta·ran·tu·la \tə'ranchələ, -'rant°lə\ *n* : large hairy usu. harmless spider

tar·dy \'tärdē\ *adj* **-di·er; -est** : late — **tar·di·ly** \'tärd°lē\ *adv* — **tar·di·ness** *n*

tar·get \'tärgət\ *n* **1** : mark to shoot at **2** : goal to be achieved ~ *vb* **1** : make a target of **2** : establish as a goal

tar·iff \'tarəf\ *n* **1** : duty or rate of duty imposed on imported goods **2** : schedule of tariffs, rates, or charges

tar·nish \'tärnish\ *vb* : make or become dull or discolored — **tarnish** *n*

tar·pau·lin \tär'pȯlən, 'tärpə-\ *n* : waterproof protective covering

¹tar·ry \'tarē\ *vb* **-ried; -ry·ing** : be slow in leaving

²tar·ry \'tärē\ *adj* : resembling or covered with tar

¹tart \'tärt\ *adj* **1** : pleasantly sharp to the taste **2** : caustic — **tart·ly** *adv* — **tart·ness** *n*

²tart *n* : small pie

tar·tan \'tärt°n\ *n* : woolen fabric with a plaid design

tar·tar \'tärtər\ *n* : hard crust on the teeth

task \'task\ *n* : assigned work

task·mas·ter *n* : one that burdens another with labor

tas·sel \'tasəl, 'täs-\ *n* : hanging ornament made of a bunch of cords fastened at one end

taste \'tāst\ *vb* **tast·ed; tast·ing** **1** : test or determine the flavor of **2** : eat or drink in small quantities **3** : have a specific flavor ~ *n* **1** : small amount tasted **2** : bit **3** : special sense that identifies sweet, sour, bitter, or salty qualities **4** : individual preference **5** : critical appreciation of quality — **taste·ful** \-fəl\ *adj* — **taste·ful·ly** *adv* — **taste·less** *adj* — **taste·less·ly** *adv* — **tast·er** *n*

tasty \'tāstē\ *adj* **tast·i·er; -est** : pleasing to the sense of taste — **tast·i·ness** *n*

tat·ter \'tatər\ *n* **1** : part torn and left hanging **2** *pl* : tattered clothing ~ *vb* : make or become ragged

tat·tle \'tat°l\ *vb* **-tled; -tling** : inform on someone — **tat·tler** *n*

tat·tle·tale *n* : one that tattles

tat·too \ta'tü\ *vb* : mark the skin with indelible designs or figures — **tattoo** *n*

taught *past of* TEACH

taunt \'tȯnt\ *n* : sarcastic challenge or insult — **taunt** *vb* — **taunt·er** *n*

taut \'tȯt\ *adj* : tightly drawn — **taut·ly** *adv* — **taut·ness** *n*

tav·ern \'tavərn\ *n* : establishment where liquors are sold to be drunk on the premises

taw·dry \'tȯdrē\ *adj* **-dri·er; -est** : cheap and gaudy — **taw·dri·ly** \'tȯdrəlē\ *adv*

taw·ny \'tȯnē\ *adj* **-ni·er; -est** : brownish orange

tax \'taks\ *vb* **1** : impose a tax on **2** : charge **3** : put under stress ~ *n* **1** : charge by authority for public purposes **2** : strain — **tax·able** *adj* — **tax·a·tion** \tak'sāshən\ *n* — **tax·pay·er** *n* — **tax·pay·ing** *adj*

taxi \'taksē\ *n, pl* **tax·is** \-sēz\ : automobile transporting passengers for a fare ~ *vb* **tax·ied; taxi·ing** *or* **taxy·ing; tax·is** *or* **tax·ies 1** : transport or go by taxi **2** : move along the ground before takeoff or after landing

taxi·cab \'taksē,kab\ *n* : taxi

taxi·der·my \'taksə,dərmē\ *n* : skill or job of stuffing and mounting animal skins — **taxi·der·mist** \-mist\ *n*

tea \'tē\ *n* : cured leaves of an oriental shrub or a drink made from these — **tea·cup** *n* — **tea·pot** *n*

teach \'tēch\ *vb* **taught** \'tȯt\; **teaching 1** : tell or show the fundamentals or skills of something **2** : cause to know the consequences **3** : impart knowledge of — **teach·able** *adj* — **teach·er** *n* — **teach·ing** *n*

teak \'tēk\ *n* : East Indian timber tree or its wood

tea·ket·tle \'tē,ket³l\ *n* : covered kettle with a handle and spout for boiling water

teal \'tēl\ *n, pl* **teal** *or* **teals** : small short-necked wild duck

team \'tēm\ *n* **1** : draft animals harnessed together **2** : number of people organized for a game or work ~ *vb* : form or work together as a team — **team** *adj* — **team·mate** *n* — **team·work** *n*

team·ster \'tēmstər\ *n* **1** : one that drives a team of animals **2** : one that drives a truck

¹**tear** \'tir\ *n* : drop of salty liquid that moistens the eye — **tear·ful** \-fəl\ *adj* — **tear·ful·ly** *adv*

²**tear** \'tar\ *vb* **tore** \'tōr\; **torn** \'tōrn\; **tear·ing 1** : separate or pull apart by force **2** : move or act with violence or haste ~ *n* : act or result of tearing

tease \'tēz\ *vb* **teased; teas·ing** : annoy by goading, coaxing, or tantalizing ~ *n* **1** : act of teasing or state of being teased **2** : one that teases

tea·spoon \\'tē͵spün\ *n* **1** : small spoon for stirring or sipping **2** : measuring spoon holding ⅙ fluid ounce — **tea·spoon·ful** \-͵fül\ *n*

teat \\'tēt\ *n* : protuberance through which milk is drawn from an udder or breast

tech·ni·cal \\'teknikəl\ *adj* **1** : having or relating to special mechanical or scientific knowledge **2** : by strict interpretation of rules — **tech·ni·cal·ly** *adv*

tech·ni·cal·i·ty \͵teknə'kalətē\ *n, pl* **-ties** : detail meaningful only to a specialist

technical sergeant *n* : noncommissioned officer in the air force ranking next below a master sergeant

tech·ni·cian \tek'nishən\ *n* : person with the technique of a specialized skill

tech·nique \tek'nēk\ *n* : manner of accomplishing something

tech·nol·o·gy \tek'näləjē\ *n, pl* **-gies** : applied science — **tech·no·log·i·cal** \͵teknə'läjikəl\ *adj*

te·dious \\'tēdēəs\ *adj* : wearisome from length or dullness — **te·dious·ly** *adv* — **te·dious·ness** *n*

te·di·um \\'tēdēəm\ *n* : tedious state or quality

tee \\'tē\ *n* : mound or peg on which a golf ball is placed before beginning play — **tee** *vb*

teem \\'tēm\ *vb* : become filled to overflowing

teen·age \\'tēn͵āj\, **teen·aged** \-͵ājd\ *adj* : relating to people in their teens — **teen·ag·er** \-͵ājər\ *n*

teens \\'tēnz\ *n pl* : years 13 to 19 in a person's life

tee·pee *var of* TEPEE

tee·ter \\'tētər\ *vb* **1** : move unsteadily **2** : seesaw — **teeter** *n*

teeth *pl of* TOOTH

teethe \\'tēth\ *vb* **teethed; teeth·ing** : grow teeth

tele·cast \\'teli͵kast\ *vb* **-cast; -cast·ing** : broadcast by television — **telecast** *n* — **tele·cast·er** *n*

tele·com·mu·ni·ca·tion \\'teləkəmyünə'kāshən\ *n* : communication at a distance (as by radio or telephone)

tele·gram \\'telə͵gram\ *n* : message sent by telegraph

tele·graph \-͵graf\ *n* : system for communication by electrical transmission of coded signals ∼ *vb* : send by telegraph — **te·leg·ra·pher** \tə'legrəfər\ *n* — **tele·graph·ic** \͵telə'grafik\ *adj*

te·lep·a·thy \tə'lepəthē\ *n* : apparent communication without known sensory means — **tele·path·ic** \ˌtelə'pathik\ *adj* — **tele·path·i·cal·ly** *adv*

tele·phone \'teləˌfōn\ *n* : instrument or system for electrical transmission of spoken words ∼ *vb* **-phoned; -phon·ing** : communicate with by telephone — **tele·phon·er** *n*

tele·scope \-ˌskōp\ *n* : tube-shaped optical instrument for viewing distant objects ∼ *vb* **-scoped; -scop·ing** : slide or cause to slide inside another similar section — **tele·scop·ic** \ˌtelə'skäpik\ *adj*

tele·vise \'teləˌvīz\ *vb* **-vised; -vis·ing** : broadcast by television

tele·vi·sion \-ˌvizhən\ *n* : transmission and reproduction of images by radio waves

tell \'tel\ *vb* **told** \'tōld\; **tell·ing** **1** : count **2** : relate in detail **3** : reveal **4** : give information or an order to **5** : find out by observing

tell·er \'telər\ *n* **1** : one that relates or counts **2** : bank employee handling money

te·mer·i·ty \tə'merətē\ *n, pl* **-ties** : boldness

temp \'temp\ *n* **1** : temperature **2** : temporary worker

tem·per \'tempər\ *vb* **1** : dilute or soften **2** : toughen ∼ *n* **1** : characteristic attitude or feeling **2** : toughness **3** : disposition or control over one's emotions

tem·per·a·ment \'tempərə-mənt\ *n* : characteristic frame of mind — **tem·per·a·men·tal** \ˌtemprə'mentᵊl\ *adj*

tem·per·ance \'temprəns\ *n* : moderation in or abstinence from indulgence and esp. the use of intoxicating drink

tem·per·ate \'tempərət\ *adj* : moderate

tem·per·a·ture \'tempərˌchùr, -prəˌchùr, -chər\ *n* **1** : degree of hotness or coldness **2** : fever

tem·pest \'tempəst\ *n* : violent storm — **tem·pes·tu·ous** \tem'peschəwəs\ *adj*

¹**tem·ple** \'tempəl\ *n* : place of worship

²**temple** *n* : flattened space on each side of the forehead

tem·po \'tempō\ *n, pl* **-pi** \-ˌpē\ *or* **-pos** : rate of speed

tem·po·ral \'tempərəl\ *adj* : relating to time or to secular concerns

tem·po·rary \'tempəˌrerē\ *adj* : lasting for a short time only — **tem·po·rar·i·ly** \ˌtempə'rerəlē\ *adv*

tempt \'tempt\ *vb* **1** : coax or persuade to do wrong **2** : attract or provoke — **tempt·er** *n*

— **tempt·ing·ly** *adv* — **tempt·ress** \'temptrəs\ *n*

temp·ta·tion \temp'tāshən\ *n* **1** : act of tempting **2** : something that tempts

ten \'ten\ *n* **1** : one more than 9 **2** : 10th in a set or series **3** : thing having 10 units — **ten** *adj or pron* — **tenth** \'tenth\ *adj or adv or n*

ten·a·ble \'tenəbəl\ *adj* : capable of being held or defended — **ten·a·bil·i·ty** \,tenə'bil-ətē\ *n*

te·na·cious \tə'nāshəs\ *adj* **1** : holding fast **2** : retentive — **te·na·cious·ly** *adv* — **te·nac·i·ty** \tə'nasətē\ *n*

ten·ant \'tenənt\ *n* : one who occupies a rented dwelling — **ten·an·cy** \-ənsē\ *n*

¹tend \'tend\ *vb* : take care of or supervise something

²tend *vb* **1** : move in a particular direction **2** : show a tendency

ten·den·cy \'tendənsē\ *n, pl* **-cies** : likelihood to move, think, or act in a particular way

¹ten·der \'tendər\ *adj* **1** : soft or delicate **2** : expressing or responsive to love or sympathy **3** : sensitive (as to touch) — **ten·der·ly** *adv* — **ten·der·ness** *n*

²tend·er \'tendər\ *n* **1** : one that tends **2** : boat providing transport to a larger ship **3** : vehicle attached to a steam locomotive for carrying fuel and water

³ten·der *n* **1** : offer of a bid for a contract **2** : something that may be offered in payment — **tender** *vb*

ten·der·ize \'tendə,rīz\ *vb* **-ized; -iz·ing** : make (meat) tender — **ten·der·iz·er** \'ten-də,rīzər\ *n*

ten·der·loin \'tender,lȯin\ *n* : tender beef or pork strip from near the backbone

ten·don \'tendən\ *n* : cord of tissue attaching muscle to bone — **ten·di·nous** \-dənəs\ *adj*

ten·dril \'tendrəl\ *n* : slender coiling growth of some climbing plants

ten·e·ment \'tenəmənt\ *n* **1** : house divided into apartments **2** : shabby dwelling

te·net \'tenət\ *n* : principle of belief

ten·nis \'tenəs\ *n* : racket-and-ball game played across a net

ten·or \'tenər\ *n* **1** : general drift or meaning **2** : highest natural adult male voice

ten·pin \'ten,pin\ *n* : bottle-shaped pin bowled at in a game (**tenpins**)

¹tense \'tens\ *n* : distinct verb form that indicates time

²tense *adj* **tens·er; tens·est** **1** : stretched tight **2** : marked by nervous tension — **tense** *vb* —

tense·ly *adv* — **tense·ness** *n* — **ten·si·ty** \'tensətē\ *n*

ten·sile \'tensəl, -ˌsīl\ *adj* : relating to tension

ten·sion \'tenchən\ *n* **1** : tense condition **2** : state of mental unrest or of potential hostility or opposition

tent \'tent\ *n* : collapsible shelter

ten·ta·cle \'tentikəl\ *n* : long flexible projection of an insect or mollusk — **ten·ta·cled** \-kəld\ *adj* — **ten·tac·u·lar** \ten'takyələr\ *adj*

ten·ta·tive \'tentətiv\ *adj* : subject to change or discussion — **ten·ta·tive·ly** *adv*

ten·u·ous \'tenyəwəs\ *adj* **1** : not dense or thick **2** : flimsy or weak — **ten·u·ous·ly** *adv* — **ten·u·ous·ness** *n*

ten·ure \'tenyər\ *n* : act, right, manner, or period of holding something — **ten·ured** \-yərd\ *adj*

te·pee \'tēˌpē\ *n* : conical tent

tep·id \'tepəd\ *adj* : moderately warm

term \'tərm\ *n* **1** : period of time **2** : mathematical expression **3** : special word or phrase **4** *pl* : conditions **5** *pl* : relations ∼ *vb* : name

ter·min·al \'tərmənᵊl\ *n* **1** : end **2** : device for making an electrical connection **3** : station at end of a transportation line — **terminal** *adj*

ter·mi·nate \'tərməˌnāt\ *vb* **-nat·ed; -nat·ing** : bring or come to an end — **ter·mi·na·ble** \-nəbəl\ *adj* — **ter·mi·na·tion** \ˌtərmə'nāshən\ *n*

ter·mi·nol·o·gy \ˌtərmə'näləjē\ *n* : terms used in a particular subject

ter·mi·nus \'tərmənəs\ *n, pl* **-ni** \-ˌnī\ *or* **-nus·es 1** : end **2** : end of a transportation line

ter·mite \'tərˌmīt\ *n* : wood-eating insect

tern \'tərn\ *n* : small sea bird

ter·race \'terəs\ *n* **1** : balcony or patio **2** : bank with a flat top ∼ *vb* **-raced; -rac·ing** : landscape in a series of banks

ter·ra–cot·ta \ˌterə'kätə\ *n* : reddish brown earthenware

ter·rain \tə'rān\ *n* : features of the land

ter·ra·pin \'terəpən\ *n* : No. American turtle

ter·rar·i·um \tə'rarēəm\ *n, pl* **-ia** \-ēə\ *or* **-i·ums** : container for keeping plants or animals

ter·res·tri·al \tə'restrēəl\ *adj* **1** : relating to the earth or its inhabitants **2** : living or growing on land

ter·ri·ble \'terəbəl\ *adj* **1** : exciting terror **2** : distressing **3** : intense **4** : of very poor quality — **ter·ri·bly** \-blē\ *adv*

ter·ri·er \'terēər\ *n* : small dog

ter·rif·ic \tə'rifik\ *adj* **1** : exciting terror **2** : extraordinary

ter·ri·fy \'terə,fī\ *vb* **-fied; -fy-ing** : fill with terror — **ter·ri-fy·ing·ly** *adv*

ter·ri·to·ry \'terə,tōrē\ *n, pl* **-ries** : particular geographical region — **ter·ri·to·ri·al** \,terə-'tōrēəl\ *adj*

ter·ror \'terər\ *n* : intense fear and panic or a cause of it

ter·ror·ism \-,izəm\ *n* : systematic covert warfare to produce terror for political coercion — **ter·ror·ist** \-ist\ *adj or n*

ter·ror·ize \-,īz\ *vb* **-ized; -iz-ing** **1** : fill with terror **2** : coerce by threat or violence

ter·ry \'terē\ *n, pl* **-ries** : absorbent fabric with a loose pile

terse \'tərs\ *adj* **ters·er; ters-est** : concise — **terse·ly** *adv* — **terse·ness** *n*

ter·tia·ry \'tərshē,erē\ *adj* : of 3d rank, importance, or value

test \'test\ *n* : examination or evaluation ∼ *vb* : examine by a test — **test·er** *n*

tes·ta·ment \'testəmənt\ *n* **1** *cap* : division of the Bible **2** : will — **tes·ta·men·ta·ry** \,testə'mentərē\ *adj*

tes·ti·cle \'testikəl\ *n* : testis

tes·ti·fy \'testə,fī\ *vb* **-fied; -fy-ing** **1** : give testimony **2** : serve as evidence

tes·ti·mo·ni·al \,testə'mōnēəl\ *n* **1** : favorable recommendation **2** : tribute — **testimonial** *adj*

tes·ti·mo·ny \'testə,mōnē\ *n, pl* **-nies** : statement given as evidence in court

tes·tis \'testəs\ *n, pl* **-tes** \-,tēz\ : male reproductive gland

tes·ty \'testē\ *adj* **-ti·er; -est** : easily annoyed

tet·a·nus \'tet°nəs\ *n* : bacterial disease producing violent spasms

tête à tête \,tātə'tāt\ *adv* : privately ∼ *n* : private conversation ∼ *adj* : private

teth·er \'tethər\ *n* : leash ∼ *vb* : restrain with a leash

text \'tekst\ *n* **1** : author's words **2** : main body of printed or written matter on a page **3** : textbook **4** : scriptural passage used as the theme of a sermon **5** : topic — **tex·tu·al** \'tekschəwəl\ *adj*

text·book \-,buk\ *n* : book on a school subject

tex·tile \'tek,stīl, 'tekst°l\ *n* : fabric

tex·ture \'tekschər\ *n* **1** : feel and appearance of something **2** : structure

than \'than\ *conj or prep* — used in comparisons

thank \'thaŋk\ *vb* : express gratitude to

thank·ful \-fəl\ *adj* : giving thanks — **thank·ful·ly** *adv* — **thank·ful·ness** *n*

thank·less *adj* : not appreciated

thanks \'thaŋks\ *n pl* : expression of gratitude

Thanks·giv·ing \thaŋks'giviŋ\ *n* : 4th Thursday in November observed as a legal holiday for giving thanks for divine goodness

that \'that\ *pron, pl* **those** \thōz\ **1** : something indicated or understood **2** : the one farther away ~ *adj, pl* **those** : being the one mentioned or understood or farther away ~ *conj or pron* — used to introduce a clause ~ *adv* : to such an extent

thatch \'thach\ *vb* : cover with thatch ~ *n* : covering of matted straw

thaw \'thȯ\ *vb* : melt or cause to melt — **thaw** *n*

the \thə, *before vowel sounds usu* thē\ *definite article* : that particular one ~ *adv* — used before a comparative or superlative

the·ater, the·atre \'thēətər\ *n* **1** : building or room for viewing a play or movie **2** : dramatic arts

the·at·ri·cal \thē'atrikəl\ *adj* **1** : relating to the theater **2** : involving exaggerated emotion

thee \'thē\ *pron, archaic objective case of* THOU

theft \'theft\ *n* : act of stealing

their \'ther\ *adj* : relating to them

theirs \'theərz\ *pron* : their one or ones

the·ism \'thē,izəm\ *n* : belief in the existence of a god or gods — **the·ist** \-ist\ *n or adj* — **the·is·tic** \thē'istik\ *adj*

them \'them\ *pron, objective case of* THEY

theme \'thēm\ *n* **1** : subject matter **2** : essay **3** : melody developed in a piece of music — **the·mat·ic** \thi'matik\ *adj*

them·selves \thəm'selvz, them-\ *pron pl* : they, them — used reflexively or for emphasis

then \'then\ *adv* **1** : at that time **2** : soon after that **3** : in addition **4** : in that case **5** : consequently ~ *n* : that time ~ *adj* : existing at that time

thence \'thens, 'thens\ *adv* : from that place or fact

the·oc·ra·cy \thē'äkrəsē\ *n, pl* **-cies** : government by officials regarded as divinely inspired — **the·o·crat·ic** \,thēə'kratik\ *adj*

the·ol·o·gy \thē'äləjē\ *n, pl* **-gies** : study of religion — **the·o·lo·gian** \,thēə'lōjən\ *n* — **the·o·log·i·cal** \-'läjikəl\ *adj*

the·o·rem \\'thēərəm, 'thirəm\\ *n* : provable statement of truth

the·o·ret·i·cal \\ˌthēə'retikəl\\ *adj* : relating to or being theory — **the·o·ret·i·cal·ly** *adv*

the·o·rize \\'thēəˌrīz\\ *vb* **-rized; -riz·ing** : put forth theories — **the·o·rist** *n*

the·o·ry \\'thēərē, 'thirē\\ *n, pl* **-ries 1** : general principles of a subject **2** : plausible or scientifically acceptable explanation **3** : judgment, guess, or opinion

ther·a·peu·tic \\ˌtherə'pyütik\\ *adj* : offering or relating to remedy — **ther·a·peu·ti·cal·ly** *adv*

ther·a·py \\'therəpē\\ *n, pl* **-pies** : treatment for mental or physical disorder — **ther·a·pist** \\-pist\\ *n*

there \\'thar\\ *adv* **1** : in, at, or to that place **2** : in that respect ~ *pron* — used to introduce a sentence or clause ~ *n* : that place or point

there·abouts, there·about \\ˌtharə'bauts, 'tharəˌ-, -'baut\\ *adv* : near that place, time, number, or quantity

there·af·ter \\thar'aftər\\ *adv* : after that

there·by \\thar'bī, 'tharˌbī\\ *adv* **1** : by that **2** : connected with or with reference to that

there·fore \\'tharˌfōr\\ *adv* : for that reason

there·in \\thar'in\\ *adv* **1** : in or into that place, time, or thing **2** : in that respect

there·of \\-'əv, -'äv\\ *adv* **1** : of that or it **2** : from that

there·upon \\'tharəˌpȯn, -ˌpän; ˌtharə'pȯn, -'pän\\ *adv* **1** : on that matter **2** : therefore **3** : immediately after that

there·with \\thar'with, -'with\\ *adv* : with that

ther·mal \\'thərməl\\ *adj* : relating to, caused by, or conserving heat — **ther·mal·ly** *adv*

ther·mo·dy·nam·ics \\ˌthərmədī'namiks\\ *n* : physics of heat

ther·mom·e·ter \\thər'mämətər\\ *n* : instrument for measuring temperature — **ther·mo·met·ric** \\ˌthərmə'metrik\\ *adj*

ther·mos \\'thərməs\\ *n* : double-walled bottle used to keep liquids hot or cold

ther·mo·stat \\'thərməˌstat\\ *n* : automatic temperature control — **ther·mo·stat·ic** \\ˌthərmə'statik\\ *adj* — **ther·mo·stat·i·cal·ly** *adv*

the·sau·rus \\thi'sȯrəs\\ *n, pl* **-sau·ri** \\-'sȯrˌī\\ *or* **-sau·rus·es** \\-'sȯrəsəz\\ : book of words and esp. synonyms

these *pl of* THIS

the·sis \\'thēsəs\\ *n, pl* **the·ses** \\'thēˌsēz\\ **1** : proposition to be argued for **2** : essay embodying results of original research

thes·pi·an \'thespēən\ *adj* : dramatic ∼ *n* : actor

they \'thā\ *pron* **1** : those ones **2** : people in general

thi·a·mine \'thīəmən, -ˌmēn\ *n* : essential vitamin

thick \'thik\ *adj* **1** : having relatively great mass from front to back or top to bottom **2** : viscous ∼ *n* : most crowded or thickest part — **thick·ly** *adv* — **thick·ness** *n*

thick·en \'thikən\ *vb* : make or become thick — **thick·en·er** \-ənər\ *n*

thick·et \'thikət\ *n* : dense growth of bushes or small trees

thick–skinned \-'skind\ *adj* : insensitive to criticism

thief \'thēf\ *n, pl* **thieves** \'thēvz\ : one that steals

thieve \'thēv\ *vb* **thieved; thiev·ing** : steal — **thiev·ery** *n*

thigh \'thī\ *n* : upper part of the leg

thigh·bone \'thīˌbōn\ *n* : femur

thim·ble \'thimbəl\ *n* : protective cap for the finger in sewing — **thim·ble·ful** *n*

thin \'thin\ *adj* **-nn-** **1** : having relatively little mass from front to back or top to bottom **2** : not closely set or placed **3** : relatively free flowing **4** : lacking substance, fullness, or strength ∼ *vb* **-nn-** : make

or become thin — **thin·ly** *adv* — **thin·ness** *n*

thing \'thiŋ\ *n* **1** : matter of concern **2** : event or act **3** : object **4** *pl* : possessions

think \'thiŋk\ *vb* **thought** \'thȯt\; **think·ing** **1** : form or have in the mind **2** : have as an opinion **3** : ponder **4** : devise by thinking **5** : imagine — **think·er** *n*

thin–skinned *adj* : extremely sensitive to criticism

third \'thərd\ *adj* : being number 3 in a countable series ∼ *n* **1** : one that is third **2** : one of 3 equal parts — **third, third·ly** *adv*

third dimension *n* : thickness or depth — **third–dimensional** *adj*

third world *n* : less developed nations of the world

thirst \'thərst\ *n* **1** : dryness in mouth and throat **2** : intense desire ∼ *vb* : feel thirst — **thirsty** *adj*

thir·teen \ˌthər'tēn\ *n* : one more than 12 — **thirteen** *adj or pron* — **thir·teenth** \-'tēnth\ *adj or n*

thir·ty \'thərtē\ *n, pl* **thirties** : 3 times 10 — **thir·ti·eth** \-ēəth\ *adj or n* — **thirty** *adj or pron*

this \'this\ *pron, pl* **these** \'thēz\ : something close or under immediate discussion

~ *adj, pl* **these** : being the one near, present, just mentioned, or more immediately under observation ~ *adv* : to such an extent or degree

this·tle \'thisəl\ *n* : tall prickly herb

thith·er \'thith̯ər\ *adv* : to that place

thong \'thȯ\ *n* : strip of leather or hide

tho·rax \'thōr͵aks\ *n, pl* **-rax-es** *or* **-races** \'thōrə͵sēz\ **1** : part of the body between neck and abdomen **2** : middle of 3 divisions of an insect body — **tho·rac·ic** \thə'rasik\ *adj*

thorn \'thȯrn\ *n* : sharp spike on a plant or a plant bearing these — **thorny** *adj*

thor·ough \'thərō\ *adj* : omitting or overlooking nothing — **thor·ough·ly** *adv* — **thor·ough·ness** *n*

thor·ough·bred \'thərə͵bred\ *n* **1** *cap* : light speedy racing horse **2** : one of excellent quality — **thoroughbred** *adj*

thor·ough·fare \'thərə͵far\ *n* : public road

those *pl of* THAT

thou \'thau̇\ *pron, archaic* : you

though \'thō\ *adv* : however ~ *conj* **1** : despite the fact that **2** : granting that

thought \'thȯt\ *past of* THINK *n* **1** : process of thinking **2** : serious consideration **3** : idea

thought·ful \-fəl\ *adj* **1** : absorbed in or showing thought **2** : considerate of others — **thought·ful·ly** *adv* — **thought·ful·ness** *n*

thought·less \-ləs\ *adj* **1** : careless or reckless **2** : lacking concern for others — **thought·less·ly** *adv*

thou·sand \'thau̇zᵊnd\ *n, pl* **-sands** *or* **-sand** : 10 times 100 — **thousand** *adj* — **thou·sandth** \-ᵊnth\ *adj or n*

thrash \'thrash\ *vb* **1** : thresh **2** : beat **3** : move about violently — **thrash·er** *n*

thread \'thred\ *n* **1** : fine line of fibers **2** : train of thought **3** : ridge around a screw ~ *vb* **1** : pass thread through **2** : put together on a thread **3** : make one's way through or between

thread·bare *adj* **1** : worn so that the thread shows **2** : trite

threat \'thret\ *n* **1** : expression of intention to harm **2** : thing that threatens

threat·en \'thretᵊn\ *vb* **1** : utter threats **2** : show signs of being near or impending — **threat·en·ing·ly** *adv*

three \'thrē\ *n* **1** : one more than 2 **2** : 3d in a set or series — **three** *adj or pron*

three·fold \'thrē͵fōld\ *adj* : triple — **three·fold** \-'fōld\ *adv*

three·score *adj* : being 3 times 20

thresh \'thresh, 'thrash\ *vb* : beat to separate grain — **thresh·er** *n*

thresh·old \'thresh,ōld\ *n* **1** : sill of a door **2** : beginning stage

threw *past of* THROW

thrice \'thrīs\ *adv* : 3 times

thrift \'thrift\ *n* : careful management or saving of money — **thrift·i·ly** \'thriftəlē\ *adv* — **thrifty** *adj*

thrill \'thril\ *vb* **1** : have or cause to have a sudden sharp feeling of excitement **2** : tremble — **thrill** *n* — **thrill·er** *n* — **thrill·ing·ly** *adv*

thrive \'thrīv\ *vb* **throve** \'thrōv\ *or* **thrived; thriv·en** \'thrivən\ **1** : grow vigorously **2** : prosper

throat \'thrōt\ *n* **1** : front part of the neck **2** : passage to the stomach — **throat·ed** *adj* — **throaty** *adj*

throb \'thräb\ *vb* **-bb-** : pulsate — **throb** *n*

throe \'thrō\ *n* **1** : pang or spasm **2** *pl* : hard or painful struggle

throne \'thrōn\ *n* : chair representing power or sovereignty

throng \'thrȯŋ\ *n or vb* : crowd

throt·tle \'thrät°l\ *vb* **-tled; -tling** : choke ~ *n* : valve regulating volume of fuel and air delivered to engine cylinders

through \'thrü\ *prep* **1** : into at one side and out at the other side of **2** : by way of **3** : among, between, or all around **4** : because of **5** : throughout the time of ~ \'thrü\ *adv* **1** : from one end or side to the other **2** : from beginning to end **3** : to the core **4** : into the open ~ *adj* **1** : going directly from origin to destination **2** : finished

through·out \thrü'aút\ *adv* **1** : everywhere **2** : from beginning to end ~ *prep* **1** : in or to every part of **2** : during the whole of

throve *past of* THRIVE

throw \'thrō\ *vb* **threw** \'thrü\; **thrown** \'thrōn\; **throw·ing** **1** : propel through the air **2** : cause to fall or fall off **3** : put suddenly in a certain position or condition **4** : move quickly as if throwing **5** : put on or off hastily — **throw** *n* — **throw·er** \'thrōər\ *n* — **throw up** *vb* : vomit

thrush \'thrəsh\ *n* : songbird

thrust \'thrəst\ *vb* **thrust; thrust·ing** **1** : shove forward **2** : stab or pierce — **thrust** *n*

thud \'thəd\ *n* : dull sound of something falling — **thud** *vb*

thug \'thəg\ *n* : ruffian or gangster

thumb \'thəm\ *n* **1** : short thick division of the hand opposing the fingers **2** : glove part for the thumb ∼ *vb* : leaf through with the thumb — **thumb·nail** *n*

thump \\'thəmp\\ *vb* : strike with something thick or heavy causing a dull sound — **thump** *n*

thun·der \\'thəndər\\ *n* : sound following lightning — **thun·der** *vb* — **thun·der·clap** *n* — **thun·der·ous** \\'thəndərəs\\ *adj* — **thun·der·ous·ly** *adv*

thun·der·bolt \\-ˌbōlt\\ *n* : discharge of lightning with thunder

thun·der·show·er \\'thəndər-ˌshaủər\\ *n* : shower with thunder and lightning

thun·der·storm *n* : storm with thunder and lightning

Thurs·day \\'thərzdā, -dē\\ *n* : 5th day of the week

thus \\'thəs\\ *adv* **1** : in this or that way **2** : to this degree or extent **3** : because of this or that

thwart \\'thwȯrt\\ *vb* : block or defeat

thy \\'thī\\ *adj, archaic* : your

thyme \\'tīm, 'thīm\\ *n* : cooking herb

thy·roid \\'thīˌrȯid\\ *adj* : relating to a large endocrine gland **(thyroid gland)**

thy·self \\thī'self\\ *pron, archaic* : yourself

ti·ara \\tē'arə, -'är-\\ *n* : decorative formal headband

tib·ia \\'tibēə\\ *n, pl* **-i·ae** \\-ēˌē\\ : bone between the knee and ankle

tic \\'tik\\ *n* : twitching of facial muscles

¹tick \\'tik\\ *n* : small 8-legged blood-sucking animal

²tick *n* **1** : light rhythmic tap or beat **2** : check mark ∼ *vb* **1** : make ticks **2** : mark with a tick **3** : operate

tick·er \\'tikər\\ *n* **1** : something (as a watch) that ticks **2** : telegraph instrument that prints on paper tape

tick·et \\'tikət\\ *n* **1** : tag showing price, payment of a fee or fare, or a traffic offense **2** : list of candidates ∼ *vb* : put a ticket on

tick·ing \\'tikiŋ\\ *n* : fabric covering of a mattress

tick·le \\'tikəl\\ *vb* **-led; -ling 1** : please or amuse **2** : touch lightly causing uneasiness, laughter, or spasmodic movements — **tickle** *n*

tick·lish \\'tiklish\\ *adj* **1** : sensitive to tickling **2** : requiring delicate handling — **tick·lish·ness** *n*

tid·al wave \\'tīdᵊl-\\ *n* : high sea wave following an earthquake

tid·bit \\'tidˌbit\\ *n* : choice morsel

tide \\'tīd\\ *n* : alternate rising and falling of the sea ∼ *vb* **tid·ed; tid·ing** : be enough to allow (one) to get by for a time — **tid·al** \ˈtīdᵊl\ *adj* — **tide·wa·ter** *n*

tid·ings \ˈtīdiŋz\ *n pl* : news or message

ti·dy \ˈtīdē\ *adj* **-di·er; -est** **1** : well ordered and cared for **2** : large or substantial — **ti·di·ness** *n* — **tidy** *vb*

tie \ˈtī\ *n* **1** : line or ribbon for fastening, uniting, or closing **2** : cross support to which railroad rails are fastened **3** : uniting force **4** : equality in score or tally or a deadlocked contest **5** : necktie ~ *vb* **tied; ty·ing** *or* **tie·ing** **1** : fasten or close by wrapping and knotting a tie **2** : form a knot in **3** : gain the same score or tally as an opponent

tier \ˈtir\ *n* : one of a steplike series of rows

tiff \ˈtif\ *n* : petty quarrel — **tiff** *vb*

ti·ger \ˈtīgər\ *n* : very large black-striped cat — **ti·ger·ish** \-gərish\ *adj* — **ti·gress** \-grəs\ *n*

tight \ˈtīt\ *adj* **1** : fitting close together esp. so as not to allow air or water in **2** : held very firmly **3** : taut **4** : fitting too snugly **5** : difficult **6** : stingy **7** : evenly contested **8** : low in supply — **tight** *adv* — **tight·en** \-ᵊn\ *vb* — **tight·ly** *adv* — **tight·ness** *n*

tights \ˈtīts\ *n pl* : skintight garments

tight·wad \ˈtītˌwäd\ *n* : stingy person

tile \ˈtīl\ *n* : thin piece of stone or fired clay used on roofs, floors, or walls ~ *vb* : cover with tiles

¹till \ˈtil\ *prep or conj* : until

²till *vb* : cultivate (soil) — **till·able** *adj*

³till *n* : money drawer

¹till·er \ˈtilər\ *n* : one that cultivates soil

²til·ler \ˈtilər\ *n* : lever for turning a boat's rudder

tilt \ˈtilt\ *vb* : cause to incline ~ *n* : slant

tim·ber \ˈtimbər\ *n* **1** : cut wood for building **2** : large squared piece of wood **3** : wooded land or trees for timber ~ *vb* : cover, frame, or support with timbers — **tim·bered** *adj* — **tim·ber·land** \-ˌland\ *n*

tim·bre \ˈtambər, ˈtim-\ *n* : sound quality

time \ˈtīm\ *n* **1** : period during which something exists or continues or can be accomplished **2** : point at which something happens **3** : customary hour **4** : age **5** : tempo **6** : moment, hour, day, or year as indicated by a clock or calendar **7** : one's experience during a particular period ~ *vb* **timed; tim·ing** **1** : arrange or set the time of **2** : determine or record the time, duration, or rate of — **time·keep·er** *n* — **time·less** *adj* — **time·less·ness** *n* — **time·li·ness** *n* — **time·ly** *adv* — **tim·er** *n*

time·piece *n* : device to show time

times \'tīmz\ *prep* : multiplied by

time·ta·ble \'tīm,tābəl\ *n* : table of departure and arrival times

tim·id \'timəd\ *adj* : lacking in courage or self-confidence — **ti·mid·i·ty** \tə'midətē\ *n* — **tim·id·ly** *adv*

tim·o·rous \'timərəs\ *adj* : fearful — **tim·o·rous·ly** *adv* — **tim·o·rous·ness** *n*

tim·pa·ni \'timpənē\ *n pl* : set of kettledrums — **tim·pa·nist** \-nist\ *n*

tin \'tin\ *n* **1** : soft white metallic chemical element **2** : metal food can

tinc·ture \'tiŋkchər\ *n* : alcoholic solution of a medicine

tin·der \'tindər\ *n* : substance used to kindle a fire

tine \'tīn\ *n* : one of the points of a fork

tin·foil \'tin,fȯil\ *n* : thin metal sheeting

tinge \'tinj\ *vb* **tinged; tinge·ing** *or* **ting·ing** \'tinjiŋ\ **1** : color slightly **2** : affect with a slight odor ∼ *n* : slight coloring or flavor

tin·gle \'tiŋgəl\ *vb* **-gled; -gling** : feel a ringing, stinging, or thrilling sensation — **tingle** *n*

tin·ker \'tiŋkər\ *vb* : experiment in repairing something — **tin·ker·er** *n*

tin·kle \'tiŋkəl\ *vb* **-kled; -kling** : make or cause to make a high ringing sound — **tinkle** *n*

tin·sel \'tinsəl\ *n* : decorative thread or strip of glittering metal or paper

tint \'tint\ *n* **1** : slight or pale coloration **2** : color shade ∼ *vb* : give a tint to

ti·ny \'tīnē\ *adj* **-ni·er; -est** : very small

¹tip \'tip\ *vb* **-pp- 1** : overturn **2** : lean ∼ *n* : act or state of tipping

²tip *n* : pointed end of something ∼ *vb* **-pp- 1** : furnish with a tip **2** : cover the tip of

³tip *n* : small sum given for a service performed ∼ *vb* : give a tip to

⁴tip *n* : piece of confidential information ∼ *vb* **-pp-** : give confidential information to

tip–off \'tip,ȯf\ *n* : indication

tip·ple \'tipəl\ *vb* **-pled; -pling** : drink intoxicating liquor esp. habitually or excessively — **tip·pler** *n*

tip·sy \'tipsē\ *adj* **-si·er; -est** : unsteady or foolish from alcohol

tip·toe \'tip‚tō\ *n* : the toes of the feet ∼ *adv or adj* : supported on tiptoe ∼ *vb* **-toed; -toe·ing** : walk quietly or on tiptoe

tip–top *n* : highest point ∼ *adj* : excellent

ti·rade \tī'rād, 'tī‚-\ *n* : prolonged speech of abuse

¹tire \'tīr\ *vb* **tired; tir·ing** **1** : make or become weary **2** : wear out the patience of — **tire·less** *adj* — **tire·less·ly** *adv* — **tire·some** \-səm\ *adj* — **tire·some·ly** *adv*

²tire *n* : rubber cushion encircling a car wheel

tired \'tīrd\ *adj* : weary

tis·sue \'tishü\ *n* **1** : soft absorbent paper **2** : layer of cells forming a basic structural element of an animal or plant body

ti·tan·ic \tī'tanik, tə-\ *adj* : gigantic

ti·ta·ni·um \tī'tānēəm, tə-\ *n* : gray light strong metallic chemical element

tithe \'tīth\ *n* : tenth part paid or given esp. for the support of a church — **tithe** *vb* — **tith·er** *n*

tit·il·late \'titᵊl‚āt\ *vb* **-lat·ed; -lat·ing** : excite pleasurably — **tit·il·la·tion** \‚titᵊl'āshən\ *n*

ti·tle \'tītᵊl\ *n* **1** : legal ownership **2** : distinguishing name **3** : designation of honor, rank, or office **4** : championship — **ti·tled** *adj*

tit·ter \'titər\ *n* : nervous or affected laugh — **titter** *vb*

tit·u·lar \'tichələr\ *adj* **1** : existing in title only **2** : relating to or bearing a title

tiz·zy \'tizē\ *n, pl* **tizzies** : state of agitation or worry

TNT \‚tē‚en'tē\ *n* : high explosive

to \'tü\ *prep* **1** : in the direction of **2** : at, on, or near **3** : resulting in **4** : before or until **5** — used to show a relationship or object of a verb **6** — used with an infinitive ∼ *adv* **1** : forward **2** : to a state of consciousness

toad \'tōd\ *n* : tailless leaping amphibian

toad·stool \-‚stül\ *n* : mushroom esp. when inedible or poisonous

toady \'tōdē\ *n, pl* **toad·ies** : one who flatters to gain favors — **toady** *vb*

toast \'tōst\ *vb* **1** : make (as a slice of bread) crisp and brown **2** : drink in honor of someone or something **3** : warm ∼ *n* **1** : toasted sliced bread **2** : act of drinking in honor of someone — **toast·er** *n*

to·bac·co \tə'bakō\ *n, pl* **-cos** : broad-leaved herb or its leaves prepared for smoking or chewing

to·bog·gan \tə'bägən\ *n* : long flat-bottomed light sled ～ *vb* : coast on a toboggan

to·day \tə'dā\ *adv* **1** : on or for this day **2** : at the present time ～ *n* : present day or time

tod·dle \'täd²l\ *vb* **-dled; -dling** : walk with tottering steps like a young child — **toddle** *n* — **tod·dler** \'täd²lər\ *n*

to–do \tə'dü\ *n, pl* **to–dos** \-'düz\ : disturbance or fuss

toe \'tō\ *n* : one of the 5 end divisions of the foot — **toe·nail** *n*

tof·fee, tof·fy \'tȯfē, 'tä-\ *n, pl* **toffees** *or* **toffies** : candy made of boiled sugar and butter

to·ga \'tōgə\ *n* : loose outer garment of ancient Rome

to·geth·er \tə'gethər\ *adv* **1** : in or into one place or group **2** : in or into contact or association **3** : at one time **4** : as a group — **to·geth·er·ness** *n*

togs \'tägz, 'tȯgz\ *n pl* : clothing

toil \'tȯil\ *vb* : work hard and long — **toil** *n* — **toil·er** *n* — **toil·some** *adj*

toi·let \'tȯilət\ *n* **1** : dressing and grooming oneself **2** : bathroom **3** : water basin to urinate and defecate in

to·ken \'tōkən\ *n* **1** : outward sign or expression of something **2** : small part repre-senting the whole **3** : piece resembling a coin

told *past of* TELL

tol·er·a·ble \'tälərəbəl\ *adj* **1** : capable of being endured **2** : moderately good — **tol·er·a·bly** \-blē\ *adv*

tol·er·ance \'tälərəns\ *n* **1** : lack of opposition for beliefs or practices differing from one's own **2** : capacity for enduring **3** : allowable deviation — **tol·er·ant** *adj* — **tol·er·ant·ly** *adv*

tol·er·ate \'tälə,rāt\ *vb* **-at·ed; -at·ing** **1** : allow to be or to be done without opposition **2** : endure or resist the action of — **tol·er·a·tion** \,tälə'rā-shən\ *n*

¹**toll** \'tōl\ *n* **1** : fee paid for a privilege or service **2** : cost of achievement in loss or suffering — **toll·booth** *n* — **toll·gate** *n*

²**toll** *vb* **1** : cause the sounding of (a bell) **2** : sound with slow measured strokes ～ *n* : sound of a tolling bell

tom·a·hawk \'tämə,hȯk\ *n* : light ax used as a weapon by American Indians

to·ma·to \tə'mātō, -'mät-\ *n, pl* **-toes** : tropical American herb or its fruit

tomb \'tüm\ *n* : house, vault, or grave for burial

tom·boy \\'täm₁bȯi\ *n* : girl who behaves in a manner usu. considered boyish

tomb·stone *n* : stone marking a grave

tom·cat \\'täm₁kat\ *n* : male cat

tome \\'tōm\ *n* : large or weighty book

to·mor·row \tə'märō\ *adv* : on or for the day after today — **to-morrow** *n*

tom–tom \\'täm₁täm\ *n* : small≠headed drum beaten with the hands

ton \\'tən\ *n* : unit of weight equal to 2000 pounds

tone \\'tōn\ *n* **1** : vocal or musical sound **2** : sound of definite pitch **3** : manner of speaking that expresses an emotion or attitude **4** : color quality **5** : healthy condition **6** : general character or quality ∼ *vb* : soften or muffle — often used with *down* — **ton·al** \-ᵊl\ *adj* — **to·nal·i·ty** \tō'nalətē\ *n*

tongs \\'täŋz, 'tȯŋz\ *n pl* : grasping device of 2 joined or hinged pieces

tongue \\'təŋ\ *n* **1** : fleshy movable organ of the mouth **2** : language **3** : something long and flat and fastened at one end — **tongued** \\'təŋd\ *adj* — **tongue·less** *adj*

ton·ic \\'tänik\ *n* : something (as a drug) that invigorates or restores health — **tonic** *adj*

to·night \tə'nīt\ *adv* : on this night ∼ *n* : present or coming night

ton·sil \\'tänsəl\ *n* : either of a pair of oval masses in the throat — **ton·sil·lec·to·my** \₁tänsə'lektəmē\ *n* — **ton·sil·li·tis** \-'lītəs\ *n*

too \\'tü\ *adv* **1** : in addition **2** : excessively

took *past of* TAKE

tool \\'tül\ *n* : device worked by hand ∼ *vb* : shape or finish with a tool

tool·bar \\'tül₁bär\ *n* : strip of icons on a computer display providing quick access to pictured functions

toot \\'tüt\ *vb* : sound or cause to sound esp. in short blasts — **toot** *n*

tooth \\'tüth\ *n, pl* **teeth** \\'tēth\ **1** : one of the hard structures in the jaws for chewing **2** : one of the projections on the edge of a gear wheel — **tooth-ache** *n* — **tooth·brush** *n* — **toothed** \\'tütht\ *adj* — **tooth-less** *adj* — **tooth·paste** *n* — **tooth·pick** *n*

tooth·some \\'tüthsəm\ *adj* **1** : delicious **2** : attractive

¹**top** \\'täp\ *n* **1** : highest part or level of something **2** : lid or covering ∼ *vb* **-pp-** **1** : cover with a top **2** : surpass **3** : go over the top of ∼ *adj* : being at the top — **topped** *adj*

²**top** *n* : spinning toy

to·paz \\'tō͟paz\ *n* : hard gem

top·coat *n* : lightweight overcoat

top·ic \\'täpik\ *n* : subject for discussion or study

top·i·cal \-ikəl\ *adj* **1** : relating to or arranged by topics **2** : relating to current or local events — **top·i·cal·ly** *adv*

top·most \\'täp͟mōst\ *adj* : highest of all

top–notch \-'näch\ *adj* : of the highest quality

to·pog·ra·phy \tə'pägrəfē\ *n* **1** : art of mapping the physical features of a place **2** : outline of the form of a place — **to·pog·ra·pher** \-fər\ *n* — **top·o·graph·ic** \͟täpə'grafik\, **top·o·graph·i·cal** \-ikəl\ *adj*

top·ple \\'täpəl\ *vb* **-pled; -pling** : fall or cause to fall

top·sy–tur·vy \͟täpsē'tərvē\ *adv or adj* **1** : upside down **2** : in utter confusion

torch \\'tȯrch\ *n* : flaming light — **torch·bear·er** *n* — **torch·light** *n*

tore *past of* TEAR

tor·ment \\'tȯr͟ment\ *n* : extreme pain or anguish or a source of this ∼ *vb* **1** : cause severe anguish to **2** : harass — **tor·men·tor** \-ər\ *n*

torn *past part of* TEAR

tor·na·do \tȯr'nādō\ *n, pl* **-does** *or* **-dos** : violent destructive whirling wind

tor·pe·do \tȯr'pēdō\ *n, pl* **-does** : self-propelled explosive submarine missile ∼ *vb* : hit with a torpedo

tor·pid \\'tȯrpəd\ *adj* **1** : having lost motion or the power of exertion **2** : lacking vigor — **tor·pid·i·ty** \tȯr'pidətē\ *n*

tor·por \\'tȯrpər\ *n* : extreme sluggishness or lethargy

torque \\'tȯrk\ *n* : turning force

tor·rent \\'tȯrənt\ *n* **1** : rushing stream **2** : tumultuous outburst — **tor·ren·tial** \tȯ'renchəl, tə-\ *adj*

tor·rid \\'tȯrəd\ *adj* **1** : parched with heat **2** : impassioned

tor·sion \\'tȯrshən\ *n* : a twisting or being twisted — **tor·sion·al** \\'tȯrshənəl\ *adj* — **tor·sion·al·ly** *adv*

tor·so \\'tȯrsō\ *n, pl* **-sos** *or* **-si** \-͟sē\ : trunk of the human body

tor·ti·lla \tȯr'tēyə\ *n* : round flat cornmeal or wheat flour bread

tor·toise \\'tȯrtəs\ *n* : land turtle

tor·tu·ous \\'tȯrchəwəs\ *adj* **1** : winding **2** : tricky

tor·ture \\'tȯrchər\ *n* **1** : use of pain to punish or force **2** : agony ∼ *vb* **-tured; -tur·ing** : inflict torture on — **tor·tur·er** *n*

toss \\'tȯs, 'täs\ *vb* **1** : move to and fro or up and down violently **2** : throw with a quick light motion **3** : move restlessly — **toss** *n*

toss–up *n* **1** : a deciding by flipping a coin **2** : even chance

tot \'tät\ *n* : small child

to·tal \'tōt°l\ *n* : entire amount ~ *vb* **-taled** *or* **-talled; -taling** *or* **-tal·ling 1** : add up **2** : amount to — **total** *adj* — **to·tal·ly** *adv*

to·tal·i·tar·i·an \tō,talə'terēən\ *adj* : relating to a political system in which the government has complete control over the people — **totalitarian** *n* — **to·tal·i·tar·i·an·ism** \-ēə,nizəm\ *n*

to·tal·i·ty \tō'talətē\ *n, pl* **-ties** : whole amount or entirety

tote \'tōt\ *vb* **tot·ed; tot·ing** : carry

to·tem \'tōtəm\ *n* : often carved figure used as a family or tribe emblem

tot·ter \'tätər\ *vb* **1** : sway as if about to fall **2** : stagger

touch \'təch\ *vb* **1** : make contact with so as to feel **2** : be or cause to be in contact **3** : take into the hands or mouth **4** : treat or mention a subject **5** : relate or concern **6** : move to sympathetic feeling ~ *n* **1** : light stroke **2** : act or fact of touching or being touched **3** : sense of feeling **4** : trace **5** : state of being in contact —

touch up *vb* : improve with minor changes

touch·down \'təch,daůn\ *n* : scoring of 6 points in football

touch·stone *n* : test or criterion of genuineness or quality

touchy \'təchē\ *adj* **touch·i·er; -est 1** : easily offended **2** : requiring tact

tough \'təf\ *adj* **1** : strong but elastic **2** : not easily chewed **3** : severe or disciplined **4** : stubborn ~ *n* : rowdy — **tough·ly** *adv* — **tough·ness** *n*

tough·en \'təfən\ *vb* : make or become tough

tou·pee \tü'pā\ *n* : small wig for a bald spot

tour \'tůr\ *n* **1** : period of time spent at work or on an assignment **2** : journey with a return to the starting point ~ *vb* : travel over to see the sights — **tour·ist** \'tůrist\ *n*

tour·na·ment \'tůrnəmənt, 'tər-\ *n* **1** : medieval jousting competition **2** : championship series of games

tour·ney \-nē\ *n, pl* **-neys** : tournament

tour·ni·quet \'tůrnikət, 'tər-\ *n* : tight bandage for stopping blood flow

tou·sle \'taůzəl\ *vb* **-sled; -sling** : dishevel (as someone's hair)

tout \'taůt, 'tüt\ *vb* : praise or publicize loudly

tow \'tō\ *vb* : pull along behind — **tow** *n*

to·ward, to·wards \'tōrd, tə-'wȯrd, 'tōrdz, tə'wȯrdz\ *prep* **1** : in the direction of **2** : with respect to **3** : in part payment on

tow·el \'tau̇əl\ *n* : absorbent cloth or paper for wiping or drying

tow·er \'tau̇ər\ *n* : tall structure ～ *vb* : rise to a great height — **tow·ered** \'tau̇ərd\ *adj* — **tow·er·ing** *adj*

tow·head \'tō,hed\ *n* : person having whitish blond hair — **tow·head·ed** \-,hedəd\ *adj*

town \'taun\ *n* **1** : small residential area **2** : city — **towns·peo·ple** \'taunz,pēpəl\ *n pl*

town·ship \'taun,ship\ *n* **1** : unit of local government **2** : 36 square miles of U.S. public land

tox·ic \'täksik\ *adj* : poisonous — **tox·ic·i·ty** \täk'sisətē\ *n*

tox·in \'täksən\ *n* : poison produced by an organism

toy \'tȯi\ *n* : something for a child to play with ～ *vb* : amuse oneself or play with something ～ *adj* **1** : designed as a toy **2** : very small

¹trace \'trās\ *vb* **traced; tracing** **1** : mark over the lines of (a drawing) **2** : follow the trail or the development of ～ *n* **1** : track **2** : tiny amount or residue — **trace·able** *adj* — **trac·er** *n*

²trace *n* : line of a harness

tra·chea \'trākēə\ *n, pl* **-che·ae** \-kē,ē\ : windpipe — **tra·che·al** \-kēəl\ *adj*

track \'trak\ *n* **1** : trail left by wheels or footprints **2** : racing course **3** : train rails **4** : awareness of a progression **5** : looped belts propelling a vehicle ～ *vb* **1** : follow the trail of **2** : make tracks on — **track·er** *n*

track–and–field *adj* : relating to athletic contests of running, jumping, and throwing events

¹tract \'trakt\ *n* **1** : stretch of land **2** : system of body organs

²tract *n* : pamphlet of propaganda

trac·ta·ble \'traktəbəl\ *adj* : easily controlled

trac·tion \'trakshən\ *n* : gripping power to permit movement — **trac·tion·al** \-shənəl\ *adj* — **trac·tive** \'traktiv\ *adj*

trac·tor \'traktər\ *n* **1** : farm vehicle used esp. for pulling **2** : truck for hauling a trailer

trade \'trād\ *n* **1** : one's regular business **2** : occupation requiring skill **3** : the buying and selling of goods **4** : act of trading ～ *vb* **trad·ed; trading** **1** : give in exchange for something **2** : buy and sell goods **3** : be a regular customer — **trades·peo·ple** \'trādz,pēpəl\ *n pl*

trade–in \'trād,in\ *n* : an item traded to a merchant at the time of a purchase

trade·mark \'trād,märk\ *n* : word or mark identifying a manufacturer — **trademark** *vb*

trades·man \'trādzmən\ *n* : shopkeeper

tra·di·tion \trə'dishən\ *n* : belief or custom passed from generation to generation — **tra·di·tion·al** \-'dishənəl\ *adj* — **tra·di·tion·al·ly** *adv*

tra·duce \trə'düs, -'dyüs\ *vb* **-duced; -duc·ing** : lower the reputation of — **tra·duc·er** *n*

traf·fic \'trafik\ *n* **1** : business dealings **2** : movement along a route ∼ *vb* : do business — **traf·fick·er** *n* — **traffic light** *n*

trag·e·dy \'trajədē\ *n, pl* **-dies** **1** : serious drama describing a conflict and having a sad end **2** : disastrous event

trag·ic \'trajik\ *adj* : being a tragedy — **trag·i·cal·ly** *adv*

trail \'trāl\ *vb* **1** : hang down and drag along the ground **2** : draw along behind **3** : follow the track of **4** : dwindle ∼ *n* **1** : something that trails **2** : path or evidence left by something

trail·er \'trālər\ *n* **1** : vehicle intended to be hauled **2** : dwelling designed to be towed to a site

train \'trān\ *n* **1** : trailing part of a gown **2** : retinue or procession **3** : connected series **4** : group of linked railroad cars ∼ *vb* **1** : cause to grow as desired **2** : make or become prepared or skilled **3** : point — **train·ee** *n* — **train·er** *n* — **train·load** *n*

trai·pse \'trāps\ *vb* **traipsed; traips·ing** : walk

trait \'trāt\ *n* : distinguishing quality

trai·tor \'trātər\ *n* : one who betrays a trust or commits treason — **trai·tor·ous** *adj*

tra·jec·to·ry \trə'jektərē\ *n, pl* **-ries** : path of something moving through air or space

tram·mel \'traməl\ *vb* **-meled** *or* **-mel·led; -mel·ing** *or* **-mel·ling** : impede — **trammel** *n*

tramp \'tramp\ *vb* **1** : walk or hike **2** : tread on ∼ *n* : beggar or vagrant

tram·ple \'trampəl\ *vb* **-pled; -pling** : walk or step on so as to bruise or crush — **trample** *n* — **tram·pler** \-plər\ *n*

tram·po·line \,trampə'lēn, 'trampə,-\ *n* : resilient sheet or web supported by springs and used for bouncing — **tram·po·lin·ist** \-ist\ *n*

trance \'trans\ *n* **1** : sleeplike condition **2** : state of mystical absorption

tran·quil \\'traŋkwəl, 'tran-\\ *adj* : quiet and undisturbed — **tran·quil·ize** \\-kwə͟līz\\ *vb* — **tran·quil·iz·er** *n* — **tran·quil·li·ty, tran·quil·i·ty** \\tran-'kwilətē, traŋ-\\ *n* — **tran·quil·ly** *adv*

trans·act \\trans'akt, tranz-\\ *vb* : conduct (business)

trans·ac·tion \\-'akshən\\ *n* **1** : business deal **2** *pl* : records of proceedings

tran·scend \\trans'end\\ *vb* : rise above or surpass — **tran·scen·dent** \\-'endənt\\ *adj* — **tran·scen·den·tal** \\͟trans͟en-'dentᵊl, -ən-\\ *adj*

tran·scribe \\trans'krīb\\ *vb* **-scribed; -scrib·ing** : make a copy, arrangement, or recording of — **tran·scrip·tion** \\trans'kripshən\\ *n*

tran·script \\'trans͟kript\\ *n* : official copy

tran·sept \\'trans͟ept\\ *n* : part of a church that crosses the nave at right angles

trans·fer \\trans'fər, 'trans͟fər\\ *vb* **-rr-** **1** : move from one person, place, or situation to another **2** : convey ownership of **3** : print or copy by contact **4** : change to another vehicle or transportation line ∼ \\'trans͟fər\\ *n* **1** : act or process of transferring **2** : one that transfers or is transferred **3** : ticket permitting one to transfer — **trans·fer·able** \\trans'fər-

əbəl\\ *adj* — **trans·fer·al** \\-əl\\ *n* — **trans·fer·ence** \\-əns\\ *n*

trans·fig·ure \\trans'figyər\\ *vb* **-ured; -ur·ing** **1** : change the form or appearance of **2** : glorify — **trans·fig·u·ra·tion** \\͟trans͟figyə'rāshən\\ *n*

trans·fix \\trans'fiks\\ *vb* **1** : pierce through **2** : hold motionless

trans·form \\-'form\\ *vb* **1** : change in structure, appearance, or character **2** : change (an electric current) in potential or type — **trans·for·ma·tion** \\͟transfər'māshən\\ *n* — **trans·form·er** \\trans'for-mər\\ *n*

trans·fuse \\trans'fyüz\\ *vb* **-fused; -fus·ing** **1** : diffuse into or through **2** : transfer (as blood) into a vein — **trans·fu·sion** \\-'fyüzhən\\ *n*

trans·gress \\trans'gres, tranz-\\ *vb* : sin — **trans·gres·sion** \\-'greshən\\ *n* — **trans·gres·sor** \\-'gresər\\ *n*

tran·sient \\'tranchənt\\ *adj* : not lasting or staying long — **transient** *n* — **tran·sient·ly** *adv*

tran·sis·tor \\tranz'istər, trans-\\ *n* : small electronic device used in electronic equipment — **tran·sis·tor·ize** \\-tə͟rīz\\ *vb*

tran·sit \\'transət, 'tranz-\\ *n* **1** : movement over, across, or through **2** : local and esp. public transportation **3** : surveyor's instrument

tran·si·tion \trans'ishən, tranz-\ *n* : passage from one state, stage, or subject to another — **tran·si·tion·al** \-'ishənəl\ *adj*

tran·si·to·ry \'transə,tōrē, 'tranz-\ *adj* : of brief duration

trans·late \trans'lāt, tranz-\ *vb* **-lat·ed; -lat·ing** : change into another language — **trans·lat·able** *adj* — **trans·la·tion** \-'lāshən\ *n* — **trans·la·tor** \-'lātər\ *n*

trans·lu·cent \trans'lüs°nt, tranz-\ *adj* : not transparent but clear enough to allow light to pass through — **trans·lu·cence** \-°ns\ *n* — **trans·lu·cen·cy** \-°nsē\ *n* — **trans·lu·cent·ly** *adv*

trans·mis·sion \-'mishən\ *n* **1** : act or process of transmitting **2** : system of gears between a car engine and drive wheels

trans·mit \-'mit\ *vb* **-tt-** **1** : transfer from one person or place to another **2** : pass on by inheritance **3** : broadcast — **trans·mis·si·ble** \-'misəbəl\ *adj* — **trans·mit·ta·ble** \-'mit-əbəl\ *adj* — **trans·mit·tal** \-'mit°l\ *n* — **trans·mit·ter** *n*

tran·som \'transəm\ *n* : often hinged window above a door

trans·par·ent \trans'parənt\ *adj* **1** : clear enough to see

through **2** : obvious — **trans·par·en·cy** \-ənsē\ *n* — **trans·par·ent·ly** *adv*

tran·spire \trans'pīr\ *vb* **-spired; -spir·ing** : take place — **tran·spi·ra·tion** \,transpə-'rāshən\ *n*

trans·plant \trans'plant\ *vb* **1** : dig up and move to another place **2** : transfer from one body part or person to another — **transplant** \'trans,-\ *n* — **trans·plan·ta·tion** \,trans-,plan'tāshən\ *n*

trans·port \trans'pōrt\ *vb* **1** : carry or deliver to another place **2** : carry away by emotion ∼ \'trans,-\ *n* **1** : act of transporting **2** : rapture **3** : ship or plane for carrying troops or supplies — **trans·por·ta·tion** \,transpər'tāshən\ *n* — **trans·port·er** *n*

trans·pose \trans'pōz\ *vb* **-posed; -pos·ing** : change the position, sequence, or key — **trans·po·si·tion** \,transpə'zi-shən\ *n*

trans·ship \tran'ship, trans-\ *vb* : transfer from one mode of transportation to another — **trans·ship·ment** *n*

trans·verse \trans'vərs, tranz-\ *adj* : lying across — **trans·verse** \'trans,vərs, 'tranz-\ *n* — **trans·verse·ly** *adv*

trap \'trap\ *n* **1** : device for catching animals **2** : something by which one is caught unawares **3** : device to allow one thing to pass through while keeping other things out ~ *vb* **-pp-** : catch in a trap — **trap-per** *n*

trap·door *n* : door in a floor or roof

tra·peze \tra'pēz\ *n* : suspended bar used by acrobats

trap·e·zoid \'trapə,zȯid\ *n* : plane 4-sided figure with 2 parallel sides — **trap·e·zoi·dal** \,trapə'zȯidᵊl\ *adj*

trap·pings \'trapiŋz\ *n pl* **1** : ornamental covering **2** : outward decoration or dress

trash \'trash\ *n* : something that is no good — **trashy** *adj*

trau·ma \'traủmə, 'trȯ-\ *n* : bodily or mental injury — **trau·mat·ic** \trə'matik, trȯ-, traủ-\ *adj*

tra·vail \trə'vāl, 'trav,āl\ *n* : painful work or exertion ~ *vb* : labor hard

trav·el \'travəl\ *vb* **-eled** *or* **-elled; -el·ing** *or* **-el·ling** **1** : take a trip or tour **2** : move or be carried from point to point ~ *n* : journey — often pl. — **trav·el·er, trav·el·ler** *n*

tra·verse \trə'vərs, tra'vərs, 'travərs\ *vb* **-versed; -vers·ing** : go or extend across — **tra·verse** \'travərs\ *n*

trav·es·ty \'travəstē\ *n, pl* **-ties** : imitation that makes crude fun of something — **travesty** *vb*

trawl \'trȯl\ *vb* : fish or catch with a trawl ~ *n* : large cone=shaped net — **trawl·er** *n*

tray \'trā\ *n* : shallow flat=bottomed receptacle for holding or carrying something

treach·er·ous \'trechərəs\ *adj* : disloyal or dangerous — **treach·er·ous·ly** *adv*

treach·ery \'trechərē\ *n, pl* **-er·ies** : betrayal of a trust

tread \'tred\ *vb* **trod** \'träd\; **trod·den** \'trädᵊn\ *or* **trod; tread·ing** **1** : step on or over **2** : walk **3** : press or crush with the feet ~ *n* **1** : way of walking **2** : sound made in walking **3** : part on which a thing runs

trea·dle \'tredᵊl\ *n* : foot pedal operating a machine — **trea·dle** *vb*

tread·mill *n* **1** : mill worked by walking persons or animals **2** : wearisome routine

trea·son \'trēzᵊn\ *n* : attempt to overthrow the government — **trea·son·able** \'trēzᵊn-əbəl\ *adj* — **trea·son·ous** \-ᵊnəs\ *adj*

trea·sure \'trezhər, 'trāzh-\ *n* **1** : wealth stored up **2** : something of great value ~ *vb* **-sured; -sur·ing** : keep as precious

trea·sur·er \'trezhərər, 'trāzh-\ *n* : officer who handles funds

trea·sury \'trezhərē, 'trāzh-\ *n, pl* **-sur·ies** : place or office for keeping and distributing funds

treat \'trēt\ *vb* **1** : have as a topic **2** : pay for the food or entertainment of **3** : act toward or regard in a certain way **4** : give medical care to ~ *n* **1** : food or entertainment paid for by another **2** : something special and enjoyable — **treat·ment** \-mənt\ *n*

trea·tise \'trētəs\ *n* : systematic written exposition or argument

trea·ty \'trētē\ *n, pl* **-ties** : agreement between governments

tre·ble \'trebəl\ *n* **1** : highest part in music **2** : upper half of the musical range ~ *adj* : triple in number or amount ~ *vb* **-bled; -bling** : make triple — **tre·bly** *adv*

tree \'trē\ *n* : tall woody plant ~ *vb* **treed; tree·ing** : force up a tree — **tree·less** *adj*

trek \'trek\ *n* : difficult trip ~ *vb* **-kk-** : make a trek

trel·lis \'treləs\ *n* : structure of crossed strips

trem·ble \'trembəl\ *vb* **-bled; -bling** **1** : shake from fear or cold **2** : move or sound as if shaken

tre·men·dous \tri'mendəs\ *adj* : amazingly large, powerful, or excellent — **tre·men·dous·ly** *adv*

trem·or \'tremər\ *n* : a trembling

trem·u·lous \'tremyələs\ *adj* : trembling or quaking

trench \'trench\ *n* : long narrow cut in land

tren·chant \'trenchənt\ *adj* : sharply perceptive

trend \'trend\ *n* : prevailing tendency, direction, or style ~ *vb* : move in a particular direction — **trendy** \'trendē\ *adj*

trep·i·da·tion \,trepə'dāshən\ *n* : nervous apprehension

tres·pass \'trespəs, -,pas\ *n* **1** : sin **2** : unauthorized entry onto someone's property ~ *vb* **1** : sin **2** : enter illegally — **tres·pass·er** *n*

tress \'tres\ *n* : long lock of hair

tres·tle \'tresəl\ *n* **1** : support with a horizontal piece and spreading legs **2** : framework bridge

tri·ad \'trī,ad, -əd\ *n* : union of 3

tri·age \trē'äzh, 'trē,äzh\ *n* : system of dealing with cases (as patients) according to priority guidelines intended to maximize success

tri·al \'trīəl\ *n* **1** : hearing and judgment of a matter in court **2** : source of great annoyance **3** : test use or experimental effort — **trial** *adj*

tri·an·gle \'trī͵aŋgəl\ *n* : plane figure with 3 sides and 3 angles — **tri·an·gu·lar** \trī'aŋgyə-lər\ *adj*

tribe \'trīb\ *n* : social group of numerous families — **trib·al** \'trībəl\ *adj* — **tribes·man** \'trībzmən\ *n* — **tribes·peo·ple** \-͵pēpəl\ *n pl*

trib·u·la·tion \͵tribyə'lāshən\ *n* : suffering from oppression

tri·bu·nal \trī'byün³l, tri-\ *n* **1** : court **2** : something that decides

trib·u·tary \'tribyə͵terē\ *n, pl* **-tar·ies** : stream that flows into a river or lake

trib·ute \'trib͵yüt\ *n* **1** : payment to acknowledge submission **2** : tax **3** : gift or act showing respect

trick \'trik\ *n* **1** : scheme to deceive **2** : prank **3** : deceptive or ingenious feat **4** : mannerism **5** : knack **6** : tour of duty ～ *vb* : deceive by cunning — **trick·ery** \-ərē\ *n* — **trick·ster** \-stər\ *n*

trick·le \'trikəl\ *vb* **-led; -ling** : run in drops or a thin stream — **trickle** *n*

tricky \'trikē\ *adj* **trick·i·er; -est** **1** : inclined to trickery **2** : requiring skill or caution

tri·cy·cle \'trī͵sikəl\ *n* : 3-wheeled bicycle

tri·dent \'trīd³nt\ *n* : 3-pronged spear

tri·en·ni·al \trī'enēəl\ *adj* : lasting, occurring, or done every 3 years — **tri·ennial** *n*

tri·fle \'trīfəl\ *n* : something of little value or importance ～ *vb* **-fled; -fling** **1** : speak or act in a playful or flirting way **2** : toy — **tri·fler** *n*

tri·fling \'trīfliŋ\ *adj* : trivial

trig·ger \'trigər\ *n* : finger-piece of a firearm lock that fires the gun ～ *vb* : set into motion — **trigger** *adj* — **trig·gered** \-ərd\ *adj*

trig·o·nom·e·try \͵trigə'näm-ətrē\ *n* : mathematics dealing with triangular measurement — **trig·o·no·met·ric** \-nə-'metrik\ *adj*

trill \'tril\ *n* **1** : rapid alternation between 2 adjacent tones **2** : rapid vibration in speaking ～ *vb* : utter in or with a trill

tril·lion \'trilyən\ *n* : 1000 billions — **trillion** *adj* — **tril·li·onth** \-yənth\ *adj or n*

tril·o·gy \'triləjē\ *n, pl* **-gies** : 3-part literary or musical composition

trim \'trim\ *vb* **-mm-** **1** : decorate **2** : make neat or reduce by cutting ～ *adj* **-mm-** : neat and compact ～ *n* **1** : state or condition **2** : ornaments — **trim·ly** *adv* — **trim·mer** *n*

trim·ming \'trimiŋ\ *n* : something that ornaments or completes

Trin·i·ty \\'trinətē\ *n* : divine unity of Father, Son, and Holy Spirit

trin·ket \\'triŋkət\ *n* : small ornament

trio \\'trēō\ *n, pl* **tri·os 1** : music for 3 performers **2** : group of 3

trip \\'trip\ *vb* **-pp- 1** : step lightly **2** : stumble or cause to stumble **3** : make or cause to make a mistake **4** : release (as a spring or switch) ~ *n* **1** : journey **2** : stumble **3** : drug-induced experience

tri·par·tite \trī'pär͵tīt\ *adj* : having 3 parts or parties

tripe \\'trīp\ *n* **1** : animal's stomach used as food **2** : trash

tri·ple \\'tripəl\ *vb* **-pled; -pling** : make 3 times as great ~ *n* : group of 3 ~ *adj* **1** : having 3 units **2** : being 3 times as great or as many

trip·let \\'triplət\ *n* **1** : group of 3 **2** : one of 3 offspring born together

trip·li·cate \\'triplikət\ *adj* : made in 3 identical copies ~ *n* : one of 3 copies

tri·pod \\'trī͵päd\ *n* : a stand with 3 legs — **tripod, tri·po·dal** \\'tripədᵊl, 'trī͵päd-\ *adj*

tri·sect \\'trī͵sekt, trī'-\ *vb* : divide into 3 usu. equal parts — **tri·sec·tion** \\'trī͵sekshən\ *n*

trite \\'trīt\ *adj* **trit·er; trit·est** : commonplace

tri·umph \\'trīəmf\ *n, pl* **-umphs** : victory or great success ~ *vb* : obtain or celebrate victory — **tri·um·phal** \trī'əmfəl\ *adj* — **tri·um·phant** \-fənt\ *adj* — **tri·um·phant·ly** *adv*

tri·um·vi·rate \trī'əmvərət\ *n* : ruling body of 3 persons

triv·et \\'trivət\ *n* **1** : 3-legged stand **2** : stand to hold a hot dish

triv·ia \\'trivēə\ *n sing or pl* : unimportant details

triv·i·al \\'trivēəl\ *adj* : of little importance — **triv·i·al·i·ty** \͵trivē'alətē\ *n*

trod *past of* TREAD

trodden *past part of* TREAD

troll \\'trōl\ *n* : dwarf or giant of folklore inhabiting caves or hills

trol·ley \\'trälē\ *n, pl* **-leys** : streetcar run by overhead electric wires

trol·lop \\'träləp\ *n* : untidy or immoral woman

trom·bone \träm'bōn, 'träm͵-\ *n* : musical instrument with a long sliding tube — **trom·bon·ist** \-'bōnist, -͵bō-\ *n*

troop \\'trüp\ *n* **1** : cavalry unit **2** *pl* : soldiers **3** : collection of people or things ~ *vb* : move or gather in crowds

troop·er \\'trüpər\ *n* **1** : cavalry soldier **2** : police officer on horseback or state police officer

tro·phy \\'trōfē\ *n, pl* **-phies** : prize gained by a victory

trop·ic \\'träpik\ *n* **1** : either of the 2 parallels of latitude one 23½ degrees north of the equator (**tropic of Cancer** \-'kansər\) and one 23½ degrees south of the equator (**tropic of Cap·ri·corn** \-'kap-rə͵kȯrn\) **2** *pl* : region lying between the tropics — **tropic, trop·i·cal** \-ikəl\ *adj*

trot \\'trät\ *n* : moderately fast gait esp. of a horse with diagonally paired legs moving together ∼ *vb* **-tt-** : go at a trot — **trot·ter** *n*

troth \\'träth, 'trȯth, 'trōth\ *n* **1** : pledged faithfulness **2** : betrothal

trou·ba·dour \\'trübə͵dȯr\ *n* : medieval lyric poet

trou·ble \\'trəbəl\ *vb* **-bled; -bling 1** : disturb **2** : afflict **3** : make an effort ∼ *n* **1** : cause of mental or physical distress **2** : effort — **trou·ble·mak·er** *n* — **trou·ble·some** *adj* — **trou·ble·some·ly** *adv*

trough \\'trȯf\ *n, pl* **troughs** \\'trȯfs, 'trȯvz\ **1** : narrow container for animal feed or water **2** : long channel or depression (as between waves)

trounce \\'traůns\ *vb* **trounced; trounc·ing** : thrash, punish, or defeat severely

troupe \\'trüp\ *n* : group of stage performers — **troup·er** *n*

trou·sers \\'traůzərz\ *n pl* : long pants — **trouser** *adj*

trous·seau \\'trüsō, trü'sō\ *n, pl* **-seaux** \-sōz, -'sōz\ *or* **-seaus** : bride's collection of clothing and personal items

trout \\'traůt\ *n, pl* **trout** : freshwater food and game fish

trow·el \\'traůəl\ *n* **1** : tool for spreading or smoothing **2** : garden scoop — **trowel** *vb*

troy \\'trȯi\ *n* : system of weights based on a pound of 12 ounces

tru·ant \\'trüənt\ *n* : student absent from school without permission — **tru·an·cy** \-ənsē\ *n* — **truant** *adj*

truce \\'trüs\ *n* : agreement to halt fighting

truck \\'trək\ *n* **1** : wheeled frame for moving heavy objects **2** : automotive vehicle for transporting heavy loads ∼ *vb* : transport on a truck — **truck·er** *n* — **truck·load** *n*

truck·le \\'trəkəl\ *vb* **-led; -ling** : yield slavishly to another

tru·cu·lent \\'trəkyələnt\ *adj* : aggressively self-assertive — **truc·u·lence** \-ləns\ *n* — **tru·cu·lent·ly** *adv*

trudge \\'trəj\ *vb* **trudged; trudg·ing** : walk or march steadily and with difficulty

true \'trü\ *adj* **tru·er; tru·est**
1 : loyal **2** : in agreement with
fact or reality **3** : genuine ∼
adv **1** : truthfully **2** : accurately
∼ *vb* **trued; true·ing** : make
balanced or even — **tru·ly** *adv*

true–blue *adj* : loyal

truf·fle \'trəfəl\ *n* **1** : edible
fruit of an underground fun-
gus **2** : ball-shaped chocolate
candy

tru·ism \'trü͵izəm\ *n* : obvious truth

trump \'trəmp\ *n* : card of a
designated suit any of whose
cards will win over other cards
∼ *vb* : take with a trump

trumped–up \'trəmpt'əp\ *adj*
: made-up

trum·pet \'trəmpət\ *n* : tubular brass wind instrument with
a flaring end ∼ *vb* **1** : blow a
trumpet **2** : proclaim loudly
— **trum·pet·er** *n*

trun·cate \'trən͵kāt, 'trən-\ *vb*
-cat·ed; -cat·ing : cut short —
trun·ca·tion \͵trən'kāshən\ *n*

trun·dle \'trənd³l\ *vb* **-dled;
-dling** : roll along

trunk \'trəŋk\ *n* **1** : main part
(as of a body or tree) **2** : long
muscular nose of an elephant
3 : storage chest **4** : storage
space in a car **5** *pl* : shorts

truss \'trəs\ *vb* : bind tightly
∼ *n* **1** : set of structural parts
forming a framework **2** : appliance worn to hold a hernia
in place

trust \'trəst\ *n* **1** : reliance on
another **2** : assured hope **3**
: credit **4** : property held or
managed in behalf of another
5 : combination of firms that
reduces competition **6** : something entrusted to another's
care **7** : custody ∼ *vb* **1** : depend **2** : hope **3** : entrust **4**
: have faith in — **trust·ful**
\-fəl\ *adj* — **trust·ful·ly** *adv*
— **trust·ful·ness** *n* — **trust-
worth·i·ness** *n* — **trust·wor·
thy** *adj*

trust·ee \͵trəs'tē\ *n* : person
holding property in trust —
trust·ee·ship *n*

trusty \'trəstē\ *adj* **trust·i·er;
-est** : dependable

truth \'trüth\ *n, pl* **truths**
\'trüthz, 'trüths\ **1** : real state
of things **2** : true or accepted
statement **3** : agreement with
fact or reality — **truth·ful**
\-fəl\ *adj* — **truth·ful·ly** *adv*
— **truth·ful·ness** *n*

try \'trī\ *vb* **tried; try·ing 1**
: conduct the trial of **2** : put to
a test **3** : strain **4** : make an effort at ∼ *n, pl* **tries** : act of
trying

try·out *n* : competitive test of
performance esp. for athletes
or actors — **try out** *vb*

tryst \'trist, 'trīst\ *n* : secret
rendezvous of lovers

tsar \'zär, 'tsär, 'sär\ *var of* CZAR

T–shirt \'tē,shərt\ *n* : collarless pullover shirt with short sleeves

tub \'təb\ *n* **1** : wide bucketlike vessel **2** : bathtub

tu·ba \'tübə, 'tyü-\ *n* : large low-pitched brass wind instument

tube \'tüb, 'tyüb\ *n* **1** : hollow cylinder **2** : round container from which a substance can be squeezed **3** : airtight circular tube of rubber inside a tire **4** : electronic device consisting of a sealed usu. glass container with electrodes inside — **tubed** \'tübd, 'tyübd\ *adj* — **tube·less** *adj*

tu·ber \'tübər, 'tyü-\ *n* : fleshy underground growth (as of a potato) — **tu·ber·ous** \-rəs\ *adj*

tu·ber·cu·lo·sis \tù,bərkyə'lō-səs, tyü-\ *n, pl* **-lo·ses** \-,sēz\ : bacterial disease esp. of the lungs — **tu·ber·cu·lar** \-'bər-kyələr\ *adj* — **tu·ber·cu·lous** \-ləs\ *adj*

tub·ing \'tübiŋ, 'tyü-\ *n* : series or arrangement of tubes

tu·bu·lar \'tübyələr, 'tyü-\ *adj* : of or like a tube

tuck \'tək\ *vb* **1** : pull up into a fold **2** : put into a snug often concealing place **3** : make snug in bed — with *in* ~ *n* : fold in a cloth

tuck·er \'təkər\ *vb* : fatigue

Tues·day \'tüzdā, 'tyüz-, -dē\ *n* : 3d day of the week

tuft \'təft\ *n* : clump (as of hair or feathers) — **tuft·ed** \'təftəd\ *adj*

tug \'təg\ *vb* **-gg-** **1** : pull hard **2** : move by pulling ~ *n* **1** : act of tugging **2** : tugboat

tug·boat *n* : boat for towing or pushing ships through a harbor

tug–of–war \,təgə'wȯr\ *n, pl* **tugs–of–war** : pulling contest between 2 teams

tu·ition \tù'ishən, 'tyü-\ *n* : cost of instruction

tu·lip \'tüləp, 'tyü-\ *n* : herb with cup-shaped flowers

tum·ble \'təmbəl\ *vb* **-bled; -bling** **1** : perform gymnastic feats of rolling and turning **2** : fall or cause to fall suddenly **3** : toss ~ *n* : act of tumbling

tum·bler \'təmblər\ *n* **1** : acrobat **2** : drinking glass **3** : obstruction in a lock that can be moved (as by a key)

tu·mid \'tüməd, 'tyü-\ *adj* : turgid

tum·my \'təmē\ *n, pl* **-mies** : belly

tu·mor \'tümər, 'tyü-\ *n* : abnormal and useless growth of tissue — **tu·mor·ous** *adj*

tu·mult \'tü,məlt, 'tyü-\ *n* **1** : uproar **2** : violent agitation of mind or feelings — **tu·mul·tu·ous** \tù'məlchəwəs, tyü-\ *adj*

tun \'tən\ *n* : large cask

tu·na \'tünə, 'tyü-\ *n, pl* **-na** *or* **-nas** : large sea food fish

tun·dra \'təndrə\ *n* : treeless arctic plain

tune \'tün, 'tyün\ *n* **1** : melody **2** : correct musical pitch **3** : harmonious relationship ~ *vb* **tuned; tun·ing 1** : bring or come into harmony **2** : adjust in musical pitch **3** : adjust a receiver so as to receive a broadcast **4** : put in first-class working order — **tun·able** *adj* — **tune·ful** \-fəl\ *adj* — **tun·er** *n*

tung·sten \'təŋstən\ *n* : metallic element used for electrical purposes and in hardening alloys (as steel)

tu·nic \'tünik, 'tyü-\ *n* **1** : ancient knee-length garment **2** : hip-length blouse or jacket

tun·nel \'tən°l\ *n* : underground passageway ~ *vb* **-neled** *or* **-nelled; -nel·ing** *or* **-nel·ling** : make a tunnel through or under something

tur·ban \'tərbən\ *n* : wound headdress worn esp. by Muslims

tur·bid \'tərbəd\ *adj* **1** : dark with stirred-up sediment **2** : confused — **tur·bid·i·ty** \,tər-'bidətē\ *n*

tur·bine \'tərbən, -,bīn\ *n* : engine turned by the force of gas or water on fan blades

tur·bo·jet \'tərbō,jet\ *n* : airplane powered by a jet engine having a turbine-driven air compressor or the engine itself

tur·bo·prop \'tərbō,präp\ *n* : airplane powered by a propeller turned by a jet engine-driven turbine

tur·bu·lent \'tərbyələnt\ *adj* **1** : causing violence or disturbance **2** : marked by agitation or tumult — **tur·bu·lence** \-ləns\ *n* — **tur·bu·lent·ly** *adv*

tu·reen \tə'rēn, tyu-\ *n* : deep bowl for serving soup

turf \'tərf\ *n* : upper layer of soil bound by grass and roots

tur·gid \'tərjəd\ *adj* **1** : swollen **2** : too highly embellished in style — **tur·gid·i·ty** \,tər-'jidətē\ *n*

tur·key \'tərkē\ *n, pl* **-keys** : large American bird raised for food

tur·moil \'tər,moil\ *n* : extremely agitated condition

turn \'tərn\ *vb* **1** : move or cause to move around an axis **2** : twist (a mechanical part) to operate **3** : wrench **4** : cause to face or move in a different direction **5** : reverse the sides or surfaces of **6** : upset **7** : go around **8** : become or cause to become **9** : seek aid from a source ~ *n* **1** : act or instance of turning **2** : change **3** : place at which something turns **4**

: place, time, or opportunity to do something in order — **turner** *n* — **turn down** *vb* : decline to accept — **turn in** *vb* **1** : deliver or report to authorities **2** : go to bed — **turn off** *vb* : stop the functioning of — **turn out** *vb* **1** : expel **2** : produce **3** : come together **4** : prove to be in the end — **turn over** *vb* : transfer — **turn up** *vb* **1** : discover or appear **2** : happen unexpectedly

turn·coat *n* : traitor

tur·nip \'tərnəp\ *n* : edible root of an herb

turn·out \'tərn,aut\ *n* **1** : gathering of people for a special purpose **2** : size of a gathering

turn·over *n* **1** : upset or reversal **2** : filled pastry **3** : volume of business **4** : movement (as of goods or people) into, through, and out of a place

turn·pike \'tərn,pīk\ *n* : expressway on which tolls are charged

turn·stile \-,stīl\ *n* : post with arms pivoted on the top that allows people to pass one by one

turn·ta·ble *n* : platform that turns a phonograph record

tur·pen·tine \'tərpən,tīn\ *n* : oil distilled from pine-tree resin and used as a solvent

tur·pi·tude \'tərpə,tüd, -,tyüd\ *n* : inherent baseness

tur·quoise \'tər,koiz, -,kwoiz\ *n* : blue or greenish gray gemstone

tur·ret \'tərət\ *n* **1** : little tower on a building **2** : revolving tool holder or gun housing

tur·tle \'tərtᵊl\ *n* : reptile with the trunk enclosed in a bony shell

tur·tle·dove *n* : wild pigeon

tur·tle·neck *n* : high close‑fitting collar that can be turned over or a sweater or shirt with this collar

tusk \'təsk\ *n* : long protruding tooth (as of an elephant) — **tusked** \'təskt\ *adj*

tus·sle \'təsəl\ *n or vb* : struggle

tu·te·lage \'tütᵊlij, 'tyüt-\ *n* **1** : act of protecting **2** : instruction esp. of an individual

tu·tor \'tütər, 'tyü-\ *n* : private teacher ∼ *vb* : teach usu. individually

tux·e·do \,tək'sēdō\ *n, pl* **-dos** *or* **-does** : semiformal evening clothes for a man

TV \,tē'vē, 'tē,vē\ *n* : television

twain \'twān\ *n* : two

twang \'twaŋ\ *n* **1** : harsh sound like that of a plucked bowstring **2** : nasal speech or resonance ∼ *vb* : sound or speak with a twang

tweak \'twēk\ *vb* : pinch and pull playfully — **tweak** *n*

tweed \'twēd\ *n* **1** : rough woolen fabric **2** *pl* : tweed clothing — **tweedy** *adj*

tweet \'twēt\ *n* : chirping note — **tweet** *vb*

twee·zers \\'twēzərz\ *n pl* : small pincerlike tool

twelve \\'twelv\ *n* **1** : one more than 11 **2** : 12th in a set or series **3** : something having 12 units — **twelfth** \\'twelfth\ *adj or n* — **twelve** *adj or pron*

twen·ty \\'twentē\ *n, pl* **-ties** : 2 times 10 — **twen·ti·eth** \-ēəth\ *adj or n* — **twenty** *adj or pron*

twen·ty–twen·ty, 20–20 *adj* : being vision of normal sharpness

twice \\'twīs\ *adv* **1** : on 2 occasions **2** : 2 times

twig \\'twig\ *n* : small branch — **twig·gy** *adj*

twi·light \\'twī,līt\ *n* : light from the sky at dusk or dawn — **twilight** *adj*

twill \\'twil\ *n* : fabric with a weave that gives an appearance of diagonal lines in the fabric

twilled \\'twild\ *adj* : made with a twill weave

twin \\'twin\ *n* : either of 2 offspring born together ~ *adj* **1** : born with one another or as a pair at one birth **2** : made up of 2 similar parts

twine \\'twīn\ *n* : strong twisted thread ~ *vb* **twined; twin·ing 1** : twist together **2** : coil about a support — **twin·er** *n* — **twiny** *adj*

twinge \\'twinj\ *vb* **twinged; twing·ing** *or* **twinge·ing** : affect with or feel a sudden sharp pain ~ *n* : sudden sharp stab (as of pain)

twin·kle \\'twiŋkəl\ *vb* **-kled; -kling** : shine with a flickering light ~ *n* **1** : wink **2** : intermittent shining — **twin·kler** \-klər\ *n*

twirl \\'twərl\ *vb* : whirl round ~ *n* **1** : act of twirling **2** : coil — **twirl·er** *n*

twist \\'twist\ *vb* **1** : unite by winding (threads) together **2** : wrench **3** : move in or have a spiral shape **4** : follow a winding course ~ *n* **1** : act or result of twisting **2** : unexpected development

twist·er \\'twistər\ *n* : tornado

¹twit \\'twit\ *n* : fool

²twit *vb* **-tt-** : taunt

twitch \\'twich\ *vb* : move or pull with a sudden motion ~ *n* : act of twitching

twit·ter \\'twitər\ *vb* : make chirping noises ~ *n* : small intermittent noise

two \\'tü\ *n, pl* **twos** **1** : one more than one **2** : the 2d in a set or series **3** : something having 2 units — **two** *adj or pron*

two·fold \\'tü,fōld\ *adj* : double — **two·fold** \-'fōld\ *adv*

two·some \\'tüsəm\ *n* : couple

-ty *n suffix* : quality, condition, or degree

ty·coon \tī'kün\ *n* : powerful and successful businessman

tying *pres part of* TIE

tyke \'tīk\ *n* : small child

tym·pa·num \'timpənəm\ *n, pl* **-na** \-nə\ : eardrum or the cavity which it closes externally — **tym·pan·ic** \tim-'panik\ *adj*

type \'tīp\ *n* **1** : class, kind, or group set apart by common characteristics **2** : special design of printed letters ~ *vb* **typed; typ·ing 1** : write with a typewriter **2** : identify or classify as a particular type

type·writ·er *n* : keyboard machine that produces printed material by striking a ribbon with raised letters — **type·write** *vb*

ty·phoid \'tī,fȯid, tī'-\ *adj* : relating to or being a communicable bacterial disease (**typhoid fever**)

ty·phoon \tī'fün\ *n* : hurricane of the western Pacific ocean

ty·phus \'tīfəs\ *n* : severe disease with fever, delirium, and rash

typ·i·cal \'tipikəl\ *adj* : having the essential characteristics of a group — **typ·i·cal·i·ty** \,tipə-'kalətē\ *n* — **typ·i·cal·ly** *adv* — **typ·i·cal·ness** *n*

typ·i·fy \'tipə,fī\ *vb* **-fied; -fy·ing** : be typical of

typ·ist \'tīpist\ *n* : one who operates a typewriter

ty·pog·ra·phy \tī'pägrəfē\ *n* **1** : art of printing with type **2** : style, arrangement, or appearance of printed matter — **ty·po·graph·ic** \,tīpə'grafik\, **ty·po·graph·i·cal** \-ikəl\ *adj* — **ty·po·graph·i·cal·ly** *adv*

ty·ran·ni·cal \tə'ranikəl, tī-\ *adj* : relating to a tyrant — **ty·ran·ni·cal·ly** *adv*

tyr·an·nize \'tirə,nīz\ *vb* **-nized; -niz·ing** : rule or deal with in the manner of a tyrant — **tyr·an·niz·er** *n*

tyr·an·ny \'tirənē\ *n, pl* **-nies** : unjust use of absolute governmental power

ty·rant \'tīrənt\ *n* : harsh ruler having absolute power

ty·ro \'tīrō\ *n, pl* **-ros** : beginner

tzar \'zär, 'tsär, 'sär\ *var of* **CZAR**

U

u \'yü\ *n, pl* **u's** *or* **us** \'yüz\ : 21st letter of the alphabet

ubiq·ui·tous \yü'bikwətəs\ *adj* : omnipresent — **ubiq·ui·tous·ly** *adv* — **ubiq·ui·ty** \-wətē\ *n*

ud·der \'ədər\ *n* : animal sac containing milk glands and nipples

ug·ly \'əglē\ *adj* **ug·li·er; -est 1** : offensive to look at **2** : mean or quarrelsome — **ug·li·ness** *n*

uku·le·le \ˌyükə'lālē\ *n* : small 4-string guitar

ul·cer \'əlsər\ *n* : eroded sore — **ul·cer·ous** *adj*

ul·cer·ate \'əlsəˌrāt\ *vb* **-at·ed; -at·ing** : become affected with an ulcer — **ul·cer·a·tion** \ˌəlsə'rāshən\ *n* — **ul·cer·a·tive** \'əlsəˌrātiv\ *adj*

ul·na \'əlnə\ *n* : bone of the forearm opposite the thumb

ul·te·ri·or \ˌəl'tirēər\ *adj* : not revealed

ul·ti·mate \'əltəmət\ *adj* : final, maximum, or extreme — **ultimate** *n* — **ul·ti·mate·ly** *adv*

ul·ti·ma·tum \ˌəltə'mātəm, -'mät-\ *n, pl* **-tums** *or* **-ta** \-ə\ : final proposition or demand carrying or implying a threat

ul·tra·vi·o·let \ˌəltrə'vīələt\ *adj* : having a wavelength shorter than visible light

um·bi·li·cus \ˌəmbə'līkəs, ˌəm-'bili-\ *n, pl* **-li·ci** \-bə'līˌkī, -ˌsī; -'biləˌkī, -ˌkē\ *or* **-li·cus-**

es : small depression on the abdominal wall marking the site of the cord (**umbilical cord**) that joins the unborn fetus to its mother — **um·bil·i·cal** \ˌəm'bilikəl\ *adj*

um·brage \'əmbrij\ *n* : resentment

um·brel·la \ˌəm'brelə\ *n* : collapsible fabric device to protect from sun or rain

um·pire \'əmˌpīr\ *n* **1** : arbitrator **2** : sport official — **umpire** *vb*

ump·teen \'əmp'tēn\ *adj* : very numerous — **ump·teenth** \-'tēnth\ *adj*

un- \ˌən, 'ən\ *prefix* **1** : not **2** : opposite of

un·ac·cus·tomed *adj* **1** : not customary **2** : not accustomed

un·af·fect·ed *adj* **1** : not influenced or changed by something **2** : natural and sincere — **un·af·fect·ed·ly** *adv*

unan·i·mous \yü'nanəməs\ *adj* **1** : showing no disagreement **2** : formed with the agreement

---

List of self-explanatory words with the prefix *un-*

unable	unadorned	unannounced
unabridged	unadulterated	unanswered
unacceptable	unafraid	unanticipated
unaccompanied	unaided	unappetizing
unaccounted	unalike	unappreciated
unacquainted	unambiguous	unapproved
unaddressed	unambitious	unarguable

of all — **una·nim·i·ty** \,yünə-'nimətē\ *n* — **unan·i·mous·ly** *adv*

un·armed *adj* : not armed or armored

un·as·sum·ing *adj* : not bold or arrogant

un·at·tached *adj* 1 : not attached 2 : not married or engaged

un·aware *adv* : unawares ∼ *adj* : not aware

un·awares \,ənə'warz\ *adv* 1 : without warning 2 : unintentionally

un·bal·anced *adj* 1 : not balanced 2 : mentally unstable

un·beat·en *adj* : not beaten

un·be·com·ing *adj* : not proper or suitable — **un·be·com·ing·ly** *adv*

un·be·liev·able *adj* 1 : improbable 2 : superlative — **un·be·liev·ably** *adv*

un·bend *vb* -bent; -bend·ing : make or become more relaxed and friendly

un·bend·ing *adj* : formal and inflexible

un·bind *vb* -bound; -bind·ing 1 : remove bindings from 2 : release

un·bolt *vb* : open or unfasten by withdrawing a bolt

un·born *adj* : not yet born

un·bo·som *vb* : disclose thoughts or feelings

un·bowed \,ən'baůd\ *adj* : not defeated or subdued

un·bri·dled \,ən'brīdᵊld\ *adj* : unrestrained

un·bro·ken *adj* 1 : not damaged 2 : not interrupted

un·buck·le *vb* : unfasten the buckle of

un·bur·den *vb* : relieve (oneself) of anxieties

un·but·ton *vb* : unfasten the buttons of

un·called–for *adj* : too harsh or rude for the occasion

un·can·ny \ən'kanē\ *adj* 1 : weird 2 : suggesting superhuman powers — **un·can·ni·ly** \-'kanᵊlē\ *adv*

un·ceas·ing *adj* : never ceasing — **un·ceas·ing·ly** *adv*

unarguably	unbearable	unchanged
unassisted	unbiased	unchanging
unattended	unbranded	uncharacteristic
unattractive	unbreakable	uncharged
unauthorized	uncensored	unchaste
unavailable	unchallenged	uncivilized
unavoidable	unchangeable	unclaimed

un·cer·e·mo·ni·ous *adj* : acting without ordinary courtesy — **un·cer·e·mo·ni·ous·ly** *adv*

un·cer·tain *adj* 1 : not determined, sure, or definitely known 2 : subject to chance or change — **un·cer·tain·ly** *adv* — **un·cer·tain·ty** *n*

un·chris·tian *adj* : not consistent with Christian teachings

un·cle \'əŋkəl\ *n* 1 : brother of one's father or mother 2 : husband of one's aunt

un·clean *adj* : not clean or pure — **un·clean·ness** *n*

un·clog *vb* : remove an obstruction from

un·coil *vb* : release or become released from a coiled state

un·com·mit·ted *adj* : not pledged to a particular allegiance or course of action

un·com·mon *adj* 1 : rare 2 : superior — **un·com·mon·ly** *adv*

un·com·pro·mis·ing *adj* : not making or accepting a compromise

un·con·cerned *adj* 1 : disinterested 2 : not anxious or upset — **un·con·cerned·ly** *adv*

un·con·di·tion·al *adj* : not limited in any way — **un·con·di·tion·al·ly** *adv*

un·con·scio·na·ble *adj* : shockingly unjust or unscrupulous — **un·con·scio·na·bly** *adv*

un·con·scious *adj* 1 : not awake or aware of one's surroundings 2 : not consciously done ~ *n* : part of one's mental life that one is not aware of — **un·con·scious·ly** *adv* — **un·con·scious·ness** *n*

un·con·sti·tu·tion·al *adj* : not according to or consistent with a constitution

un·con·trol·la·ble *adj* : incapable of being controlled — **un·con·trol·la·bly** *adv*

un·count·ed *adj* : countless

un·couth \ˌən'küth\ *adj* : rude and vulgar

un·cov·er *vb* 1 : reveal 2 : expose by removing a covering

unc·tion \'əŋkshən\ *n* 1 : rite of anointing 2 : exaggerated or insincere earnestness

unclear	uncomplimentary	unconventionally
uncleared	unconfirmed	unconverted
unclothed	unconsummated	uncooked
uncluttered	uncontested	uncooperative
uncombed	uncontrolled	uncoordinated
uncomfortable	uncontroversial	uncovered
uncomfortably	unconventional	uncultivated

unc·tu·ous \'əŋkchəwəs\ *adj* **1** : oily **2** : insincerely smooth in speech or manner — **unc·tu·ous·ly** *adv*

un·cut *adj* **1** : not cut down, into, off, or apart **2** : not shaped by cutting **3** : not abridged

un·daunt·ed *adj* : not discouraged — **un·daunt·ed·ly** *adv*

un·de·ni·able *adj* : plainly true — **un·de·ni·ably** *adv*

un·der \'əndər\ *adv* : below or beneath something ～ *prep* **1** : lower than and sheltered by **2** : below the surface of **3** : covered or concealed by **4** : subject to the authority of **5** : less than ～ *adj* **1** : lying below or beneath **2** : subordinate **3** : less than usual, proper, or desired

un·der·age \,əndər'āj\ *adj* : of less than legal age

un·der·brush \'əndər,brəsh\ *n* : shrubs and small trees growing beneath large trees

un·der·clothes \'əndər,klōz, -,klōthz\ *n pl* : underwear

un·der·cloth·ing \-,klōthiŋ\ *n* : underwear

un·der·cov·er \,əndər'kəvər\ *adj* : employed or engaged in secret investigation

un·der·cur·rent \'əndər,kərənt\ *n* : hidden tendency or opinion

un·der·cut \,əndər'kət\ *vb* **-cut; -cut·ting** : offer to sell or to work at a lower rate than

un·der·de·vel·oped \,əndərdi'veləpt\ *adj* : not normally or adequately developed esp. economically

un·der·dog \'əndər,dòg\ *n* : contestant given least chance of winning

un·der·done \,əndər'dən\ *adj* : not thoroughly done or cooked

un·der·es·ti·mate \,əndər'estə,māt\ *vb* : estimate too low

un·der·ex·pose \,əndərik'spōz\ *vb* : give less than normal exposure to — **un·der·ex·po·sure** *n*

un·der·feed \,əndər'fēd\ *vb* **-fed; -feed·ing** : feed inadequately

undamaged	undeserving	undignified
undated	undesirable	undisturbed
undecided	undetected	undivided
undeclared	undetermined	undomesticated
undefeated	undeveloped	undrinkable
undemocratic	undeviating	unearned
undependable	undifferentiated	uneducated

un·der·foot \ˌəndər'fu̇t\ *adv* **1** : under the feet **2** : in the way of another

un·der·gar·ment \'əndərˌgär-mənt\ *n* : garment to be worn under another

un·der·go \ˌəndər'gō\ *vb* **-went** \-'went\; **-gone**; **-go·ing** **1** : endure **2** : go through (as an experience)

un·der·grad·u·ate \ˌəndər-'grajəwət\ *n* : university or college student

un·der·ground \ˌəndər-'grau̇nd\ *adv* **1** : beneath the surface of the earth **2** : in secret ~ \'əndərˌ-\ *adj* **1** : being or growing under the surface of the ground **2** : secret ~ \'əndərˌ-\ *n* : secret political movement or group

un·der·growth \'əndər'grōth\ *n* : low growth on the floor of a forest

un·der·hand \'əndərˌhand\ *adv or adj* **1** : with secrecy and deception **2** : with the hand kept below the waist

un·der·hand·ed \ˌəndər-'handəd\ *adj or adv* : under-hand — **un·der·hand·ed·ly** *adv* — **un·der·hand·ed·ness** *n*

un·der·line \'əndərˌlīn\ *vb* **1** : draw a line under **2** : stress — **underline** *n*

un·der·ling \'əndərliŋ\ *n* : in-ferior

un·der·ly·ing \ˌəndərˌlīiŋ\ *adj* : basic

un·der·mine \ˌəndər'mīn\ *vb* **1** : excavate beneath **2** : weaken or wear away secretly or grad-ually

un·der·neath \ˌəndər'nēth\ *prep* : directly under ~ *adv* **1** : below a surface or object **2** : on the lower side

un·der·nour·ished \ˌəndər-'nərisht\ *adj* : insufficiently nourished — **un·der·nour·ish·ment** *n*

un·der·pants \'əndərˌpants\ *n pl* : short undergarment for the lower trunk

un·der·pass \-ˌpas\ *n* : passage-way crossing underneath another

un·der·pin·ning \'əndər-ˌpiniŋ\ *n* : support

un·der·priv·i·leged *adj* : poor

---

unemotional   unexciting   unfavorably
unending   unexplainable   unfeigned
unendurable   unexplored   unfilled
unenforceable   unfair   unfinished
unenlightened   unfairly   unflattering
unethical   unfairness   unforeseeable
unexcitable   unfavorable   unforeseen

un·der·rate \ˌəndər'rāt\ *vb* : rate or value too low

un·der·score \'əndərˌskōr\ *vb* **1** : underline **2** : emphasize — **underscore** *n*

un·der·sea \ˌəndər'sē\ *adj* : being, carried on, or used beneath the surface of the sea ~ \ˌəndər'sē\, **un·der·seas** \-'sēz\ *adv* : beneath the surface of the sea

un·der sec·re·tary *n* : deputy secretary

un·der·sell \ˌəndər'sel\ *vb* **-sold; -sell·ing** : sell articles cheaper than

un·der·shirt \'əndərˌshərt\ *n* : shirt worn as underwear

un·der·shorts \'əndərˌshòrts\ *n pl* : short underpants

un·der·side \'əndərˌsīd, ˌəndər'sīd\ *n* : side or surface lying underneath

un·der·sized \ˌəndər'sīzd\ *adj* : unusually small

un·der·stand \ˌəndər'stand\ *vb* **-stood** \-'stùd\; **-stand·ing** **1** : be aware of the meaning of **2** : deduce **3** : have a sympa-thetic attitude — **un·der·stand·able** \-'standəbəl\ *adj* — **un·der·stand·ably** \-blē\ *adv*

un·der·stand·ing \ˌəndər'standiŋ\ *n* **1** : intelligence **2** : ability to comprehend and judge **3** : mutual agreement ~ *adj* : sympathetic

un·der·state \ˌəndər'stāt\ *vb* **1** : represent as less than is the case **2** : state with restraint — **un·der·state·ment** *n*

un·der·stood \ˌəndər'stùd\ *adj* **1** : agreed upon **2** : implicit

un·der·study \'əndərˌstədē, ˌəndər'-\ *vb* : study another actor's part in order to substi-tute — **understudy** \'əndərˌ-\ *n*

un·der·take \ˌəndər'tāk\ *vb* **-took; -tak·en; -tak·ing** **1** : at-tempt (a task) or assume (a re-sponsibility) **2** : guarantee

un·der·tak·er \'əndərˌtākər\ *n* : one in the funeral business

un·der·tak·ing \'əndərˌtākiŋ, ˌəndər'-\ *n* **1** : something (as work) that is undertaken **2** : promise

---

unforgivable	ungrammatical	unimaginative
unforgiving	unharmed	unimportant
unfulfilled	unhealthful	unimpressed
unfurnished	unheated	uninformed
ungenerous	unhurt	uninhabited
ungentlemanly	unidentified	uninjured
ungraceful	unimaginable	uninsured

under–the–counter *adj* : illicit

un·der·tone \'əndər,tōn\ *n* : low or subdued tone or utterance

un·der·tow \-,tō\ *n* : current beneath the waves that flows seaward

un·der·val·ue \,əndər'valyü\ *vb* : value too low

un·der·wa·ter \-'wȯtər, -'wät-\ *adj* : being or used below the surface of the water — **underwater** *adv*

under way *adv* : in motion or in progress

un·der·wear \'əndər,war\ *n* : clothing worn next to the skin and under ordinary clothes

un·der·world \'əndər,wərld\ *n* **1** : place of departed souls **2** : world of organized crime

un·der·write \'əndər,rīt, ,əndər,-\ *vb* **-wrote; -writ·ten; -writ·ing 1** : provide insurance for **2** : guarantee financial support of — **un·der·writ·er** *n*

un·dies \'əndēz\ *n pl* : underwear

un·do *vb* **-did; -done; -do·ing 1** : unfasten **2** : reverse **3** : ruin — **un·do·ing** *n*

un·doubt·ed *adj* : certain — **un·doubt·ed·ly** *adv*

un·dress *vb* : remove one's clothes ~ *n* : state of being naked

un·due *adj* : excessive — **un·du·ly** *adv*

un·du·late \'ənjə,lāt\ *vb* **-lat·ed; -lat·ing** : rise and fall regularly — **un·du·la·tion** \,ənjə-'lāshən\ *n*

un·dy·ing *adj* : immortal or perpetual

un·earth *vb* : dig up or discover

un·earth·ly *adj* : supernatural

un·easy *adj* **1** : awkward or embarrassed **2** : disturbed or worried — **un·eas·i·ly** *adv* — **un·eas·i·ness** *n*

un·em·ployed *adj* : not having a job — **un·em·ploy·ment** *n*

un·equal *adj* : not equal or uniform — **un·equal·ly** *adv*

un·equaled, un·equalled *adj* : having no equal

---

unintelligent	**uninteresting**	**unknowing**
unintelligible	**uninterrupted**	**unknowingly**
unintelligibly	**uninvited**	**unknown**
unintended	**unjust**	**unleavened**
unintentional	**unjustifiable**	**unlicensed**
unintentionally	**unjustified**	**unlikable**
uninterested	**unjustly**	**unlimited**

un·equiv·o·cal *adj* : leaving no doubt — **un·equiv·o·cal·ly** *adv*

un·err·ing *adj* : infallible — **un·err·ing·ly** *adv*

un·even *adj* **1** : not smooth **2** : not regular or consistent — **un·even·ly** *adv* — **un·even·ness** *n*

un·event·ful *adj* : lacking interesting or noteworthy incidents — **un·event·ful·ly** *adv*

un·ex·pect·ed \ənik'spektəd\ *adj* : not expected — **un·ex·pect·ed·ly** *adv*

un·fail·ing *adj* : steadfast — **un·fail·ing·ly** *adv*

un·faith·ful *adj* : not loyal — **un·faith·ful·ly** *adv* — **un·faith·ful·ness** *n*

un·fa·mil·iar *adj* **1** : not well known **2** : not acquainted — **un·fa·mil·iar·i·ty** *n*

un·fas·ten *vb* : release a catch or lock

un·feel·ing *adj* : lacking feeling or compassion — **un·feel·ing·ly** *adv*

un·fit *adj* : not suitable — **un·fit·ness** *n*

un·flap·pa·ble \ˌən'flapəbəl\ *adj* : not easily upset or panicked — **un·flap·pa·bly** *adv*

un·fold *vb* **1** : open the folds of **2** : reveal **3** : develop

un·for·get·ta·ble *adj* : memorable — **un·for·get·ta·bly** *adv*

un·for·tu·nate *adj* **1** : not lucky or successful **2** : deplorable — **unfortunate** *n* — **un·for·tu·nate·ly** *adv*

un·found·ed *adj* : lacking a sound basis

un·freeze *vb* -**froze**; -**fro·zen**; -**freez·ing** : thaw

un·friend·ly *adj* : not friendly or kind — **un·friend·li·ness** *n*

un·furl *vb* : unfold or unroll

un·gain·ly *adj* : clumsy — **un·gain·li·ness** *n*

un·god·ly *adj* : wicked — **un·god·li·ness** *n*

un·grate·ful *adj* : not thankful for favors — **un·grate·ful·ly** *adv* — **un·grate·ful·ness** *n*

un·guent \'əŋgwənt, 'ən-\ *n* : ointment

un·hand *vb* : let go

---

unlovable	unmolested	unnoticeable
unmanageable	unmotivated	unnoticed
unmarked	unmoving	unobjectionable
unmarried	unnamed	unobservable
unmerciful	unnecessarily	unobservant
unmercifully	unnecessary	unobtainable
unmerited	unneeded	unobtrusive

un·hap·py *adj* **1** : unfortunate **2** : sad — **un·hap·pi·ly** *adv* — **un·hap·pi·ness** *n*

un·healthy *adj* **1** : not wholesome **2** : not well

un·heard–of \ˌənˈhərdəv, -ˌäv\ *adj* : unprecedented

un·hinge \ˌənˈhinj\ *vb* **1** : take from the hinges **2** : make unstable esp. mentally

un·hitch *vb* : unfasten

un·ho·ly *adj* : sinister or shocking — **un·ho·li·ness** *n*

un·hook *vb* : release from a hook

uni·cel·lu·lar \ˌyüniˈselyələr\ *adj* : having or consisting of a single cell

uni·corn \ˈyünəˌkȯrn\ *n* : legendary animal with one horn in the middle of the forehead

uni·cy·cle \ˈyüniˌsīkəl\ *n* : pedal-powered vehicle with only a single wheel

uni·di·rec·tion·al \ˌyünidəˈrekshənəl, -dī-\ *adj* : working in only a single direction

uni·form \ˈyünəˌfȯrm\ *adj* : not changing or showing any variation ∼ *n* : distinctive dress worn by members of a particular group — **uni·for·mi·ty** \ˌyünəˈfȯrmətē\ *n* — **uni·form·ly** *adv*

uni·fy \ˈyünəˌfī\ *vb* **-fied; -fy·ing** : make into a coherent whole — **uni·fi·ca·tion** \ˌyünəfəˈkāshən\ *n*

uni·lat·er·al \ˌyünəˈlatərəl\ *adj* : having, affecting, or done by one side only — **uni·lat·er·al·ly** *adv*

un·im·peach·able *adj* : blameless

un·in·hib·it·ed *adj* : free of restraint — **un·in·hib·it·ed·ly** *adv*

union \ˈyünyən\ *n* **1** : act or instance of joining 2 or more things into one or the state of being so joined **2** : confederation of nations or states **3** : organization of workers (**labor union, trade union**)

union·ize \ˈyünyəˌnīz\ *vb* **-ized; -iz·ing** : form into a labor union — **union·i·za·tion** \ˌyünyənəˈzāshən\ *n*

unique \yu̇ˈnēk\ *adj* **1** : being the only one of its kind **2** : very

---

unobtrusively	unorthodoxy	unpleasantness
unofficial	unpaid	unpopular
unopened	unpardonable	unpopularity
unopposed	unpatriotic	unposed
unorganized	unpaved	unpredictability
unoriginal	unpleasant	unpredictable
unorthodox	unpleasantly	unpredictably

unusual — **unique·ly** *adv* — **unique·ness** *n*

uni·son \\'yünəsən, -nəzən\\ *n* **1** : sameness in pitch **2** : exact agreement

unit \\'yünət\\ *n* **1** : smallest whole number **2** : definite amount or quantity used as a standard of measurement **3** : single part of a whole — **unit** *adj*

unite \\yu̇'nīt\\ *vb* **unit·ed; unit·ing** : put or join together

uni·ty \\'yünətē\\ *n, pl* **-ties** **1** : quality or state of being united or a unit **2** : harmony

uni·ver·sal \\,yünə'vərsəl\\ *adj* **1** : relating to or affecting everyone or everything **2** : present or occurring everywhere — **uni·ver·sal·ly** *adv*

uni·verse \\'yünə,vərs\\ *n* : the complete system of all things that exist

uni·ver·si·ty \\,yünə'vərsətē\\ *n, pl* **-ties** : institution of higher learning

un·kempt \\,ən'kempt\\ *adj* : not neat or combed

un·kind *adj* : not kind or sympathetic — **un·kind·li·ness** *n* — **un·kind·ly** *adv* — **un·kind·ness** *n*

un·law·ful *adj* : illegal — **un·law·ful·ly** *adv*

un·leash *vb* : free from control or restraint

un·less \\ən'les\\ *conj* : except on condition that

un·like \\ən'līk, 'ən,līk\\ *adj* **1** : not similar **2** : not equal ∼ *prep* : different from — **unlike·ly** \\ən'līklē\\ *adv* — **un·like·ness** \\-nəs\\ *n* — **un·like·li·hood** \\-lēhu̇d\\ *n*

un·load *vb* **1** : take (cargo) from a vehicle, vessel, or plane **2** : take a load from **3** : discard

un·lock *vb* **1** : unfasten through release of a lock **2** : release or reveal

un·lucky *adj* **1** : experiencing bad luck **2** : likely to bring misfortune — **un·luck·i·ly** *adv*

un·mis·tak·able *adj* : not capable of being mistaken or misunderstood — **un·mis·tak·ably** *adv*

---

unprejudiced	unproven	unreadable
unprepared	unprovoked	unready
unpretentious	unpunished	unrealistic
unproductive	unqualified	unreasonable
unprofitable	unquenchable	unreasonably
unprotected	unquestioning	unrefined
unproved	unreachable	unrelated

un·moved *adj* **1** : not emotionally affected **2** : remaining in the same place or position

un·nat·u·ral *adj* **1** : not natural or spontaneous **2** : abnormal — **un·nat·u·ral·ly** *adv* — **un·nat·u·ral·ness** *n*

un·nerve *vb* : deprive of courage, strength, or steadiness

un·oc·cu·pied *adj* **1** : not busy **2** : not occupied

un·pack *vb* **1** : remove (things packed) from a container **2** : remove the contents of (a package)

un·par·al·leled *adj* : having no equal

un·plug *vb* **1** : unclog **2** : disconnect from an electric circuit by removing a plug

un·prec·e·dent·ed *adj* : unlike or superior to anything known before

un·prin·ci·pled *adj* : unscrupulous

un·ques·tion·able *adj* : acknowledged as beyond doubt — **un·ques·tion·ably** *adv*

un·rav·el *vb* **1** : separate the threads of **2** : solve

un·re·al *adj* : not real or genuine — **un·re·al·i·ty** *n*

un·rea·son·ing *adj* : not using or being guided by reason

un·re·lent·ing *adj* : not yielding or easing — **un·re·lent·ing·ly** *adv*

un·rest *n* : turmoil

un·ri·valed, un·ri·valled *adj* : having no rival

un·roll *vb* **1** : unwind a roll of **2** : become unrolled

un·ruf·fled *adj* : not agitated or upset

un·ruly \ˌən'rülē\ *adj* : not readily controlled or disciplined — **un·rul·i·ness** *n*

un·scathed \ˌən'skāthd\ *adj* : unharmed

un·sci·en·tif·ic *adj* : not in accord with the principles and methods of science

un·screw *vb* : loosen or remove by withdrawing screws or by turning

un·scru·pu·lous *adj* : being or acting in total disregard of

unreliable	unrestrained	unsatisfactory
unremembered	unrestricted	unsatisfied
unrepentant	unrewarding	unscented
unrepresented	unripe	unscheduled
unrequited	unsafe	unseasoned
unresolved	unsalted	unseen
unresponsive	unsanitary	unselfish

conscience, ethical principles, or rights of others — **un·scru·pu·lous·ly** *adv* — **un·scru·pu·lous·ness** *n*

un·seal *vb* : break or remove the seal of

un·sea·son·able *adj* : not appropriate or usual for the season — **un·sea·son·ably** *adv*

un·seem·ly \ˌən'sēmlē\ *adj* : not polite or in good taste — **un·seem·li·ness** *n*

un·set·tle *vb* : disturb — **un·set·tled** *adj*

un·sight·ly \ˌən'sītlē\ *adj* : not attractive

un·skilled *adj* : not having or requiring a particular skill

un·snap *vb* : loosen by undoing a snap

un·speak·able \ˌən'spēkəbəl\ *adj* : extremely bad — **un·speak·ably** \-blē\ *adv*

un·sta·ble *adj* **1** : not mentally or physically balanced **2** : tending to change

un·stop *vb* **1** : unclog **2** : remove a stopper from

un·stop·pa·ble \ˌən'stäpəbəl\ *adj* : not capable of being stopped

un·strung \ˌən'strəŋ\ *adj* : nervously tired or anxious

un·sung \ˌən'səŋ\ *adj* : not celebrated in song or verse

un·tan·gle *vb* **1** : free from a state of being tangled **2** : find a solution to

un·think·able \ˌən'thiŋkəbəl\ *adj* : not to be thought of or considered possible

un·think·ing *adj* : careless — **un·think·ing·ly** *adv*

un·tie *vb* **-tied; -ty·ing** *or* **-tie·ing** : open by releasing ties

un·til \ˌən'til\ *prep* : up to the time of ～ *conj* : to the time that

un·time·ly *adj* **1** : premature **2** : coming at an unfortunate time

un·to \ˌən'tù, 'ən-\ *prep* : to

un·told *adj* **1** : not told **2** : too numerous to count

un·tow·ard \ˌən'tōrd\ *adj* **1** : difficult to manage **2** : inconvenient

---

unselfishly	unsolved	unsteadily
unselfishness	unsophisticated	unsteadiness
unshaped	unsound	unsteady
unshaven	unsoundly	unstructured
unskillful	unsoundness	unsubstantiated
unskillfully	unspecified	unsuccessful
unsolicited	unspoiled	unsuitable

un·truth *n* **1** : lack of truthfulness **2** : lie

un·used *adj* **1** \ˌənˈyüst, -ˈyüzd\ : not accustomed **2** \-ˈyüzd\ : not used

un·well *adj* : sick

un·wieldy \ˌənˈwēldē\ *adj* : too big or awkward to manage easily

un·wind *vb* **-wound; -wind·ing** **1** : undo something that is wound **2** : become unwound **3** : relax

un·wit·ting *adj* **1** : not knowing **2** : not intended — **un·wit·ting·ly** *adv*

un·wont·ed *adj* **1** : unusual **2** : not accustomed by experience

un·wrap *vb* : remove the wrappings from

un·writ·ten *adj* : made or passed on only in speech or through tradition

un·zip *vb* : zip open

up \ˈəp\ *adv* **1** : in or to a higher position or level **2** : from beneath a surface or level **3** : in or into an upright position **4** : out of bed **5** : to or with greater intensity **6** : into existence, evidence, or knowledge **7** : away **8** — used to indicate a degree of success, completion, or finality **9** : in or into parts ~ *adj* **1** : in the state of having risen **2** : raised to or at a higher level **3** : moving, inclining, or directed upward **4** : in a state of greater intensity **5** : at an end ~ *vb* **upped** *or in 1* **up; upped; up·ping; ups** *or in 1* **up** **1** : act abruptly **2** : move or cause to move upward ~ *prep* **1** : to, toward, or at a higher point of **2** : along or toward the beginning of

---

unsuitably	untreated	unwelcome
unsuited	untrue	unwholesome
unsupervised	untrustworthy	unwilling
unsupported	untruthful	unwillingly
unsure	unusable	unwillingness
unsurprising	unusual	unwise
unsuspecting	unvarying	unwisely
unsweetened	unverified	unworkable
unsympathetic	unwanted	unworthily
untamed	unwarranted	unworthiness
untanned	unwary	unworthy
untidy	unwavering	unyielding
untouched	unweaned	
untrained	unwed	

up·braid \ˌəpˈbrād\ *vb* : criticize or scold

up·bring·ing \ˈəpˌbriŋiŋ\ *n* : process of bringing up and training

up·com·ing \ˌəpˈkəmiŋ\ *adj* : approaching

up·date \ˌəpˈdāt\ *vb* : bring up to date — **update** \ˈəpˌdāt\ *n*

up·end \ˌəpˈend\ *vb* **1** : stand or rise on end **2** : overturn

up·grade \ˈəpˌgrād\ *n* **1** : upward slope **2** : increase ∼ \ˈəpˌ-, ˌəpˈ-\ *vb* : raise to a higher position

up·heav·al \ˌəpˈhēvəl\ *n* **1** : a heaving up (as of part of the earth's crust) **2** : violent change

up·hill \ˌəpˈhil\ *adv* : upward on a hill or incline ∼ \ˈəpˌ-\ *adj* **1** : going up **2** : difficult

up·hold \ˌəpˈhōld\ *vb* **-held; -hold·ing** : support or defend — **up·hold·er** *n*

up·hol·ster \ˌəpˈhōlstər\ *vb* : cover (furniture) with padding and fabric (**up·hol·stery** \-stərē\) — **up·hol·ster·er** *n*

up·keep \ˈəpˌkēp\ *n* : act or cost of keeping up or maintaining

up·land \ˈəplənd, -ˌland\ *n* : high land — **upland** *adj*

up·lift \ˌəpˈlift\ *vb* **1** : lift up **2** : improve the condition or spirits of — **up·lift** \ˈəpˌ-\ *n*

up·on \əˈpȯn, -ˈpän\ *prep* : on

up·per \ˈəpər\ *adj* : higher in position, rank, or order ∼ *n* : top part of a shoe

upper·hand *n* : advantage

up·per·most \ˈəpərˌmōst\ *adv* : in or into the highest or most prominent position — **uppermost** *adj*

up·pi·ty \ˈəpətē\ *adj* : acting with a manner of undue importance

up·right \ˈəpˌrīt\ *adj* **1** : vertical **2** : erect in posture **3** : morally correct ∼ *n* : something that stands upright — **upright** *adv* — **up·right·ly** *adv* — **up·right·ness** *n*

up·ris·ing \ˈəpˌrīziŋ\ *n* : revolt

up·roar \ˈəpˌrōr\ *n* : state of commotion or violent disturbance

up·roar·i·ous \ˌəpˈrōrēəs\ *adj* **1** : marked by uproar **2** : extremely funny — **up·roar·i·ous·ly** *adv*

up·root \ˌəpˈrüt, -ˈrut\ *vb* : remove by or as if by pulling up by the roots

up·set \ˌəpˈset\ *vb* **-set; -set·ting** **1** : force or be forced out of the usual position **2** : disturb emotionally or physically ∼ \ˈəpˌ-\ *n* **1** : act of throwing into disorder **2** : minor physical disorder ∼ *adj* : emotionally disturbed or agitated

up·shot \ˈəpˌshät\ *n* : final result

up·side down \ˌəpˌsīdˈdau̇n\ *adv* **1** : turned so that the upper and lower parts are reversed **2** : in or into confusion or disorder — **upside–down** *adj*

up·stairs \ˈəpˌsta͡rz, ˌəpˈ-\ *adv* : up the stairs or to the next floor ~ *adj* : situated on the floor above ~ *n sing or pl* : part of a building above the ground floor

up·stand·ing \ˌəpˈstandiŋ, ˈəpˌ-\ *adj* : honest

up·start \ˈəpˌstärt\ *n* : one who claims more personal importance than is warranted — **up·start** *adj*

up·swing \ˈəpˌswiŋ\ *n* : marked increase (as in activity)

up·tight \ˌəpˈtīt\ *adj* **1** : tense **2** : angry **3** : rigidly conventional

up–to–date *adj* : current — **up–to–date·ness** *n*

up·town \ˈəpˌtau̇n\ *n* : upper part of a town or city — **up·town** *adj or adv*

up·turn \ˈəpˌtərn\ *n* : improvement or increase

up·ward \ˈəpwərd\, **up·wards** \-wərdz\ *adv* **1** : in a direction from lower to higher **2** : toward a higher or greater state or number ~ *adj* : directed toward or situated in a higher place — **up·ward·ly** *adv*

up·wind \ˌəpˈwind\ *adv or adj* : in the direction from which the wind is blowing

ura·ni·um \yu̇ˈrānēəm\ *n* : metallic radioactive chemical element

ur·ban \ˈərbən\ *adj* : characteristic of a city

ur·bane \ˌərˈbān\ *adj* : polished in manner — **ur·ban·i·ty** \ˌərˈbanətē\ *n*

ur·ban·ite \ˈərbəˌnīt\ *n* : city dweller

ur·chin \ˈərchən\ *n* : mischievous youngster

–ure *n suffix* : act or process

ure·thra \yu̇ˈrēthrə\ *n, pl* **-thras** *or* **-thrae** \-ˌthrē\ : canal that carries off urine from the bladder — **ure·thral** \-thrəl\ *adj*

urge \ˈərj\ *vb* **urged; urging 1** : earnestly plead for or insist on (an action) **2** : try to persuade **3** : impel to a course of activity ~ *n* : force or impulse that moves one to action

ur·gent \ˈərjənt\ *adj* **1** : calling for immediate attention **2** : urging insistently — **ur·gen·cy** \-jənsē\ *n* — **ur·gent·ly** *adv*

uri·nal \ˈyu̇rənᵊl\ *n* : receptacle to urinate in

uri·nate \ˈyu̇rəˌnāt\ *vb* **-nat·ed; -nat·ing** : discharge urine — **uri·na·tion** \ˌyu̇rəˈnāshən\ *n*

urine \\'yu̇rən\ *n* : liquid waste material from the kidneys — **uri·nary** \-ə͵nerē\ *adj*

URL \͵yü͵är'el\ *n* : address on the Internet

urn \'ərn\ *n* **1** : vaselike or cuplike vessel on a pedestal **2** : large coffee pot

us \'əs\ *pron, objective case of* **WE**

us·able \'yüzəbəl\ *adj* : suitable or fit for use — **us·abil·i·ty** \͵yüzə'bilətē\ *n*

us·age \'yüsij, -zij\ *n* **1** : customary practice **2** : way of doing or of using something

use \'yüs\ *n* **1** : act or practice of putting something into action **2** : state of being used **3** : way of using **4** : privilege, ability, or power to use something **5** : utility or function **6** : occasion or need to use ~ \'yüz\ *vb* **used** \'yüzd; "used to" usu 'yüstə\; **us·ing** \'yüziŋ\ **1** : put into action or service **2** : consume **3** : behave toward **4** : to make use of **5** — used in the past tense with *to* to indicate a former practice — **use·ful** \'yüsfəl\ *adj* — **use·ful·ly** *adv* — **use·ful·ness** *n* — **use·less** \'yüsləs\ *adj* — **use·less·ly** *adv* — **use·less·ness** *n* — **us·er** *n*

used \'yüzd\ *adj* : not new

ush·er \'əshər\ *n* : one who escorts people to their seats ~ *vb* : conduct to a place

ush·er·ette \͵əshə'ret\ *n* : woman or girl who is an usher

usu·al \'yüzhəwəl\ *adj* : being what is expected according to custom or habit — **usu·al·ly** \'yüzhəwəlē\ *adv*

usurp \yu̇'sərp, -'zərp\ *vb* : seize and hold by force or without right — **usur·pa·tion** \͵yüsər'pāshən, -zər-\ *n* — **usurp·er** *n*

usu·ry \'yüzhərē\ *n, pl* **-ries** **1** : lending of money at excessive interest or the rate or amount of such interest — **usu·rer** \-zhərər\ *n* — **usu·ri·ous** \yu̇'zhu̇rēəs\ *adj*

uten·sil \yu̇'tensəl\ *n* **1** : eating or cooking tool **2** : useful tool

uter·us \'yütərəs\ *n, pl* **uteri** \-͵rī\ : organ for containing and nourishing an unborn offspring — **uter·ine** \-͵rīn, -rən\ *adj*

util·i·tar·i·an \yü͵tilə'terēən\ *adj* : being or meant to be useful rather than beautiful

util·i·ty \yü'tilətē\ *n, pl* **-ties** **1** : usefulness **2** : regulated business providing a public service (as electricity)

uti·lize \'yütᵊl͵īz\ *vb* **-lized; -liz·ing** : make use of — **uti·li·za·tion** \͵yütᵊlə'zāshən\ *n*

ut·most \'ət͵mōst\ *adj* **1** : most distant **2** : of the greatest or highest degree or amount — **utmost** *n*

uto·pia \yu̇'tōpēə\ *n* : place of ideal perfection — **uto·pi·an** \-pēən\ *adj or n*

ut·ter \'ətər\ *adj* : absolute ∼ *vb* : express with the voice — **ut·ter·er** \-ərər\ *n* — **ut·ter·ly** *adv*

ut·ter·ance \'ətərəns\ *n* : what one says

V

v \'vē\ *n, pl* **v's** *or* **vs** \'vēz\ : 22d letter of the alphabet

va·can·cy \'vākənsē\ *n, pl* **-cies** **1** : state of being vacant **2** : unused or unoccupied place or office

va·cant \-kənt\ *adj* **1** : not occupied, filled, or in use **2** : devoid of thought or expression — **va·cant·ly** *adv*

va·cate \-ˌkāt\ *vb* **-cat·ed; -cat·ing 1** : annul **2** : leave unfilled or unoccupied

va·ca·tion \vā'kāshən, və-\ *n* : period of rest from routine — **vacation** *vb* — **va·ca·tion·er** *n*

vac·ci·nate \'vaksəˌnāt\ *vb* **-nat·ed; -nat·ing** : administer a vaccine usu. by injection

vac·ci·na·tion \ˌvaksə'nāshən\ *n* : act of or the scar left by vaccinating

vac·cine \vak'sēn, 'vakˌ-\ *n* : substance to induce immunity to a disease

vac·il·late \'vasəˌlāt\ *vb* **-lated; -lat·ing** : waver between courses or opinions — **vac·il·la·tion** \ˌvasə'lāshən\ *n*

vac·u·ous \'vakyəwəs\ *adj* **1** : empty **2** : dull or inane — **va·cu·ity** \va'kyüətē, və-\ *n* — **vac·u·ous·ly** *adv* — **vac·u·ous·ness** *n*

vac·u·um \'vakˌyüm, -yəm\ *n, pl* **vac·u·ums** *or* **vac·ua** \-yəwə\ : empty space with no air ∼ *vb* : clean with a vacuum cleaner

vacuum cleaner *n* : appliance that cleans by suction

vag·a·bond \'vagəˌbänd\ *n* : wanderer with no home — **vagabond** *adj*

va·ga·ry \'vāgərē, və'gerē\ *n, pl* **-ries** : whim

va·gi·na \və'jīnə\ *n, pl* **-nae** \-ˌnē\ *or* **-nas** : canal that leads out from the uterus — **vag·i·nal** \'vajən°l\ *adj*

va·grant \'vāgrənt\ *n* : person with no home and no job — **va·gran·cy** \-grənsē\ *n* — **vagrant** *adj*

vague \\'vāg\\ *adj* **vagu·er; vagu·est** : not clear, definite, or distinct — **vague·ly** *adv* — **vague·ness** *n*

vain \\'vān\\ *adj* **1** : of no value **2** : unsuccessful **3** : conceited — **vain·ly** *adv*

va·lance \\'valəns, 'vāl-\\ *n* : border drapery

vale \\'vāl\\ *n* : valley

vale·dic·to·ri·an \\,valə,dik'tō-rēən\\ *n* : student giving the farewell address at commencement

vale·dic·to·ry \\-'diktərē\\ *adj* : bidding farewell — **valedictory** *n*

va·lence \\'vāləns\\ *n* : degree of combining power of a chemical element

val·en·tine \\'valən,tīn\\ *n* : sweetheart or a card sent to a sweetheart or friend on St. Valentine's Day

va·let \\'valət, 'val,ā, va'lā\\ *n* : male personal servant

val·iant \\'valyənt\\ *adj* : brave or heroic — **val·iant·ly** *adv*

val·id \\'valəd\\ *adj* **1** : proper and legally binding **2** : founded on truth or fact — **va·lid·i·ty** \\və'lidətē, va-\\ *n* — **val·id·ly** *adv*

val·i·date \\'valə,dāt\\ *vb* **-dat·ed; -dat·ing** : establish as valid — **val·i·da·tion** \\,valə'dā-shən\\ *n*

va·lise \\və'lēs\\ *n* : suitcase

val·ley \\'valē\\ *n, pl* **-leys** : long depression between ranges of hills

val·or \\'valər\\ *n* : bravery or heroism — **val·or·ous** \\'val-ərəs\\ *adj*

valu·able \\'valyəwəbəl\\ *adj* **1** : worth a lot of money **2** : being of great importance or use — **valuable** *n*

val·u·a·tion \\,valyə'wāshən\\ *n* **1** : act or process of valuing **2** : market value of a thing

val·ue \\'valyü\\ *n* **1** : fair return or equivalent for something exchanged **2** : how much something is worth **3** : distinctive quality (as of a color or sound) **4** : guiding principle or ideal — usu. pl. ∼ *vb* **val·ued; valu·ing** **1** : estimate the worth of **2** : appreciate the importance of — **val·ue·less** *adj* — **val·u·er** *n*

valve \\'valv\\ *n* : structure or device to control flow of a liquid or gas — **valved** \\'valvd\\ *adj* — **valve·less** *adj*

vam·pire \\'vam,pīr\\ *n* **1** : legendary night-wandering dead body that sucks human blood **2** : bat that feeds on the blood of animals

¹**van** \\'van\\ *n* : vanguard

²**van** *n* : enclosed truck

va·na·di·um \\və'nādēəm\\ *n* : soft ductile metallic chemical element

van·dal \'vand⁰l\ *n* : person who willfully defaces or destroys property — **van·dal·ism** \-ˌizəm\ *n* — **van·dal·ize** \-ˌīz\ *vb*

vane \'vān\ *n* : bladelike device designed to be moved by force of the air or water

van·guard \'vanˌgärd\ *n* **1** : troops moving at the front of an army **2** : forefront of an action or movement

va·nil·la \və'nilə\ *n* : a flavoring made from the pods of a tropical orchid or this orchid

van·ish \'vanish\ *vb* : disappear suddenly

van·i·ty \'vanətē\ *n, pl* **-ties 1** : futility or something that is futile **2** : undue pride in oneself **3** : makeup case or table

van·quish \'vaŋkwish, 'van-\ *vb* **1** : overcome in battle or in a contest **2** : gain mastery over

van·tage \'vantij\ *n* : position of advantage or perspective

va·pid \'vapəd, 'vāpəd\ *adj* : lacking spirit, liveliness, or zest — **va·pid·i·ty** \va'pidətē\ *n* — **vap·id·ly** \'vapədlē\ *adv* — **vap·id·ness** *n*

va·por \'vāpər\ *n* **1** : fine separated particles floating in and clouding the air **2** : gaseous form of an ordinarily liquid substance — **va·por·ous** \-pərəs\ *adj*

va·por·ize \'vāpəˌrīz\ *vb* **-ized;** **-iz·ing** : convert into vapor — **va·por·i·za·tion** \ˌvāpərə'zā-shən\ *n* — **va·por·iz·er** *n*

var·i·able \'verēəbəl\ *adj* : apt to vary — **var·i·abil·i·ty** \ˌver-ēə'bilətē\ *n* — **var·i·able** *n* — **var·i·ably** *adv*

var·i·ance \'verēəns\ *n* **1** : instance or degree of variation **2** : disagreement or dispute **3** : legal permission to build contrary to a zoning law

var·i·ant \-ənt\ *n* : something that differs from others of its kind — **variant** *adj*

vari·a·tion \ˌverē'āshən\ *n* : instance or extent of varying

var·i·cose \'varəˌkōs\ *adj* : abnormally swollen and dilated

var·ied \'verēd\ *adj* : showing variety — **var·ied·ly** *adv*

var·ie·gat·ed \'verēəˌgāted\ *adj* : having patches, stripes, or marks of different colors — **var·ie·gate** \-ˌgāt\ *vb* — **var·ie·ga·tion** \ˌverēə'gāshən\ *n*

va·ri·ety \və'rīətē\ *n, pl* **-et·ies 1** : state of being different **2** : collection of different things **3** : something that differs from others of its kind

var·i·ous \'verēəs\ *adj* : being many and unlike — **var·i·ous·ly** *adv*

var·nish \'värnish\ *n* : liquid that dries to a hard glossy protective coating ~ *vb* : cover with varnish

var·si·ty \\'värsətē\ *n, pl* **-ties** : principal team representing a school

vary \\'verē\ *vb* **var·ied; vary·ing** **1** : alter **2** : make or be of different kinds

vas·cu·lar \\'vaskyələr\ *adj* : relating to a channel for the conveyance of a body fluid (as blood or sap)

vase \\'vās, 'vāz\ *n* : tall usu. ornamental container to hold flowers

vas·sal \\'vasəl\ *n* **1** : one acknowledging another as feudal lord **2** : one in a dependent position — **vas·sal·age** \-əlij\ *n*

vast \\'vast\ *adj* : very great in size, extent, or amount — **vast·ly** *adv* — **vast·ness** *n*

vat \\'vat\ *n* : large tub- or barrel-shaped container

vaude·ville \\'vȯdvəl, 'väd-, 'vōd-, -ˌvil, -əvəl, -əˌvil\ *n* : stage entertainment of unrelated acts

¹**vault** \\'vȯlt\ *n* **1** : masonry arch **2** : usu. underground storage or burial room ~ *vb* : form or cover with a vault — **vault·ed** *adj* — **vaulty** *adj*

²**vault** *vb* : spring over esp. with the help of the hands or a pole ~ *n* : act of vaulting — **vault·er** *n*

vaunt \\'vȯnt\ *vb* : boast — **vaunt** *n*

veal \\'vēl\ *n* : flesh of a young calf

veer \\'vir\ *vb* : change course esp. gradually — **veer** *n*

veg·e·ta·ble \\'vejtəbəl, 'vejə-\ *adj* **1** : relating to or obtained from plants **2** : like that of a plant ~ *n* **1** : plant **2** : plant grown for food

veg·e·tar·i·an \ˌvejə'terēən\ *n* : person who eats no meat — **vegetarian** *adj* — **veg·e·tar·i·an·ism** \-ēəˌnizəm\ *n*

veg·e·tate \\'vejəˌtāt\ *vb* **-tat·ed; -tat·ing** : lead a dull inert life

veg·e·ta·tion \ˌvejə'tāshən\ *n* : plant life — **veg·e·ta·tion·al** \-shənəl\ *adj* — **veg·e·ta·tive** \\'vejəˌtātiv\ *adj*

ve·he·ment \\'vēəmənt\ *adj* : showing strong esp. violent feeling — **ve·he·mence** \-məns\ *n* — **ve·he·ment·ly** *adv*

ve·hi·cle \\'vēˌhikəl, 'vēəkəl\ *n* **1** : medium through which something is expressed, applied, or administered **2** : structure for transporting something esp. on wheels — **ve·hic·u·lar** \vē'hikyələr\ *adj*

veil \\'vāl\ *n* **1** : sheer material to hide something or to cover the face and head **2** : something that hides ~ *vb* : cover with a veil

vein \\'vān\ *n* **1** : rock fissure filled with deposited mineral matter **2** : vessel that carries blood toward the heart **3** : sap-carrying tube in a leaf **4** : distinctive element or style of expression — **veined** \\'vānd\ *adj*

ve·loc·i·ty \və'läsətē\ *n, pl* **-ties** : speed

ve·lour, ve·lours \və'lùr\ *n, pl* **velours** \-'lùrz\ : fabric with a velvetlike pile

vel·vet \\'velvət\ *n* : fabric with a short soft pile — **velvet** *adj* — **vel·vety** *adj*

ve·nal \\'vēnᵊl\ *adj* : capable of being corrupted esp. by money — **ve·nal·i·ty** \vi'nalətē\ *n* — **ve·nal·ly** *adv*

vend \\'vend\ *vb* : sell — **vend·ible** *adj* — **ven·dor** \\'vendər\ *n*

ven·det·ta \ven'detə\ *n* : feud marked by acts of revenge

ve·neer \və'nir\ *n* **1** : thin layer of fine wood glued over a cheaper wood **2** : superficial display ~ *vb* : overlay with a veneer

ven·er·a·ble \\'venərəbəl\ *adj* : deserving of respect

ven·er·ate \\'venə‚rāt\ *vb* **-at·ed; -at·ing** : respect esp. with reverence — **ven·er·a·tion** \‚venə'rāshən\ *n*

ve·ne·re·al disease \və'nirēəl-\ *n* : contagious disease spread through copulation

ven·geance \\'venjəns\ *n* : punishment in retaliation for an injury or offense

venge·ful \\'venjfəl\ *adj* : filled with a desire for revenge — **venge·ful·ly** *adv*

ve·nial \\'vēnēəl\ *adj* : capable of being forgiven

ven·i·son \\'venəsən, -əzən\ *n* : deer meat

ven·om \\'venəm\ *n* **1** : poison secreted by certain animals **2** : ill will — **ven·om·ous** \-əməs\ *adj*

vent \\'vent\ *vb* **1** : provide with or let out at a vent **2** : give expression to ~ *n* : opening for passage or for relieving pressure

ven·ti·late \\'ventᵊl‚āt\ *vb* **-lat·ed; -lat·ing** : allow fresh air to circulate through — **ven·ti·la·tion** \‚ventᵊl'āshən\ *n* — **ven·ti·la·tor** \\'ventᵊl‚ātər\ *n*

ven·tri·cle \\'ventrikəl\ *n* : heart chamber that pumps blood into the arteries

ven·tril·o·quist \ven'trilə‚kwist\ *n* : one who can make the voice appear to come from another source — **ven·tril·o·quism** \-‚kwizəm\ *n* — **ven·tril·o·quy** \-kwē\ *n*

ven·ture \\'venchər\ *vb* **-tured; -tur·ing** **1** : risk or take a chance on **2** : put forward (an opinion) ~ *n* : speculative business enterprise

ven·ture·some \-səm\ *adj* : brave or daring — **ven·ture·some·ly** *adv* — **ven·ture·some·ness** *n*

ven·ue \'venyü\ *n* : scene of an action or event

ve·rac·i·ty \və'rasətē\ *n, pl* **-ties** : truthfulness or accuracy — **ve·ra·cious** \və'rāshəs\ *adj*

ve·ran·da, ve·ran·dah \və'randə\ *n* : large open porch

verb \'vərb\ *n* : word that expresses action or existence

ver·bal \'vərbəl\ *adj* **1** : having to do with or expressed in words **2** : oral **3** : relating to or formed from a verb — **ver·bal·i·za·tion** \ˌvərbələ'zāshən\ *n* — **ver·bal·ize** \'vərbəˌlīz\ *vb* — **ver·bal·ly** \-ē\ *adv*

verbal auxiliary *n* : auxiliary verb

ver·ba·tim \vər'bātəm\ *adv or adj* : using the same words

ver·biage \'vərbēij\ *n* : excess of words

ver·bose \vər'bōs\ *adj* : using more words than are needed — **ver·bos·i·ty** \-'bäsətē\ *n*

ver·dant \'vərd°nt\ *adj* : green with growing plants — **ver·dant·ly** *adv*

ver·dict \'vərdikt\ *n* : decision of a jury

ver·dure \'vərjər\ *n* : green growing vegetation or its color

verge \'vərj\ *vb* **verged; verg·ing** : be almost on the point of happening or doing something ~ *n* **1** : edge **2** : threshold

ver·i·fy \'verəˌfī\ *vb* **-fied; -fy·ing** : establish the truth, accuracy, or reality of — **ver·i·fi·able** *adj* — **ver·i·fi·ca·tion** \ˌverəfə'kāshən\ *n*

ver·i·ly \'verəlē\ *adv* : truly or confidently

veri·si·mil·i·tude \ˌverəsə'miləˌtüd\ *n* : appearance of being true

ver·i·ta·ble \'verətəbəl\ *adj* : actual or true — **ver·i·ta·bly** *adv*

ver·i·ty \'verətē\ *n, pl* **-ties** : truth

ver·mi·cel·li \ˌvərmə'chelē, -'sel-\ *n* : thin spaghetti

ver·min \'vərmən\ *n, pl* **vermin** : small animal pest

ver·mouth \vər'müth\ *n* : dry or sweet wine flavored with herbs

ver·nac·u·lar \vər'nakyələr\ *adj* : relating to a native language or dialect and esp. its normal spoken form ~ *n* : vernacular language

ver·nal \'vərn°l\ *adj* : relating to spring

ver·sa·tile \'vərsət°l\ *adj* : having many abilities or uses — **ver·sa·til·i·ty** \ˌvərsə'tilətē\ *n*

¹**verse** \\'vərs\ *n* **1** : line or stanza of poetry **2** : poetry **3** : short division of a chapter in the Bible

²**verse** *vb* **versed; versing** : make familiar by experience, study, or practice

ver·sion \\'vərzhən\ *n* **1** : translation of the Bible **2** : account or description from a particular point of view

ver·sus \\'vərsəs\ *prep* : opposed to or against

ver·te·bra \\'vərtəbrə\ *n, pl* **-brae** \-,brā, -,brē\ *or* **-bras** : segment of the backbone — **ver·te·bral** \vər'tēbrəl, 'vərtə-\ *adj*

ver·te·brate \\'vərtəbrət, -,brāt\ *n* : animal with a backbone — **verte·brate** *adj*

ver·tex \\'vər,teks\ *n, pl* **ver·ti·ces** \\'vərtə,sēz\ **1** : point of intersection of lines or surfaces **2** : highest point

ver·ti·cal \\'vərtikəl\ *adj* : rising straight up from a level surface — **vertical** *n* — **ver·ti·cal·i·ty** \,vərtə'kalətē\ *n* — **ver·ti·cal·ly** *adv*

ver·ti·go \\'vərti,gō\ *n, pl* **-goes** *or* **-gos** : dizziness

verve \\'vərv\ *n* : liveliness or vividness

very \\'verē\ *adj* **veri·er; -est 1** : exact **2** : exactly suitable **3** : mere or bare **4** : precisely the same ~ *adv* **1** : to a high degree **2** : in actual fact

ves·i·cle \\'vesikəl\ *n* : membranous cavity — **ve·sic·u·lar** \və'sikyələr\ *adj*

ves·pers \\'vespərz\ *n pl* : late afternoon or evening worship service

ves·sel \\'vesəl\ *n* **1** : a container (as a barrel, bottle, bowl, or cup) for a liquid **2** : craft for navigation esp. on water **3** : tube in which a body fluid is circulated

¹**vest** \\'vest\ *vb* **1** : give a particular authority, right, or property to **2** : clothe with or as if with a garment

²**vest** *n* : sleeveless garment usu. worn under a suit coat

ves·ti·bule \\'vestə,byül\ *n* : enclosed entrance — **ves·tib·u·lar** \ve'stibyələr\ *adj*

ves·tige \\'vestij\ *n* : visible trace or remains — **ves·ti·gial** \ve'stijēəl\ *adj* — **ves·ti·gial·ly** *adv*

vest·ment \\'vestmənt\ *n* : clergy member's garment

ves·try \\'vestrē\ *n, pl* **-tries** : church storage room for garments and articles

vet·er·an \\'vetərən\ *n* **1** : former member of the armed forces **2** : person with long experience — **veteran** *adj*

Veterans Day *n* : 4th Monday in October or formerly November 11 observed as a legal holiday in commemoration of the end of war in 1918 and 1945

vet·er·i·nar·i·an \ˌvetərən-'erēən\ *n* : doctor of animals — **vet·er·i·nary** \'vetərən-ˌerē\ *adj*

ve·to \'vētō\ *n, pl* **-toes** **1** : power to forbid and esp. the power of a chief executive to prevent a bill from becoming law **2** : exercise of the veto ~ *vb* **1** : forbid **2** : reject a legislative bill

vex \'veks\ *vb* **vexed; vex·ing** : trouble, distress, or annoy — **vex·a·tion** \vek'sāshən\ *n* — **vex·a·tious** \-shəs\ *adj*

via \'vīə, 'vēə\ *prep* : by way of

vi·a·ble \'vīəbəl\ *adj* **1** : capable of surviving or growing **2** : practical or workable — **vi·a·bil·i·ty** \ˌvīə'bilətē\ *n* — **vi·a·bly** \'vīəblē\ *adv*

via·duct \'vīəˌdəkt\ *n* : elevated roadway or railway bridge

vi·al \'vīəl\ *n* : small bottle

vi·brant \'vībrənt\ *adj* **1** : vibrating **2** : pulsing with vigor or activity **3** : sounding from vibration — **vi·bran·cy** \-brənsē\ *n*

vi·brate \'vīˌbrāt\ *vb* **-brat·ed; -brat·ing** **1** : move or cause to move quickly back and forth or side to side **2** : respond sympathetically — **vi·bra·tion** \vī'brāshən\ *n* — **vi·bra·tor** \'vīˌbrātər\ *n* — **vi·bra·tory** \'vībrəˌtȯrē\ *adj*

vic·ar \'vikər\ *n* : parish clergy member — **vi·car·iate** \-ēət\ *n*

vi·car·i·ous \vī'karēəs\ *adj* : sharing in someone else's experience through imagination or sympathetic feelings — **vi·car·i·ous·ly** *adv* — **vi·car·i·ous·ness** *n*

vice \'vīs\ *n* **1** : immoral habit **2** : depravity

vice- \ˌvīs\ *prefix* : one that takes the place of

vice admiral *n* : commissioned officer in the navy or coast guard ranking above a rear admiral

vice·roy \'vīsˌrȯi\ *n* : provincial governor who represents the sovereign

vice ver·sa \ˌvīsi'vərsə, ˌvīs-'vər-\ *adv* : with the order reversed

vi·cin·i·ty \və'sinətē\ *n, pl* **-ties** : surrounding area

List of self-explanatory words with the prefix *vice-*

vice-chancellor   vice presidency   vice presidential
vice-consul   vice president   vice-regent

vi·cious \\'vishəs\ *adj* **1** : wicked **2** : savage **3** : malicious — **vi·cious·ly** *adv* — **vi·cious·ness** *n*

vi·cis·si·tude \və'sisə‚tüd, vī-, -‚tyüd\ *n* : irregular, unexpected, or surprising change — usu. used in pl.

vic·tim \\'viktəm\ *n* : person killed, hurt, or abused

vic·tim·ize \\'viktə‚mīz\ *vb* **-ized; -iz·ing** : make a victim of — **vic·tim·i·za·tion** \‚viktəmə'zāshən\ *n* — **vic·tim·iz·er** \\'viktə‚mīzər\ *n*

vic·tor \\'viktər\ *n* : winner

Vic·to·ri·an \vik'tōrēən\ *adj* : relating to the reign of Queen Victoria of England or the art, taste, or standards of her time ~ *n* : one of the Victorian period

vic·to·ri·ous \vik'tōrēəs\ *adj* : having won a victory — **vic·to·ri·ous·ly** *adv*

vic·to·ry \\'viktərē\ *n, pl* **-ries** : success in defeating an enemy or opponent or in overcoming difficulties

vict·uals \\'vit³lz\ *n pl* : food

vid·eo \\'vidē‚ō\ *adj* : relating to the television image

vid·eo·cas·sette \‚vidē‚ōkə'set\ *n* : cassette containing videotape

vid·eo·tape \\'vidēō‚tāp\ *vb* : make a recording of (a television production) on special tape — **videotape** *n*

vie \\'vī\ *vb* **vied; vy·ing** : contend — **vi·er** \\'vīər\ *n*

view \\'vyü\ *n* **1** : process of seeing or examining **2** : opinion **3** : area of landscape that can be seen **4** : range of vision **5** : purpose or object ~ *vb* **1** : look at **2** : think about or consider — **view·er** *n*

view·point *n* : position from which something is considered

vig·il \\'vijəl\ *n* **1** : day of devotion before a religious feast **2** : act or time of keeping awake **3** : long period of keeping watch (as over a sick or dying person)

vig·i·lant \\'vijələnt\ *adj* : alert esp. to avoid danger — **vig·i·lance** \-ləns\ *n* — **vig·i·lant·ly** *adv*

vig·i·lan·te \‚vijə'lantē\ *n* : one of a group independent of the law working to suppress crime

vi·gnette \vin'yet\ *n* : short descriptive literary piece

vig·or \\'vigər\ *n* **1** : energy or strength **2** : intensity or force — **vig·or·ous** \\'vigərəs\ *adj* — **vig·or·ous·ly** *adv* — **vig·or·ous·ness** *n*

vile \\'vīl\ *adj* **vil·er; vil·est** : thoroughly bad or contemptible — **vile·ly** *adv* — **vile·ness** *n*

vil·i·fy \\'vilə‚fī\ *vb* **-fied; -fy·ing** : speak evil of — **vil·i·fi-**

ca·tion \ˌviləfəˈkāshən\ *n* — **vil·i·fi·er** \ˈviləˌfīər\ *n*

vil·la \ˈvilə\ *n* : country estate

vil·lage \ˈvilij\ *n* : small country town — **vil·lag·er** *n*

vil·lain \ˈvilən\ *n* : bad person — **vil·lain·ess** \-ənəs\ *n* — **vil·lainy** *n*

vil·lain·ous \-ənəs\ *adj* : evil or corrupt — **vil·lain·ous·ly** *adv* — **vil·lain·ous·ness** *n*

vim \ˈvim\ *n* : energy

vin·di·cate \ˈvindəˌkāt\ *vb* -**cat·ed; -cat·ing 1** : avenge **2** : exonerate **3** : justify — **vin·di·ca·tion** \ˌvindəˈkāshən\ *n* — **vin·di·ca·tor** \ˈvindəˌkātər\ *n*

vin·dic·tive \vinˈdiktiv\ *adj* : seeking or meant for revenge — **vin·dic·tive·ly** *adv* — **vin·dic·tive·ness** *n*

vine \ˈvīn\ *n* : climbing or trailing plant

vin·e·gar \ˈvinigər\ *n* : acidic liquid obtained by fermentation — **vin·e·gary** \-gərē\ *adj*

vine·yard \ˈvinyərd\ *n* : plantation of grapevines

vin·tage \ˈvintij\ *n* **1** : season's yield of grapes or wine **2** : period of origin ~ *adj* : of enduring interest

vi·nyl \ˈvīnᵊl\ *n* : strong plastic

vi·o·la \vēˈōlə\ *n* : instrument of the violin family tuned lower than the violin — **vi·o·list** \-list\ *n*

vi·o·late \ˈvīəˌlāt\ *vb* -**lat·ed; -lat·ing 1** : act with disrespect or disregard of **2** : rape **3** : desecrate — **vi·o·la·tion** \ˌvīəˈlāshən\ *n* — **vi·o·la·tor** \ˈvīəˌlātər\ *n*

vi·o·lence \ˈvīələns\ *n* : intense physical force that causes or is intended to cause injury or destruction — **vi·o·lent** \-lənt\ *adj* — **vi·o·lent·ly** *adv*

vi·o·let \ˈvīələt\ *n* **1** : small flowering plant **2** : reddish blue

vi·o·lin \ˌvīəˈlin\ *n* : bowed stringed instrument — **vi·o·lin·ist** \-nist\ *n*

VIP \ˌvēˌīˈpē\ *n, pl* **VIPs** \-ˈpēz\ : very important person

vi·per \ˈvīpər\ *n* **1** : venomous snake **2** : treacherous or malignant person

vi·ra·go \vəˈrägō, -ˈrā-; ˈvirəˌgō\ *n, pl* -**goes** *or* -**gos** : shrew

vi·ral \ˈvīrəl\ *adj* : relating to or caused by a virus

vir·gin \ˈvərjən\ *n* **1** : unmarried woman **2** : a person who has never had sexual intercourse ~ *adj* **1** : chaste **2** : natural and unspoiled — **vir·gin·al** \-əl\ *adj* — **vir·gin·al·ly** *adv* — **vir·gin·i·ty** \vərˈjinətē\ *n*

vir·gule \ˈvərgyül\ *n* : mark/ used esp. to denote "or" or "per"

vir·ile \ˈvirəl\ *adj* : masculine — **vi·ril·i·ty** \vəˈrilətē\ *n*

vir·tu·al \\'vərchəwəl\ *adj* : being in effect but not in fact or name — **vir·tu·al·ly** *adv*

vir·tue \\'vərchü\ *n* **1** : moral excellence **2** : effective or commendable quality **3** : chastity

vir·tu·os·i·ty \\,vərchə'wäsətē\ *n, pl* **-ties** : great skill (as in music)

vir·tu·o·so \\,vərchə'wōsō, -zō\ *n, pl* **-sos** *or* **-si** \-,sē, -,zē\ : highly skilled performer esp. of music — **virtuoso** *adj*

vir·tu·ous \\'vərchəwəs\ *adj* **1** : morally good **2** : chaste — **vir·tu·ous·ly** *adv*

vir·u·lent \\'virələnt, -yələnt\ *adj* **1** : extremely severe or infectious **2** : full of malice — **vir·u·lence** \-ləns\ *n* — **vir·u·lent·ly** *adv*

vi·rus \\'vīrəs\ *n* **1** : tiny disease-causing agent **2** : a computer program that performs a malicious action (as destroying data)

vi·sa \\'vēzə, -sə\ *n* : authorization to enter a foreign country

vis·age \\'vizij\ *n* : face

vis·cera \\'visərə\ *n pl* : internal bodily organs esp. of the trunk

vis·cer·al \\'visərəl\ *adj* **1** : bodily **2** : instinctive **3** : deeply or crudely emotional — **vis·cer·al·ly** *adv*

vis·cid \\'visəd\ *adj* : viscous — **vis·cid·i·ty** \vis'idətē\ *n*

vis·count \\'vī,kaůnt\ *n* : British nobleman ranking below an earl and above a baron

vis·count·ess \-əs\ *n* **1** : wife of a viscount **2** : woman with rank of a viscount

vis·cous \\'viskəs\ *adj* : having a thick or sticky consistency — **vis·cos·i·ty** \vis'käsətē\ *n*

vise \\'vīs\ *n* : device for clamping something being worked on

vis·i·bil·i·ty \\,vizə'bilətē\ *n, pl* **-ties** : degree or range to which something can be seen

vis·i·ble \\'vizəbəl\ *adj* **1** : capable of being seen **2** : manifest or apparent — **vis·i·bly** *adv*

vi·sion \\'vizhən\ *n* **1** : vivid picture seen in a dream or trance or in the imagination **2** : foresight **3** : power of seeing ～ *vb* : imagine

vi·sion·ary \\'vizhə,nerē\ *adj* **1** : given to dreaming or imagining **2** : illusory **3** : not practical ～ *n* : one with great dreams or projects

vis·it \\'vizət\ *vb* **1** : go or come to see **2** : stay with for a time as a guest **3** : cause or be a reward, affliction, or punishment ～ *n* : short stay as a guest — **vis·it·able** *adj* — **vis·i·tor** \-ər\ *n*

vis·i·ta·tion \\,vizə'tāshən\ *n* **1** : official visit **2** : divine punishment or favor **3** : severe trial

vi·sor \\'vīzər\ *n* **1** : front piece of a helmet **2** : part (as on a cap or car windshield) that shades the eyes

vis·ta \\'vistə\ *n* : distant view

vi·su·al \\'vizhəwəl\ *adj* **1** : relating to sight **2** : visible — **vi·su·al·ly** *adv*

vi·su·al·ize \\'vizhəwə,līz\ *vb* **-ized; -iz·ing** : form a mental image of — **vi·su·al·i·za·tion** \,vizhəwələ'zāshən\ *n* — **vi·su·al·iz·er** \\'vizhəwə,līzər\ *n*

vi·tal \\'vīt²l\ *adj* **1** : relating to, necessary for, or characteristic of life **2** : full of life and vigor **3** : fatal **4** : very important — **vi·tal·ly** *adv*

vi·tal·i·ty \vī'talətē\ *n, pl* **-ties** **1** : life force **2** : energy

vital signs *n pl* : body's pulse rate, respiration, temperature, and usu. blood pressure

vi·ta·min \\'vītəmən\ *n* : natural organic substance essential to health

vi·ti·ate \\'vishē,āt\ *vb* **-at·ed; -at·ing** **1** : spoil or impair **2** : invalidate — **vi·ti·a·tion** \,vishē'āshən\ *n* — **vi·ti·a·tor** \\'vishē,ātər\ *n*

vit·re·ous \\'vitrēəs\ *adj* : relating to or resembling glass

vit·ri·ol \\'vitrēəl\ *n* : something caustic, corrosive, or biting — **vit·ri·ol·ic** \,vitrē'älik\ *adj*

vi·tu·per·ate \vī'tüpə,rāt, və, -'tyü-\ *vb* **-at·ed; -at·ing** : abuse in words — **vi·tu·per·a·tion** \-,tüpə'rāshən, -,tyü\ *n* — **vi·tu·per·a·tive** \-'tüpərətiv, -'tyü-, -pə,rāt-\ *adj* — **vi·tu·per·a·tive·ly** *adv*

vi·va·cious \və'vāshəs, vī-\ *adj* : lively — **vi·va·cious·ly** *adv* — **vi·va·cious·ness** *n* — **vi·vac·i·ty** \-'vasətē\ *n*

viv·id \\'vivəd\ *adj* **1** : lively **2** : brilliant **3** : intense or sharp — **viv·id·ly** *adv* — **viv·id·ness** *n*

viv·i·fy \\'vivə,fī\ *vb* **-fied; -fy·ing** : give life or vividness to

vivi·sec·tion \,vivə'sekshən, 'vivə,-\ *n* : experimental operation on a living animal

vix·en \\'viksən\ *n* **1** : scolding woman **2** : female fox

vo·cab·u·lary \vō'kabyə,lerē\ *n, pl* **-lar·ies** **1** : list or collection of words **2** : stock of words used by a person or about a subject

vo·cal \\'vōkəl\ *adj* **1** : relating to or produced by or for the voice **2** : speaking out freely and usu. emphatically

vocal cords *n pl* : membranous folds in the larynx that are important in making vocal sounds

vo·cal·ist \\'vōkəlist\ *n* : singer

vo·cal·ize \-,līz\ *vb* **-ized; -iz·ing** : give vocal expression to

vo·ca·tion \vō'kāshən\ *n* : regular employment — **vo·ca·tion·al** \-shənəl\ *adj*

vo·cif·er·ous \vō'sifərəs\ *adj* : noisy and insistent — **vo·cif·er·ous·ly** *adv*

vod·ka \'vädkə\ *n* : colorless distilled grain liquor

vogue \'vōg\ *n* : brief but intense popularity — **vogu·ish** \'vōgish\ *adj*

voice \'vȯis\ *n* **1** : sound produced through the mouth by humans and many animals **2** : power of speaking **3** : right of choice or opinion ～ *vb* **voiced; voic·ing** : express in words — **voiced** \'vȯist\ *adj*

void \'vȯid\ *adj* **1** : containing nothing **2** : lacking — with *of* **3** : not legally binding ～ *n* **1** : empty space **2** : feeling of hollowness ～ *vb* **1** : discharge (as body waste) **2** : make (as a contract) void — **void·able** *adj* — **void·er** *n*

vol·a·tile \'välət°l\ *adj* **1** : readily vaporizing at a relatively low temperature **2** : likely to change suddenly — **vol·a·til·i·ty** \,välə'tilətē\ *n* — **vol·a·til·ize** \'välət°l,īz\ *vb*

vol·ca·no \väl'kānō\ *n, pl* **-noes** *or* **-nos** : opening in the earth's crust from which molten rock and steam come out — **vol·ca·nic** \-'kanik\ *adj*

vo·li·tion \vō'lishən\ *n* : free will — **vo·li·tion·al** \-'lishənəl\ *adj*

vol·ley \'välē\ *n, pl* **-leys** **1** : flight of missiles (as arrows) **2** : simultaneous shooting of many weapons

vol·ley·ball *n* : game of batting a large ball over a net

volt \'vōlt\ *n* : unit for measuring the force that moves an electric current

volt·age \'vōltij\ *n* : quantity of volts

vol·u·ble \'välyəbəl\ *adj* : fluent and smooth in speech — **vol·u·bil·i·ty** \,välyə'bilətē\ *n* — **vol·u·bly** \'välyəblē\ *adv*

vol·ume \'välyəm\ *n* **1** : book **2** : space occupied as measured by cubic units **3** : amount **4** : loudness of a sound

vo·lu·mi·nous \və'lümənəs\ *adj* : large or bulky

vol·un·tary \'välən,terē\ *adj* **1** : done, made, or given freely and without expecting compensation **2** : relating to or controlled by the will — **vol·un·tar·i·ly** *adv*

vol·un·teer \,välən'tir\ *n* : person who offers to help or work without expecting payment or reward ～ *vb* **1** : offer or give voluntarily **2** : offer oneself as a volunteer

vo·lup·tuous \və'ləpchəwəs\ *adj* **1** : luxurious **2** : having a full and sexually attractive figure — **vo·lup·tuous·ly** *adv* — **vo·lup·tuous·ness** *n*

vom·it \\'vämət\ *vb* : throw up the contents of the stomach — **vomit** *n*

voo·doo \\'vüdü\ *n, pl* **voodoos** **1** : religion derived from African polytheism and involving sorcery **2** : one who practices voodoo **3** : charm or fetish used in voodoo — **voodoo** *adj* — **voo·doo·ism** \-ˌizəm\ *n*

vo·ra·cious \vȯ'rāshəs, və-\ *adj* : greedy or exceedingly hungry — **vo·ra·cious·ly** *adv* — **vo·ra·cious·ness** *n* — **vo·rac·i·ty** \-'rasətē\ *n*

vor·tex \\'vȯrˌteks\ *n, pl* **vor·ti·ces** \\'vȯrtəˌsēz\ : whirling liquid

vo·ta·ry \\'vōtərē\ *n, pl* **-ries** **1** : devoted participant, adherent, admirer, or worshiper

vote \\'vōt\ *n* **1** : individual expression of preference in choosing or reaching a decision **2** : right to indicate one's preference or the preference expressed ∼ *vb* **vot·ed; vot·ing** **1** : cast a vote **2** : choose or defeat by vote — **vote·less** *adj* — **vot·er** *n*

vo·tive \\'vōtiv\ *adj* : consisting of or expressing a vow, wish, or desire

vouch \\'vaȯch\ *vb* : give a guarantee or personal assurance

vouch·er \\'vaȯchər\ *n* : written record or receipt that serves as proof of a transaction

vouch·safe \vaȯch'sāf\ *vb* **-safed; -saf·ing** : grant as a special favor

vow \\'vaȯ\ *n* : solemn promise to do something or to live or act a certain way — **vow** *vb*

vow·el \\'vaȯəl\ *n* **1** : speech sound produced without obstruction or friction in the mouth **2** : letter representing such a sound

voy·age \\'vȯiij\ *n* : long journey esp. by water or through space ∼ *vb* **-aged; -ag·ing** : make a voyage — **voy·ag·er** *n*

vul·ca·nize \\'vəlkəˌnīz\ *vb* **-nized; -niz·ing** : treat (as rubber) to make more elastic or stronger

vul·gar \\'vəlgər\ *adj* **1** : relating to the common people **2** : lacking refinement **3** : offensive in manner or language — **vul·gar·ism** \-ˌrizəm\ *n* — **vul·gar·ize** \-ˌrīz\ *vb* — **vul·gar·ly** *adv*

vul·gar·i·ty \ˌvəl'garətē\ *n, pl* **-ties** **1** : state of being vulgar **2** : vulgar language or act

vul·ner·a·ble \\'vəlnərəbəl\ *adj* : susceptible to attack or damage — **vul·ner·a·bil·i·ty** \ˌvəlnərə'bilətē\ *n* — **vul·ner·a·bly** *adv*

vul·ture \\'vəlchər\ *n* : large flesh-eating bird

vul·va \\'vəlvə\ *n, pl* **-vae** \-ˌvē, -ˌvī\ : external genital parts of the female

vying *pres part of* VIE

W

w \'dəbəl‚yü\ *n, pl* **w's** *or* **ws** \-‚yüz\ : 23d letter of the alphabet

wad \'wäd\ *n* **1** : little mass **2** : soft mass of fibrous material **3** : pliable plug to retain a powder charge **4** : considerable amount ∼ *vb* **1** : form into a wad **2** : stuff with a wad

wad·dle \'wäd°l\ *vb* **-dled; -dling** : walk with short steps swaying from side to side — **waddle** *n*

wade \'wād\ *vb* **wad·ed; wading** **1** : step in or through (as water) **2** : move with difficulty — **wade** *n* — **wad·er** *n*

wa·fer \'wāfər\ *n* **1** : thin crisp cake or cracker **2** : waferlike thing

waf·fle \'wäfəl\ *n* : crisped cake of batter cooked in a hinged utensil (**waffle iron**) ∼ *vb* : vacillate

waft \'wäft, 'waft\ *vb* : cause to move lightly by wind or waves — **waft** *n*

¹wag \'wag\ *vb* **-gg-** : sway or swing from side to side or to and fro — **wag** *n*

²wag *n* : wit — **wag·gish** *adj*

wage \'wāj\ *vb* **waged; waging** : engage in ∼ *n* **1** : pay-ment for labor or services **2** : compensation

wa·ger \'wājər\ *n or vb* : bet

wag·gle \'wagəl\ *vb* **-gled; -gling** : wag — **waggle** *n*

wag·on \'wagən\ *n* **1** : 4-wheeled vehicle drawn by animals **2** : child's 4-wheeled cart

waif \'wāf\ *n* : homeless child

wail \'wāl\ *vb* **1** : mourn **2** : make a sound like a mournful cry — **wail** *n*

wain·scot \'wānskət, -‚skōt, -‚skät\ *n* : usu. paneled wooden lining of an interior wall — **wainscot** *vb*

waist \'wāst\ *n* **1** : narrowed part of the body between chest and hips **2** : waistlike part — **waist·line** *n*

wait \'wāt\ *vb* **1** : remain in readiness or expectation **2** : delay **3** : attend as a waiter ∼ *n* **1** : concealment **2** : act or period of waiting

wait·er \'wātər\ *n* : person who serves others at tables

wait·per·son \'wāt‚pərsən\ *n* : a waiter or waitress

wait·ress \'wātrəs\ *n* : woman who serves others at tables

waive \\'wāv\ *vb* **waived; waiv-ing** : give up claim to

waiv·er \\'wāvər\ *n* : act of waiving right, claim, or privilege

¹**wake** \\'wāk\ *vb* **woke** \\'wōk\; **wo·ken** \\'wōkən\; **wak·ing 1** : keep watch **2** : bring or come back to consciousness after sleep ～ *n* **1** : state of being awake **2** : watch held over a dead body

²**wake** *n* : track left by a ship

wake·ful \\'wākfəl\ *adj* : not sleeping or able to sleep — **wake·ful·ness** *n*

wak·en \\'wākən\ *vb* : wake

wale \\'wāl\ *n* : ridge on cloth

walk \\'wȯk\ *vb* **1** : move or cause to move on foot **2** : pass over, through, or along by walking ～ *n* **1** : a going on foot **2** : place or path for walking **3** : distance to be walked **4** : way of living **5** : way of walking **6** : slow 4-beat gait of a horse — **walk·er** *n*

wall \\'wȯl\ *n* **1** : structure for defense or for enclosing something **2** : upright enclosing part of a building or room **3** : something like a wall ～ *vb* : provide, separate, surround, or close with a wall — **walled** \\'wȯld\ *adj*

wal·la·by \\'wäləbē\ *n, pl* **-bies** : small or medium-sized kangaroo

wal·let \\'wälət\ *n* : pocketbook with compartments

wall·flow·er *n* **1** : mustardlike plant with showy fragrant flowers **2** : one who remains on the sidelines of social activity

wal·lop \\'wäləp\ *n* **1** : powerful blow **2** : ability to hit hard ～ *vb* **1** : beat soundly **2** : hit hard

wal·low \\'wälō\ *vb* **1** : roll about in deep mud **2** : indulge oneself excessively ～ *n* : place for wallowing

wall·pa·per *n* : decorative paper for walls — **wallpaper** *vb*

wal·nut \\'wȯl,nət\ *n* **1** : nut with a furrowed shell and adherent husk **2** : tree on which this nut grows or its brown wood

wal·rus \\'wȯlrəs, 'wäl-\ *n, pl* **-rus** *or* **-rus·es** : large seallike mammal of northern seas having ivory tusks

waltz \\'wȯlts\ *n* : gliding dance to music having 3 beats to the measure or the music — **waltz** *vb*

wam·pum \\'wämpəm\ *n* : strung shell beads used by No. American Indians as money

wan \\'wän\ *adj* **-nn-** : sickly or pale — **wan·ly** *adv* — **wan·ness** *n*

wand \\'wänd\ *n* : slender staff

wan·der \\'wändər\ *vb* **1** : move about aimlessly **2** : stray **3**

: become delirious — **wan·der·er** *n*

wan·der·lust \'wändər,ləst\ *n* : strong urge to wander

wane \'wān\ *vb* **waned; waning 1** : grow smaller or less **2** : lose power, prosperity, or influence — **wane** *n*

wan·gle \'waŋgəl\ *vb* **-gled; -gling** : obtain by sly or devious means

want \'wȯnt\ *vb* **1** : lack **2** : need **3** : desire earnestly ∼ *n* **1** : deficiency **2** : dire need **3** : something wanted

want·ing \-iŋ\ *adj* **1** : not present or in evidence **2** : falling below standards **3** : lacking in ability ∼ *prep* **1** : less or minus **2** : without

wan·ton \'wȯnt°n\ *adj* **1** : lewd **2** : having no regard for justice or for others' feelings, rights, or safety ∼ *n* : lewd or immoral person ∼ *vb* : be wanton — **wan·ton·ly** *adv* — **wan·ton·ness** *n*

wa·pi·ti \'wäpətē\ *n, pl* **-ti** *or* **-tis** : elk

war \'wȯr\ *n* **1** : armed fighting between nations **2** : state of hostility or conflict **3** : struggle between opposing forces or for a particular end ∼ *vb* **-rr-** : engage in warfare — **war·less** \-ləs\ *adj* — **war·time** *n*

war·ble \'wȯrbəl\ *n* **1** : melodious succession of low pleas-

ing sounds **2** : musical trill ∼ *vb* **-bled; -bling** : sing or utter in a trilling way

war·bler \'wȯrblər\ *n* **1** : small thrushlike singing bird **2** : small bright-colored insect-eating bird

ward \'wȯrd\ *n* **1** : a guarding or being under guard or guardianship **2** : division of a prison or hospital **3** : electoral or administrative division of a city **4** : person under protection of a guardian or a law court ∼ *vb* : turn aside — **ward·ship** *n*

¹-ward \wərd\ *adj suffix* **1** : that moves, tends, faces, or is directed toward **2** : that occurs or is situated in the direction of

²-ward, -wards *adv suffix* **1** : in a (specified) direction **2** : toward a (specified) point, position, or area

war·den \'wȯrd°n\ *n* **1** : guardian **2** : official charged with supervisory duties or enforcement of laws **3** : official in charge of a prison

ward·er \'wȯrdər\ *n* : watchman or warden

ward·robe \'wȯrd,rōb\ *n* **1** : clothes closet **2** : collection of wearing apparel

ware \'war\ *n* **1** : articles for sale — often pl. **2** : items of fired clay

ware·house \-,haùs\ *n* : place for storage of merchandise —

warehouse *vb* — **ware·house·man** \-mən\ *n* — **ware·hous·er** \-ˌhaůzər, -sər\ *n*

war·fare \'wȯrˌfar\ *n* **1** : military operations between enemies **2** : struggle

war·head \-ˌhed\ *n* : part of a missile holding the explosive material

war·like *adj* : fond of, relating to, or used in war

warm \'wȯrm\ *adj* **1** : having or giving out moderate or adequate heat **2** : serving to retain heat **3** : showing strong feeling **4** : giving a pleasant impression of warmth, cheerfulness, or friendliness ～ *vb* **1** : make or become warm **2** : give warmth or energy to **3** : experience feelings of affection **4** : become increasingly ardent, interested, or competent — **warm·er** *n* — **warm·ly** *adv* — **warm up** *vb* : make ready by preliminary activity

war·mon·ger \'wȯrˌməŋgər, -ˌmän-\ *n* : one who attempts to stir up war

warmth \'wȯrmth\ *n* **1** : quality or state of being warm **2** : enthusiasm

warn \'wȯrn\ *vb* **1** : put on guard **2** : notify in advance — **warn·ing** \-iŋ\ *n or adj*

warp \'wȯrp\ *n* **1** : lengthwise threads in a woven fabric **2** : twist ～ *vb* **1** : twist out of shape **2** : lead astray **3** : distort

war·rant \'wȯrənt, 'wär-\ *n* **1** : authorization **2** : legal writ authorizing action ～ *vb* **1** : declare or maintain positively **2** : guarantee **3** : approve **4** : justify

warrant officer *n* **1** : officer in the armed forces ranking next below a commissioned officer **2** : commissioned officer in the navy or coast guard ranking below an ensign

war·ran·ty \'wȯrəntē, 'wär-\ *n, pl* **-ties** : guarantee of the integrity of a product

war·ren \'wȯrən, 'wär-\ *n* : area where rabbits are bred and kept

war·rior \'wȯryər, 'wȯrēər; 'wärē-, 'wäryər\ *n* : man engaged or experienced in warfare

war·ship \'wȯrˌship\ *n* : naval vessel

wart \'wȯrt\ *n* **1** : small projection on the skin caused by a virus **2** : wartlike protuberance — **warty** *adj*

wary \'warē\ *adj* **war·i·er; -est** : careful in guarding against danger or deception

was *past 1st & 3d sing of* BE

wash \'wȯsh, 'wäsh\ *vb* **1** : cleanse with or as if with a liquid (as water) **2** : wet thoroughly with liquid **3** : flow along the border of **4** : flow in a stream **5** : move or remove by or as if by the action of water **6** : cover or daub lightly with a liquid **7** : undergo launder-ing ∼ *n* **1** : act of washing or being washed **2** : articles to be washed **3** : surging action of water or disturbed air — **wash-able** \-əbəl\ *adj*

wash·board *n* : grooved board to scrub clothes on

wash·bowl *n* : large bowl for water for washing hands and face

wash·cloth *n* : cloth used for washing one's face and body

washed–up \'wȯsht'əp, 'wäsht-\ *adj* : no longer capa-ble or usable

wash·er \'wȯshər, 'wäsh-\ *n* **1** : machine for washing **2** : ring used around a bolt or screw to ensure tightness or re-lieve friction

wash·ing \'wȯshiŋ, 'wäsh-\ *n* : articles to be washed

Washington's Birthday *n* : the 3d Monday in February or for-merly February 22 observed as a legal holiday

wash·out *n* **1** : washing out or away of earth **2** : failure

wash·room *n* : bathroom

wasp \'wäsp, 'wȯsp\ *n* : slen-der-bodied winged insect re-lated to the bees and having a formidable sting

wasp·ish \'wäspish, 'wȯs-\ *adj* : irritable

was·sail \'wäsəl, wä'sāl\ *n* **1** : toast to someone's health **2** : liquor drunk on festive occa-sions **3** : riotous drinking — **wassail** *vb*

waste \'wāst\ *n* **1** : sparsely settled or barren region **2** : act or an instance of wasting **3** : re-fuse (as garbage or rubbish) **4** : material (as feces) produced but not used by a living body ∼ *vb* **wast·ed; wast·ing 1** : ruin **2** : spend or use care-lessly **3** : lose substance or en-ergy ∼ *adj* **1** : wild and uninhabited **2** : being of no further use — **wast·er** *n* — **waste·ful** \-fəl\ *adj* — **waste-ful·ly** *adv* — **waste·ful·ness** *n*

waste·bas·ket \-ˌbaskət\ *n* : re-ceptacle for refuse

waste·land \-ˌland, -lənd\ *n* : barren uncultivated land

wast·rel \'wāstrəl, 'wästrəl\ *n* : one who wastes

watch \'wäch, 'wȯch\ *vb* **1** : be or stay awake intentionally **2** : be on the lookout for dan-ger **3** : observe **4** : keep one-self informed about ∼ *n* **1** : act of keeping awake to guard **2** : close observation **3** : one that watches **4** : period of duty on a ship or those on duty during this period **5** : time-piece carried on the person — **watch·er** *n*

watch·dog *n* **1** : dog kept to guard property **2** : one that protects

watch·ful \-fəl\ *adj* : steadily attentive — **watch·ful·ly** *adv* — **watch·ful·ness** *n*

watch·man \-mən\ *n* : person assigned to watch

watch·word *n* **1** : secret word used as a signal **2** : slogan

wa·ter \ˈwȯtər, ˈwät-\ *n* **1** : liquid that descends as rain and forms rivers, lakes, and seas **2** : liquid containing or resembling water ∼ *vb* **1** : supply with or get water **2** : dilute with or as if with water **3** : form or secrete watery matter

water buffalo *n* : common ox-like often domesticated Asian buffalo

wa·ter·col·or *n* **1** : paint whose liquid part is water **2** : picture made with watercolors

wa·ter·course *n* : stream of water

wa·ter·cress \-ˌkres\ *n* : perennial salad plant with white flowers

wa·ter·fall *n* : steep descent of the water of a stream

wa·ter·fowl *n* **1** : bird that frequents the water **2 waterfowl** *pl* : swimming game birds

wa·ter·front *n* : land fronting a body of water

water lily *n* : aquatic plant with floating leaves and showy flowers

wa·ter·logged \-ˌlȯgd, -ˌlägd\ *adj* : filled or soaked with water

wa·ter·mark *n* **1** : mark showing how high water has risen **2** : a marking in paper visible under light ∼ *vb* : mark (paper) with a watermark

wa·ter·mel·on *n* : large fruit with sweet juicy usu. red pulp

water moccasin *n* : venomous snake of the southeastern U.S.

wa·ter·pow·er *n* : power of moving water used to run machinery

wa·ter·proof *adj* : not letting water through ∼ *vb* : make waterproof — **wa·ter·proof·ing** *n*

wa·ter·shed \-ˌshed\ *n* : dividing ridge between two drainage areas or one of these areas

water ski *n* : ski used on water when the wearer is towed — **wa·ter–ski** *vb* — **wa·ter–skier** *n*

wa·ter·spout *n* **1** : pipe from which water is spouted **2** : tornado over a body of water

wa·ter·tight *adj* **1** : so tight as not to let water in **2** : allowing no possibility for doubt or uncertainty

wa·ter·way *n* : navigable body of water

wa·ter·works *n pl* : system by which water is supplied (as to a city)

wa·tery \ˈwȯtərē, ˈwät-\ *adj* **1** : containing, full of, or giving out water **2** : being like water **3** : soft and soggy

watt \'wät\ *n* : unit of electric power — **watt·age** \'wätij\ *n*

wat·tle \'wät³l\ *n* **1** : framework of flexible branches used in building **2** : fleshy process hanging usu. about the head or neck (as of a bird) — **wat·tled** \-³ld\ *adj*

wave \'wāv\ *vb* **waved; waving** **1** : flutter **2** : signal with the hands **3** : wave to and fro with the hand **4** : curve up and down like a wave ∼ *n* **1** : moving swell on the surface of water **2** : wave-like shape **3** : waving motion **4** : surge **5** : disturbance that transfers energy from point to point — **wave·let** \-lət\ *n* — **wave·like** *adj* — **wavy** *adj*

wave·length \'wāv,leŋth\ *n* **1** : distance from crest to crest in the line of advance of a wave **2** : line of thought that reveals a common understanding

wa·ver \'wāvər\ *vb* **1** : fluctuate in opinion, allegiance, or direction **2** : flicker **3** : falter — **waver** *n* — **wa·ver·er** *n* — **wa·ver·ing·ly** *adv*

¹wax \'waks\ *n* **1** : yellowish plastic substance secreted by bees **2** : substance like beeswax ∼ *vb* : treat or rub with wax esp. for polishing

²wax *vb* **1** : grow larger **2** : become

wax·en \'waksən\ *adj* : made of or resembling wax

waxy \'waksē\ *adj* **wax·i·er; -est** : made of, full of, or resembling wax

way \'wā\ *n* **1** : thoroughfare for travel or passage **2** : route **3** : course of action **4** : method **5** : detail **6** : usual or characteristic state of affairs **7** : condition **8** : distance **9** : progress along a course — **by the way** : in a digression — **by way of** **1** : for the purpose of **2** : by the route through — **out of the way** : remote

way·bill *n* : paper that accompanies a shipment and gives details of goods, route, and charges

way·far·er \'wā,farər\ *n* : traveler esp. on foot — **way·far·ing** \-,fariŋ\ *adj*

way·lay \'wā,lā\ *vb* **-laid** \-,lād\; **-lay·ing** : lie in wait for

way·side *n* : side of a road

way·ward \'wāwərd\ *adj* **1** : following one's own capricious inclinations **2** : unpredictable

we \'wē\ *pron* — used of a group that includes the speaker or writer

weak \'wēk\ *adj* **1** : lacking strength or vigor **2** : deficient in vigor of mind or character **3** : of less than usual strength **4** : not having or exerting authority — **weak·en** \'wēkən\ *vb* — **weak·ly** *adv*

weak·ling \-liŋ\ *n* : person who is physically, mentally, or morally weak

weak·ly \'wēklē\ *adj* : feeble

weak·ness \-nəs\ *n* 1 : quality or state of being weak 2 : fault 3 : object of special liking

wealth \'welth\ *n* 1 : abundant possessions or resources 2 : profusion

wealthy \'welthē\ *adj* **wealth·i·er; -est** : having wealth

wean \'wēn\ *vb* 1 : accustom (a young mammal) to take food by means other than nursing 2 : free from dependence

weap·on \'wepən\ *n* 1 : something (as a gun) that may be used to fight with 2 : means by which one contends against another — **weap·on·less** *adj*

wear \'war\ *vb* **wore** \'wōr\; **worn** \'wōrn\; **wear·ing** 1 : use as an article of clothing or adornment 2 : carry on the person 3 : show an appearance of 4 : decay by use or by scraping 5 : lessen the strength of 6 : endure use ~ *n* 1 : act of wearing 2 : clothing 3 : lasting quality 4 : result of use — **wear·able** \'warəbəl\ *adj* — **wear·er** *n* — **wear out** *vb* 1 : make or become useless by wear 2 : tire

wea·ri·some \'wirēsəm\ *adj* : causing weariness — **wea·ri·**

some·ly *adv* — **wea·ri·some·ness** *n*

wea·ry \'wirē\ *adj* **-ri·er; -est** 1 : worn out in strength, freshness, or patience 2 : expressing or characteristic of weariness ~ *vb* **-ried; -ry·ing** : make or become weary — **wea·ri·ly** *adv* — **wea·ri·ness** *n*

wea·sel \'wēzəl\ *n* : small slender flesh-eating mammal

weath·er \'wethər\ *n* : state of the atmosphere ~ *vb* 1 : expose to or endure the action of weather 2 : endure

weath·er–beat·en *adj* : worn or damaged by exposure to the weather

weath·er·man \-₁man\ *n* : one who forecasts and reports the weather

weath·er·proof *adj* : able to withstand exposure to weather — **weatherproof** *vb*

weather vane *n* : movable device that shows the way the wind blows

weave \'wēv\ *vb* **wove** \'wōv\ *or* **weaved; wo·ven** \'wōvən\ *or* **weaved; weav·ing** 1 : form by interlacing strands of material 2 : to make as if by weaving together parts 3 : follow a winding course ~ *n* : pattern or method of weaving — **weav·er** *n*

web \'web\ *n* 1 : cobweb 2 : animal or plant membrane 3

: network **4** *cap* : WORLD WIDE WEB ∼ *vb* **-bb-** : cover or provide with a web — **webbed** \'webd\ *adj*

web·bing \'webiŋ\ *n* : strong closely woven tape

Web site *n* : group of World Wide Web pages available online

wed \'wed\ *vb* **-dd- 1** : marry **2** : unite

wed·ding \'wediŋ\ *n* : marriage ceremony and celebration

wedge \'wej\ *n* : V-shaped object used for splitting, raising, forcing open, or tightening ∼ *vb* **wedged; wedg·ing 1** : tighten or split with a wedge **2** : force into a narrow space

wed·lock \'wed͵läk\ *n* : marriage

Wednes·day \'wenzdā, -dē\ *n* : 4th day of the week

wee \'wē\ *adj* : very small

weed \'wēd\ *n* : unwanted plant ∼ *vb* **1** : remove weeds **2** : get rid of — **weed·er** *n* — **weedy** *adj*

weeds *n pl* : mourning clothes

week \'wēk\ *n* **1** : 7 successive days **2** : calendar period of 7 days beginning with Sunday and ending with Saturday **3** : the working or school days of the calendar week

week·day \'wēk͵dā\ *n* : any day except Sunday and often Saturday

week·end \-͵end\ *n* : Saturday and Sunday ∼ *vb* : spend the weekend

week·ly \'wēklē\ *adj* : occurring, appearing, or done every week ∼ *n, pl* **-lies** : weekly publication — **weekly** *adv*

weep \'wēp\ *vb* **wept** \'wept\; **weep·ing** : shed tears — **weep·er** *n* — **weepy** *adj*

wee·vil \'wēvəl\ *n* : small injurious beetle with a long head usu. curved into a snout — **wee·vily, wee·vil·ly** \'wēvəlē\ *adj*

weft \'weft\ *n* : crosswise threads or yarn in weaving

weigh \'wā\ *vb* **1** : determine the heaviness of **2** : have a specified weight **3** : consider carefully **4** : raise (an anchor) off the sea floor **5** : press down or burden

weight \'wāt\ *n* **1** : amount that something weighs **2** : relative heaviness **3** : heavy object **4** : burden or pressure **5** : importance ∼ *vb* **1** : load with a weight **2** : oppress — **weight·less** \-ləs\ *adj* — **weight·less·ness** *n* — **weighty** \'wātē\ *adj*

weird \'wird\ *adj* **1** : unearthly or mysterious **2** : strange — **weird·ly** *adv* — **weird·ness** *n*

wel·come \'welkəm\ *vb* **-comed; -com·ing** : accept or greet cordially ∼ *adj* : received or permitted gladly ～ *n* : cordial greeting or reception

weld \\'weld\\ *vb* : unite by heating, hammering, or pressing ～ *n* : union by welding — **weld-er** *n*

wel·fare \\'wel͵far\\ *n* **1** : prosperity **2** : government aid for those in need

¹well \\'wel\\ *n* **1** : spring **2** : hole sunk in the earth to obtain a natural deposit (as of oil) **3** : source of supply **4** : open space extending vertically through floors ～ *vb* : flow forth

²well *adv* **bet·ter** \\'betər\\; **best** \\'best\\ **1** : in a good or proper manner **2** : satisfactorily **3** : fully **4** : intimately **5** : considerably ～ *adj* **1** : satisfactory **2** : prosperous **3** : desirable **4** : healthy

well–adjusted \\͵welə'jəstəd\\ *adj* : well-balanced

well–ad·vised \\͵weləd'vīzd\\ *adj* : prudent

well–balanced \\'wel'balənst\\ *adj* **1** : evenly balanced **2** : emotionally or psychologically sound

well–be·ing \\'wel'bēiŋ\\ *n* : state of being happy, healthy, or prosperous

well–bred \\-'bred\\ *adj* : having good manners

well–done *adj* **1** : properly performed **2** : cooked thoroughly

well–heeled \\-'hēld\\ *adj* : financially well-off

well–mean·ing *adj* : having good intentions

well–nigh *adv* : nearly

well–off *adj* : being in good condition esp. financially

well–read \\-'red\\ *adj* : well informed through reading

well–round·ed \\-'raúndəd\\ *adj* : broadly developed

well·spring *n* : source

well–to–do \\͵weltə'dü\\ *adj* : prosperous

welsh \\'welsh, 'welch\\ *vb* **1** : avoid payment **2** : break one's word

Welsh rabbit *n* : melted often seasoned cheese poured over toast or crackers

Welsh rare·bit \\-'rarbət\\ *n* : Welsh rabbit

welt \\'welt\\ *n* **1** : narrow strip of leather between a shoe upper and sole **2** : ridge raised on the skin usu. by a blow ～ *vb* : hit hard

wel·ter \\'weltər\\ *vb* **1** : toss about **2** : wallow ～ *n* : confused jumble

wen \\'wen\\ *n* : abnormal growth or cyst

wench \\'wench\\ *n* : young woman

wend \\'wend\\ *vb* : direct one's course

went *past of* **GO**

wept *past of* WEEP

were *past 2d sing, past pl, or past subjunctive of* BE

were·wolf \\'wer,wu̇lf, 'wir-, 'wər-\ *n, pl* **-wolves** \-,wu̇lvz\ : person held to be able to change into a wolf

west \\'west\ *adv* : to or toward the west ~ *adj* : situated toward or at or coming from the west ~ *n* **1** : direction of sunset **2** *cap* : regions to the west — **west·er·ly** \\'westərlē\ *adv or adj* — **west·ward** \-wərd\ *adv or adj* — **west·wards** \-wərdz\ *adv*

west·ern \\'westərn\ *adj* **1** *cap* : of a region designated West **2** : lying toward or coming from the west — **West·ern·er** *n*

wet \\'wet\ *adj* **-tt-** **1** : consisting of or covered or soaked with liquid **2** : not dry ~ *n* : moisture ~ *vb* **-tt-** : make or become moist — **wet·ly** *adv* — **wet·ness** *n*

whack \\'hwak\ *vb* : strike sharply ~ *n* **1** : sharp blow **2** : proper working order **3** : chance **4** : try

¹whale \\'hwāl\ *n, pl* **whales** *or* **whale** : large marine mammal ~ *vb* **whaled; whal·ing** : hunt for whales — **whale·boat** *n* — **whal·er** *n*

²whale *vb* **whaled; whal·ing** : strike or hit vigorously

whale·bone *n* : horny substance attached to the upper jaw of some large whales (**whalebone whales**)

wharf \\'hwȯrf\ *n, pl* **wharves** \\'hwȯrvz\ : structure alongside which boats lie to load or unload

what \\'hwät\ *pron* **1** — used to inquire the identity or nature of something **2** : that which **3** : whatever ~ *adv* : in what respect ~ *adj* **1** — used to inquire about the identity or nature of something **2** : how remarkable or surprising **3** : whatever

what·ev·er \hwät'evər\ *pron* **1** : anything or everything that **2** : no matter what ~ *adj* : of any kind at all

what·not \\'hwät,nät\ *pron* : any of various other things that might be mentioned

what·so·ev·er \,hwätsō'evər\ *pron or adj* : whatever

wheal \\'hwēl\ *n* : a welt on the skin

wheat \\'hwēt\ *n* : cereal grain that yields flour — **wheat·en** *adj*

whee·dle \\'hwēdᵊl\ *vb* **-dled; -dling** : coax or tempt by flattery

wheel \\'hwēl\ *n* **1** : disk or circular frame capable of turning on a central axis **2** : device of which the main part is a wheel

~ *vb* **1** : convey or move on wheels or a wheeled vehicle **2** : rotate **3** : turn so as to change direction — **wheeled** *adj* — **wheel·er** *n* — **wheel·less** *adj*

wheel·bar·row \-ˌbarō\ *n* : one=wheeled vehicle for carrying small loads

wheel·base *n* : distance in inches between the front and rear axles of an automotive vehicle

wheel·chair *n* : chair mounted on wheels esp. for the use of disabled persons

wheeze \ˈhwēz\ *vb* **wheezed; wheez·ing** : breathe with difficulty and with a whistling sound — **wheeze** *n* — **wheezy** *adj*

whelk \ˈhwelk\ *n* : large sea snail

whelp \ˈhwelp\ *n* : one of the young of various carnivorous mammals (as a dog) ~ *vb* : bring forth whelps

when \ˈhwen\ *adv* — used to inquire about or designate a particular time ~ *conj* **1** : at or during the time that **2** : every time that **3** : if **4** : although ~ *pron* : what time

whence \ˈhwens\ *adv or conj* : from what place, source, or cause

when·ev·er \hwenˈevər\ *conj or adv* : at whatever time

where \ˈhwer\ *adv* **1** : at, in, or to what place **2** : at, in, or to what situation, position, direction, circumstances, or respect ~ *conj* **1** : at, in, or to what place, position, or circumstance **2** : at, in, or to which place ~ *n* : place

where·abouts \-əˌbaůts\ *adv* : about where ~ *n sing or pl* : place where a person or thing is

where·as \hwerˈaz\ *conj* **1** : while on the contrary **2** : since

where·by *conj* : by, through, or in accordance with which

where·fore \ˈhwerˌfōr\ *adv* **1** : why **2** : therefore ~ *n* : reason

where·in \hwerˈin\ *adv* : in what respect

where·of \-ˈəv, -äv\ *conj* : of what, which, or whom

where·up·on \ˈhwerəˌpȯn, -ˌpän\ *conj* **1** : on which **2** : and then

wher·ev·er \hwerˈevər\ *adv* : where ~ *conj* : at, in, or to whatever place or circumstance

where·with·al \ˈhwerwithˌȯl, -with-\ *n* : resources and esp. money

whet \ˈhwet\ *vb* **-tt-** **1** : sharpen by rubbing (as with a stone) **2** : stimulate — **whet·stone** *n*

whether \ˈhwethər\ *conj* **1** : if it is or was true that **2** : if it is or was better **3** : whichever is the case

whey \\'hwā\ *n* : watery part of sour milk

which \\'hwich\ *adj* **1** : being what one or ones out of a group **2** : whichever ~ *pron* **1** : which one or ones **2** : whichever

which·ev·er \hwich'evər\ *pron or adj* : no matter what one

whiff \\'hwif\ *n* **1** : slight gust **2** : inhalation of odor, gas, or smoke **3** : slight trace ~ *vb* : inhale an odor

while \\'hwīl\ *n* **1** : period of time **2** : time and effort used ~ *conj* **1** : during the time that **2** : as long as **3** : although ~ *vb* **whiled; whil·ing** : cause to pass esp. pleasantly

whim \\'hwim\ *n* : sudden wish, desire, or change of mind

whim·per \\'hwimpər\ *vb* : cry softly — **whimper** *n*

whim·si·cal \\'hwimzikəl\ *adj* **1** : full of whims **2** : erratic — **whim·si·cal·i·ty** \,hwimzə-'kalətē\ *n* — **whim·si·cal·ly** *adv*

whim·sy, whim·sey \\'hwimzē\ *n, pl* **-sies** *or* **-seys** **1** : whim **2** : fanciful creation

whine \\'hwīn\ *vb* **whined; whin·ing** **1** : utter a usu. high-pitched plaintive cry **2** : complain — **whine** *n* — **whin·er** *n* — **whiny** *adj*

whin·ny \\'hwinē\ *vb* **-nied; -ny·ing** : neigh — **whinny** *n*

whip \\'hwip\ *vb* **-pp-** **1** : move quickly **2** : strike with something slender and flexible **3** : defeat **4** : incite **5** : beat into a froth ~ *n* **1** : flexible device used for whipping **2** : party leader responsible for discipline **3** : thrashing motion — **whip·per** *n*

whip·cord *n* **1** : thin tough cord **2** : cloth made of hard-twisted yarns

whip·lash *n* : injury from a sudden sharp movement of the neck and head

whip·per·snap·per \\'hwipər-,snapər\ *n* : small, insignificant, or presumptuous person

whip·pet \\'hwipət\ *n* : small swift dog often used for racing

whip·poor·will \\'hwipər,wil\ *n* : American nocturnal bird

whir \\'hwər\ *vb* **-rr-** : move, fly, or revolve with a whir ~ *n* : continuous fluttering or vibratory sound

whirl \\'hwərl\ *vb* **1** : move or drive in a circle **2** : spin **3** : move or turn quickly **4** : reel ~ *n* **1** : rapid circular movement **2** : state of commotion or confusion **3** : try

whirl·pool *n* : whirling mass of water having a depression in the center

whirl·wind *n* : whirling wind storm

whisk \\'hwisk\ *n* **1** : quick light sweeping or brushing motion

2 : usu. wire kitchen imple-ment for beating ~ *vb* **1** : move or convey briskly **2** : beat **3** : brush lightly

whisk broom *n* : small broom

whis·ker \\'hwiskər\\ *n* **1** *pl* : beard **2** : long bristle or hair near an animal's mouth — **whis·kered** \\-kərd\\ *adj*

whis·key, whis·ky \\'hwiskē\\ *n, pl* **-keys** *or* **-kies** : liquor dis-tilled from a fermented mash of grain

whis·per \\'hwispər\\ *vb* **1** : speak softly **2** : tell by whis-pering ~ *n* **1** : soft low sound **2** : rumor

whist \\'hwist\\ *n* : card game

whis·tle \\'hwisəl\\ *n* **1** : device by which a shrill sound is pro-duced **2** : shrill clear sound made by a whistle or through the lips ~ *vb* **-tled; -tling** **1** : make or utter a whistle **2** : signal or call by a whistle **3** : produce by whistling — **whis·tler** *n*

whis·tle–blow·er \\'hwisəl-ˌblōər\\ *n* : informer

whis·tle–stop *n* : brief political appearance

whit \\'hwit\\ *n* : bit

white \\'hwīt\\ *adj* **whit·er; -est** **1** : free from color **2** : of the color of new snow or milk **3** : having light skin ~ *n* **1** : color of maximum lightness **2** : white part or thing **3** : per-son who is light-skinned — **white·ness** *n* — **whit·ish** *adj*

white blood cell *n* : blood cell that does not contain hemo-globin

white·cap \\'hwīt,kap\\ *n* : wave crest breaking into white foam

white–col·lar *adj* : relating to salaried employees with duties not requiring protective or work clothing

white elephant *n* : something costly but of little use or value

white·fish \\'hwīt,fish\\ *n* : fresh-water food fish

whit·en \\'hwīt°n\\ *vb* : make or become white — **whit·en·er** \\'hwīt°nər\\ *n*

white slave *n* : woman or girl held unwillingly for purposes of prostitution — **white slavery** *n*

white·tail \\'hwīt,tāl\\ *n* : No. American deer

white·wash *vb* **1** : whiten with a composition (as of lime and water) **2** : gloss over or cover up faults or wrongdoing — **whitewash** *n*

whith·er \\'hwithər\\ *adv* **1** : to what place **2** : to what situa-tion, position, degree, or end

¹**whit·ing** \\'hwītiŋ\\ *n* : usu. light or silvery food fish

²**whiting** *n* : pulverized chalk or limestone

whit·tle \\'hwit°l\\ *vb* **-tled; -tling** **1** : pare **2** : shape by paring **3** : reduce gradually

whiz, whizz \\'hwiz\\ *vb* **-zz-** : make a sound like a speeding object — **whiz, whizz** *n*

who \\'hü\\ *pron* **1** : what or which person or persons **2** : person or persons that **3** — used to introduce a relative clause

who·dun·it \\hü'dənət\\ *n* : detective or mystery story

who·ev·er \\hü'evər\\ *pron* : no matter who

whole \\'hōl\\ *adj* **1** : being in healthy or sound condition **2** : having all its parts or elements **3** : constituting the total sum of ~ *n* **1** : complete amount or sum **2** : something whole or entire — **on the whole 1** : considering all circumstances **2** : in general — **whole·ness** *n*

whole·heart·ed \\'hōl'härtəd\\ *adj* : sincere

whole number *n* : integer

whole·sale *n* : sale of goods in quantity usu. for resale by a retail merchant ~ *adj* **1** : of or relating to wholesaling **2** : performed on a large scale ~ *vb* **-saled; -sal·ing** : sell at wholesale — **wholesale** *adv* — **whole·sal·er** *n*

whole·some \\-səm\\ *adj* **1** : promoting mental, spiritual, or bodily health **2** : healthy — **whole·some·ness** *n*

whole wheat *adj* : made of ground entire wheat kernels

whol·ly \\'hōlē\\ *adv* **1** : totally **2** : solely

whom \\'hüm\\ *pron, objective case of* WHO

whom·ev·er \\hüm'evər\\ *pron, objective case of* WHOEVER

whoop \\'hwüp, 'hwu̇p, 'hüp, 'hu̇p\\ *vb* : shout loudly ~ *n* : shout

whooping cough *n* : infectious disease marked by convulsive coughing fits

whop·per \\'hwäpər\\ *n* **1** : something unusually large or extreme of its kind **2** : monstrous lie

whop·ping \\'hwäpiŋ\\ *adj* : extremely large

whore \\'hōr\\ *n* : prostitute

whorl \\'hwȯrl, 'hwərl\\ *n* : spiral — **whorled** *adj*

whose \\'hüz\\ *adj* : of or relating to whom or which ~ *pron* : whose one or ones

who·so·ev·er \\ˌhüsō'evər\\ *pron* : whoever

why \\'hwī\\ *adv* : for what reason, cause, or purpose ~ *conj* **1** : reason for which **2** : for which ~ *n, pl* **whys** : reason ~ *interj* — used esp. to express surprise

wick \\'wik\\ *n* : cord that draws up oil, tallow, or wax to be burned

wick·ed \\'wikəd\\ *adj* **1** : morally bad **2** : harmful or troublesome **3** : very unpleasant   **4** : very impressive — **wick·ed·ly** *adv* — **wick·ed·ness** *n*

wick·er \\'wikər\\ *n* **1** : small pliant branch   **2** : wickerwork — **wicker** *adj*

wick·er·work *n* : work made of wickers

wick·et \\'wikət\\ *n* **1** : small gate, door, or window   **2** : frame in cricket or arch in croquet

wide \\'wīd\\ *adj* **wid·er; wid·est** **1** : covering a vast area   **2** : measured at right angles to the length   **3** : having a great measure across   **4** : opened fully   **5** : far from the thing in question ~ *adv* **wid·er; wid·est** **1** : over a great distance   **2** : so as to leave considerable space between   **3** : fully — **wide·ly** *adv* — **wid·en** \\'wīdᵊn\\ *vb*

wide–awake *adj* : alert

wide–eyed *adj* **1** : having the eyes wide open   **2** : amazed   **3** : naive

wide·spread *adj* : widely extended

wid·ow \\'widō\\ *n* : woman who has lost her husband by death and has not married again ~ *vb* : cause to become a widow — **wid·ow·hood** *n*

wid·ow·er \\'widəwər\\ *n* : man who has lost his wife by death and has not married again

width \\'width\\ *n* **1** : distance from side to side   **2** : largeness of extent   **3** : measured and cut piece of material

wield \\'wēld\\ *vb* **1** : use or handle esp. effectively   **2** : exert — **wield·er** *n*

wie·ner \\'wēnər\\ *n* : frankfurter

wife \\'wīf\\ *n, pl* **wives** \\'wīvz\\ : married woman — **wife·hood** *n* — **wife·less** *adj* — **wife·ly** *adj*

wig \\'wig\\ *n* : manufactured covering of hair for the head

wig·gle \\'wigəl\\ *vb* **-gled; -gling** **1** : move with quick jerky or shaking movements   **2** : wriggle — **wiggle** *n* — **wig·gler** *n*

wig·gly \\-əlē\\ *adj* **1** : tending to wiggle   **2** : wavy

wig·wag \\'wig,wag\\ *vb* : signal by a flag or light waved according to a code

wig·wam \\'wig,wäm\\ *n* : American Indian hut consisting of a framework of poles overlaid with bark, rush mats, or hides

wild \\'wīld\\ *adj* **1** : living or being in a state of nature and not domesticated or cultivated   **2** : unrestrained   **3** : turbulent   **4** : crazy   **5** : uncivilized   **6** : erratic ~ *n* **1** : wilderness   **2** : undomesticated state ~ *adv* : without control — **wild·ly** *adv* — **wild·ness** *n*

wild·cat \\-,kat\\ *n* : any of various undomesticated cats (as a lynx) ～ *adj* **1** : not sound or safe **2** : unauthorized

wil·der·ness \'wildərnəs\ *n* : uncultivated and uninhabited region

wild·fire \'wīld‚fīr\ *n* : sweeping and destructive fire

wild·fowl *n* : game waterfowl

wild·life \'wīld‚līf\ *n* : undomesticated animals

wile \'wīl\ *n* : trick to snare or deceive ～ *vb* **wiled; wil·ing** : lure

will \'wil\ *vb, past* **would** \'wu̇d\; *pres sing & pl* **will** **1** : wish **2** — used as an auxiliary verb to express (1) desire or willingness (2) customary action (3) simple future time (4) capability (5) determination (6) probability (7) inevitability or (8) a command **3** : dispose of by a will ～ *n* **1** : often determined wish **2** : act, process, or experience of willing **3** : power of controlling one's actions or emotions **4** : legal document disposing of property after death

will·ful, wil·ful \'wilfəl\ *adj* **1** : governed by will without regard to reason **2** : intentional — **will·ful·ly** *adv*

will·ing \'wiliŋ\ *adj* **1** : inclined or favorably disposed in mind **2** : prompt to act **3** : done, borne, or accepted voluntarily or without reluctance — **will·ing·ly** *adv* — **will·ing·ness** *n*

will–o'–the–wisp \‚wiləthə-'wisp\ *n* **1** : light that appears at night over marshy grounds **2** : misleading or elusive goal or hope

wil·low \'wilō\ *n* : quick= growing shrub or tree with flexible shoots

wil·lowy \'wiləwē\ *adj* : gracefully tall and slender

will·pow·er \'wil‚pau̇ər\ *n* : energetic determination

wil·ly–nil·ly \‚wilē'nilē\ *adv or adj* : without regard for one's choice

wilt \'wilt\ *vb* **1** : lose or cause to lose freshness and become limp esp. from lack of water **2** : grow weak

wily \'wīlē\ *adj* **wil·i·er; -est** : full of craftiness — **wil·i·ness** *n*

win \'win\ *vb* **won** \'wən\; **win·ning** **1** : get possession of esp. by effort **2** : gain victory in battle or a contest **3** : make friendly or favorable ～ *n* : victory

wince \'wins\ *vb* **winced; wincing** : shrink back involuntarily — **wince** *n*

winch \'winch\ *n* : machine for hoisting or pulling with a drum around which rope is wound — **winch** *vb*

¹**wind** \'wind\ *n* **1** : movement of the air **2** : breath **3** : gas in the stomach or intestines **4** : air carrying a scent **5** : intimation ~ *vb* **1** : get a scent of **2** : cause to be out of breath

²**wind** \'wīnd\ *vb* **wound** \'waund\; **wind·ing 1** : have or follow a curving course **2** : move or lie to encircle **3** : encircle or cover with something pliable **4** : tighten the spring of ~ *n* : turn or coil — **wind·er** *n*

wind·break \-ˌbrāk\ *n* : trees and shrubs to break the force of the wind

wind·break·er \-ˌbrākər\ *n* : light wind-resistant jacket

wind·fall \'wind ˌfȯl\ *n* **1** : thing blown down by wind **2** : unexpected benefit

wind instrument *n* : musical instrument (as a flute or horn) sounded by wind and esp. by the breath

wind·lass \'windləs\ *n* : winch esp. for hoisting anchor

wind·mill \'windˌmil\ *n* : machine worked by the wind turning vanes

win·dow \'windō\ *n* **1** : opening in the wall of a building to let in light and air **2** : pane in a window **3** : span of time for something **4** : area of a computer display — **win·dow·less** *adj*

win·dow–shop *vb* : look at the displays in store windows — **win·dow–shop·per** *n*

wind·pipe \'windˌpīp\ *n* : passage for the breath from the larynx to the lungs

wind·shield \'-ˌshēld\ *n* : transparent screen in front of the occupants of a vehicle

wind·up \'wīndˌəp\ *n* : end — **wind up** *vb*

wind·ward \'windwərd\ *adj* : being in or facing the direction from which the wind is blowing ~ *n* : direction from which the wind is blowing

windy \'windē\ *adj* **wind·i·er; -est 1** : having wind **2** : indulging in useless talk

wine \'wīn\ *n* **1** : fermented grape juice **2** : usu. fermented juice of a plant product (as fruit) used as a beverage ~ *vb* : treat to or drink wine

wing \'wiŋ\ *n* **1** : movable paired appendage for flying **2** : winglike thing **3** *pl* : area at the side of the stage out of sight **4** : faction ~ *vb* **1** : fly **2** : propel through the air — **winged** *adj* — **wing·less** *adj* — **on the wing** : in flight — **under one's wing** : in one's charge or care

wink \'wiŋk\ *vb* **1** : close and open the eyes quickly **2** : avoid seeing or noticing something **3** : twinkle **4** : close and open one eye quickly as a signal or hint ~ *n* **1** : brief sleep **2** : act of winking **3** : instant — **wink·er** *n*

win·ner \'winər\ *n* : one that wins

win·ning \-iŋ\ *n* **1** : victory **2** : money won at gambling ~ *adj* **1** : victorious **2** : charming

win·now \'winō\ *vb* **1** : remove (as chaff) by a current of air **2** : sort or separate something

win·some \'winsəm\ *adj* **1** : causing joy **2** : cheerful or gay — **win·some·ly** *adv* — **win·some·ness** *n*

win·ter \'wintər\ *n* : season between autumn and spring ~ *adj* : sown in autumn for harvest the next spring or summer — **win·ter·time** *n*

win·ter·green \'wintər͵grēn\ *n* : low heathlike evergreen plant with red berries

win·try \'wintrē\ *adj* **win·tri·er; -est 1** : characteristic of winter **2** : cold in feeling

wipe \'wīp\ *vb* **wiped; wip·ing 1** : clean or dry by rubbing **2** : remove by rubbing **3** : erase completely **4** : destroy **5** : pass over a surface ~ *n* : act or instance of wiping — **wip·er** *n*

wire \'wīr\ *n* **1** : thread of metal **2** : work made of wire **3** : telegram or cablegram ~ *vb* **1** : provide with wire **2** : bind or mount with wire **3** : telegraph — **wire·less** *adj*

wire·less \-ləs\ *n, chiefly Brit* : radio

wire·tap *vb* : connect into a telephone or telegraph wire to get information — **wiretap** *n* — **wire·tap·per** *n*

wir·ing \'wīriŋ\ *n* : system of wires

wiry \'wīrē\ *adj* **wir·i·er** \'wīrēər\; **-est 1** : resembling wire **2** : slender yet strong and sinewy — **wir·i·ness** *n*

wis·dom \'wizdəm\ *n* **1** : accumulated learning **2** : good sense

wisdom tooth *n* : last tooth on each half of each human jaw

¹**wise** \'wīz\ *n* : manner

²**wise** *adj* **wis·er; wis·est 1** : having or showing wisdom, good sense, or good judgment **2** : aware of what is going on — **wise·ly** *adv*

wise·crack *n* : clever, smart, or flippant remark ~ *vb* : make a wisecrack

wish \'wish\ *vb* **1** : have a desire **2** : express a wish concerning **3** : request ~ *n* **1** : a wishing or desire **2** : expressed will or desire

wish·bone *n* : forked bone in front of the breastbone in most birds

wish·ful \-fəl\ *adj* **1** : expressive of a wish **2** : according with wishes rather than fact

wishy–washy \'wishē₁wȯshē, -₁wäsh-\ *adj* : weak or insipid

wisp \'wisp\ *n* **1** : small bunch of hay or straw **2** : thin strand, strip, fragment, or streak **3** : something frail, slight, or fleeting — **wispy** *adj*

wis·te·ria \wis'tirēə\ *n* : pealike woody vine with long clusters of flowers

wist·ful \'wistfəl\ *adj* : full of longing — **wist·ful·ly** *adv* — **wist·ful·ness** *n*

wit \'wit\ *n* **1** : reasoning power **2** : mental soundness — usu. pl. **3** : quickness and cleverness in han- dling words and ideas **4** : talent for clever remarks or one noted for witty remarks — **wit·less** *adj* — **wit·less·ly** *adv* — **wit·less·ness** *n* — **wit·ted** *adj*

witch \'wich\ *n* **1** : person believed to have magic power **2** : ugly old woman ∼ *vb* : bewitch

witch·craft \'wich₁kraft\ *n* : power or practices of a witch

witch·ery \'wichərē\ *n, pl* **-er·ies** **1** : witchcraft **2** : charm

witch ha·zel \'wich₁hāzəl\ *n* **1** : shrub having small yellow flowers in fall **2** : alcoholic lotion made from witch hazel bark

witch–hunt *n* **1** : searching out and persecution of supposed witches **2** : harassment esp. of political opponents

with \'with, 'with\ *prep* **1** : against, to, or toward **2** : in support of **3** : because of **4** : in the company of **5** : having **6** : despite **7** : containing **8** : by means of

with·draw \with'drȯ, with-\ *vb* **-drew** \-'drü\; **-drawn** \-'drȯn\; **-draw·ing** \-'drȯiŋ\ **1** : take back or away **2** : call back or retract **3** : go away **4** : terminate one's participation in or use of — **with·draw·al** \-'drȯəl\ *n*

with·drawn \with'drȯn\ *adj* : socially detached and unresponsive

with·er \'withər\ *vb* **1** : shrivel **2** : lose or cause to lose energy, force, or freshness

with·ers \'withərz\ *n pl* : ridge between the shoulder bones of a horse

with·hold \with'hōld, with-\ *vb* **-held** \-'held\; **-hold·ing** **1** : hold back **2** : refrain from giving

with·in \with'in, with-\ *adv* **1** : in or into the interior **2** : inside oneself ∼ *prep* **1** : in or to the inner part of **2** : in the limits or compass of

with·out \with'aùt, with-\ *prep* **1** : outside **2** : lacking **3** : unaccompanied or unmarked by — **without** *adv*

with·stand \with'stand, with-\ *vb* **-stood** \-'stud\; **-stand·ing** : oppose successfully

wit·ness \'witnəs\ *n* **1** : testimony **2** : one who testifies **3** : one present at a transaction to testify that it has taken place **4** : one who has personal knowledge or experience **5** : something serving as proof ~ *vb* **1** : bear witness **2** : act as legal witness of **3** : furnish proof of **4** : be a witness of **5** : be the scene of

wit·ti·cism \'witə,sizəm\ *n* : witty saying or phrase

wit·ting \'witiŋ\ *adj* : intentional — **wit·ting·ly** *adv*

wit·ty \'witē\ *adj* **-ti·er; -est** : marked by or full of wit — **wit·ti·ly** \'witᵊlē\ *adv* — **wit·ti·ness** *n*

wives *pl of* WIFE

wiz·ard \'wizərd\ *n* **1** : magician **2** : very clever person — **wiz·ard·ry** \-ərdrē\ *n*

wiz·ened \'wizᵊnd\ *adj* : dried up

wob·ble \'wäbəl\ *vb* **-bled; -bling** **1** : move or cause to move with an irregular rocking motion **2** : tremble **3** : waver — **wobble** *n* — **wob·bly** \'wäbəlē\ *adj*

woe \'wō\ *n* **1** : deep suffering **2** : misfortune

woe·be·gone \'wōbi,gȯn\ *adj* : exhibiting woe, sorrow, or misery

woe·ful \'wōfəl\ *adj* **1** : full of woe **2** : bringing woe — **woe·ful·ly** *adv*

woke *past of* WAKE

woken *past part of* WAKE

wolf \'wu̇lf\ *n, pl* **wolves** \'wu̇lvz\ : large doglike predatory mammal ~ *vb* : eat greedily — **wolf·ish** *adj*

wol·fram \'wu̇lfrəm\ *n* : tungsten

wol·ver·ine \,wu̇lvə'rēn\ *n, pl* **-ines** : flesh-eating mammal related to the weasels

wom·an \'wu̇mən\ *n, pl* **wom·en** \'wimən\ **1** : adult female person **2** : womankind **3** : feminine nature — **wom·an·hood** \-,hu̇d\ *n* — **wom·an·ish** *adj*

wom·an·kind \-,kīnd\ *n* : females of the human race

wom·an·ly \-lē\ *adj* : having qualities characteristic of a woman — **wom·an·li·ness** \-lēnəs\ *n*

womb \'wüm\ *n* : uterus

won *past of* WIN

won·der \'wəndər\ *n* **1** : cause of astonishment or surprise **2** : feeling (as of astonishment) aroused by something extraordinary ~ *vb* **1** : feel surprise **2** : feel curiosity or doubt

won·der·ful \'wəndərfəl\ *adj* **1** : exciting wonder **2** : unusually good — **won·der·ful·ly** *adv* — **won·der·ful·ness** *n*

---

won·der·land \-ˌland, -lənd\ n 1 : fairylike imaginary realm 2 : place that excites admiration or wonder

won·der·ment \-mənt\ n : wonder

won·drous \'wəndrəs\ adj : wonderful — **won·drous·ly** adv — **won·drous·ness** n

wont \'wȯnt, 'wōnt\ adj : accustomed ~ n : habit — **wont·ed** adj

woo \'wü\ vb : try to gain the love or favor of — **woo·er** n

wood \'wu̇d\ n 1 : dense growth of trees usu. smaller than a forest — often pl. 2 : hard fibrous substance of trees and shrubs beneath the bark 3 : wood prepared for some use (as burning) ~ adj 1 : wooden 2 : suitable for working with wood 3 or **woods** \'wu̇dz\ : living or growing in woods — **wood·chop·per** n — **wood·pile** n — **wood·shed** n

wood·bine \'wu̇dˌbīn\ n : climbing vine

wood·chuck \-ˌchək\ n : thick-bodied grizzled animal of No. America

wood·craft n 1 : skill and practice in matters relating to the woods 2 : skill in making articles from wood

wood·cut \-ˌkət\ n 1 : relief printing surface engraved on wood 2 : print from a woodcut

wood·ed \'wu̇dəd\ adj : covered with woods

wood·en \'wu̇dᵊn\ adj 1 : made of wood 2 : lacking resilience 3 : lacking ease, liveliness or interest — **wood·en·ly** adv — **wood·en·ness** n

wood·land \-lənd, -ˌland\ n : land covered with trees

wood·peck·er \'wu̇dˌpekər\ n : brightly marked bird with a hard bill for drilling into trees

woods·man \'wu̇dzmən\ n : person who works in the woods

wood·wind \'wu̇dˌwind\ n : one of a group of wind instruments (as a flute or oboe)

wood·work n : work (as interior house fittings) made of wood

woody \'wu̇dē\ adj **wood·i·er; -est** 1 : abounding with woods 2 : of, containing, or like wood fibers — **wood·i·ness** n

woof \'wu̇f\ n : weft

wool \'wu̇l\ n 1 : soft hair of some mammals and esp. the sheep 2 : something (as a textile) made of wool — **wooled** \'wu̇ld\ adj

wool·en, wool·len \'wu̇lən\ adj 1 : made of wool 2 : relating to the manufacture of woolen products ~ n 1 : woolen fabric 2 : woolen garments — usu. pl.

wool·gath·er·ing *n* : idle daydreaming

wool·ly \'wu̇lē\ *adj* **-li·er; -est** **1** : of, relating to, or bearing wool **2** : consisting of or resembling wool **3** : confused or turbulent

woo·zy \'wüzē\ *adj* **-zi·er; -est** **1** : confused **2** : somewhat dizzy, nauseated, or weak — **woo·zi·ness** *n*

word \'wərd\ *n* **1** : brief remark **2** : speech sound or series of speech sounds that communicates a meaning **3** : written representation of a word **4** : order **5** : news **6** : promise **7** *pl* : dispute ~ *vb* : express in words — **word-less** *adj*

word·ing \'wərdiŋ\ *n* : verbal expression

word processing *n* : production of structured and printed documents through a computer program (**word processor**) — **word process** *vb*

wordy \'wərdē\ *adj* **word·i·er; -est** : using many words — **word·i·ness** *n*

wore *past of* WEAR

work \'wərk\ *n* **1** : labor **2** : employment **3** : task **4** : something (as an artistic production) produced by mental effort or physical labor **5** *pl* : place where industrial labor is done **6** *pl* : moving parts of a mechanism **7** : workmanship ~ *adj* **1** : suitable for wear while working **2** : used for work ~ *vb* **worked** \'wərkt\ *or* **wrought** \'rȯt\; **work·ing** **1** : bring to pass **2** : create by expending labor upon **3** : bring or get into a form or condition **4** : set or keep in operation **5** : solve **6** : cause to labor **7** : arrange **8** : excite **9** : labor **10** : perform work regularly for wages **11** : function according to plan or design **12** : produce a desired effect — **work·bench** *n* — **work·man** \-mən\ *n* — **work·room** *n* — **in the works** : in preparation

work·able \'wərkəbəl\ *adj* **1** : capable of being worked **2** : feasible — **work·able·ness** *n*

work·a·day \'wərkə,dā\ *adj* **1** : relating to or suited for working days **2** : ordinary

work·a·hol·ic \,wərkə'hȯlik, -'häl-\ *n* : compulsive worker

work·day \'wərk,dā\ *n* **1** : day on which work is done **2** : period of time during which one is working

work·er \'wərkər\ *n* : person who works esp. for wages

work·horse *n* **1** : horse used for hard work **2** : person who does most of the work of a group task

work·house *n* : place of confinement for persons who have committed minor offenses

work·ing \'wərkiŋ\ *adj* **1** : adequate to allow work to be done **2** : adopted or assumed to help further work or activity ∼ *n* : operation — usu. used in pl.

work·ing·man \'wərkiŋ͵man\ *n* : worker

work·man·like \-͵līk\ *adj* : worthy of a good workman

work·man·ship \-͵ship\ *n* **1** : art or skill of a workman **2** : quality of a piece of work

work·out \'wərk͵aút\ *n* : exercise to improve one's fitness

work out *vb* **1** : bring about by effort **2** : solve **3** : develop **4** : to be successful **5** : perform exercises

work·shop *n* **1** : small establishment for manufacturing or handicrafts **2** : seminar emphasizing exchange of ideas and practical methods

world \'wərld\ *n* **1** : universe **2** : earth with its inhabitants and all things upon it **3** : people in general **4** : great number or quantity **5** : class of persons or their sphere of interest

world·ly \'wərldlē\ *adj* **1** : devoted to this world and its pursuits rather than to religion **2** : sophisticated — **world·li·ness** *n*

world·ly–wise *adj* : possessing understanding of human affairs

world·wide *adj* : extended throughout the entire world — **worldwide** *adv*

World Wide Web *n* : part of the Internet accessible through a browser

worm \'wərm\ *n* **1** : earthworm or a similar animal **2** *pl* : disorder caused by parasitic worms ∼ *vb* **1** : move or cause to move in a slow and indirect way **2** : to free from worms — **wormy** *adj*

worm·wood \'wərm͵wúd\ *n* **1** : aromatic woody herb (as sagebrush) **2** : something bitter or grievous

worn *past part of* WEAR

worn–out \'wōrn'aút\ *adj* : exhausted or used up by or as if by wear

wor·ri·some \'wərēsəm\ *adj* **1** : causing worry **2** : inclined to worry

wor·ry \'wərē\ *vb* **-ried; -ry·ing 1** : shake and mangle with the teeth **2** : disturb **3** : feel or express anxiety ∼ *n, pl* **-ries 1** : anxiety **2** : cause of anxiety — **wor·ri·er** *n*

worse \'wərs\ *adj, comparative of* BAD *or of* ILL **1** : bad or evil in a greater degree **2** : more unwell ∼ *n* **1** : one that is worse **2** : greater degree of badness ∼ *adv comparative of* BAD *or of* ILL : in a worse manner

wors·en \\'wərsᵊn\\ *vb* : make or become worse

wor·ship \\'wərshəp\\ *n* **1** : reverence toward a divine being or supernatural power **2** : expression of reverence **3** : extravagant respect or devotion ∼ *vb* **-shiped** *or* **-shipped; -ship·ing** *or* **-ship·ping** **1** : honor or reverence **2** : perform or take part in worship — **wor·ship·er, wor·ship·per** *n*

worst \\'wərst\\ *adj, superlative of* BAD *or of* ILL **1** : most bad, evil, ill, or corrupt **2** : most unfavorable, unpleasant, or painful ∼ *n* : one that is worst ∼ *adv superlative of* ILL *or of* BAD *or* BADLY : to the extreme degree of badness ∼ *vb* : defeat

wor·sted \\'wustəd, 'wərstəd\\ *n* : smooth compact wool yarn or fabric made from such yarn

worth \\'wərth\\ *prep* **1** : equal in value to **2** : deserving of ∼ *n* **1** : monetary value **2** : value of something measured by its qualities **3** : moral or personal merit

worth·less \\-ləs\\ *adj* **1** : lacking worth **2** : useless — **worth·less·ness** *n*

worth·while \\-'hwīl\\ *adj* : being worth the time or effort spent

wor·thy \\'wərthē\\ *adj* **-thi·er; -est** **1** : having worth or value **2** : having sufficient worth ∼ *n, pl* **-thies** : worthy person — **wor·thi·ly** *adv* — **wor·thi·ness** *n*

would \\'wud\\ *past of* WILL — used to express **(1)** preference **(2)** intent **(3)** habitual action **(4)** contingency **(5)** probability or **(6)** a request

would–be \\'wud'bē\\ *adj* : desiring or pretending to be

¹wound \\'wünd\\ *n* **1** : injury in which the skin is broken **2** : mental hurt ∼ *vb* : inflict a wound to or in

²wound \\'waund\\ *past of* WIND

wove *past of* WEAVE

woven *past part of* WEAVE

wrack \\'rak\\ *n* : ruin

wraith \\'rāth\\ *n, pl* **wraiths** \\'rāths, 'rāthz\\ **1** : ghost **2** : insubstantial appearance

wran·gle \\'raŋgəl\\ *vb or n* : quarrel — **wran·gler** *n*

wrap \\'rap\\ *vb* **-pp-** **1** : cover esp. by winding or folding **2** : envelop and secure for transportation or storage **3** : enclose, surround, or conceal wholly **4** : coil, fold, draw, or twine about something ∼ *n* **1** : wrapper or wrapping **2** : outer garment (as a shawl)

wrap·per \\'rapər\\ *n* **1** : that in which something is wrapped **2** : one that wraps

wrap·ping *n* : something used to wrap an object

wrath \'rath\ *n* : violent anger — **wrath·ful** \-fəl\ *adj*

wreak \'rēk\ *vb* **1** : inflict **2** : bring about

wreath \'rēth\ *n, pl* **wreaths** \'rēthz, 'rēths\ : something (as boughs) intertwined into a circular shape

wreathe \'rēth\ *vb* **wreathed**; **wreath·ing** **1** : shape into or take on the shape of a wreath **2** : decorate or cover with a wreath

wreck \'rek\ *n* **1** : broken remains (as of a ship or vehicle) after heavy damage **2** : something disabled or in a state of ruin **3** : an individual who has become weak or infirm **4** : action of breaking up or destroying something ∼ *vb* : ruin or damage by breaking up

wreck·age \'rekij\ *n* **1** : act of wrecking **2** : remains of a wreck

wreck·er \-ər\ *n* **1** : automotive vehicle for removing disabled cars **2** : one that wrecks or tears down and removes buildings

wren \'ren\ *n* : small mostly brown singing bird

wrench \'rench\ *vb* **1** : pull with violent twisting or force **2** : injure or disable by a violent twisting or straining ∼ *n* **1** : forcible twisting **2** : tool for exerting a twisting force

wrest \'rest\ *vb* **1** : pull or move by a forcible twisting movement **2** : gain with difficulty ∼ *n* : forcible twist

wres·tle \'resəl, 'ras-\ *vb* **-tled**; **-tling** **1** : scuffle with and attempt to throw and pin an opponent **2** : compete against in wrestling **3** : struggle (as with a problem) ∼ *n* : action or an instance of wrestling — **wres·tler** \'reslər, 'ras-\ *n*

wres·tling \'resliŋ\ *n* : sport in which 2 opponents try to throw and pin each other

wretch \'rech\ *n* **1** : miserable unhappy person **2** : vile person

wretch·ed \'rechəd\ *adj* **1** : deeply afflicted, dejected, or distressed **2** : grievous **3** : inferior — **wretch·ed·ly** *adv* — **wretch·ed·ness** *n*

wrig·gle \'rigəl\ *vb* **-gled**; **-gling** **1** : twist and turn restlessly **2** : move along by twisting and turning — **wrig·gle** *n* — **wrig·gler** \'rigələr\ *n*

wring \'riŋ\ *vb* **wrung** \'rəŋ\; **wring·ing** **1** : squeeze or twist out moisture **2** : get by or as if by twisting or pressing **3** : twist together in anguish **4** : pain — **wring·er** *n*

wrin·kle \'riŋkəl\ *n* : crease or small fold on a surface (as in the skin or in cloth) ∼ *vb* **-kled**; **-kling** : develop or cause to develop wrinkles — **wrin·kly** \-kəlē\ *adj*

wrist \'rist\ *n* : joint or region between the hand and the arm

writ \'rit\ *n* **1** : something written **2** : legal order in writing

write \'rīt\ *vb* **wrote** \'rōt\; **writ·ten** \'rit°n\; **writ·ing** \'rītiŋ\ **1** : form letters or words on a surface **2** : form the letters or the words of (as on paper) **3** : make up and set down for others to read **4** : write a letter to — **write off** *vb* : cancel

writ·er \'rītər\ *n* : one that writes esp. as a business or occupation

writhe \'rīth\ *vb* **writhed; writh·ing** : twist and turn this way and that

writ·ing \'rītiŋ\ *n* **1** : act of one that writes **2** : handwriting **3** : something written or printed

wrong \'rȯŋ\ *n* **1** : unfair or unjust act **2** : something that is contrary to justice **3** : state of being or doing wrong ∼ *adj* **wrong·er** \'rȯŋər\; **wrong·est** \'rȯŋəst\ **1** : sinful **2** : not right according to a standard **3** : unsuitable **4** : incorrect ∼ *adv* **1** : in a wrong direction or manner **2** : incorrectly ∼ *vb* **wronged; wrong·ing 1** : do wrong to **2** : treat unjustly — **wrong·ly** *adv*

wrong·do·er \-'düər\ *n* : one who does wrong — **wrong·do·ing** \-'düiŋ\ *n*

wrong·ful \-fəl\ *adj* **1** : wrong **2** : illegal — **wrong·ful·ly** *adv* — **wrong·ful·ness** *n*

wrong·head·ed \'rȯŋ'hedəd\ *adj* : stubborn in clinging to wrong opinion or principles — **wrong·head·ed·ly** *adv* — **wrong·head·ed·ness** *n*

wrote *past of* WRITE

wrought \'rȯt\ *adj* **1** : formed **2** : hammered into shape **3** : deeply stirred

wrung *past of* WRING

wry \'rī\ *adj* **wri·er** \'rīər\; **wri·est** \'rīəst\ **1** : turned abnormally to one side **2** : twisted **3** : cleverly and often ironically humorous — **wry·ly** *adv* — **wry·ness** *n*

X

x \'eks\ *n, pl* **x's** *or* **xs** \'eksəz\ **1** : 24th letter of the alphabet **2** : unknown quantity ∼ *vb* **x–ed; x–ing** *or* **x'ing** : cancel with a series of *x*'s — usu. with *out*

xe·non \'zē,nän,'zen,än\ *n* : heavy gaseous chemical element

xe·no·pho·bia \,zenə'fōbēə, ,zēn-\ *n* : fear and hatred of foreign people and things —

xe·no·phobe \\'zenə₁fōb, 'zēn-\\ *n*

Xmas \\'krisməs\\ *n* : Christmas

x–ra·di·a·tion *n* **1** : exposure to X rays **2** : radiation consisting of X rays

x–ray \\'eks₁rā\\ *vb* : examine, treat, or photograph with X rays

X ray *n* **1** : radiation of short wavelength that is able to penetrate solids **2** : photograph taken with X rays — **X–ray** *adj*

xy·lo·phone \\'zīlə₁fōn\\ *n* : musical instrument with wooden bars that are struck — **xy·lo·phon·ist** \\-₁fōnist\\ *n*

Y

y \\'wī\\ *n, pl* **y's** *or* **ys** \\'wīz\\ : 25th letter of the alphabet

¹-y \\ē\\ *adj suffix* **1** : composed or full of **2** : like **3** : performing or apt to perform an action

²-y \\ē\\ *n suffix, pl* **-ies** **1** : state, condition, or quality **2** : activity, place of business, or goods dealt with **3** : whole group

yacht \\'yät\\ *n* : luxurious pleasure boat ∼ *vb* : race or cruise in a yacht

ya·hoo \\'yähü, 'yä-\\ *n, pl* **-hoos** : uncouth or stupid person

yak \\'yak\\ *n* : big hairy Asian ox

yam \\'yam\\ *n* **1** : edible root of a tropical vine **2** : deep orange sweet potato

yam·mer \\'yamər\\ *vb* **1** : whimper **2** : chatter — **yammer** *n*

yank \\'yaŋk\\ *n* : strong sudden pull — **yank** *vb*

Yank \\'yaŋk\\ *n* : Yankee

Yan·kee \\'yaŋkē\\ *n* : native or inhabitant of New England, the northern U.S., or the U.S.

yap \\'yap\\ *vb* **-pp-** **1** : yelp **2** : chatter — **yap** *n*

¹yard \\'yärd\\ *n* **1** : 3 feet **2** : long spar for supporting and spreading a sail — **yard·age** \\-ij\\ *n*

²yard *n* **1** : enclosed roofless area **2** : grounds of a building **3** : work area

yard·arm \\'yärd₁ärm\\ *n* : end of the yard of a square-rigged ship

yard·stick *n* **1** : measuring stick 3 feet long **2** : standard for judging

yar·mul·ke \\'yäməkə, 'yär-, -məl-\\ *n* : a small brimless cap worn by Jewish males in a synagogue

yarn \\'yärn\\ *n* **1** : spun fiber for weaving or knitting **2** : tale

yaw \\'yȯ\ *vb* : deviate erratically from a course — **yaw** *n*

yawl \\'yȯl\ *n* : sailboat with 2 masts

yawn \\'yȯn\ *vb* : open the mouth wide ~ *n* : deep breath through a wide-open mouth — **yawn·er** *n*

ye \\'yē\ *pron* : you

yea \\'yā\ *adv* **1** : yes **2** : truly ~ *n* : affirmative vote

year \\'yir\ *n* **1** : period of about 365 days **2** *pl* : age

year·book *n* : annual report of the year's events

year·ling \\'yirliŋ, 'yərlən\ *n* : one that is or is rated as a year old

year·ly \\'yirlē\ *adj* : annual — **yearly** *adv*

yearn \\'yərn\ *vb* **1** : feel desire esp. for what one cannot have **2** : feel tenderness or compassion

yearn·ing \-iŋ\ *n* : tender or urgent desire

yeast \\'yēst\ *n* : froth or sediment in sugary liquids containing a tiny fungus and used in making alcoholic liquors and as a leaven in baking — **yeasty** *adj*

yell \\'yel\ *vb* : utter a loud cry — **yell** *n*

yel·low \\'yelō\ *adj* **1** : of the color yellow **2** : sensational **3** : cowardly ~ *vb* : make or turn yellow ~ *n* **1** : color of lemons **2** : yolk of an egg — **yel·low·ish** \\'yeləwish\ *adj*

yellow fever *n* : virus disease marked by prostration, jaundice, fever, and often hemorrhage

yellow jacket *n* : wasp with yellow stripes

yelp \\'yelp\ *vb* : utter a sharp quick shrill cry — **yelp** *n*

yen \\'yen\ *n* : strong desire

yeo·man \\'yōmən\ *n* **1** : attendant or officer in a royal or noble household **2** : small farmer **3** : naval petty officer with clerical duties — **yeo·man·ry** \-rē\ *n*

-yer — see -ER

yes \\'yes\ *adv* — used to express consent or agreement ~ *n* : affirmative answer

ye·shi·va, ye·shi·vah \yə'shēvə\ *n, pl* **yeshivas** *or* **ye·shi·voth** \-ˌshē'vōt, -'vōth\ : Jewish school

yes–man \\'yes,man\ *n* : person who agrees with every opinion or suggestion of a boss

yes·ter·day \\'yestərdē\ *adv* **1** : on the day preceding today **2** : only a short time ago ~ *n* **1** : day last past **2** : time not long past

yet \\'yet\ *adv* **1** : in addition **2** : up to now **3** : so soon as now **4** : nevertheless ~ *conj* : but

yew \\'yü\ *n* : evergreen tree or shrubs with dark stiff poisonous needles

yield \\'yēld\ *vb* **1** : surrender **2** : grant **3** : bear as a crop **4** : produce **5** : cease opposition or resistance ~ *n* : quantity produced or returned

yo·del \\'yōd³l\ *vb* **-deled** *or* **-delled; -del·ing** *or* **-del·ling** : sing by abruptly alternating between chest voice and falsetto — **yodel** *n* — **yo·del·er** \\'yōd³lər\ *n*

yo·ga \\'yōgə\ *n* : system of exercises for attaining bodily or mental control and well-being

yo·gi \\'yōgē\ *n* : person who practices yoga

yo·gurt \\'yōgərt\ *n* : fermented slightly acid soft food made from milk

yoke \\'yōk\ *n* **1** : neck frame for coupling draft animals or for carrying loads **2** : clamp **3** : slavery **4** : tie or link **5** : piece of a garment esp. at the shoulder ~ *vb* **yoked; yok·ing 1** : couple with a yoke **2** : join

yo·kel \\'yōkəl\ *n* : naive and gullible country person

yolk \\'yōk\ *n* : yellow part of an egg — **yolked** \\'yōkt\ *adj*

Yom Kip·pur \\ˌyōmkiˈpu̇r, ˌyäm-, -ˈkipər\ *n* : Jewish holiday observed in September or October with fasting and prayer as a day of atonement

yon \\'yän\ *adj or adv* : yonder

yon·der \\'yändər\ *adv* : at or to that place ~ *adj* : distant

yore \\'yōr\ *n* : time long past

you \\'yü\ *pron* **1** : person or persons addressed **2** : person in general

young \\'yəŋ\ *adj* **youn·ger** \\'yəŋgər\; **youn·gest** \\'yəŋgəst\ **1** : being in the first or an early stage of life, growth, or development **2** : recently come into being **3** : youthful ~ *n, pl* **young** : persons or animals that are young — **young·ish** \-ish\ *adj*

young·ster \-stər\ *n* **1** : young person **2** : child

your \yər, 'yu̇r, 'yōr\ *adj* : relating to you or yourself

yours \\'yu̇rz, 'yōrz\ *pron* : the ones belonging to you

your·self \yərˈself\ *pron, pl* **your·selves** \-ˈselvz\ : you — used reflexively or for emphasis

youth \\'yüth\ *n, pl* **youths** \\'yü<u>th</u>z, 'yüths\ **1** : period between childhood and maturity **2** : young man **3** : young persons **4** : state or quality of being young, fresh, or vigorous

youth·ful \\'yüthfəl\ *adj* **1** : relating to or appropriate to youth **2** : young **3** : vigorous and fresh — **youth·ful·ly** *adv* — **youth·ful·ness** *n*

yowl \\'yau̇l\ *vb* : utter a loud long mournful cry — **yowl** *n*

yo–yo \\'yōˌyō\ *n, pl* **-yos** : toy that falls from or rises to the hand as it unwinds and rewinds on a string

yuc·ca \\'yəkə\ *n* : any of several plants related to the lilies that grow in dry regions

yule \\'yül\ *n* : Christmas — **yule·tide** \-ˌtīd\ *n*

yum·my \\'yəmē\ *adj* **-mi·er; -est** : highly attractive or pleasing

Z

z \\'zē\ *n, pl* **z's** *or* **zs** : 26th letter of the alphabet

za·ny \\'zānē\ *n, pl* **-nies 1** : clown **2** : silly person ~ *adj* **-ni·er; -est** : crazy or foolish — **za·ni·ly** *adv* — **za·ni·ness** *n*

zeal \\'zēl\ *n* : enthusiasm

zeal·ot \\'zelət\ *n* : fanatical partisan

zeal·ous \\'zeləs\ *adj* : filled with zeal — **zeal·ous·ly** *adv* — **zeal·ous·ness** *n*

ze·bra \\'zēbrə\ *n* : horselike African mammal marked with light and dark stripes

zeit·geist \\'tsītˌgīst, 'zīt-\ *n* : general spirit of an era

ze·nith \\'zēnəth\ *n* : highest point

zeph·yr \\'zefər\ *n* : gentle breeze

zep·pe·lin \\'zepələn\ *n* : rigid airship like a blimp

ze·ro \\'zērō\ *n, pl* **-ros 1** : number represented by the symbol 0 or the symbol itself **2** : starting point **3** : lowest point ~ *adj* : having no size or quantity

zest \\'zest\ *n* **1** : quality of enhancing enjoyment **2** : keen enjoyment — **zest·ful** \-fəl\ *adj* — **zest·ful·ly** *adv* — **zest·ful·ness** *n*

zig·zag \\'zigˌzag\ *n* : one of a series of short sharp turns or angles ~ *adj* : having zigzags ~ *adv* : in or by a zigzag path ~ *vb* **-gg-** : proceed along a zigzag path

zil·lion \\'zilyən\ *n* : large indeterminate number

zinc \\'ziŋk\ *n* : bluish white crystaline metallic chemical element

zing \\'ziŋ\ *n* **1** : shrill humming noise **2** : energy — **zing** *vb*

zin·nia \\'zinēə, 'zēnyə\ *n* : American herb widely grown for its showy flowers

¹zip \\'zip\ *vb* **-pp-** : move or act with speed ~ *n* : energy

²zip *vb* **-pp-** : close or open with a zipper

zip code *n* : number that identifies a U.S. postal delivery area

zip·per \\'zipər\ *n* : fastener consisting of 2 rows of interlocking teeth

zip·py \\'zipē\ *adj* **-pi·er; -est** : brisk

zir·con \\'zər‚kän\ *n* : zirconium-containing mineral sometimes used in jewelry

zir·co·ni·um \‚zər'kōnēəm\ *n* : corrosion-resistant gray metallic element

zith·er \\'zithər, 'zith-\ *n* : stringed musical instrument played by plucking

zi·ti \\'zētē\ *n, pl* **ziti** : short tubular pasta

zo·di·ac \\'zōdē‚ak\ *n* : imaginary belt in the heavens encompassing the paths of the planets and divided into 12 signs used in astrology — **zo·di·a·cal** \zō'dīəkəl\ *adj*

zom·bie \\'zämbē\ *n* : person thought to have died and been brought back to life without free will

zon·al \\'zōnᵊl\ *adj* : of, relating to, or having the form of a zone — **zon·al·ly** *adv*

zone \\'zōn\ *n* **1** : division of the earth's surface based on latitude and climate **2** : distinctive area ∼ *vb* **zoned; zon·ing 1** : mark off into zones **2** : reserve for special purposes — **zo·na·tion** \zō'nāshən\ *n*

zoo \\'zü\ *n, pl* **zoos** : collection of living animals usu. for public display — **zoo·keep·er** *n*

zo·ol·o·gy \zō'äləjē\ *n* : science of animals — **zo·o·log·i·cal** \‚zōə'läjikəl\ *adj* — **zo·ol·o·gist** \zō'äləjist\ *n*

zoom \\'züm\ *vb* **1** : move with a loud hum or buzz **2** : move or increase with great speed — **zoom** *n*

zuc·chi·ni \zu'kēnē\ *n, pl* **-ni** *or* **-nis** : summer squash with smooth cylindrical dark green fruits

zwie·back \\'swēbak, 'swī-, 'zwē-, 'zwī-\ *n* : biscuit of baked, sliced, and toasted bread

zy·gote \\'zī‚gōt\ *n* : cell formed by the union of 2 sexual cells — **zy·got·ic** \zī'gätik\ *adj*

Abbreviations

Most of these abbreviations have been given in one form. Variation in use of periods, in type, and in capitalization is frequent and widespread (as *mph, MPH, m.p.h., Mph*).

abbr abbreviation
AC alternating current
acad academic, academy
AD in the year of our Lord
adj adjective
adv adverb, advertisement
advt advertisement
AF air force, audio frequency
agric agricultural, agriculture
AK Alaska
aka also known as
AL, Ala Alabama
alg algebra
Alta Alberta
a.m., AM before noon
Am, Amer America, American
amp ampere
amt amount
anc ancient
anon anonymous
ans answer
ant antonym
APO army post office
approx approximate, approximately
Apr April
apt apartment, aptitude
AR Arkansas
arith arithmetic
Ariz Arizona
Ark Arkansas
art article, artificial

assn association
assoc associate, associated, association
asst assistant
ATM automated teller machine
att attached, attention, attorney
attn attention
atty attorney
Aug August
auth authentic, author, authorized
aux, auxil auxiliary
av avoirdupois
AV audiovisual
ave avenue
avg average
AZ Arizona
BA bachelor of arts
bal balance
bar barometer, barrel
bbl barrel, barrels
BC before Christ, British Columbia
BCE before Christian Era, before Common Era
bet between
biog biographer, biographical, biography
biol biologic, biological, biologist, biology
bldg building
blvd boulevard

BO backorder, best offer, body odor, box office, branch office

Brit Britain, British

bro brother, brothers

bros brothers

BS bachelor of science

Btu British thermal unit

bu bureau, bushel

c carat, cent, centimeter, century, chapter, circa, cup

C Celsius, centigrade

ca circa

CA, Cal, Calif California

cal calendar, caliber, calorie

Can, Canad Canada, Canadian

cap capacity, capital, capitalize, capitalized

Capt captain

CB citizens band

CDT central daylight time

cen central

cert certificate, certification, certified, certify

cf compare

chap chapter

chem chemistry

cir circle, circuit, circular, circumference

civ civil, civilian

cm centimeter

co company, county

CO Colorado

c/o care of

COD cash on delivery, collect on delivery

col colonial, colony, color, colored, column, counsel

Col colonel, Colorado

Colo Colorado

comp comparative, compensation, compiled, compiler, composition, compound, comprehensive, comptroller

cong congress, congressional

conj conjunction

Conn Connecticut

cont continued

contr contract, contraction

corp corporal, corporation

corr corrected, correction

cp compare, coupon

CPR cardiopulmonary resuscitation

cr credit, creditor

CSA Confederate States of America

CST central standard time

ct carat, cent, count, court

CT central time, certified teacher, Connecticut

cu cubic

cur currency, current

CZ Canal Zone

d penny

DA district attorney

dag dekagram

dal dekaliter

dam dekameter

dbl double

DC direct current, District of Columbia

DDS doctor of dental science, doctor of dental surgery

DE Delaware

dec deceased, decrease

Dec December

deg degree

Del Delaware

Dem Democrat, Democratic

dept department

det detached, detachment, detail, determine

dg decigram

dia, diam diameter

diag diagonal, diagram

dict dictionary

dif, diff difference

dim dimension, diminished

dir director

disc discount

dist distance, district

div divided, dividend, division, divorced

dl deciliter

dm decimeter

DMD doctor of dental medicine

DOB date of birth

doz dozen

DP data processing

dr dram, drive, drum

Dr doctor

DST daylight saving time

DUI driving under the influence

DWI driving while intoxicated

dz dozen

e east, eastern, excellent

ea each

ecol ecological, ecology

econ economics, economist, economy

EDT eastern daylight time

e.g. for example

EKG electrocardiogram, electrocardiograph

elec electric, electrical, electricity

elem elementary

eng engine, engineer, engineering

Eng England, English

esp especially

EST eastern standard time

ET eastern time

et al and others

etc et cetera

ex example, express, extra

exec executive

f false, female, feminine

F, Fah, Fahr Fahrenheit

Feb February

fed federal, federation

fem female, feminine

FL, Fla Florida

fl oz fluid ounce

FPO fleet post office

fr father, friar, from

Fri Friday

ft feet, foot, fort

fut future

FYI for your information

g gram

Ga, GA Georgia

gal gallery, gallon

gen general

geog geographic, geographical, geography

geol geologic, geological, geology

geom geometric, geometrical, geometry

gm gram

GMT Greenwich mean time

GOP Grand Old Party (Republican)

gov   government, governor
govt   government
GP   general practice, general practitioner
gr   grade, grain, gram
gram   grammar, grammatical
gt   great
GU   Guam
hd   head
hf   half
hgt   height
hgwy   highway
HI   Hawaii
hist   historian, historical, history
hon   honor, honorable, honorary
hr   here, hour
HS   high school
ht   height
HT   Hawaii time
hwy   highway
i   intransitive, island, isle
Ia, IA   Iowa
ICU   intensive care unit
ID   Idaho, identification
i.e.   that is
IL, Ill   Illinois
imp   imperative, imperfect
in   inch
IN   Indiana
inc   incomplete, incorporated
ind   independent
Ind   Indian, Indiana
inf   infinitive
int   interest
interj   interjection
intl, intnl   international
ital   italic, italicized
Jan   January

JD   juvenile delinquent
jour   journal, journeyman
JP   justice of the peace
jr, jun   junior
JV   junior varsity
Kan, Kans   Kansas
kg   kilogram
km   kilometer
KS   Kansas
kW   kilowatt
Ky, KY   Kentucky
l   late, left, liter, long
L   large
La   Louisiana
LA   Los Angeles, Louisiana
lat   latitude
lb   pound
lg   large, long
lib   liberal, librarian, library
long   longitude
m   male, masculine, meter, mile
M   medium
MA   Massachusetts
Man   Manitoba
Mar   March
masc   masculine
Mass   Massachusetts
math   mathematical, mathematician
max   maximum
Md   Maryland
MD   doctor of medicine, Maryland
MDT   mountain daylight time
Me, ME   Maine
med   medium
mg   milligram
mgr   manager
MI, Mich   Michigan

mid middle
min minimum, minor, minute
Minn Minnesota
misc miscellaneous
Miss Mississippi
ml milliliter
mm millimeter
MN Minnesota
mo month
Mo, MO Missouri
Mon Monday
Mont Montana
mpg miles per gallon
mph miles per hour
MRI magnetic resonance imaging
MS Mississippi
MST mountain standard time
mt mount, mountain
MT Montana, mountain time
n neuter, north, northern, noun
NA North America, not applicable
nat national, native, natural
natl national
naut nautical
NB New Brunswick
NC North Carolina
ND, N Dak North Dakota
NE, Neb, Nebr Nebraska
neg negative
neut neuter
Nev Nevada
Nfld Newfoundland
NH New Hampshire
NJ New Jersey
NM, N Mex New Mexico
no north, number
Nov November

NR not rated
NS Nova Scotia
NV Nevada
NWT Northwest Territories
NY New York
NYC New York City
O Ohio
obj object, objective
occas occasionally
Oct October
off office, officer, official
OH Ohio
OJ orange juice
OK, Okla Oklahoma
ON, Ont Ontario
opp opposite
OR, Ore, Oreg Oregon
orig original, originally
oz ounce, ounces
p page
Pa Pennsylvania
PA Pennsylvania, public address
PAC political action committee
par paragraph, parallel
part participle, particular
pass passenger, passive
pat patent
PC percent, politically correct, postcard
pd paid
PD police department
PDT Pacific daylight time
PE physical education
PEI Prince Edward Island
Penn, Penna Pennsylvania
pg page
PIN personal identification number

pk park, peak, peck
pkg package
pl place, plural
p.m., PM afternoon
PMS premenstrual syndrome
PO post office
Port Portugal, Portuguese
pos position, positive
poss possessive
pp pages
PQ Province of Quebec
pr pair, price, printed
PR public relations, Puerto Rico
prep preposition
pres present, president
prob probable, probably, problem
prof professor
pron pronoun
prov province
PS postscript, public school
PST Pacific standard time
psych psychology
pt part, payment, pint, point
PT Pacific time, physical therapy
pvt private
qr quarter
qt quantity, quart
Que Quebec
quot quotation
r right, river
rd road, rod, round
RDA recommended daily allowance, recommended dietary allowance
recd received
reg region, register, registered, regular

rel relating, relative, religion
rep report, reporter, representative, republic
Rep Republican
res residence
rev reverse, review, revised, revision, revolution
Rev reverend
RFD rural free delivery
RI Rhode Island
rm room
RPM revolutions per minute
RR railroad, rural route
RSVP please reply
rt right
rte route
s small, south, southern
SA South America
SASE self-addressed stamped envelope
Sask Saskatchewan
Sat Saturday
SC South Carolina
sci science, scientific
SD, S Dak South Dakota
secy secretary
sen senate, senator, senior
Sept, Sep September
sing singular
sm small
so south, southern
soph sophomore
sp spelling
spec special, specifically
specif specific, specifically
SPF sun protection factor
sq square
sr senior
Sr sister
SSN Social Security number

SSR Soviet Socialist Republic

st street

St saint

std standard

subj subject

Sun Sunday

supt superintendent

SWAT Special Weapons and Tactics

syn synonym

t teaspoon, temperature, ton, transitive, troy, true

T tablespoon

tbs, tbsp tablespoon

TD touchdown

tech technical, technician, technology

Tenn Tennessee

terr territory

Tex Texas

Th, Thu, Thur, Thurs Thursday

TN Tennessee

trans translated, translation, translator

tsp teaspoon

Tu, Tue, Tues Tuesday

TX Texas

UK United Kingdom

UN United Nations

univ universal, university

US United States

USA United States of America

USSR Union of Soviet Socialist Republics

usu usual, usually

UT Utah

UV ultraviolet

v verb, versus

Va, VA Virginia

var variant, variety

vb verb

VG very good

VI Virgin Islands

vol volume, volunteer

VP vice president

vs versus

Vt, VT Vermont

w west, western

WA, Wash Washington

Wed Wednesday

WI, Wis, Wisc Wisconsin

wk week, work

wt weight

WV, W Va West Virginia

WY, Wyo Wyoming

XL extra large, extra long

yd yard

yr year, younger, your

YT Yukon Territory